Conversations

SIXTH EDITION

Conversations

READINGS FOR WRITING

JACK SELZER
The Pennsylvania State University

DOMINIC DELLI CARPINI
York College of Pennsylvania

PEARSON
Longman

New York • San Francisco • Boston
London • Toronto • Sydney • Tokyo • Singapore • Madrid
Mexico City • Munich • Paris • Cape Town • Hong Kong • Montreal

Acquisitions Editor: Brandon Hight
Development Editor: Katharine Glynn
Media Supplements Editor: Jenna Egan
Marketing Manager: Alexandra Smith
Production Manager: Bob Ginsberg
Project Coordination, Text Design, and Electronic Page Makeup:
  GGS Book Services, Atlantic Highlands
Cover Design Manager: Nancy Danahy
Cover Image: © Getty, Inc.
Photo Researcher: Julie Tesser
Manufacturing Manager: Mary Fischer
Senior Manufacturing Buyer: Alfred C. Dorsey
Printer and Binder: R.R. Donnelley & Sons Company/
  Crawfordsville
Cover Printer: Coral Graphic Services, Inc.

For permission to use copyrighted material, grateful
acknowledgment is made to the copyright holders on
pp. 921–926, which are hereby made part of this copyright page.

Library of Congress Cataloging-in-Publication Data

Conversations : readings for writing / [compiled by] Jack Selzer,
Dominic Delli Carpini.
    p. cm.
    Includes bibliographical references and index.
    ISBN 0-321-31741-6 (paperback)
    1. College readers. 2. Report writing—Problems, exercises,
etc. 3. English language—Rhetoric—Problems, exercises, etc.
I. Selzer, Jack. II. Delli Carpini, Dominic.

PE1417.C6545 2005
808'.0427—dc22   2004060211

Please visit our website at http://www.ablongman.com

ISBN 0-321-31741-6

1 2 3 4 5 6 7 8 9 10—DOC—08 07 06 05

For Molly and Maggie, always their book;
For Danielle, Derek, Ariel, and Tess, inspirations all;
and
For Eben Ludlow, in our conversations from the start.

Contents

school is a building with teachers, students, headaches, tragedies, and, once in a while, a moment of shining success."

Should education focus upon preparing students for the workplace? This essay explores the promises and pitfalls of vocational education, with the premise that "the education needed for the workplace does not differ in its essentials from that needed for college or advanced technical training."

"The problem begins," this essay suggests, "when public school critics link test scores to worker productivity and the national economy."

This essay explores "a movement among school reformers who argue that size is the enemy of excellence in America's high schools and breaking up super-sized schools into smaller units is the key to improving them."

There has been much debate over whether allowing parents to choose the type of school that their children attend is a good thing. But "here's the catch": In some communities, "there is no better school."

For an increasing number of American families, home schooling has become the method of educating their children, but others fear that this movement can damage the "role of public education as the great equalizer in a democracy."

hands—could in fact serve the worst kind of antidemo-
cratic actions.

need—for liberal talk radio? A liberal talk radio show
host says yes.

"I have plowed and planted, and gathered into barns,
and no man could head me. And ain't I a woman?"

"I wasn't an enemy, in fact or feeling. I was an ally.
If I had known, then, how to tell them so, would they
have believed me?"

A murder in a small community uncovers sharp, and
persistent, divisions between the sexes.

"My experiences as a woman who does not do femininity illustrate a paradox of our two-and-only-two gender
system."

"Presumably the next step is to allow individual men or
women to legally declare themselves to be trees or
turnips."

The visual arts have long been intrigued by defining
boundaries, and the potential porousness of those boundaries. The artwork included here explores those boundaries and reminds us that much of what it means to be

male and female depends upon the visual cues that we have come to associate with gender.

organized labor, reminding us that the legacy of activism familiarized in John Steinbeck's *The Grapes of
Wrath* is far from dead.

Though activism is often associated with individualistic
acts outside the mainstream, this essay suggests that
"civic revolutionaries" can—and perhaps should be—
nurtured into a collaborative network of people with
common goals.

This U.S. senator argues "if the right to privacy means
anything, it is the right of the individual to be free from
unwarranted governmental intrusion."

Former director of the Defense Department's Information Awareness Office counters Senator Nelson's arguments against governmental intrusion by suggesting
"there are ways in which technology can help preserve
rights and protect people's privacy while helping to
make us all safer."

Drawing upon Thomas Hobbes' belief that only a
strong, authoritarian government can protect people
from disorder and dangers, this author suggests that the
United States has an obligation to become a "daddy
state," protecting the world from those who would
undermine civilization.

Rather than suggest that we should or should not allow
for gathering of information, this author suggests a

series of guidelines for collection of information that
can safeguard personal freedoms.

Among the provisions of the USA PATRIOT Act, one of
the most controversial has been one that allows government agencies to collect information on books and other
materials that individuals have borrowed from libraries.
The American Library Association responds.

"[T]here are strong grounds for arguing that the Second
Amendment is no barrier to gun control legislation."

Oh, yes, there are legal and practical barriers to gun
control: Robert Goldwin's readers strike back.

WAGC offers ammunition to women who resist gun
control.

Here's what the Constitution says about gun control—
and what it doesn't say.

These leaders of the World Health Organization's
"Tobacco Free Initiative" suggest that regulation is necessary because "tobacco companies have shown themselves to be incapable of self-regulation."

This consistent advocate of personal choice and responsibility suggests that the war against tobacco amounts
to "Nazi-like vilification tactics."

Part Six   Science and Society   795

Is Our Faith in Science Justified?   800

Rhetorical Contents

Exploratory Writing

Journal and Personal Report

Description and Narration

Process, Methods

Illustration, Example

Analysis

Cause and Effect

Definition

Argument: Categorical Proposition ("X Is in Fact Y")

Argument: Evaluation

Argument: Refutation

Irony and Satire

Visual Rhetoric

Oral Presentation

Writing from Sources

PREFACE

Imagine that you enter a parlor. You come late. When you arrive, others have long preceded you, and they are engaged in a heated discussion, a discussion too heated for them to pause and tell you exactly what it is about. In fact, the discussion had already begun long before any of them got there, so that no one present is qualified to retrace for you all the steps that had gone before. You listen for a while, until you decide that you have caught the tenor of the argument; then you put in your oar. Someone answers; you answer him; another comes to your defense; another aligns himself against you, to either the embarrassment or gratification of your opponent, depending upon the quality of your ally's assistance.

This well-known passage from Kenneth Burke's *Philosophy of Literary Form* explains the basic metaphor and the orientation of this anthology of readings for first-year college composition courses. *Conversations* contains conversations: public discourse on contemporary issues that is calculated to engage students' interests, to encourage and empower their own contributions to contemporary civic discussions, and to represent a broad cross section of the kinds of conversational styles and genres that are available to writers today.

What's Different about *Conversations*?

Conversations encourages student writing on important current civic issues. The premise of this reader is that writing is less a private act of making personal meaning out of the air than it is a public and social act of making meaning with a specific rhetorical situation—a specific situation that guides and shapes the meaning-making activity. To put the matter more simply, writing emerges from other writing, other discourse. Though nearly every anthology claims to encourage student responses, those anthologies just as often actually intimidate students because they present only one or two authoritative voices on a given issue and because those voices are given little context outside the anthology; the student reads an essay by Orwell or Baldwin or Woolf or some other eloquent writer and says to herself, "Gee, that sure seems right to me. How could I disagree with such an expert?" By contrast, instead of one or two authoritative items on an issue or topic, this reader contains "conversations" on public issues or topics, conversations-with-contexts in many familiar genres that will seem less intimidating and therefore invite student responses.

In fact, the book will encourage students to adopt a social and rhetorical model—a "conversation model"—for their own writing. Instead of seeing writing merely as private or as a point-counterpoint debate, students should sense from *Conversations* that "people are talking about this issue—and I'd like to get in on the talk somewhere." The conversation metaphor does not mean that students should "write like they talk" (since conversational informality is not always appropriate in public discourse); rather, the metaphor simply implies that students should see writing as a response to other writing or to other forms of discourse (including visual discourse). Students should be encouraged to cooperate as well as to compete with other writers, to address sub-issues as well as the main concerns, to seek consensus and new syntheses more so than victory. That is, productive writing inspires continued conversation rather than serves as the last word.

Thus, *Conversations* is organized around focused, topical, contemporary areas of public debate (e.g., media consolidation, the state of public education, the "digital divide" in computer access across classes, the role of government in the regulation of substances from guns to food, and so forth). Those public debates are contextualized within six larger thematic groupings (education, media, gender, family structure, civil liberties and civic responsibilities, and science and society) that lend additional historical and conceptual perspective. And they are further enriched with "visual conversations"—groups of images that, like the verbal debates, contribute to the public discussion on those issues.

The book includes items, both verbal and visual, that "talk to each other" both directly and indirectly. Some pieces speak directly and explicitly to each other (as with the debate over reducing federal drug sentences for crack cocaine offenders between Senator Patrick Leahy and Deputy Attorney General Larry Thompson, or the debate about single motherhood that is carried on among Iris Marion Young, Jean Bethke Elshtain, and Margaret O'Brien Steinfels). Some pieces refer only indirectly to others, as in sections on media mergers or the effect of social class upon crime and punishment. And still others comment on selections in other sections of *Conversations*: for example, selections on the use of the "new media" comment on the goals of activism and civic responsibility; those on pornography comment on governmental regulation; those on education comment on the need for civic education, and so relate to issues of civic responsibility; and, in a media-saturated culture like ours, those pieces on media consolidation—and the control of information—are omnipresent across the issues discussed. Students will find many more connections as they read. There is certainly no reason why the selections cannot be read individually, as they are in other books, without reference to other selections, especially since the headnotes orient readers to each item. And there is certainly no reason why the selections could not be read in some other order than the order in which they are presented here. Nevertheless, *Conversations* does give students a particular incentive to write because it establishes contexts for writing—contexts that individual classroom teachers can utilize and build upon to serve the course focus.

The conversation model makes the book suitable to a range of writing courses. There is plenty of expository prose here: comparisons of all kinds; careful analyses like Paul Gorski's explication of the digital divide as a multicultural issue; overviews of the home-schooling debate and the challenges to traditional notions of family; vivid descriptions of the violence inherent in pornography, of "superorganic" crops, and of the images found in wildlife photography; expositions of why media consolidation presents a problem for democracy and why embryonic stem cell research is, or isn't, the next great moment for science. Just to name a few. If you choose to develop your course around the modes of exposition or inquiry, the rhetorical table of contents can help you to do so.

But *Conversations* will also accommodate courses with an argumentative edge. This book not only includes pieces that explicitly "argue"—writing in which its clear purpose is to persuade—but tends to encourage a broadly argumentative approach to all discourse. As this book presents the writings of a wide variety of stakeholders in the public debate, it treats argument not as a polemical act but rather as a dialogical one. It is not about the harangue or the monologue in isolation, the sole voice at the bully pulpit or upon a soapbox, but instead about the dialogue that ensues all around even those monologic moments. In that sense, the goal is to give students an ear for both text and context. So *Conversations* not only includes Ron Reagan's appeal to go forward on stem cell research, but two responses to that very public moment; it not only touts the virtues of a college education, but gives voice to a college professor who suggests that "college is not for everyone." It does not merely present the many challenges that face us in relation to gender, but also questions the category of gender itself. In this way, students are asked to see the world not in black and white, but in shades and tints and colors. It asks them to hear other speakers who, rather than merely saying, "You are wrong," might also say "I see, but have you considered this as well?" In this way, the book provides a model of "argument" that leads to civil conversation about issues, not shrillness and refusal to listen. (Even though some of the pieces here *do* get shrill, the full context of the conversation tends to be more even-tempered.)

The pieces included here also will remind students that arguments have many shapes—that is, many genres. This anthology features a broad range of genres and tries to represent as fully as possible the "universe of discourse." True, essays are most prominent in *Conversations*—familiar and formal essays, academic as well as non-academic ones— because the essay is a common and important genre and because the form has important correspondences with other genres (e.g., the letter, the sermon, the report, the news story). But essays are not so prominent here as to exclude other genres. Students will find other ways of engaging in public discourse as well: through fiction, poetry, drama, letters of various kinds, public oratory, websites, posters, congressional reports and other legal documents, cartoons, and advertisements. The occasions for public discourse provided here are equally diverse and various. Students and their teachers will find weblog musings and memoirs, literary narratives and studies of cultural phenomena, laws and proposed laws, and—in acknowledgement of our increasing image-based culture—new sections that feature the many genres of visual rhetoric.

Though past editions of *Conversations* have regularly featured visual as well as alphabetic rhetoric, the "Visual Conversations" sections of this edition place increased emphasis on the role of images in the arguments we "read" and in the arguments we construct. Through these groupings of images, students will be invited to consider how pictures, like words, speak to one another. They will be asked to increase their attention to the often subtle features of these visual texts, and to "read" the images much as they would read a written text, looking for genre and nuance and audience and purpose. They might note the use of *ethos, pathos,* and *logos* in these images as they gauge the effectiveness of each. They might also consider the ethics involved in visual persuasion, as well as the responsibility of the consumer of visual rhetoric to be aware of the designs that images can have on us. And finally, they might consider the new tools that recent technologies have given them as writers—that is, how "writers" also now function as "text designers," envisioning not only manuscripts, but in some cases, finished documents that are enhanced by images, slick visual aids, and a wide array of typography.

In sum, *Conversations* assumes that students are ready, willing, and able to engage in civic, public discourses. At the same time, this book encourages students to remember that entering an ongoing discussion does not preclude the possibility for personal inventiveness—to cross genres, blend alphabetic and visual rhetoric, to bring a personal voice to academic research, and to bring public knowledge to private beliefs (and vice versa). Indeed, *Conversations* is committed to the proposition that there are many possible rhetorical stances, that there is no one "correct" way to address a reader. This anthology therefore exposes students to many rhetorical choices—from the studied erudition of John Searle to the semi-formal, "objective" voice associated with the academy; from the conversational informality of E. B. White, Frederick Douglass, and Ellen Goodman to the satiric invective of John Derbyshire and David Sally; from the thrilling and extemporaneous oratory of Sojourner Truth to the careful reasoning of Aristotle; from *The New York Times* to personal weblogs; from *The Nation* to *The Christian Science Monitor;* from *The New Yorker* to *Wired;* from Andrew Sullivan and Robert McChesney to Jonathan Swift, Alexis de Tocqueville, and Margaret Mead. Through this rich diversity of authors and contexts, mainstream authors and radical

outliers, traditionally "published" works and electronic statements that convey "I am here, too," students will learn many
conventional rhetorical maneuvers as well as many new ones
afforded by recent times. They will hear from famous professional writers and relatively anonymous but eloquent fellow
citizens; from men and women, gays and heterosexuals, majority and minority voices. *Conversations* gives students a
better chance to find their own voices because they've experienced a full range of possible voices in their reading.

   "A rhetorician," says Kenneth Burke in his essay
"Rhetoric—Old and New," "is like one voice in a dialogue.
Put several such voices together, with each voicing its own
special assertion, let them act upon one another in cooperative competition, and you get a dialectic that, properly
developed, can lead to views transcending the limitations of
each." Fostering that "co-operative competition" is the aim
of *Conversations*.

Editorial Apparatus

Substantial editorial assistance has been provided to the
users of *Conversations*. The book's introduction orients students to social motives for writing and domesticates for them
the metaphor of conversation. It also introduces students
to the notion of critical or rhetorical reading, so that they
might have a practical means of approaching every item in
Conversations—and so that they might better understand
how careful reading habits can reinforce effective writing
habits. In addition, a headnote is provided for each selection
so that students can orient themselves to the rhetoric of each
piece. The headnotes provide background on the author (especially when prior knowledge about the author affects one's
response to an item), on the topic of the selection (when the
matter requires any explanation), and on the specific occasion of the piece (especially on when and where it was originally published). The assumption of many anthologies is that
the original context of an essay or story—or whatever—
doesn't matter much, or that the anthology itself comprises
the context. *Conversations* assumes instead that careful reading must take into account the original circumstances that
prompted a given piece of writing. Writing, after all, most
often emerges in response to other writing, so situating each
item by means of the headnotes is essential to the concept of

Conversations. Each of the six major parts of the book also includes an introductory overview of the particular issues under discussion in that part. Also, as is noted previously, each part of the book acknowledges that a great deal of the public conversation is now conducted visually, and so includes a Visual Conversations section. The editorial apparatus of these sections likewise provides an overview of the issue, contextualizing the pictures within the larger conversation, and some prompts to help students start to think about how pictures as well as words can constitute a public conversation. In all these ways, the editorial apparatus judiciously provides necessary context for getting into the conversations without encumbering the selections themselves or the teacher who might use them in any number of course designs.

In other words, the text of *Conversations* assumes that students are already quite capable readers and that teachers will use this text as a support for their course, not as the course itself. On the grounds that students and teachers can handle things on their own and can appropriate readings to their own ends, the book includes no questions after selections, no suggestions for writing assignments or class discussions, no exercises, and limited footnotes. Space that might have been devoted to those matters is given instead to additional selections so that teachers might have as many selections as possible from which to choose. For those teachers who would like some ideas for using the text, however, we have provided an Instructor's Manual and a Companion Website.

Instructor's Manual

Teachers who do want additional background on unfamiliar readings or specific suggestions for making the most of *Conversations* will find plenty of help in the extensive Instructor's Manual that we have compiled. The manual contains further information on writers, overviews of the parts, discussions of each selection, some suggestions for further reading, and ideas for discussion and writing. It also offers pointers for teaching each "conversation"—for how particular selections can be used with other selections. Together, the editorial apparatus and the Instructor's Manual are designed with the conversation model of public discourse in mind and to engage the intelligence and passion of students and teachers without getting in the way of either.

Companion Website

The Companion Website (http://www.ablongman.com/selzer) offers a wealth of resources for both teachers and students. Students can access detailed part summaries, pre-writing exercises and essay activities related to the text, Web explorations, and annotated Web links for further study. New to this edition, both instructors and students will find new links and writing ideas for working with visual rhetoric. In addition, instructors will find a sample syllabus, links to further information that can be used in class planning, and the entire Instructor's Manual available for download.

Acknowledgments

This book, true to its concept, is the product of countless conversations between its two editors and among the many colleagues who have influenced our work as writing teachers (and teachers of writing teachers). This conversation began when we were teaching composition years ago at Penn State, and those conversations—about the connections between teaching writing and the advancement of democratic dialogue—have deepened over a decade. Still, as we collaborate on this edition of *Conversations*, we know our work has always been in the context of the wider conversation surrounding the teaching of writing. The present edition represents the work of numerous individuals who assisted us in finding appropriate selections and who reviewed the many drafts of previous editions. In particular, we appreciate the work of those who have assisted us in finding appropriate selections for the book, including Christine Caver, Lester Faigley, Bob Burkholder, Steven Tumino, Dana Anderson, Linda Selzer, Mike Zerbe, and Rebecca Delli Carpini. Likewise, the reviewers of past editions made excellent suggestions, as did the reviewers of this edition: Karen Krehbiel Brown, Northern Virginia Community College; Esther Godfrey, University of Tennessee, Knoxville; Jeff Harris, Somerset Community College; Roderick Hughes, St. Bonaventure University; David C. Judkins, University of Houston; Megan Knight, University of Iowa; Joan Faber McAlister, University of Iowa; Douglas McKinstry, University of Tennessee; Lisa Minnick, Georgia Institute of Technology; Rich Raymond,

University of Arkansas at Little Rock; Irving N. Rothman, University of Houston; and James Rovira, Drew University. Also, many colleagues from Penn State and York College of Pennsylvania—as well as those from the Conference on College Composition and Communication and the Council of Writing Program Administrators—continue to inform our understanding of how students learn to read, write, and engage in civic dialogue.

Thanks, too, to those involved in the production of this book. Development editor Katharine Glynn has worked closely with us throughout the project to bring it to fruition; her thoughtful suggestions and hard work are evident throughout this book. Sheila Egan Varela once again met our sometimes unreasonable deadlines for permissions, while Julie Tesser worked diligently to find appropriate visuals and secure permissions for their use. Trish Finley and the staff at GGS Book Services watched over the details of turning our manuscript into a polished product, as have Laura Owen and Jenna Egan at Longman. Teresa Ward and Stacy Dorgan have once again been instrumental in the production of the accompanying Instructor's Manual and Companion Website.

Finally, and most centrally, Eben Ludlow has from the start been a driving force behind each edition of this project. He has deeply influenced us both, not only in the production of this book but in the shape of our careers. His support will be remembered as he moves on to new challenges, and as we look forward to continuing our work with our new editor, Brandon Hight.

JACK SELZER
DOMINIC DELLI CARPINI

Conversations

Introduction

Why Write?

Why do people write?

For many reasons, of course. Sometimes the impulse to write derives from a personal need. The motive to write can come from within. Everyone needs to sort out feelings at one time or another or to make some personal sense of the world and its parts, and a good way to do such sorting is by writing. If you keep a diary or journal, or if you've shared your most intimate feelings through correspondence with a trusted friend, or if you've written essays—or notes toward an essay—in order to explore possible explanations for things, then you know what it means to write for personal reasons. (A root meaning of the word *essay* is "to try out, to experiment.") People do need a means of expressing powerful feelings and personal insights, and writing seems to provide just the tranquility required for gathering thoughts.

Other times the world itself motivates a writer. We seem to have a need to note our observations about the world, especially if those observations are indeed noteworthy—if they seem special or unique in some way. Sometimes this process of "taking note" is relatively formalized, as when a scientist records observations in a log of some kind or when you keep score at a baseball game or when a reporter transcribes "just the facts" into a news story. But just as often it is something less formal—when you take notes for a course or when you write something in your journal about your life and times. The drive "to hold the mirror up to nature," as Hamlet called it, to record our understanding about the ways of the world, accounts for much of the prose we encounter and produce each day.

The motive to write can also derive from one's occupation. Some people write because it's their life's work. They are professional writers—poets, news reporters, novelists, technical writers, screenwriters. And there are those who write to further their life's work. There are many people who might not think of themselves as writers, but who do spend a large amount of time writing—police officers, engineers, college professors, lawyers, physicians, corporate managers, teachers, and so forth. (You'd be surprised at how much time such people spend on the writing required by their jobs—just ask them!) Professional writers and professionals who write sometimes put words onto paper for the reasons named in the previous paragraphs—to express personal feelings or ideas, or to record their impressions or interpretations of their workaday worlds. But they also often think in terms of a particular kind of writing—a genre—when they compose: Newspaper employees think of themselves as writing news stories, feature stories, or editorials; poets set out to write verse; engineers or police officers spend time composing the reports they must turn in; lawyers write to produce those legal briefs that are due to the judge next week. Their sense of completing a particular writing task within a specific genre can sometimes take precedence over other motives.

Of course all these motives to write are legitimate, and seldom do these motives exist in a pure state. It is probably better to think of motives to write, instead of *a* motive, and to think of primary and secondary motives, instead of a single, all-consuming aim. When John Milton wrote *Paradise Lost*, for instance, he was certainly out to record his assessment of the nature of things and to express his most personal thoughts—and to write an epic. When Henry David Thoreau wrote *Walden*, he certainly had personal motives—the book originated in his daily journals—but he wanted "to hold the mirror up to nature" as well.

But *Walden* and *Paradise Lost* are "public" documents, too—attempts to sway public opinion and public behavior. Thoreau advertised *Walden,* after all, as his attempt to "brag as lustily as Chanticleer [the rooster] in the morning, if only to wake my neighbor up." He wanted to awaken his fellow citizens to nature and to persuade them to renew their own lives after his own example and experience. Milton's stated purpose— "to justify the ways of God to man"—was just as social. He wanted to change how people conceive of their relation to God and to detail his vision of the heroic life to be lived by every Christian—and perhaps to comment on the failure of England's Puritan revolution (an earthly "paradise" lost). Of course, just because these authors were writing to persuade doesn't mean that they weren't writing for other reasons—to discover or record thoughts, or to create a work of art in a specific genre. Indeed, writing to persuade does mean writing *about something* in a *particular genre* for reasons that can be *intensely personal.* But writing to persuade also means writing something that has designs on the hearts or minds (or both) of particular readers. This goes for John Milton who was writing about his times and for John Searle who was writing about ours. And it goes for you, too.

For though a writer may work in private, a writer is never really alone. A writer out "to wake people up" or "to justify the ways of God" to men and women is obviously anything but self-absorbed. But the persuasive writer is not alone in this: every kind of writing is social. The engineer who writes a report on a project is out to influence the project's managers. A physician's report on a patient is used by other caregivers. The lawyer's brief is meant to sway a judge. The movie reviewer's account is designed to direct people to (or away from) a film. Even "private" writing is often quite public in its uses. The letters in which you pour out your feelings get read by sympathetic and responsive friends. The essays you write to discover your version of the truth become written attempts to convert readers to that version. Even journal entries that are written just for you are shaped to an extent by the society around you, the things you experience, and the words that you hear (and part of us is always aware that someone, someday, might read those entries). In all these ways, writing is a social act. It is a primary means for touching others, and reading what others have written is a primary way of being touched in turn. The words you read and write are surrounded and shaped by the words and beliefs of the many people who share your "social context."

That social context—the world and people with whom we interact—is crucial because when you write, your reasons for writing are nearly always related to the expectations formed by that context. A friend expects a letter or waits for your screen name to appear on Instant Messenger; a supervisor at work has asked for a report; a professor assigns a paper; a job that is advertised requires a written application; a story in the paper makes you want to write a letter to the editor in response. That is why the title of this book is *Conversations*. It assumes that your writing is a response to the words or actions of others, part of a dialog.

Of course, to get in on that conversation, you have to know what others have said about the matter at hand, and you must be able to anticipate possible responses to that which you have to say. That's where this book can help. The collection of readings comprises *public* conversations— conversations on public issues that concern American society (in general and within your local community) as we contemplate a new century. Not every burning issue is represented here, of course; that would be impossible (and new ones come up every day). But this book does include conversations—give-and-take discussions—on many matters that concern you and your community. What do you want to get out of your years in college? How are you—and our country's politics—affected by the new media on the Internet? What does it mean to be a man or a woman in present-day America? Does pornography represent a threat to women's well-being, or does banning it represent a threat to our liberty? What constitutes a marriage or a family? How far should government go toward regulating various goods and substances, from guns to fast food to scientific research to who is permitted to marry? Questions like these are all around us, and affect our day-to-day lives, so people are talking about them, and writing about them. This book assumes that you'll want to get in on, and perhaps advance, some of those conversations, either nationally or within your local environs.

For while there is plenty of discussion of these matters in the national media, there is also plenty of local discussion (and electronic discussion) as well. What you read here about national trends in schools is likely mirrored by activities and events in your own school system. Discussions about gender are likely part of your campus community's decisions and perhaps even its curriculum. Debates about pornography might affect what films your school shows or what materials are available in your bookstore. Debates over gun regulation might affect the local storeowner or the neighborhood association to which you belong. And in a media-saturated society, in which so much of what we learn is filtered through television, radio, and the Internet, we are all affected by who owns the news outlets. Even if these issues do not always engage you personally, they should provide you with models of how to engage in public discussions when an issue does concern you.

There are plenty of ways to make such contributions. The contents to follow will introduce you to many different genres or kinds of writing. Essays are most prominent because the essay is a common genre and because the essay (or article) has important analogs with other forms like the letter, the sermon, the report, or the editorial. But you will experience other ways of engaging in public discourse as well—through genres like fiction, poetry, speeches, plays, interviews, e-mail exchanges, cartoons, and advertisements. There are news stories and memoirs, reports and literacy narratives, personal letters and letters to the editor and counterresponses, parodies and satires, explanations and analyses and outright arguments. And, as the Visual Conversations sections suggest, some genres, and some arguments, are comprised of images, not just words. (More about that in the last section of this introduction.)

In such a world, our choices for reading and writing are nearly infinite, making it an exciting time to engage in conversations. Of course, with many choices come many decisions, decisions that require you to use decorum to find the most appropriate forms within which to dress your thoughts. Do you want to be formal, less formal, or downright intimate with your reader? Do you want to present yourself as something of an expert on the matter or question, or as someone on the same level as your readers? Do you want to speak dispassionately, or do you want to let your feelings show? Do you want to be explicit in stating your purpose, or less direct? Do you want to compose sentences that are careful and complex and qualified, or ones that are direct and emphatic? You'll see a broad range of strategies and stylistic decisions illustrated in the following pages, a broad range that will represent the possible ways of engaging in public discourse. You'll encounter mainstream, classic items—and dissenting views. You'll see conventional presentations and startlingly inventive ones. You'll see how famous professional writers earned their fame, and you'll hear from anonymous but just-as-eloquent fellow citizens. You'll hear from women as well as men, from majority as well as minority voices. Listening to these many voices can give you a better chance of finding your voice in any given circumstance by exposing you to a range of possible voices in your reading. The idea is to empower you to engage in civic discourse—now, today—on the issues that concern you and your community.

How to Read This Book—And an Example

As the previous section explains, an answer to the question "Why write?" ultimately depends on several factors: on the writer's personal needs and motives, on the state of the world or issues within our world, on a genre or form of writing that a writer may be drawn or compelled toward, and on a reader or a community of readers that the writer wants to influence. Many times those factors, in combination, are involved in the decision to write.

All those factors, in combination, are also involved in decisions on *how* to write on any given occasion. Effective writers consider what they want to accomplish (aim), on what subject or issue, in what genre, for what particular readers. A writer's decisions on those matters comprise what rhetoricians call a writer's "rhetorical stance"—what *you* decide to say to *some audience* on a given issue in a particular *genre*. But the matter might be put more simply: Your decisions about how to write at a given time are colored by the occasion for that writing and your attitude toward that occasion. A football coach will prepare his team for a game by considering the opponent's strengths and weaknesses (audience), by thinking about his own aims (to win, of course, but also perhaps to "establish our running game" or "to get some experience for our younger players"), by assessing his own team's strengths, and so forth. Writers devise their own game plan as well, based on aim, issue, genre, and audience.

But what does all this have to do with reading—with reading this book and reading in general? Knowing these things about the way that writing and writers work can help you to distinguish between two kinds of reading that are important to your becoming a better writer.

In the first kind of reading, think of yourself as part of each writer's intended audience—someone who the writer actually hoped would read and respond to his or her message. In other words, in this first kind of reading, you read as you normally read the things that are directed at you everyday: as you would read a newspaper or an article in your favorite magazine or a personal letter from a friend. Read it as if the writer had written it just for you, and react accordingly. In most cases, this will be quite easy to do, because most of the items in *Conversations* are directed to the public—people like you—and were written quite recently to address topics of interest to us all. In some cases, you'll feel more remote from an article because it was written some time ago or because it is not addressing a topic that particularly interests you; but even then, you can behave as a member of the writer's intended audience by reading the headnote that will provide you with context on when, and why, the piece was originally written.

In the second type of reading—let's call it "critical reading" or "rhetorical reading"—you read a document not as the intended reader but as a student, as someone studying it

to appreciate the strategies and techniques used by its
writer. That is, this time you are reading in a way similar to
how a car enthusiast looks at a car or how a musician hears
a symphony or how an engineer looks at a machine; though
you still appreciate the whole thing, you also mentally take it
apart and see what's under the hood or hear the individual
notes and chords. That is, when you read rhetorically, you
not only react to the message, but you also appreciate *how*
the writing gets the job done—the craft, and sometimes the
beauty, of not only the work itself, but how well it works. In
this case, you are reading like a writer—learning new strategies by admiring or criticizing those used by others.

Of course, the two types of reading are not fully
separable—we always do a bit of each. But assuming that
you are reading this book as part of a course in writing,
thinking more about that second kind of reading can help
you to discover a great deal about the way writers do business. Reading in that way asks you to pay attention to the
same things that concerned each writer: shaping an idea to
an audience in a particular form for a particular purpose. If
you keep those things in mind, reading can help make you a
better writer. The book's headnotes can help you to read
critically, because they supply you with some context on the
writer's rhetorical stance—and so can help you consider
how, and *how well*, each author has responded to that situation. You'll hear about the writer's audience in the headnote, you'll learn more about the writer (especially when
the writer is well-known or when the writer's position affects the rhetorical stance), and you'll learn anything else
that is necessary to orient you to the original occasion of
each selection. That way, you'll be in a position to read critically and rhetorically.

Let me offer an extended example of critical, rhetorical
reading. The first item in this book is E. B. White's short
essay, "Education." What is its purpose? (If you haven't read
"Education" yet, take a few minutes to do so now; that way
you can more easily follow the rest of this introduction. I'll
wait here.)

White wrote this brief essay over half a century ago, but
you probably find it to be interesting still, in part because it
concerns a perennial question in our nation: What should
schools be like? Is education better carried out in large,
fully-equipped, but relatively impersonal settings, or in
smaller but intensely personal, schools. Which should count

for more: the efficiencies of an educational system that is "progressive" (the word comes from paragraph two), or the personal traits of the individual classroom teacher? The essay is a personal one, but the issues it raises—as is illustrated by the essays that follow it—are also very public.

What is White's position on the issue? At first it might seem that the author takes no side, that he simply wants to describe objectively the two alternatives and to record his son's experiences in each circumstance. He gives equal time to each school and seems to be in firm control of—and up front with—any personal biases ("I have always rather favored public schools"). Through his light and comic tone White implies that all will be well with his son (the little "scholar") in either circumstance, and that the two schools are to be neither favored nor feared by us. "All one can say is that the situation is different" (paragraph four), not better, in the two places.

Or is it? Many readers—including us—contend that "Education" is less an objective, neutral appraisal than it is a calculated argument that subtly favors the country school. To such readers, White's objective pose is only that—a created pose, an attempt to create a genial, sympathetic, and trustworthy speaker. By caring so obviously for his son (final paragraph), by confessing his biases, and by treating both schools with distance and detachment and reliable detail, White creates what rhetoricians call *ethos*—that quality of a piece of writing that persuades through the character of the speaker or writer. By poking gentle humor at just about everything—his son "the scholar"; his wife the prim graduate of Miss Winsor's private schools; himself "the victim of a young ceramist"; and, of course, both schools—White makes himself seem enormously sympathetic and trustworthy: fair-minded and unflappable, balanced and detached.

But is this reliable speaker arguing or describing? Those who see the essay as an argument for the ways of the country school can point to the emotional aspects of the essay—to its pathos, in other words. The image of the one-room schoolhouse, for instance, is imprinted in positive terms on the U.S. psyche, and White exploits that image for his argumentative purposes. The "scholar" walks miles through the snow to get his education; like the schoolhouse itself, he has the self-reliance and weather-resistance to care for himself and to fit into a class with children both younger and older; and he learns a practical curriculum—there is "no time at all for the esoteric"—"just as fast and as hard as he can." It is all Abraham Lincoln, *Little House on the Prairie,* and Ben Franklin arriving in Philadelphia, isn't it? And the teacher who presides over the country school appeals to the reader's emotions as only The Ideal Mother can. This teacher-mother is not only "a guardian of their health, their clothes, their habits . . . and their snowball engagements," but "she has been doing this sort of Augean task for twenty years, and is both kind and wise. She cooks for the children on the stove that heats the room, and she can cool their passions or warm their soup with equal competence."

No such individual Ideal Mother presides over the city school. Instead, that school is presided over by a staff of Educational Professionals—a bus driver, half a dozen anonymous teachers, a nurse, an athletic instructor, dieti-tians. The school itself is institutional, regimented, profes-sionalized. There the scholar is "worked on," "supervised," "pulled." Like the one-room schoolhouse, the regimented institution is ingrained in the national psyche. But in this case the emotional appeal is negative, for "The System" is something that Americans instinctively resist. True, the city school is no prison, and true, the scholar in this school learns "to read with a gratifying discernment." But the ac-complishments remain rather abstract. Faced with such an education, such a school, no wonder the students literally become ill. At least that is the implication of the end of paragraph three, where the account of the city school is concluded with an account of the networks of professional physicians that discuss diseases that never seem to appear in the country schools.

For these reasons many readers see "Education" as an ar-gument against the city school (and its "progressive" educa-tion) and an endorsement of the country one (and its "basics"). They see the essay as a comparison with an aim like most comparison essays: to show a preference. The evaluative aim is carried out by reference to specific crite-ria, namely that schools are better if they are less structured and if they make students want to attend (because moti-vated students learn better); a structured, supervised curriculum and facilities are inferior to a personalized, un-structured environment that makes students love school. Days at the country school pass "just like lightning"; to at-tend the country school the boy is willing literally to walk through snowdrifts, whereas to get to the city school he must be escorted to the bus stop—or be "pulled" there. The country school is full of "surprises" and "individual instruction," whereas the city school is full of supervision; there are no surprises in the "progressive" school. In a real sense, therefore, White persuades not only by the force of his personality or through emotional appeals but also through hard evidence, what rhetoricians call "logos." "Education" amounts to an argument by example wherein the single case—the boy scholar—stands for many such cases. This case study persuades like other case studies: by being presented as representative. White creates through his unnamed son, who is described as typical in every way, a representative example that stands for the education of Everychild. The particular details provided in the essay become not mere "concrete description" but hard evidence, summoned to support White's implicit thesis. The logic of the piece seems to go something like this: "Country schools are a bit superior to city ones. They make up for what they lack in facilities with a more personal, less authoritarian atmosphere that children respond to."

E. B. White, then, wins his reader's assent by means of ethos, pathos, and logos. But the country-school approach is also reinforced by the essay's arrangement. Notice, for example, that the essay begins and ends with favorable accounts of the country school. In other words, the emphatic first and final positions of the essay are reserved for the virtues of country schools, whereas the account of the city school is buried in the unemphatic middle of the essay. The article could easily have begun with the second paragraph (wouldn't sentence two of paragraph two have made a successful opener?), but such a strategy would have promoted the value of the city school. By choosing to add the loving vignette of the Ideal Teacher in his opening paragraph, White disposes his readers to favor country schools from the very start. Notice too that the comparison of the two schools in the body of "Education" proceeds from city to country. Again, it didn't have to be so; White could have discussed the country school first, or he could have gone back and forth from city to country more often (adopting what some handbooks call an "alternating" method of comparison as opposed to the "divided" pattern that White actually did use). By choosing to deal first with the city school, all in one lump, and then to present the country school in another lump, White furthered his persuasive aim. After all, most "preference comparisons" move from the inferior item to the superior one. In other words, writers of comparisons usually move from "this one is good" to "but this other one is even better," rather than vice versa. So when White opts to deal first with the city schools, he subtly reinforces his persuasive end through very indirect means. White's arrangement serves his purpose in two ways, then: it permits him to end with the item he wishes to prefer; and it permits him to add an introductory paragraph that places his country school in that favorable spot as well.

Even the arrangement of details within White's individual paragraphs serves his goals. It appears that the central paragraphs (three, four, and five) are arranged chronologically, that details in those paragraphs are arranged according to the rhythm of the school day. But a closer examination shows that paragraph three closes on a note of sickness. That detail could have come earlier in the paragraph, but White places the negative detail in the emphatic final position. Similarly, the two paragraphs on the country school are manipulated for rhetorical ends. Why does White divide the account of the country school into two paragraphs? (After all, he dealt with the city school in one paragraph.) By doing so he is able to give special emphasis to the first sentence of one of his paragraphs, "There is no supervised play," highlighting thereby a key difference between the two schools. (It is also possible that publication in *Harper's* called for shorter paragraphs.)

A critical reading of "Education" must also consider expression, those sentence and word choices that are sometimes equated with the style of a particular essay or author. Like most rhetoricians, we personally resist the idea that "style is the person"—that style is something inherent in a writer, that it amounts to a sort of genetic code or set of fingerprints that are idiosyncratic to each person, that it is possible to speak generically of Ben Franklin's style or Martin Luther King's style or E. B. White's style. It might be more appropriate to think of style as characteristic of a particular *occasion* for writing, as something that is as appropriate to reader and subject and genre as it is to a particular author. Words and sentences are chosen in response to rhetorical and social circumstances, and those words and sentences change as the occasion changes. If it is possible to characterize E. B. White's style or Alice Walker's style in general (and I'm not sure even of that), then it is so only with respect to certain kinds of writing that they did again and again and again. For when those writers found themselves writing outside *Harper's* or *The New Yorker* (in White's case) or outside fiction (in Walker's), they did indeed adopt different stylistic choices. It is probably wiser to focus not on the apparent idiosyncrasies associated with a Franklin or a King or a Walker or an E. B. White, but on the particular word and sentence choices at work in a particular rhetorical situation.

Take the case at hand. What stylistic choices are worthy of note in "Education"? How has White chosen particular sentence patterns and words in order to further the aims of his essay?

The sentences of White's essay are certainly appropriate for public discourse. There are roughly a thousand words and fifty sentences in "Education," so average sentence length comes to about twenty words. Many are shorter than twenty words, though (the shortest is five words), and only one forty-three-word sentence seems particularly long. The result is that this essay can probably be readily comprehended by most adults, without its sentences creating the impression of superficiality or childishness. (The sentences in White's book for children *Charlotte's Web*, by contrast, have an average length of about twelve words.)

Moreover, White's sentences are unpretentious. They move in conventional ways—from subjects and verbs to objects and modifiers. There are no sentence inversions (violations of the normal subject/verb/object order), few distracting interrupters (the parentheses and the "I suspect" in that one long sentence in paragraph two are exceptions), and few lengthy opening sentence modifiers that keep us too long from subjects and verbs. Not only that, the sentences are simple and unpretentious in another sense: White comparatively rarely uses subordinate (or modifying) clauses— clauses containing a subject and verb and beginning with *who* or *although* or *that* or *because* or the like. There are only two such modifying (or dependent) clauses in the first and third paragraphs, for instance, and just five in the second; if you don't think that is a low number, compare it to a six-hundred-word sample of your own prose. When White does add length to a sentence, he does it not by adding complex clauses that modify other clauses, but by adding independent clauses (ones that begin with *and* or *but*) and by adding phrases and modifiers in parallel series. Some examples?

The children's teacher is a guardian "of their health, their clothes, their habits, their mothers, and their snowball engagements"; the boy "learned fast, kept well, and we were satisfied"; the bus "would sweep to a halt, open its mouth, suck the boy in, and spring away." And so forth. The *ands* make White's essay informal and conversational, never remote or scholarly or full of disclaimers and qualifiers.

White uses relatively simple sentence patterns in "Education," then, but his prose is still anything but simple. Some of his sentences are beautifully parallel: "she can cool their passions or warm their soup"; "she conceives their costumes, cleans up their noses, and shares their confidences"; "in a cinder court he played games supervised by an athletic instructor, and in a cafeteria he ate lunch worked out by a dietitian"; "when the snow is deep or the motor is dead"; "rose hips in fall, snowballs in winter." These precise, mirror-image parallel structures are known as isocolons to rhetoricians. White delights in them and in the artful informality they create. He uses parallel structures and relentless coordination—*and* after *and* after *and*—to make his prose accessible to a large audience of appreciative readers. And he uses those lists of specific items in parallel series to give his writing its remarkably concrete, remarkably vivid quality.

That brings us to White's word choices. They too contributed to White's purposes. Remember the sense of detachment and generosity in White's narrative voice, the ethos of involvement and detachment apparent in the speaker? In large measure that is the result of White's word choices. For instance, White has the ability to attach mock-heroic terminology to his descriptions so that he comes across as balanced and wise, as someone who doesn't take himself or his world too seriously. The boy is a "scholar" who "sallied forth" on a "journey" to school or to "make Indian weapons of a semi-deadly nature." The gentle hyperbole fits in well with the classical allusion inherent in the word "Augean" (one of Hercules' labors was to clean the Augean stables): there is a sophistication and worldly wisdom in the speaker's voice that qualifies him to speak on this subject. And remember the discussion of whether White's aim was purely descriptive or more argumentative in character? White's metaphors underscore his argumentative aim: the city school bus "was as punctual as death," a sort of macabre monster that "would sweep to a halt, open its mouth, suck the boy in, and spring away with an angry growl"; or it is "like a train picking up a bag of mail." At the country school, by contrast, the day passes "just like lightning." If the metaphors do not provide enough evidence of White's persuasive aim, consider the connotations of words—their emotional charges, that is—that are associated with the city school: *regimented, supervised, worked on, uniforms, fevers.* And then compare these with the connotation of some words White associates with the country school: *surprises, bungalow, weather-resistant, individual instruction, guardian,* and so forth. The diction and sentence choices made by White indeed do reinforce his argumentative purpose.

This analysis by no means exhausts the full measure of rhetorical sophistication that E. B. White brings to the composition of "Education." You may have noticed other tactics at work, or you may disagree with some of the generalizations presented here. But the purpose of this discussion is not to detail the rhetoric of White's "Education." It is merely to illustrate a method of critical reading that you might employ as you read the selections in this book and the public rhetoric that you encounter in your life each day. The point has been to encourage you to read not just for *what* is said—though this is crucial—but for *how* it is said as well. For reading is as "rhetorical" an activity as is writing. It depends on an appreciation of how writer, subject, and reader are all "negotiated" through a particular document.

If you read for "how" as well as "what," the distinction between the two may begin to shorten for you. Appreciation of the rhetoric of public discourse can make you more skeptical of the arguments presented to you and to other citizens. It can make you a reader less likely to be won over on slender grounds, more likely to remain the doubter than the easy victim or trusting soul who accepts all arguments at face value. Therefore, whether or not you decide to take part in any of the particular "conversations" captured in this book, your thinking can be stimulated by critical reading.

Not only that, you'll find yourself growing as a writer; if you read critically, you'll begin to adopt and adapt for your own purposes the best rhetorical maneuvers on display in this book and elsewhere. What is a particular writer's real aim? What evidence is used to win the assent of readers? How does a particular writer establish credibility? What kind of emotional and logical appeals are at work in a given circumstance? How does the arrangement of a presentation influence its reception? How can sentence style and word choices sustain a writer's aim? By asking and answering questions like these, you can gain confidence as reader and writer. By becoming better able to understand and appreciate the conversations going on around you, you'll learn to make more powerful and sophisticated contributions to the discussions that most engage you personally. Critical reading of the selections in this book can make you a better writer, a better citizen.

Visual Conversations: Reading Images as Texts

We live in an increasingly visual world. Advertisements and political ads, the CNN television news screen and the websites we visit, newspapers and film adaptations of books like *The Lord of the Rings*, all do their work through a combination of words and images; not long ago, in many of these cases, words might have had to do the job on their own. Even music has become visual: "I don't like the way that song looks," a young girl listening to the radio blurted out, referring to the music video she had in her head. Times change. Some would even say that the images now have a greater effect than the words.

In such a world, where music *looks* a certain way and when images have messages that are at least as strong as words, being a critical reader and an effective writer—the things we've been discussing in this introduction—requires another related skill: the ability to "read" images. Like the idea of *looking at* music, *reading* images might seem like an odd concept. But you do it all the time, really. Just as you react, both viscerally (on a gut level) and analytically to that which you read, you also have gut reactions to images, reactions that can then be made more rich and thoughtful through critical "reading." Reading an image requires you to first consider that image a "text"—and in fact, many rhetoricians would define images in just that way. A text need not be just words on a page; it is anything that can be interpreted, a rhetorical act (whether it be speaking, writing, or presenting a visual image) that can be used persuasively. Defined in those ways, images can be "read" critically using techniques similar to how we "read" written texts (as discussed in the previous section).

So, reading E. B. White's "Education" as a rhetorical text requires us to pay close attention to details, to the writer's tactics and strategies in arranging the material, to the words that he chooses, and to the tone and mood that he creates. Each of those strategies of critical reading applies to the reading of images as well: we need to consider not only the choice of details in the image, but also the reasons they are included, how they are arranged on the page or screen (or sometimes in three dimensions), what relationship those images establish with the audience, and what message they seem to carry into some ongoing conversations. Not all that different, really, than reading a written text, though it requires a slightly different vocabulary: what writers call arrangement, a visual artist might call composition, for example. But despite the terminology difference, reading carefully and critically can spur responses and help you to consider strategies of persuasion that you might add to your own rhetorical repertoire.

To give you practice with reading images, in this edition of *Conversations* you'll find six sections called "Visual Conversations." These sections are a collection of images that speak to audiences—and to each other—about a particular issue, at a particular time, and for a particular purpose. Sometimes that purpose is very obvious; on other occasions, as with the example of E. B. White's "Education," that purpose might be a bit more submerged, and require your careful analysis to find it. But as with all forms of analysis, expending the energy can make you a clearer thinker, and so a better writer as well.

For example, you might consider the *Time Magazine* cover that is depicted at the beginning of Visual Conversations 1. This section collects images that illustrate some of the great variety of educational settings that exist—the places where people learn. What can we say about this particular image (reprinted on the next page)?

Let's start with that which we can observe without doing any substantial interpretation. The *Time Magazine* cover shows a woman and four children. The background seems to be a house, and the youngest child is seated at a desk with a book before her (though her attention is not on that book). And the image is accompanied by a question in large print ("Is home schooling good for America?") and a statement in smaller lettering (which reads "Like a growing number of families, the Dekkers of Texas are doing education their own

way"). Everyone is smiling and they are physically close; one boy actually has his hand on another's shoulder. Those are the basics.

Then we might consider other, more complex facets of this visual that emerge when you pay closer attention. The photograph is balanced—the leg of the desk is precisely in the middle of the photograph (creating what artists call a visual axis), and the people are framed on both sides by the green leaves of plants. In the original cover, the shirt colors also balance the photograph, using the complementary colors of blue for the woman and orange for the boy on the far right. There are also a number of horizontal elements in the photograph: the concrete line of the porch, the book, the top of the desk, the horizontal lines on the shirts of two of the boys, and the lines of mortar between the blocks on the house. There are also vertical elements: the people themselves are the most striking verticals, but the leg of the desk and lines in the mortar of the house—as well as the block typeface—are also oriented vertically.

A visual artist would tell us that this photo's composition has been stylized carefully. It creates stability and balance through the use of the horizontal and vertical elements as well as the complementary colors. That artist might also note that this effect is achieved through the design principles of unity and variety: the variety of races, ages, genders, shapes, sizes, colors, and so on are contained within the unifying elements of its concrete borders (borders that are "concrete" in more ways than one) and the structure or framed fence.

Of course, we need not be visual artists to notice these things (though having that vocabulary can help us conceptualize what we find). Nor do we need to be trained in the visual arts to notice other things: that the house seems to be suburban, that the woman seems to fit the "soccer mom" image, and that her family is well-groomed and what some might call "clean cut." (One of our editors saw this as having resemblances to the classic *American Gothic*, though at the same time parodying that well-known painting.) But just when we are ready to proclaim this family "traditional," we might notice a number of other things that subvert restrictive or traditional notions of the American family and American education: this family is not all of one race, for example, and this "school" is located outside a house rather than in a classroom, expanding or even undermining our traditional notions of what it means to be "at school." The more you look, the more you will find.

As you might have noticed, as we observe more specifics about the photo, we are moving naturally from observation to interpretation. As we interpret, we are asking questions that are similar to the ones we asked about E. B. White's "Education": Does this image present an objective look at the home-schooled family, or does it make a subtle argument about its value? That is, does it leave the question on the cover stand, or does it start to answer that question with the visuals (or perhaps even with the small print that proclaims that this "family" is "doing education their own way")? Of course, when we move from observation to interpretation, we must also consider what past experiences and attitudes we bring to those interpretations, such as our gender, our age, our own educational experiences, our values (and those of our parents), our immediate environment, our current mood or emotional state.

We can't overcome the biases we bring to interpretation, nor can we answer questions about the photographer's motives with certainty. But from the observations above, we might certainly posit that this visual seems to argue for the value of home schooling. The carefully constructed image, the pleasing colors, the smiling children (who are free of the sometimes dull walls of a classroom), the caring attitude of the mother and family members, the diversity and unity, and even the firm foundation on which this family literally stands all can be interpreted to suggest that home schooling is a viable alternative for the new American family. Could it be read in other ways as well?

This picture, and this topic, also can illustrate the ways in which the topics in *Conversations*, and the conversations that they suggest, intersect. For example, you might consider the effect of this widely distributed magazine's coverage of this topic on home schooling, and thus how media influences public opinion—a key topic of Part 2 of this book. You might consider what gender issues are raised by the fact that this picture quite accurately places the mother, not the father, "in the picture" of home schooling—an issue related to those discussed by pieces in Part 3. And as we've already noted, this picture—and this image—is deeply embedded in definitions of what constitutes a family in our culture, the center of Part 4's dialogue. You might go on to ask what this visual says about social class as it relates to home schooling, considering its depiction of what seems to be a middle- or upper-class family and home. What this suggests about equality in this country and its educational system has implications for the dialogues in both Part 1 and Part 5. (After all, is home schooling an option for single moms or families that need two incomes? How much "school choice" do they have? And what becomes of those who lack a stable family and education?) Finally, considering how much of the home schooling movement is driven by families that want to stress religious values, how might home schooling change perspectives on science—and what points of conflict are possible between science and religion in the home school curriculum (as is discussed in Part 6)?

As you "read" the images that constitute the "visual conversations" in this book, be open not only to the many topics for conversation that they introduce, but also to learning more about the ways that visual rhetoric persuades. That sensitivity can help you to become a more savvy reader of the images that bombard you daily; it can also make you a more effective communicator—because being a writer now often involves features of design as well. If you can add to your skill with words even some basic techniques of document design and visual enhancement, you will find that your rhetorical abilities—what Aristotle called your "available means of persuasion"—become significantly more diverse and extensive.

Education

Introduction

Americans have always been passionate about issues related to education. Why? For one thing, education issues affect every American in a personal way. True, there is a strong anti-intellectual strain in our national culture; but it is also true that Americans pursue with a passion the ideal of "education for all," both as a means of self-improvement and as the source of the enlightened citizenry required by democratic institutions. For another thing, education issues are decided locally and immediately. The relatively decentralized nature of our educational "system" (actually, U.S. education is hardly as monolithic as the term *system* implies) encourages continuing and passionate public discussion among citizens interested in shaping the policies and practices of local schools. Portions of three of those discussions are included in this section.

The title question that defines the first set of readings—"Is Public Education Working?"—is a risky one to ask. What if the answer is no? What are the implications of finding our educational programs inadequate, especially in a society that values education as much as we do? Despite the risk, however, it is a question that is being asked with increasing frequency and urgency; in the past decade, a number of committees and commissions launched well-publicized reform efforts aimed at everything from teacher education and accountability to classroom climate and curriculum. Frequent and high-stakes testing has been one of the most visible responses to claims that the schools *are not* working, driven by the controversial "No Child Left Behind" initiative of the Department of Education. And there have been many other efforts to jump start what are seen as failing schools over the past decade. Presidents George H. W. Bush and Clinton promoted reform efforts that they believed would invigorate U.S. education. Those calls for reform, as well as many alternative plans, can be seen in the selections included here, raising a whole host of discussion points: Is discipline a major problem in schools? Is school size the problem? What elements of the curriculum are most crucial? Should we emphasize learning skills—problem solving, critical thinking, flexibility, independent decision making—or a body of knowledge that all educated folks should know? Or should we focus on vocationalism, preparing students for their future work? Should the way that schools are funded be reconsidered, to even out differences between the "haves" and the "have-nots"? Or would that undermine a cornerstone of our educational tradition, local control? Should schools be privatized? Should citizens have more choice about what schools their children attend? Would a voucher system, or charter schools, facilitate that choice? Or would that widen the gap in educational opportunities now available to rich and poor? And what about the teachers? Are they trained adequately, paid adequately, kept current in their fields, and given enough (or too much) autonomy over their classroom? Are they held accountable? And faced with the challenges of our education systems— safety issues, issues of morality or religion, concerns about the quality of education, school and class sizes, and so on— is it reasonable for parents to opt out of public education on behalf of their children and to instead educate their children at home? The list seems endless—as are the available conversations.

The second set of readings addresses the question "What's College For?" In a country in which growing numbers of students go to college, and in which we are hearing more and more references to "K–16 education," it is a question that has a good deal of exigency. (The question likely has a great deal of personal exigency for you as well.) In broad terms, the questions can be posed this way: Is college an opportunity for personal growth and general intellectual development? Or is it a means to economic advancement? If college should foster both general education and professional specialization, then in what proportions should it do so? And through what means? Is college designed for the intellectual elite who are sophisticated enough to pursue truly advanced learning, or is it something that ought to be within reach of most high school graduates? Should all students be encouraged to go to college, or are there other, more suitable paths for some? Or would making those distinctions tend to divide the intellectual class from the working class? Do colleges hold the keys to middle-class status? And what are the obligations of educators to develop not only intellectual and professional capacities, but also civic skills and knowledge? As you read the selections here, you will no doubt also reflect on your own choices and experiences; the combination of the two can lead to some nicely balanced writing.

The third set of readings asks another key educational question: "What Does It Mean to Be Literate?" It is a question that has roots in the most basic forms of education—after all, the ability to read and write are fundamental to most parts of our education. But in a technology-saturated society, there are an increasing number of literacies that are required of us, literacies that have become part of what it means to be educated. For example, you may hear people speak of civic literacy—the knowledge of, and ability to discourse on, issues of public concern. Or you've likely heard of information literacy—the ability to access, evaluate, and incorporate the massive amounts of information available to us in a wired world. And, of course, to plug into the wired world requires technological literacy—the ability to use the most current technologies. So, while the first two essays in this section tell of two well-known Americans' struggles to achieve the literacy expected of educated individuals, the last three examine new struggles to attain information and technological literacy when access to current technologies is not available, some claim, to the economically disadvantaged. These essays explore the so-called digital divide from three differing perspectives.

And in this part's "Visual Conversations" section, you will have the opportunity to see the face of education through images. This section will ask you to consider whether the "place(s) of education"—the settings within which children learn— should also be a subject of public conversations. By "reading" these images, you will gain further insight into the challenges that face citizens as they attempt to educate their youth in all sorts of places. You'll also be asked to consider how learning is affected by the physical space in which learning occurs (or where it fails to).

Taken as a whole, this first part of *Conversations* invites you into a wider ranging set of individual, but related, discussions—discussions with which you have a great deal of knowledge and experience. If you bring those experiences to that which you read, you will no doubt have a great deal to add to this crucial set of conversations.

Is Public Education Working?

E. B. White

EDUCATION

E. B. White (1899–1985), who contributed regularly to The New Yorker *and whose work has been collected into several books, was perhaps America's most popular essayist. You may also know him as the author of the children's classic* Charlotte's Web *(1952). First published in 1939 in* Harper's *and in White's* One Man's Meat, *the following comparison of two educational philosophies remains relevant even in the twenty-first century.*

I have an increasing admiration for the teacher in the country 1
school where we have a third-grade scholar in attendance. She
not only undertakes to instruct her charges in all the subjects
of the first three grades, but she manages to function quietly
and effectively as a guardian of their health, their clothes, their
habits, their mothers, and their snowball engagements. She
has been doing this sort of Augean task for twenty years, and is
both kind and wise. She cooks for the children on the stove
that heats the room, and she can cool their passions or warm
their soup with equal competence. She conceives their costumes, cleans up their messes, and shares their confidences.
My boy already regards his teacher as his great friend, and I
think tells her a great deal more than he tells us.

The shift from city school to country school was something 2
we worried about quietly all last summer. I have always rather
favored public school over private school, if only because in
public school you meet a greater variety of children. This bias
of mine, I suspect, is partly an attempt to justify my own past
(I never knew anything but public schools) and partly an involuntary defense against getting kicked in the shins by a young

ceramist on his way to the kiln. My wife was unacquainted with public schools, never having been exposed (in her early life) to anything more public than the washroom of Miss Winsor's. Regardless of our backgrounds, we both knew that the change in schools was something that concerned not us but the scholar himself. We hoped it would work out all right. In New York our son went to a medium-priced private institution with semi-progressive ideas of education, and modern plumbing. He learned fast, kept well, and we were satisfied. It was an electric, colorful, regimented existence with moments of pleasurable pause and giddy incident. The day the Christmas angel fainted and had to be carried out by one of the Wise Men was educational in the highest sense of the term. Our scholar gave imitations of it around the house for weeks afterward, and I doubt if it ever goes completely out of his mind.

3   His days were rich in formal experience. Wearing overalls and an old sweater (the accepted uniform of the private seminary), he sallied forth at morn accompanied by a nurse or a parent and walked (or was pulled) two blocks to a corner where the school bus made a flag stop. This flashy vehicle was as punctual as death: seeing us waiting at the cold curb, it would sweep to a halt, open its mouth, suck the boy in, and spring away with an angry growl. It was a good deal like a train picking up a bag of mail. At school the scholar was worked on for six or seven hours by half a dozen teachers and a nurse, and was revived on orange juice in mid-morning. In a cinder court he played games supervised by an athletic instructor, and in a cafeteria he ate lunch worked out by a dietitian. He soon learned to read with gratifying facility and discernment and to make Indian weapons of a semi-deadly nature. Whenever one of his classmates fell low of a fever the news was put on the wires and there were breathless phone calls to physicians, discussing periods of incubation and allied magic.

4   In the country all one can say is that the situation is different, and somehow more casual. Dressed in corduroys, sweatshirt, and short rubber boots, and carrying a tin dinner pail, our scholar departs at the crack of dawn for the village school, two and a half miles down the road, next to the cemetery. When the road is open and the car will start, he makes the journey by motor, courtesy of his old man. When the snow is deep or the motor is dead or both, he makes it on the hoof. In the afternoons he walks or hitches all or part of the way home in fair weather, gets transported in foul. The schoolhouse is a two-room frame building, bungalow type, shingles stained a burnt brown with weather-resistant stain. It has a chemical

toilet in the basement and two teachers above the stairs. One takes the first three grades, the other the fourth, fifth, and sixth. They have little or no time for individual instruction, and no time at all for the esoteric. They teach what they know themselves, just as fast and as hard as they can manage. The pupils sit still at their desks in class, and do their milling around outdoors during recess.

There is no supervised play. They play cops and robbers   5
(only they call it "Jail") and throw things at one another—snowballs in winter, rose hips in fall. It seems to satisfy them. They also construct darts, pinwheels, and "pick-up-sticks" (jackstraws), and the school itself does a brisk trade in penny candy, which is for sale right in the classroom and which contains "surprises." The most highly prized surprise is a fake cigarette, made of cardboard, fiendishly lifelike.

The memory of how apprehensive we were at the beginning   6
is still strong. The boy was nervous about the change too. The tension, on that first fair morning in September when we drove him to school, almost blew the windows out of the sedan. And when later we picked him up on the road, wandering along with his little blue lunch-pail, and got his laconic report "All right" in answer to our inquiry about how the day had gone, our relief was vast. Now, after almost a year of it, the only difference we can discover in the two school experiences is that in the country he sleeps better at night—and *that* probably is more the air than the education. When grilled on the subject of school-in-country vs. school-in-city, he replied that the chief difference is that the day seems to go so much quicker in the country. "Just like lightning," he reported.

Paul E. Peterson

A LIBERAL CASE
FOR VOUCHERS

A professor of government at Harvard and Editor-in-Chief of Education Next, *Paul Peterson has studied the issue of school choice for a number of years. His research group has attempted to determine the effects of voucher systems on the education of students in Milwaukee and other cities. In October 1999, he published the following essay on vouchers in a special issue of* New Republic *magazine given over to "the future of education reform."* New Republic, *founded nearly a century ago in order to promote a liberal agenda—hence its title—is now a respected middle-of-the-road forum for discussions of politics, culture, and public policy.*

1   Perhaps you're familiar with the "skimming" argument against school vouchers. As this line of thinking goes, the parents most likely to opt for vouchers will be the ones who are already most involved with their children's education—which, on average, will mean the parents of the most motivated and gifted students. Once the best and the brightest flee to private schools, public schools will only get worse; this debilitating cycle will continue until the best students are skimmed off and the only kids left in public schools are those with the fewest skills and the least-involved parents—in other words, the students most in need of help. "Vouchers are like leeches," says North Carolina Governor Jim Hunt. "They drain the lifeblood—public support—from our schools." Bob Chase, president of the National Education Association, concurs: Establishing a system of vouchers, he says, would be like "bleeding a patient to death."

2   We liberals are sensitive to this argument because we know that needy students are now getting the short end of the educational stick. Yet, while liberals are right to be concerned about these students, new data from a privately financed voucher program in Texas suggest that we should give vouchers a second, more serious look. Far from aggravating income and racial disparities in education, vouchers may actually help to ameliorate them.

3   In April 1998, the Children's Educational Opportunity (CEO) Foundation offered vouchers to any low-income child in San Antonio's Edgewood school district. Almost all of the district's 13,490 students were eligible for the program, because Edgewood is among the poorest of the city's twelve school districts—more than 90 percent of its students are economically disadvantaged, and 93 percent are Latino. (Nonetheless, the district, which receives 90 percent of its funding from state and federal aid, spends more than $6,000 per pupil, which exceeds the state average.)

4   The vouchers were hardly paltry: Providing up to $3,600 a year for elementary school students and $4,000 a year for those in high school, they would cover tuition at most San Antonio private schools, which for voucher students averages less than

$2,000 annually. And, once a child's family decided to use vouchers, the CEO Foundation promised to continue providing them until that child graduated from high school, as long as he or she still lived in Edgewood. In addition, students could use the vouchers anywhere in San Antonio, even in public schools outside Edgewood that were willing to accept them. In the program's first year (the 1998–1999 school year), approximately 800 Edgewood students made use of the vouchers.

The Texas Federation of Teachers howled that private 5 schools would "cherry pick" the best students and predicted the program would "shorten the honor roll" in public schools. "Right now, I don't have the profile of every child," Edgewood School Superintendent Dolores Muñoz said on PBS's "News Hour with Jim Lehrer," "[but] I guarantee you that at least 80 percent will be the high-achieving students."

To make matters worse, stories of private schools shutting 6 out applicants quickly circulated. Edgewood's school board president, Manuel Garza, wrote in the *San Antonio Express News* that he had received a call from "a mother . . . for help because their application to the [Horizon program] had been denied. . . . I asked why she was denied. The mother said she was a single mom, had two jobs, and was told she was unacceptable because she could not dedicate time for extracurricular requirements, like helping out with homework and fund-raising." In other words, not only were the voucher students an unusually strong group academically, but the private schools were then allegedly winnowing their ranks even further.

But data from a recently completed evaluation (funded by 7 the Packard Foundation) that included results from tests of student achievement and questionnaires filled out by parents during testing sessions yields a more complicated, and more encouraging, picture. (Standard techniques were employed to ensure a representative sample, and Mathematica Policy Research, a well-respected evaluation firm with contracts with the Department of Education and other government agencies, collected the data.)

It's true that the private schools had only limited capacity, in 8 part because the program was unveiled in April and went into effect the very next August. Yet there is little evidence that the schools were weeding out all but the best students. For example, on the math component of the Iowa Test of Basic Skills, on which the national median score falls at the fiftieth percentile, the voucher students, upon arriving at their new schools, scored at the thirty-seventh percentile, while the students who stayed in public school scored at the thirty-fifth—a difference that is not statistically significant. In reading, voucher students scored at the thirty-fifth percentile, while public school students scored at the twenty-eighth. This difference is significant but is hardly the gaping disparity voucher opponents predicted. In addition, just 23 percent of the voucher students had been enrolled in programs for gifted students, while 29 percent of the students who stayed in public school were.

9   These results are consistent with analyses conducted by the research department at the Edgewood public schools, which compared the test scores of students who later accepted vouchers with the scores of those who remained behind. Never made public, perhaps because it directly contradicted the school superintendent's assertions, the research did not show a significant "skimming" effect. In the authors' technical language: "[F]ew statistically significant differences [in average test scores] are to be found between [the voucher] students . . . and those not . . . identified" as voucher students.

10   Apparently, families have many reasons for choosing private schools. They may be looking for better schools for children who are doing poorly just as often as they are looking for other schools for bright youngsters. But admission to private school is one thing; keeping one's place in school is another. Since private schools can suspend or expel students more easily than public schools can, critics say, they are able to weed out the worse students. Again, the numbers refute this seemingly logical argument. Suspension rates were equal for the voucher students and the Edgewood public school students—around five percent for both groups. And what about income? Average household income was nearly identical—right around $16,000. The students' ethnic background (96 percent Latino) and their levels of welfare dependency and residential stability were also extremely similar. Quite apart from suspensions, the voucher students were more likely to remain in the same school for the year and were just as likely to return to that school the next year.

11   This isn't to say that there were no distinctions whatsoever among the students. Eight percent of voucher students were enrolled in some sort of special education, while the figure for public school students was 16 percent. There were also some modest demographic differences between the two groups of parents. The average mother of a voucher student had completed twelve years of education, compared to eleven years for the average public school mother. Half of the voucher-student mothers worked full time, compared to just 37 percent of the mothers who kept their kids in public school. Only 22 percent of voucher-student mothers were on food stamps, but 33 percent of public school mothers were.

But these small distinctions are hardly enough to justify the   12
extreme resistance to vouchers. For one thing, those helped by
vouchers were far from well-off—the parents reported making
less than $16,000 a year! There are plenty of other government
programs, from Pell Grants to the Earned Income Tax Credit,
that predominantly benefit the working poor, and nobody
(well, almost nobody) protests them on the grounds that they
don't benefit people further down the economic ladder.
Support for vouchers is particularly strong among minority
families, especially those living in cities. According to a recent
survey undertaken at Stanford University, 85 percent of the
inner-city poor favor a voucher plan, compared with 59 percent of more advantaged parents who live in the suburbs.
Asked if they "strongly" favor a voucher plan, 58 percent of
poor urbanites agreed, compared to just one-third of upper-
middle-class suburbanites.

More important, though, vouchers have the potential to im-   13
prove socioeconomic and racial integration, as long as they are
generous enough to cover most of the tuition and as long as
schools are prohibited from racial or ethnic discrimination in
admissions. Remember, our public school system is *already*
plagued by vast inequalities. Because most school funding comes
through local property taxes, disparities among affluent suburban schools and city or rural schools are legendary. The story on
race is no better: Despite three decades of busing, public schools
today are more segregated, not less. In 1997, 69 percent of
African Americans attended schools composed predominantly of
minority students, up from 64 percent in 1973. For Latinos, the
increase is much steeper, from 57 percent to 75 percent over the
past 25 years. Today, despite federal interventions ranging from
Head Start to compensatory education, we have disturbingly
large test-score gaps between cities and suburbs, as well as between blacks and whites. According to one 1994 survey, only 43
percent of urban fourth-graders read at a basic level, compared
with 63 percent of students in nonurban areas.

Private schools, on the other hand, are already more racially   14
integrated than public ones. University of Texas Professor Jay
Greene estimates that private school classrooms are seven percentage points more integrated than public schools. Examining
Department of Education data, he also found more interracial
friendships in private schools than in public ones (as reported
by students) as well as less interracial fighting (as reported by
administrators, teachers, and students). And, sure enough, in
all the voucher programs for which we have been able to obtain
ethnic data, students were less likely—or at least no more
likely—to be attending segregated schools than students

remaining in public school. This isn't surprising, given that private schools can draw students from across school district boundaries, and religious schools provide a common tie that cuts across racial lines.

15   Oh, yes, and how about those voucher families in Edgewood—what do they think of their new schools? More than 60 percent say they are "very satisfied" with the schools' academic quality, compared to 35 percent of the Edgewood public school parents. Similar differences in satisfaction levels are reported by parents regarding school safety, school discipline, and quality of teaching.

16   There are, of course, many other arguments against voucher programs, from the church-and-state issue to questions about for-profit schools. I don't happen to buy those arguments, either, but I'm happy to continue letting pilot programs provide a testing ground. Given the potential of vouchers to achieve more racial and socioeconomic diversity in education—one of the great goals of education reformers since the 1960s—you'd think more liberals would be open to experimenting with them.

Martin Carnoy

DO SCHOOL VOUCHERS
IMPROVE SCHOOL
PERFORMANCE?

Martin Carnoy, a professor of education at Stanford University, has written several books, among them The Different Worlds of Urban and Suburban School Districts. *In January 2001, The* American Prospect *published the following essay, which is something of a response to the previous essay by Paul E. Peterson. The* American Prospect *publishes (every two months) essays on politics, public affairs, and contemporary culture. It is a product of the Hudson Institute, a think tank that claims not to advocate an expressed ideology or political position. According to its website, "the institution's viewpoint embodies skepticism about conventional wisdom, an appreciation of technology's role in achieving progress, optimism about solving problems, a futurist orientation, a commitment to individuality*

and free institutions, and a respect for the importance of reli-
gion, culture, and values in human affairs."

With George W. Bush's assumption of the presidency, a cam- 1
paign to provide vouchers for private schooling may gain new
life. The idea of public funding of private schools is not new, nor
does it belong exclusively to conservative free market reformers.

In the 1960s and early 1970s, academics on the left, such as 2
Christopher Jencks of Harvard University's Kennedy School of
Government, argued that vast differences between the quality
of public schooling for inner-city blacks and suburban whites
could not be resolved within the structure of a residentially
segregated public-education system. Jencks argued for a policy
concept introduced by economist Milton Friedman more than
a decade earlier. Friedman proposed to offer public funds to
families that could only be used for education, but in any educational institution, public or private. Such "vouchers" would
serve to give families increased choice about the kind of education their children received. Friedman saw vouchers as a way
to break the "monopoly" of the public sector over education,
increase consumer choice, and, hence, promote economic
well-being. Jencks saw vouchers as a way of improving educational opportunities for a historically discriminated-against
group within American society. Both shared a distrust of the
state—Friedman of the bureau-centric state interfering with
"democratic" markets, Jencks of the class-centric and race-
centric state reproducing inequality through public education.

But conditions may have changed in the last 40 years. While 3
there is still a glaring gap between the achievement of black
students and that of white students, it has been considerably
narrowed. In the last decade, however, the progress seems to
have stopped, and it is unclear what the causes of the continued disparity might be. In his latest book (co-edited with
Meredith Phillips), *The Black-White Test Score Gap*, Jencks
seems to argue that the biggest cause of the persistent gap is
differences in family characteristics over which schools, public
or private, have very little control. But he does suggest that
some school improvements, like smaller classes or better-
prepared teachers, might make a difference.

With so much attention focused on the problem, voucher ad- 4
vocates have been attempting to prove that private schools
supported by public funds actually can do a better job than
public schools of educating the children most at risk of school
failure—whether because vouchers are a route to smaller
classes and better teachers, or because private schools are superior in other respects. Over the last few years, the leading

proponent of the idea that private schools are demonstrably more effective at educating low-income African-American students has been Harvard Professor Paul Peterson.

5   In the most recent salvo in this dispute, Peterson and his colleagues (David Campbell, also of Harvard; William Howell of the University of Wisconsin, Madison; and Patrick Wolf of Georgetown University) announced last August that their voucher experiments in New York City, Washington, D.C., and Dayton, Ohio, showed that at least some pupils—African Americans—achieve better in private than in public schools. The finding was widely hailed by voucher supporters across the political spectrum as showing that private schools could solve a problem public schools apparently could not: that of raising the lagging achievement of low-income inner-city black children.

6   "This hard evidence is not what teacher unionists want to hear," William Safire noted in *The New York Times*. "The Harvard study shows Bush is on the right side of this. He should embrace the successful voucher students and joyfully join the controversy."

7   But soon after the results were presented, another member of the Peterson team, David Myers, contractor for the New York City part of the research, openly challenged Peterson's interpretation, arguing that the New York results do not show voucher students—even African Americans—with a statistically significant advantage. Earlier voucher studies in Milwaukee and Cleveland seemed to support this more skeptical view.

8   Who is right? How sanguine should we be that black, inner-city pupils would gain by switching to private schools?

9   The short answer is that the three-city study is not nearly as reliable as its authors claim. As a basis for educational policy, it should be interpreted cautiously. A more structured private-school environment with smaller classes and higher-achieving peers could possibly help African Americans make greater gains than if they stayed in public schools. It is also possible that improvements to public schools would yield comparable improvements. But that said, the Peterson results may misrepresent gains that typical low-income African-American students can make by switching to private schools. Using statistical techniques not easily understood by the media or the public, the studies' methodology is laced with potential biases. In the context of an intense ideological push for privatizing education, the question to ask is not whether this latest report overestimates private school effects, but by how much.

10   In four cities—Dayton, New York, Washington, and Charlotte, North Carolina (where data was released more recently)—the Peterson team built evaluations into the voucher

plans themselves. Evaluating these evaluations is not easy, because the researchers have not publicly released their data.

Earlier, in Milwaukee and Cleveland, the Peterson studies   11
were constructed after the fact, in response to research originally carried out by scholars not politically committed to
vouchers. The Peterson estimates in those studies have a different character. For one, the data were available to others and
thus are subject to re-analysis. More important, "experimental"
controls were nonexistent.

The Milwaukee Voucher Experiment

The longest-running voucher initiative in the United States is   12
Milwaukee's. It began in 1990–91 on the initiative of Polly
Williams, an African-American Wisconsin legislator. The
$2,500 vouchers were awarded by lottery to very-low-income
families, almost all of them African Americans, to be used only
in secular private schools. Five private schools agreed to take
1,500 voucher students.

The legislature commissioned John Witte, a professor at the   13
University of Wisconsin, Madison, to study the students who
received vouchers and compare their achievement with similar
students in public schools. Witte found high levels of satisfaction among families who received vouchers, but no significant
differences in math and reading performance between pupils
in private schools and socioeconomically similar students who
remained in public schools.

The initial voucher amount was set at roughly one-half of   14
the annual per-pupil spending in Milwaukee's public schools.
This changed quickly, with private schools demanding and getting a higher voucher payment, until it was at least as high as
(or even higher than) public costs. Of the five private schools
in the initial experiment, one subsequently closed. And of the
initial voucher takers, more than a third left the private schools
by the end of the fourth year.

In 1996 Peterson obtained the Milwaukee data and published   15
his own study, using a "quasi-experimental" design that compared achievement of students who got vouchers in the lottery
with those who did not. Results showed the pupils attending
private schools making gains in math but not reading. At the
same time, Peterson claimed that Witte had misspecified his
model by comparing private-school pupils with those who remained in public schools but had not applied for vouchers.

Witte countered that students who applied but did not get   16
vouchers included students rejected by the private schools;

they displayed falling test scores, unlike most public-school
students of similar background.

17   A third party, Princeton economist Cecilia Rouse, then took
the same data, reworked them, and found that students in private schools made small gains in math but none in reading.
A second Rouse paper found that in Milwaukee gains for low-
income public-school students in smaller classes were higher
than gains of voucher students in private schools.

18   In 1997 the Wisconsin legislature expanded the voucher program to 15,000 low-income students and included religious
schools. The Wisconsin Supreme Court upheld this legislation.
By the school year 2001–02, about 10,000 children will use
vouchers at more than 100 mostly religious private schools.
No one knows whether voucher students are performing better
because, unlike public students, they are not required to take
state-mandated tests.

The Cleveland Voucher Program

19   Cleveland's program began in 1995 with a $2,500 voucher.
Private schools have since unsuccessfully tried to increase it.
Almost all voucher students attend religious schools. On
December 11, the Sixth Circuit Court of Appeals upheld a
lower court ruling that these vouchers gave unconstitutional
aid to religious schools. The U.S. Supreme Court will decide
the program's future.

20   The Peterson group evaluated Cleveland vouchers in 1997.
The study found significant test score gains. In 1997 University
of Indiana researchers led by Kim Metcalf undertook a separate study and found no significant gains. When the Peterson
group re-analyzed Metcalf's data, it found only barely significant gains for private-school students.

21   The Peterson group's new round of research concerns efforts
by well-financed public-school opponents to fund "scholarships" (vouchers) for low-income children to attend private
schools. The programs establish lotteries for parents who
apply, give applicants a baseline test, award scholarships to applicants at random, and later test children who did and did not
receive them. Some families who get vouchers do not actually
send their children to private school, because they either cannot come up with the extra tuition or cannot find convenient
private schools to accept their children.

22   Results for Dayton, New York, and Washington show no significant test score gains for Hispanic and white voucher recipients. Gains for African Americans are found to be statistically

significant in New York and Washington, D.C., and marginally significant in reading (but not math) in Dayton. Reported gains are largest in Washington.

If the same methodology is used, the Charlotte gains are   23
found to be about 6 percentile points in reading and about 6 percentile points in math. These are not broken down by ethnic group, but 80 percent of the sample is African American.

Closer Scrutiny

Comparing students who are already in public or in private   24
schools has a major disadvantage: private-school students may come from more motivated families and may have survived selection processes. Solving this requires an "experiment": randomly assigning students to private and to public schools. But a truly blind trial, as in medical experiments in which control subjects are given a placebo and do not know whether they are receiving the treatment, is not possible, since families know whether they get a voucher. This makes education experiments subject to the so-called Hawthorne effect, whereby the participants' knowledge that they are involved in a program designed to produce a positive impact can cause them to try harder. The motivation of families whose voucher applications were rejected (that is, the control group) can also be affected.

The voucher experiments in various cities call for families to   25
apply for a voucher, give baseline tests to all applicants, and then randomly select some to get vouchers to attend private schools. But the students in these experiments are not necessarily representative of low-income urban students. Families applying for vouchers whose children attend public schools are more motivated to switch their children and more dissatisfied with public schools than are average low-income parents, most of whom do not apply. Not receiving a voucher for parents already dissatisfied with their child's schooling could have an adverse "disappointment" effect on the child's performance.

The differential gains recorded in these experiments may there-   26
fore be partly attributable to lower gains by discouraged voucher rejectees rather than to greater gains by recipients. For a better comparison, voucher experiments would also need to draw a random sample of pupils from urban public schools whose low-income parents do not apply for vouchers and give the students the initial and follow-up tests. These pupils would come from families who are probably more satisfied with their current situation.

Another problem is self-selection of who gets the follow-up   27
evaluation. Voucher researchers measure academic gains by

convincing families to bring children in on a weekend to take follow-up math and reading tests. As in medical trials, high participation rates may require inducements. For those families who received vouchers, the New York inducement was that children would have to take the test to continue getting a voucher. Researchers used only moral suasion in other cities. For those who received but did not use the voucher and for those in the control group (who did not get a voucher), the inducement was typically $20 plus eligibility for a voucher in the future. Participation rates varied: The highest rates occurred in New York (about 66 percent in the second-year follow-up), while D.C. and Dayton both experienced about 50 percent. The participation rate in Charlotte was particularly low—40 percent. All these are considerably lower than in medical trials.

28   The Peterson group deals with participation problems by estimating the probability that a student with a certain initial test score and set of family characteristics and attitudes would participate in each follow-up test; then the actual scores are weighted according to this probability. Thus, students who came back to take follow-up tests but had characteristics that made them unlikely follow-up participants were counted more heavily, so test scores would be more "representative" of the original group of students.

29   The researchers could not do much more than this to correct for no-shows. But the procedure is hardly free of potential bias. It assumes that follow-up test scores for the many who didn't take the tests would be the same as scores for those who did show up and had similar initial scores and parent characteristics. But we really don't know how follow-up scores of no-shows might be related to their not showing up. The large nonparticipation rates could easily have affected the relative gains of voucher recipients and nonrecipients.

30   Yet another problem is bias in who accepts the voucher offer. The vouchers, which range in value from $1,200 to $1,700, depending on the city, are not large enough to cover tuition at most of the available private schools. Many families that received vouchers were unable to use them. In New York, 62 percent of families whose children started out in public school used the scholarships for two years; in Dayton and Washington, 53 percent used the voucher in the first year, with an unreported drop-off in the second year.

31   Voucher takers in each city, as would be expected, have higher income than nontakers. Critics have argued that this biases results. But the researchers have made a valid attempt to deal with the problem by comparing the controls with all

students who were offered the voucher, not only those who actually used it.

In New York, the only students who made significant im-   32
provement were African Americans who switched to private schools when they were entering the fifth grade and whose gains were large enough to produce a significant average gain for the entire New York sample of African Americans.

Results for African-American students in Dayton also have   33
a strange inconsistency. Certain cohorts—those who entered second, fourth, and sixth grades in the first year of the experiment—had large gains and those in the other grades did not. The D.C. results are more consistent.

With gains so variable by cohort, it is fair to ask, as did   34
David Myers, whether one can claim that students in private schools do better than those in public schools. Shouldn't we, instead, wonder what conditions produced such large gains for some cohorts but not for others?

A final problem is erratic results. Big differences between   35
first- and second-year gains in Washington, D.C., may relate to which students failed to show up for testing in the second year. Students might have failed to participate in the second-year testing either because of negative first-year experiences in private schools or because of disappointment with the first-year testing result. For such students, the probability is higher that they would do badly again than that they would do well. If they leave the sample, that alone could drive up the second-year result.

What Have We Learned?

Voucher evaluators have made a concerted effort to eliminate   36
"selection bias" by offering vouchers to families with low incomes by lottery. In comparing pupils who receive vouchers to those who do not, bias from differential motivation and socioeconomic background is allegedly eliminated.

But this strategy does not speak to other issues. The sample   37
of low-income, urban parents seeking vouchers does not represent the average low-income urban parent with children in public school. Parents who file for vouchers are, for one thing, more dissatisfied than other parents. To argue that they are more satisfied with their child's new, private school than parents who never applied for a voucher does not measure whether private schools are better than public, even if the comparison only concerns parental satisfaction.

38   The new studies also suffer from uncorrected potential bias, including "disappointment effects" of families that do not receive vouchers, low participation rates in follow-up tests, concentration of gains in small, particular cohorts that the researchers do not attempt to explain, and possible nonrandom declines in participation between the first and second years of testing.

39   The Peterson group's model has yet another problem. Low-income urban pupils who attend private schools may do better because private schools are able to select their students, so the influence of peers on student achievement is more positive than in a public school. The ability to select students is not a feature of private education that voucher advocates care to stress. And peer effects can run out quickly as private education expands in inner cities.

40   The Peterson group could deal with this problem if they tested a random sample of students already in the private schools attended by voucher recipients, identified them by school, and estimated the peer effect (the average test score of nonvoucher students in each school) on the scores of voucher recipients attending the school. It may not be easy to convince the private schools to allow such testing, simply because they would then be subjecting themselves to evaluation. But without such information, it is difficult to understand the source of private-school advantage—if such advantage even exists.

Marc Fisher

TO EACH ITS OWN

The following essay on charter schools appeared as the cover story for the April 8, 2001 issue of the Washington Post Magazine. *That particular issue focused on education: it included articles on choosing a college, for-profit schools, adult education, and potential curricular reforms for primary grades. Marc Fisher writes a column three times a week for the* Metro *section of the* Post. *Do you think the essay shows Fisher's own opinion about the merits of charter schools?*

1   On paper, in a dream, a charter school—in essence, a privately run public school—is a way out, an answer, an engine for change.

On the street, in a kid's life, a charter school is a building   2
with teachers, students, headaches, tragedies and, once in a
while, a moment of shining success.

Nikole Richardson teaches at a charter school in   3
Washington. She is very good at what she does. She does not
feel very good about it:

"I hope [charters] are an experiment and they will succeed   4
and go away. To take out a handful of our kids and give them
something doesn't improve the lives of most of our kids.
Charters have no training, no certification. They may be dedicated to teaching black kids, but that's not enough. The advantage we have has to do with resources that the public schools
do not have, and parents who find out about the charter
schools and do whatever they need to get their kids in. What
about all the kids who don't have a family saying, 'Go here'?"

Paul Vance is superintendent of D.C. Public Schools, chief   5
target of the city's fast-growing charter system—33 schools
with about 10,000 students, or almost 15 percent of the children in the public schools. Charters are an in-your-face rebuke
to him, his teachers, his students. He wishes charters did not
have to exist, but readily concedes their advantages:

"What I've heard about the charters is that they don't have to   6
deal with insensitive bureaucracy. They have supplies and materials. They teach with few, if any, interruptions. They teach
where no one loses sight of the main thing, which is teaching
and learning. They aren't bogged down with conflicting direc-
tives from central administration. The teachers who have gone
from our schools to the charters have found the freedom and
collegiality which they were promised. There's a siphoning off
of our talented and competent teachers and administrators.
They saw an opportunity to do what they had dreamed of
doing, to become unshackled."

Washington's first charters opened in 1996, when a devastat-   7
ing report on the D.C. public schools prompted the federally
appointed financial control board to sack the superintendent
and strip authority from the elected school board. D.C.'s charters are a paradox: They were imposed on the city by school-
choice ideologues—many of them veterans of the Reagan-era
Education Department—who believe that all parents ought to
have the same options as rich folks who buy their way out of
lousy public schools. Yet in this heavily Democratic, mostly
black and low-income city, parents who often know nothing of
the conservative charter movement have embraced the schools
as an alternative to a system that chronically fails its children.

Now, with charter enrollment in the District soaring every   8
fall, the question is no longer Charters Yes or No. The question

is, what's happening in the classroom? And what comes out of the schools? Are charters a rejection of the governing philosophy of American education—an admission that the idea of a single system molding useful citizens from all walks of life has failed?

9   In his inaugural address, President Bush mentioned only a few specific goals—one was improving education, and the words he used to express his ideal were these: "common schools."

10   In a world of school choice, is there such a thing as a "common school"?

11   Charters, as Bates College professor Stacy Smith has written, "blur the boundary between public and private schools." Charters are public schools—they take public money, usually use public buildings, cannot choose their students. But the schools are free to do as they wish in the classroom.

12   Before regulators approve a charter school, they want to know how it will assess student progress, how it will hire and train teachers, what it will do with learning-disabled kids. But while the city's two school chartering boards say they indeed inquire about what's being taught, school founders say they're really on their own.

13   "The charter board looked seriously at our application only in the broadest sense," says Eric Adler, a founder of the Seed charter school in Northeast. "No one asked what in American history we were going to teach. Now, we obviously care very much about that. Some schools might not."

14   Charter advocates happily embrace the ideals of private education and the idiom of the marketplace; their language is laden with references to parents as consumers and charters as entrepreneurs. But Smith argues that charters are not simply an attempt to privatize the public system. She believes charters can make public education more democratic by educating all students to be effective citizens without forcing every child into a one-size-fits-all system.

15   Vance and other charter critics aren't buying. "There has to be a common body of knowledge," he says. "No one has convinced me that there's a better educational form than the classic and traditional education. In charter schools, there isn't a consistent philosophy. They tend to be finding their way."

16   America's public schools were founded on the notion that for a democracy to work, all children need to be able to read, write and compute, and all children must understand their responsibilities and rights as citizens. For many years, no secondary school subject was more important than history, with its curricular cousins civics and government—here, public schools

could inculcate immigrants and natives alike in the American Way, teaching the nation's roots and rationale.

But in recent decades, it's become clear that no subject is more   17 ineffectively taught than history. Amid the innumerable studies of the deficiencies of American students, history stands at the apex of Failure Mountain. National surveys repeatedly find that students get less homework in history than in most other subjects, that history is often taught from lifeless textbooks rather than from original documents, and that student interest and success in the subject decline with every year of schooling.

History is also a prime battleground in the culture wars of   18 the past 30 years: What should American teens know about their country, their world? Whose history is it, anyway?

And what will charter schools do to the ideal of a common   19 foundation? Even if charters find a better way to teach, doesn't their freedom to go their own way mean that each curriculum will be a world unto itself? Some charters set out to teach one slice of American reality—some are Afrocentric, while others focus on the military, the classics or the world of technology.

Go to a handful of charters and ask how they teach history.   20 Answer: Every which way.

Eleven students, seventh- and eighth-graders all dressed in   21 white shirts and chinos, sit opposite Mr. Lloyd, who is crisp in attire and cadence. The bell sounds in the cramped room—a converted law office—and Lloyd wastes not one second. "Which amendment says American people do not have to house soldiers in their homes?"

Five hands pop up. A boy in the back says, "Third."   22

Swiftly, a check mark goes next to the boy's name on the   23 whiteboard. Even as he's posing the next question, Lloyd moves to the back and gives the boy a two-fingered, mighty cool handshake.

"How many electoral votes does the District of Columbia   24 have?"

"Three," comes the answer, and kids are egging one another   25 on, and the atmosphere is somewhere between "It's Academic" and "Who Wants to Be a Millionaire."

"Name three duties of American citizens."   26

"Appear in court, attend school, obeying the law."   27

The teacher pauses, then slowly: "Absolutely, positively . . ."   28 Long pause. "Correct."

Over the whiteboard at the front of the room, hand-cut   29 paper letters spell out, "Move Mountains."

Felix "Brandon" Lloyd is the star of the 122-student Seed   30 school, the city's only all-residential charter school, now in its third year. He's the teacher observers are sent to watch—a charismatic, no-nonsense dynamo who connects with kids in that magical way that students remember for the rest of their lives. Even in the austere surroundings of the eighth floor of a 16th Street NW office building—Seed held classes there until it moved this winter to a site in Southeast near the Benning Road Metro station—Lloyd manages to exude warmth and firm expectations at the same time.

31   Quiz over, Lloyd explains the roots of the constitutional right to bear arms. He works without notes. "We lived far apart in those days. Demond over here, Danielle over there. And between us was cows, yarns, collard greens, corn. And we needed weapons to protect ourselves, and this is how we defended ourselves, and this led to the right to bear arms."

32   The lessons are parables, the facts infused like tea in hot water. "Terrible thing happened to me this weekend," Lloyd tells one class. "Mr. Ramirez and I were driving 90 miles per hour down 14th Street. Police stopped us and said, 'We'd like to search the car.' Which amendment protected us from that?"

33   Quizzes and games fly at the kids from all directions, at any moment. There's a five-minute detour to talk about outlining skills, a 99-second break (Lloyd sets the timer) for an impromptu discussion of whether there are limits on the right to petition. Not one head rests on a desk. Not one note gets passed from student to student. The class is highly regimented, yet students are free to check their e-mail if they finish a task early. There's a PC on every second desk.

34   Lloyd tolerates no deviation from the rules—a boy who calls out an answer without being recognized gets no credit for it— yet the teacher has given each child a street tag (Peanut, Y-Not, Kingpin, Shakespeare), and they love him for it. Lloyd requires no disciplinary tools beyond a glance of menace, a lethal shot of glare. The 75 minutes zip by, and suddenly he's asking the kids to "take good care, taaaake *good* care," and more than a handful of students linger to debate constitutional principles.

35   Brandon Lloyd never taught a minute of school before he came to Seed. He's the classic charter school hire, one who would be viewed with suspicion, if at all, by the public schools. (None of Seed's teachers came from the D.C. schools; they came from Sidwell Friends and other private schools, or from public schools in the Midwest, or from Teach for America, a sort of Peace Corps for liberal arts graduates who want to work in urban schools.) He has never taken an education course. He holds no certification in anything. Seed hired him from a city recreation center, where he taught drama and creative writing in an after-school program. He loves teaching, but what he

really wants to do is write the Great American Novel. His work in progress is titled "Shades of a Man-child." His favorite movie is "Dead Poets Society," the inspirational Robin Williams flick about the power and majesty of a traditional prep school.

Brandon Lloyd is all of 24.   36

His philosophy of teaching is "to do the opposite of the   37
teachers I had" in D.C. public schools. He credits St. John's, the private military school in upper Northwest where he went to high school, with preparing him well for Syracuse University, where he earned degrees in dramatic writing and African American studies. He designed his history and civics courses for Seed by looking at Virginia's Standards of Learning, California's standards and a bunch of textbooks—then discarding most of what he saw because "the standards were just too dense. You'd be amazed at how poor these kids' conception is of where they are. We decided that less is more." Free of the public schools' obsession with standardized tests, Seed permits Lloyd to teach what he loves and to teach it intensely.

Lloyd lived with the students in their dormitory at Trinity   38
College during Seed's first year, and he still drops by a couple of evenings a week to eat dinner or play ball. "I want to help create thinking people who are responsible citizens," he says. Toward that end, Seed students adhere to a dress code and are prohibited from watching TV. "Their music is increasingly censored" by the school, Lloyd says.

"Cultures form consciously and unconsciously," he explains.   39
"We try to direct them. I want to see these kids entering all different colleges and then being teachers and journalists, daring to be different. I want to expand their world in a way it wouldn't be in public school. If you ask them what percentage of Americans are African American, they'll say 70 percent, which is absurd, but that's their world."

Lloyd, like almost all the school's students, is black. At Seed,   40
the majority of the teaching staff is white, and Lloyd says, "That's important. The D.C. schools don't have this diversity, and the kids grow up apart from the rest of society."

Seconds after one class leaves, the next one arrives. Lloyd   41
sets an egg timer at six minutes and six seconds and starts them off with a high-energy exercise called the Instigator. "Time is wasting," he warns as he hands out questions on the Constitution and U.S. law. "Time is ticking on you, Dominique."

After the exercise, a student raises her hand. "I got a question."   42
"You *have* a question."   43
"Yeah."   44
"You *have* a question."   45

46   "I *have* a question. It's about the Seventh Amendment . . ."

47   At Cesar Chavez High School for Public Policy on Florida Avenue NW, the focus is on constitutional issues and "what students might do to change the world," says history and government teacher Andrew Touchette. So kids study District neighborhoods—Columbia Heights, Anacostia, Cleveland Park. They paint murals and produce radio shows. But they also study the Bill of Rights and engage in heated debate over how it applies to their own lives.

48   "What's great about teaching in a charter school is that each teacher designs his own course," says Touchette, whose close-cropped red hair, long sideburns, wire rims and vest make him look like a character out of Henry James. The only restriction he faces is that he must show which standards from the Modern Red Schoolhouse handbook—a favorite curriculum tool among charter schools—each of his units meets. Last year, Touchette taught in the Charles County schools, where, he says, "they just plopped a 200-page curriculum guide in front of us and said, 'Do this.' It was all about what happened on December 7, 1941, as opposed to being able to understand the concepts."

49   In Touchette's 11th-grade politics and citizenship class, the subject is the civil rights amendments. As in most classes at Chavez, blacks and Latinos—the 180-student school is almost evenly divided between the two—sit apart. (A disproportionate number of Hispanics choose charters. Six D.C. charter schools have student bodies that are 20 percent or more Hispanic, more than double the percentage in the public system.)

50   Touchette is trying to get the 15 kids to focus on the idea of equal protection and the reality of life for immigrants and minorities. But first he has to get past the kids' clean slates. To understand where the 14th Amendment came from, you need to know the basics of slavery and the Civil War. These kids don't.

51   "Did you guys ever have an American history class?" he asks after a series of questions go unanswered.

52   "Yeah, eighth grade, too long ago," Larry Peterson replies.

53   "Is there still slavery in the United States?" Touchette asks.

54   After a chorus of "Yeah" sweeps the room, he tries to distinguish between slavery and discrimination. There's a spirited discussion of a TV news broadcast about the difficulties blacks have hailing taxis on city streets. Touchette divides the class into three groups and assigns an instant essay, 15 minutes to write a memo in which you are an Alabama redneck in 1870 and you're figuring out how to sidestep the civil rights amendments, how to make the law work for you.

One of the groups is clueless; the concept eludes them en- 55
tirely. The other two struggle to get something on paper. One
parrots back what the teacher has said, but the other makes
the leap, reading out an imaginative memo in which craven
Klansmen conspire to set up a system of "separate but equal"
schools and businesses. " 'Cause it says you have to be equal
but it doesn't say you have to be together," Peterson notes.

This is the kind of moment that gives Irasema Salcido rea- 56
son to believe. A former D.C. public schools administrator who
has emerged as one of the most vibrant principals in the city's
charter schools, Salcido is Chavez's founder, and her life is a
rushing, jam-packed trainload of moments both frustrating
and fantastic.

From the start, Salcido got swept up in the high-flying rhetoric 57
of the charter movement. She and her teachers were going to
create a new kind of school, focused on involving kids in public
policy. Together, they would write a bold new curriculum.

But Chavez's new curriculum exists largely as inchoate piles 58
of paper in Salcido's office. She looks at the stacks of pulp and
she can either laugh or cry. Or she can get back out into the
hallway, corner a kid who hasn't been showing up to class, and
sit him down for a talk. She's out the door.

In theory, charters are free to teach as they wish, to experiment 59
boldly or hew to basics. In fact, charters do not brim with new
ideas about how to teach kids. An evaluation of the District's
charters by a George Washington University study team found
that most of them do not emphasize innovation and about half
offer programs barely distinguishable from the public schools'.

Chavez has turned out to be one of the most innovative char- 60
ters, even if its test scores have been unimpressive. Its students
spend weeks working as interns at Washington's think tanks,
policy shops and advocacy groups. The school's project-based
design gets kids out on the streets, exploring architecture, designing solutions to problems in their own neighborhoods.

At Chavez and many of the best charters, principals are up- 61
front about the yawning gap between the theory of charters and
the reality of opening a new school for academically struggling
kids from dysfunctional families and violent neighborhoods—
not to mention the perils of stop-and-go funding, temporary
buildings, hostility from the public system and a hunger for results from parents and regulators.

"It's not as easy as I thought it was going to be," Salcido says. 62
"We couldn't really implement the curriculum." Salcido, like
several other charter principals, has refused to promote large
numbers of students—holding back as much as half of a class.

"We underestimated the low skills of the students. We have young people who cannot do long division and have never written an essay. We want to have a rigorous curriculum, but there are no shortcuts."

63   The Washington Math, Science and Technology charter school at Waterside Mall in Southwest now expects to take at least five years to implement its new curriculum. "The biggest problem charters face is that the public school system lies to these kids by telling them that they're ninth-graders when really they read at a fifth-grade level and do math at a sixth-grade level," says Jack McCarthy, managing director of the Apple Tree Institute, which launched the school in 1998. "You risk losing your charter if you don't graduate enough kids, but if you promote socially instead of promoting mastery, then you're not doing what we all came here to do."

64   Families who choose charters clearly are searching for something better for their kids, but they are not necessarily the kind of parents who are available to help their children navigate adolescence. Salcido and other principals tell of going to great lengths to get parents to attend meetings or student performances. "I do not mail report cards," Salcido says. "You have to come and get them so I can discuss your child."

65   On the main bulletin board in Chavez's lobby, an essay is posted under "Best Student Work of the Month." It is a passionate piece of writing about a student's journey from the District's Duke Ellington high school to Chavez and from her heavy drinking and cocaine use to a no-holds-barred examination of her wayward father and a poisonous family dynamic.

66   "My true, honest, moral belief," says David Domenici, founder of the Maya Angelou School, "is that if anybody understood the level of emotional and academic needs kids come to us with, we would be having a completely different conversation about education." Angelou is a charter school that combines public money and private donations to provide all-day, year-round, nearly one-on-one instruction and counseling for troubled high school-age kids, most of whom have been in the juvenile justice system. "You cannot imagine what urban America has come to. These are kids who have spent 10 years sleeping in classrooms."

67   "We've gone back and forth on this," says Darry Strickland, a humanities teacher at the Angelou School, at Ninth and T streets NW. "What is to be valued out of all these dates, people, places and events? For me as an African American teacher teaching African American students, this is what has to be covered: slavery, the Civil War, the civil rights movement, the Harlem Renaissance. Start with that." In a three-year sequence

of courses—African American studies, American studies, world studies—Angelou uses novels and movies as well as straight-ahead history to connect major events with the lives of its almost exclusively black student body.

"For example, we'll read *Angela's Ashes* to learn not just   68
about the Irish, but the relationship between Irish and African Americans," Strickland says. "How African American maids were displaced when the Irish came.

"Is it fair that we're teaching our own version of history? I   69
think it is."

"These are topics more interesting to our students than   70
Benjamin Franklin," adds Nikole Richardson, who also teaches humanities at Angelou. "It's all a way of getting across the skills—writing, primary vs. secondary sources, thinking critically. There's a big gap between what happens on paper and what happens in the classroom. Four years ago, I would have said I want them to understand their feelings. Now I want them to be equipped with skills, and that's it."

"I'm not sure what comes through," Strickland concedes.   71
"Are we teaching them to despair? I don't think so. But they'll be in their early twenties before they can make sense of what they're reading and doing here."

The Angelou School long ago abandoned the idea of a standard   72
curriculum. With its population—two-thirds of the 65 students are just out of the justice system, many have dropped out of school at least once, most read and compute at an elementary-school level—you do what you can. Which doesn't mean you just pass them along. You push where you can, you teach individually.

The school's first-year humanities course, "Self, Family,   73
Country and Beyond," is "a very intense immersion in yourself, your neighborhood, D.C. and beyond," says founder Domenici, a lawyer and the son of Sen. Pete Domenici of New Mexico. "It's pretty much Afrocentric."

Richardson's humanities class consists of three students,   74
ages 15 and 16. If she can teach them at seventh-grade level, she'll be boosting them to new heights. The kids know it.

"If I was going to public school, I wouldn't be going to class,"   75
says Amanda Curry, who came to Angelou from Shaw Junior High School.

A timeline runs along the classroom wall, listing major   76
events in American history, but the class is just as likely to watch a Bill Cosby video and discuss methods of communication as it is to study dates and events.

Richardson is talking about monologue and dialogue, gesture   77
and inflection, the tools of a storyteller. But one student cannot pronounce "exaggeration," and so the class stops to work on

that. The student just wants to get on with it, get the focus off himself. But Richardson persists, moving close to him, leaning over, speaking softly. She pushes, prods, backs off, moves in again. Five minutes later, he's got the idea. He's relieved to get the teacher out of his face, but a moment later, he whispers the word to himself, gets it right, and smiles for no one but himself.

78   Richardson has moved on to definitions of "myth" and "custom."

79   "What's a custom?" she asks. "We don't have too many customs anymore. What would be a custom about 40 years ago if somebody got married?"

80   Jose Reyes: "Get an abortion."

81   "That's not a custom. What would be a custom?"

82   Tiara Young: "Get married."

83   "Is that a custom anymore?"

84   Jose: "Nope."

85   Tiara: "No."

86   Not in this world.

87   Domenici readily concedes, "There are a lot of D.C. Public Schools standards we are not hitting and will never meet, partly because some of them are inane, and partly because some of them our kids just cannot meet. But we're trying something different. We're spending $20,000 to $25,000 a kid [more than double what public schools spend] and just going at this for five years and we'll see where we end up. And if it works, then we can say to the public and private sectors that here we have kids who you expected to end up marginal or incarcerated, who started out reading at fifth-grade level but can now hold full-time jobs and understand long-term commitments."

88   The Angelou School has graduated eight students in its first two years. All eight went to college; seven are still enrolled.

89   Korey Brown's nine students at Marriott Hospitality charter school are spread around the room on the third floor of a D.C. government office building at Eighth and E streets NW, listening to loudly lilting, ca-chunking West African music.

90   "They're supposed to be working on knowing where every African country is," Brown says. They are not. A few work on other subjects, one dozes, two chat. "We have a lot of students who are here because their mother forced them to come, and a few who were assigned here by the courts. Most are here because their parents say the D.C. schools are wild now."

91   Marriott is anything but wild. The soft colors of the freshly painted walls are calming, and the students here are quiet and polite. With just 145 students in the high school, it's a gentle, even sleepy atmosphere. There's even a bed right next to the

principal's office—part of a mock hotel room, ready for practical lessons in bed-changing and customer service. Marriott was created by the hospitality industry in good part to train its future workers.

Brown, 24, is the school's only social studies teacher. Fresh 92 out of Vanderbilt, he is in his first year as a teacher. His ninth-grade course in world geography and D.C. history is the closest thing to a history course Marriott offers in the fall. In the spring, 10th- and 11th-graders study world and U.S. history. Brown teaches all of those courses.

"I like to deal with popular culture and not just political his- 93 tory," says Brown, who has carte blanche to set up his courses. "In the hospitality industry, you have to know how people deal with one another. In history, you see how people have related to one another in the past."

Brown relies heavily on the D.C. Public Schools curriculum. 94 His students "will learn pretty much the same information as the D.C. public students, though I will take them more to museums. I often get up in the morning and decide I want to go to the Museum of Natural History, and we just walk over at the drop of a hat."

Administrators at Marriott like Brown, and he is a friendly, 95 energetic teacher. But his superiors don't seem to know exactly what he's teaching this year, and in the classroom, the students' attention is elsewhere. It's a loose atmosphere in a school that has its heart in things nonacademic.

Depending on whom you talk to, Marriott is a training 96 school for the hotels and restaurants that helped to get it going or a comprehensive high school with a vocational option. Many students are here because they or their parents see Marriott—named for the company that is its largest private donor—as a sure route to a decent hotel job. Students, who spend half of each year in internships at local hotels and restaurants, say they want even more hotel training—cooking and catering classes—in addition to the eight hospitality courses the school already provides. School leaders are at pains to say that the school is like any other, with an emphasis on preparing graduates for college.

"We're trying to prepare people for the world of work," says 97 principal Flossie Johnson. "It's a way for the industry to boost up their workforce. We're hoping that through internships, mentoring, job shadowing, enough students will be influenced to go into the hospitality industry," not merely as desk clerks and housekeepers, but in management, personnel and marketing.

Hospitality is worked into all academic classes, says assis- 98 tant principal Sheena Reid. And former hospitality industry workers teach not only the hotel courses, but some academic classes as well. English teacher Bruce Pennington, for example, was a chef at a Washington restaurant before he came to Marriott for his first teaching job.

99   In an introductory hospitality class, students work on simulated job interviews, résumé writing and "employability skills." The problem on the whiteboard reads, "If it costs $100 to take care of a baby, how many hours would you need to work at $4 an hour?"

100   The topic in Milton Lane's 12th-grade U.S. government class at the IDEA school is the unitary form of government, taught straight from the textbook—a standard text adopted from the D.C. schools curriculum, which IDEA's principal calls "a good plan."

101   The 15 students take turns reading the text aloud, without expression, without the slightest sign of interest. They are in their chairs, in uniform, on another planet. Several talk to one another, one builds forts with his pencils, one scribbles notes to her friends, two have found solace in slumber.

102   Lane tries to draw their attention by assigning a task on the blackboard. Three students at a time must figure out the correct order of four sentences copied from the textbook and written in slightly jumbled form on the board. The students shuffle up to the board and seem genuinely stuck. Two girls write the same words over and over in chalk, then erase them and start again.

103   Teacher reads from text: "'Unitary governments tend to be inflexible.' They use the word 'inflexible.' What does that mean?"

104   "Not able to be worked around," one girl offers.

105   "Unbendable," a boy calls out.

106   Lane nods. "It can't be changed."

107   The bell rings. "We'll pick up on that point tomorrow."

108   This is Lane's first full year at IDEA (for Integrated Design Electronics Academy) after teaching at the District's Ballou High, which let him go in a downsizing. His style is gentle, low-energy. As the school's sole history teacher, he enjoys the freedom to construct his courses as he wishes. "In the public schools, I was at my wit's end," he says, "not necessarily because of the kids, but the politics. Here, the kids are motivated, or helped to be."

109   IDEA is a military high school with an emphasis on career training—electronics, drafting, construction—and an expectation that all students will graduate and go on to the military, work or college. Teachers put it to the students straight: In computer class, a whirlwind of learning in a converted closet, Brian Davis tells kids they will either master the innards of a

PC and become well-paid technicians, or rake in that minimum wage at McDonald's. In electronics shop, Gerald Bell,
who came to his first teaching job here after working for the
Florida Department of Corrections, trains kids to walk out of
IDEA and wire a house—a skill that could earn them $90,000 a
year and more. The alternative, he warns, is checking in videos
at Blockbuster.

The administrators and some teachers are real officers, re-   110
tired. They are can-do. "A kid will say, 'Well, I'm learning-
disabled,'" says Bell. "I say, 'So what? So am I.' They say, 'Well,
it's hard for me.' I say, 'Okay, work harder.'"

The students—about two-thirds of them male—wear uni-   111
forms and take part in military drills. As at many charters,
classes are longer than in public schools—85 minutes here, as
long as 100 minutes at other schools. IDEA's day is longer, too,
stretching from 8 a.m. to 4:15 p.m.

Some IDEA students chose the school; most were sent by their   112
parents, often over strenuous objections about going to a military school or having to leave their friends and neighborhood—
which in many cases was precisely their parents' reason for
picking IDEA. "They are resistant, they are angry," says Col.
William Dexter, the principal. "They hate that they have to work
hard. They hate the fact that there are no D's—we go from C to
F. You cannot slide by."

"My father felt that if I stayed in public school, I'd fall to bad   113
influences," says Alycia Walker, 17, a junior in her third year at
IDEA. "I thought, 'Oh my God, what did I get myself into?' When
I got here, I did a lot of push-ups because I broke rules, chew-
ing gum, talking out. Twenty every time, then it moved to 60
and 80, drop on the spot, right there in the classroom. It made
me a different person."

If Alycia can hit 920 on the SAT, she will qualify for an ROTC   114
college scholarship. She wants to be the first in her family to
finish college. Her father, who holds two jobs as a banquet
worker at two Washington hotels, wants his child to get there.
He knew she needed discipline to make it. And despite her initial opposition, Alycia has come around.

"My old friends make negative comments about me. They   115
see me in uniform and they're, 'Why do you have that on? Do
you think you're better than I am?' They say I don't pay attention to them. Well, they're going to graduate on a second-grade
reading level, and I'm going to go to college, so they can say
what they want."

IDEA shares space with another charter school and a day-   116
care center at what was once Carver Elementary, a decrepit,
92-year-old D.C. public school building in far Northeast. The

hallways are dark and dank, the exterior looks like it was abandoned long ago. Along the street, more buildings are boarded up than occupied.

117   IDEA's founders taught together at the public system's JROTC Career Academy, a school-within-a-school at a vocational high school. The program was funded by the Defense Department at first, but when that grant ran out, the city said there was no money to continue. So the leaders converted it into a charter.

118   The formula is small classes (as few as 10 students), no social promotion (many IDEA students repeat ninth grade) and tough discipline (drill sergeants patrol the halls). Of the school's 171 students, only eight are prepared to take geometry. "Only three students have come in at grade level in math," notes Dexter. "They come in with A's and B's and they cannot add fractions. We will not just pass them along. I had a parent come in extremely irate. Her daughter had passed algebra in the public schools and I put her in pre-algebra. I showed the mother the test paper: The child may have passed, but she didn't get the answers right."

119   A great school is a benevolent cult, led by a slightly insane visionary with an obsessive devotion to the place and its people. If you buy in—if, as student, parent or teacher, you suspend normal disbelief and adopt your school as a separate and better world than anything outside its walls—the job is halfway done.

120   In that sense, all the mountains of paper, the curricula and the applications, the test scores and evaluations, are beside the point. The GW study found that, based on test results, charter schools "are not achieving higher standards" than the public system. But teachers—about half of whom are refugees from DCPS—and students seem more satisfied at the charters. They boast not about test scores—nothing to boast about there—but about small classes and dedicated teachers, about schools where each child is known and encouraged.

121   What matters, many parents, teachers and students say, is Brian Davis at IDEA, taking kids who've never owned a computer and turning them into fact machines, fluent in the history, innards and functions of every PC ever made. What matters is Irasema Salcido creating an atmosphere at Chavez where 10th-grader Micheal Angelo Daniels can sit me down and explain that he made A's and B's when he was in the D.C. schools, but he's getting C's and D's now, and that's *good* because for the first time, teachers are making him learn, not just passing him through.

122   "Most of us come here and say, 'Oh, yeah, whatever, it's just school,'" says Brittney Morse, a 10th-grader at Chavez. "Then

you're here all the time—all day, evenings, weekends, summer—and your attitude changes."

"If we want to get something changed, like lunch, we can do it   123
if we sell our position," says Chessie Moquete, 16, a startlingly swift mind who came to Chavez from a Montgomery County school. "Try going to some big old school and saying that. They'll laugh at you." It doesn't particularly matter if that is true; the kids believe it, and so Chavez is, in their hearts, their place.

Chessie had zero desire to be torn from her friends and   124
hauled off to an inner-city school in a cruddy building, a place where, she says, "there's no foreign language, no art, no gym." But she, like many students, has found less and less time for old friendships, for hanging out in the neighborhood.

"You live your life at school," says Larry Peterson, who is   125
also 16. "School is your life."

Chavez, like Angelou, Seed and some other charters, has   126
found its edge in longer days, longer school years. "If I can have the kids most of the time, we can influence more," Salcido says. "So yes, mandatory summer school, and mandatory tutoring and the longer day, and Saturday school. And in summer vacation, I try to get them jobs so that I can pick the companies. The more I see them, the less the outside world can take hold of them."

Charter schools were supposed to initiate an intense compe-   127
tition with the public schools; the idea was that both would benefit from a robust contest of ideas and methods. Neither side has seen much of a contest; the two worlds operate almost entirely apart.

And each charter is a world unto itself, teaching its own ver-   128
sion of history. Charter advocates see America's children in tiny, school-size universes, each with its own flavor of education. That, they say, will best serve a place like Washington, where an ill-prepared student body requires specially crafted lessons.

But the content of teaching has remained deep in the back-   129
ground as public and charter schools engage in a different kind of rivalry—a political wrestling match in which both sides scramble for funding, facilities and the hearts and minds of parents. The weapons in this war are TV ads, op-ed pieces, lobbying and the spinning of test results. Every new number is taken as evidence that either the public schools or the charters are advancing beyond the enemy.

Public school administrators accuse charters of skimming—   130
stripping talented students from the public system. Charters respond by cataloguing the dysfunctions of their students.

131   Impartial studies show most of the sniping between the two systems is much ado about nothing: The populations of the city schools and the charters are nearly indistinguishable, except that charters attract a higher percentage of Hispanic children, according to the GW study, which was led by Prof. Jeffrey Henig. In both systems, about 66 percent of students are low-income. Nor are charter school parents more involved than DCPS parents.

132   But the GW study found some important differences between the two populations, notably that those parents who choose charters have nurtured more stable families and have higher educational aspirations for their children.

133   The arguments between the two sets of schools will continue as long as they operate under different rules while fighting for the same pot of tax money. While some charter advocates jealously guard their independence, a few are open to putting all public schools—regular and charter—under the superintendent, who would then be judged by his ability to promote success in both systems.

134   Superintendent Vance would like that. Vance is something new to the D.C. schools—a confident leader who knows education and does not need this job. Vance can and does tell folks to take a hike. But that is not what he's telling the charter schools.

135   Vance has watched as charters have drained students, teachers and money from his system. He has seen and even admired the TV ads for charters, the ones that show what he calls "salt of the earth, upwardly mobile black Americans—believable people who want something better for their kids." Vance came into office last year intent on reversing his predecessor's antagonistic approach to charters. Former superintendent Arlene Ackerman fought the charters at every turn—over access to facilities, over payments, over bureaucratic matters large and small. Vance has resolved to cooperate with the charters on all that, to do battle with them instead at a completely different level—in the classroom.

136   He can claim some victories there: D.C. public school test scores are rising, while preliminary numbers from many charters show flat-lining at best and depressing declines in some cases. But the charter movement has not yet peaked: Next fall, Washington will have 41 characters, up from 33. The public system, by comparison, will operate 146 schools.

137   "You would have thought by now, after two, three years, that the public schools would be asking, 'Why are kids leaving? What should we be doing?'" Salcido says. "But I don't see it. Instead, they just fight with us, and more students leave them."

138   Vance knows there is a certain romance to charters, and a reality that weighs very much on their side. "What I've seen are

excellent examples of teaching and energetic principals who are real leaders," he says, and he vows to break through the public school bureaucracy to allow the same examples to emerge there.

Can charters survive in the long run as separate worlds, as   139
an alternative to Bush's "common schools"? The GW study concludes that charters need more time to show what they can do: "It is simply not yet clear whether charter schools will lead to the revitalization of the traditional public education system or its evisceration."

Vance surveys the city's charters and sees "schools that are as   140
good as our best. I haven't seen any that are extraordinary. I believe based on my 90 years as a professional educator"—he lets slip the slightest of smiles—"that charters, like most changes in public education, will have a life of their own. Their numbers will level off and then decline, and then seek their own level. Those that survive will be those that are really exemplary. And others will not survive. And we in the public schools will need a series of small successes that help us reclaim our schools and make them acceptable again to our citizens."

W. Norton Grubb

THE NEW VOCATIONALISM: WHAT IT IS, WHAT IT COULD BE

W. Norton Grubb is the David Gardner Chair in Higher Education at the University of California, Berkeley. His research and writing, which focuses on the connection between educa-tion and employment, includes Working in the Middle: Strengthening Education and Training for the Mid-Skilled Labor Force *(1996),* Learning to Work: The Case for Re-Integrating Job Training and Education *(1996), and* Education Through Occupations in American High Schools *(1995). The essay below was originally published in 1996 in*

Phi Delta Kappan, *a respected trade journal for education specialists that advocates research-based policy reforms. Grubb's
essay outlines ways that "vocationalism"—an educational movement that makes preparing students for job success its primary
goal—can be used to make public schools vibrant. You may recognize some vocational programs used in your high school
among those discussed by Grubb. What was your experience of
such programs?*

1   Vocationalism is rampant once again. The claims that schooling ought to better prepare workers for the 21st century have
become increasingly strident since the publication of *A
Nation at Risk* more than a decade ago. Various practices to
incorporate work-related skills into the curriculum have been
proposed, and the most recent initiative of the Clinton
Administration—the School-to-Work Opportunities Act of
1994—has attracted an amazing amount of attention for what
is, after all, a piddling program. No one is proposing to resur-
rect conventional vocational education, but the notion that
public education should be more "relevant" to our country's
economic future is widespread.

2   How should education respond? The movements within the
"new vocationalism" include many odd partners with wildly
differing ideas of how to respond to economic imperatives.
Some are atavistic; others claim to have discovered such new
directions as the shift to a "high-skills economy"; still others
have rediscovered practices with long and checkered histories
in our schools, such as work-based learning. Many of these reforms have the potential to improve teaching and learning. But
the nature of these reforms, their links to vocational purposes,
and the specific ways in which they might improve learning remain murky. Moreover, many forms of the "new vocationalism" are only barely emerging.

3   In this article I disentangle the strands of renewed interest in
the occupational purposes of schooling, concentrating on the
high school—the institution that seems both the least successful and the most resistant to change. After describing five different versions of the "new vocationalism," I interpret these
changes through a matrix of approaches to pedagogy and to
academic and vocational content.

4   The penultimate section examines the economic context of
the "new vocationalism," and the final section examines the
prospects for reform. There are strong reasons to think that enduring reforms are possible, but there are equally powerful
forces that might sweep away the most innovative aspects of

the "new vocationalism." Our tasks are to identify those elements that merit widespread adoption and to institutionalize
them so that they are not blown away by the first winds of pedagogical conservatism.

Practices of the 'New Vocationalism'

A Nation at Risk, generally conceded to be the spark that ig-   5
nited the current reform movement, epitomizes the first strand
of the new vocationalism. The great threat to our country's future was "a rising tide of mediocrity" in the schools, which was
causing a decline in competitiveness with the Japanese, the
South Koreans, and the Germans. Subsequent commission reports picked up the economic rationale for education reform,
with such titles as *Higher Education and the American
Resurgence.* To be sure, the emphasis on economic roles for
schooling was leavened with a nod to the importance of
preparing a well-informed citizenry; both *A Nation at Risk* and
Higher Education and the American Resurgence approvingly
quoted Thomas Jefferson on this subject. But the connection
between education and democracy came off as an after-
thought. The dominant rationale given for schooling—indeed,
the only apparent rationale in the more utilitarian reports,
such as the report of the Secretary [of Labor]'s Commission on
Achieving Necessary Skills (SCANS), *What Work Requires of
Schools*—was the preparation of future workers.

But the content of schooling was not to change. *A Nation at*   6
Risk recommended the "New Basics": English, math, science,
social studies, and (the only novelty) half a year of computer
science. The states took up the charge and imposed higher academic standards in the form of new graduation and testing requirements and new content standards for teachers. As many
commentators noted, the dominant response was "more of the
same": the same academic curriculum that has dominated the
high school since the 19th century, taught in roughly the same
ways, though with a new sense of urgency. The only condition
that changed was that enrollments in conventional academic
subjects increased at the expense of enrollments in vocational
and remedial subjects.[1]

Of course, ever since Horace Mann the academic orthodoxy   7
has had its economic underpinnings; the only thing different
about *A Nation at Risk* was that the political, intellectual, and in-
trinsic arguments for the standard curriculum—knowledge as
its own reward, the "beauty, pleasure, surprise, personal enlightenment and enrichment at the heart of the classic liberal-arts

ideal"[2]—had been completely displaced by an economic argument. In vain might one argue that combining an occupational rationale for schooling with a conventional academic curriculum could only exacerbate a disjunction in the American high school: the high school is an inescapably vocational institution, critical to students' employment futures, while the dominant courses are those of the academic track, whose connection to later employment is obscure.[3]

8   As noted, the first round of school reform did change course-taking patterns, but otherwise mediocre performance seemed to drag on. One of many responses was the emergence of a second strand of the "new vocationalism": the argument that the changing economy requires new skills of its workers and therefore new approaches to teaching. In the widely read SCANS report, the high-skills workplace requires a range not only of basic skills (e.g., reading, writing, math, listening, speaking) but also of thinking skills (e.g., decision making, problem solving, knowing how to learn), as well as such personal qualities as responsibility, sociability, self-management, integrity, and honesty.

9   But these SCANS skills—or "workplace basics"—are not well taught through conventional didactic instruction with its emphasis on individualized rather than cooperative learning, on abstract principles and decontextualized context, and on fact acquisition rather than problem solving.[4] Thus SCANS and others have called for changing instruction through more experiential learning outside of classrooms and more contextualized teaching:

> SCANS believes that teachers and schools must begin early to help students see the relationship between what they study and its applications in real-world contexts. . . . We believe, after examining the findings of cognitive science, that the most effective way of teaching skills is "in context." Placing learning objectives within real environments is better than insisting that students first learn in the abstract what they will then be expected to apply. . . . Reading and mathematics become less abstract and more concrete when they are embedded in one or more of the competencies; that is, when the learning is "situated" in a system or a technological problem.

10   By referring to the work of cognitive scientists, the SCANS report explicitly linked the demands of employers to the claims of education reformers. The metaphor of "cognitive apprenticeship" captures this approach. Just as apprentices learn

their tasks in the context of ongoing work, so too the student-as-apprentice-learner would learn academic competencies in some meaningful context. Simpler components would be mastered before moving to more difficult tasks; the master or teacher would provide guidance ("scaffolding") at early stages and then allow the apprentice/student to do more ("fading"). The teaching would include not only a complete range of technical skills but also the interpersonal skills, the customs, and the culture of the craft.[5] As a model of teaching, this is quite different from the standard didactic approach in which learning lacks any context and the ultimate goal of instruction is either unclear or abstract.

However, while the methods of instruction may have to   11 change according to this second strand, the content of formal education could stay the same. The SCANS report suggested ways to teach various SCANS skills (e.g., interpersonal skills, systems thinking, and knowledge of technology) in such core curricular areas as English, math, and science. Recommendations for the "forgotten half" also preserved the conventional curriculum of the high school, while adding to it various forms of community-based learning.

In particular, it has been clear that the skills "employers   12 want" are not those of conventional vocational education. The Committee for Economic Development declared that "business, in general, is not interested in narrow vocationalism. It prefers a curriculum that stresses literacy and mathematical and problem-solving skills." Similarly, the National Academy of Sciences Panel on Secondary School Education for the Changing Workplace concluded:

> The education needed for the workplace does not differ in its essentials from that needed for college or advanced technical training. The central recommendation of this study is that all young Americans, regardless of their career goals, achieve mastery of this core of competencies up to their abilities.[6]

Thus the second strand of the "new vocationalism" has con-   13 tinued the economic and utilitarian emphasis of *A Nation at Risk*, giving top priority to employers and the skills they profess to need and retaining the conventional academic subjects, though with a transformed pedagogy.

The third strand of the "new vocationalism" has more di-   14 rectly addressed the deficiencies of the "old vocationalism"— traditional vocational education dating from the turn of the century, generally focusing on specific skill training for entry-level jobs. Many critics of conventional vocational education have called for occupational preparation to become broader, better connected to academic content, more accommodating of goals other than immediate employment (e.g., postsecondary education), and more critical of the current system of employment than is conventionally the case.[7] Such efforts calling for a more general form of vocational education have a long history that is linked to the deficiencies of specific vocational training on the one hand and to problems with the "irrelevance" of academic instruction on the other.[8]

15   Such improvements in vocational education have been given a substantial boost by the 1990 Amendments to the Carl Perkins Act, which funds vocational education. The amendments require that every program supported by federal funds "integrate academic and vocational education . . . through coherent sequences of courses so that students achieve both academic and occupational competencies." Other sections of the amendments support tech-prep programs that combine high school and postsecondary education (usually in community colleges) and clarify that vocational education is not a terminal program for those not destined for college. Still another provision promotes teaching students about "all aspects of the industry" they might enter, again an effort to broaden content beyond job-specific preparation.

16   In response, a large number of secondary schools have experimented with various forms of curriculum integration, and tech-prep programs—sometimes interpreted simply as curriculum integration—have proliferated. Several networks of schools have developed, including one instituted by the National Center for Research in Vocational Education and one organized by the Southern Regional Education Board. In large measure, the forms of integration adopted so far have been the simplest ones: the incorporation of more academic skills into vocational courses and the development of "applied academics" curricula that present the applications of math or writing or other "communications skills" in employment.[9] In many cases, the kinds of higher-order skills advocated by SCANS and other champions of the high-skill workplace are also included.

17   This strand of the "new vocationalism" represents a reform of vocational education by broadening its content. Unlike the more thorough forms of integrating academic and vocational education that I describe below, these practices typically focus on self-selected vocational students and continue the separation of "vocational" and "academic" tracks. By grafting academic content onto existing vocational programs, they continue

the emphasis on preparation for relatively unskilled entry-level jobs right after high school.

A fourth strand of the "new vocationalism" has emerged 18 from the new interest in school-to-work programs. Initially, such programs looked more like the German apprenticeship programs on which they were modeled.[10] That is, they were work-based programs lasting for relatively long periods of time and yielding some sort of portable credential or certificate. As this conception developed into the School-to-Work opportunities Act of 1994, it changed into a tripartite program incorporating school-based learning (in which academic and vocational education would be integrated within "career majors" and linked to at least one year of postsecondary education); a work-based component; and "connecting activities" to make school-based learning consistent with work-based learning. The school-to-work legislation also contains hints of pedagogical reform in its calls for "the use of applied teaching methods and team-teaching strategies." Thus school-to-work programs might be more contextualized and constructivist, and they can be seen to extend the reforms of the third strand of the "new vocationalism" by reemphasizing the integration of academic and vocational education while adding a work component to provide a different form of learning.

It is too early to tell what school-to-work programs will be- 19 come, since the legislation is too new, most states are still in early planning stages, and Congress will probably consolidate funding with other vocational education and job training programs. It is possible that school-to-work programs will be used as levers to shape high school reform, constructing "career majors" or clusters such as those described below.

But two other limited outcomes are possible and, in histori- 20 cal terms, seem more realistic. One is that school-to-work programs will create "work experience" programs in which some high school students—especially those considered "at risk"—spend some time in work placements of varying quality, but without changing the structure, the content, or the pedagogy of the high school one whit.[11] This approach would replicate the work experience programs that were widely supported during the 1970s without ever making much difference to high schools. Over time, we could expect such efforts to wither, as did the reforms of the 1970s. A brighter possibility is that high-quality school-to-work programs will be created for small numbers of students, leaving the college-prep track and the general track largely unchanged.[12]

A cynical (but realistic) view of the school-to-work legislation 21 is that it is an example of "piddle politics."[13] It has captured the attention of educators and business leaders not normally interested in occupationally oriented education, and it presents an image of a federal initiative devoted to building education "systems" instead of creating trifling programs that leave basic institutions unchanged. But the amounts of money—an authorization of up to $300 million a year, vanishing at the end of five years, with only $115 million appropriated for 1995—seem piddling when compared to federal vocational education funds (about $1.3 billion), federal job training funds (about $5.8 billion), total public spending for secondary education (around $85 to $90 billion), or total spending for secondary vocational education (perhaps $15 to $20 billion). Unless the federal government can promote a clear vision of school-to-work programs that will galvanize others into action with state and local resources, the school-to-work legislation seems more of a symbolic gesture than a commitment to any form of the "new vocationalism."

22   In looking across these four stands of the "new vocationalism," the differences are striking. The first has been conservative in every sense of the term, while the other three are reformist in different ways. The first two emphasize academic subjects without any incorporation of vocational content, while the third and fourth incorporate vocational content as well. They vary in their emphasis on reforming pedagogy, with the second most insistent on changing teaching methods. The fourth incorporates employment-based learning activities outside the school walls, though the second and third incorporate some of this expansiveness as well. All agree, however, in making the skills required in employment first among the goals of formal schooling, and they all continue a separation between academic programs and vocational programs.

Using Occupations to Contextualize Instruction

23   Like the third and fourth strands, a fifth strand of the "new vocationalism" has attempted to integrate academic and vocational education. But it has done so by restructuring high schools so that the opportunities for integration are more consistent. These efforts have taken three principal forms, varying in their scale.

> 1. *Career academies.* Career academies operate as schools-within-schools. Typically, four teachers collaborate: one each in math, English, science, and the occupational

area that defines the academy (health, electronics, finance, tourism, and so on). Each class of students takes all four subjects from these teachers, and they stay with the same teachers for two or three years. Students take other subjects outside the academy in the "regular" high school.

One essential element of this approach is that a group of teachers works with a group of students over a period of years. The opportunities for coordinating their courses, including special projects that cut across three or four subjects, are substantial. And because each academy is focused on a cluster of occupations, it becomes relatively natural to integrate occupational applications into academic courses.

A second essential element is a relationship with firms operating in the occupational area of an academy. These firms typically provide mentors for all students, send individuals to talk about particular aspects of their operations, give tours of their facilities, and offer summer internships for students. These opportunities represent other sources of instruction and motivation (cognitive, behavioral, and financial) in addition to those provided by teachers.[14]

Because of their small scale, academies also create communities of both students and teachers. The existence of a community of students is important to teaching methods that involve work in cooperative groups, and a community of teachers helps with curriculum integration and with identifying the problems of individual students. Since academy teachers come to know their students much better than most high school teachers can, it is less likely that their students will feel "lost."

2. *Clusters.* In some schools, students choose a cluster (or career path or "major"), often at the beginning or end of 10th grade. Like academies, clusters are usually broad occupational or industry-based groupings that reflect local labor markets and structure the curriculum of the remaining two or three years of high school accordingly. In some schools students take some coursework in the occupational area of the cluster—usually a two-period class over the entire two- or three-year period—while other subjects are taken in regular classes outside the cluster. In other schools students take some academic courses within the cluster, and a few schools have replaced conventional

discipline-based departments with departments organized along occupational lines.

The cluster organization provides focus for each student, and the required course sequence reduces the "milling around" so common in high schools.[15] Except that every student elects a cluster, clusters are much like academies. They have all the potential of academies to create a focus within which curriculum integration can take place and to develop communities of students and teachers. In addition, choosing a cluster requires an active decision on the student's part, with all the benefits associated with choice.

While there still aren't many schools that use clusters, the concept has been widely promoted at both federal and state levels. The School-to-Work Opportunities Act requires students to choose "career majors" no later than the beginning of the 10th grade. In California, the High School Task Force recommended "curricular paths" for all students; in its Educational Act for the 21st Century, Oregon defined six clusters or "focus areas" for non-college-bound young people; and a task force in New York recommended the creation of career pathways for youths not headed for college.

3. *Occupational high schools and magnet schools.* These programs emphasize preparation for vocations in a particular area. Some of these schools—such as Aviation High School, the High School of Fashion Industries, and the Murry Bergtraum High School for Business Careers in New York—have been established for a long time; others are magnet schools that were developed as mechanisms for racial desegregation, many of which have an occupational focus. Every student within an occupational school is enrolled in a curriculum incorporating courses related to the magnet's focus, though the number of these courses ranges from a trivial two or three courses in a four-year sequence to a substantial commitment of time.

Occupational high schools are similar to academies and clusters, except that the scale is schoolwide. This offers obvious advantages for curriculum integration. The incentives to incorporate applications from the school's occupational focus are strong, and the resources to do so are at hand. Occupational high schools are also excellent examples of "focus schools"—schools with clear missions, organized to pursue their educational goals, and operating with explicit social contracts that establish responsibilities for teachers, students, and parents.[16] Similar strengths are emerging in the current movement for charter schools.

Academies, schools offering clusters, and occupationally ori-   24
ented high schools share certain distinctive features. They impose some coherence on the "shopping mall high school," and
they increase opportunities for cooperation and integration
across the disciplines. Moreover, the combination of academic
and vocational content allows students to plan for postsecondary education, for employment, or for a combination of the
two. Students in magnet schools often consciously follow such
a "two-track strategy." As one senior in a magnet school commented, "This is my last year, and I'm going to get my cosme-
tology license. After I get my license, I'll just go to college for
business. If the one doesn't work out, I'll go to the other.[17]

In general, students must choose academies or clusters, and   25
in some cities they can choose among magnet schools as well.
This requires students to think, early in their high school careers, about their occupational futures. Typically, schools that
have adopted one of these ways of educating through occupations have ended up strengthening or developing more active
forms of guidance and counseling.

In theory, these practices allow for the integration of occupa-   26
tional content not only with the academic subjects considered
utilitarian—math, science, and communication skills—but
also with such subjects as literature, history, and social studies.
Indeed, an occupational focus may be a way to engage students in subjects that they generally dislike. For example, students might explore the history of technology and economic
development or the politics surrounding employment and
technological change or the themes of meaning and alienation
in work.[18] (Unfortunately, I have seen very few examples of
such practices in high schools.)

Most occupationally focused high schools have used broad   27
clusters of related occupations rather than the occupation-
specific focus of traditional vocational education—transportation rather than automotive repair or business rather than sec-
retarial and clerical occupations, for example. This approach
provides opportunities to explore a wider variety of academic
topics and avoids the problem of having modestly skilled jobs
dictate the teaching of relatively low-level academic content. It
also allows students to explore a wider variety of careers and to
understand how occupations are related to one another. If
broadly structured, clusters can reduce the class, racial, and
gender segregation common in high schools, as students from

different backgrounds with varied ambitions come together. For example, health clusters would include both would-be doctors and those who aspire to become practical nurses.

28   Finally, the use of occupational clusters provides a natural opportunity for building links with employers and with appropriate postsecondary institutions through tech-prep programs. These links need not be contrived, as they often are in comprehensive high schools, since academies, clusters, and magnet programs have already focused the curriculum on occupations of interest to postsecondary institutions and to particular employers.

29   In addition to these strengths, the movement to develop occupationally focused high schools is consistent with other strands of education reform.[19] In line with current efforts to professionalize teaching, these programs require teachers to be able to develop their own curricula, to collaborate with teachers from other disciplines, and even to work with employers. Under the best conditions, occupationally focused schools foster more student-centered, project-based, and meaning-centered instruction, partly because of their connection to traditions of vocational education that have used such methods and partly because of the interdisciplinary nature of integrated instruction. In most cases, these innovations introduce student and parental choice and encourage the development of smaller units. And these ways of shaping high schools give restructuring and local control a definition and a purpose.

30   Of course, academies, clusters, and magnet schools could have nonoccupational themes, too—e.g., the environment, math and science, or the problems of cities. Thus the advantages of academies, clusters, and magnet schools come at least partly from their focus, smaller size, and the communities of students and teachers they create—not just from the specific subjects that form their core.

31   However, there are good reasons for choosing broadly defined occupations for such a focus. John Dewey articulated several of them 80 years ago in *Democracy and Education,* when he argued that "education through occupations consequently combines within itself more of the factors conducive to learning than any other method."[20] In modern parlance, we would call such an education contextualized, and it would treat the learner as a social being rather than an isolated individual.

32   Dewey also feared that conventional vocational education would narrow the education of those preparing for lower-skilled jobs and deny them the opportunities for developing their full range of capacities. Such "trade education" would "defeat its own purpose" as changes in industry took place and

narrowly trained individuals were unable to adjust. But the broader conception of "education through occupations" would avoid these limitations. Indeed, Dewey offered examples of such a program that sound remarkably like an academy or cluster school.

Thus we can interpret the fifth strand of the new vocational-   33
ism as following a path articulated by Dewey 80 years ago. It was abandoned when the "old vocationalism"—a highly utilitarian and job-specific form of preparation for entry-level work—won the battle for federal funds and for a place in the high school. To be sure, the fifth strand incorporates many elements of the other four, including the stress on higher-order skills, the efforts to integrate academic and vocational education and to connect secondary and postsecondary education, and the potential link with employers through work-based learning. But using occupations to focus instruction—rather than maintaining the distinction between academic education and vocational education—seeks to minimize differences between the college-bound and the non-college-bound. Thus in its broadest and most Deweyan form, "education through occupations" can incorporate the entire range of political and moral purposes, rather than simply assume that the needs of employers are paramount.

NOTES

1. Richard Coley, *What Americans Study Revisited* (Princeton, N.J.: Educational Testing Service, 1994).
2. Patricia Kean, "Building a Better Beowulf: The New Assault on the Liberal Arts," *Lingua Franca, The Review of Academic Life,* May/June 1993, pp. 1–28.
3. High school students rank vocational goals higher than intellectual, personal, or social goals. However, both parents and teachers rate intellectual goals highest. See John I. Goodlad, *A Place Called School: Prospects for the Future* (New York: McGraw-Hill, 1984), chap. 2.
4. *What Work Requires of Schools* (Washington, D.C.: Secretary's Commission on Achieving Necessary Skills, 1991). See also Cathy Stasz et al., "Teaching Generic Skills," in W. Norton Grubb, ed., *Education Through Occupations in American High Schools, Volume 1: Approaches to Integrating Academic and Vocational Education* (New York: Teachers College Press, 1995).
5. Alan Collins, John Seeley Brown, and Susan Newman. "Cognitive Apprenticeship: Teaching the Craft of Reading, Writing, and Mathematics," in Lauren Resnick, ed., *Knowing, Learning, and Instruction: Essays in Honor of Robert Glaser* (Hillsdale, N.J.: Erlbaum, 1989), pp. 453–94.
6. See *Investing in Our Children: Business and the Public Schools* (New York: Committee for Economic Development, 1985), p. 15; and *National Academy of Sciences Panel on Secondary School Education for the*

Changing Workplace, High Schools amid the Changing Workplace: The Employers' View (Washington, D.C.: National Academy Press, 1984), p. 13.

7. See, for example, Charles Benson and Harold Silver, "Vocationalism in the United Kingdom and the United States," Working Paper No. 16, Institute of Education, University of London, 1991; David Spence, "Rethinking the Role of Vocational Education," *Educational Horizons*, Fall 1986, pp. 20–23; Kenneth Gray, "Vocational Education in High School: A Modern Phoenix?," *Phi Delta Kappan*, February 1991, pp. 437–45; John F. Claus, "Renegotiating Vocational Instruction," *Urban Review*, vol. 21, 1989, pp. 193–207; Roger Simon, Don Dippo, and Arleen Schenke, *Learning Work: A Critical Pedagogy of Work Education* (New York: Bergin and Garvey, 1991); Theodore Lewis, "Difficulties Attending the New Vocationalism in the USA," *Journal of Philosophy of Education*, vol. 25, 1991, pp. 95–108; Marsha Rehm, "Emancipatory Vocational Education: Pedagogy for the Work of Individuals and Society," *Journal of Education*, vol. 171, 1989, pp. 109–23; and Leonard Cantor, "The Re-Visioning of Vocational Education in the American High School," *Comparative Education*, vol. 25, 1989, pp. 125–32.

8. W. Norton Grubb, " 'The Cunning Hand, the Cultured Mind': Sources of Support for Curriculum Integration," in idem, *Education Through Occupations, Volume I*, pp. 11–25.

9. W. Norton Grubb and Cathy Stasz, *Integrating Academic and Vocational Education: Progress Under the Carl Perkins Amendments of 1990* (Berkeley: National Center for Research in Vocational Education, University of California, 1993).

10. See, for example, Stephen Hamilton, *Apprenticeship for Adulthood: Preparing Youth for the Future* (New York: Free Press, 1990).

11. Harvey Kantor, "Managing the Transition from School to Work: The False Promises of Youth Apprenticeship," *Teachers College Record*, Summer 1994, pp. 442–61; and W. Norton Grubb, "True Reform or Tired Retread? Seven Questions to Ask About School-to-Work Programs," *Education Week*, 3 August 1994, p. 68.

12. The "triple track" approach has emerged most conspicuously in the academic, vocational, and general tracks that persist (in practice, if not in name) and in the life adjustment movement, with its program of life adjustment education for the 50% of students for whom neither academic preparation for college nor vocational education is appropriate.

13. My thanks to Lorraine McDonnell for this apt phrase.

14. See David Stern, Marilyn Ruby, and Charles Dayton, *Career Academies: Partnerships for Reconstructing American High Schools* (San Francisco: Jossey-Bass, 1992); and Marilyn Ruby, "The Career Academies," in Grubb, *Education Through Occupations, Volume 1*, pp. 82–96.

15. For a variety of ways in which clusters and majors have been adopted, see W. Norton Grubb, "Coherence for All Students: High Schools with Career Clusters and Majors," in idem, *Education Through Occupations, Volume 1*, pp. 97–113.

16. On focus schools see Paul Hill, Gail Foster, and Tamar Gendler, *High Schools with Character* (Santa Monica, Calif: RAND Corporation, 1990).

17. Amy Heebner, "The Voices of Students," in Grubb, *Education Through Occupations, Volume 1*, pp. 148–66.

18. Ken Koziol and W. Norton Grubb, "Paths Not Taken: Curriculum Integration and the Political and Moral Purposes of Education," in

W. Norton Grubb, ed., *Education Through Occupations, Volume 2: The Challenges of Implementing Curriculum Integration* (New York: Teachers College Press, 1995), pp. 115–41.

19. Erika Neilsen Andrew and W. Norton Grubb, "The Power of Curricular Integration: Its Relationship to Other School Reforms," in Grubb, *Education Through Occupations, Volume 1*, pp. 39–56.

20. John Dewey, *Democracy and Education: An Introduction to the Philosophy of Education* (New York: Macmillan, 1916), p. 309.

Larry Cuban

MAKING PUBLIC SCHOOLS BUSINESS- LIKE . . . AGAIN

Though most of us would agree that one of the tasks of public education is to prepare students for their role in the workforce, there are many other purposes for education as well. Larry Cuban, an education specialist who brings 14 years of public school teaching experience to his position at Stanford University, explores the relationship between the use of schools to prepare students for work and the many other goals of public education. This essay was first published in PSOnline, *the American Political Science Association's online journal. Note the way that it uses an academic format and background research to make its argument.*

A contracting firm in New York City employed 4,900 skilled mechanics direct from Europe, paying them fifty cents per day above the union rate, because it was impossible to secure such valuable workmen in our greatest industrial center. We must not depend on Europe for our skill; *we must educate our own boys* [original italics]— Report of the Committee on Industrial Education, National Association of Manufacturers, 1905.

"Education . . . is a major economic issue," wrote John Akers, chairman of IBM, in an advertisement in the *New York Times Magazine* (1991). "If our students can't compete today, how will our companies compete tomorrow?" he asked.

1   Throughout the 20th century, business-inspired reform coali-
    tions, driven by a deep belief that strong public schools produce
    a strong economy, have changed school goals, governance,
    management, organization, and curriculum. In doing so, the
    traditional and primary collective goal of public schools build-
    ing literate citizens able to engage in democratic practices has
    been replaced by the goal of social efficiency, that is, preparing
    students for a competitive labor market anchored in a swiftly
    changing economy.

2   Akers and other business leaders, past and present, have
    not been alone in their new emphasis. In August of 2001, for
    example, then Chancellor of the New York City Public Schools
    Harold Levy—himself a corporate lawyer—had this to say
    about his goals for the public schools:

> That's the bottom line. Business has profit and loss. The
> school system has students and . . . there is nothing more
> important than our getting the children up to the levels of
> reading and math so that they can get through these exams
> and go on to successful careers. That's what this system is
> about. The minute we take our eyes off that we begin doing
> something wrong.
>
> (*New York Times* 2001)

3   As a teacher and local superintendent as well as a researcher,
    I have worked in schools for more than four decades and, re-
    cently, have studied this past century's business-inspired re-
    forms. Pushed by a broad coalition of business executives
    since the late 1970s, public officials, union leaders, and educa-
    tors, the policies, mirrored in an array of reports and commen-
    taries as well as legislation, are chiefly rooted in the following
    assumptions:[1]

    a. According to national and international test results,
       American students have insufficient knowledge and
       skills, and this mediocre performance imperils U.S.
       economic performance;
    b. These student deficits have occurred because local
       school boards and practitioners are hostile to competi-
       tion, have been unaccountable for student outcomes,
       have little managerial expertise, and have relaxed acad-
       emic standards. They lack both the political will and a
       grasp of the larger economic situation to solve these
       problems;

    c. More authority over schools must therefore be shifted
to state and federal agencies, to develop uniform academic standards, require more tests, and hold local
schools accountable while promoting parental choice
and school competition.[2]

The trouble with these assumptions, advanced by the 4
business-inspired reformers who have dominated education
policy since the 1970s, is that they are mostly mistaken.

That students from other countries outstrip U.S. students at 5
certain ages on particular tests is well known. The results for
the last three international tests in mathematics and science,
though, were mixed: U.S. students were ahead of both
European and Asian counterparts in some areas and in some
grades. For the past three decades, moreover, results on the
National Assessment of Educational Progress also have been
mixed, with alternating gains and losses in reading and mathematics performance (National Assessment of Education 2003;
Amrein and Berliner 2002). These test scores suggest, however,
that U.S. students do have a spotty record on school-learned
knowledge and skills as compared with pupils in other industrialized nations.

The problems begin, however, when public school critics 6
link test scores to worker productivity and the national economy. In 1991, for example, a U.S. Assistant Secretary of
Education said that "faltering academic achievement between
1967 and 1980 sliced billions of dollars from the U.S. gross national product." Support for such a linkage is conspicuously
underwhelming (Finn 1991).

Consider the lack of substantial evidence in three areas: 7
(1) the assumed connection between test scores and productivity; (2) the reliance on a theory of mismatched worker skills
and employer demands to explain wage differentials among
jobs and youth unemployment as well as labor productivity;
and (3) the tie between workers' supposed skill deficits and
America's global competitiveness.

1. Test Scores and Wages

Economists connect standardized test scores to hourly wages 8
by taking gains in the scores and computing corresponding
increases in dollars earned. They also use broad supervisory
ratings of employees (high, medium, and low) to estimate
worker productivity. Both measures are, of course, proxies for
actual productivity, and they certainly stretch reality. Using

standardized achievement tests, for example, assumes that these instruments measure the analytic, creative, and practical skills and positive attitudes valued by employers. Gauging the results against hourly wages assumes that pay is set by equals, by employer and worker negotiating in fully competitive markets. Furthermore, the measures require complex manipulation of data and substantial interpretation and contain many methodological problems. Little wonder that experts disagree on the worth of such data in estimating worker productivity. Yet conclusions are put forward as unadorned facts.[3]

2. Skills Deficits

9   In this argument, not only low worker productivity and decreasing global competitiveness but also youth unemployment and a widening gap between high-salary and low-wage jobs all stem from inadequate knowledge and skills that high school graduates bring to the workplace. The skills-deficit argument first appeared in the late 19th century, when industrial leaders also were deeply concerned about global competition, at that time from German and British manufacturers. In 1898, for example, the president of the National Association of Manufacturers told members at the group's annual conference:

> There is hardly any work we can do or any expenditures we can make that will yield so large a return to our industries as would come from the establishment of educational institutions which would give us skilled hands and trained minds for the conduct of our industries and our commerce (Kliebard 1999).

10   As a result, a broad coalition of civic, business, labor, and education leaders pressed district, state, and federal policy makers to introduce vocational curricula so U.S. students would be better prepared for the industrial workplace. By 1917, federal policy makers decided to subsidize high school industrial arts and home economics courses, while states and districts adopted vocational education and guidance in all schools (Kantor 1982; Lazerson and Grubb 1974).

11   Through the Great Depression, World War II, the Cold War, and Vietnam, moreover, vocational education received enormous political and economic support from business and civic elites. Yet youth unemployment, of course, still rose and fell,

remaining especially high among minority populations—and even in flush times, employers grumbled that high school graduates were unprepared for the workplace (Kliebard 1988).

Unfortunately, those who complain of skills deficits rarely specify what knowledge and skills are needed to succeed in an information-based economy, and they generally overlook the wealth of evidence showing that employers are far more concerned about applicants' attitudes and behavior than about their school-based knowledge in math or science. In fact, the supposed mismatch between worker skills and employer desires has little evidence to support it other than sturdy popular and media-amplified assertions. It is thus simply rash to suggest that students who are pressed by centralized, standards-based reforms to take more math and science courses or who do well on standardized achievement tests will succeed in entry-level jobs or in college.[4]   12

3. Global Competitiveness

Finally, the prior claims snowball into the assertion that insufficiently educated workers have slowed U.S. productivity and threatened America's position in global markets. This assertion is flawed. For one, it ignores how the United States enjoyed nearly a decade of unbroken prosperity in the 1990s. For another, U.S. productivity rates have increased (not decreased) over the past decade. For a third, even with the weaker U.S. economy of 2000–2002, the World Economic Forum found that the United States had the world's second most competitive economy, after Finland. In short, few economists or public officials doubt the predominance of the U.S. economy today.[5]   13

In light of such prosperity and competitiveness and the pivotal role that student achievement is supposed to play in U.S. economic performance, one might reasonably have expected public schools to be commended for producing graduates who contributed so much to this remarkable record. Yet no such praise has been uttered by corporate leaders, governors, policy analysts, or Oval Office occupants. Perhaps economic gains do not depend so heavily on student test scores as public school critics contend. This has, indeed, dawned on various observers. As economist Kevin Hollenbeck of the W. E. Upjohn Institute for Employment Research has put it, "The evidence seems to suggest that mediocre educational results do not threaten economic performance" (Hollenbeck 2001). In this regard,   14 note what historian Lawrence Cremin wrote in 1990 about where responsibility does lie for economic challenges:

> American economic competitiveness with Japan and other nations is to a considerable degree a function of monetary, trade and industrial policy, and of decisions made by the President and Congress, the Federal Reserve Board, and the federal Departments of the Treasury and Commerce and Labor. Therefore, to contend that problems of international competitiveness can be solved by education reform, especially education reform defined solely as school reform, is not merely utopian and millennialist, it is at best foolish and at worst a crass effort to direct attention away from those truly responsible for doing something about competitiveness and to lay the burden instead on the schools (Cremin 1990).

15   To the list of those responsible for economic performance one should add inventors of technologies that contribute significantly to improved productivity and managers (or mismanagers) of U.S. businesses, including CEOs who have been issuing so many fanciful numbers in recent years.

16   Competing with the list of those who directly influence national economic performance, however, is another list of those business-inspired reformers drawn from civic and economic elites, educators, union officials, and others who, for the past 30 years, helped shape the current purpose: insuring that public schools are little more than boot camps for future employees. Well-intentioned civic and business leaders have done what so many other reformers have been accused of in past decades: they have experimented on teachers and students for over three decades without showing much evidence of success.

17   The issue is *not* whether schools should prepare students for productive labor. They should. The issue is that the single-minded pursuit of preparing all students for college and high-paying jobs has narrowed the far broader and historic mission of civic engagement. Historically and presently, schools have been and are still expected to instill civic, social, and humanitarian attitudes and skills that will shape our democracy and influence how graduates lead their lives in their communities. Schools are expected to build student respect for differences in ideas and cultures. Schools are expected to be decent and livable places for the young to spend a large portion of their waking time. These historic and contemporary aims of public schools often have been neglected in the mistaken rush to turn schools into engines for the larger economy (Labaree 1997; Goodlad 1984).

Even more damning are the questions that have been omit-   18
ted from the current economic and political agendas shaped by
business-inspired reformers.

Consider a few of the missing questions: 19

- Do schools geared toward preparing workers also build
  literate, active, and morally sensitive citizens who carry
  out their civic duties?
- How can schools develop independently thinking citizens who earn their living in corporate workplaces?
- When the economy hiccups, unemployment increases,
  and graduates have little money to secure higher education or find a job matched to their skills, will public
  schools, now an arm of the economy, get blamed—
  as they have in the past—for creating the mismatch?

These basic questions, unasked by business-inspired reform   20
coalitions in the past three decades, go unanswered today.

NOTES

1. For details of the formation of this business-inspired coalition concentrating on school reform, see Thomas Toch, *In The Name of Excellence*
   (New York: Oxford University Press, 1991); Larry Cuban, *Why Are Good
   Schools So Hard To Get?* (New York: Teachers College Press, 2003).
   Gordon Lafer maps a sequence of events in the same quarter-century
   where employers focused on workers' lack of skills and the need for
   more training and education to equip employees for the future work-
   place. See *The Job Training Charade* (Ithaca, NY: Cornell University
   Press, 2002). Economists and widely respected analysts also produced
   best sellers in these years that judged schools as failures in teaching
   students to think and solve problems. See Ray Marshall and Marc
   Tucker, *Thinking for a Living: Education and the Wealth of Nations*
   (New York: Basic Books, 1992); Robert Reich, *The Work of Nations*
   (New York: Alfred Knopf, 1991); and Lester Thurow, *Head to Head: The
   Coming Economic Battle among Japan, Europe, and America* (New
   York: Morrow, 1992).
2. For a brief history of the movement towards standards-based reform
   with its accountability and testing, see Richard Elmore, "Building a
   New Structure for School Leadership," winter (Washington, D.C.:
   Albert Shanker Institute, 2000).
3. An example of connecting tests to wages and productivity is John
   Bishop, "Is The Test Score Decline Responsible for the Productivity
   Growth Decline?" *American Economic Review*, 1989, 74(1), 178–197.
   Bishop's answer to his question is "yes." For those who doubt these as-
   sumptions of test scores and worker productivity, see Henry Levin,
   "High-Stakes Testing and Economic Productivity," in Gary Orfield and
   Mindy Kornhaber (Eds.), *Raising Standards or Raising Barriers?*
   Inequality and High-Stakes Testing in Public Education (New York: The
   Century Foundation Press, 2001), 39–49; Robert Balfanz, "Local

Knowledge, Academic Skills, and Individual Productivity: An Alternative View," *Educational Policy*, 5(4), 1991, 343–370.

4. Levin, "High Stakes Tests and Economic Productivity"; John P. Smith, III, "Tracking the Mathematics of Automobile Production: Are Schools Failing To Prepare Students for Work?" (1999), 835–878. Also see Lafer, *The Job Training Charade*, chapters 2 and 3, for a comprehensive summary of evidence revealing how workplace demands are inconsistent with the theory and beliefs of those who argue for more well-trained graduates from high school and college. Critics of using standardized test scores as the only or best indicator of improved teaching and learning have often referred to other important measures that are either ignored or missing because of measurement difficulties. These include the quality of intellectual work in school, the linkages between classroom teaching and assessment, and other measures of student performance. The work of Lorrie Shepard is best in this regard. See "The Role of Assessment in a Learning Culture" (2000), 4–14.

5. For growth in productivity in the 1990s, see Louis Uchitelle, "Big Increases in Productivity by Workers," *New York Times*, November 13, 1999, B1; Hal Varian, "The Economic Scene," *New York Times*, June 6, 2002, C2; Michael Porter, Jeffrey Sachs, and John McArthur, *Global Competitiveness Report 2001–2002* (New York: World Economic Forum, 2002).

REFERENCES

Amrein, Audrey, and David Berliner. 2002. "High Stakes Testing, Uncertainty, and Student Learning." *Education Policy Analysis Archives* 10(18).

Balfanz, Robert. 1991. "Local Knowledge, Academic Skills, and Individual Productivity: An Alternative View." *Educational Policy* 5(4): 343–370.

Bishop, John. 1989. "Is The Test Score Decline Responsible for the Productivity Growth Decline?" *American Economic Review* 74(1): 178–197.

Cremin, Lawrence. 1990. *Popular Education and Its Discontents*. New York: Harper & Row.

Cuban, Larry. Forthcoming. "A Solution That Lost Its Problem: Why Centralized Policymaking Is Unlikely To Yield Many Classroom Gains." Denver, CO: Education Commission of States.

———. Forthcoming. *The Blackboard and the Bottom Line: Why Can't Schools Be Like Businesses?* Cambridge, MA: Harvard University Press.

———. 2003. *Why Are Good Schools So Hard To Get?* New York: Teachers College Press.

Elmore, Richard. 2000. "Building a New Structure for School Leadership." Washington, D.C.: Albert Shanker Institute.

Finn, Chester, Jr. 1991. *We Must Take Charge*. New York: Free Press.

Goodlad, John. 1984. *A Place Called School*. New York: MacMillan.

Hollenbeck, Kevin. 2001. *Education and the Economy*. W. E. Upjohn Institute for Employment Research.

Kantor, Harvey. 1982. "Vocationalism in American Education: The Economic and Political Context, 1880–1930." In *Work, Youth, and Schooling*, eds. H. Kantor and D. Tyack. Stanford: Stanford University Press, 14–44.

———. 1988. *Learning to Earn: School, Work, and Vocational Reform in California, 1880–1930*. Madison: University of Wisconsin Press.

Kliebard, Herbert. 1999. *Schooled to Work: Vocationalism and the American Curriculum, 1876–1946.* New York: Teachers College Press.

Labaree, David. 1997. "Public Goods, Private Goods: The American Struggle over Educational Goals." *American Educational Research Journal* 34(1): 39–81.

Lafer, Gordon. 2002. *The Job Training Charade.* Ithaca, NY: Cornell University Press.

Lazerson, Marvin, Norton Grubb, eds. 1974. *American Education and Vocationalism: Documents in Vocational Education, 1870–1970.* New York: Teachers College Press.

Levin, Henry. 2001. "High-Stakes Testing and Economic Productivity." In *Raising Standards or Raising Barriers? Inequality and High-Stakes Testing in Public Education,* eds. G. Orfield and M. Kornhaber. New York: The Century Foundation Press, 39–49.

Marshall, Ray, and Marc Tucker. 1992. *Thinking for a Living: Education and the Wealth of Nations.* New York: Basic Books.

National Assessment of Educational Progress. 2003. *The Nation's Report Card, Reading 2002.* Washington, D.C.: U.S. Department of Education.

Porter, Michael, Jeffrey Sachs, and John McArthur. 2002. *Global Competitiveness Report 2001–2002.* New York: World Economic Forum.

Reich, Robert. 1991. *The Work of Nations.* New York: Alfred Knopf.

Shepard, Lorrie. 2000. "The Role of Assessment in a Learning Culture." *Educational Researcher* 29(7): 4–14

Thurow, Lester. 1992. *Head to Head: The Coming Economic Battle among Japan, Europe, and America.* New York: Morrow.

Toch, Thomas. 1991. *In The Name of Excellence.* New York: Oxford University Press.

Uchitelle, Louis. 1999. "Big Increases in Productivity by Workers," *New York Times.* November 13, B1.

Varian, Hal. 2002. "The Economic Scene," *New York Times.* June 6, C2.

Thomas Toch

DIVIDE AND CONQUER

HOW BREAKING UP BIG HIGH SCHOOLS CAN BE THE KEY TO SUCCESSFUL EDUCATION REFORM

Thomas Toch, a respected education journalist for Education Week *and* U.S. News and World Report, *is the Writer-in-Residence at the National Center on Education and the Economy. This article, adapted from his latest book,* High Schools on a Human Scale: How Small Schools Can Transform American Education, *suggests that smaller schools might be the key to a better public education system.*

This essay, though quite different in form, asks questions about the way that setting affects public education, questions that are similar to those raised by E. B. White's more personal essay in this section. Toch's essay was published in May 2003 in Washington Monthly, *a "neo-liberal" journal that sees itself as a watchdog over politics in the nation's capital.*

1   High schools don't produce a lot of headlines in the national education debate. But they are arguably the weakest link in American education. International studies show that U.S. grade-school students perform reasonably well compared to their counterparts in developed countries in Europe and Asia. By junior high school, however, Americans fall behind their international peers, and plummet during the high school years. The gap is especially pronounced for kids who attend large high schools in urban areas with lots of students from low-income families.

2   A typical example of a sprawling inner-city school was the Julia Richman High School on Manhattan's Upper East Side. Though located in a high-rent neighborhood and once a prestigious school, by the early 1990s, Richman was one of the city's worst. Buffeted by a changing student population, sharp staffing cuts, and other forces, the enormous high school had degenerated into a cauldron of violence. Students tore out water fountains, destroyed bathrooms, and smashed windows, recalls John Broderick, the school's veteran engineer. Graffiti covered the hallways. Metal cages were constructed in the vice principal's office to separate belligerent students, and local cops labeled the school "Julia Riker's," after New York City's notorious Riker's Island jail. It was, says Broderick, "utter, utter chaos." The words of philosopher Francis Bacon inscribed over the building's front door, "Knowledge Is Power," seemed to be lost on everyone: The school's graduation rate was 37 percent.

3   Today, however, Julia Richman has, in Broderick's words, "turned around 500 percent." The disciplinary cages are gone, along with the metal detectors that fortified the school's entrances. Richman is bright, clean, and safe. Fights are rare. Attendance is up. Dropout rates are down substantially. And greater numbers of graduates are going on to college.

4   What produced this educational reformation at a time when the nation is lamenting the plight of urban education? A big part of the answer can be found in the two-foot-by-three-foot banners that hang largely unnoticed along the school's main corridor: Urban Academy, Vanguard, Manhattan International, Talent Unlimited, P226M, Ella Baker—these are the names of the six separate schools that collectively share what is now

known as the Julia Richman Education Complex. Richman has abandoned the American tradition of the "big high school" in favor of multiple scaled-down educational settings within the same building that engender a strong sense of community, where both students and teachers can flourish.

In recent years, there's been a movement among school re- 5
formers who argue that size is the enemy of excellence in America's high schools and breaking up super-sized schools into smaller units is the key to improving them. A decade's worth of studies comparing the merits of small high schools to large ones have revealed several clear trends: In small schools, student and teacher attendance rates are higher, disciplinary problems are fewer, graduation rates are higher, and dropout rates are lower.

But merely cleaving enormous schools into smaller units is 6
rarely enough to counter the alienating environments that plague many traditional high schools. So New York City adopted a more radical—and more productive—strategy at Julia Richman. The city began by making a clean sweep of the old high school in the early 1990s, emptying the building of students and staff and then introducing six new schools of no more than 300 students, each with its own leadership. The Richman planners made each of the new institutions "schools of choice," allowing students from across the city to attend. And to help the schools forge unique educational missions that students, parents, and teachers could understand and commit to, they gave the schools a level of autonomy over teacher selection, budgets, and instructional strategies that's rare in public education.

Assembly Line Academies

What makes the Julia Richman experiment so important is that 7
the basic blueprint of the nation's high schools hasn't changed significantly since the rise of the "comprehensive" high school nearly a century ago. At that time, high schools catered primarily to a narrow elite. But that changed in the early part of the 20th century when educators faced an influx of new students, many of them immigrants, who were thought to be ill-equipped to study academics. Leaders of the Progressive movement pushed to extend high school curricula beyond traditional academic subjects to include vocational and other nonacademic subjects that are still taught in today's schools.

Julia Richman opened as a comprehensive girls' high school 8
in the 1920s, a five-story, red-brick structure that stretches

from 67th to 68th streets on Manhattan's Upper East Side. With classrooms for 2,200 students, two gymnasiums, a swimming pool, a theater, maple floors, and brass doorknobs inscribed with the words, "Public School, City of New York," the school was not only a model of the comprehensive high school, but a source of great civic pride. Its first students studied "commercial skills," such as typing and stenography. As Greek, Latin, and other advanced subjects later entered the school's curriculum, Julia Richman grew to become one of New York City's most prestigious secondary schools.

9   This comprehensive system made sense for the industrial economy of the time. Future lawyers, accountants, and other professionals studied academics, while those headed into mills and assembly lines learned valuable practical skills. High schools essentially served as great sorting machines, preparing students very differently for very different roles in the workforce. The system was considered to be both egalitarian and efficient, deliberately applying the industrial principles of mass production to American secondary education by housing everything under one roof.

10   But just as Richman fell on hard times, so too has the idea that the large, comprehensive high schools are the best way to educate students. In today's "knowledge-based" economy, preparing students for decent-paying jobs means educating all students well enough to enter college, not just an elite few. Of course, some large high schools do that job well, just as some small schools do it poorly. But today, 60 percent of American high school students attend schools of at least 1,000 students, which places them at a disadvantage. Large schools foster the sort of apathy once seen at Julia Richman, leading to what the educator Theodore Sizer once described as a "conspiracy of the least"—an unwritten, unspoken pledge among disaffected students and teachers to put as little energy as possible into their work that produces a huge drag on the productivity of American high schools. Julia Richman's dramatic turnaround offers lessons for large urban high schools plagued by similar problems.

"Hothousing" High Schools

11   The source of the Richman concept is Deborah Meier, the founder of Central Park East Secondary School. the small, nationally acclaimed high school in East Harlem. Convinced that New York's vast comprehensive high schools were organizationally bankrupt, she and others from the Coalition of

Essential Schools, a national school reform network, in 1992 sought the permission of the New York City Board of Education to restructure one of the city's worst high schools. The board granted the request and gave Meier and her colleagues Julia Richman, which had been on New York State's list of failing schools for more than a decade.

The rechristened "Julia Richman Education Complex" 12 stopped taking new ninth graders after the 1992–93 school year, and by the summer of 1996, the last of the school's "old" students had graduated. Early on, Meier and her colleagues resolved not to found half a dozen new schools in Richman, reasoning that opening the educational complex with six schools in the throes of a start-up would likely be disastrous. Instead, several of the new high schools were "hothoused" in other locations around New York for a year, before they were imported, giving them time to work out the bugs in their school designs and establish distinct educational identities. As Herb Mack, co-director of Urban Academy and a Richman founder, puts it: "We wanted to make sure that the schools had a reason for being other than just being small." This also ensured that there would be no existing math, history, and other department heads to challenge the autonomy of the nascent schools—a problem for many high schools that merely subdivide in an effort to improve.

The first two schools to move in were Vanguard High 13 School, which serves primarily low-achieving students, and Manhattan International, which serves recent immigrants who lack a strong grasp of English. At the same time, a performing-arts program within Julia Richman known as Talent Unlimited became an autonomous school within the new complex. Urban Academy Laboratory High School, a 120-student school for teenagers who have been unsuccessful in other city high schools, moved in shortly afterward.

Urban played a key role in helping to establish the fledgling 14 schools at Richman. It had been a highly successful Manhattan school for a decade and was moved into Richman as part of the school's overhaul to serve as an "anchor" institution. Like Richman's other hothoused schools, Urban was able to bring its students to Richman under New York City's school choice program, which permits many students to select schools outside of their neighborhoods.

The results have been outstanding, to the pleasant surprise 15 of parents, the city's education leaders, and many others. The dropout rate at Vanguard, the school with the most challenging students, is only 4 percent (compared to 20 percent citywide) and Manhattan International and Urban Academy report that more than 90 percent of their students attend college after graduation. (Test score comparisons are tough because, until recently, Richman's high schools have been exempt from statewide testing; its own assessments, however, show real improvement.)

16   But remaking Julia Richman into an education "multiplex," one where the separate schools work together, was not simple. Indeed, if the creators of the Richman complex hadn't taken many steps along the way to preserve the independence of its individual schools without sacrificing the governability of the vast building, Richman wouldn't be the success it is today.

17   Urban's stature helped Richman's new high schools survive a troubled two-year coexistence with the students and teachers they were replacing. The transition generated friction between the school's old and new staffs and hurt those students whose school was being phased out. "The 700–800 exiting kids were demoralized and largely abandoned," says Ann Cook, who runs Urban Academy with Mack and who helped create the Richman complex. "The existing staff were angry and suspicious. 'Now you are fixing the place,' they would say when they saw workers doing renovations. It was horrible." Urban's leaders helped to diffuse the hostility. But they concluded that it would have been better to move the new schools into the building only after it had been vacated completely.

18   Once the new schools arrived at the Richman complex, Mack, Cook, and their colleagues went to great lengths to preserve the schools' autonomy, believing that creating a strong sense of community within each of the new schools was the best way to forge the close, respectful relationships between students and teachers that motivate students to care about their school work.

19   Students had to apply to each school in the complex separately. The majority attended schools by choice—as a result of the city's choice plan—and were thus, Meier and the others reasoned, more likely to identify with their school and work harder, even, as would prove to be the case, if many students arrived with weak academic records.

20   Richman schools are also physically distinct. Though as many as three share some floors, there are no common hallways, and the swinging double doors that connect the schools might as well be cinderblock walls; students and teachers simply don't go into other schools' space—a fact that has required a lot of instructional gerrymandering, including moving a chemistry lab to Manhattan International's wing of the building so that its students didn't have to enter Vanguard's area to go to class.

Even bathrooms, a source of discipline problems in many 21
high schools, are part of the solution at Richman. To ensure
that there aren't any public spaces where students and teachers
aren't known to each other, every bathroom in the building is
located within the boundaries of schools and is off-limits to
students from other schools—conditions that require students
and teachers at Urban to share bathrooms. There are six
schools in six different locations on six different schedules at
Richman, all of which share (at different times) a recital hall,
art gallery, gym, pool, weight room, pottery and dance studios,
cafeteria, library, an auditorium, a small theater, and a student
health clinic run by nearby Mt. Sinai Hospital. The only places
they are permitted to intermingle are the cafeteria and the
library.

A Stake in Success

In carving out distinct boundaries within the building and 22
giving the schools authority over their staffing, budgets, and
teaching strategies, Richman's organizers sought to give teachers a significant stake in their students' success. "You need autonomy for teachers for them to feel truly responsible for kids,"
says Cook. "If teachers don't feel responsible, they don't invest
themselves."

Richman's tightly knit schools, meanwhile, have engendered 23
a sense of belonging among their students that is rare in large
urban high schools. In the words of Urban Academy's Mack, a
40-year veteran of the Chicago and New York school systems,
Richman's schools "give kids a home." Urban's atmosphere is
best described as relaxed; there's little trace of the coldness and
sense of unease that pervade many traditional urban high
schools. During class breaks, Urban students hang out in
groups in stuffed chairs and old sofas in the hallway of the
school's second-floor "campus." As I sat speaking with faculty
members during a recent visit, several students dropped by to
ask them questions. They sought out teachers with no less ca-
sualness in Urban's faculty office, a large, open space with
desks pushed up against each other, as in a newsroom.

"How many teachers did you know well at Midwood?" 24
I asked Aneliese Ranzoni, a senior at Urban who had transferred from Midwood High School in Brooklyn, where there
were 3,700 students.

"Know well?" 25

"Well." 26

"None." 27

28   "How about here?"

29   "All the ones I have, and also the ones I don't have."

30   The result, says Rona Armillas, a former assistant principal at Manhattan International, is "a different type of negotiation" between students and teachers in the Richman complex. "In most high schools you approach kids as an authority figure," Armillas says. "It's a power play. And it usually doesn't work. There's no growth in students' maturity. At Richman, you know the kid and his style and there's mutual respect. Things don't escalate." As Urban science teacher Terri Grosso puts it, "It's not us versus them here."

31   Security takes on a very different meaning in such an atmosphere. Rather than a system that treats students anonymously and resorts to metal detectors and surveillance cameras, Richman's schools have become largely self-policing. Because of their small size and the building's policy of having students stay out of other schools' space, students and teachers know who belongs in their part of the building and who doesn't, and that becomes Richman's most important source of security. Students are just as likely as teachers to ask "outsiders" for identification or to report them to Richman's half dozen security guards.

32   Richman isn't completely free of disciple problems, but serious infractions like fighting, say students such as Josme Mark, a senior from Haiti via Brooklyn, are very rare. That's certainly the sense one gets at the complex's front entrance, where a mild-mannered guard with a smile and a sign-in sheet has replaced metal detectors.

33   It's hard to overstate the care with which Richman's leaders have tended to the building's social equilibrium. To discourage interschool rivalries even as they promote schools' autonomy, for example, they have sought to blend students from the sundry Richman schools in carefully chosen settings. In addition to student councils in each school, there's a building-wide student government. There are building-wide college fairs. Students represent Richman rather than their individual schools in New York City's Public School Athletic League. And Richman's athletic director has begun commingling students from the different high schools on intramural basketball teams.

34   Yet a recent event reveals both the value of the schools' autonomy and the fragile nature of the social fabric in urban high schools. Mack had given the Richman basketball teams each a classroom in Urban for pre-practice study halls. Urban students are so trusting of one another that they routinely leave expensive jackets lying around in the student lounge. But as soon as the building-wide basketball teams started coming

into Urban, the clothing began to disappear. The basketball players brought friends from other Richman schools with them to the Urban study halls who simply didn't share the same sense of community as Urban's students. When Mack subsequently moved the study halls to the Richman theater, the theft subsided.

Traffic Patterns

To protect the independence of the new Richman schools, Meier and the others resolved that the complex wouldn't have a principal, only a "building manager"—Urban co-director Herb Mack.   35

Watching the veteran educator work the building, it is easy to think he's a traditional principal. When I caught up with him at 7:15 one morning, he was speeding through Richman checking that its many doors were locked, a knot of keys bouncing up and down on his hip. He greeted the guards at the building's two student entrances, then bolted outside with a sheaf of reserved-for-staff flyers that he placed under the windshield wipers of cars parked on the school's block that didn't display school system parking permits. Back in the building he noticed that the day's newspapers weren't at the front entrance. "They've been taken again, we've got to find out who's doing it," he declared, striding toward a security guard to report the matter. By 7:45, he was welcoming students.   36

But by 8:15, Mack had changed roles. He was back at his desk in Urban Academy, talking as the school's co-director to a student about a course she needed to complete her semester's schedule. And shortly afterward, he headed down the hall to the first of the three social studies courses he teaches at Urban.   37

Mack's role also differs from that of traditional principals in other ways. He has no authority over the budgets, staffing, or instruction at Richman's various schools, other than at Urban. Rather, school-wide policies are formed by a "building council" that consists of the directors of Richman's schools and the heads of other programs housed in the building: First Steps, a child care center; the health clinic; and a teacher training center. The council convenes once a week to discuss everything from fire drills to food quality. It also gathers several times a year at the home of the director of one of Richman's schools for breakfast or lunch and a half-day's discussion. Mack leads the meetings, but he doesn't dictate their outcomes.   38

Early on, the council, then representing Richman's four high schools, decided to bring in an elementary program (the   39

300-student pre-K-through-eighth-grade Ella Baker Elementary School) and another for disabled students (P226M, serving several dozen autistic students) as a way of further tempering the adolescent environment in Richman.

40   The strategy has paid substantial dividends: Older students are more careful about what they say and do when younger children are present, and the presence of Ella Baker and P226M within the complex give the high school students ample opportunities to be tutors and teachers' aides, responsible roles they are encouraged to play. The bank of monitors that security guards at the old Richman watched 24 hours a day in a windowless second-floor office has been boxed off with plywood in what is now an Ella Baker counseling office.

41   The council reshaped Vanguard's boundaries when it realized that its original "traffic" plan had required Talent Unlimited students to go through Vanguard on their way to and from Richman's cafeteria. The result: The hallway between Talent Unlimited and the cafeteria was turned into "public" space, housing the complex's pottery and dance studios, home economics center, and distance-learning laboratory, which the building council constructed with city council funding.

42   And because many high school students in the building are parents, the council used school-system funding to turn Richman's old guidance suites into the First Steps infant-toddler child-care center, complete with an observation room and a one-way mirror for students in the building's child-development classes.

43   When I was at Richman, the building's guards were troubled by the substantial number of delivery people wandering the building. They expressed their unhappiness to the council's security subcommittee and by the next morning the council had taken action. "Delivery of food to staff and students has been a headache," Mack declared in a memo to the building's staff and students. As a result, he announced, "Any deliveries that arrive without the recipient's name and room number written on the back of the package will be sent back to the restaurant." Within a week the problem was solved.

44   But unless the welfare of Richman as a whole is at stake, the council lets schools set policies individually. When the New York City Police Department sought to ban "do rag" headwear in the city's schools to discourage gangs, the four Richman schools responded independently. Manhattan International, Vanguard, and Talent Unlimited went along with the police request. But Urban, after a student-faculty meeting where do rags were adjudged to have no gang overtones at the school, resolved to continue to let its students wear them. Richman's other three high schools respected Urban's stance.

Small Schools, Big Benefits

Despite common conception about the greater cost of small   45
schools, the Richman multiplex hasn't been expensive to operate. Skeptics frequently contend that small schools must be
less efficient than big ones because they can't spread costs over
as many students. But in many instances the Richman complex has been more efficient than the large school it replaced.
Julia Richman High School, for example, needed six extra security guards just to operate its metal detectors. Richman's
council has streamlined building-wide staffing. Schools now
require fewer counselors because teachers and administrators
know students so well. And because Richman's schools are
small, and thus more manageable, Mack and other administrators have time to teach. This has permitted the schools to focus
more of their resources on their classrooms. Eighty-seven percent of the staff in Richman's high schools teach students, for
example, compared to eighty-one percent in New York City's
high schools generally.

The cost savings of these steps have been documented by   46
Norm Fruchter and his colleagues at New York University's
Graduate School of Education, who recently examined the finances of large and small high schools nationwide and found
that the efficiencies of large high schools are largely offset by
fewer non-teaching staff and other savings in small schools.
They concluded that small schools are only about five percent
more expensive than large ones. And when the researchers
crunched the numbers from a different perspective—the cost
per graduate—the efficiency debate tilted in favor of small
schools. Because dropout rates are higher in large high
schools, Fruchter found, the cost of educating each graduate
averaged $49,578, compared to $49,554 in small high schools,
where more students stay through graduation.

Richman's schools also pool their resources. Several have   47
sought to concentrate their course offerings out of a desire to
teach fewer subjects in greater depth. Doing so has allowed
Richman's schools to hire shared staff in art, dance, and other
subjects they would be unable to teach with the enrollment-based
funding they receive from the New York City school system.

But Richman would not be run nearly as efficiently or effec-   48
tively as it is without a large measure of autonomy from New
York City's school headquarters—autonomy that the complex's
founders had to work long and hard to win, given the intensely
bureaucratic and hierarchical nature of New York's public
school system. And even with substantial independence, the

council has had to get the bureaucracy's blessing before moving on several matters. The city's superintendent of alternative schools, for example, only let the Richman council remove the building's metal detectors and surveillance cameras once it had demonstrated that parents backed the idea. Nor would Richman be the place it is today if Meier and her colleagues hadn't won the support of the 140,000-member United Federation of Teachers (UFT), the city's influential teachers union.

49   The UFT, like many teachers' unions, has the power to effectively veto school closings under job-security provisos in its contract. Thus, Meier sought the support of Sandra Feldman, the UFT president, pointing out that working conditions in the old Richman were terrible, and the multiplex was a good solution. Feldman agreed, and the UFT arranged early retirement packages and transfers to other schools for departing Richman staff.

50   Just as important was a revolutionary pact between the UFT and the New York City school board that offered the city's schools autonomy—rare in public education—over staffing, schedules, and other key aspects of school life. Under the so-called School Based Options agreement, schools with at least 70 percent of teachers backing the concept are able to abandon seniority-based staffing and other union-negotiated strictures. As a result, Richman schools can hire teachers who share their educational philosophies, which greatly strengthens the schools' sense of community.

51   Of course, replacing the nation's many dysfunctional large urban high schools with smaller, more personal educational settings doesn't guarantee students a high-quality education. Strong teaching is also a key. So Richman's new schools have sought to take advantage of their size to introduce instructional innovations that wouldn't be possible in many large schools. Urban, Vanguard, and Manhattan International, for example, use a student-evaluation system that requires every student to make oral defenses of science, social studies, math, and several other projects that they must complete in addition to their regular courses to graduate.

Bumping the Bureaucracy

52   Successfully reforming any school requires battling the bureaucracy, and Richman is no different. Despite its successes, the school is under tremendous pressure to conform to the priorities of the New York City school system in ways that threaten its stability.

The week I visited, the city's education bureaucracy assigned a   53
new guidance counselor, "bumping" Manhattan International's
existing counselor out of a job during the height of the college-
admissions season. The counselor claimed the job under a
clause in the UFT's collective-bargaining contract that permits
teachers in schools with declining enrollments to take the jobs
of less-experienced teachers in other schools. "I'm the principal
and I have no say," Ling objected at the time. But he protested to
the city's school authorities and the carpetbagger counselor was
sent elsewhere. The year before, a city school administrator sent
a patronage hire to be Richman's technology specialist, despite
the individual's having scant technology experience. The building council turned down the funding for the job rather than take
the person.

And in response to charges by the city's large, traditional   54
high schools that Richman's schools are under-populated, authorities repeatedly have sought to put more students in
Richman's high schools. "There's always pull toward the center,
toward bureaucratic control," says Mack. "What we do is not
really understandable to a bureaucracy."

Recently a group of parents sought to dismantle the Richman   55
complex completely. In a confrontation where race and class
were never far from the surface of the debate, the mostly white
and affluent parents of students at a nearby elementary school
pressed local politicians to have Richman turned into a single,
"zoned" high school available only to Upper East Side students,
a move that would have excluded from Richman the many students who now travel to the complex from Harlem, Manhattan's
Lower East Side, and the Bronx. The school fought back, led by
Ann Cook, who, as Richman's Project Director, expends as much
energy on behalf of Richman outside the complex as Mack does
inside.

Cook sought the help of Richman's "board of advisors," a   56
panel of influential lawyers, corporate executives, foundation
officers, civil rights leaders, labor unionists, and university
professors the council had assembled years earlier to help navigate New York's political waters. "Like most bureaucracies,
the New York board of education responds to outside pressure,
not to middle management," says Cook. Together, they successfully worked the city's educational and political leaders. The
parent group was "given" a building nearby.

Ultimately, Richman's leaders don't take much of anything for   57
granted when it comes to preserving the Richman complex. At
the start of every school year Mack gathers the new teachers from
throughout the complex to explain Richman and how it works.
"You have to keep building culture," he says. "It's not automatic."

58   But to engineer Broderick the results speak for themselves. "After 42 years in the business," he says of the transformation at Richman, "it's the first time I've ever had to ask teachers to leave their rooms at the end of the day so I can clean."

Alexander Russo

WHEN SCHOOL
CHOICE ISN'T

Alexander Russo is a freelance education writer and former advisor to Democratic senator Jeff Bingaman. He is a contributing editor for Catalyst, *a Chicago-based independent education reform magazine. He is the editor of* School Reform in Chicago: Lessons in Policy and Practice, 2004, *and has coauthored* Can Philanthropy Fix Our Schools? Appraising Walter Annenberg's $500 Million Gift to Public Education. *Russo has consistently advocated for equity in education across social classes, as he does in the essay below. This essay was first published in* Washington Monthly, *a left-leaning journal that examines public policies generated in our nation's capital.*

1   Central Junior High School is a typical troubled school in the down-on-its-luck working-class town of Zion, Ill. Located an hour north of Chicago near Lake Michigan on the Wisconsin border, Zion's religious origins and former glory are still apparent in the town's biblically named streets, parks, and skating rinks. In recent decades, however, the city has struggled with drugs and gang violence, and tax revenues from the nuclear power plant built here 20 years ago dried up after the plant closed in 1999.

2   Zion's schools have also struggled. Going by last year's test scores, Zion is home to four of the nearly 600 failing schools in Illinois. More than half of the town's 3,000 elementary and junior high students are poor, and more than 60 percent are minorities. Before the local bond referendum passed last year, the schools were seriously underfunded. Central, which houses more than 600 seventh- and eighth-graders from around the

district, has been "failing," and resorted to school uniforms in an attempt to limit gang and racial conflicts on campus.

Carol Suetmeyer's daughter, a student at Central, has wit-   3
nessed firsthand the school's problems, which aren't limited to academics. In one harrowing incident last year, teachers and administrators couldn't find the 14-year-old girl for several hours. She was eventually located, safe and sound, but for her mother the experience was terrifying. "I'm very protective of my daughter," she says. "Nobody knew where she was."

Like several other parents in her town, Suetmeyer would   4
love nothing better than to take her daughter out of Central and send her to another school this fall. Federal education-reform legislation passed this year—the No Child Left Behind Act—was designed by President Bush and Congress to allow parents like Suetmeyer to do just that, by giving them the option to transfer their children to better schools. But here's the catch: In Zion, there *is* no better school.

A small school district, Zion has five mostly overcrowded ele-   5
mentary schools but only one junior high school. The next closest junior high schools are not far away, in the next town over, but the new law doesn't require schools to accept transfer students from other districts. And neighboring school districts—especially wealthier ones—are no more interested in opening their doors to poor students than they were during the days of busing. As a result, Suetmeyer will be sending her daughter back to Central.

Her difficulty is a snapshot of what's likely to come this fall,   6
when the nearly 10 percent of all students who attend the nation's 8,600 "failing" public schools (4 million students in all) will have the right to choose other public schools. There are more than 14,000 school districts in the nation, but about one in three has just a single school per grade level.

"My guess is that each district will want to keep itself sepa-   7
rate," says Dennis Divoky, the principal at Central. "Community control [of schools] is the reason that there are 900 districts in Illinois."

School choice, as written into federal law, was intended to   8
provide an escape for kids stuck in lousy situations, while at the same time spurring competition for reform. It came about as a compromise between advocates and foes of private school vouchers by creating parental choice, though only within public schools. In exchange for a significant increase in federal funding, the new law demands that failing (or "persistently unsafe") schools give parents new transfer options and cover the costs of transportation to another school. To give teeth to this requirement, up to 20 percent of each district's federal funding

can be spent on transportation and such supplemental services
as after-school tutoring.

9   Zion's experience, combined with the results of a recent two-
year-old federal choice program, suggests that the impact of
school choice on school performance will be far less revolutionary than its supporters from both parties envision. As a result, if left unaddressed, the situation is likely to strengthen the
conservative argument for vouchers, which was recently bolstered by a Supreme Court decision allowing public money to
be spent on such payments to private religious schools. More
importantly, though, the choice program promises to leave
struggling parents like Suetmeyer even more frustrated, and
threatens to distract attention from the work on proven remedies to fix poorly performing schools.

Exercising Options

10   Despite its fanfare, the choice program enshrined in the new
federal law is not exactly new. It is, in fact, based closely on a
two-year-old federal program created in a compromise between the Clinton administration and House Republicans that
funneled $360 million to help improve failing schools, but
failed to provide any real choice for parents. State reports from
the program's first year revealed that remarkably few transfers
occurred. In Vermont, just 12 students transferred from two
schools in 2000–01; in North Dakota, 34 students transferred;
in Kansas, none; and in Florida, not a single school met the
state's definition of failure. The numbers didn't increase much
last year, either. In Baltimore, for example, just 22 students
changed schools.

11   As it turns out, providing viable transfer options for parents
is much harder than it sounds—especially when the program
is underfunded, poorly publicized to parents, limited to low-
performing schools, administered by unenthusiastic school officials, and full of bureaucratic loopholes. Educators raise
legions of logistical, financial, and educational objections to
giving parents more say in choosing their children's schools:
There is no other school not already overcrowded. There is no
other school not performing poorly. No neighboring district is
willing to take the complainants' children. The district can't afford to pay for transportation. Transferring students would violate class-size reduction initiatives or union contracts. The
district includes only one school per grade span. State or local
policy limits choice, or a consent decree operates to limit it.

Given these loopholes (and real difficulties), an amazing   12
number of districts were unwilling or unable to provide choice
and, thus, not required to allow or enable students to move.
However valid they may be in some cases, in many others, the
reasons offered appear to be more a function of lack of enthusiasm on the part of bureaucrats, and, more surprisingly, of
parents.

Parental Discretion

Perhaps nowhere are the limits of federally mandated choice   13
programs more apparent than in New Orleans, where fewer
than 20 of the 10,000 eligible students chose to transfer last
fall. Initially, the district claimed to "lack capacity" to provide
such choices to students attending failing schools, which
would have exempted it from the requirement under the old
law. Apparently none of the better schools in the district had
room to accept more students—at least according to those
schools' principals.

Dubious of those claims, the district then conducted a uti-   14
lization study and found almost 150 spaces at nearby
schools—not nearly enough to handle any significant move
from among the estimated 10,000 eligible students, but more
than had been expected. To make the process fair, the district
decided to set up a lottery for those slots. To the astonishment
of school administrators, no lottery was necessary. Fewer than
70 parents expressed interest in transferring their children to
other schools.

One obvious reason for the lack of interest was that the dis-   15
trict prohibited parents from choosing any of the more popular citywide enrollment schools, limiting the choices only to
other neighborhood schools that aren't considered much
better. Another was that the district had dedicated more than
$5 million in federal and local funds to provide the 11 strug-
gling schools with smaller classes, better teachers, and other
resources and improvements. The letter that New Orleans parents received notifying them of their right to transfer reads
more like an advertisement for the failing schools than an admission of their shortcomings and a listing of what other
schools might be available. "We are addressing the academic
needs of your current school in an effort to improve the quality
of instruction that your child receives," it begins, and goes on
to list 10 promised improvements in boldface, only mentioning
the choice option two paragraphs later. Even for those parents

who might be interested, the letter omits the names of the alternative schools.

16   Among educators in New Orleans and elsewhere, conventional wisdom holds that lack of space and parental preference for neighborhood schools are the major obstacles to choice programs. But lack of space has a long and notorious history as a rationale for limiting choice options for low-income students, especially when it is left to the discretion of local administrators or principals at higher-performing, typically more affluent schools. And parental interest is proportional to the type and amount of information provided about the performance of their children's school and the choices available for transfer.

17   Marie Farve, president of the New Orleans PTA, believes that most parents who haven't already moved their children aren't interested in choice anyway. Indeed, as *The Washington Monthly* documented last year (see "Student Movement," September 2001), poor public-school students change schools frequently, a fact that contradicts the basic assumption behind the choice program that poor students are "stuck" in a single bad school.

18   A General Accounting Office study found that one third-grader out of every six has attended three or more schools since entering the first grade, a problem that is even more acute in the inner city. A recent study of Chicago students revealed that fewer than half who entered school in first grade attended the same school in fourth. Some schools retained fewer than 30 percent of their first-graders. Pupils who changed schools most frequently had worse test scores than other poor students, even though one of the main reasons parents said they moved their children was to find a better school. The problem, it seems, is not the ability to switch schools, but to switch from bad schools to genuinely good ones.

Wishful Thinking

19   The Bush administration claims that the new choice requirements will break down bureaucratic barriers to choice, but many observers doubt it. True, under the new law, districts will no longer be able to claim that they lack the capacity to provide choice. Nor will they be allowed to pass local resolutions prohibiting the practice. But in a fit of wishful thinking, the new law simply erases these options, providing no clear mandate to ensure that choices actually exist. Nor does it require school administrators to arrange transfers with neighboring schools if they truly do lack capacity.

Most significantly, the law lacks any real enforcement mech-   20
anism, and the Department of Education has a long tradition
of glacially slow enforcement. In the eight years since Congress
last revisited K-12 education, the department sanctioned few
states for not meeting federal requirements. Last year, it gave
more than $200 million in second-year-choice funding to 43
states and jurisdictions, despite the widespread dearth of students who were actually transferring schools.

Already there are signs that the nation's school districts are   21
thwarting the new law's intent. This spring, in Montgomery
County, Md., one of the nation's most progressive school districts, only 102 students applied for transfers available under
the new law—fewer than 2 percent of the more than 6,000 who
attend failing schools. (Of those 102, only five fit the category
of low-performing, low-income students to whom the program
was targeted.) Some states, such as Arkansas, Virginia, and
Wyoming, have set the bar so low that they have few, if any,
"failing" schools. Others still have not released final lists of
choice schools, creating confusion and limiting interest. In
Illinois, state officials re-crunched the numbers for "failing"
schools and came up with a new list that was half as long (as
was the new list of eligible students). At the same time, state
legislators passed a new law giving districts more wiggle room
by permitting schools that are close to capacity or those with
academic specialties (such as math-and-science schools) to decline transfer students. In Chicago, that leaves only 3,000 slots
for 124,000 children whose parents are entitled to reassign
them. And after the state re-ran the data for failing schools, it
turned out, suddenly, that Zion no longer had any.

So what to do with the 8,600 schools the government has   22
identified as failing?

One option would be for the feds to force states and school   23
districts to work harder to break down educators' resistance to
transfers from failing schools, and making sure parents of kids
in failing schools know about the option and benefit of moving
their kids to better ones. Still, resistance to transferring students between different districts will always be high. Parents
are not as eager to move their children out of even the worst
schools as some in Washington imagine. And even if the government could achieve perfect compliance with the law, there
would still not be nearly enough seats in accessible, better
schools for the vast majority of entitled children who are stuck
in bad ones.

Another option that has worked well in some places, like   24
East Harlem, is "mandatory choice," where all parents are
forced actively to choose which schools their kids will attend,

creating a diversity and competition that's often lacking in places with less pressure on parents to shop around. In these programs, parents are thoroughly apprised of their options and thus lured into "shopping" for the best schools. But it's hard to know whether such programs could be replicated nationally. East Harlem had the benefit of some extraordinary administrators, who also worked hard to create many new programs within existing schools so that parents actually had something to choose from.

25   A third option would be to increase the supply of better schools through measures like vouchers and charter schools. But there are capacity and quality problems with both of these options. Given that the average voucher being touted today is worth about $2,500, poor parents would still be hard-pressed to come up with thousands of dollars of their own money to pay for tuition at most private schools. Even without vouchers (or their close cousin, tuition tax credits), affordable parochial schools in cities with substandard school systems like Washington, D.C., already have huge waiting lists that rival those for public housing. (Vouchers, incidentally, would likely go to the kids already enrolled in parochial schools rather than open new slots for kids looking to escape public schools.) Even the largest voucher programs currently being advocated would accommodate only a tiny fraction of the millions of eligible students from low-performing schools, leaving parents like Suetmeyer hardly better off than when they had no choice at all.

26   Charter schools have been launched in several big cities to try to give students an alternative to bad public schools, but their quality so far is uneven at best. In Washington, D.C., where Congress required the city to set up a charter-school system at a pace unheard of elsewhere, test scores are worse than in regular public schools, even factoring in the programs aimed at the learning disabled. And these schools have been plagued by many of the same scandals as the regular schools. (Last year, for instance, some parents discovered that one teacher was actually a former prison guard with no academic credentials.) While there may be some promise in this initiative, it will be years before it matures into anything better than what kids can get now, let alone with the capacity to accommodate millions of new students.

27   While it's worth rooting for almost any reform that truly provides better choices for students stuck in dysfunctional schools, it's hard not to conclude that the most efficient way to improve education for the millions of such children is by doing it the old-fashioned way: by fixing the schools they already attend. The vast majority of kids in failing schools are going to be stuck in those schools or others not much better. Letting the

choice issue distract from the task of finally turning those schools around would be a shame. The sooner we recognize this and start doing more of what we know can improve achievement—better teachers, higher academic expectations, summer school, smaller classes and schools—the better.

Rachel S. Cox

HOME SCHOOLING DEBATE: IS THE MOVEMENT UNDERMINING PUBLIC EDUCATION?

Rachel S. Cox, a freelance writer, lives in Washington, D.C. She earned her B.A. in English from Harvard College and has written pieces for Historic Preservation *Magazine and other publications, including* CQ Researcher, *where this piece first appeared. In keeping with the editorial policy of* CQ Researcher, *Cox attempts to present a variety of perspectives on this topic in an unbiased way. Note the ways in which the piece combines background research, interviews, and narrative in order to provide a broad picture of the debate about home schooling and its effect upon public education.*

When Jane and George Liddle's first child turned 4, they began to   1 think about her formal schooling. Living in the affluent San Francisco Bay Area community of Los Gatos, near Silicon Valley, they had access to some of California's best public schools.

But every Sunday when they attended services at the   2 Saratoga Federated Church, they couldn't help but notice how happy—and successful—the home-schooled children of fellow church members seemed to be.

"At first, I said to myself, 'I will never do this,'" recalls Jane,   3 who was a stockbroker until Caroline was born. "But we saw so many professional, well-educated people who made the choice [to home school] for educational reasons, as well as personal, philosophical ones."

4   Today, Caroline, nearly 6, starts her day by spending an hour or two working with her mother on language arts and math skills. After family devotions, they move to a classroom set up in a separate building on the rural property to study history and social studies. Two days a week, Caroline and her younger brother, William, 3, visit a home-school co-op to study and play with nearly 60 other children in class-like groupings overseen by their 12 moms.

5   School begins with the Pledge of Allegiance at the Shapiro home in Tempe, Ariz. Denise Shapiro and her husband, Aaron, a chiropractor, decided to home school to raise "very smart" children but also "biblically, morally responsible adults." At least 850,000 U.S. children are home schooled, nearly triple the number a decade ago. Public-school officials worry home schooling undercuts public education and limits students' exposure to children and adults with diverse backgrounds.

6   Jane Liddle concedes that home schooling works for her family for practical as well as philosophical reasons: The extra cost—mainly for books and other educational materials—is minimal. And with the local elementary school some distance away, she appreciates not having to spend two hours each day in her car or making Caroline ride the bus. Home schooling also improves her quality of life. "I spend such incredible time with my children," she says, "and at night when my husband is home, we really are a family. We avoid a lot of the distractions of popular culture and the pressures to arrange lots of after-school activities. We're not just chasing our tails all the time."

7   She also believes that, at least for now, home schooling offers the best possible educational experience. "I've learned that you can really shoot the moon with your child. I'm right there with her in the learning process. I know what keeps her challenged and what sabotages her. You can customize. You figure out what works for your child."

8   The Liddles' approach has grown increasingly popular over the last two decades, as a movement once considered the domain of aging hippies and religious fundamentalists increasingly has been embraced by the mainstream. But school districts complain that when parents give up on home schooling, they "dump" their children back on the public schools, which are then held accountable for the home-schoolers' performance, even if the student is lagging behind his in-school peers. Moreover, critics warn that removing children from the

public schools may threaten an essential pillar of democracy, while depriving children of vital contact with other children and adults from diverse backgrounds.

Brian D. Ray, director of the National Home Education   9
Research Institute in Salem, Ore., and a leader in the field, concedes that even as recently as five years ago home-schoolers were considered "kind of weirdo." People thought home-schoolers were all "granola eaters or Bible thumpers," he says. "But now, almost anyone you run into on the street will consider it. It's more common to find support groups, resources are more available and there's less peer pressure against it."

In 1999, the U.S. Education Department estimates, about   10
850,000 of the nation's 50 million children, ages 5 through 17, were being schooled at home—or 1.7 percent.[1] Ray puts the number at between 1.6 million and 2 million—roughly 2 per-cent of the school-age population—but his figures are gener-ally considered high.

One thing is certain: The movement has experienced robust   11
growth. Only 30 years ago, few children were being home schooled.[2] By 1991, the Department of Education estimated that up to 300,000 school-age children were being educated at home.[3] Thus, according to the department's own conservative estimates, the number of home-schooled children has nearly tripled in just 10 years.[4]

Most home-schooled children come from urban, two-parent   12
families, the study found, with one wage earner and two or more children. The parents are often well educated—a quarter have at least a bachelor's degree—and 36 percent have house-hold incomes above $50,000 per year. White families outnum-ber minorities by three to one.

Parents say they home-school for five main reasons: to give   13
their children a better education, for religious reasons, to avoid a poor school environment, for family reasons and to in-still "character/morality."[5]

"The core reasons for home schooling are very deep and sta-   14
ble," says Ray, who has studied the movement since the mid-1980s. "They want their children to learn to read, write and do arithmetic, along with some science and history. They want to individualize the curriculum for each child, meet special inter-ests or needs, provide a safe learning environment and guided social interactions for their kids, nurture strong family ties and transmit certain values and beliefs to their children."[6]

In the 1980s, he notes, the proportion of families choosing   15
home schooling for religious reasons skyrocketed, after tax-code changes forced many religious schools to close.

16   Critics long have asserted that schooling children at home impedes socialization because home-schooled kids don't learn to get along with their peers in group settings, nor are they exposed to children and adults from different backgrounds. But advocates scoff at the notion.

17   "I have nothing kind to say about the sort of socialization that occurs in schools," says Holly Albers, an economist in Washington, D.C., who home-schooled her two sons for several years when they were youngsters. "The children are thrown into single-age, often very large groups with no meaningful interactions with adults."

18   To expose their children to a wide variety of contacts, Albers and other parents organize social and educational activities with other home-schoolers and adults, who often serve as tutors in subject areas that other parents are weak in. As a result, she says, home-schoolers tend to have three advantages: closer family and sibling relationships, more friendships with different ages and genders and more friendships with adults. "There's much more positive socialization for children at home," she says.

19   In fact, studies appear to refute the argument that home-schoolers are poorly socialized. As early as 1986, John Wesley Taylor, a doctoral candidate at Andrews University, in Berrien Springs, Mich., found that half of the home-schooled children surveyed scored 47 percent higher than the average conventionally schooled child on a well-validated self-concept scale. "This answers the often-heard skepticism suggesting that home-schoolers are inferior in socialization," he concluded.[7]

20   Home-schoolers win academic kudos as well. In 2000, for instance, home-schooled children took home the top three trophies in the prestigious Scripps Howard National Spelling Bee, just a week after other home-schoolers won four of the top 10 spots at the National Geographic Society's geography bee.[8] And Buchanan, Mich., home-schooler Jeff Joyce recently scored a perfect 1600 on the College Board's Scholastic Assessment Test (SAT)—a feat accomplished by less than 0.5 percent of the students who take the test each year.[9]

21   In fact, when University of Maryland researcher Lawrence M. Rudner assessed the performance of more than 20,000 K-12 home-schooled students on standardized tests in 1999, their median scores were typically in the 70th to 80th percentile. "The achievement-test scores of this group of home school students are exceptionally high," Rudner concluded.[10]

22   But Rudner's study, which was funded and widely disseminated by home-schooling advocates, was criticized for failing to acknowledge the narrowness of its sample. The data were

gathered exclusively from parents who used the testing services of Bob Jones University, the fundamentalist Christian institution in Greenville, S.C., notorious for its history of racial discrimination. "This data simply cannot be used to reliably compare home-schoolers' achievement levels with those of the general population or to describe the demographics of home-schoolers," scholars Kariane Mari Welner and Kevin G. Welner noted.[11]

Few educators doubt the potential of a customized educa-   23
tion when a single adult is working with one child. "There's no doubt that the one-on-one work that parents can do if they're smart or well trained is amazing," says June Million, a spokeswoman for the National Association of Elementary School Principals (NAESP). But home-schooling advocates don't always tell the whole story, she suggests. "The part I never see are the ones who have returned to school after home schooling, and they're behind. It's not always a success."

NAESP President Paul Young agrees. "If families want to   24
work hard at home schooling and do it for the right reasons, they do very well. Others aren't well informed, don't follow through and get frustrated," he says.

When home schooling fails, the problem usually lands in the   25
lap of the public schools, says Young, who is principal at West Elementary School in Lancaster, Ohio. "When the parents realize they can't do it, the kids come back to public school, and then we're held responsible. In some cases these kids have been just running in the street, and the parents are not held accountable for what their children were supposed to be learning."

In addition to its concerns about the lack of adequate social-   26
ization, the NAESP worries that home schooling can deny children the full range of curriculum experiences and materials and expose students to unqualified instructors. In addition, the group says home schooling can create an extra burden for administrators responsible for enforcing compulsory-attendance laws; prevent effective assessment of statewide academic standards; violate health and safety regulations and prevent the accurate diagnosis of learning disabilities or other conditions requiring special attention.

"The public schools' greatest concern is to make sure kids   27
are actually learning," says Julie Underwood, general counsel of the National School Boards Association (NSBA). "There are very strong religious-right organizations that support very conservative [home-schooling] curricula."

Even dedicated home-schoolers acknowledge that home   28
schooling is not right for everyone. "It does require a full-time, at-home parent," Albers says, "and it is *relentless* for that parent."

29   As educators, parents and policy-makers struggle with the
peculiar mix of personal and public decision-making that
home schooling entails, these three questions frequently are
being debated:

Should the Government Regulate Home Schooling?

30   "Dog Bites System," read *The Rocky Mountain News* headline,
when a Colorado man successfully certified his miniature
schnauzer, Missy, as progressing nicely in the third grade while
being schooled at home.[12]

31   Under Colorado's home-schooling law, parents must file a
notice of intent with a local school district, then the student
must be tested or evaluated to show progress every other year,
starting in the third grade. Dog owners Nick and Cheryl
Campbell "evaluated" Missy using an evaluation form they
found on the Internet, but no one from the school district ever
tried to speak to Missy.

32   "I did it to make a point" about the laxness of the state's
oversight of home-schoolers, said Campbell, who was dis-
tressed because a 10-year-old neighbor being home schooled
had not yet learned to read.

33   Thanks to adroit lobbying by home-schooling networks,
which have access to Republican lawmakers through their
links with politically savvy religious conservatives, home
schooling is legal in every state, but requirements for eligibility
and evaluation vary widely. Thus, policymakers and educators
are debating whether local school districts should regulate
home schooling more stringently.

34   "With home schooling now firmly entrenched on the
American education scene," New Jersey attorney David Rubin
writes, "the legal battleground has shifted in recent years to
defining the rights and responsibilities of school districts and
home-schooling families."[13]

35   Many public educators believe that stricter regulation—
including testing—is needed to ensure that home-schooled
children are being adequately educated.[14] "Kentucky is very
lax on its home-school rules," says Martha Lewis, principal of
Benton Elementary in rural Marshall County, Ky. "Most of the
students that I have seen being home-schooled are ones whose
parents get disgruntled with the public school about something. They are weak students who have poor attendance.
When they come back, they are even further behind."

Requiring home-schooled students to be tested would help   36
teachers and administrators when home-schoolers return to
school, or when they take some courses in public schools, the
NSBA's Underwood says. "In some states, there are no regulations, so public school [teachers and officials] are quite
frustrated," she says. So when kids enter or return to school,
"They don't know if they're really ready. They don't have any
information."

Public educators were particularly concerned when President   37
Bush's recently enacted No Child Left Behind Act exempted
home-schooled students from the new testing requirements it
imposed on public-school students. The new law imposes serious financial consequences on schools where students test
poorly. Thus, administrators want to make sure that all students are keeping up—including returning home-schoolers.

"When children return to school, that school is held respon-   38
sible for their performance," says Young of the principals' association. "We need more specific testing requirements so there's
some accountability."

"You could have multiple forms of testing," Underwood   39
notes. "It wouldn't have to be standardized testing."

However, to home-schooling advocates like Robert Ziegler,   40
spokesman for the Home School Legal Defense Association
(HSLDA), any regulation is too much. Choosing how to educate one's children is a constitutionally protected parental
right, he says. "There should be no regulation of how parents
educate their children," he says.

To others, like home-schooling researcher Ray, it is unrea-   41
sonable to regulate a practice that receives no public financing.
"Home-schoolers don't use a single tax dollar," Ray says. "What
about children in private schools? Private schools have no regulation. Why do this to us, and not do it to private schools?"

Ray says he doesn't know of "any research suggesting that if   42
you test them, they will do better."

"If the issue is quality in education," Ziegler says, "the argu-   43
ment could be made that heavy government involvement is not
a guarantor of success."

Ziegler says stories of children who leave school and are not   44
being educated are irrelevant to debates about regulating
home schooling. "It's important to distinguish between home-
schoolers and dropouts," he says. "The horror stories are not
typical."

Home-schooling parents also point out that children   45
schooled at home can progress at their own pace, so students
who might be stigmatized as learning disabled in the public
school system often blossom when allowed to pursue their

own interests at home on their own schedule. Imposing a state-mandated testing or evaluation regimen would negate these benefits, they say.

46   Home-schooling advocates often attribute professional educators' efforts to regulate home schooling to their vested interests in keeping the numbers of schoolchildren, teachers and administrators high. "Big-government types have had a monopoly on education," Ziegler says. For teachers' unions like the American Federation of Teachers (AFT), he says, "It's a dollars-and-cents issue. Fewer jobs, fewer teachers in the union."

47   But Alex Wohl, AFT's director of public affairs, counters: "The number of home-schooled students is so small that it would never interfere with our membership, even if it were a focus, which it's not."

48   Should the public-school system support home schooling?

49   In 1999, when 13-year-old Megan Angstadt wanted to play basketball on her local middle-school's team in Williamsport, Penn., her parents obtained a one-year exception to the school-district policy excluding home-schoolers from extracurricular activities. To assure her participation the following year, they enrolled her in Western Pennsylvania Cyber Charter School, a distance-learning public school. They hoped to take advantage of a state law allowing charter school students to participate in extracurricular activities elsewhere if their charter school does not offer them.[15]

50   But the school district refused to let Megan rejoin the team. Her parents sued, contending her rights had been violated. But the district court questioned whether Megan's interest in participating in extracurricular activities rose to the level of a constitutionally protected right.

51   In a change from earlier generations, home-schooling parents like the Angstadts increasingly are augmenting their children's social and educational experiences by seeking access to public-school programs.[16]

52   And extracurricular activities are not the only public-school resources home-schoolers want to use. According to the 1999 Education Department study, about 18 percent of home schoolers attend public school part time, 11 percent use public-school books or materials and about 6 percent participate in extracurricular activities.[17]

53   States usually allow local school boards to decide whether or not to honor home-schoolers' requests to take selected courses and join extracurricular activities.

54   "We do not permit this type of smorgasbord participation in our state," says Robert Heath, principal of W. C. Sullivan Middle School in Rock Hill, S.C. "I believe this to be appropriate, as

our students must earn the right to participate in extracurricular activities through grades, behavior and so forth."

New Jersey attorney Rubin says many school districts deny such requests for a variety of reasons, including administrative inconvenience, lack of state aid and equity *vis-à-vis* other private-school students who would be denied the same opportunities.[18]   55

Legal challenges to school-district policies prohibiting home-schoolers' participation have generally been defeated. As in Megan's case, courts in Oklahoma, New York, Montana and West Virginia have held that school-district policies or state interscholastic athletic association rules that exclude home-schoolers do not violate the equal-protection rights of home-school or private-school students.[19]   56

However, a Massachusetts Superior Court ruled in 1995 that home-schooled high-school students may participate in inter-school athletics on the grounds that distinguishing between in-school and home-schooled students "was not rationally related to a legitimate state purpose."[20]   57

When stymied in the courts, home-schooling advocates have turned to the legislative arena. As of spring 2002, 14 states had laws or policies granting home-schoolers access to public-school activities, and several states have legislation pending.[21]   58

In Oregon, Washington, California, Texas and other states, some public-school districts have gone so far as to design tax-funded school-at-home programs. Local school districts receive all or part of the usual per-pupil funding, while students work off-campus and connect with the schools via computer or at learning centers with computer labs, libraries or science labs. Working closely with parents, teachers at the learning centers may offer curriculum guidance, teach some classes and provide testing and evaluation services.   59

Minorities make up only about a quarter of the nation's home-schooled students, compared with 36 percent of the children in public and private schools. Critics say home-schooled students don't have a chance to mix with students and adults from other backgrounds. Advocates respond that music, sports and other outside-the-home activities provide ample opportunities for mixing.   60

"Many public educators and the families who send their children full time to public schools . . . look askance at these programs," says Patricia D. Lines, a senior fellow at Seattle's Discovery Institute and longtime observer of home-schooling. "'It's not fair,' complained a public-school parent, 'for them to want the best of what the public school has to offer without enduring their less-popular aspects.'"[22]   61

62   In addition, many home-schoolers are wary of governmental involvement in parent-directed education, viewing it as a Trojan horse by which the state and its employees can gain control over their children's education. "Home-schoolers who get tax dollars for educational expenses will be held accountable by the state, and regulations on them will increase," *Home Education Magazine* warned recently.[23]

63   "When regulations are increased for some home-schoolers, the increased regulations are very likely to be applied to all home-schoolers, regardless of whether they are accepting tax money (or enrolling in a public e-school)," wrote home-school advocates Larry and Susan Kaseman.

64   Moreover, many home-schoolers also fear that accepting public-school services will force them to give up the religious orientation of their home program.[24]

65   But Lines believes the Trojan-horse analogy may, in fact, work the other way around, with home-schoolers subtly reforming the way public schools do business.

66   "When public schools open their doors to home-schooling families, they must operate in a very different way," she says in a recent study of school-family partnerships. "Rather than losing control over home schooling, it seems more likely that home-schoolers' ideas will influence public practices and curriculum."

67   Working with home-school families, she says, can force the public schools to adopt "a radically new service orientation toward families." Because home-schooling parents are unlikely to send their children to a conventional school, public educators will attract home-schoolers "only if they are sensitive to their needs, preferences and goals."[25]

68   Does home schooling threaten the fundamental American concept of universal public education?

69   One of the primary goals of American public education is to teach citizens how to knowledgeably participate in a democratic society. "The public doesn't realize that is one of the crucial goals of our democracy," says the NSBA's Underwood.

70   Without a well-educated citizenry, democracy cannot work and might not survive, she says. "Public education makes democracy work well. If people don't recognize that and support it, we're always at risk of losing it."

71   Home-schooling advocates argue that public-school students have no corner on citizenship, however. "Children do not have to be in the same type of school for them to be productive, kind, free-thinking citizens," says Ray, of the National Home Education Research Institute.

72   Indeed, home-schooling families tend to be more civically active than the norm, some experts say. A 1999 study based on

Education Department data found that home-schoolers were active participants in the political process. "We have reason to believe that the organizations and practices involved in private and home schooling, in themselves, tend to foster public participation in civic affairs," the authors concluded.[26]

Ziegler, of the Home School Legal Defense Association   73 (HSLDA), scoffs at the idea that home-schooling, a tiny fraction of the nation's students, undercuts public education's citizenship goals. "To the degree that having children home-schooled undermines the schools' effectiveness, the government needs to revisit how it structures its public schools."

Others ask how the public-school system can claim to be   74 promoting citizenship and democracy if it is failing to adequately educate all students. The public-school system has "failed us," says California home-school parent Jane Liddle.

Underwood acknowledges that the public schools aren't   75 perfect. "They're run by local elected officials," she says. "Sometimes wacky things happen."

Some supporters of the home-schooling movement, however,   76 believe the public-education system is more focused on producing good workers for U.S. industry than on producing good citizens. Former New York City schoolteacher John Taylor Gatto represents an extreme view of the corporate-influenced goals of state-supported schooling. His massive new book, *Underground History of American Education*, details his vision of the "deliberate transformation of American schooling, corporation-driven, which took place between 1890 and 1920, to . . . subordinate family and individual goals to the needs of 'scientific,' corporate and political managers."[27]

Others see the public schools as an authoritarian "enemy"   77 determined to undermine family values. Much of the home-school movement's literature refers to "government-controlled" or "state-run" schools and reveals grave doubts that any government-controlled agency can operate beneficently, even if the government is a democracy.

Ray himself, in a recent home-schooling guidebook, cast the   78 public schools and their supporters as enemies. "An increasing number of parents are recognizing the battle that is being waged for their children's hearts and minds—a battle that is played out in their education," he wrote.[28]

Educators worry that the home-schooling trend also could   79 jeopardize the role of public education as "the great equalizer in a democracy," in the words of Michael Roberts, a spokesman for the National Parent-Teachers Association. In school, children learn to get along with others from all minorities and all economic backgrounds, he points out, and after graduation they enter the working world equipped with the same basic education. Thus, a public education is designed to, theoretically, give each child a "level playing field" when it comes to economic opportunity and their ability to achieve success. "If we move away from that, that's detrimental."

80   Because home-schooling is not an option for poor families in which both parents must work, it tends to attract students from wealthier families, which usually are the most vocal in demanding that public schools perform better.

81   Home schooling "undermines public education's singular potential to serve as a democratic institution promoting the common good," writes Christopher Lubienski, an assistant professor of education at Iowa State University. He notes that powerful, well-organized groups are encouraging parents, especially Christian parents, to remove their children from public schools—a movement he says includes organizations with mailing lists of millions of families and a radio show with 5 million listeners (James Dobson's "Focus on the Family"). "In view of the influential groups promoting moral mandates for home schooling," Lubienski continues, home schooling should be viewed as "organized exit from public schools."[29]

82   He sees the growth of the home-schooling movement as the result of active and affluent parents pursuing "the best possible advantages for their own children even if it means hurting other children's chances."

83   By withdrawing wealthier children from the public schools, "Home schooling is a social threat to public education," Lubienski said. "It is taking some of the most affluent and articulate parents out of the system. These are the parents who know how to get things done with administrators."[30] Indeed, he writes, "Home schooling is not only a reaction to, but a cause of, declining public schools."

84   "Even self-described liberal, middle-class mothers who profess a loyalty to the idea of equality of educational opportunity are willing to negate such ideals in practice if, by doing so, they can increase educational advantages for their own children," Lubienski writes.

85   While home schooling involves less than 2 percent of the public-school population now, Underwood says, it is "one of a series of threats to public education," along with efforts to privatize schools and to provide vouchers and tax credits for private-school tuition.[31] "The underlying threat is a lack of public support for the importance of an educational system that serves all children."

86   But others point to recent polls indicating that support for the public schools is on the rise. In 2001, the annual *Phi Delta*

Kappan/Gallup poll registered the highest level of public satisfaction with local schools in the poll's 33-year history, with 51
percent grading them A or B—an 11-point increase over the
1990 rating.[32]

"Schools have clearly gotten better—there is no doubt about   87
it," said poll director Lowell C. Rose. "The 1990s have been a
decade of improvement in public schools, and the upward
trend reflects the steady increase in regard people have for the
public schools."

Moreover, the poll also showed a major rise in public accep-   88
tance of home schooling: 41 percent of respondents called it "a
good thing," up from only 15 percent in 1985; similarly, 54 percent called it "a bad thing," down from 73 percent in 1985.

"We're starting to win the battle," Ziegler says. "This may be   89
one reason that the establishment is fighting back."

NOTES

1. Stacey Bielick, Kathryn Chandler and Stephen P. Broughman,
   "Homeschooling in the United States: 1999," U.S. Department of
   Education, National Center for Education Statistics, July 2001.
2. J. Gary Knowles, Stacey E. Marlow and James A. Muchmore, "From
   Pedagogy to Ideology: Origins and Phases of Home Education in the
   United States, 1970–1990," *American Journal of Education*, Feb. 1992,
   p. 196.
3. Nola Kortner Aiex, "Home Schooling and Socialization of Children,"
   ERIC Digest, ERIC Clearinghouse on Reading, English and Communication, 1994, www.ed.gov/databases/ERIC_Digests/ed372460.html.
4. For background, see Charles S. Clark, "Home Schooling," *The CQ
   Researcher*, Sept. 9, 1994, pp. 769–792.
5. Greg Toppo, "850,000 Kids Are Being Taught at Home, Study Finds,"
   USA Today, Aug. 6, 2001, p. 5D.
6. For background, see Joan Hennessey, "Teaching Math and Science,"
   The CQ Researcher, Sept. 6, 2002, pp. 697–720.
7. Quoted in Aiex, *op. cit.*, which offers a summary of such findings.
8. Noreen S. Ahmed-Ullah, "Home-schoolers find vindication in contests,"
   The Chicago Tribune, June 21, 2001.
9. See "Home Schooled Michigan Teen Receives Perfect SAT Score," *The
   Associated Press*, June 1, 2001.
10. Lawrence M. Rudner, "Scholastic Achievement and Demographic
    Characteristics of Home School Students in 1998," *Education Policy
    Analysis Archives*, March 23, 1999.
11. Kariane Mari Welner and Kevin G. Welner, "Contextualizing
    Homeschooling Data: A Response to Rudner," *Education Policy
    Analysis Archives*, April 11, 1999.
12. Nancy Mitchell, "Dog Bites System When She Receives Progress
    Certificate," *The Rocky Mountain News*, April 30, 2002, p. 4A.
13. David Rubin, "Home Schooling, Religion and Public Schools: Striking
    a Constitutional Balance," National School Boards Association, August
    2001.

14. For background on testing, see Kenneth Jost, "Testing in Schools," *The CQ Researcher,* April 20, 2001, pp. 321–344.
15. For background, see Charles S. Clark, "Charter Schools," *The CQ Researcher,* Dec. 20, 2002, pp. 1033–1056.
16. *Ibid.*
17. Toppo, *op. cit.*
18. Rubin, *op. cit.*
19. Thomas W. Burns, "Home Schoolers: Eligibility to Participate in Public School Extracurricular Activities," *Inquiry and Analysis,* May/June 2002, p. 6.
20. *Ibid.*
21. *Ibid.* p. 7.
22. Patricia D. Lines, "When Home Schoolers Go to School: A Partnership Between Families and Schools," *Peabody Journal of Education,* January-February 2000, p. 134. Lines has served as a senior research analyst for the U.S. Department of Education and director of the Law and Education Center at the Education Commission of the States.
23. http://www.home-ed-magazine.com/HEM/196/ndtch.html (downloaded 11/12/02).
24. See Lines, *op. cit.,* p. 133.
25. *Ibid.,* p. 159.
26. Christian Smith and David Sikkink, "Is Private Schooling Privatizing?" *First Things* 92 (April 1999), www.firstthings.com/ftissues/ft9904/smith.html.
27. Online at www.JohnTaylorGatto.com.
28. Brian D. Ray, *2002–2003 Worldwide Guide to Homeschooling* (2002), p. 1.
29. Christopher Lubienski, "Whither the Common Good? A Critique of Home Schooling," *Peabody Journal of Education,* April 2000, p. 207.
30. Quoted in John Cloud, "Home Sweet School," *Time,* Aug. 27, 2001, p. 46.
31. For background on vouchers, see Kenneth Jost, "School Vouchers Showdown," *The CQ Researcher,* Feb. 15, 2002, pp. 124–144.
32. Catherine Gewertz, "Public Support for Local Schools Reaches All-Time High, Poll Finds," *Education Week,* Sept. 5, 2001.

VISUAL CONVERSATIONS 1

The Place(s) of Education: Educational Settings

As may be evident from the readings in this section, conversations on the topic of education go beyond *what* students should learn; people are also talking about *where* students should learn. "Going to school" can mean attending a large public institution or a small (and often expensive) college preparatory school. It can mean learning in an environment steeped in religious tradition, or one that strictly observes the "separation of church and state." Or it can mean simply staying at home and learning from parents, neighbors, and other students as part of the home schooling movement—a movement that, as Rachael Cox's article "Home Schooling Debate: Is the Movement Undermining Public Education?" illustrates, has enjoyed a new popularity. This section of *Conversations* invites you to observe a variety of places where students learn. As you read these "visual texts" (remember, we *read* pictures as well as words), consider not only what settings are represented, but also the ways in which these pictures make subtle arguments about the relative value of each of these settings or about the challenges we face in educating our youth. Think also about how these visual arguments interact with the issues raised in the rest of this section.

What does this image of home schoolers on the August 27, 2001 cover of *Time Magazine* suggest about its value (and the values that it supports)? How does this image portray the goals of home schooling? What conversations might these questions initiate? And what type of "family" is represented here? (You might also consider that last question in light of Part 4 of this book, which addresses family matters.)

The school environment includes not only that which is within the walls of the building or on school grounds, but that which surrounds the place—and the landscape that is altered by the influx of hundreds (or even thousands) of teenagers every day. What does this image say about those surroundings? How does it compare with other images of school settings?

What does this image of parochial school education say to you? Is it an image of the past, or does the type of education depicted here still exist? What do the details of this image say to you about religiously based educational settings, even beyond their basis in a specific faith?

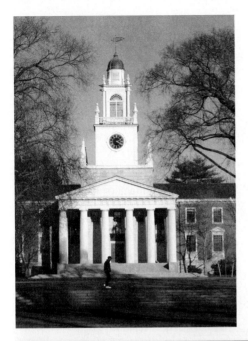

Though public education has long been one of America's cornerstones, the private school setting has a long tradition as well, both here and abroad. What specifically is it about this building and its setting that makes a statement about the type of education one could expect there and about the likely student body?

Parents...

Is GAP the right place for your child?

This advertisement for Guadalupe Alternative Programs clearly addresses a specific audience, to whom an emotionally charged question is posed. How do the image and the text work together to suggest the potential value of this program, which is designed for students who have not succeeded in traditional educational settings? What does this image suggest about this setting? More specifically, what might this visual suggest to parents of students who have struggled in other types of schools?

117

In some ways, this image depicts a typical public school setting. But do the details provide any commentary about teaching and learning methods? About the resources afforded to education? Which details do you take to be most significant? What types of arguments could this image make, either on its own or as an image accompanying a written piece?

What type of education is depicted in this photograph? What might it suggest about the way students learn? Consider not only general features of the setting, but the smaller details as well. What can we learn from the dress and expression of the students? What visual narrative is embedded in the physical features of this place and the actions that this moment suggests? Does it make an argument about what goes on in this setting—or even more generally about the goals of education?

Think back to your own experiences in elementary school, and particularly to the many lines in which you waited as a student: going to assemblies, getting ready for lunch or dismissal, preparing for a field trip, and so forth. In what ways does this picture depict similar types of experiences? In what ways is it very different? Considering those questions can also help you to think more widely about American education in relation to the education available in some developing nations.

What's College For?

Alice Walker

EVERYDAY USE

FOR YOUR GRANDMAMA

Alice Walker (born 1944) is an essayist, poet, feminist, and activist, but she is best known for her Pulitzer Prize–winning third novel, The Color Purple *(1982). Asked why she writes, she once explained, "I'm really paying homage to people I love, the people who are thought to be dumb and backward but who were the ones who first taught me to see beauty." "Everyday Use" appeared in her acclaimed collection of stories,* In Love and Trouble, *published in 1973.*

1   I will wait for her in the yard that Maggie and I made so clean and wavy yesterday afternoon. A yard like this is more comfortable than most people know. It is not just a yard. It is like an extended living room. When the hard clay is swept clean as a floor and the fine sand around the edges lined with tiny, irregular grooves anyone can come and sit and look up into the elm tree and wait for the breezes that never come inside the house.

2   Maggie will be nervous until after her sister goes: she will stand hopelessly in corners homely and ashamed of the burn scars down her arms and legs, eyeing her sister with a mixture of envy and awe. She thinks her sister has held life always in the palm of one hand, that "no" is a word the world never learned to say to her.

3   You've no doubt seen those TV shows where the child who has "made it" is confronted, as a surprise, by her own mother and father, tottering in weakly from backstage. (A pleasant surprise, of course: What would they do if parent and child came

on the show only to curse out and insult each other?) On TV mother and child embrace and smile into each other's faces. Sometimes the mother and father weep, the child wraps them in her arms and leans across the table to tell how she would not have made it without their help. I have seen these programs.

Sometimes I dream a dream in which Dee and I are sud- 4 denly brought together on a TV program of this sort. Out of a dark and soft-seated limousine I am ushered into a bright room filled with many people. There I meet a smiling, gray, sporty man like Johnny Carson who shakes my hand and tells me what a fine girl I have. Then we are on the stage and Dee is embracing me with tears in her eyes. She pins on my dress a large orchid, even though she has told me once that she thinks orchids are tacky flowers.

In real life I am a large, big-boned woman with rough, man- 5 working hands. In the winter I wear flannel nightgowns to bed and overalls during the day. I can kill and clean a hog as merci-lessly as a man. My fat keeps me hot in zero weather. I can work outside all day, breaking ice to get water for washing; I can eat pork liver cooked over the open fire minutes after it comes steaming from the hog. One winter I knocked a bull calf straight in the brain between the eyes with a sledge hammer and had the meat hung up to chill before nightfall. But of course all this does not show on television. I am the way my daughter would want me to be: a hundred pounds lighter, my skin like an uncooked barley pancake. My hair glistens in the hot bright lights. Johnny Carson has much to do to keep up with my quick and witty tongue.

But that is a mistake. I know even before I wake up. Who 6 ever knew a Johnson with a quick tongue? Who can even imag-ine me looking a strange white man in the eye? It seems to me I have talked to them always with one foot raised in flight, and my head turned in whichever way is farthest from them. Dee, though. She would always look anyone in the eye. Hesitation was no part of her nature.

"How do I look, Mama?" Maggie says, showing just enough 7 of her thin body enveloped in pink skirt and red blouse for me to know she's there, almost hidden by the door.

"Come out into the yard," I say. 8

Have you ever seen a lame animal, perhaps a dog run over by 9 some careless person rich enough to own a car, sidle up to someone who is ignorant enough to be kind to him? That is the way my Maggie walks. She has been like this, chin on chest, eyes on ground, feet in shuffle, ever since the fire that burned the other house to the ground.

10   Dee is lighter than Maggie, with nicer hair and a fuller figure. She's a woman now, though sometimes I forget. How long
ago was it that the other house burned? Ten, twelve years?
Sometimes I can still hear the flames and feel Maggie's arms
sticking to me, her hair smoking and her dress falling off her in
little black papery flakes. Her eyes seemed stretched open,
blazed open by the flames reflected in them. And Dee. I see her
standing off under the sweet gum tree she used to dig gum out
of: a look of concentration on her face as she watched the last
dingy gray board of the house fall in toward the red-hot brick
chimney. Why don't you do a dance around the ashes? I'd
wanted to ask her. She hated the house that much.

11   I used to think she hated Maggie, too. But that was before we
raised the money, the church and me, to send her to Augusta to
school. She used to read to us without pity; forcing words, lies,
other folks' habits, whole lives upon us two, sitting trapped and
ignorant underneath her voice. She washed us in a river of
make-believe, burned us with a lot of knowledge we didn't necessarily need to know. Pressed us to her with the serious way
she read, to shove us away at just the moment, like dimwits,
we seemed about to understand.

12   Dee wanted nice things. A yellow organdy dress to wear to
her graduation from high school; black pumps to match a
green suit she'd made from an old suit somebody gave me. She
was determined to stare down any disaster in her efforts. Her
eyelids would not flicker for minutes at a time. Often I fought
off the temptation to shake her. At sixteen she had a style of her
own: and knew what style was.

13   I never had an education myself. After second grade the
school was closed down. Don't ask me why: in 1927 colored
asked fewer questions than they do now. Sometimes Maggie
reads to me. She stumbles along good-naturedly but can't see
well. She knows she is not bright. Like good looks and money,
quickness passed her by. She will marry John Thomas (who
has mossy teeth in an earnest face) and then I'll be free to sit
here and I guess just sing church songs to myself. Although I
never was a good singer. Never could carry a tune. I was always
better at a man's job. I used to love to milk till I was hooked in
the side in '49. Cows are soothing and slow and don't bother
you, unless you try to milk them the wrong way.

14   I have deliberately turned my back on the house. It is three
rooms, just like the one that burned, except the roof is tin; they
don't make shingle roofs anymore. There are no real windows,
just some holes cut in the sides, like the portholes in a ship, but
not round and not square, with rawhide holding the shutters

up on the outside. This house is in a pasture, too, like the other one. No doubt when Dee sees it she will want to tear it down. She wrote me once that no matter where we "choose" to live, she will manage to come see us. But she will never bring her friends. Maggie and I thought about this and Maggie asked me, "Mama, when did Dee ever *have* any friends?"

She had a few. Furtive boys in pink shirts hanging about on   15 washday after school. Nervous girls who never laughed. Impressed with her they worshiped the well-turned phrase, the cute shape, the scalding humor that erupted like bubbles in lye. She read to them.

When she was courting Jimmy T she didn't have much time   16 to pay to us, but turned all her faultfinding power on him. He *flew* to marry a cheap gal from a family of ignorant flashy people. She hardly had time to recompose herself.

When she comes I will meet—but there they are!   17

Maggie attempts to make a dash for the house, in her shuf-   18 fling way, but I stay her with my hand. "Come back here," I say. And she stops and tries to dig a well in the sand with her toe.

It is hard to see them clearly through the strong sun. But even   19 the first glimpse of leg out of the car tells me it is Dee. Her feet were always neat-looking, as if God himself had shaped them with a certain style. From the other side of the car comes a short, stocky man. Hair is all over his head a foot long and hanging from his chin like a kinky mule tail. I hear Maggie suck in her breath. "Uhnnnh," is what it sounds like. Like when you see the wriggling end of a snake just in front of your foot on the road. "Uhnnnh."

Dee next. A dress down to the ground, in this hot weather. A   20 dress so loud it hurts my eyes. There are yellows and oranges enough to throw back the light of the sun. I feel my whole face warming from the heat waves it throws out. Earrings gold, too, and hanging down to her shoulders. Bracelets dangling and making noises when she moves her arm up to shake the folds of the dress out of her armpits. The dress is loose and flows, and as she walks closer, I like it. I hear Maggie go "Uhnnnh" again. It is her sister's hair. It stands straight up like the wool on a sheep. It is black as night and around the edges are two long pigtails that rope about like small lizards disappearing behind the ears.

"Wa-su-zo-Tean-o!" she says, coming on in that gliding way   21 the dress makes her move. The short stocky fellow with the hair to his navel is all grinning and he follows up with "Asalamalakim, my mother and sister!" He moves to hug Maggie but she falls back, right up against the back of my chair. I feel her trembling there and when I look up I see the perspiration falling off her chin.

22   "Don't get up," says Dee. Since I am stout it takes something of a push. You can see me trying to move a second or two before I make it. She turns, showing white heels through her sandals, and goes back to the car. Out she peeks next with a Polaroid. She stoops down quickly and lines up picture after picture of me sitting there in front of the house with Maggie cowering behind me. She never takes a shot without making sure the house is included. When a cow comes nibbling around the edge of the yard she snaps it and me and Maggie *and* the house. Then she puts the Polaroid in the back seat of the car, and comes up and kisses me on the forehead.

23   Meanwhile Asalamalakim is going through the motions with Maggie's hand. Maggie's hand is as limp as a fish, and probably as cold, despite the sweat, and she keeps trying to pull it back. It looks like Asalamalakim wants to shake hands but wants to do it fancy. Or maybe he don't know how people shake hands. Anyhow, he soon gives up on Maggie.

24   "Well," I say. "Dee."

25   "No, Mama," she says. "Not 'Dee,' Wangero Leewanika Kemanjo!"

26   "What happened to 'Dee'?" I wanted to know.

27   "She's dead." Wangero said. "I couldn't bear it any longer being named after the people who oppress me."

28   "You know as well as me you was named after your aunt Dicie," I said. Dicie is my sister. She named Dee. We called her "Big Dee" after Dee was born.

29   "But who was *she* named after?" asked Wangero.

30   "I guess after Grandma Dee," I said.

31   "And who was she named after?" asked Wangero.

32   "Her mother," I said, and saw Wangero was getting tired. "That's about as far back as I can trace it," I said. Though, in fact, I probably could have carried it back beyond the Civil War through the branches.

33   "Well," said Asalamalakim, "there you are."

34   "Uhnnnh," I heard Maggie say.

35   "There I was not," I said, "before 'Dicie' cropped up in our family, so why should I try to trace it that far back?"

36   He just stood there grinning, looking down on me like somebody inspecting a Model A car. Every once in a while he and Wangero sent eye signals over my head.

37   "How do you pronounce this name?" I asked.

38   "You don't have to call me by it if you don't want to," said Wangero.

39   "Why shouldn't I?" I asked. "If that's what you want us to call you, we'll call you."

40   "I know it might sound awkward at first," said Wangero.

"I'll get used to it," I said. "Ream it out again."   41

Well, soon we got the name out of the way. Asalamalakim   42
had a name twice as long and three times as hard. After I
tripped over it two or three times he told me to just call him
Hakim-a-barber. I wanted to ask him was he a barber, but I
didn't really think he was, so I didn't ask.

"You must belong to those beef-cattle peoples down the   43
road," I said. They said "Asalamalakim" when they met you,
too, but they didn't shake hands. Always too busy: feeding the
cattle, fixing the fences, putting up salt-lick shelters, throwing
down hay. When the white folks poisoned some of the herd the
men stayed up all night with rifles in their hands. I walked a
mile and a half just to see the sight.

Hakim-a-barber said, "I accept some of their doctrines, but   44
farming and raising cattle is not my style." (They didn't tell me,
and I didn't ask, whether Wangero [Dee] had really gone and
married him.)

We sat down to eat and right away he said he didn't eat col-   45
lards and pork was unclean. Wangero, though, went on through
the chitlins and corn bread, the greens and everything else. She
talked a blue streak over the sweet potatoes. Everything
delighted her. Even the fact that we still used the benches
her daddy made for the table when we couldn't afford to buy
chairs.

"Oh, Mama!" she cried. Then turned to Hakim-a-barber. "I   46
never knew how lovely these benches are. You can feel the
rump prints," she said, running her hands underneath her and
along the bench. Then she gave a sigh and her hand closed
over Grandma Dee's butter dish. "That's it!" she said. "I knew
there was something I wanted to ask you if I could have." She
jumped up from the table and went over in the corner where
the churn stood, the milk in it clabber by now. She looked at
the churn and looked at it.

"This churn top is what I need," she said. "Didn't Uncle   47
Buddy whittle it out of a tree you all used to have?"

"Yes," I said.   48

"Uh huh," she said happily. "And I want the dasher, too."   49

"Uncle Buddy whittle that, too?" asked the barber.   50

Dee (Wangero) looked up at me.   51

"Aunt Dee's first husband whittle the dash," said Maggie so   52
low you almost couldn't hear her. "His name was Henry, but
they called him Stash."

"Maggie's brain is like an elephant's," Wangero said, laugh-   53
ing. "I can use the churn top as a centerpiece for the alcove
table," she said, sliding a plate over the churn, "and I'll think of
something artistic to do with the dasher."

54   When she finished wrapping the dasher the handle stuck out. I took it for a moment in my hands. You didn't even have to look close to see where hands pushing the dasher up and down to make butter had left a kind of sink in the wood. In fact, there were a lot of small sinks; you could see where thumbs and fingers had sunk into the wood. It was beautiful light yellow wood, from a tree that grew in the yard where Big Dee and Stash had lived.

55   After dinner Dee (Wangero) went to the trunk at the foot of my bed and started rifling through it. Maggie hung back in the kitchen over the dishpan. Out came Wangero with two quilts. They had been pieced by Grandma Dee and then Big Dee and me had hung them on the quilt frames on the front porch and quilted them. One was in the Lone Star pattern. The other was Walk Around the Mountain. In both of them were scraps of dresses Grandma Dee had worn fifty and more years ago. Bits and pieces of Grandpa Jarrell's Paisley shirts. And one teeny faded blue piece, about the size of a penny matchbox, that was from Great Grandpa Ezra's uniform that he wore in the Civil War.

56   "Mama," Wangero said sweet as a bird. "Can I have these old quilts?"

57   I heard something fall in the kitchen, and a minute later the kitchen door slammed.

58   "Why don't you take one or two of the others?" I asked. "These old things was just done by me and Big Dee from some tops your grandma pieced before she died."

59   "No," said Wangero. "I don't want those. They are stitched around the borders by machine."

60   "That'll make them last better," I said.

61   "That's not the point," said Wangero. "These are all pieces of dresses Grandma used to wear. She did all this stitching by hand. Imagine!" She held the quilts securely in her arms, stroking them.

62   "Some of the pieces, like those lavender ones, come from old clothes her mother handed down to her," I said, moving up to touch the quilts. Dee (Wangero) moved back just enough so that I couldn't reach the quilts. They already belonged to her.

63   "Imagine!" she breathed again, clutching them closely to her bosom.

64   "The truth is," I said, "I promised to give them quilts to Maggie, for when she marries John Thomas."

65   She gasped like a bee had stung her.

66   "Maggie can't appreciate these quilts!" she said. "She'd probably be backward enough to put them to everyday use."

67   "I reckon she would," I said. "God knows I been saving 'em for long enough with nobody using 'em. I hope she will!" I didn't want to bring up how I had offered Dee (Wangero) a quilt when

she went away to college. Then she had told me they were old-fashioned, out of style.

"But they're *priceless!*" she was saying now, furiously; for she has a temper. "Maggie would put them on the bed and in five years they'd be in rags. Less than that!" 68

"She can always make some more," I said. "Maggie knows how to quilt." 69

Dee (Wangero) looked at me with hatred. "You just will not understand. The point is these quilts, *these* quilts!" 70

"Well," I said, stumped. "What would *you* do with them?" 71

"Hang them," she said. As if that was the only thing you *could* do with quilts. 72

Maggie by now was standing in the door. I could almost hear the sound her feet made as they scraped over each other. 73

"She can have them, Mama," she said, like somebody used to never winning anything, or having anything reserved for her. "I can 'member Grandma Dee without the quilts." 74

I looked at her hard. She had filled her bottom lip with checkerberry snuff and it gave her face a kind of dopey, hang-dog look. It was Grandma Dee and Big Dee who taught her how to quilt herself. She stood there with her scarred hands hidden in the folds of her skirt. She looked at her sister with something like fear but she wasn't mad at her. This was Maggie's portion. This was the way she knew God to work. 75

When I looked at her like that something hit me in the top of my head and ran down to the soles of my feet. Just like when I'm in church and the spirit of God touches me and I get happy and shout. I did something I never had done before: hugged Maggie to me, then dragged her on into the room, snatched the quilts out of Miss Wangero's hands and dumped them into Maggie's lap. Maggie just sat there on my bed with her mouth open. 76

"Take one or two of the others," I said to Dee. 77

But she turned without a word and went out to Hakim-a-barber. 78

"You just don't understand," she said, as Maggie and I came out to the car. 79

"What don't I understand?" I wanted to know. 80

"Your heritage," she said. And then she turned to Maggie, kissed her, and said, "You ought to try to make something of yourself, too, Maggie. It's really a new day for us. But from the way you and Mama still live you'd never know it." 81

She put on some sunglasses that hid everything above the tip of her nose and her chin. 82

Maggie smiled; maybe at the sunglasses. But a real smile, not scared. After we watched the car dust settle I asked Maggie to bring me a dip of snuff. And then the two of us sat there just enjoying, until it was time to go in the house and go to bed. 83

W. J. Reeves

COLLEGE ISN'T
FOR EVERYONE

W. J. Reeves is an English Professor at Brooklyn College, City University of New York. His essay draws on his experiences with students at this traditionally open-enrollment college—a college that accepts all students who apply. Reeves's essay raises questions not only about access to college, but also about whether college is the best path for all students. It was originally published in May 2003 in USA Today *magazine— not the newspaper of the same name, but a general-interest magazine that presents, among other things, opinion pieces on American culture. As you read, you might consider your own choice to attend college and that of others you know. Has the culture made college too much of a necessity? Are other paths better for some?*

1   Approximately 15,000,000 Americans are enrolled in college, although about half of them probably *shouldn't be*!

2   During the junior year of high school, students and, to a greater extent, their parents start to fret about getting the teenager into a college. Most of these students are unable to be admitted to first-rate schools like Williams College or the Ivy League institutions, but they and their parents believe that a college education, from any school, is necessary to succeed in the 21st century. However, Edward E. Gordon reports in an article entitled "Creating Tomorrow's Work Force" (*The Futurist,* August, 2000) that 70% of the workers in the coming decades will not need a four-year college degree, but, rather, an associate degree from a community college or some type of technical certificate. Thus, moms and dads, who foot the bill, delude themselves that going to any four-year college will make their sons and daughters literate, analytical, culturally aware, technologically advanced, and therefore employable.

3   In America today, there exists a goal that the majority of the nation's youth should go to college and that access should be the byword for higher education. On the surface, this sounds like a great idea; in reality, it is not.

4   Access in its most-extreme form—open admissions—was instituted at The City University of New York during the turmoil of the 1960s. Any student who had graduated from high

school, with no regard given to grade point average (GPA) and/or the SAT scores, was allowed into one of the CUNY schools. Today, while that policy is officially off the books, many of its aspects remain. CUNY is not alone in its attitude toward access. In every state, midrange colleges exist by some form of easy access, for access=numbers, and low numbers= low funding, and really low numbers=no college. Connected with access is *retention,* which means that, once inside the college, the students are more or less guaranteed graduation.

An examination of the relationship among access and 5 retention and preparation for the 21st-century workplace is illuminating:

Being there. It is hard to be a productive worker if one appears 6 occasionally, yet token appearances, sometimes just cameos, are tolerated in college. Jennifer Jacobson in "Rookies in the Classroom" (*The Chronicle: Career Network,* July 18, 2002) details a professor's experience with attendance: "Some of them have amazingly intricate excuses, such as one student who explained that his parent's credit card had been canceled and by the time he'd driven home to get a new card, the bookstore had sold out the texts he'd needed." In the meantime, the student had simply not come to class. One solution to this problem is to use "click-and-brick courses" (classes which combine online and in-class instruction), for being absent online is not possible.

On time. With regard to punctuality, Jacobson's article also 7 tells of a fledgling professor's encounter with a student who arrived late for class with the excuse that she'd been "caught in a traffic jam after visiting a sick grandmother." After she lamented "What was I to do?," the young professor learned after class from another student that the reason for lateness was a lie and that the person being visited was the late-to-class student's "out-of-town boyfriend."

After four years, the bad habits of not being on time and attending sporadically have become second nature. Such habits are unlikely to make for a very productive worker. 8

Cultural awareness. Most liberal arts colleges tout the virtues 9 of a well-rounded education. Becoming aware of a culture usually involves reading. In my Core Literature class that covers Western and non-Western works, the major problem is the refusal to read the assigned texts.

Teaching can be a lonely profession when the only person in 10 the classroom who has read all of *The Scarlet Letter* is the professor. In their handbooks, many moderately difficult-to-enter colleges state certain requirements, but many students spend most of their time trying to get around the requirement of reading. Their methods include shortcuts (*Cliff Notes*) and cheating (buying a paper online about an assigned work of literature). Such evasions of becoming learned are not the hallmark of the well-rounded.

11   Becoming culturally aware involves change, and change is frightening. Faced with a dilemma in a play, poem, or novel, many students become angry if pressed to offer a point of view. Expansion of vistas is not on their agenda. They want me to provide some notes, which they, or someone, will copy or record, and they expect me to produce a test, which, when graded, will produce a range of grades from A to B+. An article in *The Chronicle* (July 12, 2002), "Reports of Grade Inflation May Be Inflated," by Catherine E. Shoichet, states that "one-third of college students receive grades of C or below" and offers this number as evidence to attack the concept of grade inflation. This is skewed reasoning, for those students receiving C's in reality deserve F's, and the C is given to keep them in the college. Further, of what value is a degree with a C average from a mediocre college?

12   The end result is that students emerge from college with a diploma which the Victorian sage Matthew Arnold would characterize as "The Grand Thing without the Grand Meaning"— *i.e.*, merely a piece of paper.

13   **Literacy.** One would expect that, at the very least, colleges would not graduate students whose writing would be generously regarded as poor. One would be wrong.

14   Learning to write is supposed to be taken seriously. Sean Cavanagh, in an article entitled "Overhauled SAT Could Shake up School Curriculum" (*Education Week*, July 10, 2002), announces that the SATs will now include a writing test. Such a requirement sounds rigorous, but appearances are deceiving.

15   At one time, I scored the essay section of the GMAT, the required test for entrance into graduate schools of business where one would acquire an MBA. The test-takers were college graduates from every state and from countries around the world. Fully two-thirds of the essays I scored would not have passed my freshman composition class, yet I was expected to give a score of 4 (Passing) to such writing and, apparently, the graduate schools of business accepted such students. Access again had reared its ugly head. No graduate students=no graduate school.

16   **Diversity.** Since diversity is desired, many English-as-a-second-language (ESL) students are admitted to colleges. Once

there, they must take an English composition class. In my experience, the majority of these students speak English only when compelled to. They sit in my classes, all together, in self-imposed segregation, speaking in their native language.

Outside the class, at home, and everywhere in their existence, they converse in a language other than English. These students need to spend several years in an adult education program focused on the basics of the English language before applying to an institution of higher learning. Some of these ESL students work quite hard, but lack a basic understanding of the language. There is pressure put on professors to pass on to the world of work college graduates whose grasp of the English language is, to be kind, "shaky."   17

This is not to say that the ESL students are worse than the homegrown functional illiterates whose command of their own language is less than commanding. During the 1960s, I taught seventh-grade English in an inner-city junior high school. Now, I offer lessons on syntax and diction which I created for that junior high class to my present college classes, and I encounter failure in excess of 50%. Failing more than half of my class at the end of the semester would be asking for a public flogging. A recent case at Temple University, reported by Robin Wilson in her article, "The Teaching Equation Didn't Add Up" (*The Chronicle,* March 29, 2002), involved a tenured professor of mathematics who was fired for being an "extremely harsh grader" who was "rude" to his students. Another professor at the university remarked that "he noticed that if somebody flunks a lot of people then the administration doesn't like that, and I do what I think will not put me out on the street without a job." Translation? The inmates are running the asylum.   18

Solutions

What can be done? A college administrator could have the courage to let the word go forth that the college has admission standards and that access does not guarantee graduation. One of the state schools in New Jersey—The College of New Jersey, formerly Trenton State University—did exactly that, transforming itself from a college where admittance was rather easy into a true institution of higher learning with high admission standards. An initial dip in enrollment occurred, but today the college is listed as one of the top bargains for a quality education in the country.   19

20   I would not count on the above scenario sweeping the country. Most administrators keep their ships of education afloat by scrounging for the few dollars that come their way from full-time equivalent students. FTEs are generated by easy access and retention.

21   A more-practical solution is for parents to find a cheap apartment some distance from the family home, deposit their son or daughter in it, along with the considerable clutter accumulated during a brief lifetime, and secure enrollment in a community college. The teachers at a community college earn a living by teaching. Therefore, the students are more likely to be taught by a full-time, professional teacher.

22   In addition, community colleges offer training in the technical fields where there are jobs. In the county in New Jersey where I live, students can obtain an associate degree in radiography and get a job. It has been estimated that 1,000,000 workers in the technical fields will be needed in the coming decades. How many job offers will come the way of a graduate of a moderately difficult-to-enter, four-year college with a 2.75 GPA in English, women's studies, or history?

23   Possibly the best course of action during senior year is to participate in one of the job cooperative programs that link high schools to the world of work. One such initiative at Allentown High School in central New Jersey is entitled the Senior Practicum. It is a for-credit class in which a student explores an interest in the workplace. The program's mission is to create an opportunity for high school seniors to learn to function as responsible, contributing adults. Serving as a rite of passage, it "provides a bridge from the traditional school structure to the self-directed, self-initiated world of adults." Participation in jobs ranging from work in retail sales to positions in a pain management clinic, the local police department, law offices, and architectural firms, students learn what is expected of them by the worth of work. After graduation, some of these students gain employment in the very business where they interned and find out that the employer will pay for their further education. However, the major benefit of such school-to-work programs is the personal growth as teenagers shed their childish ways and take a major step toward becoming adults.

24   Higher education is very expensive, taxing the resources of the already overtaxed, middle-class family. In addition to the cost, the college years are a moment in time that will never return. Again and again, in my night classes, I encounter adults, now burdened with kids and dead-end jobs, who, 10 years ago,

wasted their time in college with adolescent behavior. Now, they tell me, "You know, Prof, if I had just listened to you back then, but I. . . ." I smile and nod and tune them out by repeating to myself the old saw: "If 'ifs' and 'buts' were ginger and nuts, what a Merry Christmas we'd all have."

The 19th-century novelist, and twice Prime Minister, Benjamin Disraeli wrote a book entitled *The Two Nations* which exposed the class gap in Victorian England. In 21st-century America, there is an education gap. Students with brains who have worked hard in high school can go to the top of the academic food chain and attend an Ivy League school, Stanford University, MIT, or Amherst College. Those students will lead this century. Others can receive a technical education at a local community college that will allow them to earn a good living. In his book, *Success Without a College Degree*, John T. Murphy reports that 75% of the American populace does not have a college degree, which means that those possessed of other than academic skills can find a way to succeed financially. 25

Then, there is the great, gray middle. Going to a midrange college is of value only for those students who wish to become educated and accept the fact that attendance, punctuality, and hard work are parts of the process. However, going to a college is an utter waste of time for those students who have emerged from high school neither literate nor numerate, with cultural focuses revolving around hip-hop and body piercing and with zero interest in changing their behavior. Parents should investigate one of the above solutions or invest their hard-earned dollars elsewhere while their offspring find employment in the world of the minimum wage. 26

Garry B. Trudeau
DOONESBURY

Garry B. Trudeau (born 1948) is one of America's most influential (and controversial) political and social commentators. His vehicle is the comic strip "Doonesbury," which appears in more than 850 newspapers and whose audience may top 100 million readers.

Ellen Condliffe Lagemann
THE CHALLENGE
OF LIBERTY

Ellen Condliffe Lagemann is the Dean of the Harvard University Graduate School of Education and the author of many books on educational research, including Private Power for the Public Good: A History of the Carnegie Foundation for the Advancement of Teaching *(1983), which won a Critic's Choice Award, and more recently,* An Elusive Science: The Troubling History of Education Research *(2000). The essay below was first published in the Spring 2003 edition of* Liberal Education, *the journal of the Association of American Colleges and Universities. It explores ways that the liberal arts and vocational education might work together, entering the conversations about the purpose of education found in this section as well as in the previous section on public schools.*

We live in a world that is fundamentally new—new in the often   1
fearful interconnectedness of regions, states, and people; new in both the scope of the challenges we face in finding and sustaining peace and in the consequences we face if we fail to achieve peace; and new, too, in the heterogeneity of the peoples with whom we live, work, and communicate. As globalization has changed the world we know, it has brought great opportunity and challenge and it has added renewed vigor to old, familiar questions. One such question is the one I would like to take up: What can we learn from the past to enliven our thinking about liberal education in the present and future?

Let me begin with two comments on the current situation of   2
American higher education. The first is simple. According to a recent report of the Carnegie Corporation of New York, higher education today is significantly more professional and technical in orientation than it was thirty years ago. In 1970, 50 percent of all bachelor's degrees were awarded in a liberal arts subject. In 2000, nearly 60 percent of the degrees were awarded in a pre-professional or technical field. I could multiply the statistics, but I do not think that is necessary to make the point. Today's college students do not have time or money to waste. They are careful consumers. And they are voting with their feet for more vocationally oriented programs of study.

3   My second observation derives from an essay by the journalist Nicholas Lemann, called "The Kids in the Conference
Room." It is about recent college graduates, mostly from highly
selective institutions, who are recruited to work at consulting
firms for at least a few years after graduation. As Lemann put
it, working for McKinsey & Co., or some close approximate, is
"the present-day equivalent of working for the C.I.A. in the
nineteen-fifties, or the Peace Corps in the sixties, or Ralph
Nader in the seventies, or First Boston in the eighties . . . the
job that encapsulates the Zeitgeist of the moment." Lemann
goes on to point out that working for McKinsey for a few years
is "an ideal placeholder" for bright young people, who leave college with heavy debt and no certain idea of where they want to
end up vocationally.

4   To me, there is a disturbing paradox evident in the data presented in the Carnegie Corporation's report and the observation made by Lemann. On the one hand, student course
selection indicates that they want their college education to
prepare them for careers. On the other hand, by contrast, those
students who attend our most selective institutions—all of
which, I might add, consider themselves liberal arts colleges
and universities—graduate without a clear sense of vocational
direction. At a time of extreme social challenge, we seem to
have few alternatives between clear and, inevitably, rather narrow vocational preparation and seemingly directionless programs of liberal study. This makes me wonder whether in the
challenge of our moment in history there is not a way to enliven the liberal arts by organizing them around deliberate
consideration of what it means to have a vocation.

Having a Calling

5   The word vocation implies more than earning a living or having
a career. The word vocation implies having a calling: knowing
who one is, what one believes, what one values, and where one
stands in the world. A sense of vocation is not something fully
achieved early in life. For those of us who are lucky, it grows
over time, becomes more articulate, and deepens. Granting,
then, that a sense of vocation develops over time, it is still not
unreasonable to suggest that one purpose of a college education, and a central purpose of liberal education, should be to
nurture an initial sense of vocation. This might encompass personal dispositions such as awareness of the importance of deliberate choices, individual agency, and social connection as
well as recognition, albeit initial, of the ways of thinking and

acting that seem most personally congenial. It should also include a capacity for civic intelligence. This requires that one recognize one's personal stake in public problems, global as well as domestic. It also necessitates respect for tolerance, the rights of others, evidence-based decision making, and deliberative judgment—in a word, respect for the values of due process that are essential to a democratic way of life. Vocation is not simply about an individual calling. It is about one's calling within one's society and, increasingly, across different societies around the world.

Historically, it is quite easy to see the power of vocation as a   6
driving force in the education of individual people. One might even venture that vocation, broadly defined, in the terms I have just described, tends usually to be the theme that links the different experiences that define an individual's education. Bearing in mind that I am trying to draw from history to help us think well about the liberal arts today and tomorrow, let me illustrate the importance of vocation by saying a few words about the education of some very well-known people.

Benjamin Franklin

The first person is Benjamin Franklin, who left us a wonderful   7
record of his life in his Autobiography. Franklin was born in Puritan Boston in 1706, the tenth son and fifteenth child of Josiah Franklin and his second wife, Abiah. Intended for the ministry by his father, Ben was sent to what is now called the Boston Latin School at the age of eight. He survived only a year. The tuition at Boston Latin was high, and Ben was not sufficiently pious to make a promising candidate for the ministry. His penchant for practical efficiency led him to suggest to his father that he say grace over the family's food once for the entire year rather than before every meal. A struggling candle maker, Josiah quickly realized that Ben was not suited for the church.

At that point, a search for vocation began. Nothing appealed   8
to young Ben, so, in desperation, Josiah apprenticed Ben to his older brother James, who was a printer.

It was as a printer's apprentice that Ben Franklin began quite   9
self-consciously to find ways to understand who he was as a person. He did this initially by taking on the roles of people he was not. While working for his brother James, Ben wrote fourteen essays describing the complaints of a poor rural widow, whom he named Silence Dogood. In so doing, he initiated a process of self-definition that one can also see in Poor Richard's Almanac, which Franklin wrote as a prosperous printer in

Philadelphia, or in reports and portraits of Franklin as a sea-
soned diplomat, parading around Paris dressed as a rural hick
in a coonskin cap. Repeatedly throughout his life, Ben Franklin
sought, defined, and clarified who he was in relation to others,
by juxtaposing his own persona with those of others different
from him.

Knowing Oneself

10   If what might be described as role playing was an important
part of Franklin's search for vocation, so were his various deliberate attempts at self-improvement. As a young man, for example, Ben created a chart to measure his progress toward
moral perfection. It began with fairly obvious virtues such as
"Temperance—Eat not to dullness. Drink not to elevation."
And it ended with more adventuresome ones like "Humility—
Imitate Jesus and Socrates." As a Philadelphia merchant,
Franklin organized the Junto, a discussion group that considered ways to better the city and then sponsored projects to
carry out specific reforms and improvements. Whether chart-
ing his own progress toward perfection or examining his city's
adequacy as a growing urban center, Franklin was studying
who he was, what his responsibilities were as a virtuous person or a civic leader, and, especially in the case of the Junto,
how actions taken for the public good advanced not only the
well-being of his fellow citizens of Philadelphia, but also his
own stature as a first citizen and, increasingly, as a very
wealthy printer and statesman.

11   If Franklin's own education was energized by an extraordinarily self-conscious effort constantly to find a congenial, public role
for himself—a vocation—so, too, were his writings about education predicated on the importance of vocation. Consider as an
example, the "Proposals Relating to the Education of Youth in
Pennsylvania," which was a plan for what became the University
of Pennsylvania. In this document, Franklin admitted, "It would
be well if [the youth of Pennsylvania] could be taught every
Thing that is useful and every Thing that is ornamental." But
Franklin observed: "Art is long, and [the students'] Time is short.
It is therefore propos'd that they learn those Things that are
likely to be most useful and most ornamental, regard being had
to the Professions for which they are intended." Here, subsequent occupation became an explicit guide in the selection of the
subjects to be studied.

12   In line with his emphasis on vocation, Franklin insisted that
the curriculum for the new university be modern. It was to be

free of medieval anachronism. Thus, it should include contemporary writers along with the classics. Although all students should study English grammar, instruction in foreign languages should vary by future profession. Franklin did not dispense with all traditional learning, but the curriculum he generated reflected his insistent belief that, by preparing young men for a useful role in the world, advanced learning could have greater meaning for both the individual and the society of which that individual was a part (women, it was then, of course, presumed, did not need advanced education). Having been essential to his own education, vocation became a foundation for the education Franklin recommended for others.

Jane Addams

Jane Addams's life was also inspired by a search for vocation. 13
Growing up in central Illinois, Addams greatly admired her father, a prominent local lawyer and first citizen of Cedarville, Illinois, with whom she had an especially close relationship since her mother died when she was two. She recalled in her autobiography that, as a child, she had spent many hours trying to imitate her father. But, of course, Addams could not imitate her father exactly since as a woman her occupational choices were restricted.

Rather than retreat to a traditional role, Addams instead em- 14
braced the fact of gender limitation and defined herself and her generation in opposition to traditional expectations. Speaking of changes in the education offered to women, as a student at Rockford Seminary in 1881, Addams said: "[Women's education] has passed from accomplishments and the arts of pleasing, to the development of her intellectual force, and capability for direct labor. She wishes not to be a man, nor like a man, but she claims the same right to independent thought and action. . . . As young women of the 19th century, we gladly claim these privileges, and proudly assert our independence. . . . So we have planned to be 'Breadgivers' throughout our lives; believing . . . that the only true and honorable life is now filled with good works and honest toil . . . [we will] thus happily fulfill Woman's Noblest Mission."

The articulate and self-conscious search for vocation that Jane 15
Addams was able to describe in this statement had been shaped by the formal study in which she engaged at Rockford. The curriculum, while Addams was a student there, included Latin, Greek, German, geology, astronomy, botany, medieval history, civil government, music, American literature, and evidence of

Christianity. But, as her peers recalled, "the intellectual ozone" that exuded from "her vicinity" came from her unusual determination and purpose. Jane Addams's insistent wish to find a way to express her ideals and talents, despite the limitations imposed on her as a woman, was clearly an extended and successful search for vocation.

16   That search, of course, eventually led her to the West Side of Chicago, where, with Ellen Gates Starr, she founded Hull House, a world-famous social settlement that provided social, educational, and cultural services to the diverse immigrant population of that neighborhood. Hull House's fame came, in part, from the fact that Jane Addams helped to support it by writing constantly for magazines and by lecturing. But it is important to realize that it was not merely economics that drove Jane Addams's public expressions. It was both a desire to educate the educated middle-class public about how their neighbors lived and also to continue to work out for herself what she was doing and why it mattered. Questions of vocation continued to drive Jane Addams's education even after she founded Hull House.

W.E.B. Du Bois

17   As an educated woman, Addams was constrained by the fact of her sex, and yet eager to be effective in the world. One could say that she bore the burden of what her contemporary W.E.B. Du Bois called a "double consciousness." Perhaps a sense of social marginality is always at the root of soul-searching concerning who one is and where one can contribute to the common good. Certainly that was the case for Du Bois, who, throughout his long life struggled to understand whether and how he, as a black man, could be an American. Like Addams, Du Bois turned his personal anguish about vocation into sometimes stinging, always acute social criticism. His keenest insight was probably the line that introduced the second chapter of Souls of Black Folk: "The problem of the twentieth century is the problem of the color line." However that may be, having learned as a young schoolboy in Great Barrington, Massachusetts, that he was seen as different and "a problem" by his classmates, Du Bois spent most of his ninety-five years writing about what he could and could not do as a Black American. Even at the very end of his life, when he left the United States for Ghana, Du Bois was still figuring out his place in the world.

18   Searching for vocation is a deep human need that different cultures and different historical eras have treated differently. My suggestion here is that colleges and universities today need

to acknowledge the educative drive one can see in the lives of people like W.E.B. Du Bois, Jane Addams, and Benjamin Franklin, and, recognizing the essentially vocational character of that drive, find ways to make vocational exploration central to liberal education.

Vocational Exploration and Faculty Roles

I trust that the difference I assume between vocational and oc-   19
cupational exploration is clear already. Vocational exploration is about identity formation within the context of a particular society and a particular time. Occupational exploration, by contrast, is considering one's job alternatives. Vocational exploration is, in my view, the job of the faculty; occupational exploration is a matter for the office of career services.

To make vocational exploration a more important aspect of   20
liberal education, faculty will need to re-think their roles. They will need to take seriously John Dewey's admonition that if one teaches math, history, or science in school, one must remember that it is people that one is really teaching, and not the subject matter. The subject matter is the medium through which one seeks to nurture habits of deliberation and orientations toward inquiry. It is the medium through which one helps people to learn to learn. Hopefully, the subject matter of the school curriculum is also important knowledge that is worth mastering. Still, it is worth acknowledging that teaching is not merely about furnishing the mind. It is equally, if not more importantly, about shaping, energizing, and refining the mind.

This is difficult for teachers in K-12 schools to keep in mind,   21
and it is even more difficult for professors. Virtually all professors are trained as scholars. A number are now also being trained as teachers. Even when teaching is presented to graduate students as an art to be valued and mastered, it is still one's scholarly credentials that tend to get one a job, and it is certainly one's scholarly credentials that determine whether one wins tenure. Hence, it will take determined, steady work to convince faculty members that they are, first, teaching young people, and secondly, teaching some aspect of the field they profess.

More important, giving increased primacy to overall student   22
development will also necessitate institutional reform. As we all know, colleges and universities, especially the most selective, are reluctant to modify the model that has helped them to thrive for more than fifty years. As Louis Menand recently observed in the New York Review of Books, from the end of World

War II until quite recently, universities flourished if they gave priority to research and publication and increasingly specialized knowledge. This enabled the faculty to view their teaching and advisement responsibilities as less important than their "own work," which was fairly transparent code for going to the library or laboratory to develop new ideas.

23   Giving teaching and advisement equal priority among faculty activities will be necessary to engage faculty more centrally in the lives and vocational concerns of their students. And that is not all that will need to be altered to give more emphasis to matters of vocation.

Humanistic Values

24   Generally, today, core liberal arts subjects are taught in ways that are intended to give students an introduction to characteristic ways of thinking in a discipline, to the essential elements of an area, and, more generally, to what I would call the map of knowledge in some particular domain. All that is important. But the purposes currently most commonly associated with liberal arts study represent an unnecessarily narrow conception of why one should read Shakespeare or consider the ideas of French philosophers.

25   In addition to their canonical value, subjects like these have humanistic value. They can and should encourage thought about oneself and others and about virtue and vice—the good, the bad, and the ugly. They can and should encourage thought about vocation, in the broad sense in which I am using this word. As the philosopher William James once asserted, a liberal education should "help you . . . know a good man when you see him." That is because a liberal education, at least according to James, is not a matter of taking certain specific courses, but rather of viewing any subject in terms of its "humanistic value," its value to illuminate the human condition.

26   Of course, in many liberal arts classes there is discussion of the humanistic side of things. But without neglecting canonical perspectives, which are important for helping students locate knowledge in historical or cultural perspective, the humanistic side of things could be given greater emphasis if faculty members spent more time talking with students about what they could learn and what they are learning about their own interests, values, and sense of person and place as well as what they are learning about the subject matter in question.

27   Going "meta" with students, by which I mean helping them realize that they should be learning about themselves while

reading *The Tempest* or debating Camus and not merely becoming culturally literate, is not something, at least in my experience, that faculty members tend to do systematically and on a regular basis. They tend not to do this because they tend not to have learned about meta-cognition. They tend not to know that it is pedagogically powerful to help students understand how and why they can learn what they are learning. Being subject-matter specialists as opposed to teachers, they tend not to touch upon the personal because they are instead inclined to focus on insuring an understanding of, say, the play's structure or meaning. Taking this one step further to capture in addition how and why the play connects to particular students is to take a step beyond a faculty member's role at least as traditionally configured. It would require pedagogical knowledge that many professors lack. But doing this would likely enhance a student's interest. It would offer a vital, personal reason for studying Shakespeare beyond knowing that somehow it is good to be "cultured."

Vocational interests can make the liberal arts more com-   28
pelling to students, and so can tying programs of liberal education quite directly to the world and its problems. This is happening increasingly on college campuses today as more and more institutions offer programs of service learning. More often than not, however, such programs are special courses often linked to community service of one kind or another. What I have in mind is broader.

Emerson observed that without action "thought can never   29
ripen into truth." If that is, indeed, the case, as I believe it is, then, virtually all college classes should have some kind of practicum attached to them. There is a lot of this already going on, but there needs to be more translation of classroom abstractions into action. This would enhance learning because the test of knowledge is in its application and also because constantly having opportunities to act in the world will help students develop a sense of vocation.

Having to help their students apply the models and theories   30
they were presenting in their classes would also present faculty with a salutary challenge. After all, the efficacy of a professor's ideas would be evident in his or her students' worldly competence. That is a high threshold for faculty accountability, but one that is not out of line in our times. The challenges we face domestically and globally are vast. With poverty, disease, and inequity fueling attacks on secular democracies around the world, we cannot allow colleges and universities to be home to what Alfred North Whitehead called "inert ideas." Instead, we need to encourage faculty to become engaged with the problems around

us in ways that will at once contribute to our society as well as to their students and their own competence and even wisdom as scholars.

Recalling Our Mission

31   None of what I have said is very new or original. But I believe that the problems facing all of us require recalling what our collective mission is. Colleges and universities grew up across the United States for all sorts of reasons. Many were founded to insure the continuance of a particular religious group. Some were established to increase the land values in a small town. All were intended to educate people who could provide the leadership necessary to improve society. That's why the capstone experience for nineteenth century college students at liberal arts colleges was a course in moral philosophy usually taught by the college's president. The course was intended to insure that graduates would know their responsibilities as college-educated people (actually, with few exceptions, college-educated men). It provided a last chance to inculcate values and a sense of one's self as an educated citizen. It offered a final window on the opportunities and challenges then current in the locality and the region and across the United States.

32   I do not entirely live in the past and I do not think we can revive moral philosophy classes. But I do think we need to re-embrace the logic behind them. Liberal education should establish one's sense of direction, one's knowledge of one's self as an active, effective person and citizen. Liberal education should ready one to participate in the defining issues of our times. Whether it's the AIDS epidemic in southern Africa, the chaos of states like Afghanistan that lack basic civil infrastructures, or the social anomalies we observe in our own country where there are, for example, racial achievement gaps among high school students in both wealthy, racially integrated suburbs and blighted urban areas, social challenges like these should be familiar to graduates of liberal arts colleges. They should have helped to define how graduates see themselves making a difference in the world.

33   By giving renewed emphasis to their vocational purposes, liberal arts colleges and universities can help people live productively, responsibly, and well, amidst all the confusions of the present times. By making matters of vocation central to all they do, liberal arts colleges and universities can play a more direct role in improving the world. This is not to say that detached,

seemingly idle speculation and abstract knowledge do not have value—great value—in institutions of liberal learning. They do. My concern is balance and underscoring the educative power of vocational interests. The famed social psychologist Kurt Lewin once said, "There is nothing so useful as a good theory," and following his logic, I would like to close by saying: There is nothing more liberal or liberating than education approached with matters of vocation foremost in mind. Our students seem to know that. We should give them the kind of education they want and deserve.

Ralph Ketcham
A RATIONALE FOR CIVIC EDUCATION

Among the answers to this section's title question, "What's College For?" one prominent possibility is "to educate engaged citizens." Ralph Ketcham, in the essay below, makes an argument for the centrality of civic education, an argument that is in dialogue with the discussions of liberal and vocational purposes of education found in this section. Ketcham is Professor Emeritus in the Maxwell School of Syracuse University, whose stated mission is "advancing citizenship, scholarship, and leadership around the world." He published this essay in Educational Record *in the Spring of 1992. This now-defunct journal, sponsored by the American Council on Education, published articles concerned with the broad range of issues affecting higher education aimed at colleges and universities.*

Civic education means that education required of *all* people in a   1
self-governing society, regardless of their particular calling, to execute their public office as citizen. Thomas Jefferson stated it simply in his first proposal for a national system of education that would equip all citizens "to understand their rights, to maintain them, and to exercise with intelligence their parts in self-government." Such education "would raise the mass of the people to the high ground of moral respectability necessary to their own safety, and to orderly government. . . . Worth and

genius would thus be sought out from every condition of life, and completely prepared by education for defeating the competition of wealth and birth for public trusts." To skeptics, Jefferson replied, "if we think [the people] not enlightened enough to exercise their control [over government] with a wholesome discretion, the remedy is not to take it from them, but to inform their discretion."[1]

2   Almost two centuries later, President Truman's Commission on Higher Education reported that American colleges and universities should encourage students "to develop for . . . one's personal and civic life a code of behavior . . . consistent with democratic ideas, [and] to participate actively as an informed and responsible citizen" in the nation's public life. Because "the unity of liberal education had been splintered by overspecialization," the report concluded, college graduates often "fell short of the human wholeness and civic conscience which the cooperative activities of citizenship require." Better balance was needed, therefore, between "specialized education aiming at a thousand different careers, and the transmission of a common cultural heritage toward a common citizenship."[2] Toward this goal, hundreds of colleges included under their plans of "general education" courses or programs designed to link cultural memory, critical thinking, ethical growth, and responsible citizenship.

3   Yet, in the last century, the emphasis on specialization, technical studies, and vocation that has undermined liberal education generally has taken a particular toll on civic education. A "social science" group requirement often replaced general education offerings on the grounds that it better reflected the diverse research efforts of the faculty, who, in any case, no longer had any interest or belief in the idea of a "common core of studies." Emphasis turned increasingly from the whole to the parts, resulting in the hundreds (even thousands) of courses offered at modern "multiversities." This same ethos permeated colleges, community colleges, and high schools, as "multiversity" graduates taught—or trained teachers—in the lower branches.

4   In fact, university preoccupation with the public policy dimensions of the social sciences dramatically reveals how off target such work is from the Jeffersonian ideal of "informing the discretion" of citizens-to-be. In the first place, the direction of instruction is reversed; instead of developing the informed perspective and attitude that will enable the potential citizen to address public questions, study tends to begin with a sophisticated collection of data. As the "facts" are accumulated—including, in policy analysis, the "input" of the various "actors" and of concerned special interest groups—the usual assumption is that

conclusions or policies will arise from the carefully manipulated aggregation of data. Public policy is simply the sum of the parts.

The process of arriving at policy positions is usually under- 5 taken on the basis of the "conflict-of-interest" assumption that in an open and pluralistic society, policy is best understood as the result of diverse and competitive interests. Harking back to Madison's tenth Federalist Paper, "conflict-of-interest" theory sees tyranny prevented and policy properly hammered out as a multitude of interests (the more the better) clash and interact. The process is presumed fair, and policy best determined, if access is open to all, if all then engage in vigorous self-advocacy, and if the decisions are made, after compromise, by majority vote. Justice, or the public good, is thus defined simply as the result of this open and democratic process (or at least it is presumed that one cannot do any better than that in a free society). Explicitly rejected, or perhaps simply ignored, is any notion that the public good might be defined, in Madison's terms, as the rationally determined "permanent and aggregate interests of the community."[3]

Whatever the overall merits of this approach, it seems to en- 6 tail a problematic lack of completeness in facing the full scope of political judgment and participation in a free and democratic society. Granted, it is laudably open-ended, undogmatic, fact-attentive, tolerant, diverse, and pragmatic. It is also painstakingly faithful to the scientific mode of analysis. The accumulation of data, and the rigorous application of those data to social problems, is impressive. Furthermore, a mode of leadership emphasizing accessibility and skilled brokering of interests, and a mode of citizenship keyed to effective self-advocacy and sophisticated policy analysis, receive explicit encouragement. These are worthy benefits—as far as they go. But these are a politics and a citizenship without a center, a purpose, a guiding perspective.

The social science approach is thus susceptible to use or 7 abuse, depending on what purpose or perspective, stated or implied, enlists its methods and skills. To cite an extreme illustration, Adolf Eichmann presumably had highly developed statistical analysis, policy implementation, and communication skills, but because he lacked a humane purpose and perspective, we would not regard him as an exemplary public servant.

In speaking of the merely behavioral and quantitative em- 8 phasis in contemporary social science, Leo Strauss once remarked that "it would be false to call the new political science diabolic; it has no attributes peculiar to fallen angels. . . . Nor is it Neronian. Nevertheless one may say that it fiddles while Rome burns. It is excused by two facts: it does not know that it fiddles and it does not know that Rome burns."[4] Though Strauss's judgment is not entirely fair, he does make an important point: modern social science, however effective at gathering and analyzing data, insufficiently attends to the need political decision makers have for guidance from larger, more public-spirited perspectives and purposes. And insofar as social science forgoes interest in such matters, it is incomplete training for those who participate in government.

9   If we accept that education must include "training . . . in self-government," we should then begin by regarding the citizen in a democracy as an office holder in government.[5] That is, in discussing, voting, and acting in a self-governing society, the citizen's role in government differs only in degree from that of any elected or appointed official. The essential obligations this entails (as we expect from all office holders) are a perspective and a habit that put the public interest above any private or partisan interest. In training students for the "office of citizen," we must nourish this essential, public-spirited stance. Data collection, policy analysis, and communication are important and useful skills, but by themselves they leave the political decision maker, the citizen, without guidance at crucial points. That guidance can only properly come from an enlarged and disciplined way of looking at public affairs—what Benjamin Franklin called "the virtue and public spirit of the common people."[6] Franklin believed that the essential qualification for the office of citizen was a public-spiritedness that arose not from wealth or status or class or sex or race, but from an intention, a willingness, eventually a habit, to seek the common good.

The Public Interest

10   Our sometimes cynical generation is inclined, at this point, to ask for a definition of "public spirit," or "the public interest," or even to question whether such an idea can have an objective meaning. Eighteenth-century political discourse defined the public interest as the opposite of corruption, which meant any form of self-seeking or bribery or partiality or factional spirit that opposed or ignored the well-being of the nation as a whole. Thus the public good consisted of the *intention,* first, to discern, through rational discourse, the idea of the interest of the whole, and second, to work together to give effect to that idea. Though the assumption that such an objective good did exist (it was often thought of as "natural law" or "natural right"), more directly on the agenda was the need to *seek* it, deliberately,

reasonably, and disinterestedly. It was recognized that human beings were flawed and in part indelibly selfish, but it was also widely believed that ordinary people had some potential for more noble thought and conduct.

This fundamental ambivalence, this sensing of both good   11 and bad in human nature, is still at the base of thinking about self-government, and it provides the necessary foundation for serious attention to the public education of citizens. Human beings do have the capacity to rise above narrow and self-serving states of mind, and this capacity can be nourished and educed in our public schools, colleges, and universities.

Teaching Citizenship

The teaching of such a perspective needs to be woven into   12 courses throughout a university curriculum, but it can serve equally well as the explicit focus of "participation in government" courses. For example, students can learn valuable lessons by studying the recent Supreme Court case on the right of New Jersey school authorities to search student purses.[7] Students readily understand the issue, and they are keenly alert to both the rights of students and the responsibility of authorities to maintain a safe learning environment. The facts can be grasped easily, the implications discerned quickly, and even the arguments of the Supreme Court opinions understood readily. Students need not learn the legal technicalities, nor which is the "correct" opinion, but it is critical that they understand the broad view and the careful reasoning of the justices on both sides of a split decision. That is, they must learn how to approach public questions: how to first understand the facts and issues, then see the lines of thought reasoned consideration can take, and finally move to responsible judgment. They learn primarily not which decision is "right," nor even the processes of adjudication or the principles of constitutional law, but what the proper perspective is of the participant in government. With this in mind, students are ready to "practice" it as they examine other public issues (crime, protection of the environment, arms control, etc.), as they conduct their own community research projects, and as they participate in public life.

A further important part of such education for "the office of   13 citizen" is some study of the development of responsible freedom and self-government, most notably in Western civilization. Constructive participation in free and democratic government must be grounded in some understanding of that government's evolution, principles, and practices, which define the liberal core of the public spirit. Attention to what Walter Lippmann has called "the tradition of civility," the attitudes and practices essential to the process of democracy over the centuries, the growth of free government in Anglo-America, and the ideas undergirding the U.S. Constitution, will help students understand the rich connotations of democratic citizenship.

14   Lest this approach seem unduly optimistic about the capacity of human beings to achieve a public-spirited posture, consider the possibly more foolish optimism of supposing that all is well in a democratic society when no one is expected or encouraged to achieve such a perspective. Problems of global ecology and world peace may require the forethought, reasoned approach, and concern for the good of the whole that is central to the "office of the citizen"—and that may not be amenable to a "sum-of-the-parts" approach. Our only practical option, as the twenty-first century approaches, may be to encourage human potential for a vision beyond the narrowly selfish. It is at least more practical than the dubious optimism that everything will be all right if we simply pursue our own special interests in free and open political arenas.

15   Reinhold Niebuhr once noted that "man's capacity for justice makes democracy possible; but man's inclination to injustice makes democracy necessary."[8] Though attention has focused on the hard-headed insight that the human tendency to abuse power makes its dispersal in a one-person, one-vote government the most effective way to prevent corruption and tyranny, the other part of Niebuhr's "vindication" of democracy needs equal emphasis. The capacity to sense what is fair, to understand right and wrong, to reason effectively, to exhibit compassion for others, and to act on behalf of these qualities, Niebuhr argues, is as much a part of human nature as the indelible tendencies toward greed, short-sightedness, and partiality for our own interests. In fact, the existence of both tendencies is what makes the problem of human government both complex and interesting. Niebuhr's argument precisely follows that of James Madison: "If men were angels," he observed in the *Federalist*, "no government would be necessary." Yet, if the "fundamental principle" of some human capacity for reason and good judgment were "impeached," then democracy would likely provide bad government—and a "benevolent despot" might even be better. "In framing a government . . . by men over men," Madison concluded, "auxiliary precautions" such as checks and balances and a large, pluralistic country

were useful, but a "dependence on the people [was still] the primary control on the government."[9]

The greatest wisdom in matters of government, then, is to   16
recognize the realistic way democracy prevents tyranny by encouraging a pluralism that disperses power, but to see as well the critical need to cultivate human capacities for justice, good will, reason, and public spirit. It is only mildly comforting, after all, to have a polity that, by pitting interest against interest, prevents the worst results. Indeed, this does not always happen; compromises fall between cracks, or conflicting pathologies combine into potent evil conspiracies.

At least as important, if we are to do more than merely sur-   17
vive, is to draw forth, encourage, cultivate that part of our humanity that allowed Jefferson to suppose in the Declaration of Independence that "just" government "derived from the consent of the governed." And because in a democracy there is simply no escaping this linkage of just government and responsible citizenship, its encouragement must be a prime task of American higher education. Only this is likely to provide the "common cultural heritage, . . . the human wholeness, and the civic conscience that the cooperative activities of citizenship require."[10]

NOTES

1. Thomas Jefferson, "Autobiography," 1821, in Adrienne Koch and William Peden, eds., *The Life and Selected Writings of Thomas Jefferson* (Modern Library, 1944), 52; Jefferson to John Adams, 28 October 1813 in Lester Cappon, ed., *The Adams-Jefferson Letters* (2 vols., Chapel Hill, 1959), II, 387–91; Jefferson to W. C. Jarvis, 28 September 1820, in Edward Dumbold, ed., *The Political Writings of Thomas Jefferson* (Indianapolis, 1955), 93.
2. *Higher Education for American Democracy* (6 vols., New York, 1948), I, 47–58.
3. Federalist Nos. 51 and 57; Clinton Rossiter, ed., *The Federalist Papers* (New York, 1962), 322, 350–53.
4. Leo Strauss, "Epilogue," in H. J. Storing. ed., *Essays on the Scientific Study of Politics* (New York, 1961), 327.
5. Joseph Tussman, *Obligation and the Body Politic* (New York, 1960).
6. Max Farrand, ed., *The Records of the Federal Convention* (New Haven, 1937), II, 204–05.
7. *New Jersey vs. T.L.O.*: No. 83-712 (1985).
8. Reinhold Niebuhr, *The Children of Light and the Children of Darkness* (New York, 1944), xiii.
9. Federalist Nos. 51 and 57: Clinton Rossiter, ed., *The Federalist Papers* (New York. 1962), 322, 350–53.
10. *Higher Education for American Democracy* (6 vols., New York, 1948), I, 47–58.

The ad for Hofstra University on this page appeared in several magazines and newspapers in 1989 and 1990; the ad for Seton Hall University on the next page appeared in the same places in 2001 and 2002. What does each ad imply about the purpose of a college education? Which is more persuasive?

Determination and hard work, at any age, can lead to being the best. Hofstra University, just 50 years old, is already among the top ten percent of American colleges and universities in almost all academic criteria and resources.

Professionally accredited programs in such major areas as business, engineering, law, psychology and education.

A library with over 1.1 million volumes *on campus*—a collection larger than that of 95% of American universities.

Record enrollments with students from 31 states and 59 countries— with a student-faculty ratio of only 17 to 1.

The largest, most sophisticated non-commercial television facility in the East. A high technology undergraduate teaching resource with broadcast-quality production capability.

A ranking in *Barron's Guide to the Most Prestigious Colleges*—one of only 262 colleges and universities chosen from almost 4,000.

At Hofstra, determination, inspiration and hard work are qualities our faculty demands in itself and instills in our students. These qualities are what it takes to be the best. In anything.

HOFSTRA UNIVERSITY
WE TEACH SUCCESS.

50th Anniversary
Hempstead, L.I., New York 11550

John Searle

THE CASE FOR A
TRADITIONAL LIBERAL
ARTS EDUCATION

*John Searle, who has been a professor of philosophy at the
University of California–Berkeley for many years, is best
known for his advocacy of "speech-act theory," a theory of
communication which has been both influential and roundly
debated in philosophy, linguistics, and rhetoric since it appeared in Searle's* Speech Acts: An Essay in the Philosophy of
Language *in 1969. Searle has been controversial in other ways
too, and the following essay is certainly polemical in many respects. "The Case for a Traditional Liberal Arts Education" was
originally published, interestingly enough, in* The Journal of
Blacks in Higher Education *(an academically oriented magazine specializing in articles that explore one or another aspect
of the African American experience in higher education), in the
fall of 1996. Perhaps anticipating that people might wonder
why the essay appeared there, the editor's headnote to the article explained its placement in the journal by quoting Nobel
prize winner Toni Morrison's statement that "the first gesture
of contempt for working-class students is to trivialize and devalue their need for an interest in art, languages, and culture."*

1   There is supposed to be a major debate—or even a set of
debates—going on at present concerning a crisis in the universities, specifically a crisis in the teaching of the humanities. This
debate is supposed to be in large part about whether a certain
traditional conception of liberal education should be replaced
by something sometimes called "multiculturalism." These disputes have even reached the mass media, and several best-
selling books are devoted to discussing them and related issues.
Though the arguments are ostensibly about Western civilization
itself, they are couched in a strange jargon that includes
not only "multiculturalism" but also "the canon," "political correctness," "ethnicity," "affirmative action," and even more
rebarbative expressions such as "hegemony," "empowerment,"
"poststructuralism," "deconstruction," and "patriarchalism."

2   Since I do not know of a neutral vocabulary, I will describe
the debate as between the "defenders" and the "challengers" of

the tradition. I realize that there is a great deal of variety on each side and more than one debate going on, but I am going to try to expose some common core assumptions of each side, assumptions seldom stated explicitly but which form the unstated premises behind the enthymemes that each side tends to use. Let us start by stating naively the traditionalists' view of higher education and, equally naively, the most obvious of the challengers' objections to it. This will, I hope, enable us to get into the deeper features of the debate.

Here is the traditionalists' view: There is a certain tradition   3
in American higher education, especially in the teaching of the humanities. The idea behind this tradition is that there is a body of works of philosophy, literature, history, and art that goes from the Greeks right up to the present day, and though it is not a unified tradition, there are certain family resemblances among the leading works in it, and for want of a better name, we call it the Western intellectual tradition. It extends in philosophy from Socrates to Wittgenstein or, if you like, from the pre-Socratics to Quine, in literature from the Greek poets and playwrights right up to, for example, James Joyce and Ernest Hemingway. The idea is that if you are going to be an educated person in the United States, you must have some familiarity with some of the chief works in this tradition because it defines our particular culture. You do not know who you are, in a sense, unless you have some familiarity with these works, because America is a product of this tradition, and the Constitution in particular is a product of a certain philosophical element in this tradition, the European Enlightenment. And then, too, we think that many works in this tradition, some of those by Shakespeare and Plato, for example, are really so good that they are of *universal* human interest.

So much for the naive statement of the traditionalist view.   4
There is an objection put by the challengers, and the objection, to put it in its crudest form, is as follows: If you look closely at the reading lists of this "Great Tradition," you will discover that the books are almost all by white males from Europe and North America. There are vast areas of the earth and great civilizations whose achievements are totally unrepresented in this conception of "liberal education." Furthermore, within the population of the United States as it is presently constituted, there are lots of ethnic minorities, as well as the largest minority of all, women, whose special needs, interests, traditions, and achievements are underrepresented or in some cases not represented at all in this tradition.

What is the response of the traditionalists to this objection?   5
At this point the debate already begins to get murky, because it

is hard to find traditionalist authors who address the objection directly, so I am going to interject myself and present what I think the traditionalists should say, given their other assumptions. The traditionalist should just accept this objection as a valid criticism and amend the "canon" accordingly. If great works by Asian authors, for example, have been excluded from the "canon" of great works of literature, then by all means let us expand the so-called canon to include them. Closer to home, if great women writers have been excluded, often because they are women, then let us expand membership in the list to include them as well. According to the traditionalist theory, one of the advantages of higher education is that it enables us to see our own civilization and mode of sensibility as one possible form of life among others. And one of the virtues of the tradition is the enormous variety within it. In fact, there never was a "canon." There was a set of constantly revised judgments about which books deserve close study, which deserve to be regarded as "classics." So, based on the traditionalists' own conception, there should be no objection to enlarging the list to include classics from sources outside the Western tradition and from neglected elements within it.

6   As I have presented it, the challengers are making a common-sense objection, to which the traditionalists have a common-sense answer. So it looks as if we have an obvious solution to an interesting problem and can all go home. What is there left to argue about? But it is at this point that the debate becomes interesting. What I have discovered in reading books and articles about this debate is that the objection to the so-called canon—that it is unrepresentative, that it is too exclusive—cannot be met by opening membership to include works by previously excluded elements of the population, since some people would accept such reform as adequate, but many will not. Why not? In order to answer that question I am going to try to state the usually unstated presuppositions made by both the traditionalists and the challengers. I realize, to repeat, that there is a great deal of variety on both sides, but I believe that each side holds certain assumptions, and it is important to try to make them explicit. In the debates one sees, the fundamental issues often are not coming out into the open, and as a result the debaters are talking past each other, seldom making contact. One side accuses the other of racism, imperialism, sexism, elitism, and of being hegemonic and patriarchal. The other side accuses the first of trying to destroy intellectual standards and of politicizing the university. So what is actually going on? What is in dispute?

Assumptions Behind the Tradition

I will try to state the assumptions behind the tradition as a set 7
of propositions, confining myself to half a dozen for the sake of
brevity. The first assumption is that the criteria for inclusion in
the list of "the classics" is supposed to be a combination of intellectual merit and historical importance. Some authors,
Shakespeare for example, are included because of the quality
of their work; others, Marx for example, are included because
they have been historically so influential. Some, Plato for instance, are both of high quality and historically influential.

A second assumption made by the traditionalists is that 8
there are intersubjective standards of rationality, intelligence,
truth, validity, and general intellectual merit. In our list of required readings we include Plato but not randomly selected
comic strips, because we think there is an important distinction in quality between the two, and *we think we can justify the
claim that there is a distinction*. The standards are not algorith-
mic. Making judgments of quality is not like measuring veloci-
ties, but it is not arbitrary either.

A third assumption behind the tradition is that one of the 9
things we are to do is to enable our students to overcome the
mediocrity, provincialism, or other limitations of whatever
background from which they may have come. The idea is that
your life is likely to be in large measure a product of a lot of historical accidents: the town you were born in, the community
you grew up in, the sort of values you learned in high school.
One of the aims of a liberal education is to liberate our students
from the contingencies of their backgrounds. We invite the
student into the membership of a much larger intellectual
community. This third feature of the traditional educational
theory, then, is what one might call an invitation to transcendence. The professor asks his or her students to read books that
are designed to challenge any complacencies that the students
may have brought to the university when they first arrived
there.

A fourth assumption made by the traditionalists, which is 10
related to the third, is that in the Western tradition, there is a
peculiar combination of what one might call extreme univer-
salism and extreme individualism. Again, this tends to be tacit
and is seldom made explicit. The idea is that the most precious
thing in the universe is the human individual, but that the
human individual is precious as part of the universal human
civilization. The idea is that one achieves one's maximum
intellectual *individual* potential by coming to see oneself as

part of a *universal* human species with a universal human culture.

11   A fifth feature of this tacit theory behind educational traditionalism is that a primary function of liberal education is criticism of oneself and one's community. According to this conception, the unexamined life is not worth living, and the examined life is life criticized. I do not know of any intellectual tradition that is as savagely self-critical as the Western tradition. Its hero is Socrates, and of course we all know what happened to him. "I would rather die by the present argument than live by any other," he said. This is the model we hold up to our students: the lone individual, standing out against the hypocrisy, stupidity, and dishonesty of the larger community. And that tradition goes right through to the nineteenth and twentieth centuries, through Freud, Nietzsche, Marx, and Bertrand Russell, to mention just a few. The tradition is that of the extremely critical intellectual commentator attacking the pieties and inadequacies, the inconsistencies and hypocrisies of the surrounding community.

12   I will mention a sixth and final feature. Objectivity and truth are possible because there is an independently existing reality to which our true utterances correspond. This view, called realism, has often been challenged by various forms of idealism and relativism within Western culture but it has remained the dominant metaphysical view in our culture. Our natural science, for example, is based on it. A persistent topic of debate is: How far does it extend? Is there, for example, an independently existing set of moral values that we can discover, or are we, for example, just expressing our subjective feelings and attitudes when we make moral judgments? I am tempted to continue this list but I hope that what I have said so far will give you a feel for the underlying assumptions of the traditionalist theory of liberal education.

13   I am now going to try to do the same for the challengers, but this is harder to do without distortion, simply because there is more variety among the critics of the tradition than there is in the tradition itself. Nonetheless, I am going to do my best to try to state a widely held set of core assumptions made by the challengers. Perhaps very few people, maybe no one, believe all of the assumptions I will try to make explicit, but they are those I have found commonly made in the debates. The first assumption made by the challengers is that the subgroup into which you were born—your ethnic, racial, class, and gender background—matters enormously; it is important for education. In the extreme version of this assumption, you are essentially defined by your ethnic, racial, class, and gender background. That

is the most important thing in your life. The dean of an American state university told me, "The most important thing in my life is being a woman and advancing the cause of women." Any number of people think that the most important thing in their lives is their blackness or their Hispanic identity, et cetera. This is something new in American higher education. Of course, there have always been people who were defined or who preferred to be defined by their ethnic group or by other such affiliations, but it has not been part of the theory of what the university was trying to do that we should *encourage* self-definition by ethnicity, race, gender, or class. On the contrary, as I noted in my list of the traditionalist assumptions, we were trying to encourage students to rise above the accidents of such features. But to a sizable number of American academics, it has now become acceptable to think that the most important thing in one's life is precisely these features. Notice the contrast between the traditionalists and the challengers on this issue. For the traditionalists, what matters is the individual within the universal. For the challengers, the universal is an illusion, and the individual has an identity only as a member of some subgroup.

A second feature of this alternative view is the belief that, to 14 state it crudely, all cultures are equal. Not only are they morally equal, as human beings are morally equal, but all cultures are intellectually equal as well. According to this view, the idea that we have more to learn from the representatives of one race, gender, class, or ethnic group than we do from the representatives of others is simply racism and old-fashioned imperialism. It is simply a residue of Eurocentric imperialism to suppose, as the traditionalists have been supposing, that certain works of European white males are somehow superior to the products of other cultures, classes, genders, and ethnic groups. Belief in the superiority of the Western canon is a priori objectionable because all authors are essentially representatives of their culture, and all cultures are intellectually equal.

In this alternative view, a third feature is that when it comes 15 to selecting what you should read, representativeness is obviously crucial. In a multiculturalist educational democracy, every culture must be represented. The difficulty with the prevailing system is that most groups are underrepresented, and certain groups are not represented at all. The proposal of opening up doors just to let a few superstars in is no good, because that still leaves you, in plain and simple terms, with too many dead, white, European males. Even if you include every great woman novelist that you want to include—every Jane Austen,

George Eliot, and Virginia Woolf—you are still going to have too many dead, white, European males on your list. It is part of the elitism, the hegemonism, and the patriarchalism of the existing ideology that it tries to perpetuate the same patterns of repression even while pretending to be opening up. Worse yet, the lack of diversity in the curriculum is matched by an equal lack of *diversity in the faculty.* It's no use getting rid of the hegemony of *dead* white males in the curriculum if the faculty that teaches the multicultural curriculum is still mostly *living* white males. Representativeness is crucial not only in the curriculum but even more so in the composition of the faculty.

16   I want to pause here to contrast these three assumptions of the challengers with those of the traditionalists. The traditionalists think they are selecting both reading lists and faculty members on grounds of quality and not on grounds of representation. They think they select Plato and Shakespeare, for example, because they produced works of genius, not because they are specimens or representatives of some group. The challengers think this is self-deception at best, oppression at worst. They think that since the canon consists mostly of white European males, the authors must have been selected *because* they are white European males. And they think that because most of the professors are white males, this fact by itself is proof that there is something wrong with the composition of the faculty.

17   You can see the distinction between the challengers and the traditionalists if you imagine a counterfactual situation. Suppose it was discovered by an amazing piece of historical research that the works commonly attributed to Plato and Aristotle were not written by Greek males but by two Chinese women who were cast ashore on the coast of Attica when a Chinese junk shipwrecked off the Pireaus in the late fifth century B.C. What difference would this make to our assessment of the works of Plato and Aristotle? From the traditionalist point of view, none whatever. It would be just an interesting historical fact. From the challengers' point of view, I think it would make a tremendous difference. Ms. Plato and Ms. Aristotle would now acquire a new authenticity as genuine representatives of a previously underrepresented minority, and the most appropriate faculty to teach their work would then be Chinese women. Implicit in the traditionalists' assumptions I stated is the view that the faculty member does not have to exemplify the texts he or she teaches. They assume that the works of Marx can be taught by someone who is not a Marxist, just as Aquinas can be taught by someone who is not a Catholic, and Plato by someone who is not a Platonist. But the challengers assume, for example, that women's studies should be taught by

feminist women, Chicano studies by Chicanos committed to a certain set of values, and so on.

These three points, that you are defined by your culture, that all cultures are created equal, and that representation is the criterion for selection both of the books to be read and the faculty to teach them, are related to a fourth assumption: The primary purpose of education in the humanities is political transformation. I have read any number of authors who claim this, and I have had arguments with several people, some of them in positions of authority in universities, who tell me that the purpose of education, in the humanities at least, is political transformation. For example, another dean at a big state university, herself a former Berkeley radical, has written that her academic life is just an extension of her political activities. In its most extreme version, the claim is not just that the purpose of education in the humanities *ought* to be political, but rather that all education always has been political and always will necessarily be political, so it might as well be beneficially political. The idea that the traditionalists with their "liberal education" are somehow teaching some politically neutral philosophical tradition is entirely a self-deceptive masquerade. According to this view, it is absurd to accuse the challengers of politicizing the university; it already is politicized. Education is political down to the ground. And, so the story goes, the difference between the challengers, as against the traditional approach, is that the traditional approach tries to disguise the fact that it is essentially engaged in the political indoctrination of generations of young people so that they will continue to accept a system of hegemonic, patriarchal imperialism. The challengers, on the other hand, think of themselves as accepting the inevitably political nature of the university, and they want to use it so that they and their students can be liberated into a genuine multicultural democracy. When they say that the purpose of the university is political, this is not some new proposal that they are making. They think of themselves as just facing up to the facts as they always have been.

Once you understand that the challengers regard the university as essentially political, then several puzzling features of the present debate become less puzzling. Why has radical politics migrated into academic departments of literature? In my intellectual childhood, there were plenty of radical activists about, but they tended to operate in a public political arena, or, to the extent they tended to be in universities at all, they were usually in departments of political science, sociology, and economics. Now, as far as I can tell, the leading intellectual centers of radical political activity in the United States are departments of English,

French, and comparative literature. We are, for example, in the odd situation where America's two "leading Marxists" are both professors of English. How did this come about? What would Marx think if he knew that his main impact was on literary criticism? Well, part of the reason for the migration of radical politics into literature departments is that Marxism in particular and left-wing radicalism in general have been discredited as theories of politics, society, and historical change. If ever a philosophical theory was refuted by events, it was the Marxist theory of the inevitable collapse of the capitalist economies and their revolutionary overthrow by the working class, to be followed by the rise of a classless society. Instead, it is the Marxist economies that have collapsed and the Marxist governments that have been overthrown. So, having been refuted as theories of society, these views retreated into departments of literature, where to some extent they still flourish as tools of "interpretation."

20   There is a more important reason, however. During the 1960s a fairly sizable number of leftist intellectuals became convinced that the best arena of social change was culture, that high culture in general and university departments of literature in particular could become important weapons in the struggle to overcome racism, imperialism, et cetera. We are now witnessing some of the consequences of this migration. As someone—I think it was Irving Howe—remarked, it is characteristic of this generation of radicals that they don't want to take over the country, they want to take over the English department. But, I would add, they think taking over the English department is the first step toward taking over the country.

21   So far, then, I have tried to isolate four presuppositions of the challengers: that ethnicity is important; that cultures are intellectually equal; that representativeness is crucial in the curriculum and in faculty composition; and that an important function of the humanities is political and social change. Now let me identify a fifth: There are no such things as objective standards. As one pamphlet published by the American Council of Learned Societies put it, "As the most powerful modern philosophies and theories have been demonstrating, claims of disinterest, objectivity, and universality are not to be trusted, and themselves tend to reflect local historical conditions." According to the ACLS pamphlet, such claims usually involve some power grab on the part of the person who is claiming to be objective. This presupposition, that there are no objective or intersubjective standards to which one can appeal in making judgments of quality, is a natural underpinning of the first four. The idea that there might be some objective standards of what is good and what is bad,

that you might be able to show that Shakespeare is better than Mickey Mouse, for example, threatens the concept that all cultures are equal and that representativeness must be the criterion for inclusion in the curriculum. The whole idea of objectivity, truth, rationality, intelligence, as they are traditionally construed, and distinctions of intellectual quality, are all seen as part of the same system of repressive devices.

This leads to the sixth presupposition, which is the hardest of all to state, because it is an inchoate attitude rather than a precise thesis. Roughly speaking, it involves a marriage of left-wing politics with certain antirationalist strands derived from recent philosophy. The idea is that we should stop thinking there is an objective reality that exists independently of our representations of it; we should stop thinking that propositions are true when they correspond to that reality; and we should stop thinking of language as a set of devices for conveying meanings from speakers to hearers. In short, the sixth presupposition is a rejection of realism and truth in favor of some version of relativism, the idea that all of reality is ultimately textual. This is a remarkable guise for left-wing views to take, because until recently extreme left-wing views claimed to have a scientific basis. The current challengers are suspicious of science and equally suspicious of the whole apparatus of rationality, objective truth, and metaphysical realism, which go along with the scientific attitude. 22

A seventh presupposition is this: Western civilization is historically oppressive. Domestically, its history is one of oppressing women, slaves, and serfs. Internationally, its history is one of colonialism and imperialism. It is no accident that the works in the Western tradition are by white males, because the tradition is dominated by a caste consisting of white males. In this tradition, white males are the group in power. 23

I have tried to make explicit some of the unstated assumptions of both sides, because I think that otherwise it is impossible to explain why the contestants don't seem to make any contact with each other. They seem to be talking about two different sets of issues. I believe that is because they proceed from different sets of assumptions and objectives. If I have succeeded here in articulating the two sets of assumptions, that should be enough. However, the philosopher in me insists on making a few comments about each side and stating a few assumptions of my own. I think the basic philosophical underpinnings of the challengers are weak. Let us start with the rejection of metaphysical realism. This view is derived from deconstructionist philosophers as well as from an interpretation of the works of Thomas Kuhn and Richard Rorty. The 24 idea, roughly speaking, is that Kuhn is supposed to have shown that science does not give us an account of an independently existing reality. Rather, scientists are an irrational bunch who run from one paradigm to another, for reasons with no real connection to finding objective truths. What Kuhn did for science, Rorty supposedly also did for philosophy. Philosophers don't provide accounts that mirror how the world is, because the whole idea of language as mirroring or corresponding to reality is flawed from the beginning. (The works of Kuhn and Rorty, by the way, are more admired in academic departments of literature than they are in departments in the sciences and philosophy.) Whether or not this is the correct interpretation of the works of Kuhn, Rorty, and the deconstructionists, the effect of these works has been to introduce into various humanities departments versions of relativism, anti-objectivism, and skepticism about science and the correspondence theory of truth.

25   Because of the limitation of space, I am going to be rather swift in my refutation of this view. The only defense that one can give of metaphysical realism is a transcendental argument in one of Kant's many senses of that term. We assume that something is the case and show how that metaphysical realism is a condition of possibility of its being the case. If both we and our adversaries share the assumption that something is the case and that which we assume presupposes realism, then the transcendental argument is a refutation of our adversaries' view. It seems to me obvious in this case that we as well as the antirealists assume we are communicating with each other in a public language. When the antirealists present us with an argument they claim to do so in a language that is publicly intelligible. But, I wish to argue, public intelligibility presupposes the existence of a publicly accessible world. Metaphysical realism is not a thesis; rather, it is the condition of the possibility of having theses which are publicly intelligible. Whenever we use a language that purports to have public objects of reference, we commit ourselves to realism. The commitment is not a specific theory as to *how* the world is, but rather that there is a way the world is. Thus, it is self-refuting for someone to claim in a public language that metaphysical realism is false, because a public language presupposes a public world, and that presupposition is metaphysical realism.

26   Though I will not develop it here, it seems that a similar argument applies to objective standards of rationality. Again, to put it very crudely, one can't make sense out of presenting a thesis, or having a belief, or defending a view without presupposing certain standards of rationality. The very notions of

mental and linguistic representation already contain certain logical principles built into them. For those who think that I am exaggerating the extent to which the traditional values are challenged, I suggest they read the ACLS pamphlet from which I quoted earlier.

Another fallacious move made by the challengers is to infer, from the fact that the university's educational efforts invariably have political consequences, that therefore the primary objective of the university and the primary criteria for assessing its success or failure should be political. The conclusion does not follow from the premise. Obviously, everything has political consequences, whether it's art, music, literature, sex, or gastronomy. For example, right now you could be campaigning for the next presidential election, and therefore this article has political consequences, because it prevents you from engaging in political activities in which you might otherwise be engaging. In this sense, *everything* is political. But from the fact that everything is political in this sense, it doesn't follow that our academic *objectives* are political, nor does it follow that the criteria for assessing our successes and failures are political. The argument, in short, does not justify the current attempts to use the classroom and the curriculum as tools of political transformation.

A further fallacy concerns the notion of empowerment. The most general form of this fallacy is the supposition that power is a property of groups rather than of individuals and organizations. A moment's reflection will reveal that this is not true. Most positions of power in the United States are occupied by middle-aged white males, but it does not follow that power accrues to middle-aged white males as a group. Most white males, middle-aged or otherwise, are as powerless as anyone else. In these discussions, there is a fallacy that goes as follows: People assume because most people in positions of power are white males that therefore most white males are in a position of power. I hope the fallacy is obvious.

Finally, in my list of criticisms of the challengers, I want to point out that we should not be embarrassed by the fact that a disproportionately large percentage of the major cultural achievements in our society have been made by white males. This is an interesting historical fact that requires analysis and explanation. But it doesn't in any way discredit the works of, for example, Descartes or Shakespeare that they happen to have been white males, any more than it discredits the work of Newton and Darwin that they were both English. Representativeness as such is not the primary aim in the study of the humanities. Rather, representativeness comes in as a desirable goal when there is a question of articulating the different

27

28

29

varieties of human experience. And our aim in seeking works that articulate this variety is always to find works of high quality. The problem with the predominance of white males is not that there is any doubt about the quality of the work, but that we have been excessively provincial, that great works in other cultures may have been neglected, and that, even within Western civilization, there have been groups, most notably women, whose works have been discriminated against.

30   My criticism of the traditionalists is somewhat different from my criticism of the challengers because I do not, as a matter of fact, find much that is objectionable in the assumptions behind the traditionalist philosophy of education. The difficulty is how those assumptions are being implemented in contemporary American universities.

31   There are many forms of decay and indeed corruption that have become entrenched in the actual practice of American universities, especially where undergraduate education is concerned. The most obvious sign of decay is that we have simply lost enthusiasm for the traditional philosophy of a liberal education. As our disciplines have become more specialized, as we have lost faith in the ideal of an integrated undergraduate education, we simply provide the student with the familiar cafeteria of courses and hope things turn out for the best. The problem with the traditionalists' ideology is not that it is false but that it has run out of gas. It is somewhat hypocritical to defend a traditional liberal education with a well-rounded reading list that goes from Plato to James Joyce if one is unwilling actually to attempt to educate undergraduates in this tradition. I do not, frankly, think that the challengers have superior ideas. Rather, they have something which may be more important to influencing the way things are actually done. They have more energy and enthusiasm, not to say fanaticism and intolerance. In the long run, these may be more effective in changing universities than rigorous arguments can be.

What Does It Mean to Be Literate?

Benjamin Franklin

FROM

THE AUTOBIOGRAPHY OF BENJAMIN FRANKLIN

If you have ever visited Philadelphia, you probably know quite a bit about Benjamin Franklin, for Franklin is literally that city's towering figure: Franklin was one of those versatile and energetic polymaths that we associate with the American Revolution (Thomas Jefferson and George Washington were, of course, others): in the course of his long life, he was famous as an inventor, publisher, and statesman, and his pragmatic way of life stamped itself indelibly onto the American character.

Born in Boston in 1706, he arrived in Philadelphia as a teenager to make his fortune. Finding work as a printer, he rose quickly in his profession, took over a newspaper, published Poor Richard's Almanac *(a compendium of information and commonsense advice on every topic that made his name and fortune), and took an interest in civic affairs. After 1750, he was established enough to turn the rest of his life to science—his famous kite experiment related to electricity was conducted in 1752—and to politics. Franklin played a pivotal role in the establishment of the new United States by serving in the Second Continental Congress (which developed the Declaration of Independence), by securing support from France during the war with Britain, and by helping to resolve differences during the Constitutional Convention of 1787.*

Many of the details of Franklin's life are described in his memoir, The Autobiography, *which he began in 1771, abandoned for a time, and then completed just before he died in 1790. The following excerpts, parts of a "letter to his son" that grew into the larger* Autobiography, *concern how Franklin developed his rhetorical skill. (In the passage, the references to* Pilgrim's Progress, *Bunyan's* Works, *Burton's* Historical Collections, *and so forth, all refer to well-known eighteenth-century books; the* Spectator *was an influential literary paper that was put out by Joseph Addison and Richard Steele from 1711–1712.)*

1   From a Child I was fond of Reading, and all the little Money that came into my Hands was ever laid out in Books. Pleas'd with the Pilgrim's Progress, my first Collection was of John Bunyan's Works, in separate little Volumes. I afterwards sold them to enable me to buy R. Burton's Historical Collections; they were small Chapmen's Books and cheap, 40 or 50 in all. My Father's little Library consisted chiefly of Books in polemic Divinity, most of which I read, and have since often regretted, that at a time when I had such a Thirst for Knowledge, more proper Books had not fallen in my Way, since it was now resolv'd I should not be a Clergyman. Plutarch's Lives there was, in which I read abundantly, and I still think that time spent to great Advantage. There was also a Book of Defoe's, called an Essay on Projects, and another of Dr. Mather's, call'd Essays to do Good which perhaps gave me a Turn of Thinking that had an Influence on some of the principal future Events of my Life.

2   This Bookish Inclination at length determin'd my Father to make me a Printer, tho' he had already one Son, (James) of that Profession. In 1717 my Brother James return'd from England with a Press and Letters to set up his Business in Boston. I lik'd it much better than that of my Father, but still had a Hankering for the Sea. To prevent the apprehended Effect of such an Inclination, my Father was impatient to have me bound to my Brother. I stood out some time, but at last was persuaded and signed the Indentures, when I was yet but 12 Years old. I was to serve as an Apprentice till I was 21 Years of Age, only I was to be allow'd Journeyman's Wages during the last Year. In a little time I made great Proficiency in the Business, and became a useful Hand to my Brother. I now had Access to better Books. An Acquaintance with the Apprentices of Booksellers, enabled me sometimes to borrow a small one, which I was careful to return soon and clean. Often I sat up in

my Room reading the greatest Part of the Night, when the Book was borrow'd in the Evening and to be return'd early in the Morning lest it should be miss'd or wanted. And after some time an ingenious Tradesman Mr. Matthew Adams who had a pretty Collection of Books, and who frequented our Printing House, took Notice of me, invited me to his Library, and very kindly lent me such Books as I chose to read. I now took a Fancy to Poetry, and made some little Pieces. My Brother, thinking it might turn to account encourag'd me, and put me on composing two occasional Ballads. One was called the *Light House Tragedy,* and contain'd an account of the drowning of Capt. Worthilake with his Two Daughters; the other was a Sailor Song on the Taking of *Teach* or Blackbeard the Pirate. They were wretched Stuff, in the Grubstreet Ballad Stile, and when they were printed he sent me about the Town to sell them. The first sold wonderfully, the Event being recent, having made a great Noise. This flatter'd my Vanity. But my Father discourag'd me, by ridiculing my Performances, and telling me Verse-makers were generally Beggars; so I escap'd being a Poet, most probably a very bad one. But, as Prose Writing has been of great Use to me in the Course of my Life, and was a principal Means of my Advancement, I shall tell you how in such a Situation I acquir'd what little Ability I have in that Way.

There was another Bookish Lad in the Town, John Collins by 3
Name, with whom I was intimately acquainted. We sometimes disputed, and very fond we were of Argument, and very desirous of confuting one another. Which disputacious Turn, by the way, is apt to become a very bad Habit, making People often extreamly disagreable in Company, by the Contradiction that is necessary to bring it into Practice, and thence, besides souring and spoiling the Conversation, is productive of Disgusts and perhaps Enmities where you may have occasion for Friendship. I had caught it by reading my Father's Books of Dispute about Religion. Persons of good Sense, I have since observ'd, seldom fall into it, except Lawyers, University Men, and Men of all Sorts that have been bred at Edinborough. A Question was once some how or other started between Collins and me, of the Propriety of educating the Female Sex in Learning, and their Abilities for Study. He was of Opinion that it was improper; and that they were naturally unequal to it. I took the contrary Side, perhaps a little for Dispute sake. He was naturally more eloquent, had a ready Plenty of Words, and sometimes as I thought bore me down more by his Fluency than by the Strength of his Reasons. As we parted without settling the Point, and were not to see one another again for some

time, I sat down to put my Arguments in Writing, which I copied and sent to him. He answer'd and I reply'd. Three or four Letters of a Side had pass'd, when my Father happen'd to find my Papers, and read them. Without entring into the Discussion, he took occasion to talk to me about the Manner of my Writing, observ'd that tho' I had the Advantage of my Antagonist in correct Spelling and [punctuation] (which I ow'd to the Printing House) I fell far short in elegance of Expression, in Method and in Perspicuity, of which he convinc'd me by several Instances. I saw the Justice of his Remarks, and thence grew more attentive to the *Manner* in Writing, and determin'd to endeavour at Improvement.

4   About this time I met with an odd Volume of the Spectator. It was the third. I had never before seen any of them. I bought it, read it over and over, and was much delighted with it. I thought the Writing excellent, and wish'd if possible to imitate it. With that View, I took some of the Papers, and making short Hints of the Sentiment in each Sentence, laid them by a few Days, and then without looking at the Book, try'd to compleat the Papers again, by expressing each hinted Sentiment at length and as fully as it had been express'd before, in any suitable Words, that should come to hand.

5   Then I compar'd my Spectator with the Original, discover'd some of my Faults and corrected them. But I found I wanted a Stock of Words or a Readiness in recollecting and using them, which I thought I should have acquir'd before that time, if I had gone on making Verses, since the continual Occasion for Words of the same Import but of different Length, to suit the Measure, or of different Sound for the Rhyme, would have laid me under a constant Necessity of searching for Variety, and also have tended to fix that Variety in my Mind, and make me Master of it. Therefore I took some of the Tales and turn'd them into Verse: And after a time, when I had pretty well forgotten the Prose, turn'd them back again. I also sometimes jumbled my Collections of Hints into Confusion, and after some Weeks, endeavour'd to reduce them into the best Order, before I began to form the full Sentences, and compleat the Paper. This was to teach me Method in the Arrangement of Thoughts. By comparing my work afterwards with the original, I discover'd many faults and amended them; but I sometimes had the Pleasure of Fancying that in certain Particulars of small Import, I had been lucky enough to improve the Method or the Language and this encourag'd me to think I might possibly in time come to be a tolerable English Writer, of which I was extreamly ambitious.

Frederick Douglass

FROM

THE NARRATIVE
OF THE LIFE
OF FREDERICK DOUGLASS

Frederick Douglass's rise from obscurity to prominence was even more astounding than the rise of Benjamin Franklin. Born a slave in 1818 under the name of Frederick Bailey—he never knew his father and seldom saw his mother after he was taken from her as a child—Douglass escaped to the North in 1839 and assumed a new identity. He quickly became active in abolitionist circles and, after a decade of flight, was able to purchase his freedom. Later, he began his own newspaper, The North Star, *in Rochester, New York, as a vehicle for his beliefs and causes. A prominent orator and essayist, during the Civil War he urged President Lincoln to enlist African Americans in the army, and after the war he continued to campaign for freedom, not only by advocating antilynching laws and better conditions for tenant farmers but also by supporting women's suffrage.*

Douglass gives his own account of his early life in his Narrative of the Life of Frederick Douglass, *the most famous of the hundreds of "slave narratives" (i.e., first-hand accounts of slave life) that were published in the years before the Civil War. (You may have read Toni Morrison's slave narrative,* Beloved.) *When the book was published in 1845, it established Douglass as a major voice in the antislavery movement and gave rise to images of the self that would affect the way other Americans would forever think of themselves. The following passage from Chapter 7 of the* Narrative *describes how Douglass began to learn to read and write.*

I lived in Master Hugh's family about seven years. During this   1
time, I succeeded in learning to read and write. In accomplishing this, I was compelled to resort to various stratagems. I had no regular teacher. My mistress, who had kindly commenced to instruct me, had, in compliance with the advice and direction of her husband, not only ceased to instruct, but had set

her face against my being instructed by any one else. It is due, however, to my mistress to say of her, that she did not adopt this course of treatment immediately. She at first lacked the depravity indispensable to shutting me up in mental darkness. It was at least necessary for her to have some training in the exercise of irresponsible power, to make her equal to the task of treating me as though I were a brute.

2   My mistress was, as I have said, a kind and tender-hearted woman; and in the simplicity of her soul she commenced, when I first went to live with her, to treat me as she supposed one human being ought to treat another. In entering upon the duties of a slaveholder, she did not seem to perceive that I sustained to her the relation of a mere chattel, and that for her to treat me as a human being was not only wrong, but dangerously so. Slavery proved as injurious to her as it did to me. When I went there, she was a pious, warm, and tender-hearted woman. There was no sorrow or suffering for which she had not a tear. She had bread for the hungry, clothes for the naked, and comfort for every mourner that came within her reach. Slavery soon proved its ability to divest her of these heavenly qualities. Under its influence, the tender heart be-came stone, and the lamblike disposition gave way to one of tigerlike fierceness. The first step in her downward course was in her ceasing to instruct me. She now commenced to practise her husband's precepts. She finally became even more violent in her opposition than her husband himself. She was not satis-fied with simply doing as well as he had commanded; she seemed anxious to do better. Nothing seemed to make her more angry than to see me with a newspaper. She seemed to think that here lay the *danger*. I have had her rush at me with a face made all up of fury, and snatch from me a newspaper, in a manner that fully revealed her apprehension. She was an apt woman; and a little experience soon demonstrated, to her sat-isfaction, that education and slavery were incompatible with each other.

3   From this time I was most narrowly watched. If I was in a separate room any considerable length of time, I was sure to be suspected of having a book, and was at once called to give an account of myself. All this, however, was too late. The first step had been taken. Mistress, in teaching me the alphabet, had given me the *inch*, and no precaution could prevent me from taking the *ell*.

4   The plan which I adopted, and the one by which I was most successful, was that of making friends of all the little white boys whom I met in the street. As many of these as I could, I converted into teachers. With their kindly aid, obtained at

different times and in different places, I finally succeeded in learning to read. When I was sent of errands, I always took my book with me, and by going one part of my errand quickly, I found time to get a lesson before my return. I used also to carry bread with me, enough of which was always in the house, and to which I was always welcome; for I was much better off in this regard than many of the poor white children in our neighborhood. This bread I used to bestow upon the hungry little urchins, who, in return, would give me that more valuable bread of knowledge. I am strongly tempted to give the names of two or three of those little boys, as a testimonial of the gratitude and affection I bear them; but prudence forbids;—not that it would injure me, but it might embarrass them; for it is almost an unpardonable offence to teach slaves to read in this Christian country. It is enough to say of the dear little fellows, that they lived on Philpot Street, very near Durgin and Bailey's ship-yard. I used to talk this matter of slavery over with them. I would sometimes say to them, I wished I could be as free as they would be when they got to be men. "You will be free as soon as you are twenty-one, *but I am a slave for life!* Have not I as good a right to be free as you have?" These words used to trouble them; they would express for me the liveliest sympathy, and console me with the hope that something would occur by which I might be free.

I was now about twelve years old, and the thought of being a   5 *slave for life* began to bear heavily upon my heart. Just about this time, I got hold of a book entitled "The Columbian Orator." Every opportunity I got, I used to read this book. Among much of other interesting matter, I found in it a dialogue between a master and his slave. The slave was represented as having run away from his master three times. The dialogue represented the conversation which took place between them, when the slave was retaken the third time. In this dialogue, the whole argument in behalf of slavery was brought forward by the master, all of which was disposed of by the slave. The slave was made to say some very smart as well as impressive things in reply to his master—things which had the desired though unexpected effect; for the conversation resulted in the voluntary emancipation of the slave on the part of the master.

In the same book, I met with one of Sheridan's mighty   6 speeches on and in behalf of Catholic emancipation. These were choice documents to me. I read them over and over again with unabated interest. They gave tongue to interesting thoughts of my own soul, which had frequently flashed through my mind, and died away for want of utterance. The moral which I gained from the dialogue was the power of truth over the conscience of even a slaveholder. What I got from Sheridan was a bold denunciation of slavery, and a powerful vindication of human rights. The reading of these documents enabled me to utter my thoughts, and to meet the arguments brought forward to sustain slavery; but while they relieved me of one difficulty, they brought on another even more painful than the one of which I was relieved. The more I read, the more I was led to abhor and detest my enslavers. I could regard them in no other light than a band of successful robbers, who had left their homes, and gone to Africa, and stolen us from our homes, and in a strange land reduced us to slavery. I loathed them as being the meanest as well as the most wicked of men. As I read and contemplated the subject, behold! that very discontentment which Master Hugh had predicted would follow my learning to read had already come, to torment and sting my soul to unutterable anguish. As I writhed under it, I would at times feel that learning to read had been a curse rather than a blessing. It had given me a view of my wretched condition, without the remedy. It opened my eyes to the horrible pit, but to no ladder upon which to get out. In moments of agony, I envied my fellow-slaves for their stupidity. I have often wished myself a beast. I preferred the condition of the meanest reptile to my own. Any thing, no matter what, to get rid of thinking! It was this everlasting thinking of my condition that tormented me. There was no getting rid of it. It was pressed upon me by every object within sight or hearing, animate or inanimate. The silver trump of freedom had roused my soul to eternal wakefulness. Freedom now appeared, to disappear no more forever. It was heard in every sound, and seen in every thing. It was ever present to torment me with a sense of my wretched condition. I saw nothing without seeing it, I heard nothing without hearing it, and felt nothing without feeling it. It looked from every star, it smiled in every calm, breathed in every wind, and moved in every storm.

7   I often found myself regretting my own existence, and wishing myself dead; and but for the hope of being free, I have no doubt but that I should have killed myself, or done something for which I should have been killed. While in this state of mind, I was eager to hear any one speak of slavery. I was a ready listener. Every little while, I could hear something about the abolitionists. It was some time before I found what the word meant. It was always used in such connections as to make it an interesting word to me. If a slave ran away and succeeded in getting clear, or if a slave killed his master, set fire to a barn, or did any thing very wrong in the mind of a slaveholder, it was spoken of as the fruit of *abolition*. Hearing the

word in this connection very often, I set about learning what it meant. The dictionary afforded me little or no help. I found it was "the act of abolishing;" but then I did not know what was to be abolished. Here I was perplexed. I did not dare to ask any one about its meaning, for I was satisfied that it was something they wanted me to know very little about. After a patient waiting, I got one of our city papers, containing an account of the number of petitions from the north, praying for the abolition of slavery in the District of Columbia, and of the slave trade between the States. From this time I understood the words *abolition* and *abolitionist,* and always drew near when that word was spoken, expecting to hear something of importance to myself and fellow-slaves. The light broke in upon me by degrees. I went one day down on the wharf of Mr. Waters; and seeing two Irishmen unloading a scow of stone, I went, unasked, and helped them. When we had finished, one of them came to me and asked me if I were a slave. I told him I was. He asked, "Are ye a slave for life?" I told him that I was. The good Irishman seemed to be deeply affected by the statement. He said to the other that it was a pity so fine a little fellow as myself should be a slave for life. He said it was a shame to hold me. They both advised me to run away to the north; that I should find friends there, and that I should be free. I pretended not to be interested in what they said, and treated them as if I did not understand them; for I feared they might be treacherous. White men have been known to encourage slaves to escape, and then, to get the reward, catch them and return them to their masters. I was afraid that these seemingly good men might use me so; but I nevertheless remembered their advice, and from that time I resolved to run away. I looked forward to a time at which it would be safe for me to escape. I was too young to think of doing so immediately; besides, I wished to learn how to write, as I might have an occasion to write my own pass. I consoled myself with the hope that I should one day find a good chance. Meanwhile, I would learn to write.

The idea as to how I might learn to write was suggested to me   8 by being in Durgin and Bailey's ship-yard, and frequently seeing the ship carpenters, after hewing, and getting a piece of timber ready for use, write on the timber the name of that part of the ship for which it was intended. When a piece of timber was intended for the larboard side, it would be marked thus—"L." When a piece was for the starboard side, it would be marked thus—"S." A piece for the larboard side forward, would be marked thus—"L. F." When a piece was for starboard side forward, it would be marked thus—"S. F." For larboard aft, it would be marked thus—"L. A." For starboard aft, it would be marked thus—"S. A." I soon learned the names of these letters, and for what they were intended when placed upon a piece of timber in the ship-yard. I immediately commenced copying them, and in a short time was able to make the four letters named. After that, when I met with any boy who I knew could write, I would tell him I could write as well as he. The next word would be, "I don't believe you. Let me see you try it." I would then make the letters which I had been so fortunate as to learn, and ask him to beat that. In this way I got a good many lessons in writing, which it is quite possible I should never have gotten in any other way. During this time, my copy-book was the board fence, brick wall, and pavement; my pen and ink was a lump of chalk. With these, I learned mainly how to write. I then commenced and continued copying the Italics in Webster's Spelling Book, until I could make them all without looking on the book. By this time, my little Master Thomas had gone to school, and learned how to write, and had written over a number of copy-books. These had been brought home, and shown to some of our near neighbors, and then laid aside. My mistress used to go to class meeting at the Wilk Street meeting-house every Monday afternoon, and leave me to take care of the house. When left thus, I used to spend the time in writing in the spaces left in Master Thomas's copybook, copying what he had written. I continued to do this until I could write a hand similar to that of Master Thomas. Thus, after a long, tedious effort for years, I finally succeeded in learning how to write.

Andy Carvin

MIND THE GAP: THE DIGITAL DIVIDE AS THE CIVIL RIGHTS ISSUE OF THE NEW MILLENNIUM

Andy Carvin's essay (as well as those that follow in this section) illustrate how the concept of literacy has changed— and how it has remained consistent. For Ben Franklin and

Frederick Douglass, literacy meant the ability to read and write—and to read what were considered the most influential of texts. In the twenty-first century, being "literate" also means having access to information technology and the means to use it well. Andy Carvin (acarvin@edc.org) is director of the Digital Divide Network (http://www.digitaldivide.net) at the EDC center for Media & Community in Newton, Massachusetts. He is the creator of the website EdWeb: Exploring Technology and School Reform (http://www.edwebproject.org), one of the first websites to explore the role of the Web in education. He is also the publisher of the popular blog, Andy Carvin's Waste of Bandwidth (http://www.andycarvin.com). *Carvin explores in the essay below whether all social classes have access to the stuff of twenty-first century literacy, or whether technology has left what has become known as a "digital divide" between the classes. He published this piece in* MultiMedia & Internet@ Schools, *a magazine written for and by library media specialists and other school professionals who use electronic resources with their students.*

In the years since the start of the Internet Revolution, the   1
American public has been exposed to more than its fair share
of overused catchphrases. Way back in the early '80s, then-
Senator Al Gore spoke of an Information Super Highway that
would connect the country's citizens to an overwhelming variety of telecommunications opportunities. (Okay, so he didn't
invent the Internet, but at least he gave us its most hackneyed
metaphor.) We read about the near-Messianic coming of a 500-
channel universe in which we'll be able to relish a mind-
numbing array of programming options, from The Jack Russell
Terrier Channel to Ex!, The Ex-Convicts Network. Countless
Web sites and multimedia products boast about their "interactivity" when in truth the only interactivity they offer is in
choosing which hyperlink to press next. And consider the
phrase "click here"—before the advent of the Internet it would
have been seen as a completely baffling command. (For fun try
picturing it being blurted out in a variety of awkward social settings.) Now it's the Cyber Age equivalent of a welcome mat:
Click here and enter the Web site of your dreams.

Click here and show me a way to get away from the endless   2
hype. Please!

But despite the media's penchant for beating to death any-   3
thing to do with the Internet, a new phrase has recently entered
the public's online lexicon, one that actually carries significant
societal ramifications: the digital divide. In the most basic

sense, the digital divide is the ever-growing gap between those people and communities who have access to information technology and those who do not. (In other words, to use another pedestrian metaphor courtesy of Cervantes' Sancho Panza, the have's and the have-not's.) The digital divide has been on the radar screens of those of us in the policy world for a while now, but over the course of the last five years its profile was raised as more political leaders took an interest in the subject.

4   The digital divide may seem like an intangible concept to some, but studies have begun to articulate it in no uncertain terms. Consider these statistics from the U.S. Department of Commerce's 2004 report, *A Nation Online*:

- Households earning incomes over $75,000 are nearly three times more likely to have home Internet access than those who earn $15,000 a year or less.
- Only 15.5 percent of people without a high school education have Internet access.
- People with college degrees are twice more likely to have Internet access at home than people with only a high school diploma.
- While more than 65 percent of white households have Internet access, only 45.6 percent of African American households and 37 percent of Latino households are online.

5   Such stats should not be taken lightly. The digital divide is one of the most important civil rights issues facing our modern information economy. As telecommunications increasingly entwines itself with educational, social, financial, and employment opportunities, those communities lacking access will find themselves falling further behind the rest of society. The Internet has the potential to empower its users with new skills, new perspectives, new freedoms, even new voices; those groups who remain sequestered from the technology will be further segregated into the periphery of public life.

6   In schools, of course, we've seen the digital divide tackled head-on with the implementation of the E-Rate program. Each year tens of thousands of schools receive over $2 billion in federal telecommunications subsidies to help support classroom Internet access. Though some schools still haven't felt the benefits of the E-Rate, many others have: Over 90 percent of classrooms now have Internet access. Real progress is being made.

7   Whether the issue is in schools or in communities, the digital divide is finally beginning to receive the attention it deserves. But as we try to develop a long-term strategy for

combating the divide, it begs an important question: Is the digital divide essentially an access issue? In one sense, of course, the question is a no-brainer. There is a widening gap between those who have access to information technology and those who don't; therefore, when dealing with the digital divide we need to concentrate on giving more people Internet access.

But giving people access doesn't instantly solve the manifold   8
woes of our communities and schools. If it did, every kid with Internet access would be getting straight A's and every adult with access would be gainfully employed and prosperous. It's just not that simple. Technology access is only one small piece of a much larger puzzle, a puzzle that if solved might help raise the quality of life for millions of people. None of us can rightfully say we've found all the individual pieces yet, but some of the pieces are obvious enough that we can begin to put the digital divide puzzle together:

The digital divide is about content. The value of the Internet   9
can be directly correlated to the value of its content. If all you can find online is shopping, Pokémon trading clubs, and porn, you could make a pretty good argument that it's not very important to give people access to the Internet. As anyone who's used it knows, the Internet can offer a wealth of opportunities for learning and personal enhancement, but we've only scratched the surface in terms of its potential. As more underprivileged and disenfranchised communities gain access, the Internet itself must provide the right tools so people are able to take advantage of and use it for more varied purposes, more learning styles, more languages and cultures. The Internet may feel like a diverse place, but when compared with the wealth of diversity and knowledge amongst humanity in the real world, it's still pretty weak. Until the Net contains content that has true value to all of its potential users it will remain a place for the elite.

The digital divide is about literacy. As much as we hate to admit it, functional illiteracy amongst adults is one of America's   10
dirty little secrets. Millions of adults struggle to fill out forms, follow written instructions, or even read a newspaper. The 1993 National Adult Literacy Survey suggests as many as 44 million American adults—one out of four—are functionally illiterate, while another 50 million adults are plagued by limited literacy. We often talk about the importance of information literacy when it comes to using the Internet. Information literacy is an obviously vital part of the equation, but how can we expect to conquer the digital divide when nearly half of all American adults can't even process written information competently?

Literacy must be tackled at the most basic level in order to afford more people the opportunity to use technology effectively.

11 *The digital divide is about pedagogy.* Internet access in schools isn't worth a hill of beans if teachers aren't prepared to take full advantage of technology. Research has shown that educators who are resistant to constructivist teaching practices are less likely to utilize the Internet in their lessons, while educators who are more comfortable with constructivist practices are more likely to do so. Teachers who employ more real-world interaction are thus more inclined to employ online interaction. How can professional development be reformed to take these differences into account?

12 *The digital divide is about community.* One of the greatest strengths of the Internet is in its facility for fostering communities. Communities often appear in the most low-tech of places: You can surf the Web until your knuckles implode and yet not feel like you've actually bonded with anyone, but you can subscribe to a simple e-mail listserv and join a gathering of people who have been enjoying each others' wisdom for years. It's paramount for people coming to the Internet for the first time to have opportunities to join communities and forge new communities of their own. Public spaces must be preserved online so that people can gather without feeling like direct marketing or more popular and powerful voices are crowding them out. If people can't build meaningful relationships online, how can they be expected to gravitate to it?

13   These five puzzle pieces—access, content, literacy, pedagogy and community—may not be enough to complete the entire digital divide puzzle, but they go a long way in providing us a picture of what's at stake. Giving people access to technology is important, but it's just one of many issues that need to be considered. Schools, libraries, and community centers are taking that first step in getting wired, but they must also consider the needs of the learners, the teachers, and the communities that support them.

14   We must continue fighting the scourge of illiteracy—among students, their parents, and among the community—by expanding formal and informal opportunities that improve reading and critical-thinking skills. We must demand engaging content from online producers and refuse to buy into mediocre content when it doesn't suit our teaching needs. We must encourage all learners to be creators as well, sharing their wise voices both online and offline. And we must open our schools and libraries to more connections with our communities—no

computer lab or training room should sit idly during evening and weekend hours. These are but a few examples of what the education community can do.

Solveig Singleton and Lucas Mast

HOW DOES THE EMPTY GLASS FILL?
A MODERN PHILOSOPHY OF THE DIGITAL DIVIDE

Solveig Singleton, a lawyer, currently works as senior policy analyst with the Competitive Enterprise Institute, "a non-profit public policy organization dedicated to the principles of free enterprise and limited government." Singleton is also the former director of information studies at the Cato Institute, whose mission is to "broaden the parameters of public policy debate to allow consideration of the traditional American principles of limited government, individual liberty, free markets and peace." At Cato, she specialized in privacy policy, encryption, and telecommunications law. Her articles have appeared in the Journal of Commerce, *the* Washington Post, *the* Philadelphia Inquirer, *the* Washington Times, *the* Wall Street Journal, Internet Underground, *and* HotWired. *In a 1998 article in the* Wall Street Journal, *Singleton wrote*

A country that takes the freedom of information seriously cannot properly prohibit one business from communicating information about real events and real people to other businesses. If one buys a lawn mower from Sears, the sale of the lawn mower is an actual event involving a real person. The view that information such as the purchaser's name, address, and buying habits should not be recorded and transferred without his consent conflicts with the general rule that facts and ideas, including our names and addresses, remain free for all to collect and exchange. Attempts to restrict the transfer of information thus run headlong into our rights to free speech.

*Singleton and Lucas Mast (who was at the time a research
assistant at the Cato Institute) published the article below in
the November/December 2003 issue of* Educause Review, *a
general-interest, bimonthly magazine.* Educause Review *offers
a broad look at current developments and trends in information technology and what these mean for higher education. As
you read the article below, you might consider how Singleton's
associations and beliefs may have influenced her views of the
"digital divide" in information literacy.*

1   The fuss about the "digital divide" is a testament to the power
of the human mind to take an ordinary problem and magically
transform it into a crisis threatening the future of our nation.
When all the data on digital disparities is in, there remains the
question of whether the digital glass is half empty or half full.
Even more important, is it emptying or filling? How fast is it
emptying or filling? Finally, the most important question of all
is, Why does the glass empty or fill?

2   Actually, we already know that the glass starts out empty.
Ages ago, when human beings stood up from the baked mud of
the African desert, they had nothing to their names except op-
posable thumbs and a remarkable ability to develop language.
Fast-forward to just twenty years ago: few people had cell
phones or personal computers, let alone Internet access.
The astounding thing is not that there are substantial numbers
of people without Internet access but rather that anyone has it
at all.

3   So where does wealth like computers, broadband networks,
e-mail software, and the learning represented by college diplo-
mas come from? As we will explain further below, digital
riches have come from the fiercely competitive markets typical
of the computer industry, markets that aren't regulated and
taxed to death. As we address the digital divide, the lesson
learned is to shy away from big-government solutions—in the
long run, they'll backfire.

The Digital Divide: A Glass Filling Fast

4   We have already heard the bad news about the digital divide.
Headlines tell of a "widening gap" between upper- and lower-
income groups or between single-parent and two-parent families. The Reverend Jesse Jackson calls it "classic apartheid."[1]
Falling through the Net: New Data on the Digital Divide, a report
released in 1998 by the Commerce Department's National

Telecommunications and Information Administration (NTIA), notes that although access to communications technology is "soaring," the "digital divide . . . is actually widening over time." Specifically, the report states: "The digital divide has turned into a 'racial ravine.' . . . With regard to computers, the gap between white and black households grew 39.2 percent (from a 16.8 percentage point difference to a 23.4 percentage point difference) between 1994 and 1998."

Yet a reanalysis of the NTIA's data by the Cato Institute's   5 David Boaz shows that in 1994, whites were 2.6 times as likely as blacks to have a computer and that in 1998, they were only 2.0 times as likely. From 1994 to 1998, computer ownership by whites increased 72 percent while ownership by blacks increased 125 percent. From 1994 to 1997, computer ownership by Hispanics and African-Americans increased by 117 percent in households with less than $15,000 in income. And when we control for income, blacks are more likely than whites to have access to a computer at work. "People of color are going online in droves, and we are seeing an explosion in this new medium," says David Ellington, who founded Netnoir.com, the first black online and multimedia service, in 1995. "Some of this rhetoric [regarding the digital divide] is positioning African Americans in need of help. Personally, I believe that black people have proven that when technology becomes relevant to us, we embrace it." A survey by *Cyber Dialogue* counts close to 5 million black Internet users, and the Chicago-based *Target Market News* reports that blacks spent $1.3 billion on computer-related products last year, a 143 percent increase over such spending in the previous year.[2]

The time when everyone who wants to be connected is con-   6 nected is near. Ekaterina Walsh, an Internet analyst at Forrester Research in Cambridge, Massachusetts, sums it up: "Everybody who wants to get online will have gotten online in the next five years, and it doesn't matter whether they're yellow, pink, or green."[3] It is unlikely that household penetration will ever reach 100 percent. Even for whites with household incomes over $75,000, the percentage hovers around 80 percent ownership of personal computers. People may have completely rational reasons for not owning computers: they may have unrestricted access at work, or they may simply choose to receive their information through traditional media like television and newspapers.

The digital glass isn't full yet. But it is filling fast. Internet   7 technology is spreading to the general population far faster than did automobiles, telephones, radios, electricity, television, VCRs, or microwave ovens.

The Digital Divide: Economics from Outer Space

8   According to pundits like Daniel Bell, Charles Reich, and Alvin Toffler, who warned us of the dangers of "information have-nots," the market process was not supposed to be working nearly this well. The theory goes something like this: High-tech information devices and services start out as luxury goods available only to the rich. The rich teach their offspring how to use these devices, and their offspring go out and secure the high-paying jobs that enable them to buy information technology, endlessly perpetuating the cycle. The rich get richer, and the rest of us get poorer.

9   But markets for high-tech communications equipment have acted pretty much like markets for radios, refrigerators, automobiles, and cell phones. These products all started out as luxury goods and, lo and behold, spread downward—not instantaneously but inexorably, driven by ordinary rules of supply and demand. Businesses want a mass market for their goods. Every customer that does not or cannot buy from Company A is a potential target market for Company B, C, and D. Once someone has invented the e-widget, he or she had better figure out how to capture the largest market share possible, or someone else is going to get it.

10   Generation after generation, the standards of living have been rising for the poor as well as for the rich. Even the lowest-income groups end up as a target market; take, for example, the expansion of prepaid long-distance telephone service targeted at low-income immigrants, who often need to call overseas and who may not have ordinary long-distance phone service.

The Digital Divide: An Entrepreneurial Opportunity

11   Let us put some flesh on the bones of this market theory. New businesses are springing up even in the inner city to serve the computer-deprived members of society. Whether it is the $25–$50 bargain-basement refurbished 486 computers sold by Computer Reclamation Inc. In Rockville, Maryland, or the $799 Pentium-powered units offered by Computers in the Hood (run out of a former crackhouse), entrepreneurs are recognizing the needs and opportunities that are available only while the digital divide exists. In addition to offering these computers at an

affordable and attainable price, most outfits include some type of training to get the user off and running.

Postsecondary educational institutions such as vocational   12 schools and community colleges have done an excellent job of making technology accessible to low-income groups. With low tuition, open admissions, and essential basic coursework, community colleges have long served the "have-nots" in a maturing service economy. As a path to a four-year institution or as a place to receive vocational training, community colleges are affordable options for many people—especially with the rising cost of public and private four-year colleges and universities. In a recent survey conducted by the American Association of Community Colleges, many students came from low-income households, and about one-quarter of the respondents also expressed an interest in careers involving computer/technical skills.[4]

In addition, participants in the industry that created   13 and profited from the boom in computer usage have stepped up to the plate to provide assistance to the have-nots. By providing—at little or no cost to the individual (see *<http:// www.free-pc.com>*, *<http://www.netzero.com>*, and *<http://www. freeprograms.com>*)—computers, Internet service, and software to those who presently do not have them, many arms of the computer industry can gain new customers and expose them to advertising and products in markets that go beyond technology and computers. This approach has been used over the years with tremendous success by both the alcohol and the tobacco industries; early and overwhelming brand exposure has ensured lifelong customer loyalty and new legions of customers on an ongoing basis. Even before the Internet, the services LEXIS and Westlaw provided free access to law students, hoping to develop loyal customers at the earliest possible stage in their careers.

AOL, the leading provider of online services in the United   14 States, recently announced the launch of AOL@School, a free online service that would provide schools with access to AOL's library of educational content. Additionally, Microsoft announced earlier this year the start of a five-year, $7 million philanthropic endeavor aimed at getting community colleges connected and partnered with community businesses. The glass is filling and will keep filling. By the time government programs get under way, programs such as President Clinton's plan to build community computer centers to help the information have-nots, there may no longer be any have-nots: the intended recipients may be online already. The problem we'll have then is what to do with all the obsolete equipment that our tax dollars have paid for.

Higher Education and the Digital Divide

15 From the standpoint of higher education, students who leave
high school without exposure to digital learning tools such as
the Internet will prove a much less serious problem than students who leave high school with inadequate reading or math
skills. As computer interfaces become increasingly user-
friendly, learning to use a database, a word-processor, or e-
mail will not be particularly difficult, just as was discovered by
the growing number of senior citizens who have learned to use
the Internet. For students who can read, who can figure, and
who have "learned how to learn," lack of exposure to digital
equipment in education will not be much of a handicap.

16   Many educators hope that the deployment of digital learning
tools in earlier education will help to reduce the number of
students who reach higher education with deficiencies in basic
skills such as reading. For many educators, therefore, the
problem of students who graduate from high school without
adequate reading or math skills may be perceived as linked to
the problem of getting high-tech devices into elementary and
secondary schools. Note, however, that the two are not necessarily linked. A student can learn to read and do math at very
high levels without exposure to any computer technology
whatsoever.

17   Likewise, students with virtually unlimited exposure to computers can experience no substantial improvement in basic
skills. One prime example is the Kansas City School System.
Under court order, the Kansas City School Board was told to
design a "money is no object" program to integrate the school
system and to raise the test scores of African-American students. The board added, among other new facilities, computers
everywhere, television sets and compact-disc players, television studios, and a roboties lab, and it boasted a student-
teacher ratio of 12 or 13 to 1. But the test scores of the
minority students did not rise. The board ultimately concluded
that paying more attention to hiring good teachers and firing
bad ones would have made a greater difference. Similar results
have been reported in Sausalito, California.[5]

18   The likelihood that technology alone will fail to solve the
problem of students who lack basic skills is especially high in
the absence of adequate teacher training. But even when
teachers are trained, substantial questions remain about how
much the technology can add to a student's real knowledge.
One educator was disturbed, for example, to find that when he
asked his students to determine the date on which a certain
Robert Frost poem was published, the students came back

with widely varying answers. Most of them gave their source simply as "The Internet" and seemed to have no concept that there might be Internet sources that were unreliable, and many had no idea how to use an ordinary "paper" library to get the same information. As "policy wonks," the authors can attest to a similar problem. When asked to find a document, many interns fresh out of college check first and only on the Internet. If they do not find the document there, the interns announce that the document is "not available."

The view that digital technology is either necessary or suffi-   19
cient to improve students' basic skills or their ability to engage in critical thinking, therefore, may be a dangerous distractor. The flip side is good news for educators: they may feel much less pressure to equip absolutely every learning environment with a plethora of costly gadgets destined for quick obsolescence. A school could find itself expending endless resources on technology when those resources would be better spent elsewhere in the educational system.

The deeper problem seems to be that there are more serious   20
issues plaguing elementary and high school education across the United States. Until the more fundamental problems with the educational system are fixed, throwing money into technology or into any other aspect of the educational system just will not work. This may be part of the reason that high-tech entrepreneurs such as Tim Drake and Larry Ellison of Oracle have become supporters of school vouchers.

Private or Public Sector?

Whatever differences there are in penetration levels of digital   21
communications media across various socioeconomic groups, these represent a fairly ordinary situation. The digital divide is not a fundamentally different problem from the radio divide, the automobile divide, or the air-conditioning divide of the past. It would be extraordinary to expect to see a new technology arrive for all people, in all situations across the board, simultaneously. We face no special dangers of the creation of two new social classes, one of which is doomed to fall into a hopelessly degraded state.

This is not to say that nothing need be done. Especially for   22
the desperately poor, a great deal must be done—though supplying high-tech gizmos might be rather low on the list. The heavy lifting for the greatest number of people will be accomplished, as always, by the market. We have no "crisis" or "emergency" that should be construed to justify new or special

programs of taxation and subsidy. For example, there is no need to abandon the American tradition of local and state control over schools in favor of a federal scheme such as the rather wasteful and ill-targeted e-rate program.

23   There is also the likelihood that such programs will backfire, injuring the market mechanisms that create and spread wealth. Tax-funded programs do not create new wealth. They merely move it out of one sector of the economy and into another. The e-rate program takes money from telephone consumers and companies generally and gives it to schools. Whatever gains the schools may make are offset by losses to consumers and to companies, who have less money to invest in research, network upgrades, second telephone lines, and so on.

24   Private-sector charitable efforts will always be more effective than tax mechanisms. Donors to charitable efforts, individual or corporate, are spending their own money, not that of the taxpayers. This gives them an incentive to ensure that their money is not wasted and to keep an eye on corruption. Their efforts are far more likely to be targeted where the money will do the most good. By comparison, something like the e-rate program is a massive gamble with someone else's money. Massive sums are spent long before research on how to use technology effectively in the classroom is completed or even begun.

Conclusion

25   The digital glass is filling fast as the market transforms both computers and Internet hookups from luxury goods into commonplace items. Digital wealth springs from the ordinary forces of supply and demand driven by a profit motive, just as occurred with cars and air conditioning. This process will continue to create the wealth to carry the greater mass of humanity toward a higher standard of living. Even though the market does not work perfectly, it works far better than government tax-and-spend programs. Government cannot create new wealth—it can only take existing wealth from some to give to others.

26   The success of markets in making technology more affordable is good news for educators—they are not, after all, the only thing that stands between us and a depressing future of unemployable "information have-nots." But even as more and more students get connected, schools will find they face a deeper challenge: figuring out why so many students graduate from high school without basic skills like reading. And the answer may not be on the Internet at all.

NOTES

1. Quoted in "Wrassling Dinosaurs Scare Teleco Beasts," *Communication Today* 6, no. 65 (April 6, 2000).
2. Both Ellington and the *Cyber Dialogue* survey are quoted in Hubbard Lee, "Is There Really a Digital Divide?" *New York Beacon*, April 12, 2000, 6.
3. Quoted in Alexandra Marks, "Minorities Closing Gap in High-Tech Revolution," *Christian Science Monitor*, January 26, 2000, 1.
4. American Association of Community Colleges, "Survey Shows Community Colleges Key in Technology Economy," *Headline News*, April 4, 2000, available at <http://199.75.76.25/headline/0404400head.1html> (accessed July 28, 2000).
5. Paul Clotti, "Money and School Performance: Lessons from the Kansas City Desegregation Experiment," *Cato Institute Policy Analysis*, no. 298 (March 16, 1998), available at <http://www.cato.org/pubs/pas/pa-298.html> (accessed July 28, 2000).

Paul Gorski

UNDERSTANDING THE DIGITAL DIVIDE FROM A MULTICULTURAL EDUCATION FRAMEWORK

Paul Gorski is an assistant professor in Hamline University's Graduate School of Education, where his research, personal, and civic interests focus on issues of multiculturalism. He maintains three websites, where he regularly publishes work on multiculturalism. He has also published Multicultural Education and the Internet: Intersections and Integrations *and* Multicultural Resource Series: Resources for the Multicultural Classroom. *The article below, which examines the digital divide specifically from the perspective of multiculturalism, was published on one of Gorski's websites,* The Multicultural Pavilion. *Gorski describes the mission of the site as follows: "I strive to provide resources for educators, students, and activists to explore and discuss multicultural education; facilitate opportunities for educators to work toward self-awareness and development; and provide forums for educators to interact and collaborate toward a*

critical, transformative approach to multicultural education."
Gorski also writes that

> *Multicultural Education is education that allows all stu-*
> *dents to reach their potential as learners. It produces*
> *socially active, critically thinking members of society. It*
> *respects diversity while teaching all children to become*
> *effective and participating members of a democracy. It*
> *respects individuality while promoting respect for others.*
> *It emphasizes the contributions of the various groups*
> *(e.g., ethnic, gender, religious, sexual orientation, etc.)*
> *that make up the population of the world. It focuses on*
> *how to learn rather than on learning specific informa-*
> *tion. It encourages critical analysis of all material pre-*
> *sented in the classroom, encouraging the same for*
> *material people encounter outside the classroom. It*
> *emphasizes the importance of people sharing their*
> *stories and learning from the stories of others. It makes*
> *all of us part of history, as opposed to focusing on histor-*
> *ical dates, facts, and figures. It calls for a more accurate*
> *curriculum instead of a Eurocentric one. It acknowl-*
> *edges that different children have different learning*
> *styles. It takes into consideration the learner and his or*
> *her relationship to the material. It recognizes that the*
> *measure of one's learning is not only the new informa-*
> *tion or understandings that one has gained but also*
> *includes the extent to which the learner has changed rel-*
> *ative to the material. It helps the students make sense*
> *out of their everyday life. It facilitates communication*
> *between students, their teachers and the rest of society.*

As you read the article below, consider how literacy, and in
particular, information and technological literacy, might be
affected by the so-called digital divide, and how that divide
affects the "multicultural" education Gorski envisions. (You
might also consider whether you agree with Gorski's vision of
multiculturalism.) Is the digital divide faced by those without
access to technology analogous to the literacy issues faced by
Frederick Douglass and/or Ben Franklin (whose technology
was the printing press)?

The law, in its majestic equality, forbids the rich as well as the
poor to sleep under bridges, to beg in the streets and steal bread.
                                                    —ANATOLE FRANCE

Multicultural education calls for all aspects of education 1
to be continuously examined, critiqued, reconsidered, and
transformed based on ideals of equity and social justice. This
includes instructional technology and covers its content and
delivery (or curriculum and pedagogy). That is, it is not
enough to critically examine the individual resources—in this
case, CD-ROMs, Web sites, or pieces of software—we use to
ensure inclusivity. Instead, we must dig deeper and consider
the medium itself and *how* it is being used differently in different contexts. What roles are various software titles, Web sites,
and the computers that facilitate our use of them, playing in
education? Are they contributing to education equity or supporting current systems of control and domination of those
groups already historically privileged in the United States education system (such as White people, boys and men, first language English speakers, and able-bodied people)?

The term "digital divide" has traditionally described inequali- 2
ties in access to computers and the Internet between groups of
people based on one or more social or cultural identifiers.
Under this conceptualization, researchers tend to compare
rates of access to these technologies across individuals or
schools based on race, sex, disability status, and other identity
dimensions. The "divide" refers to the difference in access rates
among groups. The racial digital divide, for example, describes
the difference in rates of access to computers and the Internet,
at home and school, between those racial groups with high
rates of access (White people and Asian and Asian-American
people) and those with lower rates of access (Black people and
Latina(o) people). Similarly, the sex or gender digital divide
refers to the gap in access rates between men and women.

So, by the end of 2000, when women surpassed men to be- 3
come a majority of the United States online population, many
people also believed the sex digital divide had disappeared. If
there were more women than men using the Internet, the logic
went, equality had been achieved. Girls and women were equally
likely to use computers and the Internet as boys and men.

Still, though the fact that more girls and women were using 4
the Internet is a meaningful step forward, a broader and deeper
look at their position in relation to the increasingly techno-
centric society and global economy reveals that equality in access is considerably different from equity in opportunity. In
fact, most of the sex and gender inequities in society and other
media are replicated online. The ever-present and ever-growing
Internet pornography industry, along with the threat of cyberstalking and the relative ease with which potential sexual
predators can attain personal information about women

online, make the Internet a hostile—and potentially dangerous—environment for many girls and women. Equally hostile to women are academic and professional pursuits of mathematics, sciences, engineering, computer sciences—all traditionally male fields that are closely linked with computers and the Internet. Research shows how women and girls are systematically steered away from these fields beginning as early as elementary school through school culture, classroom climate, traditional gender roles, and other societal pressures. Additionally, video games, largely marketed for men and boys, often depict girls and women as damsels in distress or sideshow prostitutes. Even those games, such as *Tomb Raider*, that challenge these stereotypical roles by casting strong, independent, heroic female characters in lead roles dress these big-breasted women with impossibly-dimensioned bodies in tight, revealing clothes. Most video game makers are men and most video game consumers are boys and men. So, instead of critiquing this fact and considering why it is so, the producers bow to market pressures and recycle the industry sexism. Unfortunately, a majority of information technology professionals cite video games as their initial point of interest in the field.

5   As a result of these and other socio-political, socio-historical, and socio-cultural dynamics, during the same year that women became over 50 percent of the online population, only 7 percent of all Bachelor's-level engineering degrees were conferred to women and only 20 percent of all information technology professionals were women. So, while equality in access rates reflects an important step forward, it does not, by any useful measurement, signify the end of the sex digital divide. In fact, the glaring inequities that remain despite equality in Internet access illustrate the urgency for a deeper, broader understanding of the digital divide and a deeper, broader approach for eliminating it.

6   These remaining inequities, which mirror deeply entrenched and historically cycled inequities in professional, economic, and education opportunities for women in the U.S., together serve as a clear, powerful critique of the unidimensional approach most often employed for addressing the race and class digital divides: simply providing schools and communities with more computers and more, or faster, Internet access. Again, though this is a positive step forward, it fails to address social, cultural, and political factors that will be in place with or without more machinery. For example, research indicates that, while teachers in schools with a high percentage of White students and a low percentage of students on free or reduced lunch programs are more likely to use these technologies to

engage students in creative and critical thinking activities, teachers in schools with a high percentage of Students of Color and a high percentage of students on free or reduced lunch tend to use computers and the Internet for a skills and drills approach to learning. Additionally, the growing online presence of African Americans and Latina(o)s is tempered by the growing number of white supremacy Web sites and a more intense sense of fear and vulnerability among these groups (along with Native Americans) related to the availability of personal information online.

Ultimately, the traditional understanding of the digital divide as gaps in rates of physical access to computers and the Internet fails to capture the full picture of the divide, its stronghold, and its educational, social, cultural, and economic ramifications. Meanwhile, such a narrow conceptualization of the divide serves the interests of privileged groups who can continue to critique access rates instead of thinking critically and reflectively about their personal and collective roles in cycling and recycling old inequities in a new cyber-form.   7

A new understanding of the digital divide is needed—one that provides adequate context and begins with a dedication to equity and social justice throughout education. Multicultural education—a field that enters every discussion about education with this dedication—offers an important, desperately needed framework for such an understanding. It is from that framework that I have crafted the following statement about understanding and eliminating the digital divide.   8

A multicultural education approach to understanding and eliminating the digital divide: 9

1. critiques technology-related inequities in the context of larger educational and societal inequities, keeping at the fore of the discussion the fact that those groups most disenfranchised by the digital divide are the same groups historically disenfranchised by curricular and pedagogical practices, evaluation and assessment, school counseling, and all other aspects of education (and society at large);

2. broadens the significance of "access" beyond that of physical access to computers and the Internet to include access to support and encouragement to pursue and value technology-related fields, educationally and professionally (at home, in school, in the media, by peer groups, etc.);

3. broadens the significance of "access" beyond that of physical access to computers and the Internet to include

access to non-hostile, inclusive software and Internet content;

4. critically examines not only *who* has access to computers and the Internet, but *how* these technologies are being used by various people or identity groups or by those teaching various people or groups;

5. considers, in the context of studying access rates with this broader definition of "access," the larger socio-political ramifications of, and socio-economic motivations for, the expanding significance of information technology, not only in schools, but in society at large, and how the growing merger of cyber-culture with wider U.S. culture privileges those who already have access in the broadest sense;

6. confronts capitalistic propaganda, like commercials portraying children from around the world announcing their recent arrival online, that lead people to believe that these technologies are available to everyone, everywhere, under any conditions, who want to use them;

7. rejects as simplistic and patriarchal any program that purports to "close" the divide only by providing more computers and more, or faster, Internet access, to a school, library, or other public place;

8. rejects as inadequate any solution that aims to "close" and not "eliminate" the divide; and

9. conceptualizes the elimination of the digital divide as those actions that:

   a. lead to, and maintain, a present and future in which all people, regardless of race, ethnicity, sex, gender, sexual orientation, socioeconomic class, disability status, age, education level, or any other social or cultural identity, enjoy equitable access—safe, comfortable, encouraged and encouraging, non-hostile, and valued physical, cultural, social access—to information technology including software, computers, and the Internet;

   b. lead to, and maintain, a present and future in which all people, regardless of race, ethnicity, sex, gender, sexual orientation, socioeconomic class, disability status, age, education level, or any other social or cultural identity, enjoy equitable access—safe, comfortable, encouraged and encouraging, non-hostile, and valued physical, cultural, social access—to educational pursuits in technology-related fields including mathematics, science, computer science, and engineering;

    c. lead to, and maintain, a present and future in which all people, regardless of race, ethnicity, sex, gender, sexual orientation, socioeconomic class, disability status, age, education level, or any other social or cultural identity, enjoy equitable access—safe, comfortable, encouraged and encouraging, non-hostile, and valued physical, cultural, social access—to career pursuits in technology-related fields including mathematics, science, computer science, engineering, and information technology;

    d. lead to, and maintain, a present and future in which all people, regardless of race, ethnicity, sex, gender, sexual orientation, socioeconomic class, disability status, age, education level, or any other social or cultural identity, play an equitable role in determining the socio-cultural significance of computers and the Internet and the overall social and cultural value of these technologies; and

    e. lead to, and maintain, a present and future in which all of these conditions are constantly monitored, examined, and ensured through a variety of perspectives and frameworks.

As information technology becomes more and more interwoven with all aspects of life and well-being in the United States, it becomes equally urgent to employ the complexities and critiques of multicultural education theory and practice to the problem of the digital divide. It is the next—the present—equity issue in schools and larger society with enormous social justice implications. This reframing of the digital divide can serve as a starting point for more active participation in digital divide research and action within the field of multicultural education.   10

Additionally, this conceptual piece should challenge those currently studying or working to eliminate the divide in all contexts to broaden and deepen their understandings of equity. It is crucial to recognize that the effort to eliminate the divide, while a clearly identifiable problem unto itself, must be understood as one part—albeit an immensely important one—of a larger effort toward eliminating the continuing and intensifying inequity in every aspect of education and society.   11

Media Matters

Introduction

Democracy is largely about talk—but not in the "all talk" or "just talk" sense. A well-functioning democracy, rather, is about *productive* talk—talk that allows citizens to express areas of agreement and disagreement, and so to live within an open and responsive culture. Such a culture requires a public forum within which such conversations can be heard. But in a country as large as ours, creating a public forum to which all citizens have access is difficult. This responsibility for the dissemination of information, ideas, and opinions has fallen on what we usually call "the mass media." Literally, a "medium" is an "intervening substance within which something is conveyed"; in the case of mass media, it is the mode through which the conversations that drive a democracy are rapidly conveyed to, and among, citizens.

Because the media plays such a grave role in the health of our society, it has historically not been treated as just any other business, but one that deserves special freedoms and that requires special regulations. Even the founders, who could not have imagined the speed with which news can travel, saw fit to include freedom of the press in its first Constitutional amendment. On the other hand, lawmakers who were faced with a growing and diverse set of mass media likewise felt compelled to legislate ways to keep media from mismanaging the important mission that it has. This balance between freedom and restriction is the topic of the first section in this part of *Conversations*, which asks a key question for a democratic culture: "Who Owns the News?"

Recently, that question has been much on the minds of Americans, as the Federal Communications Commission (FCC) has proposed some controversial changes to how much of the news media individual corporations can own. The FCC, which was established by the Communications Act of 1934, is an independent U.S. government agency directly responsible to Congress. It is charged with "regulating interstate and international communications by radio, television, wire, satellite and cable." One of the roles of the FCC has been to regulate ownership of media networks so as to ensure that dissemination of news, opinion, and creative productions not be centralized in the hands of a small

group. In June 2003, the FCC issued a controversial ruling
on media consolidation that

- lifted a ban on companies owning a TV station and a
  daily newspaper in the same market, except where there
  are three or fewer stations;
- allowed companies to own TV stations that as a group
  serve up to 45 percent of all households in the United
  States—up from the previous 35 percent (in the case
  of UHF stations, a single company could reach up to
  90 percent);
- eased rules on local TV ownership so that one company
  could own up to two stations in midsize markets, and
  three in large markets, as long as only one of those stations was in the top four in ratings; and
- restricted radio ownership to prevent one company
  from owning all the radio stations in a city.

After a great public outcry about the relaxation of TV and
newspaper ownership rules, their implementation was
stayed by the Third U.S. Circuit Court of Appeals and rejected by Congress. But the debate is not yet over, and it illustrates how one American ideal can clash with another.
On one hand, the FCC must insure an independent media
that provides Americans access to the full conversation, not
just the parts that specific companies and individuals allow
to be transmitted. But what about the rights of the companies? Any type of regulation, especially of media networks,
can seem counter to a free society like ours, and so the
rights of business owners and the rights of free speech are
always a counterweight to regulatory legislation—and a
source of the debates you will read about in this section.

At the same time that mass media has been consolidated
into historically few hands, more and more Americans have
gained access to the most powerful new technology for disseminating information since the printing press: the
Internet. For those of you who have grown up in an Internet
world, it is likely difficult to imagine that this technology,
first begun in 1973 by the Defense Advanced Research
Projects Agency (DARPA), has been accessible to the general
public for less than 20 years. The boom in Internet technologies over the past two decades has provided American
citizens with unprecedented access to information and
unprecedented methods of rapid communication. Some believe that these alternative or "new" media—personal and

institutional websites, e-mail, weblogs, etc.—has provided important new freedoms and reenergized grassroots democratic actions. Just about any special interest group you can think of is likely to have its own websites, discussion boards, chat rooms, etc. that bring interested people from all over the country, or world, together. Others have suggested that access to technology is still limited and overly regulated, leaving many out of the conversation. And still others suggest that the Web splinters our citizenry, developing so many private conversations and interest groups that a common discussion fails to take place. The readings in this section will ask you to think not only about the ideas and opinions expressed by these authors, but also about your own use of new media. As you read the discussion of alternative media in this section, you will be challenged to think about how these modes of communication—the "new media"—affect the way that you receive information, the way that you assess that information, and the way that you express and receive opinions.

And then there is radio. In some ways, radio is the dinosaur of electronic media. Amidst a seemingly endless stream of communication media—television, DVDs, CDs, camera phones, video messaging, instant messaging, blogging, palm pilots, etc.—radio seems rather passé. We still may have visions in our public memory from the 1940s and 1950s of families huddled around, staring at a box which gave only sound, no picture. But far from a useless and discarded technology, radio, and in particular, talk radio, has had a huge impact on the dissemination of opinions. Though talk radio has, in a sense, been around from the beginnings of commercial radio broadcasting in this country, what we consider a "talk show" has gained new popularity only recently, through the efforts of Rush Limbaugh and other largely conservative radio personalities. Attitudes toward talk radio are mixed. On the one hand, the concept of a two-way medium that allows for discussions about issues and politics of the day is precisely the type of conversations that one would encourage in a democracy—and what some suggest happens on these shows. On the other hand, some insist that talk radio is less of an open discussion, and more of an attempt to consolidate opinions—to bring together those who already agree with one another. If that is the case, is there really a conversation? The stakes in this debate about talk radio are raised further by those who claim that this medium has had a substantial effect on elections, has further divided "liberals" from "conservatives," and has encouraged speech that tends to be intolerant to differing opinions. Still, in a culture like ours that values free speech, how can talk radio be criticized for transmitting the words and ideas of any individuals, hosts and callers alike? Can those who criticize the medium for its methods of speech at the same time defend the ideals that make freedom of speech a central tenet of our country? In fact, many supporters of talk radio—some of whose words you will read in this section—suggest the detractors of this media "hate democracy in action." Perhaps the best way for you to consider the arguments made by authors in this section is to spend some time listening to this medium yourself, considering the uses of talk radio, the quality of the arguments you hear there, and the ability for a variety of voices to be heard and valued. Then you can enter into the conversation yourself.

As the part of this section on "alternative media" makes clear, the Internet is now a major player in public conversations about any number of issues. Many of those conversations are not merely in words—images such as photographs, satirical cartoons, drawings, graphs, and charts all make compelling arguments about important social issues. In this part's "Visual Conversations" section, you will find a collection of images that were gathered from various activist websites. These images comment nonverbally upon issues like the Iraqi war, media consolidation, and the role of the police in keeping the peace without violating civil liberties—issues that have a place elsewhere in this book as well. You will find that these pieces of visual rhetoric can pack a strong emotional punch; your job will be to go beyond that initial reaction and to analyze the line of argument that they present (without words), and the validity of that argument in light of the larger conversation.

Free speech, clearly, can be a dangerous business, especially when it is magnified by the technologies of mass media. But perhaps the greatest check on the dangers of free speech is the thoughtful exercise of that right—so as you read the various opinions and arguments in this section, be sure to add your voice to the conversation.

Big Media:
Who Owns the News?

Robert W. McChesney and Eric Alterman
WAGING THE MEDIA
BATTLE

Robert McChesney is perhaps the best-known opponent of media consolidation; he has written a barrage of articles and books designed to actively promote opposition to media mergers. McChesney is a Professor at the Institute of Communications Research and the Graduate School of Library and Information Science at the University of Illinois at Urbana-Champaign. He has written or edited eight books, including the influential Telecommunications, Mass Media, and Democracy: The Battle for the Control of U.S. Broadcasting, 1928–1935 *(Oxford University Press, 1993). Also among his publications are* Corporate Media and the Threat to Democracy *(Seven Stories Press, 1997) and more recently,* Rich Media, Poor Democracy: Communication Politics in Dubious Times *(New Press, 2000). He has also written over 120 journal articles. Eric Alterman is a columnist for* The Nation, *a left-leaning publication that purports to "bring to the discussion of political and social questions a really critical spirit, and to wage war upon the vices of violence, exaggeration, and misrepresentation by which so much of the political writing of the day is marred." Alterman also writes articles for many other periodicals and acts as a senior fellow of the World Policy Institute at New School University. The article below was published in* The American Prospect, *which, like* The Nation, *has an openly liberal agenda.*

1   Even if Rupert Murdoch and Sumner Redstone were to quit their jobs, change their names, and move off to New Mexico to do yoga and share a bong all day in a mountain cabin, the

operations of the News Corporation and Viacom, respectively, would not change appreciably. Whoever replaced them would follow the same cues, with more or less success. But the logic of the system would remain intact.

That system is set up to maximize profit for a relative handful   2
of large companies. The system works well for them, but it is a disaster for the communication needs of a healthy and self-governing society. So if we want to change the content and logic of the media, we have to change the system. And following my logic, we must change media content radically if we are going to have a viable self-governing society and transform this country for the better. As former Federal Communications Commission member Nicholas Johnson likes to put it: When speaking to activists and progressives, whatever your first issue of concern, media had better be your second, because without change in the media, progress in your primary area is far less likely.

Let's begin with the obvious question: Where does our media   3
system come from? In mythology, it is the result of competition between entrepreneurs duking it out in the free market. In reality, our media system is the result of a wide range of explicit government policies, regulations, and subsidies. Each of the 20 or so giant media firms that dominate the entirety of our media system is the recipient of massive government largesse—what could be regarded as corporate welfare. They receive (for free) one or more of: scarce monopoly licenses to radio and television channels, monopoly franchises to cable- and satellite-TV systems, or copyright protection for their content. When the government sets up a firm with one of these monopoly licenses, it is virtually impossible to fail. As media mogul Barry Diller put it, the only way a commercial broadcaster can lose money is if someone steals from it.

If policies establish the nature of the media system, and the   4
nature of the media system determines the nature and logic of media content, the nucleus of the media atom is the policy-making process. And it is here that we get to the source of the media crisis in the United States. Media and communication policies have been made in the most corrupt manner imaginable for generations. Perhaps the best way to capture the media policy-making process in the United States is to consider a scene from the 1974 Oscar-winning film *The Godfather II*. Roughly halfway through the movie, a bunch of American gangsters, including Michael Corleone, assemble on a Havana patio to celebrate Hyman Roth's birthday. This is 1958, pre-Fidel Castro, when Fulgencio Batista and the Mob ruled Cuba. Roth is giving a slice of his birthday cake, which has the outline of Cuba on it, to each of the gangsters. As he does so, Roth

outlines how the gangsters are divvying up the island among themselves, then triumphantly states how great it is to be in a country with a government that works with private enterprise.

5　　That is pretty much how media policies are generated in the United States. But do not think it is a conspiracy through which the corporate interests peacefully carve up the cake. In fact, as in *The Godfather II,* where the plot revolves around the Corleone-Roth battle, the big media trade associations and corporations are all slugging it out with one another for the largest slice of the cake. That is why they have such enormous lobbying arsenals and why they flood politicians with campaign donations. But, like those gangsters in Havana, there is one crucial point on which they all agree: It is their cake. Nobody else gets a slice.

6　　The solution to the media crisis now becomes evident. We need to have widespread, informed public participation in media policy-making. This will lead to better policies and a better system. There are no magic cure-all systems, and even the best policies have their weaknesses. But informed public participation is the key to seeing that the best policies emerge, the policies most likely to serve broadly determined values and objectives.

7　　Imagine, for example, that there had been a modicum of public involvement when Congress lifted the national cap on how many radio stations a single company could own in 1996. That provision—written, as far as anyone can tell, by radio-industry lobbyists—sailed through Congress without a shred of discussion and without a trace of press coverage. It is safe to say that 99.9 percent of Americans had no clue. As a result, radio broadcasting has become the province of a small number of firms that can own as many as eight stations each in a single market. The notorious Clear Channel owns more than 1,200 stations nationally.

8　　As a result of this single change in policy, competition has declined, local radio news and programming have been decimated (too expensive and much less competitive pressure to produce local content), musical playlists have less nutrition and variety than the menu at McDonald's, and the amount of advertising has skyrocketed. This is all due to a change in policy—not to the inexorable workings of the free market. "There is too much concentration in radio," John McCain said on the Senate floor in 2003. "I know of no credible person who disagrees with that."

9　　Radio has been destroyed. A medium that is arguably the least expensive and most accessible of our major media, that is ideally suited for localism, has been converted into a Wal-Mart-like profit machine for a handful of massive chains. This can only happen when policies are made under the cover of night. Welcome to Havana, Mr. Corleone.

Radio is instructive also because it highlights the propagan-   10
dists use of the term "deregulation." This term is often used to
describe the relaxation of media ownership rules, even by opponents of rules relaxation. The term deregulation implies
something good; that people will be less regulated and enjoy
more liberty. Who could oppose that? Radio broadcasting is
the classic case of a deregulated industry. But just how deregulated is it? Try testing this definition of deregulation by broadcasting on one of the 1,200 channels for which Clear Channel
has a government-enforced monopoly license. If you persist,
you will do many years in a federal penitentiary. That is very
serious regulation. In fact, all deregulation means in radio is
that firms can possess many more government-granted and
government-enforced monopoly licenses than before.

As the radio example indicates, we have a very long way to   11
go to bring widespread and informed public participation to
media-policy debates. The immediate barrier is the standard
problem facing democratic forces in the United States: The
corporate media political lobby is extraordinarily powerful and
is used to having its way on both sides of the aisle in Congress.
Moreover, corporate media power is protected from public review by a series of very powerful myths. Four of these myths in
particular need to be debunked if there is going to be any hope
of successfully infusing the public into media-policy debates.

The first myth is that the existing profit-driven U.S. media   12
system is the American way, and that there is nothing we can
do about it. The Founders, this myth holds, crafted the First
Amendment to prevent any government interference with the
free market. In fact, this could hardly be more inaccurate.
Freedom of the press was seen more as a social right belonging
to the entire population than as a commercial right belonging
to wealthy investors. The establishment of the U.S. Post Office
provides a dramatic case in point.

In the first generations of the republic, newspapers accounted   13
for between 70 percent and 95 percent of post-office traffic, and
newspapers depended upon the post office for the distribution
of much of their circulation. A key question facing Congress was
what to charge newspapers to be mailed. No one at the time was
arguing that newspapers should pay full freight, that the market
should rule; the range of debate was between those who argued
for a large public subsidy and those who argued that all postage
for newspapers should be free, to encourage the production and
distribution of a wide range of ideas. The former position won,
and it contributed to a massive flowering of print media in the
United States throughout the early 19th century. What is most
striking about this period, as Paul Starr argues in his new book,

The Creation of the Media, is that there wasn't rhetoric about free markets in the media, nor about the sacrosanct rights of commercial interests. That came later.

14   The second myth is that professional practices in journalism will protect the public from the ravages of concentrated private commercial control over the news media—and that therefore we need not worry about the media system or the policies that put it into place. The notion of professional journalism dates to the early 20th century, by which time the explicit partisanship of American newspapers had come to resemble something akin to the one-party press rule of an authoritarian society. The solution to this problem was to be professional autonomy for journalism. Trained professional journalists who were politically neutral would cover the news, and the political views of the owners and advertisers would be irrelevant (except on the editorial page). There were no schools of journalism in 1900; by 1920 many of the major schools had been established, often at the behest of major publishers.

15   Professional journalism was far from perfect, but it looked awfully good compared with what it replaced. And at its high-water mark, the 1960s and '70s, it was a barrier of sorts to commercial media ownership. But the autonomy of journalists was never written into law, and the problem today is that as media companies have grown larger and larger, the pressure to generate profit from the news has increased. That has meant slashing editorial budgets, sloughing off on expensive investigative and international coverage, and allowing for commercial values to play a larger role in determining inexpensive and trivial news topics. In short, the autonomy and integrity of U.S. journalism has been under sustained attack. This is why journalists rank among the leading proponents of media reform. They know firsthand how the media system is overwhelming their best intentions, their professional autonomy. And unless the system changes, there is not hope for a viable journalism.

16   The third myth is probably the most prevalent, and it applies primarily to the entertainment media, though with the commercialization of journalism, it is being applied increasingly there, too. This is the notion that as bad as the media system may seem to be, it gives the people what they want. If we are dissatisfied with media content, don't blame the media firms; blame the morons who demand it. This is such a powerful myth because it contains an element of truth. After all, what movie studio or TV network intentionally produces programming that people do not want to watch? The problem with it, as I detail in *The Problem of the Media*, is that it reduces a complex relationship of audience and producers to a simplistic one-way flow. In oligopolistic media markets, there is producer sovereignty, not

consumer sovereignty, so media firms give you what you want, but only within the range that generates maximum profits for them. Supply creates demand as much as demand creates supply.

And some things are strictly off-limits to consumer pressure. 17 Media content comes marinated in commercialism, although survey after survey shows that a significant percentage of Americans do not want so much advertising (65 percent, according to an April 2004 survey by Yankelovich Partners, believe they are "constantly bombarded with too much" advertising). But don't expect a mad dash by media corporations to respond to that public desire. It is difficult, if not impossible, to use the market to register opposition to hypercommercialism—that is, to the market itself. Further, the media system clearly generates many things that we do not want. Economists call these externalities—the consequences of market transactions that do not directly affect the buyer's or seller's decision to buy or sell but have a significant effect, and can level massive costs, upon society.

Media generate huge negative externalities. What we are 18 doing to children with hypercommercialization is a huge externality that will almost certainly bring massive social costs. Likewise, dreadful journalism will lead to corrupt and incompetent governance, which will exact a high cost on all of our lives, not just those who are in the market for journalism. The long and short of it is that the market cannot effectively address externalities; it will require enlightened public policy.

The fourth myth is that the Internet will set us free. Who 19 cares if Rupert Murdoch owns film studios and satellite-TV systems and TV stations and newspapers? Anyone can launch a blog or a Web site and finally compete with the big guys. It is just a matter of time until the corporate media dinosaurs disappear beneath the tidal wave of new media competition.

The Internet and the digital-communications revolution are, in 20 fact, radically transforming the media landscape, but how they do so will be determined by policies, not by magic. The Internet itself is the result of years of heavy public subsidy, and its rapid spread owed to the open-access "common carrier" policy forced upon telecommunications companies. How the Internet develops in the future will have everything to do with policies, from the copyright and the allocation of spectrum to open wireless systems to policies to assist the production of media content on the Internet. The one point that is already clear is that merely having the ability to launch a Web site does not magically transform media content. That will require public policy.

So, again, the moral of the story is clear: if we wish to 21 change the nature of media content, we have to change the system. If we wish to change the media system, we need to change media policies. And if we wish to change media policies, we have to blast open the media policy-making process and remove it from the proverbial Havana patio.

22   My sense is that the more widespread public participation there is in media policy-making, the more likely we are to have policies to encourage a more competitive and locally oriented commercial media system, as well as a much more prominent and heterogeneous nonprofit and noncommercial media sector. But if there is a legitimate public debate, I will certainly live with the results, whatever they might be.

23   From the emergence of the corporate media system more than a century ago to the present, the dominant commercial interests have done everything within their considerable power to keep people oblivious to the policies made in their name but without their informed consent. There have been a handful of key moments when media policy-making became part of the public dialogue. For example, in the Progressive Era, the corruption, sensationalism, and pro-business partisanship of much of commercial journalism produced a crisis that led to widespread criticism of capitalist control of the press, and even to movements to establish municipal or worker ownership of newspapers. In the 1930s, a fairly significant movement arose that opposed the government secretly turning over all the choice monopoly radio channels to owners affiliated with the two huge national chains—NBC and CBS—and calling for the establishment of a dominant noncommercial broadcasting system. I will not keep you in suspense: These movements failed.

24   But following World War II, media policy-making has increasingly gravitated to the Havana patio. As a result, our media system is increasingly the province of a very small number of large firms, with nary a trace of public-service marrow in their commercial bones. Regulation of commercial broadcasting degenerated to farcical proportions, as there was no leverage to force commercial broadcasters to do anything that would interfere with their ability to exploit the government-granted and enforced monopoly licenses for maximum commercial gain.

25   The prospects for challenging the corrupt policy-making process seemed especially bleak by the 1990s with the ascension of neoliberalism. Even many Democrats abandoned much of their longstanding rhetoric about media regulation in the public interest and accepted the "market uber alles" logic.

26   So when the FCC announced it would review several of its major media-ownership rules in 2002, nearly everyone thought it was a slam dunk that the commission would relax or eliminate the rules. After all, a majority of the FCC's members were on record as favoring the media firms getting bigger even before

they did any study of the matter. The media giants hated these rules and were calling in all their markers with the politicians so they could get bigger, reduce competition and risk, and get more profitable—and it didn't look as if anything could prevent them from winning.

But over the course of 2003, the FCC's review of media-ownership rules caused a spectacular and wholly unanticipated backlash from the general public. Literally millions of Americans contacted members of Congress or the FCC to oppose media concentration. By the end of 2003, members of Congress were saying that media ownership was the second-most-discussed issue by their constituents, trailing only the invasion and occupation of Iraq. It is safe to say that media issues never had cracked the congressional "top 20" list in decades. What was also striking was how much of the opposition came from the political right, as well as a nearly unified left. In September 2003, the Senate overturned the FCC's media rules changes by a 55-10-40 vote; the House leadership is currently preventing a vote among representatives, and the matter is under review in the courts.

But what drove millions of Americans to get active on media ownership in 2003 was not a belief that the status quo is quite good, or that the problem with rules changes is that they will remove the media from its exalted status. To the contrary, the movement was driven by explicit dissatisfaction with the status quo and a desire to make the system better. Years of frustration burst like an enormous boil when Americans came to the realization that the media system was not "natural" or inviolable but the result of explicit policies. Surveys showed that the more people understood media as a policy issue, the more they supported reform. Once that truth is grasped, all bets are off.

Coming off the media-ownership struggle, there is extraordinary momentum. Scores of groups have emerged over the past few years—local, national, and even global in scope—organized around a wide range of issues. In the coming few years, expect to see major progressive legislation launched to restore more competitive markets in radio and television; to have antitrust law applied effectively to media; to have copyright returned to some semblance of concern for protecting the public domain; to have viable subsidies put in place that will spawn a wide range of nonprofit and noncommercial media; to have a wireless high-speed Internet system that will be superior and vastly less expensive than what Mr. Roth and Mr. Corleone (the cable and telephone companies) have in mind; to have real limitations on advertising and commercialism, especially that aimed at children; to have protection for media workers, so they can do their work without onerous demands upon their labor by rapacious owners. The list goes on and on.

30   All of these measures would have been unthinkable just a year or two ago. Now they are in play. One of the exciting developments of the last year has been the recognition that media activism is flexible politically. Unlike campaign-finance reform, where anything short of fully publicly financed elections leaves open a crack that big money exploits to destroy the reforms, media activism allows for tangible piecemeal reforms. We may well get several hundred additional non-commercial FM stations on the dial this year, largely as a result of sustained activism. Those stations will be a tangible demonstration to people of what they can achieve, and they will spur continued activism. And media reform allows for a broad array of alliances, depending upon the issue, as the 2003 media-ownership fight demonstrated. Indeed, media activism might just be the glue to sustain a progressive democratic vision for the nation's politics.

31   But it will not be an easy fight, not at all. This is a long-term struggle, a never-ending one. What we know is that it is impossible to have a viable democracy with the current media system, and that we are capable of changing this system. The future depends upon our being successful.

Dell Champlin and Janet Knoedler
OPERATING IN
THE PUBLIC INTEREST
OR IN PURSUIT
OF PRIVATE PROFITS?
NEWS IN THE AGE OF MEDIA CONSOLIDATION

Dell Champlin is a professor of economics at Eastern Illinois University. He has published widely on the relationship of economic decisions on ethics, public policies, and worker's rights. The essay below examines those issues as regards media mergers, asking whether consolidation of media ownership serves

*public, or corporate, interests. Note the way that this carefully re-
searched and documented essay, written for an academic journal
called the* Journal of Economic Issues, *goes beyond theoretical
economics to make an argument about its effect on public policy. This is in keeping with this journal's editorial policies, which
state that the journal is meant to provide "an outlet for scholarly
articles of institutional economics . . . on major economic policies across a broad spectrum of institutional problems."*

The "synergies" created by means of the major media mergers in   1
the United States over the past decade—the combination of massive libraries of content with multiple distribution channels—
have been heralded as important benefits for consumers. The
mainstream argument is that these mergers over the past decade
have greatly increased the volume of available information and
greatly decreased the cost of delivering the news to the average
citizen. Consumers now can surf the twenty-four-hour news
channels and the ubiquitous Internet sites, or opt instead for personalized news, delivered to them daily via email.

Have these synergies really brought about an improvement   2
of consumer welfare? The media are charged with providing
an important service to their citizen-consumers—thorough
and unbiased information that will aid them in making conscious and conscientious decisions in the voting booth and in
other aspects of their consumer and citizen lives. But in the
age of media consolidation and cartelization, the quality and
even the quantity of news has deteriorated. News divisions
have become just another profit center for their conglomerate
parents that must yield the same rates of profit as the more
lucrative entertainment divisions of these media empires.
Whereas broadcast stations still are licensed to operate in "the
public interest," news in the age of media empires has become
reduced to "info-tainment." This paper will examine the current state of news in our media conglomerate age and consider,
from an institutionalist point of view, modern journalism as
the ultimate example of making money versus making "goods."

The Emergence of Media Giants

The past decade has witnessed a trend toward media concen-   3
tration, accelerated by the passage of the 1996 Telecommunications Act. As various authors have noted, concentration in
specific media sectors, already at a high level, increased
markedly during the 1990s (see Table 1). While this degree of

TABLE 1 Media Concentration

INDUSTRY	NUMBER OF TOP FIRMS	CONTROLLED BY TOP FIRMS
Book Publishing	7	"Dominate"
Cable Channels	7	75%
Cable TV Systems	6	80%
Movie Production	5	75%
Music Distribution	5	Almost all
Newspapers	6	"Dominate"
Radio Stations	4	33% (90% of revenue)

Sources: Hollings 2001, A27; McChesney, 17–19; Croteau and Hoynes 2001, 100.

concentration in specific media sectors is both unprecedented and staggering, the concomitant trend in media has been the "conglomeration of media ownership," to use McChesney's term. The alarming trend toward media consolidation and conglomeration has been especially rapid over the past two decades: in 1983, fifty corporations dominated most of the mass media in this country (Bagdikian 1997, xlvi). But today a mere handful of firms dominate our mass media (Bagdikian 2000, xii). The Big Six, as they should be called, include AOL-Time Warner, Disney, Viacom, NewsCorp, Bertelsmann, and General Electric (Bagdikian x).[1] In the largest of all recent media mergers, AOL-Time Warner combined AOL's 100 million Internet subscribers with Time Warner's 75 million cable subscribers. AOL-Time Warner is also a dominant player in cable programming, magazine publishing, movie production, book publishing, music recording, and other related ventures (McChesney, 92–93; Bagdikian, xi). Each of the other five media giants has substantial market power in most of these same areas (McChesney, 93 ff.). Moreover, the Big Six are intertwined due to ownership of stock in their fellow media empires, joint ventures, and other interlocking devices (cf. Rifkin 2000; Bagdikian; Croteau and Hoynes 2001). To quote TCI chairman John Malone, "nobody can really afford to get mad with their competitors, because they are partners in one area and competitors in another" (quoted in Rifkin 2000, 221). The firms compete vigorously in only one area, the battle for the largest share of advertising revenues (Bagdikian 2000, xxii). Ben Bagdikian predicted in 2000 that the AOL-Time Warner merger would likely bring about other media mergers (Bagdikian 2000, xi). As Bagdikian warned, "the prospect is for a giantism and concentrated power beyond anything ever seen" (Bagdikian 2000, xi).

The premise behind these mergers, estimated at $300 billion   4 in the 1990s alone (Croteau and Hoynes 2001, 71), is that conglomerate media companies can create "synergies" when combining print, broadcast, film, recording, and publishing within the "walls" of one large firm. A good example of these so-called synergies occurred with the film *Titanic*. The film was produced jointly by Twentieth Century Fox and Paramount, owned, respectively, by NewsCorp and Viacom. NewsCorp's Harper Collins published the title James Cameron's *Titanic* while its Fox television channel aired a special on the making of the film (Croteau and Hoynes 2001, 110–111). Numerous other Titanic products were spawned by this process, running the gamut from CDs to T-shirts to Broadway musicals to chocolates in the shape of Celine Dion's face.

This pursuit of synergy is, however, tending to crowd out   5 products that are not good fits for the entertainment divisions of the media giants. Croteau and Hoynes observed that "the pursuit of profits through synergistic strategies seems to be edging out the substantive ideas and discussion that would be more valuable to the health of the public sphere" (Croteau and Hoynes 2001, 162).

When, in 1999, the former CEO of Pantheon Books, Andre   6 Schiffrin, examined the spring catalogs of three major publishing houses—Harper Collins, Simon & Schuster, and Random House (belonging, respectively, to media giants NewsCorp, Viacom, and Bertelsmann)—he found, in a combined catalog of 400 titles, only four books dealing with current political issues. This synergized list instead tilted dramatically toward movie and television tie-ins. A similar process unfolds with network news: the Project for Excellence in Journalism reported this past November that 20 percent of the stories on the network morning "news" shows were devoted to some product—a book, movie, television program, music, or theme park—being produced by their corporate parent (Jaquer 2002, 20).

It is estimated that at least 90 percent of the content of prime   7 time network television originates within these conglomerates (Miller 1998, 11). The bitter irony, in this day of hundreds of cable channels and new media technologies, is that control over the access to these critical pipelines of information is more centralized than ever. Indeed, each of the media giants has moved aggressively into the Internet and is willing to take on huge losses to keep away smaller rivals. Robert McChesney observed that "For a Disney or Time Warner or Viacom to lose $200–300 million annually on the Internet is a drop in the bucket, if it means their core activities worth tens of billions of dollars are protected down the road" (McChesney 2000, 3). Rather than a proliferation of new outlets for news, to date, it is the Web sites of the big corporate TV news operations and the major newspapers that are garnering the most "hits." McChesney concluded that "the trend for online journalism is to accentuate the worst synergistic and profit-hungry attributes of commercial journalism, with its emphasis on trivia, celebrities, and consumer news" (McChesney 2000, 5). In short, we are in the grips of a media cartel that, in the words of Mark Crispin Miller, "keeps us fully entertained and permanently half-informed" (Miller 2002, 18). And it is to their duties to inform us, i.e., the "news," that we now turn.

News as a Product: Marketing and Cost Cutting

8   News in the new age of media conglomerates is in the hands of a few mega-corporations (Bagdikian 1997). Five of the media giants discussed above control a major television network news program. AOL Time Warner controls CNN and its various offspring; Disney controls ABC; Viacom controls CBS; NewsCorp controls the "fair and balanced" Fox News Channel; and GE controls NBC, CNBC, and MSNBC. Newspaper conglomerates follow closely behind the Big Six in terms of national dominance (McChesney 1999, 20), and almost all of them hold local monopolies over their local newspaper markets. With the expected relaxation of the FCC rule banning ownership of television and newspaper stations in the same town, we can look forward to complete news monopoly in many areas of the country (Ostrow 2001, E01). More importantly, the conglomeration of news divisions within ever larger corporations leads to greater pressures for these divisions to be profitable: "the larger the corporation, the more plentiful the shareholders . . . , the bigger the debt, and the greater the pressure on company managers" (Sparrow 1999, 99).

9   According to McChesney (1999), the major broadcast networks long regarded their provision of news to the public as a public service with professional journalism premised "on the notion that its content should not be shaped by the dictates of owners and advertisers, or by the biases of the editors and reporters, but rather by core public service values" (McChesney 1999, 49). This is not to say that journalism was exempt from commercial pressures up to that point (cf. Sparrow 1999, 72 ff.; Croteau and Hoynes 2001). But by the 1970s, the news divisions of the major broadcasters became important profit centers for

their corporate parents. Since that time, the news divisions have moved from being "a loss-leader and a mark of network prestige to being a major producer of network profit" (McChesney 1999, 51; Croteau and Hoynes 2001, 160).

News for profit is news that must attract ratings, and that means ratings from the demographic groups most attractive to advertisers. In other words, what a profitable news media must do to earn profits is to find and deliver the "eyeballs for sale" (Baker and Dessart 1998, 62). Broadcast media derives 100 percent of its revenue from advertisers, and cable news channels get substantial revenue from the same sources (Croteau and Hoynes). The statistical service QNBC allows NBC to analyze how the target audience responds to the news stories and advertisements, and as a result, its news division is the "'most profitable broadcast news division in the history of television'" (quoted in McChesney 1999, 51).

Of particular concern, therefore, must be the role of advertisers in determining the content of the news. In a particularly notorious example, the *LA Times* and the Staples Center in Los Angeles secretly agreed to split the advertising profits from a special edition of the Sunday magazine devoted to stories on the Staples Center. When this agreement was divulged, 300 writers for the publication signed a petition that stated their opposition to "the paper entering into hidden financial relationships with the subjects we are writing about" (quoted in Croteau and Hoynes 2001, 166). But in the internal investigation that followed, a managing editor for the newspaper revealed that "Money is always the first thing we talk about. The readers are always the last thing we talk about" (quoted in Croteau and Hoynes 2001, 166). In a similar case, journalist Barbara Walters and her cohorts on the ABC program, "The View," turned eight of their shows into "paid infomercials" for Campbell's soup (FAIR 2000, 2). Examples of stories that do not air due to advertisers' influence also, unfortunately, abound, from the decision of *60 Minutes* not to air its interview with Jeffrey Wiegand, the whistle-blowing tobacco executive, to Mobil's successful efforts to persuade the media to withhold stories unfavorable to them (Sparrow 1999, 79). While these well-known anecdotes illustrate the point, catering to advertisers' needs appears to be a widespread phenomenon. When the Project on Excellence in Journalism surveyed local TV news directors in 2000, one third suggested that they had received pressure to avoid negative stories about advertisers, while 75 percent of investigative reporters and editors at television stations reported that advertisers had tried to influence their content (FAIR 2000, 1).

12   Media consolidation has put business executives rather than journalists in charge of news divisions, and thus increased the pressure for profits (Sparrow 1999, 94–95). The unsurprising result is that the "wall" between journalism and commerce has crumbled in all areas of news reporting (Sparrow 1999, 94–95; see also Bagdikian 1997, xii).[2] Moreover, in the push for profits, synergies are exploited with depressing frequency. CBS's *Early Show* spent considerable time "interviewing" the non-survivors of its "reality" summer hit, *Survivor*. The *Early Show*'s producer later said: "Look, it's a hit show on CBS. If I didn't take advantage of it, I should be fired for malfeasance" (FAIR 2000, 10). NBC spent more time in 1996 covering stories related to the Summer Olympics, to be telecast on its network, than any other story (McChesney 1999, 53). Again in 2000, NBC's *Nightly News* devoted considerably more time than the other network news programs to news about the 2000 Sydney Olympics (FAIR 2000, 10). In a particularly egregious example, ABC news programs gave three interviews to a sock puppet: two interviews on *Good Morning America* and one on *Nightline*. As FAIR reported, though, this was "no ordinary sock—this was the corporate 'mascot' for pets.com, a . . . website that counts ABC's parent company Disney as one of its investors" (FAIR 2000, 9).

13   While the push for ratings pulls journalism toward features that appear to be commercially lucrative, it also drags it toward the lowest cost alternative and away from risky and expensive investigative work. In fact, James Fallows described much of modern journalism as being like the drunk looking for his lost keys under the streetlight rather than in the dark alley where the keys were actually lost: "much of what is in our news is there because journalists are looking where the light is. Coverage that is easy, cheap, and convenient for the news business drives out anything else" (Fallows 1996, 144). McChesney reported that the number of crime stories annually broadcast on the network news programs tripled in the first half of the 1990s (McChesney 1999, 54).

14   A blatant example was the massive coverage of the O. J. Simpson trial in 1995. CNN aired non-stop coverage of the trial, leaving other news stories, such as the question of whether North Korea would open its nuclear plants to outside inspectors, untouched. CNN's ratings increased fourfold; NBC and CBS also covered it as a major news story (Sparrow 1999, 78–79; Fallows 1996, 174). According to Croteau and Hoynes, the "all Monica, all the time" coverage by MSNBC of the Clinton impeachment story helped establish the new network as an important player in the twenty-four-hour news channels (Croteau and Hoynes 2001, 203).[3] News that is sensational is cheap and easy to cover: to quote Fallows again, "you send out

a crew, you point the camera at whatever has blown up, and the story tells itself" (Fallows 1996, 144).

There has also been a deliberate increase in soft news. In what has been referred to as the "USA Today-ization" (Sparrow 1999, 96) of news, news media now endeavor to close broadcasts with human-interest stories or to include features or attractive graphics in print. These soft news segments are increasingly promoted in advance, as a way to garner ratings. One result is the obvious homogenization of the news, from blow-dried anchors repeating similar words or interviewing the same narrow range of analysts, using theme songs and flashy graphics for their lead stories, and the constantly streaming news ticker on the news channels. A post-September 11 study of the news concluded that "while the news has become more serious, almost all of the change is focused on the war, which suggests that the networks may have simply changed subjects rather than changed their approach to the news" (quoted in Schechter 2002, 34). Catering to the public can lead to more ominous results. In their coverage of the events since September 11, Fox News Channel has relied on a mantra of "Be accurate, be fair, be American" in blatant response to the desire of their target conservative audience to hear only pro-American news (Rutenberg 2001). To quote anchor Brit Hume on their downplaying of civilian casualties in Afghanistan, "O.K., war is hell, people die.... The fact that some people are dying, is that really news?" (Rutenberg 2001).

Meanwhile, corporate malfeasance is given scant coverage by the news media: a tiny 0.6 percent of the members of the Organization of Investigative Reporters and Editors track the corporate world (Bagdikian 1997, 56). To quote former CBS president Frank Stanton, "since we are advertiser supported we must take into account the general objectives and desires of advertisers as a whole" (Sparrow 1999, 80). The scant coverage of corporate actions becomes completely mute when reporting on the activities of the media corporate parents. Arthur Kent, a former journalist for NBC, reported on GE's opposition to any investigation of its business activities by its corporate child (McChesney 1999, 52). ABC suppressed a report on labor and safety abuses at Disney World (McChesney) and terminated the radio program of Jim Hightower when he began to criticize the network's corporate parent. Two ABC insiders who chose to remain anonymous reported that the network's news magazine *20/20* had considered a special report on executive compensation but "the idea was dropped because no one wanted to draw attention to the extraordinarily rich pay package of Disney's chairman, Michael Eisner" (FAIR 2000, 10).

17   The broader implications of the media merger wave have
largely gone unreported by the news divisions of these media
conglomerates. Most of the coverage of the Viacom-CBS merger
was done by business reporters (Solomon 2000, 58), with the reporting strictly along business lines rather than giving consideration to the broader implications of the story. At times, any
semblance of reporting gives way to flattery and sycophancy:
when the *Tribune* company acquired the *Times Mirror* company,
the *LA Times* praised its new owner as receiving "high marks for
using cost-cutting and technology improvements throughout
the corporation to generate a profit margin that's among the industry's highest" (Solomon 2000, 59).

18   Of course, the other way to increase profits by reporting the
news is to cut the costs of providing the news. Evidence of cost
cutting and other methods of cheapening the product is replete.
In the wake of the Capital Cities–ABC merger in the 1980s, the
ABC news division had to meet the same profit goals as the new
firm's entertainment divisions. One fifth of the news division
was subsequently laid off (Croteau and Hoynes 2001, 43). This
pattern was repeated at CBS and NBC in the mid 1980s and
again at all the news networks in the mid 1990s (Croteau and
Hoynes 2001, 80; McChesney 1999, 54). A distinctive feature of
the cost cutting is the closing, or significant reduction in staff,
of foreign news bureaus and thus of foreign news coverage.
Coverage of international news was cut in half over the period
1988 to 1996 (Sparrow 1999, 85; cf. Bagdikian 2000, xxx).

19   Domestic news resources have also been cut: Sparrow noted
that the sizes of the Washington bureaus have also been reduced, and bureaus in major cities have been cut back or eliminated (Sparrow 1999, 87). The reduction of staff has led in
turn to a reduction of the number of investigative reporters:
one NBC reporter was quoted as saying that "we don't have the
researchers or the time to dig, except on the most important
stories" (quoted in Sparrow 1999, 87). The pressure to keep
costs down has led to an over-reliance on pre-packaged "news":
press conferences or press releases, pooling of news gathering
resources, de-emphasis on investigative reporting (Croteau
and Hoynes 2001, 163–64). The now infamous presidential
election exit-polling consortium was initiated in 1990 by ABC
as part of an effort to increase profit margins for their news divisions (Mazzocco 1994, 131).

20   In short, news in the age of media is increasingly a practice
aimed at enriching the corporate parent rather than enriching
the public debate. The line between news and entertainment
grows ever thinner, indeed, if Steve Friedman, producer of
CBS's *Early Show*, was correct when he said, "That line is long

gone. Now you can lament and say it's terrible. You can say it's over, the civilization is over. You know what, to compete you've got to compete. And we are in this to win. And we will use this show to help us win" (FAIR 2000, 10).

Conclusion: Veblen and the Public Interest View of Broadcasting

It was Secretary of Commerce Herbert Hoover who first made   21
the case for a public interest standard for the fledgling broadcasting industry: "The emphasis must be first and foremost on the interest, the convenience, and the necessity of the listening public, and not on the interest, convenience, or necessity of the individual broadcaster or the advertiser" (quoted in Jaquet 1998, 13). This principle was later codified in the Communications Act of 1934 (Croteau and Hoynes 2001, 55). But this principle of public interest is endangered in our present age of media consolidation by absent regulators and corporate commercial interests. The nation's chief regulator of media, Michael Powell, chairman of the FCC, recently sounded off about the notion of public interest in breezy terms: "It's an empty vessel into which people pour whatever their preconceived views or biases are" (quoted in Miller 2002, 39). As for the corporate titans, Gerald Levin, head of the former Time Warner corporation, offered a scary insight into their thinking about public interest when he declared that

> [g]lobal media . . . is fast becoming the predominant business of the 21st century, and we're in a new economic age, and what may happen, assuming that's true, is it's more important than government. It's more important than educational institutions and nonprofits. So what's going to be necessary is that we're going to need to have these corporations redefined as instruments of public service because they have the resources, they have the reach, they have the skill base. (Quoted in Solomon 2000, 58)

Levin's attempt to redefine public service is troubling but not   22
surprising. As Thorstein Veblen observed, "The motives of the business man are pecuniary motives, inducements in the way of pecuniary gain to him or to the business enterprise with which he is identified. . . . Serviceability, industrial advisability, is not the decisive point" (Veblen 1988, 36–39). In other words, modern media firms are following the pecuniary aims of their

predecessors and making money, not making news. Dire as the consequences of pecuniary management of the industrial processes were during the bricks-and-mortar stage of capitalism, in the point-and-click stage, they are even more troubling. When monopoly and oligopoly restrict consumer choice for automobiles or deodorant, consumers must purchase the products available or do without. It is a loss of consumer welfare, as we intone in our economics classes. But when a media cartel narrows the spectrum of opinions in the public airwaves, crowding out news of public importance with fluff or irrelevant nonsense or pandering flag waving, the larger welfare of society is endangered. We may be able to reverse this trend, but it will take both greater awareness on the part of the media-consuming public and stronger support for antitrust enforcement. Given the fact that media conglomerates, themselves, to a large extent direct and influence public awareness and opinion, we are not optimistic.

NOTES

1. The Nation includes ten firms in the media cartel—these six and AT&T, Sony, Liberty Media, and Vivendi. See "What's Wrong with This Picture?," *The Nation*, January 7–14, 2002: 18–22.
2. The commercial success of CBS's venerable *60 Minutes* program is seen as one of the pivotal events that changed television journalism, for "one simple reason," according to James Fallows: "It made money" (1996, 55). The program's success in turn led to a slew of imitation programs on other networks, "most of which failed in both journalistic and commercial terms" (Croteau and Hoynes 2001, 160). One casualty of the influx of news magazines programs has been the longer, and more costly to produce, news documentary.
3. Is crime and sensationalism what the public really wants? A Pew research poll found that even at the peak of the Monica–Bill story, only 36 percent of respondents were "very interested" in the story, and only 16 percent of the public was "very interested" in the round-the-clock coverage of the Gary Condit–Chandra Levy story this past summer (Anon. 2001, 60).

BIBLIOGRAPHY

Anonymous. "Not Everyone Wants 'Tabloid TV.'" *The Quill*, September 2001: 60.
Bagdikian, Ben. *The Media Monopoly*. Boston: Beacon Press, 2000.
———. *The Media Monopoly*. Boston: Beacon Press, 1997.
Baker, William F., and George Dessart. *Down the Tube: An Inside Account of the Failure of American Television*. New York: Basic Books, 1998.
Croteau, David, and William Hoynes. *The Business of Media: Corporate Media and the Public Interest*. Thousand Oaks, California: Pine Forge Press, 2001.
FAIR. "Fear and Favor 2000: How Power Shapes the News." Internet: http://www.fair.org/ff2000.html.

Fallows, James. *Breaking the News*. New York: Pantheon Books, 1996.

Gans, Herbert. *Deciding What's News*. New York: Pantheon Books, 1979.

Herman, Edward S. "The Media Mega-Mergers." *Dollars and Sense*, May/June 1996: 8–13.

Hollings, Ernest F., and Byron Dorgan. "Your Local Station, Signing Off." *The Washington Post*, June 20, 2001: A27.

Jaquet, Janine. "Taking Back the People's Air." *The Nation*, June 8, 1998: 13–16.

———. "The Wages of Synergy." *The Nation*, January 7–14, 2002: 20.

Lewis, Justin. *Constructing Public Opinion*. New York: Columbia UP, 2001.

Mazzocco, Dennis W. *Networks of Power: Corporate TV's Threat to Democracy*. Boston, Mass.: South End Press, 1994.

McChesney, Robert W., and John Nichols. "Getting Serious about Media Reform." *The Nation*, January 7/14, 2002: 11–17.

McChesney, Robert. *Rich Media, Poor Democracy*. Urbana, Ill.: U of Urbana P, 1999.

———. "The Titanic Sails On." Extra!, March/April 2000. Internet: http://www.fair.org/extra/0003/aol-mcchesney.html: 1–7.

Miller, Mark Crispin. "Free the Media." *The Nation*, June 3, 1996: 9–15.

———. "TV: The Nature of the Beast." *The Nation*, June 8, 1998: 11–13.

———. "What's Wrong with This Picture." *The Nation*, January 7/14, 2002: 18–22.

Ostrow, Joanne. "Stand By for Strange Bedfellows." *Denver Post*, June 17, 2001: E01.

Rifkin, Jeremy. *The Age of Access*. New York: Jeremy P. Tarcher/Putnam, 2000.

Rutenberg, Jim. "Fox Portrays a World of Good and Evil, and Many Applaud." *New York Times*, December 3, 2001.

Schechter, Danny. "Take This Media . . . Please." *The Nation*, January 7/14, 2002: 35.

Solomon, Norman. "Coverage of Media Mergers." *Nieman Reports* 54, no. 2 (summer 2000): 57–59.

Sparrow, Bartholomew H. *Uncertain Guardians*. Baltimore: The Johns Hopkins UP, 1999.

Veblen, Thorstein. *The Theory of Business Enterprise*. New Brunswick, New Jersey: Transaction Publishers, 1988.

Tom Goldstein

DOES BIG MEAN BAD?

Though "media consolidation" or "media mergers" immediately strike many members of the American public as dangerous, because a free press might be endangered if it is in control of a small group of people who control the dissemination of information, the essay below reminds us not to make snap judgments. Tom Goldstein, former dean of the reputed Columbia University School of Journalism, wrote this essay to remind readers of the need to fully examine the situation before a rush to judgment. It was published in the Columbia Journalism Review, *which calls itself "America's premier media monitor." (CJR also maintains an extensive website that monitors issues such as media consolidation.) Though Goldstein held an academic position, he has also published in many venues that have a wide, nonspecialist readership such as* Rolling Stone, The New York Times Magazine, The Nation, Columbia Law Review, Washington Journalism Review, The Washington Post, The Philadelphia Inquirer, The San Francisco Chronicle, *and* The Buffalo News. *How is the style and tone of this piece different from and/or similar to the essay by Dell Champlin and Janet Knoedler that precedes it?*

1   The journalist's fear of the concentrated power of the big media companies is almost instinctual. Yet what do we fear exactly? Is it the potential for misuse of journalistic properties to benefit other arms of a corporation? Is it the undercurrent of corporate values that we think we sense flowing through and shaping some news? Or do we fear mere phantoms, the anti-monopoly sentiments of a century that is passing into history?

2   In my last incarnation, as dean of the Graduate School of Journalism at the University of California at Berkeley, I once lobbied a top recruiter for a major newspaper chain to hire students from the school. The recruiter then explained why her company had not interviewed anyone from Berkeley for many years. The reason was simple: "Bagdikian."

3   I protested. Ben Bagdikian, the media critic and my predecessor there as dean, is a self-effacing giant in the field. I was missing the point, the recruiter told me. She was convinced that we drilled our students with Ben's anti-chain views, that like some kind of witch doctor he was initiating students into the dark arts of skepticism toward media power. (In fact, in no course did we assign Ben's influential book, *The Media Monopoly*. Shame on us.) Ultimately, the recruiter shed her remarkably thin skin and began hiring Berkeley students.

4   In the honorable ideological tradition of Will Irwin, Upton Sinclair, George Seldes, and I. F. Stone, Bagdikian contends that no commercial power should dominate the news—just as no state power should. The media giants make up, in the haunting phrase he coined, a "private ministry of information."

In the first edition of *Media Monopoly*, in 1984, Bagdikian   5
bemoaned that just fifty corporations controlled more than
half of the media outlets in this country. He was writing when
CNN was in its infancy, when most journalists still used type-
writers, and long before the Internet. By 1997, in the book's
fifth edition, Bagdikian pegged the "number of media corporations with dominant power in society" at closer to ten. The
"new communications cartel," he wrote, has the power to "surround almost every man, woman, and child in the country
with controlled images and words." With that power comes the
"ability to exert influence that in many ways is greater than
that of schools, religion, parents and even government itself."

Bagdikian's role as a media gadfly is gradually being taken   6
over by a new generation, including Mark Crispin Miller, a
forceful and original thinker now teaching at New York
University. At a duPont-Columbia University Forum called "Is
This News?" earlier this year, Miller pointed to "increasing evidence of direct and conscious manipulation of the news
process by higher corporate powers and by advertisers generally." Worse, said Miller, is "a system in which the mere fact of
ratings anxiety and declining news budgets and the scramble
for promotions, simple careerism inside the news business—
all these things combine to help produce a kind of seamless
trivial spectacle that really doesn't tell us anything."

Miller's words are potent, but they are not the last on the   7
subject of the effects of media concentration. Nor are
Bagdikian's.

The financial markets have certainly spoken. They have   8
richly rewarded some media-company mergers and made
stockholders—including journalists—happy folks. Walk into the
lobby of a big newspaper these days and you might be confronted with the latest stock price of the paper's parent company.

While few have written compellingly in favor of media giants   9
gobbling up other media giants, some thoughtful observers
have made arguments that question the validity of the traditional way of looking at media concentration. In a recent issue
of *Newsweek*, columnist Robert Samuelson mulled a survey by
the Pew Research Center for the People & the Press document-
ing the shrinking audience for the television networks' nightly
news programs. That survey, combined with the success that
his brother, an innkeeper, reaped from advertising on his own
Web site, led Samuelson to rethink some basic assumptions.

"The notion of a media elite, if ever valid, requires that peo-   10
ple get news and entertainment from a few sources dominated
by a handful of executives, editors, anchors, reporters, and
columnists," Samuelson wrote. "As media multiply, the elite

becomes less exclusive. Smaller audiences give them less prominence and market power (i.e. salaries)."

11   Writing two years ago in the extraordinary issue of *The Nation* that contained a spider-like chart illustrating the holdings of the four dominant members of "the national entertainment state," Michael Arlen, an uncommonly astute commentator, argued that the specter of a vast, monolithic, all-pervading media has been wildly overdrawn. George Orwell's vision of Big Brother in *1984* was a resoundingly false prophecy. "How disappointing it would have been to Orwell to observe the actual play-out of this romantic drama," Arlen wrote. As proof, he pointed to "the emergence over the past several decades of a startling cacophony of market-crazed citizens all over the world, with their insistence on two-way communication and their appetite for fragmentation of broadcast authority."

12   These competing views of media power (and there are many, many more) do not cancel each other out. They just underscore that we have no unitary explanation of the extent and impact of media concentration. If journalism is just another business, then the primary scorecard of success is justifiably the verdict of the financial markets.

13   Because of the First Amendment protection it enjoys, journalism is more than another business. Still, we need to know more about what differentiates media concentration from consolidation in other commercial enterprises. We see consolidation among the airlines, military suppliers, banks, brokerage firms, and telephone companies. Look at accounting firms. For years there was the Big Eight. Then, the Big Six. And now, the Big Four.

14   Why do efficiencies of scale work for some businesses and not, say, for journalistic enterprises? With big media ownership in fewer hands, what barriers to entry actually have been erected? (It has been quite a while since anyone tried to start a major metropolitan newspaper. Many have tried recently to start new television networks, but these latter-day broadcasting pioneers are among the very behemoths that so trouble Bagdikian and Miller.) Why is the much-touted buzzword of the early 1990s—synergy—now viewed with such distrust by journalists? Having moved from an age of media scarcity to one of media babble, what new ways do we need to analyze media concentration?

15   For all the Matt Drudges churning away in small rooms, there are signs that the Internet may come to be dominated by big media. In June, Disney agreed to buy a large portion of the search engine company Infoseek. NBC purchased a share of

CNET and its online search engine, Snap! These new investments, wrote Matt Welch in the *Online Journalism Review* (www.ojr.org), "further confused the already byzantine web of ownership, business alliances, and competition among the parent companies of the biz/tech sites."

In the Internet Age, media concentration bears even closer watching. Ownership needs to be demystified. Customers are entitled to know what corporate entity is responsible for bringing them their news. And this is now getting harder to know, with the emergence of a crop of big media companies not normally associated with journalism. In the next century, will Softbank dominate? Or Vulcan? Or Zapata? Or Intel?   16

Too often, commentary on media concentration has been fragmentary or anecdotal. We need to recast the debate, which shows signs of stagnating. We need to add new perspectives. That is why we should welcome fresh efforts at understanding media concentration. . . . With hard data and hard analysis will come answers to the vital questions that need to be asked about media concentration.   17

Ronnie Dugger

CORPORATE TAKEOVER
OF THE MEDIA

Ronnie Dugger is the editor of the Texas Observer, *a publication founded in 1954 by Frankie Randolph to cover issues ignored by other publications such as race, class, and the struggles of the working class. In 1994, Dugger made the observer part of the nonprofit Texas Democracy Foundation in order to further promote this mission. Dugger is the founding director of the Progressive Populist Movement, which is "not a political party," and which [seeks] to, in the words of its mission statement, "end corporate domination, to establish true political democracy, and to build a just society with a sustainable, equitable economy." As you read the essay below, you might consider the author's political and social goals, and consider why media issues are so crucial for him and the organizations to which he is committed.*

1   No anti-democratic trend in the United States during the past
    quarter-century is more threatening to freedom than the
    takeover and control of mainstream journalism by gigantic
    corporations. Under the Bush administration, the government
    is preparing a crackdown on the public interest in broadcast-
    ing such as we have not seen since the Reagan administration
    abolished the Fairness Doctrine.

2   Consider some recent events. The Federal Communications
    Commission (FCC) voted October 11, 2001, to let public televi-
    sion stations run commercial advertisements on some of the
    five or six new digital channels that Congress stole from the
    people and gave, absolutely free, to each of the licensed broad-
    casters under the 1996 telecommunications law. Public televi-
    sion has already been corrupted by commercials mislabeled as
    "underwriting announcements." Now the FCC is going all out,
    and openly, to ruin public broadcasting.

3   Under the 1996 law, which former Senator Bob Dole labeled
    a $70-billion giveaway, Congress enabled just one corporation
    to own every radio station in the United States. Before that
    law, the largest radio group owned thirty-nine stations; now
    the largest group owns 1,100 of them. Big-corporate broad-
    casting companies are winning federal court rulings that hold,
    contrary to common sense, that antitrust limits on them vio-
    late their rights of free speech. These same corporations are
    pressuring the FCC to abolish the present rules, already pitiful
    on their face, which provide that no corporation can beam
    television programs to more than 35 percent of the American
    population; no cable corporation can control more than 30
    percent of the cable market; and no corporation can own a
    television station and a newspaper in the same market. The
    Bush-whacked FCC looks ready to buckle, evidently reasoning
    that, since CBS/Viacom already reaches 41 percent of U.S.
    households and Tribune Co., Gannett, and News Corp. already
    operate television stations and newspapers in the same mar-
    kets, who needs the old limits?

4   George W. Bush's new chair of the FCC, Michael Powell, has
    attacked the federal statute, relied upon and illuminated in
    seventy years of case law, which requires that the FCC consider
    "the public interest." Powell told the American Bar Association
    earlier this year that the public-interest standard "is about as
    empty a vessel as you can accord a regulatory agency."
    Evidently Michael Powell is about as empty a vessel as you can
    find to occupy the chairmanship of an agency established to
    serve the public good.

5   The deep root of this trouble for democracy is a long line of
    Supreme Court decisions, starting in 1886, that have bestowed

all of the constitutional rights of persons on corporations except (so far) the right to vote and protection under the Fifth Amendment. By these decisions these nine people in black robes have elevated corporations to the status of Super-Citizens, and reduced us mere people to Sub-Citizens. Work on the production line of a major corporation and you'll find out soon enough what has free speech (the corporation) and who doesn't (you). Freedom of the press, which was meant to protect freedom of speech, instead protects big corporations' selling for profit. Democracy has been turned upside down. In effect and outcome, it's a counterrevolution.

Newspapers and radio and television stations have been   6
bought up and linked together under a few powerful conglomerates. In 1945, about 80 percent of U.S. daily newspapers were independently owned; by 1989, about 80 percent were owned by corporate chains. Huge corporations own the four major television networks and run the networks' news divisions.

On the Sunday morning political talk shows, according to a   7
recent study, topics loosely related to corporate power made up only four percent of the discussion topics. When your employer is owned by a just-indicted worldwide price-fixer, how much airtime do you give the story, if any? When your boss is a weapons merchant, what do you report, if anything, about the case against the war?

"The Founders didn't count on the rise of mega-media," Bill   8
Moyers has written. "They didn't count on huge private corporations that would own not only the means of journalism but also vast swaths of the territory that journalism should be covering." As media philosopher Ben Bagdikian writes, "It is normal for all large businesses to make serious efforts to influence the news. . . . Now they own most of the news media they wish to influence."

The big-corporate domination of the media is a mortal   9
threat to democracy. Without a freely and robustly informed people, democracy is an illusion. Day and night the few men at the top of the giant media corporations control what the people are invited to think about—and more important, what they are not invited to think about. Corporate censorship and self-censorship happen. Around the world, too, the means for the mass dissemination of expression are being gobbled up by media-wielding conglomerates. A few media barons are acquiring what may already be, or on present trends will certainly become, the control of mainstream discourse and expression among most of the people of the world. There's never been anything like it.

10   The power of the major media to make and un-make the
news is manifest in the way it handled the question of the legitimacy of the present Bush presidency. In January a consortium
of U.S. news organizations, including the *New York Times*, the
Washington Post, the *Wall Street Journal*, the Associated Press,
Newsweek, CNN, and several others hired the University of
Chicago's National Opinion Research Center to examine
180,000 uncounted Florida ballots from the presidential election last year. This examination was finished in August and reporters and editors from the sponsoring media prepared to
review the survey and attempt to say who won Florida: Bush or
Gore. But after the mass murders on September 11, the consortium decided to postpone the study "indefinitely." The
major media quietly "spiked" the major story of the legitimacy
of the Bush presidency. Astoundingly patriotism trumped the
biggest story in American democracy since the impeachment
of Richard Nixon. The "war on terrorism" trumped the question of who should be the president. Then, on November 12,
the consortium served up a slanted interpretation of the survey. Another column would be needed to deal with it.

11   Yet the worst is just surfacing. The electromagnetic spectrum,
"the airwaves," is public property in every country in the world.
It is a global commons. But thirty-seven economists proposed to
the FCC last February that the licensed corporate broadcasters,
who pay nothing for their billion-dollar licenses, be permitted to
lease the airwaves and sell and lease them in secondary markets.
As Jeremy Rifkin described in an article in the *Guardian* of
London, the plan is now afoot to give ownership and control of
the world's airwaves to a few global corporations.

12   Congress and both major U.S. political parties are beholden
at the top to the corporations and multi-millionaires who finance their elections. We need people to run for high public office as rebels—whether as Democrats, Republicans, Greens,
Independents, who cares—rebels who will make corporate
control of the mainstream media a sizzling political issue and
who will hold forth the vision of a truly public broadcasting
system as the keystone of a nonprofit national and local
telecommunications information consortium. This consortium, as former NBC News president Lawrence Grossman conceives it, would "serve all of the people, all of the time."

13   "The ultimate goal," according to communications professor
and writer Robert McChesney, "must be to have the public service sector be the dominant component of the broadcasting
and media system. Hence the struggle for public service broadcasting cannot avoid direct confrontation and conflict with the
existing corporate media giants."

Nick Gillespie
THE MYTH OF MEDIA
MONOPOLY

Reason Online, *which first published this essay by its editor,*
Nick Gillespie, is published by the Reason Foundation, an or-
ganization that states as its mission "to advance a free society
by developing, applying, and promoting libertarian principles,
including free markets, individual liberty, and the rule of law."
Libertarians subscribe to a philosophy very much like that of
Henry David Thoreau, whose essay "Civil Disobedience" is in-
cluded in Part 5 of Conversations: *"That government is best*
which governs least." Gillespie, who holds a Ph.D. in English
literature from SUNY Buffalo, is a frequent commentator for
political talk shows on National Public Radio, Fox News, and
C-Span. In what ways do Gillespie's political views seem to in-
fluence the essay below? Considering his views, and those of
the Reason Foundation, why might he hold the opinions to-
ward corporate consolidation of the media that he does?

Does Rupert Murdoch Control the Media?
Does Anyone?

As the power behind News Corp., the Fox broadcast network,   1
the Fox News Channel, *The Weekly Standard*, and more,
Murdoch seems every inch a latter-day William Randolph
Hearst, controlling a media empire that many believe exercises
tyrannical, ideologically driven control over the nation's news
and entertainment.

Liberals and leftists fume especially at the popular success of   2
the Fox News Channel. As Robert McChesney, co-author of *Our*
Media, Not Theirs: The Democratic Struggle Against Corporate
Media, has thundered, Fox News "does virtually no journalism
at all." For their part, conservatives wink at Fox News' self-
evidently ironic "fair and balanced" mantra, preferring to forget
that only a few years ago Murdoch was an arch villain to them.
In 1999 professional moralist "Lucky Bill" Bennett teamed up
with current Democratic presidential hopeful Joe Lieberman to
present the Aussie-born magnate a "Silver Sewer Award," an
honor the dyspeptic duo used to bestow annually upon the nation's top "cultural polluter." By creating TV shows such as

Married . . . With Children and *The Simpsons*, Murdoch supposedly had "done more than any other programmer in television to
foul the public airwaves and define our cultural norms down."

3   So does Murdoch—or anyone else—control the media? As
media researcher Ben Compaine underscores in "Domination
Fantasies," the answer is no. In an age when the right and the
left shrilly insist that the other is consolidating total control
over the planet's airwaves, publishing houses, and newspapers,
Compaine argues persuasively that fears about "galloping concentration" in the media are about as compelling as the quickly
canceled Fox series *Skin*.

4   As far as major industries go, the media are not particularly
concentrated, nor have they become much more so during the
last 10 or 20 years. Compaine explains how deregulation and
market forces—viewed suspiciously by liberals and conservatives alike—help ensure a diversity of viewpoints. "Most important," writes Compaine, "there is no compelling evidence that
the current level of media concentration has had negative consequences for consumers, culture, or democracy." Indeed,
these days any individual can "easily and inexpensively have
access to a huge variety of news, information, opinion, culture,
and entertainment, whether from 10, 50, or 3,000 sources."

5   That's the sort of liberating outcome people used to wish for
in the dread age of three broadcast channels, a few dominant
print outlets, and no Internet. And it's one that those of us who
can now communicate far more easily and effectively to whole
new audiences find positively thrilling.

Pew Research Center

BOTTOM-LINE
PRESSURES NOW
HURTING COVERAGE,
SAY JOURNALISTS

The Pew Research Center for the People and the Press, one arm
of Pew Charitable Trusts, is an independent research organiza-
tion that measures public opinion on the press, public policy,
and politics. Because of its scholarly base and independent
status, the organization and its studies enjoy a great deal of

credibility. The essay below was based on interviews with 547 reporters, editors, producers, and so forth involved in journalism in the United States. As you read, consider the ways in which the quantitative numbers—the survey figures—are introduced and interpreted by the writers of this piece. You might compare this use of quantitative figures with other essays in this section that rely less on numbers, or other essays in Conversations *that likewise use demographic information. What is the effect of statistics in bolstering a case? What are their limitations?*

Overview

Journalists are unhappy with the way things are going in their profession these days. Many give poor grades to the coverage offered by the types of media that serve most Americans: daily newspapers, local TV, network TV news and cable news outlets. In fact, despite recent scandals at the *New York Times* and *USA Today*, only national newspapers—and the websites of national news organizations—receive good performance grades from the journalistic ranks.

Profit Pressures Hurting Coverage

	National			Local		
	1995 %	*1999* %	*2004* %	*1995* %	*1999* %	*2004* %
Effect of bottom-line pressure on news coverage						
Hurting	41	49	66	33	46	57
Just changing	38	40	29	50	46	35
Other/DK	_21_	_11_	_5_	_17_	_8_	_8_
	100	100	100	100	100	100
Reporting is increasingly sloppy and error-prone						
Valid criticism	30	40	45	40	55	47
Not valid	65	58	54	59	42	52
Don't know	5	2	1	1	3	1

Roughly half of journalists at national media outlets (51%), and about as many from local media (46%), believe that journalism is going in the wrong direction, as significant majorities of journalists have come to believe that increased bottom-line pressure is "seriously hurting" the quality of news coverage. This is the view of 66% of national news people and 57% of the local journalists questioned in this survey.

3   Journalists at national news organizations generally take a dimmer view of the state of the profession than do local journalists. But both groups express considerably more concern over the deleterious impact of bottom-line pressures than they did in polls taken by the Center in 1995 and 1999. Further, both print and broadcast journalists voice high levels of concern about this problem, as do majorities working at nearly all levels of news organizations.

4   The notable dissent from this opinion comes from those at the top of national news organizations. Most executives at national news organizations (57%) feel increased business pressures are "mostly just changing the way news organizations do things" rather than seriously undermining quality.

5   The survey of journalists—conducted March 10–April 20 among 547 national and local reporters, editors and executives by the Pew Research Center for the People and the Press in collaboration with the Project for Excellence in Journalism and the Committee of Concerned Journalists—also finds increased worries about economic pressures in the responses to an open-ended question about the biggest problem facing journalism today. As was the case in the 1999 survey, problems with the quality of coverage were cited most frequently. Underscoring these worries, the polling finds a continuing rise in the percentage of journalists believing that news reports are full of factual errors. In the national media, this view increased from 30% in 1995 to 40% in 1999 to 45% in the current survey.

6   When asked about what is going well in journalism these days, print and broadcast journalists have strikingly different things to say. TV and radio journalists most often mention the speed of coverage—the ability to respond quickly to breaking news stories—while print journalists emphasize the quality of coverage and the watchdog role the press plays as the profession's best features.

7   Journalists whose own newsrooms have undergone staff reductions are among the most worried that bottom-line pressures are undermining quality. Fully three-quarters of national and local journalists who have experienced staff cuts at their workplace say bottom-line pressures are seriously hurting the quality of news coverage. Those not reporting staff reductions are far more likely to say business pressures are just changing newsgathering techniques.

Beyond the stress of shrinking workplaces, there are a num- 8
ber of specific criticisms of the news media that are closely associated with the view that bottom-line pressure is hurting the
quality of news coverage. First, there is almost universal agreement among those who worry about growing financial pressure that the media is paying too little attention to complex
stories. In addition, the belief that the 24-hour news cycle is
weakening journalism is much more prevalent among this
group than among news people who do not view financial
pressure as a big problem, and a majority says news reports
are increasingly full of factual errors and sloppy reporting. And
most journalists who worry about declining quality due to
bottom-line pressures say that the press is "too timid" these days.

Views of Journalists Concerned About Bottom-Line Pressures

	YES, CONCERNED %	*NOT CONCERNED* %	*DIFFERENCE*
Percent citing as valid criticisms . . .			
News avoids complex issues	86	64	+22
24/7 cycle weakens journalism	50	26	+24
The press is too timid	56	31	+25
Increasingly sloppy reporting	52	36	+16

Based on national journalists.

In that regard, the poll finds that many journalists—especially 9
those in the national media—believe that the press has not been
critical enough of President Bush. Majorities of print and broadcast journalists at national news organizations believe the press
has been insufficiently critical of the administration. Many local
print journalists concur. This is a minority opinion only among
local news executives and broadcast journalists. While the press
gives itself about the same overall grade for its coverage of
George W. Bush as it did nine years ago for its coverage of Bill
Clinton (B− among national journalists, C+ from local journalists), the criticism in 1995 was that the press was focusing too
much on Clinton's problems, and too little on his achievements.

Press Treatment of Bush

	GENERAL PUBLIC* %	NAT'L PRESS %	LOCAL PRESS %
Too critical	34	8	19
Not critical enough	24	55	37
Fair	35	35	42
Don't know	7	2	2
	100	100	100

*Public figures from May 2004 Pew Media Believability Study (N = 1,800)

10   There are significant ideological differences among news people in attitudes toward coverage of Bush, with many more self-described liberals than moderates or conservatives faulting the press for being insufficiently critical. In terms of their overall ideological outlook, majorities of national (54%) and local journalists (61%) continue to describe themselves as moderates. The percentage identifying themselves as liberal has increased from 1995: 34% of national journalists describe themselves as liberals, compared with 22% nine years ago. The trend among local journalists has been similar—23% say they are liberals, up from 14% in 1995. More striking is the relatively small minority of journalists who think of themselves as politically conservative (7% national, 12% local). As was the case a decade ago, the journalists as a group are much less conservative than the general public (33% conservative).

11   The strong sentiment in favor of a more critical view of White House coverage is just one way the climate of opinion among journalists has changed since the 1990s. More generally, there has been a steep decline in the percentage of national and local news people who think the traditional criticism of the press as too cynical still holds up. If anything, more national news people today fault the press for being too timid, not too cynical.

12   Not only do many national news people believe the press has gone too soft in its coverage of President Bush, they express considerably less confidence in the political judgment of the American public than they did five years ago. Since 1999, the percentage saying they have a great deal of confidence in the public's election choices has fallen from 52% to 31% in the national sample of journalists.

13   Nonetheless, journalists have at least as much confidence in the public's electoral judgments as does the public itself. In addition, the growing distrust in the public's electoral decisions is not being driven by negative feelings about President Bush.

Journalists who think the press is not critical enough of Bush are no more likely than others to express skepticism about the public's judgments.

Confidence in the Public's Electoral Judgment

	PUBLIC	NATIONAL PRESS		LOCAL PRESS	
	2004*	1999	2004	1999	2004
	%	%	%	%	%
A great deal	20	52	31	28	22
A fair amount	48	41	51	56	54
Not very much	24	6	15	13	21
None at all	5	1	2	3	2
Don't know	3	–	1	–	1
	100	100	100	100	100

*Public figures from May 2004 Pew Media Believability Study (N = 1,800)

By more than three-to-one, national and local journalists be- 14
lieve it is a bad thing if some news organizations have a "decidedly ideological point of view" in their news coverage. And
more than four-in-ten in both groups say journalists too often
let their ideological views show in their reporting. This view is
held more by self-described conservative journalists than moderates or liberals.

At the same time, the single news outlet that strikes most jour- 15
nalists as taking a particular ideological stance—either liberal or
conservative—is Fox News Channel. Among national journalists, more than twice as many could identify a daily news
organization that they think is "especially conservative in its
coverage" than one they believe is "especially liberal" (82% vs.
38%). And Fox has by far the highest profile as a conservative
news organization; it was cited unprompted by 69% of national
journalists. The *New York Times* was most often mentioned as
the national daily news organization that takes a decidedly liberal point of view, but only by 20% of the national sample.

The survey shows that journalists continue to have a positive 16
opinion of the Internet's impact on journalism. Not only do majorities of national (60%) and local journalists (51%) believe the
Internet has made journalism better, but they give relatively
high grades for the websites of national news organizations.

News people also acknowledge a downside to the Internet— 17
solid majorities of both national and local journalists think the
Internet allows too much posting of links to unfiltered material.
In addition, sizable numbers in the national (42%) and local

samples (35%) say the Internet has intensified the deadline pressure they face. The changing media environment is generally having an impact on journalists' workloads—pluralities of national and local news people say they are increasingly rewriting and repackaging stories for multiple uses.

18   While journalists voice increasing concern over sloppy and error-filled news reports, there is no evidence that recent scandals like those at *USA Today* and the *New York Times* are having a significant impact on the way journalists view the profession. The number of journalists who cite "ethics and standards" as the biggest problem facing journalism has not grown since 1999. And most say that while plagiarism may be getting more attention these days, it is actually no more prevalent today than in the past.

Brent Cunningham

ACROSS THE GREAT
DIVIDE: CLASS

Among the many things that influence access to, and the attention of, media, social class is crucial. Brent Cunningham's essay explores the ways in which journalists tend to ignore those on the other side of what he calls "the great divide." You might also consider how social class affects other parts of being an American—like digital literacy (Part 1) and criminal prosecution (Part 5). Cunningham is the managing editor of the Columbia Journalism Review, *a publication that acts as a watchdog on media issues. He is also a faculty member at the Graduate School of Journalism at Columbia University, and has worked as a reporter and researcher for several publications including* Life Magazine. *In what ways does his work experience as a reporter and magazine editor increase his credibility on this issue? Can it affect his credibility in any negative ways?*

1   In the January 19 issue of *The New Yorker*, Karl Rove told the writer Ken Auletta that President Bush thinks the press is "elitist," that "the social and economic backgrounds of most reporters have nothing in common with those of most Americans."

For decades now, the political Right has made considerable hay out of the liberal elite bogeyman, and such a sentiment from Bush might be dismissed as mere culture-war blather. But class, which is what the president really means, *will* play a role in the coming election: tax cuts, unemployment, corporate greed, health care, the echo of John Edwards's "two Americas."

And Bush is right. Sort of. The class divide between journal- 2 ists and the poor and working-class Americans many of us claim to write for and about is real, though it has little to do with political ideology and is more complicated than the faux populists of the Right would have us believe. Russell Baker, the former *New York Times* columnist, got closer to the mark in the December 18 issue of *The New York Review of Books*. "Today's top-drawer Washington newspeople . . . belong to the culture for which the American political system works exceedingly well," he wrote. "The capacity for outrage had been bred out of them."

So much for comforting the afflicted and afflicting the com- 3 fortable. As Baker points out, we *are* the comfortable. The de- mographics confirm it. We are part of the professional class, reasonably affluent and well educated. By 1996, for example, the last time the American Society of Newspaper Editors con- ducted a broad survey of the U.S. newsroom, 89 percent of journalists had finished college. Meanwhile, only 27 percent of all Americans have four or more years of college, according to the latest census.

Yet numbers alone can't explain the uneven and often subtle 4 contours of this story. The press has the power to shape how people think about what's important, in effect to shape reality. But whose reality is being depicted? This is how the class di- vide between journalists and a large swath of the populace comes into play. Just one example: Andrew Tyndall, a media analyst who began measuring the evening newscasts of ABC, CBS, and NBC in 1987, finds that since then coverage of eco- nomic issues has steadily skewed away from stories of poverty and toward stories concerning wealth. Thus, the poor have become increasingly invisible. The Catholic Campaign for Human Development, the social justice arm of the U.S. Conference of Catholic Bishops, reported in 2002 that its an- nual survey of American attitudes toward poverty showed that "the general public substantially underestimates the dimen- sions of poverty in the United States." Most respondents, it said, "maintained that poverty affects some one million people in this country." The real number is thirty-five million.

This divide, this inability of one America to see and under- 5 stand the other Americas, has something to do with the collec- tive howl from the mainstream press over the "offshoring" of white-collar jobs—turning Lou Dobbs into a protectionist—after years of writing off blue-collar job losses as the price of progress. And with why the Democratic candidates' anti-poverty policies were all but ignored, despite the fact that both John Edwards and John Kerry had extensive "urban America" proposals on their Web sites. And with why Philip Hersh, a *Chicago Tribune* sportswriter, wrote in January that the disgraced skater Tonya Harding "grew up in an environment that . . . reeked of white trash," and when called on it by a reader and the *Tribune's* public editor, replied that he had "thought long and hard before using it. The term fit Tonya Harding perfectly." The divide helps explain why Frank Gilliam, a political scientist at UCLA who studies issues of race and local TV news, was told by residents in both a poor black neighborhood and a poor white neighborhood in Indianapolis that the press "only focused on the bad stuff, that they had no access to the media, and were not treated with respect by the media." It also helps explain the growth of ethnic newspapers. And it has something to do with why Abby Scher, who runs the New York Office of the Independent Press Association, got the following response from a magazine editor in Chicago when she told him, after graduating from college in the eighties, that she couldn't afford to take a job for $8,500 a year: "Can't your parents help you out?"

6   We in the press have a responsibility to engage everyone, not just those readers and viewers with whom we share cultural and economic touchstones. The good news is that the best reporters and serious news outlets find ways to bridge this divide. The bad news is that we don't do it often enough, and our reluctance to talk about class—in the newsroom and elsewhere—makes it hard to change the equation. There are consequences to the fact that millions of people in this country see little of themselves and their lives in the media, unless they are connected somehow to a problem. It may have something to do with why the press is so disliked and distrusted; or why daily newspaper circulation has been in decline for twenty years. Every reporter has his blind spots. But when we all share many of the same blind spots, it makes it difficult to see the forty-four million people who lack health insurance in this country, for example, as anything but the face of failed social policies—important but abstract.

In Search of the Working Class

7   Anthony DePalma, who has been a national correspondent and a foreign correspondent for *The New York Times*, and now covers environmental issues, says that for years he felt as though

he had "snuck my way into the paper." DePalma grew up the son of a longshoreman in Hoboken, New Jersey. He recalls seeing his father sitting at the kitchen table at the end of a workday, in T-shirt and reading glasses, paging through the *Jersey Journal*. "I never saw my dad read anything else, but he would spend forty-five minutes with the *Journal* every day," DePalma says. "It sent a semiconscious message about a newspaper's ability to reach a wide audience."

DePalma graduated from Seton Hall in 1975 (the first in his   8 family to go to college), married, and went to work unloading trucks for UPS on the overnight shift. During the day, he freelanced. In 1986, after doing quite a bit of work for the *Times* over the years, he was hired as a reporter in the real estate section. "The lowest rung, the backdoor, whatever you want to call it," he says. Inside, DePalma felt the divide. "The Pulitzers, the Ivy Leagues. I felt it very strongly," he says. "You have to understand, the *Times* never crossed the threshold at our house, growing up."

The very idea of class makes Americans, including journal-   9 ists, uncomfortable. It grates against the myth, so firmly ingrained in our national psyche, that ours is a society of self-made men, with bootstraps. This idea persists even though upward mobility, in any broad sense, is becoming a myth. It adds a moral tinge to discussions of poverty, a notion that the poor must shoulder much of the blame for their plight, and the corollary, that the wealthy should be credited for their success.

Class is also difficult to discuss because it has become so con-   10 nected to the polarizing issue of race. When Alexis Patterson, a black seven-year-old from Milwaukee, and Elizabeth Smart, a fourteen-year-old white girl from Salt Lake City, vanished within a month of each other in 2002, the press turned Smart into a national crusade while few people outside of Milwaukee ever heard of Patterson. Race had something to do with why, as did the circumstances of each case; Elizabeth's abduction from her bed, which was witnessed by her terrified little sister, arguably made for a better story than Alexis, who vanished on her way to school. But class played a role, too. Patterson came from a poor neighborhood, and her stepfather had done time on a drug charge. Smart's father is a real-estate broker, and her uncle a photographer with the local newspaper.

Class is problematic, too, because we don't agree on how to   11 define it. Is it about education? Income? Where do the swelling ranks of the working poor fit in? Under the headline WHAT IS RICH? a *Houston Chronicle* article last year illustrated how "in one of the world's most affluent countries, few seem to see themselves as rich, even if they're in the upper-income brackets." Michael Zweig, an economist at the State University of

New York at Stony Brook who directs the Center for Study of Working Class Life, defines class based on power. Using data from the census bureau and the Bureau of Labor Statistics, he designated occupations as working class, middle class, or capitalist class by the relative power each job affords. A truck driver is working class, for example, but a truck driver who owns his own rig is an independent contractor and is therefore middle class. By this measure, Zweig says, 62 percent of the country's workforce is actually working class. "That's eighty-five million people, hardly a special interest group," he says.

12   Zweig's formula resonated with Paul Solman, an economics reporter on *The NewsHour with Jim Lehrer*, on PBS. In the spring of 2003, Solman was doing a series of reports on the jobless recovery, and he interviewed Zweig. With the camera rolling, Solman said to Zweig, "By your measure, I am middle class, right?" Zweig agreed, then nodded to the cameraman behind Solman, "And he is working class." Solman looked over his shoulder at his well-paid cameraman, "Is that true, Kevin?" Kevin thought for a minute and said that it was. "Why?" Solman asked. Kevin answered, "Because I can't say 'cut.' "

13   Says Solman: "I was struck by that because it suggested that the variable wasn't income, but power, and to a lesser extent security."

14   Yet in our national discourse, we are a middle-class country, period. In polls people tend to identify as middle class, regardless of what they do or how much money they make. (Zweig notes that poll respondents are rarely given the choice of "working class," but when they are more choose that than "middle class.") From a journalistic standpoint, the working class has historically been linked to organized labor. As labor's numbers, and thus its political power, declined, so did our coverage of it. With its most important public countenance fading, the working-class perspective largely disappeared, too.

15   DePalma recently got a taste of just how difficult it can be to recapture that perspective in any consistent way. When the *Times* began its "Portraits of Grief" project on those killed in the World Trade Center, DePalma volunteered. "They were people I knew," he says, "and I realized that this is a world I had been running away from all these years." DePalma wrote a portrait of someone who had gone to his high school. He wrote six portraits of fellow Seton Hall graduates. Afterward, he discussed his experience writing portraits with Jonathan Landman, then the paper's Metro editor. "Jon said there are all these people out there who we never write about," DePalma recalls. "People who basically play by the rules, don't make huge demands on public services. We ignore them except when they

die in a tower." Together they decided that DePalma would take on a new beat that sought to fill this gap in the coverage, a working-class beat.

From June 2002 to August 2003, only two of DePalma's sto- 16
ries from this mini-beat—he was still a general assignment reporter—made page one. The centerpiece was a series about a block in Ozone Park, Queens. DePalma wrote about Rosemere and Danny Messina, who were struggling to save ten dollars a week to celebrate their son's first Holy Communion; about Joseph Raia, retired on permanent disability, who agonized over whether to raise the rent on his long-time tenants—a couple with two young children whom Raia is close to—in the face of the city's property tax increase; about Antoinette Francisco's frustrating effort to care for a neglected tree, which the city eventually cut down.

In September of last year, DePalma got a fellowship at Notre 17
Dame, and handed the beat off to a fellow reporter to tend in her spare time until he got back. When he returned in January, no stories had been done, Landman had been promoted, and interest in the working-class beat seemed lacking. "It had tremendous support from the Metro desk, but it is hard to see how that support was carried out more broadly in the paper," DePalma says. "I always took that to mean there was a discomfort with terms like 'working class', and attempts to define class in meaningful ways." DePalma chose to move on.

Landman, now an assistant managing editor, disputes the no- 18
tion that the beat had little support beyond Metro. "I never heard anybody express or signal discomfort with the idea of reporting on class," he said via e-mail, noting that "support in Metro is what you need to succeed in Metro," anyway. As for why the beat was dropped, Landman says that DePalma asked for the environmental beat when he returned from Notre Dame.

For his part, DePalma doesn't hide his disappointment. 19

"The idea was to expose our readers to a world we normally 20
ignore, the same way we would with villagers in, say, Suriname," he says. "It is fairly pitiful to compare the working class in this country to villagers in Suriname, but they are almost equally unknown."

"A Secure Lodgment"

Contrary to the comforting notion of the press standing firmly 21
behind the little guy, there was never a Golden Age when American journalism consistently sided with the powerless

against the powerful. By 1927, H. L. Mencken was already lashing the press for what he saw as its upwardly mobile ambitions. "A good reporter," he wrote, "used to make as much as a bartender or a police sergeant; he now makes as much as the average doctor or lawyer, and probably a great deal more. His view of the world he lives in has thus changed. He is no longer a free-lance in human society, thumbing his nose at its dignitaries; he has got a secure lodgment in a definite stratum, and his wife, if he has one, maybe has social ambitions."

22   There was once, though, a prominent strain of American journalism that was much more organically connected to the poor and the working class. In the first two decades of the twentieth century, for instance, *Appeal to Reason*, a socialist weekly out of Kansas, drew hundreds of thousands of readers with its scathing indictments of the inequities of unfettered capitalism by the likes of Upton Sinclair and Eugene Debs. In the 1940s, the short-lived New York paper, *PM*, was a more mainstream incarnation of this same spirit. Its motto: "*PM* is against people who push other people around." In the years before Rupert Murdoch bought it in 1976, the *New York Post* made something of a last stab at bottom-up journalism. By the 1960s, though, TV was on its way to becoming the dominant journalistic force, the newspaper business began hitching its star to Wall Street, and the age of corporate media was under way. The path to a journalism job led, increasingly, through journalism school, and thus began a new round of professionalization in the business.

23   Meanwhile, in the late 1960s the Republican Party began recasting itself as the party of the hardhats, those angry white men (mostly)—real Americans—who resented the decade's emphasis on the struggles of blacks, the poor, and the spoiled hippies who were against the Vietnam war. Part of this strategy was to portray the press as members of a liberal elite, the New Class, that was out of touch with these real Americans. This charge, remarkably, has kept the press more or less on its heels ever since. The soul-searching on display in a column Joseph Kraft wrote in the wake of the 1968 Democratic National Convention—"Most of us in what is called the communications field are not rooted in the great mass of ordinary Americans . . . "—echoes today in the press's paralyzing fear of being accused of liberal bias. By the time Ronald Reagan was elected and began vilifying the poor, the press—increasingly corporate and cowed—was in no position to resist.

24   In the 1980s, the gap between the haves and the have-nots widened—and journalists were increasingly among the haves. The middle class split, as blue-collar manufacturing jobs disappeared and were replaced by a tide of low-paying, insecure service sector jobs and an expansion of the professional class.

Under Reagan, the country sprinted into the ample arms of a shiny new money culture, offering salvation through free markets (and later through technology). Media deregulation launched a leap-frogging series of media mergers that culminated—for the time being—in the ill-fated AOL purchase of Time Warner in 2001. So as journalists joined a broader professional elite, the companies they worked for swelled into corporate behemoths.

In the 1990s, the Internet economy and its overnight million-   25
aires sharpened the wage envy of the new generation of journalists for their professional-class counterparts. David Denby's new book, *American Sucker*, about his own sad money chase, lays bare this phenomenon of irrational exuberance. So many journalists either bolted for the Internet ether or threatened to that some newspapers began offering stock options to hang on to their talent. The divide got a little wider. "A world where money is a marker and all comparisons are directed upward makes it hard to understand people for whom a million dollars would be a fortune, or those for whom $10,000 would be the difference between affording college or not, not to mention those for whom $246 is a full week's earnings, before tax, at the minimum wage," wrote James Fallows in an essay called "The Invisible Poor," published in the March 19, 2000 issue of *The New York Times Magazine*. Later in that same piece, he wrote, "Compared with the software elite, the professional-class American finds it easier to imagine financial ruin . . . . But there is a great similarity between the view from the top and the view from the next few tiers: the increasing haziness and 'Oh, yes, now that you remind me' nature of the view of the poor."

The evolution of journalism as a profession—with its higher   26
ethical standards and emphasis on expertise, good writing, and analysis—was crucial for the press to keep pace with the world. But it came at a cost. When the barriers to entry into journalism were lower, newsrooms were open to people who brought a wider range of life experiences to their reporting and editing than we have today. To be sure, that era had its problems. It was inhabited almost exclusively by white men, for one. But an interesting thing about that ASNE survey, mentioned earlier, is how so many attitudes cut across age, race, gender, or ethnic lines. What diversity there is, it seems, is only skin deep.

Empathy and Imagination

The opening scene in Alex Kotlowitz's 1991 book, *There Are No*   27
Children Here, offers a hint as to how we might begin to bridge this divide. It starts with a group of boys from a Chicago public

housing project hunting for garter snakes in the weeds beside some train tracks. Even for someone who didn't grow up in public housing, this is a familiar scene. And that, says Kotlowitz, is the point. "The obvious place to open it is with a scene of violence, because there is violence all through the book," he says. "But instead I began with this benign moment, to show that even kids whose lives are so precarious find refuge in some of the same things we all did."

28   Kotlowitz's subjects were poor, not working class, and in some ways the press does a better job of covering poor people and their issues. The poor have agencies and policies and activists to create pegs for stories. We have a public discourse about poverty in a way we don't about the working class. Still, that discourse is too often one-dimensional: the poor are a problem, victims and perpetrators, the face of failed social policies. Such stories need to be done, of course; news is often about problems, things that are broken. Yet for those of us who are lucky enough to have health care, plenty to eat, a home, and a job that gives us discretionary income, the news has a lot to offer besides problems. We see our lives reflected in the real estate section, the travel section, the food section, the business section. When was the last time you read a story about how to buy a good used car for less than a thousand dollars?

29   The press has difficulty seeing, as Kotlowitz puts it, what is familiar about the poor. "There are so few reporters who spend time in these communities, that when they are there it seems exotic and foreign," he says. "We are so appalled by what we see that we are only looking for what is unfamiliar." This makes it hard to empathize.

30   Fear, too, makes it difficult to see what is familiar about the poor. Most people working in journalism today grew up in a society that taught us that housing projects were only dangerous places to be avoided. As Jamie Kalven, a Chicago-based writer and public housing activist, put it in *Slate* in 2002, fear "blocks our capacity for perception, for learning. When mediated by fear, ignorance can coexist with knowledge, blindness with vision. As a result, decent people find it possible to support indecent policies." In an interview, Kalven amplifies the point. Fear, he says, makes us hostage to a "one-dimensional moral geography" composed of good places and bad places, and "somehow people who are decent and morally sensitive are able to read *The New York Times* and listen to NPR every day and still hold this notion."

31   This flattened coverage is evident in the press's treatment of Chicago's massive "transformation plan," which began in 1996 and involves razing all of the city's public housing highrises

and replacing them with mixed-income developments. The plan represents a fundamental shift in the way the city houses its poor, and a number of cities around the country are following Chicago's lead. There has been a fair amount of coverage over the last seven years, both local and national, and some of it has been important and thoughtful. For example, a series by the *Chicago Tribune* in 1998 showed how, contrary to the goals of the plan, many displaced public housing residents were ending up in neighborhoods that were just as solidly poor and racially monochrome as the ones they left.

But much of the coverage is top-down, focused on the problems and the process, and heavy with official sources. It is full of middle-class assumptions and fears, including this from a November 10, 1999, *USA Today* piece on the new mixed-income developments: "The wealthier families bring a greater work ethic and sense of community pride to once-desolate neighborhoods, officials say."   32

Against this backdrop, Mary Schmich's columns in the *Tribune* on Cabrini-Green, one of Chicago's most famous projects, stand out. Since May 2000, Schmich, a Metro columnist, has written two dozen columns on various characters tied to the closing of Cabrini. Those characters—from three black girls saying goodbye to their old school and hello to a new one, to a young white couple who bought into the new, mixed-income Cabrini community—spring from the page fully formed. As one of the schoolgirls, referring to her anxieties about going to school with white kids for the first time, said to Schmich, "We the same kind of people inside." It was impossible not to feel a connection to these people, partly because Schmich refused to romanticize their situations. But she also showed us their insecurities, their prejudices, their joy. "Too often reporters who want to write about public housing have very fixed ideas of how to write these stories," she says. "They have the characters in their heads, because they watch too much *Law & Order.*"   33

Schmich, who has been at the *Tribune* since 1985, says three things allowed her to feel as if she weren't writing about "someplace else" when doing the Cabrini columns. For starters, she lives in an affluent neighborhood that abuts Cabrini, and has been "hanging out" around Cabrini for ten years. She also grew up in Georgia near people who were poor and black, and her own father had, as Schmich says, "numerous jobs and we were often broke. The differences between me and the people in Cabrini is that there were patches in my childhood when I wasn't so poor, my parents were educated, and I was white, people helped me out," she says. "When I did   34

these columns it wasn't anthropology, but rather from a sense
that these were my neighbors."

35   Her main criticism of how her paper covers the poor in
Chicago is really a criticism of journalism broadly. "I think this
paper has a very deep commitment to covering the whole range
of people and issues in Chicago," Schmich says. "But it is a
question of how we do it. We bite off a huge project every few
years, and that has the effect of reducing the poor to a problem.
Then they disappear largely until the next big project."

"What If?"

36   There are consequences to covering the poor in this one-
dimensional way, consequences that the more affluent subjects
of news stories can avoid. "You're dealing with a population
that has extremely limited resources for self-representation,"
says Jamie Kalven. "They have no mechanism for holding folks
accountable." In a *Newsweek* article on the Chicago transformation plan from May 15, 2000, for instance, Mayor Richard
M. Daley is quoted as saying, "What people want is education,
jobs and job training." But in a survey that Kalven's organization did in 2000 that asked residents of the Stateway Gardens
housing project what they most wanted for their neighborhood, three of the top five answers were related to better
health care, but the other two were "more activities for children" and "more cultural activities," like theater and music.
Says Kalven: "These people were asserting their dignity as human beings. Our entire discourse defines them as problems,
and they quietly resist it, but no one is listening."

37   All this would seem to suggest that if we want more nuanced
coverage of the poor and the working class, then we should
hire more reporters and editors who come from poor and
working class backgrounds. But, as many good reporters continue to prove, you don't have to be a coal miner's daughter to
write well about Appalachia. Kotlowitz, for example, grew up
comfortably middle class on New York's Upper West Side. In
fact, being an insider can bring some unexpected problems.
Wil Cruz, a *Newsday* reporter who was born and raised in the
LaGuardia Houses, a public housing project on New York's
Lower East Side, knows something of this. "If you and I were
to go cover a story in the south Bronx, they would see you as
official and treat you with some respect," he says. "They would
be more comfortable with me, but I'm not sure that works to
my advantage. They might see me as showing off my success."

Reporters do, however, need to be motivated to get beyond   38
our assumptions. To do that it helps, as the *St. Paul Pioneer
Press*'s Maja Beckstrom says, to be able to imagine "What if?"
An interesting thing emerged as I interviewed reporters for this
piece: a large number of them were raised by single mothers,
including Beckstrom, the author David Shipler, *The Washington
Post*'s Anne Hull, and *The Guardian's* Gary Younge. All said
something similar, that experiencing the fragility of a broken
family—no matter how quickly or comfortably things settled—
allowed them to imagine how close they are to those in society
whose lives seem, from the outside, to be nothing but problems.
Hull, a national features writer at the *Post*, isn't sure just how
her background shaped her as a reporter, but says this: "I'm
much more comfortable around these people than I am being
at, say, the courthouse, or places where everyone wears a suit.
Maybe I'm intimidated by power. I don't know."

"These people" Hull refers to include the young immigrants   39
and children of immigrants in Atlanta whom she wrote about
in a four-part series in late 2002. The original idea, not surprisingly, was a piece on the growth of Latino gangs in Atlanta—a
problem. But Hull came back with a richer story about kids
who were caught between their desire to escape the world of
their parents and an American society that often failed them,
either in the classroom or on the streets. "A lot of writing about
immigrants today is really precious, and reduces them to a single dimension: hardworking," Hull says. "But they're real people, with flaws. They make bad decisions."

It takes time for outsiders to write these stories; Hull spent   40
sixteen months on her Atlanta series. That may be an extreme,
but to do these stories right requires that such coverage be a
newsroom priority.

Obstacles

Spurred by its 1998 project on poverty, the *Pioneer Press* cre-   41
ated a poverty beat and gave it to Maja Beckstrom. In 2002 she
went on maternity leave and the beat died, a victim, she says,
of the paper's "effort to rethink priorities of coverage given a
tight budget." Once back at work, she was given the choice of a
twenty-something lifestyle beat or one on parenting and families. Beckstrom chose the latter.

Even if reporters are attuned to the complexities of life for   42
the poor and the working class, they face a number of obstacles to getting those stories in the paper or on the air. The

profit expectations of newspapers and television news operations have had a dramatic and well-known effect on the quality
of journalism: shorter stories, fewer reporters, and a focus on
those readers who appeal to advertisers. "There aren't too
many publishers who come striding into the newsroom demanding more coverage of the ghetto," says Walker Lundy,
a former editor of the *Pioneer Press* and *The Philadelphia
Inquirer*, who is now retired. "You can't sell many ads when
your readers don't have credit cards, and thus some readers are
worth more than others."

43   The priorities of corporate media aside, the very ways we define and deliver news today works against the kind of coverage
Hull, Schmich, and the others are after. Our devotion to the
ideal of objectivity produces too many stories that are so concerned with "balance" that they end up saying very little. The
pace of the news cycle, as well as the shrinking newshole, foster a way of thinking about the news that doesn't lend itself to
nuance and complexity. We are trained to find the quick hit,
not to connect the various dots and reach conclusions. For example, a new study of how New York City's daily newspapers
covered the city's post-9/11 budget crisis, commissioned by the
nonprofit Drum Major Institute for Public Policy, found that
the coverage failed "to clarify the stakes of policy decisions on
various socioeconomic classes." The coverage, the study concluded, suggested that "everyone's interests are identical." Not
surprisingly, the sources used to delineate and explain those interests were mostly politicians and government officials.

44   For David Shipler, the former *New York Times* correspondent
whose latest book is about the working poor, it took a newsroom strike to free him of the confines of daily journalism. "I
was in Moscow with the *Times* when we went on strike in
1978," he says. "For three months I didn't have to write for the
paper, and I stopped thinking in terms of the seven-hundred-
word story. I began to notice things that I hadn't stopped to
consider, to see patterns and connections. That's why I was
able to write a book. I got a different lens. When your antennae
are highly tuned for the 'good story,' these things go by you.
Unless a paper is willing to give reporters the freedom to not
write every day, then it will be hard for them to find a new
lens."

45   Dale Maharidge, who won a Pulitzer for his 1989 book *And
Their Children After Them*, about rural poverty, never found it
difficult to see the world from the bottom up. Since taking his
first journalism job at *The Gazette of Medina* in Cleveland, his
hometown, in 1977, Maharidge has been referred to by editors,
somewhat derisively, he says, as the "bum writer." He was the

son of a steelworker who had a side business at home, grinding cutting tools for industrial use. "I literally grew up breathing steel dust," says Maharidge. His new book, *Homeland*, due out July 4, is about an undercurrent of working-class—really working-poor—anger that Maharidge says predates 9/11. The book highlights the kinds of stories the press misses because of this "lens" problem Shipler talks about.

Among the people Maharidge introduces us to are a mother   46 and son who live together in Bridgeview, a blue-collar neighborhood in Chicago, where, following the terrorist attacks on New York and Washington, a white mob marched on a local mosque, threatening to burn it down. In 2002, on the first anniversary of the attacks, there was another march in Bridgeview, and Maharidge was there for it. He saw the mother and son, carrying an American flag, being chased off by the police, and he followed them and got their names and address. A few days later he went to their house. Two hours later he had a deeper understanding of the anger on display in that march, and it wasn't as much about anti-Muslim bigotry as press accounts surmised. The son, who was in his mid-thirties, couldn't work because of a heart condition. He showed Maharidge a grocery bag full of medical bills—$200,000 worth, the son said—that he had no way to pay. The mother, who needed knee-replacement surgery that she couldn't afford, lifted her shirt to show him a pain patch on her back. She worked for seven dollars an hour at J.C. Penney, but had no insurance. "Would they have still been racists if they had jobs and insurance?" Maharidge says. "Sure. But would they have been out there marching? Maybe not."

Outrage

There are things that we could do to address this class divide   47 and get a news report that is, as the Columbia sociologist Herbert Gans put it, "multiperspectival." The most obvious is to broaden our diversity recruitment programs to include a specific focus on class. Efforts to bring racial and ethnic diversity to the newsroom have struggled, and this one wouldn't be any easier. But Tim Rutten, a columnist for the *Los Angeles Times*, cautions against fatalism on the question of building socioeconomic diversity. "I worked with the first black in the *L.A. Times* newsroom, the first Latino, the first woman editor, and the first woman on the masthead," he says. "All those things are commonplace now in journalism, but there was a time when each seemed an impossible social barrier."

48   Editors might do more to encourage reporters like *Newsday's*
Wil Cruz as he struggles to figure out how to use his
background—he dropped out of high school before eventually
getting a degree from New York's City College—to inform his reporting on his new beat, education. "I don't know if it gives me
power," he says of his atypical path to journalism. "If it does, I
haven't been able to channel that advantage into my stories. But
I need to, because I see it as a responsibility to do it right."

49   Newspapers need to play to their strengths, and stop trying
to compete with the electronic media on every breaking story.
The ability of even the sharpest journalism to effect real
change is incremental at best, but the stories that have a shot—
the scoops that matter—are those that go deep and tell us important things about the world, that challenge the way we
think about something. David Barstow and Lowell Bergman's
Pulitzer-winning articles last year in *The New York Times* said
something important about worker safety in this country, but
they took seventeen months to complete and involved a dozen
reporters, researchers, producers, and editors. As important as
those stories were, though, they are indicative of how the press
approaches the poor and the working class. As Mary Schmich
says, we embrace the big project, then ignore them until time
for the next big project. Day to day, their perspectives and concerns are missing from the media.

50   A bit of outrage would help, too. Russell Baker says that outrage has been "bred" out of us, that we come from a class for
whom the system has largely worked, and he's right. The working class has all but disappeared from our pages and no one
seems to notice. We report on the poor, but do little to empower the poor. That's what makes the recent crusade by the
New York *Daily News* to raise the state's minimum wage so
noteworthy. Not only did the paper have a reporter dogging the
issue from the field, but its editorial page hammered away at it
for months.

51   Anthony DePalma says that the outrage is still with us, but
that it takes a crisis—a pair of kids starving to death in Newark,
an innocent man being shot forty-one times by the police in the
Bronx—to draw it to the surface. Well, how about this for a
crisis: We are the richest country in the history of the world,
and we tolerate thirty-five million of our fellow Americans living in poverty; we tolerate forty-four million without health insurance. Meanwhile, Gannett pays Larry Miller, its outgoing
CFO, $600,000 a year for an open-ended "consulting" contract,
in addition to a car and golf club membership.

Alternative Media: A New Free Press?

Diane Owen
EFFECTS OF
ELECTRONIC MEDIA ON
DEMOCRATIC ATTITUDES

Although the "media" used to be synonymous with print, radio, and television journalism, the Internet and other electronic media have greatly expanded that definition. As such, many researchers, including Diane Owen, have become interested in measuring how this so-called new media affects political attitudes in the United States. Owen is a professor of political science at Georgetown University, where she focuses on American politics as well as political psychology/sociology. She is the coauthor of New Media, American Politics *and* Media Messages in American Presidential Elections, *and numerous articles on the political implications of the Internet, including the piece below. This piece was first delivered as a paper at the Democracy and the Globalization of Politics and the Economy International Conference. As you read, you might consider how Owen supports her claims about the influence of the new media—and what that form of support suggests about her intended audience.*

The past decade has witnessed fundamental changes in the American mass media environment. Contemporary media technologies and format innovations have created new ways of communicating and reaching audiences. New actors, such as talk show hosts and tabloid reporters, have entered the political communications environment, altering the rules by which journalists, leaders, and citizens negotiate the public sphere. The nature of the political media product has changed, becoming almost inextricably infused with entertainment content. In sum, the United States has entered a "new media" age.

2   Electronic media dominate in the "new media" era even more than in the recent past. Technologies, such as the Internet, have rendered print communication electronic, as traditional news organizations establish online counterparts to their newspapers and magazines. Further, the substance, form, and style of electronic communication has been altered radically. New-style electronic formats, such as Internet discussion groups and chat rooms, create new public spaces and provide unprecedented opportunities for political discourse. It is clear that the transformation of the American media system has important implications for democratic citizenship, especially as audiences' relationships to mass communication have been influenced significantly. However, perspectives on the prospects for democratic political systems in the "new media" era vary widely.

3   The first goal of this paper is to present an overview of the current political communication environment with a focus on establishing the context within which citizen attitudes and orientations are shaped. Alternative perspectives will be articulated. The second objective is to examine how electronic media shape political attitudes. Finally, we will speculate about the effect of electronic media on the socialization of young citizens. In particular, we will examine young people's evaluations of the President and government in light of the Clinton/Lewinsky matter. The paper uses the United States as a case study in the relationship between electronic media and democratic attitudes. It is the author's hope that the American case study will provide a segue for a discussion of the modern media-citizenship connection in other nations.

The "New Media" World and Citizenship Orientations

4   Some observers have heralded the coming of the "new media" age as the catalyst that has instigated a populist political movement where citizens have greater access to the political world than ever before (Abramson, Arterton, and Orren, 1988). The most optimistic articulation of this view posits that mass media serve to stimulate political interest and activism among the mass public. Ordinary citizens are able to establish meaningful and effective roles for themselves in the political arena that has been

primarily the domain of elites. Talk radio, for example, can provide an unstructured outlet for public expression (Herbst, 1995).

There is some evidence that this kind of populism is not an   5
impossibility in the current media environment. There is more
political information disseminated today through a vast diversity of sources than at any time in history. Political news is
available for general audiences through network evening newscasts, real time news broadcasts, including CNN and MSNBC,
morning news/entertainment programs, like the *Today* show,
and televised news magazines, such as *Dateline* and *20/20*. The
wide range of available formats also permits information to be
targeted at specific audience segments, including those who
traditionally have been under-represented in the political
world. Cable television, call-in radio forums, and Internet plat-
forms, in particular, allow citizens to receive information that
is relevant to them personally, and to make contact with others
who have similar social and political orientations. As opposed
to the "sound-bite" journalism that characterizes much mainstream political media, newer forums have more time and
space for the presentation of contextual and historical material
as well as extended discussions of issues, actors, and events.

One of the primary characteristics of the "new media" age is   6
the interactivity that communications technologies facilitate
among citizens, public officials, and media personnel. Rather
than merely being the passive recipients of political information, it is now possible for citizens to make their political presence and opinions known, and to play a more visible role in
political events. For example, televised news chat programs regularly feature citizen call-ins, news magazines present instanta-
neous online polls of citizens' opinions about political events
and issues, and average people ask questions of candidates during televised debates. Political elites keep abreast of talk radio
discussions as a gauge of public opinion. Further, record numbers of citizens are joining political organizations other than
parties, especially those associated with particular issues. This
involvement has been aided by media publicity and interactive
communication forums which allow people to express their
opinions, ask for and obtain information quickly, and receive
instructions about how to take action (Schudson, 1998).

Computer networks have gained particular attention for   7
their potential to translate democratic ideals into reality.
Visionaries predict that as computers become more fully integrated in society, the public will be linked by horizontal networks that will facilitate conversations between citizens and
elites. The closer proximity of the mass public to decision-
makers will allow greater citizen input into the policy arena

(Neuman, 1991). Further, journalists will be more likely to publicize citizen opinions beyond the snapshot of polls. There is already evidence that the general public is becoming a greater resource for news stories, as reporters will go online to solicit ideas and reactions to events and issues.

8   More realistic assessments contend that the infrastructure for mass media to foster greater civic involvement is in place, but the communications environment has been allowed to develop haphazardly. Citizens and leaders need to carefully consider the opportunities offered by electronic media to foster democratic ideals, and take steps, including legislative efforts, to assure that these goals are met (Grossman, 1995). As it stands, the "new media" environment has failed to provide the public with quality political information, to accommodate meaningful discourse, or to encourage political engagement.

9   The imperative behind political communication in the current era is profit, and not a sense of public service which was at least in the back of reporters' minds in the pre-"new media" period (Schudson, 1978). As such, the content of political news and information has become increasingly entertainment-oriented. Traditional news sources, including the network newscasts, have adopted reporting strategies that sometimes resemble those of supermarket tabloids. The overall tenor of political news is negative, if not downright uncivil and vitriolic. Journalists operate under the credo that only bad news is worth reporting where politics is concerned. Citizens are rarely treated to stories about how political institutions are functional or how government officials are admirable public servants, although in reality this is a large part of the story. Instead, news media highlight political discord, malfeasance, and scandal (Bennett, 1996). Further, heavily reported scandals involving public officials today, in keeping with the dominant entertainment news frame, are more likely to involve personal issues than policy problems, as was the case during a prior era of "watchdog journalism" (Sabato, 1991).

10   The public is clearly dissatisfied with the current political media offerings. While many Americans consider themselves to be "news junkies" and express a strong need to keep informed, they don't trust many news sources. A majority of citizens believe that the news is unduly influenced by powerful business and political interests who play into the media's own desire to make profits. Further, they consider the news to be too sensational and scandal-ridden. The public feels that the press is intrusive, and goes too far in invading people's personal lives in the interest of getting a story. Audience members are concerned about the accuracy of reporting, especially as media organizations compete to be the first with a breaking

story (Freedom Forum, 1997; Pew Research Center, 1998). In fact, journalist norms of sourcing and fact-checking largely have become a thing of the past, as the pace of news reporting has accelerated. The credibility of political news is challenged further as questionable sources emerge from the depths of cyberspace to drive the media agenda, as was the case with Matt Drudge during the Clinton/Lewinsky affair.

In addition, the tone and content of political discourse in the 11
forums that promote citizen participation, such as call-in programs and Internet chat rooms, are hardly civil or constructive. Encouraged by hosts driven by audience ratings, political talk has become, in large part, an opportunity for venting rather than an effective discussion forum (Davis, 1997; Owen, 1995). Some scholars, including political theorist Benjamin Barber, go so far as to contend that the electronic "public square" breeds faction, disaffection, and discontent (Starobin, 1996).

It is often difficult in the "new media" age for citizens to sort 12
through the profusion of political material and decide what is useful and what is not. Faced with "data glut," the public tunes out. Frequently, there is much news, but few stories, as multifarious press organizations dwell upon a single theme (Reeves, 1999). In addition, the traditional hierarchy of media organizations, where it was possible to establish the quality of information by the brand name associated with it, is eroding. Political scandals that break in the tabloid press go on to grace the front page of *The New York Times*.

The "new media" environment is still the bastion of society's 13
more privileged members, and has done little to encourage participation among the traditionally unengaged. The newer communication formats, such as talk radio and the Internet, attract audiences from higher socio-economic and educational groups who tend to be politically active in other ways (Graber, 1997; Davis and Owen, 1998). Even as the Internet user base increases[1] and becomes more "ordinary" (Pew Research Center, 1999), it still is not available to millions of citizens without the resources and skills to take part. In some ways, the Internet has widened the political information and participation gap between societal "have's" and "have-not's."

While some observers view the enhanced ability to target 14
particular audiences for political media in the current environment to be an advantage, others consider the increased segmentation of the media market to be problematic. Audience segmentation creates discrete communities of special interests who may lose sight of the greater societal good. Discussion remains confined to separate media spheres of like-minded participants, lessening the ability for a multitude of voices to be heard (Thelen, 1996).

15   For the most part, political and media elites still control the agenda of media forums, and will only go so far to stimulate public discussion and feedback. Call-in radio and television programs frequently use citizen callers as props designed to spark commentary by hosts and guest elites. Political leaders and candidates regularly establish Web sites to publicize their activities and campaigns. These sites contain lots of information, but far fewer opportunities for citizen interaction. Campaign sites, in particular, routinely include mechanisms for recruiting volunteers online and providing updates to interested parties. Few campaign sites contain email or discussion forums, as candidates do not want to address controversial issues that online users might raise.

16   In sum, the "new media" environment offers novel opportunities for democratic politics. "New media" forums have the ability to spark citizen interest, increase awareness and knowledge of public affairs, and prompt political participation. There are signs that this is occurring, as a significant number of people seek out political information online and take part in discussions in electronic space. Still, the democratizing potential of the current mass media system is largely unrealized. Rather than encourage the public to become politically attentive and engaged, the media environment may actually deter involvement. The content and presentational style of much news turns the public off to politics, as the political world appears trivial, scandalous, and nasty.

17   It may be the case that media politics even may be a deterrent to actual political participation. Communications scholar Roderick Hart argues that watching governance has become a substitute for engaging in politics for many people. Electronic communications today leave citizens with the false impression that they are close to politicians, and that taking real steps to gain the attention of elites is unnecessary (Hart, 1994). Similarly, political scientist Robert Putnam contends that attending to media, political or otherwise, takes time away from engaging in other activities, especially community affairs (Putnam, 1995).

Electronic Media and Citizen Attitudes

18   Having examined the current political media context, we now turn to the question of the effects on democratic attitudes. Specifically, we will examine the relationship between electronic communication and citizen knowledge, support for government, and sense of political efficacy. While the jury is still

out, preliminary evidence suggests that electronic media formats, especially those that involve citizen interaction, influence political attitudes in both positive and negative ways.

It has been widely observed that American citizens are traditionally poorly informed about political affairs. The apparent abundance of political information has not translated generally into greater civic knowledge. Nor has the increase in educational attainment over the past three decades corresponded to a commensurate gain in knowledge (Delli Carpini and Keeter, 1996). A variety of reasons have been offered as explanations for this phenomenon. People are too busy to monitor politics. They do not consider politics a priority, as they fail to see the connection to their daily lives. Government and Washington appear remote and are run by political insiders.

Media-related explanations also have been suggested. The news product may be unsuitable to fostering political learning. Even when people are exposed to political news, they process a minuscule amount of information and forget the little that registers within a very short period of time. Political information frequently is presented in a fragmented style which includes little substantive information or context. The negative character and entertainment focus of political news undercuts its significance. Further, sources of political information that present more detailed and substantive perspectives on politics frequently are pitched at more educated and elite audiences, and have an insider orientation.

There is, however, an indication that some citizens may be exhibiting increased levels of political interest and knowledge as a result of their use of newer communication formats. Regular talk radio listeners and callers as well as users of online media resources are significantly more politically informed than the general public (Davis and Owen, 1998). While it may be the case that talk radio and online media audience members are naturally more inclined to seek information, their use of these media enhances the depth and breadth of their knowledge. Talk radio and online media users are more likely to hold more sophisticated and detailed opinions on public policy issues than other citizens. Talk radio listeners, in particular, acknowledge that they gain information from their use of the medium. The talk radio audience also tends to hold more extreme and conservative political views than nonlisteners (Barker, 1998).

Mass communications, particularly electronic media, also have been linked to public evaluations of political institutions and leaders, especially government in Washington. Trust in government had been declining since the 1960s, with a minor reprieve in the early 1980s. Americans' political trust reached

19

20

21

22

historical lows in the 1990s, although confidence in government has begun to climb (Moore, 1999). The high levels of public cynicism have generated concern, as lack of trust can undermine democratic values, weaken community ties, and erode social capital (Putnam, 1995).

23   While not the sole culprit, media have been blamed for exacerbating public distrust of government and politicians, and for diminishing faith in the democratic process. As we have discussed in the previous section, news media give an inordinate amount of attention to political scandal, infighting, and corruption to the exclusion of positive information or issue content. Communications scholars Joseph Cappella and Kathleen Hall Jamieson provide empirical validation of these conjectures. They demonstrate that the press frames political news in terms of political strategies, conflict, and politicians' motives, which are rarely portrayed as legitimate. These standard news frames encourage citizens to question politicians' values and actions, and lead to increased political cynicism (Cappella and Jamieson, 1997).

24   It is reasonable to speculate that the audiences for particular forms of electronic media, especially television and radio call-in programs and online political discussion groups, might be more cynical about government than the general public.

25   The content of these media forums is especially dense with negative messages about government and scathing personal attacks on public officials. President Clinton, in the wake of the bombing of the federal building in Oklahoma City, publically denounced talk radio for promoting a culture of intolerance. However, users of these media are no more likely to distrust government and political leaders than others in society (Davis and Owen, 1998).

26   The final political attitude we examine is political efficacy, which refers to an individual's belief that she or he can influence the political process and successfully reach political leaders. The concept of efficacy is frequently considered in terms of two distinct dimensions. Internal efficacy indicates people's perceptions that they personally have the skills necessary to navigate the political realm successfully. External efficacy deals with whether people believe that the government is responsive to attempts by ordinary citizens like themselves to affect government (Abramson, 1983). Efficacy is closely linked to political trust, as those who are most supportive of government are more likely to believe they can influence the political world. Citizens who have a strong sense of political efficacy also are more inclined to participate in public affairs and to take part in community service activities.

As is the case with trust in government, Americans' collective   27
sense of political efficacy, both internal and external, has been
on the decline since the Watergate era. Individuals do not believe that they can make a difference in politics. They perceive
that politics is too complicated for them to understand. They
do not feel that their vote counts. Further, the public senses
that the government doesn't care what the people think, and
that average citizens have no say in political affairs.

Considering whether citizens' sense of political efficacy is in   28
any way influenced by the "new media" environment is an interesting proposition, especially in light of the populist potential of particular media formats. Several scenarios are possible.
It may be the case that citizens who already are strongly effica-
cious will be attracted to interactive media and use them to enhance their political presence. Alternatively, these formats may
appeal to people who do not feel that they can influence government or political leaders via conventional channels, such as
voting, letter writing, or circulating petitions. They may turn to
mass media forums out of a sense of frustration. They may
perceive that the interactive forums will be receptive to political outsiders like themselves. It is also possible that the "new
media" environment may have little to do with fostering or undermining citizens' sense of efficacy.

There is some support for the contention that interactive   29
communication formats may heighten political efficacy. People
who regularly go online and participate in political discussions
have a more positive view of their ability to play a meaningful
role in politics than the general public. However, participants
in online political discussions may begin with a strong sense of
efficacy, and their participation serves to reinforce this predisposition. Studies of the talk radio audience permit a more direct test of electronic media's ability to enhance efficacy.
Research conducted in 1993 indicated that talk radio callers
and listeners had a strong sense of civic duty and commitment,
but lower levels of political efficacy than other citizens (Owen,
1996). By 1996, the talk radio audience's feelings of internal efficacy far exceeded those of nonlisteners. Talk radio devotees
also evidenced an increase in their sense of external efficacy.
Over time, regular talk radio listeners acquired a more favorable view of their own political power through their experience
with the medium (Davis and Owen, 1998). Talk radio hosts do
much to instill this perception in their listeners. Audience
members' appreciation for the power of political talk is further
reinforced by the fact that political leaders will appear as
guests on talk radio programs and publicly acknowledge their
significance.

The Next Generations' Attitudes

30   We have explored the effects of the "new media" age on adult
     political attitudes. The final issue we will address is: What in-
     fluence does electronic media have on young people's political
     orientations? In the current media environment, the prolifera-
     tion of communication sources coupled with the conflation of
     political and entertainment content renders it more likely that
     children and adolescents will be exposed to political informa-
     tion, either deliberately or inadvertently. Further, the nature of
     this content paints an unflattering picture of government and
     political leaders. Is this media-defined negativity reflected in
     young people's attitudes?

31   An analysis of the effects of the Clinton/Lewinsky affair on
     young people's attitudes provides some insights into the
     media's role in socializing citizens to politics. Early studies of
     children's relationship to the political world indicated that
     their impressions about the President played a central role in
     constructing their images of government, and formed the basis
     of general support for the democratic polity. However, children
     are able to make distinctions between the presidential person-
     ality and the presidential role. This distinction became clear
     during Watergate, as children maintained respect for govern-
     ment, while registering their disappointment in President
     Nixon (Easton and Dennis, 1969).

32   Young people's attitudes toward the President and the politi-
     cal system are substantially more negative in the wake of the
     events surrounding the Clinton impeachment than they have
     been at any time during this century. In fact, children evalu-
     ated President Clinton far more harshly than did their parents,
     as only 43% of the youth sample of a Gallup poll held a favor-
     able view compared to 55% of their parents. Further, young
     people strongly believed that President Clinton's conduct was
     wrong, and that the Senate should have voted to remove him
     from office. This perception again diverged from that of adults,
     as 47% of young people felt that Clinton should not remain as
     President as opposed to 36% of adults.[2]

33   Young people received most of their information about
     Watergate from personal sources—parents, teachers, and
     sometimes peers. In contrast, parents reported overwhelm-
     ingly that their children received most of their information
     about the Clinton/Lewinsky matter from television. The media
     set the agenda for interpersonal discussion, as children's expo-
     sure to press reports prompted them to raise the issue with
     parents and teachers.[3] The media's pervasive, sensational,

tabloid-style coverage of the Clinton affair made it difficult to shelter children from the scandal. Some children were attentive to the news coverage because of its similarity to entertainment television programs and films. Children's interest in the event was amplified by the personal nature of the scandal. Further, the Clinton impeachment was framed by the media as a matter of the President lying, an issue to which young people could relate (Owen and Dennis, 1999).

While young people had highly negative opinions of   34 President Clinton, their evaluations of government were somewhat more generous. However, young people's views of government and politics today are markedly more negative than during Watergate. These findings are not encouraging, as support for political institutions and processes tends to dissipate with age. Young people have come to accept that scandalous behavior is the norm for political leaders. In addition, few children and adolescents dream of becoming President. Only 26% of young people polled by Gallup had presidential aspirations, which is far lower than the figure for prior generations.

Conclusion

In weighing the benefits and detriments of the effects of elec-   35 tronic media on democratic attitudes, it would appear that the bad transcends the good. There appear to be some gains in political knowledge and efficacy among segments of the public, particularly those who have regular experiences with the most populist and interactive forms of media. However, the audience profile for talk radio and online media users, especially, indicates that these are people from the higher economic and educational echelons who already are politically engaged in other ways. The "new media" environment does little to reach those whose political voice is muffled.

More troubling is the evidence that the current media envi-   36 ronment appears to undermine citizens' faith in government officials and political institutions, as well as in the democratic political process. This trend is suggested for both young people and adults. While it is important, indeed essential, for citizens to maintain a healthy skepticism about government to assure that officials do not abuse power, unbridled cynicism is detrimental to democracy. That this cynicism is couched in terms of the politics of scandal as presented by mass media is cause for concern.

NOTES

1. Recent reports indicate that approximately one third of American homes have direct access to the Internet. Approximately forty percent of the public has access to the Internet at work, twenty percent at school, and fifteen percent someplace else. Two thirds of all households have access to the Internet in some location. Those who do not have access, who mostly hail from the lower social classes, report feeling left out and at a disadvantage (Withlin Worldwide, 1999).
2. The survey consisted of 1,022 adults and 305 young people aged 11 to 17, and was conducted by the Gallup organization on February 4–8, 1999.
3. The Pew Research Center for the People & the Press conducted a survey of parents' reaction to the Clinton/Lewinsky scandal on September 19–23, 1998. The sample consisted of 597 parents with children between the ages of 8 and 17.

REFERENCES

Abramson, Jeffrey, F. Christopher Arterton, and Gary R. Orren. 1988. *The Electronic Commonwealth: The Impact of New Media Technologies on Democratic Policies* (New York, NY: Basic Books).

Abramson, Paul R. 1983. *Political Attitudes in America* (San Francisco, CA: W. H. Freeman).

Barker, David C. "Rush to Action: Political Talk Radio and Health Care (un)Reform," *Political Communication*, vol. 15, pp. 83–98.

Bennett, W. Lance. 1996. *News: The Politics of Illusion*, 3rd edition (White Plains, NY: Longman).

Cappella, Joseph C., and Kathleen Hall Jamieson. 1997. *Spiral of Cynicism* (New York, NY: Oxford UP).

Craig, Stephen C. 1996. "The Angry Voter and Popular Discontent in the 1990s," in Stephen C. Craig, ed. *Broken Contract: Changing Relationships Between Americans and Their Government* (Boulder, CO: Westview Press), pp. 46–66.

Davis, Richard, and Diana Owen. 1998. *New Media and American Politics* (New York, NY: Oxford UP).

Davis, Richard. 1997. "Understanding Broadcast Political Talk," *Political Communication*, vol. 14: 323–332.

Delli Carpini, Michael X., and Scott Keeter. 1996. *What Americans Know About Politics and Why It Matters* (New Haven, CT: Yale UP).

Easton, David, and Jack Dennis. 1969. *Children in the Political System: The Origins of Political Legitimacy* (New York, NY: McGraw-Hill Book Company).

Freedom Forum. 1997. "News Junkies, News Critics: How Americans Use the News and What They Think About It," *Presswatch*, March 7 (New York, NY: Freedom Forum Media Studies Center).

Graber, Doris A. 1997. "Media as Opinion Resources: Are the 1990s a New Ball Game?" In Barbara Norrander and Clyde Wilcox, eds. *Understanding Public Opinion* (Washington, D.C.: CQ Press).

Grossman, Larry K. 1995. *The Electronic Commonwealth* (New York, NY: Penguin Books).

Hart, Roderick P. 1994. *Seducing America* (New York, NY: Oxford UP).

Herbst, Susan. 1995. "On Electronic Public Space: Talk Shows in Theoretical Perspective," *Political Communication*, 12, 3, pp. 263–274.

Moore, David W. 1999. "Public Trust in Federal Government Remains High," *Gallup News Service*, January 8 (www.gallup.com/poll/releases/pr990108.asp).

Neuman, W. Russell. 1991. *The Future of the Mass Audience* (New York, NY: Cambridge University Press).

Owen, Diana. 1995. "Who's Talking? Who's Listening? The New Politics of Radio and Television Talk Shows," in Stephen C. Craig, ed. *Broken Contract: Changing Relationships Between Citizens and Their Government* (Boulder, CO: Westview Press).

Owen, Diana, and Jack Denni. 1999. "The Clinton Legacy for Preadult Political Learning," *The Public Perspetive*, June.

Pew Research Center for the People & the Press. 1998. "Event-Driven News Audiences/Internet News Takes Off: Annual Media Consumption Survey," April (Washington, D.C.: Pew Research Center).

Pew Research Center for the People & the Press. 1999. "The Internet News Audience Goes Ordinary," January 14 (Washington, D.C.: Pew Research Center).

Putnam, Robert D. 1995. "Bowling Alone: America's Declining Social Capital," *Journal of Democracy*, 6, pp. 65–78.

Reeves, Richard. 1999. "Dumbing Down the News," *Uexpress*, Universal Press Syndicate (www.uexpress.com).

Sabato, Larry J. *Feeding Frenzy: How Attack Journalism Has Transformed American Politics* (New York, NY: The Free Press).

Schudson, Michael. 1978. *Discovering the News* (New York, NY: Basic Books).

Schudson, Michael. 1998. *The Good Citizen* (New York, NY: The Free Press).

Starobin, Paul. 1996. "On the Square," *National Journal*, May 25, pp. 1145–49.

Thelen, David. 1996. *Becoming Citizens in the Age of Television* (Chicago, IL: U of Chicago P).

Wirthlin Worldwide. 1999. "The Internet: How Are You Connected?" *The Wirthlin Report*, February, 1999.

Kimberly Meltzer, Brett A. Mueller,
and Russell M. Tisinger

ENGAGING THE ELECTRONIC ELECTORATE

Though in one sense, "media" are just the forms used to dis-seminate ideas, it is important to remember that the type of medium used certainly affects the way we receive those ideas.

*That is the starting point for this essay by Kimberly Meltzer,
Brett A. Mueller, and Russell M. Tisinger, who investigate how
people interact with the information that they gather online.
The essay below, written by three graduate students at the
Annenberg School of Communication, was first presented at
the International Communication Association. As you read,
you might note not only the results that these researchers at-
tained, but also the methods that they used to assure a valid
study. These methods of collecting and interpreting data are
typical of the social sciences, so thinking more about the ways
in which this quantitative data is handled, and how it is incorporated into the article's argument, can teach you a great deal
about writing in this field. You might also consider how this
information contributes to the wider conversation about new
media's influence on political attitudes.*

1   The Internet has been hailed as a medium with the potential
for increasing both citizen information about and participation in politics. Not only does it facilitate interaction with others across long distances, but it also offers a convenient way of
searching for and obtaining information. Two of the chief reasons that people use the Internet to get political information
are to obtain guidance about and to surveil candidates.[1]

2   This research resonates with the results of surveys of voters
in both the 2000 and the 2002 elections. In October and
November of 2000, nearly seven in ten of those who went online for election news sought information on the candidates'
positions on the issues.[2] In 2002, 79 percent of those who used
the Internet for politics sought information about candidates'
records. A majority of voters who went online for political information wanted to compare candidates' stances on specific
issues of interest. Fifty-seven percent of those who used the
Internet for politics visited Web sites that provided them with
information about specific issues such as the environment,
gun control, abortion, and health care.[3]

3   As more people obtain information from the Internet (on a
typical day in December 2000, fifty-eight million Americans
were logging on—an increase of nine million people from six
months earlier, according to the Pew Internet and American
Life Project),[4] it becomes important to understand how citizens
interact with political information online. Political information
conveyed on the Internet, like political information transmitted
through any medium, is most helpful when it is both engaging
and educational. Social scientists are starting to understand
how people interact with political information online but have

not developed clear guidelines for presenting online political information that effectively informs and engages people.

In trying to increase the public's knowledge about politics 4 and participation in civic life, previous research indicated that the local level was an appropriate place to begin. Friedland argues for starting at the community level, and building democracy upward and outward from there.[5] Kaniss also has studied the role of the media in the construction of local identity in the modern American city and claims that "local media are driven to focus on issues with the symbolic capital necessary to unite a fragmented metropolitan audience that comprises the extremely different urban environments of city and suburb."[6] This claim suggests that local television newscasts might be in a unique position to reach citizens at the level where information about politics and civic activity will resonate in the community.

How can local broadcasters use the Internet to engage their 5 audiences in civic issues? Results from the Covering Politics On-Air and Online project, a partnership among ten local broadcast stations across the country, the Annenberg Public Policy Center (APPC) at the University of Pennsylvania, and the Radio-Television News Directors Foundation, and made possible by a grant from the Pew Charitable Trusts, offer some direction.

The Project

The ten stations that participated in the project were 6 WFAA, Dallas; KCNC, Denver; KCCI, Des Moines; WCCO, Minneapolis; WKMG, Orlando; WCAU, Philadelphia; WTAE, Pittsburgh; KGW, Portland, Oregon; KTVU, San Francisco and Oakland; and KELO, Sioux Falls, South Dakota. Another project preceded this one and involved a 944-person experiment administered by Northwest Data Services in Eugene, Oregon, as part of the Engaging the Electronic Electorate (E3) project of the Annenberg Public Policy Center. This project resulted in the development and refinement of a number of online election templates that subjects found most likeable and informative.

These templates, some of which were variations of formats 7 used by the Web sites of the Center for Public Integrity, Democracy Net, National Journal, the Center for Responsive Politics, and state governments during the 2000 presidential election, were made available to partner stations for use on their Web sites. APPC staff programmed the templates and offered technical assistance and support to stations as they put the templates online. The APPC encouraged partner stations to consider using at least four templates and to conduct a moderated online chat. The four templates the APPC most encouraged stations to use were the issue grid (a matrix comparing candidates on relevant issues), the ad watch (an examination of the claims within a political advertisement), the candidate biography, and the National Voter Registration form. In many cases, stations also chose to use several other templates, including a campaign finance template, an election-knowledge quiz template, a template with standardized information about how to judge and pick candidates, and a template describing how to use the voting machines installed in each market.

8   Stations were required to integrate their on-air and online election coverage. They did this most noticeably by conducting ad watches both on-air and online. When some stations discovered that the ad watch template could be used to analyze claims made in debates, they created "debate watch" features that ran on-air and online as well (see Appendix). Stations were required to promote their improved online election coverage during their newscasts. Some of the innovative and interesting ways in which they did this coincided with bumps in Web site traffic.

What Worked Best

9   Data were collected from both prewave and postwave surveys conducted in three of the ten markets. The surveys were administered to participants by random digit dialing in Nielsen-identified demographic market areas in Philadelphia, Pittsburgh, and Minneapolis by LHK Partners. Table 1 provides data on sample size, response rates, and recontact rates. Focus groups were also conducted in two of those markets. The study identified design features for political information that encourage learning and engagement.

10   Three basic formats emerged as most engaging and enlightening: (1) single-page side-by-side comparisons, (2) conventional Web site designs, and (3) streaming video of political advertisements accompanied by fact-checked reviews of the advertisements (ad watches). (See examples of these features in the Appendix.) The results complement a growing literature on how people interact with different presentation formats online. There is evidence that Internet users gravitate to information that facilitates comparison and contrast,[7] is presented in a relatively simple format that is easy to use,[8] and verifies the accuracy of claims in political advertising.[9]

11   Data from the experiment in which we tested our templates revealed that overall subjects preferred and were engaged by

TABLE 1 Sample Size, Response Rates, and Recontact
Rates for Participants in Prewave and Postwave Surveys

	PHILADELPHIA	PITTSBURGH	MINNEAPOLIS	MINNEAPOLIS INDEPENDENT SAMPLE
Prewave sample size	1,449	1,393	1,354	
Prewave response rate	20.3%	24.7%	33.4%	
Postwave sample size	920	723	761	332
Postwave recontact rate	71.2%	62.7%	65.8%	31.1% (response rate)

the single-page issue grid format.[10] In contrast to the multi-page formats, subjects rated the issue grid content higher, said they were less bored by the issue grid, and said they were more likely to return to it when online. These findings resonate with the Covering Politics On-Air and Online data gleaned from focus groups and surveys of voters during the 2002 campaign. Without prompting and before viewing stations' Web sites, viewers expressed a desire for a grid format to allow easy comparison of candidates across issues. Younger participants wanted a format that would allow them to look only at topics about which they were concerned. They stressed their interest in using the grid to educate themselves about political issues. They wanted the grid format because it would allow simple and easy comparisons.

The highest percentage of survey respondents in all three markets (34.5 percent in Philadelphia, 33.1 percent in Pittsburgh, and 32.6 percent in Minneapolis) also said that of eleven types of political information available online, they were most likely to access a candidate's stance on specific issues. This was also the number one feature respondents reported actually visiting online. In at least two cases (KCNC in Denver and WCCO in Minneapolis) issue grids were the most visited features on station Web sites, as measured by page views.

12

13   (The stations with whom we worked were contractually-
obligated to provide daily homepage and election page traffic
for the period from September 1 through November 14. The
APPC hosted part or all of the election sections of KTVU,
WCCO, and KCNC on its server. Due to this in-house server
hosting, we were able to obtain detailed breakdowns of traffic
to the individual templates and features used on these stations'
election sites. Traffic to the election sites the APPC hosted on
its server were calculated by hand from detailed lists of hits to
URL addresses. This hand-calculation was intended to "clean"
the data on traffic hits to images, thus making the daily tallies
as equal as possible to the page view calculations used by the
other stations. Differences in how accurate the stations were in
reporting page views could not be controlled.)

14   Web traffic analysis showed increases in home page and politics page traffic on partner stations as election day approached.
Home page traffic increases were generally gradual, while most
stations experienced sharp increases in politics page traffic.
Spikes in politics page traffic were generally noted around the
time of major political events such as candidate debates, presidential visits to the state, primary elections, and in one case, the
death of a candidate. We also found traffic increases to coincide
with the promotion of politics page features that appeared during on-air broadcasts. For instance, most stations experienced
uncharacteristically high Web traffic near and on the voter registration deadline for their states. Most stations promoted their
online voter registration feature in the days approaching this
deadline. It is not intuitive that a local broadcast station Web
site would carry online voter registration forms. This suggests
that the increase in Web traffic that accompanied voter registration deadlines was attributable in large part to the promotion and presence of voter registration forms on the stations'
Web sites.

15   It is also noteworthy that politics page Web traffic generally
did not return to its previous levels following increases attributable to political events and promotions but rather plateaued
at a higher level than before. It appears that political events
and promotions may act as gateways to getting users interested in the politics section of a station's Web site. That is,
some users respond positively to finding useful one-time information on a Web site by returning for more information in the
future. That trend, coupled with a general interest in the election, contributed to the steady increases seen on stations' politics pages through late September and October, as election day
approached. Analysis of individual template use on the four

stations' sites for which these data were available revealed that traffic to particular templates peaked with events of particular interest. For example, senate and gubernatorial debates coincided with increased traffic to candidate issue grids and candidate biographies. And unsurprisingly, voter registration deadlines coincided with higher traffic to voter registration form templates.

Individual template use varied by market: 16

KCNC site users in Denver were particularly interested in candidate biographies and issue grids and accessed the voter registration template in high numbers. 17

Minneapolis users visited WCCO's campaign finance information with greater frequency than did users who accessed that type of information in other markets, and they visited candidate issue grids in high numbers. 18

Portland users came to KGW's site for polling information in high numbers. San Francisco user traffic suggests a particular interest in KTVU's presentation of ballot issues. We hypothesize that these variations in individual template traffic by market reflect: differences in user interests attributable to demographics and regional culture, differences in the interest some races generated (for instance, California's governor race was widely considered uncompetitive, so users turned their attention to ballot issues), variations in features provided by some stations (KGW was one of only a handful of stations to conduct polling), and differences in how strongly stations promoted particular features during their broadcasts. 19

In addition to the APPC templates, other innovations that stations made seemed to be well-received, such as KTVU's ballot initiative pages and KGW's polling feature, KCCI's quiz, WFAA's voter registration card guide, and WKMG's polling place locator. Although template level traffic is not available for these innovations, they fit our normative ideals for online political features in that they were simply designed and they presented straightforward, useful information that presumably met their audiences' political information needs and interests. 20

More Good News for Broadcasters

Survey data regarding media use were analyzed prior to and immediately following the 2002 midterm elections to determine whether television was being displaced by the Internet as a source of political information. In analyzing the relationship between television use and the use of online sources, evidence 21 did not suggest that displacement was occurring for political information over the course of the election, despite increased on-air cross-promotion efforts. There was no relationship between the use of television and the use of the Internet for obtaining political information.[11]

Building on the Successes Achieved

22   A normative desire to extend solid political coverage to the periods between election seasons, coupled with the discovery of a great interest on the part of station audiences in candidate issue stances, led the APPC to propose involving four partner stations in a postelection addition to the project that would track the progress of promises made by winning candidates during the 2002 election. The stations selected—KCNC in Denver, KCCI in Des Moines, WKMG in Orlando, and KTVU in San Francisco and Oakland—were charged with designing and programming a promise-tracking Web site feature, and with researching candidate promises and progress on those promises.

23   Partner stations were encouraged to develop these promise-tracking feature designs independently, whereas in the Covering Politics On-Air and Online project, stations were limited to presenting information in the templates the APPC had designed. This allowed the partner stations to innovate and design features that they felt would best meet the needs and desires of their particular audiences, given the preliminary research they had from us suggesting the use of single-page side-by-side comparisons, conventional designs, and the integration of streaming video into reporters' fact-checking of candidate statements as good places to start.

24   Analysis of the effectiveness of these features is just beginning, but early observations suggest that this might be a viable way to keep news organizations and audiences interested in and informed about politics throughout the down time between elections.

25   KTVU has had plenty to present in its feature, given the recall news in California, while KCNC and WKMG have tried innovative design strategies in line with the principles that evolved from our preliminary research suggestions.

26   Local broadcasters have a number of tools and ideas at their disposal for engaging audiences in politics and other civics activities. The results of our research indicate that there might be some basic principles local broadcasters and others can use to

guide their selection of engaging material and the best ways to present it, both on-air and online.

NOTES

1. Kaye, B. K., and Johnson, T. J. "Online and in the Know: Uses and Gratifications of the Web for Political Information." *Journal of Broadcasting & Electronic Media*, 2002, *46*(1), 54–76.
2. "What Americans Think: Election Information via the Internet." *Spectrum: The Journal of State Government*, Jan. 1, 2001, pp. 30–31.
3. Hotline. "Internet Politicking: You've Got E-Mail." Mar. 21, 2003.
4. Web site of the Pew Internet & American Life Project [www. Pewinternet.org].
5. Friedland, L. A. "Communication, Community, and Democracy: Toward a Theory of the Communicatively Integrated Community." *Communication Research*, 2001, 28(4), 464–506.
6. Kaniss, P. *Making Local News*. University of Chicago Press: 1991.
7. Jamieson, K. H. *Everything You Think You Know About Politics and Why You're Wrong*. (2nd ed.) New York: Basic Books, 2000; Lau, R., and Redlawsk, D. "An Experimental Study of Information Search, Memory, and Decision-Making During a Political Campaign." In J. Kuklinski (ed.), *Citizens and Politics: Perspectives from Political Psychology*. New York: Cambridge University Press, 2001; Einhorn, H. J. "Use of Nonlinear, Noncompensatory Models as a Function of Task and Amount of Information." *Organizational Behavior and Human Performance*, 1971, *6*, 1–27; Abelson, R. P., and Levi, A. "Decision Making and Decision Theory." In G. Lindzey and E. Aronson (eds.), *The Handbook of Social Psychology* (3rd ed., vol. 1). New York: Random House, 1985.
8. Nielsen, J. "What is Usability?" [http://www.zdnet.com/devhead/ stories/articles/0,4413,2137671,00.html], Sept. 29, 1998; Nielsen, J. *Designing Web Usability: The Practice of Simplicity*. New York: New Riders, 1999; Humphreys, L. "Usability: Analysis, Critique and Recommendations." Unpublished manuscript, Annenberg School for Communication, University of Pennsylvania, Philadelphia, 2001; Palmer, J. "Designing for Web Site Usability." *Computer*, 2002, *35*(7), 102.
9. Cappella, J., and Jamieson, K. H. *Spiral of Cynicism: The Press and the Public Good*. New York: Oxford University Press, 1997.
10. Tisinger, R., Meltzer, K., Jomini, T., Mueller, B., and Gans, R. "The Effective Presentation of Political Information on the Internet." Unpublished manuscript, Annenberg Public Policy Center, University of Pennsylvania, Philadelphia, Aug. 2003.
11. Jomini, T., Mueller, B., Meltzer, K., Tisinger, R., and Gans, R. "Displacement Between the Internet and Television." Unpublished manuscript, Annenberg Public Policy Center, University of Pennsylvania, Philadelphia, Aug. 2003.

APPENDIX

Following are examples of online election coverage features used by the stations that participated in the Covering Politics On-Air and Online project.

Ad watch. Political advertisements accompanied by fact-checked reviews of claims.
Source: *KCCI-TV Des Moines. Reprinted with permission.*

Debate watch. Candidates' most important claims, accuracy ratings, and links to sources that helped viewers research relevant issues, listed by KCCI after the first debate of the Iowa Senate race.
Source: *KCCI-TV Des Moines. Reprinted with permission.*

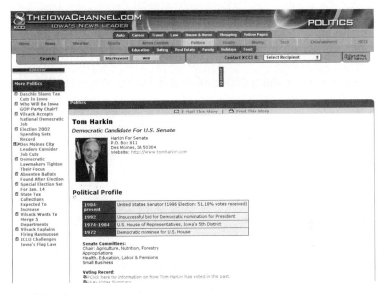

Candidate bio.
Source: *KCCI-TV Des Moines. Reprinted with permission.*

Matt Welch

BLOGWORLD
AND ITS GRAVITY

A weblog or "blog" is an online discussion board. It is different than a chat room or Instant Messenger because it is "asynchronous"—that is, the participants in the discussion don't have to all be engaged in the conversation at the same time. It is, rather, a type of electronic bulletin board, where people go to read messages left by others and then respond with their own thoughts. Those messages are usually "threaded" by topic, so that someone entering the conversation can read through the whole interchange that preceded them before jumping in; much like the story of the parlor by Kenneth Burke discussed in the Preface to *this book, when one enters a blog, one usually lays back for a while and listens (or "lurks," to use the Internet lingo) before chiming in. In the essay below, Matt Welch investigates the ways that "blogs" have influenced the dissemination of information and opinions in a post-9/11 world. The* Columbia Journalism Review, *where this was first published, studies all aspects of the media to keep the public informed about its influence. Welch, who authored this essay, is also the associate editor for the online publication* Reason Magazine. *The ways in which weblogs and other activist websites use visual, as well as verbal, persuasion can be explored in the "Visual Conversations" section included in this part of the book.*

1   This February, I attended my first Association of Alternative Newsweeklies conference, in the great media incubator of San Francisco. It's impossible to walk a single block of that storied town without feeling the ghosts of great contrarian media innovators past: Hearst and Twain, Hinckle and Wenner, Rossetto and Talbot. But after twelve hours with the AAN, a much different reality set in: never in my life have I seen a more conformist gathering of journalists.

2   All the newspapers looked the same—same format, same fonts, same columns complaining about the local daily, same sex advice, same five-thousand-word hole for the cover story. The people were largely the same, too: all but maybe 2 percent of the city-slicker journalists in attendance were white; the vast majority were either Boomer hippies or Gen X slackers. Several asked me the exact same question with the same suspicious looks on their faces: "So . . . what's your alternative experience?"

3   At the bar, I started a discussion about what specific attributes qualified these papers, and the forty-seven-year-old publishing genre that spawned them, to continue meriting the adjective "alternative." Alternative to what? To the straight-laced "objectivity" and pyramid-style writing of daily newspapers? New Journalists and other narrative storytellers crashed those gates long ago. Alternative to society's oppressive intolerance toward deviant behavior? Tell it to the Osbournes, as they watch *Queer Eye for the Straight Guy*. Something to do with corporate ownership? Not unless "alternative" no longer applies to *Village Voice Media* (owned in part by *Goldman Sachs*) or the New Times chain (which has been involved in some brutal acquisition and liquidation deals). Someone at the table lamely offered up "a sense of community," but Fox News could easily clear that particular bar.

4   No, it must have something to do with political slant—or, to be technically accurate, political correctness. Richard Karpel,

the AAN executive director, joined the conversation, so I put him on the spot: Of all the weeklies his organization had rejected for membership on political grounds, which one was the best editorially? The *Independent Florida Sun*, he replied. Good-looking paper, some sharp writing but, well, it was just too friendly toward the church. "And if there's anything we all agree on," Karpel said with a smile, "it's that we're antichurch."

I assumed he was joking—that couldn't be all we have left   5
from the legacy of Norman Mailer, Art Kunkin, Paul Krassner, and my other childhood heroes, could it? Then later I looked up the AAN's Web site to read the admission committee's rejection notes for the *Florida Sun* (which was excluded by a vote of 9–2). "The right-wing church columnist has no place in AAN," explained one judge. "All the God-and-flag shit disturbs me," wrote another. "Weirdly right-wing," chimed a third.

The original alternative papers were not at all this politically   6
monochromatic, despite entering the world at a time when Lenny Bruce was being prosecuted for obscenity, Tom Dooley was proselytizing for American intervention in Vietnam, and Republicans ruled the nation's editorial pages. Dan Wolf, cofounder of the trailblazing *Village Voice*, loved to throw darts at what he called "the dull pieties of official liberalism," and founding editors like Mailer were forever trying to tune their antennae to previously undetected political frequencies.

The dull pieties of official progressivism is one of many at-   7
tributes that show how modern alt weeklies have strayed from what made them alternative in the first place. The papers once embraced amateur writers; now they are firmly established in the journalistic pecking order, with the salaries and professional standards to match. They once championed the slogan "never trust anyone over thirty"; now their average reader is over forty and aging fast. They have become so ubiquitous in cities over a certain size, during decades when so many other new media formats have sprung up (cable television, newsletters, talk radio, business journals, Web sites), that the very notion that they represent a crucial "alternative" to a monolithic journalism establishment now strains credulity.

But there still exists a publishing format that manages to em-   8
body all these lost qualities, and more—the Weblog. The average blog, needless to say, pales in comparison to a 1957 issue of the *Voice*, or a 1964 *Los Angeles Free Press*, or a 2003 Lexington, Kentucky, *ACE Weekly*, for that matter. But that's missing the point. Blogging technology has, for the first time in history, given the average Jane the ability to write, edit, design, and publish her own editorial product—to be read and responded to by millions of people, potentially—for around $0 to $200 a

year. It has begun to deliver on some of the wild promises about the Internet that were heard in the 1990s. Never before have so many passionate outsiders—hundreds of thousands, at minimum—stormed the ramparts of professional journalism.

9   And these amateurs, especially the ones focusing on news and current events, are doing some fascinating things. Many are connecting intimately with readers in a way reminiscent of old-style metro columnists or the liveliest of the New Journalists. Others are staking the narrowest of editorial claims as their own—appellate court rulings, new media proliferation in Tehran, the intersection of hip-hop and libertarianism—and covering them like no one else. They are forever fact-checking the daylights out of truth-fudging ideologues like Ann Coulter and Michael Moore, and sifting through the biases of the *BBC* and Bill O'Reilly, often while cheerfully acknowledging and/or demonstrating their own lopsided political sympathies. At this instant, all over the world, bloggers are busy popularizing under-appreciated print journalists (like *Chicago Sun-Times* columnist Mark Steyn), pumping up stories that should be getting more attention (like the Trent Lott debacle), and perhaps most excitingly of all, committing impressive, spontaneous acts of decentralized journalism.

Blogging's Big Bang

10   Every significant new publishing phenomenon has been midwifed by a great leap forward in printing technology. The movable-type printing press begat the Gutenberg Bible, which begat the Renaissance. Moving from rags to pulp paved the way for Hearst and Pulitzer. The birth of alternative newspapers coincided almost perfectly with the development of the offset press. Laser printers and desktop publishing ushered in the newsletter and the 'zine, and helped spawn the business journal.

11   When it burst onto the scene just ten years ago, the World Wide Web promised to be an even cheaper version of desktop publishing. And for many people it was, but you still had to learn HTML coding, which was inscrutable enough to make one long for the days of typesetting and paste-up. By the late 1990s, I owned a few Web domains and made a living writing about online journalism, yet if I really needed to publish something on my own, I'd print up a Word file and take it down to the local copy shop. Web publishing was theoretically possible and cheap (if you used a hosting service like Tripod), but it just wasn't easy for people as dull-witted as I.

12   In August 1999, Pyra Labs changed all that, with a product called Blogger (responsible, as much as anything, for that terrible four-letter word). As much of the world knows by now,

"Weblog" is usually defined as a Web site where information is updated frequently and presented in reverse chronological order (newest stuff on top). Typically, each post contains one and often several hyperlinks to other Web sites and stories, and usually there is a standing list of links to the author's favorite bookmarks. Pyra labs, since bought out by *Google*, had a revolutionary insight that made all this popular: every technological requirement of Web publishing—graphic design, simple coding for things like links, hosting—is a barrier to entry, keeping non-techies out; why not remove them? Blogger gave users a for-dummies choice of templates, an easy-to-navigate five-minute registration process, and (perhaps best of all) Web hosting. All for free. You didn't even need to buy your own domain; simply make sure joesixpack.blogspot.com wasn't taken, pick a template, and off you go.

The concept took off, and new blogging companies like   13
Livejournal, UserLand, and Movable Type scrambled to compete. Blogger cofounders Evan Williams, Paul Bausch, and Meg Hourihan, along with Web designer Jason Kottke, and tech writer Rebecca Blood—these were the stars of the first major mainstream-media feature about blogging, a November 2000 *New Yorker* story by Rebecca Mead, who christened the phenomenon "the CB radio of the Dave Eggers generation."

Like just about everything else, blogging changed forever   14
on September 11, 2001. The destruction of the World Trade Center and the attack on the Pentagon created a huge appetite on the part of the public to be part of The Conversation, to vent and analyze and publicly ponder or mourn. Many, too, were unsatisfied with what they read and saw in the mainstream media. Glenn Reynolds, proprietor of the wildly popular InstaPundit.com blog, thought the mainstream analysis was terrible. "All the talking heads . . . kept saying that 'we're gonna have to grow up, we're gonna have to give up a lot of our freedoms,'" he says. "Or it was the 'Why do they hate us' sort of teeth-gnashing. And I think there was a deep dissatisfaction with that." The daily op-ed diet of Column left and Column Right often fell way off the mark. "It's time for the United Nations to get the hell out of town. And take with it CNN war-slut Christiane Amanpour," the *New York Post*'s Andrea Peyser seethed on September 21. "We forgive you; we reject vengeance," Colman McCarthy whimpered to the terrorists in the *Los Angeles Times* September 17. September 11 was the impetus for my own blog (mattwelch.com/warblog.html). Jeff Jarvis, who was trapped in the WTC dust cloud on September 11, started his a few days later. "I had a personal story I needed to tell," said Jarvis, a former *San Francisco Examiner* columnist, founding editor of *Entertainment Weekly*, and current

president and creative director of Advance.net, which is the Internet wing of the Conde Nast empire. "Then lo and behold! I discovered people were linking to me and talking about my story, so I joined this great conversation."

15   He wasn't alone. Reynolds, a hyper-kinetic University of Tennessee law professor and occasional columnist who pro-duces techno records in his spare time, had launched InstaPundit the month before. On September 11, his traffic jumped from 1,600 visitors to almost 4,200; now it averages 100,000 per weekday. With his prolific posting pace—dozens of links a day, each with comments ranging from a word to sev-eral paragraphs—and a deliberate ethic of driving traffic to new blogs from all over the political spectrum, Reynolds quickly became the "Blogfather" of a newly coined genre of sites: the warblogs. "I think people were looking for context, they were looking for stuff that wasn't dumb," he said. "They were looking for stuff that seemed to them to be consistent with how Americans ought to respond to something like this."

16   There had been plenty of news-and-opinion Weblogs previously—from political journalists such as Joshua Micah Marshall, Mickey Kaus, Andrew Sullivan, and Virginia Postrel; not to mention "amateurs" like Matt Drudge. But September 11 drew unpaid nonprofessionals into the current-events fray. And like the first alternative publishers, who eagerly sought out and formed a network with like-minded mavericks across the coun-try, the post-September 11 Webloggers spent considerable energy propping up their new comrades and encouraging their readers to join the fun. I'd guess 90 percent of my most vocal early read-ers have gone on to start sites of their own. In April 2002 Reynolds asked InstaPundit readers to let him know if he had in-spired any of them to start their own blogs. Nearly two hundred wrote in. (Imagine two hundred people deciding to become a columnist just because Maureen Dowd was so persuasive.) Meanwhile, Blogger alone has more than 1.5 million registered users, and Livejournal reports 1.2 million. No one knows how many active blogs there are worldwide, but Blogcount (yes, a blog that counts blogs) guesses between 2.4 million and 2.9 million. Freedom of the press belongs to nearly 3 million people.

What's the Point?

17   So what have these people contributed to journalism? Four things: personality, eyewitness testimony, editorial filtering, and uncounted gigabytes of new knowledge.

"Why are Weblogs popular?" asks Jarvis, whose company   18
has launched four dozen of them, ranging from beachcams on
the Jersey shore to a temporary blog during the latest Iraq war.
"I think it's because they have something to say. In a media
world that's otherwise leached of opinions and life, there's so
much life in them."

For all the history made by newspapers between 1960   19
and 2000, the profession was also busy contracting, standard-
izing, and homogenizing. Most cities now have their monopo-
list daily, their alt weekly or two, their business journal.
Journalism is done a certain way, by a certain kind of people.
Bloggers are basically oblivious to such traditions, so reading
the best of them is like receiving a bracing slap in the face. It's
a reminder that America is far more diverse and iconoclastic
than its newsrooms.

After two years of reading Weblogs, my short list of favorite   20
news commentators in the world now includes an Air Force
mechanic (Paul Palubicki *ofsgtstryker.com*), a punk rock singer-
songwriter (Dr. Frank of *doktorfrank.com*), a twenty-four-year-
old Norwegian programmer (Bjorn Staerk of *http://bearstrong.
net/warblog/index.html*), and a cranky libertarian journalist
from Alberta, Canada (Colby Cosh). Outsiders with vivid writing styles and unique viewpoints have risen to the top of the
blog heap and begun vaulting into mainstream media. Less
than two years ago, Elizabeth Spiers was a tech-stock analyst
for a hedge fund who at night wrote sharp-tongued observations about Manhattan life on her personal blog; now she's
the It Girl of New York media, lancing her colleagues at
Gawker.com, while doing free-lance work for the *Times*, the
New York Post, *Radar*, and other publications. Salam Pax, a
pseudonymous young gay Iraqi architect who made hearts
flutter with his idiosyncratic personal descriptions of Baghdad
before and after the war, now writes columns for *The Guardian*
and in July signed a book deal with Grove/Atlantic. Steven Den
Beste, a middle-aged unemployed software engineer in San
Diego, has been spinning out thousands of words of international analysis most every day for the last two years; recently
he has been seen in the online edition of *The Wall Street
Journal*.

With personality and an online audience, meanwhile, comes   21
a kind of reader interaction far more intense and personal than
anything comparable in print. Once, when I had the poor taste
to mention in my blog that I was going through a rough financial period, readers sent me more than $1,000 in two days. Far
more important, the intimacy and network effects of the blog-
world enable you to meet people beyond your typical circle

and political affiliation, sometimes with specialized knowledge of interest to you. "It exposes you to worlds that most people, let alone reporters, never interact with," says Jarvis, whose personal blog (*buzzmachine.com*) has morphed into a one-stop shop for catching up on Iranian and Iraqi bloggers, some of whom he has now met online or face to face.

22   Such specialization and filtering is one of the form's key functions. Many bloggers, like the estimable Jim Romenesko, with his popular journalism forum on Poynter's site, focus like a laser beam on one microcategory, and provide simple links to the day's relevant news. There are scores dealing with ever-narrower categories of media alone, from a site that obsesses over the *San Francisco Chronicle* (*ChronWatch.com*), to one that keeps the heat on newspaper ombudsmen (*OmbudsGod. blogspot.com*). Charles Johnson, a Los Angeles Web designer, has built a huge and intensely loyal audience by spotting and vilifying venalities in the Arab press (*littlegreenfootballs. com/weblog*). And individual news events, such as the Iraq war, spark their own temporary group blogs, where five or ten or more people all contribute links to minute-by-minute breaking news. Sometimes the single most must-see publication on a given topic will have been created the day before.

23   Besides introducing valuable new sources of information to readers, these sites are also forcing their proprietors to act like journalists: choosing stories, judging the credibility of sources, writing headlines, taking pictures, developing prose styles, dealing with readers, building audience, weighing libel considerations, and occasionally conducting informed investigations on their own. Thousands of amateurs are learning how we do our work, becoming in the process more sophisticated readers and sharper critics. For lazy columnists and defensive gate-keepers, it can seem as if the hounds from a mediocre hell have been unleashed. But for curious professionals, it is a marvelous opportunity and entertaining spectacle; they discover what the audience finds important and encounter specialists who can rip apart the work of many a generalist. More than just A. J. Liebling-style press criticism, journalists finally have something approaching real peer review, in all its brutality. If they truly value the scientific method, they should rejoice. Blogs can bring a collective intelligence to bear on a question.

24   And when the decentralized fact-checking army kicks into gear, it can be an impressive thing to behold. On March 30, veteran British war correspondent Robert Fisk, who has been accused so often of anti-American bias and sloppiness by bloggers that his last name has become a verb (meaning, roughly, "to disprove loudly, point by point"), reported that a bomb

hitting a crowded Baghdad market and killing dozens must have been fired by U.S. troops because of some Western numerals he found on a piece of twisted metal lying nearby. Australian blogger Tim Blair, a free-lance journalist, reprinted the partial numbers and asked his military-knowledgeable readers for insight. Within twenty-four hours, more than a dozen readers with specialized knowledge (retired Air Force, former Naval Air Systems Command employees, others) had written in describing the weapon (U.S. high-speed antiradiation missile), manufacturer (*Raytheon*), launch point (F-16), and dozens of other minute details not seen in press accounts days and weeks later. Their conclusion, much as it pained them to say so: Fisk was probably right.

In December 2001 a University of New Hampshire Econom-   25 ics and Women's Studies professor named Marc Herold published a study, based mostly on press clippings, that estimated 3,767 civilians had died as a result of American military action in Afghanistan. Within a day, blogger Bruce Rolston, a Canadian military reservist, had already shot holes through Herold's methodology, noting that he conflated "casualties" with "fatalities," double-counted single events, and depended heavily on dubious news sources. Over the next two days, several other bloggers cut Herold's work to ribbons. Yet for the next month, Herold's study was presented not just as fact, but as an understatement, by the *Guardian*, as well as the *New Jersey Star-Ledger*, *The Hartford Courant*, and several other newspapers. When news organizations on the ground later conducted their surveys of Afghan civilian deaths, most set the number at closer to 1,000.

But the typical group fact-check is not necessarily a   26 matter of war. Bloggers were out in the lead in exposing the questionable research and behavior of gun-studying academics Michael Bellesiles and John Lott Jr. (the former resigned last year from *Emory University* after a blogger-propelled investigation found that he falsified data in his antigun book, *Arming America*; the latter, author of the pro-gun book, *More Guns, Less Crime*, was forced by bloggers to admit that he had no copies of his own controversial self-defense study he had repeatedly cited as proving his case, and that he had masqueraded in online gun-rights discussions as a vociferous John Lott supporter named "Mary Rosh"). The fact-checking bloggers have uncovered misleading use of quotations by opinion columnists, such as Maureen Dowd, and jumped all over the inaccurate or irresponsible comments of various 2004 presidential candidates. They have become part of the journalism conversation.

Breathing in Blogworld

27   Which is not to say that 90 percent of news-related blogs aren't crap. First of all, 90 percent of any new form of expression tends to be mediocre (think of band demos, or the cringe-inducing underground papers of years gone by), and judging a medium by its worst practitioners is not very sporting. Still, almost every criticism about blogs is valid—they often are filled with cheap shots, bad spelling, the worst kind of confirmation bias, and an extremely off-putting sense of self-worth (one that this article will do nothing to alleviate). But the "blogosphere," as many like to pompously call it, is too large and too varied to be defined as a single thing, and the action at the top 10 percent is among the most exciting new trends the profession has seen in a while. Are bloggers journalists? Will they soon replace newspapers?

28   The best answer to those two questions is: those are two really dumb questions; enough hot air has been expended in their name already.

29   A more productive, tangible line of inquiry is: Is journalism being produced by blogs, is it interesting, and how should journalists react to it? The answers, by my lights, are "yes," "yes," and "in many ways." After a slow start, news organizations are beginning to embrace the form. Tech journalists, such as the *San Jose Mercury News's* Dan Gillmor, launched Weblogs long before "blogger" was a household word. Beat reporting is a natural fit for a blog—reporters can collect standing links to sites of interest, dribble out stories and anecdotes that don't necessarily belong in the paper, and attract a specific like-minded readership. One of the best such sites going is the recently created California Insider blog by the *Sacramento Bee's* excellent political columnist, Daniel Weintraub, who has been covering the state's wacky recall news like a blanket. Blogs also make sense for opinion publications, such as the *National Review, The American Prospect*, and my employer, *Reason*, all of which have lively sites.

30   For those with time to notice, blogs are also a great cheap farm system for talent. You've got tens of thousands of potential columnists writing for free, fueled by passion, operating in a free market where the cream rises quickly.

31   Best of all, perhaps, the phenomenon is simply entertaining. When do you last recall reading some writer and thinking "damn, he sure looks like he's having fun"? It's what buttoned-down reporters thought of their long-haired brethren back in the 1960s. The 2003 version may not be so immediately identifiable on sight—and that may be the most promising development of all.

Andrew Boyd
THE WEB REWIRES
THE MOVEMENT

Andrew Boyd, who wrote the essay below, is a lecturer at New York University. This essay, published in a politically liberal publication called The Nation, *explores the potential held by the Internet to organize and mobilize grassroots political and social movements—a contention that is questioned in the essay by Joshua Kurlantzick that follows. You might also consider how this use of new media raises topics of conversation with the essays in Part 5 that consider whether activism is an act of citizenship.*

The Battle in Seattle brought to the world's attention a new   1
global resistance movement that was not only made possible
by the Internet but, as Naomi Klein has deftly pointed out, was
shaped in its image. Sharing the Internet's architecture of in-
terconnected hubs and spokes, the new movement was a coalition of coalitions, a decentralized network of campaigns
"intricately and tightly linked to one another."

The net allows large mobilizations to unfold with minimal   2
bureaucracy and hierarchy. "Forced consensus and labored
manifestoes are fading into the background," Klein wrote in
2000, "replaced instead by a culture of constant, loosely structured, and sometimes compulsive information-swapping."

But if Seattle was the birth of this new kind of organizing,   3
last February 15's global peace demonstration marked its coming of age. That day, some 400,000 people turned out onto the
streets of New York to protest Bush's impending war on Iraq,
and close to 10 million more turned out in cities across the
globe. It was arguably the single largest day of protest in world
history; the *New York Times* dubbed its participants "the other
superpower."

The day sent a clear message about the grassroots organiz-   4
ing power of the net: It enabled the antiwar movement to
turn out its base quickly and cheaply, do an end run around
corporate-controlled media and reach into the politically disaffected American mainstream. The coming months and years
will test how deeply the new movement can tap this potential,
and to what extent "nets roots" organizing will be adopted by
more established political players, liberal and conservative alike.

5   Given this deepening embrace of the net by movement culture, it is fitting that the website of United for Peace and Justice
(UFPJ), the national coalition at the heart of the February 15
protest, not only anchored the massive mobilization but preceded the existence of the organization and helped it to coa-
lesce. In December, UFPJ did not have an office or a paid staff.
The website, however, was already a one-stop shop for the many
disparate strands of the peace movement. Launched the previous October, it was getting hundreds of thousands of hits a day.

6   "At the beginning, we had almost no money, not even enough
to do a major mailing," says L. A. Kauffman, a staff organizer
for UFPJ. The Internet allowed UFPJ to start serious organizing with only $5,000 to $10,000. "We pulled off a demo in five
weeks that would normally take five or six months," she says.

7   Providing one place for UFPJ's hundreds of member organizations to list their actions and report their activities, the website
quickly became an antiwar hub. Organizers put campaign materials and action kits online, and 15,000 copies of the February 15
flier were downloaded. People could easily find and plug into
local peace activities in their towns or states, and time local
events to coordinate with broader efforts. In the end, 793 protests
happened around the world on that day, including more than 200
across the United States and Canada, with paid organizers put to
work only on the biggest, in New York. All the others were self-
organized by UFPJ affiliates—local church, labor and peace
groups who used the website to facilitate their own coordination.

8   When I asked Leda Dederich, UFPJ's web director, where her
organization would be without the Internet, she said, "Mostly,
we wouldn't be."

9   A follow-up demonstration, on March 16, on the eve of the invasion of Iraq, was even more a creature of the web. A wave of
candlelight vigils, following the dusk west across the Earth, involved an estimated 1 million people in more than 6,000 gath-
erings in 130 countries and every state in the nation. This
global action was put together in even less time—six days—by
an organization with only five staff people, MoveOn. What
MoveOn did have was a nearly 1.5-million-person e-mail list
and a piece of web software known as "the meeting tool."

10   The meeting tool allows anyone anywhere to propose a
meeting time and place in his or her own neighborhood—and
makes it easy for others to sign up. The day before that Sunday
in March, I went to the MoveOn website, entered my ZIP code
and learned that three vigils had been scheduled in my neighborhood of Park Slope, Brooklyn, including one outside the
apartment of prowar Senator Chuck Schumer. The website

told me how many of my neighbors had signed up for each. It was already well into the hundreds, and I made it one more.

That Sunday evening, I joined 1,500 of my neighbors. 11
Someone handed me a candle and lit it for me; at some point a rabbi and a pastor spoke to the crowd. But otherwise, there was no obvious leadership, and it didn't seem to matter. There had been no meetings, no leaflets, no clipboards, no phone calls—we were all there, essentially, because of an e-mail we trusted.

The global vigils were but one of a string of Internet-enabled 12
antiwar actions facilitated by UFPJ and MoveOn. MoveOn itself was founded well before the war, or even Bush's presidency, as an effort during Bill Clinton's impeachment to push Congress to censure the President and "move on." The petition went viral, gathering half a million signatures in a few weeks. After that, the group used its list to raise money for progressive Democrats, and by the time Bush was threatening war, MoveOn had become a well-oiled machine. The group raised millions of dollars online to run national TV spots and print ads, delivered a petition of 1 million signatures to the UN Security Council and got 200,000 people to call Washington on a single day. MoveOn facilitated leafleting efforts in cities and small towns across the country and coordinated volunteer-led accountability sessions with almost every member of Congress. None of this stopped the war, but it did help put antiwar sentiment squarely on the political map—and made the case for how powerful the net can be in mobilizing social protest.

"You could say that MoveOn has a postmodern organizing 13
model," says Eli Pariser, the organization's 22-year-old campaigns director. "It's opt-in, it's decentralized, you do it from your home." MoveOn makes it easy for people to participate or not with each solicitation—an approach that embraces the permission-based culture of the Internet, and consumer culture itself. "If Nike hadn't already taken it," Pariser says, "our motto would be 'Just Do It.'" MoveOn has set the threshold for involvement so low that it has provoked skepticism among some activists—and jokes on *The Daily Show*. Nevertheless, this organizing model has allowed MoveOn to play an important role as a campaign aggregator—inviting people in on one issue—say, the war—and then introducing them to additional issues, from Bush's tax plan to the deregulation of media ownership. "We're helping to overcome the single-issue balkanization of the progressive movement," Pariser says.

By now, many well-funded advocacy groups (Common Cause, 14
Environmental Defense) have developed e-mail lists topping 100,000, which they typically use to run traditional, tightly

controlled campaigns, using e-mail as they would direct mail or a phone bank to mobilize their base to lobby legislators. Within the more radical global justice movement, on the other hand, there are a multitude of resource-poor grassroots groups whose e-mail lists are relatively small (5,000 to 50,000), but who use their websites to foster self-organizing—putting their organizing kit online and trusting their activist base to run with it. "What MoveOn has done," says Tom Matzzie, 28, the AFL-CIO's online mobilization manager, "is to bring the core elements of these two models together for the first time." MoveOn has a huge list that it carefully manages, and it also provides web tools that enable members to organize themselves. In the past eight months, as antiwar organizing exploded, their membership more than doubled, to a global total of more than 2.1 million.

15   A good e-mail list is not something you can buy or borrow. "Every MoveOn member comes to us with the personal endorsement of someone they trust," Pariser says. It is word-of-mouth organizing—in electronic form. E-mail is cheap, fast and easy to use, and it has made mixing the personal and the political more socially acceptable. Casually passing on a high-content message to a social acquaintance feels completely natural in a way handing someone a leaflet at a cocktail party never could.

16   This "tell a friend" phenomenon is key to how organizing happens on the net. It gives people who feel alienated from politics something valuable to contribute: their unique credibility within their particular circle of acquaintances. A small gesture to these friends can contribute to a massive multiplier effect. It is a grassroots answer to the corporate consolidation of media, which has enabled an overwhelmingly conservative punditry to give White House spin real political momentum, and the semblance of truth, simply through intensity of repetition.

17   MoveOn is often criticized from the left for not attempting to build permanent local structures or on-the-ground leadership. "They're great at getting new people involved, but it's not true self-organizing," says UFPJ's Dederich. The criticism is fair, but MoveOn's strength lies elsewhere, in providing a home for busy people who may not want to be part of a chapter-based organization with regular meetings. And given what MoveOn is doing—activating people on two or three different issues at a time, often for short durations as legislative targets change— it's hard to imagine a more appropriate model. By combining a nimble entrepreneurial style with a strong ethic of listening to its members—via online postings and straw polls—MoveOn has built a responsive, populist and relatively democratic virtual community.

Although MoveOn does not track member demographics,   18
anecdotal evidence suggests that its base is disproportionately
white. (Al Sharpton and Carol Moseley Braun, for example,
fared poorly in the group's recent "primary.") This reflects the
persevering digital divide, in which, according to a recent Pew
survey, a full 24 percent of Americans are totally offline, and
those who are online still tend to be younger, whiter, suburban,
better-off and better educated. But defying online trends, the
majority of MoveOn's active volunteers are female. And staffers
says its members are diverse in other ways, with thousands in
each state, ranging in age and income.

Zack Exley, a former SEIU organizer and MoveOn's organiz-   19
ing director, says that the group reaches deep into politically
disaffected middle-class constituencies—what he calls America's
"silenced majority." Unlike the traditional left, he says, "we
trust people. We don't think Americans are crazy or stupid or
brainwashed or apathetic. We're not trying to drag them kick-
ing and screaming over to our view. We know that there are
millions of Americans in every community and walk of life who
already know that something is terribly wrong with our country
and who are as angry as we are and who are mostly just looking
for a meaningful way to do something about it."

According to Pariser, most MoveOn members do not define   20
themselves as activists. Rather, MoveOn is often their first step
into political action—and what brings them to take that step is
usually an e-mail message. "A lot of 'Take action now' e-mails
feel like they were written by a focus-group e-newsletter
robot," says Madeline Stanionis, who as a senior consultant for
San Francisco–based Donordigital has developed scores of online advocacy campaigns. "MoveOn e-mails feel personal and
fresh. They write from their hearts." The e-mails about the
global vigil came directly from Pariser. His voice was strong yet
level-headed. There were no ideological digressions. He got to
the point early and kept it action-oriented. It was easy to trust.

Pariser says he crafts his messages with an eye toward tak-   21
ing MoveOn members on a journey, by providing a narrative
that connects them to an ongoing social movement. As each
campaign proceeds, short e-mail updates ("50,000 of you have
already signed up . . . here's a typical response from a schoolteacher in New Mexico . . .") build excitement and a sense of
community. This feedback loop is an example of how the
Internet, when well used, can extend the shoulder-to-shoulder
solidarity one feels on the street to fellow participants across
the nation and around the globe.

22   Returning to the MoveOn website a couple of days after the global vigil, I was able to browse through photographs and personal commentaries from vigils all over the world—Kazakhstan, Korea and Kenya, as well as the one I attended in Park Slope. All in all, some 10,000 photographs were uploaded that week. Through the Internet we had found our way into the streets, and the streets had then found their way right back onto the Internet. Our local protest was immediately reflected back to us as part of a larger story of national and global resistance.

23   Now that the war on Iraq—or one phase of it—is over, last winter's intense outpouring of antiwar sentiment feels like a distant episode. The peace movement is collectively catching its breath and wondering what to do next. At a June convention in Chicago, UFPJ consolidated its far-flung coalition by forging a unifying program for a new wave of movement-building. Many in the peace movement are looking to the 2004 elections, when MoveOn's fundraising and outreach muscle—the group seeks to raise tens of millions of dollars and mobilize a million volunteers—could be a factor. In a much-debated experiment in online democracy, MoveOn challenged the power of pundits and wealthy campaign donors to wield control over the presidential nomination process, by asking its 1.5 million American members to vote on which Democratic candidate the organization should endorse. Howard Dean and Dennis Kucinich, the top two vote-getters, have both emerged as magnets for antiwar Democrats disaffected by the party's tepid opposition to Bush's extreme agenda. But Dean, who outfundraised his competitors last quarter through a torrent of small online donations, is the only one of the pair to have caught the Internet wave. His campaign manager, Joe Trippi, sees the net as the missing element that will make Dean's 2004 run a "perfect storm." (It couldn't hurt that MoveOn was a paid technical adviser to Dean's campaign, prompting charges of partiality from the Gephardt and Edwards campaigns during the MoveOn primary. Exley says other Democrats declined such assistance, but wouldn't say which ones.)

24   "Whether it has coalesced around the outsider candidacies of Ross Perot or Jerry Brown, grassroots disaffection and energy have always been there," Trippi says. "What's changed this time around is the maturity of the Internet as a peer-to-peer tool."

25   Dean enthusiasts have made great use of a free web service, meetup.com (a commercial cousin of MoveOn's meeting tool). It allows users to identify and then meet face to face with like-minded locals who might share an interest in knitting, motorcycles or, say, Howard Dean for President. Anyone who joins a meet-up can volunteer as a "host," someone who shows up a

half-hour early to meet and greet. Members vote on a public venue for the get-togethers from a preapproved list in their area.

Tim Cairl, 28, a financial consultant whose only previous po- 26
litical involvement had been to call his Congressperson a few times when prompted by MoveOn, put himself forward as host of the Atlanta Dean meet-up when it was first coming together. In March, forty-two Dean fans crowded together in the back room of a downtown restaurant. The group was mostly white but ranged widely in age and occupation; the majority were new to political involvement of any kind. The typical attendee—upset about the war, and curious about Dean after seeing him on TV—had browsed his campaign website, and then found her way to meetup.com. "Meetup.com gets us in the same room," Cairl says. "We have to take it from there."

The feeling was social, almost fraternal. The agenda was sim- 27
ple: introductions, then, What do we like about Dean? What should we do? What the group did, given that no campaign organization yet existed in their late-primary state, was create one, appointing county leaders, scheduling tabling and showing up to local Democratic Party meetings. Subsequent meet-ups became a way to funnel new volunteers into this work; attendance grew to sixty-five in April, 150 by May, and soon meetings sprang up in cities across Georgia. Nationally, the 500 people who had signed up for Dean meet-ups in January grew to 60,000 by mid-July.

Trippi says traditional campaign structures run on a military 28
model—from the national campaign director down to local precinct captains—are deadly for an Internet strategy. Indeed, the more typical Kerry and Edwards campaigns have only 5,600 and 1,000 members, respectively, on meetup.com. "The other campaigns see this Internet activity as chaos. They can't control it, so they don't want to waste time on it. We trust our members to be good representatives of their own views. Instead of trying to control the chaos, we feed it and give it a little direction."

Matzzie says all this activity is impressive, but could prove 29
irrelevant in the general election if it doesn't take place in the right precincts. He notes that in 2002 only 94,000 well-placed votes would have given the Democrats control of Congress. He quotes recent studies from Yale's Institution for Social and Policy Studies showing that e-mail on its own—just like direct mail and commercial phone banking—does not increase voter turnout. "Anyone who gives you his e-mail is already with you," says Matzzie. "The trick is to get those people to talk to their neighbors, friends and colleagues offline. Those are the people we need to mobilize." He's been growing the AFL-CIO e-mail list by hundreds of thousands in the past few months

with this goal in mind. But he'll combine online work with shoe leather and door-knocking. Stanionis says the discussion among online advocacy experts is similar—how to get beyond the just-send-an-e-mail consumer model to "escalate the ask" and achieve more real-world involvement.

30   Matzzie is keeping a close eye on how the two major parties leverage technology in the months ahead: The Republican National Committee recently launched an "on-line toolbox for Republican activists" at GOPTeamLeader.com, and the Democrats will be bringing a similar site online soon. The net does not favor left or right, but it may favor outsiders who don't have access to the power of incumbency, and progressives seem to have been quickest at putting it to use. For the moment the biggest and best-managed e-mail lists are in the hands of liberal advocates who are allies of the Democrats. But the Republicans, Matzzie says, have the stronger field organization, once a Democratic strength.

31   Matzzie is not the only organizer rejecting Internet hype for a more measured view of its capabilities. "The Internet has been an enormous boon to grassroots mobilizations," says UFPJ's Kauffman. "But it can't replace old-fashioned face-to-face organizing, especially when you're trying to build something as delicate as a multiracial coalition." The polarizing debate about how to take up the issue of Palestine, for example, which roiled the UFPJ listserv in May, was handily resolved in the more goal-oriented and accountable setting of the coalition's June conference. E-mail is a notoriously bad way to resolve serious disputes over contentious issues, since it easily leads to harsh tones and misunderstandings. The Internet is best for pulling together a coalition when there is already a broad base of agreement—as there was for UFPJ and MoveOn around the Iraq war. And fault lines in the MoveOn consensus may yet emerge if a prowar Democrat gets the nomination.

32   Thenmozhi Soundararajan, executive director of Third World Majority, a digital media collective, says the racial skew to who's online further limits the usefulness of using e-mail to hash out political disputes. With only 3 percent of the world's population online, the divide is even more pronounced in international campaigns. "When you're online," she says, "a whole lot of people are not in the room." Kauffman says that UFPJ organizers, conscious of these demographics, were careful to use a mix of outreach strategies for the February 15 mobilization, distributing 1.2 million pieces of literature in six languages in every corner of New York City.

33   In some ways, the debate over whether online organizing is as "real" or as effective as face-to-face organizing misses the point.

What's interesting about meetup.com, the UFPJ website and MoveOn's meeting tool is how they leverage the Internet to get people together face to face in ways (and at speeds and costs) that were simply not possible before. As with the phone, the television or computer-generated direct mail, the Internet won't replace traditional organizing, but it does alter the rules in important ways. Because e-mail is near-instantaneous and costs just fractions of a penny, one can communicate very quickly with a lot of people at the speed of word of mouth. Because it is browsable from home, at any hour, it provides a much easier first point of contact between a campaign and interested participants. Because it is a peer-to-peer tool open to all, it allows geographically dispersed people to find each other easily and coordinate. Because it is still an open-publishing model, free from the constraints of corporate-owned media, it can carry the channels of alternative information essential for sustaining social movements.

34   Although it replaces some organizing structures (e-mail makes for a far better phone tree than phones ever did) and invents whole new ones, like the campaign web hub or the meeting tool, the Internet is no silver bullet. But what organizing tool ever is? Rather, contemporary social movements will, more and more, straddle both worlds, in a synthetic feedback loop, at once real and virtual, online and off.

35   Last December in South Korea—the most densely wired country on the planet—a grassroots revolt streaming rich media across high-bandwidth connections helped elect an outsider human rights activist as president. Where will our own Internet-fueled movements take us?

36   In the first month after MoveOn installed its meeting tool on the Dean campaign website, supporters self-organized more than a thousand local events—testament, perhaps, to the stirrings of a democratic revival, in which large swaths of disaffected Americans are finding forms of political participation that feel fulfilling, effective and connected. MoveOn's Zack Exley asks us to imagine a political landscape, five years from now, with fifty MoveOns, each tapping different political currents, with a whole new ability to mobilize grassroots power. In June, United for Peace and Justice announced plans for a protest during the Republican National Convention in August 2004. But unlike the Philadelphia demonstrations in 2000, this protest will go global. Such plans are a sign of activists' growing confidence, post–February 15, in the potentially explosive convergence of common global concerns and the wide reach of the Net.

37   Whatever else it has done, the Internet has helped to level the playing field between an entrenched government and corporate and media power, and an insurgent citizenry. The future might indeed be up for grabs.

Joshua Kurlantzick
DICTATORSHIP.COM

Joshua Kurlantzick is the foreign editor of The New Republic, *a well-known middle-of-the-road publication that aspires to "cover issues before they become mainstream." Kurlantzick has also written about economics and trade issues for* U.S. News and World Report, *and worked as a correspondent in Southeast Asia for* The Economist. *He has published frequently in magazines and journals including* Foreign Affairs, The Washington Quarterly, World Policy Journal, The Atlantic Monthly, *and* Current History. *In the essay below, Kurlantzick questions received opinions about the potential of the Internet to allow for grassroots activism and open political discussions. Consider this essay's contentions in relation to the claims made by Andrew Boyd in the previous essay as well as in terms of the larger questions about new media raised in this section.*

1   Last spring, during a trip to Laos, I visited an Internet café in the capital, Vientiane. Inside, the scene reminded me more of the West Village than the heart of a backward, communist nation. Though Laotians threshed rice by hand just a few miles away, the café itself was thoroughly modern. Tourists and local teenagers surfed the Internet on relatively new PCs. On a large screen on one wall, music videos featured Madonna gyrating half-naked. Below, kids seated at a row of computers logged onto pop-culture sites like MTV.com.

2   Yet, despite its trendiness and high-tech appearance, the Internet joint conspicuously lacked one element usually associated with café life: any discussion of current events. Virtually no one in the café spoke with anyone else. Except for the tourists, no one seemed to venture onto news Web pages—this, despite the fact that many Laotians can read Thai and could have accessed uncensored information on news sites based in neighboring (and democratic) Thailand. When I attempted to access the Web pages of exile groups opposed to the authoritarian Vientiane regime, I received an error message saying the pages were not accessible.

3   My experience in the Vientiane café was a sobering antidote to a pervasive myth: that the Internet is a powerful force for democracy. For years, a significant subset of the democratization industry—that network of political scientists, think tanks, and policymakers—has placed its bets (and, in many cases, its

money) on the Web's potential to spread liberal ideas in illib-
eral parts of the world. Whereas once American politicians and
democratization groups focused on older technologies, such as
radio, today their plans to spread democracy rest in considerable part on programs for boosting Internet access. In early
March, Secretary of State Colin Powell told Congress that a
crucial part of the Bush administration's democratization initiative will be establishing "American corners" in libraries
overseas, complete with Internet kiosks where locals can surf
the Web. In the Middle East, American diplomats have touted
their recent online interactions with locals, such as Web dialogue between the American consul in Jeddah and Saudis.

But world leaders, journalists, and political scientists who   4
tout the Internet as a powerful force for political change are
just as wrong as the dot-com enthusiasts who not so long ago
believed the Web would completely transform business. While
it's true that the Internet has proved itself able to disseminate
pop culture in authoritarian nations—not only Laos, but China,
Singapore, Saudi Arabia, and elsewhere—to date, its political
impact has been decidedly limited. It has yet to topple—or even
seriously undermine—its first tyrannical regime. In fact, in
some repressive countries the spread of the Internet actually
may be helping dictatorships remain in power.

Ever since the Internet became a mass medium in the mid-   5
'90s, its advocates have been touting its political potential.
In a 1996 appearance at the World Economic Forum in Davos,
John Perry Barlow, co-founder of one of the leading Internet
freedom organizations, delivered an address titled "Declaration
of the Independence of Cyberspace." In it, he announced,
"The global social space we are building" will "be naturally independent of the tyrannies [that governments] impose on us."
Other leading political theorists, such as Harvard's Joseph Nye,
argued that, by increasing information flows within and between countries and providing a space for political organization, the Internet would threaten dictators.

With the gauntlet laid down, the Internet became a new focus   6
of America's foreign policy elite. Political science departments
began hiring faculty with backgrounds in both political theory
and computer science. The National Democratic Institute and
other democratization groups in Washington made seminars
on utilizing the Web for political discourse a central part of
their agenda. In a 1995 study, the Pentagon predicted the
Internet would prove a "strategic threat to authoritarian
regimes." In 2000, President Clinton told reporters that, "in
the new century, liberty will spread by . . . cable modem" and

memorably warned that, if China's leaders attempted to crack down on the Web, they would find it as difficult as "trying to nail Jell-O to the wall." In 1999, then–presidential candidate George W. Bush confidently predicted that, if the Internet were to take hold in China, "freedom's genie will be out of the bottle."

7   Since taking office, the Bush administration has focused on programs to expand Web access in the Middle East, such as funding for Internet connections in Arab schools. Margaret Tutwiler, undersecretary of state for public diplomacy and public affairs, recently told Congress that such efforts would help provide people in the Middle East with "a window on the world. . . . It opens up a whole lot of avenues that I think are in our self-interest." Edward Djerejian, chairman of the White House advisory group on public diplomacy, testified that, "given the strategic importance of information technologies, a greater portion of the budget should be directed to tap the resources of the Internet."

8   Academics and journalists, too, have bought into the idea, frequently pointing to increased Internet usage as de facto evidence of political liberalization. "The Internet and globalization," wrote *The New York Times'* Thomas Friedman in 2000, "are acting like nutcrackers to open societies and empower Arab democrats." A year later, when Bashar Assad became president of Syria, the fact that he had once headed a Syrian computer group was taken as evidence that he might be a liberalizer. Saudi Arabia is the most recent beneficiary of this kind of misunderstanding, with media reports crediting the desert kingdom with liberalization based on its burgeoning Internet culture. This March, *The Economist* enthused, "The Internet, the mobile phone and satellite television are all eroding the [Saudi] authorities' control."

9   But little of this excitement is predicated on empirical research. It's true, of course, that Internet usage has surged in many authoritarian nations. In China, the number of people accessing the Web on a regular basis has risen from fewer than one million in 1997 to almost 70 million in 2003. In the Middle East, Internet penetration has nearly doubled in the past five years. It's also true that this increased access has provided some citizens of dictatorships more access to the outside world and helped loosen restrictive cultural norms. By prompting more open discussion of sexuality, for instance, foreign websites may make it easier for Southeast Asian youngsters to talk frankly about sex—a life-and-death proposition in a region decimated by HIV/AIDS.

10   Yet the growth of the Internet has not substantially altered the political climate in most authoritarian countries. In quasi-authoritarian Singapore, where more than 50 percent of

the population has regular Internet access, the ruling People's Action Party actually increased its political stranglehold in the last election, winning more than 95 percent of the seats in the legislature. In Malaysia, another country where Internet access is much higher than in most of the developing world, the ruling United Malays National Organization, which has been in power for over two decades, dominated this week's national elections. The State Department's March report on human rights in Burma says, "The Government's extremely poor human rights record worsened. . . . Citizens still did not have the right to change their government." And its annual report on human rights in China, also released in March, said that last year saw "backsliding on key human rights issues" by Beijing—such significant backsliding that the United States is considering censuring China at the U.N. Human Rights Commission. Indeed, nearly all the Chinese political science professors I have spoken with agree that the mainland Chinese democracy movement is weaker now than it was a decade ago. Nor is this unhappy trend limited to the Far East. Since March 2003, the Cuban government has initiated its biggest crackdown on dissent in years. Neither Cuba nor such Middle Eastern nations as Saudi Arabia, Egypt, and Syria have made any recent progress toward democracy, according to Freedom House's 2004 ranking of countries around the world.

Why has the Web failed to transform such regimes? In part   11
because, as a medium, the Web is in many ways ill-suited for expressing and organizing dissent. And, even more significantly, because, as a technology, it has proved surprisingly easy for authoritarian regimes to stifle, control, and co-opt.

Many Internet advocates forget that, on the most basic level,   12
the Web is a vehicle merely for disseminating information. Someone, in other words, first needs to have access to the information and a willingness to share it. In practice, this means the impact of the Web depends to a certain degree on local resources—specifically, the existence of opposition networks able to provide evidence of government wrongdoing. This limitation is evident when one compares Malaysia with Singapore. "The Internet has had more impact on politics in Malaysia than in Singapore," says Cherian George, who is writing a book on Internet usage in Southeast Asia. There are several nongovernmental organizations (NGOs) in Malaysia committed to investigating the government; in Singapore, there are virtually none. As a consequence, when activists in Malaysia want to use the Web to highlight human rights abuses, George says, they can draw upon the information amassed by the NGOs from their networks of sources. Singaporeans, by contrast, have no such

resources. This is part of the reason James Gomez, founder of the well-known Singaporean dissident website ThinkCentre.org, admits that his organization has not significantly altered local politics by using the Internet.

13   Another shortcoming of the Internet is that it lends itself to individual rather than communal activities. It "is about people sitting in front of a terminal, barely interacting," says one Laotian researcher. The Web is less well-suited to fostering political discussion and debate because, unlike radio or even television, it does not generally bring people together in one house or one room. In Rangoon, the capital of Burma—one of the most repressive nations on earth—groups of men often crowd around radios in tea shops to clandestinely listen to news from the BBC's Burmese service and then discuss what they've heard. Similarly, in bars and cafés in China, people gather around televisions to watch and discuss the news. But, while restaurateurs in the developing world can afford to use a radio or television to lure customers who might have a snack while listening or watching, owners of Internet cafés have to recoup their much higher capital investments. They do this by dividing their establishments into individual terminals and charging each user separately. In fact, in nearly every Internet café I have visited, in Vientiane last year and in Rangoon this winter (as well as in New York and in London), I have watched the same scenes of people sitting in front of individual computer terminals, barely talking to each other.

14   Add to this a still more simple fact about the Internet—that, unlike television or radio, it generally requires users to be literate—and it's not hard to see why democracy advocates in authoritarian countries (and some authoritarian leaders) consider older, broadcast media to be a more effective means of disseminating information and fostering debate. Wang Dan, a well-known Chinese democracy activist, has argued that television and radio are still the best means for communicating dissident messages within China. Western diplomats in Laos concur, telling me that Thai television, available to many Laotians, has more potential than the Internet to subvert the authoritarian Laotian government. Likewise, in the Middle East, Islamist organizations—the only groups that have had much success challenging authoritarian regimes in the region—have largely disdained the Web, relying instead on clandestine videos and audiocassettes, which can be watched communally and then passed along from mosque to mosque.

15   In addition to lending itself primarily to individual use, the Internet also fosters a kind of anarchy inimical to an effective opposition movement. Singaporean dissident Gomez says the

Web empowers individual members of a political movement, rather than the movement as a whole. Opposition members can offer dissenting opinions at will, thus undermining the leadership and potentially splintering the organization. In combating an authoritarian regime, in other words, there's such a thing as too much democracy. Two of the most successful opposition movements of the last few decades—the South African opposition led by Nelson Mandela and the Burmese resistance led by Aung San Suu Kyi—relied upon charismatic, almost authoritarian leaders to set a message followed by the rest of the movement. The anti-globalization movement, by contrast, has been a prime example of the anarchy that can develop when groups utilize the Web to organize. Allowing nearly anyone to make a statement or call a meeting via the Web, the anti-globalizers have wound up with large but unorganized rallies in which everyone from serious critics of free trade to advocates of witches and self-anointed saviors of famed death-row convict Mumia Abu Jumal have their say. To take just one example, at the anti-globalization World Social Forum held in Mumbai in January, nuanced critics of globalization like former World Bank chief economist Joseph Stiglitz shared space with, as *The New York Times* reported, "a long list of regional causes," including anti-Microsoft and anti–Coca Cola activists.

But the Internet's inherent flaws as a political medium are only part of the reason for its failure to spread liberty. More significant has been the ease with which authoritarian regimes have controlled and, in some cases, subverted it. The most straightforward way governments have responded to opposition websites has been simply to shut them down. In Singapore, for example, an online political forum called Sintercom became popular in the mid-'90s as one of the only places where citizens could express political opinions relatively openly. But, following government pressure, Sintercom was shut down in 2001. Since then, according to Shanthi Kalathil and Taylor C. Boas, authors of the recent comprehensive book *Open Networks, Closed Regimes: The Impact of the Internet on Authoritarian Rule*, the scope of online political discussion in Singapore has shrunk. In Malaysia, too, many of the anti-government websites that formed in the mid-'90s have been shuttered, enabling the regime to beat back a liberal reform movement that sprang up five years ago. 16

But nowhere has a regime's ability to corral the Internet been more apparent than in China, the world's largest authoritarian state. Despite President Clinton's prediction, Beijing has proved that it can, in fact, nail Jell-O to the wall. A 2003 study by 17

Jonathan Zittrain and Benjamin Edelman, two Harvard researchers, found that China has created the most extensive system of Internet censorship in the world and has almost completely controlled the impact of the Web on dissent. It has done this, they note, by mandating that all Web traffic go through government-controlled servers and by constructing an elaborate system of firewalls—which prevent access to certain websites—and online monitoring by state security agents. Censored sites include much of the Western media and sites related to Taiwan, democratization, and other sensitive topics. (*The New York Times* won a reprieve only when its former editor appealed personally to former President Jiang Zemin.) In their book, Kalathil and Boas note that Saudi Arabia has constructed similarly comprehensive systems to limit online dissent, expanding their "censorship mechanism to keep pace with the burgeoning sources of objectionable content." What's more, various authoritarian regimes have collaborated with one another to improve their ability to control the Web. As Kalathil and Boas note, China is formally advising Cuba on its Internet policies, while several Middle Eastern states have looked to Singapore as an example in controlling their citizens' Web usage.

18   In such efforts, authoritarian regimes have also benefited from the willingness of Western companies to sell the latest censorship technology. Cybersecurity companies, such as San Jose–based Secure Computing, have competed intensely to sell Web-filtering and -monitoring technology to Riyadh, Beijing, and other repressive governments. One vice president of Websense, a San Diego company that competed for the Saudi contract, told the *Times* in 2001 that it would "be a terrific deal to win." Unsurprisingly, these companies have not made a similar effort to provide cash-poor dissidents in these nations with technology that could enable them to overcome firewalls or conceal their online identities. In a 2002 study, Michael Chase and James Mulvenon, two RAND researchers, found that the Chinese authorities were able to prevent Internet users from accessing anti-monitoring technology 80 percent of the time.

19   China also has co-opted its own local Internet content providers. In 2002, the country's leading Web entrepreneurs signed a pledge vowing to promote self-discipline in Web usage and encourage "the elimination of deleterious information [on] the Internet." Some of these Internet entrepreneurs are former dissidents who fled China after the 1989 Tiananmen uprising but have since abandoned their political activism, returning to China seeking Web fortune. In fact, as Kalathil and Boas note, "Many of China's up-and-coming Internet entrepreneurs see a substantial . . . role for the government in the

Internet sector. . . . [They] have visions for Chinese Internet development that are inherently pragmatic and complementary to state strategy." So much for Barlow's idea that technology workers will reject the "tyrannies" of government.

In the past two years, as authoritarian regimes have become   20
more sophisticated in controlling the Web, many of them have been able to leverage that control to create climates of online self-censorship. According to Nina Hachigian, an expert on China at the Pacific Council on International Policy, the knowledge that the Chinese government monitors online activity, combined with Internet laws so broad they could apply to almost any Web surfer, effectively scare most users into avoiding political sites altogether. As Gary Rodan, a Southeast Asia specialist at Murdoch University in Australia, notes in an essay on Singapore in *Political Science Quarterly*, "When extensive networks of political surveillance are already in place and a culture of fear about such practices exists, the impact of monitoring is likely to be strong."

To maintain this fear, Internet cops in China launch periodic   21
crackdowns on the Web, arresting and prosecuting Chinese citizens for posting Web items related to democracy or to helping people evade firewalls. Beijing also has shuttered thousands of Internet cafés over the past four years. On a visit to Shanghai in 1999, I noticed numerous new cafés. By 2003, many had been closed. Other authoritarian regimes have used similar bullying tactics to foster climates of self-censorship online. Singapore also has drafted broad Internet laws that could implicate many Web users and, Kalathil and Boas report, has reinforced citizens' paranoia by occasionally arresting people for posting articles critical of the government and by periodically reminding the public that the country's one Internet service provider, which is connected to the government, snoops through users' Web accounts. The Vietnamese government has made owners of Internet cafés responsible for anything users post online and has made a series of arrests over the past two years of people who posted dissident articles. In January, Hanoi sentenced a man who used the Web to criticize the Vietnamese government to seven years in prison.

Even beyond its failure to live up to democratizers' dreams, the   22
Web may actually be helping to keep some dictatorships in power. Asian dissidents have told me that the Web has made it easier for authoritarian regimes to monitor citizens. In Singapore, Gomez says, the government previously had to employ many security agents and spend a lot of time to monitor activists who were meeting with each other in person. But, with the advent of the Web, security agents can easily use

government-linked servers to track the activities of activists and dissidents. In fact, Gomez says, in recent years opposition groups in Singapore have moved away from communicating online and returned to exchanging information face-to-face, in order to avoid surveillance.

23   In China, the Web has similarly empowered the authorities. In the past two decades, Beijing's system of monitoring the population by installing informers into businesses, neighborhoods, and other social institutions has broken down—in part because the Chinese population has become more transient and in part because the regime's embrace of capitalism has meant fewer devoted Communists willing to spy for the government. But Beijing has replaced these legions of informers with a smaller group of dedicated security agents who monitor the Internet traffic of millions of Chinese. "The real problem with groups trying to use the Internet is that you are actually more easily monitored if you use online forms of communication than if you just meet in person in secret," one specialist in Chinese Internet usage told me. Indeed, in May 2003 Beijing's security services imprisoned four people for "inciting the overthrow of the Chinese government"; press reports suggested the authorities learned about the dissidents' movements through reports on pro-democracy websites. Later, in February of this year, Beijing charged Du Daobin, a well-known Internet dissident, with "inciting subversion of state power and the overthrow of China's socialist system."

24   In the Middle East, security services have used the Internet in similar ways. In Egypt, police once had to conduct time-consuming stakeouts of bars and clubs to find gay men breaking the laws against homosexuality. Yet, in 2002, the Associated Press reported that a group of state security agents went "online masquerading as gay men . . . [and] arrested men . . . who responded to the ads." In its most recent annual report on human rights in Egypt, the State Department noted, "Egyptian police have continued to target homosexuals using Internet-based sting operations."

25   What's more, authoritarian regimes have begun flooding the Web with their own content, using high-profile websites to actually increase support for the government. Kalathil and Boas report that e-government services "are likely to boost regime legitimacy, particularly in countries [like Singapore and China] where the state has traditionally offered extensive services [such as social welfare programs] in exchange for political support." Singapore has indeed developed one of the most extensive e-government sites in the world, and Hachigian's research shows that nearly one-tenth of all sites in China are directly

related to the Beijing regime. Some of these sites, such as the e-government sites for Beijing municipality, are very sophisti-cated and include sections in which citizens can e-mail Beijing's mayor with suggestions. (There is little evidence, however, that the mayor feels any need to respond to or even read the submissions.)

Dictators also have poured money into the websites of state-linked media outlets, helping to make them more appealing than their independent competitors. Gomez says that *The Straits Times*, the government-linked newspaper in Singapore with the most sophisticated and comprehensive website, is where nearly everyone in Singapore goes for news. Similarly, the *People's Daily*, a leading party publication in China, now has a very sophisticated Internet presence and has become a leading source of news for wired Chinese. Its chat rooms have become notorious for their nationalistic sentiment—partly the consequence of security bureau Beijing agents logging into the rooms and posting xenophobic statements. Indeed, during crises like the China-U.S. spy-plane incident in 2001 and the run-up to last week's election in Taiwan, Beijing has utilized these chat rooms to whip up patriotic sentiment.   26

In the long run, the Internet may fulfill some of its hype as an engine of liberalization. Gomez told me that small civil society groups that do not attract as much attention from state security agents—professional organizations, charities, religious groups—are where the Internet's true potential is likely to be. Not, in other words, with groups pushing for regime change. Chinese environmental organizations provide an example of how smaller groups can benefit: These single-issue groups, which normally focus on one environmental problem, have used the Web to coordinate meetings. What's more, by empowering small companies, the Web may decrease state control of the economy. In *New Media, New Politics? From Satellite Television to the Internet in the Arab World*, a recent study of technology in the Middle East, Jon Alterman reports that, in countries like the Persian Gulf states, the spread of the Web may allow small, nim-ble entrepreneurs to challenge the massive, state-linked compa-nies that have been the foundations of autocratic regimes.   27

While recognizing that the Internet is not developing into the political tool many had predicted, governments and private companies could help promote the Web's gradual emergence as a force for change. In the House of Representatives, Christopher Cox has sponsored legislation to allow U.S. com-panies to more easily export encryption technology, which lets Internet users send coded messages that cannot be monitored   28 by central governments. Other legislators have proposed a U.S. Office of Global Internet Freedom designed to facilitate the reform of Internet policies around the world. Most important, the private sector could push regimes not to crack down on Internet freedoms. Such an idea is not wishful thinking. China, Malaysia, Singapore, and other authoritarian states desperately want to prove that they are modern, First World nations, and mastering the Internet is essential to this image. Malaysia has built a massive "Multimedia Super Corridor" in an attempt to create a local version of Silicon Valley, while Singapore has promoted itself as an "Intelligent Island" hardwired into the Web. Consequently, foreign companies can have some influence over dictators, since, without their assistance, authoritarian regimes cannot realize their pretensions of modernity. According to *The New York Times*, John Kamm, the former head of Hong Kong's American Chamber of Commerce, once gave a speech at a banquet for Zhou Nan, Beijing's senior representative in the city, in which he asked Zhou to push for the release of a prominent student detained during the Tiananmen Square protest. Though in public Zhou reacted icily to Kamm's request, a month later the student was released.

29   But neither Western governments nor Western companies seem likely to step up to the plate. Since the war on terrorism began, the Bush administration has been at pains not to ruffle Beijing's feathers. (Indeed, in an ironic twist, the White House is now considering Web-surveillance techniques similar to those utilized by the Chinese government.) Meanwhile, as the information-technology sector continues to struggle, most tech companies are unwilling to risk alienating potential clients, such as the Chinese government. In part, this eagerness to jump into bed with Beijing and Riyadh reflects the economic reality of a sector no longer in a state of permanent expansion. And, in part, it represents the transition of the Web from a technology run by civil-libertarian geeks like Barlow to one dominated by relatively conservative, large corporations. "In the mid-1990s, there was this feeling among the Web's early users that it had to be a medium to promote freedom," says author George. "But companies like AOL, they don't share that commitment—they focus on entertainment." Indeed, Yahoo! and America Online have both willingly censored their news content to please authoritarian regimes like China. "I haven't seen any businesses pushing governments in this way," Gomez told me. "People are giving up on the idea of the Internet as a frontier for freedom."

VISUAL CONVERSATIONS **2**

Virtual Communities, Real Politics in the New Media

As some of the essays in this part of *Conversations* suggest, "alternative" media are much more accessible to individuals who wish to have their voices heard than "Big Media" (media owned by individual corporations). In particular, websites and weblogs (or "blogs") administered by special-interest and activist groups have provided anyone with access to the Internet with a way of beginning or joining conversations conducted on local, national, and international scales. Some of those conversations are free-flowing and undirected. Some are focused and directed at a particular social or political goal. But two things are clear: lots of people are turning to the Internet to find a community with which to share their political beliefs, and the Internet is responding with sites devoted to just about any political opinion you can imagine. And people are not only acting as consumers of these political messages; more and more are joining in on these online conversations or setting up their own media network by developing personal or organization-based websites. In fact, research done by Pew Charitable Trusts media group noted recently that 44 percent of U.S. Internet users have contributed their thoughts to the online world. That's a lot of conversation. What does all this mean for our understanding of "media," which until recently was largely a one-way dissemination of information?

Though an "alternative press" is, in some ways, nothing new, two aspects of the virtual communities that are out there are very new. First, the speed with which people can disseminate views and communicate within these virtual communities is unprecedented. And second, that communication is no longer only in words. Activist and special-interest websites—sites that bring together groups who share common goals for political action—use visuals very effectively to make their case and to invite others into the conversation. Below are some examples of visuals taken from activist websites. As you view these images and words, consider the arguments that each picture makes, examining both the overall impact and the small details.

You should also consider the methods of persuasion—that is, the types of rhetoric—that each piece employs. You might consider, for example, whether each piece's argument is mainly based in *ethos* (establishing a strong character), *logos* (based upon the "facts" of the case), or *pathos* (drawing us in with emotions). You should also consider the context and rhetorical situation for each piece, as you would with a piece of writing: its intended audience, the purpose it is meant to serve, and the exigency for this argument—what makes it timely and important. Think also about the medium—how does each piece lend itself to use in an electronic medium?

ARE YOU WILLING TO KILL
HER TO GET SADDAM?

STOP THE WAR ON IRAQ

Tell the White House what you think (202)456-1111
www.NoMoreVictims.org
A bomb dropped by a U.S. plane south of Basra, Iraq, blew off this little girl's arm.

First developed by nomorevictims.org, this image has appeared on many antiwar websites. Consider details of the photo that make it such a powerful image, as well as the ways that the image and the words work together. You might also consider the ethics of this type of *pathos* (emotion) based appeal. Does it also allow for reasonable discussions? What types of conversations is it likely to spur?

The website from which this photo was taken is devoted to supporting the work of U.S. troops in Iraq. What story does this photo tell visually? What details and contrasts help support its argument? How does it present an alternative voice to images on antiwar sites like the one included above.

Run by women, CodePink4Peace is a liberal activist website that also sponsors street rallies and protests. The image shown here is used as a link to the "Peaceful New York Police" program. What features of this graphic develop its message? What argument is it attempting to make?

What commentary about the effect of media, and of television in particular, does this cartoon make? How do the small details in this cartoon contribute to that overall message and to your understanding of media as it is discussed in this part of *Conversations*?

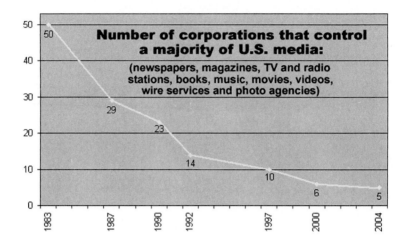

Since this graph originally appeared on a website with a particular purpose, try to determine that purpose by thinking about specific features of the graph. Here are some things to consider:

- What affect does the title of the graph have? Does it have a persuasive purpose in and of itself?
- How is media defined for the purposes of the graph? What affect does that definition have on the results presented?
- Why was a line graph chosen as opposed to a pie chart or bar graph? What effect might changing the type of graph have? How are such choices made?

You might also consider the effect of visual aids in general, as well as the purpose of this one in particular, by asking some other questions:

- Would the information have been more effective or less effective if it had been presented as a chart or table rather than a graph?
- Would the presentation have been more or less effective if it was summarized in paragraph form?
- How can we assure that the quantitative information that we are presenting, or that is being presented to us, is accurately portraying the information? (That is a difficult question, but one worth pondering.)

Those questions are just a start—there are many more visual elements you might consider as you analyze the way facts, figures, and statistics are presented visually.

Two-Way Media: Is Talk Radio Good for Democracy?

American Demographics

OPENING UP THE CONVERSATION

The essay below was first published in American Demographics, *a magazine that since 1978 has studied and published trends in American culture, largely for the purpose of providing information to marketing specialists. "Demographics," literally the characteristics of various human groups, are used not only by marketers, but by political analysts and parties as well. The essay below explores the phenomenon of talk radio, a two-way medium that has itself become a source of political conversations, by providing the demographics of talk radio listeners—their age groups, political inclinations, gender, and so forth. What statistical information about talk radio listeners might be particularly important in understanding the effect of this media on the public conversation? Do the demographics reported here square with your experience of this medium and its listeners?*

Has the heyday of talk radio come and gone? Clinton's ratings-friendly scandals have died down, Howard Stern's marriage collapsed, Rush Limbaugh seems to have lost his buzz along with his weight and Dr. Laura Schlessinger was swiftly booed off TV. On the surface, it seems the radio babblers have been unceremoniously shushed. 1

Not so fast. Talk radio is still tremendously popular, capturing 17 percent of all listeners during a given quarter-hour period, a share that has remained stable over the past few years. Radio talk show hosts wield enormous influence. Witness the 2 success of former radio stars on television: Larry King, Sean Hannity and Alan Colmes all rose through the ranks of radio. Limbaugh and Schlessinger still host the No. 1 and No. 2 radio shows in America. And five days into office, Vice President Dick Cheney awarded his first radio interview to Oliver North, syndicated host on Common Sense Radio.

3   But talk radio today goes beyond conservative political bluster. The format is veering in multiple directions—trying to target younger audiences, Hispanics and women—with variations like "hot talk," infotalk, sports talk, consumer and personal finance talk, and all-Spanish news. "The biggest trend taking place in talk radio is similar to what music radio went through during the '70s and '80s," explains Michael Harrison, editor and publisher of Talkers magazine. "We're seeing a broadening and expansion of talk into a number of niches—in terms of format, subject matter and demographic targets."

4   Advertisers have long underestimated radio's reach. The RAB Media Facts Book reports that consumers currently spend 85 percent of their time with ear-oriented media like radio and television, compared with 15 percent on print formats. Yet advertisers spend 55 percent of their dollars on eye-media, such as newspapers and magazines, and only 45 percent on ear-media. Talk radio is a particularly strong form of ear-media because it requires a high level of involvement from the listener. Unlike music, which tends to fade into the background, talk radio demands a listener's full attention. Furthermore, most programs rely on a high degree of interactivity through guests and listener call-ins. If a program's topic doesn't prove immediately popular with call-in listeners, the subject is changed, placing listeners in charge of content.

5   Talk radio seems to fit right in with our changing society— mobile, impatient and self-obsessed. Talk is most popular during weekday mornings, with the highest average quarter-hour rating (AQR) share of any format during the 6 a.m. and 10 a.m. commute—also the time slot with the largest radio audience overall. The rise of cell phones has aided talk's popularity during the morning drive time, allowing listeners to call in from their traffic-stalled vehicles. Radio listeners also tend to be loyal, tuning in to two or three different stations, but generally remaining true to one favorite.

6   Recent ratings back up the fact that listeners have their ears cocked. According to Interep, a New York City–based radio advertising and sales company, nine of the top 10 metro areas currently feature a talk format among their top 10 ranked stations. Arbitron, an international media research firm that measures radio audiences, shows the AQR for the news/talk/information

category was up to 16.9 in the fall of 2000, from 16.4 in the fall of 1998 and a low of 15.6 in spring 2000. With nearly 17 percent of radio listeners in any given quarter-hour period tuning in to talk, it's the most popular radio format on the air. Moreover, all-talk formats have been steadily increasing, from an AQR of 1.6 in 1998 to an AQR of 2.2 in 2000. In 1983, only 53 radio stations had talk/news formats. (There were also fewer radio stations back then—8,748 total in 1980—but the proportion of talk formats was, nonetheless, miniscule.) Today, 1,724 of the 13,307 radio stations in America—or 13 percent—are devoted to news/talk/information.

Talk radio is not only one of the earliest examples of media   7
providing connectivity, it's also one of the most effective. Advertisements are often integrated into the programming, with products hawked by its popular hosts, who create a "just between you and me" kind of pitch. The result is a highly successful illustration of one-to-one marketing.

Talk programs also tend to be more expensive for advertisers   8
than music formats. One measure used to track radio revenue by format is the "power radio," which compares share of audience to share of revenue. Historically, talk has had a power ratio of about 1.4, which means there's a 40 percent premium for talk radio above and beyond its strict audience share, according to George Nadel Rivin, partner in charge of broadcast services at North Hollywood, Calif.–based Miller, Kaplan, Arase & Co., a certified public accounting firm specializing in radio. "Talk has consistently been among the top three formats in terms of converting audience share to revenue share," explains Nadel Rivin.

At the same time, talk has a bad reputation. Critics say the for-   9
mat has evolved from a dispassionate discussion of public affairs into an incendiary forum for extremist opinions. They charge on-air hosts with inciting hate, undermining public debate and spreading harmful lies. This image dates back to the FCC's repeal of the "fairness doctrine" in 1987, which required stations to give equal time to both sides of any issue. As a result, talk ricocheted to the political right and rocketed in the ratings. Limbaugh was launched into national syndication from Sacramento's WFBK in 1986, followed by other right wing hosts like G. Gordon Liddy, Alan Keyes and Schlessinger, all of whom give talk radio an extremist reputation. Their defenders claim that such hosts simply understand how verbal theatrics translate into high ratings. They also like to point out that talk radio listeners are not all right wing, but are rather diverse politically.

They're correct—to a certain extent. The stereotypical   10
talk radio listener is the angry white male fuming along to

Don Imus while stuck in rush hour traffic or gramps puffing on his pipe to Limbaugh's latest aural rampage. In fact, it's true that radio skews male and older. Fifty-eight percent of listeners are men, age 18 and older, compared with 42 percent of same age women. According to Arbitron, three out of 10 listeners are seniors over age 65. For adults ages 55 to 64, the news/talk/information format remains one of the most popular, along with stations that play classical music and adult standards, such as Frank Sinatra and Cole Porter.

11   But in other ways, the stereotype of the talk radio listener is inaccurate. "Talk radio is much more diverse than you would think," says Tom Taylor, editor of the Nashville, Tenn.–based M Street Daily newsletter. "Radio changes to reflect the demographics and tastes of America." The demographics of radio audiences are beginning to shift: talk radio listeners are no longer exclusively conservative. Most talk show hosts say that even for political programs, the core value is entertainment, not policy. "Politics has to have something exciting going on, otherwise it's just policy and people tune out," Talkers' Harrison explains. Moreover, listening does not signify agreement. Harrison points out that liberals and moderates will listen to conservative radio, but not vice versa. In the effort to gain a larger audience, it can make sense for a station to choose a right wing host.

12   At the same time, new voices are breaking out of the Limbaugh mold. One example is "the Lone Liberal," a frequent anonymous talk show guest who skewers traditional talk radio conventions. Another is Dave Barber, a popular host carried statewide by the Michigan Talk Radio Network. Tom Leykis, syndicated nationally by Westwood One, opens his shows with the line, "I'm not a conservative wacko or a convicted felon."

13   "The mind-numbing conformity pervading talk radio" is one impetus to this broadening spectrum, according to Holland Cooke, a news talk specialist with McVay Media, a radio programming consulting firm based in Cleveland. He adds that, "Everyone became Rush Limbaugh wannabes and what you lost was interactivity and spontaneity." According to Cooke, the result has been a renewed search for fresh formats and hosts.

14   A variety of up-and-coming talkers are creating a new picture of talk radio's potential. One growing area is personal finance, where syndicated hosts like Dave Ramsey, Ken and Daria Dolan, Tom Martino and Clark Howard (the nation's No. 3 talk show host after Limbaugh and Schlessinger) together draw over 11 million listeners a week. Dr. Joy Browne's discussions of relationships attracts a core group of women ages 25 to 54. And Premiere Radio's Phil Hendrie attracts up to

1 million listeners with his satirical mockery of traditional radio talk shows.

The talk audience is not only becoming more open-minded, it's getting younger. Over the past three years, the number of listeners age 35 to 44 increased to 25 percent from 22 percent of the talk audience, while the 65 and over age group fell by 5 percentage points to 6 percent. "Talk is successfully attracting a younger audience," says Walter Sabo, president of New York–based radio consulting company SaboMedia. "In Orlando, WTKS FM targets the 28-year-old man and focuses on what he talks about over lunch—annoyances at work, trouble with the girlfriend, what to do over the weekend—and it's the No. 1 station with men 18 to 34. It beats every music station. That's revolutionary." 15

This shift toward a younger audience can partly be tied to a slow move over the past six years from AM to FM, as talk radio has begun to infiltrate the FM dial. With more people switching to FM from AM (1 percent to 2 percent of listeners move over every year; and the number of FM stations has more than tripled over the past 30 years, while the number of AM stations has remained constant), talk radio has started to shift as well. The move has not been dramatic for a couple of reasons: First, there is still the presumption that FM is music and AM is talk, limiting the extent to which investors are willing to plunge into FM talk. Second, there are regulatory statutes that almost force station owners in metro areas to push talk to AM, by stipulating the number of formats and stations per metropolitan area. Nonetheless, five years ago, there were about five full-fledged talk stations on FM; today there are 35. And more music stations are broadening their formats to include talk. 16

In fact, advertisers' desire for young listeners has led radio stations to offer a proliferation of new formats. An increase in shows such as the recently syndicated "Opie and Anthony" and its predecessor, "Howard Stern," lure young males with so-called "hot talk" or "shock talk." Indeed, talk show personalities tend to be controversial, crude and full of attitude because those attributes appeal to young males. Sports talk radio like WFAN, the No. 1 billing station in terms of advertising revenue in America, also brings in a younger, mostly male, demographic. "Understand that for a 40-year-old guy listening to that WFAN—which has news and talk—that is his news/talk/information station," says Sabo. "That's a major new trend. And those stations do really well." 17

Michael Packer, president of Rochester Hills, Mich.–based Packer Talk Radio Consulting, says that talk is splintering into new formats to serve two very different psychographic types. 18

The first type, "intuitive feelers," are the traditional talk base. "They want the inside story, the dirt, the emotional side," he explains. The second type, "analytical thinkers," believe that "talk show hosts are the dumbest people in the world. They want the facts, the news, the useful information," he adds. The result is a split between the old-fashioned Limbaugh format and variations on the "news you can use" format.

19   Talkers' Harrison believes talk radio is still missing tremendous opportunities to target women. "Talk radio is in the habit of programming to men—old and young," he explains. With programming created by and for men, it's no wonder advertisers think of talk as a male medium. Cooke agrees. "The missing quotient in talk radio today is . . . the opposite of Rush Limbaugh. It's Annabelle Gurwitch—this gangly, wisecracking young woman who hosts a show on TBS. What if we sought out a young woman instead of an angry old man and see what happens?"

20   One area that talk is becoming increasingly reflective of America's diversity is Spanish language programming. Ten years ago, there were only a few Hispanic stations; today there are over 60 programs nationwide exclusively in Spanish. Miami-based Radio Unica, the first 24/7 news station aimed at Hispanics, launched three years ago; it features Hispanic media stars on 59 affiliate stations across the country. The largest Spanish language broadcaster is Hispanic Broadcasting based in Dallas, which owns and operates over 40 stations in 12 of the top 15 Hispanic markets. "When the census figures get plugged into Arbitron's system later this year, it's going to be a revelation," predicts Taylor. "Hispanics spend an enormous amount of time listening to radio. It's a real connection to their culture. In Mexico and other Latin American countries, radio is ubiquitous, and that's the usage pattern Hispanics are bringing to the States."

21   Targeted talk radio is clearly the future of the format. The new talk hones in on Hispanic, black, female, young male or older male interests and delves into personal finance, consumer affairs, relationships, gardening or old-fashioned politics. In short, talk radio is going through the expansive proliferation of niche markets that has already hit almost every other form of media—television, movies, magazines and music radio.

22   The key is getting local and getting specific. "When I program a new talk station, I bake from scratch," explains Sabo. "I create a station for a particular group of people in a particular city at a particular point in time. The result is completely different in each case—and it should be."

Sara O'Sullivan

THE ILLUSION
OF CONSUMER
PARTICIPATION: THE
CASE OF TALK RADIO

Sara O'Sullivan teaches at University College, Dublin, where her fields of research and special interest include sociology of the media and sociology of health and illness. She is a member of the editorial board of the Irish Journal of Sociology, *where she has also acted as a guest editor of a special edition on media issues. The article included here examines whether talk radio is truly a two-way medium that allows for audience participation, using the example of a popular Irish talk radio show. You might consider to what degree the issues raised in regard to this Irish show relate to American talk radio as well. This piece was first published in October 2001 in* Media/Culture Journal, *an online publication that accepts both academic essays and essays written by members of the wider public. This editorial policy is a purposeful attempt to conduct its debates and conversations among a larger segment of society rather than limiting them to only experts in media and cultural analysis. In what ways does O'Sullivan's essay accommodate that wider audience? How might it do so more effectively?*

Introduction

Talk radio is the term used to refer to those radio programmes   1
that allow members of the public to participate in on-air debate and discussion. It allows the audience an audible presence on-air and so creates at least an illusion of access to the airwaves. In this paper I draw on my Ph.D. research (O'Sullivan, 2000), a qualitative case study of an Irish talk radio show *The Gerry Ryan Show* (go to *www.2fm.ie* to hear today's show). A key feature of *The Gerry Ryan Show* is the access it offers to the audience. The audience are continuously addressed by the host as potential callers. Before nearly every advertising or music break he repeats his "catch-phrase" "1850 85 22 22 the RyanLine is Open."

2   The major component of the show is caller's stories about themselves and their everyday lives. Topics cover both mundane and extraordinary aspects of everyday experience. Routine activities like going to the supermarket or the dentist, driving and getting up in the morning are all packaged into entertaining stories by callers to the show. This involves the "entrepreneurship of the self," that is monitoring one's own everyday experience for stories suitable for *The Gerry Ryan Show*, getting through to the show and successfully selling the story to the production team, and finally performing the story live on-air when called upon to do so. These stories also include more bizarre topics, for example "my pet is crazy . . . he eats concrete slabs" and "I was abducted by aliens," stories which are easier to perform.

3   Many commentators have argued that talk radio performs an important democratic function because of the access offered to "ordinary" citizens who can participate in on-air debate and discussion (see for example Wright, Crittenden, Hofstetter et al., Annenberg Public Policy Center). The resultant forum has been described as "perhaps, the epitome of participatory democracy" (Rehm 70). More recently a public sphere framework has been used by some writers to understand the possible contribution made to democratic debate and discussion by talk radio and talk television shows (see for example O'Sullivan, 1997; Page and Tannenbaun, Livingstone and Lunt).

4   Habermas (158–62) identifies a move from a culture-debating to a culture-consuming public where involvement replaces discussion. The public sphere becomes a mass and people withdraw into a private sphere (Habermas 159). The "transmogrified" public sphere becomes a sphere of cultural consumption. Subjectivity is shaped by leisure activities rather than debate and discussion in the private sphere. Critical discussion gives way to "exchanges about tastes and preferences" (Habermas 171). The press no longer transmits "the rational-critical debate of private people assembled into a public" but shapes the debate from the outset (Habermas 188). The result is a "staged display"; "even arguments are transmuted into symbols to which again one cannot respond by arguing but only by identifying with them" (Habermas 206).

5   *The Gerry Ryan Show* exhibits many features of a transmogrified public sphere. Rather than communication and understanding there is performance and publicity; appearance is more important than rational-critical debate. The audience are positioned as, and respond as, consumers rather than citizens. The production team limit and control access to *The Gerry*

Ryan Show, despite the illusion of open access. Callers use *The Gerry Ryan Show* for self-presentation rather than any critical discussion of social and political issues. Performativity is a factor here, as in any public forum.

The production team exercise control over the content of *The*   6
Gerry Ryan Show in a number of ways. Topics are usually predefined rather than open-ended. Calls are pre-selected and there is limited access to the airways available. Getting on-air requires an understanding of the style of *The Gerry Ryan Show*, and orienting your contribution accordingly. A key issue is to be entertaining and to avoid being boring. Callers are aware of these requirements and are also aware of the constraints or limitations to the participation offered by the show. The power of the host is another key factor (see Moss and Higgins 1981, Moss and Higgins 1992, Liddicoat et al.).

Performative Aspect of Calling

All public sphere fora involve an audience. This holds whether   7
you are talking about the bourgeois public sphere of the eighteenth century, or contemporary talk radio shows. Interaction involves the presentation of the self (Goffman). Callers to *The Gerry Ryan Show* orient to the transmogrified public sphere as an arena for self-presentation, that is as a stage. Goffman argues that individuals use both defensive and protective techniques to safeguard the impressions they give off. Goffman (43) also argues that in different circumstances individuals will be more or less concerned "to make an effective showing." In relation to a public forum like *The Gerry Ryan Show* it would appear to be likely that an individual would be concerned about their on-air performance given the presence of a large audience.

However, a good performance is difficult. First of all the in-   8
stitutional nature of on-air talk means that there are external factors affecting the performance that are out of the individual's control. The setting is "fixed." For the majority of callers, going on-air is a new part that has to be performed. A concern about errors and mistakes is seen as central to the performance (Goffman 52). It is not surprising to find that, for some respondents, calling the show created anxiety. Callers were very aware of the public nature of their call to the show and calling was seen as potentially dangerous to the self.

> You're aware that other people are em listening to you
> [(yeah)] (. . .) so from that point of view it is intimidating.
> You're not, you're not always going to come across with the

perfect English or express yourself as you would in a totally relaxed setting, you know [(uhum, uhum)] (. . .) you are afraid because you're on national radio you are afraid that there are people listening to it that you do know [(uhum)] that you're going to say something thick.

Conclusion

9   *The Gerry Ryan Show* exhibits many features of a transmogrified public sphere. The audience are positioned as, and respond as, consumers rather than citizens. The production team limit and control access to *The Gerry Ryan Show*, despite the illusion of open access. Callers use *The Gerry Ryan Show* for self-presentation rather than any critical discussion of social and political issues. Performativity is a factor here, as in any public forum.

10   Talk radio can provide a unique space for audience participation. However, talk shows exist primarily to attract and maintain large audiences. Market criteria require callers' stories to be entertaining or they will not make it through the screening process. Callers have to monitor and survey their biographies for suitable material. Callers also have to know how to package them in the appropriate manner. I would argue that this limits the participation offered by talk radio.

WORKS CITED

Annenberg Public Policy Center. *Call-In Political Talk Radio: Background, Content, Audiences, Portrayal in Mainstream Media* under the direction of Joseph N. Capella, Joseph Turow and Kathleen Hall Jamieson, presented at the 1996 Annual Meeting of the American Political Science Association, San Francisco, California, 1996.

Crittenden, J. "Democratic Functions of the Open Mike Radio Forum." *Public Opinion Quarterly* 35.2 (1971): 200–10.

Goffman, Erving. *The Presentation of the Self in Everyday Life*. London: Pelican, 1971.

Habermas, Jurgen. *The Structural Transformation of the Public Sphere: An Inquiry into a Category of Bourgeois Society* translated by Thomas Burger. Cambridge: Polity Press, 1989.

Hofstetter, C. R., M. C. Donovan, M. R. Klauber, A. Cole, C. J. Huie and T. Yuasa. "Political Talk Radio: A Stereotype Reconsidered." *Political Research Quarterly* 47.2 (1994): 467–79.

Liddicoat, Anthony, Susanne Dopke, Kristina Love and Anne Brown. "Presenting a point of view: Callers' contributions to talkback radio in Australia." *Journal of Pragmatics* 22 (1994): 139–56.

Livingstone, Sonia and Peter Lunt. *Talk on Television: Audience Participation and Public Debate*. London and New York: Routledge, 1994.

Moss, Peter and Christine Higgins. "A Discourse Analysis of Talk-Back Radio: Some Cultural Implications." *Australian Review of Applied Linguistics* 4 (1981): 32–47.

Moss, Peter and Christine Higgins. *Sounds Real: Radio in Everyday Life.* St. Lucia: University of Queensland Press, 1982.

O'Sullivan, Sara. "The Ryanline is Now Open." pp. 167–90 in Mary J. Kelly and Barbara O'Connor (eds.) *Media Audiences in Ireland: Power and Cultural Identity.* Dublin: UCD Press, 1997.

O'Sullivan, Sara. *Understanding Irish Talk Radio: A Qualitative Case Study of The Gerry Ryan Show.* Unpublished Ph.D. thesis, 2000.

Page, Benjamin I. and Jason Tannenbaum. "Populistic Deliberation and Talk Radio." *Journal of Communication,* Spring (1996): 33–54.

Rehm, Diane. "Talking Over America's Electronic Backyard Fence." pp. 69–73 in Edward C. Pease and Everette E. Dennis (eds.), *Radio: The Forgotten Medium.* New Brunswick, N.J.: Transaction Publishers, 1995.

Wright, Anthony. *Local Radio and Local Democracy: A Study in Political Education.* London: IBA, 1983.

L. Brent Bozell III

TALK RADIO: MEDIA HATE "DEMOCRACY IN ACTION"

Though talk radio has many critics, as the first essay in this section suggests, it still has a great many devotees who find in this medium like-minded others with whom to converse publicly. The essay below responds to those who have stressed the negatives of talk radio. Its author, Brent Bozell III, is the president of the Media Research Center, Parents Television Council, and the Conservative Communications Center. A lecturer and syndicated columnist as well as a businessman, publisher and activist, Bozell is a leader in the conservative movement. This piece was first published in 1996 by Media Research Center, a politically conservative organization that was founded "to bring balance and responsibility to the news media" because, according to its website, "leaders of America's conservative movement have long believed that within the national news media a strident liberal bias existed that influenced the public's understanding of critical issues." In what ways does this article support the conservative argument about media in general, and talk radio specifically? How does it engage the arguments made by others about talk radio in this section?

1   It is the conventional wisdom of the elitist national news media that talk radio is one of those unfortunate casualties of the democratic process, wherein freedom of speech allows for demagogic hatemongers to pollute with nonsense the minds of the poor, uneducated, and easy to command.

2   As usual, the enlightened press corps is wrong.

3   The Annenberg School for Communication at the University of Pennsylvania, headed up by professor Kathleen Hall Jamieson (no conservative, she), has released a year-long study of talk radio that included listening to hundreds of hours of talk radio as well as reading 2,647 print stories on talk radio over a two-year period. Among their findings:

> 1. "Political talk radio listeners are more likely than nonlisteners to consume all news media other than TV news, to be more knowledgeable, and to be involved in political activities. This is true regardless of the ideology of the hosts of the programs to which they listen."

4   In shorthand: The talk radio listener is smarter than the average American.

5   This confounds the snooty liberal cocktail banter that inevitably becomes the stuff of published establishment thought. In a *Washington Post* book review, former CBS newsman Marvin Kalb sniffed: "Cut off the funding for NPR, or gradually reduce its funding to the point where it becomes a mere shadow of its usual robust, sensible self, and the American people may find themselves left with nothing much more than Rush and his dozens of mini-clones for information about the world. For Limbaugh's 'ditto-heads,' this may be the most splendid of tomorrows, but for other more thoughtful listeners, it may be the bleakest of forecasts." NBC's Bob Faw once put it another way, asking whether "talk radio is not democracy in action, but democracy run amok."

> 2. "The mainstream media tend to portray political talk radio superficially and as powerful, pernicious, and homogeneous." The study found not only that "the homogeneity of political talk radio is overstated," but that "By focusing on extreme moments of talk radio

without indicating how typical they are of the most widely heard shows, mainstream news may invite the inference that political talk is routinely uncivil at best, dangerous at worst."

In shorthand: Critics of talk radio are misleading the public.   6

The Annenberg report might have included *Time's* Richard   7
Lacayo writing after the Oklahoma City bombing: "In a nation that has entertained and appalled itself for years with hot talk on the radio and the campaign trail, the inflamed rhetoric of the '90s is suddenly an unindicted co-conspirator in the blast."

Or *Los Angeles Times* reporter Nina Easton: "The Oklahoma   8
City attack on federal workers and their children also alters the once-easy dynamic between charismatic talk show and adoring audience. Hosts who routinely espouse the same anti-government themes as the militia movement now must walk a fine line between inspiring their audience—and inciting the most radical among them."

Or Dan Rather, who defamed talk radio this way: "Even after   9
Oklahoma City, you can turn on your radio in any city and still dial up hate talk: extremist, racist, and violent rhetoric from the hosts and those who call in."

> 3. "In 61 percent of the cases that the host was mentioned, the host's program was not mentioned . . . Articles where talk show hosts appeared virtually ignored audiences, callers, guests, and advertisers."

The Annenberg School study found Limbaugh came up in 74   10
percent of print stories mentioning talk show hosts, more than one in three of them unfavorable. But the study's authors argue Limbaugh is a different animal than most of talk radio: "Limbaugh spends more time than other hosts arguing to his audience that they should assume personal responsibility and can make a difference . . . It promotes a fundamental value of personal responsibility and efficacy in support of political involvement."

Further, "His ongoing attempts to teach his listeners how to   11
'interpret' the 'liberal' press are rarely mentioned in the nearly 3,000 articles we read. Yet one can make a case that from the standpoint of the general press, and perhaps the entire political process, these daily lessons are one of the most far-reaching consequences of his program."

In shorthand: Limbaugh performs a public service, extolling   12
his listeners not only to think for themselves, but to practice democracy through involvement in the political process.

13   The Annenberg study proves what conservatives have said all along: far from enlightened, the national news media are ignorant about, and therefore unqualified to judge, talk radio. Far from objective, their slant is leftist, arrogant, mean-spirited—and wrong.

14   Need more proof? Every network newscast has run stories getting it wrong about Rush Limbaugh at one point or another; every network refused to report this study. For the print press, more of the same: with the exception of *The Washington Times* and the briefest of mentions in *USA Today*, not one national newspaper or news magazine gave the study consideration.

15   We rest our case.

José Márquez
TALK, RADIO
AND DEMOCRACY

José Néstor Márquez was born in Havana, Cuba, the son of a man who spent ten years in prison for his opposition to Fidel Castro. After studying political science and religion, he worked in public broadcasting and other media. This piece, self-published on Márquez's website in April 2004, examines the phenomenon of talk radio in light of the "civil society" to which America claims. This essay illustrates, both in form and in its mode of publication, the entry of "new media" into the way that we receive information and opinions. You might consider how the Internet, which allows for the free publication of opinions, allows for a greater voice of individuals like Márquez. You might also consider the possible dangers of, and restrictions to, that free publication venue that are raised by other authors in this part of Conversations.

When the Soviets took power, the communications technology they favored wasn't telephone networks, but the loudspeaker.
—*NICHOLAS LEMANN*

As it becomes more difficult to reach across the party line, campaigns are devoting more energy to firing up their hard-core

supporters. For voters in the middle, this election may aggravate their feeling that politics no longer speaks to them, that it has become a dialogue of the deaf, a rant of uncompromising extremes.
— *"POLITICAL SPLIT IS PERVASIVE," THE WASHINGTON POST*

I recently had the opportunity to interview, via email, the astute editor of a magazine devoted to talk radio.   1

Early on in our email exchange, the interviewee quoted   2
Shakespeare to say "All the world is a stage," and talk radio, though it claims to offer political advice, is primarily a form of entertainment.

To which I responded: If talk radio is mostly entertainment,   3
then it need not be faithful to the democratic process.

In other words, if talk shows hosts are merely entertainers   4
they have no obligation to defend their statements through a dialogue with expert detractors.

Perhaps, their entertaining but not necessarily truthful de-   5
piction of political matters, left unexamined, might negatively affect our society's ability to engage in democracy. (Mind you, this applies to liberals as much as conservatives.)

My concern, as a Cuban refugee and an American citizen *by*   6
choice, is the anti-democratic effect of the populist demagogue. As I see it, when monologuists set the tone for public debate, dialogue is often very difficult—and democracy relies on dialogue.

But, the editor of the talk radio industry magazine countered   7
that politics is actually war by peaceful means and no one side need give the other the opportunity to speak.

He went on to say that the occasion for a rebuttal is made   8
possible by the "Freedom of Speech" protections in the U.S. Constitution and it ultimately falls to the marketplace of ideas and enlightened consumers to sort out competing claims.

Respectfully and joyfully, I disagreed, on several points.   9

First, while the definition of politics as "war by other means"   10
has a long historical tradition, from Machiavelli to Clausewitz to Karl Rove, it is not the only definition of the political process.

From the time of Plato, there has been a countervailing defi-   11
nition which holds that, unlike war, politics is a deliberative process where the preferred outcome is not necessarily known beforehand.

In this tradition, people enter into politics not only to estab-   12
lish a particular order (as they would through war) but, rather, to investigate and determine what the best possible order might be.

13   Furthermore, the marketplace of ideas (or goods) is not inherently transparent and has, on many occasions, been manipulated at the expense of the consumer; whether purchasing fruit or buying into an idea.

14   And while the First Amendment protects the right to rebutt claims, it does not provide for the means to do so in a public square ostensibly dominated by private soapboxes.

15   Finally, "What's entertainment?" For if talk radio is the domain of monologuists, it is also a deviation from the tradition of Shakespeare, novels, movies and other forms of popular storytelling.

16   In most of these genres, the best stories include not one but multiple perspectives and voices. Almost always, the better realized the villain, the more compelling the story.

17   For the record, my nerdy response led to a snippy riposte (his), a puzzled apology (mine) and a conciliatory gesture (his). We ended our email exchange shortly thereafter, with a perfunctory: "We will agree to disagree."

18   Later on that same day, I caught an episode of The Charlie Rose show devoted to the Sadr militia revolt in Iraq. As the guests on this television talk show pointed out, winning the war in Iraq proved very easy—but establishing a democracy will be far more difficult.

19   One guest on the program drew a parallel to the Western democracies, saying: It took us one thousand years, from the signing of the Magna Carta, to develop our democratic institutions. It took the Japanese five to seven years after World War II to create their democracy. In conclusion, Why would we think we can create a democracy in Iraq in less than 12 months?

20   And that's when it hit me.

21   If, as the shrewd talk tadio expert had said, politics and war are two sides of the same concern, then there should be no problem in Iraq: the winner takes all.

22   But, in fact, there is a tremendous problem in Iraq. For war and politics—by which I have always assumed one means democracy—are not one and the same.

23   And so the U.S. must now slowly, painstakingly, use military means to create the conditions for a democracy in what was formerly a dictatorship—to fashion a society where dialogue rather than monologue reigns supreme.

24   This last week, that march towards democracy was ambushed by a charismatic and, I would imagine, highly entertaining figure: Muqtada al-Sadr. Note that what al-Sadr says is beyond refutation—although he is but a student, he has used his father's legacy as a member of the clergy to issue proclamations that allow for no rebuttal.

Furthermore, in the chain of events that triggered his power   25
play—his military act—the turning point may have come
when the U.S. occupying forces closed down his newspaper,
al-Hawzah, last week.

Why was the *al-Hawzah* newspaper closed down? Because it   26
was printing stories that often had little to no basis in reality.
Instead, like entertaining opinions, they painted sensational
pictures of U.S. misdeeds.

One could argue that the U.S. was censoring *al-Hawzah*,   27
but censorship is only meaningful in the context of a civil society, where institutions—like the legal system—exist to hash out
the validity of claims. No such institutions exist at the moment
in Iraq.

al-Hawzah and al-Sadr tell stories and offer observations that   28
are ostensibly entertaining, popular and compelling. Yet, the
expression of same has been found to be a threat for democracy
in Iraq, most likely because al-Sadr has no intentions of sharing
the stage or engaging in dialogue with his detractors.

Naturally, I don't mean to imply the popular talk show hosts   29
are the American equivalent of firebrand clerics like al-Sadr.
But, the parallels are intriguing.

In order to dismiss this comparison, one would have to suc-   30
cesfully argue that democracy in the U.S. is nowhere near as
fragile as it is in Iraq.

Our legal system and our constitution are, without a doubt, a   31
solid guarantee of democracy. Our schools and media are, similarly, both varied, stable and in many ways independent.

But how healthy is our civil society?   32

Thom Hartmann

TALKING BACK
TO TALK RADIO—
FAIRNESS, DEMOCRACY,
AND PROFITS

*Talk radio has historically been dominated by conservative
hosts and listeners, as most experiments with left-leaning talk*

shows have not proved successful. Still, new liberal talk radio shows have begun to re-emerge, including one hosted by the author of the essay below, Thom Hartmann. Hartmann is a best-selling author, a teacher, and a psychotherapist. His books include Unequal Protection: The Rise of Corporate Dominance and the Theft of Human Rights. *In the essay included here Hartmann makes an argument for the importance of liberal talk radio despite its past failures. The article was published on a liberal activist website,* Common Dreams, *which describes itself as "a national non-profit citizens' organization working to bring progressive Americans together to promote progressive visions for America's future." The organization is "committed to being on the cutting-edge of using the Internet as a political organizing tool and creating new models for internet activism." How does the venue in which this essay was published affect your reading of it?*

1   "All Democrats are fat, lazy, and stupid," the talk-show host said in grave, serious tones as if he were uttering a sacred truth.

2   We were driving to Michigan for the holidays, and I was tuning around, listening for the stations I'd worked for two and three decades ago. I turned the dial. "It's a Hannity For Humanity house," a different host said, adding that the Habitat For Humanity home he'd apparently hijacked for his own self-promotion would only be given to a family that swears it's conservative. "No liberals are going to get this house," he said.

3   Turning the dial again, we found a convicted felon ranting about the importance of government having ever-more powers to monitor, investigate, and prosecute American citizens without having to worry about constitutional human rights protections. Apparently the combining of nationwide German police agencies (following the terrorist attack of February 1933 when the Parliament building was set afire) into one giant Fatherland Security Agency answerable only to the Executive Branch, the Reichssicherheitshauptamt and its SchutzStaffel, was a lesson of history this guy had completely forgotten. Neither, apparently, do most Americans recall that the single most powerful device used to bring about the SS and its political master was radio.

4   Is history repeating itself?

5   Setting aside the shrill and nonsensical efforts of those who suggest the corporate-owned media in America is "liberal," the situation with regard to talk radio is particularly perplexing: It doesn't even carry a pretense of political balance. While the

often-understated Al Gore recently came right out and said
that much of the corporate-owned media are "part and parcel
of the Republican Party," those who listen to talk radio know it
has swung so far to the right that even Dwight Eisenhower or
Barry Goldwater would be shocked.

Average Americans across the nation are wondering how 6
could it be that a small fringe of the extreme right has so captured the nation's airwaves? And done it in such an effective
fashion that when they attack folks like Tom Daschle, he and
his family actually get increased numbers of death threats?
How is it that ex-felons like John Poindexter's protégée Ollie
North and Nixon's former burglar G. Gordon Liddy have become stars? How is it that ideologues like Rush Limbaugh can
openly promote hard-right Republicans, and avoid a return of
the dead-since-Reagan Fairness Doctrine (and get around the
desire of the American public for fairness) by claiming what
they do is "just entertainment"?

And, given the domination of talk radio by the fringe hard- 7
right that represents the political views of only a small segment
of America, why is it that the vast majority of talk radio stations across the nation never run even an occasional centrist or
progressive show in the midst of their all-right, all-the-time
programming day?

Even within the radio industry itself, there's astonishment. 8

Program directors and station managers I've talked with claim 9
they have to program only hard-right hosts. They point out that
when they insert even a few hours of a centrist or progressive
talk host into a typical talk-radio day, the station's phone lines
light up with angry, flaming reactions from listeners; even advertisers get calls of protest. Just last month, a talk-radio station
manager told me solemnly, "Only right-wingers listen to AM
radio any more. The lefties would rather read."

How could this be? After all, an "environmentalist" 10
Democrat—Al Gore—won the majority of the popular vote in
the last presidential election, with a half-million more votes
than any other presidential candidate (of any party) in the entire history of the nation. How could it be that there are only
two Democratic or progressive voices in major national radio
syndication, and only a small handful in partial syndication or
on local shows?

The issue is important for two reasons. 11

First, in a nation that considers itself a democratic republic, 12
the institutions of democracy are imperiled by a lack of balanced national debate on issues of critical importance. As both
Nazi Germany and Stalinist Russia learned, a steady radio
drumbeat of a single viewpoint—from either end of the political

spectrum—is not healthy for democracy when opposing voices are marginalized.

13   Second, what's happened recently in the radio industry represents a business opportunity of significant proportions. The station manager I talked with is wrong, because of something in science known as "sample bias." He was assuming his radio listeners represent all radio listeners, a critical error.

14   Here's why the talk radio scene is so dominated by the right, and how it can become more democratic. First, a very brief history:

15   When radio first became a national force in the 1920s and 1930s, most stations programmed everything. Country/Western music would be followed by Big Band, followed by Mozart, followed by drama or comedy. Everything was jumbled together, and people needed the newspaper program guides to know when to listen to what.

16   As the market matured, and drama and comedy moved to television, radio stations realized there were specific market segments and niches within those segments to which they could program. And they realized that people within those niches had very specific tastes. Country/Western listeners only wanted to hear Country/Western—Big Band put them off, and classical music put them to sleep. Classical music fans, on the other hand, became irritated when Country/Western or the early versions of Rock 'n Roll came on the air. And Rock fans clicked off the moment Frank Sinatra came on.

17   So, as those of us who've worked in the business saw, stations began to program into these specific musical niches, and it led to a new renaissance (and profit windfall) in the radio business.

18   But to make money in the new world of radio that emerged in the 1950s, you had to be true to your niche.

19   When I was a Country/Western DJ, if I had tried to drop in a song from The Rolling Stones, my listeners would have gone ballistic, calling in and angrily complaining. Similarly, when I was doing morning drive-time Rock, it would have been suicide to drop in four minutes of Mozart. Smart programmers know to always hold true to their niche and their listeners.

20   At first, radio talk shows were seen as a way of fulfilling FCC community service requirements. In the late 1960s and early 1970s, when I was a reporter and news anchor at WITL-AM/FM in Lansing, Michigan, we had an afternoon talk show that ran from 2 to 3 p.m. Usually hosted by the station's general manager, the late Chuck Drake, and sometimes fill-in hosted by us in the news staff, the show was overtly run to satisfy the FCC's mandate that stations "serve the public interest." Thus, our talk show focused mostly on public-interest issues, from

local and national politics to lost dog reports, and we tried
hard to present all viewpoints fairly (as was then required by
the FCC's Fairness Doctrine).

In that, we were following a long radio tradition. Modern talk   21
radio as a major force in America started in 1926, when
Catholic priest Father Charles E. Coughlin took to the airwaves.
By the mid-1930s, as many as a full third of the entire nation—
an estimated 45 million people—listened to his weekly broadcasts. His downfall, and the end of the 15-year era of talk radio
he'd both created and dominated, came in the early 1940s when
the nation was at war and Hitler was shipping millions of Jews
to the death camps. For reasons still unknown (Alzheimer's is
suspected), Coughlin launched into hard-right anti-Semitic
tirades in his broadcasts, blaming an international Jewish conspiracy for communism, the Great Depression, World War II,
and most of the world's other ills. His sudden shift to the radical
right disgusted his listeners, and led his superiors in the
Catholic Church to demand he retire from radio and return to
his parish duties where he died in relative obscurity.

Many say the Fairness Doctrine came about in part because   22
of Coughlin.

A generation later, a new Father Coughlin emerged in the   23
form of Rush Limbaugh, an articulate and talented talk-show
host out of Sacramento. Joe Pyne (a conservative who almost
always had a liberal with him on the air) was dead, and conservative investors and programmers were looking to unseat the
fabulously popular liberal talker Alan Berg and bring "balance"
to America's airwaves. (In June of 1984, the year Rush began
"issues talk" on Sacramento's KFBK, Berg was machine-
gunned to death by right-wingers claiming they were from the
Aryan Nation.) Within four years, Rush rose to national status
by offering his program free of charge to stations across the
nation. Station managers, not being business dummies, laid
off local talent and picked up Rush's free show, leading to a national phenomena: the Limbaugh show was one of America's
greatest radio success stories, spreading from state to state
faster than any modern talk show had ever done. (Such free or
barter offerings are now standard in the industry.)

And, station managers discovered, there is a loyal group of   24
radio listeners (around 20 million occasional listeners, with
perhaps one to five million who consider themselves
"dittoheads") who embraced Rush's brand of overt hard-right
spin, believing every word he says even though he claims
his show is "just entertainment" to avoid a reemergence of
the Fairness Doctrine and the political-activity provisions of
McCain/Feingold. The sudden success of Rush led local radio

station programmers to look for more of the same: there was a sudden demand for Rush-clone talkers who could meet the needs of the nation's Rush-bonded listeners, and the all-right-wing-talk radio format emerged, dominated by Limbaugh and Limbaugh-clones in both style and political viewpoint.

25   Thus, the extreme fringe of the right wing dominates talk radio not because all radio listeners are right-wingers, but, instead, because the right wingers and their investors were the first to the market with a consistent and predictable programming slant, making right-wing-talk the first large niche to mature in the newly emergent talk segment of the radio industry. Listeners always know what they'll get with Rush or one of his clones, and programming to a loyal and identifiable audience is both the dream and the necessity of every radio station's management.

26   Which brings us to the opportunity this represents for Democrats, progressives, radio stations, and those interested in supporting democracy by bringing balance to the nation's airwaves.

27   Going back to the music radio programming analogy, think of Rush and Rush-clone-right-wing-talk as if it were Country/Western music. It's unique, instantly recognizable, and has a loyal and definable audience, just like any of the specific music niches. This explains why it's nearly impossible to successfully program progressive talk in the halfway fashion that's often been tried (and often failed) up to today.

28   The rules are the same as in music programming: any competent radio station program director knows they'll get angry listeners if they drop an hour of Rock or Rap into a Country/Western programming day. It's equally easy to predict that if you were to drop an hour or three of a progressive talker like Mike Malloy or Peter Werbe into a day dominated by Rush and his clones, the listeners will be outraged. After all, those particular listeners thought they were tuned into an all-right-wing station.

29   But that response doesn't mean—as conservatives in the radio industry suggest—that there is no market for progressive talk radio. What it means is that there's not yet an awakening in the broadcast industry to the reality that they're missing a huge unserved market. But, like with right-wing talk, for balanced or progressive talk radio to succeed it must be programmed consistently throughout the day (and with talent as outrageous and interesting as Rush and his most successful clones).

30   Most stations who today identify themselves as "talk radio" stations are really programming the specific niche of "hard-right-Republican-talk-radio," and the niche of "progressive-and-Democratic-talk-radio" (which would speak to an equal sized market) is just beginning to emerge and mature. Only a

small handful of stations have made a serious effort to program progressive talk, and the only national network to offer any of it in a serious fashion, the "i.e. America Network," hasn't yet made the distinction between "progressive talk" and "soft/advice talk," and, thus, doesn't offer a full day and night's lineup of "hard" progressive talkers along with their "soft" talkers who break up the day.

The key to success for both radio stations and networks is to realize that talk radio isn't a monolithic niche—it's matured into a category, like music did in the 1950s—and within that category there are multiple niches, including the very large demographic niches of conservative talk, relationship-advice talk, progressive talk, and sports talk, and smaller niches of travel talk, investment talk, medical talk, local talk, etc.   31

The station programmers I've talked with who've tried a progressive or centrist talker for an hour or two, only to get angry responses from dittoheads, think this means only extreme-right-wing talkers (and, ideally, convicted felons or those who "declare war on liberals") will make money for their station. And, because they've already carved out the hard-right-Republican-talk niche and alienated the progressive/Democrat niche, they're right.   32

But for stations who want to get into talk in a market already dominated by right-wing talkers on competing stations, the irrefutable evidence of national elections and polls shows that believing only right-wingers will bring listeners (and advertisers) is a mistake. All they need do is what anybody with music programming experience would recommend: identify their niche and stick with it. (Cynics say stations won't program Democrats because owners and management are all "rich Republicans": to this, I say they should listen to some of the music being profitably produced and programmed by America's largest publishing and broadcasting corporations. Profits, for better or worse, are relatively opinion-free.)   33

By running Democratic/progressive-talk in a programming day free of right-wing talkers, stations will open up a new niche and ride it to success. This is a particularly huge opportunity for music stations who look with envy at the success of talk stations in their market, but haven't been willing to jump in because all the best right-wing talkers are already on the competition: all they need do is put on progressive talkers, and they'll open a new, unserved, and profitable niche.   34

And, with right-wing ideologues now in charge of our government, the time has never been better: as Rush showed during the Clinton years (the peak of his success), "issues" talk thrives best in an underdog environment. It's in the American   35 psyche to give a fair listen to people challenging the party in power.

36   Those stations that take the plunge into progressive talk will serve democracy by offering a loyal opposition (which Americans always appreciate), and earn healthy revenues in an industry where it's increasingly difficult to find a profitable niche. And whichever network is first to realize this simple reality and provide stations with solid progressive or Democrat talk programming will build a strong, viable, and financially healthy business.

37   It's time to revitalize democracy and rational political discourse by returning balance to our nation's airwaves, and the profits to be made in this huge unfilled niche may be just the catalyst to bring it about.

3

Gender

Introduction

Of the many ways that we define ourselves, gender is among the most basic. Whether a biological category, a cultural one, or both, what it means to be a "man" or a "woman"— and how the two genders do and should interact—has been a perennial topic of conversation. Gender issues obviously apply to *both* genders. But most recent conversations about gender have been driven by feminism, because until very recently, it was men that defined women, mostly in a misogynist (women-hating) tradition that is deeply seated in Western culture. The fact that women are now involved in defining gender roles has not effaced the tradition of misogyny; nor has it ended discussion of those roles. Just what form will the future of feminist revolution take? (And it is nothing short of a revolution, if one stands back and looks at changes over the last half century.) Just what is it that defines the essential natures of women and men? Beyond reproductive differences, are there inevitable distinctions between the sexes in terms of emotions, sexuality, physiology, morals, values, and so forth? Are all such distinctions the result of social conditioning—social conditioning that might be altered—or are there biological, genetic differences that define not only primary sex characteristics, but behaviors? These questions are all raised by the issues discussed in this section. And although most of the selections primarily address women's concerns, each one has direct and indirect implications for men as well. The readings in this section will first ask you to consider definitional questions (What does it mean to be a man or a woman?) and then to become part of two related facets of that conversation: (1) how gender attitudes might be affected by the language we use and (2) whether pornography can affect male attitudes toward women, or women's attitudes about themselves, or even lead to violence against women.

The first section, "How Can Gender Be Defined?" asks a question that at first glance might seem to be ridiculously obvious. We don't really need to think too deeply to tell the difference between a man and a woman. Or do we? Are these categories as simple as choosing the right clothing department or restroom? Sometimes, it is the concepts that are closest to us that cause the least reflection. The readings in this section will help you to hear (and see) some of the

conversations surrounding gender and sex roles in our culture, and to hear how definitions of the concept differ in
various fields of study as well. Of course, we should not beg
the larger question suggested by this section: *Can* gender be
defined? Beginning from this more inscrutable point of inquiry, which asks whether gender is a concept that can be
hemmed in enough to put into words, is a fine way to generate ideas. After all, even if the answer to that question is
"not definitively," the process of trying to wrap our minds
around the concept of gender is likely to breed many important conversations. More specifically, the readings in this
section allow you to listen in to writers (or in the case of
Sojourner Truth, speakers) who are trying to come to grips
with the same question that we are: how can we define the
experience of being a man or a woman, both personally and
as a group? That question is addressed by the readings in
this section in a number of written styles or "genres": the
transcript of an informal speech, a play, a personal essay, a
science-based essay that draws on personal experience, and
a satire that reminds us not to take ourselves too seriously.

Though sex is, on the one hand, clearly a biological category, few would deny that social conditioning plays at least
some role in what it means to be a man or a woman. (In
fact, for some, social conditioning is considered much more
important than physiological difference.) And few things
have more of an impact on our social conditioning than
language. We learn about the world through experience; but
we conceive of that experience in language—both that
which we speak and write, and that which we hear and
read. With that in mind, it is clear that the ways that language constructs gender norms is worth consideration. As
the reading selections and cartoon printed in this section
disclose, the English language can favor some groups at the
expense of others—particularly men at the expense of
women. To what extent does English, as the product of a
culture dominated by males, demean and delimit women?
To what extent does English perpetuate outworn cultural
assumptions about women? In other words, to what extent
is English itself sexist? And what can be done about it?
Those are the questions taken up in this section. For some,
the argument for gender neutrality in language is a matter
of fairness, and suggests that the way we frame something
in language—the way we write or talk about it—affects our
own and others' perspectives on it. So, if we use "he" as a

pronoun meant to refer to all people, are we at the same
time suggesting that men are more central than women? Do
words (such as doctor/nurse, confirmed bachelor/spinster)
carry with them gender stereotypes? Others, however, suggest that such close scrutiny of language is just a matter of
"political correctness" or the acts of a "language police."
The arguments made on this issue can provide you a way of
entering into this cultural conversation.

The third section in this part of *Conversations* asks another gender-based question: "Does Pornography Cause
Harm to Women?" Of course, we might (and implicitly do)
ask the parallel question—does it cause harm to men? After
all, pornography is sought by both men and women. But
men are much more likely to use pornography regularly;
about 28 percent of men claim to be exposed to porn almost
every day, whereas only 6 percent of women view porn
daily. And in general, pornography is more a part of the
male culture than the female. (Consider, for example, that
we have "strippers" and "male strippers"—no need to define
the first category as "female.") With that in mind, as a gender issue, we might ask how consumption of pornography
effects male perspectives on women, male–female relations,
and in the extreme, the safety of women. Those are the conversations that you'll be entering in this section of the book.
The readings included range widely across time, and feature a sometimes pointed set of conversations among those
who differ on this question: you will hear both the majority
and minority reports on the President's Commission on
Pornography from 1967. You will read an exchange on the
issue of pornography that crosses genders and that pits the
right to free speech against what some authors claim is
the physical harm that takes precedence over free speech in
this case—because, as the old adage goes, free speech does
not give one the right to yell fire in a crowded theater. Free
speech, most suggest, must be limited to that which does
not impose on the rights of others. Hence the question of
this section: Does pornography cause harm to women? And
lest you think that this issue is split purely along gender
lines, you will read an essay by a woman defending the
right to publish pornography and by a man who wants to
see it eliminated.

Since manhood and womanhood are such perennial subjects of conversation, and since they play such an important
role in our identities, it is no surprise that these concepts

have been subject to the imaginations of a wide variety of artists. This part's "Visual Conversations" section asks you to consider the ways that gender and gender roles have been depicted in the arts and the effect of those renderings upon our cultural notions of gender. From artists whose work conveys the gender attitudes of the times, to artists whose intent is to critique those attitudes—or to preserve them—the images in this section will challenge you to think (and to rethink) about what it means to be a man or a woman. Think about the ways that these pictures speak to one another as well as to their audiences. These visuals will also give you the opportunity to consider how the attitudes toward gender that are discussed in this part's readings appear in the images we see everyday on television, on the Internet, and in advertising.

So, can gender be defined? Not likely—at least not in any way that will bring consensus. But the conversation surrounding that question can be an extremely useful one for considering our society's policies and your own judgments and actions as a gendered individual.

How Can Gender
Be Defined?

Sojourner Truth
AIN'T I A WOMAN?

Sojourner Truth's story is fascinating and moving. Born into slavery in Ulster County, New York, around 1797 and given the name Isabella, she was sold three times before she turned twelve. Perhaps sexually abused by one of her owners, she fled to freedom in 1827, a year before slavery was outlawed in New York. In New York City she worked as a domestic and fell in with an evangelical preacher who encouraged her efforts to convert prostitutes. Though illiterate, she managed to negate the sale of her son Peter to the South when her former "owner" tried to accomplish the sale. In 1843, inspired by mystical visions, she took the name Sojourner Truth and set off alone and undeterred by her illiteracy to preach and sing about religion and the abolition of slavery. By 1850, huge crowds were coming to witness the oratory of the ex-slave with the resounding voice and message. During the Civil War she was presented to President Lincoln at the White House. After the war she spoke out for women's suffrage, but she never gave up her spiritual and racial themes—or her humor and exuberance. She continued to lecture until near her death in Battle Creek, Michigan, in 1883.

Sojourner Truth accepted neither the physical inferiority of women nor the idea that they should be placed on pedestals; nor did she subordinate women's rights to the pursuit of racial equality. At a women's rights convention in May 1851, Sojourner Truth rose extemporaneously to rebut speakers who had impugned the rights and capabilities of women. According to an eyewitness who recorded the scene in his diary, this is what she said:

Well, children, where there is so much racket there must be   1
something out of kilter. I think that 'twixt the negroes of the
South and the women at the North, all talking about rights, the
white men will be in a fix pretty soon. But what's all this here
talking about?

That man over there says that women need to be helped into   2
carriages, and lifted over ditches, and to have the best place
everywhere. Nobody ever helps me into carriages, or over
mud-puddles, or gives me any best place! And ain't I a woman?
Look at me! Look at my arm! I have ploughed and planted, and
gathered into barns, and no man could head me! And ain't I a
woman? I could work as much and eat as much as a man—
when I could get it—and bear the lash as well! And ain't I a
woman? I have borne thirteen children, and seen them most
all sold off to slavery, and when I cried out with my mother's
grief, none but Jesus heard me! And ain't I a woman?

Then they talk about this thing in the head; what's this they   3
call it? [Intellect, someone whispers.] That's it, honey. What's
that got to do with women's rights or negro's rights? If my cup
won't hold but a pint, and yours holds a quart, wouldn't you be
mean not to let me have my little half-measure full?

Then that little man in black there, he says women can't have   4
as much rights as men, 'cause Christ wasn't a woman! Where
did your Christ come from? Where did your Christ come from?
From God and a woman! Man had nothing to do with Him.

If the first woman God ever made was strong enough to turn   5
the world upside down all alone, these women together ought
to be able to turn it back, and get it right side up again! And
now they is asking to do it, the men better let them.

Obliged to you for hearing on me, and now old Sojourner   6
ain't got nothing more to say.

Scott Russell Sanders

THE MEN WE CARRY
IN OUR MINDS

*Scott Russell Sanders (born 1945 in Memphis) grew up in
rural Ohio and Tennessee. Active in the environmental movement through organizations such as the Nature Conservancy,*

the Audubon Society, and the Wilderness Society, he has the
ability to cross between the so-called two cultures (science and
the humanities) in his fiction, science fiction, and essays. A
member of the faculty at Indiana University and the author of
many books, he recently told the editors of Contemporary
Authors *that "a writer should be a servant of language, com-*
munity, and nature."

1   "This must be a hard time for women," I say to my friend
Anneke. "They have so many paths to choose from, and so
many voices calling them."

2   "I think it's a lot harder for men," she replies.

3   "How do you figure that?"

4   "The women I know feel excited, innocent, like crusaders in
a just cause. The men I know are eaten up with guilt."

5   "Women feel such pressure to be everything, do everything,"
I say. "Career, kids, art, politics. Have their babies and get back
to the office a week later. It's as if they're trying to overcome a
million years' worth of evolution in one lifetime."

6   "But we help one another. And we have this deep-down sense
that we're in the *right*—we've been held back, passed over,
used—while men feel they're in the wrong. Men are the ones
who've been discredited, who have to search their souls."

7   I search my soul. I discover guilty feelings aplenty—toward
the poor, the Vietnamese, Native Americans, the whales, an
endless list of debts. But toward women I feel something more
confused, a snarl of shame, envy, wary, tenderness, and amaze-
ment. This muddle troubles me. To hide my unease I say,
"You're right, it's tough being a man these days."

8   "Don't laugh," Anneke frowns at me. "I wouldn't be a man for
anything. It's much easier being the victim. All the victim has
to do is break free. The persecutor has to live with his past."

9   How deep is that past? I find myself wondering. How much
of an inheritance do I have to throw off?

10 When I was a boy growing up on the back roads of
Tennessee and Ohio, the men I knew labored with their bodies.
They were marginal farmers, just scraping by, or welders, steel-
workers, carpenters; they swept floors, dug ditches, mined
coal, or drove trucks, their forearms ropy with muscle; they
trained horses, stoked furnaces, made tires, stood on assembly
lines wrestling parts onto cars and refrigerators. They got up
before light, worked all day long whatever the weather, and
when they came home at night they looked as though somebody had been whipping them. In the evenings and on weekends they worked on their own places, tilling gardens that were

lumpy with clay, fixing broken-down cars, hammering on houses that were always too drafty, too leaky, too small.

The bodies of the men I knew were twisted and maimed in   11 ways visible and invisible. The nails of their hands were black and split, the hands tattooed with scars. Some had lost fingers. Heavy lifting had given many of them finicky backs and guts weak from hernias. Racing against conveyor belts had given them ulcers. Their ankles and knees ached from years of stand-ing on concrete. Anyone who had worked for long around ma-chines was hard of hearing. They squinted, and the skin of their faces was creased like the leather of old work gloves. There were times, studying them, when I dreaded growing up. Most of them coughed, from dust or cigarettes, and most of them drank cheap wine or whiskey, so their eyes looked blood-shot and bruised. The fathers of my friends always seemed older than the mothers. Men wore out sooner. Only women lived into old age.

As a boy I also knew another sort of men, who did not sweat   12 and break down like mules. They were soldiers, and so far as I could tell they scarcely worked at all. But when the shooting started, many of them would die. This was what soldiers were *for*, just as a hammer was for driving nails.

Warriors and toilers; those seemed, in my boyhood vision, to   13 be the chief destinies for men. They weren't the only destinies, as I learned from having a few male teachers, from reading books, and from watching television. But the men on television—the politicians, the astronauts, the generals, the savvy lawyers, the philosophical doctors, the bosses who gave orders to both soldiers and laborers—seemed as remote and unreal to me as the figures in Renaissance tapestries. I could no more imagine grow-ing up to become one of these cool, potent creatures than I could imagine becoming a prince.

A nearer and more hopeful example was that of my father,   14 who had escaped from a red-dirt farm to a tire factory, and from the assembly line to the front office. Eventually he dressed in a white shirt and tie. He carried himself as if he had been born to work with his mind. But his body, remembering the earlier years of slogging work, began to give out on him in his fifties, and it quit on him entirely before he turned 65.

A scholarship enabled me not only to attend college, a rare   15 enough feat in my circle, but even to study in a university meant for the children of the rich. Here I met for the first time young men who had assumed from birth that they would lead lives of comfort and power. And for the first time I met women who told me that men were guilty of having kept all the joys and privi-leges of the earth for themselves. I was baffled. What privileges?

What joys? I thought about the maimed, dismal lives of most of the men back home. What had they stolen from their wives and daughters? The right to go five days a week, 12 months a year, for 30 or 40 years to a steel mill or a coal mine? The right to drop bombs and die in war? The right to feel every leak in the roof, every gap in the fence, every cough in the engine as a wound they must mend? The right to feel, when the layoff comes or the plant shuts down, not only afraid but ashamed?

16   I was slow to understand the deep grievances of women. This was because, as a boy, I had envied them. Before college, the only people I had ever known who were interested in art or music or literature, the only ones who read books, the only ones who ever seemed to enjoy a sense of ease and grace were the mothers and daughters. Like the menfolk, they fretted about money, they scrimped and made do. But, when the pay stopped coming in, they were not the ones who had failed. Nor did they have to go to war, and that seemed to me a blessed fact. By comparison with the narrow, ironclad days of fathers, there was an expansiveness, I thought, in the days of mothers. They went to see neighbors, to shop in town, to run errands at school, at the library, at church. No doubt, had I looked harder at their lives, I would have envied them less. It was not my fate to become a woman, so it was easier for me to see the graces. I didn't see, then, what a prison a house could be, since houses seemed to me brighter, handsomer places than any factory. I did not realize—because such things were never spoken of—how often women suffered from men's bullying. Even then I could see how exhausting it was for a mother to cater all day to the needs of young children. But if I had been asked, as a boy, to choose between tending a baby and tending a machine, I think I would have chosen the baby. (Having now tended both, I know I would choose the baby.)

17   So I was baffled when the women at college accused me and my sex of having cornered the world's pleasures. I think something like my bafflement has been felt by other boys (and by girls as well) who grew up in dirt-poor farm country, in mining country, in black ghettos, in Hispanic barrios, in the shadows of factories, in Third World nations—any place where the fate of men is just as grim and bleak as the fate of women.

18   When the women I met at college thought about the joys and privileges of men, they did not carry in their minds the sort of men I had known in my childhood. They thought of their fathers, who were bankers, physicians, architects, stockbrokers, the big wheels of the big cities. They were never laid off, never short of cash at month's end, never lined up for welfare. These fathers made decisions that mattered. They ran the world.

The daughters of such men wanted to share in this power,   19
this glory. So did I. They yearned for a say over their future, for
jobs worthy of their abilities, for the right to live at peace, un-
molested, whole. Yes, I thought, yes yes. The difference between me and these daughters was that they saw me, because
of my sex, as destined from birth to become like their fathers,
and therefore as an enemy to their desires. But I knew better. I
wasn't an enemy, in fact or in feeling. I was an ally. If I had
known, then, how to tell them so, would they have believed
me? Would they now?

Susan Glaspell
TRIFLES

*Susan Glaspell (1882–1948), an Iowan by birth and educa-
tion, moved east in 1911. A Pulitzer Prize–winning dramatist
and a prolific fiction writer, she cofounded the Provincetown
Playhouse on Cape Cod in 1915, which became a center for experimental and innovative drama. In 1916, she wrote* Trifles,
*the one-act play reprinted here; then she adapted it a few
months later into the story "A Jury of Her Peers."*

Characters
GEORGE HENDERSON, *County Attorney*
HENRY PETERS, *Sheriff*
LEWIS HALE, *A Neighboring Farmer*
MRS. PETERS
MRS. HALE

SCENE
The kitchen in the now abandoned farmhouse of JOHN WRIGHT, *a*   1
*gloomy kitchen, and left without having been put in order—
unwashed pans under the sink, a loaf of bread outside the breadbox, a dish towel on the table—other signs of incompleted work.
At the rear the outer door opens and the* SHERIFF *comes in followed by the* COUNTY ATTORNEY *and* HALE. *The* SHERIFF *and* HALE
are men in middle life, the COUNTY ATTORNEY *is a young man; all*

*are much bundled up and go at once to the stove. They are fol-
lowed by two women—the* SHERIFF'S *wife first; she is a slight wiry
woman with a thin nervous face.* MRS. HALE *is larger and would
ordinarily be called more comfortable looking, but she is disturbed now and looks fearfully about as she enters. The women
have come in slowly, and stand close together near the door.*

2 COUNTY ATTORNEY. [*Rubbing his hands.*] This feels good. Come
up to the fire, ladies.

3 MRS. PETERS. [*After taking a step forward.*] I'm not—cold.

4 SHERIFF. [*Unbuttoning his overcoat and stepping away from the
stove as if to mark the beginning of official business.*] Now,
Mr. Hale, before we move things about, you explain to Mr.
Henderson just what you saw when you came here yesterday morning.

5 COUNTY ATTORNEY. By the way, has anything been moved? Are
things just as you left them yesterday?

6 SHERIFF. [*Looking about.*] It's just the same. When it dropped
below zero last night I thought I'd better send Frank out this
morning to make a fire for us—no use getting pneumonia
with a big case on, but I told him not to touch anything except the stove—and you know Frank.

7 COUNTY ATTORNEY. Somebody should have been left here
yesterday.

8 SHERIFF. Oh—yesterday. When I had to send Frank to Morris
Center for that man who went crazy—I want you to know I
had my hands full yesterday. I knew you could get back
from Omaha by today and as long as I went over everything
here myself—

9 COUNTY ATTORNEY. Well, Mr. Hale, tell just what happened when
you came here yesterday morning.

10 HALE. Harry and I had started to town with a load of potatoes.
We came along the road from my place and as I got here I
said, "I'm going to see if I can't get John Wright to go in with
me on a party telephone." I spoke to Wright about it once
before and he put me off, saying folks talked too much anyway, and all he asked was peace and quiet—I guess you
know about how much he talked himself; but I thought
maybe if I went to the house and talked about it before his
wife, though I said to Harry that I didn't know as what his
wife wanted made much difference to John—

11 COUNTY ATTORNEY. Let's talk about that later, Mr. Hale. I do want
to talk about that, but tell now just what happened when
you got to the house.

12 HALE. I didn't hear or see anything; I knocked at the door, and
still it was all quiet inside. I knew they must be up, it was

past eight o'clock. So I knocked again, and I thought I heard somebody say, "Come in." I wasn't sure, I'm not sure yet, but I opened the door—this door [*Indicating the door by which the two women are still standing*] and there in that rocker—[*Pointing to it.*] sat Mrs. Wright. [*They all look at the rocker.*]

COUNTY ATTORNEY. What—was she doing?   13

HALE. She was rockin' back and forth. She had her apron in her   14
hand and was kind of—pleating it.

COUNTY ATTORNEY. And how did she—look?   15

HALE. Well, she looked queer.   16

COUNTY ATTORNEY. How do you mean—queer?   17

HALE. Well, as if she didn't know what she was going to do next. 18
And kind of done up.

COUNTY ATTORNEY. How did she seem to feel about your coming?   19

HALE. Why, I don't think she minded—one way or other. She did-   20
n't pay much attention. I said, "How do, Mrs. Wright, it's cold,
ain't it?" And she said, "Is it?"—and went on kind of pleating
at her apron. Well, I was surprised; she didn't ask me to come
up to the stove, or to set down, but just sat there, not even
looking at me, so I said, "I want to see John." And then she—
laughed. I guess you would call it a laugh. I thought of Harry
and the team outside, so I said a little sharp: "Can't I see
John?" "No," she says, kind o' dull like. "Ain't he home?" says
I. "Yes," says she, "he's home." "Then why can't I see him?" I
asked her, out of patience. "'Cause he's dead," says she.
"*Dead?*" says I. She just nodded her head, not getting a bit excited, but rockin' back and forth. "Why—where is he?" says I,
not knowing what to say. She just pointed upstairs—like that
[*Himself pointing to the room above.*] I got up, with the idea of
going up there. I walked from there to here—then I says,
"Why, what did he die of?" "He died of a rope round his neck,"
says she, and just went on pleatin' at her apron. Well, I went
out and called Harry. I thought I might—need help. We went
upstairs and there he was lyin'—

COUNTY ATTORNEY. I think I'd rather have you go into that up-   21
stairs, where you can point it all out. Just go on now with
the rest of the story.

HALE. Well, my first thought was to get that rope off. It looked . . . 22
[*Stops, his face twitches.*] . . . but Harry, he went up to him,
and he said, "No, he's dead all right, and we'd better not
touch anything." So we went back downstairs. She was still
sitting that same way. "Has anybody been notified?" I asked.
"No," says she, unconcerned. "Who did this, Mrs. Wright?"
said Harry. He said it businesslike—and she stopped pleatin'
of her apron. "I don't know," she says. "You don't *know*?"
says Harry. "No," says she. "Weren't you sleepin' in bed with

him?" says Harry. "Yes," says she, "but I was on the inside."
"Somebody slipped a rope round his neck and strangled him
and you didn't wake up?" says Harry. "I didn't wake up," she
said after him. We must 'a looked as if we didn't see how
that could be, for after a minute she said, "I sleep sound."
Harry was going to ask her more questions but I said maybe
we ought to let her tell her story first to the coroner, or the
sheriff, so Harry went fast as he could to Rivers' place,
where there's a telephone.

23 COUNTY ATTORNEY. And what did Mrs. Wright do when she knew
    that you had gone for the coroner?

24 HALE. She moved from that chair to this one over here
    [*Pointing to a small chair in the corner.*] and just sat there
    with her hands held together and looking down. I got a feel-
    ing that I ought to make some conversation, so I said I had
    come in to see if John wanted to put in a telephone, and at
    that she started to laugh, and then she stopped and looked
    at me—scared. [*The* COUNTY ATTORNEY, *who has had his note-
    book out, makes a note.*] I dunno, maybe it wasn't scared. I
    wouldn't like to say it was. Soon Harry got back, and then
    Dr. Lloyd came, and you, Mr. Peters, and so I guess that's all
    I know that you don't.

25 COUNTY ATTORNEY. [*Looking around.*] I guess we'll go upstairs
    first—and then out to the barn and around there. [*To the*
    SHERIFF] You're convinced that there was nothing important
    here—nothing that would point to any motive.

26 SHERIFF. Nothing here but kitchen things. [*The* COUNTY ATTOR-
    NEY, *after again looking around the kitchen, opens the door of
    a cupboard closet. He gets up on a chair and looks on a shelf.
    Pulls his hand away, sticky.*]

27 COUNTY ATTORNEY. Here's a nice mess.
    [*The women draw nearer.*]

28 MRS. PETERS. [*To the other woman.*] Oh, her fruit; it did freeze. [*To
    the* COUNTY ATTORNEY.] She worried about that when it turned
    so cold. She said the fire'd go out and her jars would break.

29 SHERIFF. Well, can you beat the woman! Held for murder and
    worryin' about her preserves.

30 COUNTY ATTORNEY. I guess before we're through she may have
    something more serious that preserves to worry about.

31 HALE. Well, women are used to worrying over trifles. [*The two
    women move a little closer together.*]

32 COUNTY ATTORNEY. [*With the gallantry of a young politician.*] And
    yet, for all their worries, what would we do without the
    ladies? [*The women do not unbend. He goes to the sink, takes
    a dipperful of water from the pail and pouring it into a basin,
    washes his hands. Starts to wipe them on the roller towel,
    turns it for a cleaner place.*] Dirty towels! [*Kicks his foot*

against the pans under the sink.] Not much of a housekeeper, would you say, ladies?

MRS. HALE. [*Stiffly.*] There's a great deal of work to be done on a   33
farm.

COUNTY ATTORNEY. To be sure. And yet [*With a little bow to her.*] I   34
know there are some Dickson county farmhouses which do
not have such roller towels.
[*He gives it a pull to expose its full length again.*]

MRS. HALE. Those towels get dirty awful quick. Men's hands   35
aren't always as clean as they might be.

COUNTY ATTORNEY. Ah, loyal to your sex, I see. But you and Mrs.   36
Wright were neighbors. I suppose you were friends, too.

MRS. HALE. [*Shaking her head.*] I've not seen much of her of late   37
years. I've not been in this house—it's more than a year.

COUNTY ATTORNEY. And why was that? You didn't like her?   38

MRS. HALE. I liked her all well enough. Farmers wives have their   39
hands full, Mr. Henderson. And then—

COUNTY ATTORNEY. Yes—?   40

MRS. HALE. [*Looking about.*] It never seemed a very cheerful place.   41

COUNTY ATTORNEY. No—it's not cheerful. I shouldn't say she had   42
the homemaking instinct.

MRS. HALE. Well, I don't know as Wright had, either.   43

COUNTY ATTORNEY. You mean that they didn't get on very well?   44

MRS. HALE. No, I don't mean anything. But I don't think a   45
place'd be any cheerfuller for John Wright's being in it.

COUNTY ATTORNEY. I'd like to talk more of that a little later. I   46
want to get the lay of things upstairs now.
[*He goes to the left, where three steps lead to a stair door.*]

SHERIFF. I suppose anything Mrs. Peters does'll be all right. She   47
was to take in some clothes for her, you know, and a few little things. We left in such a hurry yesterday.

COUNTY ATTORNEY. Yes, but I would like to see what you take,   48
Mrs. Peters, and keep an eye out for anything that might be
of use to us.

MRS. PETERS. Yes, Mr. Henderson.   49
[*The women listen to the men's steps on the stairs, then look
about the kitchen.*]

MRS. HALE. I'd hate to have men coming into my kitchen, snoop-   50
ing around and criticising.
[*She arranges the pans under sink which the* COUNTY ATTORNEY
had shoved out of place.]

MRS. PETERS. Of course it's no more than their duty.   51

MRS. HALE. Duty's all right, but I guess that deputy sheriff that   52
came out to make the fire might have got a little of this on.
[*Gives the roller towel a pull.*] Wish I'd thought of that
sooner. Seems mean to talk about her for not having things
slicked up when she had to come away in such a hurry.

53   MRS. PETERS. [*Who has gone to a small table in the left rear corner of the room, and lifted one end of a towel that covers a pan.*] She had bread set.
[*Stands still.*]

54   MRS. HALE. [*Eyes fixed on a loaf of bread beside the breadbox, which is on a low shelf at the other side of the room. Moves slowly toward it.*] She was going to put this in there. [*Picks up loaf, then abruptly drops it. In a manner of returning to familiar things.*] It's a shame about her fruit. I wonder if it's all gone. [*Gets up on the chair and looks.*] I think there's some here that's all right, Mrs. Peters. Yes—here; [*Holding it toward the window.*] this is cherries too. [*Looking again.*] I declare I believe that's the only one. [*Gets down, bottle in her hand. Goes to the sink and wipes it off on the outside.*] She'll feel awful bad after all her hard work in the hot weather. I remember the afternoon I put up my cherries last summer. [*She puts the bottle on the big kitchen table, center of the room. With a sigh, is about to sit down in the rocking-chair. Before she is seated realizes what chair it is; with a slow look at it, steps back. The chair which she has touched rocks back and forth.*]

55   MRS. PETERS. Well, I must get those things from the front room closet. [*She goes to the door at the right, but after looking into the other room, steps back.*] You coming with me, Mrs. Hale? You could help me carry them.
[*They go in the other room; reappear,* MRS. PETERS *carrying a* dress and skirt, MRS. HALE *following with a pair of shoes.*]

56   MRS. PETERS. My, it's cold in there.
[*She puts the clothes on the big table, and hurries to the stove.*]

57   MRS. HALE. [*Examining her skirt.*] Wright was close. I think maybe that's why she kept so much to herself. She didn't even belong to the Ladies Aid. I suppose she felt she couldn't do her part, and then you don't enjoy things when you feel shabby. She used to wear pretty clothes and be lively, when she was Minnie Foster, one of the town girls singing in the choir. But that—oh, that was thirty years ago. This all you was to take in?

58   MRS. PETERS. She said she wanted an apron. Funny thing to want, for there isn't much to get you dirty in jail, goodness knows. But I suppose just to make her feel more natural. She said they was in the top drawer in this cupboard. Yes, here. And then her little shawl that always hung behind the door. [*Opens stair door and looks.*] Yes, here it is.
[*Quickly shuts door leading upstairs.*]

59   MRS. HALE. [*Abruptly moving toward her.*] Mrs. Peters?

60   MRS. PETERS. Yes, Mrs. Hale?

61   MRS. HALE. Do you think she did it?

62   MRS. PETERS. [*In a frightened voice.*] Oh, I don't know.

MRS. HALE. Well, I don't think she did. Asking for an apron and   63
her little shawl. Worrying about her fruit.

MRS. PETERS. [*Starts to speak, glances up, where footsteps are*   64
heard in the room above. In a low voice.] Mr. Peters says it
looks bad for her. Mr. Henderson is awful sarcastic in a
speech and he'll make fun of her sayin' she didn't wake up.

MRS. HALE. Well, I guess John Wright didn't wake when they   65
was slipping that rope under his neck.

MRS. PETERS. No, it's strange. It must have been done awful   66
crafty and still. They say it was such a—funny way to kill a
man, rigging it all up like that.

MRS. HALE. That's just what Mr. Hale said. There was a gun in   67
the house. He says that's what he can't understand.

MRS. PETERS. Mr. Henderson said coming out that what was   68
needed for the case was a motive; something to show anger,
or—sudden feeling.

MRS. HALE. [*Who is standing by the table.*] Well, I don't see any   69
signs of anger around here. [*She puts her hand on the dish
towel which lies on the table, stands looking down at table,
one half of which is clean, the other half messy.*] It's wiped to
here. [*Makes a move as if to finish work, then turns and looks
at loaf of bread outside the breadbox. Drops towel. In that
voice of coming back to familiar things.*] Wonder how they
are finding things upstairs. I hope she had it a little more
red-up up there. You know, it seems kind of *sneaking.*
Locking her up in town and then coming out here and trying to get her own house to turn against her!

MRS. PETERS. But Mrs. Hale, the law is the law.   70

MRS. HALE. I s'pose 'tis. [*Unbuttoning her coat.*] Better loosen up   71
your things, Mrs. Peters. You won't feel them when you go out.
[MRS. PETERS *takes off her fur tippet, goes to hang it on hook at
back of room, stands looking at the under part of the small
corner table.*]

MRS. PETERS. She was piecing a quilt.   72
[*She brings the large sewing basket and they look at the bright
pieces.*]

MRS. HALE. It's log cabin pattern. Pretty, isn't it? I wonder if she   73
was goin' to quilt it or just knot it?
[*Footsteps have been heard coming down the stairs. The*
SHERIFF *enters followed by* HALE *and the* COUNTY ATTORNEY.]

SHERIFF. They wonder if she was going to quilt it or just knot it!   74
[*The men laugh; the women look abashed.*]

COUNTY ATTORNEY. [*Rubbing his hands over the stove.*] Frank's   75
fire didn't do much up there, did it? Well, let's go out to the
barn and get that cleared up.
[*The men go outside.*]

76 MRS. HALE. [*Resentfully.*] I don't know as there's anything so strange, our takin' up our time with little things while we're waiting for them to get the evidence. [*She sits down at the big table smoothing out a block with decision.*] I don't see as it's anything to laugh about.

77 MRS. PETERS. [*Apologetically.*] Of course they've got awful important things on their minds.
[*Pulls up a chair and joins* MRS. HALE *at the table.*]

78 MRS. HALE. [*Examining another block.*] Mrs. Peters, look at this one. Here, this is the one she was working on, and look at the sewing! All the rest of it has been so nice and even. And look at this! It's all over the place! Why, it looks as if she didn't know what she was about!
[*After she has said this they look at each other, then start to glance back at the door. After an instant* MRS. HALE *has pulled at a knot and ripped the sewing.*]

79 MRS. PETERS. Oh, what are you doing, Mrs. Hale?

80 MRS. HALE. [*Mildly.*] Just pulling out a stitch or two that's not sewed very good. [*Threading a needle.*] Bad sewing always made me fidgety.

81 MRS. PETERS. [*Nervously.*] I don't think we ought to touch things.

82 MRS. HALE. I'll just finish up this end. [*Suddenly stopping and leaning forward.*] Mrs. Peters?

83 MRS. PETERS. Yes, Mrs. Hale?

84 MRS. HALE. What do you suppose she was so nervous about?

85 MRS. PETERS. Oh—I don't know. I don't know as she was nervous. I sometimes sew awful queer when I'm just tired. [MRS. HALE *starts to say something, looks at* MRS. PETERS, *then goes on sewing.*] Well, I must get these things wrapped up. They may be through sooner than we think. [*Putting apron and other things together.*] I wonder where I can find a piece of paper, and string.

86 MRS. HALE. In that cupboard, maybe.

87 MRS. PETERS. [*Looking in cupboard.*] Why, here's a birdcage. [*Holds it up.*] Did she have a bird, Mrs. Hale?

88 MRS. HALE. Why, I don't know whether she did or not—I've not been here for so long. There was a man around last year selling canaries cheap, but I don't know as she took one; maybe she did. She used to sing real pretty herself.

89 MRS. PETERS. [*Glancing around.*] Seems funny to think of a bird here. But she must have had one, or why would she have a cage? I wonder what happened to it.

90 MRS. HALE. I s'pose maybe the cat got it.

91 MRS. PETERS. No, she didn't have a cat. She's got that feeling some people have about cats—being afraid of them. My cat

got in her room and she was real upset and asked me to take it out.

MRS. HALE. My sister Bessie was like that. Queer, ain't it?   92

MRS. PETERS. [*Examining the cage.*] Why, look at this door. It's   93
broke. One hinge is pulled apart.

MRS. HALE [*Looking too.*] Looks as if someone must have been   94
rough with it.

MRS. PETERS. Why, yes.   95

[*She brings the cage forward and puts it on the table.*]

MRS. HALE. I wish if they're going to find any evidence they'd be   96
about it. I don't like this place.

MRS. PETERS. But I'm awful glad you came with me, Mrs. Hale.   97
It would be lonesome for me sitting here alone.

MRS. HALE. It would, wouldn't it? [*Dropping her sewing.*] But I   98
tell you what I do wish, Mrs. Peters. I wish I had come over
sometimes when *she* was here. I—[*Looking around the
room.*]—wish I had.

MRS. PETERS. But of course you were awful busy, Mrs. Hale—   99
your house and your children.

MRS. HALE. I could've come. I stayed away because it weren't   100
cheerful—and that's why I ought to have come. I—I've never
liked this place. Maybe because it's down in a hollow and
you don't see the road. I dunno what it is but it's a lonesome
place and always was. I wish I had come over to see Minnie
Foster sometimes. I can see now—[*Shakes her head.*]

MRS. PETERS. Well, you mustn't reproach yourself, Mrs. Hale.   101
Somehow we just don't see how it is with other folks until—
something comes up.

MRS. HALE. Not having children makes less work—but it makes a   102
quiet house, and Wright out to work all day, and no company
when he did come in. Did you know John Wright, Mrs. Peters?

MRS. PETERS. Not to know him; I've seen him in town. They say   103
he was a good man.

MRS. HALE. Yes—good; he didn't drink, and kept his word as   104
well as most, I guess, and paid his debts. But he was a hard
man, Mrs. Peters. Just to pass the time of day with him—
[*Shivers.*] Like a raw wind that gets to the bone. [*Pauses, her
eye falling on the cage.*] I should think she would'a wanted a
bird. But what do you suppose went with it?

MRS. PETERS. I don't know, unless it got sick and died. [*She   105
reaches over and swings the broken door, swings it again.
Both women watch it.*]

MRS. HALE. You weren't raised round here, were you? [MRS.   106
PETERS *shakes her head.*] You didn't know—her?

MRS. PETERS. Not till they brought her yesterday.   107

108   MRS. HALE. She—come to think of it, she was kind of like a bird
        herself—real sweet and pretty, but kind of timid and—
        fluttery. How—she—did—change. [*Silence; then as if struck
        by a happy thought and relieved to get back to everyday
        things.*] Tell you what, Mrs. Peters, why don't you take the
        quilt in with you? It might take up her mind.

109   MRS. PETERS. Why, I think that's a real nice idea, Mrs. Hale.
        There couldn't possibly be any objection to it, could there?
        Now, just what would I take? I wonder if her patches are in
        here—and her things.
        [*They look in the sewing basket.*]

110   MRS. HALE. Here's some red. I expect this has got sewing things
        in it. [*Brings out a fancy box.*] What a pretty box. Looks like
        something somebody would give you. Maybe her scissors
        are in here. [*Opens box. Suddenly puts her hand to her nose.*]
        Why—[MRS. PETERS *bends nearer, then turns her face away.*]
        There's something wrapped up in this piece of silk.

111   MRS. PETERS. Why, this isn't her scissors.

112   MRS. HALE. [*Lifting the silk.*] Oh, Mrs. Peters—its—[MRS. PETERS
        bends closer.]

113   MRS. PETERS. It's the bird.

114   MRS. HALE. [*Jumping up.*] But, Mrs. Peters—look at it! Its neck!
        Look at its neck! It's all—other side *to*.

115   MRS. PETERS. Somebody—wrung—its—neck.
        [*Their eyes meet. A look of growing comprehension, of horror.
        Steps are heard outside.* MRS. HALE *slips box under quilt
        pieces, and sinks into her chair. Enter* SHERIFF *and* COUNTY
        ATTORNEY. MRS. PETERS *rises.*]

116   COUNTY ATTORNEY. [*As one turning from serious things to little
        pleasantries.*] Well, ladies, have you decided whether she
        was going to quilt it or knot it?

117   MRS. PETERS. We think she was going to—knot it.

118   COUNTY ATTORNEY. Well, that's interesting, I'm sure. [*Seeing the
        birdcage.*] Has the bird flown?

119   MRS. HALE. [*Putting more quilt pieces over the box.*] We think
        the—cat got it.

120   COUNTY ATTORNEY. [*Preoccupied.*] Is there a cat?
        [MRS. HALE *glances in a quick covert way at* MRS. PETERS.]

121   MRS. PETERS. Well, not *now*. They're superstitious, you know.
        They leave.

122   COUNTY ATTORNEY. [*To* SHERIFF PETERS, *continuing an interrupted
        conversation.*] No sign at all of anyone having come from
        the outside. Their own rope. Now let's go up again and go
        over it piece by piece. [*They start upstairs.*] It would have to
        have been someone who knew just the—[MRS. PETERS *sits
        down. The two women sit there not looking at one another,*

*but as if peering into something and at the same time holding
back. When they talk now it is in the manner of feeling their
way over strange ground, as if afraid of what they are saying,
but as if they cannot help saying it.*]

MRS. HALE. She liked the bird. She was going to bury it in that   123
pretty box.

MRS. PETERS. [*In a whisper.*] When I was a girl—my kitten—   124
there was a boy took a hatchet, and before my eyes—and before I could get there—[*Covers her face an instant.*] If they
hadn't held me back I would have—[*Catches herself, looks
upstairs where steps are heard, falters weakly.*]—hurt him.

MRS. HALE. [*With a slow look around her.*] I wonder how it   125
would seem never to have had any children around. [*Pause.*]
No, Wright wouldn't like the bird—a thing that sang. She
used to sing. He killed that, too.

MRS. PETERS. [*Moving uneasily.*] We don't know who killed the   126
bird.

MRS. HALE. I knew John Wright.   127

MRS. PETERS. It was an awful thing was done in this house that   128
night, Mrs. Hale. Killing a man while he slept, slipping a
rope around his neck that choked the life out of him.

MRS. HALE. His neck. Choked the life out of him.   129

[*Her hand goes out and rests on the birdcage.*]

MRS. PETERS. [*With rising voice.*] We don't know who killed him.   130
We don't know.

MRS. HALE. [*Her own feeling not interrupted.*] If there'd been   131
years and years of nothing, then a bird to sing to you, it
would be awful—still, after the bird was still.

MRS. PETERS. [*Something within her speaking.*] I know what still-   132
ness is. When we homesteaded in Dakota, and my first baby
died—after he was two years old, and me with no other then—

MRS. HALE. [*Moving.*] How soon do you suppose they'll be   133
through, looking for the evidence?

MRS. PETERS. I know what stillness is. [*Pulling herself back.*] The   134
law has got to punish crime, Mrs. Hale.

MRS. HALE. [*Not as if answering that.*] I wish you'd seen Minnie   135
Foster when she wore a white dress with blue ribbons and
stood up there in the choir and sang. [*A look around the
room.*] Oh, I *wish* I'd come over here once in a while! That
was a crime! That was a crime! Who's going to punish that?

MRS. PETERS. [*Looking upstairs.*] We mustn't—take on.   136

MRS. HALE. I might have known she needed help! I know how   137
things can be—for women. I tell you, it's queer, Mrs. Peters.
We live close together and we live far apart. We all go through
the same things—it's all just a different kind of the same
thing. [*Brushes her eyes; noticing the bottle of fruit, reaches out*

for it.] If I was you I wouldn't tell her her fruit was gone. Tell her it *ain't.* Tell her it's all right. Take this in to prove it to her. She—she may never know whether it was broke or not.

138 MRS. PETERS. [*Takes the bottle, looks about for something to wrap it in; takes petticoat from the clothes brought from the other room, very nervously begins winding this around the bottle. In a false voice.*] My, it's a good thing the men couldn't hear us. Wouldn't they just laugh! Getting all stirred up over a little thing like a—dead canary. As if that could have anything to do with—with—wouldn't they *laugh!*

[*The men are heard coming downstairs.*]

139 MRS. HALE. [*Under her breath.*] Maybe they would—maybe they wouldn't.

140 COUNTY ATTORNEY. No, Peters, it's all perfectly clear except a reason for doing it. But you know juries when it comes to women. If there was some definite thing. Something to show—something to make a story about—a thing that would connect up with this strange way of doing it—[*The women's eyes meet for an instant. Enter* HALE *from outer door.*]

141 HALE. Well, I've got the team around. Pretty cold out there.

142 COUNTY ATTORNEY. I'm going to stay here a while by myself. [*To the* SHERIFF.] You can send Frank out for me, can't you? I want to go over everything. I'm not satisfied that we can't do better.

143 SHERIFF. Do you want to see what Mrs. Peters is going to take in? [*The* COUNTY ATTORNEY *goes to the table, picks up the apron, laughs.*]

144 COUNTY ATTORNEY. Oh, I guess they're not very dangerous things the ladies have picked out. [*Moves a few things about, disturbing the quilt pieces which cover the box. Steps back.*] No, Mrs. Peters doesn't need supervising. For that matter, a sheriff's wife is married to the law. Ever think of it that way, Mrs. Peters?

145 MRS. PETERS. Not—just that way.

146 SHERIFF. [*Chuckling.*] Married to the law. [*Moves toward the other room.*] I just want you to come in here a minute, George. We ought to take a look at these windows.

147 COUNTY ATTORNEY. [*Scoffingly.*] Oh, windows!

148 SHERIFF. We'll be right out, Mr. Hale.

[HALE *goes outside. The* SHERIFF *follows the* COUNTY ATTORNEY *into the other room. Then* MRS. HALE *rises, hands tight together, looking intensely at* MRS. PETERS, *whose eyes make a slow turn, finally meeting* MRS. HALE'S. *A moment* MRS. HALE *holds her, then her own eyes point the way to where the box is concealed. Suddenly* MRS. PETERS *throws back quilt pieces and tries to put the box in the bag she is wearing. It is too big. She opens box, starts to take bird out, cannot touch it, goes to pieces, stands there helpless. Sound of a knob turning in the other room.* MRS. HALE *snatches the box and puts it in the pocket of her big coat. Enter* COUNTY ATTORNEY *and* SHERIFF.]

COUNTY ATTORNEY. [*Facetiously.*] Well, Henry, at least we found   149
out that she was not going to quilt it. She was going to—
what is it you call it, ladies?

MRS. HALE. [*Her hand against her pocket.*] We call it—knot it,   150
Mr. Henderson.

CURTAIN

Betsy Lucal

WHAT IT MEANS TO BE GENDERED ME: LIFE ON THE BOUNDARIES OF A DICHOTOMOUS GENDER SYSTEM

The borders of gender, for some, are not easy to find. The same can be said about writing. The writing that you do might be divided up into personal, professional, and academic. But sometimes those borders are not so easy to maintain, nor are they always useful. In this essay by Betsy Lucal, a professor of sociology who specializes in issues of gender, we find those borders blurred. On the one hand, this is an "academic" essay—one that is written by an expert and that uses substantial research to make its case. Yet it is Lucal's masculine physical appearance that gives her first-hand experience with the boundary between male and female, which she explores in this essay; she, to quote one of its subtitles, uses "my self as data." It was first published in Gender and Society, *a journal that publishes peer-reviewed articles on issues of gender and feminism that cut across many academic disciplines such as anthropology, women's studies, history, and political science.*

AUTHOR'S NOTE: *I thank the journal's reviewers, my writing group (Linda Chen, Louise Collins, April Lidinsky, Margarete Myers, Monica Tetzlaff, and Becky Torstrick), Heather Bulan, and Linda Fritschner for their helpful comments on earlier versions of this article.*

1   I understood the concept of "doing gender" (West and
    Zimmerman 1987) long before I became a sociologist. I have
    been living with the consequences of inappropriate "gender
    display" (Goffman 1976; West and Zimmerman 1987) for as
    long as I can remember.

2   My daily experiences are a testament to the rigidity of gender
    in our society, to the real implications of "two and only two"
    when it comes to sex and gender categories (Garfinkel 1967;
    Kessler and McKenna 1978). Each day, I experience the conse-
    quences that our gender system has for my identity and interac-
    tions. I am a woman who has been called "Sir" so many times
    that I no longer even hesitate to assume that it is being directed
    at me. I am a woman whose use of public restrooms regularly
    causes reactions ranging from confused stares to confronta-
    tions over what a man is doing in the women's room. I regularly
    enact a variety of practices either to minimize the need for oth-
    ers to know my gender or to deal with their misattributions.

3   I am the embodiment of Lorber's (1994) ostensibly paradoxical
    assertion that the "gender bending" I engage in actually might
    serve to preserve and perpetuate gender categories. As a feminist
    who sees gender rebellion as a significant part of her contribution
    to the dismantling of sexism, I find this possibility disheartening.

4   In this article, I examine how my experiences both support
    and contradict Lorber's (1994) argument using my own experi-
    ences to illustrate and reflect on the social construction of gen-
    der. My analysis offers a discussion of the consequences of
    gender for people who do not follow the rules as well as an ex-
    amination of the possible implications of the existence of people
    like me for the gender system itself. Ultimately, I show how life
    on the boundaries of gender affects me and how my life, and the
    lives of others who make similar decisions about their participa-
    tion in the gender system, has the potential to subvert gender.

5   Because this article analyzes my experiences as a woman who
    often is mistaken for a man, my focus is on the social construc-
    tion of gender for women. My assumption is that, given the gen-
    dered nature of the gendering process itself, men's experiences
    of this phenomenon might well be different from women's.

The Social Construction of Gender

6   It is now widely accepted that gender is a social construction,
    that sex and gender are distinct, and that gender is something
    all of us "do." This conceptualization of gender can be traced to
    Garfinkel's (1967) ethnomethodological study of "Agnes."[1] In
    this analysis, Garfinkel examined the issues facing a male who

wished to pass as, and eventually become, a woman. Unlike individuals who perform gender in culturally expected ways, Agnes could not take her gender for granted and always was in danger of failing to pass as a woman (Zimmerman 1992).

This approach was extended by Kessler and McKenna (1978)   7 and codified in the classic "Doing Gender" by West and Zimmerman (1987). The social constructionist approach has been developed most notably by Lorber (1994, 1996). Similar theoretical strains have developed outside of sociology, such as work by Butler (1990) and Weston (1996). Taken as a whole, this work provides a number of insights into the social processes of gender, showing how gender(ing) is, in fact, a process.

We apply gender labels for a variety of reasons; for example,   8 an individual's gender cues our interactions with her or him. Successful social relations require all participants to present, monitor, and interpret gender displays (Martin 1998; West and Zimmerman 1987). We have, according to Lorber, "no social place for a person who is neither woman nor man" (1994, 96); that is, we do not know how to interact with such a person. There is, for example, no way of addressing such a person that does not rely on making an assumption about the person's gender ("Sir" or "Ma'am"). In this context, gender is "omnirelevant" (West and Zimmerman 1987). Also, given the sometimes fractious nature of interactions between men and women, it might be particularly important for women to know the gender of the strangers they encounter; do the women need to be wary, or can they relax (Devor 1989)?

According to Kessler and McKenna (1978), each time we en-   9 counter a new person, we make a gender attribution. In most cases, this is not difficult. We learn how to read people's genders by learning which traits culturally signify each gender and by learning rules that enable us to classify individuals with a wide range of gender presentations into two and only two gender categories. As Weston observed, "Gendered traits are called attributes for a reason: People attribute traits to others. No one possesses them. Traits are the product of evaluation" (1996, 21). The fact that most people use the same traits and rules in presenting genders makes it easier for us to attribute genders to them.

We also assume that we can place each individual into one of   10 two mutually exclusive categories in this binary system. As Bem (1993) notes, we have a polarized view of gender; there are two groups that are seen as polar opposites. Although there is "no rule for deciding 'male' or 'female' that will always work" and no attributes "that always and without exception are true of only one gender" (Kessler and McKenna 1978, 158, 1), we operate under the assumption that there are such rules and attributes.

11   Kessler and McKenna's analysis revealed that the fundamental schema for gender attribution is to "See someone as female
only when you cannot see [the person] as male" (1978, 158).
Individuals basically are assumed to be male/men until proven
otherwise, that is, until some obvious marker of conventional
femininity is noted. In other words, the default reading of a
nonfeminine person is that she or he is male; people who do
not deliberately mark themselves as feminine are taken to be
men. Devor attributed this tendency to the operation of gender
in a patriarchal context: "Women must mark themselves as
'other',," whereas on the other hand, "few cues [are required] to
identify maleness" (1989, 152). As with language, masculine
forms are taken as the generically human; femininity requires
that something be added. Femininity "must constantly reassure its audience by a willing demonstration of difference"
(Brownmiller 1984, 15).

12   Patriarchal constructs of gender also devalue the marked
category. Devor (1989) found that the women she calls "gender
blenders" assumed that femininity was less desirable than
masculinity; their gender blending sometimes was a product of
their shame about being women. This assumption affects not
only our perceptions of other people but also individuals'
senses of their own gendered selves.

13   Not only do we rely on our social skills in attributing genders
to others, but we also use our skills to present our own genders
to them. The roots of this understanding of how gender operates lie in Goffman's (1959) analysis of the "presentation of self
in everyday life," elaborated later in his work on "gender display" (Goffman 1976). From this perspective, gender is a performance, "a stylized repetition of acts" (Butler 1990, 140,
emphasis removed). Gender display refers to "conventional-
ized portrayals" of social correlates of gender (Goffman 1976).
These displays are culturally established sets of behaviors, appearances, mannerisms, and other cues that we have learned
to associate with members of a particular gender.

14   In determining the gender of each person we encounter and
in presenting our genders to others, we rely extensively on
these gender displays. Our bodies and their adornments provide us with "texts" for reading a person's gender (Bordo 1993).
As Lorber noted, "Without the deliberate use of gendered
clothing, hairstyles, jewelry, and cosmetics, women and men
would look far more alike" (1994, 18–19). Myhre summarized
the markers of femininity as "having longish hair; wearing
makeup, skirts, jewelry, and high heels; walking with a wiggle;
having little or no observable body hair; and being in general
soft, rounded (but not too rounded), and sweet-smelling"

(1995, 135). (Note that these descriptions comprise a Western conceptualization of gender.) Devor identified "mannerisms, language, facial expressions, dress, and a lack of feminine adornment" (1989, x) as factors that contribute to women being mistaken for men.

A person uses gender display to lead others to make attribu-   15
tions regarding her or his gender, regardless of whether the presented gender corresponds to the person's sex or gender self-identity. Because gender is a social construction, there may be differences among one's sex, gender self-identity (the gender the individual identifies as), presented identity (the gender the person is presenting), and perceived identity (the gender others attribute to the person).[2] For example, a person can be female without being socially identified as a woman, and a male person can appear socially as a woman. Using a feminine gender display, a man can present the identity of a woman and, if the display is successful, be perceived as a woman.

But these processes also mean that a person who fails to es-   16
tablish a gendered appearance that corresponds to the person's gender faces challenges to her or his identity and status. First, the gender nonconformist must find a way in which to construct an identity in a society that denies her or him any legitimacy (Bem 1993). A person is likely to want to define herself or himself as "normal" in the face of cultural evidence to the contrary. Second, the individual also must deal with other people's challenges to identity and status—deciding how to respond, what such reactions to their appearance mean, and so forth.

Because our appearances, mannerisms, and so forth con-   17
stantly are being read as part of our gender display, we do gender whether we intend to or not. For example, a woman athlete, particularly one participating in a nonfeminine sport such as basketball, might deliberately keep her hair long to show that, despite actions that suggest otherwise, she is a "real" (i.e., feminine) woman. But we also do gender in less conscious ways such as when a man takes up more space when sitting than a woman does. In fact, in a society so clearly organized around gender, as ours is, there is no way in which to not do gender (Lorber 1994).

Given our cultural rules for identifying gender (i.e., that   18
there are only two and that masculinity is assumed in the absence of evidence to the contrary), a person who does not do gender appropriately is placed not into a third category but rather into the one with which her or his gender display seems most closely to fit; that is, if a man appears to be a woman, then he will be categorized as "woman," not as something else. Even if a person does not want to do gender or would like to do

a gender other than the two recognized by our society, other people will, in effect, do gender for that person by placing her or him in one and only one of the two available categories. We cannot escape doing gender or, more specifically, doing one of two genders. (There are exceptions in limited contexts such as people doing "drag" [Butler 1990; Lorber 1994].)

19   People who follow the norms of gender can take their genders for granted. Kessler and McKenna asserted, "Few people besides transsexuals think of their gender as anything other than 'naturally' obvious"; they believe that the risks of not being taken for the gender intended "are minimal for non-transsexuals" (1978, 126). However, such an assertion overlooks the experiences of people such as those women Devor (1989) calls "gender blenders" and those people Lorber (1994) refers to as "gender benders." As West and Zimmerman (1987) pointed out, we all are held accountable for, and might be called on to account for, our genders.

20   People who, for whatever reasons, do not adhere to the rules, risk gender misattribution and any interactional consequences that might result from this misidentification. What are the consequences of misattribution for social interaction? When must misattribution be minimized? What will one do to minimize such mistakes? In this article, I explore these and related questions using my biography.

21   For me, the social processes and structures of gender mean that, in the context of our culture, my appearance will be read as masculine. Given the common conflation of sex and gender, I will be assumed to be a male. Because of the two-and-only-two genders rule, I will be classified, perhaps more often than not, as a man—not as an atypical woman, not as a genderless person. I must be one gender or the other; I cannot be neither, not can I be both. This norm has a variety of mundane and serious consequences for my everyday existence. Like Myhre (1995), I have found that the choice not to participate in femininity is not one made frivolously.

22   My experiences as a woman who does not do femininity illustrate a paradox of our two-and-only-two gender system. Lorber argued that "bending gender rules and passing between genders does not erode but rather preserves gender boundaries" (1994, 21). Although people who engage in these behaviors and appearances do "demonstrate the social constructedness of sex, sexuality, and gender" (Lorber 1994, 96), they do not actually disrupt gender. Devor made a similar point: "When gender blending females refused to mark themselves by publicly displaying sufficient femininity to be recognized as women, they were in no way challenging patriarchal gender assumptions"

(1989, 142). As the following discussion shows, I have found that my own experiences both support and challenge this argument. Before detailing these experiences, I explain my use of my self as data.

My Self As Data

This analysis is based on my experiences as a person whose appearance and gender/sex are not, in the eyes of many people, congruent. How did my experiences become my data? I began my research "unwittingly" (Krieger 1991). This article is a product of "opportunistic research" in that I am using my "unique biography, life experiences, and/or situational familiarity to understand and explain social life" (Riemer 1988, 121; see also Riemer 1977). It is an analysis of "unplanned personal experience," that is, experiences that were not part of a research project but instead are part of my daily encounters (Reinharz 1992).   23

This work also is, at least to some extent, an example of Richardson's (1994) notion of writing as a method of inquiry. As a sociologist who specializes in gender, the more I learned, the more I realized that my life could serve as a case study. As I examined my experiences, I found out things—about my experiences and about theory—that I did not know when I started (Richardson 1994).   24

It also is useful, I think, to consider my analysis an application of Mills's (1959) "sociological imagination." Mills (1959) and Berger (1963) wrote about the importance of seeing the general in the particular. This means that general social patterns can be discerned in the behaviors of particular individuals. In this article, I am examining portions of my biography, situated in U.S. society during the 1990s, to understand the "personal troubles" my gender produces in the context of a two-and-only-two gender system. I am not attempting to generalize my experiences; rather, I am trying to use them to examine and reflect on the processes and structure of gender in our society.   25

Because my analysis is based on my memories and perceptions of events, it is limited by my ability to recall events and by my interpretation of those events. However, I am not claiming that my experiences provide the truth about gender and how it works. I am claiming that the biography of a person who lives on the margins of our gender system can provide theoretical insights into the processes and social structure of gender. Therefore, after describing my experiences, I examine how they illustrate and extend, as well as contradict, other work on the social construction of gender.   26

Gendered Me

27   Each day, I negotiate the boundaries of gender. Each day, I face
the possibility that someone will attribute the "wrong" gender
to me based on my physical appearance.

28   I am six feet tall and large-boned. I have had short hair for
most of my life. For the past several years, I have worn a crew
cut or flat top. I do not shave or otherwise remove hair from
my body (e.g., no eyebrow plucking). I do not wear dresses,
skirts, high heels, or makeup. My only jewelry is a class ring, a
"men's" watch (my wrists are too large for a "women's" watch),
two small earrings (gold hoops, both in my left ear), and (occasionally) a necklace. I wear jeans or shorts, T-shirts, sweaters,
polo/golf shirts, button-down collar shirts, and tennis shoes or
boots. The jeans are "women's" (I do have hips) but do not look
particularly "feminine." The rest of the outer garments are
from men's departments. I prefer baggy clothes, so the fact that
I have "womanly" breasts often is not obvious (I do not wear a
bra). Sometimes, I wear a baseball cap or some other type of
hat. I also am white and relatively young (30 years old).[3]

29   My gender display—what others interpret as my presented
identity—regularly leads to the misattribution of my gender.
An incongruity exists between my gender self-identity and the
gender that others perceive. In my encounters with people I do
not know, I sometimes conclude, based on our interactions,
that they think I am a man. This does not mean that other people do not think I am a man, just that I have no way of knowing what they think without interacting with them.

Living with It

30   I have no illusions or delusions about my appearance. I know
that my appearance is likely to be read as "masculine" (and
male) and that how I see myself is socially irrelevant. Given
our two-and-only-two gender structure, I must live with the
consequences of my appearance. These consequences fall into
two categories: issues of identity and issues of interaction.

31   My most common experience is being called "Sir" or being referred to by some other masculine linguistic marker (e.g., "he,"
"man"). This has happened for years, for as long as I can remember, when having encounters with people I do not know.[4] Once, in
fact, the same worker at a fast-food restaurant called me "Ma'am"
when she took my order and "Sir" when she gave it to me.

32   Using my credit cards sometimes is a challenge. Some clerks
subtly indicate their disbelief, looking from the card to me and

back at the card and checking my signature carefully. Others challenge my use of the card, asking whose it is or demanding identification. One cashier asked to see my driver's license and then asked me whether I was the son of the cardholder. Another clerk told me that my signature on the receipt "had better match" the one on the card. Presumably, this was her way of letting me know that she was not convinced it was my credit card.

My identity as a woman also is called into question when I   33
try to use women-only spaces. Encounters in public rest rooms are an adventure. I have been told countless times that "This is the ladies' room." Other women say nothing to me, but their stares and conversations with others let me know what they think. I will hear them say, for example, "There was a man in there." I also get stares when I enter a locker room. However, it seems that women are less concerned about my presence there, perhaps because, given that it is a space for changing clothes, showering, and so forth, they will be able to make sure that I am really a woman. Dressing rooms in department stores also are problematic spaces. I remember shopping with my sister once and being offered a chair outside the room when I began to accompany her into the dressing room.

Women who believe that I am a man do not want me in   34
women-only spaces. For example, one woman would not enter the rest room until I came out, and others have told me that I am in the wrong place. They also might not want to encounter me while they are alone. For example, seeing me walking at night when they are alone might be scary.[5]

I, on the other hand, am not afraid to walk alone, day or night.   35
I do not worry that I will be subjected to the public harassment that many women endure (Gardner 1995). I am not a clear target for a potential rapist. I rely on the fact that a potential attacker would not want to attack a big man by mistake. This is not to say that men never are attacked, just that they are not viewed, and often do not view themselves, as being vulnerable to attack.

Being perceived as a man has made me privy to male-male in-   36
teractional styles of which most women are not aware. I found out, quite by accident, that many men greet, or acknowledge, people (mostly other men) who make eye contact with them with a single nod. For example, I found that when I walked down the halls of my brother's all-male dormitory making eye contact, men nodded their greetings at me. Oddly enough, these same men did not greet my brother; I had to tell him about making eye contact and nodding as a greeting ritual. Apparently, in this case I was doing masculinity better than be was!

I also believe that I am treated differently, for example, in   37
auto parts stores (staffed almost exclusively by men in most

cases) because of the assumption that I am a man. Workers there assume that I know what I need and that my questions are legitimate requests for information. I suspect that I am treated more fairly than a feminine-appearing woman would be. I have not been able to test this proposition. However, Devor's participants did report "being treated more respect-fully" (1989, 132) in such situations.

38   There is, however, a negative side to being assumed to be a man by other men. Once, a friend and I were driving in her car when a man failed to stop at an intersection and nearly crashed into us. As we drove away, I mouthed "stop sign" to him. When we both stopped our cars at the next intersection, he got out of his car and came up to the passenger side of the car, where I was sitting. He yelled obscenities at us and pounded and spit on the car window. Luckily, the windows were closed. I do not think be would have done that if he thought I was a woman. This was the first time I realized that one of the implications of being seen as a man was that I might be called on to defend myself from physical aggression from other men who felt challenged by me. This was a sobering and somewhat frightening thought.

39   Recently, I was verbally accosted by an older man who did not like where I had parked my car. As I walked down the street to work, he shouted that I should park at the university rather than on a side street nearby. I responded that it was a public street and that I could park there if I chose. He contin-ued to yell, but the only thing I caught was the last part of what he said: "Your tires are going to get cut!" Based on my appear-ance that day—I was dressed casually and carrying a back-pack, and I had my hat on backward—I believe he thought that I was a young male student rather than a female professor. I do not think he would have yelled at a person he thought to be a woman—and perhaps especially not a woman professor.

40   Given the presumption of heterosexuality that is part of our system of gender, my interactions with women who assume that I am a man also can be viewed from that perspective. For example, once my brother and I were shopping when we were "hit on" by two young women. The encounter ended before I re-alized what had happened. It was only when we walked away that I told him that I was pretty certain that they had thought both of us were men. A more common experience is realizing that when I am seen in public with one of my women friends, we are likely to be read as a heterosexual dyad. It is likely that if I were to walk through a shopping mall holding hands with a woman, no one would look twice, not because of their open-mindedness toward lesbian couples but rather because of their

assumption that I was the male half of a straight couple. Recently, when walking through a mall with a friend and her infant, my observations of others' responses to us led me to believe that many of them assumed that we were a family on an outing, that is, that I was her partner and the father of the child.

Dealing with It

Although I now accept that being mistaken for a man will be a   41 part of my life so long as I choose not to participate in femininity, there have been times when I consciously have tried to appear more feminine. I did this for a while when I was an undergraduate and again recently when I was on the academic job market. The first time, I let my hair grow nearly down to my shoulders and had it permed. I also grew long fingernails and wore nail polish. Much to my chagrin, even then one of my professors, who did not know my name, insistently referred to me in his kinship examples as "the son." Perhaps my first act on the way to my current stance was to point out to this man, politely and after class, that I was a woman.

More recently, I again let my hair grow out for several   42 months, although I did not alter other aspects of my appearance. Once my hair was about two and a half inches long (from its original quarter inch), I realized, based on my encounters with strangers, that I had more or less passed back into the category of "woman." Then, when I returned to wearing a flat top, people again responded to me as if I were a man.

Because of my appearance, much of my negotiation of interac-   43 tions with strangers involves attempts to anticipate their reactions to me. I need to assess whether they will be likely to assume that I am a man and whether that actually matters in the context of our encounters. Many times, my gender really is irrelevant, and it is just annoying to be misidentified. Other times, particularly when my appearance is coupled with something that identifies me by name (e.g., a check or credit card) without a photo, I might need to do something to ensure that my identity is not questioned. As a result of my experiences, I have developed some techniques to deal with gender misattribution.

In general, in unfamiliar public places, I avoid using the rest   44 room because I know that it is a place where there is a high likelihood of misattribution and where misattribution is socially important. If I must use a public rest room, I try to make myself look as nonthreatening as possible. I do not wear a hat, and I try to rearrange my clothing to make my breasts more obvious. Here, I am trying to use my secondary sex characteristics to make my gender more obvious rather than the usual use of gender to make sex obvious. While in the rest room, I never make eye contact, and I get in and out as quickly as possible. Going in with a woman friend also is helpful; her presence legitimizes my own. People are less likely to think I am entering a space where I do not belong when I am with someone who looks like she does belong.[6]

45   To those women who verbally challenge my presence in the rest room, I reply, "I know," usually in an annoyed tone. When they stare or talk about me to the women they are with, I simply get out as quickly as possible. In general, I do not wait for someone I am with because there is too much chance of an unpleasant encounter.

46   I stopped trying on clothes before purchasing them a few years ago because my presence in the changing areas was met with stares and whispers. Exceptions are stores where the dressing rooms are completely private, where there are individual stalls rather than a room with stalls separated by curtains, or where business is slow and no one else is trying on clothes. If I am trying on a garment clearly intended for a woman, then I usually can do so without hassle. I guess the attendants assume that I must be a woman if I have, for example, a women's bathing suit in my hand. But usually, I think it is easier for me to try the clothes on at home and return them, if necessary, rather than risk creating a scene. Similarly, when I am with another woman who is trying on clothes. I just wait outside.

47   My strategy with credit cards and checks is to anticipate wariness on a clerk's part. When I sense that there is some doubt or when they challenge me, I say, "It's my card." I generally respond courteously to requests for photo ID, realizing that these might be routine checks because of concerns about increasingly widespread fraud. But for the clerk who asked for ID and still did not think it was my card, I had a stronger reaction. When she said that she was sorry for embarrassing me, I told her that I was not embarrassed but that she should be. I also am particularly careful to make sure that my signature is consistent with the back of the card. Faced with such situations, I feel somewhat nervous about signing my name—which, of course, makes me worry that my signature will look different from how it should.

48   Another strategy I have been experimenting with is wearing nail polish in the dark bright colors currently fashionable. I try to do this when I travel by plane. Given more stringent travel regulations, one always must present a photo ID. But my experiences have shown that my driver's license is not necessarily convincing. Nail polish might be. I also flash my polished nails when I enter airport rest rooms, hoping that they will provide a clue that I am indeed in the right place.

There are other cases in which the issues are less those of identity than of all the norms of interaction that, in our society, are gendered. My most common response to misattribution actually is to appear to ignore it, that is, to go on with the interaction as if nothing out of the ordinary has happened. Unless I feel that there is a good reason to establish my correct gender, I assume the identity others impose on me for the sake of smooth interaction. For example, if someone is selling me a movie ticket, then there is no reason to make sure that the person has accurately discerned my gender. Similarly, if it is clear that the person using "Sir" is talking to me, then I simply respond as appropriate. I accept the designation because it is irrelevant to the situation. It takes enough effort to be alert for misattributions and to decide which of them matter; responding to each one would take more energy than it is worth. 49

Sometimes, if our interaction involves conversation, my first verbal response is enough to let the other person know that I am actually a woman and not a man. My voice apparently is "feminine" enough to shift people's attributions to the other category. I know when this has happened by the apologies that usually accompany the mistake. I usually respond to the apologies by saying something like "No problem" and/or "It happens all the time." Sometimes, a misattributor will offer an account for the mistake, for example, saying that it was my hair or that they were not being very observant. 50

These experiences with gender and misattribution provide some theoretical insights into contemporary Western understandings of gender and into the social structure of gender in contemporary society. Although there are a number of ways in which my experiences confirm the work of others, there also are some ways in which my experiences suggest other interpretations and conclusions. 51

What Does It Mean?

Gender is pervasive in our society. I cannot choose not to participate in it. Even if I try not to do gender, other people will do it for me. That is, given our two-and-only-two rule, they must attribute one of two genders to me. Still, although I cannot choose not to participate in gender, I can choose not to participate in femininity (as I have), at least with respect to physical appearance. 52

That is where the problems begin. Without the decorations of femininity, I do not look like a woman. That is, I do not look 53 like what many people's commonsense understanding of gender tells them a woman looks like. How I see myself, even how I might wish others would see me, is socially irrelevant. It is the gender that I *appear* to be (my "perceived gender") that is most relevant to my social identity and interactions with others. The major consequence of this fact is that I must be continually aware of which gender I "give off" as well as which gender I "give" (Goffman 1959).

54   Because my gender self-identity is "not displayed obviously, immediately, and consistently" (Devor 1989, 58), I am somewhat of a failure in social terms with respect to gender. Causing people to be uncertain or wrong about one's gender is a violation of taken-for-granted rules that leads to embarrassment and discomfort; it means that something has gone wrong with the interaction (Garfinkel 1967; Kessler and McKenna 1978). This means that my nonresponse to misattribution is the more socially appropriate response; I am allowing others to maintain face (Goffman 1959, 1967). By not calling attention to their mistakes, I uphold their images of themselves as competent social actors. I also maintain my own image as competent by letting them assume that I am the gender I appear to them to be.

55   But I still have discreditable status; I carry a stigma (Goffman 1963). Because I have failed to participate appropriately in the creation of meaning with respect to gender (Devor 1989), I can be called on to account for my appearance. If discredited, I show myself to be an incompetent social actor. I am the one not following the rules, and I will pay the price for not providing people with the appropriate cues for placing me in the gender category to which I really belong.

56   I do think that it is, in many cases, safer to be read as a man than as some sort of deviant woman. "Man" is an acceptable category; it fits properly into people's gender worldview. Passing as a man often is the "path of least resistance" (Devor 1989; Johnson 1997). For example, in situations where gender does not matter, letting people take me as a man is easier than correcting them.

57   Conversely, as Butler noted, "We regularly punish those who fail to do their gender right" (1990, 140). Feinberg maintained, "Masculine girls and women face terrible condemnation and brutality—including sexual violence—for crossing the boundary of what is 'acceptable' female expression" (1996, 114). People are more likely to harass me when they perceive me to be a woman who looks like a man. For example, when a group of teenagers realized that I was not a man because one of their mothers identified me correctly, they began to make derogatory comments when I passed them. One asked, for example, "Does she have a penis?"

Because of the assumption that a "masculine" woman is a les-   58
bian, there is the risk of homophobic reactions (Gardner 1995;
Lucal 1997). Perhaps surprisingly, I find that I am much more
likely to be taken for a man than for a lesbian, at least based on
my interactions with people and their reactions to me. This
might be because people are less likely to reveal that they have
taken me for a lesbian because it is less relevant to an encounter
or because they believe this would be unacceptable. But I think
it is more likely a product of the strength of our two-and-only-
two system. I give enough masculine cues that I am seen not as
a deviant woman but rather as a man, at least in most cases. The
problem seems not to be that people are uncertain about my
gender, which might lead them to conclude that I was a lesbian
once they realized I was a woman. Rather, I seem to fit easily
into a gender category—just not the one with which I identify.

In fact, because men represent the dominant gender in our   59
society, being mistaken for a man can protect me from other
types of gendered harassment. Because men can move around
in public spaces safely (at least relative to women), a "masculine" woman also can enjoy this freedom (Devor 1989).

On the other hand, my use of particular spaces—those desig-   60
nated as for women only—may be challenged. Feinberg provided
an intriguing analysis of the public rest room experience. She
characterized women's reactions to a masculine person in a public rest room as "an example of genderphobia" (1996, 117), viewing such women as policing gender boundaries rather than
believing that there really is a man in the women's rest room. She
argued that women who truly believed that there was a man in
their midst would react differently. Although this is an interesting perspective on her experiences, my experiences do not lead to
the same conclusion.[7] Enough people have said to me that "This
is the ladies' room" or have said to their companions that "There
was a man in there" that I take their reactions at face value.

Still, if the two-and-only-two gender system is to be main-   61
tained, participants must be involved in policing the categories
and their attendant identities and spaces. Even if policing
boundaries is not explicitly intended, boundary maintenance is
the effect of such responses to people's gender displays.

Boundaries and margins are an important component of both   62
my experiences of gender and our theoretical understanding of
gendering processes. I am, in effect, both woman and not-
woman. As a woman who often is a social man but who also is a
woman living in a patriarchal society, I am in a unique position
to see and act. I sometimes receive privileges usually limited to
men, and I sometimes am oppressed by my status as a deviant
woman. I am, in a sense, an outsider-within (Collins 1991).

Positioned on the boundaries of gender categories, I have developed a consciousness that I hope will prove transformative (Anzaldua 1987).

63   In fact, one of the reasons why I decided to continue my nonparticipation in femininity was that my sociological training suggested that this could be one of my contributions to the eventual dismantling of patriarchal gender constructs. It would be my way of making the personal political. I accepted being taken for a man as the price I would pay to help subvert patriarchy. I believed that all of the inconveniences I was enduring meant that I actually was doing something to bring down the gender structures that entangled all of us.

64   Then, I read Lorber's (1994) *Paradoxes of Gender* and found out, much to my dismay, that I might not actually be challenging gender after all. Because of the way in which doing gender works in our two-and-only-two system, gender displays are simply read as evidence of one of the two categories. Therefore, gender bending, blending, and passing between the categories do not question the categories themselves. If one's social gender and personal (true) gender do not correspond, then this is irrelevant unless someone notices the lack of congruence.

65   This reality brings me to a paradox of my experiences. First, not only do others assume that I am one gender or the other, but I also insist that I *really am* a member of one of the two gender categories. That is, I am female; I self-identify as a woman. I do not claim to be some other gender or to have no gender at all. I simply place myself in the wrong category according to stereotypes and cultural standards; the gender I present, or that some people perceive me to be presenting, is inconsistent with the gender with which I identify myself as well as with the gender I could be "proven" to be. Socially, I display the wrong gender; personally, I identify as the proper gender.

66   Second, although I ultimately would like to see the destruction of our current gender structure, I am not to the point of personally abandoning gender. Right now, I do not want people to see me as genderless as much as I want them to see me as a woman. That is, I would like to expand the category of "woman" to include people like me. I, too, am deeply embedded in our gender system, even though I do not play by many of its rules. For me, as for most people in our society, gender is a substantial part of my personal identity (Howard and Hollander 1997). Socially, the problem is that I do not present a gender display that is consistently read as feminine. In fact, I consciously do not participate in the trappings of femininity. However, I do identify myself as a woman, not as a man or as someone outside of the two-and-only-two categories.

Yet, I do believe, as Lorber (1994) does, that the purpose of   67
gender, as it currently is constructed, is to oppress women.
Lorber analyzed gender as a "process of creating distinguishable social statuses for the assignment of rights and responsibilities" that ends up putting women in a devalued and
oppressed position (1994, 32). As Martin put it, "Bodies that
clearly delineate gender status facilitate the maintenance of
the gender hierarchy" (1998, 495).

For society, gender means difference (Lorber 1994). The ero-   68
sion of the boundaries would problematize that structure.
Therefore, for gender to operate as it currently does, the category "woman" *cannot* be expanded to include people like me.
The maintenance of the gender structure is dependent on the
creation of a few categories that are mutually exclusive, the
members of which are as different as possible (Lorber 1994). It
is the clarity of the boundaries between the categories that allows gender to be used to assign rights and responsibilities as
well as resources and rewards.

It is that part of gender—what it is used for—that is most   69
problematic. Indeed, is it not *patriarchal*—or, even more specifically, *heteropatriarchal*—constructions of gender that are actually the problem? It is not the differences between men and
women, or the categories themselves, so much as the meanings
ascribed to the categories and, even more important, the hierarchical nature of gender under patriarchy that is the problem
(Johnson 1997). Therefore, I am rebelling not against my fe-
maleness or even my womanhood; instead, I am protesting
contemporary constructions of femininity and, at least indirectly, masculinity under patriarchy. We do not, in fact, know
what gender would look like if it were not constructed around
heterosexuality in the context of patriarchy.

Although it is possible that the end of patriarchy would   70
mean the end of gender, it is at least conceivable that something like what we now call gender could exist in a postpatriar-
chal future. The two-and-only-two categorization might well
disappear, there being no hierarchy for it to justify. But I do not
think that we should make the assumption that gender and
patriarchy are synonymous.

Theoretically, this analysis points to some similarities and dif-   71
ferences between the work of Lorber (1994) and the works of
Butler (1990), Goffman (1976, 1977), and West and Zimmerman
(1987). Lorber (1994) conceptualized gender as social structure,
whereas the others focused more on the interactive and proces-
sual nature of gender. Butler (1990) and Goffman (1976, 1977)
view gender as a performance, and West and Zimmerman
(1987) examined it as something all of us do. One result of this

difference in approach is that in Lorber's (1994) work, gender comes across as something that we are caught in—something that, despite any attempts to the contrary, we cannot break out of. This conclusion is particularly apparent in Lorber's argument that gender rebellion, in the context of our two-and-only-two system, ends up supporting what it purports to subvert. Yet, my own experiences suggest an alternative possibility that is more in line with the view of gender offered by West and Zimmerman (1987): If gender is a product of interaction, and if it is produced in a particular context, then it can be changed if we change our performances. However, the effects of a performance linger, and gender ends up being institutionalized. It is institutionalized, in our society, in a way that perpetuates inequality, as Lorber's (1994) work shows. So, it seems that a combination of these two approaches is needed.

72   In fact, Lorber's (1994) work seems to suggest that effective gender rebellion requires a more blatant approach—bearded men in dresses, perhaps, or more active responses to misattribution. For example, if I corrected every person who called me "Sir," and if I insisted on my right to be addressed appropriately and granted access to women-only spaces, then perhaps I could start to break down gender norms. If I asserted my right to use public facilities without being harassed, and if I challenged each person who gave me "the look," then perhaps I would be contributing to the demise of gender as we know it. It seems that the key would be to provide visible evidence of the nonmutual exclusivity of the categories. Would *this* break down the patriarchal components of gender? Perhaps it would, but it also would be exhausting.

73   Perhaps there is another possibility. In a recent book, *The Gender Knot*, Johnson (1997) argued that when it comes to gender and patriarchy, most of us follow the paths of least resistance; we "go along to get along," allowing our actions to be shaped by the gender system. Collectively, our actions help patriarchy maintain and perpetuate a system of oppression and privilege. Thus, by withdrawing our support from this system by choosing paths of greater resistance, we can start to chip away at it. Many people participate in gender because they cannot imagine any alternatives. In my classroom, and in my interactions and encounters with strangers, my presence can make it difficult for people not to see that there *are* other paths. In other words, following from West and Zimmerman (1987), I can subvert gender by doing it differently.

74   For example, I think it is true that my existence does not have an effect on strangers who assume that I am a man and never learn otherwise. For them, I do uphold the two-and-only-two system. But there are other cases in which my existence

can have an effect. For example, when people initially take me for a man but then find out that I actually am a woman, at least for that moment, the naturalness of gender may be called into question. In these cases, my presence can provoke a "category crisis" (Garber 1992, 16) because it challenges the sex/gender binary system.

The subversive potential of my gender might be strongest in   75
my classrooms. When I teach about the sociology of gender, my students can see me as the embodiment of the social construction of gender. Not all of my students have transformative experiences as a result of taking a course with me; there is the chance that some of them see me as a "freak" or as an exception. Still, after listening to stories about my experiences with gender and reading literature on the subject, many students begin to see how and why gender is a social product. I can disentangle sex, gender, and sexuality in the contemporary United States for them. Students can begin to see the connection between biographical experiences and the structure of society. As one of my students noted, I clearly live the material I am teaching. If that helps me to get my point across, then perhaps I am subverting the binary gender system after all. Although my gendered presence and my way of doing gender might make others— and sometimes even me—uncomfortable, no one ever said that dismantling patriarchy was going to be easy.

NOTES

1. Ethnomethodology has been described as "the study of commonsense practical reasoning" (Collins 1988, 274). It examines how people make sense of their everyday experiences. Ethnomethodology is particularly useful in studying gender because it helps to uncover the assumptions on which our understandings of sex and gender are based.

2. I thank an anonymous reviewer for suggesting that I use these distinctions among the parts of a person's gender.

3. I obviously have left much out by not examining my gendered experiences in the context of race, age, class, sexuality, region, and so forth. Such a project clearly is more complex. As Weston pointed out, gender presentations are complicated by other statuses of their presenters: "What it takes to kick a person over into another gendered category can differ with race, class, religion, and time" (1996, 168). Furthermore, I am well aware that my whiteness allows me to assume that my experiences are simply a product of gender (see, e.g., hooks 1981; Lucal 1996; Spelman 1988; West and Fenstermaker 1995). For now, suffice it to say that it is my privileged position on some of these axes and my more disadvantaged position on others that combine to delineate my overall experience.

4. In fact, such experiences are not always limited to encounters with strangers. My grandmother, who does not see me often, twice has mistaken me for either my brother-in-law or some unknown man.

5. My experiences in rest rooms and other public spaces might be very different if I were, say, African American rather than white. Given the stereotypes of African American men, I think that white women would react very differently to encountering me (see, e.g., Staples [1986] 1993).

6. I also have noticed that there are certain types of rest rooms in which I will not be verbally challenged; the higher the social status of the place, the less likely I will be harassed. For example, when I go to the theater, I might get stared at, but my presence never has been challenged.

7. An anonymous reviewer offered one possible explanation for this. Women see women's rest rooms as their space; they feel safe, and even empowered, there. Instead of fearing men in such space, they might instead pose a threat to any man who might intrude. Their invulnerability in this situation is, of course, not physically based but rather socially constructed. I thank the reviewer for this suggestion.

REFERENCES

Anzaldua, G. 1987. *Borderlands/La Frontera*. San Francisco: Aunt Lute Books.

Bem, S. L. 1993. *The lenses of gender*. New Haven, CT: Yale University Press.

Berger, P. 1963. *Invitation to sociology*. New York: Anchor.

Bordo, S. 1993. *Unbearable weight*. Berkeley: University of California Press.

Brownmiller, C. 1984. *Femininity*. New York: Fawcett.

Butler, J. 1990. *Gender trouble*. New York: Routledge.

Collins, P. H. 1991. *Black feminist thought*. New York: Routledge.

Collins, R. 1988. *Theoretical sociology*. San Diego: Harcourt Brace Jovanovich.

Devor, H. 1989. *Gender blending: Confronting the limits of duality*. Bloomington: Indiana University Press.

Feinberg, L. 1996. *Transgender warriors*. Boston: Beacon.

Garber, M. 1992. *Vested interests: Cross-dressing and cultural anxiety*. New York: HarperPerennial.

Gardner, C. B. 1995. *Passing by: Gender and public harassment*. Berkeley: University of California.

Garfinkel, H. 1967. *Studies in ethnomethodology*. Englewood Cliffs, NJ: Prentice Hall.

Goffman, E. 1959. *The presentation of self in everyday life*. Garden City, NY: Doubleday.

———.1963. *Stigma*. Englewood Cliffs, NJ: Prentice Hall.

———.1967. *Interaction ritual*. New York: Anchor/Doubleday.

———.1976. Gender display. *Studies in the Anthropology of Visual Communication* 3:69–77.

———.1977. The arrangement between the sexes. *Theory and Society* 4:301–31.

hooks, b. 1981. *Ain't I a woman: Black women and feminism*. Boston: South End Press.

Howard, J. A., and J. Hollander. 1997. *Gendered situations, gendered selves*. Thousand Oaks, CA: Sage.

Kessler, S. J., and W. MeKenna. 1978. *Gender: An ethnomethodological approach*. New York: John Wiley.

Krieger, S. 1991. *Social science and the self*. New Brunswick, NJ: Rutgers University Press.

Johnson, A. G. 1997. *The gender knot: Unraveling our patriarchal legacy*. Philadelphia: Temple University Press.

Lorber, J. 1994. *Paradoxes of gender*. New Haven, CT: Yale University Press.

———.1996. Beyond the binaries: Depolarizing the categories of sex, sexuality, and gender. *Sociological Inquiry* 66:143–59.

Lucal, B. 1996. Oppression and privilege: Toward a relational conceptualization of race. *Teaching Sociology* 24:245–55.

———. 1997. "Hey, this is the ladies' room!": Gender misattribution and public harassment. *Perspectives on Social Problems* 9:43–57.

Martin, K. A. 1998. Becoming a gendered body: Practices of preschools. *American Sociological Review* 63:494–511.

Mills, C. W. 1959. *The sociological imagination*. London: Oxford University Press.

Myhre, J.R.M. 1995. One bad hair day too many, or the hairstory of an androgynous young feminist. In *Listen up: Voices from the next feminist generation*, edited by B. Findlen. Seattle, WA: Seal Press.

Reinharz, S. 1992. *Feminist methods in social research*. New York: Oxford University Press.

Richardson, L. 1994. Writing: A method of inquiry. In *Handbook of Qualitative Research*, edited by N. K. Denzin and Y. S. Lincoln. Thousand Oaks, CA: Sage.

Riemer, J. W. 1977. Varieties of opportunistic research. *Urban Life* 5:467–77.

———.1988. Work and self. In *Personal sociology*, edited by P. C. Higgins and J. M. Johnson. New York: Praeger.

Spelman, E. V. 1988. *Inessential woman: Problems of exclusion in feminist thought*. Boston: Beacon.

Staples, B. 1993. Just walk on by. In *Experiencing race, class, and gender in the United States*, edited by V. Cyrus. Mountain View, CA: Mayfield. (Originally published 1986)

West. C., and S. Fenstermaker. 1995. Doing difference. *Gender & Society* 9:8–37.

West, C., and D. H. Zimmerman. 1987. Doing gender. *Gender & Society* 1:125–51.

Weston, K. 1996. *Render me, gender me*. New York: Columbia University Press.

Zimmerman, D. H. 1992. They were all doing gender, but they weren't all passing: Comment on Rogers. *Gender & Society* 6:192–98.

John Derbyshire

THE ABOLITION OF SEX
DON'T WORRY—ONLY IN THE LAW. ONLY!

Though many in the biological and social sciences continue to illustrate ways that gender lines are thin, and perhaps somewhat arbitrary, others find the breaching of these boundaries to be problematic. The essay below satirizes legal attempts to make definitions of gender and sexuality less strict. Its author,

John Derbyshire, is a critic, commentator, novelist, and columnist for the politically conservative publication The National Review, *in which the article included here was published. He writes in many genres. He is the author of* Prime Obsession, *a nonfiction story about struggles to solve a crucial mathematical equation; two novels,* Fire from the Sun *and* Seeing Calvin Coolidge in a Dream; *and a collection of poems recorded on CD.*

1   With recent events in Massachusetts and California, homosexual marriage—an idea that seems not to have occurred to anyone at all in the entire span of human history until about five years ago—is now a daily topic in our newspapers and TV programs. While there is certainly a great deal to be said about homosexual marriage, I have come to believe that this issue is merely an epiphenomenon, the visible manifestation of some deeper trend. To be precise, I think that what is under way here is a program to purge the very notion of sex from all our laws. This is not just a campaign to permit men to marry men, and women women; it is a campaign for the abolition of sex. Nor is it the homosexuals who are in the vanguard here, but the *trans*sexualists—persons who wish to be not the sex Nature, in forming their bodies, intended them to be, but the other one.

2   I had better clarify my usage. I don't mean that we are witnessing an attempt to stamp out the intimate act. Probably nothing could be further from the minds of the activists promoting this revolution. No: Here I am using "sex" in the first of the senses offered by Merriam-Webster's *Third*: "one of the two divisions of organic, especially human, beings respectively designated male or female." In what passes for academic literature in this field, the word "gender" is now commonly used with this denotation. If I were more modern-minded I would say "the abolition of gender." However, when I have used "gender" in this sense in the past, I have got angry letters and e-mails from fellow conservatives. After reading through several dozen of these, I have concluded that my correspondents are correct. Furthermore, if you read much of the propaganda of transsexualist agitators, you realize that there is, for them, a key distinction between "sex" and "gender." "Sex" is what someone else thinks you are, based on some objective criterion (visual inspection, chromosome count, biochemical analysis); "gender" is *what you feel yourself to be*, tests and evidences notwithstanding. The latter notion, being subjective, is of course good; the former is correspondingly bad. See how the wheel has turned: "Sex" is once again a dirty word!

So my argument is that these recent shenanigans at top right   3
and bottom left of our country are the first battles in a much
broader war, a war to expunge sex from the public sphere
altogether.

This came to me in a flash of understanding while I was   4
reading the Gender Recognition Bill, which was passed by
Britain's House of Lords last month. This bill, the fruit of many
years' lobbying by transsexualist groups, is a remarkable document. The essence of it is that if you are a man who wishes to
be known as a woman (or, of course, vice versa), the public authorities will oblige you. They will even issue you a new birth
certificate, with your new sex written in. You will thenceforth
be a woman, for all legal and political purposes.

There will be some formalities to be gone through. The bill re-   5
quires that you present yourself to a Gender Recognition Panel,
armed with a certificate from either "a registered medical prac-
titioner practising in the field of gender dysphoria, or . . . a chartered psychologist practising in that field." You must offer some
evidence that you have been living as a member of your new sex
for two years. You do not, however, need to have undergone sex-
reassignment surgery. A man with a full set of tackle can now be
a woman under British law. He and another man, similarly
equipped, could present themselves as man and woman at a
church, and be married. You see why I believe the homosexual-
marriage issue to be a secondary phenomenon here.

This bill has, as I said, passed the House of Lords. The de-   6
bates were not without some droll moments.

LORD TEBBIT: Clause 16 provides that if an Earl re-registers
  himself as a woman, he fortunately does not have to become
  a Countess. That is a most liberal part of the Bill; for such
  small mercies we should be grateful. I therefore presume
  that if a King should undertake gender reassignment,
  he could rule as a woman, but he would still be a King. I
  must say that that would raise some curious thoughts.
EARL FERRERS: My Lords, my noble friend's speech is so fascinating that it has stimulated my thoughts. What happens if an
  Earl becomes a woman? Does his son then become the Earl?
LORD TEBBIT: My Lords, I really do not know. Presumably, as he
  would remain an Earl rather than becoming a Countess, his
  son would have other problems on his mind than whether
  he would immediately succeed to the title.
BARONESS O'CATHAIN: My Lords, let us hope that my noble
  friend is not going to do it.
LORD TEBBIT: Indeed, my Lords, we hope that my noble friend's
  interest in the matter is not entirely personal.

7   At the time this issue of NATIONAL REVIEW goes to press, the bill, having passed the House of Lords, is being debated in Commons.

8   Baroness O'Cathain attempted to introduce an amendment to the bill, specifying that "a body which exists for the purposes of organised religion may prohibit or restrict the participation in its religious activities or ceremonies of persons whose gender has become the acquired gender under this Act . . . if the prohibition is necessary to comply with the doctrines of the religion." This amendment was defeated on a vote, 144 to 149. (Nobody who follows Church of England affairs will be much surprised to learn that opposition to this amendment was led by the Right Reverend Peter Selby, Bishop of Worcester.)

9   Another amendment was proposed by old Thatcherite warhorse Lord Tebbit, specifying that "no two persons each possessing XX chromosomes nor each possessing XY chromosomes, nor each possessing genitalia appropriate to the same sex, may be married the one to the other." That one went down 46 to 121. Not only does the Gender Recognition Bill open the door to homosexual marriage, it effectively prohibits a clergyman from refusing to conduct such a marriage. And if, after conducting a marriage between two people he assumed to be of opposite biological sex, the clergyman discovers that they were, in fact, of the same sex, he may not tell anyone of his discovery. Should he do so, he will have broken the law, and will face a £5,000 fine!

10   In line with the thinking of most British citizens, while religion was given short shrift by the assembled peers, sport occupied a great deal of their time. If Hulk Hogan were to get himself "recognized" as a woman in British law, could a women's wrestling team exclude him without opening itself to a discrimination lawsuit? Their lordships pondered mightily before passing a subtle amendment permitting sports bodies to make their own determinations of sex, where considerations of safety or fair competition might otherwise be compromised. You could practically hear Britain's swelling legion of trial attorneys rubbing their hands with glee at this point.

11   As an American friend remarked when I explained the bill to him: "Presumably the next step is to allow individual men or women to legally declare themselves to be trees or turnips." Presumably so; though that step will of course require parliament to first pass a Species Recognition Bill.

Images of Gender in the Arts

Although issues of gender are amply illustrated in words throughout this part of the book, one might argue that gender is perhaps best understood in images—images that both *reflect* and *create* the vision of gender that we incorporate into our own self-image. For this reason, artists have perennially explored gender and its boundaries, and have done so in a wide variety of genres and media. As you study the pieces below, consider the varied perspectives on gender and gender boundaries that each portrays—and the conversations that those images might spur about the roles of men and women in our culture.

Albrecht Dürer's *The Fall of Man*, 1504, uses classical images of the male and female forms to depict Adam and Eve, perhaps the most widely known Western icons of gender. What does this painting suggest about gender, the relationship between the genders, and gender roles? How does it interact with the narrative of Adam and Eve?

These three images provide a wide range of perspectives on maleness (clockwise from top left): the iconic photo of Marlon Brando in his role as Stanley Kowalski in the 1951 film version of *A Streetcar Named Desire*, Andy Warhol's silkscreen image of John Wayne, and the classical sculpture of *David* by Michaelangelo. What does each piece suggest about the male gender? In what ways are these images similar in their presentation of maleness? How are they different? How do those images compare with other images of being a man or a woman that are presented in this section?

Barbara Kruger, "Untitled" (Your body is a battleground), 112″ × 112″, photographic silkscreen/vinyl, 1989. Collection: The Broad Art Foundation, Santa Monica. Courtesy: Mary Boone Gallery, New York.

What it means to be female has been explored throughout the history of art in ways that go beyond the idealized images we see in the media. How do the varied styles—from relatively realistic to abstract, from two dimensional to three dimensional—affect the message of each, and the conversations they are likely to spur? Clockwise from top: Barbara Kruger, *Untitled* (1989); Alice Neel, *Self-Portrait* (1980); Edgar Degas, *Bathers on the Grass* (1886–90).

Romaine Brooks' *Self-Portrait* (1923) (top) and Andy Warhol's *Self-Portrait in Fright Wig* (1987) (bottom) each ask us to extend our conventional notions of gender. What physical characteristics of gender do they portray and/or distort? What messages do they seem to emit about the male gender and its relationship to the female gender? And, since each piece is a self-portrait, you might also ask what notions of selfhood, especially as related to gender, each suggests. In what ways are their depictions of self androgynous?

Is English Sexist?

Beverly Gross

BITCH

Salmagundi, a quarterly magazine of the humanities and so-cial sciences that is produced at Skidmore College, carries po-etry, fiction, critical essays, and social analyses on a variety of issues. In the summer of 1994, it published the following med-itation on language by Beverly Gross, a professor of English at City University of New York.

We were discussing Mary McCarthy's *The Group* in a course 1
called Women Writers and Literary Tradition. McCarthy's biog-rapher Carol Gelderman, I told the class, had been intrigued by how often critics called Mary McCarthy a bitch. I read a few ci-tations. "Her novels are crammed with cerebration and bitchi-ness" (John Aldridge). "Her approach to writing [is] reflective of the modern American bitch" (Paul Schlueter). Why McCarthy? a student asked. Her unrelenting standards, I ventured, her tough-minded critical estimates—there was no self-censoring, appeasing Angel in the House of Mary McCarthy's brain. Her combativeness (her marital battles with Edmund Wilson be-came the stuff of academic legend). Maybe there were other factors. But the discussion opened up to the more inclusive issue of the word bitch itself. What effect does that appellation have on women? What effect might it have had on McCarthy? No one ever called Edmund Wilson a bitch. Do we excuse, even pay respect when a man is critical, combative, assertive? What is the male equivalent of the word bitch, I asked the class.

"Boss," said Sabrina Sims. 2

This was an evening class at a branch of the City University 3
of New York. Most of the students are older adults trying to fit

a college education into otherwise busy lives. Most of them
have fulltime jobs during the day. Sabrina Sims works on Wall
Street, is a single mother raising a ten year old daughter, is
black, and had to take an Incomplete in the course because she
underwent a kidney transplant in December.

4   Her answer gave us all a good laugh. I haven't been able to
get it out of my mind. I've been thinking about bitch, watching
how it is used by writers and in conversation, and have explored its lexical history. "A name of reproach for a woman" is
how Doctor Johnson's Dictionary dealt with the word in the
eighteenth century, as though anticipating the great adaptability of this particular execration, a class of words that tends toward early obsolescence. Not bitch, however, which has been
around for a millennium, outlasting a succession of definitions.
Its longevity is perhaps attributable to its satisfying misogyny.
Its meaning matters less than its power to denounce and subju-
gate. Francis Grose in *A Classical Dictionary of the Vulgar
Tongue* (1785) considered bitch "the most offensive appellation
that can be given to an English woman, even more provoking
than that of whore." He offered as evidence "a low London
woman's reply on being called a bitch" in the late eighteenth
century: "I may be a whore but can't be a bitch!" The meaning
of bitch has changed over the centuries but it remains the word
that comes immediately to the tongue, still "the most offensive
appellation" the English language provides to hurl at a woman.

5   The *Oxford English Dictionary* records two main meanings
for the noun bitch up through the nineteenth century:

1. The female of the dog

2. Applied opprobriously to a woman; strictly a lewd or sensual woman. Not now in decent use.

6   It was not until the twentieth century that bitch acquired its
opprobrious application in realms irrespective of sensuality.
The Supplement to the *OED* (1972) adds:

2a: "In mod. use, esp. a malicious or treacherous woman."

7   Every current desk dictionary supplies some such meaning:

A spiteful, ill-tempered woman [*World Book Dictionary*]

   A malicious, unpleasant, selfish woman, esp. one who stops
at nothing to reach her goal. [*Random House Dictionary*]

But malice and treachery only begin to tell the story.   8
The informal questionnaire that I administered to my students
and a number of acquaintances elicited ample demonstration
of the slippery adaptability of bitch as it might be used
these days:

a conceited person, a snob
a self-absorbed woman
a complainer
a competitive woman
a woman who is annoying, pushy, possibly underhanded (in
    short, a man in a woman's body)
someone rich, thin and free!

"A word used by men who are threatened by women" was   9
one astute response. Threat lurks everywhere: for women the
threat is in being called a bitch. "Someone whiny, threatening,
crabby, pestering" is what one woman offered as her definition. "Everything I try hard not to be," she added, "though it
seeps through." I offer as a preliminary conclusion that bitch
means to men whatever they find threatening in a woman and
it means to women whatever they particularly dislike about
themselves. In either case the word functions as a misogynistic
club. I will add that the woman who defined bitch as everything she tries hard not to be when asked to free associate
about the word came up immediately with "mother." That
woman happens to be my sister. We share the same mother,
who was often whiny and crabby, though I would never have
applied the word bitch to her, but then again, I don't consider
whiny, crabby and pestering to be prominent among my own
numerous flaws.

Dictionaries of slang are informative sources, in touch as   10
they are with nascent language and the emotive coloration of
words, especially words of abuse. A relatively restrained definition is offered by the only female lexicographer I consulted for
whom bitch is "a nasty woman" or "a difficult task" (Anita
Pearl, *Dictionary of Popular Slang*). The delineations of bitch
by the male lexicographers abound with such cascading hostility that the compilers sometimes seem to be reveling in their
task. For example, Howard Wentworth and Stuart Berg Flexner
in *Dictionary of American Slang*:

A woman, usu., but not necessarily, a mean, selfish,
malicious, deceiving, cruel, or promiscuous woman.

11   Eugene E. Landy's *The Underground Dictionary* (1971) offers:

> 1. Female who is mean, selfish, cruel, malicious, deceiving. a.k.a. cunt.
> 2. Female. See Female.

I looked up the entry for "Female" (Landy, by the way, provides no parallel entry for "Male"):

> beaver, bird, bitch, broad, bush, cat, chick, crack, cunt, douche, fish, fox, frail, garbage can, heffer, pussy, quail, ruca, scag, snatch, stallion, slave, sweet meat, tail, trick, tuna. See GIRLFRIEND; WIFE.

12   Richard A. Spear's *Slang and Euphemism* comments on the derivative adjective:

> bitchy 1. pertaining to a mood wherein one complains incessantly about anything. Although this applies to men or women, it is usually associated with women, especially when they are menstruating. Cf. DOG DAYS

13   Robert L. Chapman's definition in *Thesaurus of American Slang* starts off like a feminist analysis:

> bitch. 1 n. A woman one dislikes or disapproves of.

Followed, however, by a sobering string of synonyms: "broad, cunt, witch."

And then this most interesting note:

> Female equivalents of the contemptuous terms for men, listed in this book under "asshole," are relatively rare. Contempt for females, in slang, stresses their putative sexual promiscuity and weakness rather than their moral vileness and general odiousness. Some terms under "asshole," though, are increasingly used of women.

14   "See ball-buster." Chapman suggests under his second definition for bitch ("anything arduous or very disagreeable"). I looked up "ball-buster":

> n. Someone who saps or destroys masculinity.
> ball-whacker

bitch

nut-cruncher.

Some*thing* has become some*one*. The ball-buster is not a dis-   15
agreeable thing but a disagreeable (disagreeing?) person. A female person. "A woman one dislikes or disapproves of." For
someone so sensitive to the nuances of hostility and verbal put-
down, Chapman certainly takes a circuitous route to get to the
underlying idea that no other dictionary even touches: Bitch
means ball-buster.

What one learns from the dictionaries: there is no classifi-   16
able thing as a bitch, only a label produced by the act of name-
calling. The person named is almost always a female. The
name-calling refers to alleged faults of ill-temper, selfishness,
malice, cruelty, spite, all of them faults in the realm of interpersonal relating—women's faults: it is hard to think of a put-
down word encompassing these faults in a man. "Bastard" and
even "son of a bitch" have bigger fish to fry. And an asshole is
an asshole in and of himself. A bitch is a woman who makes
the name-caller feel uncomfortable. Presumably that name-
caller is a man whose ideas about how a woman should behave
toward him are being violated.

"Women," wrote Virginia Woolf, "have served all these cen-   17
turies as looking-glasses possessing the magic and delicious
power of reflecting the figure of man at twice its natural size."
The woman who withholds that mirror is a bitch. Bitchiness is
the perversion of womanly sweetness, compliance, pleasant-
ness, ego-building. (Male ego-building, of course, though that
is a virtual tautology; women have egos but who builds them?)
If a woman is not building ego she is busting balls.

Ball-buster? The word is a nice synecdoche (like asshole)   18
with great powers of revelation. A ball-buster, one gathers, is a
demanding bitch who insists on overexertion from a man to
satisfy her sexual or material voraciousness. "The bitch is
probably his wife." But balls also bust when a disagreeable
woman undermines a guy's ego and "saps or destroys masculinity." The bitch could be his wife, but also his boss, Gloria
Steinem, the woman at the post office, the woman who spurns
his advances. The familiar Freudian delineation of the male-
female nexus depicts male sexuality as requiring the admiration, submission and subordination of the female. The ultimate threat of (and to) the back-talking woman is male
impotence.

Bitch, the curse and concept, exists to insure male potency   19
and female submissiveness. Men have deployed it to defend
their power by attacking and neutralizing the upstart. "Bitch"

is admonitory, like "whore," like "dyke." Borrowing something from both words, "bitch" is one of those verbal missiles with the power of shackling women's actions and impulses.

20   The metamorphosis of bitch from the context of sexuality (a carnal woman, a promiscuous woman) to temperament (an angry woman, a malicious woman) to power (a domineering woman, a competitive woman) is a touchstone to the changing position of women through this century. As women have become more liberated, individually and collectively, the word has taken on connotations of aggressive, hostile, selfish. In the old days a bitch was a harlot; nowadays she is likely to be a woman who won't put out. Female sensuality, even carnality, even infidelity, have been supplanted as what men primarily fear and despise in women. Judging by the contemporary colorations of the word bitch, what men primarily fear and despise in women is power.

21   Some anecdotes:
1) Barbara Bush's name-calling of Geraldine Ferraro during the 1984 presidential election: "I can't say it but it rhymes with 'rich.'"

22   How ladylike of the future First Lady to avoid uttering the unmentionable. The slur did its dirty work, particularly among those voters disturbed by the sudden elevation of a woman to such unprecedented political heights. In what possible sense did Barbara Bush mean that Geraldine Ferraro is a bitch? A loose woman? Hardly. A nasty woman? Not likely. A pushy woman? Almost certainly. The unspoken syllable was offered as a response to Ferraro's lofty ambitions, potential power, possibly her widespread support among feminists. Imagine a woman seeking to be vice-president instead of vice-husband.

23   The ascription of bitchery seems to have nothing to do with Ferraro's bearing and behavior. Certainly not the Ferraro who wrote about the event in her autobiography:

> Barbara Bush realized what a gaffe she had made . . .
>
> "I just want to apologize to you for what I said," she told me over the phone while I was in the middle of another debate rehearsal. "I certainly didn't mean anything by it."
>
> "Don't worry about it," I said to her. "We all say things at times we don't mean. It's all right."
>
> "Oh," she said breathlessly. "You're such a lady."
>
> All I could think of when I hung up was: Thank God for my convent school training.

2) Lady Ashley at the end of *The Sun Also Rises:* "It makes one   24
feel rather good, deciding not to be a bitch." The context here is
something like this: a bitch is a woman who ruins young heroic
bullfighters. A woman who is propelled by her sexual drive, desires and vanity. The fascination of Brett Ashley is that she lives
and loves like a man: her sexuality is unrepressed and she does-
n't care much for monogamy. (Literary critics until the 1960s
commonly called her a nymphomaniac.) She turns her male ad-
mirers into women—Mike becomes a self-destructive alcoholic,
Robert a moony romantic, Pedro a sacrificial virgin, and Jake a
frustrated eunuch. At her entrance in the novel she is surrounded by an entourage of twittering fairies. Lady Ashley is a
bitch not because she is nasty, bossy or ill-tempered (she has
lovely manners and a terrific personality). And perhaps not
even because of her freewheeling, strident sexuality. She is a
bitch because she overturns the male/female nexus. What could
be a more threatening infraction in a Hemingway novel?

2a) Speaking of Hemingway: After his falling out with Gertrude   25
Stein who had made unflattering comments about his writing in
The Autobiography of Alice B. Toklas, Hemingway dropped her off
a copy of his newly published *Death in the Afternoon* with the
handwritten inscription. "A bitch is a bitch is a bitch."

[Q.] Why was Gertrude Stein a bitch?
[A.] For no longer admiring Hemingway. A bitch is a woman
    who criticizes.

3) "Ladies and gentlemen. I don't believe Mrs. Helmsley is   26
charged in the indictment with being a tough bitch" is how her
defense lawyer Gerald A. Feffer addressed the jury in Leona
Helmsley's trial for tax fraud and extortion. He acknowledged
that she was "sometimes rude and abrasive," and that she
"may have overcompensated for being a woman in a hard-
edged men's business world." Recognizing the difficulty of defending what the New York *Post* called "the woman that
everyone loves to hate," his tactic was to preempt the prosecution by getting there first with "tough bitch." He lost.

4) *Esquire* awarded a Dubious Achievement of 1990 to Victor   27
Kiam, owner of the New England Patriots football team, for
saying "he could never have called Boston *Herald* reporter Lisa
Olson 'a classic bitch' because he doesn't use the word classic."
Some background on what had been one of that year's most
discussed controversies: Olson aroused the ire of the Patriots
for showing up in their locker room with the male reporters
after a game. Members of the Patriots, as *Esquire* states,

surrounded her, "thrusting their genitals in her face and daring her to touch them."

28   Why is Lisa Olson a bitch? For invading the male domain of sports reportage and the male territory of the locker room? For telling the world, instead of swallowing her degradation, pain and anger? The club owner's use of "bitch" seems meant to conjure up the lurking idea of castrating female. Seen in that light the Patriots' act of "thrusting their genitals in her face" transforms an act of loutishness into a position of innocent vulnerability.

29   5) Bumper sticker observed on back of pickup truck:

> Impeach Jane Fonda, American Traitor Bitch

The bumper sticker seemed relatively new and fresh. I observed it a full two decades after Jane Fonda's journey to North Vietnam which is the event that surely inspired this call to impeachment (from what? aerobics class?). Bitch here is an expletive. It originates in and sustains anger. Calling Jane Fonda a "traitor" sounds a bit dated in the 1990s, but adding "bitch" gives the accusation timelessness and does the job of rekindling old indignation.

30   6) Claude Brown's account in *Manchild in the Promised Land* of how he learned about women from a street-smart older friend:

> Johnny was always telling us about bitches. To Johnny, every chick was a bitch. Even mothers were bitches. Of course there were some nice bitches, but they were still bitches. And a man had to be a dog in order to handle a bitch.
>
> Johnny said once. "If a bitch ever tells you she's only got a penny to buy the baby some milk, take it. You take it, 'cause she's gon git some more. Bitches can always git some money." He really knew about bitches. Cats would say, "I saw your sister today, and she is a fine bitch." Nobody was offended by it. That's just the way things were. It was easy to see all women as bitches.

31   Bitch in black male street parlance seems closer to its original meaning of a female breeder—not a nasty woman and not a powerful woman, but the biological bearer of litters. The word is likely to be used in courting as well as in anger by males seeking the sexual favor of a female, and a black female addressed as bitch by an admirer is expected to feel not insulted but honored by the attention. (Bitch signifies something

different when black women use it competitively about other black women.) But even as an endearment, from male to female, there is no mistaking the lurking contempt.

A *Dictionary of Afro-American Slang* compiled by Clarence   32
Major (under the imprint of the leftist International Publishers) provides only that bitch in black parlance is "a mean, flaunting homosexual," entirely omitting any reference to its rampant use in black street language as the substitute word for woman. A puzzling omission. Perhaps the word is so taken for granted that its primary meaning is not even recognized as black vernacular.

Bitch, mama, motherfucker—how frequently motherhood   33
figures in street language. Mothers are the object of insults when playing the dozens. The ubiquitous motherfucker simultaneously strikes out at one's immediate foe as well as the sanctity of motherhood. Mama, which Clarence Major defines as "a pretty black girl," is an endearment that a man might address to a sexy contemporary. "Hey mama" is tinged with a certain sweetness. "Hey bitch" has more of an edge, more likely to be addressed to a woman the man no longer needs to sweet-talk. It is hard to think of white males coming on by evoking motherhood or of white women going for it. A white male addressing a woman as bitch is not likely to be expecting a sexual reward. She will be a bitch behind her back and after the relationship is over or didn't happen.

The widespread use of bitch by black men talking to black   34
women, its currency in courting, and its routine acceptance by women are suggestive of some powerful alienation in male-female relations and in black self-identity. Although there may be the possibility of ironic inversion, as in calling a loved one nigger, a black man calling a loved one bitch is expressing contempt for the object of his desire with the gratuitous fillip of associative contempt for the woman who gave him life. Bitch, like motherfucker, bespeaks something threatening to the male sense of himself, a furious counter to emasculation in a world where, as the young Claude Brown figured out, mothers have all the power. It is not hard to see that the problem of black men is much more with white racism than it is with black women. Whatever the cause, however, the language sure doesn't benefit the women. Here is still one more saddening instance of the victim finding someone even more hapless to take things out on. (Does this process explain why Clarence Major's only reference for bitch is to the "mean, flaunting homosexual"?)

7) "Do you enjoy playing that role of castrating bitch" is a ques-   35
tion put to Madonna by an interviewer for *The Advocate*. Madonna's answer: "I enjoy expressing myself. . . ."

36   A response to another question about the public's reaction to
her movie *Truth or Dare:* "They already think I'm a cunt bitch,
they already think I'm Attila the Hun. They already compare
me to Adolf Hitler and Saddam Hussein."

37   Bitch has lost its power to muzzle Madonna. Unlike other female celebrities who have cringed from accusations of bitchi-
ness (Joan Rivers, Imelda Marcos, Margaret Thatcher, Nancy
Reagan), Madonna has made her fortune by exploiting criticism. Her career has skyrocketed with the media's charges of
obscenity and sacrilege; she seems to embrace the bitch label
with the same eager opportunism.

38   "I enjoy expressing myself" is not merely the explanation for
why Madonna gets called bitch; "I enjoy expressing myself" is
the key to defusing the power of bitch to fetter and subdue.
Madonna has appropriated the word and turned the intended
insult to her advantage. This act of appropriation, I predict,
will embolden others with what consequences and effects it is
impossible to foresee.

Deborah Tannen
CROSSTALK

*Deborah Tannen, a professor of linguistics at Georgetown
University in Washington, D.C., published* You Just Don't
Understand: Women and Men in Conversation *in 1990. This
exploration of the complexities of communication between
men and women became a national best-seller. The following
selection from the book has been printed elsewhere as a self-
contained piece.*

1   A woman who owns a bookstore needed to have a talk with the
store manager. She had told him to help the bookkeeper with
billing, he had agreed, and now, days later, he still hadn't done
it. Thinking how much she disliked this part of her work, she
sat down with the manager to clear things up. They traced the
problem to a breakdown in communication.

2   She had said, "Sarah needs help with the bills. What do you
think about helping her out?" He had responded, "OK," by

which he meant, "OK, I'll think about whether or not I want to help her." During the next day, he thought about it and concluded that he'd rather not.

This wasn't just an ordinary communication breakdown that could happen between any two people. It was a particular sort of breakdown that tends to occur between women and men.   3

Most women avoid giving orders. More comfortable with decision-making by consensus, they tend to phrase requests as questions, to give others the feeling they have some say in the matter and are not being bossed around. But this doesn't mean they aren't making their wishes clear. Most women would have understood the bookstore owner's question, "What do you think about helping her out?" as assigning a task in a considerate way.   4

The manager, however, took the owner's words literally. She had asked him what he thought; she hadn't told him to *do* anything. So he felt within his rights when he took her at her word, thought about it and decided not to help Sarah.   5

Women in positions of authority are likely to regard such responses as insubordination: "He knows I am in charge, and he knows what I want; if he doesn't do it, he is resisting my authority."   6

There may be a kernel of truth in this view—most men are inclined to resist authority if they can because being in a subordinate position makes them intensely uncomfortable. But indirect requests that are transparent to women may be genuinely opaque to men. They assume that people in authority will give orders if they really want something done.   7

These differences in management styles are one of many manifestations of gender differences in how we talk to one another. Women use language to create connection and rapport; men use it to negotiate their status in a hierarchical order. It isn't that women are unaware of status or that men don't build rapport, but that *the genders tend to focus on different goals*.   8

The Source of Gender Differences

These differences stem from the way boys and girls learn to use language while growing up. Girls tend to play indoors, either in small groups or with one other girl. The center of a girl's social life is her best friend, with whom she spends a great deal of time sitting, talking and exchanging secrets. It is the telling of secrets that makes them best friends. Boys tend to play outdoors, in larger groups, usually in competitive games. It's doing things together that makes them friends.   9

10   Anthropologist Marjorie Harness Goodwin compared boys
and girls at play in a black inner-city neighborhood in
Philadelphia. Her findings, which have been supported by researchers in other settings, show that the boys' groups are hierarchical: high-status boys give orders, and low-status boys
have to follow them, so they end up being told what to do.
Girls' groups tend to be egalitarian: girls who appeared "better" than others or gave orders were not countenanced and in
some cases were ostracized.

11   So while boys are learning to fear being "put down" and
pushed around, girls are learning to fear being "locked out."
Whereas high-status boys establish and reinforce their authority by giving orders and resisting doing what others want, girls
tend to make suggestions, which are likely to be taken up by
the group.

Cross-Gender Communication in the Workplace

12   The implications of these different conversational habits and
concerns in terms of office interactions are staggering. Men
are inclined to continue to jockey for position, trying to resist
following orders as much as possible within the constraints of
their jobs.

13   Women, on the other hand, are inclined to do what they
sense their bosses want, whether or not they are ordered to. By
the same token, women in positions of authority are inclined
to phrase their requests as suggestions and to assume they will
be respected because of their authority. These assumptions are
likely to hold up as long as both parties are women, but they
may well break down in cross-gender communication.

14   When a woman is in the position of authority, such as the
bookstore owner, she may find her requests are systematically
misunderstood by men. And when a woman is working for a
male boss, she may find that her boss gives bald commands that
seem unnecessarily imperious because most women would
prefer to be asked rather than ordered. One woman who
worked at an all-male radio station commented that the way
the men she worked for told her what to do made her feel as if
she should salute and say, "Yes, boss."

15   Many men complain that a woman who is indirect in making requests is manipulative: she's trying to get them to do
what she wants without telling them to do it. Another common
accusation is that she is insecure: she doesn't know what she
wants. But if a woman gives direct orders, the same men might
complain that she is aggressive, unfeminine or worse.

Women are in a double bind: *If we talk like women, we are*   16
not respected. If we talk like men, we are not liked.

We have to walk a fine line, finding ways to be more direct   17
without appearing bossy. The bookstore owner may never be
comfortable by directly saying, "Help Sarah with the billing
today," but she might find some compromise such as, "Sarah
needs help with the billing. I'd appreciate it if you would make
some time to help her out in the next day or two." This request
is clear, while still reflecting women's preferences for giving
reasons and options.

What if you're the subordinate and your boss is a man who's   18
offending you daily by giving you orders? If you know him well
enough, one potential solution is "metacommunication"—that
is, talk about communication. Point out the differences between women and men, and discuss how you could accommodate to each other's styles. (You may want to give him a copy of
this article or my book.)

But if you don't have the kind of relationship that makes   19
metacommunication possible, you could casually, even jok-
ingly, suggest he give orders another way. Or just try to remind
yourself it's a cross-cultural difference and try not to take his
curtness personally.

How to Handle a Meeting

There are other aspects of women's styles that can work   20
against us in a work setting. Because women are most comfortable using language to create rapport with someone they
feel close to, and men are used to talking in a group where they
have to prove themselves and display what they know, a formal
meeting can be a natural for men and a hard nut to crack for
women. Many women find it difficult to speak up at meetings;
if they do, they may find their comments ignored, perhaps
later to be resuscitated by a man who gets credit for the idea.
Part of this is simply due to the expectation that men will have
more important things to contribute.

But the way women and men tend to present themselves can   21
aggravate this inequity. At meetings, men are more likely to
speak often, at length and in a declamatory manner. They may
state their opinions as fact and leave it to others to challenge
them.

Women, on the other hand, are often worried about appear-   22
ing to talk too much—a fear that is justified by research showing that when they talk equally, women are perceived as talking
more than men. As a result, many women are hesitant to speak

at a meeting and inclined to be succinct and tentative when they do.

Developing Options

23   Working on changing your presentational style is one option; another is to make your opinions known in private conversation with the key people before a meeting. And if you are the key person, it would be wise to talk personally to the women on your staff rather than assuming all participants have had a chance to express themselves at the meeting.

24   Many women's reticence about displaying their knowledge at a meeting is related to their reluctance to boast. They find it more humble to keep quiet about their accomplishments and wait for someone else to notice them. But most men learn early on to display their accomplishments and skills. And women often find that no one bothers to ferret out their achievements if they don't put them on display. Again, a woman risks criticism if she talks about her achievements, but this may be a risk she needs to take, to make sure she gets credit for her work.

25   I would never want to be heard as telling women to adopt men's styles across the board. For one thing, there are many situations in which women's styles are more successful. For example, the inclination to make decisions by consensus can be a boon to a woman in a managerial position. Many people, men as well as women, would rather feel they have influence in decision-making than be given orders.

26   Moreover, recommending that women adopt men's styles would be offensive, as well as impractical, because women are judged by the norms for women's behavior, and doing the same thing as men has a very different, often negative, effect.

A Starting Point

27   Simply knowing about gender differences in conversational style provides a starting point for improving relations with the women and men who are above and below you in a hierarchy.

28   The key is *flexibility*; a way of talking that works beautifully with one person may be a disaster with another. If one way of talking isn't working, try another, rather than trying harder to do more of the same.

29   Once you know what the parameters are, you can become an observer of your own interactions, and a style-switcher when you choose.

Sherryl Kleinman

WHY SEXIST LANGUAGE MATTERS

Though sexist language is sometimes considered no more than "political correctness" or a method of controlling free speech, Sherryl Kleinman, a sociologist, essayist, and poet, argues here that sexist language does matter. As you read, consider how her background as a sociologist influences her methods of argument and the evidence she presents. To what alternative views does her title and the essay itself, first published in Qualitative Sociology *in 2002, seem to be responding? Kleinman has taught at UNC-Chapel Hill since 1980, offering courses in social psychology, race, class and gender, and social and economic justice. Her books include* Equals before God: Seminarians as Humanistic Professionals *(1984),* Emotions and Fieldwork *(with Martha Copp, 1993), and* Opposing Ambitions: Gender and Identity in an Alternative Organization *(1996).*

For eleven years I've been teaching a sociology course at the University of North Carolina on gender inequality. I cover such topics as the wage gap, the "second shift" (the disproportionate amount of housework and child care that heterosexual women do at home), the equation of women's worth with physical attractiveness, the sexualizing of women in the media, lack of reproductive rights for women (especially poor women), sexual harassment, and men's violence against women. But the issue that both female and male students have the most trouble understanding—or, as I see it, share a strong unwillingness to understand—is sexist language. 1

I'm not referring to such words as "bitch," "whore," and "slut." What I focus on instead are words that most people consider just fine: male (so-called) generics. Some of these words refer to persons occupying a position: postman, chairman, freshman, congressman, fireman. Other words refer to the entire universe of human beings: "mankind" or "he." Then we've got manpower, man-made lakes, and "Oh, man, where did I leave my keys?" There's "manning" the tables in a country where we learn that "all men are created equal." 2

The most insidious, from my observations, is the popular expression "you guys." People like to tell me it's a regional term. But 3

I've heard it in Chapel Hill, New York, Chicago, San Francisco, and Montreal. I've seen it in print in national magazines, newsletters, and books. I've heard it on television and in films. And even if it were regional, that doesn't make it right. I bet we can all think of a lot of practices in our home regions we'd like to get rid of.

4   Try making up a female-based generic, such as "freshwoman," and using it with a group of male students, or calling your male boss "chairwoman." Then again, don't. There could be serious consequences for referring to a man as a woman—a term that still means "lesser" in our society. If not, why do men get so upset at the idea of being called women?

5   What's the big deal? Why does all this "man-ning" and "guysing" deserve a place on my list of items of gender inequality?

6   The answer is because male-based generics are another indicator—and, more importantly, a *reinforcer*—of a system in which "man" in the abstract and men in the flesh are privileged over women. Some say that language merely reflects reality and so we should ignore our words and work on changing the unequal gender arrangements that are reflected in our language. Well, yes, in part.

7   It's no accident that "man" is the anchor in our language and "woman" is not. And of course we should make social change all over the place. But the words we use can also reinforce current realities when they are sexist (or racist or heterosexist). Words are the tools of thought. We can use words to maintain the status quo or to think in new ways—which in turn creates the possibility of a new *reality*. It makes a difference if I think of myself as a "girl" or a "woman"; it makes a difference if we talk about "Negroes" or "African Americans." Do we want a truly inclusive language or one that just pretends?

8   For a moment, imagine a world—as the philosopher Douglas R. Hofstadter did in his 1986 satire on sexist language—where people used generics based on race rather than gender. In that world, people would use "freshwhite," "chairwhite," and, yes, "you whiteys." People of color would hear "all whites are created equal"—and be expected to feel included. In an addendum to his article, Hofstadter says that he wrote "A Person Paper on Purity in Language" to shock readers: Only by substituting "white" for "man" does it become easy to see the pervasiveness of male-based generics and to recognize that using "man" for all human beings is wrong. Yet, women are expected to feel flattered by "freshman," "chairman," and "you guys."

9   And why do so many women cling to "freshman," "chairman," and "you guys?"

10   I think it's because women want to be included in the term that refers to the higher-status group: men. But while being

labeled "one of the guys" might make women *feel* included, it's only a guise of inclusion, not the reality. If women were really included we wouldn't have to disappear into the word "guys."

At the same time that women in my classes throw around   11
"you guys"—even here in the southern United States, where "y'all" is an alternative—they call themselves "girls." I'm not sure if this has gotten worse over the years or I've just noticed it more. When I was an undergraduate in the early to mid 1970s, we wanted to be women. Who would take us seriously at college or at work if we were "girls"? To many of my students today, "woman" is old enough to be "over the hill." A "girl" is youthful and thus more attractive to men than a "woman." Since they like the term so much, I suggest that we rename Women's Studies "Girls' Studies." And since the Women's Center on campus provides services for them, why not call it "The Girls' Center." They laugh. "Girls" sounds ridiculous, they say. The students begin to see that "girl"—as a label for twenty-one-year-olds—is infantilizing, not flattering.

"Girl" and "you guys" aren't the only linguistic problems on   12
campus. A few years ago Bob, a student in my class, said that his fraternity is now open to women as well as men and that a controversy had erupted over whether to continue to use the term "brother" to refer to all fraternity members, or to use "sister" for female members. Almost all the women in his fraternity, he said, voted to be called brother rather than sister. As with "you guys," the women wanted to take on the word that has more value. Yet the practice of using "brother" reinforces the idea that a real member of the group is a brother (i.e., a man). I asked what would happen if he had suggested that all fraternity members be called sisters rather than brothers, or that they rename the fraternity a sorority. Everyone laughed at the absurdity of this suggestion. Exactly. Yet it is not absurd, but acceptable, to call women by the term "guys" or "brothers."

Since the "fraternity" Bob referred to is no longer exclusively   13
male, and since gender is no longer a criterion for membership, I asked him how he thought others might react if he suggested they substitute "association" or "society" for "fraternity." Perhaps they could call both men and women "members," or, if students preferred a more informal term, "friends"?

"Yes, that makes sense." Bob told us. "But, I just don't think   14
they'll go for it." He paused. "I'm not sure why."

We talked as a class about why this simple solution might   15
meet with resistance. We concluded that many men would resist losing these linguistic signifiers of male superiority, and

many women would resist losing the valued maleness implied by "brother" and "fraternity." "Member" would feel like a drop in status for both women and men!

16   The students, like most people who use male "generics," don't have bad intentions. But as sociologists, we know that it's important to look at the *consequences*. All those "man" words—said many times a day by millions of people every day—cumulatively reinforce the message that men are the standard and that women should be subsumed by the male category.

17   I worry about what people with the best of intentions are teaching our children. A colleague's five-year-old daughter recently left her classroom crying after a teacher said, "What do you guys think?" She thought the teacher didn't care about what *she* thought. When the teacher told her that of course she was included, her tears stopped. But what was the lesson? She learned that her opinion as a girl mattered only when she's a guy. She learned that men are the norm.

18   A friend's six-year-old son refused to believe that the female firefighter who came to his school to talk to the class—dressed in uniform—actually fought fires. The firefighter repeatedly referred to herself as a "fireman." Despite the protests of the teacher and the firefighter, the boy would not be convinced. "A fire*man* can't be a woman," he said. His mother, who is fastidious in her use of nonsexist language, had a tough time doing damage control.

19   So, is it any surprise that the worst insult a boy can hurl at another boy is "girl"?

20   We know from history that making a group invisible makes it easier for the powerful to do what they want with members of that group. Perhaps that's why linguists use the strong language of "symbolic annihilation" to refer to the disappearance of women into male-based terms. And we know, from too many past and current studies, that far too many men are doing "what they want" with women. Most of us can see a link between calling women "sluts" and "whores" and men's sexual violence against women. We need to recognize that making women linguistically a subset of man/men through terms like "mankind" and "guys" also makes women into objects. If we, as women, aren't worthy of such true generics as "first-year," "chair," or "you all," then how can we expect to be paid a "man's wage," be respected as people rather than objects (sexual or otherwise) on the job and at home, be treated as equals rather than servers or caretakers of others, be considered responsible enough to make our own decisions about reproduction, and

define who and what we want as sexual beings? If we aren't even deserving of our place in humanity in language, why should we expect to be treated as decent human beings otherwise?

Some people tell me that making English nonsexist is a slip-   21
pery slope. As one colleague said to me, "Soon we'll have to say 'waitperson,' which sounds awful. We won't be able to 'man' the table at Orientation. And we'll become 'fellowpersons' at the Institute!" I told him that "server" works well. We can "staff" the table. And why not use "scholars" instead of "fellows"? We've got a big language to roam in. Let's have fun figuring out how to speak and write without making "man" the center. If sliding down that slope takes us to a place where we speak non-sexist English, I'm ready for the ride.

And this doesn't mean that every word with "m-e-n" in it is a   22
problem. Menstruation and mending are fine. Making amends is good, too. There's only a problem when "men," as part of a word, is meant to refer to everyone (freshmen, chairmen, and so on).

Now and then someone says that I should work on more im-   23
portant issues—like men's violence against women—rather than on "trivial" issues like language. Well, I work on lots of is-sues. But that's not the point. Working against sexist language *is* working against men's violence against women. It's one step. If we cringe at "freshwhite" and "you whiteys" and would protest such terms with loud voices, then why don't we work as hard at changing "freshman" and "you guys"? Don't women de-serve it? That women primarily exist in language as "girls" (children), "sluts" (sex objects) and "guys" (a subset of men) makes it less of a surprise that we still have a long list of gen-dered inequalities to fix.

We've got to work on *every* item on the list. Language is one   24
we can work on right now, if we're willing. It's easier to start saying "you all," "y'all" or "you folks" instead of "you guys" than to change the wage gap tomorrow.

And what might help us make changes in our language?   25
About a year ago I was complaining, as usual, about the "you guys" problem. "What we need is a card that explains why we don't want to be called guys!" Smita Varia, a veteran of my gen-der course, said. "Let's write one."

And so we did. Smita enlisted T. Christian Helms, another   26
former student, to design a graphic for the card. You can ac-cess the layout of this business-sized card from our website: www.youall.freeservers.com. Make lots of copies. Give the cards to friends and ask them to think about sexist language. Leave one with a big tip after you've been "you guysed" during a meal. The card explains the problem and offers alternatives.

"Hey, You Guys!"

Imagine someone walking up to a group of guys and saying, "Hey, girls, how're ya doing?" We doubt they'd be amused! So isn't it weird that women are supposed to accept—even like—being called "one of the guys"? We're also supposed to like "freshman," "chairman" and "mankind."

Get over it, some people say. Those words are generic. They apply to everyone. But then how come so-called generics are always male?

What if generics ended in "white"? Freshwhite, chairwhite, and "hey, you whiteys!" Would people of color like being called "one of the whites"? We don't think so.

The terms "guys" makes women invisible by lumping them in with men. Let's quit doing that. When you're talking to a group of customers, gender doesn't really matter, so why not replace "you guys" with "you all," "folks," or "y'all." Or simply say "what can I get you?" That would take care of us all.

Thanks for your help.

27   And institutional change is also possible. Some universities have adopted "first-year student" (instead of "freshman") because some students and faculty got angry about the male-based generics embedded in university documents. The American Psychological Association has a policy of using only inclusive language in their publications. Wherever you work or play, get together with other progressive people and suggest that your organization use "chair" instead of "chairman," "Ms." instead of "Mrs." or "Miss," "humankind" instead of "mankind," and "she or he" instead of "he." In my experience, members of some activist groups think sexist language is less important than other issues. But if we're going to work on social change, shouldn't we start by practicing nonsexist English among ourselves? Let's begin creating *now* the kind of society we want to live in later.

28   Nonsexist English is a resource we have at the tip of our tongues. Let's start using it.

REFERENCE

Hofstadter, D. R. (1986). A person paper on purity in language. In D. R. Hofstadter, *Metamagical themas: A questing for the essence of mind and pattern* (pp. 159–167). New York: Bantam.

David F. Sally
GENDERATOR I.I:
A MODISH PROPOSAL

David Sally (born 1960) teaches courses in management at the business school at Cornell University. He is especially interested in how language functions within organizations and the impact of bias on organizational behavior. In 1999 he published the following spoof in Georgia Review, *a quarterly magazine of the arts and culture that publishes fiction, poetry, reviews, and scholarly articles.*

Dear *person*⊗[1] or *individual*⊗[6],

Remember the last time you were writing and somehow, despite all your best attempts to keep your analysis structural and your text within bounds, you found yourself describing a given categorical, individual human being? Then, after following a single phrase down this path, you faced a second that, for efficiency's sake, demanded a personal pronoun? Take, for example, this sentence from a recent issue of the *American Journal of Politics*: "The death of the American voter paradoxically implies that in a Chicagonian fashion, [————] will be able to vote twice." What do you put in the blank? How do you refer to the prototypical voter? Is *he* a *he* or *not a he* ♂[8]?* You are confronted with the need to put on what we here at the Neuter Corporation refer to as the GENDERATION CAP™. When you wear this cap you are not just picking a personal pronoun, you are making a political statement.   1

God knows, using language is getting harder all the time. Let's look at the current options you have in the sentence above. If you use *he*, then every reader can only guess where on the right wing you are positioned: are you a fascist Neanderthal willing to promulgate the continued oppression of women through the biased use of language, or an uncaring conservative who ignores the deleterious effects of conventional personal pronouns in favor of preserving tradition? On the other hand, if you use *she*, then you imperfectly signal to the reader that you are located on the left somewhere between   2

---

*This question has been genderated. As you read further here you will notice how much more meaningful it is and how much more you learn about the author!

a sensitive, caring liberal capable of achieving even more enlightenment than you already have, and a rabid communist
who names a daughter Karla and a dog Barx.

3   If you are a political independent, you are even more out of
luck. *It* is unavailable. The constructions, *he or she* or *she/he* or
she or he or *he or she*, require that one gender take spatial/
temporal precedence. A footnote attached to your first use of a
personal pronoun explaining your deep concern about this
issue and your numerous reasons for choosing either *he* or *she*
will be ignored by many readers in light of your apparent political bias; random selection of a pronoun cannot be verified by
the reader and hence can never be trusted.

4   Everyone loses! Those who wish to be unlabeled cannot be,
and those who wish to wear their ideological hearts on their
rhetorical sleeves may be mislabeled. And it's not just pronouns:
other words—verbs, adjectives, and even prepositions—are suf-
fused with meanings that you have a hard time controlling.

5   Now, the Neuter Corporation is proud to introduce a word processing tool/utensil that will make all your gender worries vanish in the night—GENDERATOR I.I®!

6   GENDERATOR I.I is fully compatible with Windows 98, works
seamlessly with all major word processing and desktop publishing programs, and uses only 50k of EWE ♀ [10]. GENDERATOR I.I will
almost certainly be approved shortly by all the major journals
in literary criticism and sociology, and by many in political science, art history, psychology, and history.[*]

7   You will never find another syntactic program this easy to
use. Once you are done typing a document, you simply click on
the Genderator icon ⚥, specify a particular set of options based
either on provided labels or on custom menus, and then let the
powerful and sensitive search-and-replace engine do its work
in the blink of an eye. Each and every nominal change initiated
by the program is italicized and marked with an appropriate
icon (♀ and ♂ or left and right, respectfully respectively; ⊗ for
neutrality). The icon is then given a specific numerical exponent to indicate fervor and seriousness (you can find examples
throughout this brochure). We like to say, "Be a proponent—
use the exponent!"

---

[*]We are hopeful that within the next few months the *American Economic
Review* and the *Journal of Theoretical Biology* will become new clients.
There are unresolved problems in chemistry and zoology due to such
proper nouns as *maleate, hymenopteron,* and *myna*.

For professional publication we suggest that you use one of 8
the packaged options that allows your editors and readers to
be fully informed with regard to your ideological preferences.
The program will automatically print, either within the title/
author footnote or within the author's *acknowledgmynts* ♀^{5}, the
phrase "Genderated @————and guaranteed by the Neuter
Corporation," with the blank being filled by one of the preset
package names such as "really random," "revolutionary red,"
"burning Burke," or "flaming Foucault." To learn more about
specific features of GENDERATOR I.I, find your category in the
ideological spectrum that follows:

Liberal. No longer will you have to be tormented by the thought 9
of your reader not appreciating just how sensitive and enlightened you are. If confusion about your own reality, identity, and
gender has led you to refer to yourself only through third person
pronouns, then think how the female side of (what might be) you
will be comforted, knowing that the "wicked Woolf" level of
GENDERATOR I.I is doing all the expressing. At sensitivity levels of
♀^{7} and above, this program is capable of spotting crossword,
anagrammatic, and homonymic insensitivity: "Wilbur's pen is
home to a variety of animals" would become "The enclosure of
Wilbur is . . ."; Dorothy's quest would take her to the "Efemerald
City"; and the automatic replacement of "penal code" by "the set
of statutes dealing with crimes and punishments" will finally un-
fetter the field of feminist criminal studies.

Among the Liberal preset packages offered is "mocking 10
MacKinnon," an option designed especially for humorous
pieces. Watch as "mocking MacKinnon" works wonders in
combining the magic of power, gender, and laughter in this
passage from Jonathan Swift's infamous essay:

> I, *being the oppressive male that I am* ♀^{3}, think it is agreed by
> all parties that this prodigious number of children in the
> arms, or on the backs, or at the heels of their mothers, *i.e.,*
> *postsocietally transmuted womyn* ♀^{8}, and frequently of their
> fathers, *i.e., postsocietally transmuted worms* ♀^{8}, is in the
> present deplorable state of the kingdom a very great addi-
> tional grievance; and, therefore, whoever could find out a
> fair, cheap, and easy method of making these children
> sound, useful members of the commonwealth, would
> deserve so well of the public as to have his statue set up for a
> preserver of the nation, *as if I even need to comment on the*
> *obvious connections among patriarchy, statuary, and phony*
> *phalluses* ♀^{7}.

11   Just think: if GENDERATOR I.I can cut this decrepit Brobdingnagian down to size, obviously it can help you turn the rest of the so-called Literary Canon into mere fodder!

12   *Unrepentant Conservative.* You are tired of all the games people play with the English language, and you want those people to know it. If *he* was good enough for the Greeks and the Romans and the Bible, it is good enough for you and for everybody else. Why waste any time even thinking about this issue? GENDERATOR I.I gives you this freedom from thought. Just use the simple, pull-down windows to reveal "Doctor Johnson," for example, or some other conservative guardian of English, and rest assured that your document will boldly satisfy every convention. At levels of rigidity of $\male^7$ and above, this program will even suggest ways in which your prose can be altered to transform third-person-plural phrases to singular ones, to utilize phallic metaphors and symbols, and to employ telling anagrams such as "spineless."

13   The only socially constructed roles you believe in are the ones from Pillsbury that your wife pops in the over for dinner. Imagine the pleasure of improving Shakespeare by combining the "full-well Falwell" content option with the "Ouayle quality" grammatical option, as in this dramatic monologue:

> *Oh* Romeo, Romeo, are *you therefor* Romeo?
> Deny *your* father, *who works so hard to provide for you and*
>   *your mother* $\male^6$, and refuse *your* name;
> *swear, but not with the Lord's name* $\male^4$, to   Or, if *you* will not,
>   be my love,
> And I'll no longer be a Capulet,
> *But a Montague, since I will take your last name as all good*
>   *wives should* $\male^8$.

14   Moreover, you can count your blessings that after the plot is generated at "full-well Falwell," Romeo never lays his hands on Juliet's balcony until after they are married!

15   Modern language, orthodox pronouns, and good old-fashioned family values . . . GENDERATOR I.I lets you have it all!

16   *Independent.* It used to be that if you didn't want to get involved, you could just say so. But times have changed. Uninvolvement requires its own language of meaning and a new passion. Think of GENDERATOR I.I as the soap and water that allow you to wash your hands of the controversy over biased language, your neutrality expressible in two ways: first, there is a special icon, $(\female)$, the Spinning Randogenderator[©], that will randomly produce either masculine or feminine pronominal

forms. The reputation of the Neuter Corporation stands behind the stochasticity of this function, and assures the reader that you had no idea what you were writing.

Second, depending on the level of neutrality you specify, common nouns such as *human being, person,* and *individual* will fill the role of personal pronouns. These substitutes appear on a pop-up menu and change as your need for impartiality increases: at $\otimes^2$, *humyn* is a possible selection; at $\otimes^4$, *per offspring* may be chosen; at the maximal level of uninvolvement, the only term available is *individual*, which receives a subscript, e.g., "The tension within Henry Fielding between licentious convention and conventional license is revealed in *Tom Jones*: '*Individual$_1$'s* intentions were strictly honourable, as the phrase is; that is, to rob an *individual$_2$* of *individuals$_2$'s* fortune by way of marriage $\otimes^{10}$.'"* With GENDERATOR I.I, your honorable intent to stay well out of the fray can finally be recognized!

Best of all, no matter what your position on objective reality, GENDERATOR I.I is now available at a special low price for all academic users. Don't let the new standard in language processing pass you by. Depending on how you employ it, GENDERATOR I.I can allow you to spend a lot more time on substance and a lot less on form or, a lot more on form and a lot less on substance. It's up to the individual, and the way *she* wants to use *his* time ⊂♀⊃.

Our guarantee to you, our valued customer, is to keep you fully *achest* $\otimes^5$ of the latest refinements in social language. As more labels are attached to more words, we promise to *mail* ♂^{1} to your *residential postal location* ♀^{3} frequent updates of GENDERATOR software, including special offers on future versions that *speak directly to* ♀^{3} such areas as:

Race
Generational Conflict
Ethnicity
Sexual Orientation.

Please call 1-800-NEUTRAL to reserve your new trial copy of GENDERATOR I.I. We guarantee your satisfaction, and we hope that you will continue to look to the Neuter Corporation for all your sensitive, social, syntactic software needs.

17

18

19

20

---

*Yoon, S. H. 1996. "Fielding's *Tom Jones*: Woe, woe, woe, is he a lady?" *Critical Review of Canonical Literature*, v. 2:235–48. Note that this journal was one of the first to make GENDERATOR I.I obligatory.

This cartoon appeared in The New Yorker, *famous for its very funny and rather sophisticated cartoons. Is the cartoon just for fun, or does it make a serious point?*

"You'll just love the way he handles."

Drawing by Bernard Schoenbaum; © 1991 The New Yorker Magazine, Inc.

Does Pornography Cause Harm to Women?

President's Commission on Obscenity and Pornography
MAJORITY REPORT

*In 1967, Congress by law established an eighteen-member spe-
cial commission (appointed by President Nixon) to study the
impact of obscenity and pornography on American life. After
gathering testimony, reviewing research, and conferring at
length, the commission in 1970 recommended against legislation that would restrain pornography. A minority of the members of the commission, feeling differently, submitted their own
dissenting report. Excerpts from both follow.*

Discussions of obscenity and pornography in the past have   1
often been devoid of fact. Popular rhetoric has often contained
a variety of estimates of the size of the "smut" industry and assertions regarding the consequences of the existence of these
materials and exposure to them. Many of these statements,
however, have had little anchoring in objective evidence.
Within the limits of its time and resources, the Commission
has sought, through staff and contract research, to broaden the
factual basis for future continued discussion. The Commission
is aware that not all issues of concern have been completely researched nor all questions answered. It also recognizes that the
interpretations of a set of "facts" in arriving at policy implications may differ even among men of good will. Nevertheless,
the Commission is convinced that on most issues regarding
obscenity and pornography the discussion can be informed by
important and often new facts. It presents its Report, hopeful
that it will contribute to this discussion at a new level. . . .

Exposure to erotic stimuli appears to have little or no effect on   2
already established attitudinal commitments regarding either

sexuality or sexual morality. A series of four studies employing a large array of indicators found practically no significant differences in such attitudes before and after single or repeated exposures to erotica. One study did find that after exposure persons became more tolerant in reference to other persons' sexual activities although their own sexual standards did not change. One study reported that some persons' attitudes toward premarital intercourse became more liberal after exposure, while other persons' attitudes became more conservative, but another study found no changes in this regard. The overall picture is almost completely a tableau of no significant change. . . .

3   Statistical studies of the relationship between availability of erotic materials and the rates of sex crimes in Denmark indicate that the increased availability of explicit sexual materials has been accompanied by a decrease in the incidence of sexual crime. Analysis of police records of the same types of sex crimes in Copenhagen during the past 12 years revealed that a dramatic decrease in reported sex crimes occurred during this period and that the decrease coincided with changes in Danish law which permitted wider availability of explicit sexual materials. Other research showed that the decrease in reported sexual offenses cannot be attributed to concurrent changes in the social and legal definitions of sex crimes or in public attitudes toward reporting such crimes to the police, or in police reporting procedures.

4   Statistical studies of the relationship between the availability of erotic material and the rates of sex crimes in the United States presents a more complex picture. During the period in which there has been a marked increase in the availability of erotic materials, some specific rates of arrest for sex crimes have increased (e.g., forcible rape) and others have declined (e.g., overall juvenile rates). For juveniles, the overall rate of arrests for sex crimes decreased even though arrests for nonsexual crimes increased by more than 100%. For adults, arrests for sex offenses increased slightly more than did arrests for nonsex offenses. The conclusion is that, for America, the relationship between the availability of erotica and changes in sex crime rates neither proves nor disproves the possibility that availability of erotica leads to crime, but the massive overall increases in sex crimes that have been alleged do not seem to have occurred. . . .

I. Non-Legislative Recommendation

5   The Commission believes that much of the "problem" regarding materials which depict explicit sexual activity stems from the inability or reluctance of people in our society to be open and direct in dealing with sexual matters. . . .

The Commission believes that accurate, appropriate sex infor-   6
mation provided openly and directly through legitimate channels and from reliable sources in healthy contexts can compete
successfully with potentially distorted, warped, inaccurate, and
unreliable information about clandestine, illegitimate sources;
and it believes that the attitudes and orientations toward sex
produced by the open communication of appropriate sex information from reliable sources through legitimate channels will
be normal and healthy, providing a solid foundation for the
basic institutions of our society.

The Commission, therefore, . . . *recommends that a massive*   7
sex education effort be launched. . . . The Commission feels that
such a sex education program would provide a powerful positive approach to the problems of obscenity and pornography.
By providing accurate and reliable sex information through
legitimate sources, it would reduce interest in and dependence
upon clandestine and less legitimate sources. By providing
healthy attitudes and orientations toward sexual relationships,
it would provide better protection for the individual against
distorted and warped ideas he may encounter regarding sex.
By providing greater ease in talking about sexual matters in
appropriate contexts, the shock and offensiveness of encounters with sex would be reduced. . . .

II. Legislative Recommendation

The Commission recommends that federal, state, and local legis-   8
lation prohibiting the sale, exhibition, or distribution of sexual
materials to consenting adults should be repealed. . . .
Our conclusion is based upon the following considerations:

1. Extensive empirical investigation, both by the Commis-   9
sion and by others, provides no evidence that exposure to
or use of explicit sexual materials plays a significant role in
causation of social or individual harms such as crime, delinquency, sexual or nonsexual deviancy or severe emotional
disturbances. . . . Empirical investigation thus supports the
opinion of a substantial majority of persons professionally
engaged in the treatment of deviancy, delinquency and antisocial behavior, that exposure to sexually explicit materials has
no harmful causal role in these areas. Studies show that a
number of factors, such as disorganized family relationships
and unfavorable peer influences, are intimately related to
harmful sexual behavior or adverse character development.
Exposure to sexually explicit materials, however, cannot be
counted as among these determinative factors.

10   2. On the positive side, explicit sexual materials are sought
as a source of entertainment and information by substantial
numbers of American adults. At times, these materials also
appear to serve to increase and facilitate constructive communication about sexual matters within marriage. The most
frequent purchaser of explicit sexual materials is a college-
educated, married male, in his thirties or forties, who is of
above average socio-economic status. Even where materials
are legally available to them, young adults and older adolescents do not constitute an important portion of the purchasers
of such materials.

11   3. Society's attempts to legislate for adults in the area of
obscenity have not been successful. Present laws prohibiting
the consensual sale or distribution of explicit sexual materials
to adults are extremely unsatisfactory in their practical application. The Constitution permits material to be deemed
"obscene" for adults only if, as a whole, it appeals to the "prurient" interest of the average person, is "patently offensive" in
light of "community standards," and lacks "redeeming social
value." These vague and highly subjective aesthetic, psychological and moral tests do not provide meaningful guidance for
law enforcement officials, juries or courts. As a result, law is
inconsistently and sometimes erroneously applied and the distinctions made by courts between prohibited and permissible
materials often appear indefensible. Errors in the application
of the law and uncertainty about its scope also cause interference with the communication of constitutionally protected
materials.

12   4. Public opinion in America does not support the imposi-
tion of legal prohibitions upon the right of adults to read or see
explicit sexual materials. While a minority of Americans favors
such prohibitions, a majority of the American people presently
are of the view that adults should be legally able to read or see
explicit sexual materials if they wish to do so.

13   5. The lack of consensus among Americans concerning
whether explicit sexual materials should be available to adults
in our society, and the significant number of adults who wish
to have access to such materials, pose serious problems regarding the enforcement of legal prohibitions upon adults,
even aside from the vagueness and subjectivity of present law.
Consistent enforcement of even the clearest prohibitions upon
consensual adult exposure to explicit sexual materials would
require the expenditure of considerable law enforcement resources. In the absence of a persuasive demonstration of damage flowing from consensual exposure to such materials, there
seems no justification for thus adding to the overwhelming

tasks already placed upon the law enforcement system. Inconsistent enforcement of prohibitions, on the other hand, invites discriminatory action based upon considerations not directly relevant to the policy of the law. The latter alternative also breeds public disrespect for the legal process.

6. The foregoing considerations take on an added signifi-   14
cance because of the fact that adult obscenity laws deal in the realm of speech and communication. Americans deeply value the right of each individual to determine for himself what books he wishes to read and what pictures or films he wishes to see. Our traditions of free speech and press also value and protect the right of writers, publishers, and booksellers to serve the diverse interests of the public. The spirit and letter of our Constitution tell us that government should not seek to interfere with these rights unless a clear threat of harm makes that course imperative. Moreover, the possibility of the misuse of general obscenity statutes prohibiting distributions of books and films to adults constitutes a continuing threat to the free communication of ideas among Americans—one of the most important foundations of our liberties.

7. In reaching its recommendation that government should   15
not seek to prohibit consensual distributions of sexual materials to adults, the Commission discussed several arguments which are often advanced in support of such legislation. The Commission carefully considered the view that adult legislation should be retained in order to aid in the protection of young persons from exposure to explicit sexual materials. We do not believe that the objective of protecting youth may justifiably be achieved at the expense of denying adults materials of their choice. It seems to us wholly inappropriate to adjust the level of adult communication to that considered suitable for children. Indeed, the Supreme Court has unanimously held that adult legislation premised on this basis is a clearly unconstitutional interference with liberty. . . .

8. The Commission has also taken cognizance of the con-   16
cern of many people that the lawful distribution of explicit sexual materials to adults may have a deleterious effect upon the individual morality of American citizens and upon the moral climate in America as a whole. This concern appears to flow from a belief that exposure to explicit materials may cause moral confusion which, in turn, may induce antisocial or criminal behavior. As noted above, the Commission has found no evidence to support such a contention. Nor is there evidence that exposure to explicit sexual materials adversely affects character or moral attitudes regarding sex and sexual conduct. . . .

President's Commission on
Obscenity and Pornography

MINORITY REPORT

Overview

1   The Commission's majority report is a Magna Carta for the pornographer. . . . The fundamental "finding" on which the entire report is based is: that "empirical research" has come up with "no reliable evidence to indicate that exposure to explicit sexual materials plays a significant role in the causation of delinquent or criminal behavior among youth or adults." The inference from this statement, i.e., pornography is harmless, is not only insupportable on the slanted evidence presented; it is preposterous. How isolate one factor and say it causes or does not cause criminal behavior? How determine that one book or one film caused one man to commit rape or murder? A man's entire life goes into one criminal act. No one factor can be said to have caused that act.

2   The Commission has deliberately and carefully avoided coming to grips with the basic underlying issue. The government interest in regulating pornography has always related primarily to the prevention of moral corruption and *not* to prevention of overt criminal acts and conduct, or the protection of persons from being shocked and/or offended. The basic question is whether and to what extent society may establish and maintain certain moral standards. If it is conceded that society has a legitimate concern in maintaining moral standards, it follows logically that government has a legitimate interest in at least attempting to protect such standards against any source which threatens them. . . .

3   Sex education, recommended so strongly by the majority, is the panacea for those who advocate license in media. The report suggests sex education, with a plaint for the dearth of instructors and materials. It notes that three schools have used "hard-core pornography" in training potential instructors. The report does not answer the question that comes to mind immediately: Will these instructors not bring the hard-core pornography into the grammar schools? Many other questions are left unanswered: How assure that the instructor's moral or ethical code (or lack of same) will not be communicated to children? Shouldn't parents, not children, be the recipients of sex education courses?

Children cannot grow in love if they are trained with pornog-   4
raphy. Pornography is loveless; it degrades the human being,
reduces him to the level of animal. And if this Commission majority's recommendations are heeded, there will be a glut of
pornography for teachers and children.

In contrast to the Commission report's amazing statement   5
that public opinion in America does not support the imposi-
tion of legal prohibitions upon the consensual distribution of
pornography to adults, we find, as a result of public hearings
conducted by two of the undersigned in eight cities throughout
the country, that the majority of the American people favor
tighter controls. Twenty-six out of twenty-seven witnesses at
the hearing in New York City expressed concern and asked for
remedial measures. Witnesses were a cross section of the
community, ranging from members of the judiciary to members of women's clubs. This pattern was repeated in the cities
of New Orleans, Indianapolis, Chicago, Salt Lake City, San
Francisco, Washington, D.C., and Buffalo. . . . Additionally, law
enforcement officers testifying at the Hill-Link hearings were
unanimous in declaring that the problem of obscenity and
pornography is a serious one. . . . We point also to the results of
a Gallup poll, published in the summer of 1969. Eighty-five out
of every 100 adults interviewed said they favored stricter state
and local laws dealing with pornography sent through the
mails, and 76 of every 100 wanted stricter laws on the sort of
magazines and newspapers available on newsstands. . . .

Some have argued that because sex crimes have apparently   6
declined in Denmark while the volume of pornography has increased, we need not be concerned about the potential effect in
our country of this kind of material (because, essentially, of
Denmark's benign experience). However two considerations
must be noted. First we are a different culture with a greater
commitment to the Judeo-Christian tradition; and secondly,
we are actually only a year or so behind Denmark in the distribution and sale of pornography. Hardcore written pornography can be purchased anywhere in the U.S. now. Hardcore still
pictures and movies can now be purchased over the counter
in some cities. Anything can be purchased through the mails.
And in a few cities people can attend hard-core pornographic
movies. About the only thing we don't have, which Denmark
has, are live sex shows. What is most relevant are sex crime
statistics in this country, not Denmark. . . :

Reported Rapes (verified)
   Up 116% 1960–69 (absolute increase)
   Up 93% 1960–69 (controlled for Pop. Growth)

Rape Arrests
Up 56.6% all ages 1960–69
Up 85.9% males under 18 1960–69

7   However, it should be stated that conclusively proving causal relationships among social science type variables is extremely difficult if not impossible. Among adults whose life histories have included much exposure to pornography it is nearly impossible to disentangle the literally hundreds of causal threads or chains that contributed to their later adjustment or maladjustment. Because of the extreme complexity of the problem and the uniqueness of the human experience it is doubtful that we will ever have absolutely convincing scientific proof that pornography is or isn't harmful. And the issue isn't restricted to, "Does pornography cause or contribute to sex crimes?" The issue has to do with how pornography affects or influences the individual in his total relationship to members of the same as well as opposite sex, children and adults, with all of its ramifications.

Susan Brownmiller

LET'S PUT PORNOGRAPHY BACK IN THE CLOSET

Susan Brownmiller is a journalist, novelist, women's rights activist, and a founder of Women against Pornography. Her book Against Our Will: Men, Women, and Rape, *published in 1975, articulates a position on pornography that has been developed by later feminists. The following essay originally appeared in* Newsday, *a Long Island newspaper, in 1979 and a year later in* Take Back the Night, *a collection of essays against pornography.*

1   Free speech is one of the great foundations on which our democracy rests. I am old enough to remember the Hollywood Ten, the screenwriters who went to jail in the late 1940s because they refused to testify before a congressional committee about their political affiliations. They tried to use the First Amendment as a defense, but they went to jail because in those

days there were few civil liberties lawyers around who cared to champion the First Amendment right to free speech, when the speech concerned the Communist Party.

The Hollywood Ten were correct in claiming the First 2 Amendment. Its high purpose is the protection of unpopular ideas and political dissent. In the dark, cold days of the 1950s, few civil libertarians were willing to declare themselves First Amendment absolutists. But in the brighter, though frantic, days of the 1960s, the principle of protecting unpopular political speech was gradually strengthened.

It is fair to say now that the battle has largely been won. 3 Even the American Nazi Party has found itself the beneficiary of the dedicated, tireless work of the American Civil Liberties Union. But—and please notice the quotation marks coming up—"To equate the free and robust exchange of ideas and political debate with commercial exploitation of obscene material demeans the grand conception of the First Amendment and its high purposes in the historic struggle for freedom. It is a misuse of the great guarantees of free speech and free press."

I didn't say that, although I wish I had, for I think the words 4 are thrilling. Chief Justice Warren Burger said it in 1973, in the United States Supreme Court's majority opinion in *Miller* v. *California*. During the same decades that the right to political free speech was being strengthened in the courts, the nation's obscenity laws also were undergoing extensive revision.

It's amazing to recall that in 1934 the question of whether 5 James Joyce's *Ulysses* should be banned as pornographic actually went before the Court. The battle to protect *Ulysses* as a work of literature with redeeming social value was won. In later decades, Henry Miller's *Tropic* books, *Lady Chatterley's Lover* and the *Memoirs of Fanny Hill* also were adjudged not obscene. These decisions have been important to me. As the author of *Against Our Will*, a study of the history of rape that does contain explicit sexual material, I shudder to think how my book would have fared if James Joyce, D. H. Lawrence and Henry Miller hadn't gone before me.

I am not a fan of *Chatterley* or the *Tropic* books, I should 6 quickly mention. They are not to my literary taste, nor do I think they represent female sexuality with any degree of accuracy. But I would hardly suggest that we ban them. Such a suggestion wouldn't get very far anyway. The battle to protect these books is ancient history. Time does march on, quite methodically. What, then, is unlawfully obscene, and what does the First Amendment have to do with it?

In the Miller case of 1973 (not Henry Miller, by the way, but 7 a porn distributor who sent unsolicited stuff through the mails), the Court came up with new guidelines that it hoped would strengthen obscenity laws by giving more power to the states. What it did in actuality was throw everything into confusion. It set up a three-part test by which materials can be adjudged obscene. The materials are obscene if they depict patently offensive, hard-core sexual conduct; lack serious scientific, literary, artistic or political value; and appeal to the prurient interest of an average person—as measured by contemporary community standards.

8   "Patently offensive," "prurient interest" and "hard-core" are indeed words to conjure with. "Contemporary community standards" are what we're trying to redefine. The feminist objection to pornography is not based on prurience, which the dictionary defines as lustful, itching desire. We are not opposed to sex and desire, with or without the itch, and we certainly believe that explicit sexual material has its place in literature, art, science and education. Here we part company rather swiftly with old-line conservatives who don't want sex education in the high schools, for example.

9   No, the feminist objection to pornography is based on our belief that pornography represents hatred of women, that pornography's intent is to humiliate, degrade and dehumanize the female body for the purpose of erotic stimulation and pleasure. We are unalterably opposed to the presentation of the female body being stripped, bound, raped, tortured, mutilated and murdered in the name of commercial entertainment and free speech.

10   These images, which are standard pornographic fare, have nothing to do with the hallowed right of political dissent. They have everything to do with the creation of a cultural climate in which a rapist feels he is merely giving in to a normal urge and a woman is encouraged to believe that sexual masochism is healthy, liberated fun. Justice Potter Stewart once said about hard-core pornography, "You know it when you see it," and that certainly used to be true. In the good old days, pornography looked awful. It was cheap and sleazy, and there was no mistaking it for art.

11   Nowadays, since the porn industry has become a multimillion dollar business, visual technology has been employed in its service. Pornographic movies are skillfully filmed and edited, pornographic still shots using the newest tenets of good design artfully grace the covers of *Hustler, Penthouse* and *Playboy*, and the public—and the courts—are sadly confused.

12   The Supreme Court neglected to define "hard-core" in the Miller decision. This was a mistake. If "hard-core" refers only to explicit sexual intercourse, then that isn't good enough. When women or children or men—no matter how artfully—are shown tortured or terrorized in the service of sex, that's

obscene. And "patently offensive," I would hope, to our "contemporary community standards."

Justice William O. Douglas wrote in his dissent to the Miller   13
case that no one is "compelled to look." This is hardly true. To
buy a paper at the corner newsstand is to subject oneself to a
forcible immersion in pornography, to be demeaned by an
array of dehumanized, chopped-up parts of the female
anatomy, packaged like cuts of meat at the supermarket. I happen to like my body and I work hard at the gym to keep it in
good shape, but I am embarrassed for my body and for the
bodies of all women when I see the fragmented parts of us so
frivolously, and so flagrantly, displayed.

Some constitutional theorists (Justice Douglas was one)   14
have maintained that any obscenity law is a serious abridgement of free speech. Others (and Justice Earl Warren was one)
have maintained that the First Amendment was never intended
to protect obscenity. We live quite compatibly with a host of
free-speech abridgements. There are restraints against false
and misleading advertising or statements—shouting "fire"
without cause in a crowded movie theater, etc.—that do not
threaten, but strengthen, our societal values. Restrictions on
the public display of pornography belong in this category.

The distinction between permission to publish and permission to display publicly is an essential one and one which   15
I think consonant with First Amendment principles. Justice
Burger's words which I quoted above support this without
question. We are not saying "Smash the presses" or "Ban the
bad ones," but simply "Get the stuff out of our sight." Let the
legislatures decide—using realistic and humane contemporary
community standards—what can be displayed and what cannot. The courts, after all, will be the final arbiters.

John Irving

PORNOGRAPHY
AND THE NEW PURITANS

If you saw the films The World According to Garp *or* The
Cider House Rules, *you have had some experience with
the work of John Irving (born 1942), for he is the author of the*

*novels on which both films were based as well as seven other
novels. He contributed the following essay to the New York
Times Book Review in March 1992. Notice that a response to
the article, also printed in the Times Book Review, is reprinted
right after it.*

1   These are censorial times. I refer to the pornography victims'
compensation bill, now under consideration by the Senate
Judiciary Committee—that same bunch of wise men who dis-
patched such clearheaded, objective jurisprudence in the
Clarence Thomas hearings. I can't wait to see what they're going
to do with this maladroit proposal. The bill would encourage
victims of sexual crimes to bring civil suits against publishers
and distributors of material that is "obscene or constitutes child
pornography"—*if* they can prove that the material was "a substantial cause of the offense," *and if* the publisher or distributor
should have "foreseen" that such material created an "unreasonable risk of such a crime." If this bill passes, it will be the first
piece of legislation to give credence to the unproven theory that
sexually explicit material actually *causes* sexual crimes.

2   At the risk of sounding old-fashioned, I'm still pretty sure
that rape and child molestation predate erotic books and
pornographic magazines and X-rated videocassettes. I also
remember the report of the two-year, $2 million President's
Commission on Obscenity and Pornography (1970), which
concluded there was "no reliable evidence . . . that exposure to
explicit sexual material plays a significant role in the causation
of delinquent or criminal sexual behavior." In 1986, not satisfied with that conclusion, the Meese commission on pornography and the Surgeon General's conference on pornography
also failed to establish such a link. Now, here they go again.

3   This time, it's Republican Senators Mitch McConnell of
Kentucky, Charles Grassley of Iowa and Strom Thurmond of
South Carolina; I can't help wondering if they read much.
Their charmless bill is a grave mistake for several reasons; for
starters, it's morally reprehensible to shift the responsibility for
any sexual crime onto a third party—namely, *away* from the
actual perpetrator.

4   And then, of course, there's the matter of the bill running
counter to the spirit of the First Amendment of the United
States Constitution; this bill is a piece of back-door censorship,
plain and simple. Moreover, since the laws on obscenity differ
from state to state, and no elucidation of the meaning of obscenity is presented in the bill, how are the publishers or distributors
to know in advance if their material is actionable or not? It is my

understanding, therefore, that the true intent of the bill is to make the actual creators of this material think very conservatively—that is, when their imaginations turn to sex and violence.

I recall that I received a lot of unfriendly mail in connection with a somewhat explicit scene in my novel *The World According to Garp*, wherein a selfish young man loses part of his anatomy while enjoying oral sex in a car. (I suppose I've always had a fear of rear-end collisions.) But thinking back about that particular hate mail, I don't recall a single letter from a young woman saying that she intended to rush out and *do* this to someone; and in the 14 years since that novel's publication, in more than 35 foreign languages, no one who actually *has done* this to someone has written to thank me for giving her the idea. Boy, am I lucky!

In a brilliant article on the Op-Ed page of *The New York Times*, Teller, of those marvelous magicians Penn & Teller, had this to say about the pornography victims' compensation bill: "The advocates of this bill seem to think that if we stop showing rape in movies people will stop committing it in real life. Anthropologists call this 'magical thinking.' It's the same impulse that makes people stick pins in voodoo dolls, hoping to cripple an enemy. It feels logical, but it does not work." (For those of you who've seen these two magicians and are wondering which is Penn and which is Teller, Teller is the one who never talks. He *writes* very well, however.) "It's a death knell for creativity, too," Teller writes. "Start punishing make-believe, and those gifted with imagination will stop sharing it." He adds, "We will enter an intellectual era even more insipid than the one we live in."

Now *there's* a scary idea! I remember when the film version of Günter Grass's novel *The Tin Drum* was banned in Canada. I always assumed it was the eel scene that offended the censors, but I don't know. In those days, a little naked sex—in the conventional position—was permissible, but unpleasant suggestiveness with eels was clearly going too far. But now, in the light of this proposed pornography victims' compensation bill, is there any evidence to suggest that there have been *fewer* hellish incidents of women being force-fed eels in Canada than in those countries where the film was available? Somehow, I doubt it. I know that they're out there—those guys who want to force-feed eels to women—but I suspect they're going to do what they're going to do, unaided by books or films. The point is: let's do something about *them*, instead of trying to control what they read or see.

It dismays me how some of my feminist friends are hot to ban pornography. I'm sorry that they have such short memories. It wasn't very long ago when a book as innocent and valuable as *Our Bodies, Ourselves* was being banned by school boards and public libraries across the country. The idea of this good book was that women should have access to detailed information about their bodies and their health, yet the so-called feminist ideology behind the book was thought to be subversive; indeed, it was (at that time) deplored. But many writers and writers' organizations (like PEN) wrote letters to those school boards and those public libraries. I can't speak to the overall effectiveness of these letters in regard to reinstating the book, but I'm aware that some of the letters worked; I wrote several of those letters. Now here are some of my old friends, telling me that attitudes toward rape and child molestation can be changed only if we remove the offensive *ideas*. Once again, it's ideology that's being banned. And although the movement to ban pornography is especially self-righteous, it looks like blacklisting to me.

9   Fascism has enjoyed many name changes, but it usually amounts to banning something you dislike and can't control. Take abortion, for example. I think groups should have to apply for names; if the Right to Life people had asked me, I'd have told them to find a more fitting label for themselves. It's morally inconsistent to manifest such concern for the poor fetus in a society that shows absolutely no pity for the poor child after it's born.

10   I'm also not so sure that these so-called Right to Lifers are as fired up about those fetuses as they say. I suspect what really makes them sore is the idea of women having sex and somehow not having to *pay* for it—pay in the sense of suffering all the way through an unwanted pregnancy. I believe this is part of the loathing for promiscuity that has always fueled those Americans who feel that a life of common decency is slipping from their controlling grasp. This notion is reflected in the unrealistic hope of those wishful thinkers who tell us that sexual abstinence is an alternative to wearing a condom. But I say how about *carrying* a condom, just in case you're moved to *not* abstain?

11   No one is coercing women into having abortions, but the Right to Lifers want to coerce women into having babies; that's why the pro-choice people are well named. It's unfortunate, however, that a few of my pro-choice friends think that the pornography victims' compensation bill is a good idea. I guess that they're really not entirely pro-choice. They want the choice to reproduce or not, but they *don't* want too broad a choice of things to read and see; they know what *they* want to read and see, and they expect other people to be content with what they want. This sounds like a Right to Life idea to me.

Most feminist groups, despite their vital advocacy of full en-   12
forcement of laws against violence to women and children,
seem opposed to Senate Bill 1521. As of this writing, both the
National Organization for Women in New York State and in
California have written to the Senate Judiciary Committee in
opposition to the bill, although the Los Angeles chapter of
NOW states that it has "no position." I admit it is perverse of
me even to imagine what Tammy Bruce thinks about the
pornography victims' compensation bill; I hope Ms. Bruce is
not such a loose cannon as she appears, but she has me worried. Ms. Bruce is president of L.A. NOW, and she has lately
distinguished herself with two counts of knee-jerk overreac-
tion. Most recently, she found the Academy of Motion Picture
Arts and Sciences to be guilty of an "obvious exhibition of sexism" in not nominating Barbra Streisand for an Oscar for best
director. Well, maybe. Ms. Streisand's other talents have not
been entirely overlooked; I meekly submit that the academy
might have found *The Prince of Tides* lacking in directorial
merit—it wouldn't be the first I've heard of such criticism. (Ms.
Bruce says the L.A. chapter received "unrelenting calls" from
NOW members who were riled up at the perceived sexism.)

Most readers will remember Tammy Bruce for jumping all   13
over that nasty novel by Bret Easton Ellis. To refresh our memories: Simon & Schuster decided at the 11th hour not to publish *American Psycho* after concluding that its grisly content
was in "questionable taste." Now please don't get excited and
think I'm going to call that censorship; that was merely a
breach of contract. And besides, Simon & Schuster has a right
to its own opinion of what questionable taste is. *People* magazine tells us that Judith Regan, a vice president and senior editor at Simon & Schuster, recently had a book idea, which she
pitched to Madonna. "My idea was for her to write a book of
her sexual fantasies, her thoughts, the meanderings of her
erotic mind," Ms. Regan said. The pity is, Madonna hasn't delivered. And according to Mitchell Fink, author of the Insider column for *People*, "Warner Books confirmed it is talking about a
book—no word on what kind—with Madonna." I don't know
Madonna, but maybe she thought the Simon & Schuster book
idea was in questionable taste. Simon & Schuster, clearly, sub-
scribes to more than one opinion of what questionable taste *is*.

But only two days after Mr. Ellis's book was dropped by   14
Simon & Schuster, Sonny Mehta, president of Alfred A. Knopf
and Vintage Books, bought *American Psycho*, which was published in March 1991. Prior to the novel's publication,
Ms. Bruce called for a boycott of all Knopf and Vintage titles—
except for books by feminist authors, naturally—until *American*

Psycho was withdrawn from publication (it wasn't), or until the end of 1991. To the charge of censorship, Ms. Bruce declared that she was *not* engaged in it; she sure fooled me.

15   But Ms. Bruce wasn't alone in declaring what *wasn't* censorship, nor was she alone in her passion; she not only condemned Mr. Ellis's novel—she condemned its availability. And not only the book itself *but its availability* were severely taken to task in the very pages in which I now write. In December 1990—three months *before American Psycho* was published, and at the urging of *The Book Review*—Roger Rosenblatt settled Mr. Ellis's moral hash in a piece of writing prissy enough to please Jesse Helms. According to Mr. Rosenblatt, Jesse Helms has never engaged in censorship, either. For those of us who remain improperly educated in regard to what censorship actually *is*, Mr. Rosenblatt offers a blanket definition. "Censorship is when a government burns your manuscript, smashes your presses and throws you in jail," he says.

16   Well, as much as I may identify with Mr. Rosenblatt's literary taste, I'm of the opinion that there are a few forms of censorship more subtle than that, and Mr. Rosenblatt has engaged in one of them. If you slam a book when it's published, that's called book reviewing, but if you write about a book three months in advance of its publication and your conclusion is "don't buy it," your intentions are more censorial than critical.

17   And it *is* censorship when the writer of such perceived trash is not held *as* accountable as the book's publisher; the pressure that was brought to bear on Mr. Mehta was totally censorial. *The Book Review* is at its most righteous in abusing Mr. Mehta, who is described as "clearly as hungry for a killing as Patrick Bateman." (For those of you who don't know Mr. Ellis's book, Patrick Bateman is the main character and a serial killer.) Even as reliable a fellow as the editorial director of *Publisher's Weekly*, John F. Baker, described *American Psycho* as a book that "does transcend the boundaries of what is acceptable in mainstream publishing."

18   It's the very idea of making or keeping publishing "acceptable" that gives *me* the shivers, because that's the same idea that lurks behind the pornography victims' compensation bill—making the *publisher* (not the perpetrator of the crime or the writer of the pornography) responsible for what's "acceptable." If you want to bash Bret Easton Ellis for what he's written, go ahead and bash him. But when you presume to tell Sonny Mehta, or any other publisher, what he can or can't—or should or shouldn't—*publish*, that's when you've stepped into dangerous territory. In fact, that's when you're knee-deep in blacklisting, and you ought to know better—all of you.

Mr. Rosenblatt himself actually says, "No one argues that a   19
publishing house hasn't the right to print what it wants. We
fight for that right. But not everything is a right. At some point,
someone in authority somewhere has to look at Mr. Ellis's rat
and call the exterminator." Now this is interesting, and perhaps
worse than telling Sonny Mehta what he should or shouldn't
publish—because that's exactly what Mr. Rosenblatt *is* doing
while he's *saying* that he isn't.

Do we remember that tangent of the McCarran-Walter Act of   20
1952, that finally defunct business about ideological exclusion? That was when we kept someone from coming into our
country because we perceived that the person had *ideas* that
were in conflict with the "acceptable" ideas of our country.
Under this act of exclusion, writers as distinguished as
Graham Greene and Gabriel Garcia Márquez were kept out of
the United States. Well, when we attack what a publisher has
the right to publish, we are simply applying the old ideological
exclusion act at home. Of all people, those of us in the idea
business should know better than that.

As for the pornography victims' compensation bill, the vote in   21
the Senate Judiciary Committee will be close. As of this writing,
seven senators have publicly indicated their support of the bill;
they need only one more vote to pass the bill out of committee.
Friends at PEN tell me that the committee has received a lot of
letters from women saying that support of the bill would in
some way "make up for" the committee's mishandling of the
Clarence Thomas hearings. Some women are putting the decision to support Justice Thomas alongside the decision to find
William Kennedy Smith innocent of rape; these women think
that a really strong antipornography bill will make up for what
they perceive to be the miscarriage of justice in both cases.

The logic of this thinking is more than a little staggering.   22
What would these women think if lots of men were to write the
committee and say that because Mike Tyson has been found
guilty of rape, what we need is *more* pornography to make up
for what's happened to Iron Mike? This would make a lot of
sense, wouldn't it?

I conclude that these are not only censorial times; these are   23
stupid times. However, there is some hope that opposition to
Senate Bill 1521 is mounting. The committee met on March 12
but the members didn't vote on the bill. Discussion was brief, yet
encouraging. Colorado Senator Hank Brown told his colleagues
that there are serious problems with the legislation; he should
be congratulated for his courageous decision to oppose the
other Republicans on the committee, but he should also be
encouraged not to accept any compromise proposal. Ohio

Senator Howard Metzenbaum suggested that imposing third-party liability on producers and distributors of books, magazines, movies and recordings raises the question of whether the bill shouldn't be amended to cover the firearms and liquor industries as well.

24　　It remains to be seen if the committee members will resist the temptation to *fix* the troubled bill. I hope they will understand that the bill cannot be fixed because it is based on an erroneous premise—namely, that publishers or distributors should be held liable for the acts of criminals. But what is important for us to recognize, even if this lame bill is amended out of existence or flat-out defeated, is that *new* antipornography legislation will be proposed.

25　　Do we remember Nancy Reagan's advice to would-be drug users? ("Just say no.") As applied to drug use, Mrs. Reagan's advice is feeble in the extreme. But writers and other members of the literary community *should* just say no to censorship in any and every form. Of course, it will always be the most grotesque example of child pornography that will be waved in front of our eyes by the Good Taste Police. If we're opposed to censorship, they will say, are we in favor of filth like this?

26　　No; we are not in favor of child pornography if we say no to censorship. If we disapprove of reinstating public hangings, that doesn't mean that we want all the murderers to be set free. No writer or publisher or *reader* should accept censorship in any form; fundamental to our freedom of expression is that each of us has a right to decide what is obscene and what isn't.

27　　But lest you think I'm being paranoid about the iniquities and viciousness of our times, I'd like you to read a description of Puritan times. It was written in 1837—more than 150 years ago—and it describes a scene in a Puritan community in Massachusetts that you must imagine taking place more than 350 years ago. This is from a short story by Nathaniel Hawthorne called "Endicott and the Red Cross," which itself was written more than 10 years before Hawthorne wrote *The Scarlet Letter*. This little story contains the germ of the idea for that famous novel about a woman condemned by Puritan justice to wear the letter A on her breast. But Hawthorne, obviously, had been thinking about the iniquities and viciousness of early New England morality for many years.

28　　Please remember, as you read what Nathaniel Hawthorne thought of the Puritans, that the Puritans are not dead and gone. We have many new Puritans in our country today; they are as dangerous to freedom of expression as the old Puritans ever were. An especially sad thing is, a few of these new Puritans are formerly liberal-thinking feminists.

"In close vicinity to the sacred edifice [the meeting-house] ap-   29
peared that important engine of Puritanic authority, the whip-
ping-post—with the soil around it well trodden by the feet of
evil doers, who had there been disciplined. At one corner of the
meeting-house was the pillory, and at the other the stocks; . . .
the head of an Episcopalian and suspected Catholic was
grotesquely incased in the former machine; while a fellow-
criminal, who had boisterously quaffed a health to the king,
was confined by the legs in the latter. Side by side, on the meeting-house steps, stood a male and a female figure. The man was
a tall, lean, haggard personification of fanaticism, bearing on
his breast this label,—A WANTON GOSPELLER,—which beto-
kened that he had dared to give interpretations of Holy Writ un-
sanctioned by the infallible judgment of the civil and religious
rulers. His aspect showed no lack of zeal . . . even at the stake.
The woman wore a cleft stick on her tongue, in appropriate retribution for having wagged that unruly member against the elders of the church; and her countenance and gestures gave
much cause to apprehend that, the moment the stick should be
removed, a repetition of the offence would demand new inge-
nuity in chastising it.

"The above-mentioned individuals had been sentenced to   30
undergo their various modes of ignominy, for the space of one
hour at noonday. But among the crowd were several whose
punishment would be life-long; some, whose ears had been
cropped, like those of puppy dogs; others, whose cheeks had
been branded with the initials of their misdemeanors; one,
with his nostrils slit and seared; and another, with a halter
about his neck, which he was forbidden ever to take off, or to
conceal beneath his garments. Methinks he must have been
grievously tempted to affix the other end of the rope to some
convenient beam or bough. There was likewise a young
woman, with no mean share of beauty, whose doom was to
wear the letter A on the breast of her gown, in the eyes of all
the world and her own children. And even her own children
knew what that initial signified. Sporting with her infamy, the
lost and desperate creature had embroidered the fatal token in
scarlet cloth, with golden thread and the nicest art of needle-
work; so that the capital A might have been thought to mean
Admirable, or anything rather than Adulteress.

"Let not the reader argue, from any of these evidences of in-   31
iquity, that the times of the Puritans were more vicious than
our own."

In my old-fashioned opinion, Mr. Hawthorne sure got that   32
right.

Andrea Dworkin
REPLY TO JOHN IRVING

*As she notes in the following reply, Andrea Dworkin (born
1947) has written (with University of Michigan law professor
Catherine MacKinnon) antipornography ordinances for
Minneapolis, Indianapolis, and other cities. (The ordinances
later were overturned by the courts.) A successful and controversial essayist and fiction writer, she has also written*
Pornography: Men Possessing Women *(1988) and* Pornography and Civil Rights *(1988), both of which argue in favor
of the kinds of laws that she advocates.*

To the Editor:

1   As a woman determined to destroy the pornography industry, a writer of 10 published books and someone who reads,
perhaps I should be the one to tell John Irving ("Pornography
and the New Puritans," March 29) who the new Puritan is. The
old Puritans wouldn't like her very much; but then, neither
does Mr. Irving.

2   I am 45 years old now. When I was a teen-ager, I baby-sat. In
any middle-class home one could always find the dirty books—
on the highest shelf, climbing toward God, usually behind a
parched potted plant. The books themselves were usually
"Ulysses," "Tropic of Cancer" or "Lady Chatterley's Lover."
They always had as a preface or afterword the text of an obscenity decision in which the book was exonerated and art
extolled. Or a lawyer would stand in for the court to tell us that
through his mighty efforts law had finally vindicated a perse-
cuted genius.

3   Even at 15 and 16, I noticed something strange about the
special intersection of art, law and sex under the obscenity
rubric: some men punished other men for producing or publishing writing that caused arousal in (presumably) still other
men. Although Mrs. Grundy got the blame, women didn't
make these laws or enforce them or sit on juries to deliberate
guilt or innocence. This was a fight among men—but about
what?

4   Meanwhile, my life as a woman in prefeminist times went
on. This means that I thought I was a human being with rights.
But before I was much over 18, I had been sexually assaulted
three times. Did I report these assaults (patriarchy's first question, because surely the girl must be lying)?

When I was 9, I told my parents. To protect me, for better or   5
worse, they did not call the police.

The second time, beaten as well as raped, I told no one. I was   6
working for a peace group, and I heard jokes about rape day in
and day out. What do you tell the draft board when they ask you
if you would kill a Nazi who was going to rape your sister? "I'd
tell my sister to have a good time" was the answer of choice.

The third time, I was 18, a freshman in college, and I had   7
been arrested for taking part in a sit-in outside the United
Nations to protest the Vietnam War. It was February of 1965.
This time, my experience was reported in *The New York Times*,
newspapers all around the world and on television: girl in
prison—New York's notorious Women's House of Detention—
says she was brutalized by two prison doctors. Forced entry
with a speculum—for 15 days I had vaginal bleeding, a vagina
so bruised and ripped that my stone-cold family doctor burst
into tears when he examined me.

I came out of the Women's House of Detention mute. Speech   8
depends on believing you can make yourself understood: a
community of people will recognize the experience in the
words you use and they will care. You also have to be able to
understand what happened to you enough to convey it to others. I lost speech. I was hurt past what I had words for. I lived
out on the streets for several days, not having a bed of my own,
still bleeding; and finally spoke because Grace Paley convinced
me that she would understand and care. Then I spoke a lot. A
grand jury investigated. Columnists indicted the prison. But
neither of the prison doctors was charged with sexual assault
or sexual battery. In fact, no one ever mentioned sexual assault.
The grand jury concluded that the prison was fine. In despair, I
left the country—to be a writer, my human dream.

A year later I came back. I have since discovered that what   9
happened to me is common: homeless, poor, still sexually trau-
matized, I learned to trade sex for money. I spent a lot of years
out on the street, living hand to mouth, these New York streets
and other streets in other hard cities. I thought I was a real
tough woman, and I was: tough-calloused; tough-numb; tough-
desperate; tough-scared; tough-hungry; tough-beaten by men
often; tough-done it every which way including up. All of my
colleagues who fight pornography with me know about this. I
know about the lives of women in pornography because I lived
the life. So have many feminists who fight pornography.
Freedom looks different when you are the one it is being practiced on. It's his, not yours. Speech is different, too. Those sexy
expletives are the hate words he uses on you while he is using
you. Your speech is an inchoate protest never voiced.

10   In my work, fiction and nonfiction, I've tried to voice the protest against a power that is dead weight on you, fist and penis organized to keep you quiet. I would do virtually anything to get women out of prostitution and pornography, which is mass-produced, technologized prostitution. With pornography, a woman can still be sold after the beatings, the rapes, the pain, the humiliation have killed her. I write for her, on behalf of her. I know her. I have come close to being her.

11   I read a lot of books. None of them ever told me the truth about what happens to women until feminists started writing and publishing in this wave, over these last 22 years. Over and over, male writers consider prostituted women "speech"—their speech, their right. Without this exploitation, published for profit, the male writer feels censored. The woman lynched naked on a tree, or restrained with ropes and a ball gag in her mouth, has what? Freedom of what?

12   I lost my ability to speak—became mute—a second time in my life. I've written about being a battered wife: I was beaten and tortured over a period of a few years. Amnesty International never showed up. Toward the end, I lost all speech. Words were useless to the likes of me. I had run away and asked for help— from friends, neighbors, the police—and had been turned away many times. My words didn't seem to mean anything, or it was O.K. to torture me.

13   Taken once by my husband to a doctor when hurt, I risked asking for help. The doctor said he could write me a prescription for Valium or have me committed. The neighbors heard the screaming, but no one did anything. So what are words? I have always been good with them, but never good enough to be believed or helped. No, there were no shelters then.

14   But I am talking about speech: it isn't easy for me. I come to speech from under a man, tortured and tormented. What he did to me took away everything; he was the owner of everything. He hurt all the words out of me, and no one would listen anyway. I come to speech from under the brutalities of thousands of men. For me, the violence of marriage was worse than the violence of prostitution; but this is no choice. Men act out pornography. They have acted it out on me. Women's lives become pornography. Mine did. And so for 20 years now I have been looking for the words to say what I know.

15   But maybe liberal men—so open-minded and intellectually curious—can't find the books that would teach them about women's real lives. Maybe, while John Irving and PEN are defending *Hustler*, snuff films and *Deep Throat*, the direct product of the coercion of Linda Marchiano, political dissidents like

myself are anathema—especially to the free-speech fetishists—not because the publishing industry punishes prudes but because dissenters who mean it, who stand against male power over women, are pariahs.

Maybe Mr. Irving and others do not know that in the world   16
of women, pornography is the real geography of how men use us and torment us and hate us.

With Catharine A. MacKinnon, I drafted the first civil law   17
against pornography. It held pornographers accountable for what they do: they traffic women (contravening the United Nations Universal Declaration of Human Rights and the Convention on the Elimination of All Forms of Discrimination Against Women); they eroticize inequality in a way that materially promotes rape, battery, maiming and bondage; they make a product that they know dehumanizes, degrades and exploits women; they hurt women to make the pornography, and then consumers use the pornography in assaults both verbal and physical.

Mr. Irving refers to a scene in *The World According to Garp* in   18
which a woman bites off a man's penis in a car when the car is accidentally rammed from behind. This, he says, did not cause women to bite off men's penises in cars. I have written (in my novels, *Ice and Fire* and *Mercy*, and in the story "The New Woman's Broken Heart") about a woman raped by two men sequentially, the first aggressor routed by the second one, to whom the woman, near dead, submits; he bites viciously and repeatedly into her genitals. When I wrote it, someone had already done it—to me. Mr. Irving uses his imagination for violent farce. My imagination can barely grasp my real life. The violence, as Mr. Irving must know, goes from men to women.

Women write to me because of our shared experiences. In   19
my books they find their lives—until now beyond the reach of language. A letter to me dated March 11 says in part: "The abuse was quite sadistic—it involved bestiality, torture, the making of pornography. Sometimes, when I think about my life, I'm not sure why I'm alive, but I'm always sure about why I do what I do, the feminist theory and the antipornography activism." Another letter, dated March 13, says: "It was only when I was almost [raped] to pieces that I broke down and learned to hate. . . . I have never stopped resenting the loss of innocence that occurred the day I learned to hate."

Male liberals seem to think we fight pornography to protect   20
sexual innocence, but we have none to protect. The innocence we want is the innocence that lets us love. People need dignity to love.

21   Mr. Irving quoted Hawthorne's condemnation of Puritan orthodoxy in the short story "Endicott and the Red Cross"—a graphic description of public punishments of women: bondage, branding, maiming, lynching. Today pornographers do these things to women, and the public square is a big place—every newsstand and video store. A photograph shields rape and torture for profit. In defending pornography as if it were speech, liberals defend the new slavers. The only fiction in pornography is the smile on the woman's face.

Nadine Strossen

THE PERILS
OF PORNOPHOBIA

Nadine Strossen's essay on pornography appeared in The Humanist *in the spring of 1995. Strossen, a member of the faculty at New York Law School, is president of the American Civil Liberties Union, an organization famous for defending the constitutional rights of U.S. citizens. Her essay was adapted from her 1995 book* Defending Pornography: Free Speech, Sex, and the Fight for Women's Rights.

1   In 1992, in response to a complaint, ficials at Pennsylvania State University unceremoniously removed Francisco de Goya's masterpiece, *The Nude Maja*, from a classroom wall. The complaint had not been lodged by Jesse Helms or some irate member of the Christian Coalition. Instead, the complainant was a feminist English professor who protested that the eighteenth-century painting of a recumbent nude woman made her and her female students "uncomfortable."

2   This was not an isolated incident. At the University of Arizona at Tucson, feminist students physically attacked a graduate student's exhibit of photographic self-portraits. Why? The artist had photographed *herself* in her *underwear*. And at the University of Michigan Law School feminist students who had organized a conference on "Prostitution: From Academia to Activism" removed a feminist-curated art exhibition held in conjunction with the conference. Their reason? Conference

speakers had complained that a composite videotape containing interviews of working prostitutes was "pornographic" and therefore unacceptable.

What is wrong with this picture? Where have they come 3 from—these feminists who behave like religious conservatives, who censor works of art because they deal with sexual themes? Have not feminists long known that censorship is a dangerous weapon which, if permitted, would inevitably be turned against them? Certainly that was the irrefutable lesson of the early women's rights movement, when Margaret Sanger, Mary Ware Dennett, and other activists were arrested, charged with "obscenity" and prosecuted for distributing educational pamphlets about sex and birth control. Theirs was a struggle for freedom of sexual expression and full gender equality, which they understood to be mutually reinforcing.

Theirs was also a lesson well understood by the second wave 4 of feminism in the 1970s, when writers such as Germaine Greer, Betty Friedan, and Betty Dodson boldly asserted that women had the right to be free from discrimination not only in the workplace and in the classroom but in the bedroom as well. Freedom from limiting, conventional stereotypes concerning female sexuality was an essential aspect of what we then called "women's liberation." Women should not be seen as victims in their sexual relations with men but as equally assertive partners, just as capable of experiencing sexual pleasure.

But it is a lesson that, alas, many feminists have now forgot- 5 ten. Today, an increasingly influential feminist pro-censorship movement threatens to impair the very women's rights movement it professes to serve. Led by law professor Catharine MacKinnon and writer Andrea Dworkin, this faction of the feminist movement maintains that sexually oriented *expression*— not sex-segregated labor markets, sexist concepts of marriage and family, or pent-up rage—is the preeminent cause of discrimination and violence against women. Their solution is seemingly simple: suppress all "pornography."

Censorship, however, is never a simple matter. First, the of- 6 fense must be described. And how does one define something so infinitely variable, so deeply personal, so uniquely individualized as the image, the word, and the fantasy that cause sexual arousal? For decades, the U.S. Supreme Court has engaged in a Sisyphean struggle to craft a definition of *obscenity* that the lower courts can apply with some fairness and consistency. Their dilemma was best summed up in former Justice Potter Stewart's now famous statement: "I shall not today attempt further to define [obscenity]; and perhaps I could never succeed in intelligibly doing so. But I know it when I see it."

7   The censorious feminists are not so modest as Justice Stewart.
They have fashioned an elaborate definition of *pornography* that
encompasses vastly more material than does the currently recognized law of *obscenity*. As set out in their model law (which has
been considered in more than a dozen jurisdictions in the United
States and overseas, and which has been substantially adopted in
Canada), pornography is "the sexually explicit subordination of
women through pictures and/or words." The model law lists
eight different criteria that attempt to illustrate their concept of
"subordination," such as depictions in which "women are presented in postures or positions of sexual submission, servility, or
display" or "women are presented in scenarios of degradation,
humiliation, injury, torture . . . in a context that makes these conditions sexual." This linguistic driftnet can ensnare anything
from religious imagery and documentary footage about the mass
rapes in the Balkans to self-help books about women's health.
Indeed, the Boston Women's Health Book Collective, publisher
of the now-classic book on women's health and sexuality, *Our
Bodies, Ourselves*, actively campaigned against the MacKinnon-
Dworkin model law when it was proposed in Cambridge,
Massachusetts, in 1985, recognizing that the book's explicit text
and pictures could be targeted as pornographic under the law.

8   Although the "MacDworkinite" approach to pornography
has an intuitive appeal to many feminists, it is *itself* based
on subordinating and demeaning stereotypes about women.
Central to the pornophobic feminists—and to many traditional
conservatives and right-wing fundamentalists, as well—is the
notion that *sex* is inherently degrading to women (although
not to men). Not just sexual expression but sex itself—even
consensual, nonviolent sex—is an evil from which women, like
children, must be protected.

9   MacKinnon puts it this way: "Compare victims' reports of
rape with women's reports of sex. They look a lot alike. . . . The
major distinction between intercourse (normal) and rape (ab-
normal) is that the normal happens so often that one cannot
get anyone to see anything wrong with it." And from Dworkin:
"Intercourse remains a means or the means of physiologically
making a woman inferior." Given society's pervasive sexism,
she believes, women cannot freely consent to sexual relations
with men; those who do consent are, in Dworkin's words, "collaborators . . . experiencing pleasure in their own inferiority."

10   These ideas are hardly radical. Rather, they are a reincarna-
tion of disempowering puritanical, Victorian notions that feminists have long tried to consign to the dustbin of history:
woman as sexual victim; man as voracious satyr. The
MacDworkinite approach to sexual expression is a throwback

to the archaic stereotypes that formed the basis for nineteenth-century laws which prohibited "vulgar" or sexually suggestive language from being used in the presence of women and girls.

In those days, women were barred from practicing law and   11
serving as jurors lest they be exposed to such language. Such "protective" laws have historically functioned to bar women from full legal equality. Paternalism always leads to exclusion, discrimination, and the loss of freedom and autonomy. And in its most extreme form, it leads to purdah, in which women are completely shrouded from public view.

The pro-censorship feminists are not fighting alone. Although   12
they try to distance themselves from such traditional "family-values" conservatives as Jesse Helms, Phyllis Schlafly, and Donald Wildmon, who are less interested in protecting women than in preserving male dominance, a common hatred of sexual expression and fondness for censorship unite the two camps. For example, the Indianapolis City Council adopted the MacKinnon-Dworkin model law in 1984 thanks to the hard work of former council member Beulah Coughenour, a leader of the Indiana Stop ERA movement. (Federal courts later declared the law unconstitutional.) And when Phyllis Schlafly's Eagle Forum and Beverly LaHaye's Concerned Women for America launched their "Enough Is Enough" anti-pornography campaign, they trumpeted the words of Andrea Dworkin in promotional materials.

This mutually reinforcing relationship does a serious disser-   13
vice to the fight for women's equality. It lends credibility to and strengthens the right wing and its anti-feminist, anti-choice, homophobic agenda. This is particularly damaging in light of the growing influence of the religious right in the Republican Party and the recent Republican sweep of both Congress and many state governments. If anyone doubts that the newly empowered GOP intends to forge ahead with anti-woman agendas, they need only read the party's "Contract with America" which, among other things, reintroduces the recently repealed "gag rule" forbidding government-funded family-planning clinics from even discussing abortion with their patients.

The pro-censorship feminists base their efforts on the largely   14
unexamined assumption that ridding society of pornography would reduce sexism and violence against women. If there were any evidence that this were true, anti-censorship feminists—myself included—would be compelled at least to reexamine our opposition to censorship. But there is no such evidence to be found.

A causal connection between exposure to pornography and   15
the commission of sexual violence has never been established.

The National Research Council's Panel on Understanding and Preventing Violence concluded in a 1993 survey of laboratory studies that "demonstrated empirical links between pornography and sex crimes in general are weak or absent." Even according to another research literature survey that former U.S. Surgeon General C. Everett Koop conducted at the behest of the staunchly anti-pornography Meese Commission, only two reliable generalizations could be made about the impact of "degrading" sexual material on its viewers: it caused them to think that a variety of sexual practices was more common than they had previously believed, and to more accurately estimate the prevalence of varied sexual practices.

16   Correlational studies are similarly unsupportive of the pro-censorship cause. There are no consistent correlations between the availability of pornography in various communities, states, and countries and their rates of sexual offenses. If anything, studies suggest an inverse relationship: a greater availability of sexually explicit material seems to correlate not with higher rates of sexual violence but, rather, with higher indices of gender equality. For example, Singapore, with its tight restrictions on pornography, has experienced a much greater increase in rape rates than has Sweden, with its liberalized obscenity laws.

17   There *is* mounting evidence, however, that MacDworkinite-type laws will be used against the very people they are supposed to protect—namely, women. In 1992, for example, the Canadian Supreme Court incorporated the MacKinnon-Dworkin concept of pornography into Canadian obscenity law. Since that ruling, in *Butler* v. *The Queen*—which MacKinnon enthusiastically hailed as "a stunning victory for women"— well over half of all feminist bookstores in Canada have had materials confiscated or detained by customs. According to the *Feminist Bookstore News*, a Canadian publication, "The *Butler* decision has been used . . . only to seize lesbian, gay, and feminist material."

18   Ironically but predictably, one of the victims of Canada's new law is Andrea Dworkin herself. Two of her books, *Pornography: Men Possessing Women* and *Women Hating*, were seized, customs officials said, because they "illegally eroticized pain and bondage." Like the MacKinnon-Dworkin model law, the *Butler* decision makes no exceptions for material that is part of a feminist critique of pornography or other feminist presentation. And this inevitably overbroad sweep is precisely why censorship is antithetical to the fight for women's rights.

19   The pornophobia that grips MacKinnon, Dworkin, and their followers has had further counterproductive impacts on the

fight for women's rights. Censorship factionalism within the feminist movement has led to an enormously wasteful diversion of energy from the real cause of and solutions to the ongoing problems of discrimination and violence against women. Moreover, the "porn-made-me-do-it" defense, whereby convicted rapists cite MacKinnon and Dworkin in seeking to reduce their sentences, actually impedes the aggressive enforcement of criminal laws against sexual violence.

A return to the basic principles of women's liberation would   20
put the feminist movement back on course. We women are entitled to freedom of expression—to read, think, speak, sing, write, paint, dance, dream, photograph, film, and fantasize as we wish. We are also entitled to our dignity, autonomy, and equality. Fortunately, we can—and will—have both.

Robert Jensen

THE PAINFUL TRUTH ABOUT TODAY'S PORNOGRAPHY—AND WHAT MEN CAN DO ABOUT IT

Robert Jensen is a professor in the School of Journalism at the University of Texas, Austin. His research interests include gender issues (on his homepage, he describes himself as a feminist) and issues related to pornography and women—the topic of the essay included here. He has published widely on social issues and activism, including Citizens of the Empire: The Struggle to Claim Our Humanity *(2004),* Writing Dissent: Taking Radical Ideas from the Margins to the Mainstream *(2001),* Pornography: The Production and Consumption of Inequality *(1998), and* Freeing the First Amendment: Critical Perspectives on Freedom of Expression *(1995). He has also served on the editorial board of* Violence Against Women. *The essay below graphically describes scenes from pornographic films. As you read, you might consider why Jensen decided to include these descriptions, their likely effect on readers, and whether it makes for an effective rhetorical strategy.*

1   After an intense three hours, the workshop on pornography is winding down. The 40 women present all work at a center that serves battered women and rape survivors. These are the women on the front lines, the ones who answer the 24-hour hotlines and deal directly with victims. These women have heard and seen it all, and there is no way to one-up them with stories of male violence. But after three hours discussing the commercial heterosexual pornography industry, many of these women are drained. Sadness hangs over the room.

2   One women has held back throughout the workshop, her arms wrapped tightly around herself. Now, finally, she speaks. "This hurts," she says. "It just hurts so much."

3   Everyone is quiet as the words sink in. Slowly the conversation restarts, but her words hang in the air:

4   It hurts.

5   It hurts to know that no matter who you are, you can be reduced to a thing to be penetrated, and that men will buy movies about that, and that in many of those movies your humiliation will be the central theme. It hurts to know that so much of the pornography men buy fuses sexual desire with cruelty.

6   Even women who cope daily with those injured by male violence struggle with this knowledge. It's one thing to deal with overt acts; it's another to face the thoughts and fantasies that fuel so many men's sexual lives.

7   People routinely assume that pornography is such a difficult and divisive issue because it's about sex. I think that's wrong. This culture struggles unsuccessfully with pornography because it is also about men's cruelty to women, and about the pleasure that men sometimes take in that cruelty. And that is much more difficult for everyone to face.

8   There are different pornographic genres, but my studies of pornographic videos over the past seven years have focused on the stories told in mainstream heterosexual pornography. By that I mean the videos and DVDs that are widely available in the United States, marketed as sexually explicit (what is commonly called "hardcore"), rented and purchased primarily by men, and depict sex primarily between men and women. The sexual activity is not simulated: What happens on the screen happened in the world. This mainstream pornography does not include overt bondage and sadomasochism, explicit violence, urination or defecation, although such material is widely available in shops, through the mail, or on the Internet.

(There's also, of course, an underground market for child pornography—the only porn clearly illegal everywhere in the United States.)

To obtain mainstream pornographic videos for study, I vis- 9 ited stores that sold "adult product" (the industry's preferred term) and asked clerks and managers to help me select the most commonly rented and purchased tapes. I wanted to avoid the accusation that feminists analyzing pornography only pick out the worst examples, the most violent material, to critique.

While many may find what is described here to be disturb- 10 ing, these are not aberrations. These tapes are broadly representative of the 11,303 new hardcore titles that were released in 2002, according to *Adult Video News*, the industry's trade magazine. They are standard fare from a pornography industry with an estimated $10 billion in annual sales. They are what brothers and fathers and uncles are watching, what boyfriends and husbands and, in many cases, male children are watching.

What kind of stories does this mainstream pornography tell 11 the all-American boy—and what does that mean for the girl next door? Here are three examples:

- The 2003 film "Sopornos 4" was produced by VCA Pictures, one of the "high-end" companies that create films for the "couples market." These films, sometimes called "features," typically attempt some plot and character development. The industry claims these films appeal to women as well as men.

  The plot of "Sopornos" is a takeoff on the popular HBO series about New Jersey mobsters. In the last of six sex scenes, the mob boss's wife has sex with two of his men. Moving through the standard porn progression—oral sex and then vaginal sex—one of the men prepares to penetrate her anally. She tells him: "That fucking cock is so fucking huge. . . . Spread [my] fucking ass. . . . Spread it open." He penetrates her. Then, she says, in a slightly lower tone, "Don't go any deeper." She seems to be in pain. At the end of the scene, she requests the men's semen ("Two cocks jacking off in my face. I want it.") and opens her mouth. The men ejaculate onto her at the same time.

- "Two in the Seat #3," a 2003 "gonzo" release (meaning, there is no attempt to create characters or story lines) from Red Light District, contains six scenes in which two men have sex with one woman, culminating in a double-penetration (the woman is penetrated vaginally and anally at the same time). In one scene, 20-year-old Claire, her hair in pigtails, says she has been in the industry for three months. Asked by the off-camera interviewer what will happen in the scene, she replies, "I'm here to get pounded." The two men then enter the scene and begin a steady stream of insults, calling her "a dirty, nasty girl," "a little fucking cunt," "a little slut." After oral and vaginal sex, she asks one to "Please put your cock in my ass." During double-penetration on the floor, her vocalizations sound pained. She's braced against the couch, moving very little. The men spank her, and her buttock is visibly red. One man asks, "Are you crying?"

Claire: "No, I'm enjoying it."

Man: "Damn, I thought you were crying. It was turning me on when I thought you were crying."

Claire: "Would you like me to?"

Man: "Yeah, give me a fucking tear. Oh, there's a fucking tear."

- Finally, there's "Gag Factor 10," a 2002 release from JM Productions also in the "gonzo" category. One of the 10 sex scenes involves a woman and man having a picnic in a park. While she sits on the blanket, he stands and thrusts his penis into her mouth. Two other men who walk by join in. One man grabs her hair and pulls her head into his penis in what his friend calls "the jackhammer."

  At this point the woman is grimacing and seems in pain. She then lies on the ground, and the men approach her from behind. "Eat that whole fucking dick. . . . You little whore, you like getting hurt," one says. After they all ejaculate into her mouth, the semen flows out onto her body. She reaches quickly for the wine glass, takes a large drink, looks up at her boyfriend, and says, "God, I love you, baby." Her smile fades to a pained look of shame and despair.

12   I can't know exactly what the women in these films were feeling, physically or emotionally. But here is what BellaDonna, one of the women who appeared in "Two in the Seat #3," told a television interviewer about such sex scenes: "You have to really prepare physically and mentally for it. I mean, I go through a process from the night before. I stop eating at 5 p.m. I do, you know, like two enemas, and then the next morning I don't eat anything. It's so draining on your body."

13   Even if the pain shown in the above scenes is acted and not real, why don't directors edit *out* pained expressions? I see only two possible answers: either they view such pain as being of no consequence to the viewers' interest—and hence to the goal of

maximizing film sales—or they believe viewers enjoy seeing the women's pain. So why, then, do some men find the infliction of pain on women during sex either not an obstacle to their ability to achieve sexual pleasure or a factor that can *enhance* their pleasure?

I believe it's all about the edge.   14

There are only so many ways that human beings can, in me-   15
chanical terms, have sex. There are a limited number of body parts and openings, a limited number of ways to create the friction that produces the stimulation and sensations. That's why stories about sexuality generally tap into something beyond the mechanical. When most nonpornographic films deal with sex, they draw, at least in part, on the emotions most commonly connected with sex: love and affection. But pornography doesn't have that option, since my research has shown that men typically consume it to *avoid* love and affection and go straight to sexual release.

And that means pornography, without emotional variation,   16
will become repetitive and uninteresting, even to men watching primarily to facilitate masturbation. So pornography needs an edge.

When the legal restrictions on pornography gradually loos-   17
ened in the 1970s and '80s, anal sex captured that edge, because it was seen as something most women don't want. Then, as anal sex became routine in pornography, the gonzo genre started routinely adding double-penetrations and gag-inducing oral sex—again, acts that men believe women generally do not want. These days, pornography has become so normalized and so mainstream in our culture that the edge keeps receding. As Jerome Tanner put it during a pornography directors' roundtable discussion featured in *Adult Video News*, "People just want it harder, harder, and harder, because . . . what are you gonna do next?"

It's not surprising that the new edge more and more involves   18
overt cruelty—an easy choice given that the dynamic of male domination and female submission is already in place in patriarchy. All people are capable of being cruel, of course. But contemporary mainstream heterosexual pornography forces the question: Why has cruelty become so sexualized for some men?

Feminist research long ago established that rape involves the   19
sexualization of power, the equation in men's imaginations of sexual pleasure with domination and control. The common phrase "rape is about power, not sex" misleads, though; rape is about the fusion of sex and domination, about the eroticization of control. And in this culture, rape is normal. That is, in a culture where the dominant definition of sex is the taking of

pleasure from women by men, rape is an expression of the sexual norms of the culture, not violations of those norms. Sex is a sphere in which men are trained to see themselves as naturally dominant and women as naturally passive. Rape is both nominally illegal and completely normal at the same time.

20   By extension, there should be nothing surprising about the fact that some pornography includes explicit images of women in pain. But my question is: Wouldn't a healthy society want to deal with that? Why aren't more people, men or women, concerned?

21   Right-wing opponents of pornography offer a moralistic critique that cannot help us find solutions, because typically those folks endorse male dominance (albeit not these particular manifestations of it). Conversely, some feminists want us to believe that the growing acceptance of pornography is a benign sign of expanding sexual equality and freedom. Meanwhile, feminist critics of pornography have been marginalized in political and intellectual arenas. And all the while, the pornographers are trudging off to the bank with bags of money.

22   I think this helps explain why even the toughest women at rape crisis centers find the reality of pornography so difficult to cope with. No matter how hard it may be to face rape, at least our society still brands it as a crime. Pornography, however, is not only widely accepted, but sold to us as liberation.

23   I don't pretend to speak for women; my focus is on men. And I believe that the task for men of conscience is to define ourselves and our sexuality outside of the domination/submission dynamic. It is not easy: Like everyone, we are products of our culture and have to struggle against it. But as a man, I at least have considerable control over the conditions in which I live and the situations in which I function. Women sometimes do not have that control. They're at far more risk of sexual violence, and they have to deal with men who disproportionately hold positions of power over them. Mainstream pornography tips that power balance even further.

24   For example, when a female student has a meeting about a research project with a male college professor who the night before was watching "Gag Factor 10," who will she be to him? Or when a woman walks into a bank to apply for a loan from a male loan officer who the night before was watching "Two in the Seat #3," what will he be thinking? And when a woman goes in front of a male judge who the night before was watching "Sopornos 4," will she be judged fairly?

25   But some will argue: How can you assume that just because men watch such things they will act in a callous and cruel manner, sexually or otherwise? It is true that the connection between mass-media exposure and human behavior is complex,

and social scientists argue both sides. But taken together, the laboratory evidence, the research on men who abuse, and the voluminous testimony of women clearly indicate that in some cases pornography influences men's sexual behavior. Pornography may not *cause* abuse, but it can be implicated as an accessory to the crime.

If we could pretend that these images are consumed by some   26
small subset of deviant men, then we could identify and isolate those aberrant men, maybe repair them. But men who consume these images are everywhere: men who can't get a date and men who have all the dates they want. Men who live alone and men who are married. Men who grew up in liberal homes where pornography was never a big deal and men who grew up in strict religious homes where no talk of sex was allowed. Rich men and poor men, men of all colors and creeds.

When I critique pornography, I am often told to lighten up.   27
Sex is just sex, people say, and I should stop trying to politicize pornography. But pornography offers men a politics of sex and gender—and that politics is patriarchal and reactionary. In pornography, women are not really people; they are three holes and two hands. Women in pornography have no hopes, no dreams, and no value apart from the friction those holes and hands can produce on a man's penis.

As with any political issue, successful strategies of resis-   28
tance, I would suggest, must be collective and public rather than solely personal and private. Pornographers know that to be true—which is why they try to cut off the discussion. When we critique pornography, we typically are accused of being people who hate freedom, sexually dysfunctional prudes who are scared of sex, or both.

Pornographers also want to derail any talk of sexual ethics.   29
They, of course, have a sexual ethic: Anything—and they mean anything—goes, and consenting adults should be free to choose. I agree that choice is crucial. But in a society in which power is not equally distributed, "anything goes" translates into "anything goes for men, while some women and children will suffer for it."

There are many controversial issues in the pornography de-   30
bate, but there should be nothing controversial about this: To critique pornography is not repressive. We should be free to talk about our desire for an egalitarian intimacy and for sexuality that rejects pain and humiliation. That is not prudishness or censorship. It is at attempt to claim the best parts of our common humanity: love, caring, empathy. To do that is not to limit anyone. It is to say, simply, that women count as much as men.

4

Revolutions in Marriage and Family

Introduction

Marriage and family matters have long been a cornerstone of our culture's values. Traditionally, the family has been synonymous with successful relationships: Colleges and businesses like to describe themselves as families. We count it as a compliment when a friend says that we are "like family." Blood, we are told, is thicker than water. And the commonplaces go on. This chapter will challenge you to examine those assumptions about family. The readings ask you to consider the various ways that families have been traditionally defined, and how they might be defined in our own time. You will also be asked to consider how the social unit of the family fits, or should fit, within the larger social units that define American culture. And you will even be asked to consider whether family is itself as productive and positive a unit as we have come to believe.

Marriage and family, despite their individual and personal roots, are also issues taken up by public policy. One need only look at the 1996 Defense of Marriage Act or proposed state and federal constitutional amendments designed to preserve what some call "traditional family values" to see that. Politically, it is impossible to be antifamily. After all, what politician is apt to suggest that he is against a value so close to our center? Indeed, political campaigns are often built on defense of family values. But those values still differ because families are *defined* differently: For example, President George W. Bush supports a constitutional amendment that would define marriage to be only between a man and a woman; his opponent in the 2004 presidential election, democratic candidate John Kerry, did not. But neither would claim to be antifamily. During the 1996 presidential campaign, likewise, both Bob Dole and Bill Clinton promised to sustain vigorous efforts to protect the American family, as did both Al Gore and George W. Bush in 2000. No doubt you have heard the general concerns mentioned again and again—concerns about the state of the family during a time of increasing divorce and out-of-wedlock births; concerns about child support that ought to be honored by absent partners, but isn't; concerns about teenage crime, suicide, pregnancy, substance abuse, and truancy that seem to be associated with broken homes; concerns about the effectiveness of day care, necessitated by

two working parents; concerns about child abuse. Moreover, you have likely heard a great deal of recent conversation about revolutionary concepts in family and marriage
that have come about due to new social customs and developments in reproductive technology—about who should
have custody of children in cases of divorce and about
whether single-sex couples should be able to marry and/or
adopt children—or in the case of lesbian women, give birth
to children through artificial insemination. Without a doubt,
conversations about marriage and family are everywhere;
the readings in this section provide just a sampling of that
conversation.

Despite the inability of politicians to take any stance
about family values other than being in favor of them—in
some form—that is not true for all. The readings in the first
section of this part of *Conversations* not only ask the definitional question, "What is a marriage?" (as does the third
section on same-sex marriage). Some of the authors ask a
wider, more controversial, question: Is marriage still a useful institution? Driven by feminist ideas and changing economic realities, some have suggested that the demise of
marriage is not necessarily a bad thing—that perhaps it has
outlived its usefulness. For many, perhaps including you,
such a contention is nothing short of heresy. But no matter
where you stand, asking definitional questions about marriage and its purposes can lead to some extremely important conversations. In fact, teachers of oratory have always
used the consideration of opposite opinions as a way to
tease out the available arguments on any given issue. Here,
too, as you read the wide variety of opinions about marriage and its effects, you can generate a great many ideas
for your own writing.

Likewise, the readings in the second section of this part,
"What Is a Family?" do not beg the question of whether a
family is still a good and useful thing. Just the title of Ellen
Willis's "Why I'm Not Pro-Family," for example, may raise
your interest—or your ire. And you would not be alone.
Family values are a flashpoint for many Americans who feel
that our whole culture is built on this institution. An example: Many years ago, a public debate about family values
erupted, oddly enough, because of an episode of a situation
comedy starring Candice Bergen as Murphy Brown. On
that show, the title character—a strong and independent-
minded woman—decided to parent a child herself rather

than within a marriage. This fictional scenario gave rise to an actual civic debate when then Vice President Dan Quayle assailed this character's decision as a bad example of America's family values (as is discussed in Barbara Dafoe Whitehead's essay, included in this section). The debate about family has grown even wider recently, as gay marriage and gay adoption issues have entered the public conversation, along with feminist questions about what they see as a patriarchal system rooted in the traditional family. Still, many Americans find the traditional family structure worth defending on many economic, religious, and sociological grounds. As the readings included here make amply clear, the American family continues to be a key subject of conversation even as changes occur all around us.

Perhaps one of the most impassioned conversations regarding family that our culture faces currently is whether marriage has a foundational core of one man and one woman. For many Americans, marriage is among our most basic institutions. That legislators have proposed that the traditional understanding of marriage as a pact between one man and one woman needs to be defended by a federal Constitutional amendment, by the passage in 1996 of the Defense of Marriage Act, and by the passage of two state constitutional amendments (with 12 more state amendments pending) gives us a good idea of how fundamental this issue can be for many. But there are a great many other perspectives that surround this topic as well, conversations that remind us that there are a great many more than two perspectives—for or against—on a topic.

As such, the third section of this part of *Conversations* asks whether America is ready to extend its definition of two of its most venerable institutions—marriage and family—to include same-sex couples. In some ways, the growth of gay marriage and families (as Dan Gilgoff's essay chronicles) suggests that it is; after all, gay marriages and families are already here. But will they be accepted? Will there be backlash against the growing acceptance of same-sex unions? And even if same-sex unions are accepted, should they be defined as marriage, an institution that has both civil and religious implications? Once again, the conversation is not as simple as pro and con; in fact, if you listen carefully, you will hear a polyphony of voices on this topic that can help you to see all the way around this complex issue, and then to respond with your own thoughts and writing. And you will likely need to engage with these essays not only intellectually but emotionally, because questions of family carry with them a great deal of *pathos* for most of us.

Though the issue of same-sex marriage has been with us for some time, 2004 brought this topic to the center of our national consciousness in unprecedented, and very visual, ways. The "Visual Conversations" section included in this part of the book gives you a glimpse at key moments in San Francisco, where the mayor issued marriage licenses to gay couples despite a state resolution against such actions, and in Massachusetts, where gay marriage was legalized. In both of these specific times and places, the issue ceased being theoretical and exploded into action—action that was reported not only in words, but in images that caused gay love to be more visible than perhaps at any other time in American history. As a result, the conversations surrounding same-sex marriage have become all the more impassioned— as is also depicted in these photographs. As you view the images in this section, you should consider the role that pictures like these play in adding exigency to this heated national debate; and more generally, you might consider how *seeing* as well as hearing about news somehow raises the stakes. (What effect, for example, did having "embedded journalists" make in the first days of the Iraqi war? How did those still and video images change the country's view of the war?)

All in all, this part of *Conversations* allows you to hear varied and impassioned discussions surrounding a set of values that are among the most revered in our culture, but which are undergoing a period of radical changes. For some, change means abandoning those values; for others, it means widening access to them; and for still others, it is the values themselves that need to change. Without a doubt, it is a conversation that will ask you to examine your own values as well.

What Is a Marriage?

David Masci

IS TRADITIONAL MATRIMONY GOING OUT OF STYLE?

Congressional Quarterly, *the publication where this article first appeared, is published by a nonprofit organization. It attempts to provide extensive research on current topics and "to advance the quality of reporting about government, helping elected officials and citizens alike understand and improve our democracy." It purports to do so by providing even-handed accounts of issues, giving equal time to many perspectives. As you read the excerpt from David Masci's 2004 essay, which surveys changes to "traditional matrimony" in recent years, you might consider whether this piece does achieve a balanced portrayal of the topic, and if so, how it maintains that objectivity. The author, Masci, has written for* CQ Researcher *since 1996 and specializes in foreign affairs, religion, and social policy. He has degrees in history and law.*

1   For Washington-area lawyers Melissa Jurgens and Jim Reed, their four years of marriage has meant greater happiness and stability than they have ever known.

2   "After I married Jim, I had someone I could talk to all the time and who could support me in ways that my friends, as wonderful as they are, just can't," Jurgens says. "He's more than a friend: He's committed to me, like I am to him, and that makes all the difference. We're going to be living together for the next 50 years, and so he needs to ensure that I'm OK and happy."

Marriage has been equally transforming for Reed. "I was 35 at   3
the time and had already been a lawyer for 10 years," he says.
"But I didn't really feel established until I married my wife.
Marrying Melissa committed me to certain things—like my career path and staying here in Washington . . . [in part] because
we want to have children."

But Dimitra Hengen, a successful businesswoman in   4
Alexandria, Va., wants no part of the institution. "A lot of people do much better living on their own rather than in a marriage," says Hengen, who divorced her husband in 2001 after
18 years of marriage. "I'm not saying that we don't need companionship, but you need to assess this need against the things
you have to give up when you marry, like your independence—
and I don't want to give those things up."

Instead, she sees herself having long-term relationships that   5
may be permanent, but will never lead to matrimony. "I have a
wonderful boyfriend right now, and he wants to marry me, but
I don't even want to live with him," she says. "I want to be able
to come and go as I please, to travel, to see friends and family,
all without the compromises that come with marriage. I don't
need marriage."

Hengen is among a growing number of Americans who see   6
marriage as more of an option than a necessity, according to
Laura Kipnis, a professor of media studies at Northwestern
University and author of *Against Love: A Polemic*. "As the economic necessity of it has become less pressing, people have
discovered that they no longer need marriage," she says. "It restricts our choices and is too confining, which is why fewer
people are marrying."

Indeed, in the last 50 years, the percentage of American   7
households headed by married couples has fallen from
nearly 80 percent to an all-time low of 50.7 percent, according
to the Census Bureau. Meanwhile, the percentage of marriages
that end in divorce jumped from roughly 25 percent to 45
percent.

As a result of the changing marriage and divorce statistics,   8
married couples with children now comprise only 25 percent
of all American households. The number is expected to fall to
20 percent by 2010. By that time, the bureau predicts, single
adults will make up 30 percent of all households.[1]

Nonetheless, many marriage scholars argue that despite cur-   9
rent trends, marriage will never really go out of style.

"We're a pair-bonding species, and we have a deep need at   10
the species level to love and be loved by another and a need to
pass on a part of ourselves to the next generation," says David
Blankenhorn, founder and president of the Institute for

American Values, a marriage advocacy group. "Marriage is the institution that encompasses these two great needs."

11   The case for marriage is further bolstered by research showing that married men and women are healthier, wealthier and happier than their single or divorced counterparts, Blankenhorn says. Children, too, are more likely to do better in school and less likely to have disciplinary trouble if they live in homes with married parents, he says.[2]

12   Marriage advocates note there is already some evidence to support the institution's resiliency, pointing out that divorce rates, for instance, have leveled off and even declined slightly in recent years.

13   And compared with Northern Europeans, Americans are still marriage fanatics. In Denmark, for instance, 60 percent of all children are born out of wedlock, compared to 34 percent in the United States.[3]

14   But many experts worry that the United States eventually will become more like Europe, with cohabitation and single parenthood replacing marriage as the dominant social institution. They point out that between 1996 and 2002 the number of cohabiting couples rose from 2.8 million to nearly 4.3 million, a trend that is expected to continue in the coming years.

15   Marriage advocates say that increasing rates of cohabitation can and should be stopped with education and other measures. They support a recent $1.5 billion Bush administration proposal to promote marriage among the poor, who are more likely to have children outside wedlock than middle-class Americans.

16   But critics of the initiative, which is part of a planned reauthorization of the nation's welfare law, argue that marriage-promotion schemes are unlikely to work. And even if they did prove successful, they say, the money could better be spent on education or job training, which help women become more self-sufficient and less in need of a husband.

17   The Bush administration also has promoted marriage by rewriting the tax code to eliminate the so-called marriage penalty—which required some married couples to pay higher taxes together than if they had remained single. The penalty was eliminated when Congress passed the first Bush tax cuts in 2001, but the provisions expire at the end of the year. On April 28, the House passed legislation making the elimination of the penalty permanent. However, prospects in the Senate are uncertain.[4]

18   The drive to promote marriage, especially through taxes or benefits, has angered many singles. Unmarried workers, for instance, complain that pension and health benefits favor those with spouses and children. If the percentage of single employees in America were to surpass the percentage of married

employees, singles could begin demanding equal treatment with regard to employee benefits and other government policies that currently favor married workers. Already, 40 percent of the nation's largest 500 companies have reexamined their "marriage-centric" benefit policies. For instance, Bank of America has redefined "family" to include non-traditional household members—such as domestic partners or adult children living at home.[5]

At the same time, many widows and widowers feel that they can't afford to remarry because they will lose health, pension and other benefits tied to their deceased spouses.   19

Ironically, concerns over the state of heterosexual marriage come as more gay couples are forming families by adopting children, and national debate flares over whether same-sex partners should be allowed to wed. While most polls show that roughly two-thirds of Americans oppose same-sex unions, several state courts in recent years have expanded marriage rights for homosexuals—ranging from civil unions now allowed in Vermont to matrimony approved by the Massachusetts Supreme Court in November. In addition, mayors and other public officials in several cities—notably San Francisco and Portland, Ore.—have issued thousands of marriage licenses to gay couples.[6]   20

Social conservatives have responded by proposing an amendment to the U.S. Constitution defining marriage as the union of a man and a woman—effectively banning same-sex marriages. Supporters of the amendment, including President Bush, argue a constitutional amendment is needed to prevent liberal judges and officials from watering down the millennia-old definition of marriage until it loses all meaning and significance.   21

But the amendment's critics, including gay-rights groups and even some conservatives, note that the Constitution is usually changed to expand rights rather than take them away.   22

As the experts debate the future of one of the most important social institutions in human history, here are some of the questions they are asking: 23

Is the Future Bleak for Traditional Marriage?

Nearly half of all American marriages end in divorce, according to the U.S. Census Bureau. Meanwhile, the nation's marriage rate has been steadily dropping, from an annual rate of 9.9 marriages per thousand population in 1987 to 8.4 per thousand in 2001.[7] Today, just over 50 percent of all households are headed by married couples, compared with three-quarters of the same group 40 years ago.   24

25   At the same time, the number of households with unmarried
couples has risen dramatically. In 1977, only 1 million Americans
were cohabiting; today, it's 5 million. The percentage of children
raised in single-parent households also has jumped, tripling in the
last 40 years—from 9.4 percent in 1960 to 28.5 percent in 2002.

26   Some scholars say that while traditional marriage will not disappear, it will never again be the country's pre-eminent social
arrangement. "Ozzie and Harriet are moving out of town, and
they're not coming back," says Stephanie Coontz, a professor of
history at The Evergreen State College in Olympia, Wash., and
author of the upcoming *A History of Marriage.* "Americans now
have too many choices—due to new technologies and economic
and social opportunities—and it would take a level of repression
unacceptable to nearly everyone to force us to begin marrying
and stay married at the same levels we once did."

27   Coontz argues that marriage thrived during more socially
and economically restricted times. "For thousands of years,
marriage has been humanity's most important economic and
social institution," she says. "It gave women economic security
and helped men financially, through dowry payments and
socially by connecting them to another family."

28   However, Coontz continues, the recent expansion of individual wealth and freedom—especially among women—makes
the economic argument for marriage much less compelling.
"We no longer need a spouse for economic security or to [fi-
nancially] take care of us when we get old," she says. "We can
do these things for ourselves now."

29   Northwestern's Kipnis agrees. "Look, marriage has essentially
been an economic institution with some romantic aspects tacked
onto it," she says. "Once you take away the economic need,
marriage becomes different, and for many people it becomes
confining."

30   Indeed, only 38 percent of Americans in first marriages say
that they are happy, Kipnis says, citing a 1999 survey by the
National Marriage Project at Rutgers University.[8] "What does
that say about everyone else?" she asks.

31   Some of the unhappiness may be stoked by a consumer culture that emphasizes choice and happiness, raising unrealistic
expectations, she says. "Our emotional and physical needs have
expanded a lot, and people now expect that the person they are
with is going to meet those needs," Kipnis says. "That makes it
much harder to find someone else they feel they can marry."

32   It also increases the likelihood of divorce, says Diane Sollee,
founder and director of the Coalition for Marriage, Family and
Couples Education, in Washington. "There are a lot of unnecessary divorces because when married people feel unhappy,

they assume that they married the wrong person. So they find someone new, and when that person doesn't make them happy, they move on to the next one."

But supporters of marriage believe that the institution is begin-   33 ning to make a comeback, in part because of the very changes that the pessimists cite. "All of this mobility and freedom also means that we're living in an increasingly impersonal mass society," says William Doherty, director of the Marriage and Family Therapy Program at the University of Minnesota in St. Paul. "Marriage will continue to be important. We will continue to need someone who is permanently and unquestionably in our corner."

Others argue that marriage will survive and thrive because it   34 is still the best way to organize society on a personal level. "People are beginning to see how much we need marriage, because it is the only effective way to raise children," says Tom Minnery, vice president of public policy at Focus on the Family, a Christian-oriented advocacy group in Colorado Springs. "And this isn't something that just religious people are saying; it's accepted by the scientific community too."

There are already signs of a reverse in the trend away from   35 marriage, Minnery says. He points out, for instance, that the annual divorce rate has dropped, from five per 1,000 people in 1982 to four in 2002.[9]

In addition, the upward trend toward working motherhood   36 has halted, Minnery says, noting that the percentage of working mothers (72 percent) has held steady since 1997, after rising dramatically during the previous 20 years.[10]

Optimists also contend that young people today take mar-   37 riage more seriously than people did 20 or 30 years ago. "I actually think the institution of marriage is going to become more stable in the future," Doherty says. "People are becoming more sober and serious about marriage and doing more to prepare themselves for it, like taking marriage-education classes before they wed."

He attributes the trend, in part, to painful memories. "The   38 children of divorce are keen to not make the same mistakes as their parents," he says. "Even those whose parents stayed together feel this way, because they were able to witness the divorce revolution in other families."

"When you look at young people, they're more conservative   39 and religious than their parents," Minnery agrees. "Just like the Baby Boomers rebelled against what their parents did, the children of Baby Boomers are rebelling against their parents and their lifestyle choices."

Finally, marriage optimists say the institution will endure be-   40 cause it fulfills basic human needs. "There's still a great hunger for stable, loving, intimate relationships," Doherty says, "and marriage is still the best way to have them."

Would President Bush's Initiative to Promote Marriage Improve Poor People's Lives?

41   In 2001, President Bush proposed a new initiative to promote marriage for lower-income Americans as part of the reauthorization of the federal government's welfare program. Recently, the president expanded his proposal.

42   Bush's new Healthy Marriage Initiative would provide $1.5 billion over five years in grants to states, local governments and private charities for a variety of activities, including establishing marriage-education programs in schools and community centers and advertising pro-marriage messages. Funds could also be spent to teach marriage skills to people preparing to tie the knot or to mentor troubled married couples.[11]

43   The proposal was included in the massive Welfare Reform Reauthorization bill passed by the House last year. But the measure stalled in the Senate in March after legislators could not agree on several issues unrelated to the marriage proposal.[12] No new date has been set for the Senate to revisit the bill.

44   The University of Minnesota's Doherty says Bush's initiative is "well worth the effort" because research shows that marriage can dramatically improve the physical and emotional health of adults and especially children. "We know that the best way to raise children is in a healthy marriage, and yet our welfare policy hasn't reflected that," he says.

45   Blankenhorn agrees. "We know that in most cases children do better in a home where their biological parents are married," he says. "So we have a real interest in seeing that people with children marry and making those marriages work."

46   But opponents of the initiative contend it will neither be effective nor do much social good.

47   "You can't really push people into a decision this big, absent fraud or coercion," Evergreen State's Coontz says. "This will change a few minds, but not many."

48   Moreover, says Barbara Risman, a sociology professor at North Carolina State University in Raleigh, changing minds in one direction should not be the focus of federal efforts. Instead, she says, the government should better equip people to make their own decisions.

49   "The focus on marriage, as opposed to self-sufficiency, is a negative issue for women," she says. "The government shouldn't

promote marriage. It should promote the ability of anyone to live with the kind of families they want to have."

There are better ways to spend welfare funds, critics like 50
Risman and Coontz add. "No matter what [supporters] say, this is going to divert funds, because at the end of the day you only have so much welfare money to spend," Coontz says. "And we have such pressing needs in child care, health and in so many other areas."

In fact, opponents say, marriage promotion could do more 51
harm than good, in part because the pool of good husbands is likely to be much smaller among the group the administration would target—poor women. "Poor people have a lot of barriers in their lives, like economic instability, substance abuse and a history of being on the giving or receiving end of domestic violence," says Lisalyn Jacobs, vice president for government relations at the National Organization for Women's (NOW) Legal Defense and Education Fund, a women's-rights group. "It may not be such a great idea to get or keep some of these people together, because they're not very stable."

Marriage also might not be such a good idea if the potential 52
marriage partner is abusive, she adds. "Sixty percent of all women on welfare have been victims of domestic violence at some time in their lives," Jacobs says, "so encouraging people to stay together might put many of them at greater risk of injury."

But Sollee disputes that argument. "Women generally get 53
beat up when they're single or in a cohabiting relationship," she says, pointing to the National Crime Victimization Survey, which shows that two-thirds of the violence against women is not committed by husbands but by casual dating partners.[13] "Marriage stabilizes relationships and makes domestic violence much less likely."

Indeed, the idea that those on welfare are different with regard 54
to marriage is "insulting to the poor," she says. "Poor people pair up for the same reason everyone else does: Because they're human, and they want to form love relationships. Given that, we need to give them the skills needed to make the right choices."

Should the Constitution Be Amended to Define Marriage as the Union of a Man and a Woman?

After months of pressure from religious and conservative 55
groups alarmed at what they saw as a rising tide of same-sex marriages, President Bush on Feb. 24 publicly endorsed amending the U.S. Constitution to define marriage as the

union of a man and a woman. Bush said the decision had been forced upon him by "activist judges and local officials" in Massachusetts, California and elsewhere, who had made "an aggressive attempt" to redefine marriage.

56   "On a matter of such importance, the voice of the people must be heard," the president said at a White House press conference announcing his support for the amendment. "Activist courts have left the people with one recourse. If we are to prevent the meaning of marriage from being changed forever, our nation must enact a constitutional amendment to protect marriage in America."

57   The federal government had addressed the issue in 1996, when Congress passed, and President Bill Clinton signed, the Defense of Marriage Act, which defined marriage as being between a man and a woman for purposes of federal law. It explicitly prevents any jurisdiction from being forced to accept another's definition of marriage. In other words, if Massachusetts legalizes same-sex unions and marries two men, New York is not required to acknowledge the marriage if the couple subsequently moves there.

58   But because the Constitution's Full Faith and Credit Clause requires each state to recognize the lawful actions of other states, Bush and gay marriage opponents say federal courts might overrule the law and require other states to recognize gay marriages performed outside their jurisdiction.

59   The amendment, proposed by Colorado Republicans Sen. Wayne Allard and Rep. Marilyn M. Musgrave, would still allow states to pass civil-union or domestic-partnership laws that could grant same-sex partners and others the same rights as married couples. But marriage would be strictly limited to heterosexual couples.

60   Gay-rights activists, civil-liberties organizations and even some conservatives and libertarians oppose the amendment, albeit for different reasons.

61   "It's a perversion to use our founding document to discriminate against a group of people when it has traditionally been used to expand liberties and rights," says Kevin M. Cathcart, executive director of the Lambda Legal Defense and Education Fund, a gay-rights group in New York. "It's ironic that on the 50th anniversary of the *Brown v. Board of Education* decision, which struck down the doctrine of 'separate but equal,' we're on the verge of writing it back into the Constitution."[14]

62   Other opponents of gay marriage say a Constitutional amendment is heavy-handed and unnecessary. Former Rep. Bob Barr, who as a conservative Republican from Georgia helped write the 1996 Defense of Marriage Act, calls the

amendment an unwarranted intrusion into an area traditionally left to the states.

"Changing the Constitution is just unnecessary—even after   63
the Massachusetts decision, the San Francisco circus and the
Oregon licenses," Barr told the House Judiciary Subcommittee
on the Constitution on March 30. "We have a perfectly good law
on the books that defends marriage on the federal level and protects states from having to dilute their definitions of marriage by
recognizing other states' same-sex marriage licenses."[15]

Opponents also call the administration's claim that the amend-   64
ment process was "forced" on them by activist judges and mayors a cynical election-year ploy. "I don't think this is really about
gay marriage at all, but is a distraction meant to focus attention
away from the [Iraq] war and the deficit and all of the other
problems this administration is dealing with," Cathcart says.

Moreover, by trying to amend the Constitution, they say, con-   65
servatives are trying to cut off the emerging national debate on
same-sex marriage. "You know, we're really just beginning this
debate all over the country, and already they want to amend
the Constitution," Cathcart says. "They accuse liberals of trying to use the courts and local officials to circumvent debate,
but that's actually what they're doing."

"Amending the Constitution is something that you tradition-   66
ally do when you've run out of remedies," agrees NOW's
Jacobs. "It seems to me that we've only just begun to try to
work this one out."

But supporters point out that to become law any constitu-   67
tional amendment must first win the support of two-thirds of
Congress and three-quarters of the nation's state legislatures.
"This would be a wonderful way to debate the issue, given all
of the hurdles that have to be jumped before it became part of
the Constitution," says Minnery of Focus on the Family. "There
would be a debate in Congress and then in every state legislature in the country. That seems pretty thorough to me."

And while proponents admit the amendment process has   68
traditionally been about expanding rights, they argue that gay
marriage presents a unique challenge to American society that
calls for a unique solution.

"Our founding documents, like the Declaration of Indepen-   69
dence, tell us that our rights have come from our creator or,
to put it another way, they are part of natural law," says Ed
Vitagliano, pastor of Harvester Church in Pontotoc, Miss., and a
spokesman for the conservative American Family Association.
"When you talk about redefining marriage, you're really talking
about an overthrow of this natural order or natural law, because
marriage is something that predates government. So this is a big

deal, a once-in-a-lifetime debate about whether to overturn the natural order upon which our rights are based. That requires a big response."

Changes in Marriage

70   The 20th century witnessed unparalleled changes in married life, at least in rich countries. In the United States, Europe and elsewhere, a trend away from obligations to parents, community and other forms of collective responsibility gave way to more of an emphasis on individual choice. People had more freedom to decide whom to marry and whether to stay in that marriage.

71   Many scholars predict even more dramatic changes for married life in the coming decades. "People will view their marriages more and more as a private relationship, rather than as a public institution as they did in the past," Blankenhorn of the Institute for American Values says. "You already see this happening, as, for instance, many couples no longer speak the traditional vows but write their own."

72   Blankenhorn contends that the "privatization of marriage," as he calls it, will make marriages less stable, because the built-in guideposts and expectations that once accompanied married life are disappearing. "Without a set of public expectations—like permanence or total commitment to each other—people are more on their own, and that's more risky."

73   The University of Minnesota's Doherty agrees that marriage will continue shifting from a public to a private institution. But he sees a positive side to such a change: Future marriages, to some degree, will be on a more equal footing. "Men will look more and more at a woman's earning potential when they decide on a mate and be less interested in women as homemakers," Doherty says. "They're going to want someone who can bring in as much as they do or just a little less. This will bring a new level of gender equality to marriage."

74   Still, Doherty adds, husbands will continue to want to make at least as much as their wives. "Men are hardwired by evolution to be 'providers,' and this is still backed up by our culture," he says. "So a man who makes less than his wife will still feel 'inadequate.'"

75   However, some scholars see few, if any, additional changes occurring in married life—at least in the United States. "We've had so much happen in the last 100 years that I think we're entering a period of stability," North Carolina State's Risman

says. "We're going to spend the next 50 years absorbing the changes of the last 50."

Risman says several trends bolster her belief. "The divorce rate has stabilized over the last few decades, which to me is a sign that the rate of change has slowed significantly." Moreover, things don't seem to be changing all that much for women at home, she points out.

"Housework remains women's work, and there is no sign that that is changing." The fact that the number of women staying at home with their children and putting off a career is holding steady is a sign that "women still don't think they can have it all, because their husbands still haven't been told that they can't have it all."

Evergreen State's Coontz agrees that marriage won't change too much in the immediate future, but neither will it remain static. "We're going to spend the next few decades sorting through the enormous changes we've seen in marriage."

In particular, she says, couples will have to work through the consequences of gender equality in marriage. "Men can no longer count on being the boss anymore," she says. "So, we're going to see more efforts to develop new habits, new emotional expectations, new time schedules and new negotiating skills as we sort out the details of this new reality."

NOTES

1. Figures cited at www.census.gov/population/www/socdemo/ms-la.html.
2. For background, see David Masci, "Children and Divorce," *The CQ Researcher*, Jan. 19, 2001, pp. 25–40.
3. Figures cited in *National Vital Statistics Reports*, Centers for Disease Control and Prevention, Vol. 52, No. 10, Dec. 17, 2003, p. 1.
4. Amy Fagen, "Permanent Tax Cut OK'd," *The Washington Times*, April 29, 2004, p. A1.
5. Michelle Conlin, "Unmarried America," *Business Week*, Oct. 20, 2003, p. 106.
6. For background, see Kenneth Jost, "Gay Marriage," *The CQ Researcher*, Sept. 5, 2003, 721–748.
7. Figures cited in *National Vital Statistics Reports*, Centers for Disease Control and Prevention, Vol. 50, No. 14, Sept. 11, 2002, p. 1.
8. Barbara Defoe Whitehead and David Popenoe, "The State of Our Unions: The Social Health of Marriage in America," National Marriage Project, Rutgers University, 1999.
9. Figures cited in *National Vital Statistics Reports, op. cit.*, and "U.S. Per Capita Divorce Rates Every Year: 1940–1990," Centers for Disease Control and Prevention, www.cdc.gov/nchs/fastats/pdf/43-9s-t1.pdf.
10. Figures cited in Claudia Wallis, "The Case for Staying at Home," *Time*, March 22, 2004, p. 51. See also Sarah Glazer, "Mothers' Movement," *The CQ Researcher*, April 4, 2003, pp. 297–320.
11. Amy Fagen, "Senate Mulls Pro-Marriage Funds," *The Washington Times*, April 1, 2004, p. A5.

76

77

78

79

12. Bill Swindell, "Welfare Reauthorization Becomes Another Casualty in Congress' Partisan Crossfire," *CQ Weekly*, April 3, 2004, p. 805.
13. Figures cited in Ronet Bachman and Linda E. Saltzman, "Violence Against Women: Estimates from the Redesigned Survey," *National Crime Victimization Survey Special Report*, August 1996, p. 4.
14. For background, see Kenneth Jost, "School Desegregation," *The CQ Researcher*, April 23, 2004, pp. 345–372.
15. Barr's testimony available at www.house.gov/judiciary/barr033004.pdf.

Margaret Mead

CAN MARRIAGE
BE FOR LIFE?

Margaret Mead, who died in 1978, was a well-known anthropologist. The daughter of two social scientists, she was one of the first anthropologists to conduct psychologically oriented research—an instrumental moment in pushing the social science toward interdisciplinary work. She specialized in (among other things) what she called "conditioning of the social personalities of both sexes." Mead did field research in the South Pacific and lectured widely in the United States and elsewhere, becoming a public as well as an academic figure. (In September 1977, Mead was called as a witness before the Select Committee on Aging of the House of Representatives, discussing age stereotyping and television.) Though her writing includes a wide variety of topics, she was a consistent defender of family and children. In the excerpt from her 1970 book, Male and Female, *Mead discusses the impact of the wider availability of divorce on marriage mores. Consider how much of what Mead suggests here has played itself out in the more than three decades since this piece was written.*

1   An ethics that is peculiarly American has arisen in the United States, to support a marriage-and-divorce code of great contradictoriness. Young people are still encouraged to marry as if they could count on marriage's being for life, and at the same time they are absorbing a knowledge of the great frequency of

divorce and the ethics that may later enjoin divorce upon them. There has been much inveighing from the pulpit and the bench which assumes that all those who get divorces are self-ish, self-indulgent creatures. But as long as divorce was limited to the selfish and the self-indulgent, there were very few di-vorces, and it was safe to encourage young people to think of divorce as something that could happen to other people, but not to them. Divorce has now been so absorbed into our ethics that husbands or wives lie sleepless and torn, wondering, "Ought I to get a divorce? Would she be happier with some-body else? Would he develop more with somebody else? Am I spoiling his life? Am I spoiling her life? Isn't it wrong to stay with some one out of mere loyalty? What will happen to the children if this goes on? Isn't it bad for the children to live in a home with this much friction?" Not only the possibility that any marriage except the marriage where *both* partners are deeply committed to some religious orthodoxy may end in di-vorce, but the phrasing of divorce as something that at least one of the partners in an imperfect marriage *ought* to get, is permeating the whole country, altering our expectations, mak-ing marriage many times more difficult.

It is difficult on two counts: because the expectation of per-manency is still great enough to brand every impermanence as a failure, if not a sin, and also because to all the other insecuri-ties of American life insecurity about marriage is added. In the United States, where all status is relative, where all jobs can be lost, where men are judged by how much they continue to ad-vance, sometimes a little by how far they have advanced, but never simply by where they are—here marriage in former gen-erations offered one refuge from this eternal uncertainty, this endless incitement to anxious effort. Whether a man suc-ceeded or failed, his wife was there, and whether a woman was an invalid, a failure at housekeeping, an incompetent mother, or a paragon, her husband was there—in most cases, in enough cases to reassure every healthy person that here was one harbour in which his ship could ride at anchor where the winds of success and failure blew less harshly. It was safe to be romantic when there was no real danger that new romances could tempt you away. 2

> When I should be her lover forever and a day,
> And she my faithful sweetheart till the golden hair was gray;
> And we should be so happy that when either's lips were
>   dumb
> They would not smile in Heaven till the other's kiss had
>   come.

3   These were verses that could be appropriately written into a
poem about one's wife entitled "That Old Sweetheart of Mine."
The romance need not be scrutinized too carefully where there
was no other choice; after the altar it was never again put to
the test.

4   But to-day, with the growing recognition that divorce may
come to any marriage, no matter how devoted, how conscientious, how much in love each spouse originally was, a marriage
is something that has to be worked at each day. As the husband
has to face the possibility of losing his job, so also the wife has
to face the possibility of losing hers, of finding herself compan-
ionless, out of the job she chose, often with small children to
care for alone. Both husband and wife face the need to re-
choose each other, to reassert and re-establish the never permanent claim of one upon the other's choice. The wife in
curl-papers is replaced by a wife who puts on lip-stick before she
wakes her husband, and the husband with a wandering eye
finds that his eye wanders less happily because at any moment it
may light on some one whom he will choose instead of his wife.
As it is her obligation to make herself continuingly desirable, so
it is his obligation not to put himself in positions where other
women may become desirable to him. This means never going
out in mixed company without his wife. It means that all casual
flirtations take on a menacing quality that Europeans newly
come to America find it very difficult to understand. Where
there is freedom to divorce, there is less freedom for either casual relationships or passionate extramarital love of any sort.

5   Yet the implied expectation of permanency, still based of
course on statistics—for frequent as divorces are in some age-
groups, most marriages are still permanent marriages—not
only does not protect the new marriage, it actually compromises it. For American behaviour in marriage, the behaviour
that young people have learned in their own homes, from their
own and their friends' parents, is behaviour that depends on
the finality of marriage. Quarrelling, sulking, neglectfulness,
stubbornness, could be indulged very differently within a
frame that could not be broken. But now over every quarrel
hang the questions: "Do you want a divorce? Do I want a divorce? Does she want a divorce? Will that be the end of this? Is
that where we are going?"

6   There is no reason why we cannot develop manners and customs appropriate to the greater fragility of marriage in the
United States; they are very badly needed. For it seems unlikely
that the other solution, tightening up on divorce laws, is likely to
occur. Once freedom of divorce has become part of our ethics,
as it has for many segments of the United States, simply going

back becomes a genuinely retrogressive step. The very reasons that made divorce necessary, the enormous heterogeneity of our population and the great chances of maladjustment under our system of free marital choice, would remain. Rather the more likely development would seem to be forward to a new pattern of behaviour that fits the new conditions. And there are signs that such a new pattern of behaviour is developing.

In a pattern for marriage which accepts the fact that marriage *may* be for life, *can* be for life, but also may not be, it is possible to set to work to find ways of establishing that permanence which is most congruent with bringing up children, who are defined as immature until the early twenties. Although it is possible to argue and bring together much evidence that children are more damaged when they live in an unhappy home, resonant with the spoken and unspoken resentments of at least one parent, than when they live in a better relationship with just one parent, it is not possible at present to claim that children are better-off in a broken than in a whole home. One of the most important learnings for every human child is how to be a full member of its own sex and at the same time fully related to the opposite sex. This is not an easy learning, it requires the continuing presence of a father and a mother to give it reality. If the child is to know how to hold a baby in its arms, it must be held, and if it is to know how a member of the opposite sex holds a child, it must be held by both parents. It must watch both parents meet its springing impulse, watch both parents discipline and mould their own impulses so that the child is protected, and at adolescence be set free by both parents to go out into the world. Ideally, both parents will be there to bless and define the marriage, and to help their grown children assume the parental role by the way in which they take their grandparenthood. This is the way is which human lives have been given full stature, and as yet we know no better way. 7

We do know, however, that this continuity is of a different order in a changing society than it is in a stable one, and in a heterogeneous society than it is in a homogeneous one. In a changing society like ours the models can never be so perfect, and they must be far less detailed. Daughters do not learn to make the bread that mother used to make; at best they learn to enjoy feeding their families, with different food, differently prepared. The picture of how one will look and feel, act and think, at seventy cannot be filled in by concrete details of Grandmother's gold-rimmed spectacles and Grandfather's tapping cane. At best something of the vigour with which they set out on journeys at eighty, or the placidity with which they sit in the sun and remember the hymns they sang in childhood, may become part of the 8 child's faith in the life that he will live. There is need of developing forms of education, forms that supplement the particularness of the single family, that will make it possible for the child to learn ways of feeling and acting which can be used in a world yet unborn, a world that the imagination of the elders is powerless to anticipate. The world will be the poorer if children learn patterns of behaviour so concrete and particular that twenty years later, as adults, they must wander homeless in nostalgia for a lost way of life. We now know a great deal about how to do this, how a nursery-school can translate and broaden the child's own home experience and make the experience of each child available to the others, how parental precepts can shift from the sureness of "Never eat on the street," "Never ring a door-bell more than three times," "Never accept a present from a man that you can't use up at once or return," to a different kind of teaching which includes the recognition that eating must always be disciplined to make it possible for people to enjoy eating in each other's company, that social fictions are useful and worth respecting, and that relations between the sexes need some kind of patterning to protect those who participate in them. But it is a complicated thing to learn how to transmit a pattern in such a way that the next generation may have its protection without making that protection a prison, may have its delicate discriminations without the inability to make new discriminations, may in fact neither simply repeat nor complete it, but develop a new pattern of their own. The casualties are bound to be greater than in those old traditional societies where five generations played hide-and-seek under the same apple-tree, were born and died in the same high bed.

9   One of the particular characteristics of a changing society is the possibility of deferred maturity, of later and later shifts in the lives of the most complex, the most flexible individuals. In very simple societies children have completed their acceptance of themselves and their rôles in life by the time they are six or seven, and then must simply wait for physical maturity to assume a complete rôle. But in most societies, adolescence is a period of re-examination, and possible re-orientation of the self towards the expressed goals of society. In cultures like ours, there may be a second or a third adolescence, and the most complex, the most sensitive, may die still questing, still capable of change, starting like Franz Boas at seventy-seven to re-read the folk-lore of the world in the light of new theoretical developments. No one who values civilization and realizes how men have woven the fabric of their lives from their own imaginations as they played over the memory of the past, the experience of the present, and the hope of the future, can count this postponed maturity, this possibility of recurrent adolescent crises and change of life-plan, as anything but gain.

But a world in which people may reorient their whole lives at   10
forty or fifty is a world in which marriage for life becomes much
more difficult. Each spouse is given the right to and the means
for growth. Either may discover a hidden talent and begin to
develop it, or repudiate a paralyzing neurotic trend and begin
anew. Ever since women have been educated, marriages have
been endangered by the possible development or failure to
develop of both husbands and wives. "He outgrew her," or less
common but with increasing frequency, "She outgrew him." In a
society where mobility is enjoined on every citizen and each
man should die a long distance from the class he comes from—
or devote his life to preventing downward movement, the only
recourse left to the upper class—the danger that spouses will get
out of step is very great. To all the other exorbitant requirements
for a perfect mate, chosen from all the world yet in all things like
the self, or complementary on a trivial basis, must be added "capacity to grow." Arapesh parents perform anxious little magical
tricks to keep the girl who grows too fast smaller than her young
husband, lest the marriage be ruined by the disparity. But
American lovers have neither divinatory methods nor precautionary magic to ensure them that they will grow and change in
step. Only the recognition of the problem itself can help to solve
it, to make young people pause in their choices as they evaluate
whether he or she will make a life companion, add to their other
criteria "capacity to grow at something like the same rate." And
they need to be able to treat failures to grow as tragedies, but
not as personal betrayals. Some day a discovered and intractable discrepancy in rate of growth may seem a really legitimate reason for divorce, and one that both couples can accept
as simply as do those peoples who accept childlessness as a reason for ending a marriage. Once there is recognition that change
in rate of growth is simply a function of living in a complex
modern world, then the marriage that is developing a dangerous
discrepancy may be given professional help, just as the childless
may seek the advice of the sterility clinic. And as in the sterility
clinic, some of those who seek for help can and some cannot be
helped. But the whole way of looking at life will be changed. For
thousands of years men and women have blamed ghosts and
demons, witches and elves and the sorcery of the next tribe, and
most of all each other's inferiority or malice, for childlessness.
But to-day it is possible to seek expert help from physiologist or
psychiatrist, and the needless tragedies can be averted, and
those which cannot be averted can be accepted gently by both.
For just as there is no good marriage in which each does not
wholly choose it, so there is no good divorce that is not chosen
by both partners. Among the Negrito people of the Philippines,
where vigorous little men and women obey their chief implicitly

in a society that seems rather like the childhood of the world, when both partners agree on a divorce it is granted at once; there simply is no marriage. The acceptance of a religious faith that includes the ideal and the promise of indissoluble marriage carries with it dignity for man. But a civil marriage that marries any pair who choose each other and can show no legal impediment, and then will not permit them to choose to end that choice, is a travesty of all the values of human dignity. There are at best something like 71,000,000 church members in the United States, and many of these are no longer guaranteed by their faith that they will be able to stay married for life. For the other 61,000,000 a pattern must be found that will make it possible for them to treat divorce when it does occur with dignity and regret, and so make it possible for each married pair to work openly to keep and keep on keeping their marriages safe.

11   There are signs that a vigorous younger generation are doing just that. They are learning to handle the unprecedented and contradictory premarital freedom that they have been accorded by society so that they know the rules and can keep them. They are learning to guard their expectancies of falling in love so that the chance-met girl in the railroad station who becomes one's fate will stay more in the movies, where she belongs, and less in real life, where she is more likely to be a disappointment. They are developing new patterns of learning to know each other, to replace the outmoded long engagement, with its stylizations that now seem artificial and lacking in sincerity. For the old theory that a girl would somehow become "awakened after marriage," and the later compensatory demand for trial marriages, new methods of getting acquainted and demonstrating confidence are being worked out. These include more stages of partial commitment, the slow involvement of more friends in the possible marriage, provision for more retreats with unimpaired dignity for each partner. They are making more realistic demands on the personality of the future partner, partly under a sobering recognition of how many marriages in the war generation have gone to pieces under pressures of absence, housing, and so on, revealing a lack of what it takes to stay married in the United States to-day.* Meanwhile the society as a whole is becoming more conscious of the terrific strains that have been placed on marriages, and of the need for a variety of new measures, pre-marriage counselling, marriage counselling, nursery-schools, housekeeping services, and so on, to reduce the strain on each young couple asked to build single-handed a whole

---

*Postwar divorces in 1945 were one for every three marriages, and will probably, according to William F. Ogburn, drop to one for every five or six.

way of life in a world in which neither they, nor any one else, have ever lived. For the careful protective care that kinship groups and tribal elders, family councils and parents, once gave young people, wider social institutions that will serve the same function in a new fashion are springing into being, slowly, and against great resistance, but surely.

Meanwhile, young married people seem to be, if anything, more anxious to have children than they have been in our immediate past. Children are regarded neither as an inescapable part of life nor as a penalty of marriage, but as a value that can be consciously sought and worked for, a value that makes life worth living. The demand for symmetry between husband and wife is of course being felt here, the demand that each share in the choice made, in the planning for the children, and in the enjoyment and care of the children. As working-hours are cut down and a free Saturday becomes an American institution, many of the evils of the household that lived in a suburb for the children's sake, and so Father never got home in time to see the children, and was too tired on Sunday, can be overcome. Two free days out of seven provide enough leeway so that even very tired, overstrained men can first relax, loosen their belts and kick off their shoes, and when rested, be ready to start something sizable with the children. The definition of children as joy rather than as duty is spreading rapidly, though with all the hazards that a duty-ridden people will then ask, "Am I enjoying my children enough?" and "Are my children really enjoying me?" 12

But whatever the possibilities for anxiety, marriage that is a responsible, chosen, and joyous way of life seems a more possible goal for the descendants of Puritans than the mere unhappy reaction to a loss of orthodoxy in which duty to some unnamed entity pathetically and inappropriately replaces a duty to God. To the extent that all marriage and all parenthood become more responsible, the religiously orthodox will also be safer, less threatened by the disintegrating standards of a society where so many live without even missing religion. 13

But if such responsible new patterns are to develop, then it is crucial that in theory, and in practice, the fact that divorce may come to any marriage—except where the religion of both partners forbids it—must be faced. The stigma of failure and of sin must be removed, the indignities of divorce laws that demand either accusation or collusion must be done away with. Social practices must be developed so that the end of a marriage is announced, soberly, responsibly, just as the beginning of a marriage is published to the world. This means a sort of coming-to-terms with sorrow that Americans have been finding difficult to practice in regard to death as well as divorce. We jubilate over 14 birth and dance at weddings, but more and more hustle the dead off the scene without ceremony, without an opportunity for young and old to realize that death is as much a fact of life as is birth. A world in which one really says, "Let the dead bury the dead," is an ugly world in which corpses lie rotting on the streets and the living have to flee for their lives. A dead marriage is sad, a marriage that is broken by death is also infinitely sad (in 1947 of every 100 families, 12 were broken, 9 by widowhood, 1 by divorce and 2 by separation). Both are part of life. If we recognize that we live in a society where marriage is terminable, and in some cases should be terminable, we can then give every newly married pair, and every old married pair, a chance to recognize the hazards they face, and to make genuine efforts to survive them. Marriage was once a harbour from which some marriages set sail safely, some lay in it and rotted, some were simply wrecked on the shore. It is now a voyage in the open sea, with no harbour at any point, and each partner is committed to vigilance and deep concern if the ship is to sail at all. Each form of marriage can be dignified and rewarding, if men choose to make it so.

15   As long as divorce is something disgraceful, for which however no one is punished, something to be hidden and yet something available to any one, we may expect an increasing number of irresponsible marriages in which one or both partners simply say, "Oh well, if it doesn't work, we'll get a divorce." From such an attitude, many divorces are the expected crop. But if young people can say instead, "Knowing every hazard, we will work to keep our marriage," then the number of irresponsible marriages and irresponsible divorces may begin to fall. But society must recognize and honour those who try again, recognize the belief in marriage so well summed up in the movie title *This Time, for Keeps*.

Steven L. Nock

THE PROBLEM
WITH MARRIAGE

Steven L. Nock teaches sociology at the University of Virginia. His special area of interest is the family, and he has written widely on the subject—as for example in his recent book

*Marriage in Men's Lives and "The Social Cost of Dein-
stitutionalizing Marriage," in Revitalizing the Institution of
Marriage for the Twenty-First Century (2002). The following
essay by Nock appeared in 1999 in Society, a magazine devoted to social issues (broadly considered), along with several
other articles that describe a "moral crisis" in America associated with the decline of the family. Together the contributors
represented The Council on Civil Society (CCS), a nonpartisan
group of social scientists jointly sponsored by the Institute
for American Values and the University of Chicago Divinity
School. CCS is committed to the health of America's civic institutions and concerned about challenges to the health of the
family. In 1999 the group (which includes Jean Bethke
Elshtain, Cornel West, and Senator Joseph Lieberman) issued
a formal Call to Civil Society, which called attention to a range
of social ills related to families and children.*

A Call to Civil Society warns that the institutions most critical   1
to democratic society are in decline. "What ails our democracy
is not simply the loss of certain organizational forms, but also
the loss of certain organizing ideals—moral ideals that authorize our civic creed, but do not derive from it. At the end of this
century, our most important challenge is to strengthen the
moral habits and ways of living that make democracy possible." I suggest that American institutions have traditionally been
organized around gender and that the loss of this organizing
principle explains many of the trends discussed in the report.
Specifically, the continued centrality of gender in marriage—
and its growing irrelevance everywhere else—helps explain
many contemporary family problems. The solution is to restore
marriage to a privileged status from which both spouses gain
regardless of gender.

The family trends we are now seeing reflect a conflict between   2
the ideals central to marriage and those that define almost all
other institutions. Growing numbers of Americans reject the
idea that adults should be treated differently based on their gender. But it is difficult to create a new model of marriage based
on such a premise. For many people, assumptions about gender
equality conflict with the reality of their marriages. It may
hardly matter if one is male or female in college, on the job, at
church, in the voting booth, or almost anywhere else in public.
But it surely matters in marriage. The family, in short, is still
organized around gender while virtually nothing else is.
Alternatively, marriage has not been redefined to accommodate
the changes in male–female relations that have occurred

elsewhere. This, I believe, is the driving force behind many of the problematic trends identified in *A Call to Civil Society*.

3   Stable marriages are forged of extensive dependencies. Yet trends toward gender equality and independence have made the traditional basis of economic dependency in marriage increasingly problematic. The challenge is to reinvent marriage as an institution based on dependency that is not automatically related to gender. Both partners, that is, must gain significantly from their union, and both must face high exit costs for ending it.

4   Despite dramatic changes in law and public policy that have erased (or minimized) distinctions between men and women, married life has changed more slowly and subtly. In the last four decades, the percentage of married women in the paid labor force increased from 32 percent to 59 percent, and the number of hours that wives commit to paid labor increased apace. While men do not appear to be doing much more housework today than they did two decades ago, women are doing less in response to their commitments to paid labor. Women did 2.5 times as much household labor as their husbands in 1975. By 1987, the ratio was 1.9. Wives' share of total (reported) household income increased marginally, from 35 percent in 1975–1980 to 38 percent in 1986–1991. In such small ways, husbands and wives are increasingly similar. Still, marriages are hardly genderless arrangements. My research for *Marriage in Men's Lives* showed that most marriages in America resemble a traditional model, with husbands as heads of households, and wives who do most of the housework and child care. Given the pace at which gender distinctions have been, or are being, eliminated from laws, work, school, religion, politics, and other institutions, the family appears to be curiously out of step.

5   One reason gender is still a central motif in marriage is because masculinity (and possibly, femininity) are defined by, and displayed in marriage. As the title of Sara Berk's book proclaimed, the family is *The Gender Factory*. Consider the consequences of unemployment for husbands. If spouses were economically rational, then the unemployed (or lower-paid) partner would assume responsibility for housework. Sociologist Julie Brines found just the opposite. After a few months of unemployment, husbands actually *reduced* their housework efforts. The reason is that housework is much more than an economic matter. It is also symbolic. "Men's" work means providing for the family and being a "breadwinner," whereas "women's" work means caring for the home and children. Such assumptions are part of our cultural beliefs. Doing housework, earning a living, providing for the family, and caring for children are ways of demonstrating masculinity or femininity. When

wives are economically dependent on their husbands, doing housework is consistent with traditional assumptions about marriage. Such women conform to cultural understandings about what it means to be a wife, or a woman. However, a dependent husband departs from customary assumptions about marriage and men. Were he to respond by doing more housework, his deviance would be even greater. Marriage is still the venue in which masculinity and femininity are displayed.

The husband and wife who construct a new model of marriage that doesn't include gender as a primary organizing principle will face challenges. The husband who decides to be the primary child-care provider or the wife who elects to be the sole wage earner will find these unusual marital roles difficult but not impossible to sustain. Relationships with parents may be awkward. Friends may struggle to understand the arrangement if it differs from their own. Employers may also find such an arrangement difficult to understand and accept. Yet as difficult as it may be to forge a new model of marriage, it seems certain that some change is necessary if marriage is to endure. 6

The title of Goldscheider and Waite's recent book asks a stark question: *New Families, or No Families?* In "new" families, husbands and wives will share family economic responsibilities *and* domestic tasks equitably. The alternative, according to these authors, is "no" families. Quite simply, marriage must be redefined to reflect the greater gender equality found everywhere else, or women will not marry. Or those who do will face increasing difficulties reconciling their public and private lives. Indeed, young women today value marriage less than young men do. Three in four (75 percent) never-married men under age 30 described getting married as important for their lives in 1993. A smaller percentage (66 percent) of comparable women replied that way (1993 General Social Survey). 7

Research confirms that most women who marry today desire marriages that differ importantly from those of their grandmothers because women's lives have changed in so many other ways in recent decades. However, though the options available to women have expanded in other respects, the basic pattern of marriage is pretty much the same as it has been for decades. The revolution in gender has not yet touched women's marriages. Part of the reason is that men have been excluded from the gender revolution. While almost any young woman today will notice enormous differences between her life options and those of her great-grandmother, the differences between men and their great-grandfathers are minimal, at most. The script for men in America has not changed. In short, despite enormous changes in what it means to be a woman, 8 marriage does not yet incorporate those changes. Neither men nor women have yet figured out how to fashion "new" families.

9 Many of our problems are better seen as the result of institutional change than of individual moral decline. The *personal problems* that lead to family decline are also legitimate *public issues*. Institutions like the family are bigger than any individual. So when large numbers of people create new patterns of family life, we should consider the collective forces behind such novel arrangements. And if some of those innovations are harmful to adults or children, fixing them will require more than a call for stronger moral habits (though there is certainly nothing wrong with such advice). Fixing them will require restructuring some basic social arrangements.

10 Since *A Call to Civil Society* focuses on *institutional* decline, I want to consider the meaning of an institution. A society is a cluster of social institutions, and institutions are clusters of *shared* ideals. Only when people agree about how some core dimension of life should be organized is there a social institution. The family is a good example.

11 Although individual families differ in detail, collectively they share common features as a result of common problems and tested solutions. In resolving and coping with the routine challenges of family life such as child care, the division of household labor, or relations with relatives, individuals draw on conventional (i.e., shared) ideals. As disparate individuals rely on shared answers to questions about family life, typical patterns emerge that are understood and recognized—mother, father, son, daughter, husband, and wife. To the extent that such ideals are widely shared, the family is a social institution. Were individuals left completely on their own to resolve the recurring problems of domestic life, there would be much less similarity among families. Alternatively, were there no conventional values and beliefs to rely on, the family would not be an institution. The family, as an institution, differs in *form* from one culture to another. Yet everywhere, it consists of patterned (i.e., shared and accepted) solutions to the problems of dependency (of partners, children, and the elderly).

12 The problem today is that an assumption that was once central to all social institutions is no longer so compelling. Beliefs about gender have long been an organizing template that guided behaviors in both public and private. Yet while gender has become increasingly unimportant in public, neither women nor men have fully adjusted to these changes in their private married lives. If men and women are supposed to be indistinguishable at work or school, does the same standard apply in marriage? Americans have not yet agreed about the

answer. As a result, the institution of the family (the assumptions about how married life should be organized) no longer complements other social arrangements. Increasingly, the family is viewed as a problem for people because the assumptions about domestic life no longer agree with those in other settings. When husbands and wives return home from work, school, church, or synagogue, they often struggle with traditional ideals about marriage that do not apply in these other areas. No matter what her responsibilities at work, the married mother will probably be responsible for almost all child care at home, for instance. Responsibilities at work are unlikely to be dictated by whether the person is male or female. But responsibilities at home are. This contradiction helps explain the trends identified in *A Call to Civil Society*.

High rates of divorce, cohabitation, and unmarried child-   13
bearing are documented facts, and all have clearly increased this century. Do such trends suggest that the family is losing its institutional anchor? In fact, the traditional arrangements that constitute the family are less compelling today than in the past. In this respect, the institution of the family is weaker. To understand why, I now consider the traditional basis of the family, legal marriage.

Legal Marriage and the Institution of the Family

The extent to which the family *based on legal marriage* is an in-   14
stitution becomes obvious when one considers an alternative way that adult couples arrange their intimate lives. Certainly there is no reason to believe that two people cannot enjoy a harmonious and happy life without the benefit of legal marriage. In fact, growing numbers of Americans appear to believe that unmarried *cohabitation* offers something that marriage does not. One thing that cohabitation offers is freedom from the rules of marriage because there are no widely accepted and approved boundaries around cohabitation. Unmarried partners have tremendous freedom to decide how they will arrange their legal and other relationships. Each partner must decide how to deal with the other's parents, for example. Parents, in turn, may define a cohabiting child's relationship as different from a married child's. Couples must decide whether vacations will be taken together or separately. Money may be pooled or held in separate accounts. If children are born, cohabiting parents must decide about the appropriate (non-legal) obligations each incurred as a result. In such small ways, cohabiting couples and their associates must *create* a relationship. Married

couples may also face decisions about some of these matters. However, married spouses have a pattern to follow. For most matters of domestic life, marriage supplies a template. This is what cohabiting couples lack. They are exempt from the vast range of marriage norms and laws in our society.

15   A man can say to his wife: "I am your husband. You are my wife. I am expected to do certain things for you, and you likewise. We have pledged our faithfulness. We have promised to care for one another in times of sickness. We have sworn to forego others. We have made a commitment to our children. We have a responsibility and obligation to our close relatives, as they have to us." These statements are not simply personal pledges. They are also enforceable. Others will expect these things of the couple. Laws, religion, and customs bolster this contract. When this man says to someone, "I would like you to meet my wife," this simple declaration says a great deal.

16   Compare this to an unmarried couple living happily together. What, if any, are the conventional assumptions that can be made? What are the limits to behavior? To whom is each obligated? Who can this couple count on for help in times of need? And how do you complete this introduction of one's cohabiting partner: "I would like you to meet my . . ."? The lack of a word for such a partner is a clear indication of how little such relationships are governed by convention. Alternatively, we may say that such a relationship is *not* an institution, marriage is. I believe this helps explain why cohabiting couples are less happy, and less satisfied with their relationships than married couples.

17   Almost all worrisome social trends in regard to the *family* are actually problems related to *marriage*: declining rates of marriage, non-marital fertility, unmarried cohabitation, and divorce. Any understanding of the family must begin with a consideration of marriage. I now offer a *normative definition of marriage*; a statement of what Americans agree it *should* be, the assumptions and taken-for-granted notions involved. In so doing, I will lay the foundation for an explanation of family decline.

18   In *Marriage in Men's Lives*, I developed the details of normative marriage by consulting three diverse sources. First, I examined large national surveys conducted repeatedly over the past two decades. Second, I read domestic relations law, including state and federal appellate decisions. Finally, I consulted sources of religious doctrine, especially the Bible. Throughout, my goal was to identify all aspects of marriage that are widely shared, accepted as legitimate, and broadly viewed as compelling.

19   A normative definition of marriage draws attention to the central idea that marriage is more than the sum of two spouses. As an institution, marriage includes rules that originate outside

the particular union that establish boundaries around the relationship. Those boundaries are the understood limits of behavior that distinguish marriage from all other relationships. Married couples have something that all other couples lack; they are heirs to a system of shared principles that help organize their lives. If we want to assess changes in the family, the starting point is an examination of the institutional foundation of marriage. Six ideals define legal marriage in America.

1) *Individual Free Choice.* Mate selection is based on roman- 20
tic love. In the course of a century, parents have come to play a smaller and smaller role in the choice of married partners. Dating supplanted courtship as compatibility, attractiveness, and love replaced other bases for matrimony. National surveys show that "falling in love" is the most frequently cited reason for marrying one's spouse, and that the most important traits in successful marriages are thought to be "satisfying one another's needs" and "being deeply in love." Western religious ceremonies admonish partners to love one another until death, and every state permits a legal divorce when love fails ('incompatibility', 'irreconcilable differences' or similar justifications). Love is associated with feelings of security, comfort, companionship, erotic attraction, overlooking faults, and persistence. Since love and marriage are so closely related, people expect all such feelings from their marriages.

2) *Maturity.* Domestic relations law defines an age at which 21
persons may marry. Throughout the U.S., the minimum is 18, though marriage may be permitted with approval by parents or the court at earlier ages. Parental responsibilities for children end with legal *emancipation* at age 18. Thus, marriage may occur once parents are released from their legal obligations to children, when children are legally assumed to be mature enough to enter binding contracts, and once children are assumed able to become self-sufficient and able to provide for offspring. Traditional religious wedding ceremonies celebrate a new form of maturity as Genesis states: "A man leaves his father and mother and cleaves to his wife and they become one flesh."

3) *Heterosexuality.* Traditionally, and legally, the only accept- 22
able form of sex has been with one's spouse. Sex outside of marriage (fornication or adultery) is still illegal in half of U.S. states. And sexual expression within marriage has traditionally been legally restricted to vaginal intercourse (sodomy laws). Though such laws are rarely enforced even where they exist, they remind us of the very close association of marriage and conventional forms of heterosexual sexuality. Recent efforts to legalize homosexual marriage have been strenuously resisted. Since the full-faith-and-credit clause of the Constitution

requires that marriages conducted legally in one state be recognized as legal in others, the possibility of legal homosexual
marriage in Hawaii prompted an unprecedented federal
"Defense of Marriage Act" in September 1996. This law will
allow states to declare homosexual Hawaiian marriages void in
their jurisdiction. Despite growing acceptance of homosexuality, there is very little support for homosexual marriages. The
1990 General Social Survey showed that only 12 percent of
Americans believe homosexuals should be allowed to marry.

23   4) *Husband as Head*. Though Americans generally endorse
equality between the sexes, men and women still occupy different roles in their marriages. Even if more and more couples
are interested in egalitarian marriages, large numbers of people aren't. The 1994 General Social Survey shows that adults
are almost evenly divided about whether both spouses should
contribute to family income (57 percent approve of wives
working, and in fact, 61 percent of wives are employed). Four
in ten adults endorse a very traditional division of roles, where
the wife takes care of the home and family, and the husband
earns all the income. Traditional religious wedding ceremonies
ask women to "honor and obey" their husbands. In reality,
most husbands have more authority than their wives do. The
spouse who is primarily responsible for income enjoys more
authority, and in the overwhelming majority of American marriages, that is the husband. Demands made of husbands at
work are translated into legitimate demands made on the family. So most husbands have more authority than their wives do,
regardless of professed beliefs.

24   5) *Fidelity and Monogamy*. In law, sexual exclusivity is the
symbolic core of marriage, defining it in more obvious ways
than any other. Husbands and wives have a legal right to engage in (consensual) sex with one another. Other people may
not have a legal right to engage in sex with either married partner. Adultery is viewed as sufficiently threatening to marriages
that homicides provoked by the discovery of it may be treated
as manslaughter. Extramarital sex is viewed as more reprehensible than any other form, including sex between young
teenagers, premarital sex, and homosexual sex. Eight in ten
adults in the 1994 General Social Survey described extramarital sex as "always wrong." Adultery, in fact, is rare. Recent research reported by Laumann and his colleagues in *The Social
Organization of Sexuality* revealed that only 15 percent of married men and 5 percent of married women have ever had extramarital sex. Among divorced people these percentages are only
slightly higher, 25 percent for men and 10 percent for women.
Monogamy is closely related to fidelity because it restricts all

sexual expression to one married partner. With the exception of Utah where some Mormons practice polygamy (against the canons of the Mormon Church), monogamy has gone largely unchallenged in the United States since 1878 when the U.S. Supreme Court upheld the conviction of a Mormon who practiced polygamy.

6) *Parenthood*. With rare exceptions, married people become   25 parents. Despite high rates of unmarried fertility, there is little to suggest that married couples are less likely to have, or desire to have, children today than they were several decades ago. Only 13 percent of ever-married women aged 34 to 45 are childless today. Two decades ago, the comparable figure was 7 percent. The six-point difference, however, is due to delayed fertility, rather than higher childlessness. Overall completed cohort fertility (i.e., the total number of children born to women in their lifetime) has remained stable since the end of the Baby Boom. And while the legal disabilities once suffered by illegitimate children have been declared unconstitutional, marital and nonmarital fertility differ in important respects. Unmarried fathers may, through legal means, obtain the custody of their children, although few do. Indeed, a vast legal apparatus exists to enforce the parental obligations of men who do not voluntarily assume them. On the other hand, married men are automatically presumed to be the legal father of their wife's children, and nothing (except the absence of "unfitness") is required of them to establish custody.

Challenges to Normative Marriage

This ensemble of behaviors and beliefs describes how most   26 Americans understand marriage. Even if particular marriages depart in some ways from this model, this should be the starting point when attempting to assess family change. If "the family" has declined, then such change will be obvious in one or more of the foregoing dimensions. Widespread attempts to change normative marriage, or wholesale departures from it, are evidence that Americans do not agree about the institution. I now briefly review three obvious challenges to the normative model of marriage just outlined. High divorce rates, late ages at marriage, and declining rates of remarriage are a reflection of an underlying theme in such challenges. That theme is the importance of gender in marriage.

The increasingly common practice of unmarried *cohabitation*   27 is an example of a challenge to normative marriage. In 1997, 4.1 million opposite-sex cohabiting couples were counted by the U.S. Bureau of the Census, the majority of whom (58 percent) have never married, and one in five of whom (22 percent) is under 25 years old. Research on cohabiting partners has identified a central theme in such relationships. Cohabiting individuals are more focused on gender equality in economic and other matters than married spouses. They are also less likely to have a gender-based division of tasks in most forms of household labor except the care of infants.

28　　Yet another challenge to normative marriage is unmarried childbearing. One in three children in America is born to an unmarried woman; six in ten of those children were conceived outside of marriage (the balance were conceived prior to a divorce or separation). The historical connection between sexual intercourse and marriage weakened once effective contraception and abortion became available. Without contraception, married women became pregnant if fecund. There was no reason to ask a married woman why, or when she would have a child. Parenthood in an era of universal contraception, however, is a choice. It is now possible to ask *why* someone had a child. Since childbearing is thought to be a choice, it is viewed as a decision made chiefly by women. And the type of woman who chooses to have children differs from the childless woman because motherhood now competes with many other legitimate roles in a woman's life. Research has shown that women who choose motherhood give occupational and income considerations lower priority than childless women.

29　　By the late 1960s, feminists who argued that wives should not be completely dependent on husbands joined this critique of the exclusive breadwinner role of husbands. Just as the exclusive breadwinner role for men was criticized, the exclusive homemaker-mother role for married women was identified as oppressive. And, of course, such women are the statistical exception today. Maternity must be balanced with many other adult roles in women's lives, and traditional marriage is faulted as creating a "second shift" for women who return home from work only to assume responsibility for their households with little help from their husbands.

30　　All significant challenges to marriage focus on various aspects of gender. The traditional assignment of marital roles based on sex (i.e., husband as head of household) is the core problem in marriage. Other dimensions of normative marriage are less troublesome. There is little evidence of widespread disagreement about the ideas of free choice of spouses, fidelity, monogamy, heterosexual marriage, maturity, or parenthood.

31　　Whether Americans are now less committed to common moral beliefs than in the past is an empirical question. Values (i.e., moral beliefs) are researchable issues, and it would be possible to investigate their role in matters of family life. Increases in divorce, cohabitation, illegitimacy, or premarital sex are certainly evidence that some beliefs are changing. However, social scientists have yet to identify all the various causes of these family trends. Undoubtedly there are many, including demographic (e.g., longer life, lower fertility), technological (e.g., contraception, public health) and cultural (e.g., shifting patterns of immigration). Changing values about gender are but one cause of family change. Still, I suspect they are the most important. When something as basic and fundamental as what it means to be a man or woman changes, virtually everything else must change accordingly. Now we must incorporate such new ideas into the institution of marriage.

New Families

It is easy to imagine how a new model of marriage would look.   32
None of the basic elements of normative marriage are likely to change except the gender assumptions about who heads the family. Husbands and wives are already familiar with this new model of marriage, even if we have yet to acknowledge it. In 1995, virtually all (95 percent) of married men with children in the household were employed. Two-thirds (65 percent) of wives in such families were employed. Husbands are still breadwinners, but so are wives. While employment does not typically eliminate a wife's dependency on her husband, it does mean that husbands are also dependent on wives. Most American marriages now involve a pooling of incomes. The resulting lifestyle, therefore, is produced jointly by wives and husbands. Income pooling has increasingly replaced the breadwinner/homemaker pattern.

These new economic realities of married life have not been   33
fully incorporated into the institution of normative marriage—the way we think about marriage. Husbands and wives have yet to reconcile their joint economic dependency with the routine of married life. Even if most married couples today depend on one another's earnings, traditional patterns of domestic responsibilities persist. Such gendered marriages are a problem because they do not fit with the assumptions about men and women in all other spheres of their lives.

The trends in the family that worry us might better be viewed   34
as a consequence of redefining the institution. We are now struggling to resolve ideas about what is proper in our marriages with ideas about what is proper outside of them.

Repeated studies have shown that conflicts over gender (Should the wife work? Who should do what?) are leading causes of divorce. Growing numbers of women find it difficult to live in marriages that appear to devalue their roles as breadwinners. On the other hand, full-time housewives feel that housework is devalued. Growing numbers of couples opt for "informal" marriage, or cohabitation, as a way to live without strict gender assumptions. Large numbers of women decide to pursue parenthood without the limitations and restrictions that would be imposed by marriage. It is easy to see why people make these choices. But though understandable, they are costly. Adults and children thrive in stable, nuclear families, even if they are not always happy. No feasible alternative comes close in its economic or emotional benefits for children or adults.

35   But the solution is not complete independence in marriage. Cohabitation has taught us that two soloists do not make a very good duet. Such equal partnerships do not last very long, and cohabiting couples report low levels of happiness and satisfaction. That is probably because nothing binds cohabiting couples together except love and affection. As desirable as those emotions are, they are a flimsy basis for an enduring relationship without alternative bonds. Stable, enduring marriages must be forged of extensive dependencies. Each person must depend on the other for many things. But such dependencies need not be inequitable or unfair.

36   What is the problem with marriage? The problem is the role of gender in the institution. More accurately, the problem is how to deal with widespread social change in matters of gender. But there is good reason to believe that we will come to terms with such challenges. Few boys today will grow up with mothers who are not employed. Young men are unlikely to inherit their fathers' or grandfathers' traditional views about marriage or women. Fewer men work with colleagues who openly view women and wives in traditional restricted roles. More and more of the youthful life course is spent in nontraditional families or outside of families altogether. Children, especially boys, who experience such childhoods (employed mothers, divorce, non-family living) are more accepting of women's new roles and options and are willing to perform more housework. It is not, therefore, a dramatic change in the basic institution of normative marriage that we need. Rather, it is a recognition and accommodation to the changes in women's lives and patience for intergenerational (cohort) change to catch up with current expectations. And men must become a part of the gender revolution. Even if this is not a fundamental redefinition of marriage, it will have profound

consequences for how marriage is experienced because the tension between public and private lives will be reduced.

Marriage and Public Policy

Social institutions can be changed intentionally, but not easily,   37
not quickly, and not without widespread discussion and debate. I have been studying covenant marriage in Louisiana for the past year. In that state (and in Arizona) couples may elect one of two marriage regimes; the traditional one based on no-fault divorce rules, and covenant marriage which requires premarital counseling, and is governed by traditional fault-grounds for divorce. Covenant marriage laws are the first in over 200 years in America designed explicitly to make *marriage more permanent and divorce more restrictive*. Not surprisingly, therefore, they are extremely controversial. It is much too early to know if this legal innovation will affect divorce rates. But one thing is clear. The passage of more restrictive divorce laws, even if optional, has provoked intense debate and discussion about the meaning of marriage and the role of the state in family affairs. Covenant marriage is discussed and debated almost weekly in the Louisiana media. A public discussion about marriage has begun in that state. Only through such *megalogues*, as Etzioni calls them, will institutions change. Social change is not being legislated. It is simply being encouraged, debated, and discussed.

Proposals that marriage be recognized, promoted, and pro-   38
tected by revisions in federal tax codes, increased use of premarital counseling, and revisions in divorce laws are a good start. I believe we must go further, however, to create and reinforce dependencies in marriage. Dependency based automatically on gender will eventually be purged from marriage, as it is now being purged from work, school, and other public realms. The transition is clearly difficult and painful as we now can see. But what will bind couples to such new families? The answer is that bases of dependency other than gender must be created. Significant benefits must flow from the marriage, and significant exit costs must exist for both partners.

The most sensible, though controversial way to achieve these   39
goals is for states to establish a preference for married couples in the distribution of discretionary benefits. My research on covenant marriage has convinced me that any attempt to privilege marriage over other statuses will be controversial and resisted, especially by those who see traditional marriage as unfair to women. Since the inequities in marriage are being resolved, I would focus on ways to privilege marriage by granting

significant economic benefits to couples willing to commit to a restrictive regime. The purpose would be to create a new distinction between married and unmarried persons, though not one automatically based on gender. If marriage is to thrive, significant benefits *other than emotional ones* must flow from the status. And men and women alike must benefit from the status of marriage.

40   Marriage has traditionally been founded on dependencies of many types. But unequal (i.e. women's) economic dependencies are the most obvious (and often the source of inequity). In a world where men and women may each be economically independent, the benefits of pooled incomes may not suffice to sustain couples during those inevitable times when love fades. What the authors of *A Call to Civil Society* refer to as "the philosophy of expressive individualism"—a belief in the "sovereignty of the self"—here too is fostered by gender equality and individual economic independence. In the absence of unequal economic dependencies, marriage must become a privileged status again, or else divorce rates will remain high, and marriage rates will continue to fall. To make it a privileged status, we should establish significant economic incentives. To the extent that people benefit economically in obvious and large ways by virtue of their marriages (and to the extent that such benefits are not available to unmarried people), each spouse is dependent on *the union, per se* (dependency is typically measured by the costs of exiting a relationship).

41   The state has an enormous economic interest in promoting stable marriages. Strangely, the *macroeconomic* costs of divorce are rarely discussed in deliberations about public policy. Yet the *microeconomic* consequences are well known. Divorce and single-parenthood take a toll on earnings, educational attainment, labor-force attachment, subsequent marital stability, and the likelihood of poverty for the adults and the children involved. The aggregate consequences of all such individual losses are vast, even if unknown. Promoting marriage makes very good economic sense, beyond any other benefits to children or adults.

42   There are many ways we might promote marriage. Here I offer one example. We should consider significant tax credits for some married couples to create an economic interest in the marital union and significant exit costs for both partners. Americans will not tolerate mandatory family policy, so states should follow the lead of Louisiana in offering couples the option of two marriage regimes. Any couple could elect to be married under the customary no-fault divorce system without requirements for pre-marital and marital counseling. The more restrictive marriage regime would require premarital and marital counseling (as a prerequisite for a divorce), and would apply

prevailing "best interests of the child" custody standards in granting a divorce. Divorce would be denied if the court determined that it was not in the best interest of the child (or children) involved. ("Best interests of the child" divorce proposals have been considered in several states, though never enacted.)

Couples who marry under the more restrictive marriage   43
regime would qualify for very significant tax credits. Such credits must be quite large—$2,500 or $3,500 a year—sufficient to offset the costs of a college education for the children of married parents, or to underwrite the costs of a home, for example. Such tax credits would create a financial interest in the marriage *per se*, a benefit that flows to married couples by virtue of their marital status and nothing else. It also creates a significant exit cost at divorce. Both partners benefit so long as they remain married, both lose at divorce. How will we pay for such generous benefits? In fact, it is not certain that there would be net costs. A more appropriate question is how we will continue to pay for single parenthood and divorce.

Such a proposal seeks to restore marriage to a privileged sta-   44
tus. It also addresses the need for a new basis of dependency in modern marriages where both spouses are likely to be breadwinners. It is intended to foster higher rates of marriage, lower rates of unmarried childbearing, and delays in divorce. Were any policy to be partially successful in having these consequences, the long-term economic ledgers (i.e., costs and benefits) may balance. Even if they didn't, such proposals would surely provoke discussion and debate about the importance of marriage in America. *A Call to Civil Society* asks us to begin such a debate about the loss of organizing ideals. Let's start with a consideration of the centrality of gender to the problem with marriage.

Jennifer Marshall

MARRIAGE: WHAT SOCIAL SCIENCE SAYS AND DOESN'T SAY

Jennifer Marshall is the director of domestic policy studies at The Heritage Foundation, a conservative think tank that describes its mission as the formulation and promotion of

*"conservative public policies based on principles of free enter-
prise, limited government, individual freedom, traditional
American values, and a strong national defense." As you read
Marshall's piece, which was published in the "Research" section of Heritage's website, you might consider how it serves
that organization's mission—and how it uses "research" and
"social science" to bolster its argument.*

1   Social science data indicate that the intact family—defined as
a man and a woman who marry, conceive, and raise their children together—best ensures the current and future welfare of
children and society when compared with other common
forms of households. As alternative family forms have become
more prevalent since the 1960s, social science research and
government surveys have indicated an accompanying rise in a
number of serious social problems.

2   Government's interest in marriage has been based primarily
on its interest in the welfare of the next generation. Among the
many types of social relationships, marriage has always had a
special place in all legal traditions, our own included, because
it is the essential foundation of the intact family, and no other
family form has been able to provide a commensurate level of
social security.

3   In all other common family and household forms, the risk
of negative individual outcomes and family disintegration is
much greater, increasing the risk of dependence on state services. A free society requires a critical mass of individuals in
stable households who are not dependent on the state. The
most stable and secure household, the available research
shows, is the intact family. Therefore, the state has an interest
in protecting the intact family and we should be cautious
about facilitating other forms of household, the effects of
which are either deleterious or unknown.

4   Compared with counterparts in other common household
arrangements, adolescents in intact families have better health,
are less likely to be depressed, are less likely to repeat a grade in
school, and have fewer developmental problems, data show. By
contrast, national surveys reveal that, as a group, children in
other family forms studied are more likely to experience
poverty, abuse, behavioral and emotional problems, lower academic achievement, and drug use. These surveys illustrate

   • Adolescents in intact families, as a group, are the least
     likely to feel depressed compared to those with divorced,
     step-, cohabiting, or single parents; (National Longitu-
     dinal Survey of Adolescent Health)

- The national average grade-point scores of children in intact families is 2.98, compared to 2.79 for children of cohabiting parents and 2.71 for children living in stepfamilies; (National Longitudinal Survey of Adolescent Health)
- The rate of youth incarceration is significantly greater for children raised in single-mother and stepfamily homes than for those raised in intact families, even after controlling for parental income and education; (National Longitudinal Survey of Youth)
- Children in non-intact families are three times as likely to have children outside of marriage; (National Longitudinal Survey of Youth) and
- Rates of engaging in problem behaviors such as lying, stealing, drunkenness, and violence are sharply higher for children of divorce compared to children in intact families. (National Longitudinal Survey of Adolescent Health)

During the 1990s, a serious public policy debate resulted when 5 emerging social science data showed the consequences of several decades of experimentation with family forms. Out of this increased awareness grew a movement for policy and cultural changes to reinforce and restore marriage in America. Policy decisions—such as welfare reform—were grounded in these data. We have seen some of the fruit of those efforts in declining rates of teen sex and childbearing.

By contrast, the current debate over same-sex marriage is 6 not anchored in sound research, and data on the consequences of children being brought up by same-sex couples remains scarce. Same-sex couples with children constitute a new form of household that has not been carefully studied. Nor has the objective of this policy discussion been clearly defined as the interest of children or the future of the nation's families.

Same-sex marriage advocates propose that we institutional- 7 ize a social experiment in its early stages by elevating it in law to the status of the oldest of institutions: marriage. That experiment is the same-sex coupling and parenting recently taking place around us. To be sure, Americans have become more accepting of other types of sexual experimentation—sex outside of marriage, cohabitation, single parenting—but do not equate them with or see them as a substitute for marriage. None of these experiments has been regarded in law as the equivalent of the intact family. Yet this is precisely the proposal before us on the question of same-sex marriage: that we institutionalize in law an experiment about which we have very little knowledge.

8   The data on the homosexual household is extremely limited. We know relatively little about the long-term effects of homosexual relationships on partners and even less about the children that will be raised in such households. Such an absence of data should give us pause before reconfiguring the basic institution of society. Thus we should study the results of the current experiment in homosexual households with children rather than forcing communities at large to accept, by law, same-sex marriage and parenting.

9   We should also further explore what it is about marriage that sets the intact family apart in the current research. Many would contend that the unique natures and contributions of a male and a female constitute the critical characteristic of marriage, and that the distinctive sexual nature and identity of each parent, along with their number (two rather than one) and relationship status (marriage rather than cohabitation), gives the intact family the exceptional quality it exhibits. This needs to be examined carefully, to determine how having two parents of opposite sexes contributes to the upbringing of a child.

10   In the meantime, with the policy debate forced by same-sex marriage advocates beyond the conclusions of existent social science research, we must look to the best evidence currently available about family forms and their social impacts. What we know about alternative family forms is a good indicator of what we might expect from this variant.

11   Modern policymaking should be informed by the realities of available empirical evidence. In time, the data will be forthcoming on this newest form of experimentation, same-sex partnering and parenting, and its effects on homosexual men and women and on those who live with them. In the meantime America's marriage and family law should stay the course based on what we *do* know.

Shere Hite

BRINGING
DEMOCRACY HOME

In the spring of 1995, Ms. *magazine carried the following excerpt from Shere Hite's book* The Hite Report on the Family: Growing Up under Patriarchy *(1995), the product of her study of several thousand families. Hite has made a reputation not only on this report but also on her books* The Hite Report: A Nationwide Study of Female Sexuality *(1976) and* The Hite Report: A Study of Male Sexuality *(1981)—both controversial, widely discussed titles. Hite is a cultural historian specializing in psychosexual behavior and gender relations. She has worked as an instructor of female sexuality at New York University and has lectured at a number of universities worldwide, including the Sorbonne, Harvard, Columbia, Cambridge, Oxford, the London School of Economics and others. She directed the National Organization for Women's feminist sexuality project from 1972 to 1978.*

1   Love and anger, love and obedience, love and power, love and hate. These are all present in family relationships. It's easy to say that they are inevitable, that stresses and strains are unavoidable, given "human nature." To some extent this is true, but these stresses and strains are exaggerated by a tense and difficult family system that is imposed upon our emotions and our lives, structuring them to fit its own specified goals.

2   Is the family as we have known it for so long the only way to create safe, loving, and caring environments for people? The best way? To understand the family in Western tradition, we must remember that much of what we see, say, and think about it is based on the archetypal family that is so pervasive in our society—Jesus, Mary, and Joseph. There is no daughter icon. This is the "holy family" model that we are expected, in one way or another, to live up to. But is this model really the right one for people who believe in equality and justice? Does it teach a good understanding of love and the way to make relationships work when we become adults?

3   One constantly hears that the family is in trouble, that it doesn't work anymore, that we must find ways to help it. If the family doesn't work, maybe there is something wrong with its structure. People must have reasons for fleeing the nuclear family: human rights abuses and the battering of women are well documented in many governments' statistics.

4   The family is changing because only in recent decades has the process of democratization, which began in Western political life more than two centuries ago, reached private life. Although John Stuart Mill wrote in favor of women's rights in the egalitarian democratic theory he helped develop, the family and women's role in the world were left out of most discussions of democracy, left in the "sacred" religious domain. Women and nonproperty owners, as well as "minorities," did not have the vote when democracy first began. Men made a

fatal mistake. The democracy they thought they could make work in the public sphere would not really work without democracy in private life.

5   Some people, of course, are alarmed by changes in the family. Reactionary fundamentalist groups have gone on the offensive to try to stop this process. Yet most people are happier with their personal lives today than people were 50 years ago. Women especially have more choices and freedom than they did in the past. There is a positive new diversity springing up in families and relationships today in Western society. This pluralism should be valued and encouraged: far from signaling a breakdown of society, it is a sign of a new, more open and tolerant society springing up, a new world being born out of the clutter of the old.

6   Democracy could work even better if we changed the aggressive personality that is being created by the patriarchal family system. Children brought up with choice about whether to accept their parents' power are more likely to be confident about believing in themselves and their own ideas, less docile or habituated to bending to power. Such a population would create and participate in public debate very differently. And there are many more advances we are on the threshold of achieving: naming and eliminating emotional violence, redefining love and friendship, progressing in the areas of children's rights and in men's questioning of their own lives.

7   My work salutes the gentler and more diverse families that seem to be arising. They are part of a system that does not keep its members in terror: fathers in terror lest they not be "manly" and able to support it all; mothers in terror lest they be beaten in their own bedrooms and ridiculed by their children; children in terror of being forced to do things against their will and having absolutely no recourse, no door open to them for exit.

8   What I am offering is a new interpretation of relationships between parents and children, a new theory of the family. My interpretation of the data from my questionnaires takes into account not only the individual's unique experiences, as is done in psychology, but also the cultural backdrop—the canvas of social "approval" or "disapproval" against which children's lives are lived. This interdisciplinary theory also takes into account the historical ideology of the family; those who took part in my research are living in a world where perception of "family" is filtered through the Christian model of the "holy family" with its reproductive icons of Jesus, Mary, and Joseph. But no matter how beautiful it appears (especially in its promise of "true love"), this family model is an essentially repressive one,

teaching authoritarian psychological patterns, meekness in
women, and a belief in the unchanging rightness of male
power. In this hierarchical family, love and power are inextricably linked, a pattern that has damaging effects not only on
all family members but on the politics of the wider society.
How can there be successful democracy in public life if there is
an authoritarian model in private life?

So used have we become to these symbols that we continue   9
to believe—no matter what statistics we see in the newspapers
about divorce, violence in the home, mental breakdown—that
the icons and the system they represent are right, fair, and just.
We assume without thinking that this model is the only "natural" form of family, and that if there are problems it must be
the individual who is at fault, not the institution.

We need a new interpretation of what is going on. We may   10
be at one of the most important turning points of the Western
world, the creation of a new social base that will engender an
advanced and improved democratic political structure.

What Is the Family All About?

Creating new, more democratic families means taking a clear   11
and rational look at our institutions. We tend to forget that the
family was created in its current form in early patriarchy for
political, not religious, reasons. The new political order had to
solve a specific problem: How could lineage or inheritance
flow through men (and not women as it had previously) if men
do not bear children?

The modern patriarchal family was created so that each man   12
would "own" a woman who would reproduce for him. He then
had to control the sexuality of "his" woman, for how else could
he be sure that "his" child was really his? Restrictions were
placed on women's lives and bodies by men; women's imprisonment in marriage was made a virtue, for example, through the
later archetype of the self-sacrificing Mary, who was happy to
be of service, never standing up for herself or her own rights.
Mary, it is important to note, is a later version of a much earlier
Creation Mother goddess. In her earlier form, she had many
more aspects, more like the Indian goddess Kali than the
"mother" whom the Christian patriarchal system devised.

Fortunately, the family is a human institution: humans made   13
it and humans can change it. My research indicates that the extreme aggression we see in society is not a characteristic of biological "human nature" (as Freud concluded), nor a result of

hormones. "Human nature" is a psychological structure that is carefully implanted in our minds—for life—as we learn the love and power equations of the family. Power and love are combined in the family structure: in order to receive love, most children have to humiliate themselves, over and over again, before power.

14   In our society, parents have the complete legal, economic, and social "right" to control children's lives. Parents' exclusive power over children creates obedience. Children are likely to take on authoritarian emotional, psychological, and sexual patterns, and to see power as one of the central categories of existence.

15   Love is at the heart—so to speak—of our belief in the importance of the family. The desire for love is what keeps us returning to the icons. Even when they don't seem to work in our lives, we try and try again. We are told that we will never find love if we don't participate in the family. We hear repeatedly that the only place we will ever be able to get security, true acceptance, and understanding is in the family; that we are only "half a family" or a "pretend family" if we create any other human group; that without being a member of the family we will be forever "left out," lonely, or useless. No one would want to deny the importance of love, or of lasting relationships with other people. But the violent, distorted definitions of love created by the patriarchal family make it difficult for love to last, and to be as profound as it could be.

16   How confusing it is for children, the idea of being loved! They are so often told by their parents, "Of course we love you, why do you even ask?" It is easy for children to believe that the emotion they feel when faced with a powerful person is "love"—or that the inscrutable ways of a person who is sometimes caring and friendly, and other times punitive and angry, are loving. The problem then is that, since the parents are still the providers and "trainers" of the children, legally and economically the "owners" of the children, they exercise incredible power over the children—the very power of survival itself.

17   Children must feel gratitude, and so, in their minds, this gratitude is mixed with love. How much of the love they feel is really supplication before the power of the parents? How will they define love later in life? Won't they be highly confused by passion (either emotional or physical) and what it means, unable to connect it with other feelings of liking and concern? Of course, long-term caring for others is something positive that can also be learned in families, but it can be learned in other kinds of families, not just the nuclear model.

Does "Love" Include Sex? The Body?

And what definition of love do children learn from the way   18
their parents relate physically? Isn't it strange to think of your
parents having sex? Finding parents in any kind of physical
embrace comes as a fascinating shock to most children: 83 percent of children in my research say their parents seem completely asexual.

It would be logical if children drew the conclusion that "real   19
love" is never sexual, or even physically affectionate. But isn't
affection a great part of what love is? If parents don't hug and
kiss each other, is the definition of adult "love" different? And
if so, what is it? Why do parents feel that they shouldn't touch
each other in front of the children? Because the children
would be jealous? Because it would give the children sexual
feelings and ideas? Or, do many parents really not want to
touch each other? Children wonder, if the parents don't want to
be affectionate, why exactly are they together? If they are only
together "for the sake of the children," this puts an awfully big
burden on the children to be "worth it" or to "make their parents happy," thus confusing the definitions of love even further.

Another way children learn that power and domination are   20
part of love is through observing the relationship of their parents. Gender tension and especially second-class treatment of
the mother by the father is reported by the majority of people
from two-parent families in this study. Girls in particular find
this gender inequality mixed with "love" confusing, even psychologically violent and terrifying. Why? Because for girls it
means coming to terms with what this power relationship will
mean for them: Will they inherit this gender inequality? Can
they avoid being considered lesser beings when they become
women? How can they love a father who represents this system? Or a mother who lets herself participate in it?

Are Single-Parent Families Bad for Children?

There are very few carefully controlled studies of the effects of   21
single-parent families on children. Today, much popular journalism assumes that the two-parent family is better for children. My data show that there are beneficial effects for the
majority of children living in single-parent families. It is more
positive for children not to grow up in an atmosphere poisoned
by gender inequality.

22   Do girls who grow up with "only" their mother have a better relationship with her? According to my study, 49 percent of such girls felt that it was a positive experience; 20 percent did not like it; and the rest had mixed feelings. Mothers in one-parent families are more likely to feel freer to confide in daughters because no "disloyalty to the spouse" is implied. Daughters in such families are less likely to see the mother as a "wimp"—she is an independent person.

23   Boys who grow up with "only" their mother experience less pressure to demonstrate contempt for things "feminine" and for nonaggressive parts of themselves. In *The Hite Report on Men and Male Sexuality*, I was surprised to find that boys who grew up with their mother alone were much more likely to have good relationships with women in their adult lives: 80 percent of men from such families had formed strong, lasting ties with women (in marriage or long-term relationships), as opposed to only 40 percent from two-parent families. This does not mean that the two-parent family cannot be reformed so that it provides a peaceful environment for children— indeed this is part of the ongoing revolution in the family in which so many people today are engaged.

24   Single-parent families are mostly headed by mothers, yet there is an increasing number of single-father families. Many single fathers don't take much part in child care but instead hire female nannies or ask their mothers, sisters, or girlfriends to take care of the children. Men could change the style of families by taking more part domestically, and by opening up emotionally and having closer contact with children. My research highlights men's traumatizing and enforced split from women at puberty. . . .

25   Healing this is the single most important thing we as a society could do to bridge the distance men feel from "family."

Democracy of the Heart: A New Politics

26   If you listen to people talk about their families, it becomes clear that we must give up on the outdated notion that the only acceptable families are nuclear families. We should not see the new society that has evolved over the last 40 years as a disaster simply because it is not like the past.

27   The new diversity of families is part of a positive pluralism, part of a fundamental transition in the organization of society that calls for open-minded brainstorming by all of us: What do we believe "love" and "family" are? Can we accept that the many people fleeing the nuclear family are doing so for valid

reasons? If reproduction is no longer the urgent priority that it was when societies were smaller, before industrialization took hold, then the revolt against the family is not surprising. Perhaps it was even historically inevitable. It is not that people don't want to build loving, family-style relationships, it is that they do not want to be forced to build them within one rigid, hierarchical, heterosexist, reproductive framework. Diversity in family forms can bring joy and enrichment to a society: new kinds of families can be the basis for a renaissance of spiritual dignity and creativity in political as well as personal life.

Continuing this process of bringing private life into an ethical and egalitarian frame of reference will give us the energy and moral will to maintain democracy in the larger political sphere. We can create a society with a new spirit and will—but politics will have to be transformed. We can use the interactive frame of reference most often found today in friendships between women. Diversity in families can form the basic infrastructure for a new and advanced type of political democracy to be created, imagined, developed—a system that suits the massive societies that communications technology today has made into one "global village."   28

One cannot exaggerate the importance of the current debate: there has been fascism in societies before; it could certainly emerge again, alongside fascism in the family. If we believe in the democratic, humanist ideals of the last 200 years, we have the right, almost the duty, to make out family system a more just one; to follow our democratic ideals and make a new, more inclusive network of private life that will reflect not a preordained patriarchal structure, but our belief in justice and equality for all—women, men, and children. Let's continue the transformation, believe in ourselves, and go forward with love instead of fear. In our private lives and in our public world, let's hail the future and make history.   29

Gregory Corso
MARRIAGE

Gregory Corso (1930–2001) was a key member of the so-called Beat movement in poetry, which had a great effect on the youth of the rebellious 1960s and 1970s America. The Beat movement's

*most famous voice, Allen Ginsberg, called Corso an "awakener
of youth." Corso worked variously at a number of manual
labor positions and as a writer for the* Los Angeles Times.
*Consider how the rebelliousness of the Beat movement can be
seen in Corso's poetic treatment of the institution of marriage.
How is humor used here? Is there anything like a serious message behind this poem, or is it just good fun?*

Should I get married? Should I be good?
Astound the girl next door with my velvet suit and faustus
hood?
Don't take her to movies but to cemeteries
tell all about werewolf bathtubs and forked clarinets
then desire her and kiss her and all the preliminaries   5
and she going just so far and I understanding why
not getting angry saying You must feel! It's beautiful to
feel!
Instead take her in my arms lean against an old crooked
tombstone
and woo her the entire night the constellations in the sky—

When she introduces me to her parents   10
back straightened, hair finally combed, strangled by a tie,
should I sit knees together on their 3rd degree sofa
and not ask Where's the bathroom?
How else to feel other than I am.
often thinking Flash Gordon soap—   15
O how terrible it must be for a young man
seated before a family and the family thinking
We never saw him before! He wants our Mary Lou!
After tea and homemade cookies they ask What do you do
      for a   20
        living?
Should I tell them? Would they like me then?
Say All right get married, we're losing a daughter
but we're gaining a son—
And should I then ask Where's the bathroom?   25

O God, and the wedding! All her family and her friends
and only a handful of mine all scroungy and bearded
just wait to get at the drinks and food—
And the priest! he looking at me as if I masturbated
asking me Do you take this woman for your lawful
wedded wife?   30

And I trembling what to say say Pie Glue!
I kiss the bride all those corny men slapping me on the
back

She's all yours, boy! Ha-ha-ha!
And in their eyes you could see some obscene honeymoon
    going   35
        on—
Then all that absurd rice and clanky cans and shoes
Niagara Falls! Hordes of us! Husbands! Wives!
    Flowers!
        Chocolates!   40
All streaming into cozy hotels
All going to do the same thing tonight
The indifferent clerk he knowing what was going to
happen
The lobby zombies they knowing what
The whistling elevator man he knowing   45
The winking bellboy knowing
Everybody knowing! I'd be almost inclined not to do
anything!
    Stay up all night! Stare that hotel clerk in the eye!
    Screaming: I deny honeymoon! I deny honeymoon!
    running rampant into those almost climactic suites   50
    yelling Radio belly! Cat shovel!
    O I'd live in Niagara forever! in a dark cave beneath the
Falls
    I'd sit there the Mad Honeymooner
    devising ways to break marriages, a scourge of bigamy
    a saint of divorce—   55

But I should get married I should be good
How nice it'd be to come home to her
and sit by the fireplace and she in the kitchen
aproned young and lovely wanting my baby
and so happy about me she burns the roast beef   60
and comes crying to me and I get up from my big papa
chair
    saying Christmas teeth! Radiant brains! Apple deaf!
    God what a husband I'd make! Yes, I should get
married!
    So much to do! like sneaking into Mr. Jones' house late at
night
    and cover his golf clubs with 1920 Norwegian books   65

Like hanging a picture of Rimbaud[1] on the lawnmower
like pasting Tannu Tuva postage stamps all over the picket
fence
like when Mrs Kindhead comes to collect for the
Community Chest
grab her and tell her There are unfavorable omens in the
sky!
And when the mayor comes to get my vote tell him   70
When are you going to stop people killing whales!
And when the milkman comes leave him a note in the
bottle
Penguin dust, bring me penguin dust, I want penguin
dust—

Yet if I should get married and it's Connecticut
and snow
and she gives birth to a child and I am sleepless, worn,   75
up for nights, head bowed against a quiet window, the
past
        behind
            me,
finding myself in the most common of situations a
trembling man
knowledged with responsibility not twig-smear   80
nor Roman
        coin
            soup—
O what would that be like!
Surely I'd give it for a nipple a rubber Tacitus
For a rattle a bag of broken Bach records   85
Tack Della Francesca[2] all over its crib
Sew the Greek alphabet on its bib
And build for its playpen a roofless Parthenon

No, I doubt I'd be that kind of father
not rural not snow no quiet window   90
but hot smelly tight New York City
seven flights up, roaches and rats in the walls

---

[1]*Rimbaud:* Arthur Rimbaud (1854–1891), French poet whose work is
characterized by dramatic and imaginative vision, especially in the realm
of hallucination.
   [2]*Della Francesco:* Italian painter and mathematician (1420?–1492).

a fat Reichian[3] wife screeching over potatoes Get a job!
And five nose running brats in love with Batman
And the neighbors all toothless and dry haired   95
like those hag masses of the 18th century
all wanting to come in and watch TV
The landlord wants his rent
Grocery store Blue Cross Gas & Electric Knights of
Columbus
Impossible to lie back and dream Telephone snow,   100
ghost parking—
   No! I should not get married I should never get married!
   But—imagine If I were married to a beautiful
sophisticated woman
   tall and pale wearing an elegant black dress and long
black gloves
   holding a cigarette holder in one hand and a highball in
the other
   and we lived high up in a penthouse with a huge   105
window
   from which we could see all of New York and ever
     farther on
       clearer days
   No, can't imagine myself married to that pleasant prison
dream—

   O but what about love? I forget love   110
   not that I am incapable of love
   it's just that I see love as odd as wearing shoes—
   I never wanted to marry a girl who was like my mother
And Ingrid Bergman was always impossible
And there's maybe a girl now but she's already   115
married
And I don't like men and—
but there's got to be somebody!
Because what if I'm 60 years old and not married,
   all alone in a furnished room with pee stains on my
underwear
   and everybody else is married! All the universe   120
married but me!

---

[3]*Reichian:* after Wilhelm Reich (1897–1957), Austrian psychiatrist and
biophysicist who believed the universe to be permeated by a primal, mass-
free phenomenon called *orgone energy;* the failure to release this energy
through natural sexual intercourse he believed to be the genesis of individual and collective neuroses.

Ah, yet well I know that were a woman possible as I am
possible
   then marriage would be possible—
   Like SHE in her lonely alien gaud waiting her Egyptian
lover
   so I wait—bereft of 2,000 years and the bath of life.

What Is a Family?

Ellen Willis

WHY I'M NOT "PRO-FAMILY"

Ellen Willis, author of No More Nice Girls; Countercultural
Essays *(1992), teaches journalism at NYU. The article published here originally appeared in* Glamour *(October 1994),
a national magazine devoted to fashions, cultural matters,
careers, nutrition, and civic issues interesting to women.*

In 1992, "Family Values" bombed in Houston. Right-wingers at   1
the Republican convention, sneering at career women and single
mothers, turned voters off. Now the Democrats are in power—
yet ironically, the family issue has reemerged, more strongly than
ever. Last year New York's influential Democratic senator, Daniel
Patrick Moynihan, suggested that in relaxing the stigma against
unmarried childbearing, we had laid the groundwork for the
burgeoning crime rate. Then *The Atlantic* published a cover story
provocatively titled: "Dan Quayle Was Right." Its author, social
historian Barbara Dafoe Whitehead, invoked recent research to
argue that high rates of divorce and single parenthood hurt children and underlie "many of our most vexing social problems."

The article hit a nerve. It provoked an outpouring of mail,   2
was condensed for *Reader's Digest* and won an award from the
National Women's Political Caucus. Commentators both conservative and liberal praised it in newspapers across the country. Together, Moynihan's and Whitehead's salvos launched a
national obsession with "the decline of the family." President
Clinton joined the bandwagon: "For 30 years," he declared in
his State of the Union message, "family life in America has
been breaking down."

3   The new advocates of the family seem more sympathetic to
women than their right-wing precursors. They know women
are in the workforce to stay; they are careful to talk about the
time pressures faced by "parents"—not "mothers"—with jobs,
and they put an unaccustomed emphasis on men's family obligations, such as contributing their fair share of child support.
Some advocate liberal reforms ranging from antipoverty programs to federally funded child care to abortion rights, arguing
that such measures are pro-family because they help existing
families. (A recent Planned Parenthood fund-raising letter proclaims, "Pro-choice is pro-family.")

4   I'm all for reforms that make it easier to give children the
care they need, and I'm certainly in favor of men's equal participation in childrearing. My quarrel is with the underlying
terms of the discussion, especially the assumption that anyone
who cares about children must be "pro-family." I grew up in
the fifties, in a family with two committed parents—the kind of
home the pro-familists idealize. I had security; I had love. Yet
like many of my peers, especially women, I saw conventional
family life as far from ideal and had no desire to replicate it. It
wasn't only that I didn't want to be a housewife like my
mother; I felt that family life promoted self-abnegation and
social conformity while stifling eroticism and spontaneity. I
thought the nuclear family structure was isolating, and that
within it, combining childrearing with other work would be exhausting, even if both parents shared the load—impressions I
can now confirm from experience.

5   To me the alternative that made the most sense was not single parenthood—we needed *more* parents, not fewer, to share
the daily responsibilities of childrearing and homemaking. In
the seventies, a number of people I knew were bringing up
children in communal households, and I imagined someday
doing the same. But by the time my companion and I had a
child ten years ago, those experiments and the counterculture
that supported them were long gone.

6   From my perspective, the new champions of the family are
much like the old. They never consider whether the current instability of families might signal that an age-old institution is
failing to meet modern needs and ought to be reexamined. The
idea that there could be other possible structures for domestic
life and childrearing has been excluded from the conversation—
so much so that cranks like me who persist in broaching the
subject are used to getting the sort of tactful and embarrassed
reaction accorded, say, people who claim to have been kid-
napped by aliens. And the assumption that marriage is the self-
evident solution to single parents' problems leads to impatience

and hostility toward anyone who can't or won't get with the nuclear-family program.

Consider the hottest topic on the pro-family agenda: the 7 prevalence of unwed motherhood in poor black communities. For Moynihan and other welfare reformers, the central cause of inner-city poverty and crime is not urban economic collapse, unemployment or racism, but fatherless households. Which means the solution is to bring back the stigma of "illegitimacy" and restrict or eliminate welfare for single mothers. Clinton has proposed requiring welfare recipients to leave the rolls after two years and look for work, with temporary government jobs as a backup (where the permanent jobs are supposed to come from, in an economy where massive layoffs and corporate shrinkage are the order of the day, is not explained).

As the reformers profess their concern for poor children 8 (while proposing to make them even poorer), the work ethic (as jobs for the unskilled get even scarcer) and the overburdened taxpayer, it's easy to miss their underlying message—that women have gotten out of hand. They may pay lip service to the idea that men too should be held responsible for the babies they father. But in practice there is no way to force poor, unemployed men to support their children or to stigmatize men as well as women for having babies out of wedlock. This is, after all, still a culture that regards pregnancy as the woman's problem and childrearing as the woman's job. And so, predictably, women are the chief targets of the reformers' punitive policies and rhetoric. It's women who will lose benefits; women who stand accused of deliberately having babies as a meal ticket; women who are (as usual) charged with the social failures of their sons. Given the paucity of decently paying jobs available to poor women or the men they're likely to be involved with, demanding that they not have children unless they have jobs or husbands to support them is tantamount to demanding that they not have children at all. (Note the logic: Motherhood is honorable work if supported by a man but parasitic self-indulgence if supported by the public.) Put that demand together with laws restricting abortion for poor women and teenagers, and the clear suggestion is that they shouldn't have sex either.

While this brand of misogyny is specifically aimed at poor 9 black women, it would be a mistake to think the rest of us are off the hook. For one thing (as Whitehead and other pro-familists are quick to remind us), it's all too easy in this age of high divorce and unemployment rates for a woman who imagined herself securely middle-class to unexpectedly become an impoverished single mother. Anyway, there is a thin line between fear and loathing of welfare mothers and moral distaste for unmarried mothers per se. Secretary of Health and Human Services Donna Shalala, a feminist and one of the more liberal members of the Clinton cabinet, has said, "I don't like to put this in moral terms, but I do believe that having children out of wedlock is just wrong." The language the welfare reformers use—the vocabulary of *stigma* and *illegitimacy*—unnervingly recalls the repressive moral climate of my own teenage years.

10   I can't listen to harangues about illegitimacy without getting posttraumatic flashbacks. Let's be clear about what the old stigma meant: a vicious double standard of sexual morality for men and women; the hobbling of female sexuality with shame, guilt and inhibition; panic over dislodged diaphragms and late periods; couples trapped into marriages one or both never wanted; pregnant girls barred from school and hidden in homes for unwed mothers; enormous pressure on women to get married early and not be too picky about it.

11   Is it silly to worry that in the post-*Roe* v. *Wade*, post-Pill nineties some version of fifties morality could reassert itself? I don't think so. Activists with a moral cause can be very persuasive. Who would have imagined a few years ago that there would be a public debate about restricting cigarettes as an addictive drug? Abortion may still be legal, but its opponents have done a good job of bringing back its stigma (ironically, this is one reason a lot of pregnant teenagers decide to give birth).

12   Many pro-familists, above all those who call themselves communitarians, are openly nostalgic for a sterner moral order. They argue that we have become a society too focused on rights instead of duties, on personal freedom and happiness instead of sacrifice for the common good. If the welfare reformers appeal to people's self-righteousness, the communitarians tap an equally potent emotion—guilt. In our concern for our own fulfillment, they argue, we are doing irreparable harm to our children.

13   Whitehead's *Atlantic* article cites psychologist Judith Wallerstein and other researchers to support her contention that while adults have benefited from the freedom to divorce and procreate outside marriage, children have suffered. Children in single-parent families, Whitehead warns, are not only at great risk of being poor but are more likely to have emotional and behavioral problems, drop out of school, abuse drugs. She calls on Americans to recognize that our experiment with greater freedom has failed and to "act to overcome the legacy of family disruption."

14   I don't doubt that the fragility of today's family life is hard on kids. It doesn't take a social scientist to figure out that a lone parent is more vulnerable than two to a host of pressures, or that children whose familial world has just collapsed need support

that their parents, depleted by the struggle to get their own lives in order, may not be able to give. But Whitehead's response, and that of communitarians generally, amounts to lecturing parents to pull up their socks, stop being selfish, and do their duty. This moralistic approach does not further a discussion of what to do when adults' need for satisfying relationships conflicts with children's need for stability. It merely stops the conversation.

Women, of course, are particularly susceptible to guilt mon-   15
gering: If children are being neglected, if marriages are failing, whose fault can it be but ours? And come on now, who is that "parent" whose career is really interfering with family life? (Hint: It's the one who gets paid less.) While the children Judith Wallerstein interviewed were clearly miserable about their parents' breakups, she made it equally clear that the parents weren't self-indulgent monsters, only people who could no longer stand the emotional deadness of their lives. Are we prepared to say that it's too bad, but their lives simply don't matter?

This is the message I get from David Blankenhorn, coeditor   16
of a pro-family anthology and newsletter, who exhorts us to "analyze the family *primarily* through the eyes of children" (my emphasis). I think this idea is profoundly wrongheaded. Certainly we need to take children seriously, which means empathizing with their relatively powerless perspective and never unthinkingly shifting our burdens to their weaker backs. On the other hand, children are more narcissistic than most adults ever dream of being—if my daughter had her way, I'd never leave the house. They too have to learn that other people's needs and feelings must be taken into account.

Besides, children are the next generation's adults. There's   17
something tragic about the idea that parents should sacrifice their own happiness for the sake of children who will grow up to sacrifice in turn (in my generation, that prospect inspired pop lyrics like, "Hope I die before I get old"). Instead of preaching sacrifice, we should be asking what it is about our social structure that puts adults and children at such terrible odds, and how we might change this. Faced with a shortage of food, would we decide parents have to starve so their kids can eat— or try to figure out how to increase food production?

Intelligent social policy on family issues has to start with a   18
deeper understanding of why marriage and the two-parent family are in trouble: not because people are more selfish than they used to be but because of basic—and basically desirable— changes in our culture. For most of history, marriage has not been primarily a moral or an emotional commitment but an economic and social contract. Men supported women and children and had unquestioned authority as head of the household.

Women took care of home, children, and men's personal and sexual needs. Now that undemocratic contract, on which an entire social order rested, is all but dead. Jobs and government benefits, along with liberalized sexual mores, allow women and their children to survive (if often meagerly) outside marriage; as a result, women expect more of marriage and are less willing to put up with unsatisfying or unequal relationships. For men, on the other hand, traditional incentives to marry and stay married have eroded.

19   What's left when the old contract is gone is the desire for love, sexual passion, intimate companionship. But those desires are notoriously inadequate as a basis for domestic stability. Human emotions are unpredictable. People change. And in the absence of the social compulsion exerted by that contract, moral platitudes about sacrifice count for little. Nor is it possible to bring back the compulsion without restoring inequality as well. Restrict divorce? Men who want out will still abandon their families as they did in the past; it's women with young children and less earning power who are likely to be trapped. Punish single parenthood? Women will bear the brunt.

20   The dogmatic insistence that only the two-parent family can properly provide for children is a self-fulfilling prophecy. As even some pro-familists recognize, the larger society must begin to play an active part in meeting the economic and social needs the family once fulfilled. This means, first of all, making a collective commitment to the adequate support of every child. Beyond that, it means opening our minds to the possibility of new forms of community, in which children have close ties with a *number* of adults and therefore a stable home base that does not totally depend either on one vulnerable parent or on one couple's emotional and sexual bond.

21   Of course, no social structure can guarantee permanence: In earlier eras, families were regularly broken up by death, war and abandonment. Yet a group that forms for the specific purpose of cooperative child-rearing might actually inspire more long-term loyalty than marriage, which is supposed to provide emotional and sexual fulfillment but often does not. The practical support and help parents would gain from such an arrangement—together with the greater freedom to pursue their own personal lives—would be a strong incentive for staying in it, and the inevitable conflicts and incompatibilities among the group members would be easier to tolerate than the intense deprivation of an unhappy marriage.

22   It's time, in other words, to think about what has so long been unthinkable, to replace reflexive dismissiveness with questions. What, for instance, can we learn from the kibbutz—how might

some of its principles be adapted to Americans' very different circumstances? What worked and didn't work about the communal experiments of the sixties and seventies? What about more recent projects, like groups of old people moving in together to avoid going to nursing homes? Or the "co-housing" movement of people who are buying land in the suburbs or city apartment buildings and dividing the space between private dwellings and communal facilities such as dining rooms and child-care centers?

I'm not suggesting that there's anything like an immediate   23 practical solution to our present family crisis. What we can do, though, is stop insisting on false solutions that scapegoat women and oversimplify the issues. Perhaps then a real discussion— worthy of Americans' inventiveness and enduring attraction to frontiers—will have a chance to begin.

Claudia Wallis
THE CASE FOR STAYING HOME

Although the role of women in our culture has changed dramatically in the last half-century, some women have opted to return to the role of motherhood on a full-time basis. The essay by Claudia Wallis that is included below explores this phenomenon. It was written for the "society" section of the news weekly Time Magazine. *Claudia Wallis is the editor-at-large for* Time, *and specializes in stories about health and science, women's and children's issues, and education. She was the third woman in the magazine's history to be named editor and has written over 20 cover stories for this well-known and influential publication, including the cover stories "Who was Jesus?" (1988), "Adoption" (1989), "Vitamins" (1992), "The Ice Man" (1992), "Dinosaurs" (1993), "The Info Highway" (1993), and "Sex in America" (1993). In 1990, she coordinated* TIME's *special issue "Women: The Road Ahead," which received an award from the National Women's Political Caucus. As you read this piece, you might consider how Wallis's interest in women's*

causes squares with what might, at first glance, seem to be a re-
turn to a time when women had fewer choices. How does the
writer negotiate that difficult rhetorical situation?

1   It's 6:35 in the morning, and Cheryl Nevins, 34, dressed for
work in a silky black maternity blouse and skirt, is busily tending to Ryan, 2½, and Brendan, 11 months, at their home in the
leafy Edgebrook neighborhood of Chicago. Both boys are sob-
bing because Reilly, the beefy family dog, knocked Ryan over.
In a blur of calm, purposeful activity, Nevins, who is 8 months
pregnant, shoves the dog out into the backyard, changes Ryan's
diaper on the family-room rug, heats farina in the microwave
and feeds Brendan cereal and sliced bananas while crooning
Open, Shut Them to encourage the baby to chew. Her husband
Joe, 35, normally out the door by 5:30 a.m. for his job as a finance manager for Kraft Foods, makes a rare appearance in
the morning muddle. "I do want to go outside with you," he
tells Ryan, who is clinging to his leg, "but Daddy has to work
every day except Saturdays and Sundays. That stinks."

2   At 7:40, Vera Orozco, the nanny, arrives to begin her 10½-
hour shift at the Nevinses'. Cheryl, a labor lawyer for the
Chicago board of education, hands over the baby and checks
her e-mail from the kitchen table. "I almost feel apprehensive
if I leave for work without logging on," she confesses. Between
messages, she helps Ryan pull blue Play-Doh from a container,
then briefs Orozco on the morning's events: "They woke up
early. Ryan had his poop this morning, this guy has not."
Throughout the day, Orozco will note every meal and activity
on a tattered legal pad on the kitchen counter so Nevins can
stay up to speed.

3   Suddenly it's 8:07, and the calm mom shifts from cruise control into hyperdrive. She must be out the door by 8:10 to make
the 8:19 train. Once on the platform, she punches numbers
into her cell phone, checks her voice mail and then leaves a
message for a co-worker. On the train, she makes more calls
and proofreads documents. "Right now, work is crazy," says
Nevins, who has been responsible for negotiating and administering seven agreements between the board and labor unions.

4   Nevins is "truly passionate" about her job, but after seven
years, she's about to leave it. When the baby arrives, she will
take off at least a year, maybe two, maybe five. "It's hard. I'm
giving up a great job that pays well, and I have a lot of respect
and authority," she says. The decision to stay home was a
tough one, but most of her working-mom friends have made
the same choice. She concludes, "I know it's the right thing."

Ten, 15 years ago, it all seemed so doable. Bring home the 5
bacon, fry it up in a pan, split the second shift with some sensitive New Age man. But slowly the snappy, upbeat work-life
rhythm has changed for women in high-powered posts like
Nevins. The U.S. workweek still averages around 34 hours,
thanks in part to a sluggish manufacturing sector. But for
those in financial services, it's 55 hours; for top executives in
big corporations, it's 60 to 70, says Catalyst, a research and
consulting group that focuses on women in business. For dual-
career couples with kids under 18, the combined work hours
have grown from 81 a week in 1977 to 91 in 2002, according to
the Families and Work Institute. E-mail, pagers and cell
phones promised to allow execs to work from home. Who
knew that would mean that home was no longer a sanctuary?
Today BlackBerrys sprout on the sidelines of Little League
games. Cell phones vibrate at the school play. And it's back
to the e-mail after *Goodnight Moon*. "We are now the workaholism capital of the world, surpassing the Japanese," laments
sociologist Arlie Hochschild, author of *The Time Bind: When
Work Becomes Home and Home Becomes Work*.

Meanwhile, the pace has quickened on the home front, where 6
a mother's job has expanded to include managing a packed
schedule of child-enhancement activities. In their new book
The Mommy Myth, Susan Douglas, a professor of communication studies at the University of Michigan, and Meredith
Michaels, who teaches philosophy at Smith College, label the
phenomenon the New Momism. Nowadays, they write, our
culture insists that "to be a remotely decent mother, a woman
has to devote her entire physical, psychological, emotional,
and intellectual being, 24/7, to her children." It's a standard of
success that's "impossible to meet," they argue. But that sure
doesn't stop women from trying.

For most mothers—and fathers, for that matter—there is lit- 7
tle choice but to persevere on both fronts to pay the bills.
Indeed, 72% of mothers with children under 18 are in the work
force—a figure that is up sharply from 47% in 1975 but has
held steady since 1997. And thanks in part to a dodgy economy,
there's growth in another category, working women whose husbands are unemployed, which has risen to 6.4% of all married
couples.

But in the professional and managerial classes, where higher 8
incomes permit more choices, a reluctant revolt is under way.
Today's women execs are less willing to play the juggler's game,
especially in its current high-speed mode, and more willing to
sacrifice paychecks and prestige for time with their family.
Like Cheryl Nevins, most of these women are choosing not so

much to drop out as to stop out, often with every intention of returning. Their mantra: You can have it all, just not all at the same time. Their behavior, contrary to some popular reports, is not a June Cleaver-ish embrace of old-fashioned motherhood but a new, nonlinear approach to building a career and an insistence on restoring some kind of sanity. "What this group is staying home from is the 80-hour-a-week job," says Hochschild. "They are committed to work, but many watched their mothers and fathers be ground up by very long hours, and they would like to give their own children more then they got. They want a work-family balance."

9   Because these women represent a small and privileged sector, the dimensions of the exodus are hard to measure. What some experts are zeroing in on is the first-ever drop-off in workplace participation by married mothers with a child less than 1 year old. That figure fell from 59% in 1997 to 53% in 2000. The drop may sound modest, but, says Howard Hayghe, an economist at the Bureau of Labor Statistics, "that's huge," and the figure was roughly the same in 2002. Significantly, the drop was mostly among women who were white, over 30 and well educated.

10   Census data reveal an uptick in stay-at-home moms who hold graduate or professional degrees—the very women who seemed destined to blast through the glass ceiling. Now 22% of them are home with their kids. A study by Catalyst found that 1 in 3 women with M.B.A.s are not working full-time (it's 1 in 20 for their male peers). Economist and author Sylvia Ann Hewlett, who teaches at Columbia University, says she sees a brain drain throughout the top 10% of the female labor force (those earning more than $55,000). "What we have discovered in looking at this group over the last five years," she says, "is that many women who have any kind of choice are opting out."

11   Other experts say the drop-out rate isn't climbing but is merely more visible now that so many women are in high positions. In 1971 just 9% of medical degrees, 7% of law degrees and 4% of M.B.A.s were awarded to women; 30 years later, the respective figures were 43%, 47% and 41%.

The Generation Factor

12   For an older group of female professionals who came of age listening to Helen Reddy roar, the exodus of younger women can seem disturbingly regressive. Fay Clayton, 58, a partner in a small Chicago law firm, watched in dismay as her 15-person

firm lost three younger women who left after having kids, though one has since returned part time. "I fear there is a generational split and possibly a step backwards for younger women," she says.

Others take a more optimistic view. "Younger women have 13 greater expectations about the work-life balance," says Joanne Brundage, 51, founder and executive director of Mothers & More, a mothers' support organization with 7,500 members and 180 chapters in the U.S. While boomer moms have been reluctant to talk about their children at work for fear that "people won't think you're a professional," she observes, younger women "feel more entitled to ask for changes and advocate for themselves." That sense of confidence is reflected in the evolution of her organization's name. When Brundage founded it in Elmhurst, Ill., 17 years ago, it was sheepishly called FEMALE, for Formerly Employed Mothers at Loose Ends.

Brundage may be ignoring that young moms can afford to 14 think flexibly about life and work while pioneering boomers first had to prove they could excel in high-powered jobs. But she's right about the generational difference. A 2001 survey by Catalyst of 1,263 men and women born from 1964 to 1975 found that Gen Xers "didn't want to have to make the kind of trade-offs the previous generation made. They're rejecting the stresses and sacrifices," says Catalyst's Paulette Gerkovich. "Both women and men rated personal and family goals higher than career goals."

A newer and larger survey, conducted late last year by the 15 Boston-area marketing group Reach Advisors, provides more evidence of a shift in attitudes. Gen X (which it defined as those born from 1965 to 1979) moms and dads said they spent more time on child rearing and household tasks than did boomer parents (born from 1945 to 1964). Yet Gen Xers were much more likely than boomers to complain that they wanted more time. "At first we thought, Is this just a generation of whiners?" says Reach Advisors president James Chung. "But they really wish they had more time with their kids." In the highest household-income bracket ($120,000 and up), Reach Advisors found that 51% of Gen X moms were home full time, compared with 33% of boomer moms. But the younger stay-at-home moms were much more likely to say they intended to return to work: 46% of Gen Xers expressed that goal, compared with 34% of boomers.

Chung and others speculate that the attitude differences can 16 be explained in part by forces that shaped each generation. While boomer women sought career opportunities that were unavailable to their mostly stay-at-home moms, Gen Xers were the latchkey kids and the children of divorce. Also, their careers have bumped along in a roller-coaster, boom-bust economy that may have shaken their faith in finding reliable satisfaction at work.

17   Pam Pala, 35, of Salt Lake City, Utah, is in some ways typical. She spent years building a career in the heavily male construction industry, rising to the position of construction project engineer with a big firm. But after her daughter was born 11 months ago, she decided to stay home to give her child the attention Pala had missed as a kid. "I grew up in a divorced family. My mom couldn't take care of us because she had to work," she says. "We went to baby-sitters or stayed home alone and were scared and hid under the bathroom counter whenever the doorbell rang." Pala wants to return to work when her daughter is in school, and she desperately hopes she won't be penalized for her years at home. "I have a feeling that I'll have to start lower on the totem pole than where I left," she says. "It seems unfair."

Maternal Desire and Doubts

18   Despite such misgivings, most women who step out of their careers find expected delights on the home front, not to mention the enormous relief of no longer worrying about shortchanging their kids. Annik Miller, 32, of Minneapolis, Minn., decided not to return to her job as a business-systems consultant at Wells Fargo Bank after she checked out day-care options for her son Alex, now 11 months. "I had one woman look at me honestly and say she could promise that my son would get undivided attention eight times each day—four bottles and four diaper changes," says Miller. "I appreciated her honesty, but I knew I couldn't leave him."

19   Others appreciate a slower pace and being there when a child asks a tough question. In McLean, Va., Oakie Russell's son Dylan, 8, recently inquired, out of the blue, "Mom, who is God's father?" Says Russell, 45, who gave up a dream job at PBS: "So, you're standing at the sink with your hands in the dishwater and you're thinking, 'Gee, that's really complicated. But I'm awfully glad I'm the one you're asking.' "

20   Psychologist Daphne de Marneffe speaks to these private joys in a new book, *Maternal Desire* (Little Brown). De Marneffe argues that feminists and American society at large have ignored the basic urge that most mothers feel to spend meaningful time with their children. She decries the rushed fragments of quality time doled out by working moms trying to do it all. She writes, "Anyone who has tried to 'fit everything in' can attest to how excruciating the five-minute wait at the

supermarket checkout line becomes, let alone a child's slow-motion attempt to tie her own shoes when you're running late getting her to school." The book, which puts an idyllic gloss on staying home, could launch a thousand resignations.

What de Marneffe largely omits is the sense of pride and meaning that women often gain from their work. Women who step out of their careers can find the loss of identity even tougher than the loss of income. "I don't regret leaving, but a huge part of me is gone," says Bronwyn Towle, 41, who surrendered a demanding job as a Washington lobbyist to be with her two sons. Now when she joins her husband Raymond, who works at the U.S. Chamber of Commerce, at work-related dinners, she feels sidelined. "Everyone will be talking about what they're doing," says Towle, "and you say, 'I'm a stay-at-home mom.' It's conference-buzz kill."   21

Last year, after her youngest child went to kindergarten, Towle eased back into the world of work. She found a part-time job in a forward-thinking architectural firm but hopes to return to her field eventually. "I wish there was more part-time or job-sharing work," she says. It's a wish expressed by countless formerly working moms.   22

Building On-Ramps

Hunter College sociologist Pamela Stone has spent the past few years interviewing 50 stay-at-home mothers in seven U.S. cities for a book on professional women who have dropped out. "Work is much more of a culprit in this than the more rosy view that it's all about discovering how great your kids are," says Stone. "Not that these mothers don't want to spend time with their kids. But many of the women I talked to have tried to work part time or put forth job-sharing plans, and they're shot down. Despite all the family-friendly rhetoric, the workplace for professionals is extremely, extremely inflexible."   23

That's what Ruth Marlin, 40, of New York City found even at the family-friendly International Planned Parenthood Federation. After giving birth to her second child, 15 months ago, she was allowed to ease back in part time. But Marlin, an attorney and a senior development officer, was turned down when she asked to make the part-time arrangement permanent. "With the job market contracted so much, the opportunities just aren't there anymore," says Marlin, who hates to see her $100,000 law education go to waste. "Back in the dotcom days, people just wanted employees to stay. There was more flexibility. Who knows? Maybe the market will change."   24

25   There are signs that in some corners it is changing. In industries that depend on human assets, serious work is being done to create more part-time and flexible positions. At PricewaterhouseCoopers, 10% of the firm's female partners are on a part-time schedule, according to the accounting firm's chief diversity officer, Toni Riccardi. And, she insists, it's not career suicide: "A three-day week might slow your progress, but it won't prohibit you" from climbing the career ladder. The company has also begun to address the e-mail ball and chain. In December PWC shut down for 11 days over the holidays for the first time ever. "We realize people do need to rejuvenate," says Riccardi. "They don't, if their eye is on the BlackBerry and their hand is on a keyboard."

26   PWC is hardly alone. Last month economist Hewlett convened a task force of leaders from 14 companies and four law firms, including Goldman Sachs and Pfizer, to discuss what she calls the hidden brain drain of women and minority professionals. "We are talking about how to create off-ramps and on-ramps, slow lanes and acceleration ramps" so that workers can more easily leave, slow down or re-enter the work force, she explains.

27   "This is a war for talent," says Carolyn Buck Luce, a partner at the accounting firm Ernst & Young, who co-chairs the task force. Over the past 20 years, half of new hires at Ernst & Young have been women, she notes, and the firm is eager not only to keep them but to draw back those who have left to tend their children. This spring Deloitte Touche Tohmatsu will launch a Personal Pursuits program, allowing above-average performers to take up to five years of unpaid leave for personal reasons. Though most benefits will be suspended, the firm will continue to cover professional licensing fees for those on leave and will pay to send them for weeklong annual training sessions to keep their skills in shape. Such efforts have spawned their own goofy jargon. Professionals who return to their ex-employers are known as boomerangs, and the effort to reel them back in is called alumni relations.

28   One reason businesses are getting serious about the brain drain is demographics. With boomers nearing retirement, a shortfall of perhaps 10 million workers appears likely by 2010. "The labor shortage has a lot to do with it," says Melinda Wolfe, managing director and head of Goldman Sachs' global leadership and diversity.

29   Will these programs work? Will part-time jobs really be part time, as opposed to full-time jobs paid on a partial basis? Will serious professionals who shift into a slow lane be able to pick up velocity when their kids are grown? More important, will corporate culture evolve to a point where employees feel

genuinely encouraged to use these options? Anyone who re-
members all the talk about flex time in the 1980s will be
tempted to dismiss the latest ideas for making the workplace
family-friendly. But this time, perhaps, the numbers may be on
the side of working moms—along with many working dads
who are looking for options.

On-ramps, slow lanes, flexible options and respect for all   30
such pathways can't come soon enough for mothers eager to
set examples and offer choices for the next generation. Terri
Laughlin, 38, a stay-at-home mom and former psychology professor at the University of Nebraska at Lincoln, was alarmed a
few weeks ago when her daughters Erin, 8, and Molly, 6, announced their intentions to marry men "with enough money so
we can stay at home." Says Laughlin: "I want to make sure
they realize that although it's wonderful staying at home, that's
only one of many options. What I hope to show them is that at
some point I can re-create myself and go back to work."

Barbara LeBey

AMERICAN FAMILIES
ARE DRIFTING APART

*By any measure, the traditional American family is, as the title
of this piece suggests, "drifting apart." As other essays in this
section suggest, of course, our assessment of the impact of that
fact is based at least partially—and perhaps to a great degree—
on how we define "family." This essay focuses on changes to
the whole "landscape" of marriage and family. Its author,
Barbara LeBey, is an attorney and former judge. She has authored two books on issues related to the American family:*
Family Estrangements: How They Begin, How to Mend
Them, How to Cope with Them *(2001) and* Remarried with
Children: Ten Secrets for Successfully Blending & Extending
Your Family *(2004).*

A variety of reasons—from petty grievances to deep-seated prej-   1
udices, misunderstandings to all-out conflicts, jealousies, sibling

rivalry, inheritance feuds, family business disputes, and homosexual outings—are cause for families to grow apart. Family estrangements are becoming more numerous, more intense, and more hurtful. When I speak to groups on the subject, I always ask: Who has or had an estrangement or knows someone who does? Almost every hand in the room goes up. Sisters aren't speaking to each other since one of them took the silver when Mom died. Two brothers rarely visit because their wives don't like each other. A son alienates himself from his family when he marries a woman who wants to believe that he sprung from the earth. Because Mom is the travel agent for guilt trips, her daughter avoids contact with her. A family banishes a daughter for marrying outside her race or religion. A son eradicates a divorced father when he reveals his homosexuality. And so it goes.

2   The nation is facing a rapidly changing family relationship landscape. Every assumption made about the family structure has been challenged, from the outer boundaries of single mothers raising out-of-wedlock children to gay couples having or adopting children to grandparents raising their grandchildren. If the so-called traditional family is having trouble maintaining harmony, imagine what problems can and do arise in less-conventional situations. Fault lines in Americans' family structure were widening throughout the last 40 years of the 20th century. The cracks became evident in the mid 1970s when the divorce rate doubled. According to a 1999 Rutgers University study, divorce has risen 30% since 1970; the marriage rate has fallen faster, and just 38% of Americans consider themselves happy in their married state, a drop from 53% 25 years ago. Today, 51% of all marriages end in divorce.

3   How Americans managed to alter their concept of marriage and family so profoundly during those four decades is the subject of much scholarly investigation and academic debate. In a May, 2000, *New York Times Magazine* article titled "The Pursuit of Autonomy," the writer maintains that "the family is no longer a haven; all too often a center of dysfunction, it has become one with the heartless world that surrounds it." Unlike the past, the job that fits you in your 20s is not the job or career you'll likely have in your 40s. This is now true of marriage as well—the spouse you had in your 20s may not be the one you will have after you've gone through your midlife crisis.

4   In the 1960s, four main societal changes occurred that have had an enormous impact on the traditional family structure. The sexual revolution, women's liberation movement, states' relaxation of divorce laws, and mobility of American families have converged to foster family alienation, exacerbate old family rifts, and create new ones. It must be emphasized, however,

that many of these changes had positive outcomes. The nation experienced a strengthened social conscience, women's rights, constraints on going to war, and a growing tolerance for diversity, but society also paid a price.

The 1960s perpetuated the notion that we are first and fore- 5 most *entitled* to happiness and fulfillment. It's positively unAmerican *not* to seek it! This idea goes back to that early period of our history when Thomas Jefferson dropped the final term from British philosopher John Locke's definition of human rights—"life, liberty, and . . . property"—and replaced it with what would become the slogan of our new nation: "the pursuit of happiness." In the words of author Gail Sheehy, the 1960s generation "expressed their collective personality as idealistic, narcissistic, anti-establishment, hairy, horny and preferably high."

Any relationship that was failing to deliver happiness was 6 being tossed out like an empty beer can, including spousal ones. For at least 20 years, the pharmaceutical industry has learned how to cash in on the American obsession with feeling good by hyping mood drugs to rewire the brain circuitry for happiness through the elimination of sadness and depression.

Young people fled from the confines of family, whose mem- 7 bers were frantic, worrying about exactly where their adult children were and what they were doing. There were probably more estrangements between parents and adult children during the 1960s and early 1970s than ever before.

In the wake of the civil rights movement and Pres. Lyndon 8 Johnson's Great Society came the women's liberation movement, and what a flashy role it played in changing perceptions about the family structure. Women who graduated from college in the late 1960s and early 1970s were living in a time when they could establish and assert their independent identities. In Atlanta, Emory Law School's 1968 graduating class had six women in it, the largest number ever to that point, and all six were in the top 10%, including the number-one graduate. In that same period, many all-male colleges opened their doors to women for the first time. No one could doubt the message singer Helen Reddy proclaimed: "I am woman, hear me roar." For all the self-indulgence of the "hippie" generation, there was an intense awakening in young people of a recognition that civil rights must mean equal rights for everyone in our society, and that has to include women.

Full equality was the battle cry of every minority, a status 9 that women claimed despite their majority position. As they had once marched for the right to vote, women began marching for sexual equality and the same broad range of career and job opportunities that were always available to men. Financial independence gave women the freedom to walk away from unhappy marriages. This was a dramatic departure from the puritanical sense of duty that had been woven into the American fabric since the birth of this nation.

10   For all the good that came out of this movement, though, it also changed forever traditional notions of marriage, motherhood, and family unity, as well as that overwhelming sense of children first. Even in the most-conservative young families, wives were letting their husbands know that they were going back to work or back to school. Many women had to return to work either because there was a need for two incomes to maintain a moderate standard of living or because they were divorced and forced to support their offspring on their own. "Don't ask, don't tell" day-care centers proliferated where overworked, undertrained staff, and two-income yuppie parents, ignored the children's emotional needs—all in the name of equality and to enable women to reclaim their identities. Some might say these were the parents who ran away from home.

11   Many states began to approve legislation that allowed no-fault divorce, eliminating the need to lay blame on spouses or stage adulterous scenes in sleazy motels to provide evidence for states that demanded such evidence for divorces. The legal system established procedures for easily dissolving marriages, dividing property, and sharing responsibility for the children. There were even do-it-yourself divorce manuals on bookstore shelves. Marriage had become a choice rather than a necessity, a one-dimensional status sustained almost exclusively by emotional satisfaction and not worth maintaining in its absence. Attitudes about divorce were becoming more lenient, so much so that the nation finally elected its first divorced president in 1980—Ronald Reagan.

12   With divorced fathers always running the risk of estrangement from their children, this growing divorce statistic has had the predictable impact of increasing the number of those estrangements. Grandparents also experienced undeserved fallout from divorce, since, almost invariably, they are alienated from their grandchildren.

13   The fourth change, and certainly one of the most pivotal, was the increased mobility of families that occurred during those four decades. Family members were no longer living in close proximity to one another. The organization man moved to wherever he could advance more quickly up the corporate ladder. College graduates took the best job offer, even if it was 3,000 miles away from where they grew up and where their family still lived.

Some were getting out of small towns for new vistas, new ad-   14
ventures, and new job opportunities. Others were fleeing the
overcrowded dirty cities in search of cleaner air, a more reasonable cost of living, and retirement communities in snow-
free, warmer, more-scenic locations. Moving from company to
company had begun, reaching what is now a crescendo of job-
hopping. Many young people chose to marry someone who
lived in a different location, so family ties were geographically
severed for indeterminate periods of time, sometimes forever.

According to Lynn H. Dennis' *Corporate Relocation Takes Its*   15
Toll on Society, during the 10 years from 1989 to 1999, more
than 5,000,000 families were relocated one or more times by
their employers. In addition to employer-directed moves, one
out of five Americans relocated at least once, not for exciting adventure, but for economic advancement and/or a safer
place to raise children. From March, 1996, to March, 1997,
42,000,000 Americans, or 16% of the population, packed up
and moved from where they were living to another location.
That is a striking statistic. Six million of these people moved
from one region of the country to another, and young adults
aged 20 to 29 were the most mobile, making up 32% of the
moves during that year. This disbursement of nuclear families
throughout the country disconnected them from parents,
brothers, sisters, grandparents, aunts, uncles, and cousins—
the extended family and all its adhesive qualities.

Today, with cell phones, computers, faxes, and the Internet,   16
the office can be anywhere, including in the home. Therefore,
we can *live* anywhere we want to. If that is the case, why aren't
more people choosing to live in the cities or towns where they
grew up? There's no definitive answer. Except for the praise
heaped on "family values," staying close to family no longer
plays a meaningful role in choosing where we reside.

These relocations require individuals to invest an enormous   17
amount of time to reestablish their lives without help from
family or old friends. Although nothing can compare to the experience of immigrants who left their countries knowing they
probably would never see their families again, the phenomenon of Americans continually relocating makes family relationships difficult to sustain.

Our culture tends to focus on the individual, or, at most, on   18
the nuclear family, downplaying the benefits of extended families, though their role is vital in shaping our lives. The notion
of "moving on" whenever problems arise has been a time-
honored American concept. Too many people would rather
cast aside some family member than iron out the situation and
keep the relationship alive. If we don't get along with our

father or if our mother doesn't like our choice of mate or our way of life, we just move away and see the family once or twice a year. After we're married, with children in school, and with both parents working, visits become even more difficult. If the family visits are that infrequent, why bother at all? Some children grow up barely knowing any of their relatives. Contact ceases; rifts don't resolve; and divisiveness often germinates into a full-blown estrangement.

19   In an odd sort of way, the more financially independent people become, the more families scatter and grow apart. It's not a cause, but it is a facilitator. Tolerance levels decrease as financial means increase. Just think how much more we tolerate from our families when they are providing financial support. Look at the divorced wife who depends on her family for money to supplement alimony and child support, the student whose parents are paying all college expenses, or the brother who borrows family money to save his business.

20   Recently, a well-known actress being interviewed in a popular magazine was asked, if there was one thing she could change in her family, what would it be? Her answer was simple: "That we could all live in the same city." She understood the importance of being near loved ones and how, even in a harmonious family, geographical distance often leads to emotional disconnectedness. When relatives are regularly in each other's company, they will usually make a greater effort to get along. Even when there is dissension among family members, they are more likely to work it out, either on their own or because another relative has intervened to calm the troubled waters. When rifts occur, relatives often need a real jolt to perform an act of forgiveness. Forgiving a family member can be the hardest thing to do, probably because the emotional bonds are so much deeper and usually go all the way back to childhood. Could it be that blood is a thicker medium in which to hold a grudge?

21   With today's families scattered all over the country, the matriarch or patriarch of the extended family is far less able to keep his or her kin united, caring, and supportive of one another. In these disconnected nuclear families, certain trends—workaholism, alcoholism, depression, severe stress, isolation, escapism, and a push toward continuous supervised activity for children—are routinely observed. What happened to that family day of rest and togetherness? We should mourn its absence.

22   For the widely dispersed baby boomers with more financial means than any prior generation, commitment, intimacy, and family togetherness have never been high on their list of priorities. How many times have you heard of family members

trying to maintain a relationship with a relative via e-mail and answering machines? One young man now sends his Mother's Day greeting by leaving a message for his mom on *his* answering machine. When she calls to scold him for forgetting to call her, she'll get a few sweet words wishing her a happy Mother's Day and his apology for being too busy to call or send a card! His sister can expect the same kind of greeting for her birthday, but only if she bothers to call to find out why her brother hadn't contacted her.

Right now, and probably for the forseeable future, we will be searching for answers to the burgeoning problems we unwittingly created by these societal changes, but don't be unduly pessimistic. Those who have studied and understood the American psyche are far more optimistic. The 19th-century French historian and philosopher Alexis de Tocqueville once said of Americans, "No natural boundary seems to be set to the effort of Americans, and in their eyes what is not yet done, is only what they have not yet attempted to do." Some day, I hope this mindset will apply not to political rhetoric on family values, but to bringing families back together again.   23

Barbara Dafoe Whitehead

DAN QUAYLE
WAS RIGHT

The Atlantic Monthly, *a respected left-of-center magazine of current affairs and opinion, received more letters in response to the following excerpted essay by Barbara Dafoe Whitehead than it has ever received in response to an article. When it was published in April 1993, its title was alluding to former Vice President Dan Quayle's controversial opposition to the family arrangements of TV character Murphy Brown. Whitehead, a native of Wisconsin (born 1944) and co-director of The National Marriage Project at Rutgers University, in part defends a position that she expressed in an earlier article in the* Washington Post, *which helped motivate the vice president to make family issues central to the 1992 presidential campaign.*

1   Divorce and out-of-wedlock childbirth are transforming the lives of American children. In the postwar generation more than 80 percent of children grew up in a family with two biological parents who were married to each other. By 1980 only 50 percent could expect to spend their entire childhood in an intact family. If current trends continue, less than half of all children born today will live continuously with their own mother and father throughout childhood. Most American children will spend several years in a single-mother family. Some will eventually live in stepparent families, but because stepfamilies are more likely to break up than intact (by which I mean two-biological parent) families, an increasing number of children will experience family breakup two or even three times during childhood.

2   According to a growing body of social-scientific evidence, children in families disrupted by divorce and out-of-wedlock birth do worse than children in intact families on several measures of well-being. Children in single-parent families are six times as likely to be poor. They are also likely to stay poor longer. Twenty-two percent of children in one-parent families will experience poverty during childhood for seven years or more, as compared with only two percent of children in two-parent families. A 1988 survey by the National Center for Health Statistics found that children in single-parent families are two to three times as likely as children in two-parent families to have emotional and behavioral problems. They are also more likely to drop out of high school, to get pregnant as teenagers, to abuse drugs, and to be in trouble with the law. Compared with children in intact families, children from disrupted families are at a much higher risk for physical or sexual abuse.

3   Contrary to popular belief, many children do not "bounce back" after divorce or remarriage. Difficulties that are associated with family breakup often persist into adulthood. Children who grow up in single-parent or stepparent families are less successful as adults, particularly in the two domains of life— love and work—that are most essential to happiness. Needless to say, not all children experience such negative effects. However, research shows that many children from disrupted families have a harder time achieving intimacy in a relationship, forming a stable marriage, or even holding a steady job.

4   Despite this growing body of evidence, it is nearly impossible to discuss changes in family structure without provoking angry protest. Many people see the discussion as no more than an attack on struggling single mothers and their children: Why blame single mothers when they are doing the very best they can? After all, the decision to end a marriage or a relationship

is wrenching, and few parents are indifferent to the painful burden this decision imposes on their children. Many take the perilous step toward single parenthood as a last resort, after their best efforts to hold a marriage together have failed. Consequently, it can seem particularly cruel and unfeeling to remind parents of the hardships their children might suffer as a result of family breakup. Other people believe that the dramatic changes in family structure, though regrettable, are impossible to reverse. Family breakup is an inevitable feature of American life, and anyone who thinks otherwise is indulging in nostalgia or trying to turn back the clock. Since these new family forms are here to stay, the reasoning goes, we must accord respect to single parents, not criticize them. Typical is the view expressed by a Brooklyn woman in a recent letter to *The New York Times:* "Let's stop moralizing or blaming single parents and unwed mothers, and give them the respect they have earned and the support they deserve."

Such views are not to be dismissed. Indeed, they help to explain why family structure is such an explosive issue for Americans. The debate about it is not simply about the social-scientific evidence, although that is surely an important part of the discussion. It is also a debate over deeply held and often conflicting values. How do we begin to reconcile our long-standing belief in equality and diversity with an impressive body of evidence that suggests that not all family structures produce equal outcomes for children? How can we square traditional notions of public support for dependent women and children with a belief in women's right to pursue autonomy and independence in childbearing and child-rearing? How do we uphold the freedom of adults to pursue individual happiness in their private relationships and at the same time respond to the needs of children for stability, security, and permanence in their family lives? What do we do when the interests of adults and children conflict? These are the difficult issues at stake in the debate over family structure.

In the past these issues have turned out to be too difficult and too politically risky for debate. In the mid-1960s Daniel Patrick Moynihan, then an assistant secretary of labor, was denounced as a racist for calling attention to the relationship between the prevalence of black single-mother families and the lower socioeconomic standing of black children. For nearly twenty years the policy and research communities backed away from the entire issue. In 1980 the Carter Administration convened a historic White House Conference on Families, designed to address the growing problems of children and families in America. The result was a prolonged, publicly subsidized quarrel over the definition of "family." No President since has tried to hold a national family conference. Last year, at a time when the rate of out-of-wedlock births had reached a historic high, Vice President Dan Quayle was ridiculed for criticizing Murphy Brown. In short, every time the issue of family structure has been raised, the response has been first controversy, then retreat, and finally silence.

7   Yet it is also risky to ignore the issue of changing family structure. In recent years the problems associated with family disruption have grown. Overall child well-being has declined, despite a decrease in the number of children per family, an increase in the educational level of parents, and historically high levels of public spending. After dropping in the 1960s and 1970s, the proportion of children in poverty has increased dramatically, from 15 percent in 1970 to 20 percent in 1990, while the percentage of adult Americans in poverty has remained roughly constant. The teen suicide rate has more than tripled. Juvenile crime has increased and become more violent. School performance has continued to decline. There are no signs that these trends are about to reverse themselves.

8   If we fail to come to terms with the relationship between family structure and declining child well-being, then it will be increasingly difficult to improve children's life prospects, no matter how many new programs the federal government funds. Nor will we be able to make progress in bettering school performance or reducing crime or improving the quality of the nation's future work force—all domestic problems closely connected to family breakup. Worse, we may contribute to the problem by pursuing policies that actually increase family instability and breakup.

From Death to Divorce

9   Across time and across cultures, family disruption has been regarded as an event that threatens a child's well-being and even survival. This view is rooted in a fundamental biological fact: unlike the young of almost any other species, the human child is born in an abjectly helpless and immature state. Years of nurture and protection are needed before the child can achieve physical independence. Similarly, it takes years of interaction with at least one but ideally two or more adults for a child to develop into a socially competent adult. Children raised in virtual isolation from human beings, though physically intact, display few recognizably human behaviors. The social arrangement that

has proved most successful in ensuring the physical survival and promoting the social development of the child is the family unit of the biological mother and father. Consequently, any event that permanently denies a child the presence and protection of a parent jeopardizes the life of the child.

The classic form of family disruption is the death of a parent.   10 Throughout history this has been one of the risks of childhood. Mothers frequently died in childbirth, and it was not unusual for both parents to die before the child was grown. As recently as the early decades of this century children commonly suffered the death of at least one parent. Almost a quarter of the children born in this country in 1900 lost one parent by the time they were fifteen years old. Many of these children lived with their widowed parent, often in a household with other close relatives. Others grew up in orphanages and foster homes.

The meaning of parental death, as it has been transmitted   11 over time and faithfully recorded in world literature and lore, is unambiguous and essentially unchanging. It is universally regarded as an untimely and tragic event. Death permanently severs the parent-child bond, disrupting forever one of the child's earliest and deepest human attachments. It also deprives a child of the presence and protection of an adult who has a biological stake in, as well as an emotional commitment to, the child's survival and well-being. In short, the death of a parent is the most extreme and severe loss a child can suffer.

Because a child is so vulnerable in a parent's absence, there   12 has been a common cultural response to the death of a parent: an outpouring of support from family, friends, and strangers alike. The surviving parent and child are united in their grief as well as their loss. Relatives and friends share in the loss and provide valuable emotional and financial assistance to the bereaved family. Other members of the community show sympathy for the child, and public assistance is available for those who need it. This cultural understanding of parental death has formed the basis for a tradition of public support to widows and their children. Indeed, as recently as the beginning of this century widows were the only mothers eligible for pensions in many states, and today widows with children receive more generous welfare benefits from Survivors Insurance than do other single mothers with children who depend on Aid to Families With Dependent Children.

It has taken thousands upon thousands of years to reduce the   13 threat of parental death. Not until the middle of the twentieth century did parental death cease to be a commonplace event for children in the United States. By then advances in medicine had dramatically reduced mortality rates for men and women.

14   At the same time, other forms of family disruption—separation, divorce, out-of-wedlock birth—were held in check by
powerful religious, social, and legal sanctions. Divorce was
widely regarded both as a deviant behavior, especially threatening to mothers and children, and as a personal lapse:
"Divorce is the public acknowledgment of failure," a 1940s sociology textbook noted. Out-of-wedlock birth was stigmatized,
and stigmatization is a powerful means of regulating behavior,
as any smoker or overeater will testify. Sanctions against nonmarital childbirth discouraged behavior that hurt children and
exacted compensatory behavior that helped them. Shotgun
marriages and adoption, two common responses to nonmarital
birth, carried a strong message about the risks of premarital
sex and created an intact family for the child.

15   Consequently, children did not have to worry much about
losing a parent through divorce or never having had one because of nonmarital birth. After a surge in divorces following
the Second World War, the rate leveled off. Only 11 percent of
children born in the 1950s would by the time they turned eighteen see their parents separate or divorce. Out-of-wedlock
childbirth barely figured as a cause of family disruption. In the
1950s and early 1960s, five percent of the nation's births were
out of wedlock. Blacks were more likely than whites to bear
children outside marriage, but the majority of black children
born in the twenty years after the Second World War were
born to married couples. The rate of family disruption reached
a historic low point during those years.

16   A new standard of family security and stability was established in postwar America. For the first time in history the vast
majority of the nation's children could expect to live with married biological parents throughout childhood. Children might
still suffer other forms of adversity—poverty, racial discrimination, lack of educational opportunity—but only a few would be
deprived of the nurture and protection of a mother and a father. No longer did children have to be haunted by the classic
fears vividly dramatized in folklore and fable—that their parents would die, that they would have to live with a stepparent
and stepsiblings, or that they would be abandoned. These were
the years when the nation confidently boarded up orphanages
and closed foundling hospitals, certain that such institutions
would never again be needed. In movie theaters across the
country parents and children could watch the drama of
parental separation and death in the great Disney classics, secure in the knowledge that such nightmare visions as the death
of Bambi's mother and the wrenching separation of Dumbo
from his mother were only make-believe.

In the 1960s the rate of family disruption suddenly began to   17
rise. After inching up over the course of a century, the divorce
rate soared. Throughout the 1950s and early 1960s the divorce
rate held steady at fewer than ten divorces a year per 1,000
married couples. Then, beginning in about 1965, the rate increased sharply, peaking at twenty-three divorces per 1,000
marriages by 1979. (In 1974 divorce passed death as the leading cause of family breakup.) The rate has leveled off at about
twenty-one divorces per 1,000 marriages—the figure for 1991.
The out-of-wedlock birth rate also jumped. It went from five
percent in 1960 to 27 percent in 1990. In 1990 close to 57 percent of births among black mothers were nonmarital, and
about 17 percent among white mothers. Altogether, about one
out of every four women who had a child in 1990 was not married. With rates of divorce and nonmarital birth so high, family
disruption is at its peak. Never before have so many children
experienced family breakup caused by events other than death.
Each year a million children go through divorce or separation
and almost as many more are born out of wedlock.

Half of all marriages now end in divorce. Following divorce,   18
many people enter new relationships. Some begin living together. Nearly half of all cohabiting couples have children in the
household. Fifteen percent have new children together. Many
cohabiting couples eventually get married. However, both cohabiting and remarried couples are more likely to break up
than couples in first marriages. Even social scientists find it
hard to keep pace with the complexity and velocity of such
patterns. In the revised edition (1992) of his book *Marriage,
Divorce, Remarriage*, the sociologist Andrew Cherlin ruefully
comments: "If there were a truth-in-labeling law for books, the
title of this edition should be something long and unwieldy
like *Cohabitation, Marriage, Divorce, More Cohabitation, and
Probably Remarriage*."

Under such conditions growing up can be a turbulent experi-   19
ence. In many single-parent families children must come to
terms with the parent's love life and romantic partners. Some
children live with cohabiting couples, either their own unmarried parents or a biological parent and a live-in partner. Some
children born to cohabiting parents see their parents break up.
Others see their parents marry, but 56 percent of them (as compared with 31 percent of the children born to married parents)
later see their parents' marriages fall apart. All told, about three
quarters of children born to cohabiting couples will live in a
single-parent home at least briefly. One of every four children
growing up in the 1990s will eventually enter a stepfamily.
According to one survey, nearly half of all children in stepparent

families will see their parents divorce again by the time they reach their late teens. Since 80 percent of divorced fathers remarry, things get even more complicated when the romantic or marital history of the noncustodial parent, usually the father, is taken into account. Consequently, as it affects a significant number of children, family disruption is best understood not as a single event but as a string of disruptive events: separation, divorce, life in a single-parent family, life with a parent and live-in lover, the remarriage of one or both parents, life in one stepparent family combined with visits to another stepparent family, the breakup of one or both stepparent families. And so on. This is one reason why public schools have a hard time knowing whom to call in an emergency.

20   Given its dramatic impact on children's lives, one might reasonably expect that this historic level of family disruption would be viewed with alarm, even regarded as a national crisis. Yet this has not been the case. In recent years some people have argued that these trends pose a serious threat to children and to the nation as a whole, but they are dismissed as declinists, pessimists, or nostalgists, unwilling or unable to accept the new facts of life. The dominant view is that the changes in family structure are, on balance, positive.

A Shift in the Social Metric

21   There are several reasons why this is so, but the fundamental reason is that at some point in the 1970s Americans changed their minds about the meaning of these disruptive behaviors. What had once been regarded as hostile to children's best interests was now considered essential to adults' happiness. In the 1950s most Americans believed that parents should stay in an unhappy marriage for the sake of the children. The assumption was that a divorce would damage the children, and the prospect of such damage gave divorce its meaning. By the mid-1970s a majority of Americans rejected that view. Popular advice literature reflected the shift. A book on divorce published in the mid-1940s tersely asserted: "Children are entitled to the affection and *association* of two parents, not one." Thirty years later another popular divorce book proclaimed just the opposite: "A two-parent home is not the only emotional structure within which a child can be happy and healthy. . . . The parents who take care of themselves will be best able to take care of their children." At about the same time, the long-standing taboo against out-of-wedlock childbirth also collapsed. By the mid-1970s three fourths of Americans said that

it was not morally wrong for a woman to have a child outside marriage.

Once the social metric shifts from child well-being to adult   22
well-being, it is hard to see divorce and nonmarital birth in anything but a positive light. However distressing and difficult they may be, both of these behaviors can hold out the promise of greater adult choice, freedom, and happiness. For unhappy spouses, divorce offers a way to escape a troubled or even abusive relationship and make a fresh start. For single parents, remarriage is a second try at marital happiness as well as a chance for relief from the stress, loneliness, and economic hardship of raising a child alone. For some unmarried women, nonmarital birth is a way to beat the biological clock, avoid marrying the wrong man, and experience the pleasures of motherhood. Moreover, divorce and out-of-wedlock birth involve a measure of agency and choice; they are man- and woman-made events. To be sure, not everyone exercises choice in divorce or nonmarital birth. Men leave wives for younger women, teenage girls get pregnant accidentally—yet even these unhappy events reflect the expansion of the boundaries of freedom and choice.

This cultural shift helps explain what otherwise would be   23
inexplicable: the failure to see the rise in family disruption as a severe and troubling national problem. It explains why there is virtually no widespread public sentiment for restigmatizing either of these classically disruptive behaviors and no sense—no public consensus—that they can or should be avoided in the future. . . .

Dinosaurs Divorce

It is true that many adults benefit from divorce or remarriage.   24
According to one study, nearly 80 percent of divorced women and 50 percent of divorced men say they are better off out of the marriage. Half of divorced adults in the same study report greater happiness. A competent self-help book called *Divorce and New Beginnings* notes the advantages of single parenthood: single parents can "develop their own interests, fulfill their own needs, choose their own friends and engage in social activities of their choice. Money, even if limited, can be spent as they see fit." Apparently, some women appreciate the opportunity to have children out of wedlock. "The real world, however, does not always allow women who are dedicated to their careers to devote the time and energy it takes to find—or be found by—the perfect husband and father wannabe," one

woman said in a letter to *The Washington Post*. A mother and chiropractor from Avon, Connecticut, explained her unwed maternity to an interviewer this way: "It is selfish, but this was something I needed to do for me."

25   There is very little in contemporary popular culture to contradict this optimistic view. But in a few small places another perspective may be found. Several racks down from its divorce cards, Hallmark offers a line of cards for children—To Kids With Love. These cards come six to a pack. Each card in the pack has a slightly different message. According to the package, the "thinking of you" messages will let a special kid "know how much you care." Though Hallmark doesn't quite say so, it's clear these cards are aimed at divorced parents. "I'm sorry I'm not always there when you need me but I hope you know I'm always just a phone call away." Another card reads: "Even though your dad and I don't live together anymore, I know he's still a very special part of your life. And as much as I miss you when you're not with me, I'm still happy that you two can spend time together."

26   Hallmark's messages are grounded in a substantial body of well-funded market research. Therefore it is worth reflecting on the divergence in sentiment between the divorce cards for adults and the divorce cards for kids. For grown-ups, divorce heralds new beginnings (A HOT NEW SINGLE). For children, divorce brings separation and loss ("I'm sorry I'm not always there when you need me").

27   An even more telling glimpse into the meaning of family disruption can be found in the growing children's literature on family dissolution. Take, for example, the popular children's book *Dinosaurs Divorce: A Guide for Changing Families* (1986), by Laurene Krasny Brown and Marc Brown. This is a picture book, written for very young children. The book begins with a short glossary of "divorce words" and encourages children to "see if you can find them" in the story. The words include "family counselor," "separation agreement," "alimony," and "child custody." The book is illustrated with cartoonish drawings of green dinosaur parents who fight, drink too much, and break up. One panel shows the father dinosaur, suitcase in hand, getting into a yellow car.

28   The dinosaur children are offered simple, straightforward advice on what to do about the divorce. *On custody decisions*: "When parents can't agree, lawyers and judges decide. Try to be honest if they ask you questions; it will help them make better decisions." *On selling the house*: "If you move, you may have to say good-bye to friends and familiar places. But soon your new home will feel like the place you really belong." *On the economic impact of divorce*: "Living with one parent almost

always means there will be less money. Be prepared to give up some things." *On holidays:* "Divorce may mean twice as much celebrating at holiday times, but you may feel pulled apart." *On parents' new lovers:* "You may sometimes feel jealous and want your parent to yourself. Be polite to your parents' new friends, even if you don't like them at first." *On parents' remarriage:* "Not everyone loves his or her stepparents, but showing them respect is important."

These cards and books point to an uncomfortable and gener- 29 ally unacknowledged fact: what contributes to a parent's happiness may detract from a child's happiness. All too often the adult quest for freedom, independence, and choice in family relationships conflicts with a child's developmental needs for stability, constancy, harmony, and permanence in family life. In short, family disruption creates a deep division between parents' interests and the interests of children.

One of the worst consequences of these divided interests is a 30 withdrawal of parental investment in children's well-being. As the Stanford economist Victor Fuchs has pointed out, the main source of social investment in children is private. The investment comes from the children's parents. But parents in disrupted families have less time, attention, and money to devote to their children. The single most important source of disinvestment has been the widespread withdrawal of financial support and involvement by fathers. Maternal investment, too, has declined, as women try to raise families on their own and work outside the home. Moreover, both mothers and fathers commonly respond to family breakup by investing more heavily in themselves and in their own personal and romantic lives.

Sometimes the tables are completely turned. Children are 31 called upon to invest in the emotional well-being of their parents. Indeed, this seems to be the larger message of many of the children's books on divorce and remarriage. *Dinosaurs Divorce* asks children to be sympathetic, understanding, respectful, and polite to confused, unhappy parents. The sacrifice comes from the children: "Be prepared to give up some things." In the world of divorcing dinosaurs, the children rather than the grown-ups are the exemplars of patience, restraint, and good sense.

Three Seventies Assumptions

As it first took shape in the 1970s, the optimistic view of family 32 change rested on three bold new assumptions. At that time, because the emergence of the changes in family life was so recent, there was little hard evidence to confirm or dispute these assumptions. But this was an expansive moment in American life.

33   The first assumption was an economic one: that a woman could now afford to be a mother without also being a wife. There were ample grounds for believing this. Women's workforce participation had been gradually increasing in the postwar period, and by the beginning of the 1970s women were a strong presence in the workplace. What's more, even though there was still a substantial wage gap between men and women, women had made considerable progress in a relatively short time toward better-paying jobs and greater employment opportunities. More women than ever before could aspire to serious careers as business executives, doctors, lawyers, airline pilots, and politicians. This circumstance, combined with the increased availability of child care, meant that women could take on the responsibilities of a breadwinner, perhaps even a sole breadwinner. This was particularly true for middle-class women. According to a highly regarded 1977 study by the Carnegie Council on Children, "The greater availability of jobs for women means that more middle-class children today survive their parents' divorce without a catastrophic plunge into poverty."

34   Feminists, who had long argued that the path to greater equality for women lay in the world of work outside the home, endorsed this assumption. In fact, for many, economic independence was a stepping-stone toward freedom from both men and marriage. As women began to earn their own money, they were less dependent on men or marriage, and marriage diminished in importance. In Gloria Steinem's memorable words, "A woman without a man is like a fish without a bicycle."

35   This assumption also gained momentum as the meaning of work changed for women. Increasingly, work had an expressive as well as an economic dimension: being a working mother not only gave you an income but also made you more interesting and fulfilled than a stay-at-home mother. Consequently, the optimistic economic scenario was driven by a cultural imperative. Women would achieve financial independence because, culturally as well as economically, it was the right thing to do.

36   The second assumption was that family disruption would not cause lasting harm to children and could actually enrich their lives. *Creative Divorce: A New Opportunity for Personal Growth*, a popular book of the seventies, spoke confidently to this point: "Children can survive any family crisis without permanent damage—and grow as human beings in the process. . . ." Moreover, single-parent and stepparent families created a more extensive kinship network than the nuclear family. This network

would envelop children in a web of warm and supportive relationships. "Belonging to a stepfamily means there are more people in your life," a children's book published in 1982 notes. "More sisters and brothers, including the step ones. More people you think of as grandparents and aunts and uncles. More cousins. More neighbors and friends. . . . Getting to know and like so many people (and having them like you) is one of the best parts of what being in a stepfamily . . . is all about."

The third assumption was that the new diversity in family   37
structure would make America a better place. Just as the nation has been strengthened by the diversity of its ethnic and racial groups, so it would be strengthened by diverse family forms. The emergence of these brave new families was but the latest chapter in the saga of American pluralism.

Another version of the diversity argument stated that the   38
real problem was not family disruption itself but the stigma still attached to these emergent family forms. This lingering stigma placed children at psychological risk, making them feel ashamed or different; as the ranks of single-parent and stepparent families grew, children would feel normal and good about themselves.

These assumptions continue to be appealing, because they   39
accord with strongly held American beliefs in social progress. Americans see progress in the expansion of individual opportunities for choice, freedom, and self-expression. Moreover, Americans identify progress with growing tolerance of diversity. Over the past half century, the pollster Daniel Yankelovich writes, the United States has steadily grown more open-minded and accepting of groups that were previously perceived as alien, untrustworthy, or unsuitable for public leadership or social esteem. One such group is the burgeoning number of single-parent and stepparent families.

The Education of Sara McLanahan

In 1981 Sara McLanahan, now a sociologist at Princeton   40
University's Woodrow Wilson School, read a three-part series by Ken Auletta in *The New Yorker*. Later published as a book titled *The Underclass*, the series presented a vivid portrait of the drug addicts, welfare mothers, and school dropouts who took part in an education-and-training program in New York City. Many were the children of single mothers, and it was Auletta's clear implication that single-mother families were contributing to the growth of an underclass. McLanahan was taken

aback by this notion. "It struck me as strange that he would be viewing single mothers at that level of pathology."

41   "I'd gone to graduate school in the days when the politically correct argument was that single-parent families were just another alternative family form, and it was fine," McLanahan explains, as she recalls the state of social-scientific thinking in the 1970s. Several empirical studies that were then current supported an optimistic view of family change. (They used tiny samples, however, and did not track the well-being of children over time.)

42   One, *All Our Kin*, by Carol Stack, was required reading for thousands of university students. It said that single mothers had strengths that had gone undetected and unappreciated by earlier researchers. The single-mother family, it suggested, is an economically resourceful and socially embedded institution. In the late 1970s McLanahan wrote a similar study that looked at a small sample of white single mothers and how they coped. "So I was very much of that tradition."

43   By the early 1980s, however, nearly two decades had passed since the changes in family life had begun. During the intervening years a fuller body of empirical research had emerged: studies that used large samples, or followed families through time, or did both. Moreover, several of the studies offered a child's-eye view of family disruption. The National Survey on Children, conducted by the psychologist Nicholas Zill, had set out in 1976 to track a large sample of children aged seven to eleven. It also interviewed the children's parents and teachers. It surveyed its subjects again in 1981 and 1987. By the time of its third round of interviews the eleven-year-olds of 1976 were the twenty-two-year-olds of 1987. The California Children of Divorce Study, directed by Judith Wallerstein, a clinical psychologist, had also been going on for a decade. E. Mavis Hetherington, of the University of Virginia, was conducting a similar study of children from both intact and divorced families. For the first time it was possible to test the optimistic view against a large and longitudinal body of evidence.

44   It was to this body of evidence that Sara McLanahan turned. When she did, she found little to support the optimistic view of single motherhood. On the contrary. When she published her findings with Irwin Garfinkel in a 1986 book, *Single Mothers and Their Children*, her portrait of single motherhood proved to be as troubling in its own way as Auletta's.

45   One of the leading assumptions of the time was that single motherhood was economically viable. Even if single mothers did face economic trials, they wouldn't face them for long, it was argued, because they wouldn't remain single for long: single

motherhood would be a brief phase of three to five years, followed by marriage. Single mothers would be economically re-
silient: if they experienced setbacks, they would recover quickly.
It was also said that single mothers would be supported by informal networks of family, friends, neighbors, and other single
mothers. As McLanahan shows in her study, the evidence de-
molishes all these claims.

For the vast majority of single mothers, the economic spec-   46
trum turns out to be narrow, running between precarious and
desperate. Half the single mothers in the United States live below
the poverty line. (Currently, one out of ten married couples with
children is poor.) Many others live on the edge of poverty. Even
single mothers who are far from poor are likely to experience
persistent economic insecurity. Divorce almost always brings a
decline in the standard of living for the mother and children.

Moreover, the poverty experienced by single mothers is no   47
more brief than it is mild. A significant number of all single
mothers never marry or remarry. Those who do, do so only
alter spending roughly six years, on average, as single parents.
For black mothers the duration is much longer. Only 33 percent of African-American mothers had remarried within ten
years of separation. Consequently, single motherhood is hardly
a fleeting event for the mother, and it is likely to occupy a third
of the child's childhood. Even the notion that single mothers
are knit together in economically supportive networks is not
borne out by the evidence. On the contrary, single parenthood
forces many women to be on the move, in search of cheaper
housing and better jobs. This need-driven restless mobility
makes it more difficult for them to sustain supportive ties to
family and friends, let alone other single mothers.

Single-mother families are vulnerable not just to poverty but   48
to a particularly debilitating form of poverty: welfare dependency. The dependency takes two forms: First, single mothers,
particularly unwed mothers, stay on welfare longer than other
welfare recipients. Of those never-married mothers who receive
welfare benefits, almost 40 percent remain on the rolls for ten
years or longer. Second, welfare dependency tends to be passed
on from one generation to the next. McLanahan says, "Evidence
on intergenerational poverty indicates that, indeed, offspring
from [single-mother] families are far more likely to be poor and
to form mother-only families than are offspring who live with
two parents most of their pre-adult life." Nor is the intergenerational impact of single motherhood limited to African-
Americans, as many people seem to believe. Among white
families, daughters of single parents are 53 percent more likely
to marry as teenagers, 111 percent more likely to have children

as teenagers, 164 percent more likely to have a premarital birth, and 92 percent more likely to dissolve their own marriages. All these intergenerational consequences of single motherhood increase the likelihood of chronic welfare dependency.

49   McLanahan cites three reasons why single-mother families are so vulnerable economically. For one thing, their earnings are low. Second, unless the mothers are widowed, they don't receive public subsidies large enough to lift them out of poverty. And finally, they do not get much support from family members—especially the fathers of their children. In 1982 single white mothers received an average of $1,246 in alimony and child support, black mothers an average of $322. Such payments accounted for about 10 percent of the income of single white mothers and for about 3.5 percent of the income of single black mothers. These amounts were dramatically smaller than the income of the father in a two-parent family and also smaller than the income from a second earner in a two-parent family. Roughly 60 percent of single white mothers and 80 percent of single black mothers received no support at all.

50   Until the mid 1980s, when stricter standards were put in place, child-support awards were only about half to two-thirds what the current guidelines require. Accordingly, there is often a big difference in the living standards of divorced fathers and of divorced mothers with children. After divorce the average annual income of mothers and children is $13,500 for whites and $9,000 for nonwhites, as compared with $25,000 for white nonresident fathers and $13,600 for non-white nonresident fathers. Moreover, since child-support awards account for a smaller portion of the income of a high-earning father, the drop in living standards can be especially sharp for mothers who were married to upper-level managers and professionals.

51   Unwed mothers are unlikely to be awarded any child support at all, partly because the paternity of their children may not have been established. According to one recent study, only 20 percent of unmarried mothers receive child support.

52   Even if single mothers escape poverty, economic uncertainty remains a condition of life. Divorce brings a reduction in income and standard of living for the vast majority of single mothers. One study, for example, found that income for mothers and children declines on average about 30 percent, while fathers experience a 10 to 15 percent increase in income in the year following a separation. Things get even more difficult when fathers fail to meet their child-support obligations. As a result, many divorced mothers experience a wearing uncertainty about the family budget: whether the check will come in or not; whether new sneakers can be bought this month or not; whether the electric bill will be paid on time or not. Uncertainty

about money triggers other kinds of uncertainty. Mothers and children often have to move to cheaper housing after a divorce. One study shows that about 38 percent of divorced mothers and their children move during the first year after a divorce. Even several years later the rate of moves for single mothers is about a third higher than the rate for two-parent families. It is also common for a mother to change her job or increase her working hours or both following a divorce. Even the composition of the household is likely to change, with other adults, such as boyfriends or babysitters, moving in and out.

All this uncertainty can be devastating to children. Anyone who knows children knows that they are deeply conservative creatures. They like things to stay the same. So pronounced is this tendency that certain children have been known to request the same peanut-butter-and-jelly sandwich for lunch for years on end. Children are particularly set in their ways when it comes to family, friends, neighborhoods, and schools. Yet when a family breaks up, all these things may change. The novelist Pat Conroy has observed that "each divorce is the death of a small civilization." No one feels this more acutely than children. 53

Sara McLanahan's investigation and others like it have helped to establish a broad consensus on the economic impact of family disruption on children. Most social scientists now agree that single motherhood is an important and growing cause of poverty, and that children suffer as a result. (They continue to argue, however, about the relationship between family structure and such economic factors as income inequality, the loss of jobs in the inner city, and the growth of low-wage jobs.) By the mid-1980s, however, it was clear that the problem of family disruption was not confined to the urban underclass, nor was its sole impact economic. Divorce and out-of-wedlock childbirth were affecting middle- and upper-class children, and these more privileged children were suffering negative consequences as well. It appeared that the problems associated with family breakup were far deeper and far more widespread than anyone had previously imagined. 54

The Missing Father

Judith Wallerstein is one of the pioneers in research on the long-term psychological impact of family disruption on children. The California Children of Divorce Study, which she directs, remains the most enduring study of the long-term effects of divorce on children and their parents. Moreover, it represents the best-known effort to look at the impact of divorce on middle-class children. The California children entered the 55 study without pathological family histories. Before divorce they lived in stable, protected homes. And although some of the children did experience economic insecurity as the result of divorce, they were generally free from the most severe forms of poverty associated with family breakup. Thus the study and the resulting book (which Wallerstein wrote with Sandra Blakeslee), *Second Chances: Men, Women, and Children a Decade After Divorce* (1989), provide new insight into the consequences of divorce which are not associated with extreme forms of economic or emotional deprivation.

56   When, in 1971, Wallerstein and her colleagues set out to conduct clinical interviews with 131 children from the San Francisco area, they thought they were embarking on a short-term study. Most experts believed that divorce was like a bad cold. There was a phase of acute discomfort, and then a short recovery phase. According to the conventional wisdom, kids would be back on their feet in no time at all. Yet when Wallerstein met these children for a second interview more than a year later, she was amazed to discover that there had been no miraculous recovery. In fact, the children seemed to be doing worse.

57   The news that children did not "get over" divorce was not particularly welcome at the time. Wallerstein recalls, "We got angry letters from therapists, parents, and lawyers saying we were undoubtedly wrong. They said children are really much better off being released from an unhappy marriage. Divorce, they said, is a liberating experience." One of the main results of the California study was to overturn this optimistic view. In Wallerstein's cautionary words, "Divorce is deceptive. Legally it is a single event, but psychologically it is a chain—sometimes a never-ending chain—of events, relocations, and radically shifting relationships strung through time, a process that forever changes the lives of the people involved."

58   Five years after divorce more than a third of the children experienced moderate or severe depression. At ten years a significant number of the now young men and women appeared to be troubled, drifting, and underachieving. At fifteen years many of the thirtyish adults were struggling to establish strong love relationships of their own. In short, far from recovering from their parents' divorce, a significant percentage of these grownups were still suffering from its effects. In fact, according to Wallerstein, the long-term effects of divorce emerge at a time when young adults are trying to make their own decisions about love, marriage, and family. Not all children in the study suffered negative consequences. But Wallerstein's research presents a sobering picture of divorce. "The child of divorce faces

many additional psychological burdens in addition to the normative tasks of growing up," she says.

Divorce not only makes it more difficult for young adults to   59
establish new relationships. It also weakens the oldest primary
relationship: that between parent and child. According to
Wallerstein, "Parent-child relationships are permanently altered by divorce in ways that our society has not anticipated."
Not only do children experience a loss of parental attention at
the onset of divorce, but they soon find that at every stage of
their development their parents are not available in the same
way they once were. "In a reasonably happy intact family,"
Wallerstein observes, "the child gravitates first to one parent
and then to the other, using skills and attributes from each in
climbing the developmental ladder." In a divorced family, children find it "harder to find the needed parent at needed times."
This may help explain why very young children suffer the most
as the result of family disruption. Their opportunities to engage in this kind of ongoing process are the most truncated
and compromised.

The father-child bond is severely, often irreparably, damaged   60
in disrupted families. In a situation without historical precedent, an astonishing and disheartening number of American
fathers are failing to provide financial support to their children. Often, more than the father's support check is missing.
Increasingly, children are bereft of any contact with their fathers. According to the National Survey of Children, in disrupted families only one child in six, on average, saw his or her
father as often as once a week in the past year. Close to half did
not see their father at all in the past year. As time goes on, contact becomes even more infrequent. Ten years after a marriage
breaks up, more than two thirds of children report not having
seen their father for a year. Not surprisingly, when asked to
name the "adults you look up to and admire," only 20 percent
of children in single-parent families named their father, as
compared with 52 percent of children in two-parent families. A
favorite complaint among Baby Boom Americans is that their
fathers were emotionally remote guys who worked hard, came
home at night to eat supper, and didn't have much to say to or
do with the kids. But the current generation has a far worse father problem: many of their fathers are vanishing entirely.

Even for fathers who maintain regular contact, the pattern   61
of father-child relationships changes. The sociologists Andrew
Cherlin and Frank Furstenberg, who have studied broken families, write that the fathers behave more like other relatives
than like parents. Rather than helping with homework or carrying out a project with their children, nonresidential fathers

are likely to take the kids shopping, to the movies, or out to dinner. Instead of providing steady advice and guidance, divorced fathers become "treat" dads.

62   Apparently—and paradoxically—it is the visiting relationship itself, rather than the frequency of visits, that is the real source of the problem. According to Wallerstein, the few children in the California study who reported visiting with their fathers once or twice a week over a ten-year period still felt rejected. The need to schedule a special time to be with the child, the repeated leave-takings, and the lack of connection to the child's regular, daily schedule leaves many fathers adrift, frustrated, and confused. Wallerstein calls the visiting father a parent without portfolio.

63   The deterioration in father-child bonds is most severe among children who experience divorce at an early age, according to a recent study. Nearly three quarters of the respondents, now young men and women, report having poor relationships with their fathers. Close to half have received psychological help, nearly a third have dropped out of high school, and about a quarter report having experienced high levels of problem behavior or emotional distress by the time they became young adults.

Long-Term Effects

64   Since most children live with their mothers after divorce, one might expect that the mother-child bond would remain unaltered and might even be strengthened. Yet research shows that the mother-child bond is also weakened as the result of divorce. Only half of the children who were close to their mothers before a divorce remained equally close after the divorce. Boys, particularly, had difficulties with their mothers. Moreover, mother-child relationships deteriorated over time. Whereas teenagers in disrupted families were no more likely than teenagers in intact families to report poor relationships with their mothers, 30 percent of young adults from disrupted families have poor relationships with their mothers, as compared with 16 percent of young adults from intact families. Mother-daughter relationships often deteriorate as the daughter reaches young adulthood. The only group in society that derives any benefit from these weakened parent-child ties is the therapeutic community. Young adults from disrupted families are nearly twice as likely as those from intact families to receive psychological help.

65   Some social scientists have criticized Judith Wallerstein's research because her study is based on a small clinical sample and does not include a control group of children from intact families. However, other studies generally support and strengthen

her findings. Nicholas Zill has found similar long-term effects on children of divorce, reporting that "effects of marital discord and family disruption are visible twelve to twenty-two years later in poor relationships with parents, high levels of problem behavior, and an increased likelihood of dropping out of high school and receiving psychological help." Moreover, Zill's research also found signs of distress in young women who seemed relatively well adjusted in middle childhood and adolescence. Girls in single-parent families are also at much greater risk for precocious sexuality, teenage marriage, teenage pregnancy, nonmarital birth, and divorce than are girls in two-parent families.

Zill's research shows that family disruption strongly affects 66 school achievement as well. Children in disrupted families are nearly twice as likely as those in intact families to drop out of high school; among children who do drop out, those from disrupted families are less likely eventually to earn a diploma or a GED. Boys are at greater risk for dropping out than girls, and are also more likely to exhibit aggressive, acting-out behaviors. Other research confirms these findings. According to a study by the National Association of Elementary School Principals, 33 percent of two-parent elementary school students are ranked as high achievers, as compared with 17 percent of single-parent students. The children in single-parent families are also more likely to be truant or late or to have disciplinary action taken against them. Even after controlling for race, income, and religion, scholars find significant differences in educational attainment between children who grow up in intact families and children who do not. In his 1992 study *America's Smallest School: The Family*, Paul Barton shows that the proportion of two-parent families varies widely from state to state and is related to variations in academic achievement. North Dakota, for example, scores highest on the math-proficiency test and second highest on the two-parent-family scale. The District of Columbia is second lowest on the math test and lowest in the nation on the two-parent-family scale.

Zill notes that "while coming from a disrupted family signifi- 67 cantly increases a young adult's risks of experiencing social, emotional or academic difficulties, it does not foreordain such difficulties. The majority of young people from disrupted families have successfully completed high school, do *not* currently display high levels of emotional distress or problem behavior, and enjoy reasonable relationships with their mothers." Nevertheless, a majority of these young adults do show maladjustment in their relationships with their fathers.

These findings underscore the importance of both a mother 68 and a father in fostering the emotional well-being of children. Obviously, not all children in two-parent families are free from emotional turmoil, but few are burdened with the troubles that accompany family breakup. Moreover, as the sociologist Amitai Etzioni explains in a new book, *The Spirit of Community*, two parents in an intact family make up what might be called a mutually supportive education coalition. When both parents are present, they can play different, even contradictory, roles. One parent may goad the child to achieve, while the other may encourage the child to take time out to daydream or toss a football around. One may emphasize taking intellectual risks, while the other may insist on following the teacher's guidelines. At the same time, the parents regularly exchange information about the child's school problems and achievements, and have a sense of the overall educational mission. However, Etzioni writes,

> The sequence of divorce followed by a succession of boy or girlfriends, a second marriage, and frequently another divorce and another turnover of partners often means a repeatedly disrupted educational coalition. Each change in participants involves a change in the educational agenda for the child. Each new partner cannot be expected to pick up the previous one's educational post and program. . . . As a result, changes in parenting partners mean, at best, a deep disruption in a child's education, though of course several disruptions cut deeper into the effectiveness of the educational coalition than just one. . . .

Poverty, Crime, Education

69   Family disruption would be a serious problem even if it affected only individual children and families. But its impact is far broader. Indeed, it is not an exaggeration to characterize it as a central cause of many of our most vexing social problems. Consider three problems that most Americans believe rank among the nation's pressing concerns: poverty, crime, and declining school performance.

70   More than half of the increase in child poverty in the 1980s is attributable to changes in family structure, according to David Eggebeen and Daniel Lichter, of Pennsylvania State University. In fact, if family structure in the United States had remained relatively constant since 1960, the rate of child poverty would be a third lower than it is today. This does not bode well for the future. With more than half of today's children likely to live in single-parent families, poverty and associated welfare costs threaten to become even heavier burdens on the nation.

Crime in American cities has increased dramatically and   71
grown more violent over recent decades. Much of this can be
attributed to the rise in disrupted families. Nationally, more
than 70 percent of all juveniles in state reform institutions
come from fatherless homes. A number of scholarly studies
find that even after the groups of subjects are controlled for income, boys from single-mother homes are significantly more
likely than others to commit crimes and to wind up in the juvenile justice, court, and penitentiary systems. One such study
summarizes the relationship between crime and one-parent
families in this way: "The relationship is so strong that controlling for family configuration erases the relationship between
race and crime and between low income and crime. This conclusion shows up time and again in the literature." The nation's
mayors, as well as police officers, social workers, probation
officers, and court officials, consistently point to family breakup
as the most important source of rising rates of crime.

Terrible as poverty and crime are, they tend to be concentrated   72
in inner cities and isolated from the everyday experience of many
Americans. The same cannot be said of the problem of declining
school performance. Nowhere has the impact of family breakup
been more profound or widespread than in the nation's public
schools. There is a strong consensus that the schools are failing
in their historic mission to prepare every American child to be a
good worker and a good citizen. And nearly everyone agrees that
the schools must undergo dramatic reform in order to reach that
goal. In pursuit of that goal, moreover, we have suffered no shortage of bright ideas or pilot projects or bold experiments in school
reform. But there is little evidence that measures such as curricular reform, school-based management, and school choice will
address, let alone solve, the biggest problem schools face: the rising number of children who come from disrupted families.

The great educational tragedy of our time is that many   73
American children are failing in school not because they are
intellectually or physically impaired but because they are emotionally incapacitated. In schools across the nation principals
report a dramatic rise in the aggressive, acting-out behavior
characteristic of children, especially boys, who are living in
single-parent families. The discipline problems in today's suburban school—assaults on teachers, unprovoked attacks on
other students, screaming outbursts in class—outstrip the problems that were evident in the toughest city schools a generation ago. Moreover, teachers find many children emotionally
distracted, so upset and preoccupied by the explosive drama of
their own family lives that they are unable to concentrate on
such mundane matters as multiplication tables.

74   In response, many schools have turned to therapeutic reme-
diation. A growing proportion of many school budgets is
devoted to counseling and other psychological services. The
curriculum is becoming more therapeutic: children are taking
courses in self-esteem, conflict resolution, and aggression
management. Parental advisory groups are conscientiously debating alternative approaches to traditional school discipline,
ranging from teacher training in mediation to the introduction
of metal detectors and security guards in the schools. Schools
are increasingly becoming emergency rooms of the emotions,
devoted not only to developing minds but also to repairing
hearts. As a result, the mission of the school, along with the
culture of the classroom, is slowly changing. What we are seeing, largely as a result of the new burdens of family disruption,
is the psychologization of American education.

75   Taken together, the research presents a powerful challenge to
the prevailing view of family change as social progress. Not a
single one of the assumptions underlying that view can be sustained against the empirical evidence. Single-parent families
are not able to do well economically on a mother's income. In
fact, most teeter on the economic brink, and many fall into
poverty and welfare dependency. Growing up in a disrupted
family does not enrich a child's life or expand the number of
adults committed to the child's well-being. In fact, disrupted
families threaten the psychological well-being of children and
diminish the investment of adult time and money in them.
Family diversity in the form of increasing numbers of single-
parent and stepparent families does not strengthen the social
fabric. It dramatically weakens and undermines society, placing new burdens on schools, courts, prisons, and the welfare
system. These new families are not an improvement on the nuclear family, nor are they even just as good, whether you look
at outcomes for children or outcomes for society as a whole. In
short, far from representing social progress, family change
represents a stunning example of social regress.

The Two-Parent Advantage

76   All this evidence gives rise to an obvious conclusion: growing
up in an intact two-parent family is an important source of advantage for American children. Though far from perfect as a
social institution, the intact family offers children greater security and better outcomes than its fast-growing alternatives:
single-parent and stepparent families. Not only does the intact

family protect the child from poverty and economic insecurity; it also provides greater noneconomic investments of parental time, attention, and emotional support over the entire life course. This does not mean that all two-parent families are better for children than all single-parent families. But in the face of the evidence it becomes increasingly difficult to sustain the proposition that all family structures produce equally good outcomes for children.

Curiously, many in the research community are hesitant 77 to say that two-parent families generally promote better outcomes for children than single-parent families. Some argue that we need finer measures of the extent of the family-structure effect. As one scholar has noted, it is possible, by disaggregating the data in certain ways, to make family structure "go away" as an independent variable. Other researchers point to studies that show that children suffer psychological effects as a result of family conflict preceding family breakup. Consequently, they reason, it is the conflict rather than the structure of the family that is responsible for many of the problems associated with family disruption. Others, including Judith Wallerstein, caution against treating children in divorced families and children in intact families as separate populations, because doing so tends to exaggerate the differences between the two groups. "We have to take this family by family," Wallerstein says.

Some of the caution among researchers can also be attrib- 78 uted to ideological pressures. Privately, social scientists worry that their research may serve ideological causes that they themselves do not support, or that their work may be misinterpreted as an attempt to "tell people what to do." Some are fearful that they will be attacked by feminist colleagues, or, more generally, that their comments will be regarded as an effort to turn back the clock to the 1950s—a goal that has almost no constituency in the academy. Even more fundamental, it has become risky for anyone—scholar, politician, religious leader— to make normative statements today. This reflects not only the persistent drive toward "value neutrality" in the professions but also a deep confusion about the purposes of public discourse. The dominant view appears to be that social criticism, like criticism of individuals, is psychologically damaging. The worst thing you can do is to make people feel guilty or bad about themselves.

When one sets aside these constraints, however, the case 79 against the two-parent family is remarkably weak. It is true that disaggregating data can make family structure less significant as a factor, just as disaggregating Hurricane Andrew into wind, rain, and tides can make it disappear as a meteorological phenomenon. Nonetheless, research opinion as well as common sense suggests that the effects of changes in family structure are great enough to cause concern. Nicholas Zill argues that many of the risk factors for children are doubled or more than doubled as the result of family disruption. "In epidemiological terms," he writes, "the doubling of a hazard is a substantial increase. . . . the increase in risk that dietary cholesterol poses for cardiovascular disease, for example, is far less than double, yet millions of Americans have altered their diets because of the perceived hazard."

80   The argument that family conflict, rather than the breakup of parents, is the cause of children's psychological distress is persuasive on its face. Children who grow up in high-conflict families, whether the families stay together or eventually split up, are undoubtedly at great psychological risk. And surely no one would dispute that there must be societal measures available, including divorce, to remove children from families where they are in danger. Yet only a minority of divorces grow out of pathological situations; much more common are divorces in families unscarred by physical assault. Moreover, an equally compelling hypothesis is that family breakup generates its own conflict. Certainly, many families exhibit more conflictual and even violent behavior as a consequence of divorce than they did before divorce.

81   Finally, it is important to note that clinical insights are different from sociological findings. Clinicians work with individual families, who cannot and should not be defined by statistical aggregates. Appropriate to a clinical approach, moreover, is a focus on the internal dynamics of family functioning and on the immense variability in human behavior. Nevertheless, there is enough empirical evidence to justify sociological statements about the causes of declining child well-being and to demonstrate that despite the plasticity of human response, there are some useful rules of thumb to guide our thinking about and policies affecting the family.

82   For example, Sara McLanahan says, three structural constants are commonly associated with intact families, even intact families who would not win any "Family of the Year" awards. The first is economic. In intact families, children share in the income of two adults. Indeed, as a number of analysts have pointed out, the two-parent family is becoming more rather than less necessary, because more and more families need two incomes to sustain a middle-class standard of living.

83   McLanahan believes that most intact families also provide a stable authority structure. Family breakup commonly upsets

the established boundaries of authority in a family. Children are often required to make decisions or accept responsibilities once considered the province of parents. Moreover, children, even very young children, are often expected to behave like mature adults, so that the grown-ups in the family can be free to deal with the emotional fallout of the failed relationship. In some instances family disruption creates a complete vacuum in authority; everyone invents his or her own rules. With lines of authority disrupted or absent, children find it much more difficult to engage in the normal kinds of testing behavior, the trial and error, the failing and succeeding, that define the developmental pathway toward character and competence. McLanahan says, "Children need to be the ones to challenge the rules. The parents need to set the boundaries and let the kids push the boundaries. The children shouldn't have to walk the straight and narrow at all times."

Finally, McLanahan holds that children in intact families   84
benefit from stability in what she neutrally terms "household personnel." Family disruption frequently brings new adults into the family, including stepparents, live-in boyfriends or girlfriends, and casual sexual partners. Like stepfathers, boyfriends can present a real threat to children's, particularly to daughters', security and well-being. But physical or sexual abuse represents only the most extreme such threat. Even the very best of boyfriends can disrupt and undermine a child's sense of peace and security, McLanahan says. "It's not as though you're going from an unhappy marriage to peacefulness. There can be a constant changing until the mother finds a suitable partner."

McLanahan's argument helps explain why children of wid-   85
ows tend to do better than children of divorced or unmarried mothers. Widows differ from other single mothers in all three respects. They are economically more secure, because they receive more public assistance through Survivors Insurance, and possibly private insurance or other kinds of support from family members. Thus widows are less likely to leave the neighborhood in search of a new or better job and a cheaper house or apartment. Moreover, the death of a father is not likely to disrupt the authority structure radically. When a father dies, he is no longer physically present, but his death does not dethrone him as an authority figure in the child's life. On the contrary, his authority may be magnified through death. The mother can draw on the powerful memory of the departed father as a way of intensifying her parental authority: "Your father would have wanted it this way." Finally, since widows tend to be older than divorced mothers, their love life may be less distracting.

86   Regarding the two-parent family, the sociologist David Popenoe, who has devoted much of his career to the study of families, both in the United States and in Scandinavia, makes this straightforward assertion:

> Social science research is almost never conclusive. There are always methodological difficulties and stones left unturned. Yet in three decades of work as a social scientist, I know of few other bodies of data in which the weight of evidence is so decisively on one side of the issue: on the whole, for children, two-parent families are preferable to single-parent and stepfamilies.

The Regime Effect

87 The rise in family disruption is not unique to American society. It is evident in virtually all advanced nations, including Japan, where it is also shaped by the growing participation of women in the work force. Yet the United States has made divorce easier and quicker than in any other Western nation with the sole exception of Sweden—and the trend toward solo motherhood has also been more pronounced in America. (Sweden has an equally high rate of out-of-wedlock birth, but the majority of such births are to cohabiting couples, a long-established pattern in Swedish society.) More to the point, nowhere has family breakup been greeted by a more triumphant rhetoric of renewal than in America.

88   What is striking about this rhetoric is how deeply it reflects classic themes in American public life. It draws its language and imagery from the nation's founding myth. It depicts family breakup as a drama of revolution and rebirth. The nuclear family represents the corrupt past, an institution guilty of the abuse of power and the suppression of individual freedom. Breaking up the family is like breaking away from Old World tyranny. Liberated from the bonds of the family, the individual can achieve independence and experience a new beginning, a fresh start, a new birth of freedom. In short, family breakup recapitulates the American experience.

89   This rhetoric is an example of what the University of Maryland political philosopher William Galston has called the "regime effect." The founding of the United States set in motion a new political order based to an unprecedented degree on individual rights, personal choice, and egalitarian relationships. Since then these values have spread beyond their original

domain of political relationships to define social relationships as well. During the past twenty-five years these values have had a particularly profound impact on the family.

Increasingly, political principles of individual rights and choice shape our understanding of family commitment and solidarity. Family relationships are viewed not as permanent or binding but as voluntary and easily terminable. Moreover, under the sway of the regime effect the family loses its central importance as an institution in the civil society, accomplishing certain social goals such as raising children and caring for its members, and becomes a means to achieving greater individual happiness—a lifestyle choice. Thus, Galston says, what is happening to the American family reflects the "unfolding logic of authoritative, deeply American moral-political principles."

One benefit of the regime effect is to create greater equality in adult family relationships. Husbands and wives, mothers and fathers, enjoy relationships far more egalitarian than past relationships were, and most Americans prefer it that way. But the political principles of the regime effect can threaten another kind of family relationship—that between parent and child. Owing to their biological and developmental immaturity, children are needy dependents. They are not able to express their choices according to limited, easily terminable, voluntary agreements. They are not able to act as negotiators in family decisions, even those that most affect their own interests. As one writer has put it, "a newborn does not make a good 'partner.'" Correspondingly, the parental role is antithetical to the spirit of the regime. Parental investment in children involves a diminished investment in self, a willing deference to the needs and claims of the dependent child. Perhaps more than any other family relationship, the parent-child relationship—shaped as it is by patterns of dependency and deference—can be undermined and weakened by the principles of the regime.

More than a century and a half ago Alexis de Tocqueville made the striking observation that an individualistic society depends on a communitarian institution like the family for its continued existence. The family cannot be constituted like the liberal state, nor can it be governed entirely by that state's principles. Yet the family serves as the seedbed for the virtues required by a liberal state. The family is responsible for teaching lessons of independence, self-restraint, responsibility, and right conduct, which are essential to a free, democratic society. If the family fails in these tasks, then the entire experiment in democratic self-rule is jeopardized.

To take one example: independence is basic to successful functioning in American life. We assume that most people in

America will be able to work, care for themselves and their families, think for themselves, and inculcate the same traits of independence and initiative in their children. We depend on families to teach people to do these things. The erosion of the two-parent family undermines the capacity of families to impart this knowledge; children of long-term welfare-dependent single parents are far more likely than others to be dependent themselves. Similarly, the children in disrupted families have a harder time forging bonds of trust with others and giving and getting help across the generations. This, too, may lead to greater dependency on the resources of the state.

94   Over the past two and a half decades Americans have been conducting what is tantamount to a vast natural experiment in family life. Many would argue that this experiment was necessary, worthwhile, and long overdue. The results of the experiment are coming in, and they are clear. Adults have benefited from the changes in family life in important ways, but the same cannot be said for children. Indeed, this is the first generation in the nation's history to do worse psychologically, socially, and economically than its parents. Most poignantly, in survey after survey the children of broken families confess deep longings for an intact family.

95   Nonetheless, as Galston is quick to point out, the regime effect is not an irresistible undertow that will carry away the family. It is more like a swift current, against which it is possible to swim. People learn; societies can change, particularly when it becomes apparent that certain behaviors damage the social ecology, threaten the public order, and impose new burdens on core institutions. Whether Americans will act to overcome the legacy of family disruption is a crucial but as yet unanswered question.

Iris Marion Young

MAKING SINGLE
MOTHERHOOD NORMAL

Iris Marion Young, a philosopher by trade and a leading feminist who now teaches at the University of Chicago, has written Throwing Like a Girl and Other Essays in Feminist

*Philosophy and Social Theory (1990), Justice and the Politics
of Difference (1990), and Intersecting Voices: Dilemmas of
Gender, Political Philosophy, and Policy (1997). She contributed the following essay in the winter of 1994 to Dissent, a
very progressive bimonthly journal of public affairs. A few
months later her essay was answered in Dissent by Jean Bethke
Elshtain, a prominent political scientist also from the
University of Chicago who has a particular interest in family issues. Margaret O'Brien Steinfels, at the time the editor of
Commonweal magazine (a liberal publication on public affairs
loosely associated with Catholicism—and another place where
Elshtain places some of her work), also responded in the same
issue of Dissent to Young's essay, right after Elshtain's piece.
Iris Young then responded to both Elshtain and Steinfels. Their
entire exchange is reprinted here.*

When Dan Quayle denounced Murphy Brown for having a   1
baby without a husband in May 1992, most liberals and leftists
recognized it for the ploy it was: a Republican attempt to win
an election by an irrational appeal to "tradition" and "order."
To their credit, American voters did not take the bait. The
Clinton campaign successfully turned the family values
rhetoric against the GOP by pointing to George Bush's veto of
the Family and Medical Leave Act and by linking family well-
being to economic prosperity.

Nonetheless, family values rhetoric has survived the elec-   2
tion. Particularly disturbing is the fact that the refrain has
been joined by people who, by most measures, should be called
liberals, but who can accept only the two-parent heterosexual
family. Communitarians are leading the liberal chorus de-
nouncing divorce and single motherhood. In *The Spirit of
Community*, Amitai Etzioni calls for social measures to privilege two-parent families and encourage parents to take care of
young children at home. Etzioni is joined by political theorist
William Galston—currently White House adviser on domestic
policy—in supporting policies that will make divorce more difficult. Jean Bethke Elshtain is another example of a social
liberal—that is, someone who believes in state regulation of
business, redistributive economic policies, religious toleration
and broad principles of free speech—who argues that not all
kinds of families should be considered equal from the point of
view of social policy or moral education. William Julius
Wilson, another academic who has been close to Democratic
party policy makers, considers out-of-wedlock birth to be a

symptom of social pathology and promotes marriage as one solution to problems of urban black poverty.

3   Although those using family values rhetoric rarely mention gays and lesbians, this celebration of stable marriage is hardly good news for gay and lesbian efforts to win legitimacy for their lives and relationships. But I am concerned here with the implications of family values rhetoric for another despised and discriminated-against group: single mothers. Celebrating marriage brings a renewed stigmatization of these women, and makes them scapegoats for social ills of which they are often the most serious victims. The only antidote to this injustice is for public policy to regard single mothers as normal, and to give them the social supports they need to overcome disadvantage.

4   Most people have forgotten another explicit aim of Dan Quayle's appeal to family values: to "explain" the disorders in Los Angeles in May 1992. Unmarried women with children lie at the source of the "lawless social anarchy" that sends youths into the streets with torches and guns. Their "welfare ethos" impedes individual efforts to move ahead in society.

5   Liberal family values rhetoric also finds the "breakdown" of "the family" to be a primary cause of all our social ills. "It is not an exaggeration," says Barbara Dafoe Whitehead in the *Atlantic* (April 1993) "to characterize [family disruption] as a central cause of many of our most vexing social problems, including poverty, crime, and declining school performance." Etzioni lays our worst social problems at the door of self-indulgent divorced or never-married parents. "Gang warfare in the streets, massive drug abuse, a poorly committed workforce, and a strong sense of entitlement and a weak sense of responsibility are, to a large extent, the product of poor parenting." Similarly, Galston attributed fearsome social consequences to divorce and single parenthood. "The consequences of family failure affect society at large. We all pay for systems of welfare, criminal justice, and incarceration, as well as for physical and mental disability; we are all made poorer by the inability or unwillingness of young adults to become contributing members of society; we all suffer if our society is unsafe and divided."

6   Reductionism in the physical sciences has faced such devastating criticism that few serious physicists would endorse a theory that traced a one-way causal relationship between the behavior of a particular sort of atom and, say, an earthquake. Real-world physical phenomena are understood to have many mutually conditioning forces. Yet here we have otherwise subtle and intelligent people putting forward the most absurd social reductionism. In this simplistic model of society, the

family is the most basic unit, the first cause that is itself uncaused. Through that magical process called socialization, families cause the attitudes, dispositions, and capacities of individual children who in turn as adults cause political and economic institutions to work or not work.

The great and dangerous fallacy in this imagery, of course, is   7
its implicit assumption that non-familial social processes do not cause family conditions. How do single-mother families "cause" poverty, for example? Any sensible look at some of these families shows us that poverty is a cause of their difficulties and failures. Doesn't it make sense to trace some of the conflicts that motivate divorce to the structure of work or to the lack of work? And what about all the causal influences on families and children over which parents have very little control—peer groups, dilapidated and understaffed schools, consumer culture, television and movie imagery, lack of investment in neighborhoods, cutbacks in public services? Families unprotected by wide networks of supportive institutions and economic resources are bound to suffer. Ignoring the myriad social conditions that affect families only enables the government and the public to escape responsibility for investing in the ghettos, building new houses and schools, and creating the millions of decent jobs that we need to restore millions of people to dignity.

Family-values reductionism scapegoats parents, and espe-   8
cially single parents, and proposes a low-cost answer to crime, poverty, and unemployment: get married and stay married.

Whitehead, Galston, Etzioni, and others claim that there is   9
enough impressive evidence that divorce harms children emotionally to justify policies that discourage parents from divorcing. A closer look at the data, however, yields a much more ambiguous picture. One meta-analysis of ninety-two studies of the effects of divorce on American children, for example, finds statistically insignificant differences between children of divorced parents and children from intact families in various measures of well-being. Many studies of children of divorce fail to compare them to children from "intact" families, or fail to rule out predivorce conditions as causes. A ten-year longitudinal study released in Australia last June found that conflict between parents—whether divorced or not—is a frequent cause of emotional distress in children. This stress is mitigated, however, if the child has a close supportive relationship with at least one of the parents. Results also suggest that Australia's stronger welfare state and less adversarial divorce process may partly account for differences with U.S. findings.

Thus the evidence that divorce produces lasting damage   10
to children is ambiguous at best, and I do not see how the

ambiguities can be definitively resolved one way or the other. Complex and multiple social causation makes it naive to think we can conclusively test for a clear causal relationship between divorce and children's well-being. Without such certainty, however, it is wrong to suggest that the liberty of adults in their personal lives should be restricted. Galston and Etzioni endorse proposals that would impose a waiting period between the time a couple applied for divorce and the beginning of divorce proceedings. Divorce today already often drags on in prolonged acrimony. Children would likely benefit more from making it easier and less adversarial.

11 Although many Americans agree with me about divorce, they also agree with Quayle, Wilson, Galston, and others that single motherhood is undesirable for children, a deviant social condition that policy ought to try to correct. Etzioni claims that children of single parents receive less parental supervision and support than do children in two-parent families. It is certainly plausible that parenting is easier and more effective if two or more adults discuss the children's needs and provide different kinds of interactions for them. It does not follow, however, that the second adult must be a live-in husband. Some studies have found that the addition of any adult to a single-mother household, whether a relative, lover, or friend, tends to offset the tendency of single parents to relinquish decision making too early. Stephanie Coontz suggests that fine-tuned research on single-parent families would probably find that they are better for children in some respects and worse in others. For example, although adults in single-parent families spend less time supervising homework, single parents are less likely to pressure their children into social conformity and more likely to praise good grades.

12 Much less controversial is the claim that children in single-parent families are more often poor than those in two-parent families. One should be careful not to correlate poverty with single-parenthood, however; according to Coontz, a greater part of the increase in family poverty since 1979 has occurred in families with both spouses present, with only 38 percent concentrated in single-parent families. As many as 50 percent of single-parent families are likely to be poor, which is a shocking fact, but intact two-parent families are also increasingly likely to be poor, especially if the parents are in their twenties or younger.

13 It is harder to raise children alone than with at least one other adult, and the stresses of doing so can take their toll on children. I do not question that children in families that depend primarily on a woman's wage-earning ability are often

disadvantaged. I do question the conclusion that getting single mothers married is the answer to childhood disadvantage.

Conservatives have always stated a preference for two- 14 parent families. Having liberals join this chorus is disturbing because it makes such preference much more mainstream, thus legitimizing discrimination against single mothers. Single mothers commonly experience credit and employment discrimination. Discrimination against single mothers in renting apartments was legal until 1988, and continues to be routine in most cities. In a study of housing fairness in Pittsburgh in which I participated, most people questioned said that rental housing discrimination is normal in the area. Single mothers and their children also face biases in schools.

There is no hope that discrimination of this sort will ever 15 end unless public discourse and government policy recognize that female-headed families are a viable, normal, and permanent family form, rather than something broken and deviant that policy should eradicate. Around one-third of families in the United States are headed by a woman alone; this proportion is about the same world-wide. The single-mother family is not going to fade away. Many women raise children alone because their husbands left them or because lack of access to contraception and abortion forced them to bear unwanted children. But many women are single mothers by choice. Women increasingly initiate divorces, and many single mothers report being happier after divorce and uninterested in remarriage, even when they are poorer.

Women who give birth out of wedlock, moreover, often have 16 chosen to do so. Discussion of the "problem" of "illegitimate" births commonly assumes the image of the irresponsible and uneducated teenager (of color) as the unwed mother. When citing statistics about rising rates of out-of-wedlock birth, journalists and scholars rarely break them down by the mother's age, occupation, and so on. Although the majority of these births continue to be to young mothers, a rising proportion are to mid-life women with steady jobs who choose to have children. Women persist in such choices despite the fact that they are stigmatized and sometimes punished for them.

In a world where it can be argued that there are already too 17 many people, it may sometimes be wrong for people to have babies. The planned birth of a third child in a stable two-parent family may be morally questionable from this point of view. But principles of equality and reproductive freedom must hold that there is nothing *more* wrong with a woman in her thirties with a stable job and income having a baby than with a similar married couple.

18   If teen pregnancy is a social problem, this is not because the mothers are unmarried, but because they are young. They are inexperienced in the ways of the world and lack the skills necessary to get a job to support their children; once they become parents, their opportunities to develop those skills usually decrease. But these remain problems even when the women marry the young men with whom they have conceived children. Young inexperienced men today are just as ill prepared for parenting and just as unlikely to find decent jobs.

19   Although many young unmarried women who bear children do so because they are effectively denied access to abortions, many of these mothers want their babies. Today the prospects for meaningful work and a decent income appear dim to many youth, and especially to poor youth. Having a baby can give a young woman's life meaning, earn her respectful attention, make her feel grown up, and give her an excuse to exit the "wild" teenager scene that has begun to make her uncomfortable. Constructing an education and employment system that took girls as seriously as boys, that trained girls and boys for meaningful and available work would be a far more effective antidote to teen birth than reprimanding, stigmatizing, and punishing these girls.

20   Just as we should examine the assumption that something is wrong with a mid-life woman having a child without a husband, so we ought to ask a more radical question: just what *in principle* is *more* wrong in a young woman's bearing a child without a husband than in an older woman's doing so? When making their reproductive decisions, everyone ought to ask whether there are too many people in the world. Beyond that, I submit that we should affirm an unmarried young woman's right to bear a child as much as any other person's right.

21   There is reason to think that much of the world, including the United States, has plural childbearing cultures. Recently I heard a radio interview with an eighteen-year-old African American woman in Washington, D.C. who had recently given birth to her second child. She affirmed wanting both children, and said that she planned to have no more. She lives in a subsidized apartment and participates in a job training program as a condition for receiving AFDC. She resisted the interviewer's suggestion that there was something morally wrong or at least unfortunate with her choices and her life. She does not like being poor, and does not like having uncertain child care arrangements when she is away from her children. But she believes that in ten years, with hard work, social support, and good luck, she will have a community college degree and a decent job doing something she likes, as does her mother, now thirty-four.

There is nothing in principle wrong with such a pattern of   22
having children first and getting education and job training
later. Indeed, millions of white professional women currently in
their fifties followed a similar pattern. Most of them, of course,
were supported by husbands, and not state subsidy, when they
stayed home to take care of their young children. Our racism,
sexism, and classism are only thinly concealed when we praise
stay-at-home mothers who are married, white, and middle
class, and propose a limit of two years on welfare to unmarried,
mostly non-white, and poor women who do the same thing.
From a moral point of view, is there an important difference between the two kinds of dependence? If there is any serious commitment to equality in the United States, it must include an
equal respect for people's reproductive choices. In order for
children to have equal opportunities, moreover, equal respect
for parents, and especially mothers, requires state policies that
give greater support to some than others.

If we assume that there is nothing morally wrong with single-   23
mother families, but that they are often disadvantaged by lack of
child care and by economic discrimination and social stigma,
then what follows for public policy? Some of the answers to this
question are obvious, some not so obvious, but in the current
climate promoting a stingy and punitive welfare state, all bear
discussion. I will close by sketching a few proposals.

1. *There is nothing in principle any more wrong with a teenage*   24
woman's choice to have a child than with anyone else's. Still, there
is something wrong with a society that gives her few alternatives
to a mothering vocation and little opportunity for meaningful
job training. If we want to reduce the number of teenage women
who want to have babies, then education and employment policies have to take girls and women much more seriously.

2. *Whether poor mothers are single because they are divorced or*   25
because they never married, it is wrong for a society to allow moth-
ers to raise children in poverty and then tell them that it's their fault
when their children have deprived lives. Only if the economy offered women decent-paying jobs, moreover, would forcing welfare women to get jobs lift them out of poverty. Of course, with
good job opportunities most of them would not need to be forced
off welfare. But job training and employment programs for girls
and women must be based on the assumption that a large proportion of them will support children alone. Needless to say,
there is a need for massive increases in state support for child
care if these women are to hold jobs. Public policy should, however, also acknowledge that taking care of children at home is

work, and then support this work with unstigmatized subsidy where necessary to give children a decent life.

26   3. *The programs of schools, colleges, and vocational and professional training institutions ought to accommodate a plurality of women's life plans, combining childbearing and child-rearing with other activities.* They should not assume that there is a single appropriate time to bear and rear children. No woman should be disadvantaged in her education and employment opportunities because she has children at age fifteen, twenty-five, thirty-five, or forty-five (for the most part, education and job structures are currently such that each of these ages is the "wrong time").

27   4. *Public policy should take positive steps to dispel the assumption that the two-parent heterosexual nuclear family is normal and all other family forms deviant.* For example, the state should assist single-parent support systems, such as the "mothers' houses" in some European countries that provide spaces for shared child minding and cooking while at the same time preserving family privacy.

28   5. *Some people might object that my call for recognizing single motherhood as normal lets men off the hook when it comes to children.* Too many men are running out on pregnant women and on the mothers of their children with whom they have lived. They are free to seek adventure, sleep around, or start new families, while single mothers languish in poverty with their children. This objection voices a very important concern, but there are ways to address it other than forcing men to get or stay married to the mothers of their children.

29   First, the state should force men who are not poor themselves to pay child support for children they have recognized as theirs. I see nothing wrong with attaching paychecks and bank accounts to promote this end. But the objection above requires more than child support. Relating to children is a good thing in itself. Citizens who love and are committed to some particular children are more apt than others to think of the world in the long term, and to see it from the perspective of the more vulnerable people. Assuming that around one-third of households will continue to be headed by women alone, men should be encouraged to involve themselves in close relationships with children, not necessarily their biological offspring.

30   6. *More broadly, the American public must cease assuming that support and care for children are the responsibility of their parents alone, and that parents who require social support have somehow failed.* Most parents require social support, some more than others. According to Coontz, for a good part of American history this fact was assumed. I am not invoking a Platonic vision of communal childrearing; children need particular significant

others. But non-parents ought to take substantial economic and social responsibility for the welfare of children.

After health care, Clinton's next big reform effort is likely to be   31
aimed at welfare. Condemning single mothers will legitimate harsh welfare reforms that will make the lives of some of them harder. The left should press instead for the sorts of principles and policies that treat single mothers as equal citizens.

Jean Bethke Elshtain

SINGLE MOTHERHOOD

A RESPONSE TO IRIS YOUNG

What I found most surprising in Iris Young's analysis ("Making   1
Single Motherhood Normal," Winter 1994) is the radical disconnection between her policy proposals and the constraints and possibilities of our current situation. She calls for "massive increases in state support for child care" when state budgets are strapped, cutbacks are being ordered across the board, and new initiatives in health care will gobble up whatever additional revenues are available. (Presumably she supports universal health care and favors moves in that direction.) She calls for "public policy" to dispel any notion of "normality" in family structure. But, surely, we have already conducted that experiment and it has failed. It has failed for the very people it was designed to help—single mothers and their children. I will offer up evidence on this score—evidence Young systematically overlooks.

She calls for states to "force men" to "pay child support for   2
children they have recognized as theirs." She claims men shouldn't be let off the hook where their responsibilities are concerned. But her formulation continues to put the onus for child-rearing and child "recognition," if you will, on women. In fact, startlingly, her argument is a call for a return to a particularly rigid form of "separate spheres," something I thought feminists had a strong stake in criticizing and reforming. Once again we are in a world of "women and children only," where a woman can do it all by herself, thank you. A man could easily bypass Young's requirement by refusing to recognize a child as "his." Who is to compel this recognition if the institutional framework within which it has taken place historically—the two-parent family—has been entirely dismantled as a "norm"

or "ideal" of any sort? There are no "fathers" or "daddies" in Young's universe with direct, daily responsibility for child care and family sustenance, something not reducible to a paycheck. Still, Young would "encourage" men to "involve themselves in close relationships with children, not necessarily their biological offspring." How? Why? What institutional forms will nurture and sustain such relationships? Are we to see forlorn bands of disconnected men roaming neighborhoods, knocking on doors, and asking if there is a baby inside they can "bond" with for a few hours? Young's rhetorical demolition of what she takes to be onerous tradition combined with her wholly abstract, vague pleas for connection and responsibility shows us again that politics of denunciation and sentimentalism that undermined much of 1960s radicalism. (I know: I was there.)

3   Let's enter the real world. For Young misses altogether what is at stake in the travail of the present moment. She reverts to the claim that "poverty" is the cause of all other troubles. This is curious because Young thrashes reductionism before rapidly moving to her own reductionist formula, namely, that any "sensible look" at the plight of poor families reveals that "poverty" is the cause of, well, being poor. Here she reproduces the very "one-way" causal claims she attacked just a few sentences earlier. The problem, of course, is that matters are far more complex than this. The mountain of evidence now available from reputable scholars tells us that cultural changes—alterations in norms and values—are not mere epiphenomenal foam on the causal sea but are themselves vectors of economic trouble. We know that poverty is associated with single parents. This means mothers, often very young mothers (those "babies having babies" Jesse Jackson talks about) in a father-absent situation. We also know, from the National Commission on Children, the Center for the Study of Social Policy, the U.S. Department of Health and Human Services, and dozens of other reliable sources that children growing up in single-parent households are at greater risk on every index of well-being (crime, violence, substance abuse, mental illness, dropping out of school, and so on).

4   But mark this: there is no compelling evidence that a decline in government spending accounts for the past several decades' burgeoning litany of risks to children. Economists Victor Fuchs and Diane Reklis have shown that the well-being of children worsened in a period when "purchases of goods and services for children by government rose very rapidly, as did real household income per child, and the poverty rate of children plummeted. Thus, we must seek explanations for the rising problems of that period in the cultural realm." The period to which Fuchs and Reklis refer is the 1960–1970 decade. If you continue to track direct government expenditures per child up to the present

moment you find no compelling correlation between government support and child well-being per se. Indeed, we are spending more for children today in the public sphere than ever before. The sad truth is that our public investment in children is being outstripped by "private disinvestment," in other words, the breakup of the two-parent home. If you control for all other factors, *including* economic status, you learn that father absence is the single most important risk factor for children, whether one is talking about poor health or poverty or behavioral problems (the latter being a euphemistic way of gesturing toward drug addiction, being the victim or perpetrator of violence, adolescent out-of-wedlock birth, and so on). Do we change all of this by making a one-parent family suddenly "normal"? That won't stop children from suffering. That won't help a child find security and trust and safety. Of course, we should do our best for all children. But that means doing our best to create situations that do best for children, not continuing to try to patch things up when we *know*, because the evidence is in, that some familial arrangements are better for children than others.

The *Kids Count Data Book*, published by the liberal Center 5 for the Study of Social Policy, one of the most widely accepted scholarly sources in this area, offers up annual "Profiles of Child Well-Being." The most recent profile included the following startling information. Researchers looked at two groups and compared them: couples who completed high school, married, and waited until age twenty to have their first child against couples who did none of the above—they neither married nor finished school, and in which the girl gave birth before age twenty. In the first group, the number of children who fell below the poverty line was 8 percent. In the second group, the number of children who fell below the poverty line was a startling 79 percent. What this suggests is that marriage, somewhat delayed child-bearing, and high school completion—cultural and educational factors—fuel economic outcomes. It is high time we set aside economic reductionism of the sort Young oddly endorses and looked to the dissolution of the fabric of families and communities, a tragedy entangled with the repudiation of those "norms" for male and female responsibility for children that Young finds oppressive because they "stigmatize" single mothers. The stigma attached to single motherhood has virtually disappeared, if we trust the survey data, but the problems associated with the children of single parents do not go away so readily.

If we are to see investment "in the ghettos," the building of 6 new houses and schools, the creation of "millions of decent jobs," no less, we need people capable of holding jobs; we need secure social institutions; we need children who are compelled by parents to stay in school; we need all the things Young blithely ignores. The most successful organizing for change over the past fifty years has come from poor and working-class communities who form broad-based coalitions to work for housing, jobs, schools, in the most devastated urban areas—from Brownsville to San Antonio. I have in mind, for example, the activities of the Industrial Areas Foundation. If Young wants to see revitalization of communities in action she should check out the work of the East Brooklyn Congregations (EBC) and their Nehemiah Homes project or Baltimoreans United in Leadership Development (BUILD), a group that has made significant strides in school reform in the inner city. There are dozens and dozens of such examples. The organizing base is families and churches—the remnants of intact institutions—for you cannot make lasting, meaningful change of any kind outside institutions.

7   Civic philosophy dies when academics, in the name of radicalism, in the name, heaven help us, of that democratic socialism for which this journal has traditionally stood, endorse values that erode the only possible bases for creating and sustaining community institutions over time—calling for more individualism (hence Young's celebration of an individual woman's "choice" to have a baby whether she is thirteen years old or fifty, as if that choice and not any consideration of the child's well-being were the only value at stake); more vast government projects, hence more clientage; normlessness as a norm; and on and on. It is depressing to see these old nostrums refurbished as radical or reformist when they could scarcely be more conformist—to the naively anti-institutionalist, hyperindividualist tendencies of our time, with a heavy dollop of "separate spheres with a feminist face" thrown in for good measure.

Margaret O'Brien Steinfels

RIGHTS AND RESPONSIBILITIES

A RESPONSE TO IRIS YOUNG

1   Fully achieved, Iris Young's proposals would be a disaster for women and children, probably for men too, and certainly for liberal and left politics.

She is wrong on three points, at least: single mothers are *not*   2
despised; liberals don't view single mothers as the sole source
of our social ills; liberalism has *not* abandoned its heritage by
rallying to the two-parent family.

If only *Time* magazine had made Marla Maples—an unwed   3
mother—the woman of the year, we would fully realize that
a mother's unwedded state is no bar to celebrity or social
lionizing—and a kiss on the cheek from (former) Mayor David
Dinkins. The press and television treat single motherhood as a
variant of the American family. I suspect that teachers, principals, social workers, acquaintances, and neighbors don't ask
and don't care. That changes when the individual choice of single motherhood becomes a collective responsibility. It is women
who have children that they can't support or get fathers to support that exercise tax-paying Americans, at least some of whom
are single-mother families themselves! Plain and simple, the
problem is not single mothers but single mothers who depend
on the rest of us to support them and their children.

The Reagan administration and accompanying pundits con-   4
vinced the American electorate that the welfare system now
functions as a dowry system for adolescent girls, who, becoming
pregnant, are launched into motherhood and adulthood with
food stamps, child support, housing allowances, and Medicaid
long before they are ready to be good mothers. And it doesn't end
there, the critics go on: rather than supporting people in need
until they can get back on their feet, the system is failing children
and undermining young men's sense of responsibility for their
children. Conservatives think that welfare is hurting poor people.
Among others, a lot of poor people agree with them.

This analysis has penetrated the thinking of Democrats and   5
other liberals. Some speak of job training, of community service in return for welfare. Some speak of two-year limits; others of withholding aid for infants born when a woman is
already on welfare; all stand behind that once unthinkable policy of dunning delinquent dads for court-ordered child support. Even Wisconsin, with its tradition of progressive politics,
is bailing out of the federal welfare system in order to limit and
control its own expenditures.

Should these be counted traitors to the liberal cause?   6

Those old enough to remember will recall that liberals created   7
the welfare system to keep families together, to help tide over
those in temporary trouble, and to help widows maintain a
household. Aid to Families with Dependent Children (AFDC)
and other welfare measures were never meant to support
teenage moms or help their boyfriends elude the responsibilities
of fatherhood; nor were they intended to make up for missing

child-support payments. The system has been adapted to meet these needs on the assumption that women with children often have no other recourse. Often they do not. When, however, the system itself seems to encourage unwed motherhood or male abandonment and to contribute to family breakdown, reasonable people ask their politicians why. To their credit some liberals are reconsidering the merits of the two-parent family. Were two-parent families to come back into vogue, our social ills would not disappear. But there is reason to expect that children would have saner, more secure, and—boys especially—more disciplined upbringings. These would be a good in themselves.

8   Iris Young wants us to assume that "there is nothing morally wrong with single-mother families." What does she mean? Women of any age, educational attainment, income level, or marital status should be able to bear and raise a child. I agree. At least I agree that no one else—the state, the father, the woman's relatives—has a right to force a woman to get an abortion if she is pregnant. Or force her to use contraception. Or, barring abusive or seriously neglectful behavior, take her child from her. In that sense the mother-child relationship is sacrosanct; the right to conceive and bear a child is basic.

9   But not every exercise of a "right" adds up to a moral good. Nations have a right to protect their sovereignty; not every act in pursuit of that right is moral. Individuals in our society have a right to free speech; not every sentence uttered in exercising that right constitutes a moral good. The analogy applies to childbearing decisions: it may be a right, but that does not make it a moral good. Single motherhood—though not wrong in and of itself—can undermine the well-being of others.

10   First, there is the child and his or her need for care, comfort, and stability—constant attention as an infant and consistent attention as a child and adolescent. Even with two (or more) adults, this is an arduous undertaking spanning more than two decades. Can single-mother families really meet this responsibility? Many do; many others do not.

11   Then, consider alternative child-care support systems. There is the woman's own family, which may be her surest recourse. But what if this, too, is a single-mother family? or siblings need attention? or husband and wife both work? A single mother's need may be great, but families have limits. Other child-caring facilities—day-care centers, schools, camps—are available, but they may be overwhelmed with the needs of materially and emotionally deprived children. Young believes more money and more personnel are the answer. But can a single mother (or father) act on the assumption that they are?

And from where do these additional and abundant new resources come?

This brings us to the question of the common good and the   12
implicit social contract on which it rests. Young refers to the
"state" and the "welfare state" as if these were entities capable
of delivering goods and services at will. The United States is a
democracy that eventually comes to reflect—if only imperfectly—
the views of its citizens. Underlying at least some of the critical
views of welfare—which Young thinks stingy—is a sense of
quid pro quo: Social responsibility ought to encourage individual responsibility, not undermine or replace it. Is that unreasonable? The reservoirs of social responsibility that Young
wants to draw upon will be swiftly depleted in a society whose
citizens, women and men alike, do not habitually feel and exercise responsibility for themselves and their families.

Our social experiment in single motherhood over the last   13
twenty-five years is failing great numbers of women and children while corroding the bonds that tie men to familial responsibilities. In the name of reform, we should not take from them
the admittedly meager resources provided by the current system. But neither can opinion makers, academics, or intellectual elites, feminist and otherwise, go on arguing that this
situation is normal, and will be made even "more normal" by
increased welfare payments and better support systems.

The communitarians have a slogan that we might all take to   14
heart: strong rights entail strong responsibilities—that goes for
the right to bear and raise children.

Iris Marion Young

RESPONSE TO ELSHTAIN
AND STEINFELS

Jean Elshtain and Margaret Steinfels and I agree at least on   1
one thing: too many children are poor, badly educated, at risk
of being un- or underemployed, becoming substance dependent, criminal, or dead. What we disagree on are the solutions
to these problems. Indeed, for all their strong language, I find

neither offering any action. Calls for "secure institutions," restoring the "fabric of families," and living up to "strong responsibilities" are empty exhortations unless we specify just who should take responsibility to do what. The form of the rhetoric, moreover, leaves the impression that it's "they" and not "we" who have shirked responsibilities. This vague rhetoric seems to function as an excuse not only for doing nothing, but for not even thinking about what to do.

2   Elshtain and Steinfels both claim that "we" have undertaken a "social experiment" in single motherhood that has "failed." What odd phrasing! Who are "we" who designed such a cruel "experiment"? But, of course, no one designed the patchwork of plural family living arrangements in the United States today. In some respects, it has always been with us. There is no question, however, that the last two decades have seen more divorce and less marriage, though the rate of teenage pregnancy has not in fact increased.

3   What do Elshtain and Steinfels propose that we do about the lives of children? We should, in the words of Elshtain, "create situations that do best for children," that is, promote intact two-parent families. But how shall we do that? It is hard to believe that Elshtain and Steinfels would forbid divorce. Perhaps they favor making divorce more difficult, as some recommend, with a waiting period. This assumes that couples now rush into divorce without thinking, which is for the most part not so. Since divorce in the United States is already painful and costly, especially when there are children, making divorce more difficult is not likely to reduce appreciably the number of divorces.

4   And what shall we do about women who give birth without being married? Again, Elshtain and Steinfels would not force abortions, and I suspect that they would not force men to marry and live with the women they have impregnated. Would they recommend punishing women who give birth out of wedlock as a deterrent to others, or punishing fathers who do not marry them? This alternative is frighteningly close to the minds of some people in the current debate, but it doesn't sound like Elshtain or Steinfels. Perhaps the carrot is a better idea: cash awards and medals for couples who get and stay married.

5   The most that Elshtain's and Steinfels's calls for restoration of family values and responsibilities can mean practically is that public discussion promote the idea that intact two-parent families are better than other families; churches, schools, community groups, perhaps occasional television ad campaigns should send out this message. If such a society-wide educational campaign were implemented, it might indeed have some measurable impact on marriage and divorce rates, but I submit

not very much. Thus I find Elshtain and Steinfels recommending virtually no social action to improve the lives of children.

Their insistence that although women have a "right" to parent alone, their family lives are less valuable, moreover, is an affront to the worth and dignity of women who have tried marriage and found it wanting, are out on their own with their children, and are not interested in a new husband. Is a liberal society really to condemn these women, and if it does can it claim it is respecting them as equal citizens?   6

With the communitarian refrain, "strong rights entail strong responsibilities," Steinfels suggests that it's about time the parents of those children did something, instead of sitting around waiting for handouts from the state. Elshtain, too, suggests a kind of quid pro quo: if we are to see investment in dilapidated neighborhoods, building of new schools and houses, we need secure social institutions and children who are compelled by their parents to stay in school. Once parents get off their duffs and build these institutions and discipline their children, then maybe we can talk about social support.   7

Are Elshtain and Steinfels really suggesting that single mothers (not all of whom are poor) or poor people (not all of whom are in families with one parent) are, as a group, more irresponsible than other people? When middle-class, married couples refuse to support the local school system through a tax increase, complain about the quality of the schools, and enroll their kids in private school, are they behaving responsibly? When bank executives refuse to make loans to homeowners and businesses in poor neighborhoods and invest instead in risky tourism ventures on the other side of the country, are they behaving responsibly? I submit that irresponsibility is randomly distributed across race, class, gender, and family form, and I agree that there is far too much of it. But I also submit that most people most of the time are trying to meet their responsibilities to their families, friends, and coworkers. Less often, perhaps, do people think about and meet their responsibilities to distant strangers, but here responsibility increases with social privilege. We live in a time of a "responsibility deficit," some say, but I don't know the measure of responsibility levels. If the measure for single mothers is the income level of their children and the state of the schools, health clinics, and parks in the neighborhoods where they live, then this is a most unforgivable example of blaming the victims.   8

I completely agree with Elshtain that a vigorous and just society depends on the active participation of citizens in civic institutions of their own making, either not connected or only loosely connected to the state—neighborhood cleanup crews,   9

parent councils in schools, volunteer social services, community arts and culture centers, cooperatives, political advocacy
organizations. Despite communitarian complaints, I find no
evidence that this sort of volunteer community organizing
and service provision has waned in the United States in the last
two decades. The heroic activities of organizations like the
Industrial Areas Foundation or the Cabrini Green Tenants
Association, which Elshtain applauds, are very often led by
single mothers. Other such volunteer civic activities are led by
the "forlorn bands of disconnected men" Elshtain imagines
"roaming neighborhoods." Many men run athletic and cultural
programs for children, or volunteer in tutoring centers, drug-
prevention, and skills-building workshops. Despite what I regard as a healthy level of civic activity in the United States
among people of both genders and all races and classes, there
is certainly need for more. Public expenditures on street lighting and better transportation, along with private corporate decisions to reduce working hours without reducing pay, might
enable more people to engage in more self-defined civic activities to improve their lives and their neighborhoods.

10   It is Elshtain and Steinfels who have their heads in the sand if
they think that "private disinvestment" in the two-parent family
has destroyed our schools and taken jobs away from the neighborhoods. American society has been severely damaged by three
decades of private and public disinvestment in basic manufacturing, new and rehabilitated housing, bridges and rail lines,
public education, adult retraining, and social services such as
preventive health care and libraries. Volunteers can only barely
begin to fill these gaping holes in the American dream.

11   Elshtain and Steinfels write as though I have called for more
of the same tired old welfare policies in order to respond to the
stresses of single motherhood and the economic disadvantage
many children suffer. But my policy principles call for social
investment (this word that Elshtain seems to find so hyper-
bolic), not draining handouts. Private industry should bear as
much responsibility for this investment, moreover, as government does. Elshtain suggests that a condition for the creation
of decent jobs is that children be motivated to stay in school.
Only a little reflection should suggest that precisely the reverse
is true. She accuses me of resuscitating a separate spheres ideology that would keep women at home caring for children, yet
scoffs at my call for the massive increases in state support for
child care that would enable more mothers—and fathers—to
work outside the home and volunteer, knowing that their children were cared for. Steinfels suggests that parents cannot assume that more money and personnel will make quality child

care more available and affordable. I do not understand why we cannot assume that it would help a great deal.

Neither Elshtain nor Steinfels mentions the single most im-   12 portant cause of the economic disadvantage in which children of many single mothers live: low wages for women's work. Coupled with the scarcity or expense of child care, low wages make it rational for many women to stay on welfare. Millions of single mothers nevertheless take jobs that enable them and their children only barely to escape poverty, if that. We do not have to accept as given the sex segregation of women's work that helps keep those wages low. It is simple sexism to decide that the only way to pull the children of single mothers out of poverty is to get them live-in fathers; it is also an unrealistic expectation, since male unemployment rates have been steadily rising in the last decade, and male wage rates have been falling. Public and private programs should be devoted to training women for higher wage jobs and raising the wages of traditionally female jobs. This is not a wasteful handout; it is justice.

Decent schools, housing, infrastructure, decent jobs for all   13 able to work, wage equalization, and affordable child care can come about only through significant levels of public spending combined with both coerced and voluntary efforts of private capital. Elshtain and Steinfels throw up their hands at the absurdity of such a statement in these days "when state budgets are strapped, cutbacks are being ordered across the board." Are these facts of nature? If caring progressives treat them as such, then we are certainly doomed. Americans must engage in a serious and prolonged discussion of public and private spending and taxation, with the aim of shifting resources from waste and quick profits to investment in people and neighborhoods.

Topping the agenda for such discussion must be the fat pub-   14 lic larder where we still see very little in the way of cutbacks: military spending. According to the Center for Defense Information, Clinton's 1994 budget contains $340 billion in military spending, only $10 billion lower than Bush's 1993 budget. Compare this to $54 billion for education and social services, or $11 billion for community and regional development. In his State of the Union Address, Clinton vowed not to cut another dime from military spending. Surely this is madness. I wouldn't say that we should leave ourselves defenseless, or even unable to fight one imperialist war at a time; let's just take *half* of that $340 billion over the next five years and rechannel it into job-creating schools, day-care centers, new houses and apartments, steel, clean trains, parks, libraries, bridges and roads, and, yes, community organizing clearinghouses.

Will America Accept Gay Marriages and Gay Families?

Dan Gilgoff

THE RISE
OF THE GAY FAMILY

U.S. News and World Report, *which first published this essay in May 2004, is a general news magazine that leans toward conservative views and readership. Thus, in such a venue, an article entitled "The Rise of the Gay Family" is likely to be scrutinized carefully. As you read Gilgoff's essay, you might consider the ways in which the author attempts to provide an objective report on this phenomenon—and whether he succeeds. Dan Gilgoff is a journalist who publishes frequently in* U.S. News *as well as several other print and online publications.*

1   "We were afraid people out here would be skeptical of us," says Sheri Ciancia, sipping a glass of iced tea outside the four-bedroom house she and her partner bought last fall in Tomball, Texas, a half-hour's drive from Houston. "Afraid they wouldn't let their kids play with ours."

2   "But we've got to take chances," adds Stephanie Caraway, Ciancia's partner of seven years, sitting next to her on their concrete patio as their 8-year-old daughter, Madison, attempts to break her own record for consecutive bounces on a pogo stick. "We're not going to live in fear."

3   A trio of neighborhood boys pedal their bikes up the driveway, say hello to the moms, and ask Madison if they can use her bike ramp. The boys cruise up and down the ramp's shallow slopes while Madison continues bouncing, the picture of suburban serenity. Despite their misgivings about relocating

from Houston to this tidy subdivision, the family has yet to encounter hostility from their neighbors. "We have to give straight
people more credit," Caraway says with a wry smile. "I'm working on that."

Tomball—its roads lined with single-room Baptist churches   4
and the occasional sprawling worship complex, known to
some locals as "Jesus malls"—may seem an unlikely magnet
for gay couples raising kids. A year before Caraway and
Ciancia moved here, activists in the neighboring county got a
popular children's book that allegedly "tries to minimize or
even negate that homosexuality is a problem" temporarily removed from county libraries. So imagine Caraway's and
Ciancia's surprise when, shortly after moving in, their daughter
met another pair of moms rollerblading down their block: a
lesbian couple who had moved into the neighborhood with
their kids just a few months earlier.

Growing. Gay families have arrived in suburban America, in   5
small-town America, in Bible Belt America—in all corners of
the country. According to the latest census data, there are now
more than 160,000 families with two gay parents and roughly a
quarter of a million children spread across some 96 percent
of U.S. counties. That's not counting the kids being raised by
single gay parents, whose numbers are likely much higher—
upwards of a million, by most estimates, though such households aren't tracked.

This week, the commonwealth of Massachusetts will recharge   6
the gay-marriage debate by becoming the first state to offer
marriage licenses to same-sex couples. The move has raised
the ire of conservatives who believe gay marriage tears at the
fabric of society—and earned support from progressives who
think gay men and lesbians deserve the same rights as heterosexuals. But the controversy is not simply over the bond between two men or two women; it's about the very nature of the
American family.

Gay parents say their families are much like those led by   7
their straight counterparts. "I just say I have two moms," says
Madison, explaining how she tells friends about her parents
(whom she refers to as "Mom" and "Mamma Sheri"). "They're
no different from other parents except that they're two girls. It's
not like comparing two parents with two trees. It's comparing
two parents with two other parents."

Many of today's gay parents, who grew up with few gay-   8
parent role models, say their efforts have helped introduce a culture of family to the gay community. "In the straight community,
adoption is a secondary choice," says Rob Calhoun, 35, who

adopted a newborn daughter with his partner 20 months ago. "But in the gay community, it's like, 'Wow, you've achieved the ultimate American dream.'"

9   The dream has not been without cost, though. Gay parents and their kids in many parts of the country frequently meet with friction from the outside world, in the form of scornful family members, insensitive classmates, and laws that treat same-sex parents differently from straight parents. In general, Americans are split on the subject. A national poll this winter found that 45 percent believe gays should have the right to adopt; 47 percent do not.

10   Many traditional-marriage advocates argue that marriage is first and foremost about procreation. "It is the reason for marriage," Pennsylvania Sen. Rick Santorum said last summer. "Marriage is not about affirming somebody's love for somebody else. It's about uniting together to be open to children." Other critics call gay and lesbian couples who are raising kids—whether from previous marriages, adoption, or artificial insemination—dangerously self-centered. "It's putting adult desires above the interest of children," says Bill Maier, psychologist in residence at Focus on the Family and coauthor of the forthcoming *Marriage on Trial: The Case Against Same-Sex Marriage and Parenting.* "For the first time in history, we're talking about intentionally creating permanently motherless and fatherless families."

11   *Evidence?* Three decades of social science research has supplied some ammunition for both sides of the gay-parent debate. Many researchers say that while children do best with two parents, the stability of the parents' relationship is much more important than their gender. The American Psychological Association, the American Academy of Pediatrics, the National Association of Social Workers, and the American Bar Association have all released statements condoning gay parenting. "Not a single study has found a difference [between children of gay and straight parents] that you can construe as harmful," says Judith Stacey, a professor of sociology, gender, and sexuality at New York University and a gay-rights advocate.

12   Stacey and other researchers even suggest that gay and lesbian parents who form families through adoption, artificial insemination, or surrogacy may offer some advantages over straight parents. "In the lesbian and gay community, parents are a self-selecting group whose motivation for parenthood is high," says Charlotte Patterson, a psychologist and researcher at the University of Virginia. But studies on the subject have so

far examined relatively few children (fewer than 600, by some counts) and virtually no kids of gay dads.

One study coauthored by Stacey and widely cited by both supporters and opponents of gay parenting found that children of lesbians are more likely to consider homosexual relationships themselves (though no more likely to identify as homosexuals as adults) and less likely to exhibit gender-stereotyped behavior. "If we could break down some of society's gender stereotypes, that would be a good thing," says Ellen Perrin, professor of pediatrics at the Floating Hospital for Children at Tufts–New England Medical Center. Focus on the Family's Maier disagrees: "They don't have rigid gender stereotypes? That's gender identity confusion."

While the debate continues, the number of kids with gay parents keeps growing. According to Gary Gates, an Urban Institute demographer, 1 in 3 lesbian couples was raising children in 2000, up from 1 in 5 in 1990, while the number of male couples raising kids jumped from 1 in 20 to 1 in 5 during the same period. The uptick is partly due to changes in the census itself, which in 1990 tabulated most same-sex couples that identified themselves as married on census forms as straight married couples. In the 2000 census, though, those couples were tabulated as gay and lesbian partners. But the leap in such couples with children is large enough to suggest a real spike. And because gay and lesbian couples are sometimes reluctant to identify themselves as such on census forms, actual figures could be much higher.

Moving in. What's perhaps most surprising is that gay- and lesbian-headed families are settling in some of the most culturally conservative parts of the country. According to the *Gay and Lesbian Atlas,* published earlier this month by the Urban Institute, Alaska, Arizona, Georgia, Louisiana, and New Mexico are among the 10 states with the largest number of gay families—along with more historically gay-friendly New York, California, and Vermont. States where gay and lesbian couples are most likely to have children (relative to the state's total number of gay couples) are Mississippi, South Dakota, Alaska, South Carolina, and Louisiana, in that order. "Same-sex couples who live in areas where all couples are more likely to have children" may simply be more likely to have children themselves, according to the atlas. And couples with children—regardless of their sexual orientation—are looking for good schools, safe streets, and outdoor green space. "It's gay couples who don't have kids whose behavior tends to be different: They live in more-distressed areas of cities, with higher crime and

13

14

15

more racial diversity," says Gates. "But a large portion of gay people own their homes, live in the suburbs, and are raising two children."

16   Most of these children are the products of previous heterosexual relationships. Madison, for one, is Caraway's daughter by a former boyfriend. Caraway says the pregnancy forced her to come to terms with her homosexuality; she started dating Ciancia soon after her daughter's birth. "If you stay in a relationship but you're not in love or committed to the person, children sense that," says Caraway, now 31. "What kind of message does that send?"

17   But as these children enter middle and high school, their peers are more likely to inquire about their parents' sexuality—and not always politely. The Tufts–New England Medical Center's Perrin, who authored the American Academy of Pediatrics' policy on gay parenting, says that children of same-sex parents "get stigmatized because of who their parents are. It's the biggest problem they face by far." Just like many gays and lesbians themselves, children of homosexuals speak of "coming out" as a long and often difficult ordeal. "You are, on a day-to-day basis, choosing if you're out or if you're going to be hiding the whole truth," says Abigail Garner, author of the recently released *Families Like Mine*, about children of homosexuals. "Is she your mom's roommate or your aunt or your mom's friend?"

18   During middle school and part of high school, A. J. Costa, now a freshman at Texas Lutheran University outside San Antonio, kept his mother's relationship with a live-in partner secret. He grew close to his mom's partner, even preferred the arrangement to his mom's previous marriage, which ended when he was 7, but never invited friends to the house. "I didn't want anyone to make fun of me," says Costa. "Nobody was going to mess with my family."

19   Costa's fears were reinforced by some classmates who did find out and referred to his moms as "dykes." But in the summer before his junior year in high school, Costa visited Provincetown, Mass., for "Family Week," an annual gathering of gay parents and their children. "I couldn't get over how many families there were, all like mine," he recalls. "I realized that it wasn't about whether I have two gay moms. It was that I have two *moms*. It was getting past the fact that they're gay."

20   **Support.** In recent years, support networks for children of gay parents and for parents themselves have expanded dramatically. Children of Lesbians and Gays Everywhere, or COLAGE, has chapters in 28 states. The Family Pride Coalition, whose dozens of local affiliate organizations attract gay parents who

want their kids to meet other children of gays and lesbians, has doubled its member and volunteer base in the past five years, to 17,000. Vacation companies like Olivia, founded 30 years ago for lesbian travelers, now offer packages specifically for gays and lesbians with children, and R Family Vacations, underwritten by former talk-show host Rosie O'Donnell, will launch its inaugural cruise this summer. Tanya Voss, a 36-year-old college professor in Austin who, with her partner, has two young boys through artificial insemination, plans to attend the first Family Pride Coalition weekend at Disney World next month. Kids need environments where "they don't have to explain their families," she says, "a safe place where they could just be."

Still, neither COLAGE nor Family Pride Coalition has affiliate   21
groups in Mississippi, South Dakota, or Alaska, the states where gay and lesbian couples are most likely to have kids. ("The way you manage in a more hostile environment," says Gates, "is to go about your business and not draw much attention to yourself.") Many such states also present the highest legal hurdles for those families. Roughly two thirds of children with same-sex parents live in states where second-parent or joint adoptions—which allow the partner of a child's biological or adoptive parent to adopt that child without stripping the first parent of his or her rights, much like stepparent adoption—has been granted only in certain counties or not at all.

Absent such arrangements, a biological or adoptive parent's   22
partner could be powerless to authorize emergency medical treatment or denied custody if the other parent dies. When Voss and her partner were planning to have their first child, they decided Voss wouldn't carry the baby because her parents—who disapprove of Voss's homosexuality—would have likely claimed custody in the event that their daughter died during childbirth.

Gay-rights advocates argue that it's often children who end up   23
suffering from laws restricting gay parenting—and same-sex marriage. If a parent without a legal relationship with his or her partner's child dies, a 10-year-old child whose nonlegal parent was earning $60,000 at the time of death, for example, would forgo nearly $140,000 in Social Security survivor benefits paid to children of married couples, according to the Urban Institute and the Human Rights Campaign. That's on top of the more than $100,000 in Social Security paid to a widow—but not a gay partner—whose spouse earned $60,000. And without laws recognizing them as legitimate parents, nonlegal parents are unlikely to be required to pay child support if they leave their partner.

Recently, some states have further restricted adoption. Earlier   24
this year, a federal appeals court upheld Florida's ban on homosexuals' adopting children, the only one of its kind in the nation.

Arkansas now bans gay foster parenting, Mississippi bans same-sex couples from adopting, and Utah bans adoptions by all unmarried couples. "State legislatures that opposed gay marriage are going to push to replicate what Florida has done," says lawyer John Mayoue, author of *Balancing Competing Interests in Family Law*. "We'll see more of this as part of the backlash against gay marriage."

25   Even so, more gay couples—especially male couples—are adopting than ever before. A study last year found that 60 percent of adoption agencies accept applications from homosexuals, up from just a few a decade ago. The 2000 census showed that 26 percent of gay male couples with children designate a stay-at-home parent, compared with 25 percent of straight parents. "When you have children, whether you're gay or straight, you spend lots of time wondering how good a job you're doing for your kids; you lose sleep over it," says Mark Brown, 49, whose partner stays home with their two young adopted kids. "It doesn't leave much time to worry about how we're being perceived by straight society."

Rick Santorum

AMERICANS MUST PRESERVE INSTITUTION OF MARRIAGE

Rick Santorum, the junior Republican Senator from Pennsylvania and an outspoken advocate for the traditional family, has consistently opposed same-sex marriage. The essay included here was written for USA Today, *a national newspaper with a daily readership of nearly 5.4 million. As you read, consider the ways in which Santorum's status as a U.S. senator affects his rhetorical situation—his credibility, his relationship with audience, his purposes, and so forth.*

1   The majority of Supreme Court justices may not be willing to admit it, but everyone else seems eager to acknowledge that

the greatest near-term consequence of the *Lawrence v. Texas* anti-sodomy ruling could be the legalization of homosexual marriage.

Although the court's majority opinion attempts to distance the ruling from the marriage debate, the dissenting justices say, "Do not believe it." Major Web sites such as America Online's home page, as well as newspapers and TV commentators, have signaled that the decision puts the gay-marriage debate in high gear. *The Washington Post's* front page trumpeted, "A debate on marriage, and more, now looms." And *Newsweek's* July 7 cover asks: "Is Gay Marriage Next?"

Before, the right to privacy in sexual matters was limited primarily to married couples. Now the court in its sweeping decision expanded constitutional privacy protection to consensual acts of sodomy, striking down anti-sodomy laws in Texas and 12 other states.

The court's majority opinion telegraphed unmistakably its position on the question of homosexual marriage. It listed "personal decisions relating to marriage" among the areas in which homosexuals "may seek autonomy," just as heterosexuals may.

The dissenting justices, including Chief Justice William Rehnquist, noted: "Today's opinion dismantles the structure of constitutional law that has permitted a distinction to be made between heterosexual and homosexual unions, insofar as formal recognition in marriage is concerned."

After the ruling, Senate Majority Leader Bill Frist, R-Tenn., expressed concern over the court's encroaching upon Americans' right to protect the family and joined the majority of Americans in backing a proposed constitutional amendment to ban homosexual marriage. I also would support a constitutional amendment to affirm traditional marriage.

In fact, I believe that Congress has an obligation to take action to defend the legal status of marriage before the Supreme Court or individual state supreme courts take away the public's ability to act.

Every civilization since the beginning of man has recognized the need for marriage. This country and healthy societies around the world give marriage special legal protection for a vital reason—it is the institution that ensures the society's future through the upbringing of children. Furthermore, it's just common sense that marriage is the union of a man and a woman.

There is an ocean of empirical data showing that the union between a man and a woman has unique benefits for children and society. Moreover, traditional family breakdown is the single biggest social problem in America today. In study after study, family breakdown is linked to an increase in violent crime, youth crime, teen pregnancy, welfare dependency and child poverty.

10   Marriage has already been weakened. The out-of-wedlock childbirth rate is at a historically high level, while the divorce rate remains unacceptably high. Legalization of gay marriage would further undermine an institution that is essential to the well-being of children and our society. Do we need to confuse future generations of Americans even more about the role and importance of an institution that is so critical to the stability of our country?

11   The last thing we should do is destroy the special legal status of marriage. But galvanized by the Supreme Court victory, proponents of removing that status are out in force. Ruth Harlow, lead attorney representing the plaintiffs in the *Texas* case, said, "The ruling makes it much harder for society to continue banning gay marriages."

12   That is where we are today, thanks to the *Texas* ruling. But the majority of Americans will have the final say in the battle to preserve the institution of marriage.

13   I hope elected leaders will rally behind the effort to defend the legal status of marriage from a non-elected group of justices, and I urge you to join those elected leaders in this vital case.

Adam Tenney

WHOSE FAMILY VALUES?

As you can tell from the many perspectives on marriage and family included in this part of Conversations, *any issue clearly has more than "two sides." Indeed, the question asked by the title of the essay included below is one that readers might keep in mind as they read any of the pieces in this section. In particular, the essay by Adam Tenney that is reprinted here is informed by Marxist social values and appeared in the Marxist publication,* Political Affairs. *As you read, consider how the author uses the issues of family and "family values" to critique the capitalist culture that Marxists tend to oppose. Is this piece*

meant for a general audience, or just for those who already ac-
cept Marxist ideals? Does it participate in the conversation
with other specific pieces in this section?

The struggle for gay rights is moving into a pivotal moment. 1
Over the past year, there have been many victories and much
to celebrate. In June, the Supreme Court struck down Texas'
sodomy law that made sexual acts between people of the same
gender illegal. Over the rest of the summer, shows like *Queer*
Eye for the Straight Guy and *Boy Meets Boy* brought gay culture
and life to the homes of millions. In November, the
Massachusetts Supreme Court ruled that the state could not
bar gay couples from marriage.

However, at each of these victories has come a price. The 2
ultra right has launched a vicious counterattack on the gay
rights movement. After each of the court cases, the ultra right
lined up its spokespeople to rant and rave these rulings were
spelling the end of the family and our country. After the
Supreme Court ruling, Republicans in Congress introduced a
bill that would amend the Constitution to define marriage as
between one man and one woman. Bush gave his approval of
the bill during his State of the Union address last January. The
ultra right is pushing for another round of the "culture wars"
and is putting the issue of gay marriage and gay equality at the
center of this year's presidential election.

At this critical time, it is important for us to examine the 3
ultra right's tactics and rhetoric. We must understand why they
are so obsessed with fighting against gay rights and gay marriage. If we are to continue to advance the struggle for both, we
must be able to articulate a sound rebuttal.

The ultraright has put the issue of the family at the center of its 4
battle cry, conjuring up the image of the "homosexual menace"
in order to frighten people to vote against gay marriage. The
right tells the masses that homosexuals are out to destroy families, recruit their children and end society as we know it. As ambitious as this agenda may be, it simply is not true. Conservatives
have created this rather frightening and far-fetched lie in order to
cover the crisis they have put the family in.

In order for us to make sense of the right's argument, we 5
must take it apart in two pieces. First, we must search for the
reason why they feel the family needs saving. To find our answer, we must look at the development of the family under capitalism. This will create a basis for our understanding of the
current crisis the family is in. Second, we must look at how the
ultra right's policies have influenced the family. By analyzing

their policies, we will be able to see how "family friendly" they really are.

The Family under Capitalism

6   Capitalist development created a contradiction in the family when it moved society from one centered on household production to one based on commodity production. Historian John D'Emilio has described the erosion of the family due to capitalist development. He argues that in the early stages of capitalism, men and women were dependent on each other for many basic needs. Within the family, men provided the economic necessities while the women raised the children and provided most of the needs of the home such as cooking and clothes making. As capitalism became more developed, factory produced materials eventually replaced those created within the home. Gradually, capitalism ended the economic necessity that forced many men and women into marriage. By the late 1800s capitalism had produced the conditions that allowed some men and women to live on their wages instead of within the traditional family setting.

7   While the interdependence between the husband and wife for economic and household production has fallen apart, child rearing is still an important factor in forming a family. Even though capitalism was undermining the material basis for the family, it still needed an institution to raise children in. Instead of marriage being an economic and social necessity, it was transformed into a deeply personal necessity. In order to justify the continued existence of the nuclear family, capitalist society created an ideology that put marriage as the place where the human desire for intimacy occurs. Heterosexual marriage became the way men and women fulfilled their deepest personal wants and needs. With this ideology in place, capitalist society was able to keep the nuclear family intact.

8   This brief analysis allows us to start thinking of how the family is in crisis. While it was mostly men at first that were able to live outside of marriage, women have been able to make strides towards economic independence. Even though women are still hindered by institutional sexism in access to employment and education, they are able to choose if and when they want to get married. In addition to creating the false myth that heterosexual marriage fulfills our intimate desires, the right has moved to a reactionary position when it comes to the definition of the family. The right, in its mission to "save the family," has created an extreme view of the family and a social agenda to support their position.

The Right and the Family

In our society, the nuclear family has two roles. First is the re-   9
production of children. Second, is the socialization of children
into the norms and morals of our society. It is the role of socialization that the family plays that the ultra right has focused
on. The ultra right wants to create families that reproduce sexist and heterosexist attitudes about gender relations. Within
the ultra right's view of the family, women are to be forced into
the role of the submissive wife while the husband is cast as the
domineering economic provider. Within this framework, children are raised with a sexist view on the roles of men and
women within society and the heterosexist notion that heterosexuality is the "natural" arrangement of women and men.

In order to push away criticisms of their warped view of the   10
family, the ultra right has created scapegoats out of groups of
people that challenge their notion of the family. It demonizes
single mothers, feminists and gays as the root cause of many of
the problems with youth and society. Conservatives have tried
to make it impossible for single mothers to raise children by
cutting back on welfare, job training and other social services
that many single mothers use to provide for their families.
While cutting these social services, the right attacks single
mothers as being inadequate at raising their own children.
They continue to make the argument that children that grow
up in a single mother household end up as problem children.

The right has attacked feminism because it wants to alter the   11
basic relationship between men and women and calls for greater
access for women in the job market. Women are now able to put
off having a family until they are ready, instead of that decision
being made by their husbands. The right opposes gay marriage
and gay rights because it does redefine what makes a family and
creates a situation where heterosexuality is not the norm.

Fighting Back

With an understanding of the type of family that the ultra right   12
is really the protector of, we can begin to break apart the anti-
family rhetoric the right launches at the movement for gay
marriage. We know that gay marriage is not seeking to destroy
the nuclear family. Instead, it is advocating that there are other
equally healthy ways to create loving relationships and raise
children outside of heterosexual marriage. Gay marriage,
along with other types of marital arrangements, redefine what
makes a family. We already know that many of the families in

our country do not fit into the archetypal version that the right supports. Many families are made of single mothers, foster parents, grandparents raising grandchildren and other familial arrangements. We also know that these families do not always produce "problem children" as the right would like us to believe. Yet, this does not mean that our society is falling apart. It means that we are admitting what is already in front of us: that the nuclear family is not the only way to raise a child.

13   Most importantly, we know that those that are supposedly working to save it are putting the family under a tremendous strain. The right continuously institutes policies that have a negative effect on working families. By cutting welfare, funds for public education and daycare, the right makes it extremely difficult for working families who depend on these institutions to raise children. The massive unemployment that has plagued this country due to the policies of the Bush administration has put added strain on the family. Another strain on the family comes from the criminalization of our society. With people going to prison younger and for longer sentences (especially men of color), it puts an extreme burden on the functioning of the family.

14   To deflect attention from the effects of these anti-family policies, the right turns criticism toward those who live in or advocate the normality of alternative family situations, especially toward families with same-sex partners. We should be clear that it is the policies of the right and not gay marriage that undermines the family. By articulating how the policies of the ultra right, and not gay marriage, undermine the family, we can begin to dismantle the right's attack and advance the fight for gay marriage and equality.

Ellen Goodman

SHOWING US THE POWER OF MARRIAGE

Ellen Goodman is a Pulitzer prize–winning columnist who began with the Boston Globe *and whose work is now nationally syndicated. In addition to her regular columns on issues spanning a wide variety of social issues, she has published a book on social change,* Turning Points, *and five collections of her essays. She has also won the American Society of Newspaper*

Editors Distinguished Writing Award, the President's Award from the National Women's Political Caucus, and Women's Research and Education Institute's American Woman Award. In 1996, Goodman was a visiting professor at Stanford University. The essay included here was published in The Boston Globe *in May 2004, soon after the rush of marriages in Massachusetts.*

Let's just say that the man selling newspapers at the entrance   1
of the government center subway station hadn't yet caught the spirit of the day. Marriage comes with three rings, he was telling a customer, "engagement ring, wedding ring, suffering." But the headline in the paper he was hawking had a different take on this historic moment. It announced simply: "Free to marry."

Monday was the first day in which gay couples in   2
Massachusetts could tie the legal knot. "Free to marry" may sound like a contradiction in terms—liberated to be committed?—but not among those lined up to get licenses.

Men and men, women and women formed an ad hoc recep-   3
tion line snaking out of Boston City Hall as the media walked up and down with pens and cameras.

Rebecca Priest and Madonna Berry wanted to tell me they   4
had met through a newspaper personals ad eight years ago— "fortysomething, independent, loves the movies."

Mark Strickland and Tread Pearson wanted to be sure that I   5
knew they were being married by a [United Church of Christ] minister. Abha Agrawal and Vijay Sharina, a doctor and biologist, said they had come here a dozen years ago from India "to a place they could be together happily."

Those I met had been together anywhere from one year to   6
18. Some shared houses. Others shared children. Most said they already felt married. Yet when the chance came to be married, it was different.

Janet Deegan and Constance Cervone, who share a mortgage   7
and a real estate business and a 12-year relationship—how much more committed can you get?—shared something else: a case of the premarital jitters.

A decade ago, a few hamlets in liberal pockets of America   8
tested out the idea of "domestic partnership." When a gay couple in Hawaii sued for marriage, saying "we want the whole enchilada," many gay rights leaders were leery of even putting marriage on the agenda. In 2000, the first civil unions were legalized in Vermont and the citizens reacted as if the sky were falling and the maple sap had stopped running.

Now after a historic court ruling, same-sex couples in   9
Massachusetts are—for now at least—marriage material. As the

stickers from GLAD, the Gay and Lesbian Advocates and Defenders, boasted: "We do the courting, you do the marrying."

10   So put aside for a moment the controversy. Put aside the folks who believe that same-sex marriage will destroy traditional marriage. In their shared jitters, the couples "free to marry" in Massachusetts reinforce the power of a somewhat battered institution.

11   What seems so radical from a distance seems conservative when close-up and personal. Not just because we have extended old rights to a new category of citizens. Not just because the marriage debate has turned the face of gay America into an image of two dads, two moms, a kid, a golden retriever, and a soccer schedule.

12   It's conservative because it presents and upholds marriage itself as the official gold standard of relationships, the socially accepted test of commitment that gay couples too now face.

13   Marriage in America has been sorely tested. Half of all marriages end in divorce. In 2000, 5.5 million unmarried couples lived together—and nearly 5 million of them were heterosexual. We've developed a whole in-between set of rights and benefits for the not-exactly-married.

14   As gay couples are allowed to legally wed, ironically, the line that separates marriage from partnership may be redefined. As marriage becomes possible, every gay couple will face "the conversation" common to straight couples: Where are we going? What does commitment mean? Is marriage the "whole enchilada"?

15   These couples want a license to join, not to destroy, marriage. Two by two, they are reminders of the importance of marriage as a passage, a public commitment and a support system. They are even reminders of the power of tradition.

16   At 9:30 Monday morning, a few subway stops away, up the tulle-wrapped staircase of Cambridge City Hall, I watched Tanya McCloskey and Marcia Kadish take each other "to be my spouse." They promised "My friendship, my support, and my love."

17   Yes, these veterans of an 18-year-old relationship were already committed for better or for worse. Yet they too confessed to "shaking" before the justice of the peace. Just like newlyweds.

18   Meanwhile down in Provincetown, two men—one of them a divorce attorney—said they were getting married because, as one told a TV reporter, "I know one thing will be definite—it will be him."

19   Engagement ring, wedding ring, suffering? There are few cynics applying for licenses in this wedding week. In Massachusetts, same sex couples are now choosing and celebrating the freedom—of commitment.

Barbara Findlen
IS MARRIAGE
THE ANSWER?

Barbara Findlen is the former executive editor of **Ms.** *magazine, the famous feminist publication that carried the following article in the May/June 1995 issue. Findlen also edited the
influential collection of feminist essays,* Listen Up: Voices
from the Next Feminist Generation.

In December 1990, Ninia Baehr and Genora Dancel applied for 1
a marriage license at their local health department office in
Honolulu. When the license was denied because they are both
women, they—along with two other same-sex couples who applied for marriage licenses on the same day—sued the state of
Hawaii on the grounds of discrimination. The three couples—
two lesbian and one gay male—were well prepared: before applying for the licenses, they'd already determined that they
might have a shot at changing Hawaii's marriage laws.

And indeed, by May 1993, the Hawaii Supreme Court ruled 2
that prohibiting members of the same sex from marrying constitutes sex discrimination and is therefore a violation of the state
constitution, which includes an equal rights amendment. The
supreme court then proceeded to send the case back to a lower
court, ordering the state to show a "compelling interest" in
maintaining the discrimination. Remarkably, most observers believe that, barring a change in the makeup of the court or some
other extreme circumstance, the couples will triumph when the
case is finally decided sometime within the next 18 months.

The case is significant, not just for the future of gay mar- 3
riage, but also for the fate of domestic partnership agreements,
which give benefits such as health insurance coverage to unmarried couples. Some activists are wondering, for example,
what will become of the dozens of domestic partnership policies that have sprung up over the last decade, many of which
also benefit unmarried heterosexual couples. If gay marriage
were to become legal, entities that currently offer these policies
might decide that since anyone can marry, benefits should be
offered only to spouses. Domestic partnership policies would
therefore be seen as unnecessary. Many of those who favor
domestic partnership policies over marriage espouse the arguably radical notion that *no* rights or benefits should be

based on marriage. Other critics would even prefer to see marriage, with its patriarchal trappings, abolished altogether.

4   While some people might view lesbian and gay marriage as a radical development because it would at last put homosexual relationships on a par with heterosexual ones, domestic partnership advocates view it as conservative because it upholds the basic primacy of marriage as the foundation of the family and marginalizes people who are outside that unit. Notes Paula L. Ettelbrick, a legislative counsel at New York's Empire State Pride Agenda: "The marriage campaign has moved our community to a more conservative, middle-of-the-road political perspective. It has taken people out of the broader, social justice view of family."

5   But there are different agendas among those who advocate domestic partnership, acknowledges Matt Coles, the director of the ACLU Lesbian and Gay Rights Project and coauthor of one of the first domestic partnership policies ever proposed in the U.S. (for the city of San Francisco in 1980). Some view domestic partnership as a straightforward equal-pay-for-equal-work issue: employment benefits that are offered to employees' legal spouses should be offered to partners of unmarried employees. For others, it's a way station en route to lesbian and gay marriage. Still others see it as a way to begin to fundamentally redefine the legal meaning of "family," thus undermining the power of the patriarchal nuclear family.

6   Melinda Paras, executive director of the National Gay and Lesbian Task Force (NGLTF), is aiming for the latter. "Part of our struggle," she says, "is to fight for a broader definition of families. Domestic partners shouldn't have to be gay or lesbian. They shouldn't have to be having sex. They can be two adults sharing a home and sharing commitment, responsible to each other."

7   Currently, about 35 municipalities and scores of private companies, educational institutions, and nonprofit organizations offer some kind of policy that bestows benefits on unmarried cohabiting couples—gay *and* straight. There are two kinds of domestic partnership policies—those offered by the private sector, which generally do not provide benefits to unmarried heterosexuals, and municipal policies created by city governments, which cover both same-sex and opposite-sex partners. A typical municipal policy might well define domestic partners in terms similar to those of Paras. In Madison, Wisconsin, for example, they can be any two unrelated adults "in a relationship of mutual support, caring, and commitment." In Seattle, the partners must "have a close and personal relationship" and share "basic living expenses." In many cities, more straight couples than gay couples register as domestic partners. Municipalities establish a registry, and city employees who file are usually given a

certificate that validates their domestic partnership and often provides access to spousal equivalent benefits (health insurance, bereavement leave, and other benefits granted to married employees). People who don't work for the city may also receive a certificate. Though organizations in the private sector, such as auto clubs or health clubs, may honor this municipal certificate as a basis for providing benefits, it's strictly optional, and the benefits offered by the city to nonemployees are limited— perhaps access to family memberships at a museum or a gym, or the right to hospital or jail visitation.

Private sector policies tend to be much narrower than municipal policies. Most apply only to same-sex partners. The major benefit is usually health insurance, and some policies even stop short of that, offering only bereavement or family care leave, use of recreational facilities, access to married faculty or student housing—benefits that cost the institution little. 8

The rationale behind most private sector plans is: lesbian and gay employees can't marry, so as a matter of workplace equity, they should have access to benefits they would have if they could marry. Nancy Polikoff, a law professor whose work has focused on lesbian and gay families, cites the policy at her own institution, American University, which applies only to same-sex domestic partners. "What happens when there's gay and lesbian marriage?" she says. "That's the end of domestic partnership benefits. We will be told, 'Get married.' What does that say about the notion that we can choose not to get married?" 9

What about a corporation like Levi Strauss & Co., which offers benefits to unmarried heterosexual partners? It's hard to predict whether policies like that will disappear, but it seems likely that the possibility of same-sex marriage would remove a lot of the impetus behind the domestic partnership movement. Although the policies often benefit straight people, the initiative has mostly come from lesbians and gay men, who don't have access to marriage rights. 10

"My big fear," says Ettelbrick, "is that if gay people were allowed to marry tomorrow, I know that we would lose a substantial part of our community that is working on domestic partner benefits. The point is that neither straight people nor gay people should have to get married in order to have some very basic protections for the families that they've chosen. I don't think we have a unified sense of social reform anymore. We have a piece-by-piece approach—we'll make change where we can. We no longer have bigger picture items on our agendas." 11

Domestic partnership, like many other issues that now concern this country, is curiously tied to health care. The word "benefit," after all, is often synonymous with health insurance. 12

And why, many ask, is health insurance coverage tied to marital, couple, *or* employment status? "If universal health care were available, no one would be forced to say, 'I want to be able to get married to take advantage of my partner's health insurance benefits,'" says Polikoff. "What we ought to do is let every employee designate a person to receive co-benefits. That person could be your sexual partner, best friend, aunt, or sister. Why are we making people's sexual partners more important than others with whom they share their lives? This kind of arrangement would be my way station to uncoupling all of these benefits from marriage and creating a world in which the things that are now considered components of marriage become social entitlements or can be designated by individuals."

13   Adds Robin Kane, NGLTF's communications director: "We could wait for universal health care coverage to be enacted by Congress. We could wait for the Hawaii marriage ruling to come down and then for every state to battle out whether or not they'll recognize it. But in the meantime, there are people who are actually getting health insurance for their partners through domestic partner benefits."

14   But domestic partnership policies don't hold a candle to the entitlements that come with marriage. It is already possible to approximate some of the rights granted automatically to married people—inheritance can be addressed through wills, the right to make health care decisions through durable powers of attorney. Compare these with the rights that come with a marriage license and cannot be exercised by unmarried couples, no matter where they live or what agreements they have made: the right to joint parenting, through birth or adoption; the right to file joint income tax returns; legal immigration and residency for partners from other countries; benefits such as annuities, pensions, and Social Security for surviving spouses; wrongful death benefits for surviving partners; immunity from having to testify in court against a spouse.

15   Jane, a health club manager, and Beth, a teacher in suburban New York (not their real names), know the consequences of not having those rights. Five years ago, Jane gave birth to a daughter conceived via insemination by an anonymous donor. When a married couple have a baby in this way, the husband is automatically declared the father. Beth's application to legally adopt their daughter was denied on the grounds that the couple, who have been together for 18 years, were not married. "I'm considered her mother by our community, day care, school, and families," says Beth, "but I have no legal rights as her mother."

16   Whether or not lesbians and gay men should fight for the right to marry has been a subject of debate in the gay community for

years. In 1989, the lesbian and gay magazine *Outlook* published opposing articles, "Since When Is Marriage a Path to Liberation?" by Paula Ettelbrick, and "Why Gay People Should Seek the Right To Marry," by Thomas B. Stoddard. Both authors are lawyers who were working for the Lambda Legal Defense and Education Fund at the time. "Marriage runs contrary to two of the primary goals of the lesbian and gay movement: the affirmation of gay identity and culture, and the validation of many forms of relationships," argued Ettelbrick. Answered Stoddard: "The issue is not the desirability of marriage, but rather the desirability of the right to marry."

Even Beth and Jane aren't sure they would exercise that   17
right. "It's for heterosexuals," says Jane. "Our union doesn't need that ceremony. We would only do it for legal protection."

Feminists have long criticized the institution of marriage   18
as a place of oppression, danger, and drudgery for women. Nineteenth-century feminists protested that a woman's legal identity literally disappeared upon marriage. Even in 1969, a New York City organization called the Feminists declared: "All the discriminatory practices against women are patterned and rationalized by this slavery-like practice. We can't destroy the inequities between men and women until we destroy marriage." These days the uneasiness is due to marriage's power as the singular definer of family, a reinforcer of sex roles, and an institution of heterosexual privilege. Karen Lindsey has been thinking about different forms of family for more than 15 years. Her 1981 book, *Friends as Family*, begins, "The traditional family isn't working," and goes on to explore workplace families, "honorary kin," and chosen families. "In my ideal world, there would be no such thing as marriage," she says today. "What there would be is individuals choosing to live together on whatever terms meet their needs, and then appropriate legal connections to address those needs."

"People say that there are all these goodies that go with   19
being married and why shouldn't gay people get to have them," agrees Polikoff. "My vision is one in which the goodies are not tied to marriage."

As feminists, Ninia Baehr and Genora Dancel, two of the   20
Hawaii plaintiffs, are well aware of these arguments. But for them, the decision to marry was an emotional, not a political, one. Baehr, who was the codirector of the women's center at the University of Hawaii when the suit was filed, says: "If I had sat down and planned my career as a feminist years ago, I would never have said, 'The most important thing I can do is legalize marriage for lesbian and gay people.' But the reality is that when I met Genora, I thought, 'My God, she's the one that

I've been dreaming about.' I wanted to get married. I wanted to be able to say at the end of my life that I had loved someone really well for a long time."

21   Hawaii state legislators meanwhile are doing whatever they can to keep Baehr and Dancel and the other two couples from legally tying the knot. Alarmed at the prospect of their state being the first to allow gay marriage, they passed a law last year that explicitly defines marriage as being between a man and a woman. However, this legislation will presumably be subject to the same "compelling interest" requirement as the previous policy, so it's unlikely that the law will change the outcome of the case. A few legislators have proposed amending the state constitution to exclude same-sex marriage—the one sure way around the state supreme court—but these proposals have failed.

22   Although the Hawaii court ruling would apply only to marriages performed in that state, the decision could spark legal chaos all over the country. Lesbian and gay couples will likely flock to Hawaii to marry, then return to their home states and try to file joint tax returns, sign up for spousal health insurance coverage, or adopt children together. Currently every state recognizes marriages performed in other states. Couples who are denied recognition of their legal same-sex marriages granted in Hawaii will have grounds to sue their home states.

23   "There will be litigation in many states for years to come," says Evan Wolfson, cocounsel for the three Hawaii couples and director of the Lambda Legal Defense and Education Fund's Marriage Project. The dozens of expected cases could implicate even the federal government, which relies on the states to determine who is married for purposes of taxes, Social Security benefits, immigration, and other matters. And though all marriage laws are state laws, the question potentially could be settled by the U.S. Supreme Court. If that happened, lawyers for the couples would likely base their arguments on the provision of the U.S. Constitution that requires states to give "full faith and credit" to the lawful marriages of other states.

24   And these other states are keeping an anxious eye on Hawaii. The state legislature of Utah has passed legislation that would refuse recognition of any same-sex marriage performed in another state. South Dakota also tried, but failed, to pass such a law.

25   The ACLU's Matt Coles thinks one significant result of the pending Hawaii ruling will be a proliferation of domestic partnership protections for lesbians and gay men as states try—by offering spousal equivalent benefits—to avoid the need to recognize gay marriage.

26   NGLTF's Paras says: "I think we will end up with marriage and domestic partnership as simultaneously existing legal

constructs. Marriage will be a huge battle that will mostly be lost for a long time. In the meantime, domestic partnership practices are expanding and will become a much larger body of law and policy. By the time equality finally gets won universally, we'll be in a whole other place about the definition of family, and gay marriage may become almost irrelevant."

Tom Toles

THE TROUBLE
WITH GAYS

Tom Toles's sharpwitted cartoons regularly appear in the conservative U.S. News & World Report *as well as in many newspapers. He created this one in June 2000.*

Andrew Sullivan
HERE COMES
THE GROOM

Andrew Sullivan (born 1963) is one of the leading commentators on gay, lesbian, and bisexual issues in the nation. Openly gay, devotedly Catholic, critical of certain aspect of the gay community, and outspokenly iconoclastic, he advocates the full intergration of gays, lesbians, and bisexuals into American life. In 1996, Sullivan disclosed that he was receiving treatment for AIDS. He entered graduate school at Harvard to study government and resigned from his position as an associate editor at New Republic, *which had published the argument that follows in 1989. In addition to many articles, he is the author of* Virtually Normal: An Argument about Homosexuality *(1995) and* Love Undetectable: Notes on Friendship, Sex, and Survival *(1999). He also maintains a popular website called The Daily Dish at www.andrewsullivan.com, where he publishes some of his writing.*

1   Last month in New York, a court ruled that a gay lover had the right to stay in his deceased partner's rent-control apartment because the lover qualified as a member of the deceased's family. The ruling deftly annoyed almost everybody. Conservatives saw judicial activism in favor of gay rent control: three reasons to be appalled. Chastened liberals (such as the *New York Times* editorial page), while endorsing the recognition of gay relationships, also worried about the abuse of already stretched entitlements that the ruling threatened. What neither side quite contemplated is that they both might be right, and that the way to tackle the issue of unconventional relationships in conventional society is to try something both more radical and more conservative than putting courts in the business of deciding what is and is not a family. That alternative is the legalization of civil gay marriage.

2   The New York rent-control case did not go anywhere near that far, which is the problem. The rent-control regulations merely stipulated that a "family" member had the right to remain in the apartment. The judge ruled that to all intents and purposes a gay lover is part of his lover's family, inasmuch as a "family" merely means an interwoven social life, emotional commitment, and some level of financial interdependence.

It's a principle now well established around the country. 3
Several cities have "domestic partnership" laws, which allow
relationships that do not fit into the category of heterosexual
marriage to be registered with the city and qualify for benefits
that up till now have been reserved for straight married couples. San Francisco, Berkeley, Madison, and Los Angeles all
have legislation, as does the politically correct Washington,
D.C., suburb, Takoma Park. In these cities, a variety of interpersonal arrangements qualify for health insurance, bereavement leave, insurance, annuity and pension rights, housing
rights (such as rent-control apartments), adoption and inheritance rights. Eventually, according to gay lobby groups, the
aim is to include federal income tax and veterans' benefits as
well. A recent case even involved the right to use a family member's accumulated frequent-flier points. Gays are not the only
beneficiaries; heterosexual "live-togethers" also qualify.

There's an argument, of course, that the current legal advan- 4
tages extended to married people unfairly discriminate against
people who've shaped their lives in less conventional arrangements. But it doesn't take a genius to see that enshrining in the
law a vague principle like "domestic partnership" [DP] is an invitation to qualify at little personal cost for a vast array of entitlements otherwise kept crudely under control.

To be sure, potential DPs have to prove financial interdepen- 5
dence, shared living arrangements, and a commitment to mutual caring. But they don't need to have a sexual relationship or
even closely mirror old-style marriage. In principle, an elderly
woman and her live-in nurse could qualify. A couple of une-
uphemistically confirmed bachelors could be DPs. So could
two close college students, a pair of seminarians, or a couple of
frat buddies. Left as it is, the concept of domestic partnership
could open a Pandora's box of litigation and subjective judicial
decision-making about who qualifies. You either are or are not
married; it's not a complex question. Whether you are in a "domestic partnership" is not so clear.

More important, the concept of domestic partnership chips 6
away at the prestige of traditional relationships and undermines
the priority we give them. This priority is not necessarily a product of heterosexism. Consider heterosexual couples. Society has
good reason to extend legal advantages to heterosexuals who
choose the formal sanction of marriage over simply living together. They make a deeper commitment to one another and to
society; in exchange, society extends certain benefits to them.
Marriage provides an anchor, if an arbitrary and weak one,
in the chaos of sex and relationships to which we are all prone.
It provides a mechanism for emotional stability, economic

security, and the healthy rearing of the next generation. We rig the law in its favor not because we disparage all forms of relationship other than the nuclear family, but because we recognize that not to promote marriage would be to ask too much of human virtue. In the context of the weakened family's effect upon the poor, it might also invite social disintegration. One of the worst products of the New Right's "family values" campaign is that its extremism and hatred of diversity has disguised this more measured and more convincing case for the importance of the marital bond.

7   The concept of domestic partnership ignores these concerns, indeed directly attacks them. This is a pity, since one of its most important objectives—providing some civil recognition for gay relationships—is a noble cause and one completely compatible with the defense of the family. But the decision to go about it is not to undermine straight marriage; it is to legalize old-style marriage for gays.

8   The gay movement has ducked this issue primarily out of fear of division. Much of the gay leadership clings to notions of gay life as essentially outsider, antibourgeois, radical. Marriage, for them, is co-optation into straight society. For the Stonewall generation, it is hard to see how this vision of conflict will ever fundamentally change. But for many other gays—my guess, a majority—while they don't deny the importance of rebellion 20 years ago and are grateful for what was done, there's now the sense of a new opportunity. A need to rebel has quietly ceded to a desire to belong. To be gay and to be bourgeois no longer seems such an absurd proposition. Certainly, since AIDS, to be gay and to be responsible has become a necessity.

9   Gay marriage squares several circles at the heart of the domestic partnership debate. Unlike domestic partnership, it allows for recognition of gay relationships, while casting no aspersions on traditional marriage. It merely asks that gays be allowed to join in. Unlike domestic partnership, it doesn't open up avenues for heterosexuals to get benefits without the responsibilities of marriage, or a nightmare of definitional litigation. And unlike domestic partnership, it harnesses to an already established social convention the yearnings for stability and acceptance among a fast-maturing gay community.

10   Gay marriage also places more responsibilities upon gays: it says for the first time that gay relationships are not better or worse than straight relationships, and that the same is expected of them. And it's clear and dignified. There's a legal benefit to a clear, common symbol of commitment. There's also a personal benefit. One of the ironies of domestic partnership is

that it's not only more complicated than marriage, it's more demanding, requiring an elaborate statement of intent to qualify. It amounts to a substantial invasion of privacy. Why, after all, should gays be required to prove commitment before they get married in a way we would never dream of asking of straights?

Legalizing gay marriage would offer homosexuals the same   11
deal society now offers heterosexuals: general social approval and specific legal advantages in exchange for a deeper and harder-to-extract-yourself-from commitment to another human being. Like straight marriage, it would foster social cohesion, emotional security, and economic prudence. Since there's no reason gays should not be allowed to adopt or be foster parents, it could also help nurture children. And its introduction would not be some sort of radical break with social custom. As it has become more acceptable for gay people to acknowledge their loves publicly, more and more have committed themselves to one another for life in full view of their families and their friends. A law institutionalizing gay marriage would merely reinforce a healthy social trend. It would also, in the wake of AIDS, qualify as a genuine public health measure. Those conservatives who deplore promiscuity among some homosexuals should be among the first to support it. Burke could have written a powerful case for it.

The argument that gay marriage would subtly undermine the   12
unique legitimacy of straight marriage is based upon a fallacy. For heterosexuals, straight marriage would remain the most significant—and only legal—social bond. Gay marriage could only delegitimize straight marriage if it were a real alternative to it, and this is clearly not true. To put it bluntly, there's precious little evidence that straights could be persuaded by any law to have sex with—let alone marry—someone of their own sex. The only possible effect of this sort would be to persuade gay men and women who force themselves into heterosexual marriage (often at appalling cost to themselves and their families) to find a focus for their family instincts in a more personally positive environment. But this is clearly a plus, not a minus: gay marriage could both avoid a lot of tortured families and create the possibility for many happier ones. It is not, in short, a denial of family values. It's an extension of them.

Of course, some would claim that any legal recognition of   13
homosexuality is a de facto attack upon heterosexuality. But even the most hardened conservatives recognize that gays are a permanent minority and aren't likely to go away. Since persecution is not an option in a civilized society, why not coax gays into traditional values rather than rail incoherently against them?

14   There's a less elaborate argument for gay marriage: it's good
for gays. It provides role models for young gay people who,
after the exhilaration of coming out, can easily lapse into
short-term relationships and insecurity with no tangible goal
in sight. My own guess is that most gays would embrace such a
goal with as much (if not more) commitment as straights.
Even in our society as it is, many lesbian relationships are virtual textbook cases of monogamous commitment. Legal gay
marriage could also help bridge the gulf often found between
gays and their parents. It could bring the essence of gay life—a
gay couple—into the heart of the traditional straight family in
a way the family can most understand and the gay offspring
can most easily acknowledge. It could do as much to heal the
gay-straight rift as any amount of gay rights legislation.

15   If these arguments sound socially conservative, that's no accident. It's one of the richest ironies of our society's blind spot
toward gays that essentially conservative social goals should
have the appearance of being so radical. But gay marriage is
not a radical step. It avoids the mess of domestic partnership;
it is humane; it is conservative in the best sense of the word.
It's also practical. Given the fact that we already allow legal gay
relationships, what possible social goal is advanced by framing
the law to encourage those relationships to be unfaithful, un-
developed, and insecure?

Hadley Arkes
THE CLOSET STRAIGHT

*Hadley Arkes (born 1944) is a professor of law at Amherst
College in Massachusetts. His response (following) to the argu-
ments of Andrew Sullivan originally appeared in 1993 in the*
National Review, *which maintains a conservative editorial
stance. Arkes's essay counters not the previous essay in*
Conversations *by Sullivan but a similar one, entitled "The
Politics of Homosexuality," that Sullivan wrote in 1993.*

1   John Courtney Murray once observed that the atheist and the
theist essentially agree in their understanding of the problem:

The atheist does not mean to reject the existence of God only in Staten Island; he means to reject God universally, as a necessary truth. He accepts the same framework of reference, and he makes the same move to a transcendent standard of judgment. In a thoughtful, extended essay, Andrew Sullivan, the young, gay editor of *The New Republic*, has made a comparable concession for the advocate of "gay rights." For Sullivan has put into place, as the very ground and framework of his argument, a structure of understanding that must call into question any claims for the homosexual life as a rival good.

"The Politics of Homosexuality" confirms, at length, what 2 anyone who has been with Andrew Sullivan can grasp within five minutes: he regards his erotic life as the center of his being, but he also conveys the most powerful need to seek that erotic fulfillment within a framework of domesticity, of the normal and the *natural*. The most persisting thread of anguish in the essay is the pain of awareness and reconciliation in his own family, with the recurring memory of his father weeping when Andrew declared, as he says, his sexuality. Sullivan reserves some of his most stinging words for the producers of a "queer" politics, aimed at "cultural subversion." That brand of politics would simply confirm the strangeness of homosexuals, and deepen the separation from their families. Ironically, says Sullivan, "queer" politics "broke off dialogue with the heterosexual families whose cooperation is needed in every generation, if gay children are to be accorded a modicum of dignity and hope."

The delicacy barely conceals that "cooperation is needed in 3 every generation" precisely because "homosexual families" cannot produce "gay children." Gay children must come into being through the only kind of family that nature knows. Those who wish to preserve, say, a Jewish people, know that Jews need to reproduce and raise their children as Jews. But what would be the comparable path of obligation for the person who is committed to the preservation of a "gay community"? Sullivan is convinced that there is something in our biology or chemistry that "determines" our sexuality, and in that case, the tendency to gay sex may be passed along to the next generation, as readily as temperament and allergies. The person who wishes to preserve, for the next generation, a gay community may be tempted then to render the ultimate service: For the good of the cause, he may cross the line and enter another domain of sex. But in crossing that line, he makes a decisive concession: implicitly, but unmistakably, he is compelled to acknowledge that homosexuality cannot even pretend to stand on the same plane as the way of life it would displace.

We do not really find two kinds of "families" carrying out transactions with one another. But rather, we come to recognize again the primacy of "sexuality" in the strictest sense, the only sexuality that can produce "another generation."

4   It is evidently important to Sullivan to insist that homosexuality is rooted in "nature," that it is determined for many people by something in their makeup quite beyond their control. He would wish to draw to his side a certain strand of natural law to suggest that anything so rooted in nature cannot be wrong. And yet, he falls there into an ancient mistake. As the great expounders of natural law explained, we do not make our way to the "natural" simply by generalizing upon the mixed record of our species: by that reckoning, incest and genocide would be in accord with natural law, since they seem to form an intractable part of the human experience. And even if we could show, say, that some of us carried a gene for "arson," that would not settle the moral question on arson. We might not be as quick to blame the bearers of these genes, but we would expect them to exert more self-control, and we would hardly waive our moral reservations about arson.

5   In a passage of searing candor, Sullivan acknowledges that discrimination has not affected gays with the same kinds of deprivations that have been visited upon blacks. "[Gay] men and lesbians suffer no discernible communal economic deprivations and already operate at the highest levels of society." But when they call to their aid the levers of the law, they cultivate the sense of themselves as vulnerable and weak, in need of protection, and they perpetuate, among gays, the tendencies to self-doubt. They suggest that the things most needful to gays are in the hands of other people to confer. In the sweep of his own conviction, Sullivan would soar past those demands altogether. He would stop demanding laws, which confer, upon straight people, the franchise of confirming, or discounting, the worth of gays.

Love and Marriage

6   Except for one, notable thing. What Andrew Sullivan wants, most of all, is marriage. And he wants it for reasons that could not have been stated more powerfully by any heterosexual who had been raised, as Sullivan was, in the Catholic tradition and schooled in political philosophy. "[T]he apex of emotional life," says Sullivan, "is found in the marital bond." The erotic interest may seek out copulation, but the fulfillment of eros depends on the integrity of a bond woven of sentiment and confirmed by law. Marriage is more than a private contract; it

is "the highest public recognition of our personal integrity." Its equivalent will not be supplied by a string of sensual nights, accumulated over many years of "living together." The very existence of marriage "premises the core of our emotional development. It is the architectonic institution that frames our emotional life."

No one could doubt for a moment: as much as any of the   7
"guys" in the Damon Runyon stories, the man who wrote those lines is headed, irresistibly, for marriage. What he craves— homosexual marriage—would indeed require the approval conferred by law. It would also require a benediction conferred by straight people, who would have to consent to that vast, new modeling of our laws. That project will not be undertaken readily, and it may not be undertaken at all. Still, there is something, rooted in the nature of Andrew Sullivan, that must need marriage.

But as Mona Charen pointed out, in an encounter with   8
Sullivan at the National Review Institute conference this winter, it is not marriage that domesticates men; it is women. Left to themselves, these forked creatures follow a way of life that George Gilder once recounted in its precise, chilling measures: bachelors were 22 times more likely than married men to be committed to hospitals for mental disease (and 10 times more likely to suffer chronic diseases of all kinds). Single men had nearly double the mortality rate of married men and 3 times the mortality rate of single women. Divorced men were 3 times more likely than divorced women to commit suicide or die by murder, and they were 6 times more likely to die of heart disease.

We have ample reason by now to doubt that the bipeds de-   9
scribed in these figures are likely to be tamed to a sudden civility if they are merely arranged, in sets of two or three, in the same house. I had the chance to see my own younger son, settled with three of his closest friends in a townhouse in Georgetown during his college years. The labors of the kitchen and the household were divided with a concern for domestic order, and the abrasions of living together were softened by the ties of friendship. And yet, no one, entering that house, could doubt for a moment that he was in a camp occupied for a while by young males, with their hormones flowing.

This is not to deny, of course, that men may truly love men,   10
or commit themselves to a life of steady friendship. But many of us have continued to wonder just why any of these relations would be enhanced in any way by adding to them the ingredients of penetration—or marriage. The purpose of this alliance, after all, could not be the generation of children, and a marriage would not be needed then as the stable framework for

welcoming and sheltering children. For gays, the ceremony of marriage could have the function of proclaiming to the world an exclusive love, a special dedication, which comes along with a solemn promise to forgo all other, competing loves. In short, it would draw its power from the romance of monogamy. But is that the vision that drives the movement for "gay rights"? An excruciating yearning for monogamy?

11   That may indeed be Andrew Sullivan's own yearning, but his position is already marking him as a curious figure in the camp of gay activists. When Sullivan commends the ideal of marriage for gays, he would seem to be pleading merely for the inclusion of gay "couples" in an institution that is indeed confined to pairs, of *adults*, in monogamous unions. But that is not exactly the vision of gay sex.

12   For many activists and connoisseurs, Sullivan would represent a rather wimpish, constricted view of the world they would open to themselves through sexual liberation. After all, the permissions for this new sexual freedom have been cast to that amorphous formula of "sexual orientation": the demand of gay rights is that we should recede from casting moral judgments on the way that people find their pleasure in engagements they regard as "sexual." In its strange abstraction, "sexual orientation" could take in sex with animals or the steamier versions of sado-masochism. The devotees of S&M were much in evidence during the recent march in Washington, but we may put aside for a moment these interests, to consider others which are even more exotic yet. There is, for example, the North American Man-Boy Love Association, a contingent of gay activists who identify themselves, unashamedly, as pedophiles. They insist that nothing in their "sexual orientation" should disqualify them to work as professional counselors, say, in the schools of New York, and to counsel young boys. And since they respect themselves, they will not hold back from commending their own way of life to their young charges. If there is to be gay marriage, would it be confined then only to adults? And if men are inclined to a life of multiple partners, why should marriage be confined to two persons? Why indeed should the notion of gay marriage be scaled down to fit the notions held by Andrew Sullivan?

Sullivan's Dilemma

13   The sources of anguish run even deeper here than Sullivan may suspect, for his dilemma may be crystallized in this way: If he would preserve the traditional understanding of marriage

and monogamy, he would not speak for much of a constituency among gays. But if the notion of "marriage" were enlarged and redefined—if it could take in a plurality of people and shifting combinations—it could hardly be the kind of marriage that Sullivan devoutly wishes as "the apex of emotional life" and "the highest public recognition of our personal integrity."

In traditional marriage, the understanding of monogamy   14
was originally tied to the "natural teleology" of the body—to the recognition that only two people, no more and no fewer, can generate children. To that understanding of a union, or a "marriage," the alliance of two men would offer such an implausible want of resemblance that it would appear almost as a mocking burlesque. It would be rather like confounding, as Lincoln used to say, a "horse chestnut" and a "chestnut horse." The mockery would be avoided if the notion of marriage could be opened, or broadened, to accommodate the varieties of sexual experience. The most notable accommodation would be the acceptance of several partners, and the change could be readily reckoned precisely because it would hardly be novel: the proposal for gay marriage would compel us to look again— to look anew with eyes unclouded by prejudice—to the ancient appeal of polygamy. After all, there would be an Equal Protection problem now: we could scarcely confine this new "marital" arrangement only to members of one gender. But then, once the arrangement is opened simply to "consenting adults," on what ground would we object to the mature couplings of aunts and nephews, or even fathers and daughters— couplings that show a remarkable persistence in our own age, even against the barriers of law and sentiment that have been cast up over centuries? All kinds of questions, once placed in a merciful repose, may reasonably be opened again. They become live issues once we are willing to ponder that simple question, Why should marriage be confined, after all, to couples, and to pairs drawn from different sexes?

That question, if it comes to be treated as open and problem-   15
atic, will not readily be closed, or not at least on the terms that Andrew Sullivan seeks. The melancholy news then is this: We cannot deliver to him what he wants without introducing, into our laws, notions that must surely undercut the rationale and the justification for marriage. The marriage that he wants, he cannot practicably have; but in seeking it, he runs the risk of weakening even further the opinion that sustains marriage as "the architectonic institution that frames our emotional life."

But for marriage so understood, Sullivan does not seem to   16
command a large following, or even a substantial interest, among gays. New York City must surely contain one of the

largest concentrations of accomplished, successful gay men. Since March, New York has allowed the registering of "domestic partners," and by the first of June, 822 couples had come forth to register. By the unofficial estimate of people in the bureau, those couples have been just about evenly distributed between gays and lesbians. Four hundred gay couples would not be a trivial number, but in a city like New York, it does rather suggest that the craving for this public recognition may not be widely diffused. If all of the couples registered under the new law were collected in Yankee Stadium, they would hardly be noticeable in the crowd. Their numbers would not exactly suggest that there is a strong political constituency out there for gay marriage.

Unintended Consequence

17   In making then his own, heartfelt case for marriage, Andrew Sullivan is swept well past the interests and enthusiasms that mark most other people who now make up the "gay community." And he may earnestly put this question to himself: In the sweep of his own convictions, in the sentiment that draws him, powerfully, to marriage, has he not in fact swept past, and discarded, the rationales that sustain the homosexual life?

18   What comes through the writing, finally, is a man who finds his eros in domesticity, who will find pleasure in driving his own children to their soccer games on Saturday mornings. He will explain again to his friends that we must "cooperate" with heterosexual families; that if we would protect gay children we must raise them, and even produce them. There may be winks all around, and the sense that he is doing something for "the cause." But as Andrew Sullivan appreciates, "queer" politics always seeks to take "shame-abandonment to a thrilling conclusion." And what could be more exquisite and subtle than this reversal upon a reversal?: A man lives a highly visible public life as a homosexual, but he enters a marriage, which is taken as a kind of charade, and he is content to abet the jest with knowing glances. But the secret that dare not speak its name is that he really is, after all, a domesticated man, settled in his marriage. As a writer and a man, Andrew Sullivan is committed to an understanding of political life that finds its ground in nature. And he takes, as the core of our civic life, marriage and the laws that sustain marriage. For all of that, we here, composed, as we are, of eros and dust, love him.

Anna Quindlen
EVAN'S TWO MOMS

Anna Quindlen (born 1955) for a number of years wrote a widely praised, syndicated column for the New York Times *and many other newspapers. She won a Pulitzer Prize for commentary in 1992 and she now contributes an essay to* Newsweek *every other week. Her work has been collected in several books, including* Thinking Out Loud: On the Personal, the Political, the Public, and the Private *(1993) and* Loud and Clear *(2004). The following essay comes from that collection.*

Evan has two moms. This is no big thing. Even has always had two moms—in his school file, on his emergency forms, with his friends. "Ooooh, Evan, you're lucky," they sometimes say. "You have two moms." It sounds like a sitcom, but until last week it was emotional truth without legal bulwark. That was when a judge in New York approved the adoption of a six-year-old boy by his biological mother's lesbian partner. Evan. Evan's mom. Evan's other mom. A kid, a psychologist, a pediatrician. A family.

The matter of Evan's two moms is one in a series of events over the last year that lead to certain conclusions. A Minnesota appeals court granted guardianship of a woman left a quadriplegic in a car accident to her lesbian lover, the culmination of a seven-year battle in which the injured woman's parents did everything possible to negate the partnership between the two. A lawyer in Georgia had her job offer withdrawn after the state attorney general found out that she and her lesbian lover were planning a marriage ceremony; she's brought suit. The computer company Lotus announced that the gay partners of employees would be eligible for the same benefits as spouses.

Add to these public events the private struggles, the couples who go from lawyer to lawyer to approximate legal protections their straight counterparts take for granted, the AIDS survivors who find themselves shut out of their partners' dying days by biological family members and shut out of their apartments by leases with a single name on the dotted line, and one solution is obvious.

Gay marriage is a radical notion for straight people and a conservative notion for gay ones. After years of being sledgehammered by society, some gay men and lesbian women are deeply suspicious of participating in an institution that seems to have "straight world" written all over it.

5   But the rads of twenty years ago, straight and gay alike, have other things on their minds today. Family is one, and the linchpin of family has commonly been a loving commitment between two adults. When same-sex couples set out to make that commitment, they discover that they are at a disadvantage: No joint tax returns. No health insurance coverage for an uninsured partner. No survivor's benefits from Social Security. None of the automatic rights, privileges, and responsibilities society attaches to a marriage contract. In Madison, Wisconsin, a couple who applied at the Y with their kids for a family membership were turned down because both were women. It's one of those small things that can make you feel small.

6   Some took marriage statutes that refer to "two persons" at their word and applied for a license. The results were court decisions that quoted the Bible and embraced circular argument: marriage is by definition the union of a man and a woman because that is how we've defined it.

7   No religion should be forced to marry anyone in violation of its tenets, although ironically it is now only in religious ceremonies that gay people can marry, performed by clergy who find the blessing of two who love each other no sin. But there is no secular reason that we should take a patchwork approach of corporate, governmental, and legal steps to guarantee what can be done simply, economically, conclusively, and inclusively with the words "I do."

8   "Fran and I chose to get married for the same reasons that any two people do," said the lawyer who was fired in Georgia. "We fell in love; we wanted to spend our lives together." Pretty simple.

9   Consider the case of *Loving* v. *Virginia*, aptly named. At the time, sixteen states had laws that barred interracial marriage, relying on natural law, that amorphous grab bag for justifying prejudice. Sounding a little like God throwing Adam and Eve out of paradise, the trial judge suspended the one-year sentence of Richard Loving, who was white, and his wife, Mildred, who was black, provided they got out of the State of Virginia.

10   In 1967 the Supreme Court found such laws to be unconstitutional. Only twenty-five years ago and it was a crime for a black woman to marry a white man. Perhaps twenty-five years from now we will find it just as incredible that two people of the same sex were not entitled to legally commit themselves to each other. Love and commitment are rare enough; it seems absurd to thwart them in any guise.

Victoria A. Brownworth
THE LIMITS OF FAMILY

Narrative—storytelling—is a powerful way to attract and move an audience. In the personal essay below, Victoria Brownworth uses a personal tragedy, the death of her mother, to argue for the rights of same-sex couples and families. Brownworth is the author of seven books and frequent essays for publications including Ms., The Nation, The Village Voice, Out, The Philadelphia Inquirer, *and* The Baltimore Sun. *Much of her writing, like the piece included here, focuses on the experience of being a lesbian. She teaches writing and film at the University of the Arts in Philadelphia.*

My mother died this summer, unexpectedly, after a brief ill- 1
ness. Her death certificate lists "complications of aspiration pneumonia" as the cause of death, a catchall diagnosis used by doctors when a patient has suffocated from lack of oxygen.

Had I been asked to fill out my mother's death certificate, I 2
would have listed poverty as the cause of her death, with com-plications from gender. My mother died well before her pro-jected life expectancy because she had been poverty-stricken for most of her life. Poverty had damaged her health, assaulted her well-being. Being poor is stressful. Being a poor woman is acutely stressful.

Ethereally beautiful in her youth, my mother had a mind to 3
match her looks. Had she been born now rather than in the 1930s, her intellectual desire and acumen would have pro-pelled her forward, could have mitigated the pall of poverty. She could have grown into a successful woman with power and position. She could have used her knowledge of languages (she spoke several), literature (she was an omnivorous reader who passed that trait on to me), music (she never forgot a piece of music or its notation once she heard it) and politics (she was a socialist who worked tirelessly in the black civil-rights movement when I was a child and taught me the impor-tance of social justice and equity) to do more than teach her children the value of the mind and heart.

I don't like to think of my mother as a victim. But she clearly 4
was: of her time, her gender, her penury and the lifelong de-pression that accompanied her inability to escape those lim-itations. My last conversations with my mother before her

final illness were about politics: the recent Supreme Court decisions, the war on Iraq, the perils of a right-wing agenda. The substance and verve of those conversations belied the circumstances of my mother's life and in no way augured her death.

5   Regret accompanies most death. For my sister and myself, our mother's death was a tragedy—not just of her immediate passing but of her largely unfulfilled life. My sister and I lament never 'having recorded our mother's compelling life history, from her own involvement in political movements to that of our grandmother, who, bitter over not having been allowed to attend college, fought for women's suffrage and was one of the original "bloomer girls."

6   As I waited for my mother to die, waited as paralysis subsumed the agonizing pain that preceded it, waited as she shuddered with each breath, I had time to think about family and all it embodies. In my mother's hospital room, I spoke to her about our shared history as mother and daughter, about my sister's three lovely children, about my deceased but still-missed grandparents. My mother's delft blue eyes were open and she looked right at me, but hourly shots of morphine kept her sedated. Even with the mask, her breathing was too shallow to get much oxygen to her lungs, blood and brain. I don't know if she heard that final, one-sided conversation.

7   My sister and I had to make many decisions to ease my mother's dying, decisions difficult and painful. Yet since my mother's death, that burden has been revealed as fortunate, for us and for her. We made my mother's passing easier. Our legal status as her daughters allowed us to help her die free from unnecessary and unhelpful interventions, allowed us free access to her bedside as she lay dying.

8   But imagine if my mother had been, as are many of my friends and many of you reading this, the non-biological parent in a lesbian family. My sister and I might have played no role in her dying, might even have been barred from her bedside. We would have been erased as her daughters, just as she would have been erased as our mother.

9   Political discourse on the right to queer marriage and, by extension, the rights of queer families has exploded since the U.S. Supreme Court overturned sodomy laws last June. Queer marriage isn't "necessary," argue many, including liberals. But when queers are denied the right to marry and the concomitant right to legalize their families, their children grow up into an unwilling and unwitting generation of bastards, children for whom one parent is always a legal nonentity, a social cipher, someone who can be excised from their lives by a court or a vindictive lover.

One of the first people to call me to extend her condolences   10
over my mother's death was an old friend who spent six years
embroiled in a custody suit with her lesbian lover. Jane and her
partner Liz had a daughter in the 10th year of their relationship, a child Liz bore through artificial insemination. When
the child was 2, the couple split; a battle soon ensued over custody arrangements. Jane was represented by the National
Center for Lesbian Rights and Liz hired a homophobic lawyer
to argue that Jane, the woman with whom she had spent
12 years of her life and borne a child, should have nothing to
do with their daughter. Not shared custody, as Jane requested,
but no involvement whatsoever.

Jane lost her fight to share custody of her daughter, which   11
has scarred her irreparably, as losing a child can do. The lack
of legal constructs for queer families allowed Liz to take their
daughter away from Jane, something she never could have
done to a male partner, whose parental rights would have been
protected by law.

Lesbians deserve the rights that accrue to every heterosexual   12
in our society. My mother's life was shaped by her poverty and
her gender, and she suffered because of it, but feminism has
garnered change; today, her life could have been better. My life
is shaped by my sexual orientation. Conversely, my heterosexual sister and her children are granted a social status that my
and my lover's children can never have under current law.

Queers deserve better. We deserve the right to be present at   13
the births of our children, the deaths of our parents, at all the
events that comprise and embody family. We should not be
kept from those occasions by a homophobic definition of what
family is. Nor should we be allowed, as Liz and many other biological lesbian parents have been, to abdicate our responsibility to our lesbian families by utilizing homophobic laws when
they suit our needs.

It was painful to witness my mother's agonizing passing.   14
Had I been barred from her bedside as she lay dying, I would
have sustained a wound that would never have healed, a wound
like Jane has sustained in being barred from her daughter's
life. This, finally, is what our rights come down to: autonomy.
Claiming our families as our own, legally as well as emotionally. That is the equity we must struggle to achieve, for ourselves, our children and our future.

VISUAL CONVERSATIONS **4**

Gay Marriage Comes Out of the Closet and into the Public Eye

Though the effects of allowing same-sex marriages have been debated for many years, the conversation surrounding gay marriage had two particularly important—and very public—moments in 2004. In February of that year, the newly elected mayor of San Francisco, Gavin Newsom, ordered the issuance of marriage licenses to same-sex couples. This action defied California's Proposition 22, accepted by 61 percent of California voters in 2000, which defined marriage as exclusively between one man and one woman. (See the images of citizens on both sides of this vote on the next page.) Gay couples rushed to obtain licenses, seizing what they knew would be a short-lived chance to marry. Then, on May 17, 2004, Massachusetts became the first state to legally sanction gay marriage, an action that was met with great fanfare and great protest. As couples married that day many conversations—informal, political, legal— ensued as individuals and groups asserted their views. All over the United States, people saw images that are burned into our public memory (a sampling of which are included here). Though the weddings soon ceased, the conversation prompted by not only this issue, but the pictures that accompanied it, promises to continue for a long time. As you examine the images below, consider the place that they, and visual rhetoric more generally, play in public conversations.

The photographs on this page visually depict public conversations—assertions, refutations, use of evidence and authority, and so forth. Consider the interaction of ideas that is developed as these various perspectives are brought into dialogue with one another—and how a variety of value systems are used in support of contrary arguments in this very public, and very visual, set of arguments.

Among the ways that the images of gay marriage that accompanied 2004's events affected public perceptions were the extremely emotional moments that were captured in the media coverage of those marriages. What message does the image of a recently married lesbian couple above portray? What about the image of Ross Ladouceur, shown in tears after learning that he and his partner, Stuart Sanders, had missed their chance to be wed before the issuance of licenses in San Francisco was halted? What stories do these pictures tell, and how do these stories affect the public conversation on this topic?

What types of visual arguments do these images make? In what ways do they attempt to link the debate over gay marriage to other American ideals? (The top image was published by the National Organization of Women; the other two were published by the American Family Association.) Consider the logic of both the words and images, and how they support the overall point made by each. In what ways do these ads appeal to the emotions and logic of citizens? What argument do they make? What purpose do they serve?

5

Civil Liberties and Civic Responsibilities

Introduction

This chapter brings together two key ingredients of a civil society: the liberties that we can expect as citizens and the responsibilities that our government has to make laws that (as the preamble of our Constitution reminds us) "secure the blessings of liberty to ourselves and our posterity." About most of this we can agree. But, as they say, the devil is in the details. How much liberty is too much liberty? What is the role of government in balancing our liberties with regulations that at once restrict and protect those liberties? Is civic responsibility a duty or a choice? Does being a citizen mean that it is our responsibility to follow the rules, even when they might seem wrong to us personally? Or does being a citizen mean exercising our right to make reasonable choices about laws, and so to disobey those that we find unjust? And how has that balance changed in an age of global terrorism, when freedom can also lead to vulnerability? As you can imagine, these questions do not have easy answers; but they do lead to a great many conversations about the relationship between our rights as individual members of a society and our responsibilities as citizens of that society.

All of these conversations arise from the foundational writings of our democratic culture. Indeed, a basic premise of *Conversations* is that writing typically emerges from other writing. As a demonstration of that premise, consider some very basic texts in our political history. Consider, for instance, the words of the First Amendment to the Constitution:

> Congress shall make no laws respecting an establishment of religion, or prohibiting the free exercise thereof; or abridging the freedom of speech, or of the press; of the right of the people peaceably to assemble, and to petition the Government for a redress of grievances.

Or consider section one of the Fourteenth Amendment, ratified in 1868:

> All persons born or naturalized in the United States, and subject to the jurisdiction thereof, are citizens of the United States and of the State wherein they reside. No State shall make or enforce any law which shall abridge the privileges or immunities of citizens of the United States; nor shall any State deprive any person of life, liberty, or property, without

due process of law; nor deny to any person within its jurisdiction the equal protection of the laws.

Or this fragment from the Declaration of Independence:

We hold these truths to be self-evident, that all Men are created equal, that they are endowed by their Creator with certain inalienable Rights, that among these are Life, Liberty,
and the Pursuit of Happiness. That to secure these rights,
Governments are instituted among Men. . . .

Or the Preamble to our Constitution:

We the People of the United States, in Order to form a more
perfect Union, establish Justice, insure domestic Tranquility,
provide for the common defense, promote the general
Welfare, and secure the Blessings of Liberty to ourselves and
our Posterity, do ordain and establish this Constitution for
the United States of America.

The readings in Part 5 explore some of the implications of
these seminal passages from our heritage, first by reviewing
some basic premises of a democratic culture and the expectations of its citizens, and then by looking at the issues we
face in contemporary America.

The first section is entitled "Conformity and Activism:
What Does Democratic Citizenship Require?" First a note
about the section's title. Though we considered calling this
section "Conformity OR Activism," we settled on "and" because we did not want to suggest that conformity to the
laws and customs of our land necessarily stood in opposition to activism—which sometimes requires one to stand
against those laws and customs on behalf of one's larger
beliefs. True, at its most basic, membership in any group
tends to demand one's willingness to obey the rules of that
group. But is that always the case? Is it unpatriotic to suggest
that one's city's, state's, or country's rules are so unjust that
one ought not follow them? Does disobedience and activism
violate our membership in a community ("Love it or leave
it")? Why do we count some who disobey rules as criminals,
and others—like Gandhi or Martin Luther King—heroes? As
you can tell, the conversations surrounding this topic can be
both rich and complex. You'll hear from some foundational
voices in the American tradition of activism as well as from

some who remain committed to the individual's right to disagree with the mainstream opinions of a culture.

The conflict between the individual and society is central to culture in the United States, because we value both the dignity of the private individual and the importance of public institutions sanctioned through the democratic process. Faced with the dilemma of paying taxes to support a popular war, which he disagreed with, Henry David Thoreau proposed civil disobedience—a private act of personal conscience against what Alexis de Tocqueville (whose *Democracy in America* is excerpted in this section) called "the tyranny of the majority." Later in history, Mahatma Gandhi and Martin Luther King Jr. refined civil disobedience into an effective tactic for achieving public justice and political equality. Were they right to do so? What is civil disobedience or activism anyway? Is it a legitimate political tool or an invitation to anarchy that would destroy the principles of democratic rule? What should people do when "higher laws" put them in conflict with majority rule? Can such a majority be a "tyranny," or is it the resistance to legitimate, democratic authority that is arrogant and tyrannical? Could activism even exist in a truly tyrannical society, one without a free press (as discussed in Part 2 of *Conversations*) and trial by jury, one in which political minorities disappear in the middle of the night? And how has access to the rapid communication available through the Internet affected the ability of activist groups to form and execute their resistance activities? The selections in this section articulate and debate the question of activism, first by examining some foundational documents in the American tradition of civil disobedience, and then by readings that detail specific recent efforts by individuals committed to their causes. These examples can help you to contextualize the theoretical debate about activism through specific actions.

Liberty, the freedom to disagree—and even to disobey—is clearly at the heart of our American culture. But even those who are strong advocates for individual liberties find themselves in dilemmas on the scope of governmental regulation. For example, many liberal citizens find themselves on the one hand arguing for free speech, on the other for gun control, and on another (it takes many hands, sometimes, to be a thinking American) for the regulation or banning of pornography, especially child pornography. How do all these perspectives square? The two sections on government regulation in this part of *Conversations* ask you to take on a series of difficult questions by reading the views of citizens on the scope of government legislation.

First, you will read a series of perspectives on government's attempts to "promote the general welfare" by protecting us from terrorist activities, by gun control, and by the regulation of tobacco. Do you envision that individuals on the individual liberty side would agree that all three should be free of government regulation? Conversely, do you imagine that those who suggest that surveillance is necessary to protect us in a post-9/11 world would necessarily also suggest that we need to control guns, so as to keep them away from terrorists? Would they necessarily wish to have the "general welfare" promoted by antismoking legislation? Clearly, the various freedoms and restrictions are often dealt with on a case-by-case basis, and so can lead to intriguing conversations about the general topic of civil liberties when you bring them together.

One specific case of governmental regulation involves a substance that until recently seemed anything but dangerous: food. Due to recent reports by the National Institute of Health and the Surgeon General, which labeled obesity a national health crisis, there have been moves toward new regulation of fast-food and other industries that produce our food. For some, this is a responsible action of a country concerned about its nation's health—and a reasonable way to combat the advertising of companies that profit by "supersizing" that which we eat (and in too many cases, us). This concern has been exacerbated by books like Eric Schlosser's *Fast Food Nation* and Greg Critser's *Fat Land: How Americans Became the Fattest People in the World.* But for others, teaching personal responsibility is a much more reasonable approach to this health issue; they cite many reasons why governmental regulation is neither wise nor useful. For those against measures to regulate the food-service industry, this is more than a question of calories; it is a question of personal freedoms and responsibilities and of limiting government's reach.

This conversation among those who tend toward wide civil liberties and those who tend toward government's role in "promoting the general welfare" share a central belief in the foundations of civil and civic actions—even in the case of civil disobedience. But what of those who step outside of society's laws, and do so in ways that demand punishment? How does, or should, a free society react to those individuals? The last section of Part 5 asks a specific question about our society, in which "all men are created equal": "How Does Social Class Affect Crime and Punishment?" The readings in this section, written by a wide variety of individuals—from an anarchist revolutionary to academic researchers to U.S. legislators—form a wide-ranging discussion about the ways in which our law enforcement systems can equally protect the rights of all individuals, no matter their social class. According to our founding documents, that is the intent of a constitution based on equality under law. The readings here ask how well we have lived up to the intent.

All of the various conversations about civil rights and civic responsibilities, of course, can't always solve the problems that arise when private interests, the interests of various groups, and opinions about what constitutes the public interest collide. In those cases, political activism sometimes becomes civil disobedience. And civil disobedience is very much about memorable pictures—pictures of brave individuals, angry individuals, resistance, and repression. And though we might *read* about such acts of bravery (like the Chinese student who stood in front of tanks in Tiananmen Square or Rosa Parks sitting in the front seat of that bus), *seeing* those moment carries a much more emotional impact. The images of protest and activism found in this part's "Visual Conversations" will challenge you to think about how pictures influence our conversations about rights, responsibilities, and maintaining order in a civil society.

The conversations in which this discussion of civil liberties and civic responsibilities engages you can illustrate the diversity of ways that citizenship affects you—from what you eat to what you have the right to know, from the government's responsibility to protect your freedoms to its rights to take rights from you in the process. There is perhaps nothing more fundamental to being human than being part of a society; the readings in this section will help you to explore what that participation requires of you.

Conformity and Activism: What Does Democratic Citizenship Require?

Aristotle

FROM POLITICS

Aristotle was a fourth-century B.C.E. *Greek philosopher, rhetorician, and scientist (areas of study that were not as widely separated as they are in our own times), and his name still controls a powerful* ethos. *Aristotle's* Politics, *from which the brief excerpt below is taken, is an examination of various forms of government and the relative strengths and weaknesses of each. This excerpt examines the value and weaknesses of democracy; it can provide a framework for some of the discussions that follow.*

Book 5, Part II

The basis of a democratic state is liberty; which, according to the common opinion of men, can only be enjoyed in such a state; this they affirm to be the great end of every democracy. One principle of liberty is for all to rule and be ruled in turn, and indeed democratic justice is the application of numerical not proportionate equality; whence it follows that the majority must be supreme, and that whatever the majority approve must be the end and the just. Every citizen, it is said, must have equality, and therefore in a democracy the poor have more power than the rich, because there are more of them, and the will of the majority is supreme. This, then, is one note of liberty which all democrats affirm to be the principle of

1

617

their state. Another is that a man should live as he likes. This, they say, is the privilege of a freeman, since, on the other hand, not to live as a man likes is the mark of a slave. This is the second characteristic of democracy, whence has arisen the claim of men to be ruled by none, if possible, or, if this is impossible, to rule and be ruled in turns; and so it contributes to the freedom based upon equality.

2   Such being our foundation and such the principle from which we start, the characteristics of democracy are as follows the election of officers by all out of all; and that all should rule over each, and each in his turn over all; that the appointment to all offices, or to all but those which require experience and skill, should be made by lot; that no property qualification should be required for offices, or only a very low one; that a man should not hold the same office twice, or not often, or in the case of few except military offices: that the tenure of all offices, or of as many as possible, should be brief, that all men should sit in judgment, or that judges selected out of all should judge, in all matters, or in most and in the greatest and most important—such as the scrutiny of accounts, the constitution, and private contracts; that the assembly should be supreme over all causes, or at any rate over the most important, and the magistrates over none or only over a very few. Of all magistracies, a council is the most democratic when there is not the means of paying all the citizens, but when they are paid even this is robbed of its power; for the people then draw all cases to themselves, as I said in the previous discussion. The next characteristic of democracy is payment for services; assembly, law courts, magistrates, everybody receives pay, when it is to be had; or when it is not to be had for all, then it is given to the law-courts and to the stated assemblies, to the council and to the magistrates, or at least to any of them who are compelled to have their meals together. And whereas oligarchy is characterized by birth, wealth, and education, the notes of democracy appear to be the opposite of these—low birth, poverty, mean employment. Another note is that no magistracy is perpetual, but if any such have survived some ancient change in the constitution it should be stripped of its power, and the holders should be elected by lot and no longer by vote. These are the points common to all democracies; but democracy and demos in their truest form are based upon the recognized principle of democratic justice, that all should count equally; for equality implies that the poor should have no more share in the government than the rich, and should not be the only rulers, but that all should rule equally according to their numbers. And in this

way men think that they will secure equality and freedom in their state.

Book 5, Part III

Next comes the question, how is this equality to be obtained? Are 3 we to assign to a thousand poor men the property qualifications of five hundred rich men? and shall we give the thousand a power equal to that of the five hundred? or, if this is not to be the mode, ought we, still retaining the same ratio, to take equal numbers from each and give them the control of the elections and of the courts?—Which, according to the democratical notion, is the juster form of the constitution—this or one based on numbers only? Democrats say that justice is that to which the majority agree, oligarchs that to which the wealthier class; in their opinion the decision should be given according to the amount of property. In both principles there is some inequality and injustice. For if justice is the will of the few, any one person who has more wealth than all the rest of the rich put together, ought, upon the oligarchical principle, to have the sole power—but this would be tyranny; or if justice is the will of the majority, as I was before saying, they will unjustly confiscate the property of the wealthy minority. To find a principle of equality which they both agree we must inquire into their respective ideas of justice.

Now they agree in saying that whatever is decided by the ma- 4 jority of the citizens is to be deemed law. Granted: but not without some reserve; since there are two classes out of which a state is composed—the poor and the rich—that is to be deemed law, on which both or the greater part of both agree; and if they disagree, that which is approved by the greater number, and by those who have the higher qualification. For example, suppose that there are ten rich and twenty poor, and some measure is approved by six of the rich and is disapproved by fifteen of the poor, and the remaining four of the rich join with the party of the poor, and the remaining five of the poor with that of the rich; in such a case the will of those whose qualifications, when both sides are added up, are the greatest, should prevail. If they turn out to be equal, there is no greater difficulty than at present, when, if the assembly or the courts are divided, recourse is had to the lot, or to some similar expedient. But, although it may be difficult in theory to know what is just and equal, the practical difficulty of inducing those to forbear who can, if they like, encroach, is far greater, for the weaker are always asking for equality and justice, but the stronger care for none of these things.

Book 5, Part V

5 The mere establishment of a democracy is not the only or principal business of the legislator, or of those who wish to create such a state, for any state, however badly constituted, may last one, two, or three days; a far greater difficulty is the preservation of it. The legislator should therefore endeavor to have a firm foundation according to the principles already laid down concerning the preservation and destruction of states; he should guard against the destructive elements, and should make laws, whether written or unwritten, which will contain all the preservatives of states. He must not think the truly democratical or oligarchical measure to be that which will give the greatest amount of democracy or oligarchy, but that which will make them last longest. The demagogues of our own day often get property confiscated in the law-courts in order to please the people. But those who have the welfare of the state at heart should counteract them, and make a law that the property of the condemned should not be public and go into the treasury but be sacred. Thus offenders will be as much afraid, for they will be punished all the same, and the people, having nothing to gain, will not be so ready to condemn the accused. Care should also be taken that state trials are as few as possible, and heavy penalties should be inflicted on those who bring groundless accusations; for it is the practice to indict, not members of the popular party, but the notables, although the citizens ought to be all attached to the constitution as well, or at any rate should not regard their rulers as enemies.

6 Now, since in the last and worst form of democracy the citizens are very numerous, and can hardly be made to assemble unless they are paid, and to pay them when there are no revenues presses hardly upon the notables (for the money must be obtained by a property tax and confiscations and corrupt practices of the courts, things which have before now overthrown many democracies); where, I say, there are no revenues, the government should hold few assemblies, and the law-courts should consist of many persons, but sit for a few days only. This system has two advantages: first, the rich do not fear the expense, even although they are unpaid themselves when the poor are paid; and secondly, causes are better tried, for wealthy persons, although they do not like to be long absent from their own affairs, do not mind going for a few days to the law-courts. Where there are revenues the demagogues should not be allowed after their manner to distribute the surplus; the poor are always receiving and always wanting more and more, for such help is like water poured into a leaky cask. Yet the true

friend of the people should see that they be not too poor, for extreme poverty lowers the character of the democracy; measures therefore should be taken which will give them lasting prosperity; and as this is equally the interest of all classes, the proceeds of the public revenues should be accumulated and distributed among its poor, if possible, in such quantities as may enable them to purchase a little farm, or, at any rate, make a beginning in trade or husbandry. And if this benevolence cannot be extended to all, money should be distributed in turn according to tribes or other divisions, and in the meantime the rich should pay the fee for the attendance of the poor at the necessary assemblies; and should in return be excused from useless public services. By administering the state in this spirit the Carthaginians retain the affections of the people; their policy is from time to time to send some of them into their dependent towns, where they grow rich. It is also worthy of a generous and sensible nobility to divide the poor amongst them, and give them the means of going to work. The example of the people of Tarentum is also well deserving of imitation, for, by sharing the use of their own property with the poor, they gain their good will. Moreover, they divide all their offices into two classes, some of them being elected by vote, the others by lot; the latter, that the people may participate in them, and the former, that the state may be better administered. A like result may be gained by dividing the same offices, so as to have two classes of magistrates, one chosen by vote, the other by lot.

Alexis de Tocqueville

DEMOCRACY IN AMERICA

In 1831, French statesman Alexis de Tocqueville visited the United States with the express purpose of studying American democracy, since his own country was moving toward democratization as well. Four years later, de Tocqueville published his famous tome, Democracy in America. *Because it was written by an outsider, this work provides American readers with a uniquely anthropological perspective on our culture, which he studied in great detail; it has become a standard text for political science students and scholars. The excerpts in-cluded here discuss the relationship among law, freedom, and rule by the majority, which forms the basis of many questions about civil rights, civic responsibilities, and in some cases, the need for civil disobedience.*

Respect for Law in the United States

American respect for law. Paternal affection they feel for it. Personal interest of everybody in increasing the law's strength.

1   It is not always feasible to call on the whole people, either directly or indirectly, to take its part in lawmaking, but no one can deny that when that can be done the law derives great authority therefrom. This popular origin, though often damaging to the wisdom and quality of legislation, gives it peculiar strength.

2   There is prodigious force in the expression of the wills of a whole people. When it stands out in broad daylight, even the imagination of those who would like to contest it is somehow smothered.

3   Parties are well aware of this truth.

4   For that reason, whenever possible they cast doubts on the majority's validity. Having failed to gain a majority from those who voted, they claim it among those who abstained from voting, and if that fails them, they claim a majority among those who have no right to vote.

5   In the United States, except for slaves, servants, and paupers fed by the township, no one is without a vote and, hence, an indirect share in lawmaking. Therefore those who would like to attack the laws are forced to adopt ostensibly one of two courses: they must either change the nation's opinion or trample its wishes under foot.

6   There is a second reason, too, more direct and powerful in its effect, namely, that every American feels a sort of personal interest in obeying the laws, for a man who is not today one of the majority party may be so tomorrow, and so he may soon be demanding for laws of his choosing that respect which he now professes for the lawgiver's will. Therefore, however annoying a law may be, the American will submit to it, not only as the work of the majority but also as his own doing; he regards it as a contract to which he is one of the parties.

7   So in the United States there is no numerous and perpetually turbulent crowd regarding the law as a natural enemy to fear

and to suspect. On the contrary, one is bound to notice that all classes show great confidence in their country's legislation, feeling a sort of paternal love for it.

I am wrong in saying all classes. As in America, the [8] European ladder of power has been turned upside down; the wealthy find themselves in a position analogous to that of the poor in Europe: it is they who often mistrust the law. As I have said elsewhere, the real advantage of democratic government is not that it guarantees the interests of all, as is sometimes claimed, but just that it does protect those of the greatest number. In the United States, where the poor man rules, the rich have always some fear that he may abuse his power against them.

This state of mind among the wealthy may produce a [9] silent discontent, but it creates no violent trouble for society, for the same reason which prevents the rich man from trusting the lawgiver also prevents him from defying his commands. Because he is rich he does not make the law, and because of his wealth he does not dare to break it. Among civilized nations it is generally only those with nothing to lose who revolt. Hence, though democratic laws may not always deserve respect, they are almost always respected, for those who usually break the laws cannot fail to obey those they have made and from which they profit, and those citizens who might have an interest in infringing them are impelled both by character and by circumstance to submit to the lawgiver's will, whatever it may be. Moreover, in America the people obey the law not only because it is their work but also because they can change it if by any chance it does injure them; they submit to it primarily as a self-imposed evil, and secondly as a passing one.

Activity Prevailing in All Parts of the Political Body in the United States; the Influence Thereby Exerted on Society

The political activity prevailing in the United States is harder to conceive than the freedom and equality found there. The continual feverish activity of the legislatures is only an episode and an extension of a movement that is universal. How difficult an American finds it to be occupied with his own business only. Political agitation spills over into civil society. The industrial activity of the Americans is in part due to this. Indirect advantages derived by society from democratic government.

10   When one passes from a free country into another which is not so, the contrast is very striking: there, all is activity and bustle; here all seems calm and immobile. In the former, betterment and progress are the questions of the day; in the latter, one might suppose that society, having acquired every blessing, longs for nothing but repose in which to enjoy them. Nevertheless, the country which is in such a rush to attain happiness is generally richer and more prosperous than the one that seems contented with its lot. And considering them one by one, it is hard to understand how this one daily discovers so many new needs, while the other seems conscious of so few.

11   While this remark applies to free countries that have preserved the forms of monarchy and to those dominated by an aristocracy, it is even more true of democratic republics. In them it is not only one section of the people that undertakes to better the state of society, for the whole nation is concerned therewith. It is not just the necessities and comforts of one class that must be provided for, but those of all classes at once.

12   It is not impossible to conceive the immense freedom enjoyed by the Americans, and one can also form an idea of their extreme equality, but the political activity prevailing in the United States is something one could never understand unless one had seen it.

13   No sooner do you set foot on American soil than you find yourself in a sort a tumult; a confused clamor rises on every side, and a thousand voices are heard at once, each expressing some social requirements. All around you everything is on the move: here the people of a district are assembled to discuss the possibility of building a church; there they are busy choosing a representative; further on, the delegates of a district are hurrying to town to consult about some local improvements; elsewhere it's the village farmers who have left their furrows to discuss the plan for a road or a school. One group of citizens assembles for the sole object of announcing that they disapprove of the government's course, while others unite to proclaim that the men in office are the fathers of their country. And here is yet another gathering which regards drunkenness as the main source of ills in the state and has come to enter into a solemn undertaking to give an example of temperance.[1]

---

[1]Temperance societies are associations whose members undertake to abstain from strong drink. At the time of my visit temperance societies already counted more than 270,000 members, and consequently, in the state of Pennsylvania alone the consumption of strong liquors had fallen by 500,000 gallons a year.

The great political movement which keeps American legisla-   14
tures in a state of continual agitation, and which alone is noticed from outside, is only an episode and a sort of extension of
the universal movement, which begins in the lowest ranks of
the people and thence spreads successively through all classes
of citizens. No one could work harder to be happy.

It is hard to explain the place filed by political concerns in   15
the life of an American. To take a hand in the government of
society and to talk about it is his most important business and,
so to say, the only pleasure he knows. That is obvious even in
the most trivial habits of his life; even the women often go to
public meetings and forget household cares while they listen to
political speeches. For them clubs to some extent take the
place of theaters. An American does not know how to converse,
but he argues; he does not talk, but expatiates. He always
speaks to you as if addressing a meeting, and if he happens to
get excited, he will say "Gentlemen" when addressing an audience of one.

The inhabitant in some countries shows a sort of repug-   16
nance in accepting the political rights granted to him by the
law; it strikes him as a waste of time to spend it on communal
interests, and he likes to shut himself up in a narrow egoism,
of which four ditches with hedges on top define the precise
limits.

But if an American should be reduced to occupying himself   17
with his own affairs, at that moment half his existence would
be snatched from him; he would feel it as a vast void in his life
and would become incredibly unhappy.[2]

I am convinced that if despotism ever came to be established   18
in the United States it would find it even more difficult to overcome the habits that have sprung from freedom than to conquer the love of freedom itself.

That constantly renewed agitation introduced by democratic   19
government into political life passes, then, into civil society.
Perhaps, taking everything into consideration, that is the greatest advantage of democratic government, and I praise it much
more on account of what it causes to be done than for what it
does.

It is incontestible that the people often manage public affairs   20
very badly, but their concern therewith is bound to extend their

---

[2]The same fact was already noted at Rome under the first Caesars.
Montesquieu remarks somewhere that nothing equals the despair of certain Roman citizens who after the excitements of a political existence suddenly return to the calm of private life.

mental horizon and shake them out of the rut of ordinary routine. A man of the people, when asked to share the task of governing society, acquires a certain self-esteem. Since he then has power, the brains of very enlightened people are put at his disposal. Constant efforts are made to enlist his support, and he learns from a thousand different efforts to deceive him. In politics he takes a part in undertakings he has not thought of, and they give him a general taste for enterprise. Daily new improvements to communal property are suggested to him, and that starts him wishing to improve his own. He may not be more virtuous or happier than his forebears, but he is more enlightened and active. I have no doubt that democratic institutions, combined with the physical nature of the land, are the indirect reason, and not, as is often claimed, the direct one, for the prodigious industrial expansion seen in the United States. It is not the laws' creation, but the people have learned to achieve it by making the laws.

21   When the enemies of democracy claim that a single man does his appointed task better than the government of all, I think they are right. There is more consistency in one man's rule than in that of a multitude, assuming equal enlightenment on either side; one man is more persevering, has more idea of the whole problem, attends more closely to details, and is a better judge of men. Anyone who denies that either has never seen a democratic republic or bases his view on too few examples. Democracy, even when local circumstances and the character of the people allow it to maintain itself, does not display a regular or methodical form of government. That is true. Democratic freedom does not carry its undertakings through as perfectly as an intelligent despotism would; it often abandons them before it has reaped the profit, or embarks on perilous ones; but in the long run it produces more; each thing is less well done, but more things are done. Under its sway it is not especially the things accomplished by the public administration that are great, but rather those things done without its help and beyond its sphere. Democracy does not provide a people with the most skillful of governments, but it does that which the most skillful government often cannot do: it spreads throughout the body social a restless activity, superabundant force, and energy never found elsewhere, which, however little favored by circumstance, can do wonders. Those are its true advantages.

22   In this century, when the destinies of the Christian world seem in suspense, some hasten to assail democracy as a hostile power while it is still growing; others already worship this new deity emerging from chaos. But both parties have an imperfect

knowledge of the object of their hate or their desire; they fight in the dark and strike at random.

What do you expect from society and its government? We 23
must be clear about that.

Do you wish to raise mankind to an elevated and generous 24
view of the things of this world? Do you want to inspire men with a certain scorn of material goods? Do you hope to engender deep convictions and prepare the way for acts of profound devotion?

Are you concerned with refining mores, elevating manners, 25
and causing the arts to blossom? Do you desire poetry, renown, and glory?

Do you set out to organize a nation so that it will have a pow- 26
erful influence over all others? Do you expect it to attempt great enterprises and, whatever be the result of it efforts, to leave a great mark on history?

If in your view that should be the main object of men in soci- 27
ety, do not support democratic government; it surely will not lead you to that goal.

But if you think it profitable to turn man's intellectual and 28
moral activity toward the necessities of physical life and use them to produce well-being, if you think that reason is more use to men than genius, if your object is not to create heroic virtues but rather tranquil habits, if you would rather contemplate vices than crimes and prefer fewer transgressions at the cost of fewer splendid deeds, if in place of a brilliant society you are content to live in one that is prosperous, and finally, if in your view the main object of government is not to achieve the greatest strength or glory for the nation as a whole but to provide for every individual therein the utmost well-being, protecting him as far as possible from all afflictions, then it is good to make conditions equal and to establish a democratic government.

But if there is no time left to make a choice, and if a force be- 29
yond human control is already carrying you along regardless of your desires toward one of these types of government, then at least seek to derive from it all the good that it can do; understanding its good instincts as well as its evil inclinations, try to restrain the latter and promote the former.

Tyranny of the Majority

How the principle of the sovereignty of the people should be understood. Impossibility of conceiving a mixed government. Sovereign power must be placed somewhere. Precautions which one should take to moderate its action. These precautions have not been taken in the United States. Result thereof.

30   I regard it as an impious and detestable maxim that in matters of government the majority of a people has the right to do everything, and nevertheless I place the origin of all powers in the will of the majority. Am I in contradiction with myself?

31   There is one law which has been made, or at least adopted, not by the majority of this or that people, but by the majority of all men. That law is justice.

32   Justice therefore forms the boundary to each people's right.

33   A nation is like a jury entrusted to represent universal society and to apply the justice which is its law. Should the jury representing society have greater power than that very society whose laws it applies?

34   Consequently, when I refuse to obey an unjust law, I by no means deny the majority's right to give orders; I only appeal from the sovereignty of the people to the sovereignty of the human race.

35   There are those not afraid to say that in matters which only concern itself a nation cannot go completely beyond the bounds of justice and reason and that there is therefore no need to fear giving total power to the majority representing it. But that is the language of a slave.

36   What is a majority, in its collective capacity, if not an individual with opinions, and usually with interests, contrary to those of another individual, called the minority? Now, if you admit that a man vested with omnipotence can abuse it against his adversaries, why not admit the same concerning a majority? Have men, by joining together, changed their character? By becoming stronger, have they become more patient of obstacles?[3] For my part, I cannot believe that, and I will never grant to several that power to so everything which I refuse to a single man.

37   It is not that I think that in order to preserve liberty one can mix several principles within the same government in such a way that they will be really opposed to one another.

38   I have always considered what is called a mixed government to be a chimera. There is in truth no such thing as a mixed

---

[3]No one would wish to maintain that a nation cannot abuse its power against another nation. But parties form something like little nations within the nation, and the relations between them are like those of strangers.

If it is agreed that a nation can be tyrannical toward another nation, how can one deny that a party can be so toward another party?

government (in the sense usually given to the words), since in any society one finds in the end some principle of action that dominates all the others.

Eighteenth-century England, which has been especially cited   39
as an example of this type of government, was an essentially aristocratic state, although it contained within itself great elements of democracy, for laws and mores were so designed that the aristocracy could always prevail in the long run and manage public affairs as it wished.

The mistake is due to those who, constantly seeing the inter-   40
ests of the great in conflict with those of the people, have thought only about the struggle and have not paid attention to the result thereof, which was more important. When a society really does have a mixed government, that is to say, one equally shared between contrary principles, either a revolution breaks out or that society breaks up.

I therefore think it always necessary to place somewhere one   41
social power superior to all others, but I believe that freedom is in danger when that power finds no obstacle that can restrain its course and give it time to moderate itself.

Omnipotence in itself seems a bad and dangerous thing. I   42
think that its exercise is beyond man's strength, whoever he be, and that only God can be omnipotent without danger because His wisdom and justice are always equal to His power. So there is no power on earth in itself so worthy of respect or vested with such a sacred right that I would wish to let it act without control and dominate without obstacles. So when I see the right and capacity to do all given to any authority whatsoever, whether it be called people or king, democracy or aristocracy, and whether the scene of action is a monarchy or a republic, I say: the germ of tyranny is there, and I will go look for other laws under which to live.

My greatest complaint against democratic government as   43
organized in the United States is not, as many Europeans make out, its weakness, but rather its irresistible strength. What I find most repulsive in America is not the extreme freedom reigning there but the shortage of guarantees against tyranny.

When a man or a party suffers an injustice in the United   44
States, to whom can he turn? To public opinion? That is what forms the majority. To the legislative body? It represents the majority and obeys it blindly. To the executive power? It is appointed by the majority and serves as its passive instrument. To the police? They are nothing but the majority under arms. A jury? The jury is the majority vested with the right to pronounce judgment; even the judges in certain states are elected

by the majority. So, however iniquitous or unreasonable the measure which hurts you, you must submit.[4]

45   But suppose you were to have a legislative body so composed that it represented the majority without being necessarily the slave of its passions, an executive power having a strength of its own, and a judicial power independent of the other two authorities; than you would still have a democratic government, but there would be hardly any remaining risk of tyranny.

46   I am not asserting that at the present time in America there are frequent acts of tyranny. I do say that one can find no guarantee against it there and that the reasons for the government's gentleness must be sought in circumstances and in mores rather than in the laws.

[4]At Baltimore during the War of 1812 there was a striking example of the excesses to which despotism of the majority may lead. At that time the war was very popular at Baltimore. A newspaper which came out in strong opposition to it aroused the indignation of the inhabitants. The people assembled, broke the presses, and attacked the house of the editors. An attempt was made to summon the militia, but it did not answer the appeal. Finally, to save the lives of these wretched men threatened by the fury of the public, they were taken to prison like criminals. This precaution was useless. During the night the people assembled again; the magistrates having failed to bring up the militia, the prison was broken open; one of the journalists was killed on the spot and the others left for dead; the guilty were brought before a jury and acquitted.

I once said to a Pennsylvanian: "Please explain to me why in a state founded by Quakers and renowned for its tolerance, freed Negroes are not allowed to use their rights as citizens? They pay taxes; is it not right that they should vote?"

"Do not insult us," he replied, "by supposing that our legislators would commit an act of such gross injustice and intolerance."

"So, with you, Negroes do have the right to vote?"

"Certainly."

"Then how was it that at the electoral college this morning I did not see a single one of them in the meeting?"

"That is not the fault of the law," said the American. "It is true that Negroes have the right to be present at elections, but they voluntarily abstain from appearing."

"That is extraordinarily modest of them."

"Oh! It is not that they are reluctant to go there, but they are afraid they may be maltreated. With us it sometimes happens that the law lacks force when the majority does not support it. Now, the majority is filled with the strongest prejudices against Negroes, and the magistrates do not feel strong enough to guarantee the rights granted to them by the lawmakers."

"What! The majority, privileged to make the law, wishes also to have the privilege of disobeying the law?"

Henry David Thoreau
CIVIL DISOBEDIENCE

Henry David Thoreau (1817–1862) is best know for his classic
Walden *(1854), an autobiographical, satiric, spiritual, scien-*
tific, and naturalistic "self-help book" based on his two years'
stay at Walden Pond, near Boston. A friend of Ralph Waldo
Emerson and other transcendentalists, Thoreau expressed his
idealism in a number of concrete ways, for example, in his op-
position to slavery and the Mexican War. His refusal to pay
taxes to support the Mexican War inspired his essay "Civil
Disobedience" (1849). First delivered as a lecture in 1848,
"Civil Disobedience" influenced the thinking of Mahatma
Gandhi and Martin Luther King Jr.

I heartily accept the motto,—"That government is best which   1
governs least"; and I should like to see it acted up to more
rapidly and systematically. Carried out, it finally amounts to
this, which also I believe,—"That government is best which
governs not at all"; and when men are prepared for it, that will
be the kind of government which they will have. Government
is at best but an expedient; but most governments are usually,
and all governments are sometimes, inexpedient. The objections which have been brought against a standing army, and
they are many and weighty, and deserve to prevail, may also at
last be brought against a standing government. The standing
army is only an arm of the standing government. The government itself, which is only the mode which the people have chosen to execute their will, is equally liable to be abused and
perverted before the people can act through it. Witness the present Mexican war, the work of comparatively a few individuals
using the standing government as their tool; for, in the outset,
the people would not have consented to this measure.

This American government—what is it but a tradition,   2
though a recent one, endeavoring to transmit itself unimpaired
to posterity, but each instant losing some of its integrity? It has
not the vitality and force of a single living man; for a single
man can bend it to his will. It is a sort of wooden gun to the
people themselves. But it is not the less necessary for this; for
the people must have some complicated machinery or other,
and hear its din, to satisfy that idea of government which they
have. Government show thus how successfully men can be imposed on, even impose on themselves, for their own advantage.

It is excellent, we must all allow. Yet this government never of itself furthered any enterprise, but by the alacrity with which it got out of its way. *It* does not keep the country free. *It* does not settle the West. *It* does not educate. The character inherent in the American people has done all that has been accomplished; and it would have done somewhat more, if the government had not sometimes got in its way. For government is an expedient by which men would fain succeed in letting one another alone; and, as has been said, when it is most expedient, the governed are most let alone by it. Trade and commerce, if they were not made of India-rubber, would never manage to bounce over the obstacles which legislators are continually putting in their way; and, if one were to judge these men wholly by the effects of their actions and not partly by their intentions, they would deserve to be classed and punished with those mischievous persons who put obstructions on the railroads.

3   But, to speak practically and as a citizen, unlike those who call themselves no-government men, I ask for, not at once no government, but *at once* a better government. Let every man make known what kind of government would command his respect, and that will be one step toward obtaining it.

4   After all, the practical reason why, when the power is once in the hands of people, a majority are permitted, and for a long period continue, to rule is not because they are most likely to be in the right, nor because this seems fairest to the minority, but because they are physically the strongest. But a government in which the majority rule in all cases cannot be based on justice, even as far as men understand it. Can there not be a government in which majorities do not virtually decide right and wrong, but conscience?—in which majorities decide only those questions to which the rule of expediency is applicable? Must the citizen ever for a moment, or in the least degree, resign his conscience to the legislator? Why has every man a conscience, then? I think that we should be men first, and subjects afterward. It is not desirable to cultivate a respect for the law, so much as for the right. The only obligation which I have a right to assume is to do at any time what I think right. It is truly enough said, that a corporation has no conscience; but a corporation of conscientious men is a corporation *with* a conscience. Law never made men a whit more just; and, by means of their respect for it, even the well-disposed are daily made the agents of injustice. A common and natural result of an undue respect for law is, that you may see a file of soldiers, colonel, captain, corporal, privates, powder-monkeys, and all, marching in admirable order over hill and dale to the wars, against their will, ay, against their common sense and consciences, which makes it very steep marching

indeed, and produces a palpitation of the heart. They have no doubt that it is a damnable business in which they are concerned; they are all peaceably inclined. Now, what are they? Men at all? or small movable forts and magazines, at the service of some unscrupulous man in power? Visit the Navy-Yard, and behold a marine, such a man as an American government can make, or such as it can make a man with its black arts,—a mere shadow and reminiscence of humanity, a man laid out alive and standing, and already, as one may say, buried under arms with funeral accompaniments, though it may be,—

> "Not a drum was heard, not a funeral note,
>   As his corse to the rampart we hurried;
> Not a soldier discharged his farewell shot
>   O'er the grave where our hero we buried."[1]

The mass of men serve the state thus, not as men mainly, but   5
as machines, with their bodies. They are the standing army, and the militia, jailers, constables, posse comitatus, etc. In most cases there is no free exercise whatever of the judgment or of the moral sense; but they put themselves on a level with wood and earth and stones; and wooden men can perhaps be manufactured that will serve the purpose as well. Such command no more respect than men of straw or a lump of dirt. They have the same sort of worth only as horses and dogs. Yet such as these even are commonly esteemed good citizens. Others—as most legislators, politicians, lawyers, ministers, and office-holders—serve the state chiefly with their heads; and, as they rarely make any moral distinctions, they are as likely to serve the Devil, without *intending* it, as God. A very few, as heroes, patriots, martyrs, reformers in the great sense, and *men*, serve the state with their consciences also, and so necessarily resist it for the most part; and they are commonly treated as enemies by it. A wise man will only be useful as a man, and will not submit to be "clay," and "stop a hole to keep the wind away," but leave that office to his dust at least:—

> "I am too high-born to be propertied,
> To be a secondary at control,
> Or useful serving-man and instrument
> To any sovereign state throughout the world."[2]

---

[1] From "Burial of St. John Moore at Corunna" by Charles Wolfe (1817).
[2] The line before the quotation is from *Hamlet* V. i. 236–37; the quotation is from Shakespeare's *King John* V. ii. 79–82.

6   He who gives himself entirely to his fellow-men appears to them useless and selfish; but he who gives himself partially to them is pronounced a benefactor and philanthropist.

7   How does it become a man to behave toward this American government to-day? I answer, that he cannot without disgrace be associated with it. I cannot for an instant recognize that political organization as *my* government which is the *slave's* government also.

8   All men recognize the right of revolution; that is, the right to refuse allegiance to, and to resist, the government, when its tyranny or its inefficiency are great and unendurable. But almost all say that such is not the case now. But such was the case, they think, in the Revolution of '75. If one were to tell me that this was a bad government because it taxed certain foreign commodities brought to its ports, it is most probable that I should not make an ado about it, for I can do without them. All machines have their friction; and possibly this does enough good to counterbalance the evil. At any rate, it is a great evil to make a stir about it. But when the friction comes to have its machine, and oppression and robbery are organized, I say, let us not have such a machine any longer. In other words, when a sixth of the population of a nation which has undertaken to be the refuge of liberty are slaves, and a whole country is unjustly overrun and conquered by a foreign army, and subjected to military law, I think that it is not too soon for honest men to rebel and revolutionize. What makes this duty the more urgent is the fact that the country so overrun is not our own, but ours is the invading army.

9   Paley,[3] a common authority with many on moral questions, in his chapter on the "Duty of Submission to Civil Government," resolves all civil obligation into expediency; and he proceeds to say, "that so long as the interest of the whole society requires it, that is, so long as the established government cannot be resisted or changed without public inconveniency, it is the will of God that the established government be obeyed, and no longer. . . . This principle being admitted, the justice of every particular case of resistance is reduced to a computation of the quantity of the danger and grievance on the one side, and of the probability and expense of redressing it on the other." Of this, he says, every man shall judge for himself. But Paley appears never to have contemplated those cases to which the rule of expediency does not apply, in which a people, as well as an individual, must do justice, cost what it may. If I

---

[3]William Paley (1743–1805), English theologian.

have unjustly wrested a plank from a drowning man, I must restore it to him though I drown myself. This, according to Paley,
would be inconvenient. But he that would save his life, in such
a case, shall lose it. This people must cease to hold slaves, and
to make war on Mexico, though it cost them their existence as
a people.

In their practice, nations agree with Paley; but does any one   10
think that Massachusetts does exactly what is right at the present crisis?

> "A drab of state, a cloth-o'-silver slut,
> To have her train borne up, and her soul trail in the dirt."

Practically speaking the opponents to a reform in Massachusetts are not a hundred thousand politicians at the South,
but a hundred thousand merchants and farmers here, who
are more interested in commerce and agriculture than they
are in humanity, and are not prepared to do justice to the slave
and to Mexico, *cost what it may*. I quarrel not with far-off
foes, but with those who, near at home, coöperate with, and do
the bidding of, those far away, and without whom the latter
would be harmless. We are accustomed to say, that the mass
of men are unprepared; but improvement is slow, because the
few are not materially wiser or better than the many. It is not
so important that many should be as good as you, as that there
be some absolute goodness somewhere; for that will leaven
the whole lump. There are thousands who are *in opinion*
opposed to slavery and to the war, who yet in effect do nothing
to put an end to them; who, esteeming themselves children of
Washington and Franklin, sit down with their hands in their
pockets, and say that they know not what to do, and do nothing; who even postpone the question of freedom to the question of free-trade, and quietly read the prices-current along
with the latest advices from Mexico, after dinner, and, it may
be, fall asleep over them both. What is the price-current of an
honest man and patriot to-day? They hesitate, and they regret,
and sometimes they petition; but they do nothing in earnest
and with effect. They will wait, well disposed, for others to
remedy the evil, that they may no longer have it to regret. At
most, they give only a cheap vote, and a feeble countenance
and Godspeed, to the right, as it goes by them. There are nine
hundred and ninety-nine patrons of virtue to one virtuous
man. But it is easier to deal with the real possessor of a thing
than with the temporary guardian of it.

All voting is a sort of gaming, like checkers or backgammon,   11
with a slight moral tinge to it, a playing with right and wrong,

with moral questions; and betting naturally accompanies it. The character of the voters is not staked. I cast my vote, perchance, as I think right; but I am not vitally concerned that that right should prevail. I am willing to leave it to the majority. Its obligation, therefore, never exceeds that of expediency. Even voting *for the right* is *doing* nothing for it. It is only expressing to men feebly your desire that it should prevail. A wise man will not leave the right to the mercy of chance, nor wish it to prevail through the power of the majority. There is but little virtue in the action of masses of men. When the majority shall at length vote for the abolition of slavery, it will be because they are indifferent to slavery, or because there is but little slavery left to be abolished by their vote. *They* will then be the only slaves. Only *his* vote can hasten the abolition of slavery who asserts his own freedom by his vote.

12   I hear of a convention to be held at Baltimore, or elsewhere, for the selection of a candidate for the Presidency, made up chiefly of editors, and men who are politicians by profession; but I think, what is it to any independent, intelligent, and respectable man what decision they may come to? Shall we not have the advantage of his wisdom and honesty, nevertheless? Can we not count upon some independent votes? Are there not many individuals in the country who do not attend conventions? But no: I find that the respectable man, so called, has immediately drifted from his position, and despairs of his country, when his country has more reason to despair of him. He forthwith adopts one of the candidates thus selected as the only *available* one, thus proving that he is himself *available* for any purpose of the demagogue. His vote is of no more worth than that of any unprincipled foreigner or hireling native, who may have been bought. O for a man who is a *man*, and, as my neighbor says, has a bone in his back which you cannot pass your hand through! Our statistics are at fault: the population has been returned too large. How many *men* are there to a square thousand miles in this country? Hardly one. Does not America offer any inducement for men to settle here? The American has dwindled into an Odd Fellow,—one who may be known by the development of his organ of gregariousness, and a manifest lack of intellect and cheerful self-reliance; whose first and chief concern, on coming into the world, is to see that the Almshouses are in good repair; and, before yet he has lawfully donned the virile garb, to collect a fund for the support of the widows and orphans that may be; who, in short, ventures to live only by the aid of the Mutual Insurance company, which has promised to bury him decently.

13   It is not a man's duty, as a matter of course, to devote himself to the eradication of any, even the most enormous wrong; he may

still properly have other concerns to engage him; but it is his duty, at least, to wash his hands of it, and, if he gives it no thought longer, not to give it practically his support. If I devote myself to other pursuits and contemplations, I must first see, at least, that I do not pursue them sitting upon another man's shoulders. I must get off him first, that he may pursue his contemplations too. See what gross inconsistency is tolerated. I have heard some of my townsmen say, "I should like to have them order me out to help put down an insurrection of the slaves, or to march to Mexico;—see if I would go"; and yet these very men have each, directly by their allegiance, and so indirectly, at least, by their money, furnished a substitute. The soldier is applauded who refuses to serve in an unjust war by those who do not refuse to sustain the unjust government which makes the war; is applauded by those whose own act and authority he disregards and sets at naught; as if the state were penitent to that degree that it hired one to scourge it while it sinned, but not to that degree that it left off sinning for a moment. Thus, under the name of Order and Civil Government, we are all made at last to pay homage to and support our own meanness. After the first blush of sin comes its indifference; and from immoral it becomes, as it were, *un*moral, and not quite unnecessary to that life which we have made.

The broadest and most prevalent error requires the most dis- 14
interested virtue to sustain it. The slight reproach to which the virtue of patriotism is commonly liable, the noble are most likely to incur. Those who, while they disapprove of the character and measures of a government, yield to it their allegiance and support are undoubtedly its most conscientious supporters, and so frequently the most serious obstacles to reform. Some are petitioning the state to dissolve the Union, to disregard the requisitions of the President. Why do they not dissolve it themselves,—the union between themselves and the state,— and refuse to pay their quota into its treasury? Do not they stand in the same relation to the state that the state does to the Union? And have not the same reasons prevented the state from resisting the Union which have prevented them from resisting the state?

How can a man be satisfied to entertain an opinion merely, 15
and enjoy *it*? Is there any enjoyment in it, if his opinion is that he is aggrieved? If you are cheated out of a single dollar by your neighbor, you do not rest satisfied with knowing that you are cheated, or with saying that you are cheated, or even with petitioning him to pay you your due; but you take effectual steps at once to obtain the full amount, and see that you are never cheated again. Action from principle, the perception and the performance of right, changes things and relations; it is

essentially revolutionary, and does not consist wholly with anything which was. It not only divides states and churches, it divides families; ay, it divides the *individual,* separating the diabolical in him from the divine.

16   Unjust laws exist: shall we be content to obey them, or shall we endeavor to amend them, and obey them until we have succeeded, or shall we transgress them at once? Men generally, under such a government as this, think that they ought to wait until they have persuaded the majority to alter them. They think that, if they should resist, the remedy would be worse than the evil. But it is the fault of the government itself that the remedy *is* worse than the evil. *It* makes it worse. Why is it not more apt to anticipate and provide for reform? Why does it not cherish its wise minority? Why does it cry and resist before it is hurt? Why does it not encourage its citizens to be on the alert to point out its faults, and *do* better than it would have them? Why does it always crucify Christ, and excommunicate Copernicus and Luther, and pronounce Washington and Franklin rebels?

17   One would think, that a deliberate and practical denial of its authority was the only offense never contemplated by government; else, why has it not assigned its definite, its suitable and proportionate penalty? If a man who has no property refuses but once to earn nine shillings for the state, he is put in prison for a period unlimited by any law that I know, and determined only by the discretion of those who place him there; but if he should steal ninety times nine shillings from the state, he is soon permitted to go at large again.

18   If the injustice is part of the necessary friction of the machine of government, let it go, let it go; perchance it will wear smooth,—certainly the machine will wear out. If the injustice has a spring, or a pulley, or a rope, or a crank, exclusively for itself, then perhaps you may consider whether the remedy will not be worse than the evil; but if it is of such a nature that it requires you to be the agent of injustice to another, then, I say, break the law. Let your life be a counter friction to stop the machine. What I have to do is to see, at any rate, that I do not lend myself to the wrong which I condemn.

19   As for adopting the ways which the state has provided for remedying the evil, I know not of such ways. They take too much time, and a man's life will be gone. I have other affairs to attend to. I came into this world, not chiefly to make this a good place to live in, but to live in it, be it good or bad. A man has not everything to do, but something; and because he cannot do *everything*, it is not necessary that he should do *something* wrong. It is not my business to be petitioning the Governor or the Legislature any more than it is theirs to

petition me; and if they should not hear my petition, what should I do then? But in this case the state has provided no way; its very Constitution is the evil. This may seem to be harsh and stubborn and unconciliatory; but it is to treat with the utmost kindness and consideration the only spirit that can appreciate or deserves it. So is all change for the better, like birth and death, which convulse the body.

I do not hesitate to say, that those who call themselves   20
Abolitionists should at once effectually withdraw their support, both in person and property, from the government of Massachusetts, and not wait till they constitute a majority of one, before they suffer the right to prevail through them. I think that it is enough if they have God on their side, without waiting for that other one. Moreover, any man more right than his neighbors constitutes a majority of one already.

I meet this American government, or its representative, the   21
state government, directly, and face to face, once a year—no more—in the person of its tax-gatherer; this is the only mode in which a man situated as I am necessarily meets it; and it then says distinctly, Recognize me; and the simplest, the most effectual, and, in the present posture of affairs, the indispensablest mode of treating with it on this head, of expressing your little satisfaction with and love for it, is to deny it then. My civil neighbor, the tax-gatherer, is the very man I have to deal with,—for it is, after all, with men and not with parchment that I quarrel,—and he has voluntarily chosen to be an agent of the government. How shall he ever know well what he is and does as an officer of the government, or as a man, until he is obliged to consider whether he shall treat me, his neighbor, for whom he has respect, as a neighbor and well-disposed man, or as a maniac and disturber of the peace, and see if he can get over this obstruction to his neighborliness without a ruder and more impetuous thought or speech corresponding with his action. I know this well, that if one thousand, if one hundred, if ten men whom I could name,—if ten *honest* men only,—ay, if *one* HONEST man, in this State of Massachusetts, *ceasing to hold slaves*, were actually to withdraw from this copartnership, and be locked up in the county jail therefor, it would be the abolition of slavery in America. For it matters not how small the beginning may seem to be; what is once well done is done forever. But we love better to talk about it: that we say is our mission. Reform keeps many scores of newspapers in its service, but not one man. If my esteemed neighbor, the State's ambassador, who will devote his days to the settlement of the question of human rights in the Council Chamber, instead of being threatened with the prisons of Carolina, were to sit down the

prisoner of Massachusetts, that State which is so anxious to foist the sin of slavery upon her sister,—though at present she can discover only an act of inhospitality to be the ground of a quarrel with her—the Legislature would not wholly waive the subject the following winter.

22   Under a government which imprisons any unjustly, the true place for a just man is also a prison. The proper place today, the only place which Massachusetts has provided for her freer and less desponding spirits, is in her prisons, to be put out and locked out of the State by her own act, as they have already put themselves out by their principles. It is there that the fugitive slave, and the Mexican prisoner on parole, and the Indian come to plead the wrongs of his race should find them; on that separate, but more free and honorable ground, where the State places those who are not *with* her, but *against* her,—the only house in a slave State in which a free man can abide with honor. If any think that their influence would be lost there, and their voices no longer afflict the ear of the State, that they would not be as an enemy within its walls, they do not know by how much truth is stronger than error, nor how much more eloquently and effectively he can combat injustice who has experienced a little in his own person. Cast your whole vote, not a strip of paper merely, but your whole influence. A minority is powerless while it conforms to the majority; it is not even a minority then; but it is irresistible when it clogs by its whole weight. If the alternative is to keep all just men in prison, or give up war and slavery, the State will not hesitate which to choose. If a thousand men were not to pay their tax-bills this year, that would not be a violent and bloody measure, as it would be to pay them, and enable the State to commit violence and shed innocent blood. This is, in fact, the definition of a peaceable revolution, if any such is possible. If the tax-gatherer, or any other public officer, asks me, as one has done, "But what shall I do?" my answer is, "If you really wish to do anything, resign your office." When the subject has refused allegiance, and the officer has resigned his office, then the revolution is accomplished. But even suppose blood should flow. Is there not a sort of blood shed when the conscience is wounded? Through this wound a man's real manhood and immortality flow out, and he bleeds to an everlasting death. I see this blood flowing now.

23   I have contemplated the imprisonment of the offender, rather than the seizure of his goods,—though both will serve the same purpose,—because they who assert the purest right, and consequently are most dangerous to a corrupt State, commonly have not spent much time in accumulating property. To

such the State renders comparatively small service, and a slight tax is wont to appear exorbitant, particularly if they are obliged to earn it by special labor with their hands. If there were one who lived wholly without the use of money, the State itself would hesitate to demand it of him. But the rich man— not to make any invidious comparison—is always sold to the institution which makes him rich. Absolutely speaking, the more money, the less virtue; for money comes between a man and his objects, and obtains them for him; and it was certainly no great virtue to obtain it. It puts to rest many questions which he would otherwise be taxed to answer; while the only new question which it puts is the hard but superfluous one, how to spend it. Thus his moral ground is taken from under his feet. The opportunities of living are diminished in proportion as what are called the "means" are increased. The best thing a man can do for his culture when he is rich is to endeavor to carry out those schemes which he entertained when he was poor. Christ answered the Herodians according to their condition. "Show me the tribute-money," said he;—and one took a penny out of his pocket;—if you use money which has the image of Caesar on it, and which he has made current and valuable, that is, *if you are men of the State,* and gladly enjoy the advantages of Caesar's government, then pay him back some of his own when he demands it. "Render therefore to Caesar that which is Caesar's, and to God those things which are God's,"—leaving them no wiser than before as to which was which; for they did not wish to know.

When I converse with the freest of my neighbors, I perceive that, whatever they may say about the magnitude and seriousness of the question, and their regard for the public tranquillity, the long and the short of the matter is, that they cannot spare the protection of the existing government, and they dread the consequences to their property and families of disobedience to it. For my own part, I should not like to think that I ever rely on the protection of the State. But, if I deny the authority of the State when it presents its tax-bill, it will soon take and waste all my property, and so harass me and my children without end. This is hard. This makes it impossible for a man to live honestly, and at the same time comfortably, in outward respects. It will not be worth the while to accumulate property; that would be sure to go again. You must hire or squat somewhere, and raise but a small crop, and eat that soon. You must live within yourself, and depend upon yourself always tucked up and ready for a start, and not have many affairs. A man may grow rich in Turkey even, if he will be in all respects a good subject of the Turkish government. Confucius

24

said: "If a state is governed by the principles of reason, poverty and misery are subjects of shame; if a state is not governed by the principles of reason, riches and honors are the subjects of shame." No: until I want the protection of Massachusetts to be extended to me in some distant Southern port, where my liberty is endangered, or until I am bent solely on building up an estate at home by peaceful enterprise, I can afford to refuse allegiance to Massachusetts, and her right to my property and life. It costs me less in every sense to incur the penalty of disobedience to the State than it would to obey. I should feel as if I were worth less in that case.

25   Some years ago, the State met me in behalf of the Church, and commanded me to pay a certain sum toward the support of a clergymen whose preaching my father attended, but never I myself. "Pay," it said, "or be locked up in the jail." I declined to pay. But, unfortunately, another man saw fit to pay it. I did not see why the schoolmaster should be taxed to support the priest, and not the priest the schoolmaster; for I was not the State's schoolmaster, but I supported myself by voluntary subscription. I did not see why the lyceum should not present its tax-bill, and have the State to back its demand, as well as the Church. However, at the request of the selectmen, I condescended to make some such statement as this in writing;— "Know all men by these presents, that I, Henry Thoreau, do not wish to be regarded as a member of any incorporated society which I have not joined." This I gave to the town clerk; and he has it. The State, having thus learned that I did not wish to be regarded as a member of that church, has never made a like demand on me since; though it said that it must adhere to its original presumption that time. If I had known how to name them, I should then have signed off in detail from all the societies which I never signed on to; but I did not know where to find a complete list.

26   I have paid no poll-tax[4] for six years. I was put into jail once on this account, for one night; and, as I stood considering the walls of solid stone, two or three feet thick, the door of wood and iron, a foot thick, and the iron grating which strained the light, I could not help struck with the foolishness of that institution which treated me as if I were mere flesh and blood and bones, to be locked up. I wondered that it should have concluded at length that this was the best use it could put me to,

[4]Tax assessed against a person (not property); payment was frequently prerequisite for voting.

and had never thought to avail itself of my services in some way. I saw that, if there was a wall of stone between me and my townsmen, there was still a more difficult one to climb or break through before they could get to be as free as I was. I did not for a moment feel confined, and the walls seemed a great waste of stone and mortar. I felt as if I alone of all my townsmen had paid my tax. They plainly did not know how to treat me, but behaved like persons who are underbred. In every threat and in every compliment there was a blunder; for they thought that my chief desire was to stand the other side of that stone wall. I could not but smile to see how industriously they locked the door on my meditations, which followed them out again without let or hindrance, and *they* were really all that was dangerous. As they could not reach me, they had resolved to punish my body; just as boys, if they cannot come at some person against whom they have a spite, will abuse his dog. I saw that the State was half-witted, that it was timid as a lone woman with her silver spoons, and that it did not know its friends from its foes, and I lost all my remaining respect for it, and pitied it.

Thus the State never intentionally confronts a man's sense, intellectual or moral, but only his body, his senses. It is not armed with superior wit or honesty, but with superior physical strength. I was not born to be forced. I will breathe after my own fashion. Let us see who is the strongest. What force has a multitude? They only can force me who obey a higher law than I. They force me to become like themselves. I do not hear of *men* being *forced* to live this way or that by masses of men. What sort of life were that to live? When I meet a government which says to me, "Your money or your life," why should I be in haste to give it my money? It may be in a great strait, and not know what to do; I cannot help that. It must help itself; do as I do. It is not worth the while to snivel about it. I am not responsible for the successful working of the machinery of society. I am not the son of the engineer. I perceive that, when an acorn and a chestnut fall side by side, the one does not remain inert to make way for the other, but both obey their own laws, and spring and grow and flourish as best they can, till one, perchance, overshadows and destroys the other. If a plant cannot live according to its nature, it dies; and so a man.   27

The night in prison was novel and interesting enough. The prisoners in their shirt-sleeves were enjoying a chat and the evening air in the doorway, when I entered. But the jailer said "Come, boys, it is time to lock up;" and so they dispersed, and I heard the sound of their steps returning into the hollow   28 apartments. My room-mate was introduced to me by the jailer as "a first-rate fellow and a clever man." When the door was locked, he showed me where to hang my hat, and how he managed matters there. The rooms were whitewashed once a month; and this one, at least, was the whitest, most simply furnished, and probably the neatest apartment in the town. He naturally wanted to know where I came from, and what brought me there; and, when I had told him, I asked him in my turn how he came there, presuming him to be an honest man, of course; and, as the world goes, I believe he was. "Why," said he, "they accuse me of burning a barn; but I never did it." As near as I could discover, he had probably gone to bed in a barn when drunk, and smoked his pipe there; and so a barn was burnt. He had the reputation of being a clever man, had been there some three months waiting for his trial to come on, and would have to wait as much longer; but he was quite domesticated and contented, since he got his board for nothing, and thought that he was well treated.

29   He occupied one window, and I the other; and I saw that if one stayed there long, his principal business would be to look out the window. I had soon read all the tracts that were left there, and examined where former prisoners had broken out, and where a grate had been sawed off, and heard the history of the various occupants of that room; for I found that even here there was a history and a gossip which never circulated beyond the walls of the jail. Probably this is the only house in the town where verses are composed, which are afterward printed in a circular form, but not published. I was shown quite a long list of verses which were composed by some young men who had been detected in an attempt to escape, who avenged themselves by singing them.

30   I pumped my fellow-prisoner as dry as I could, for fear I should never see him again; but at length he showed me which was my bed, and left me to blow out the lamp.

31   It was like traveling into a far country, such as I had never expected to behold, to lie there for one night. It seemed to me that I never had heard the town-clock strike before, nor the evening sounds of the village; for we slept with the windows open, which were inside the grating. It was to see my native village in the light of the Middle Ages, and our Concord was turned into a Rhine Stream, and vision of knights and castles passed before me. They were the voices of old burghers that I heard in the streets. I was an involuntary spectator and auditor of whatever was done and said in the kitchen of the adjacent village-inn,—a wholly new and rare experience to me. It was a closer view of my native town. I was fairly inside of it. I never

had seen its institutions before. This is one of its peculiar institution; for it is a shire town. I began to comprehend what its
inhabitants were about.

In the morning, our breakfasts were put through the hole in   32
the door, in small oblong-square tin pans, made to fit, and holding a pint of chocolate, with brown bread, and an iron spoon.
When they called for the vessels again, I was green enough to
return what bread I had left; but my comrade seized it, and said
that I should lay that up for lunch or dinner. Soon after he was
let out to work at haying in a neighboring field, whither he
went every day, and would not be back till noon; so he bade me
good-day, saying that he doubted if he should see me again.

When I came out of prison—for some one interfered, and   33
paid that tax,—I did not perceive that great changes had taken
place on the common, such as he observed who went in a
youth and emerged a tottering and gray-headed man; and yet a
change had to my eyes come over the scene,—the town, and
State, and country,—greater than any that mere time could effect. I saw yet more distinctly the State in which I lived. I saw
to what extent the people among whom I lived could be trusted
as good neighbors and friends; that their friendship was for
summer weather only; that they did not greatly propose to do
right; that they were a distinct race from me by their prejudices and superstitions, as the Chinamen and Malays are; that
in their sacrifices to humanity they ran no risks, not even to
their property; that after all they were not so noble but they
treated the thief as he had treated them, and hoped, by a certain outward observance and a few prayers, and by walking in
a particular straight though useless path from time to time, to
save their souls. This may be to judge my neighbors harshly;
for I believe that many of them are not aware that they have
such an institution as the jail in their village.

It was formerly the custom in our village, when a poor debtor   34
came out of jail, for his acquaintances to salute him, looking
through their fingers, which were crossed to represent the grating of a jail window, "How do ye do?" My neighbors did not thus
salute me, but first looked at me, and then at one another, as if I
had returned from a long journey. I was put into jail as I was
going to the shoemaker's to get a shoe which was mended. When
I was let out the next morning, I proceeded to finish my errand,
and, having put on my mended shoe, joined a huckleberry party,
who were impatient to put themselves under my conduct; and in
half an hour,—for the horse was soon tackled,—was in the midst
of a huckleberry field, on one of our highest hills, two miles off,
and then the State was nowhere to be seen.

This is the whole history of "My Prisons."   35

Mahatma Gandhi
LETTER TO LORD IRWIN

Mahatma Gandhi (Mahatma means "of great soul") was born in India in 1869, studied law in London, and in 1893 went to South Africa, where he opposed discriminatory legislation against Indians, was exposed to the writing of Henry David Thoreau, and carried on a famous correspondence with the Russian novelist Leo Tolstoy concerning civil disobedience. In 1914 he returned to India, and about 1920 began a lifetime of committed support for India's independence from England—notably through the practice and encouragement of nonviolent resistance (satyagraha). After a decade of sporadic civil dis-obedience and periodic imprisonments, Gandhi in 1930 pre-pared a Declaration of Independence for India and soon after led a remarkable (and famous) 200-mile march to the sea to collect salt in symbolic defiance of the English government's monopoly on that product; by the end of the year, more than 100,000 people were jailed in the campaign. India of course did finally achieve independence, in 1947. The following year, while trying to calm tensions between Hindus and Moslems, Gandhi was assassinated.

The following letter was sent by Gandhi to the British viceroy in India, Lord Irwin, in March 1930, just ten days be-fore the salt march was to begin. It was sent from Satyagraha Ashram, a community established to practice Gandhi's method of nonviolent resistance.

Satyagraha Ashram, Sabarmati,
March 2, 1930

Dear Friend,

1   Before embarking on civil disobedience and taking the risk I have dreaded to take all these years, I would fain approach you and find a way out.

2   My personal faith is absolutely clear. I cannot intentionally hurt anything that lives, much less fellow human beings, even though they may do the greatest wrong to me and mine. Whilst, therefore, I hold the British rule to be a curse, I do not intend harm to a single Englishman or to any legitimate inter-est he may have in India.

I must not be misunderstood. Though I hold the British rule   3
in India to be a curse, I do not, therefore, consider Englishmen
in general to be worse than any other people on earth. I have
the privilege of claiming many Englishmen as dearest friends.
Indeed much that I have learnt of the evil of British rule is due
to the writings of frank and courageous Englishmen who have
not hesitated to tell the unpalatable truth about that rule.

And why do I regard the British rule as a curse?   4

It has impoverished the dumb millions by a system of pro-   5
gressive exploitation and by a ruinously expensive military and
civil administration which the country can never afford.

It has reduced us politically to serfdom. It has sapped the foun-   6
dations of our culture. And, by the policy of cruel disarmament,
it has degraded us spiritually. Lacking the inward strength, we
have been reduced, by all but universal disarmament, to a state
bordering on cowardly helplessness.

In common with many of my countrymen, I had hugged the   7
fond hope that the proposed Round Table Conference might
furnish a solution. But, when you said plainly that you could
not give any assurance that you or the British Cabinet would
pledge yourselves to support a scheme of full Dominion Status,
the Round Table Conference could not possibly furnish the
solution for which vocal India is consciously, and the dumb
millions are unconsciously, thirsting.

It seems as clear as daylight that responsible British states-   8
men do not contemplate any alteration in British policy that
might adversely affect Britain's commerce with India or require an impartial and close scrutiny of Britain's transactions
with India. If nothing is done to end the process of exploitation
India must be bled with an ever increasing speed. The Finance
Member regards as a settled fact the 1/6 ratio which by a stroke
of the pen drains India of a few crores.[1] And when a serious attempt is being made through a civil form of direct action, to
unsettle this fact, among many others, even you cannot help
appealing to the wealthy landed classes to help you to crush
that attempt in the name of an order that grinds India to
atoms.

Unless those who work in the name of the nation understand   9
and keep before all concerned the motive that lies behind the
craving for independence, there is every danger of independence coming to us so changed as to be of no value to those
toiling voiceless millions for whom it is sought and for whom it
is worth taking. It is for that reason that I have been recently
telling the public what independence should really mean.

[1]In Indian currency, a crore is equivalent to ten million rupees.

10   Let me put before you some of the salient points.

11   The terrific pressure of land revenue, which furnishes a large part of the total, must undergo considerable modification in an independent India. Even the much vaunted permanent settlement benefits the few rich zamindars,[2] not the ryots.[3] The ryot has remained as helpless as ever. He is a mere tenant at will. Not only, then, has the land revenue to be considerably reduced, but the whole revenue system has to be so revised as to make the ryot's good its primary concern. But the British system seems to be designed to crush the very life out of him. Even the salt he must use to live is so taxed as to make the burden fall heaviest on him, if only because of the heartless impartiality of its incidence. The tax shows itself still more burdensome on the poor man when it is remembered that salt is the one thing he must eat more than the rich man both individually and collectively.

12   The iniquities sampled above are maintained in order to carry on a foreign administration, demonstrably the most expensive in the world. Take your own salary. It is over Rs. 21,000 per month, besides many other indirect additions. The British Prime Minister gets £5,000 per year, i.e., over Rs. 5,400 per month at the present rate of exchange. You are getting over Rs. 700 per day against India's average income of less than annas 2 per day. The Prime Minister gets Rs. 180 per day against Great Britain's average income of nearly Rs. 2 per day. Thus you are getting much over five thousand times India's average income. The British Prime Minister is getting only ninety times Britain's average income. On bended knees I ask you to ponder over this phenomenon. I have taken a personal illustration to drive home a painful truth. I have too great a regard for you as a man to wish to hurt your feelings. I know that you do not need the salary you get. Probably the whole of your salary goes for charity. But a system that provides for such an arrangement deserves to be summarily scrapped.

13   If India is to live as a nation, if the slow death by starvation of her people is to stop, some remedy must be found for immediate relief. The proposed Conference is certainly not the remedy. It is not a matter of carrying conviction by argument. The matter resolves itself into one of matching forces. Conviction or no conviction, Great Britain would defend her Indian commerce and interests by all the forces at her command. India must consequently evolve force enough to free herself from that embrace of death.

[2] A zamindar is a landowner.
[3] A ryot is a tenant farmer.

It is common cause that, however disorganized and, for the   14
time being, insignificant it may be, the party of violence is
gaining ground and making itself felt. Its end is the same as
mine. But I am convinced that it cannot bring the desired relief
to the dumb millions. And the conviction is growing deeper
and deeper in me that nothing but unadulterated non-violence
can check the organized violence of the British Government.
Many think that non-violence is not an active force. My experience, limited though it undoubtedly is, shows that non-
violence can be an intensely active force. It is my purpose to set
in motion that force as well against the organized violent force
of the British rule as [against] the unorganized violent force of
the growing party of violence. To sit still would be to give rein
to both the forces above mentioned. Having an unquestioning
and immovable faith in the efficacy of non-violence as I know
it, it would be sinful on my part to wait any longer.

This non-violence will be expressed through civil disobedi-   15
ence, for the moment confined to the inmates of the
Satyagraha Ashram, but ultimately designed to cover all those
who choose to join the movement with its obvious limitations.

I know that in embarking on non-violence I shall be running   16
what might fairly be termed a mad risk. But the victories of
truth have never been won without risks, often of the gravest
character. Conversion of a nation that has consciously or unconsciously preyed upon another, far more numerous, far
more ancient and no less cultured than itself, is worth any
amount of risk.

I have deliberately used the word "conversion." For my am-   17
bition is no less than to convert the British people through
non-violence, and thus make them see the wrong they have
done to India. I do not seek to harm your people. I want to
serve them even as I want to serve my own. I believe that I have
always served them. I served them up to 1919 blindly. But
when my eyes were opened and I conceived non-cooperation,
the object still was to serve them. I employed the same weapon
that I have in all humility successfully used against the dearest
members of my family. If I have equal love for your people
with mine it will not long remain hidden. It will be acknowledged by them even as the members of my family acknowledged it after they had tried me for several years. If the people
join me as I expect they will, the sufferings they will undergo,
unless the British nation sooner retraces its steps, will be
enough to melt the stoniest hearts.

The plan through civil disobedience will be to combat such   18
evils as I have sampled out. If we want to sever the British connection it is because of such evils. When they are removed the

path becomes easy. Then the way to friendly negotiation will be open. If the British commerce with India is purified of greed, you will have no difficulty in recognizing our independence. I respectfully invite you then to pave the way for immediate removal of those evils, and thus open a way for a real conference between equals, interested only in promoting the common good of mankind through voluntary fellowship and in arranging terms of mutual help and commerce equally suited to both. You have unnecessarily laid stress upon the communal problems that unhappily affect this land. Important though they undoubtedly are for the consideration of any scheme of government, they have little bearing on the greater problems which are above communities and which affect them all equally. But if you cannot see your way to deal with these evils and my letter makes no appeal to your heart, on the 11th day of this month, I shall proceed with such co-workers of the Ashram as I can take, to disregard the provisions of the salt laws. I regard this tax to be the most iniquitous of all from the poor man's standpoint. As the independence movement is essentially for the poorest in the land the beginning will be made with this evil. The wonder is that we have submitted to the cruel monopoly for so long. It is, I know, open to you to frustrate my design by arresting me. I hope that there will be tens of thousands ready, in a disciplined manner, to take up the work after me, and, in the act of disobeying the Salt Act to lay themselves open to the penalties of a law that should never have disfigured the Statute-book.

19   I have no desire to cause you unnecessary embarrassment, or any at all, so far as I can help. If you think that there is any substance in my letter, and if you will care to discuss matters with me, and if to that end you would like me to postpone publication of this letter, I shall gladly refrain on receipt of a telegram to that effect soon after this reaches you. You will, however, do me the favour not to deflect me from my course unless you can see your way to conform to the substance of this letter.

20   This letter is not in any way intended as a threat but is a simple and sacred duty peremptory on a civil resister. Therefore I am having it specially delivered by a young English friend who believes in the Indian cause and is a full believer in non-violence and whom Providence seems to have sent to me, as it were, for the very purpose.

I remain,
Your sincere friend,
M. K. Gandhi

PUBLIC STATEMENT
BY EIGHT ALABAMA
CLERGYMEN

Born in Atlanta and educated at Morehouse College, Crozer Theological Seminary (near Philadelphia), and Boston University, Martin Luther King Jr. (1929–1968) was the most visible leader of the civil rights movement of the 1960s. An ordained minister with a doctorate in theology from Boston University, he worked especially in the South and through nonviolent means to overturn segregation statutes, to increase the number of African American voters, and to support other civil rights initiatives. Reverend King won the Nobel Peace Prize in 1964. When he was assassinated in 1968, all America mourned.

On April 12, 1963, in order to have himself arrested on a symbolic day (Good Friday), Reverend Martin Luther King Jr. disobeyed a court injunction forbidding demonstrations in Birmingham, Alabama. (See the photo on the next page.) That same day, eight leading white Birmingham clergymen (Christian and Jewish) published a letter in the Birmingham News *calling for the end of protests and exhorting protesters to work through the courts for the redress of their grievances. On the morning after his arrest, while held in solitary confinement, King began his response to these clergymen— his famous "Letter from Birmingham Jail." Begun in the margins of newspapers and on scraps of paper and finished by the following Tuesday, the letter was widely distributed and later became a central chapter in King's* Why We Can't Wait *(1964).*

April 12, 1963

We the undersigned clergymen are among those who, in   1
January, issued "An Appeal for Law and Order and Common
Sense," in dealing with racial problems in Alabama. We expressed understanding that honest convictions in racial matters could properly be pursued in the courts, but urged that

decisions of those courts should in the meantime be peacefully
obeyed.

2   Since that time there had been some evidence of increased
forbearance and a willingness to face facts. Responsible citizens have undertaken to work on various problems which
cause racial friction and unrest. In Birmingham, recent public
events had given indication that we all have opportunity for a
new constructive and realistic approach to racial problems.

3   However, we are now confronted by a series of demonstrations by some of our Negro citizens, directed and led in
part by outsiders. We recognize the natural impatience of people who feel that their hopes are slow in being realized. But we
are convinced that these demonstrations are unwise and
untimely.

4   We agree rather with certain local Negro leadership which
has called for honest and open negotiation of racial issues in
our area. And we believe this kind of facing of issues can best

be accomplished by citizens of our own metropolitan area, white and Negro, meeting with their knowledge and experience of the local situation. All of us need to face that responsibility and find proper channels for its accomplishment.

Just as we formerly pointed out that "hatred and violence 5 have no sanction in our religious and political traditions," we also point out that such actions as incite to hatred and violence, however technically peaceful those actions may be, have not contributed to the resolution of our local problems. We do not believe that these days of new hope are days when extreme measures are justified in Birmingham.

We commend the community as a whole, and the local 6 news media and law enforcement officials in particular, on the calm manner in which these demonstrations have been handled. We urge the public to continue to show restraint should the demonstrations continue, and the law enforcement officials to remain calm and continue to protect our city from violence.

We further strongly urge our own Negro community to withdraw support from these demonstrations, and to unite locally in working peacefully for a better Birmingham. When rights are consistently denied, a cause should be pressed in the courts and in negotiations among local leaders, and not in the streets. We appeal to both our white and Negro citizenry to observe the principles of law and order and common sense. Signed by:

C. C. J. Carpenter, D.D., LL.D.,
Bishop of Alabama
Joseph A. Durick, D.D.,
Auxiliary Bishop, Diocese of Mobile, Birmingham
Rabbi Milton L. Grafman,
Temple Emanu-El, Birmingham, Alabama
Bishop Paul Hardin,
Bishop of the Alabama-West Florida Conference of the
  Methodist Church
Bishop Nolan B. Harmon,
Bishop of the North Alabama Conference of the
  Methodist Church
George M. Murray, D.D., LL.D.,
Bishop Coadjutor, Episcopal Diocese of Alabama
Edward V. Ramage,
Moderator, Synod of the Alabama Presbyterian Church
  in the United States
Earl Stallings,
Pastor, First Baptist Church, Birmingham, Alabama

Martin Luther King Jr.

LETTER FROM BIRMINGHAM JAIL

April 16, 1963

1 My Dear Fellow Clergymen:

While confined here in the Birmingham city jail, I came across your recent statement calling my present activities "unwise and untimely." Seldom do I pause to answer criticism of my work and ideas. If I sought to answer all the criticisms of my work and ideas. If I sought to answer all the criticisms that cross my desk, my secretaries would have little time for anything other than such correspondence in the course of the day, and I would have no time for constructive work. But since I feel that you are men of genuine good will and that your criticisms are sincerely set forth, I want to try to answer your statement in what I hope will be patient and reasonable terms.

2 I think I should indicate why I am here in Birmingham, since you have been influenced by the view which argues against "outsiders coming in." I have the honor of serving as president of the Southern Christian Leadership Conference, an organization operating in every southern state, with headquarters in Atlanta, Georgia. We have some eighty-five affiliated organizations across the South, and one of them is the Alabama Christian Movement for Human Rights. Frequently we share staff, educational and financial resources with our affiliates. Several months ago the affiliate here in Birmingham asked us to be on call to engage in a nonviolent direct-action program if such were deemed necessary. We readily consented, and when the hour came we lived up to our promise. So I, along with several members of my staff, am here because I was invited here. I am here because I have organizational ties here.

3 But more basically, I am in Birmingham because injustice is here. Just as the prophets of the eighth century B.C. left their villages and carried their "thus saith the Lord" far beyond the boundaries of their home towns, and just as the Apostle Paul left his village of Tarsus and carried the gospel of Jesus Christ to the far corners of the Greco-Roman world, so am I compelled to carry the gospel of freedom beyond my own home town. Like Paul, I must constantly respond to the Macedonian call for aid.

4 Moreover, I am cognizant of the interrelatedness of all communities and states. I cannot sit idly by in Atlanta and not

be concerned about what happens in Birmingham. Injustice anywhere is a threat to justice everywhere. We are caught in an inescapable network of mutuality, tied in a single garment of destiny. Whatever affects one directly, affects all indirectly. Never again can we afford to live with the narrow, provincial "outside agitator" idea. Anyone who lives inside the United States can never be considered an outsider anywhere within its bounds.

You deplore the demonstrations taking place in Birmingham.   5
But your statement, I am sorry to say, fails to express a similar concern for the conditions that brought about the demonstrations. I am sure that none of you would want to rest content with the superficial kind of social analysis that deals merely with effects and does not grapple with underlying causes. It is unfortunate that demonstrations are taking place in Birmingham, but it is even more unfortunate that the city's white power structure left the Negro community with no alternative.

In any nonviolent campaign there are four basic steps: collec-   6
tion of the facts to determine whether injustices exist; negotiation; self-purification; and direct action. We have gone through all these steps in Birmingham. There can be no gainsaying the fact that racial injustice engulfs this community. Birmingham is probably the most thoroughly segregated city in the United States. Its ugly record of brutality is widely known. Negroes have experienced grossly unjust treatment in the courts. There have been more unsolved bombings of Negro homes and churches in Birmingham than in any other city in the nation. These are the hard, brutal facts of the case. On the basis of these conditions, Negro leaders sought to negotiate with the city fathers. But the latter consistently refused to engage in good-faith negotiation.

Then, last September, came the opportunity to talk with lead-   7
ers of Birmingham's economic community. In the course of the negotiations, certain promises were made by the merchants— for example, to remove the stores' humiliating racial signs. On the basis of these promises, the Reverend Fred Shuttlesworth and the leaders of the Alabama Christian Movement for Human Rights agreed to a moratorium on all demonstrations. As the weeks and months went by, we realized that we were the victims of a broken promise. A few signs, briefly removed, returned; the others remained.

As in so many past experiences, our hopes had been blasted,   8
and the shadow of deep disappointment settled upon us. We had no alternative except to prepare for direct action, whereby we would present our very bodies as a means of laying our case before the conscience of the local and the national community. Mindful of the difficulties involved, we decided to undertake a process of self-purification. We began a series of workshops on nonviolence, and we repeatedly asked ourselves: "Are you able

to accept blows without retaliating?" "Are you able to endure the ordeal of jail?" We decided to schedule our direct-action program for the Easter season, realizing that except for Christmas, this is the main shopping period of the year. Knowing that a strong economic-withdrawal program would be the by-product of direct action, we felt that this would be the best time to bring pressure to bear on the merchants for the needed change.

9   Then it occurred to us that Birmingham's mayoral election was coming up in March, and we speedily decided to postpone action until after election day. When we discovered that the Commissioner of Public Safety, Eugene "Bull" Connor, had piled up enough votes to be in the run-off, we decided again to postpone action until the day after the run-off so that the demonstrations could not be used to cloud the issues. Like many others, we waited to see Mr. Connor defeated, and to this end we endured postponement after postponement. Having aided in this community need, we felt that our direct action program could be delayed no longer.

10   You may well ask: "Why direct action? Why sit-ins, marches and so forth? Isn't negotiation a better path?" You are quite right in calling for negotiation. Indeed, this is the very purpose of direct action. Nonviolent direct action seeks to create such a crisis and foster such a tension that a community which has constantly refused to negotiate is forced to confront the issue. It seeks so to dramatize the issue that it can no longer be ignored. My citing the creation of tension as part of the work of the nonviolent-resister may sound rather shocking. But I must confess that I am not afraid of the word "tension." I have earnestly opposed violent tension, but there is a type of constructive, nonviolent tension which is necessary for growth. Just as Socrates felt that it was necessary to create a tension in the mind so that individuals could rise from the bondage of myths and half-truths to the unfettered realm of creative analysis and objective appraisal, so must we see the need for nonviolent gadflies to create the kind of tension in society that will help men rise from the dark depths of prejudice and racism to the majestic heights of understanding and brotherhood.

11   The purpose of our direct-action program is to create a situation so crisis-packed that it will inevitably open the door to negotiation. I therefore concur with you in your call for negotiation. Too long has our beloved Southland been bogged down in a tragic effort to live in monologue rather than dialogue.

12   One of the basic points in your statement is that the action that I and my associates have taken in Birmingham is untimely. Some have asked: "Why didn't you give the new city administration time to act?" The only answer that I can give to this

query is that the new Birmingham administration must be prod-
ded about as much as the outgoing one, before it will act. We are
sadly mistaken if we feel that the election of Albert Boutwell
as mayor will bring the millennium to Birmingham. While
Mr. Boutwell is a much more gentle person than Mr. Connor,
they are both segregationists, dedicated to maintenance of the
status quo. I have hope that Mr. Boutwell will be reasonable
enough to see the futility of massive resistance to desegregation.
But he will not see this without pressure from devotees of civil
rights. My friends, I must say to you that we have not made a
single gain in civil rights without determined legal and nonviolent pressure. Lamentably, it is an historical fact that privileged
groups seldom give up their privileges voluntarily. Individuals
may see the moral light and voluntarily give up their unjust posture; but, as Reinhold Niebuhr has reminded us, groups tend to
be more immoral than individuals.

We know through painful experience that freedom is never   13
voluntarily given by the oppressor; it must be demanded by the
oppressed. Frankly, I have yet to engage in a direct-action campaign that was "well timed" in the view of those who have not
suffered unduly from the disease of segregation. For years now
I have heard the word "Wait!" It rings in the ear of every Negro
with piercing familiarity. This "Wait" has almost always meant
"Never." We must come to see, with one of our distinguished
jurists, that "justice too long delayed is justice denied."

We have waited for more than 340 years for our constitu-   14
tional and God-given rights. The nations of Asia and Africa are
moving with jetlike speed toward gaining political independence, but we still creep at horse-and-buggy pace toward gaining a cup of coffee at a lunch counter. Perhaps it is easy for
those who have never felt the stinging darts of segregation to
say, "Wait." But when you have seen vicious mobs lynch your
mothers and fathers at will and drown your sisters and brothers
at whim; when you have seen hate-filled policemen curse, kick
and even kill your black brothers and sisters; when you see the
vast majority of your twenty million Negro brothers smothering
in an airtight cage of poverty in the midst of an affluent society;
when you suddenly find your tongue twisted and your speech
stammering as you seek to explain to your six-year-old daughter
why she can't go to the public amusement park that has just
been advertised on television, and see tears welling up in her
eyes when she is told that Funtown is closed to colored
children, and see ominous clouds of inferiority beginning to
form in her little mental sky, and see her beginning to distort
her personality by developing an unconscious bitterness toward
white people; when you have to concoct an answer for a

five-year-old son who is asking: "Daddy, why do white people treat colored people so mean?"; when you take a cross-country drive and find it necessary to sleep night after night in the uncomfortable corners of your automobile because no motel will accept you; when you are humiliated day in and day out by nagging signs reading "white" and "colored"; when your first name becomes "nigger," your middle name becomes "boy" (however old you are) and your last name becomes "John," and your wife and mother are never given the respected title "Mrs."; when you are harried by day and haunted by night by the fact that you are a Negro, living constantly at tiptoe stance, never quite knowing what to expect next, and are plagued with inner fears and outer resentments; when you are forever fighting a degenerating sense of "nobodiness"—then you will understand why we find it difficult to wait. There comes a time when the cup of endurance runs over, and men are no longer willing to be plunged into the abyss of despair. I hope, sirs, you can understand our legitimate and unavoidable impatience.

15   You express a great deal of anxiety over our willingness to break laws. This is certainly a legitimate concern. Since we so diligently urge people to obey the Supreme Court's decision of 1954 outlawing segregation in the public schools, at first glance it may seem rather paradoxical for us consciously to break laws. One may well ask: "How can you advocate breaking some laws and obeying others?" The answer lies in the fact that there are two types of laws: just and unjust. I would be the first to advocate obeying just laws. One has not only a legal but a moral responsibility to obey just laws. Conversely, one has a moral responsibility to disobey unjust laws. I would agree with St. Augustine that "an unjust law is no law at all."

16   Now, what is the difference between the two? How does one determine whether a law is just or unjust? A just law is a man-made code that squares with the moral law or the law of God. An unjust law is a code that is out of harmony with the moral law. To put it in the terms of St. Thomas Aquinas: An unjust law is a human law that is not rooted in eternal law and natural law. Any law that uplifts human personality is just. Any law that degrades human personality is unjust. All segregation statutes are unjust because segregation distorts the soul and damages the personality. It gives the segregator a false sense of superiority and the segregated a false sense of inferiority. Segregation, to use the terminology of the Jewish philosopher Martin Buber, substitutes an "I–it" relationship for an "I–thou" relationship and ends up relegating persons to the status of things. Hence segregation is not only politically, economically and sociologically unsound, it is morally wrong and sinful. Paul Tillich has

said that sin is separation. Is not segregation an existential expression of man's tragic separation, his awful estrangement, his terrible sinfulness? Thus it is that I can urge men to obey the 1954 decision of the Supreme Court, for it is morally right; and I can urge them to disobey segregation ordinances, for they are morally wrong.

Let us consider a more concrete example of just and unjust laws. An unjust law is a code that a numerical or power majority group compels a minority group to obey but does not make binding on itself. This is *difference* made legal. By the same token, a just law is a code that a majority compels a minority to follow and that it is willing to follow itself. This is *sameness* made legal. 17

Let me give another explanation. A law is unjust if it is inflicted on a minority that, as a result of being denied the right to vote, had no part in enacting or devising the law. Who can say that the legislature of Alabama which set up that state's segregation laws was democratically elected? Throughout Alabama all sorts of devious methods are used to prevent Negroes from becoming registered voters, and there are some counties in which, even though Negroes constitute a majority of the population, not a single Negro is registered. Can any law enacted under such circumstances be considered democratically structured? 18

Sometimes a law is just on its face and unjust in its application. For instance, I have been arrested on a charge of parading without a permit. Now, there is nothing wrong in having an ordinance which requires a permit for a parade. But such an ordinance becomes unjust when it is used to maintain segregation and to deny citizens the First-Amendment privilege of peaceful assembly and protest. 19

I hope you are able to see the distinction I am trying to point out. In no sense do I advocate evading or defying the law, as would the rabid segregationist. That would lead to anarchy. One who breaks an unjust law must do so openly, lovingly, and with a willingness to accept the penalty. I submit that an individual who breaks a law that conscience tells him is unjust, and who willingly accepts the penalty of imprisonment in order to arouse the conscience of the community over its injustice, is in reality expressing the highest respect for law. 20

Of course, there is nothing new about this kind of civil disobedience. It was evidenced sublimely in the refusal of Shadrach, Meshach and Abednego to obey the laws of Nebuchadnezzar, on the ground that a higher moral law was at stake. It was practiced superbly by the early Christians, who were willing to face hungry lions and the excruciating pain of chopping blocks rather than submit to certain unjust laws of the Roman 21

Empire. To a degree, academic freedom is a reality today because Socrates practiced civil disobedience. In our own nation, the Boston Tea Party represented a massive act of civil disobedience.

22   We should never forget that everything Adolf Hitler did in Germany was "legal" and everything the Hungarian freedom fighters did in Hungary was "illegal." It was "illegal" to aid and comfort a Jew in Hitler's Germany. Even so, I am sure that, had I lived in Germany at the time, I would have aided and comforted my Jewish brothers. If today I lived in a Communist country where certain principles dear to the Christian faith are suppressed, I would openly advocate disobeying that country's anti-religious laws.

23   I must make two honest confessions to you, my Christian and Jewish brothers. First, I must confess that over the past few years I have been gravely disappointed with the white moderate. I have almost reached the regrettable conclusion that the Negro's great stumbling block in his stride toward freedom is not the White Citizen's Counciler or the Ku Klux Klanner, but the white moderate, who is more devoted to "order" than to justice; who prefers a negative peace which is the absence of tension to a positive peace which is the presence of justice; who constantly says: "I agree with you in the goal you seek, but I cannot agree with your methods of direct action"; who paternalistically believes he can set the timetable for another man's freedom; who lives by a mythical concept of time and who constantly advises the Negro to wait for a "more convenient season." Shallow understanding from people of good will is more frustrating than absolute misunderstanding from people of ill will. Lukewarm acceptance is much more bewildering than outright rejection.

24   I had hoped that the white moderate would understand that law and order exist for the purpose of establishing justice and that when they fail in this purpose they become the dangerously structured dams that block the flow of social progress. I had hoped that the white moderate would understand that the present tension in the South is a necessary phase of the transition from an obnoxious negative peace, in which the Negro passively accepted his unjust plight, to a substantive and positive peace, in which all men will respect the dignity and worth of human personality. Actually, we who engage in nonviolent direct action are not the creators of tension. We merely bring to the surface the hidden tension that is already alive. We bring it out in the open, where it can be seen and dealt with. Like a boil that can never be cured so long as it is covered up but must be opened with all its ugliness to the natural medicines of air and light, injustice must be exposed,

with all the tension its exposure creates, to the light of human conscience and the air of national opinion before it can be cured.

In your statement you assert that our actions, even though peaceful, must be condemned because they precipitate violence. But is this a logical assertion? Isn't this like condemning a robbed man because his possession of money precipitated the evil act of robbery? Isn't this like condemning Socrates because his unswerving commitment to truth and his philosophical inquires precipitated the act by the misguided populace in which they made him drink hemlock? Isn't this like condemning Jesus because his unique God-consciousness and never ceasing devotion to God's will precipitated the evil act of crucifixion? We must come to see that, as the federal courts have consistently affirmed, it is wrong to urge an individual to cease his efforts to gain his basic constitutional rights because the quest may precipitate violence. Society must protect the robbed and punish the robber.

I had also hoped that the white moderate would reject the myth concerning time in relation to the struggle for freedom. I have just received a letter from a white brother in Texas. He writes: "All Christians know that the colored people will receive equal rights eventually, but it is possible that you are in too great a religious hurry. It has taken Christianity almost two thousand years to accomplish what it has. The teachings of Christ take time to come to earth." Such an attitude stems from a tragic misconception of time, from the strangely irrational notion that there is something in the very flow of time that will inevitably cure all ills. Actually, time itself is neutral; it can be used either destructively or constructively. More and more I feel that the people of ill will have used time much more effectively than have the people of good will. We will have to repent in this generation not merely for the hateful words and actions of the bad people but for the appalling silence of the good people. Human progress never rolls in on wheels of inevitability; it comes through the tireless efforts of men willing to be co-workers with God, and without this hard work, time itself becomes an ally of the forces of social stagnation. We must use time creatively, in the knowledge that time is always ripe to do right. Now is the time to make real the promise of democracy and transform our pending national elegy into a creative psalm of brotherhood. Now is the time to lift our national policy from the quicksand of racial injustice to the solid rock of human dignity.

You speak of our activity in Birmingham as extreme. At first I was rather disappointed that fellow clergymen would see my nonviolent efforts as those of an extremist. I began thinking

25

26

27

about the fact that I stand in the middle of two opposing forces in the Negro community. One is a force of complacency, made up in part of Negroes who, as a result of long years of oppression, are so drained of self-respect and a sense of "somebodiness" that they have adjusted to segregation; and in part of a few middle-class Negroes who, because of a degree of academic and economic security and because in some ways they profit by segregation, have become insensitive to the problems of the masses. The other force is one of bitterness and hatred, and it comes perilously close to advocating violence. It is expressed in the various black nationalist groups that are springing up across the nation, the largest and best-known being Elijah Muhammad's Muslim movement. Nourished by the Negro's frustration over the continued existence of racial discrimination, this movement is made up of people who have lost faith in America, who have absolutely repudiated Christianity, and who have concluded that the white man is an incorrigible "devil."

28   I have tried to stand between these two forces, saying that we need emulate neither the "do-nothingism" of the complacent nor the hatred and despair of the black nationalist. For there is the more excellent way of love and nonviolent protest. I am grateful to God that, through the influence of the Negro church, the way of nonviolence became an integral part of our struggle.

29   If this philosophy had not emerged, by now many streets of the South would, I am convinced, be flowing with blood. And I am further convinced that if our white brothers dismiss as "rabble-rousers" and "outside agitators" those of us who employ nonviolent direct action, and if they refuse to support our nonviolent efforts, millions of Negroes will, out of frustration and despair, seek solace and security in black-nationalist ideologies—a development that would inevitably lead to a frightening racial nightmare.

30   Oppressed people cannot remain oppressed forever. The yearning for freedom eventually manifests itself, and that is what has happened to the American Negro. Something within has reminded him of his birthright of freedom, and something without has reminded him that it can be gained. Consciously or unconsciously, he has been caught up by the *Zeitgeist*, and with his black brothers of Africa and his brown and yellow brothers of Asia, South America and the Caribbean, the United States Negro is moving with a sense of great urgency toward the promised land of racial justice. If one recognizes this vital urge that has engulfed the Negro community, one should readily understand why public demonstrations are taking place. The Negro has many pent-up resentments and latent frustrations, and he must release them. So let him march; let him make prayer pilgrimages to the

city hall; let him go on freedom rides—and try to understand why he must do so. If his repressed emotions are not released in nonviolent ways, they will seek expression through violence; this is not a threat but a fact of history. So I have not said to my people: "Get rid of your discontent." Rather, I have tried to say that this normal and healthy discontent can be channeled into the creative outlet of nonviolent direct action. And now this approach is being termed extremist.

But though I was initially disappointed at being categorized   31 as an extremist, as I continued to think about the matter I gradually gained a measure of satisfaction from the label. Was not Jesus an extremist for love: "Love your enemies, bless them that curse you, do good to them that hate you, and pray for them which despitefully use you, and persecute you." Was not Amos an extremist for justice: "Let justice roll down like waters and righteousness like an ever-flowing stream." Was not Paul an extremist for the Christian gospel: "I bear in my body the marks of the Lord Jesus." Was not Martin Luther an extremist: "Here I stand; I cannot do otherwise, so help me God." And John Bunyan: "I will stay in jail to the end of my days before I make a butchery of my conscience." And Abraham Lincoln: "The nation cannot survive half slave and half free." And Thomas Jefferson: "We hold these truths to be self-evident, that all men are created equal . . ." So the question is not whether we will be extremists, but what kind of extremists we will be. Will we be extremists for hate or for love? Will we be extremists for the preservation of injustice or for the extension of justice? In that dramatic scene on Calvary's hill three men were crucified. We must never forget that all three were crucified for the same crime—the crime of extremism. Two were extremists for immorality, and thus fell below their environment. The other, Jesus Christ, was an extremist for love, truth and goodness, and thereby rose above his environment. Perhaps the South, the nation and the world are in dire need of creative extremists.

I had hoped that the white moderate would see this need.   32 Perhaps I was too optimistic; perhaps I expected too much. I suppose I should have realized that few members of the oppressor race can understand the deep groans and passionate yearnings of the oppressed race, and still fewer have the vision to see that injustice must be rooted out by strong, persistent and determined action. I am thankful, however, that some of our white brothers in the South have grasped the meaning of this social revolution and committed themselves to it. They are still all too few in quantity, but they are big in quality. Some—such as Ralph McGill, Lillian Smith, Harry Golden, James McBride Dabbs, Ann Braden and Sarah Patton Boyle—have written about our struggle in eloquent and prophetic terms. Others have marched with us down nameless streets of the South. They have languished in filthy, roach-infested jails, suffering the abuse and brutality of policemen who view them as "dirty nigger-lovers." Unlike so many of their moderate brothers and sisters, they have recognized the urgency of the moment and sensed the need for powerful "action" antidotes to combat the disease of segregation.

33   Let me take note of my other major disappointment. I have been so greatly disappointed with the white church and its leadership. Of course, there are some notable exceptions. I am not unmindful of the fact that each of you has taken some significant stands on this issue. I commend you, Reverend Stallings, for your Christian stand on this past Sunday, in welcoming Negroes to your worship service on a nonsegregated basis. I commend the Catholic leaders of this state for integrating Spring Hill College several years ago.

34   But despite these notable exceptions, I must honestly reiterate that I have been disappointed with the church. I do not say this as one of those negative critics who can always find something wrong with the church. I say this as a minister of the gospel, who loves the church; who was nurtured in its bosom; who has been sustained by its spiritual blessings and who will remain true to it as long as the cord of life shall lengthen.

35   When I was suddenly catapulted into the leadership of the bus protest in Montgomery, Alabama, a few years ago, I felt we would be supported by the white church. I felt that the white ministers, priests and rabbis of the South would be among our strongest allies. Instead, some have been outright opponents, refusing to understand the freedom movement and misrepresenting its leaders; all too many others have been more cautious than courageous and have remained silent behind the anesthetizing security of stained-glass windows.

36   In spite of my shattered dreams, I came to Birmingham with the hope that the white religious leadership of this community would see the justice of our cause and, with deep moral concern, would serve as the channel through which our just grievances could reach the power structure. I had hoped that each of you would understand. But again I have been disappointed.

37   I have heard numerous southern religious leaders admonish their worshipers to comply with a desegregation decision because it is the law, but I have longed to hear white ministers declare: "Follow this decree because integration is morally right and because the Negro is your brother." In the midst of blatant injustices inflicted upon the Negro, I have watched white churchmen stand on the sideline and mouth pious

irrelevancies and sanctimonious trivialities. In the midst of a mighty struggle to rid our nation of racial and economic injustice, I have heard many ministers say: "Those are social issues, with which the gospel has no real concern." And I have watched many churches commit themselves to a completely other-worldly religion which makes a strange, un-Biblical distortion between body and soul, between the sacred and the secular.

I have traveled the length and breadth of Alabama, Mississippi   38
and all the other southern states. On sweltering summer days and crisp autumn mornings I have looked at the South's beautiful churches with their lofty spires pointing heavenward. I have beheld the impressive outlines of her massive religious-education buildings. Over and over I have found myself asking: "What kind of people worship here? Who is their God? Where were their voices when the lips of Governor Barnett dripped with words of interposition and nullification? Where were they when Governor Wallace gave a clarion call for defiance and hatred? Where were their voices of support when bruised and weary Negro men and women decided to rise from the dark dungeons of complacency to the bright hills of creative protest?"

Yes, these questions are still in my mind. In deep disappoint-   39
ment I have wept over the laxity of the church. But be assured that my tears have been tears of love. There can be no deep disappointment where there is not deep love. Yes, I love the church. How could I do otherwise? I am in the rather unique position of being the son, the grandson and the great-grandson of preachers. Yes, I see the church as the body of Christ. But, oh! How we have blemished and scarred that body through social neglect and through fear of being non-conformists.

There was a time when the church was very powerful—in the   40
time when the early Christians rejoiced at being deemed worthy to suffer for what they believed. In those days the church was not merely a thermometer that recorded the ideas and principles of popular opinion; it was a thermostat that transformed the mores of society. Whenever the early Christians entered a town, the people in power became disturbed and immediately sought to convict the Christians for being "disturbers of the peace" and "outside agitators." But the Christians pressed on, in the conviction that they were "a colony of heaven," called to obey God rather than man. Small in number, they were big in commitment. They were too God-intoxicated to be "astronomically intimidated." By their effort and example they brought an end to such ancient evils as infanticide and gladiatorial contests.

Things are different now. So often the contemporary church   41
is a weak, ineffectual voice with an uncertain sound. So often it is an arch-defender of the status quo. Far from being

disturbed by the presence of the church, the power structure of the average community is consoled by the church's silent—and often even vocal—sanction of things as they are.

42   But the judgment of God is upon the church as never before. If today's church does not recapture the sacrificial spirit of the early church, it will lose its authenticity, forfeit the loyalty of millions, and be dismissed as an irrelevant social club with no meaning for the twentieth century. Every day I meet young people whose disappointment with the church has turned into outright disgust.

43   Perhaps I have once again been too optimistic. Is organized religion too inextricably bound to the status quo to save our nation and the world? Perhaps I must turn my faith to the inner spiritual church, the church within the church, as the true *ekklesia* and the hope of the world. But again I am thankful to God that some noble souls from the ranks of organized religion have broken loose from the paralyzing chains of conformity and joined us as active partners in the struggle for freedom. They have left their secure congregations and walked the streets of Albany, Georgia, with us. They have gone down the highways of the South on tortuous rides for freedom. Yes, they have gone to jail with us. Some have been dismissed from their churches, have lost the support of their bishops and fellow ministers. But they have acted in the faith that right defeated is stronger than evil triumphant. Their witness has been the spiritual salt that has preserved the true meaning of the gospel in these troubled times. They have carved a tunnel of hope through the dark mountain of disappointment.

44   I hope the church as a whole will meet the challenge of this decisive hour. But even if the church does not come to the aid of justice, I have no despair about the future. I have no fear about the outcome of our struggle in Birmingham, even if our motives are at present misunderstood. We will reach the goal of freedom in Birmingham and all over the nation, because the goal of America is freedom. Abused and scorned though we may be, our destiny is tied up with America's destiny. Before the pilgrims landed at Plymouth, we were here. Before the pen of Jefferson etched the majestic words of the Declaration of Independence across the pages of history, we were here. For more than two centuries our forebears labored in this country without wages; they made cotton king; they built the homes of their masters while suffering gross injustice and shameful humiliation—and yet out of a bottomless vitality they continued to thrive and develop. If the inexpressible cruelties of slavery could not stop us, the opposition we now face will surely fail. We will win our freedom because the sacred heritage of our nation and the eternal will of God are embodied in our echoing demands.

Before closing I feel impelled to mention one other point in   45
your statement that has troubled me profoundly. You warmly
commended the Birmingham police force for keeping "order"
and "preventing violence." I doubt that you would have so
warmly commended the police force if you had seen its dogs
sinking their teeth into unarmed, nonviolent Negroes. I doubt
that you would so quickly commend the policemen if you were
to observe their ugly and inhumane treatment of Negroes here
in the city jail; if you were to watch them push and curse old
Negro women and young Negro girls; if you were to see them
slap and kick old Negro men and young boys; if you were to
observe them, as they did on two occasions, refuse to give us
food because we wanted to sing our grace together. I cannot
join you in your praise of the Birmingham Police Department.

It is true that the police have exercised a degree of discipline   46
in handling the demonstrators. In this sense they have conducted themselves rather "nonviolently" in public. But for
what purpose? To preserve the evil system of segregation. Over
the past few years I have consistently preached that nonviolence demands that the means we use must be as pure as the
ends we seek. I have tried to make clear that it is wrong to use
immoral means to attain moral ends. But now I must affirm
that it is just as wrong, or perhaps even more so, to use moral
means to preserve immoral ends. Perhaps Mr. Connor and his
policemen have been rather nonviolent in public, as was Chief
Pritchett in Albany, Georgia, but they have used the moral
means of nonviolence to maintain the immoral end of racial
injustice. As T. S. Eliot has said: "The last temptation is the
greatest treason: To do the right deed for the wrong reason."

I wish you had commended the Negro sit-inners and demon-   47
strators of Birmingham for their sublime courage, their willingness to suffer and their amazing discipline in the midst of great
provocation. One day the South will recognize its real heroes.
They will be the James Merediths, with the noble sense of purpose that enables them to face jeering and hostile mobs, and
with the agonizing loneliness that characterizes the life of the
pioneer. They will be old, oppressed, battered Negro women,
symbolized in a seventy-two-year-old woman in Montgomery,
Alabama, who rose up with a sense of dignity and with her people decided not to ride segregated buses, and who responded
with ungrammatical profundity to one who inquired about her
weariness: "My feets is tired, but my soul is at rest." They will
be the young high school and college students, the young ministers of the gospel and a host of their elders, courageously and
nonviolently sitting in at lunch counters and willingly going to
jail for conscience sake. One day the South will know that when
these disinherited children of God sat down at lunch counters,

they were in reality standing up for what is best in the American dream and for the most sacred values in our Judaeo-Christian heritage, thereby bringing our nation back to those great wells of democracy which were dug deep by the founding fathers in their formulation of the Constitution and the Declaration of Independence.

48   Never before have I written so long a letter. I'm afraid it is much too long to take your precious time. I can assure you that it would have been much shorter if I had been writing from a comfortable desk, but what else can one do when he is alone in a narrow jail cell, other than write long letters, think long thoughts and pray long prayers?

49   I hope this letter finds you strong in the faith. I also hope that circumstances will soon make it possible for me to meet each of you, not as an integrationist or a civil rights leader but as a fellow clergyman and a Christian brother. Let us all hope that the dark clouds of racial prejudice will soon pass away and the deep fog of misunderstanding will be lifted from our fear-drenched communities, and in some not too distant tomorrow the radiant stars of love and brotherhood will shine over our great nation with all their scintillating beauty.

> Yours for the cause of Peace and Brotherhood,
> Martin Luther King, Jr.

Christine Woyshner

MOTHERHOOD, ACTIVISM, AND SOCIAL REFORM

Christine Woyshner is assistant professor of education at Temple University. Her research interests center on the role of volunteer organizations in educational settings in the twentieth century. She also is concerned with issues surrounding women's education and women's role in social reform— the topic of the essay included here as well as of her edited collection, Minding Women: Reshaping the Educational Realm.

Interestingly, it is Alexis de Tocqueville, whose work is ex-cerpted in this section of Conversations, *that Woyshner cites at the opening of her review article, "The Education of Women for Wifehood":*

> *The American woman . . . never falls into the bonds of marriage as into a trap set for her simplicity and igno-rance. She has been taught in advance what is expected of her, and she freely places herself in the yoke on her own. She tolerates her new condition courageously because she has chosen it.*
>
> *—ALEXIS DE TOCQUEVILLE, 1840*

In the essay included below, Woyshner discusses the largely untold story of mothers in activist activities. This piece was published in USA Today Magazine *in March 2002.*

Mothers are sometimes the least likely candidates to spearhead   1
social movements. However, a closer look reveals more than
meets the eye. On my way to work each day, I pass a billboard
promoting the platform of the Million Mom March organization.
The black-and-white photograph depicts a diverse group of
women, all staring at the onlooker. Some have their arms folded,
others have their hands at their sides, but not one has a hand
raised in response to the query, "Anyone not in favor of stricter
gun laws raise your hand." With the rise of youth violence, the
billboard makes it clear that if you are not in favor of stricter gun
laws, you are acting in opposition to all that mothers represent.

The members of this national grassroots organization are   2
not the first mothers to take a stand. Throughout U.S. history,
women—whether or not they were mothers—have used
Americans' collective sentiment and ideology regarding mothers and motherhood in social reform. Essentially, this belief
holds that mothers are selfless, caring, and nurturing people.
They bear the physical pain of labor and tend to their offspring. They are considered to be a youngster's first teacher.
Some individuals even believe that mothers possess an instinctual proclivity for children's needs. Such notions are part of
Americans' collective consciousness, and mothers' influence is
reinforced with the commonplace usage of such aphorisms as
"The hand that rocks the cradle rules the world."

Indeed, mothers appear to be more active today than ever. In   3
addition to working full- or part-time jobs, they volunteer at
houses of worship and schools and are involved in political
campaigns. Then there are the national crusades, such as

Mothers Against Drunk Driving and the Million Mom March, which borrowed its name from the African-American movement. It would be facile, if not paradoxical, to assume that with the women's liberation movement in the 1970s, mothers have become more politically active and outspoken. In fact, a much-more intense period of maternal activism occurred a century ago. While females today enjoy more rights and greater freedoms (suffrage being the most obvious), mothers of the late 19th and early 20th centuries were organized, vocal, and effective, if only for a short period of time.

4   The origins of political motherhood can be found after the American Revolution and the ratification of the Constitution, when the Founding Fathers were faced with a central concern regarding the education of the citizenry. Within the framework of popular sovereignty, how could order be maintained within a free society? One popular solution was the notion that it would become women's responsibility—and not that of the masses—to educate the nation's sons for the role of virtuous citizen. Since that time, the notion of mother as civic guardian has remained.

5   Over the course of the 19th century, the effects of industrialization, immigration, and urbanization created new roles for men and women. Their spheres of activity, particularly of the white middle class, become more circumscribed, with males belonging to the public world of work and females increasingly relegated to the home. Such clearly defined gender roles necessitated that women—if they were to have a public role at all— use their motherhood as a lever in establishing rights and fomenting social change.

6   During this time, based on assumptions about the importance and purity of mothers' love, middle-class women were barraged with advice literature which told them how to be ladies and mothers. Catharine Beecher, a popular writer of this era, argued for the importance of women's domestic sphere, despite their lower status in the new democratic nation. Accepting rather than challenging gender roles, she claimed that the separate duties of males and females better served the work that society was to undertake. Beecher's position was effective in allowing women to leave the home for paid employment in at least one respect. Her suggestion that it was woman's responsibility as caretaker of children led to the widespread acceptability of females in teaching beginning in the 1830s and 1840s.

7   By the end of the 19th century, maternal activism reached its apex with the widespread acceptance and growth of women's national associations and Progressive reform fervor. In order to understand the motives and accomplishments of

women at the turn of the 20th century, it is important to remember that it was a time when they did not have the vote; *de jure* and *de facto* segregation were the norm; and white, middle-class women were seen as higher moral beings whose primary responsibility was caring for the young. Women took this assumed caretaking role and made it a national, public concern.

Two theories defined female activism in the public arena.   8 First, the notion of maternalism held that all women were mothers, or at least potential ones, and therefore needed to act on behalf of all children for the betterment of society. In the years prior to the 1920 ratification of the Nineteenth Amendment, maternalist rhetoric was employed by women at various points on the political spectrum. The language of maternalism was so pervasive that even the single, college-educated, liberal women of the settlement houses considered themselves "public mothers."

Another common understanding of the early 20th century—   9 municipal housekeeping—went hand-in-hand with maternalism. Women of this era were able to enter the public world, despite the widely held belief that they belonged at home, by arguing the community, city, or town was an extension of the walls of their homes. Women's and mothers' clubs around the nation established playgrounds and parks, raised money for new schools, and petitioned for child labor laws. It was an era in which females were to mother other people's children despite the obvious rub that white, middle-class women were imposing their values and expectations on a culturally, ethnically, and religiously diverse group of people. Americanization efforts dovetailed with these activities, as maternal reformers sought to promote the value of cleanliness, thrift, and temperance to the immigrants and lower classes.

These reforms were not scattered attempts, but were united   10 through women's national associations. Among the largest and most influential were the Woman's Christian Temperance Union, General Federation of Women's Clubs, National Association of Colored Women (NACW), and National Congress of Mothers (NCM). Figures on national membership reached into the millions.

In the 1910s, women's clubs saw through the short-lived mothers' pensions that provided income for widows so they would not   11 have to get jobs. Based on the belief that woman's most important role was as mother, the stipends were at one time available in 40 states. In what scholars consider to be a major political coup and precursor to New Deal legislation, women's clubs fought for the Sheppard-Towner Act, passed in 1921 and repealed in 1929. The legislation provided Federal funds for states to establish clinics to distribute advice and literature on pregnancy and childbirth with the goal of decreasing infant mortality rates. It was defeated as private physicians assumed the role of dispensing advice and providing maternal health care.

12   Perhaps the most-well-known maternal activist association was the National Congress of Mothers, today known as the National Parent-Teacher Association (PTA). The association was a major force behind the mothers' pensions and Sheppard-Towner Act. Alice Birney, the founder of the association, helped popularize the notion of motherhood as women's highest calling. She maintained that bonds of motherhood united females regardless of their race, class, or religion. During the years of the rise of women's college attendance, Birney insisted that education for motherhood took precedence over a college education. Her vision of the "highest and holiest of missions" was embraced by popular factions who wished to further relegate women to the home and a particular role during a time of suffrage agitation. After the 1920s, the NCM enjoyed its greatest growth spurt as it transformed to the National PTA and focused its energies on the public schools. After 1925, the rhetoric of motherhood was used less frequently as a political position by women throughout U.S. society.

13   Despite the liberal rhetoric of Progressive-era women reformers like Birney, white women in general did not actively involve black ones in their associations. At best, black women were to be helped, but not included. Nonetheless, black women engaged in separate yet parallel maternal reforms, but with the added challenge of racial discrimination. African-American females had their own organizations to address their own set of worries. For instance, during this era, they were five times as likely to work outside the home. Black women activists had little hope of influencing white institutions and policymakers, so they focused on community reform efforts and self-help. Their clubs engaged in a kind of social motherhood that provided much-needed services to the community, such as old-age homes, orphanages, day nurseries (the early 20th-century version of day care centers), and funds to help bury black friends, neighbors, and relatives.

14   African-American mothers had an additional burden, not only to raise their children to be good citizens, but to teach them to live in a racist society. Poverty, racial animosity, and violence, in addition to the belief that black women were immortal and prone to promiscuity, hindered them at every turn. Black females during the Progressive era challenged this view, and they, too, used the language of "highest womanhood" and "true motherhood" in their efforts at racial uplift. One key

difference between white and black women's clubs was that, unlike white females, who valued the stay-at-home mother, African-Americans were accepting of the black working mother out of necessity. Therefore, black female leaders valued the working mother as one who was worthy of respect.

The National Association of Colored Women was formed in 1896 to coordinate philanthropic and self-improvement efforts. Mary Eliza Church Terrell, a key figure nationally and in the NACW, was an outspoken advocate for racial understanding, and she used motherhood rhetoric to this end. Under Terrell's leadership, the NACW asserted black women sameness with all females, yet it worked for racial uplift. In so doing, Terrell linked motherhood to the condition of all African-Americans as she relied on images of mothers and children in her speeches and writings, thus speaking of the NACW in maternalist terms. Despite local successes, the NACW had little national influence within the context of Jim Crow segregation and as racial unrest increased as the 20th century wore on. 15

It strikes me as ironic that, prior to suffrage, women may have had greater political leverage since they were united as an oppressed class. To add yet another irony, suffrage eventually was won based on the contention that women's more-virtuous ways would clean up party politics, rather than on an argument about their equality to men. After 1920, the female voting bloc never materialized, as women in subsequent decades splintered into various factions and faced many different struggles and challenges. 16

Major ideological shifts took place after 1920. In the post-World War I and post-woman suffrage era, exemplary mothers were those who focused on their husbands and children. With this shift came the responsibility of the individual mother for children's problems. This is a stark contrast to the Progressive era emphasis on social factors of poverty and unhealthful conditions. 17

From the 1920s through the 1960s, mothers' activism retreated from the national stage. It appears to have taken place largely in local PTAs and other conservative venues. After 1970, as the women's movement gained intensity, females became further divided along political ideology. One major area of debate pitted mothers against nonmothers and working vs. nonworking mothers. Prior to 1920, all women were viewed as mothers or had the leverage to use maternalist rhetoric in their social reform efforts. These days, the status as a biological mother gives a woman that foundation for political change, as long as the issue connects to the care of children. 18

Nevertheless, something is wrong with both Progressive era and contemporary pictures. Men are absent from the equation. 19

The assumption that the care of children is the purview of women or that men are not caretakers hinders reform efforts in such areas as violence and poverty, as well as family issues like maternity/paternity leaves and adequate and affordable day care. While marginal advances in thinking about and accepting men's nurturer role can be noted since the 1970s, a major shift in thinking still needs to occur. The transformation would include men—as biological fathers or not—as those who have a stake in the care and development of children at home and in society at large. Men and women of different races and classes thus would work together for a better society.

Julie Quiroz-Martínez

IMMIGRANTS HIT THE ROAD FOR CIVIL RIGHTS

Julie Quiroz-Martínez is the associate director of the Center for Third World Organizing in Oakland, California. According to its website, the Center for Third World Organizing is "a racial justice organization dedicated to building a social justice movement led by people of color." Dedicated to promoting a multicultural society, this group works to bring about social change by using activist methods. The essay included here describes some of these methods; you might consider whether these types of activism are useful to a democratic culture as discussed by other authors in this section.

1   In 1961, 19-year-old Ruby Doris Smith arrived in Rock Hill, South Carolina, fully expecting the violent racist fury that awaited her and the other black students on her bus. At the time, the term "Freedom Ride" had not yet come into use. But everyone, including the menacing white thugs in the bus station, understood that these young people had come to challenge the oppressive state segregation laws that had been struck down, at least on paper, by the U.S. Supreme Court. So prepared for danger were the riders that some had given sealed letters to friends to mail in case they were killed.

I'm thinking of Ruby Doris Smith as I roll down Highway 80   2
in the brilliant Nevada sunshine, an Afghan homecare worker
on my right, a Chinese hotel housekeeper on my left, an
African-American custodian in the seat ahead. Each of these
women has taken her seat on the bus as part of the Immigrant
Workers Freedom Ride (IWFR) of 2003. Although theirs is far
from the same world confronted by Ruby Doris four decades
ago, the powerful moral example of the original riders embold-
ens them all.

The IWFR sprang from the imagination of organized labor,   3
which has recognized that its future depends on recruiting new
immigrant members. The IWFR's ambitious five-point agenda
reflects the demands of a diverse immigrant constituency: a new
legalization process for undocumented workers, an accessible
"path to citizenship," a commitment to family reunification for
immigrants waiting for relatives abroad, extension of labor protections to all workers and strengthening of civil rights and liberties to insure equal treatment of immigrants. For two weeks,
buses from ten cities—Seattle, Los Angeles, Houston, Chicago,
Minneapolis, Miami, San Francisco, Las Vegas, Boston and
Portland, Oregon—hit the road, bound for Washington, DC,
then a rally in Flushing Meadows, Queens, on October 4, where
the crowd surged to 100,000, according to organizers.

It's 6 P.M. on September 23 when my bus pulls up to a local   4
park in Reno, where hundreds of Latino families have gathered
to welcome the riders with a barbecue and soccer tournament.
The event's speakers include Raul, a Mexican day laborer from
San Jose, who describes the harassment of immigrants whose
only crime is "looking for work," and Maria, a hotel employee
who has not seen her children in El Salvador for fourteen years.

Bob Fulkerson, the fair-haired director of the Progressive   5
Leadership Alliance of Nevada, is elated by the turnout. "In
Reno, nothing has ever happened on this scale. Around here
the Department of Motor Vehicles will call in the INS when
people go to register their car."

In my nine hours on the IWFR bus, I heard a diverse range of   6
stories from the riders, underscoring the breadth of their needs
and interests. Many are union members. Most are foreign-born,
representing the whole spectrum of immigration status categories, from those without any documents to legal residents to
fully naturalized citizens. Olia tells me about how she fled
Afghanistan when the Taliban came to power, leaving behind
three children. "I never forget," she says, carefully crafting a
sentence in English. "I do job eighteen hours every day and save
all my money. After four years, my children come."

7   Or Helen, who speaks to me through an interpreter, and tells of migrating from Hong Kong to take a job as a seamstress in a sweatshop where she "couldn't even make minimum wage." Now she works at the San Francisco Marriott, where she helped lead her Chinese, Latino and Filipino co-workers through a successful six-year union contract fight.

8   There's Antonia (not her real name), who hesitates before she explains that she is an undocumented Mexican immigrant and a lesbian. She speaks softly in Spanish about her decision not to maintain a heterosexual facade for immigration officials scrutinizing her marriage to a U.S. citizen. "I had to sacrifice the opportunity for 'papers,'" she tells me, "because of my sexual identity."

9   Then there's Doretha, who talks energetically about what it's like to be a black woman and union steward at her predominantly immigrant worksite. "When you have a language barrier or anything they can put over on you, they'll use it," says Doretha. "It took me a long time to get it," she confesses. "The way they treat immigrants is how they treated us in the sixties."

10   Who, I wonder, are "they" now?

11   Of course, there are still traces of the "they" the 1960s Freedom Riders faced: the violent white mobs whose ugliness was captured forever in grainy black-and-white photos. On our bus, I've heard talk that white supremacists will be descending on Little Rock, where one of the IWFR buses is set to stop. I'm concerned, but know it's easy to become preoccupied with isolated flash points, harder to grapple with the insidious structures of racism that mold so much of the daily experience of immigrants and African-Americans.

12   "The Freedom Rides of the 1960s challenged the racist policies that were central to how the United States functioned," says Bill Fletcher Jr., who left a top-level job at the AFL-CIO to head the TransAfrica Forum. "Through the civil rights movement we won an end to legal racial segregation. But while the 'colored only' signs are gone," notes Fletcher, "racism has taken a different form. Back then, laws prevented blacks from buying certain homes. Now, it's that we can't get a loan, or that a realtor won't show us the house. The enemy is no longer as clear as when you had a George Wallace standing out there."

13   The vast diversity of today's immigrants further complicates the picture. It's no small task to forge a political identity among Haitians in Miami, Arabs in Chicago, Mexicans in Atlanta and Vietnamese in San Jose. To satisfy so many constituencies, the IWFR agenda needed to respond to a variety of concerns, with legalization topping Latinos' list of priorities and family reunification dominant among Asians' worries.

In the IWFR, as its name would suggest, the unifying experi- 14
ence emphasized is that of workers, though the riders describe a
struggle for both economic and racial justice. "In the eyes of the
dominant white culture and the federal government," asserts
observer Arnoldo Garcia of the National Network for Immigrant
and Refugee Rights, "'immigrant' has become a racialized category. The Immigrant Workers Freedom Ride is a complex call
for a new civil rights charter that includes the foreign-born."

Employers are often the frontline enemy in this racialized 15
reality. In the 1960s, and throughout U.S. history, employers
have used racial and ethnic differences to divide workers and
weaken their organizing. Today, as Doretha and others confirm, the strategy is still the same, though new tactics are
emerging. "Employers try to separate people," she says, "like
we don't have a common issue."

In recent years, the arsenal available to employers aiming to ex- 16
ploit divisions among workers has been expanding. For example,
in its *Hoffman Plastic Compounds, Inc. v. NLRB* decision last year,
the Supreme Court found that José Castro, an undocumented
worker illegally fired for his union organizing activities, could not
receive back pay because he was unauthorized to work. While the
ruling itself was quite narrow, its impact has been broad.
According to a recent report by the Mexican American Legal
Defense and Educational Fund and the National Employment
Law Project, "It has encouraged unscrupulous employers to engage in retaliation against unauthorized workers who claim violations of their workplace rights, and to make more claims that
these workers are unprotected by any labor laws. This in turn has
a chilling effect on workers' enforcement of their remaining
workplace rights." In other words, employees are seizing on the
ruling as a way to undermine worker unity by isolating and
threatening undocumented employees engaged in union activity.

Standing at the front of a bus in Richmond, Virginia, the 17
president of the Hotel Employees and Restaurant Employees
International Union (HERE), John Wilhelm, tackled this issue
head-on. "The Immigrant Workers Freedom Rides are telling
this country that we're not going to fall for divide and conquer
anymore," proclaimed Wilhelm to the busload of riders. "We
will not be divided by the color of our skin, nor by what country we come from, nor by the first language we learned. We
will not be divided into who the U.S. government says is 'illegal' and who the U.S. government says is 'legal.'" Listening to
the rally over a cell phone, I hear the riders cheering wildly.
"No human being is 'illegal!'" shouts Wilhelm, the riders breaking into thunderous applause.

18   Of all the differences between 1961 and now, the most striking is the relationship of the federal government to the riders.
Then, federal law was on the side of the Freedom Riders as
they set out to dismantle Southern Jim Crow laws. But today,
U.S. law is part of the problem. According to Cecilia Muñoz
of the National Council of La Raza, "The people on the
Immigrant Workers Freedom Ride are taking very serious
risks. Under the current legal regime, the attack could come
from the federal government."

19   Those fears were fulfilled all too vividly in Sierra Blanca,
Texas, when two IWFR buses were stopped at an INS check-
point. Speaking via cell phone, Kat Rodriguez tells me how the
Border Patrol boarded the buses, asking everyone, "Are you a
U.S. citizen?" After each rider presented cards asserting their
right to remain silent, the Border Patrol ordered the riders to
leave the bus one at a time. As they descended, loudly singing
"We Shall Overcome," Rodriguez could see "cars with blond
Anglos getting waved through without even being stopped."

20   "I was afraid," says Rodriguez, who works for the Coalition
for Human Rights/Indigenous Alliance Without Borders, in
Tucson, Arizona. "When one of the Border Patrol agents pointed
to me and said, 'Take this one too!' I didn't know if they were
going to bus some of us to a detention center." Instead, the riders were divided into groups and locked into 9 by 10 rooms
where, despite Border Patrol claims to the contrary, no one received water or food.

21   Rodriguez knew that under the Patriot Act the riders—
regardless of their place of birth or immigration status—could
have been detained it the government had somehow deemed
their mission subversive. "The Patriot Act took policies that have
long been used against immigrants," says Rodriguez, "and expanded them to citizens." According to Isabel Garcia, director of
the Pima County Legal Defender's Office and a Coalition for
Human Rights board member, "In theory, taking action against
the riders would have required showing some basis for suspicion. But, if we had been under some elevated 'terrorist alert,' a
whole other scenario would certainly have been possible."

22   To the riders' surprise, after four hours they were let go. "We
found out later that people were flooding the Border Patrol
with phone calls and faxes," Rodriguez explains. "People even
contacted the Department of Homeland Security and the
President. Unlike with the 147 migrants who have died at the
U.S.-Mexico border this year, we knew the whole world was
watching our bus."

23   This tug of war between fear and determination to fight reminds me of Nabil, the 23-year-old son of Indian immigrants,

with whom I rode to Reno. Nabil is a volunteer with the Council on American-Islamic Relations (CAIR), who asked him to represent them on the IWFR. "I have friends who say, 'Being a young Muslim male you should avoid getting into political issues.' They say, 'You're putting yourself in jeopardy of being profiled by the government in the future.' It's a real possibility."

Very real. In fact, since 9/11, more than 83,000 Arab, Middle   24
Eastern and Asian men have voluntarily complied with new "Special Registration" requirements that include fingerprinting and monitoring. This past June the federal government quietly began taking action to seek deportation of 13,000 of these men, none of whom had been found to have terrorist ties. Mohamed Nimer, research director at CAIR, describes "a climate of fear and apprehension" among Arabs and Muslims, "where people don't know who is going to be next. We're seeing search and seizure tactics targeting people who don't fully agree with government policy."

At the core of the IWFR is an evolving and sometimes rocky   25
relationship between organized labor and the broader immigrant rights community, which have strong common interests but also some different priorities. For example, unions would surely go to the mat for repeal of laws sanctioning employees for hiring undocumented workers, and are likely to oppose any kind of temporary guest worker program. Immigrant rights groups, however, might see demilitarization of the border or access to higher education as the first order of business, and might be open to some forms of temporary work if accompanied by significant rights and protections. "These relationships are being made up as we go along," observes Cecilia Muñoz. "You have to remember that the AFL has only been on the right side of the issue for three years," she says, referring to the labor federation's February 2000 decision to actively support the rights of undocumented workers. "It's amazing progress," Muñoz concludes. "But there are growing pains."

Those growing pains are being felt in Nevada, as Bob Fulkerson   26
attests. "Here in Reno, labor has been willing to work in coalition, to make shared decisions. But labor is still the 800-pound gorilla in the room. They're the most powerful political entity around. They've got 50,000 members. They do mailings in five languages. But there's not one immigrant rights group in the whole state." Nonetheless, a labor/immigrant rights alliance makes strategic sense. "The immigrant rights movement has been doing heroic work on nothing but fumes," says Frank Sharry, executive director of the National Immigration Forum. "A real commitment from labor is like putting a turbocharged engine on a canoe."

But, Sharry cautions, the IWFR should not count on sweep-   27
ing legislative changes in the short term. "The only things that

have a real chance of passing in 2004 are the 'Dream Act' and the farmworker deal. One is legalization for college kids and the other is legalization for a sector of farmworkers."

28   Chung-Wha Hong, advocacy director for the New York Immigration Coalition, is braced for storms ahead. Hong points out that while bipartisan support exists for some form of legalization, "Republicans are going to want to exchange it for more enforcement—along the lines of a national ID card." Hong admits, "Since the IWFR doesn't have a specific legislative agenda, there have been times when we've wondered, 'What are we really supporting?' But the whole point is to create a new political environment, to build new relationships and an infrastructure for when there is legislation." As Sharry notes, "The collective goal is really about building a movement that succeeds no matter who is President in 2005." Ultimately, the IWFR is less about legislative politics than about envisioning an ideal of justice and compelling the public to recognize it. In the words of former Freedom Rider and Congressional Black Caucus member John Lewis, "The most important purpose of this ride is to establish a coalition conscience."

Douglas Henton, John Melville, and Kim Walesh

THE RISE OF THE NEW CIVIC REVOLUTIONARIES: ANSWERING THE CALL TO STEWARDSHIP IN OUR TIMES

This article represents not only a collaborative writing effort, but collaborative business projects sponsored by the organization for which all three work, Collaborative Economics. Doug Henton has worked for over 20 years to bring industry, government, education, research, and community leaders together around specific collaborative projects to improve regional competitiveness. John Melville is an expert in collaborative theory and has worked to bring that theory to policy initiatives in the public and private sector. Kim Walesh works to help public and private leaders to develop and implement collaborative strategies to create better communities. In this article, the three express the need for "new civic revolutionaries." How does their definition of "revolutionaries" square with those of such leaders as Martin Luther King or Mahatma Gandhi?

In the mid-1700s, a grassroots movement began as leaders in small communities across the American colonies recognized their common destiny as an independent nation that was based on the revolutionary principle of liberty. Coming together through "committees of correspondence," future leaders of the American Revolution, including Ben Franklin, John Adams, and Thomas Jefferson, began to share their thoughts. The voices of Virginia, Pennsylvania, Massachusetts, and other colonies joined; they spoke first through the Declaration of Independence and later through the Constitution and *The Federalist Papers*. These leaders from local communities were not looking for greatness, but greatness was thrust upon them at a critical moment. We remember the heritage of these American revolutionaries. 1

Similar grassroots movements have occurred periodically in American history. Local leaders first discuss ideas in their communities and then join together to create sweeping change for the nation. This practice was true during the debate about slavery before the U.S. Civil War and the debates about the role of trusts before the Progressive era of the early 1900s. The civil rights movement was preceded by community organizing across the South in the 1950s. The environmental movement was inspired by Rachael Carson's book *Silent Spring* in the 1960s and local efforts to fight pollution. 2

A new grassroots movement is under way in the regions of the United States today. Once again, a movement is beginning in communities across the nation, urged ahead by leaders who see the need for fundamental change in how their regions define and solve problems and ultimately how they are governed. They represent a new kind of regional civic leadership attuned to the economic and social realities of our times. Traditional, top-down leadership styles and stovepipe government models simply do not work in the fast-paced, global economy and diverse society of today. Business, civic, and government leaders know that the old way of governing is simply not working anymore in solving critical economic, social, and environmental challenges, especially as these issues become more interdependent. Although the old model is failing, new models have not yet fully emerged to take their place. We are in an uncertain 3 time of transition, similar to the 1760s, 1850s, 1900s, and 1950s, just before major change.

4   In particular, a generation born after World War II—tempered by the social turmoil of the 1960s, the political disruptions of the 1970s, and the economic turbulence of the 1980s and 1990s—must now rise to the challenge. Many people who are part of the large baby boom generation have a commitment to place that is based on the communitarian values of the 1960s, combined with an entrepreneurial spirit forged by the realities of the emerging new economy. Many people of this generation are responsible for igniting the beginning of the grassroots revolution in the regions of America during the 1990s.

5   Just as Franklin, Adams, and Jefferson found each other to forge the American Revolution; just as Abraham Lincoln melded the forces of antislavery to save the Union; just as Teddy Roosevelt rallied the elements of an emerging progressive movement to fight the trusts; and just as Martin Luther King, Jr., coalesced the civil rights movement, the next decade may find the coming together of new civic revolutionaries to write the next chapter in the American story. We may need new "committees of correspondence" among our regional civic leaders, a "Regionalist Papers" to marshal the intellectual arguments for new forms of distributed governance, and new kinds of dialogue with lasting impact—like that of Abraham Lincoln and Stephen Douglas, who debated slavery, or like that of generations of civil rights leaders who raised the consciousness of the nation at important times during American history.

6   This time, new "regional stewards" may seek to achieve the moral imperatives of freedom, equality, and opportunity through more decentralized means than through centralized national government because conditions have changed. We need flexible, innovative responses rooted in collaboration that meet real community needs, rather than the simple top-down, "mainframe," one-size-fits-all models of the earlier Progressive era. In fact, centralized means left over from that era have themselves become captive of special interests, often leading to gridlock. Although the ends may remain the same, the means must change to meet new economic and social realities.

7   In our book *Civic Revolutionaries: Igniting the Passion for Change in America's Communities,* we describe the journey of some of these new civic revolutionaries, working on promising experiments in regional stewardship. They are practicing a new style of civic leadership because it is working. As "visionary pragmatists," they see the value in working more collaboratively to solve complex problems on the basis of fundamental principles and shared values. Together, they may change how our country solves problems—one region at a time, and then

joining together as streams become rivers, building to a tidal wave of change across America.

Guiding Principles for Civic Revolutionaries: Reconciling Competing American Values

Following the example of the nation's founders and subsequent 8 generations, these new civic revolutionaries are grappling with the timeless tensions of the American Experience. The struggle between competing, positive values (such as the individual and the community) is as old as the nation itself, but every generation must address it anew. The task of every generation is to seek and find the "points of reconciliation" between these competing values—enabling the American Experiment to move forward.

The new civic revolutionaries are driving promising experi- 9 ments in regions across the country—efforts to reconcile important American values in their communities in our time. Taken together, these efforts are clarifying the practical challenges and the type of transformation necessary to achieve reconciliation among these American values. Their work is beginning to help us answer the question, "What does success look like for our time?" In other words, what are the guiding principles for reconciliation of important American values? Given their experience so far, the work of these new civic revolutionaries suggests a number of principles for reconciliation, an answer to the question of what success may look like.

Create Common Purpose, to Reconcile the Values of Individual and Community

- People voluntarily exercise their freedom to build a community of place, believing they will gain more in social benefits than they give up in individual liberty.
- Competing interests form working relationships that are based on complementary values and roles.
- Complex problems transform into manageable tasks, and independent efforts are channeled into collaborative action grounded in simple but elegant guiding principles

Build Webs of Responsibility, to Reconcile the Values of Trust and Accountability

- Both strong expectations and authentic opportunities exist to participate in civic affairs through open and influential organizations as well as inclusive and catalytic processes.

- Written agreements formalize the basic lines of accountability among stakeholders, creating a foundation for
  building trust and confidence in the system.

Strengthen the Vital Cycle, to Reconcile the Values of Economy and Society

- Businesses prosper as part of the fabric of communities
  by being both globally competitive and deeply rooted to
  place.
- The economy is considered an essential part of the community and operates in a productive relationship with
  people and the environment.
- The economy is an expanding source of opportunity and
  mobility for all, rather than a fixed source of opportunity for some and not for others.

Make the Creative Connection, to Reconcile the Values of People and Place

- People and places are on a shared pathway to better living standards.
- People and places feed off each other in a creative interaction that fuels economic and community vitality.

Create a Vigilance for Renewal, to Reconcile the Values of Change and Continuity

- The community expects constant, dynamic change,
  seeking to leaven the negative impacts and leverage the
  positive benefits while preserving core values.
- The community is purposeful about filling its leadership
  pipeline, expanding the sources of leaders and excusing
  no one from service.

Build a Resilience of Place, to Reconcile the Values of Idealism and Pragmatism

- The community generates powerful ideas that renew
  core values in light of current circumstances, providing
  the glue that joins idealism and pragmatism.
- The community has an environment that encourages
  individuals leaders from all walks of life to answer the
  call to stewardship, to make a long-term commitment to
  place and play their role in the continuing American
  Experiment.

Practical Roles for Civic Revolutionaries: Igniting the Passion for Community Change

Civic Revolutionaries explores sets of competing American val-   10
ues, from their historic revolutionary roots to their contemporary effects, and shows how the current generation is trying to
reconcile them for our time. We do not presume to offer an exclusive list of competing values, nor offer a set of choices between "good and evil." Although clear-cut, black-and-white
choices will always exist, much of what happens in communities today is more complex, operating in a gray area where no
one can stake claim to the moral high ground, where reasonable people can disagree. However, even in this gray area, a
case could be made for other sets of competing values—and it
should be made if those values need to be reconciled for a
community or region to move forward.

   Our purpose, instead, is to suggest that Americans can find   11
ample common ground in the process of reconciling positive
American values—values that compete with each other and
can clash in a struggle for supremacy, creating a cascade of
negative consequences for people and communities. By focusing on how to reconcile and maximize the positive impacts of
these American values, civic revolutionaries can ignite the passion for community change.

   Our purpose is also to identify practical insights from the field   12
of experimentation, strategies and techniques that might be useful to civic revolutionaries in regions across the country. On the
basis of these experiences, and rooted in the experience of the nation's founders, we believe there are three major roles that civic
revolutionaries play in igniting the passion for change and navi-
gating the process of experimentation in their communities.
These roles mirror the experience and beliefs of John W. Gardner,
for whom life was a continuous cycle of reflection, decision, and
action. For today's civic revolutionaries, like those before them,
change is a continuous cycle of *discovery, decision,* and *action.*

Discover: They Build a Convincing Case for Change

Civic revolutionaries build a convincing case for change in their   13
communities, accumulating information, ideas, and allies in the
process. They diagnose the challenges facing their communities,
the tensions between competing values that must be addressed
in new ways. They creatively describe, reframe, measure, and
connect issues and root causes. They try to understand what is
working, what is not working, and what might work. They seek
out the experiences of other communities, to expand the view of

what's possible and to find other civic revolutionaries who might be able to help them frame problems or develop solutions. At the same time, they seek out and discover allies in their communities, individuals who can help make the case and become part of the coalition for change.

Decide: They Make Critical Choices in Experimentation

14   Civic revolutionaries use what they learn from the discovery process to make decisions. They make choices from among the many actions they could take to tackle their challenges. Although they may consult with those in other communities and tap into national sources of research and ideas to consider options for action, they themselves sort through different ideas and decide on how best to apply what they have learned. They decide about focus, scope, and priority in designing experiments in community change—immediate actions connected to an overall vision (or story) of change that will create opportunities for continuous feedback and adaptation.

Drive: They Mobilize Allies for Change

15   Civic revolutionaries are relentless in their drive for change. They are thoughtful and reflective in preparation and in decision making about what to do, but they neither succumb to "paralysis by analysis" nor engage in an endless search for the perfect solution. They embody the spirit of experimentation; they reflect, decide, and act, then reflect on initial results, make more decisions, pursue new actions, and start the process again. They drive a realistic, opportunistic, and adaptable experimentation process.

Renewing America's Social Compact to Meet the Challenges of a New Era

16   By playing a practical role to advance core principles of reconciliation, today's civic revolutionaries are, in effect, renewing America's social compact. Through their actions, they are redefining the relationship between Americans and their communities, regions, and nation—to better meet the challenges of a new era. In fact, we may have reached a stage similar to the period before the American Revolution, the Civil War, the Progressive Era, and the civil rights movement where a new social compact will emerge from experimentation at the grass roots. What shifts have to be made to create a new social compact that is founded on the promising experiments of civic

revolutionaries across America? They are redefining the relationship between the values of:

- *Individuals and community*—shifting from compromise, conflict, and chaos to choice, complementarity, and cohesion
- *Trust and accountability*—shifting from skeptical bystanders and unclear responsibilities to engaged shareholders and mutual accountability
- *Economy and society*—shifting from short-term speculation to long-term investment, from uneven access to universal mobility
- *People and place*—shifting from separate paths to shared destinies, from common places to creative environments
- *Change and continuity*—shifting from stability as an expectation to change as a given, from leadership roulette to leadership renewal
- *Idealism and pragmatism*—shifting from wishful thinking to visionary pragmatism, from diverse leaders to regional stewards

To complete these shifts in turn requires additional changes: 17
movement from top-down to decentralized solutions, interest group politics to public engagement, and widening inequality to shared prosperity. It won't happen overnight, and it won't be easy. But the seeds are germinating in communities across America. A new social compact will have to include both rights and responsibilities; as John W. Gardner was fond of saying, "Freedom and responsibility, liberty and duty. That's the deal." Harvard professor Michael J. Sandel claims that a new political movement requires a new public philosophy, one that draws on stronger notions of citizenship and civic virtue than those informing present politics. Central among these notions is an emphasis on the civic consequences of economic arrangements, what he calls the political economy of citizenship.[1] Such a public philosophy would be driven by a set of simple rules, based on ethical principles, that help guide complex behavior to address the economic and social challenges of today.

Are we on our way to a new compact? In the 1990s, we went 18
too far with our faith in the marketplace, losing touch with Adam Smith's original vision of the importance of "moral sentiments" (or sympathy for others) as a guiding principle behind the invisible hand of markets. According to author Peter Dougherty, a new civic economics is emerging, one that involves "the construction of a civic infrastructure that attracts and stimulates markets, the economics of large scale public

enterprises (such as the G.I. Bill) without large bureaucracies, the economics of expanded assets and property ownership."[2]

19   Perhaps the new compact will hark back to the famous nineteenth-century Cambridge University economist Alfred Marshall, who pronounced in an address to the Royal Economic Society in 1907 that the "age of chivalry is not over. . . . No one can lay his head on his pillow at peace with himself, who is not giving some time and substance to diminish the number of those who cannot earn a reasonable income and thus have an opportunity of living a noble life."[3]

20   What makes the creation of a new social compact possible? The American Revolution, the U.S. Civil War, the Vietnam War and other conflicts have helped to mobilize the nation and bring forth new leaders. Ben Franklin, John Adams, Thomas Jefferson, George Washington, Alexander Hamilton, James Madison, and others were not heroes prior to the Revolutionary War, but they found each other during those fateful years and created a nation based on fundamental principles that constitute the foundation for the American social compact. The Civil War brought forth the wisdom of Abraham Lincoln, who reconciled the promise of the Declaration of Independence with the practicality of the Constitution and renewed the nation's social compact.

21   Economic crises and excesses can also spur change, as with the downturns of the late 1800s and 1930s, which stimulated new progressive movements and the environmental movement in the 1970s. Demographic shifts and social forces can also stimulate change; they helped give rise to the civil rights movement of the 1950s and 1960s, and the women's movement of the 1970s. According to Ted Halstead of the New America Foundation:

> America has so far experimented with three social contracts, each of which reflected the political forces of its time. The purpose of the first . . . was to found the nation. The goal of the second was to put it back together after the Civil War. The third—first articulated in FDR's New Deal and later expanded in Lyndon B. Johnson's Great Society—sought to build a mass middle-class society by relying on ambitious government programs and new economic regulation. It is now time for a fourth American social contract. To fit the post-industrial age, it must be able to reconcile competing demands of flexibility and fairness [and] will require new roles and responsibilities for all three parties to the contract: government, business, and citizenry.[4]

In the early years of the twenty-first century, a series of dis- 22
ruptions have opened a window for change. In rapid succession, we experienced the implosion of the Internet bubble,
followed by the hard new realities of economic slowdown.
These events created a wake-up call after a decade of prosperity. The events of September 11, 2001, have stimulated a new
sense of communal urgency, while the collapse of Enron and
other corporate scandals have created a crisis of confidence in
business. Taken together, these disruptions may stimulate a
new willingness to leave behind old structures and experiment
with new approaches grounded in core values. It could hasten
the renewal of America's social compact.

Renewing America's social compact was a core concern of 23
John W. Gardner during his long and distinguished life. It is in
his memory and with the purpose of continuing his work that
the national Alliance for Regional Stewardship has launched
the John W. Gardner Academy for Regional Stewardship. The
purpose of the academy is much like that of Plato's Academy
and Aristotle's Lyceum—it will explicitly link principles with
practice, reflection with action. It will be based on the idea
that public philosophy should be an active way of life, not simply a way of thinking or discourse. Along with others, it will
help civic revolutionaries renew America's social compact—
first community by community and region by region, and then
ultimately between Americans and their nation. Near the end
of his life, Gardner issued this call to action:

> Most Americans welcome the voice that lifts them out of
> themselves. They want to be better people. They want to help
> make this a better country . . . what you can do is to awaken
> them to the possibilities within themselves. Awaken them to
> what *they* can do for their country, the country of their chil-
> dren and their children's children.
>
> So those who have not succumbed to the contemporary
> disaffection and alienation must speak the world of life to
> their fellow Americans. It is not a liberal or conservative
> issue. It is not Democrat versus Republican. It is a question
> of whether we are going to settle into a permanent state of
> self-absorption or show the vigor and purpose that becomes
> us. We don't want it said that after a couple of great cen-
> turies we let the American Experiment disintegrate.[5]

Following in the footsteps of the founders and later civic 24
revolutionaries of the nineteenth and twentieth centuries, the

time has come for this generation of Americans to take its
place as stewards of the American Experiment.

NOTES

1. Sandel, M. J. "The Political Economy of Citizenship." In S. Greenberg
   and T. Skocpol Yale (eds.), *The New Majority*. New Haven, Conn.: Yale
   University Press, 1997.
2. Dougherty, P. *Who's Afraid of Adam Smith? How the Market Got Its
   Soul*. New York: Wiley, 2002, p. 16.
3. Marshall, A. "The Social Possibilities of Chivalry." (Address to the
   Royal Economic Society, London, 1907.)
4. Halstead, T. "The American Paradox." *Atlantic Monthly*, Jan. 2003,
   p. 124.
5. O'Connell, B. *Civil Society: The Underpinnings of American Democracy*.
   Hanover, N.H.: University Press of New England, 1999, p. xv.

What Is the Scope of Government Regulation I? Legislating Information, Guns, and Tobacco

Bill Nelson

THE RIGHT TO PRIVACY

Bill Nelson is a Democratic Senator for the state of Florida, first elected in 2000. He has also served as member of the House of Representatives and as a member of the Armed Forces and Committee on Foreign Relations, where he works with the subcommittee on Operations and Terrorism. For this reason, his thoughts on the relationship between the need for security regulations and procedures and the need to protect individual freedoms of Americans is particularly exigent and informed. This essay was first published as part of a pro/con debate presented in Congressional Digest, *a periodical that informs readers of current issues by giving "both sides of important public policy controversies." (Of course, there are often more than two sides—always room for you to join the conversation with an alternative viewpoint.) The contrary viewpoint in this case is taken by John Poindexter, former director of the Information Awareness Office; his essay is also included.*

I realize that in this technologically advanced age, in order to go after the bad guys, in order to be able to stop them before they hit us, clearly there has to be the clandestine means of penetrating the communications that are going on. That is very important to the defense of this country and our citizens. At the same time, the constitutional rights of privacy must always be foremost in our minds as we battle this new, elusive kind of enemy called the terrorist.

2   I start, first, with words from a very famous American who had something significant to say about privacy, Justice Louis Brandeis, in which he argued, in a 1928 case, that the Framers of our Constitution—and I will quote Justice Brandeis—". . . sought to protect Americans in their beliefs, their thoughts, their emotions, and their sensations." Justice Brandeis went on, that the Framers of the Constitution had ". . . conferred, as against the government, the right to be let alone—the most comprehensive of rights and the right most valued by civilized man."

3   Now, Justice Brandeis wrote those words in a dissenting opinion in a 1928 case involving a liquor dealer who was convicted by evidence gathered through a wiretap, way back then, early in the last century. That case arose because technology had granted the government an increased ability to peer inside people's private lives—then, in 1928, a wiretap.

4   The technology increased governmental authority, forcing the Supreme Court to evaluate and redefine the boundaries between freedom and governmental power. The technological advances also stimulated an important national debate about the balance between individual freedom and the legitimate needs of law enforcement.

5   Now we are at a similar crossroads, and those words ring out to us today as we go about trying to balance the rights between individual freedom and the legitimate needs of the government to penetrate terrorist cells.

6   Technology has advanced faster than the Nation's norms and the laws for managing them. Modern technology makes possible unprecedented intrusions into the private lives of American people. This ability, coupled with increasing governmental demands to use that technology, poses a grave threat to personal privacy and personal freedom.

7   This past week, I was riveted by the news of the revelations about how the Department of Defense is developing a computer system to grant intelligence and law enforcement authorities the power to secretly access ordinary citizens' private information, including email, financial statements, and medical records—to access that private information without the protections of a court order.

8   Clearly, in this post-9/11 world, we need to develop tools that will enable our government to keep us safe from terrorists by disrupting their operations. But these tools need to be balanced against the protection of innocent people's right to privacy. If the right to privacy means anything, it is the right of the individual to be free from unwarranted governmental intrusion.

So what riveted my attention were reports, first in the *New* 9
York Times, the *Washington Post*, and then in the *Washington*
Times, that the so-called Total Information Awareness
program—located in DARPA [Defense Advanced Research
Projects Agency], deep inside the Department of Defense—
would make possible unwarranted governmental intrusions
such as we have never seen before.

It is disturbing that we are developing a research system 10
that, if ever used, would violate the Privacy Act as well as a lot
of other Federal laws on unreasonable searches of private information without probable cause, which is the typical standard that needs to be met. That is why we go to a judge to get
an order allowing us to intrude on such things as searches, as
seizures, on such things as wiretaps.

I have a serious concern about whether this type of program, 11
called Total Information Awareness, can be used responsibly. So
while we investigate and learn more about it, I intend to speak
out to the Congress and to the committees on which I am privileged to serve—including the Armed Services Committee—to
speak out that we need to oversee this program to ensure that
there is no abuse of law-abiding individuals' privacy.

It has been reported that this program is authorized or en- 12
dorsed by the homeland security legislation pending now in the
Senate. And that does not appear to be the case. While it doesn't
specifically tend to be the case, this legislation, the Homeland
Security Department, does include a provision creating a research division within the new Homeland Security Department.
It would develop, among other things, information technologies
similar to the Total Information Awareness Program.

While I strongly support funding for new research, and I cer- 13
tainly believe that we must use our technological advantage to
defeat our enemies, at the same time I think we better take a
breath, be very cautious that any new research done in the
Defense Department or within the new proposed Department of
Homeland Security does not threaten our personal freedoms.

I also have grave concerns that this information awareness 14
program is being directed by someone who is very controversial: Retired Rear Admiral [John] Poindexter, the former
Reagan Administration official who was convicted in, you remember, the Iran-Contra story. There is a very legitimate question about whether or not he is the appropriate person to head
such a sensitive program.

When I first came here, I became concerned that, back in 15
1999, we allowed banks and insurance companies to merge,
but we didn't protect individuals' privacy. It would shock people to know that if you go have a physical exam in order to get
a life insurance policy and if that life insurance company is

acquired by a bank, that the access to those individually identifiable medical records is unlimited, without your personal consent, to anywhere within that bank holding company.

16   You might also be interested to know that recently we had the issuance of rules by the Bush Administration on medical record privacy, but there was a huge omission in that pharmaceutical companies could go to drugstore chains, pay the drugstore chain for the names and ability to communicate to individual people who had prescriptions, and then that pharmaceutical chain could contact that individual patient, asking them, soliciting them to change their medication to a different kind of medication, one that would be within the generic equivalent or a different brand name than the one that the physician had prescribed for them.

17   That is an invasion of personal privacy. Yet it is allowed under the rules of the new Administration.

18   Take, for example, the case two weeks ago in Fort Myers, Florida. Suddenly a dumpster was overflowing with tax records, bank records, Social Security numbers, all kinds of personally identifiable financial information not properly disposed of by the bank subsidiary. The bank says there is no such law. So I filed a bill to protect individuals' personal financial privacy. Lo and behold, another invasion of privacy, identity theft, more recently, in Orlando, Florida—another dumpster. Now all of a sudden, one of the two large pharmaceutical drugstore chains dumps all of the prescriptions in the dumpster, along with the bottles. As a result, the personally identifiable medical information is there for the public to see from someone pilfering the dumpster. Privacy is something we better be concerned about.

John Poindexter
THE NEED FOR INFORMATION AWARENESS

At the time that John Poindexter wrote the essay included here in the point/counterpoint discussion for Congressional Digest *in April 2003, he was the director of the Information*

Awareness Office. Poindexter, in a presentation about his work, noted that

> *The Information Awareness Office at DARPA is about creating technologies that would permit us have both security and privacy. More than just making sure that different databases can talk to one another, we need better ways to extract information from those unified databases, and to ensure that the private information on innocent citizens is protected. The main point is that we need a much more systematic approach. A variety of tools, processes and procedures will be required to deal with the problem, but they must be integrated by a systems approach built around a common architecture to be effective. Total Information Awareness—a prototype system—is our answer. We must be able to detect, classify, identify, and track terrorists so that we may understand their plans and act to prevent them from being executed.*

Soon after the essay below was published, however, Poindexter resigned his post at the Information Office (in August 2003). In his letter of resignation, he wrote:

> *The United States and free-world continue to face an enormous threat to our freedom and way of life by those who choose to use terrorism to destroy what we cherish—the ultimate threat to our privacy. The Senate version of the Defense Appropriations Bill going into conference with the House on September 2 eliminates funding for most of the counter terrorism programs of my office—both the non-controversial as well as the controversial. I hope a compromise can be reached that will permit a continuation of at least the non-controversial parts. It is my sincerest hope that our country's children and grandchildren can understand that, in my opinion, the complex issues facing this nation today may not be solved using historical solutions and rhetoric that has been applied in the past, and that it may be useful to explore complex solutions that sometimes involve controversial technical concepts in order to rediscover the privacy foundations of this nation's strength and the basis for its freedoms. (You can view the full letter at http://www.washingtonpost.com/wp-srv/ nation/transcripts/poindexterletter.pdf.)*

Poindexter's remarks on both occasions lay out his belief that information collection is crucial to protect our society. This conversation, between the right to privacy and the exigencies of protecting our country against terrorism, is likely to go on for a long time.

1   The world has changed dramatically since the Cold War when there existed two superpowers. During the years I was in the White House, it was relatively simple to identify our intelligence collection targets. It was sometimes hard to collect the intelligence, but the targets were clear.

2   Today, we are in a world of asymmetries. The most serious asymmetric threat facing the United States is terrorism, a threat characterized by collections of people loosely organized in shadowy networks that are difficult to identify and define and whose goals are the destruction of our way of life.

3   The intelligence collection targets are thousands of people whose identities and whereabouts we do not always know. It is somewhat analogous to the antisubmarine warfare problem of finding submarines in an ocean of noise—we must find the terrorists in a world of noise, understand what they are planning, and develop options for preventing their attacks. If we are to preserve our national security, we must figure out a way of combating this threat.

4   I think the solution is largely associated with information technology. We must become much more efficient and more clever in the ways we find new sources of data, mine information from the new and old, generate information, make it available for analysis, convert it to knowledge, and create actionable options.

5   We must also break down the stovepipes—at least punch holes in them. By this, I mean we must share and collaborate between agencies, and create and support high-performance teams operating on the edges of existing organizations. Tools are needed to facilitate these collaborations, and to support these teams that work to ensure our security.

6   The Information Awareness Office at DARPA is about creating technologies that would permit us to have both security and privacy. More than just making sure that different databases can talk to one another, we need better ways to extract information from those unified databases, and to ensure that the private information on innocent citizens is protected.

7   The main point is that we need a much more systematic approach. A variety of tools, processes, and procedures will be required to deal with the problem, but they must be integrated

by a systems approach built around a common architecture to be effective.

Total Information Awareness—a prototype system—is our answer. We must be able to detect, classify, identify, and track terrorists so that we may understand their plans and act to prevent them from being executed. To protect our rights, we must ensure that our systems track the terrorists and those that mean us harm.   8

IAO programs are focused on making Total Information Awareness, TIA, real. This is a high-level, visionary, functional view of the worldwide system—somewhat oversimplified. One of the significant new data sources that needs to be mined to discover and track terrorists is the transaction space. If terrorist organizations are going to plan and execute attacks against the United States, their people must engage in transactions and they will leave signatures in this information space.   9

Currently, terrorists are able to move freely throughout the world, to hide when necessary, to find sponsorship and support, to operate in small, independent cells, and to strike infrequently, exploiting weapons of mass effects and media response to influence governments. We are painfully aware of some of the tactics that they employ. This low-intensity/ low-density form of warfare has an information signature. We must be able to pick this signal out of the noise.   10

Certain agencies and apologists talk about connecting the dots, but one of the problems is to know which dots to connect. The relevant information extracted from these data must be made available in large-scale repositories with enhanced semantic content for easy analysis to accomplish this task. The transactional data will supplement our more conventional intelligence collection.   11

While our goal is total information awareness, there will always be uncertainty and ambiguity in trying to understand what is being planned. That's why our tools have to build models of competing hypotheses. That is, we need to bring people with diverse points of view together in a collaborative environment where there is access to all source data, discovery tools, and model-building tools.   12

Collaboration has not been so important in the past when problems were less complex, but now it is essential. And tools have to make the analysis process more efficient, to properly explore the multiple possibilities.   13

This is the analytical environment. I could have called it the intelligence community, but in the case of counterterrorism, it is broader to include law enforcement, friendly allies, outside experts, etc. A similar environment exists for the policy and   14

operations community, but the functions and tools are different. The mission here is to take the competing hypotheses from the analytical environment and estimate a range of plausible futures. The objective is to identify common nodes, representing situations that could occur, and to explore the probable impact of various actions or interventions that authorities might make in response to these situations.

15   The Information Awareness Office has a number of ongoing projects to address the functional requirements of this vision, and we will be starting new projects to complete the picture.

16   The overarching program that binds IAO's efforts together is the Total Information Awareness system. The primary goal of TIA is the integration and assured transition of components developed in the programs Genoa, Genoa II, Genisys, EELD [Evidence Extraction and Link Discovery], WAE [Wargaming the Asymmetric Environment], TIDES [Translingual Information, Detection, Extraction, and Summarization], HumanID, and Bio-Surveillance.

17   TIA will develop a modular system architecture using open standards that will enable a spiral development effort that will allow the insertion of new components when they are available. We will produce a complete, end-to-end, closed-loop prototype system in a realistic environment.

18   To accomplish this, we will supplement the programs in IAO with commercial and other government components to rapidly implement early versions of the TIA system at our R&D [research and development] laboratory. We have already begun a spiral development and experiment program in conjunction with Army partners. Over the next few years we will continuously add functionality to the system as components become available.

19   Where will IAO's projects get data in order to develop their algorithms? To proceed with development, without intruding on domestic or foreign concerns, we are creating a database of synthetic transactions using a simulation model. This will generate billions of transactions constituting realistic background noise. We will insert into this noise simulated transactions by a red team acting as a terrorist organization to see if we can detect and understand this activity.

20   In the Genisys program we will be investigating the problem of developing technologies that can give us the capability to detect foreign terrorist activities in this transaction space and achieve enhanced privacy for the innocents.

21   There are significant information policy issues related when considering data mining in actual transaction spaces. The United States, and other countries as well, have just begun to

consider some of the issues and consequences. There are ways in which technology can help preserve rights and protect people's privacy while helping to make us all safer. We are taking a number of steps to begin a reasoned discussion of the policy issues, imbued with knowledge of technology capabilities.

DARPA's Information Systems and Technology (ISAT) panel has been tasked with a summer study on how we can achieve the necessary security we need and still have privacy. Discussions have been started with the National Academy of Sciences to do a longer-range study on Information Policy for the InfoSpace of the Future.   22

We believe that total information awareness is a very difficult problem and in the tradition of the very hard problems that DARPA has addressed in the past. We think we have some very good ideas about how to solve the problem. IAO has an open BAA [broad agency announcement] that was issued last March and will be open for a year. We will be funding some of the good ideas that we have already received, but if you have good ideas that we haven't seen yet, please tell us about them. The BAA is on the DARPA website.   23

I believe the ultimate solution to countering terrorism requires a co-evolution in four areas: technology, process/operations, policy, and culture. Our focus is on developing the technology, the first area, and making sure that decisions in the other areas, such as policy, are knowledgeable about what is possible and what isn't. It's an exciting area, and I am proud of the contributions that we will all be collectively making to national security.   24

Paul Starobin

DAWN OF THE
DADDY STATE

Paul Starobin writes for, among others, the Columbia Journalism Review, *the* National Journal, *and* The Atlantic Monthly. *In 2004, he completed a four-year assignment as Moscow Bureau Chief for* Business Week, *where he wrote a series of articles on the Russian economy. The piece included here was published in June 2004 in* The Atlantic Monthly, *which describes its mission as follows: "to provide a considered look at all aspects of our national life; to write, as well, about matters that are not strictly American; to emphasize the big story that lurks, untold, behind the smaller ones that do get told; to write with intelligence and perspective about matters such as marriage, morals, and the mind that are important but aren't necessarily "news"; to shun the bandwagon; and to spread the conclusions of our authors to people who need to know."* The Atlantic *also notes a commitment to "beauty" ("Many of life's nobler and more satisfying pursuits are not, as we all know, practical and utilitarian") and to serve a purpose "not unlike that of a liberal education." Clearly, this publication has set very high standards for its work. As you read this essay by Paul Starobin, which enters the conversation on the relationship between freedom and regulation, see whether you can distinguish a style and tone that fit the editorial mission of this publication. You might also consider whether Starobin's four years away from the United States might have influenced his views.*

1   Last fall, on the occasion of the twentieth anniversary of the National Endowment for Democracy, a federally funded agency chartered to spread liberty around the world, President George W. Bush delivered a speech holding out some "essential principles" as "common to every successful society in every culture." The first of these, the President declared, is that "successful societies limit the power of the state and the power of the military so that governments respond to the will of the people and not the will of the elite." That was what America had learned in its 200-year "journey" on the road to perfecting its democracy, Bush observed, by way of encouraging less mature works in progress—namely, post-Taliban Afghanistan and post-Saddam Iraq—to follow this tried and true path.

2   The rhetoric may seem unexceptionable. But in the context of our age—an age in which certain dark forces, most prominently terrorism, confront the state with the elemental task of maintaining security and civic order—the principles Bush named are not just irrelevant but almost precisely the opposite of the ones we should be dedicating ourselves to. Leaving aside the question of military power, the necessary response to terrorism is not to limit the power of the state but, rather, to bolster it, so as to preserve the basic order without which the defenseless citizen has no prospect of enjoying the splendors

of liberty. In the wake of Madrid, in the wake of 9/11, in the wake of suicide bombings in Moscow subway stations and Jerusalem cafés, the state is impelled to become even more intrusive and muscular than it already is. How well today's leaders meet this obligation to construct more-vigilant states is very likely to stand as one of history's most important criteria for assessing their stewardship.

An authoritarian push is often seen as coming from above, forced on an unsuspecting public by would-be autocrats. But today's global trend toward what might be called the Daddy State is propelled by the anxious demands of majority blocs of citizens. The Russians recently re-elected Vladimir Putin, a former KGB colonel, with 71 percent of the vote, handing him a mandate to continue his crackdown on Chechen terrorists. The Israelis are demanding the Fence—envisioned as a sniper-patrolled, electrified national barrier aimed at keeping out Palestinian suicide bombers. Not only do Americans broadly support Bush's Patriot Act, but women—who worry more than men do that they or someone close to them will fall victim to terrorism—tend to view the measure as not tough enough, according to a recent Gallup poll. Europeans are demanding closer policing of their rapidly growing Muslim minority, which now stands at 15 million in the EU.   3

In short, we are at the dawn of a popularly sanctioned movement toward greater authoritarianism in the domain of what is now fashionably called "homeland security." As Thomas Hobbes explained in his mid-seventeenth-century treatise *Leviathan* (a work that can be read as a primer on homeland security), there is no real contradiction in the idea of authoritarianism as a choice. In a proverbial state of nature, man willingly gives up some portion of his liberty to a sovereign as the only conceivable protector of his life and property. During times of relative quiet and prosperity it is easy to forget that this sort of bargain exists—but in times of danger, woe to the sovereign that neglects its duty to protect.   4

To say that we are at the beginning of an authoritarian age is not, of course, to end the conversation but to begin it. The challenge is to get authoritarianism right, and it's important to identify what could go wrong as we try to meet the demands of this new era. One obvious danger, fascism, already lurks at the door of Russia, a humiliated country whose color has shifted from red to brown since the collapse of the Soviet Union, in 1991. Putin is proving to be a manipulative paternalist, exploiting fears of Chechen terrorists and thuggish business oligarchs to nourish nationalist sentiment and his own cult of personality in the Kremlin.   5

6   Nor is Putin respecting the prudent boundaries of a Daddy State. There is no popular demand for an increase in state power over the market or the media—yet the Putin regime is exerting greater control in those areas, too. (All major television stations are now state-controlled.) With democratic institutions so weakly grounded in Russia, there is likely to be no check on Putin's impulses without pressure from Western governments.

7   America illustrates the hazards of the opposite problem: too many constraints on the Daddy State. In particular, Congress— the body positioned between the executive and the people— is proving a serious hindrance. For example, just after 9/11 alarmed legislators sensibly created a Transportation Security Agency, with broad powers to improve airport security. But since then Congress has hamstrung the agency's effort to develop a computerized profiling system that would help identify potentially dangerous passengers—in part because of pressure from airlines worried that travelers inconvenienced by "false positives" would blame them for missed flights. Such is the classic defect of legislatures, which reliably respond to the will of the majority in emergencies but afterward tend to succumb to the predations of well-entrenched lobbies.

8   Homeland security in the United States probably isn't going to improve unless those responsible for formulating and administering protection policies are insulated from the legislature. That was the painful lesson taught by a wave of bombings in France and other European countries in the 1980s; after the bombings France improved its counterterrorism capabilities by endowing an elite group of Paris-based magistrates with investigative powers that far outstrip those given to John Ashcroft's Justice Department in the Patriot Act. The former White House counterterrorism chief Richard Clarke recommends establishing an elite unit modeled on M15, the internal British Security Service, and subject to oversight by a blue-ribbon board of prominent citizens. The United States has its own model of sorts in the Federal Reserve, which is protected from congressional encroachment and is one of the nation's most effective government institutions.

9   For both Europe and Israel the Daddy State poses a tricky cultural challenge: to extend the bargain envisioned by Hobbes—a partial sacrifice of personal liberty in return for the state's protection—to isolated and distrusted Muslim minorities that have historically been overlooked or discriminated against. Continuing to neglect this imperative for greater civic inclusion is especially dangerous now that Muslim communities are more closely scrutinized for terrorist ties (as they must be). Shorn of the occupied territories by fortified barriers, Israel proper would

still have an Arab minority of some 20 percent. Moshe Arens, Israel's hard-line former Defense Minister, has in intriguing suggestion: subject Israeli Arabs to the requirement of military service, from which all except Druze Arabs are currently exempt. If any institution in Israeli society can instill in the Arab minority a sense of belonging, it is the military, which is not only Israel's chief cultural melting pot but also a prime source of contacts for those seeking to build careers in business and other areas.

The French government is trying to promote cultural   10
integration—and to prove itself a caring paternalist—by banning Muslim girls from wearing headscarves in public schools, on the principle that many girls are being forced to do so by religious radicals. But such policies risk being seen as discriminatory. Compulsory civic education would offer a better avenue for acculturating Muslims living in ghettos on the outskirts of metropolises such as Paris, London, and Madrid. Britain has made a good start by insisting that immigrants attend citizenship classes and pass an English-language test as a condition of receiving a passport—a tough-love sort of idea that is a limited, reasonable invasion of personal autonomy.

Although "Leviathan" denotes a scary sea monster, Hobbes him-   11
self was in fact one of the modernizing West's great early humanists. His central aim was to find a formula for ending the civil wars, inflamed by religious passions, that were consuming the England of his time. Today's Islamic *jihadis* now threaten something like a global civil war, as opposed to a conventional war between states; their transnational armies occupy stealth bases on every continent except Antarctica. Were he alive today, Hobbes might argue not for a planet of Daddy States but for a Daddy Planet—a single Leviathan, or World Sovereign, to which all of us would be made to submit, for our own security. At the very least a modern Hobbesian would be likely to favor the establishment of an EU-wide antiterrorism czar—a step that jealous guardians of national sovereignty have been resisting.

Life in a Daddy State global order promises to be a some-   12
what mixed affair. Life will be best for majority groups in well-fortified but not overly heavy-handed Daddy States. As ever, life will be rough for anyone under the boot-heel of an unconstrained autocrat. But perhaps the most terrible fate awaits those trapped in the primeval chaos, without any sort of state protection. That condition of extreme vulnerability is borne by, for instance, Palestinians living in the Israeli-occupied West Bank and Gaza Strip. And should state-building fail in Afghanistan and Iraq, their peoples, too, will inhabit this sort of limbo, in which, as Hobbes memorably wrote, "there is no

place for Industry . . . no Arts; no Letters; no Society; and which is worst of all, continuall feare, and danger of violent death; And the life of man, solitary, poore, nasty, brutish, and short."

Ray C. Spencer

CAN WE CURB
THE PRIVACY INVADERS?

This essay first appeared in March 2002 in USA Today Magazine, *a general-interest monthly that publishes informational and opinion pieces on a wide variety of topics from American culture. Its author, Ray C. Spencer, is coordinator of research programs in political economy and public policy at the University of Illinois at Urbana-Champaign, where he also works in the Disability Research Institute. This essay approaches the topics of privacy and surveillance by laying out a series of criteria that might help distinguish necessary from unnecessary surveillance. You might consider how this method of analysis can help to build an argument on a topic that asks a writer to make judgments.*

1   When the time came for John—the executive vice-president who had devoted his 20-year career to one of the nation's top Fortune 500 companies—to be appointed president, events took a surprising turn. The incumbent president was retiring in four months, and a committee of the board of directors had been designated to make the formal recommendation for his successor. John fully expected to be promoted to the position. To the shock of John and his colleagues, when the announcement was officially made, the selection turned out to be the second vice-president, a man with far fewer credentials and less time with the company.

2   All explanations by the board spokesman rang hollow, and John was determined to get the full story. He hired an attorney, who subpoenaed the files of the selection committee. Those files revealed a complete copy of his medical records maintained by his personal physician. In his physician's scrawled

handwriting was the notation, "patient seems to have trouble managing his finances." The notation was made at a time when John was having persistent headaches and his doctor was probing all possible causes, including mental pressures.

John's case is not unique. Countless Americans have been 3 denied credit, insurance, jobs, or other opportunities on the basis of inaccurate, irrelevant, or outdated information gathered haphazardly, stored in computers, and passed along from one organization to another.

Indeed, "the right to be let alone," as Supreme Court Justice 4 Louis Brandeis said some 80 years ago, may still be "the right most valued by civilized men." To achieve that valued goal in our society, though, an individual would have to become a hermit, with no income, job, or fixed address. Accordingly, few of us would be willing to sacrifice our normal social and economic relationships for perfect privacy. To hold a job, receive medical care, be granted credit, buy insurance, and/or get an education, we must strike a series of bargains whereby we give up pieces of our personal privacy in exchange for society's benefits.

Today, we must examine these everyday exchanges and de- 5 termine whether a new balance needs to be struck between the individual's right to keep his or her personal information private and the need of public and private institutions for personal information that helps them perform their functions.

Let us examine how our right to be left alone has been 6 eroded over the years—and why the present and potential threats are so alarming. Our need for information grew along with the population explosion after World War II, which, in turn, caused an explosion of goods and services and the expansion of government's role in our private lives:

In 1950, total public aid expenditures were $2,500,000,000; 7 by 1989, $127,500,000,000. In 1950, 651,000 Americans received payments through Aid to Families with Dependent Children; by 1991, 2,300,000,000 did. In 1949, 62,000,000 workers were covered under government social insurance programs; by 1990, 126,000,000 were.

The social consequences of these explosions have been pro- 8 found. The growth of urbanization and an increasingly mobile population have depersonalized what were once face-to-face transactions. The small-town America of 60 years ago had little need for formal records. You *knew* whom you were lending money to or to whom you were selling equipment. Those personal encounters are being replaced by records that have assumed an ever-increasing importance as our country has moved from a cash to a credit economy. The combined result of all these forces has been an avalanche of paperwork, which, in turn, gave birth to the computerization of personal information.

9   The computer itself is not the villain. Government agencies and private businesses that found it necessary to computerize their records because their manual systems were inadequate did not set out to create data systems that would intrude on our privacy. Quite the contrary. Record-keeping practices were merely carried over from the old manual, index card days— practices that few people objected to because they had never been exposed to public scrutiny.

10   The point ought to be made that, in precomputer days, personal information sought by private business was much more intrusive than it is today. For example, consider this note taken from a history of the Ford Motor Company:

11   "Ford established a sociological department staffed with 100 investigators who were empowered to go into the workers' homes to make sure that no one was drinking too much, that everyone's sex life was without blemish, that leisure time was profitably spent, that houses were clean and neat, and so on. An employee who did not measure up lost his claim to the five-dollar day."

12   A typical employment application of the 1920s inquired whether the applicant smoked, gambled, used slang, had been divorced, or swore. "Who is your political leader?" was a common question.

13   In precomputer days, the prohibitive costs of maintaining, storing, retrieving, and disseminating manual records were a powerful deterrent to widespread abuse of personal information. In the computer era, however, the economic pressures work just the opposite way. It may be cheaper to maintain and store computerized record than to destroy them; a computerized record can be retrieved in a matter of seconds; and the exchange and conjoining of computerized records from one data system to other compatible systems is a low-cost, high-efficiency operation.

14   While data banks in the private sector play an ever-increasing role in determining who is eligible for credit, insurance, and employment, government data banks do so in decisions about who is eligible for Social Security, welfare, and government employment, as well as who should be subject to law enforcement actions.

15   What has caused concern about the privacy aspects of government and private record systems is not only the increased capacity of computers, but the changing perceptions of social organization in America. The struggle of minorities, including blacks, women, Hispanics, homosexuals, the aged, and the

physically handicapped, for an equal place in America's social, political, and economic life has overturned the 200-year-old notion that only the so-called "right" people—church-going, monogamous, white Protestant males—are entitled to reap rewards, both here and in the hereafter.

Although equality, not personal information privacy, is the principal goal of these movements, the consequences of some of their demands are reflected in legislation that prohibits the collection of racial, sexual, religious, and ethnic information that might be used in a discriminatory way. This, in turn, has raised the public's consciousness about personal information privacy in general, and there have been some encouraging responses to this new awareness. In the public sector, the government has reexamined its record-keeping practices and eliminated requests for information that are intrusive or irrelevant, while taking steps to safeguard confidential private information. Several private businesses, too, have voluntarily undertaken privacy protection programs to guard their employees' records.   16

By and large, though, the haphazard collection, retention, and dissemination of personal information continues unregulated on an unprecedented scale—largely concealed from the individuals whose data is being used. Privacy, therefore, is a challenge to the corporate leadership of our country. What is done to protect the individual's right to personal privacy can have a profound impact on all Americans. Three basic privacy standards can be applied to record-keeping, whether it be in credit, banking, insurance, employment, medical care, education, or government: 17

Is the information being gathered relevant to the purpose for which it is being collected? Obviously, what is relevant in one circumstance may not be so in another. It is certainly reasonable, for example, for one's psychiatrist to inquire deeply into marital or sexual affairs. However, it is irrelevant and intrusive for an auto insurance company to do so and deny car insurance to an applicant with a perfect driving record who cohabits with someone outside of marriage.   18

Is the information accurate? Some personal information that goes into data systems originates with private investigative companies that interview neighbors and past associates, but whose reports do not distinguish between documented facts and gossip. For instance, a respected newspaper editor's credit report contained evidence that he was lacking in judgment and unable to discipline his children properly. It turned out that the source of these false allegations was an elderly neighbor who didn't appreciate the editor's children.   19

20   An element of relevance and accuracy is timeliness, a special problem of computerized information systems with their capacity for longtime storage at little incremental cost. Grammar school records, medical records of long-cured ailments, old financial records, and old arrest records not followed by convictions should not be maintained to haunt the individual into perpetuity, and a generally accepted schedule of disposal should be implemented.

21   *Is information kept confidential when the individual has an expectation of confidentiality?* The answer to that question is generally "no." This is especially true of medical and financial records. Indeed, 35% of Fortune 500 companies responding to a University of Illinois survey said medical records are used in making employment-related decisions and, in nine out of 10 cases, the employees are not informed.

22   It is important to remember that personal information sought by private business is not a new phenomenon. Historian Sharon Salinger points out that indentured servants of the 18th century were displayed like cattle. Prospective buyers felt their muscles, checked their teeth and health, verified occupations, inquired about their background, and, if satisfied, paid the master the cost and took the servant home.

23   While today's workers are spared such scrutiny, giving employers full access to applicants' medical records may be just as intrusive. The way to make certain that personal health information remains private is for every segment of society— government, private industry, and individuals—to take an active part in ensuring that personal privacy is respected in every information transaction.

24   Next to medical records, most people consider their financial records as most deserving of confidentiality, but that expectation, too, is illusory. Government agencies are given free and easy access to financial and credit records. Even when government agents go to the trouble of getting a court order to inspect an individual's bank records or credit records, and the bank or company duly notifies the depositor or customer of the court order, the individual is powerless to prevent inspection of his or her records. In addition, with electronic funds transfer fully operational throughout the nation, the debit purchases of all Americans with bank accounts is stored in massive data banks, available to anyone having access to an appropriate terminal.

25   Paradoxically, confidentiality problems are most severe in the area where legislation designed to guard confidentiality already exists. The Fair Credit Reporting Act is meant to give individuals notification when they are denied credit, employment, or

other benefits because of adverse information before it is disseminated. Yet, this legislation, while an important step forward in privacy protection, has some serious defects. An individual who is the subject of an investigative report is not told what will be collected, from whom the information will be sought, how it will be used, and to whom it will subsequently be disseminated. The subject does not have to be shown a copy of an adverse report, only told its substance, and the source of the adverse information does not have to be revealed.

Avoiding Abuses

These and other privacy problems in our information society   26
can be avoided if a few general principles are applied to most
information systems:

• To ensure relevance, government and private institutions should collect just that personal information necessary to perform their service or fulfill their function. Legally established guidelines limiting the collection of irrelevant personal information are needed. For instance, questions about applicants' marital status, organizational memberships, lifestyle, medical history, etc., can be eliminated from employment application forms. Where such information is required after employment, it should be sequestered in the appropriate department—that is, marital information is kept confidential in the accounting department and used just to determine benefits and tax deductions, while medical information is sequestered in the medical department and utilized only to pay claims or limit work not suitable for an individual's physical condition. Such information is never shared with the employee's supervisors and plays no role in determining promotions. Such respect for employee privacy can boost workplace morale and foster increased productivity. Some private businesses have reviewed their information practices and already adopted such guidelines voluntarily.
• To ensure fairness, certain information-gathering techniques should be banned—among them, pretext interviews (those conducted under false pretenses) and psychological or honesty tests administered as a condition of employment. The latter are offensive for two reasons. First, they often ask deeply probing questions not related to the aim of the test, thus eliciting information that an individual normally would not volunteer. Second, by its very nature, psychological testing is coercive. As a practical matter, the accuracy and reliability of these tests are open to question.

- To ensure accuracy, the subject of the record should be given access to it, including the right to correct misstatements and challenge the sources used to update the record. This right should be made available to everyone as a matter of course. As a further contribution to accuracy and fairness, government and private organizations should adopt disposal schedules where appropriate.
- To ensure confidentiality, the individual subject should be a participating source. The use of blanket consent forms should be eliminated. Instead, the individual should be informed in advance of each proposed transfer of personal information. If that proposed transfer does not serve the original purpose for which the information was first given, then the individual should have the right to refuse to authorize the transfer. Each subsequent transfer should be made only with the informed consent of the individual. Obviously, exceptions should be provided for. Epidemic diseases must be reported to protect the health of the entire community, for example, whether or not the individual wishes his or her disease to be reported. At the very least, however, in such circumstances, the information transfer should be made known to the individual, even though it must take place without consent. Moreover, organizations that violate confidentiality rules should be liable for civil damages.

27   Improper relationships between record-keeping practices and individuals can result in substantial harm to the persons concerned. Inaccurate, unfair, or outdated records have caused individuals to be denied jobs, housing, insurance, education, and other benefits. Irrelevant or discriminatory records can unfairly penalize the individual. Circulation of information that the individual regards as sensitive and confidential, even if it does not cause loss of benefits, may result in severe psychological damage. These should be reasons enough for our country to take legislative action on privacy protection.

28   There is also a compelling reason—beyond harm to a particular individual—to put our record-keeping practices in order, and that is harm to society as a whole. Secret record systems, intrusive information-gathering practices, dossiers that record an individual's political and private associations, data systems that reduce individuals to an identifying number—all of these unravel the fabric of our democratic society. They induce a feeling of powerlessness and a lack of control over one's life.

29   Even when their purposes are benign, secret record systems, or those created without the consent or knowledge of their subjects, heighten fears that benign purposes will be subverted and the information misused. They evoke images of totalitarian societies, citizens kept under constant surveillance, networks of

informants, personal dossiers locked away in government files, and secret police. The way to make certain that this doesn't happen in the U.S. is for every segment of our society—government, private industry, and individuals—to take an active part in constraining some of our personal information record practices, to ensure that personal privacy is respected in every information transaction and the rights of individuals are not sacrificed to the informational needs of the state and other institutions.

American Library Association

RESOLUTION ON THE USA PATRIOT ACT AND RELATED MEASURES THAT INFRINGE ON THE RIGHTS OF LIBRARY USERS

The USA PATRIOT Act (an acronym for Uniting and Strengthening America by Providing Appropriate Tools Required to Intercept and Obstruct Terrorism) was passed soon after the September 11, 2001, attacks on the World Trade Towers—so soon after that event that some groups felt that its effects upon civil liberties were not carefully enough considered. One such group, the American Library Association, passed the following resolution on January 29, 2003. Consider this resolution in light of the ALA's stated mission to "ensure access to information for all." What parts of the USA PATRIOT Act might conflict with this group's mission enough to prompt this public response?

WHEREAS, The American Library Association affirms the responsibility of the leaders of the United States to protect and preserve the freedoms that are the foundation of our democracy; and   1

   WHEREAS, Libraries are a critical force for promoting the free flow and unimpeded distribution of knowledge and information for individuals, institutions, and communities; and   2

3   WHEREAS, The American Library Association holds that suppression of ideas undermines a democratic society; and

4   WHEREAS, Privacy is essential to the exercise of free speech, free thought, and free association; and, in a library, the subject of users' interests should not be examined or scrutinized by others; and

5   WHEREAS, Certain provisions of the USA PATRIOT Act, the revised Attorney General Guidelines to the Federal Bureau of Investigation, and other related measures expand the authority of the federal government to investigate citizens and noncitizens, to engage in surveillance, and to threaten civil rights and liberties guaranteed under the United States Constitution and Bill of Rights; and

6   WHEREAS, The USA PATRIOT Act and other recently enacted laws, regulations, and guidelines increase the likelihood that the activities of library users, including their use of computers to browse the Web or access e-mail, may be under government surveillance without their knowledge or consent; now, therefore, be it

7   RESOLVED, That the American Library Association opposes any use of governmental power to suppress the free and open exchange of knowledge and information or to intimidate individuals exercising free inquiry; and, be it further

8   RESOLVED, That the American Library Association encourages all librarians, library administrators, library governing bodies, and library advocates to educate their users, staff, and communities about the process for compliance with the USA PATRIOT Act and other related measures and about the dangers to individual privacy and the confidentiality of library records resulting from those measures; and, be it further

9   RESOLVED, That the American Library Association urges librarians everywhere to defend and support user privacy and free and open access to knowledge and information; and, be it further

10   RESOLVED, That the American Library Association will work with other organizations, as appropriate, to protect the rights of inquiry and free expression; and, be it further

11   RESOLVED, That the American Library Association will take actions as appropriate to obtain and publicize information about the surveillance of libraries and library users by law enforcement agencies and to assess the impact on library users and their communities; and, be it further

12   RESOLVED, That the American Library Association urges all libraries to adopt and implement patron privacy and record retention policies that affirm that "the collection of personally identifiable information should only be a matter of routine or policy when necessary for the fulfillment of the mission of the

library" (ALA Privacy: An Interpretation of the Library Bill of
Rights); and, be it further

RESOLVED, That the American Library Association consid-   13
ers sections of the USA PATRIOT Act a present danger to the
constitutional rights and privacy rights of library users and
urges the United States Congress to:

1. provide active oversight of the implementation of the
   USA PATRIOT Act and other related measures, and the
   revised Attorney General Guidelines to the Federal
   Bureau of Investigation;
2. hold hearings to determine the extent of the surveillance on library users and their communities; and
3. amend or change the sections of these laws and the
   guidelines that threaten or abridge the rights of inquiry
   and free expression; and, be it further

RESOLVED, That this resolution be forwarded to the   14
President of the United States, to the Attorney General of
the United States, to Members of both Houses of Congress, to
the library community, and to others as appropriate.

Adopted by the ALA Council, January 29, 2003

Robert Goldwin
GUN CONTROL
IS CONSTITUTIONAL

*Goldwin is a scholar affiliated with the American Enterprise
Institute, a conservative research institute. He contributed the
following to the* Wall Street Journal, *the conservative busi-
ness-news daily, in December 1991. The letters published after
it and responding to it appeared a few weeks later in the same
newspaper.*

Congress has been dismayingly inconsistent in its voting on   1
gun-control legislation this year, first passing the Brady Bill,
then moving in the opposite direction by defeating a provision
to ban certain assault weapons and ammunition. But in one
respect members of Congress are consistent: they demand
respect for our "constitutional right to own a gun." They cite

the Constitution's Second Amendment and argue it prohibits effective national regulation of the private ownership of guns.

2   But there are strong grounds for arguing that the Second Amendment is no barrier to gun-control legislation. In my opinion, it even provides a solid constitutional basis for effective national legislation to regulate guns and gun owners.

3   The best clues to the meaning of the key words and phrases are in debates in the First Congress of the United States. The Members of that Congress were the authors of the Second Amendment. A constitutional amendment calling for the prohibition of standing armies in time of peace was proposed by six state ratifying conventions. Virginia's version, later copied by New York and North Carolina, brought together three elements in one article—affirmation of a right to bear arms, reliance on state militia, and opposition to a standing army.

4   "That the people have a right to keep and bear arms; that a well regulated militia, composed of the body of the people trained to arms, is the proper, natural, and safe defense of a free state; that standing armies, in times of peace, are dangerous to liberty, and therefore ought to be avoided. . . ."

5   The purpose was to limit the power of the new Congress to establish a standing army, and instead to rely on state militias under the command of governors. The Constitution was ratified without adopting any of the scores of proposed amendments. But in several states ratification came only with solemn pledges that amendments would follow.

6   Soon after the First Congress met, James Madison, elected as a congressman from Virginia on the basis of such a pledge, proposed a number of amendments resembling yet different from articles proposed by states. These eventually became the Bill of Rights. In the version of the arms amendment he presented, Madison dropped mention of a standing army and added a conscientious objector clause.

7   "The right of the people to keep and bear arms shall not be infringed, a well armed and well regulated militia being the best security of a free country, but no person religiously scrupulous of bearing arms shall be compelled to render military service in person."

8   In this version, "bearing arms" must mean "to render military service," or why else would there have to be an exemption for religious reasons? What right must not be infringed? The right of the people to serve in the militia.

9   This militia amendment was referred to a congressional committee and came out of committee in this form:

10   "A well regulated militia, composed of the body of the people, being the best security of a free state, the right of the people to

keep and bear arms shall not be infringed; but no person religiously scrupulous shall be compelled to bear arms."

Two significant changes had been made: first, the phrase "to   11
render military service in person" was replaced by the phrase,
"to bear arms," again indicating that they are two ways to say
the same thing; second, an explanation was added that the
"militia" is "composed of the body of the people."

The House then debated this new version in committee of   12
the whole and, surprisingly, considering the subsequent history of the provision, never once did any member mention the
private uses of arms, for self-protection, or hunting, or any
other personal purpose. The debate focused exclusively on the
conscientious objector provision. Eventually the committee's
version was narrowly approved. The Senate in turn gave it its
final form: briefer, unfortunately more elliptical, and with the
exemption for conscientious objectors deleted:

"A well-regulated militia, being necessary to the security of a   13
free state, the right of the people to keep and bear arms, shall
not be infringed."

Certain explanations were lost or buried in this legislative   14
process: that the right to bear arms meant the right to serve in
the militia; that just about everybody was included in the militia; and that the amendment as a whole sought to minimize if
not eliminate reliance on a standing army by emphasizing the
role of the state militia, which would require that everyone be
ready to be called to serve.

But what about the private right "to keep and bear arms," to   15
own a gun for self-defense and hunting? Isn't that clearly protected by the amendment? Didn't just about everyone own a gun
in 1791? Wouldn't that "right" go without saying? Yes, of course,
it would go without saying, especially then when there were no
organized police forces and when hunting was essential to the
food supply.

But such facts tell us almost nothing relevant to our question.   16
Almost everyone also owned a dog for the same purposes. The
Constitution nevertheless says nothing about the undeniable
right to own a dog. There are uncountable numbers of rights not
enumerated in the Constitution. These rights are neither denied
nor disparaged by not being raised to the explicit constitutional
level. All of them are constitutionally subject to regulation.

The right to bear arms protected in the Second Amendment   17
has to do directly with "a well-regulated militia." More evidence
of the connection can be found in the Militia Act of 1792.

"Every free able-bodied white male citizen" (it was 1792,   18
after all) was required by the act to "enroll" in the militia for
training and active service in case of need. When reporting for

service, every militiaman was required to provide a prescribed rifle or musket, and ammunition.

19   Here we see the link of the private and public aspects of bearing arms. The expectation was that every man would have his own firearms. But the aspect that was raised to the level of constitutional concern was the public interest in those arms.

20   What does this mean for the question of gun control today? Well, for example, it means that Congress has the constitutional power to enact a Militia Act of 1992, to require every person who owns a gun or aspires to own one to "enroll" in the militia. In plain 1990s English, if you want to own a gun, sign up with the National Guard.

21   Requiring every gun owner to register with the National Guard (as we require 18-year-olds to register with the Selective Service) would provide the information about gunowners sought by the Brady and Staggers bills, and much more. Standards could be set for purchase or ownership of guns, and penalties could be established.

22   Restoring a 200-year-old understanding of the Constitution may be difficult, but there isn't time to dawdle. Americans now own more than 200 million guns, and opinion polls show Americans want gun control. Why not avail ourselves of the Second Amendment remedy? Call in the militia, which is, after all, "composed of the body of the people."

Responses to Robert Goldwin: Letters to the Editor of the Wall Street Journal

1   In his "Gun Control Is Constitutional" the American Enterprise Institute's Robert A. Goldwin's principal concern, it seems, is to deny that the right to keep and bear arms precludes the power to regulate gun ownership and use. Few would disagree. Even activities protected by the First Amendment may be regulated when they threaten the rights of others.

2   But Mr. Goldwin also writes that "The right to bear arms protected in the Second Amendment has to do directly with 'a well regulated militia'"; thus, arguably, he continues, "if you

want to own a gun, sign up with the National Guard." Clearly, this goes well beyond regulating to protect the rights of others. This would condition the "right" to keep and bear arms on joining the National Guard.

Mr. Goldwin's mistake stems from his having confused a 3 necessary with a sufficient condition. The Second Amendment, in its language and its history, makes plain that the need for a well-regulated militia is a *sufficient* condition for the right to keep and bear arms. Yet Mr. Goldwin treats it as a *necessary* condition, which enables him to conclude that Congress could deny an individual the right to own a gun if he did not join the National Guard.

Mr. Goldwin makes this mistake, in turn, because he has 4 misread Madison's original version of the Second Amendment, which exempted conscientious objectors from military service. Thus he says that "In this version, 'bearing arms' must mean 'to render military service', or why else would there have to be an exemption for religious reasons? What right must not be infringed? The right of the people to serve in the militia."

Plainly, any conscientious objector provision would arise 5 not from a *right* but from a *duty* to serve in the militia. Yet Mr. Goldwin believes the amendment means, as he later says, "that the right to bear arms meant the right to serve in the militia." Thus does he reduce the first of these rights to the second, when clearly it is much broader.

> Roger Pilon
> *Senior Fellow and Director*
> *Center for Constitutional Studies*
> *CATO Institute*

The militia is not the National Guard but rather the people 1 of the original states. In Ohio, we have an Ohio militia that is not a part of the National Guard. The fear of standing armies and the control these armed men gave a central government was foremost in the Framers' minds when writing the Bill of Rights. Thomas Jefferson moved to prevent this type of power in a few people's hands by the Second Amendment. He stated, "No free man shall ever be debarred the use of arms."

The addition in the early drafts of a conscientious-objector 2 clause was added for the preservation of religious freedoms, which the Colonists had not had in England. It is unfortunate today's "scholars" seem to spend their time picking apart history and the great thoughts of the visionary men who formed this country.

3   In my personal celebration of this 200-year-old document, I have pledged the following: I will give up my freedom of speech when they cut out my tongue; I will give up my right to worship when they have slain my God and myself; I will assemble with the people of my choice even when they are imprisoned, and I will give up my rifle when they pry my cold dead fingers from around it.

Samuel R. Bush III

1   Let those who want guns join the National Guard, says Mr. Goldwin. Ah, the sanctimonious arrogance of it. What gives Mr. Goldwin the right to deny mine when I abide by the laws?

2   He stresses the differences between the world of 1791 and today to suit his prejudice. He studiously ignores other major differences between 1791 and today.

3   In 1791, punishment was swifter and surer. Plea bargaining was not epidemic; judges did not provide revolving doors on prisons. There was no army of drug dealers and junkies preying on the public. If anything, the reasons for citizens to own weapons for self-defense are more compelling today than they were in 1791.

4   Let Mr. Goldwin show us how he would make us safer in our homes and we might understand his wish to strip away our only sure defense.

Carl Roessler

1   Mr. Goldwin suggests gun control via enlistment in the National Guard. Swell idea. Updating the right to bear arms from 1791 to 1991, when I report for service, I'll bring, as required, a few items consistent with the current infantryman's inventory: a Barett Light .50 semiautomatic sniper rifle, so I can reach out and touch people half a mile away: a Squad Automatic Weapon firing 5.56mm rounds at the rate of a whole lot per second out of 30-round clips or hundred-round belts; a 40mm grenade launcher . . . but you get the idea. Then, as a thoroughly modern, well-regulated militiaman, I'll take my weapons home, just as did Morgan's riflemen, and the musket bearers of Lexington and Concord, and the Colonial light artillerists.

Andrew L. Isaac

Below is the website for an organization known as Women Against Gun Control (WAGC). The site mounts an argument in support of the right to bear arms, but what are the specific visual elements on the website that contribute to that argument? A stringer running across the top reads "The Second Amendment is the Equal Rights Amendment." And the far right-hand margin includes two scrolls: one with the names Rosie O'Donnell, Janet Reno, Diane Feinstein, and Hillary Clinton, and a motto reading "Let's Blow Holes in Their Arguments"; and one with a picture of a burglar and a motto reading "If women are disarmed, a rapist will never hear STOP OR I'LL SHOOT!"

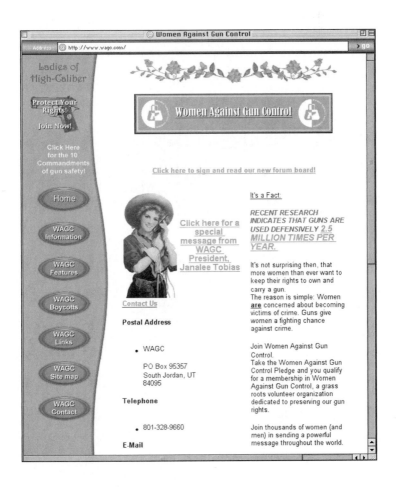

National Rifle Association
DON'T EDIT THE BILL
OF RIGHTS

*The ad printed on these two pages, developed and paid for by
the National Rifle Association Institute for Legislative Action,
appeared in* USA Today *and many other newspapers in
December 1991—on the 200th anniversary of the ratification
of the Bill of Rights.*

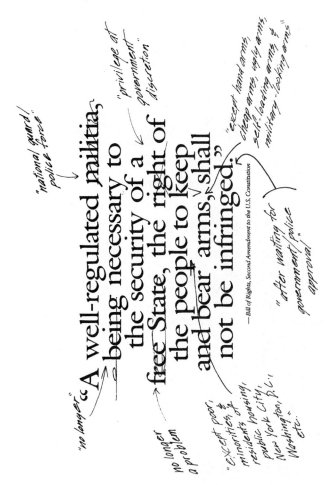

Before anyone edits the Bill of Rights, the authors would like a word with you:

"No free man shall ever be debarred the use of arms."

THOMAS JEFFERSON

"Arms in the hands of citizens may be used at individual discretion... in private self-defense."

JOHN ADAMS

"[The Constitution preserves] the advantage of being armed which Americans possess over the people of almost every other nation... [where] the governments are afraid to trust the people with arms."

JAMES MADISON

"...arms discourage and keep the invader and plunderer in awe, and preserve order in the world as well as property.... Horrid mischief would ensue were [the law-abiding] deprived of the use of them."

THOMAS PAINE

"Laws that forbid the carrying of arms... disarm only those who are neither inclined nor determined to commit crimes.... Such laws make things worse for the assaulted and better for the assailants; they serve rather to encourage than to prevent homicides, for an unarmed man may be attacked with greater confidence than an armed man."

THOMAS JEFFERSON, quoting Cesare Beccaria

"A militia, when properly formed, are in fact the people themselves... and include all men capable of bearing arms.... To preserve liberty it is essential that the whole body of the people always possess arms and be taught alike... how to use them."

RICHARD HENRY LEE

"The Constitution shall never be construed to prevent the people of the United States who are peaceable citizens from keeping their own arms."

SAMUEL ADAMS

"I ask, sir, what is the militia? It is the whole people.... To disarm the people is the best and most effectual way to enslave them..."

GEORGE MASON

A message on celebration of the 200th Anniversary of the Ratification of the Bill of Rights, December 15, 1791. Paid for by the National Rifle Association Institute for Legislative Action. For more information or call 202-828-6130.

Douglas Bettcher and Chitra Subramaniam

THE NECESSITY
OF GLOBAL TOBACCO
REGULATIONS

Douglas Bettcher and Chitra Subramaniam work for the World Health Organization's "Tobacco Free Initiative." The World Health Organization has been since 1948 the United Nations specialized agency for health. WHO's objective, as set out in its Constitution, is "the attainment by all peoples of the highest possible level of health," which it defines as "a state of complete physical, mental and social well-being and not merely the absence of disease or infirmity." You might read the essay below with that mission in mind (as well as the specific work of a "Tobacco Free Initiative"). How does the writing of these two individuals also serve the organization for which they work?

1   While multinational tobacco companies market high tar and nicotine cigarettes worldwide, in developing countries they advertise these products with techniques that are banned in their home countries.[1] Of the 8.4 million deaths that tobacco is expected to cause by 2020, 70% will occur in transitional countries.[2]

2   Global legislation must hold tobacco companies to the same standards of safety in developing markets that they are held to in their industrialized home markets. To create such global legislation, the World Health Organisation's (WHO's) 191 member states are currently negotiating a legally binding international agreement, the Framework Convention on Tobacco Control (FCTC), which may include legally binding rules on tobacco smuggling, international standardization, disclosure of product contents, and package design and labeling.[3]

3   The ethical basis of the FCTC is the principle that a multinational corporation has a nondelegable duty to protect citizens from harm caused by its products. This includes the duty to ensure that all activities are conducted with the highest standards of safety and to provide all necessary information and warnings regarding the activity involved.[4] In addition, the "negative harm" principle of business ethics requires that, in their operations abroad, corporations have an obligation not to add to the suffering and deprivation of people.

4   Tobacco companies have argued that people should be allowed to consume products of their choice freely.[5] However, a recent

World Bank report cites three ways in which the choice to buy tobacco products differs from the purchase of other consumer goods. First, many smokers are not aware of the high probability of disease and premature death their choice to smoke entails, and thus, their consent to be exposed to harm is uninformed. Children and teenagers in particular may not have the capacity to assess properly information on the health effects of smoking. Second, the highly addictive nature of nicotine, particularly as it is delivered in a manufactured cigarette, limits the tobacco user's freedom to choose not to smoke.[6] Third, smokers impose both direct and indirect costs on other non-consenting individuals. These failures to meet "free" market standards provide a rationale for demand-reduction interventions.[7]

Beyond this theoretical justification for action, there is also 5 a practical one. Tobacco companies have shown themselves to be incapable of self-regulation.[8] Despite the fact that cigarette smoke contains some 4000 different constituents, 60 of which are known carcinogens,[9] there is evidence that tobacco companies have failed to perform inhouse smoking and health research, and that this failure was, in part, the result of tobacco company efforts to mislead the public about the health effects of smoking.[10]

The tobacco companies have deliberately increased the ad- 6 dictive potential of cigarettes through their well-documented strategy of manipulating nicotine levels. Furthermore, a WHO committee concluded that tobacco companies had conspired to undermine the agency's tobacco control programs around the world. The committee made 58 recommendations to protect against the subterfuge of the tobacco industry.[11]

During a global public hearing in October 2000, the WHO 7 supported measures and policies to restrict youth access to tobacco. Recently, three major tobacco companies proposed weak voluntary global marketing standards, but such measures are known to have only limited impact on youth and adult consumption of tobacco.[12] At the same time, tobacco companies opposed comprehensive advertising bans and price increases, interventions that have had a measurable and sustained impact to decrease tobacco use.

Tobacco companies have an ethical responsibility to mini- 8 mize the harm caused by their products in developing countries and to adhere to the same safety standards in developing countries that they use in their home countries.

They have proven themselves unwilling or unable to meet 9 this responsibility voluntarily, and the cost of this failure is enormous. The kind of legally binding global regulation of dangerous practices that the FCTC could provide has become necessary.

NOTES

1. Giddens, A. Globalization. Available at: news.bbc.co.uk/hi/english/ static/events/reith_99/week1/week1/week1.htm. Accessed November 14, 2001.
2. Murray, C. L., and Lopez, A. D. Alternative projections of mortality and disability by cause 1990–2020: Global Burden of Disease Study. *Lancet.* 1997;349;1498–1504.
3. Taylor, A. L., and Bettcher, D. W. WHO Framework Convention on Tobacco Control: A global "good" for public health. *Bull World Health Organ.* 2000;78:920–929.
4. Finzen, B. A., and Walburn, R. B. *Union Carbide Corporation's Liability for the Bhopal Disaster. Multinational Enterprise Liability.* Westport, Conn: Quorom Books; 1990:145–150.
5. British American Tobacco. Answer to frequently asked question: "How can you justify being in the business of selling a product that is harmful to people's health?" Available at: http://www.bat.com. Accessed November 14, 2001.
6. Hurt, R. D., and Robertson, C. R. Prying open the tobacco industry's secrets about nicotine. *JAMA.* 1998;280:1173–1181.
7. Jha, P., and Chaloupka, F. J., eds. *Curbing the Epidemic: Governments and the Economics of Tobacco Control.* Washington, DC: World Bank; 1999:3–4.
8. Richards, J. W., Tye, J. B., and Fischer, P. M. The tobacco industry's code of advertising in the United States: Myth and reality. *Tob Control.* 1996; 5:295–311.
9. Shopland, D. Machine Testing for constituent levels in cigarettes. Monograph: *Advancing Knowledge on Regulating Tobacco Products.* Paper presented at International Conference: Advancing Knowledge on Regulating Tobacco Products, Oslo, Norway, 9–11 February 2000.
10. Zeltner, T., Kessler, D., Martiny, A., and Randera, F. *Tobacco Company Strategies to undermine Tobacco Control Activities at the World Health Organization.* Report of the Committee of Experts on Tobacco Industry Documents, July 2000:229–243.
11. Goldman, L. K., and Glantz, S. A. Evaluation of antismoking advertising campaigns. *JAMA.* 1998;279:772–777.
12. Philip Morris' comments on the Framework Convention for Tobacco Control for the Public Hearings on the FCTC, October 12–13, 2000. Available at: http://www3.who.int/whosis/fctc/fctc.cfm. Accessed November 14, 2001.

Walter E. Williams
NAZI TACTICS

Walter E. Williams has served on the faculty of George Mason University in Fairfax, Virginia, as John M. Olin Distinguished Professor of Economics, since 1980. He is the author of over 150 publications, which have appeared in scholarly journals such as Economic Inquiry, American Economic Review, Georgia Law Review, Journal of Labor Economics, Social Science Quarterly, *and* Cornell Journal of Law and Public Policy. *He has also written for a popular audience, with work appearing in publications such as* Newsweek, National Review, Reader's Digest, Cato Journal, Policy Review, *and* Ideas on Liberty, *a generally conservative publication, which in 2003 first published the piece reprinted here. He has also authored six books:* America: A Minority Viewpoint; The State Against Blacks, *which was later made into the PBS documentary "Good Intentions,"* All It Takes Is Guts; South Africa's War Against Capitalism, *which was later revised for South African publication;* Do the Right Thing: The People's Economist Speaks; *and* More Liberty Means Less Government. *Williams has appeared frequently on radio and television, and has served as an occasional substitute host for the "Rush Limbaugh" show. You might consider how the piece included here uses an analogy with "Nazi tactics" to make its case—what are the implications and emotions that such a parallel suggests? You can also compare Williams's views here with those he takes on the regulation of food in "Whose Business Is It?" also included in this part of* Conversations.

Prior to the 1930s, Germany was Europe's most hospitable   1
country for Jews. While Jews were only 1 percent of the population, they were one-fourth of Germany's law and medical
students. In some German cities, Jews were the majority of
doctors. While Jews were only 5 percent of the Berlin
Population in 1905, they paid 31 percent of all income taxes
collected. For Germany as a whole, Jewish income was more
than three times the national average. In his book, *Migration
and Cultures*, Thomas Sowell adds that Jews were so highly integrated into German economic and social life that in nearly
half of all Jewish marriages during the 1920s one of the
spouses was gentile. During World War I, Jewish-American
publications were investigated and prosecuted by the U.S. government for writing favorably about Germany, a nation at war
with the United States.

Much of German history has been one of racial toleration.   2
This is partially seen by their anti-slavery positions in Brazil
and the United States. In the United States, Germans had a
large hand in assisting runaway slaves by way of the "underground railroad." Germans also had an established reputation
of getting along well with American Indians.

3   So why the story about pre-Nazi Germany? I think examining it raises an interesting question that few bother to answer; namely, if Germany was so hospitable to Jews, relative to other countries, how in the world did the Holocaust happen? There are several alternative explanations, such as Hitler's massive consolidation of government power. Then there's the fact that German culture places high values on regimentation and obedience to authority. An important part of the answer of how Germans came to accept Jewish persecution was a massive and successful Nazi Jewish-vilification program. Teaching Germans to think of Jews as inferiors and as responsible for the post–World War I economic devastation made it possible for Germans to accept the mistreatment of Jews.

4   You say, "Okay, you're right, but what's the relevance to us?" There are about 40 million Americans who smoke cigarettes. Prior to the 1980s, all efforts to curb tobacco use relied on arguments pertaining to the health risks borne by smokers. The only way to achieve today's level of sustained attack on smokers and tobacco companies was to create an argument that tobacco smoke harmed not only smokers but others as well. Thanks to a fraudulent Environmental Protection Agency study on secondhand smoke, "Respiratory Health Effects of Passive Smoking," we have today's tobacco regulations. This is despite devastating evidence that EPA's study made subjective judgments, failed to account for important factors that could bias the results, and relaxed a crucial scientific standard to achieve the result the researchers were looking for.

5   The "relaxed" scientific standard was the EPA's lowering of the confidence interval applied to its analysis from the more standard 95 percent to 90 percent—in effect, doubling the chance of error. A federal court in *Flue-Cured Tobacco Cooperative Stabilization Corporation v. EPA* added that the EPA "disregarded information and made findings based on selective information . . .; deviated from its risk assessment guidelines; failed to disclose important [opposition] findings and reasoning; and left significant questions without answers."

6   As a result of both official and non-official fraudulent claims about the health effects, as well as the health-care costs, of smoking, there has been widely successful vilification of cigarette smokers and tobacco manufacturers. Lawmakers have little hesitation in imposing confiscatory tobacco taxes, in some jurisdictions of one to three dollars per pack. Zealous lawmakers and other public officials have attempted to ban smoking on streets and in parks. In at least a couple of jurisdictions there have been attempts to outlaw smoking in one's own home or apartment under the flimflam reasoning that

neighbors are injured by secondhand smoke. Americans don't mind at all seeing their fellow Americans huddled in the winter outside their workplaces in order to have a cigarette. In the state of Washington, a condemned prisoner was denied a last request for a cigarette. Last summer, California banned smoking in some of its prisons.

None of this could have happened during a much more civi-   7
lized era in our country. Nazi-like vilification tactics had to be employed to convince decent Americans that smokers and tobacco companies deserved any harsh treatment.

All Should Be Concerned

I'm by no means suggesting that smokers are headed off to   8
concentration camps and gas chambers, although they might have been in Germany because Hitler was a rabid anti-cigarette zealot. Instead, I'm suggesting that the cigarette-smoker vilification campaign is something about which we all should be concerned, whether we smoke cigarettes or not. These people who want to control our lives are almost finished with smokers; but never in history has a tyrant arisen one day and then decided to tyrannize no more. The nation's tyrants have now turned their attention to the vilification of fast-food chains such as McDonald's, Burger King, Wendy's, and KFC, charging them with having created an addiction to fatty foods. Thus, the tyrants claim, fast-food chains have contributed to obesity-related problems and growing health-care costs. Like the anti-tobacco zealots, they call for regulation, compensation for injury, and taxes on foods they deem to be nonnutritious. In addition to fast-food chains, these tyrants have targeted soft drink and candy manufacturers. Chinese and Mexican restaurants are also in their sights because they have meal servings deemed to be too large.

In their campaign against fast-food chains, restaurants, and   9
soda and candy manufacturers, the nation's food Nazis always refer to the anti-tobacco campaign as the model for their agenda.

VISUAL CONVERSATIONS 5

The Varied Faces of Activism

"The pen is mightier than the sword," is a phrase that has long inspired those who have sought to bring about change by peaceful means. But for those who attempt to win support for their causes, another aphorism also applies: "A picture is worth a thousand words." By definition, activists attempt to bring about social change; and they do so by putting things that they believe need public conversation in "the public eye," using both words and images to get people talking. For that reason, both public demonstration and the dissemination of the images that these public displays create are one of the most effective ways for activists to get their message out there. As you examine the images below—some of which have become ingrained in our national and international consciousness—consider how both the participants in these moments and the photographic artists who chronicled them use visual rhetoric to spur public debate.

Perhaps one of the most familiar images of resistance, this photograph depicts a moment from the famous Tiananmen Square revolt in 1989. What about this image explains the large affect that it had on international opinion? Was it the action or the image that caused that response?

Images of resistance to government actions or social policies that citizens find to be unjust are part of American history as well. The images on this page illustrate the courage necessary—and the cost that some have been willing to pay—to protest those actions or policies. They present two of the most memorable moments of protest in this country. The top image depicts Rosa Parks' refusal to move from the front of a Montgomery, Alabama, bus—the part reserved for "whites only"—in December 1955. The bottom photograph reminds us that political activism is not always quiet and reserved. Consider how the perspective of the photograph presents a specific vision of activism, especially in contrast to the depiction of Rosa Parks. Consider also how the issue—here the USA PATRIOT Act (discussed in the American Library Association resolution in the preceding section)—changes the rhetorical situation.

Civic activism can take many forms. At times it is symbolic and non-violent, meant to bring to public consciousness actions that individuals or groups find unjust (as with the protestors in the top photo demonstrating against the use of inhumane bear traps). Sometimes, however, protests are very real and can turn violent. This was the case when rioting broke out in Los Angeles in 1965 after an African-American man was beaten during a traffic stop. What do the details of the image of the "Watts Riots" as it was depicted on the cover of *Life* magazine (bottom photo) say about that moment in history—and about the dangers of civil disobedience? How does it compare with the image of the animal rights activists?

The peaceful methods of protest and resistance discussed in the pieces by Mahatma Gandhi and Martin Luther King in this part of *Conversations,* and the brave acts by civil rights leaders like Rosa Parks as depicted earlier in this section, are generally treated by history as acts of patriotism. But there are moments of protest that remain more problematic, even as time wears on. The top image depicts American athletes Tommie Smith and John Carlos giving the "black power" sign at the 1968 Olympics—in protest against American racism. The bottom image shows riot police confronting a rebellious demonstrator at the WTO protests in Seattle. How can we "read" these moments through the details of the images that recall them? Do they change your views on civil disobedience, activism, or American citizenship?

What Is the Scope of Government Regulation II? Who Is Watching What We Eat?

Eric Schlosser

FAST FOOD NATION

"Fast Food Nation," the title of this essay, is also the title of Eric Schlosser's best-selling first book. Schlosser, a correspondent for the Atlantic Monthly, *received great acclaim for that work, and subsequently appeared on 60 Minutes, CNN, CBS Evening News, NBC Nightly News, FOX News, The O'Reilly Factor, and Extra!, and has been interviewed on NPR and for* Entertainment Weekly, USA Today, *and the* New York Times. *His indictment of the fast-food industry, along with National Institute of Health and Surgeon General's warnings about obesity in this country, has touched a nerve. But others fear the regulation of food that may be imminent because of these reports, preferring to let businesses and individuals take responsibility and to self-regulate. As you read Schlosser's work, you might consider whether he makes a compelling enough case to warrant governmental regulation, especially in light of the other arguments about regulation made in this part of* Conversations.*

This essay was published in April 2004, in The Ecologist, *a widely read environmental magazine that is published on four continents and read by over 200,000 people in 150 countries. It considers itself an activist journal as well, describing itself as a "key player in major environmental campaigns against GM [genetically modified] crops, rainforest destruction, climate change and the impact of globalization." You might consider why an environmental journal such as this decided to publish Schlosser's piece on fast food.*

In February a report by George W. Bush's Council of Economic   1
Advisers (CEA) suggested that fast food workers might in the
future be classified as manufacturing workers. A CEA report
asked: "When a fast-food restaurant sells a hamburger, for example, is it providing a 'service,' or is it combining inputs to
'manufacture' a product?"

Reclassifying fast-food restaurants as 'factories' would have a   2
number of benefits for the Bush administration. It would, in a
single stroke, add about 3.5 million manufacturing jobs to the
U.S. economy, at a time when such jobs are rapidly being exported overseas. From a statistical point of view, it would make
the U.S. seem like an industrial powerhouse once again, instead
of an ageing superpower threatened by low-cost competitors.
And it would allow the fast-food industry, a strong backer of
the Republican Party, to enjoy the tax breaks provided to U.S.
manufacturers.

The CEA's chairman N. Gregory Mankiw was derided and   3
ridiculed in the press for making the proposal, and his plan is
likely to go nowhere. Yet there was an underlying logic to it.
Fast food is indeed factory food, perhaps the most heavily
processed food on the planet, and the low-paid workers who
defrost, reheat and reconstitute it have jobs as boring, highly
regimented and strictly supervised as the workers in a 19th
century textile mill would have had. Moreover, the founding fathers of the industry probably wouldn't have minded the manufacturing label at all. Bringing the philosophy of the assembly
line to the commercial restaurant kitchen was the simple innovation responsible for Ronald McDonald's global conquest.

The fast-food industry began in 1948. Richard and Maurice   4
McDonald were growing tired of running their successful
drive-in restaurant in San Bernadino, California. They were
tired of constantly hiring new carhops, the teenaged girls who
took food to customers waiting in parked automobiles. They
were tired of replacing the dishes and glasses broken by their
adolescent customers. But most of all, they were tired of paying the high wages demanded by skilled short-order cooks.

So the McDonalds decided to shut down their drive-in and   5
replace it with a revolutionary new form of restaurant. The
McDonald brothers started by firing all their car-hops and short-
order cooks. They simplified the menu, hired unskilled workers
and made each worker perform the same task again and again.
One person only made french fries. Another only made shakes.
Another only flipped burgers. By getting rid of skilled workers, by
serving food and drinks in paper cups and plates, by demanding
that customers wait in line for their own meals, the new 'Speedee
Service System' allowed the brothers to serve fast, cheap food.

6   The new restaurant was an instant success. It fitted perfectly with the new culture emerging in post-war southern California— a car culture that worshipped speed, convenience and the latest technology. Ray Kroc, the milk shake machine salesman who bought out the McDonald brothers in the early 1960s and later exported their Speedee system around the world, embraced a blind faith in science: a Disneyesque vision of society transformed through chemistry and families living happily in plastic homes and travelling in sleek, nuclear-powered cars.

7   Kroc also believed fervently in the ethic of mass production. A philosophy of uniformity, conformity and total control that had long dictated the manufacture of steel wire was now applied not only to food, but to the people who prepared the food. "We have found out . . . that we cannot trust some people who are non-conformists," Kroc declared. "We will make conformists out of them in a hurry . . . The organisation cannot trust the individual; the individual must trust the organisation."

8   For the first two decades of its existence, the McDonald's operating system had little impact on the way people lived and ate. In 1968 there were only 1,000 McDonald's restaurants, all of them in the U.S. The chain bought fresh ground beef and potatoes from hundreds of local suppliers. But the desire for rapid growth and the desire for everything to taste exactly the same at thousands of different locations transformed not only the McDonald's supply system, but also the agricultural economy of the entire U.S.

9   McDonald's switched entirely to frozen hamburger patties and frozen fries, relying on a handful of large companies to manufacture them. Other fast food chains spread nationwide at the same time, helping to drive local restaurants, small suppliers, independent ranchers and farmers out of business. And by the 1970s McDonald's began to expand overseas, taking with it a mentality perfectly expressed years later in one of the company's slogans—One taste worldwide.

10   Half a century after Richard and Maurice McDonald decided to fire their carhops, the world's food supply is dominated by an agro-industrial complex in which the fast-food chains occupy the highest rung. Monsanto developed genetically-modified potatoes to supply McDonald's with perfectly uniform French fries—and then halted production of the "New Leaf GM Potato" when McDonald's decided, for publicity reasons, not to buy it. When the fast-food industry wants something, the major food processors rush to supply it.

11   Although many of the foods we eat look the same as the ones we ate a generation ago, they have been fundamentally changed. They have become industrial commodities, with

various components (flavour, colour, fats) manufactured and assembled at different facilities. If you bought a hamburger in the U.S. 30 years ago, it would most probably have contained meat from one steer or cow, which would have been processed at a local butcher shop or small meat-packing plant. Today a typical fast-food hamburger patty contains meat from more than 1,000 different cattle, raised in as many as five different countries. It looks like an old-fashioned hamburger, but is a fundamentally different thing.

Here is a partial list of what fast food and the fast-food men-   12 tality have recently brought us: the homogenisation of culture, both regionally and worldwide; the malling and sprawling of the landscape; the feeling that everywhere looks and feels the same; a low-wage, alienated service-sector workforce; a low-wage, terribly exploited meat-packing workforce; a widening gap between rich and poor; concentration of economic power; the control of local and national government by agribusiness; an eagerness to aim sophisticated mass marketing at children; a view of farm animals as industrial commodities; unspeakable cruelty toward those animals; the spread of factory farms; extraordinary air and water pollution; the rise of foodborne illnesses; antibiotic resistance; BSE; soaring obesity rates that have caused soaring rates of asthma, heart disease and early-onset diabetes; reduced life expectancy; a cloying, fake, manipulative, disposable, plastic worldview, the sole aim of which is to make a buck.

None of this was inevitable. The triumph of the fast-food sys-   13 tem was aided at almost every step by government subsidies, lack of proper regulation, misleading advertisements, and a widespread ignorance of how fast, cheap food is actually produced. This system is not sustainable. In less than three decades it has already done extraordinary harm. When the fast-food industry is made to bear the costs it is now imposing on the rest of society, it will collapse. The alternative to fast food now seems obvious: slow food.

By "slow food" I do not mean precious, gourmet food, sold   14 by celebrity chefs and prepared according to recipes in glossy cookbooks. I mean food that is authentic, that has been grown and prepared using methods that are local, organic and sustainable. Most slow foods are peasant foods. Somehow mankind existed for thousands of years without Chicken McNuggets. And I'd argue that our future survival depends on living without them.

What's the difference between fast food and slow food?   15

Here are the ingredients you need to make a strawberry milk   16 shake the old-fashioned, slow-food way: milk, cream, sugar, ice, vanilla beans and strawberries.

17   And here are the ingredients you need to make a fast-food strawberry milk shake: milk-fat, non-fat milk, sugar, sweet whey, high-fructose corn syrup, corn syrup, guar gum, mono- and diglycerides, cellulose gum, sodium phosphate, carrageenan, citric acid, sodium benzoate, red colouring #40 and artificial strawberry flavour (amyl acetate, amyl butyrate, amyl valerate, anethol, anisyl formate, benzyl acetate, benzyl isobutyrate, butyric acid, cinnamyl isobutyrate, cinnamyl valerate, cognac essential oil, diacetyl, dipropyl kentone, ethyl acetate, ethyl amylketone, ethyl butyrate, ethyl cinnamate, ethyl heptanoate, ethyl heptylate, ethyl lactate, ethyl methylphenylglycidate, ethyl nitrate, ethyl propionate, ethyl valerate, heliotropin, hydroxyphenyl-2-bulanone, xionone, isobutyl anthranilale, isobutyl anthranilate, isobutyl butyrate, lemon essential oil, maltol, 4-methylacetophenone, methyl anthranilate, methyl benzoate, methyl cinnamate, methyl heptine carbonate, methyl naphthyl ketone, methyl salicylate, mint essential oil, neroli essential oil, nerolin, neryl isobutyrate, orris butter, phenethyl alcohol, rose, rum ether, yundecalactone, vannilin and solvent).

Charles Stein

In Supersized World, Regulatory Indigestion

The complexity of an issue like the regulation of food is illustrated in Charles Stein's conflicted essay, where he describes the process of changing his mind from one side of the issue to another. As you read, you might think about what including that rethinking process does for readers of this piece. Charles Stein is a columnist for the Boston Globe, *where he writes regular pieces on financial issues in a feature called* Boston Capital. *He is a former Bagehot Fellow, an award granted each year to ten journalists who spend a year studying business at Columbia University. How might Stein's role as a business writer influence his views? Do any of his views seem contrary to what you would expect from a businessperson?*

We're a supersized nation. We drive supersized cars and eat su- 1
persized portions of food, both of which cause big problems. Our
love affair with SUVs clogs the roads, creates pollution, and
makes us dependent on Middle East oil. The french fries and
giant sodas we crave lead to obesity, diabetes, and heart disease.
As a free market guy, my position on both these issues has been
the same: No one puts a gun to our heads and makes us buy SUVs
or Big Macs. In short, we are responsible for what we consume.

But after the publication of two new books, one on SUVs, 2
the other on food, I'm beginning to thing I've been putting the
blame in the wrong place. The two books make one thing
abundantly clear: These harmful products didn't just drop
from the sky. Neither did consumers one day announce, "Gee, I
wish I could have a car that gets lousy mileage or food that
makes me grossly fat." The products were created by American
corporations after considerable thought and effort and sold
with all the skill the companies can muster.

In the case of SUVs, much of that effort went into lobbying. 3
According to Keith Bradsher, author of "High and Mighty," the
automakers got Congress to classify SUVs as light trucks
rather than cars. As trucks, SUVs don't have to meet the requirements for mileage, emissions, or safety that apply to cars.
And they don't meet them. SUVs get dismal mileage, emit a
disproportionate amount of the pollution that produces smog,
and are prone to roll-over accidents. Whenever reformers have
tried to change the rules, Detroit and its union allies have held
the line, fearful that change would cut into the fat profits SUVs
generate. Somehow this information is omitted from SUV
commercials, which focus instead on how useful SUVs can be
on the days you need to scale snowcapped mountains.

In the food industry, writes Greg Critser, author of "Fat 4
Land," supersizing was born of a simple but brilliant insight:
People are a lot like dogs. If you put more food in their dish—
or their cups and containers—they will eat and drink more. A
lot more. At McDonald's, you used to be able to order a small
white bag with a reasonable number of french fries. Today all
you can get is a large red container with enough french fries to
feed a small country. Since the cost of raw materials in food is
minimal, bigger portions translate into bigger profits.

The search for bigger profits is as American as hamburgers 5
and frequently results in innovative products and services.
"But sometimes innovation plays to people's darker sides and
their weaker impulses," said John Fay, who teaches management at Boston College.

If the automakers and foodmakers knew what they were 6
doing, it seems only fair to hold them partly responsible for the

harm their products have inflicted on the environment and the public's health. The next step is tougher: What do you do about it? Is the appropriate response government action or can the marketplace solve the problem?

7   On the auto side, since government rules contributed to the trouble, changing government rules seems like a good remedy. Tell the carmakers they have five years to make SUVs comply with all the regulations that govern cars. Let them use their innovative skills on making better vehicles, not on lobbying. On food, the answer is less clear. Do we really want laws mandating the number of french fries in a package?

8   Some business watchers say the marketplace is already enforcing a certain amount of discipline. Lawyers are suing fast-food restaurants on behalf of obese clients. Customers and investors can vote with their feet if they don't like the way companies are behaving. "Companies today are increasingly being held to a standard that has both moral and financial dimensions," writes Harvard Business School professor Lynn Sharp Paine in a new book called "Value Shift." Maybe that kind of pressure will be enough. If not, the government may have to step in. I'm guessing about 50 french fries per package is the right number.

Ninos P. Malek

FAST FOOD AND PERSONAL RESPONSIBILITY

The issue of governmental regulation involves not only questions about freedom versus law, but also the question of personal responsibility. That is the issue raised by Ninos Malek in the article reprinted here from Ideas on Liberty, *a conservative publication that favors a more hands-off policy regarding government. Ninos Malek, who wrote this piece in 2003, teaches economics at San Jose State University, De Anza College, and Valley Christian High School.*

1   By now everyone knows that the fast-food chains are being sued because they allegedly contribute to obesity. On Fox's

"Hannity and Colmes" program last July, Samuel Hirsch, the attorney who filed lawsuits against McDonald's, Burger King, Wendy's, and KFC on behalf of his client who blames them for his poor health, admitted that the restaurants are not completely to blame. But he added that their failure to post warnings about nutrition content and their sophisticated marketing strategies make them partly culpable.

Hirsch's claim that nutrition information is not available is false. Every one of these companies has its nutrition information available on its website, and I have seen nutrition-content posters at several fast-food establishments. But even if the restaurant provided no information, it is easy enough to learn from books, the Internet, television, and radio that certain foods can promote heart disease, diabetes, and high blood pressure. To hear Hirsch tell it, "working" parents must be stupid because they don't know what they are buying. With his use of the term "working" he was setting himself up as the champion of the "common man."   2

The ridiculous claim that corporations are responsible for people's health problems is nothing new. Remember the lawsuits against the tobacco companies? If you smoke let me ask you this: did an employee from one of the tobacco companies put a gun to your head and make you smoke a cigarette? I didn't think so. People who are dying because of smoking-related illnesses have nobody to blame but themselves. And it's the same for people who eat poorly. I have never seen Ronald McDonald with an M-16 forcing people to buy Big Macs. A person has to drive to McDonald's, order a Big Mac, and eat it on his own.   3

The lack of personal responsibility has even my high school students blaming their poor diets on the school cafeteria. Granted, our cafeteria sells burritos and pizza, but they also sell salads and other healthy food. And if that weren't good enough, I would tell them to wake up earlier and make their own healthy lunches. But that would involve a cost—waking up earlier. So I tell them to stop complaining and that they need to understand a simple economic concept—actions are what count. Obviously the benefit of eating their "bad" lunches outweighs the cost of waking up earlier or taking the time to make their lunches the night before. Eating unhealthy lunches is their choice.   4

Will ice cream companies be next? What about candy companies? And, God forbid, Starbucks! Caffeine may be bad for us, right? And all that whipped cream and caramel syrup in those Frappuccinos can't be good for us.   5

Thomas DiLorenzo and James T. Bennett in their book *From Pathology to Politics: Public Health in America* (2000) correctly   6 predicted this absurd litigation. Their book also points out that many public-health "experts" are not so concerned about health as they are about politics and their social agenda, which means more government control over our lives. Even before lawyer Hirsch came on the scene, there were those who advocated "fat taxes." Not flat taxes, as supported by supply-side economists, but a tax on fat. In other words, foods that are considered "bad" will be taxed and foods that are considered "good" will be subsidized.

It's Your Life

7   Look, I am a "health nut" myself. I do not eat fast food (maybe once in a while), and I do not smoke cigarettes. I make a choice to eat that Subway sandwich with no cheese and no mayonnaise, rather than that juicy hamburger or large fries. I make the choice to go to the gym and lift weights and run. Get the picture? It's called personal responsibility. Those notorious restaurants exist because consumers want them to exist. While I may think smokers and people who live on fast food (like many of my friends) are unwise, it's their lives. They have to weigh their own costs and benefits. No company is forcing them to do anything.

8   At the end of the "Hannity and Colmes" show, both conservative Sean Hannity and "liberal" law professor and guest-host Susan Estrich agreed that it is up to the person to choose what to eat. They both laughed at Hirsch, who responded by saying, "In five to ten years you won't be laughing."

9   I think he's right. Unfortunately, I believe the laws will be changed to "protect" people from these evil companies. I tell my students that in ten years Starbucks will have bouncers at their door checking for IDs (and eventually Starbucks will be shut down because caffeine will be illegal). No more Jolt Cola or Mountain Dew for you high school students either unless you are 18. And cigars and cigarettes? I think we will see a new Prohibition on tobacco. The public-health movement will have a role in this socialist plot. As DiLorenzo and Bennett write in their book:

> The denial of individual responsibility for one's own life and well-being has become the keystone of the public health movement. For if individuals are responsible for their own health, who needs the "public" health establishment's political agenda? The very word "public" in this regard is a

euphemism for "socialized." And once our health is socialized, then all behavior becomes the "legitimate" province of state control and regulation. But once it is agreed that the state has a "right" to control any and all behavior that might possibly have a negative effect on "public" health, then we are on the road to losing all of our privacy and our freedom.

Milton Friedman made the simple statement in his "Free to   10
Choose" television series that a voluntary exchange will not take place unless both parties believe they will benefit. Every time you buy cigarettes or unhealthy food, and every time you do not buy food that's good for you, you are weighing your own costs and benefits. I give credit to those who keep quiet about personal health risks. It's the whiners and people who cannot accept responsibility that are irritating. As F. A. Hayek wrote in *The Constitution of Liberty:* "Liberty and responsibility are inseparable."

Susan Llewelyn Leach

THOSE EXTRA POUNDS—ARE THEY GOVERNMENT'S BUSINESS?

Susan Llewelyn Leach is a staff writer for the Christian Science Monitor, *an international daily newspaper founded in 1908. Though it is sponsored by a church, its editorial policy suggests that it is "a real newspaper" in scope and objectivity, not a religious newspaper. This publication is also proud of its independence: "In an age of corporate conglomerates dominating news media, the* Monitor's *combination of church ownership, a public-service mission, and commitment to covering the world (not to mention the fact that it was founded by a woman shortly after the turn of the century, when U.S. women didn't yet have the vote!) gives the paper a uniquely independent voice in journalism." You might consider that claim in light of the discussion of media consolidation in Part 2 of* Conversations. *The 2004 essay included here provides a collection of opinions on the topics of obesity and food regulation; you might think about ways that the article attempts to maintain its objective stance on the topic—and whether it does so.*

1   As America's waistline expands and the anti-obesity movement gains momentum, what you eat may soon slip out of the private domain and into the public. Nobody will be regimenting your diet, but the government may start offering more pointed advice and regulating what goes into preprepared foods, among other things. Proposals include a tax on high-fat, low-nutrition food; better school meals; and nutrition labels on restaurant menus.

2   Having the government in your kitchen wouldn't be the first time private habits have come under outside scrutiny. Tobacco, alcohol, and drugs have all gone that route at various points in U.S. history. But where did personal responsibility fall off the bandwagon?

3   The shift of private behavior to public oversight, with new legislation to enforce it, happens in a quantifiable way, says Rogan Kersh, political scientist at Syracuse University's Maxwell School, who is writing a book on the politics of obesity.

4   The first and most significant of several triggers, he explains, is social disapproval. For instance, "it used to be sexy and desirable to smoke. . . . [Now] you're committing some grave moral wrong."

5   As disapproval gains momentum, he says, "public health crusades start to build around these behaviors": Sometimes the science is accurate (the medical establishment is unanimous on the evils of smoking); sometimes the science is a mixed bag (some studies suggest that alcohol isn't as dangerous as the Prohibitionists claimed); and sometimes the science is completely spurious (Victorian physicians warned that too much sex would maim, blind, or kill).

6   Despite almost two thirds of Americans being overweight, the U.S. is paradoxically one of the most antifat biased countries in the world. And that bias has only intensified in recent decades. Only a couple of brief periods in the 20th century showed a return to the acceptance of corpulence, Professor Kersh says, and both were after the world wars when Americans had undergone deprivation.

With social disapproval already widespread, medical science 7
is reinforcing that view. Numerous studies and articles, some
more alarmist that others, point to the health consequences of
being heavy.

The message is no longer that being overweight is not good 8
for you. It's now, "you're killing yourself through your obesity
and the government must help you" to change, Kersh says.

That sort of shift in reasoning, reframing the problem in 9
terms of a toxic food environment rather than weak will and
failing personal responsibility, is key to the government stepping in. The individual is no longer blamed for not pushing
back from the table. It's now a social problem.

What has helped accelerate that redefinition is the medical 10
bill for dealing with weight-related illnesses, which reached
$117 billion last year, according to the U.S. surgeon general,
and may soon surpass the toll on healthcare taken by smoking.
"When something becomes an economic problem in this country, government tends to act in a more urgent way than if it's a
different kind of problem like constitutional rights."

"The point is, even though I'm not obese I'm paying for peo- 11
ple who are. This really burns Americans and they want their
policymakers to act in response," Kersh says. Already, more
than 140 anti-obesity laws have been introduced in state legislatures this year.

But Sandie Sabo-Russo disputes the health-bill figure. "If a 12
person is large-sized and goes to the doctor for something that
has nothing to do with their size, it's often trumped up to be
obesity related," says Ms. Sabo-Russo, a member of the board
of NAAFA, the National Association to Advance Fat Acceptance
and the largest obesity-rights organization in the U.S. "I don't
trust what we're getting on that information."

She also points out the complexity of the issue. Being obese, 13
or overweight, she says, is not always about food, "There are as
many reasons as to how or why people are fat as there are fat
people."

As for studies on obesity and its consequences, she questions 14
their accuracy because many come from sources with a vested
interest. "The first thing we try to look at when a new study
comes out is who funded it. If it's funded by Weight Watchers
International [for example], I'm not sure I'm going to believe
what it says."

As societal pressure builds, and government reluctantly eyes 15
new legislation, the courts are already grappling with obesity
issues. More and more class-action lawsuits are taking aim at
the food industry. And of the 10 major cases filed so far, mostly

consumer protection suits, five have had some success. McDonald's, for example, had to fork over $12 million for not disclosing that its fries were cooked in beef fat. Pirates Booty paid $4 million over a cheese snack that misstated the amount of fat it contained.

16   Even though no personal-injury suits have yet won in court, a case brought against McDonald's elicited an unusual response from the judge. A man who sued the fast-food chain when he gained large amounts of weight lost his case twice. But the judge spelled out what the plaintiff could have done to make the case stronger and suggested ways obesity cases could be argued.

17   "With judges doing that, trial lawyers are catching on and it's only a matter of time before they strike," says Kersh. The class-action suit, Kersh adds, has its roots in social movements that once took to the streets to demand change. Now large numbers of people can gather together through the courts.

18   Another historical pattern Kersh has identified in this gradual shift away from personal responsibility is the self-help movement. Twelve-step programs which usually spring up in response to medical warnings—Alcoholics Anonymous, Nicotine Anonymous, Overeaters Anonymous and so on—encourage Americans to live healthier lives. When that encouragement doesn't bear fruit fast enough, the users (in this case, the fat) tend to get "demonized" and so do the producers—the food and restaurant industries, who throw temptation the public's way.

19   The government has responded to public concern by telling people to exercise more and eat less—noncontroversial advice, as critics have noted, which won't rock the boat with the food lobby.

20   With the demonization of big tobacco fresh in memory, however, McDonald's and others are trying to minimize their liability by cutting portion sizes, ending supersizing, eliminating school marketing, and offering more salads. The fast-food industry is still big on individual choice, and even NAAFA's Sabo-Russo doesn't want the government legislating menus.

21   The danger of this growing push to trim the fat, Kersh says, is that it takes such a head of steam to change laws that the momentum often carries action beyond what's necessary. He cites Prohibition's 15-year fiasco and the zero-tolerance drug sentencing of the 1980s that is now being rolled back.

22   "Demonization makes very powerful politics, but it makes miserable public policy. You get these all out prohibitions, zero-tolerance policies which in practice are unrealistic and quite unjust," he says.

Walter E. Williams

WHOSE BUSINESS IS IT?

The essay reprinted here first appeared in a publication called Human Events. *That publication explains its title, and its mission, as follows:*

> *The Declaration of Independence begins: "When in the course of human events. . . ." In reporting the news,* Human Events *is objective; it aims for accurate presentation of all the facts. But it is not impartial. It looks at events through eyes that favor limited constitutional government, local self-government, private enterprise and individual freedom. These are the principles that inspired our Founding Fathers. We think that today the same principles will preserve freedom in America.*

This publication makes no claims to "impartiality," but instead makes the protection of conservative policies its major aim. You might consider whether such an admission is admirable in its honesty, or whether it undermines the quality of the content as you read Walter Williams's piece on fast-food regulation. You might also compare his argument here (where he likens regulation to fascism) to the argument about tobacco regulation also included in this section (where he likens regulation to Nazism). (See the headnote to Williams's essay "Nazi Tactics" for biographical information on the author.)

Fitness Fascists Go After Food Companies

My health and other aspects of my wellbeing are the business 1
of whom?

I'm simply asking whose business is it if I don't adequately 2
plan for retirement or save money for my child's education? If I
don't wear a seatbelt while driving or a helmet while biking,
whose business is it? What if I don't get enough sleep or don't
exercise enough for good health—should government force
me to, under the pain of punishment? In other words, should
Congress have the power to force people to do what's in their
own health, safety and welfare interests?

I'm afraid that most Americans believe that government 3
should be able to force people to do what's in their health,

safety and welfare interests. Their reasoning might be that if I don't wear a helmet while biking or a seatbelt while driving, I might have an accident, become a vegetable and become a burden on other Americans as taxpayers.

4   That reasoning fueled much of the anti-tobacco zealotry, confiscatory cigarette taxes, and federal, state and local government lawsuits against tobacco companies in the name of recouping tobacco-related healthcare costs.

5   Emboldened by their dramatic success in their war against smokers, America's neo-Nazis have now turned their attention to the food industry, with lawsuits against McDonald's, Burger King, Wendy's and KFC, alleging that they have created an addiction to fatty foods.

6   Fast-food chains are alleged to have contributed to obesity-related health problems and increased healthcare costs. Like the tobacco Nazis, the food Nazis are calling for government regulation and taxes on foods they deem non-nutritious. Already timid CEOs of fastfood chains, like their tobacco-industry counterparts, are beginning to cave to legal hustlers.

7   Should the fact that if I become injured by not wearing a seatbelt or sick from eating and smoking too much, and become a burden on taxpayers, determine whether I'm free to not wear a seatbelt or puff cigarettes and gorge myself? Is there a problem with freedom? I say no, it's a problem of socialism.

8   There is absolutely no moral case for government's taking another American's earnings, through taxes, to care for me for any reason whatsoever. Doing so is simply a slightly less offensive form of slavery. Allowing government to be in the business of caring for people for any reason moves us farther down the road to serfdom. After all, if government is going to take care of us, it will assume it has a right to dictate how we live.

9   Right now, the government has successfully attacked cigarette smokers. They are well on their way, with the help of crooked lawyers and judges, to doing the same thing to fast-food companies, soda manufacturers, candy-makers and other producers of foods deemed fattening or non-nutritious.

10   When these people finish with food producers, what might be next on their agenda? Numerous health studies have shown that sedentary lifestyles and lack of exercise also contribute to healthcare costs. I wouldn't be surprised at all if America's neo-Nazis call for government mandates requiring morning exercises, biking, jogging and fitness facility memberships.

11   You say, "Williams, that's stretching it!" That's exactly what an American who might have died in 1950 would have said about the attack on smokers and fast-food restaurants.

James Matorin

OBESITY AWARENESS CAMPAIGN NEEDED, BUT REGULATIONS WON'T CURB FAST-FOOD APPETITE

While many of the things we write are expressions of our selves, and so "come from the heart," writing is also a way of representing an institutional perspective—a perspective that is meant to defend values that affect our work. James Matorin, the author of this article, is an entrepreneur in the restaurant industry in Philadelphia, and so has a large stake in decisions made about the government's regulation of food. This piece was published in 2001 in Nation's Restaurant News, *a trade publication for professionals in the food service industry. Why is this an apt venue for Matorin's piece? How might we read it differently from the outside?*

Anyone who took time to peruse the story "Feds chew fat on U.S. diet" in the March 26 issue of this publication has to be concerned about its implications. The article was about obesity in the United States and what the government plans to do about it. 1

Here's my read of it: 2

Surgeon General David Satcher to conduct hearings on obesity? Fantastic! The hearings to take about a year? Given the government's history of time-management, that sounds about right. 3

One of the items on the agenda? "Fat" taxes on certain foods! Now that, folks, sets my imagination running wild. What foods get taxed? What kinds of meals get taxed—staples such as butter and lard? Combo meals of double cheeseburgers, super-sized with french fries and bottomless cups of soda? Refried beans? Fettucine Alfredo? Beer? Martinis? 4

Talk about an issue the nutrition police really can sink their teeth into: That one they'll chew on like a dog with a bone. Michael Jacobson, the executive director of the Center for Science in the Public Interest, already is drooling. As reported in this journal, he thinks it's dandy idea that "the caloric content of food [be] placed on menus with the same prominence as prices." 5

6   Now, don't get me wrong. Even though I've always believed that my body is my temple and that I'm free to do whatever I want to it—either to revere it or to desecrate it—I do applaud Satcher's efforts.

7   And, even though I always thought that what I eat is my business and not that of the government, I'm inclined to think that a discussion that raises the awareness of obesity, avoiding at all costs the temptation to legislate diet, is a good idea. Speaking of which, residing as I do in Philadelphia, I may be more aware of obesity than most. After all, wasn't it *Men's Health* magazine that rated my city, along with Houston and Detroit, as one of the fattest in the country? Could that be attributed to the fact that we're the cheesesteak capital of the universe? In the wake of that report, my mayor, John Street, appointed a fitness cabinet member to spearhead a citywide weight-loss program. I'll spare you the whimsy of the program. Suffice it to say that it has something to do with the city's NBA team, the 76ers, and 76 tons of weight loss for all of the city's fat people in 76 days. Are the San Francisco 49ers listening?

8   Let's look at the alarming facts. According to the latest study published by the National Institute of Health, 20 percent of the population is thought to be obese. Fifty-four percent—that's 97 million people—are overweight. The NIH says that results in an estimated $238 billion a year in medical costs—a lot of it traceable to obesity, diabetes, cardiovascular disease, stroke, hypertension and asthma.

9   So, all right already, I'll support an obesity "awareness" plan. I understand its ramifications, its consequences, its implications. I just hope that the industry groups and businesses that participate in the study do so realistically, not emotionally, and that they understand how the "new law of supply and demand" has exacerbated the problem.

10   Let me explain: the multithousands of quick-service restaurants, and many of their midscale derivatives, didn't surface because their owners thought it a great idea to snatch up prime pieces of real estate. Having first conditioned generations of kids to accept their products as the greatest food groups since sliced breads, they moved on to the next phase: creating an irresistible affection for, an awareness of and a subsequent addiction to, their products. That compelled the quick-service chains to add units to meet the demand. See? Supply and demand. Johns Hopkins University reports that the average kid, age 8 to 16, sees 10,000 food ads a year on TV.

11   So here's a plan I offer both to the government and to Surgeon General Satcher, free of charge: If you mitigate the supply, you'll affect the demand. All in favor of that plan,

please raise your hands. That's what I thought. OK. Does someone have a better idea?

Will the government's "action plan" to improve our lives   12
work? I doubt it. Unless it plans to alleviate much of the stress
associated with our careers at the same time. Listen up,
Surgeon General Satcher: we multitask, we eat while we work,
we power-lunch, we eat while we drive, fly, walk and run. Ergo:
we demand convenience, which just happens to be one more
piece of evidence to support the demand side of the equation
mentioned above. Supply side? According to the NRA, to feed
that demand for convenience, quick-service sales are expected
to exceed $111.9 billion this year. That's 28 percent of the in-
dustry's total food and beverage sales.

Add to all of that my contention that we have no idea what   13
we're eating. We inhale our food. Thirty-seven percent of all
quick-service occasions occur at the drive-thru. Who has time
to stop and eat? In light of all that, Surgeon General Satcher
ought to launch a subsidiary program to study the American
digestive system.

Bottom line? Obesity is a major issue. It's good that the gov-   14
ernment is looking into it. We need to develop an action—sorry
about that—an awareness plan to show Americans how to
improve their diets. I don't think, however, that the nutritional
police need to retard the process with a lot of intellectual banter and demands that restaurant menus take on the heft of
encyclopedias.

Fat tax? Talk about opening up a can of Spam! Whoever be-   15
comes involved with the Fed's program must consider that
obesity largely is a result of the American lifestyle at work and
at play: eat and run, gulp and gobble, call it what you will.
Curb that appetite and there won't be any need for a fat tax.

Awareness? Of course. Regulations? Don't think that's too   16
smart. We are what we eat and will continue to eat what we
like despite the government's efforts to impose absolutes. Just
ask the cigarette smokers of America.

How Does Social Class Affect Crime and Punishment?

Ed Mead

REFLECTIONS ON CRIME AND CLASS

Ed Mead, the author of this piece, spent 18 years in prison after his illegal activities with the so-called George Jackson Brigade in the 1970s. The George Jackson Brigade was a Marxist/anarchist urban guerrilla group active in the Pacific Northwest in the 1970s. According to Brigade veteran Bo Brown, "We were not all anything, we were pretty diverse actually. Half of us were women. Half of those women were lesbians. We were probably 90% working class, 75% ex-convicts, and we were tired of armchair revolutionaries who read great books and made predictions and attempted to become the leadership of various movements but didn't really do anything." Mead and his supporters tend to call him a political prisoner who had "expropriated" a bank; legal authorities might call him a revolutionary, an anarchist, and/or a bank robber. Mead has become an antiprison advocate in the San Francisco Bay area. The essay included here, written after Mead's release from prison and first published in 2000 by Social Justice, *explores the relationship between crime and class in America. As you read, you might consider the* ethos *(i.e., character) that Mead portrays as well as the* ethos *that he brings with him as an ex-convict and/or an advocate for social justice. Do his views on crime and class hold weight despite, or even because of, his criminal record? You might also consider whether the actions of a radical group like the George Jackson Brigade falls under the category of "civil disobedience" as discussed in the earlier part of* Conversations, *or whether it has crossed a line—and where that line is.*

Walk around town in any major U.S. city today and one can't 1
help but notice the huge and seemingly growing number of
homeless people living on the streets. This sight is particularly
unnerving to me, a modern-day Rip Van Winkle. I went into
prison for political crimes back in the mid-1970s and came out
nearly 20 years later to a very different world. Before I went to
prison, a person could hitchhike from place to place without
a second thought. In one trip I hitched from Buffalo, New
York, to San Francisco, California, and then on up to Seattle,
Washington, and in the process met a wonderful culture of
people who traveled around the country in this way. Back in
those days we could happily talk to people we passed on the
streets. We even had the luxury to smile and speak to children
we didn't know. Today, I can safely speak to a dog passing me
on the sidewalk, but not to the person walking the animal. I
shudder to think about the possible consequences of speaking
to some stranger's child. If this country's poverty and fear have
gotten this bad since the mid-1970s, how bad will it become in
another 20 years?

When I was a youthful revolutionary, I was prepared to risk 2
imprisonment or worse to bring about a better world. My
peers and I felt the risks were a better alternative than continuing to live under the boot of capitalism's culture of death.
Today that culture is far worse. The system is considerably
more vicious, the nation's citizens more confused, and the level
of social atomization has never been greater. One of the state's
primary mechanisms for isolating us from each other is fear.
The fear of crime is the greatest fear of all, and no domestic
segment of society is more demonized than the one consisting
of criminals. The alleged offender is no longer a part of "us,"
but has suddenly become one of "them" (the other upon whom
any evil can justly be visited). Not only is this demonized person politically disenfranchised and held behind bars under
constitutionally sanctioned conditions of slavery, the hapless
offender is also subjected to endless forms of torture.

The first step in getting a better grasp of the crime/fear dy- 3
namic is to understand the dialectical processes involved—not
the ongoing, media-driven hysteria. What constitutes a crime
is not some fixed set of proscribed behaviors; rather, these behaviors change with time and the class nature of the existing
social order. Ancient Greece and Rome, for example, were societies based upon the state-supported economic system of slavery. A slave owner during that period would be perfectly within

his legal rights to murder one or more of his slaves. He could premeditatedly kill them as punishment or for the mere pleasure of watching them die. The law of the day protected his right to dispose of his property in any way he saw fit.

4   Today, getting rich from the surplus value created by your employees is looked upon as one of bourgeois society's highest virtues. In tomorrow's working-class social order, on the other hand, that sort of behavior will be criminally repugnant. Just as what we call first-degree premeditated murder was behavior protected by the power of the state under the system of slavery, so too, in a future social order, acts seen as virtuous today will be looked upon as criminal behavior. Indeed, in a future communist society it would rightfully be a crime for one person to materially profit from the labor of another.

5   Just as the definitions of crime can change with the class basis of the existing social order, so too can its punishments. Today's capitalist system engenders myriad schemes for separating the working class from its hard-earned money, ranging from telemarketing scams to the usury committed by banks and credit card companies. Some of these are legal and some are not. When such crimes are punished, the punishment is light, usually a fine of some sort. The same is true for punishments against corporations and wealthy individuals. Indeed, a rich person has never been executed in all of American history. Yet in all class societies to the present, the crimes of the poor are punished far more harshly. This disparity in punishment is applied with a vengeance during periods of social instability. In feudal England, for example, committing such petty offenses as killing a rabbit on private land, chopping down a tree on a public lane, or picking a pocket were crimes punishable by death. These draconian punishments have never worked. History records groups of pickpockets gleefully plying their trade on crowds gathered to watch the hanging of fellow pickpockets.

6   When General Licinius Crassus impaled the heads of Spartacus and thousands of rebellious followers on spikes along the road to Rome, his doing so did not save the system of slavery or the Roman Empire that lived off it. Nor did murdering hapless pickpockets save the British monarchy from the onslaught of capitalist productive relations. Similarly, the adoption of harsh three-strikes legislation, the gutting of constitutional protections, and the ongoing expansion of the death penalty will not save the moribund system of international capitalism. Yet, if history is any teacher, we can expect ever-harsher punishments and still fewer legal safeguards for accused criminals or others who seek to implement a radical transformation of existing class relations.

Although the ruling class makes good use of the existence of   7
crime (by keeping people isolated by fear from one another),
they do not desire the presence of crime any more than we do.
Nobody wants crime. Still, in a social order in which one-half
of one percent of the population owns more than 90% of the
nation's property, resources, and productive capacity (not to
mention control of the means of education and information), it
is understandable that those who have the least will take some
stumbling steps to restore a more natural balance of wealth.

The rich fully understand that crime is a force, not unlike   8
that of electricity or running water, and as such it will follow
the path of least resistance. It even has a natural direction,
too—against property (90% of all crimes are against property).
By increasing the effort required to attack their property interests, the ruling class effectively channels the force of crime
back onto the poor. The rich live in remote, gated communities; their banks have armed guards, sophisticated alarm systems, and are protected by the jurisdiction of the federal courts
and the investigative techniques of the FBI.

Since crime tends to follow the course of least resistance, the   9
social effect of these and other security measures is to rechan-
nel the force of crime toward the poor. Hence, the dramatic increase in the level and intensity of poor-on-poor crime. With
the advent of increasingly less expensive and more available
surveillance mechanisms and alarm systems, the force of
crime is being steadily pushed further into our poorest minority communities. We can expect this trend to continue until
every home (or car), whose owner can afford it, will be an electronic fortress.

How are progressives to respond to this situation? A starting   10
point would be to organize our communities so as to redirect
the force of crime back up against those elements responsible
for its development—the rich. We cannot today implement the
economically just society necessary for the ultimate elimination of crime. Without that foundation, without control of the
means of information and education, we can only work to redirect the force of crime against those who created the conditions for its development.

The political consciousness of the under-culture needs to be   11
raised to a point that makes preying on the poor uncool or
even dangerous for those confused victims of capitalism who
steal from or otherwise victimize their neighbors. The message
must be: "Rather than ripping off that old woman for her
monthly sustenance check, take your needs to those who can
better afford to pay." Prisoners should especially be involved
in this process. Their lack of class-consciousness is clearly

reflected by the fact that there is currently no stigma attached if you are in prison for cannibalizing your own community. There must be the same stigma for stealing a welfare mother's check as there is for being a rapist or a child molester. Indeed, these predatory cannibals who prey on their own class are the very lowest of the low. It must be made clear to them that class considerations are always primary.

12   On the outside, we can start laying the foundation for dual power by policing our communities (without collaboration with the state's apparatus of repression). Taking control of our neighborhoods is an important part of increasing the resistance that will ultimately direct crime against the rich. When the movement finally develops again, class-conscious ex-convicts would take leadership in this community-protection process. Those still on the inside would hold study groups for their peers on issues of class, race, and the various manifestations of sexism. Although we can't yet eliminate crime, we can at least start the process of making it more class conscious.

13   Maybe one day I will be able to walk down the street and smile and say hello to the person walking his dog, and to give a warm greeting and a pat on the head to those children who need a whole community to love them. Maybe I can stick out my thumb and meet many new friends as I travel the land. Although a revolution is necessary, right now I would be happy to get back to the mind frame of the late 1960s and early 1970s. Of course, back then I thought things were so bad that I risked death and a life of imprisonment to try and overthrow the system. In those days we were optimists. We knew that the object was to win.

Christian Parenti

CRIME AS SOCIAL CONTROL

Christian Parenti is the author of The Soft Cage: Surveillance in America from Slavery to the War on Terror *and a fellow at City University of New York's Center for Place, Culture, and Politics. He has also written many articles on social policies regarding crime and punishment, including "Policing the Color Line," "Big Brother's Corporate Cousin," and "D.C.'s Virtual Panopticon," and has been a visiting fellow at CUNY's Center for Place, Culture, and Politics. In an interview with the* Baltimore Sun, *Parenti noted, apropos to the conversation in this section's essays, that "we need to remember that, while the police may get kittens out of trees and enhance public safety, their social-control function has been at the heart of the job from the beginning, even though it's not most of what they do.... Though the poor were not rebelling, they were still a threat. Poor people threaten the system's legitimacy in that they make the social structure appear unjust. They also pose an aesthetic threat, scaring and disturbing the moneyed classes by showing up in inconvenient places. And whether or not poor people are, at the moment, organized and rebelling, there's always the threat that they will." As you read the essay that follows, first printed in* Social Justice *in Fall 2000, you might consider whether he has made this case adequately.*

Is crime proto-revolutionary—a pre-political form of rebellion? 1 Or is crime a form of social control? Is it the "auto-repression" of communities that have throughout history rebelled in organized and unorganized ways? It is often alleged that during the late 1960s and early 1970s, many on the Left romanticized "street crime" as proto-revolutionary rebellion. To some extent this position had currency among elements of the white ultra-Left. However, mainstream criminologists and historians of the 1960s have overemphasized this (Cummins, 1994).

To the extent that there was romanticization of crime, it was 2 based, in part, on a warped reading of Fanon's ideas about the psychologically salubrious and politically heuristic effects of revolutionary violence and his casting of the lumpen classes in colonial towns as potential militants, rather than as the declasse and dangerous dross white Marxists often took them to be. Yet, to be fair, Left valorization of crime as proto-political was neither common nor even very important in shaping left politics around criminal justice; any back issue of this journal's earliest incarnations will attest to that.

So what is a radical reading of crime? By crime, I mostly 3 mean the "index offenses" or interpersonal violence, such as murder, rape, and assault, along with noncorporate theft like burglary and strong-arm robbery. To some extent, however, we can throw in the violence associated with addiction and street-level narcocapitalism.

4   A look at the real impacts of street crime begins to reveal that crime and the fear of crime are forms of social control. Strong-arm robbery, rape, homicide, and general thuggery in poor communities leave people scared, divided, cynical, and politically confused; ultimately these acts drive the victims of capitalism, racism, and sexism into the arms of a racist, probusiness, sexist state. In short, crime justifies state violence and even creates popular demand for state repression. Thus, it helps to liquidate or at least neutralize a whole class of potential rebels. Crime also short-circuits the social cohesion necessary for radical mobilization.

5   As one community organizer in San Francisco put it: "How do you think they get all the police in here? Without bad guys, there's no so-called good guys."[1] Foucault recognized this point in *Discipline and Punish*. Commenting on the politics of crime in France at the end of the 18th century, Foucault summed up the political benefits of crime—then and now—as follows:

> Crime was too useful for them [the authorities] to dream of anything as crazy—or ultimately as dangerous—as a society without crime. No crime means no police. What makes the presence and control of the police tolerable for the population, if not fear of the criminal? This institution of the police, which is so recent and so oppressive, is only justified by that fear. If we accept the presence in our midst of these uniformed men, who have exclusive right to carry arms, who demand our papers, who come and prowl on our doorsteps, how would any of this be possible if there were no criminals? And if there weren't articles every day in the newspaper telling us how numerous and dangerous our criminals are (Foucault, 1980: 47)?

6   How, then, does crime function as social control in the U.S. today? A comparison of crime with the most extreme example of state terrorism, death squads, is instructive. What were the hallmarks and political impacts of state terror in Central America in the 1980s? State violence against popular movements was systematic, but also deliberately random and spectacularly arbitrary—all of which helped to spread ubiquitous fear. People simply "disappeared" forever or, after being captured, showed up on public roads mutilated, their corpses serving as political advertisements. Such tactics caused thousands of activists to give up on politics completely and to retreat into their private lives. Other comrades, particularly survivors of

torture, often became pathological and difficult to work with. Most destructive of all, though, was the fact that the best and the brightest were just gone—dead.

As a result, many potential activists were simply too scared   7
to attend meetings or read radical literature or go to demonstrations. State terror, most graphically embodied in the death squads, scrambled the everyday patterns upon which organizing depended. Street crime in America does the same.

There are three primary ways in which crime acts as social   8
control: it creates fear and demoralization, absorbs "bodies" and human energy that might be harassed by rebellion, and drives poor and oppressed people into the arms of the state. Very directly, crime frightens people away from meetings and keeps community members isolated and voluntarily locked up, not in cells, but in their homes. Moreover, violence and addiction corrode basic social structures, such as friendship and family, upon which political mobilization depends.

In East New York, a once super-bloody, but still violent   9
neighborhood at the end of the old IRT in New York City, an organizer with the United Community Centers reports that it is difficult, if not impossible, to have meetings or events in the evening. Women, who make up the bulk of the community activists, and many men, are too scared to venture outdoors in their neighborhoods after dark for fear of being robbed or brutalized.[2] Housing activists in San Francisco's Bayview/ Hunters Point neighborhood tell a similar story. As one activist who works in Section-Eight public housing explained:

Knocking on doors is a basic part of organizing, right? And in some of the projects where we work—not all, but some— our staff or volunteers are scared to go out and knock on doors. I mean, I've had bottles and rocks thrown at me when I ride through some of these projects. And with the residents it's the same: they live in constant fear of who is on the other side of the door.

He goes on to add: 10

I am not talking about your neighborhood thugs on the corner. In some of these projects you've got crews that are into really heavy skit; activities that involve regularly killing people, organized crime stuff. A body was just dumped in one of these developments. And it's not just propaganda: there are units that have been taken over by some of the serious gangs for dealing. It's not a joke; people have got legitimate fears.[3]

11   Other community activists from the same neighborhood relate similar stories of the corroding effect of crime on social bonds, as it creates chaos and sows fear, all of which undermine political organizing.

12   The whole drug scene creates mistrust. If you're a consumer, you're caught up in your addiction. You can't be responsible, go to meetings, and all that. If you're a dealer, you're busy getting that money and just trying to stay alive. Then the addiction and dealing lead to street crime: killing, robbing. So everybody else is scared to go out at night.[4]

13   Beyond affecting "the community," crime damages family cohesion, a key element in rendering communities disorganized and politically docile. For example, consider the political implications of these comments from a 17-year-old gangster in Phoenix, Arizona, who talked about his relationship with his brother who lives across town and claims a different set:

> It's crazy because we are like from different gangs; only me and my cousin are from the same gang. Like my brother, I always disrespect him because he's from Camelback and skit, they did a drive-by on my house and skit, and then he called me. I was like, "Fuck you, motherfucker, fuck your barrio and skit," and he was like, "Don't disrespect," and I was like, "Fuck you." That's the only thing bad about it if you decide to join the wrong gang.

14   In the same study, another youth commented on his relationship with his uncles:

> They are from different gangs, though . . . but I don't care about them because they be trying to shoot at us all the time. My own uncle shot at me; one of them tried to kill me already, but that's alright (Zatz and Portillos, 2000: 46–47).

15   Communities fighting themselves have a difficult time fighting City Hall. More specifically, crime leads to a collapse in what social psychologists call "neighborhood social ties"—the "glue which makes a collection of unrelated neighbors into a neighborhood" and therefore into a likely platform for community organization (Kuo et al., 1998). This dynamic has a spatial angle as well as the more obvious cultural/psychological ones. When community spaces are dominated by signs of neglect and anonymity, or have become dangerous, social relations soon decline as well.

Common spaces are, in a very literal sense, the platform upon which communities and their movements are built.

The hard Right capitalizes on a similar point with its much-vaunted Broken Windows theory. For the Right, such signs of anomie and community dysfunction indicate a lack of social control. However, the Left could use evidence of crime's damage to neighborhood social ties in theorizing crime as auto-oppression, as social control, or as useful in reproducing capitalism and white supremacy.   16

Fear and social breakdown are not the only politically useful effects produced by street crime in poor and racially oppressed areas. Although crime—particularly the drug trade—scares some, it seduces others, siphoning off people who might otherwise become politically active. As one organizer put it: "We're competing with drugs for the same employees, if you will. People that we try to organize to demand social and economic justice are often pulled into the drug trade."[5] Many of the same folks soon get packed away to prison, or the morgue. As one Hunters Point activist put it: "If you've got a hassle, if you're in the game, you've got to keep your head down. You're compromised." Activists say this is particularly true vis-a-vis intimate and immediate oppressors such as private landlords, the housing authority, or HUD, while going down to City Hall is less frightening because it is a more anonymous conflict entailing less risk of retribution. A new federal policy called "one strike" makes this fear of political conflict true even for people who are only "involved" by association.   17

Since the early 1990s, automatic eviction is the fate of anyone living in public housing whose family member, or even guest, is arrested for selling or using drugs. In Oakland, the housing authority even tried to evict an elderly man whose homecare attendant was using drugs. Almost everyone in public housing thus lives with the constant threat of eviction and activists have noted that this has a definite chilling effect on resident activism, particularly when it comes to facing off against their housing authority landlords.   18

Crime absorbs activists and entire organizations as well. When crime is a pressing issue, community mobilization frequently focuses on "stopping the violence" rather than on broader questions of social justice and economic redistribution. Thus, the women who started groups like Mothers Against Gangs might have under different conditions started "Mothers Against Landlords."   19

The absorption effect of crime segues into the third, and perhaps most powerful, way in which crime operates as social control. That is by driving poor and working-class people into the   20 arms of the state—a state that through most of its policies co-operates with capital to exploit and marginalize the majority. Community activists in Los Angeles and the Bay Area mention, without prompting, that one of the first and most consistent demands from the impoverished communities in which they work is "more cops." Throughout California, the many racist, get-tough anticrime ballot propositions of the 1990s have received healthy support from poor and working-class people of color.

21   This final, doubly pernicious, angle on the issue is that nothing produces crime and violence like sending young people to prison. (Prison as a finishing school for criminals is one of the oldest and most consistent criticisms against that institution.) Thus, incarceration returns us to square one: it helps produce the predator class that frightens and disorganizes potentially rebellious communities.

22   In recent years, residents in some public housing projects have organized to address crime, but the "solutions" have only made things more difficult for organizers. Most anticrime measures have involved poorly paid and trained security guards who are ultimately unaccountable to the residents.

23   As the housing activist explains: "The private security are scared, they're not gonna mess with the West Mob or Big Block [two infamous gangs in Hunters Point]. So they just stay in their security booths all night. And then to look proactive they start harassing people for little stuff." Picking on "easy targets" can go as far as summary evictions. Inevitably, say activists, the very residents who worked to bring in private security are targeted by those forces. The result is more fear, further demoralization, and further militarization.

24   If private security doesn't work, what about the police? East New York offers a particularly chilling example of what this can mean. Activists and residents interviewed by the press said that cops from the local precinct—shown by the 1994 Mollen Commission to be massively corrupt—were never there when needed. When they did arrive, they acted like an occupying army, treating everyone with massive contempt. As a result, East New York was like a war zone. Between the waves of police occupation, the neighborhood was under siege by many of its own youth who, driven by racism and poverty, had plunged headlong into the lethal front lines of the drug trade. Thus, fear comes in waves, one wearing uniforms, one not.

25   Whatever this analysis of crime as social control may mean for shaping a Left response to crime, one thing is certain: community power and empowerment are at the heart of any real anticrime agenda. Thus, the pro-peace culture emerging among

urban youth of color should be embraced not just as a marketable, hip niche for nonprofits to embrace, but as an example of anticrime measures rooted in popular power. Likewise, police accountability should be constructed not simply as a human rights issue, but as an anticrime issue. Police will be effective at deactivating and preventing violence when they are accountable, and that will only happen when they are subject to the sorts of radically democratic structures of community control that were proposed in the 1970s in the Bay Area and other regions. (Those plans called for community-elected local "police councils," an elected police commission, and a recall process for officers who abused their power. Officers were also required to live within their "police districts.")

As many community organizers are already doing, we might   26
articulate the struggle for public services and community economic development (such as sanitation, street maintenance, housing, rehabilitation, education, and health care) as anticrime measures. During the Clinton era, just the opposite was true: policing was dressed up as "community development." Community Development Block Grants were even handed over to cops in a few cities. We need the opposite.

One could also imagine the proliferation of unarmed, preven-   27
tive, locally organized forms of community safety, such as escort services for the elderly and peace patrols trained—not to be the state's "eyes and ears" or vigilantes—but to intervene and defuse tense situations through mediation. In addition, community-controlled "target hardening," like adequate streetlights and the removal of abandoned cars, should be worked into broader Left strategies of mobilization, self-determination, and economic justice. It is not enough to get good lighting; rather, the whole question of crime control should be increasingly subordinated to a political discourse of community development. (It is noteworthy that such grassroots anticrime activities have often been directly attacked by the police.)

The discussion of crime control is currently so poisonous   28
and monopolized by the Right as to taint any contemplation of a Left response to crime. Yet a realistic (not realist) approach to crime from the Left must be fashioned. This approach must particularly take into account that imprisonment causes crime and thus argue against the overuse of incarceration.

NOTES

1. Interview, with Michael Green, Field Organizer, Housing Rights Committee Organizer, 2000.
2. Interview with Mel Grizer, Executive Director, United Community Centers, 1995.

3. Rob Eshelman, Housing Rights Committee, 2000.
4. Interview with Michael Green.
5. Interview with Carlos Fresco, Organizer, United Community Centers, 1995.

REFERENCES

Cummins, Eric. 1994. *The Rise and Fall of California's Radical Prison Movement*. Stanford: Stanford University Press.

Foucault, Michel. 1980. *Power/Knowledge: Selected Interviews and Other Writings, 1972–1977*. New York: Pantheon.

Kuo, Frances E., William C. Sullivan, Rebekah Levine Coley, and Liesette Brunson. 1998. "Fertile Ground for Community: Inner-City Neighborhood Common Spaces." *American Journal of Community Psychology* 26, 6 (December 1).

Terry, Don. 1990. "Bronx Clash with Police Angers Citizen's Patrol." *New York Times* (September 12).

Zatz, Marjorie S. and Edwardo L. Portillos. 2000. "Voices from the Barrio: Chicano/a Gangs, Families, and Communities." *Criminology* 38, 2 (May 1).

Patrick Leahy

CONGRESS SHOULD PASS LEGISLATION TO LOWER FEDERAL CRACK COCAINE SENTENCES

One of the debates about the relationship of crime and punishment to issues of class surrounds sentencing rules for possession of crack cocaine and powder cocaine. Some have contended that the laws and their enforcement are biased against minorities, and especially against young African Americans. According to The Sentencing Project, though the effects of cocaine in both forms are similar, the following differences exist in laws surrounding them:

- *For powder cocaine, a conviction with intent to distribute 500 grams of powder cocaine carries a five-year sentence; for*

> *crack cocaine, only 5 grams leads to a five-year sentence. This is a 100:1 ratio.*
> - *Approximately two-thirds of crack users are white or Hispanic, but in 1994, 85 percent of those convicted of possession were African American, and 88 percent of those convicted for trafficking were African American.*
> - *Fifty-eight percent of convictions for powder cocaine involved white defendants; 27 percent were African American.*

Although these statistics point to possible racial and class biases in drug penalties, some suggest that the higher sentence for crack is warranted, since it is more addictive. The debate about this issue was brought to Congress in 1995 and is reflected in the piece below and the one that follows by Larry Thompson. Patrick Leahy is a democratic Senator from Vermont, first elected in 1974. The piece below is excerpted from testimony presented before the Senate Judiciary Committee's Subcommittee on Crime and Drugs in 2002. It was published in 2003 in Congressional Digest, *a journal that features pro/con interchanges on current issues. The opposite view is taken in Thompson's article, which follows in this section.*

Few of our criminal laws have created more controversy over the last 15 years than the laws governing cocaine sentencing. The wide disparity between sentences for crack and powder cocaine has fed a debate about racial bias in our justice system, and harmed the ability of law enforcement officers to do their jobs in minority communities. Even as the crack epidemic of the 1980s has receded, and as the crime rate has dropped dramatically, we in Congress have been unwilling to revisit this issue in a serious way. I hope that today's hearing indicates a change in focus for this Committee from the demagogic battles we fought over cocaine sentencing during the 1990s. 1

The Sentencing Commission has released a report to Congress that provides a comprehensive review of our cocaine sentencing policies, and the Commission's unanimous recommendations about how those policies can be improved. This is an important report and it deserves the attention of all the members of this Committee, and of the Congress as a whole. It shows that the principles that guided Congress in 1986 were 2 often uninformed or improperly implemented, and offers a better approach.

3   Under current law, someone who is apprehended with five grams of crack cocaine faces the same five-year mandatory minimum sentence as someone with 500 grams of powder cocaine. This 100:1 disparity in threshold quantity creates a gulf between sentences for powder and crack cocaine offenses.

4   For example, the Commission reports that in 2000, the average sentence for a crack cocaine offense was nearly four years longer than the average sentence for a powder cocaine offense, 118 months to 74 months. This has swelled our prisons, and has had a disproportionate impact on African Americans, who make up 85 percent of the defendants facing crack cocaine penalties.

5   This disparate impact on African Americans would be troubling enough if we believed our cocaine sentencing policy was working. But it is particularly disturbing when one considers that the penalties Congress created in 1986 have proven poorly suited to the concerns Congress sought to address.

6   In 1986, Congress wanted to crack down on those who were bringing crack into our neighborhoods, in response to overwhelming public concern about the effect of the crack epidemic on our urban areas and our young people. The supporters of severe crack penalties said they wanted to focus on major traffickers, but the results have not reflected that intention. The Sentencing Commission reports that two-thirds of Federal crack cocaine offenders are street-level dealers, not the "serious" or "major" traffickers the 1986 Anti-Drug Abuse Act was targeting. In other words, the policy has not had its intended effect.

7   During the 1986 debate, there was a substantial focus on crack babies. Congress believed that our Nation was in the midst of, or at least on the verge of, an epidemic, and that prenatal exposure to crack was far more devastating than exposure to other harmful substances. This belief was a powerful prod toward increasing penalties for crack far beyond those for cocaine and other drugs. According to the commission, we now know that the negative effects of prenatal crack cocaine exposure are identical to the effects of prenatal powder cocaine exposure, and less severe than the negative effects of prenatal alcohol exposure.

8   The Commission's recommendations provide a roadmap for Congress toward a fairer, more proportionate drug sentencing system. The Commission would increase the five-year mandatory minimum threshold quantity for crack cocaine offenses

from five grams to at least 25 grams, and the 10-year threshold from 50 grams to at least 250 grams, while leaving the threshold quantities for powder cocaine untouched. This would reduce the 100:1 disparity to 20:1, a substantial change that should greatly reduce perceptions of racial bias in our criminal justice system.

At the same time, the Commission recommends additional 9 sentencing enhancements that would ensure that we provide longer sentences to the criminals who should be our most important targets, including drug importers, drug offenders who use weapons or violence, and dealers who sell to kids. These enhancements would apply to all drugs, including powder cocaine, so that the worst offenders are punished more severely than they sometimes are today.

Indeed, I have not heard anyone make the argument that 10 powder cocaine sentences under current law are insufficient. Although the Justice Department has suggested lowering powder cocaine thresholds, Deputy Attorney General [Larry D.] Thompson testified before the Sentencing Commission that he was not aware of any evidence that existing powder cocaine penalties are too low. In other words, the Administration's only rationale for increasing penalties for powder cocaine is to reduce the disparity between powder and crack without decreasing crack penalties.

The Administration's failure to support even the slightest 11 modification of crack penalties has been a surprise and a deep disappointment. Two days before taking office, President Bush said that we should address this problem "by making sure the powder cocaine and the crack cocaine sentences are the same." He also said, "I don't believe we ought to be discriminatory."

Given the context in which he made the remarks—he was 12 speaking about his concerns that we imprison too many people for too long for drug offenses—it defies belief that the President's aim was to equalize penalties for crack and powder cocaine through a dramatic increase in powder penalties that would further overcrowd our prisons. Yet his Justice Department has decided that that is the only acceptable way to equalize crack and powder penalties. Thankfully, neither the Republicans nor the Democrats on the Sentencing Commission accepted the Administration's view, and instead were unanimous in their recommendation to us today.

I urge my colleagues to embrace that recommendation and 13 make it law. It is long past time for us to do something about this issue.

Larry D. Thompson

CONGRESS SHOULD NOT LOWER FEDERAL CRACK COCAINE SENTENCES

As is discussed in the headnote to the previous essay by Patrick Leahy, there have been many questions raised about the disparity in sentencing guidelines for possession and sale of powder and crack cocaine—a disparity that some have seen as based on race and social class biases. Larry Thompson, the Deputy Attorney General, here argues that the disparity exists for good reasons. This piece was published as a counterpoint to Leahy's argument; both were published in 2003 in Congressional Digest.

1   The Commission has asked for specific comments on whether Federal cocaine sentencing policy should be amended. For the reasons I will lay out in detail, we believe the current Federal sentencing policy and guidelines for crack cocaine offenses are proper, and that it would be more appropriate to address the differential between crack and powder cocaine by recommending that penalties for powder cocaine be increased. Moreover, we will oppose any effort by the Commission to issue guidelines that do not adhere to the congressionally enacted statutes that define and prescribe penalties for Federal cocaine offenses.

2   We are guided in all of our work on drug policy by the President's comprehensive national strategy to fight illegal drug use. The strategy seeks to expand the national drug treatment system while recognizing the vital role of law enforcement in interdiction programs. The strategy recognizes that the individual consequences of drug use can be deadly to the user and that the consequences for society are no less serious.

3   Unfortunately, drug use continues to plague this country at unacceptably high levels. According to estimates generated by the National Household Survey on Drug Abuse, 2.8 million Americans are dependent on illegal drugs. An additional 1.5 million are nondependent abusers.

4   In the year 2000, Americans spent almost $63 billion on drugs. Of that, approximately $36 billion was spent on cocaine alone.

We understand that the Commission is considering lowering 5
penalties for crack offenders. After thorough study and internal debate, we have concluded that the current Federal policy
and guidelines for sentencing crack cocaine offenses are
proper. It would therefore be more appropriate to address the
differential between crack and power cocaine by recommending that penalties for powder cocaine be increased.

Current research shows that crack is an extremely danger- 6
ous substance for many reasons. The most common routes of
administration for crack and powder cause crack to be the
more psychologically addictive of the substances. This makes
crack cocaine more dangerous, resulting in far more emergency room episodes and public facility treatment admissions
than powder cocaine, despite the fact that powder cocaine is
much more widely used.

Further, crack can easily be broken down and packaged into 7
small and inexpensive quantities for distribution, sometimes
as little as single-dose quantities for just a few dollars, making
it particularly attractive to some of the more vulnerable members of our society.

As [Harvard Law] Professor Randall Kennedy has noted, be- 8
cause it is relatively inexpensive, crack has had the dubious
achievement of helping tremendously to democratize cocaine
use. Crack dealers have fulfilled its promise by marketing it to
these vulnerable groups.

Additionally, the open-air street markets and crack houses 9
used for the distribution of crack cocaine contribute heavily to
the deterioration of neighborhoods and communities. Both the
scale of marketing and its open and notorious nature enable
many who would not previously have had access to cocaine
powder to purchase, use, and become addicted to crack cocaine.

The present crack market is associated with violent crime to 10
a greater extent than that of cocaine powder. Crack offenders
are more frequently associated with weapons use than powder
cocaine offenders.

For example, in the year 2000, weapons were involved in 11
approximately 10.6 percent of Federal powder convictions and
21 percent of Federal crack convictions. Federal crack offenses
are also more frequently associated with violence and bodily
injury than powder offenses.

Although the Commission has proposed separate enhance- 12
ment for offenders who employ weapons, violence by offenders
themselves is only a portion of the crime that crack causes and
thus would not reflect the dangers and the true nature of the
use and distribution of this drug. Crack is linked to robbery
and assault by customers seeking to finance their habit. Crack

is strongly linked to prostitution as well. In one recent study, almost 87 percent of women surveyed were not involved in prostitution in the year before starting crack use. And fully one-third became involved in prostitution in the year after they began to use crack.

13   Women who were already involved in prostitution dramatically increased their involvement, with rates nearly four times higher than before beginning crack use. And because of the incidents of prostitution among crack users to finance their habit, crack cocaine smokers have been found to have rates of HIV infection as high as those among IV drug users.

14   Another recent study found that women who use crack cocaine had much higher than average rates of victimization than woman who did not. Among an Ohio sample of 171 adult female crack users, 62 percent had been physically attacked since the onset of crack use. Rape was reported by 32 percent of the women since they began using crack. And among these, 83 percent reported being high on crack when the rape occurred, as were an estimated 57 percent of the perpetrators.

15   These and many other statistics and studies tell the story of the devastation that cocaine and crack cocaine specifically bring to the Nation, especially its minority communities. Lowering crack penalties would simply send the wrong message—the message that we care more about crack dealers than we do about the people and the communities victimized by crack. That is something we simply cannot support.

16   Further, lowering crack penalties is inconsistent with a rejuvenated national fight against illegal drug use. As we indicate in the national drug strategy, effective drug control policy reduced to its barest essentials has two elements: (1) modifying individual behavior to discourage and reduce drug use and addiction, and (2) disrupting the market for illegal drugs. We think lowering crack penalties fails on both counts.

17   Now, we recognize that this Commission and others have expressed legitimate and strong concerns that the current Federal cocaine sentencing policy tacitly directs Federal enforcement resources toward lower-level drug traffickers. With this in mind, today the Attorney General announced a new Federal drug enforcement strategy that seeks to identify and target the most significant drug and money-laundering organizations operating across the country for Federal investigation and prosecution.

18   And as part of this strategy, I will personally be coordinating all of the Department's drug enforcement efforts, which will place increased emphasis on intelligence-based targeting to

reach the most significant drug trafficking organizations. We think that this new strategy, together with existing sentencing mechanisms, such as the safety valve and substantial assistance departures, will go a long way toward addressing the concerns over low-level offenders and Federal drug sentencing policy.

If the Commission decides to amend the penalty structure   19
for crack and powder cocaine, we strongly urge you to make only recommendations to Congress and not to issue guideline amendments. By issuing guidelines the Commission would, we believe, effectively decouple the guidelines from the mandatory minimums passed by Congress.

The Department of Justice opposes and has historically op-   20
posed departing from the penalty scheme established by Congress for two principal reasons.

First, a sentencing system consisting of guidelines that are   21
inconsistent with Federal statutes could produce potentially a rash of sentences providing a 10-year sentence under the mandatory minimum statute for a defendant who trafficked in 50 grams of crack, while providing a far lesser sentence for an individual who trafficked in 1/100th of a gram less.

Such a system would fail to honor the congressional man-   22
date set forth in the Commission's organic statute to avoid unwarranted disparities among defendants with similar records.

Second and more fundamentally, decoupling would disre-   23
gard Congress's express wishes. The current mandatory minimums are the law of the land. The Commission should not ignore the law and impose its own will in the face of clear congressional action. By changing the guidelines before any change in the existing provisions, the Commission would be doing just that, ignoring the existing law.

In our constitutional system, we believe the Sentencing   24
Commission exists to effectuate the express will of Congress. The Supreme Court's decision upholding the constitutionality of the Sentencing Reform Act is fundamentally premised on the belief that Congress had appropriately dealt with the commission and set forth the commission's discretion.

We appreciate the chance to share our views with the   25
Commission. We think the Commission should be guided by the words of President Bush, and I'd like to read them to you. "We must reduce drug use for one great moral reason. Over time drugs rob men, women, and children of their dignity and of their character. Illegal drugs are the enemies of ambition and hope. When we fight against drugs, we fight for the souls of our fellow Americans."

Jeffrey Reiman
FROM THE RICH GET RICHER AND THE POOR GET PRISON

Jeffrey Reiman, the William Fraser McDowell Professor of Philosophy at the American University, has for many years researched the relationship between crime and social class. His influential book, The Rich Get Richer and the Poor Get Prison, *an excerpt of which is included here, is now in its seventh edition. In his introduction to* Criminal Justice Ethics, *Reiman wrote*

> *By "morality" is meant the standards of rightness and goodness by which we judge human behavior: fairness, non-malevolence, tolerance, and truthfulness are such standards. In contrast, "ethics" means the philosophical study of morality, the search for principles that justify the moral standards that we seek to apply. And second, "ethics" means those moral standards that are appropriate to particular occupations (so we speak of legal ethics or medical ethics, rather than of legal or medical morality). In both these senses, the study of whether and how criminal justice is moral is rightly called* criminal justice ethics: *It is a philosophical undertaking, and it seeks to understand and justify those moral standards that are appropriate to the occupations that comprise the criminal justice system.*

As you read Reiman's account of the criminal justice system in America, you might consider his definitions of "morality" and "ethics," and how they might inform professionals in the field of criminal justice, for whom both books were primarily written. You might also ask how it can inform the wider questions about civil liberties and responsibilities that are addressed by the works in this section.

Arrest and Charging

The problem with most official records of who commits crime   1
is that they are really statistics on who gets arrested and convicted. If, as I will show, the police are more likely to arrest
some people than others, these official statistics may tell us
more about police than about criminals. In any event, they give
us little reliable data about those who commit crimes and do
not get caught. Some social scientists, suspicious of the bias
built into official records, have tried to devise other methods of
determining who has committed a crime. Most often, these
methods involve an interview or questionnaire in which the re-
spondent is assured of anonymity and asked to reveal whether
he or she has committed any offenses for which he or she
could be arrested and convicted. Techniques to check reliability of these self-reports also have been devised; however, if
their reliability is still in doubt, common sense dictates that
they would understate rather than overstate the number of individuals who have committed crimes and never come to official notice. In light of this, the conclusions of these studies are
rather astounding. It seems that crime is the national pastime.
The President's Crime Commission conducted a survey of
10,000 households and discovered that "91 percent of all
Americans have violated laws that could have subjected them
to a term of imprisonment at one time in their lives."[1]

A number of other studies supports the conclusion that seri-   2
ous criminal behavior is widespread among middle- and
upper-class individuals, although these individuals are rarely, if
ever, arrested. Some of the studies show that there are no significant differences between economic classes in the incidence
of criminal behavior.[2] The authors of a recent review of literature on class and delinquency conclude that "Research published since 1978, using both official and self-reported data
suggests ... that there is no pervasive relationship between
SES [socioeconomic status] and delinquency."[3] This conclusion is echoed by Dunaway, Cullen, Burton and Evans, who
conclude, from a study based on questionnaires given to 550
adults in a midwestern urban area, that "direct class impact on
general crime is relatively weak."[4]

Others conclude that while lower-class individuals do com-   3
mit more than their share of crimes, arrest records overstate
their share and understate that of the middle and upper
classes.[5] Still other studies suggest that some forms of serious
crime—forms usually associated with lower-class youth—show
up *more frequently* among higher-class persons than among

lower.[6] For instance, Empey and Erikson interviewed 180 white males aged 15 to 17 who were drawn from different economic strata. They found that "virtually all respondents reported having committed not one but a variety of different offenses." Although youngsters from the middle classes constituted 55 percent of the group interviewed, they admitted to 67 percent of the instances of breaking and entering, 70 percent of the instances of property destruction, and an astounding 87 percent of all the armed robberies admitted to by the entire sample.[7]

4   Even those who conclude "that more lower status youngsters commit delinquent acts more frequently than do higher status youngsters"[8] also recognize that lower-class youth are significantly overrepresented in official records. Gold writes that "about five times more lowest than highest status boys appear in the official records; if records were complete and unselective, we estimate that the ratio would be closer to 1.5:1."[9] The simple fact is that for the same offense, *a poor person is more likely to be arrested and, if arrested charged, than a middle- or upper-class person.*[10]

5   This means, first of all, that poor people are more likely to come to the attention of the police. Furthermore, once apprehended, the police are more likely to formally charge a poor person and release a higher-class person *for the same offense.* Gold writes that

> boys who live in poorer parts of town and are apprehended by police for delinquency are four to five times more likely to appear in some official record than boys from wealthier sections who commit the same kinds of offenses. These same data show that, at each stage in the legal process from charging a boy with an offense to some sort of disposition in court, boys from different socioeconomic backgrounds are treated differently, so that those eventually incarcerated in public institutions, that site of most of the research on delinquency, are selectively poorer boys.[11]

From a study of self-reported delinquent behavior, Gold finds that, when individuals were apprehended, "if the offender came from a higher status family, police were more likely to handle the matter themselves without referring it to the court."[12]

6   Terence Thornberry reached a similar conclusion in his study of 3,475 delinquent boys in Philadelphia. Thornberry found that among boys arrested *for equally serious offenses* and who had *similar prior offense records,* police were more likely to refer the lower-class youths than the more affluent ones to

juvenile court. The police were more likely to deal with the wealthier youngsters informally, for example, by holding them in the station house until their parents came rather than instituting formal procedures. Of those referred to juvenile court, Thornberry found further that, for *equally serious offenses* and with *similar prior records*, the poorer youngsters were more likely to be institutionalized than were the affluent ones. The wealthier youths were more likely to receive probation than the poorer ones. As might be expected, Thornberry found the same relationships when comparing the treatment of black and white youths apprehended for equally serious offenses.[13]

Recent studies continue to show similar effects. For example, Sampson found that, for the same crimes, juveniles in lower-class neighborhoods were more likely to have some police record than those in better-off neighborhoods. Again, for similar crimes, lower-class juveniles were more likely to be referred to court than better-off juveniles. If you think these differences are not so important because they are true only of young offenders, remember that this group accounts for much of the crime problem. Moreover, other studies not limited to the young tend to show the same economic bias. McCarthy found that, in metropolitan areas, for similar suspected crimes, unemployed people were more likely to be arrested than employed people.[14]   7

As I indicated above, I take racial bias as either a form of bias against the poor or a means to the same result. And blacks are more likely to be suspected or arrested than whites. A 1988 *Harvard Law Review* overview of studies on race and the criminal process concludes that "most studies . . . reveal what many police officers freely admit: that police use race as an independently significant, if not determinative, factor in deciding whom to follow, detain, search, or arrest."[15] "A 1994 study of juvenile detention decisions found that African American and Hispanic youths were more likely to be detained at each decision point, even after controlling for the influence of offense seriousness and social factors (e.g., single-parent home). Decisions by both police and the courts to detain a youngster were highly influenced by race."[16] The study states that "[n]ot only were there direct effects of race, but indirectly, socioeconomic status was related to detention, thus putting youth of color again at risk for differential treatment."[17] Reporting the results of University of Missouri criminologist Kimberly Kempf's study of juvenile justice in 14 Pennysylvania counties, Jerome Miller says that "Black teenagers were more likely to be detained, to be handled formally, to be waived to adult court, and to be adjudicated delinquent."[18] And there is some   8

evidence that charges against blacks are thrown out more frequently than charges against whites because blacks are arrested on the basis of less evidence.[19]

9   There is also the disturbing finding that many black people
are apparently arrested for the crime of "driving while black."
John Lamberth of Temple University set out to study whether
the police arrest black drivers on the New Jersey Turnpike out
of proportion to their percentage in the driving population and
to their rate of committing traffic violations. Lamberth and his
team "recorded data on more that forty-two thousand cars."
They found that

> blacks and whites violated the traffic laws at almost exactly
> the same rate; there was no statistically significant differ-
> ence in the way they drove. Thus, driving behavior alone
> could not explain differences in how police might treat black
> and white drivers. With regard to arrests, 73.2 percent of
> those stopped and arrested were black, while only 13.5 per-
> cent of the cars on the road had a black driver or passenger.
> Lamberth notes that the disparity between these two num-
> bers is 'statistically vast.'[20]

Similar studies, with similar results, were carried out in
Maryland and Ohio.

10   For reasons mentioned earlier, a disproportionately large
percentage of the casualties in the recent war on drugs are
poor inner-city minority males. Michael Tonry writes that, "according to National Institute on Drug Abuse (1991) surveys of
Americans' drug use, [Blacks] are not more likely than Whites
ever to have used most drugs of abuse. Nonetheless, the . . .
number of drug arrests of Blacks more than doubled between
1985 and 1989, whereas White drug arrest increased only by
27 percent."[21] A study conducted by the Sentencing Project,
based mainly on Justice Department statistics, indicates that
"Blacks make up 12 percent of the United States' population
and constitute 13 percent of all monthly drug users . . . , but
represent 35 percent of those arrested for drug possession, 55
percent of those convicted of drug possession and 74 percent
of those sentenced to prison for drug possession."[22]

11   The greater likelihood of arrest that minorities face is
matched by a greater likelihood of being charged with a
serious offense. For example, Huizinga and Elliott report:
"Minorities appear to be at greater risk for being charged with
more serious offenses than whites when involved in comparable levels of delinquent behavior."[23] Bear in mind that, once an

individual has a criminal record, it becomes harder for that person to obtain employment, thus increasing the likelihood of future criminal involvement and more serious criminal charges.

Numerous studies of police use of deadly force show that blacks are considerably more likely than whites or Hispanics to be shot by the police. For example, using data from Memphis, Tennessee, covering the years from 1969 through 1974, James Fyfe found that blacks were 10 times more likely than whites to have been shot at unsuccessfully by police, 18 times more likely to have been wounded, and 5 times more likely to have been killed."[24] A nation that has watched the brutal treatment meted out to Rodney King by California police officers will not find this surprising. Does anyone think this would have happened if King were a white man?   12

Any number of reasons can be offered to account for the differences in police treatment of poor versus well-off citizens. Some argue that they reflect that the poor have less privacy.[25] What others can do in their living rooms or backyards, the poor do on the street. Others argue that a police officer's decision to book a poor youth and release a middle-class youth reflects either the officer's judgment that the higher-class youngster's family will be more likely and more able to discipline him or her than the lower-class youngster's, or differences in the degree to which poor and middle-class complainants demand arrest. Others argue that police training and police work condition police officers to be suspicious of certain kinds of people, such as lower-class youth, blacks, Mexicans, and so on,[26] and thus more likely to detect their criminality. Still others hold that police mainly arrest those with the least political clout,[27] those who are least able to focus public attention on police practices or bring political influence to bear, and these happen to be the members of the lowest social and economic classes.   13

Regardless of which view one takes, and probably all have some truth in them, one conclusion is inescapable: One of the reasons the offender "at the end of the road in prison is likely to be a member of the lowest social and economic groups in the country" is that the police officers who guard the access to the road to prison make sure that more poor people make the trip than well-to-do people.   14

Likewise for prosecutors. A recent study of prosecutors' decisions shows that lower-class individuals are more likely to have charges pressed against them than upper-class individuals.[28] Racial discrimination also characterizes prosecutors' decisions to charge. The *Harvard Law Review* overview of studies on race   15 and the criminal process asserts: "Statistical studies indicate that prosecutors are more likely to pursue full prosecution, file more severe charges, and seek more stringent penalties in cases involving minority defendants than in cases involving nonminority defendants."[29] One study of whites, blacks, and Hispanics arrested in Los Angeles on suspicion of having committed a felony found that, among defendants with equally serious charges and prior records, 59 percent of whites had their charges dropped at the initial screening, compared with 40 percent of blacks and 37 percent of Hispanics.[30]

16   The *weeding out of the wealthy* starts at the very entrance to the criminal justice system: The decision about whom to investigate, arrest, or charge is not made simply on the basis of the offense committed or the danger posed. It is a decision distorted by a systematic economic bias that works to the disadvantage of the poor.

17   This economic bias is a two-edged sword. Not only are the poor arrested and charged out of proportion to their numbers for the kinds of crimes poor people generally commit— burglary, robbery, assault, and so forth—but when we reach the kinds of crimes poor people almost never have the opportunity to commit, such as antitrust violations, industrial safety violations, embezzlement, and serious tax evasion, the criminal justice system shows an increasingly benign and merciful face. The more likely that a crime is the type committed by middle- and upper-class people, the less likely it is that it will be treated as a criminal offense. When it comes to crime in the streets, where the perpetrator is apt to be poor, he or she is even more likely to be arrested and formally charged. When it comes to crime in the suites, where the offender is apt to be affluent, the system is most likely to deal with the crime noncriminally, that is, by civil litigation or informal settlement. When it does choose to proceed criminally, as we will see in the section on sentencing, it rarely goes beyond a slap on the wrist. Not only is the main entry to the road to prison held wide open to the poor, the access routes for the wealthy are largely sealed off. Once again, we should not be surprised at whom we find in our prisons.

18   Many writers have commented on the extent and seriousness of "white-collar crime," so I will keep my remarks to a minimum. Nevertheless, for those of us trying to understand how the image of crime is created, four points should be noted.

> 1. White-collar crime is costly; it takes far more dollars from our pockets than all the FBI Index crimes combined.

2. White-collar crime is widespread, probably much more so than the crimes of the poor.
3. White-collar criminals are rarely arrested or charged; the system has developed kindlier ways of dealing with the more delicate sensibilities of its higher-class clientele.
4. When white-collar criminals are prosecuted and convicted, their sentences are either suspended or lenient when judged by the cost their crimes have imposed on society.

The first three points will be discussed here . . .

Everyone agrees that the cost of white-collar crime is enormous. In 1985, *U.S. News & World Report* reported that "Experts estimate that white-collar criminals rake in a minimum of $200 billion annually."[31] Marshall Clinard also cites the $200 billion estimate in his recent book, *Corporate Corruption: The Abuse of Corporate Power*.[32] Nonetheless, $200 billion probably underestimates the actual cost. Some experts place the cost of white-collar crime for firms doing business in the government sector alone at $500 billion a year.[33] Tax evasion alone has been estimated to cost from 5 to 7 percent of the gross national product. For 1997, that would be between $403 and $564 billion.[34] A survey conducted by the National White Collar Crime Center between January and April 1999 found that one in three American households had been the victim of white-collar crime.[35]

In some areas of the economy, white-collar crime is growing dramatically. For example, the North American Securities Administrators Association conducted a survey of state enforcement actions and found that $400 million had been lost to investors as a result of fraud and abuse in the financial planning industry during the period from 1986 to 1988. Most striking, however, was their finding that "the number of state actions against financial planners rose 155 percent and the amount of lost investor funds climbed 340 percent" since their previous survey in 1985.[36] Then, of course, there was the outbreak of fraud in the savings and loan industry . . .

We need a rough estimate of the cost of white-collar crime so that we can compare its impact with that of the crimes reported on by the FBI. For this purpose, we can use the conservative estimates in the U.S. Chamber of Commerce's *A Handbook on White-Collar Crime*.[37] Because the *Handbook* was issued in 1974, we will have to adjust its figures to take into account both inflation and growth in population to compare these figures with losses reported for 2000 by the FBI. (In light of the avalanche of statistics the government puts out on street crimes, it's worth wondering why the Chamber has not seen fit

19

20

21

to revise its 29-year-old figures, and why no other private or public institution—neither the FBI nor the U.S. Department of Commerce—keeps up-to-date statistics on the overall cost of white-collar crime.) In some categories, I shall modify the Chamber's figures in light of more recent estimates. As usual, I use conservative estimates when there is a choice. The result will be a rough estimate of the costs of different categories of white-collar crime, as well as of the overall total.

22   First, the modifications: As might be expected, the cost of computer crime is far beyond the $0.1 billion estimated by the Chamber in 1974. A report from ZDNet News says: "No comprehensive records on computer-related crime are public, but it is estimated to drain as much as $11 billion per year from consumers and corporations in the U.S. alone."[38] I will use this $11 billion estimate for computer crime. Telemarketing fraud alone is said to cost consumers $40 billion a year.[39] I will use this figure as a conservative estimate for the cost of consumer fraud, though it represents only one among many forms that such fraud can take.[40] As for business victims of consumer fraud, illegal competition and deceptive practices, "figures ranging between $50 and $240 billion have been posited as the amounts 'lost' in the United States through industrial espionage."[41] I will use the low estimate here—$50 billion—noting again that it covers only one form of illegal competition. Government revenue loss has also outstripped the Chamber's estimate of $12 billion annually. An article in *U.S. News & World Report* maintains that "25 percent of Americans admit to tax cheating which costs $100 billion annually."[42] Because this doesn't include defense and other procurement fraud, we can take $100 billion as a conservative estimate.

23   Credit card fraud has also exceeded the Chamber's expectations, with several sources estimating its annual cost at over $1 billion, a figure we can safely use.[43] According to *The New York Times*, "Mastercard International alone experienced $526 million in fraudulent transactions last year [1998]."[44] "The FBI estimates that if commercial banks and other institutions combined their check fraud losses, the total would be $12 to $15 billion annually."[45] I will use the $12 billion figure.

24   The cost of pilferage has increased as well. "The Bureau of National Affairs estimates total employee theft at $15 billion to $25 billion, while the U.S. Chamber of Commerce [recently] says it may be as high as $20 billion to $40 billion. And that's not including theft by government workers, which can be significant."[46] I'll use the low end of the range recently given by the Chamber.

25   Insurance fraud has also gone far beyond the Chamber's 1974 estimates. The Coalition Against Insurance Fraud estimates

that insurance fraud costs more than $85 billion a year and is still growing.[47] I will use the $85 billion figure, which is surely an underestimate in light of government estimates of $100 billion a year in health care fraud—much of which is insurance fraud.[48] It will also come as no surprise, after the era of Boesky and Milken (two stockbrokers who served time in prison for illegal stock manipulations), that security thefts and frauds have far outstripped the Chamber's 1974 estimate of $4 billion. The FBI's Economic Crimes Unit estimates the cost of securities and commodities fraud at $40 billion,[49] and there is now a new category, not even dreamt of by the Chamber in 1974: theft of cellular phone services, estimated to cost $1 billion a year.[50]

For the remainder of the Chamber's figures, I will assume   26
that the rate of white-collar crime relative to the population remained constant from 1974 to 2000 and that its real dollar value remained constant as well (two conservative assumptions in light of the evidence just cited, which shows considerable growth in many white-collar crimes). Thus, I will simply adjust these figures to reflect the growth in population and inflation since 1974. Between 1974 and 2000, the population of the United States increased 32 percent, and the Consumer Price Index increased 250 percent. (That is, 2000's population is 132 percent of 1974's, and 2000's prices are 350 percent of 1974's.) Thus, we can bring the Chamber of Commerce's figures up-to-date by multiplying them by 4.62 (1.32 × 3.5 = 4.62). This, taken together with the modifications indicated in the previous paragraph, gives us an estimated total cost of white-collar crime in 2000 of *$404 billion* (almost ten times higher than the Chamber's 1974 estimated total cost of $41.78 billion). (See Table 1 for the total cost and the breakdown into costs per category of white-collar crime.) The figure $404 billion jibes with the estimates quoted earlier, but it is surely on the conservative side. Nonetheless, it is more than *25 times* the $16 billion that the FBI states is the total amount stolen in all property crimes reported in the *Uniform Crime Reports* for 2000.[51]

In addition to the standard forms of white-collar crime by   27
individuals, corporate crime is also rampant. Sutherland, in a study published in 1949 that has become a classic, analyzed the "behavior" of 70 of the 200 largest U.S. corporations over a period of some 40 years:

> The records reveal that every one of the seventy corporations had violated one or more of the laws, with an average of about thirteen adverse decisions per corporation and a range of from one to fifty adverse decisions per corporation. . . .

TABLE 1 The Cost of White-Collar Crime (in billions of dollars), 2000

Bankruptcy fraud		$ 0.37
Bribery, kickbacks, and payoffs		13.86
Computer- and Internet-related crime		11.00
Consumer fraud, illegal competition, deceptive practices		190.00
Consumer victims	$ 40.00	
Business victims	50.00	
Government revenue loss	100.00	
Credit card and check fraud		13.00
Credit card	1.00	
Check	12.00	
Embezzlement and pilferage		33.86
Embezzlement	13.86	
(cash, goods, services)		
Pilferage	20.00	
Insurance fraud		85.00
Receiving stolen property		16.17
Securities thefts and frauds		40.00
Cellular phone fraud		1.00
	Total (billions)	$404.26

Source: Chamber of Commerce of the United States, *Handbook on White-Collar Crime, 1974* (figures adjusted for inflation and population growth through 2000, and supplemented from other sources documented in the text).

Thus, generally, the official records reveal that these corporations violated the trade regulations with great frequency. The "habitual criminal" laws of some states impose severe penalties on criminals convicted the third or fourth time. If this criterion were used here, about 90 percent of the large corporations studied would be considered habitual white-collar criminals.[52]

28   Nevertheless, corporate executives almost never end up in jail, where they would find themselves sharing cells with poorer persons who had stolen less from their fellow citizens. What Sutherland found in 1949 continues up to the present. In his 1990 book, *Corporate Corruption: The Abuse of Power*, Marshall Clinard writes:

Many government investigations, both federal and state, have revealed extensive law violations in such industries as oil, autos, and pharmaceuticals. . . . [O]ver one two-year period, the federal government charged nearly two-thirds of the Fortune 500 corporations with law violations; half were charged with a serious violation. . . . According to a 1982 *U.S. News & World Report* study, more than one out of five of the *Fortune 500* companies had been convicted of at least one major crime or had paid civil penalties for serious illegal behavior between 1970 and 1979.[53]

A recent study of offenders convicted of federal white-collar 29 crimes found "that white-collar criminals are often repeat offenders."[54] As for the treatment of these repeat offenders, Clinard says "a large-scale study of sanctions imposed for corporate law violations found that administrative [that is, non-criminal] penalties were employed in two-thirds of serious corporate law violations, and that slightly more than two-fifths of the sanctions . . . consisted simply of a warning to the corporation not to commit the offense again."[55]

The continued prevalence of these practices is confirmed in 30 a recent study of white-collar crime prosecutions by Susan Shapiro, titled "The Road Not Taken: The Elusive Path to Criminal Prosecution for White-Collar Offenders." Focusing on the enforcement practices of the Securities and Exchange Commission (SEC), Shapiro writes that:

> while criminal dispositions are often appropriate, they are rarely pursued to the sentencing stage. Out of every 100 suspects investigated by the SEC, 93 have committed securities violations that carry criminal penalties. Legal action is taken against 46 of them, but only 11 are selected for criminal treatment. Six of these are indicted; 5 will be convicted and 3 sentenced to prison. Thus, for Securities and Exchange Commission enforcement, criminal prosecution most often represents the road not taken. Of those found to have engaged in securities fraud, 88 percent never have to contend with the criminal justice system at all.[56]

Russell Mokhiber reports that "less than one half of one percent (250) of the criminal indictments brought by the Department [of Justice] in 1994 involved environmental crimes, occupational safety and health crimes, and crimes involving product and consumer safety issues."[57] With upper-class lawbreakers, the authorities prefer to sue in civil court for damages or for an injunction rather than treat the wealthy as common criminals. Judges have, on occasions, stated in open court that they would not make criminals of reputable businessmen. One would think it would be up to the businessmen to make criminals of themselves by their actions, but, alas, this privilege is reserved for the lower classes.

31   Examples of reluctance to use the full force of the criminal process for crimes not generally committed by the poor can be multiplied ad nauseam. We shall see later that a large number of potential criminal cases arising out of the savings and loan scandals has been dismissed by federal law enforcement agencies because they lack the personnel to pursue them, even as we hire 100,000 new police officers to fight street crime.

32   Let me close with one final example that typifies this particular distortion of criminal justice policy. Embezzlement is the crime of misappropriating money or property entrusted to one's care, custody, or control. Because the poor are rarely entrusted with tempting sums of money or valuable property, this is predominantly a crime of the middle and upper classes. The U.S. Chamber of Commerce estimate of the annual economic cost of embezzlement, adjusted for inflation and population growth, is $13.86 billion, more than three-quarters of the total value of all property and money stolen in all FBI Index property crimes in 2000. (Don't be fooled into thinking that this cost is imposed only on the rich or on big companies with lots of resources. They pass on their losses—and their increased insurance costs—to consumers in the form of higher prices. Embezzlers take money out of the very same pockets that muggers do: yours!) Nevertheless, the FBI reports that, in 2001, when there were 1,120,346 arrests for property crimes, there were 13,836 arrests for embezzlement nationwide.[58] Although their cost to society is comparable, the number of arrests for property crimes was *more than 80 times greater* than the number of arrests for embezzlement. Roughly, this means there was one property crime arrest for every $14,000 stolen, and one embezzlement arrest for every $898,000 "misappropriated": Note that even the language becomes more delicate as we deal with a "better" class of crook.

33   The clientele of the criminal justice system forms an exclusive club. Entry is largely a privilege of the poor. The crimes they commit are the crimes that qualify one for admission, and they are admitted in greater proportion than their share of those crimes. Curiously enough, the crimes the affluent commit are not the kind that easily qualify one for membership in the club.

34   And as we have seen, the reluctance to use the full force of the criminal justice system in pursuit of white-collar criminals is matched by a striking reluctance to use the full force of current public and private research organizations to provide up-to-date estimates of its cost. This coincidence is worth pondering

by anyone interested in how criminal justice policy gets made and how research and statistics function in the process.

NOTES

1. Isidore Silver, "Introduction" to the Avon edition of *The Challenge of Crime in a Free Society* (New York: Avon, 1968), p. 31.
2. This is the conclusion of Austin L. Porterfield, *Youth in Trouble* (Fort Worth, Tex.: Leo Potishman Foundation, 1946); Fred J. Murphy, M. Shirley, and H. L. Witmer, "The Incidence of Hidden Delinquency," *American Journal of Orthopsychiatry* 16 (October 1946), pp. 686–96; James F. Short, Jr., "A Report on the Incidence of Criminal Behavior, Arrests, and Convictions in Selected Groups," *Proceedings of the Pacific Sociological Society, 1954*, pp. 110–18, published as vol: 22, no. 2 of *Research Studies of the State College of Washington* (Pullman: State College of Washington, 1954); F. Ivan Nye, James F. Short, Jr., and Virgil J. Olson, "Socioeconomic Status and Delinquent Behavior," *American Journal of Sociology* 63 (January 1958), pp. 381–89; Maynard L. Erickson and Lamar T. Empey, "Class Position, Peers and Delinquency," *Sociology and Social Research* 49 (April 1965), pp. 268–82; William J. Chambliss and Richard H. Nagasawa, "On the Validity of Official Statistics: A Comparative Study of White, Black, and Japanese High-School Boys," *Journal of Research in Crime and Delinquency* 6 (January 1969), pp. 71–77; Eugene Doleschal, "Hidden Crime," *Crime and Delinquency Literature* 2, no. 5 (October 1970), pp. 546–72; Nanci Koser Wilson, *Risk Ratios in Juvenile Delinquency* (Ann Arbor, Mich.: University Microfilms, 1972); and Maynard L. Erikson, "Group Violations, Socioeconomic Status, and Official Delinquency," *Social Forces* 52, no. 1 (September 1973), pp. 41–52.
3. Charles R. Tittle and Robert F. Meier, "Specifying the SES/Delinquency Relationship," *Criminology* 28, no. 2 (1990), p. 292.
4. R. Gregory Dunaway, Francis Cullen, Velmer Burton, Jr., and David Evans, "The Myth of Social Class and Crime Revisited: An Examination of Adult and Class Criminality," *Criminology* 38, no. 2 (2002), p. 600.
5. This is the conclusion of Martin Gold, "Undetected Delinquent Behavior," *Journal of Research in Crime and Delinquency* 3, no. 1 (1966), pp. 27–46; and of Sutherland and Cressey, *Criminology*, pp. 137, 220.
6. Cf. Larry Karacki and Jackson Toby, "The Uncommitted Adolescent: Candidate for Gang Socialization," *Sociological Inquiry* 32 (1962), pp. 203–15; William R. Arnold, "Continuities in Research—Scaling Delinquent Behavior," *Social Problems* 13, no. 1 (1965), pp. 59–66; Harwin L. Voss, "Socio-economic Status and Reported Delinquent Behavior," *Social Problems*, 13, no. 3 (1966), pp. 314–24; LaMar Empey and Maynard L. Erikson, "Hidden Delinquency and Social Status," *Social Forces* 44, no. 4 (1966), pp. 546–54; Fred J. Shanley, "Middle-Class Delinquency as a Social Problem," *Sociology and Social Research* 51 (1967), pp. 185–98; Jay R. Williams and Martin Gold, "From Delinquent Behavior to Official Delinquency," *Social Problems* 20, no. 2 (1972), pp. 209–29.
7. Empey and Erikson, "Hidden Delinquency and Social Status," pp. 549, 551. Nye, Short, and Olson also found destruction of property to be committed most frequently by upper-class boys and girls, "Socioeconomic Status and Delinquent Behavior," p. 385.
8. Gold, "Undetected Delinquent Behavior," p. 37.

9. Ibid., p. 44.

10. Comparing socioeconomic status categories, "scant evidence is found that would support the contention that group delinquency is more characteristic of the lower-status levels than other socioeconomic status levels. In fact, only arrests seem to be more characteristic of the low-status category than the other categories." Erikson, "Group Violations, Socioeconomic Status and Official Delinquency," p. 15.

11. Gold, "Undetected Delinquent Behavior," p. 28 (emphasis added).

12. Ibid., p. 38.

13. Terence P. Thornberry, "Race, Socioeconomic Status and Sentencing in the Juvenile Justice System," *Journal of Criminal Law and Criminology* 64, no. 1 (1973), pp. 90–98.

14. Robert Sampson, "Effects of Socioeconomic Context on Official Reaction to Juvenile Delinquency," *American Sociological Review* 51 (December 1986), pp. 876–85: Belinda R. McCarthy, "Social Structure, Crime, and Social Control: An Examination of Factors Influencing Rates and Probabilities of Arrest," *Journal of Criminal Justice* 19, (1991), pp. 19–29.

15. Note, "Developments in the Law—Race and the Criminal Process," *Harvard Law Review* 101 (1988), p. 1496.

16. Jerome Miller, *Search and Destroy: African-American Males in the Criminal Justice System* (New York: Cambridge University Press, 1996), p. 76. The study reported is M. Wordes, T. Bynum, and C. Corley, "Locking up Youth: The Impact of Race on Detention Decisions," *Journal of Research in Crime and Delinquency* 31, no. 2 (May 1994).

17. M. Wordes et al., "Locking up Youth," p. 164: quoted in Miller, *Search and Destroy*, pp. 76–77

18. Miller, *Search and Destroy*, p. 72. The study reported is Kimberly L. Kempf, *The Role of Race in Juvenile Justice Processing in Pennsylvania*, Study Grant #89–90/J/01/3615, Pennsylvania Commission on Crime and Delinquency, August 1992.

19. Free, "Racial Bias and the American Criminal Justice System," p. 209.

20. Cited in David A. Harris, "The Stories, the Statistics, and the Law: Why 'Driving While Black' Matters," *Minnesota Law Review* 84 (1999), pp. 265–326, available at http://academic.udayton.edu/race/03/justice/dwb03/htm

21. Michael Tonry, "Racial Politics, Racial Disparities, and the War on Crime," *Crime & Delinquency* 40, no. 4 (October 1994), p. 483.

22. Fox Butterfield, "More Blacks in Their 20s Have Trouble with the Law," *The New York Times*, October 5, 1995, p. A8.

23. David Huizinga and Delbert Elliott, "Juvenile Offenders: Prevalence, Offender Incidence and Arrest Rates by Race," paper presented at Meeting on Race and the Incarceration of Juveniles, Racine, Wisconsin, December 1986, University of Colorado, Boulder, Institute of Behavioral Science, National Youth Survey; reported in Miller, *Search and Destroy*, p. 73.

24. James Fyfe, "Blind justice: Police Shootings in Memphis," *Journal of Criminal Law and Criminology* 73 (1982), pp. 707, 718–20.

25. See, for example, D. Chapman, "The Stereotype of the Criminal and the Social Consequences," *International Journal of Criminology and Penology* 1 (1973), p. 24.

26. This view is widely held, although the degree to which it functions as a self-fulfilling prophecy is less widely recognized. Versions of this view

can be seen in *Challenge*, p. 79; Jerome Skolnick, *Justice without Trial* (New York: Wiley, 1966), pp. 45–48, 217–18; and Jessica Mitford, *Kind and Usual Punishment*, p. 53. Piliavin and Briar write in "Police Encounters with Juveniles":

> *Compared to other youths, Negroes and boys whose appearance matched the delinquent stereotype were more frequently stopped and interrogated by patrolmen—often even in the absence of evidence that an offense had been committed—usually were given more severe dispositions for the some violations. Our data suggest, however, that these selective apprehension and disposition practices resulted not only from the intrusion of long-held prejudices of individual police officers but also from certain job-related experiences of law-enforcement personnel. First, the tendency of police to give more severe dispositions to Negroes and to youths whose appearance correspond to that which police associated with delinquents partly reflected the fact, observed in this study, that these youths also were much more likely than were other types of boys to exhibit the sort of recalcitrant demeanor which police construed as a sign of the confirmed delinquent. Further, officers assumed, partly on the basis of departmental statistics, that Negroes and juveniles who "look tough" (e.g., who wear chinos, leather jackets, boots, etc.) commit crimes more frequently than do other types of youths [p. 212].*

Cf. Albert Reiss, *The Police and the Public* (New Haven, Conn.: Yale University Press, 1971). Reiss attributes the differences to the differences in the actions of complainants.

27. Richard J. Lundman, for example, found higher arrest rates to be associated with "offender powerlessness." "Routine Police Arrest Practices: A Commonwealth Perspective," *Social Problems* 22, no. 1 (October 1974), pp. 127– 41.
28. William Bales, "Race and Class Effects on Criminal Justice Prosecution and Punishment Decisions" (unpublished Ph.D. dissertation, Florida State University, Tallahassee, Fla., 1987).
29. Note, "Developments in the Law—Race and the Criminal Process," *Harvard Law Review* 101 (1988), p. 1520.
30. Cassia Spohn, John Gruhl, and Susan Welch, "The Impact of the Ethnicity and Gender of Defendants on the Decision to Reject or Dismiss Felony Charges," *Criminology* 25 (1987), pp. 175, 180, 185.
31. "Stealing $200 Billion the Respectable Way," *U.S. News & World Report*, May 20, 1985, p. 83.
32. Marshall B. Clinard, *Corporate Corruption: The Abuse of Corporate Power* (New York: Praeger, 1990), p. 15.
33. August Bequai, "High-Tech Security and the Failings of President Clinton's Commission on Critical Infrastructure Protection," *Computers and Security* 17 (1998), pp. 19–21.
34. Michael Levi, *Regulating Fraud: white-Collar Crime and the Criminal Process* (London: Tavistock, 1987), p. 33; *StatAbst–1998*, p. 456, Table 721.
35. National White Collar Crime Center, "National Public Survey on White Collar Crime," available at: http://www.nw3c.org/surveyresults.htm
36. North American Securities Administrators Administration, The NASAA Survey of Fraud and Abuse in the Financial Planning Industry—Report to the U.S. Senate Subcommittee on Consumer Affairs, Committee on

Banking, Housing and Urban Affairs (Washington, D.C., July 1988), pp. 1–2.

37. Chamber of Commerce of the United States, *A Handbook on White Collar Crime* (Washington, D.C., 1974), p. 6. Copyright © 1974 by the Chamber of Commerce of the United States. Table reprinted by permission of the Chamber of Commerce of the United States.

38. Sandeep Junnarkar, "Online Banks: Prime Targets for Attacks," *ZDNet News*, April 30, 2002; available at: http://zdnet.com.com/2100-1106-895079.html.

39. National White Collar Crime Center, White Collar Crime Topic papers, "Telemarketing Fraud," available at: http://www.nw3c.org/topics_intro.htm.

40. It is essential to be conservative in estimating costs of various white-collar crimes due to the possibility of overlap in the estimates. For example, telemarketing fraud might count some credit card or computer fraud, and vice versa. Nonetheless, working with such partial numbers as we have, we can be quite confident that we are far from overestimating the actual costs—indeed.

41. Peter Grabosky, Russell Smith, Gillian Dempsey, *Electronic Theft: Unlawful Acquisition in Cyberspace* (Cambridge: Cambridge University Press, 2001), p. 143.

42. Harrison Rainies, "The State of Greed,"*U.S News & World Report*, June 17, 1996, p. 64.

43. Margaret Webb Pressler, "Signs of Fraud Go Beyond Signature: Credit Card Companies Use Artificial Intelligence to Thwart Thieves," *The Washington Post*, July 21, 2002, p. H5.

44. Steve Barnes, "A Credit Card Loophole Can Ensnare Retailers," *The New York Times*, August 15, 1999, p.BU4. One observer maintains that 1989 credit card fraud in the United States already exceeded $1 billion. Jerry Godfrey, "The Three 'Rs' of Credit Card Fraud," *Target Marketing* 13, no. 6 (June 1990), p. 28.

45. National White Collar Crime Center, White Collar Crime Topic Papers, "Check Fraud," available at: http://www.nw3c.org/topics_intro.htm

46. Robert McGough and Elicia Brown, "Thieves at Work," *Financial World* 159 (December 11, 1990), p. 18.

47. Coalition Against Insurance Fraud, "Insurance Fraud—The Hidden Tax," available at www.insurancefraud.org

48. "It has been estimated by the General Accounting Office that fraud accounts for up to 10 percent of total health care expenditures"—which amounts to $100 billion. See National White Collar Crime Center, White Collar Crime Topic Papers: Health Care Fraud, available at http://www.nw3c.org/topics_intro.htm

49. FBI Economic Crimes Unit," Securities/Commodities Fraud," available at http://fbi.gov/hq/cid/fc/ec/about/about_scf.htm

50. "Numbers Game: A High-Tech Arrest Gives Unusual Glimpse of Cell-Phone Fraud," *The Wall Street Journal*, April 29, 1996, p. A1:6

51. *Sourcebook–1998*, p. 284, Table 3.124; *UCR–1997*, p. 36.

52. Sutherland and Cressey, *Criminology*, p. 41 (emphasis added).

53. Marshall B. Clinard, *Corporate Corruption: The Abuse of Power* (New York: Praeger, 1990), p. 15.

54. David Weisburd, Ellen F. Chayet, and Elin J. Waring, "White-Collar Crime and Criminal Careers: Some Preliminary Findings," *Crime & Delinquency* 36, no. 3 (July 1990), p. 352.

55. Clinard, *Corporate Corruption: The Abuse of Power*, p. 15.
56. Susan Shapiro, "The Road Not Taken: The Elusive Path to Criminal Prosecution for White-Collar Offenders," *Law and Society Review* 19, no. 2 (1985), p. 182.
57. Russell Mokhiber, "Underworld, U.S.A.," *In These Times*, April 1, 1996, p. 15.
58. *UCR–2001*, p. 235, Table 30.

Richard Johnston

THE BATTLE AGAINST
WHITE-COLLAR CRIME

Though any division of crime into "white collar" and other types (blue collar? violent? victimless? corporate? cyber?) is necessarily limited, Richard Johnston has for many years studied the phenomenon known as "white-collar crime"—crime committed by and often within companies, usually economic and technologically based. Though inexact, part of the reason for the term is to label those ethical breaches in conduct that attain a specific threshold of illegality as actual "crimes." Johnston retired in 2004 as director of the National White Collar Crime Center after 11 years of service in that position. Johnston began his 34-year career in criminal justice with the Bureau of Alcohol, Tobacco, and Firearms and became Deputy Director of the Louisville-Jefferson County Crime Commission in Kentucky and later, Director of Drug Enforcement Training at the Virginia Department of Criminal Justice Services. Johnston's essay was first published in USA Today, *a general-interest magazine on current American issues. As an informational essay, it largely attempts to help nonexpert readers understand the key issues surrounding the topic. But does it make an implicit argument, or take a position, on the issues of crime and class discussed by the readings in this section as well?*

One in three American households are victims of white-collar   1
crime, yet just 41% actually report it. Of those reported, a mere
21% made it into the hands of a law enforcement or consumer
protection agency. This means that less than eight percent of
white-collar crimes reached the proper authorities, according

to the National Public Survey on White Collar Crime, a groundbreaking survey conducted by the National White Collar Crime Center (NW3C), a nonprofit, Federally funded organization that supports state and local police in their efforts to prevent, investigate, and prosecute economic and high-tech crime. For consumers and businesses alike, these statistics are unsettling as the threat of white-collar crimes invades our new, high-tech society.

2   Why do Americans fail to report these crimes that are costing the nation hundreds of billions of dollars every year? Our statistics show that there is a wide disparity between how people believe they will react when they are victimized and how they do so when they actually are. One reason may be that they may not have initially considered the offenses to them as crimes; they may have been uncertain about which agency to contact; or they may have a lack of faith that the offenders would be apprehended.

3   White-collar crimes come in many different forms, including money laundering; credit card, health care, insurance, securities, and/or telecommunications fraud; intellectual property and computer crimes; and identity theft. The growth of the information age and the globalization of Internet communication and commerce have impacted significantly upon the manner in which economic crimes are committed, their frequency, and the difficulty in apprehending the perpetrators.

4   According to the National Fraud Center statistics, economic crime cost the nation $5,000,000,000 in 1970, $20,000,000,000 in 1980, and $100,000,000,000 in 1990. As businesses and financial transactions become more and more computer and Internet dependent, the reality of increased economic crime grows exponentially, fueled by the rapid growth of technology.

5   The Federal Bureau of Investigation's Uniform Crime Reports national arrest statistics for the period 1988–97 show that, while arrests for most index crimes of violence (*e.g.*, murder, nonnegligent manslaughter, rape) and property crimes (robbery, burglary, motor vehicle theft) have declined, those for fraud and embezzlement have risen significantly.

6   Considering the amount of government funding allocated to the control of "street crime," there has been relatively little money set aside for dealing with white-collar crime. This is due in part to a long-standing belief that the public is apathetic towards white-collar offenses and offenders.

7   The aim of the NW3C in administering the National Public Survey on White Collar Crime was to add broader and more-current information to the insights furnished by prior surveys. Rather than limiting our focus to any one aspect, we touched

upon several perception dimensions to present a comprehensive picture of what the average American thinks about white-collar crime. We were interested in obtaining answers to questions such as: How serious do you believe white-collar crime is? How safe do you feel from white-collar crime? Have you or someone in your household been victimized by white-collar crime? If so, did you report the victimization? What type of person do you believe the average white-collar crime victim is? We also asked about participation in risk behaviors associated with white-collar crime victimization, perceptions of the control of white-collar crime, and opinions on workplace theft.

The results proved informative to the law enforcement com- 8
munity, consumer protection organizations, and victim advocacy groups, as well as to criminologists. Statistics to the contrary, the results uncovered a deep concern with white-collar crime and how effectively the criminal justice system deals with such offenses.

Upon assessing the survey results, a multilayered picture 9
materialized. We found the public is becoming well acquainted with theft by deception (as its victims) and tends to view the commission of such crime with an increasingly jaundiced eye. We were able to conclude that the level of victimization is high when compared to earlier studies. Relying on the survey results alone, it is difficult to explain the underlying reasons for the high incidence of victimization. The FBI's Uniform Crime Reports indicate that arrests for fraud, embezzlement, and forgery have risen nationally over the last several years. The incidence of white-collar crime victimizations culled from our survey may simply be a reflection of a rise in activity in this area. On the other hand, the number of victimizations might be a sign that the people may not be sufficiently aware of their vulnerability to being victimized.

Combating White-Collar Crime

Several channels have contributed to combating economic and 10
high-tech crime:

Independent corporations and private-sector industry coali- 11
tions. As a result of limited law enforcement resources, corporations on their own or in cooperation with industry coalitions, such as BITS, the technology group for the Financial Services Roundtable, have had to initiate strategic economic crime-management plans and investigative groups.

There is a growing level of frustration among these corporations, because the monetary thresholds for law enforcement
even to investigate a case, let alone prosecute, can be very high,
depending on the jurisdiction. Coupled with this is increased
legislation requiring corporations to institute anti-fraud
programs and compliance departments. While protection of
corporate assets and their consumers should be their responsibility, there are several consequences to this arrangement.
Many economic crimes go unreported; fewer prosecutions of
these offenses occur; and perpetrators tend to be fired rather
than prosecuted, leaving them free to move on to another organization and continue their victimizing.

12 *Law enforcement.* On the Federal level, numerous regulatory
and law enforcement agencies are authorized to combat
specific economic crimes, including the Federal Bureau of
Investigation, Secret Service, Postal Inspection Service, Securities and Exchange Commission, and Customs. Local law enforcement capabilities for combating economic crime vary,
depending on the size and location of the department and the
allocation of resources. Some larger municipalities and state
law enforcement agencies have formed economic and computer crime units. As resources, training, and awareness of the
intensity of the problem increase, it is likely and necessary that
more of these units will be formed.

13 *National White Collar Crime Center.* The NW3C provides programs geared to meet the specific investigative support needs of
state and local law enforcement agencies in their fight against
economic and high-tech criminal activity. In addition, new projects include the development of the National Fraud Complaint
Management Center to leverage technology in the management
of economic crime complaints. A significant part of this project
is the establishment of the Internet Fraud Complaint Center in
partnership with the FBI. (Learn more at www.nw3c.org.)

14 *Internet Fraud Complaint Center.* The IFCC is a resource established *for* law enforcement *by* law enforcement. For victims
of Internet fraud, it provides a convenient and easy way to
alert authorities of a suspected violation. For law enforcement
and regulatory agencies, the IFCC offers a central repository
for complaints related to Internet fraud, uses the information
to quantify patterns, and provides timely statistical data of current fraud trends. The key to its success lies in its ability to re-
lay timely and complete information to the appropriate local,

state, and/or Federal law enforcement agencies. By facilitating the flow of information between law enforcement and victims of fraud, the IFCC streamlines the case initiation effort on behalf of both the victim and law enforcement agencies.

National Cybercrime Training Partnership. Developed by the   15
Department of Justice and managed by the NW3C, the NCTP provides guidance and assistance to local, state, and Federal law enforcement agencies in an effort to ensure that the law enforcement community is properly trained to address electronic and high-technology crime.

Coalition for the Prevention of Economic Crime. A nonprofit   16
organization established in 1996, CPEC provides support services to businesses in their fight against economic crime. Its mission is to raise awareness of such offences and their impact on businesses. CPEC works closely with law enforcement through a partnership with the NW3C. Current training programs include instruction on fraud management; operational and strategic fraud management techniques; financial investigations practical skills, examination, and analysis; basic data recovery and analysis; and instruction on how to use the Internet for investigations and research.

Needs and Challenges

As a nation, we are faced with an irrefutable challenge to find   17
solutions to the growing threat of white-collar crime. Law enforcement training is key. Preventing, detecting, investigating, and prosecuting economic crimes must become a priority in order to lessen their impact on the economy and the public's confidence. Law enforcement, as it stands now, is in danger of slipping further behind highly sophisticated criminals.

Specialized training in the areas of economic and computer   18
crime, as well as computer forensics, needs to be continued for law enforcement personnel at the Federal, state, and local levels. This is especially important as nearly all white-collar crime now involves computers.

Laws, regulations, and reporting systems are crucial solu-   19
tions. In the U.S., all levels of government have allowed self-regulation of the Internet. Government regulation, for the most part, has focused on cybercrimes that are not economic ones, such as child pornography and cyberstalking. That attitude appears to be changing. There are numerous bills pending

in Congress that address criminal frauds committed on the Internet, identity theft, and issues involving Internet security and attacks upon websites.

20   Public-private partnerships are essential in this battle. Since no one group will be able to solve the complex problems, coalitions of private and public groups must work together to combat economic and cybercrime. As more of these alliances develop, there will be added resources available to reverse the trend of economic crime. Colleges and universities need to revamp their existing programs to create new ones to meet the changing needs of society in this area.

21   What makes the solutions a challenge is based on several factors. First, classifying white-collar crimes is difficult. Lack of clear definitions make it hard for categories to be formed and accurate statistics kept. For example, many individuals use the term white-collar crime, financial crime, and computer crime interchangeably, thus complicating the recording methods of each crime.

22   Another challenge is getting law enforcement and private security professionals to take advantage of the training resources available to them. The reasons this may be occurring include insufficient funding, lack of awareness of the opportunities for training, and a shortage of appropriate staff.

23   Finally, a big block in the road to solving the white-collar crime threat is the fact that the public perception of fraud and its seriousness has not yet been heightened to an appropriate level of concern. Consumers, businesses, and the nation's lawmakers must be persuaded of the importance of recognizing how high-tech and economic crime affects and impacts on society.

24   The NCTP has conducted several focus group meetings revealing that electronic crime is having a profound effect on law enforcement and that no agency is escaping it. At the meetings, a nationwide survey of 31 state and local law enforcement representatives who impact a training base of more than 84,000 persons concluded that program coordination, fast-track initiatives implementation, and skills training are the keys to fighting this growing concern.

25   With a purposeful concentration on the state and local police experience, the following issues were raised during the sessions as a needs list for combating cybercrime:

- Public awareness, to educate individuals, elected officials, and businesses about the impact of electronic crime
- Data and reporting, to understand the extent and impact of electronic crime

- Uniform training and certification courses, to train the police to do their jobs
- On-site management assistance for electronic crime units and task forces, to give help in developing properly equipped computer investigation units
- Updated laws applied at the Federal and state levels, in order to keep pace with electronic crime
- Cooperation with the high-tech industry, to control electronic crime and to protect the nation's critical infrastructure
- Special research and publications, to give investigators a comprehensive directory of training and expert resources to aid them in combating electronic crime
- Management awareness and support, to help senior staffers to understand the impact of electronic crime and to support the expertise and tools needed to investigate and prosecute electronic crime cases
- Investigative and forensic tools, to provide the police with up-to-date technology and the tools necessary to conduct electronic crime investigations
- Structuring of a computer crime unit, to establish best practices on how to create a police unit that can investigate and analyze electronic evidence.

The NCTP has already begun training programs to address many of these concerns and is giving law enforcement professionals across the nation a place to turn to help consumers with the cybercrime problem. Current initiatives include the development and delivery of electronic and high-technology crime training. The NW3C has developed and deployed computer crime training in the last year alone that has benefited more than 1,400 agencies throughout the U.S. That number continues to grow. 26

Specialized law enforcement training has had an impact. NCTP training efforts have reached officers on the front lines, forensic specialists, detectives, prosecutors, and others in need of formal training at either an entry or advanced level, depending on their case involvement. 27

The Internet Fraud Complaint Center has proven its worth to America's fraud victims, referring large and small complaints to law enforcement agencies nationwide. The IFCC conducted a takedown initiative, code named Operation Cyber Loss, which included efforts by the FBI and numerous state and local police departments. They brought charges against 90 individuals and companies, who face a variety of Federal and state criminal charges, which include fraud by wire, mail fraud, bank fraud, 28 money laundering, and intellectual property rights violations. The schemes exposed as part of this operation represent over 56,000 victims who suffered cumulative losses in excess of $117,000,000.

29   The IFCC is in a unique position to identify training needs for law enforcement. The NW3C is responding to state and local law enforcement's training requests through its role as Operations Center for the NCTP. The IFCC also continues to expand its capabilities to accommodate the needs of businesses better, as it has begun the work of creating the appropriate channels that will enable regular communication with representatives from private industry across the nation. We continue to invite input from companies to refine the process of how data at the IFCC is collected and quantified.

30   The exponential growth of technology and the use of computers have triggered a purposeful rethinking of the tools needed by law enforcement organizations to address Internet-related crime. Law enforcement professionals have voiced their concern regarding adequate training in order to be effective in apprehending and prosecuting criminals who use the Internet to facilitate their crimes. State and local police, through their affiliation with the National White Collar Crime Center, have tasked us to help them meet this challenge.

31   Most individuals are unaware of the extent to which their lives, financial status, businesses, families, or privacy might be affected by electronic crime. Unless individuals, companies, and government officials are informed of the increase in crimes committed using the Internet, cybercriminals will continue to steal people's money, identities, and property.

Science and Society

Introduction

No one doubts that science and technology have become central enterprises in our culture. Some scientists would like to have it otherwise, actually; they would like to insulate science as much as possible from social pressures. But that would be impossible: It is not only impossible to keep scientific developments in medicine, genetic engineering, evolutionary biology, supercolliders, space exploration, and environmental science away from public scrutiny, but also not in our best interest to do so. For ultimately science and technology are themselves social creations, carried out through very human means for human purposes; that has already been made quite clear through the conversations about digital literacy in Part 1 and about "new media" in Part 2. Scientific enterprises have always involved ethical and moral dimensions; to dehumanize them is to diminish them. And as the fruits of these fields become more central to our culture, conflicts between science and technology (on the one hand) and society (on the other) will become more important, more frequent, and more complicated.

The first section of this part explores what Dorothy Nelkin calls "the scientific mystique," examining the ways that science uses language to create its special *ethos*. As the topics that science addresses become more complex and as the concepts and technologies that support science's studies have become more specialized, the language used to express those complex concepts has become equally specialized. As a result, the conversation around science can take on a mystique that calls for faith in its goals and progress, rather than real understanding. For example, you may have heard someone ask "Where's the science behind your claims?", suggesting that the only defensible arguments are ones that have "science" behind them—and conversely, that if there *is* good "science," then the assertion it supports stands. In his last book, *The Demon-Haunted World*, Carl Sagan asked us to consider whether this strong reliance on science amounts to just another form of faith, to "worshipping at the altar of science." Though Sagan suggests it does not, the question remains a poignant one. Have we placed too much faith in science? Does the complex language surrounding scientific discovery keep nonexperts in awe, but out of the real conversation? Do we always believe that science will find an answer to humanity's problems? Or does science move us toward a more reasonable, and hence greater, society? These are the topics of conversation in the readings in this section, topics that you will find have gone on for some time—as evidenced by Jonathan Swift's eighteenth-century work, *Gulliver's Travels*, which is excerpted in this section.

The next section in this part of *Conversations* examines a more specific example of the interrelationship between science and society, the important topic of genetic engineering. Whenever scientists delve into the basic building blocks of life—as with cloning, engineering of agricultural products, stem cell research, the Human Genome project—their work raises impassioned arguments. One of the perennial critiques of giving too much authority to science is that doing so is "playing God." Whether we look to fictional stories like *Frankenstein* or *Dr. Jekyll and Mr. Hyde* or to debates about whether cloning is dangerous and ethically suspect, searching for the limits of what science *should do* amidst the broader scope of what it potentially *can do* leads to some important conversations. The essays in this section focus on genetic engineering, both of animal and plant life. They also examine whether science has a moral obligation to stay within limits, or a moral obligation to push as far as it can in the service of humanity. As you read, you might apply these questions to the many other questions that are raised by new biotechnologies—stem cell research, animal-to-human transplants, cosmetic surgery, and so forth. You will also find that even scientists disagree among themselves about just where the boundaries of science's turf lie.

The third section turns to another crucial scientific issue—the protection of our environment. Although many have enough faith in science to believe that any environmental disaster can be staved off by it, others argue that such a disaster is not far off—and that there can come a time that is simply too late for science to fix. There are many other key questions as well: Is the relationship between people and the environment inevitably adversarial? Is nature inevitably at odds with technology? Do we have a custodial responsibility to nature that derives from morality and from our long-term prospects for self-preservation? The readings in this section provide an historical survey of the environmental movement in this country, a movement that arose as population growth and our economic expansion began to threaten our wilderness, a wilderness that is very much at the heart of American ideals. But just because the wilderness is a shared ideal, clearly no one is anti-environment. Still, it does not follow that all agree about how, or when, it needs protection: some make the protection of the wilderness their primary task, whereas others believe that focusing on the wilderness masks the more important job of watching over our own environment—the one in our backyard, our town, our city. Rachel Carson's *Silent Spring* made environmentalism a political issue in the 1960s, influencing President Nixon to create the Environmental Protection Agency in 1973. But long before that, in the nineteenth century, Americans were drawn to the green world, were sanctifying it in their art and literature, and were beginning to think about preservation. But even as some Americans were revering the land as a special landscape that sustained them morally and spiritually, pioneers moving westward were subduing it for their own economic purposes, in the process spoiling rivers and air and virgin forests—and native peoples—in the name of development. Are science and technology friends or foes of the environment? What is a suitable balance between resource development and resource protection? To what extent should we devote scarce resources to the protection of little-known species? How can poorer nations develop economically without environmental repercussions? And what is the role of the United States, as part of the world community, to participate in global environmental efforts like the Kyoto Treaty? Questions like these are debated every day, especially since organized environmental groups are legion— Earth First, The Sierra Club, The Nature Conservancy; and so *Conversations* includes an exchange about the meaning of "wilderness."

Our concept of the wilderness is also very much dependent upon the experience of wild-spaces and wildlife in pictures. From the cute and cuddly animals that show up on talk shows or in advertisements to supposed depictions of the brutality of life in the wild we see on television, for those who live far from the wilderness, the experience is largely through images. But, as with all visual art, the subject is changed by the eye of the artist—through selection, composition, lens choice (for photographers) or palette (for painters), and so forth. Some believe that building affection for nature through these visuals is crucial for those detached from it; others (like William Cronon) find that these distortions of actual nature can do more harm than good. As you "read" the images included in this part's "Visual Conversations," consider how our understanding of, and relationship with, nature is affected by the renderings of landscape and wildlife that you find there—and those that we experience every day.

This issue, and the myriad conversations about science and its boundaries have raised many impassioned arguments on both sides. The passion, of course, comes from the deeply emotional investment we all have in the scientific enterprise. Science, after all, is inseparable from society. The words and images presented in this section invite you to consider your own position in this conversation.

Is Our Faith in Science Justified?

Jonathan Swift

FROM *GULLIVER'S TRAVELS*, PART III: A VOYAGE TO LAPUTA, BALNIBARBI, LUGGNAGG, GLUBBDUBDRIB, AND JAPAN

You are likely quite familiar with the first book of Gulliver's Travels, *the classic work by Irish writer Jonathan Swift, in which Gulliver visits Liliput, the land of the little people. But there are three other books as well, which feature other strange lands visited by Gulliver as a result of the continuing mishaps that befell his ships. In Book 3, from which the piece below is excerpted, Gulliver visits Laputa, where he encounters those who make learning and science their central concerns. Swift uses this narrative to raise questions about his own culture's growing faith in science; do these questions still apply today?*

Chapter II

The Humours and Dispositions of the *Laputians* described. An Account of their Learning. Of the King and his Court. The Author's Reception there. The Inhabitants subject to Fears and Disquietudes. An Account of the Women.

At my alighting I was surrounded by a Crowd of People, but 1
those who stood nearest seemed to be of better Quality. They
beheld me with all the Marks and Circumstances of wonder;
neither indeed was I much in their Debt; having never till then
seen a Race of Mortals so singular in their Shapes, Habits, and
Countenances. Their Heads were all reclined either to the
Right, or the Left; one of their Eyes turned inward, and the
other directly up to the Zenith. Their outward Garments were
adorned with the Figures of Suns, Moons, and Stars, interwoven with those of Fiddles, Flutes, Harps, Trumpets, Guittars,
Harpsichords, and many more Instruments of Musick, unknown to us in *Europe*. I observed here and there many in the
Habit of Servants, with a blown Bladder fastned like a Flail to
the End of a short Stick, which they carried in their Hands. In
each Bladder was a small Quantity of dried Pease, or little
Pebbles, (as I was afterwards informed.) With these Bladders
they now and then flapped the Mouths and Ears of those who
stood near them, of which Practice I could not then conceive
the Meaning. It seems the Minds of these People are so taken
up with intense Speculations, that they neither can speak, nor
attend to the Discourses of others, without being rouzed by
some external Taction upon the Organs of Speech and
Hearing; for which Reason those Persons who are able to
afford it always keep a *Flapper* (the Original is *Climenole*) in
their Family, as one of their Domesticks; nor ever walk abroad
or make Visits without him. And the Business of this Officer is,
when two or more Persons are in Company, gently to strike
with his Bladder the Mouth of him who is to speak, and
the right Ear of him or them to whom the Speaker addresses
himself. This *Flapper* is likewise employed diligently to attend
his Master in his Walks, and upon Occasion to give him a soft
Flap on his Eyes; because he is always so wrapped up in
Cogitation, that he is in manifest Danger of falling down every
Precipice, and bouncing his Head against every Post; and in
the Streets, of jostling others, or being jostled himself into the
Kennel.

It was necessary to give the Reader this Information, with- 2
out which he would be at the same Loss with me, to understand the Proceedings of these People, as they conducted me
up the Stairs, to the Top of the Island, and from thence to the
Royal Palace. While we were ascending, they forgot several
Times what they were about, and left me to my self, till their
Memories were again rouzed by their *Flappers*; for they appeared altogether unmoved by the Sight of my foreign Habit
and Countenance, and by the Shouts of the Vulgar, whose
Thoughts and Minds were more disengaged.

3   At last we entered the Palace, and proceeded into the Chamber
of Presence; where I saw the King seated on his Throne, attended
on each Side by Persons of prime Quality. Before the Throne, was
a large Table filled with Globes and Spheres, and Mathematical
Instruments of all Kinds. His Majesty took not the least Notice of
us, although our Entrance were not without sufficient Noise, by
the Concourse of all Persons belonging to the Court. But he was
then deep in a Problem, and we attended at least an Hour, before
he could solve it. There stood by him on each Side, a young Page,
with Flaps in their Hands; and when they saw he was at Leisure,
one of them gently struck his Mouth, and the other his right Ear;
at which he Started like one awakened on the sudden, and looking towards me and the Company I was in, recollected the
Occasion of our coming, whereof he had been informed before.
He spoke some Words, whereupon immediately a young Man
with a flap came up to my Side, and flapped me gently on the
Right Ear; but I made Signs, as well as I could, that I had no
Occasion for such an Instrument; which, as I afterwards found,
gave his Majesty and the whole Court a very mean Opinion of my
Understanding. The King, as far as I could conjecture, asked me
several Questions, and I addressed my self to him in all the
Languages I had. When it was found, that I could neither understand nor be understood, I was conducted by the King's Order to
an Apartment in his Palace, (this Prince being distinguished
above all his Predecessors for his Hospitality to Strangers,) where
two Servants were appointed to attend me. My Dinner was
brought, and four Persons of Quality, whom I remembered to
have seen very near the King's Person, did me the Honour to dine
with me. We had two Courses, of three Dishes each. In the first
Course, there was a Shoulder of Mutton, cut into an AEquilateral
Triangle; a Piece of Beef into a Rhomboides; and a Pudding into a
Cycloid. The second Course was two Ducks, trussed up into the
Form of Fiddles; Sausages and Puddings resembling Flutes and
Haut-boys, and a Breast of Veal in the Shape of a Harp. The
Servants cut our Bread into Cones, Cylinders, Parallelograms,
and several other Mathematical Figures.

4   While we were at Dinner, I made bold to ask the Names of
several Things in their Language; and those noble Persons, by
the Assistance of their *Flappers,* delighted to give me Answers,
hoping to raise my Admiration of their great Abilities, if I
could be brought to converse with them. I was soon able to call
for Bread and Drink, or whatever else I wanted.

5   After Dinner my Company withdrew, and a Person was sent
to me by the King's Order, attended by a *Flapper.* He brought
with him Pen, Ink, and Paper, and three or four Books; giving
me to understand by Signs, that he was sent to teach me the

Language. We sat together four Hours, in which Time I wrote down a great Number of Words in Columns, with the Translations over against them. I likewise made a Shift to learn several short Sentences. For my tutor would order one of my Servants to fetch something, to turn about, to make a Bow, to sit, or stand, or walk, and the like. Then I took down the Sentence in Writing. He shewed me also in one of his Books, the Figures of the Sun, Moon, and Stars, the Zodiack, the Tropics, and Polar Circles, together with the Denominations of many Figures of Planes and Solids. He gave me the Names and Descriptions of all the Musical Instruments, and the general Terms of Art in playing on each of them. After he had left me, I placed all my Words with their Interpretations in alphabetical Order. And thus in a few Days, by the help of a very Faithful Memory, I got some Insight into their Language.

The Word, which I interpret the *Flying* or *Floating Island*, is in 6 the Original *Laputa*; whereof I could never learn the true Etymology. *Lap* in the old obsolete Language signifieth *High*, and *Untuh* a *Governor;* from which they say by Corruption was derived *Laputa*, from *Lapuntuh*. But I do not approve of this Derivation, which seems to be a little strained. I ventured to offer to the Learned among them a Conjecture of my own, that *Laputa* was *quasi Lap outed; Lap* signifying properly the dancing of the Sun Beams in the Sea; and *outed* a Wing, which however I shall not obtrude, but submit to the judicious Reader.

Those to whom the King had entrusted me, observing how ill I 7 was clad, ordered a Taylor to come next Morning, and take my Measure for a Suit of Cloths. This Operator did his Office after a different Manner from those of his Trade in *Europe*. He first took my Altitude by a Quadrant, and then with Rule and Compasses, described the Dimensions and Out-Lines of my whole Body; all which he entered upon Paper, and in six Days brought my Cloths very ill made, and quite out of Shape, by happening to mistake a Figure in the Calculation. But my Comfort was, that I observed such Accidents very frequent, and little regarded.

During my Confinement for want of Cloaths, and by an 8 Indisposition that held me some Days longer, I much enlarged my Dictionary; and when I went next to Court, was able to understand many Things the King spoke, and to return him some Kind of Answers. His Majesty had given Orders that the Island should move North-East and by East, to the vertical Point over *Lagado*, the Metropolis of the whole Kingdom, below upon the firm Earth. It was about Ninety Leagues distant, and our Voyage lasted four Days and an Half. I was not in the least sensible of the progressive Motion made in the Air by the Island. On the second Morning, about Eleven o'Clock, the King himself in Person, attended by his Nobility, Courtiers, and Officers, having prepared all their Musical Instruments, played on them for three Hours without Intermission; so that I was quite stunned with the Noise; neither could I possibly guess the Meaning, till my Tutor informed me. He said, that the People of their Island had their Ears adapted to hear the Musick of the Spheres, which always played at certain Periods; and the Court was now prepared to bear their Part in whatever Instrument they most excelled.

9   In our Journey towards *Lagado* the Capital City, his Majesty ordered that the Island should stop over certain Towns and Villages, from whence he might receive the Petitions of his Subjects. And to this Purpose, several Packthreads were let down with small Weights at the Bottom. On these Packthreads, the People strung their Petitions, which mounted up directly like the Scraps of Paper fastned by School-boys at the End of the String that holds their Kite. Sometimes we received wine and Victuals from below, which were drawn up by Pullies.

10   The Knowledge I had in Mathematicks gave me great Assistance in acquiring their Phraseology, which depended much upon that Science and Musick; and in the latter I was not unskilled. Their Ideas are perpetually conversant in Lines and Figures. If they would, for Example, praise the Beauty of a Woman, or any other Animal, they describe it by Rhombs, Circles, Parallelograms, Ellipses, and other Geometrical Terms; or by Words of Art drawn from Musick, needless here to repeat. I observed in the King's Kitchen all sorts of Mathematical and Musical Instruments, after the Figures of which they cut up the Joynts that were served to his Majesty's Table.

11   Their Houses are very ill built, the Walls bevil without one right Angle in any Apartment; and this Defect ariseth from the Contempt they bear to practical Geometry; which they despise as vulgar and mechanick, those Instructions they give being too refined for the Intellectuals of their Workmen; which occasions perpetual Mistakes. And although they are dextrous enough upon a Piece of Paper in the Management of the Rule, the Pencil, and the Divider, yet in the common Actions and Behaviour of Life, I have not seen a more clumsy, awkward, and unhandy People, nor so slow and perplexed in their Conceptions upon all other Subjects, except those of Mathematicks and Musick. They are very bad Reasoners, and vehemently given to Opposition, unless when they happen to be of the right Opinion, which is seldom their Case. Imagination, Fancy, and Invention, they are wholly Strangers to, nor have any Words in their Language by which those Ideas can be expressed; the whole Compass of their Thoughts and Mind, being shut up within the two forementioned Sciences.

Most of them, and especially those who deal in the Astronomi-   12
cal Part, have great Faith in judicial Astrology, although they are
ashamed to own it publickly. But, what I chiefly admired, and
thought altogether unaccountable, was the strong Disposition I
observed in them towards News and Politicks, perpetually en-
quiring into public Affairs, giving their Judgments in Matters of
State; and passionately disputing every Inch of a Party Opinion.
I have indeed observed the same Disposition among most of
the Mathematicians I have known in *Europe;* although I could
never discover the least Analogy between the two Sciences; unless those People suppose, that because the smallest Circle hath
as many Degrees as the largest, therefore the Regulation and
Management of the World require no more Abilities than the
handling and turning of a Globe. But, I rather take this Quality to
spring from a very common Infirmity of human Nature, inclin-
ing us to be more curious and conceited in Matters where we
have least Concern, and for which we are least adapted either by
Study or Nature.

These People are under continual Disquietudes, never enjoy-   13
ing a Minute's Peace of Mind; and their Disturbances proceed
from Causes which very little affect the rest of Mortals. Their
Apprehensions arise from several Changes they dread in the
Celestial Bodies. For Instance; that the Earth by the continual
Approaches of the Sun towards it, must in Course of Time be
absorbed or swallowed up. That the Face of the Sun will by
Degrees be encrusted with its own Effluvia, and give no more
Light to the World. That, the Earth very narrowly escaped a
Brush from the Tail of the last Comet, which would have infal-
libly reduced it to Ashes; and that the next, which they have
calculated for One and Thirty Years hence, will probably de-
stroy us. For, if in its Perihelion it should approach within a
certain Degree of the Sun, (as by their Calculations they have
Reason to dread) it will conceive a Degree of Heat ten
Thousand Times more intense than that of red hot glowing
Iron; and in its Absence from the Sun, carry a blazing Tail Ten
Hundred Thousand and Fourteen Miles long; through which
if the Earth should pass at the Distance of one Hundred
Thousand Miles from the *Nucleus* or main Body of the Comet,
it must in its Passage be set on Fire, and reduced to Ashes.
That the Sun daily spending its Rays without any Nutriment to
supply them, will at last be wholly consumed and annihilated;
which must be attended with the Destruction of this Earth,
and of all the Planets that receive their Light from it.

They are so perpetually alarmed with the Apprehensions of   14
these and the like impending Dangers, that they can neither
sleep quietly in their Beds, nor have any Relish for the common

Pleasures or Amusements of Life. When they meet an Acquain-
tance in the Morning, the first Question is about the Sun's
Health; how he looked at his Setting and Rising, and what
Hopes they have to avoid the Stroak of the approaching Comet.
This conversation they are apt to run into with the same
Temper that boys discover, in delighting to hear terrible Stories
of Sprites and Hobgoblins, which they greedily listen to, and
dare not go to Bed for fear.

15   The Women of the Island have Abundance of Vivacity:
they contemn their Husbands, and are exceedingly fond of
Strangers, whereof there is always a considerable Number from
the Continent below, attending at Court, either upon Affairs of
the several Towns and Corporations, or their own particular
Occasions; but are much despised, because they want the same
Endowments. Among these the Ladies chuse their Gallants: But
the Vexation is, that they act with too much Ease and Security;
for the Husband is always so rapt in Speculation, that the
Mistress and Lover may proceed to the greatest Familiarities
before his Face, if he be but provided with Paper and
Implements, and without his *Flapper* at his Side.

16   The Wives and Daughters lament their Confinement to the
Island, although I think it the most delicious Spot of Ground in
the World; and although they live here in the greatest Plenty
and Magnificence, and are allowed to do whatever they please:
They long to see the World, and take the Diversions of the
Metropolis, which they are not allowed to do without a particular Licence from the King; and this is not easy to obtain, because the People of Quality have found by frequent Experience,
how hard it is to persuade their Women to return from below. I
was told, that a great Court Lady, who had several Children, is
married to the prime Minister, the richest Subject in the
Kingdom, a very graceful Person, extremely fond of her, and
lives in the finest Palace of the Island; went down to *Lagado*, on
the Pretense of Health, there hid herself for several Months, till
the King sent a Warrant to search for her; and she was found in
an obscure Eating-House all in rags, having pawned her Cloths
to maintain an old deformed Footman, who beat her every Day,
and in whose Company she was taken much against her Will.
And although her Husband received her with all possible
Kindness, and without the least Reproach; she soon after contrived to steal down again with all her Jewels, to the same
Gallant, and has not been heard of since.

17   This may perhaps pass with the Reader rather for an
European or *English* Story, than for one of a Country so remote. But he may please to consider, that the Caprices of
Womankind are not limited by any Climate or Nation; and that
they are much more uniform than can be easily imagined.

In about a Month's Time I had made a tolerable Proficiency 18
in their Language, and was able to answer most of the King's
Questions, when I had the Honour to attend him. His Majesty
discovered not the least Curiosity to enquire into the Laws,
Government, History, Religion, or Manners of the Countries
where I had been; but confined his Questions to the State of
Mathematicks, and received the Account I gave him with great
Contempt and Indifference, though often rouzed by his *Flapper*
on each Side.

Dorothy Nelkin
THE SCIENTIFIC
MYSTIQUE

*Dorothy Nelkin, who died in 2003, was a sociologist in the
Faculty of Arts and Sciences since 1988 and holder of one of
NYU's highest ranks, University Professor. Nelkin's research examined the interplay among science, technology, society, and—
in* Selling Science: How the Press Covers Science and
Technology *(from which the essay below is excerpted)—
rhetoric. Nelkin has been praised for bringing a great deal of
thoughtful reflection to scientific practices, and for reminding
American culture about the limitations of science in the face of
its becoming almost an object of faith. She was also concerned
about the potential for civil liberties abuses that technology
and the use of DNA analyses brought with it—an issue that is
raised by many of the readings in Part 5 of* Conversations. *The
edition of* Selling Science *from which this piece was excerpted
was published in 1995, revised from the 1987 first edition.*

The public conceives of science as a "variant of the black art," 1
wrote the editor of the *Nation* in January 1902. To the public,
scientists are wizards and magicians, socially isolated from the
society: "The scientist appears akin to the medicine man . . .
the multitude thinks of him as a being of quasisupernatural
and romantic powers. . . . There is in all this little resemblance
to Huxley's definition of science as simply organized and
trained common sense."[1]

2   In the 1990s science still appears in the press as an arcane
and incomprehensible subject, far from organized common
sense. And scientists still appear to be remote but superior wizards, culturally isolated from the mainstream of society. Such
heroic images are most apparent in press reports about prestigious scientists, especially Nobel laureates. But the mystique
of science as a superior culture is also conveyed in the coverage of scientific theories, and even in stories about scientific
misconduct and fraud. This distanced and lofty image is useful
for a community seeking public funds with limited public accountability. But far from enhancing public understanding,
such media images create a distance between scientists and
the public that, paradoxically, obscures the importance of science and its critical effect on our daily lives.

The Scientist as Star

3   Each year the media devotes considerable attention to winners
of the Nobel Prize. With stunning regularity, stories of the
Nobelists focus on their national affiliations and stellar qualities, using language recycled from reports of the Olympic
Games: "Another strong U.S. show"; "Americans again this
year receive a healthy share of the Nobel Prizes"; "U.S. showed
it is doing something right by scoring a near sweep of the
Prize"; "The winning American style."

4   Just as the papers count Olympic medals, so they keep a running count of the Nobel awards: one year "Americans won eight
of eleven"; in another, "Eight Americans were recognized, tying a
record set in 1972." "Since 1941," *U.S. News and World Report*
announced to its readers in 1980, "the U.S. has had 26 Nobel
winners in science, more than double the number won by second
place Britain." In 1993 Nobel coverage, a *Boston Globe* reporter
worried that the "American dynasty may falter in the future because the prizes . . . were for work done in the 1970s when basic
science had more government support."[2] These stories describe
nations as rivals somehow competing in a Nobel race for national pride, ignoring the international cooperation that is supposed to, and often does, characterize scientific endeavors.

5   Following the style of sports writing or reports of the
Academy Awards, journalists emphasize the honor, the glory,
and the supreme achievement of the prize: "The most prestigious prizes in the world. . . . They bring instant fame, flooding
winners with speaking invitations, job offers, book contracts,
and honorary degrees," runs a typical comment. In 1979 *Time*
printed a large picture of the gold medal: "The Nobel Prize

Winners are called to Mount Olympus; the recipients have worldwide respect."

Local or regional papers cover Nobel winners like sports or   6 movie stars, seeking to find a local angle, however remote. Consider Roald Hoffmann, who received the 1981 prize in chemistry. A Rochester, New York, paper mentioned that he was a "Kodak consultant." The *New York Daily News* reported that he had graduated from Stuyvesant High School in New York City and printed his picture from the high school yearbook. Columbia University claimed Hoffmann as one of 39 laureates among its former faculty and alumni.

In one important respect, though, reports of Nobel awards   7 differ markedly from sports writing. Coverage of sports stars often includes analyses of their training, their techniques, and the details of their accomplishments. However, except in the *New York Times* and specialized science journals, stories about Nobel scientists seldom provide details on the nature of the prizewinner's research or its scientific significance. Rather, when the research is described, it appears as an esoteric, mysterious activity that is beyond the comprehension of normal human beings. "How many people could identify with Mr. Hoffman's lecture subject: 'coupling carbenes and carbynes on mono-, di-, and tri-nuclear transmission metal centers'"?[3] Reinforcing the presentation of science as abstruse are photographs of scientists standing before blackboards that are covered with complicated equations.

In interviews with journalists, scientists themselves reinforce   8 the mystification of science by emphasizing the extraordinary complexity of their work. Physicist Val Fitch described his research: "It's really quite arcane." "I find it difficult to convey to my family just what it is I've been doing," said physicist James Cronin in an interview with a *Time* reporter in 1980. *Time* cited the words of a member of the Nobel committee to describe Cronin's work: "Only an Einstein could say what it means."[4]

Just as science is described as divorced from normal activity,   9 so the scientist, at least the male scientist, is portrayed in popular newspapers and magazines as socially removed, above most normal human preoccupations—"on the mountaintop," as the 1990 winner in medicine was described. Science appears to be the activity of lonely geniuses whose success reflects their combination of inspiration and dedication to their work. One scientist sees "in a most passive looking object" a "veritable cauldron of activity" that the rest of us are unaware of. Another "stumbled" on his find but then spent a year "probing" for errors. A frequent image is the scientist who spends twelve hours a day, seven days a week, at his work. Prizewinning scientists are part of "an inner circle of scientific giants" who talk about science "the way other people talk about ball games." Being with them is "like sitting in a conversation with the angels." How will the prize affect the lives of such dedicated people? A journalist from *Time* notes that Sir Godfrey Hounsfield, one of the 1979 winners in medicine, "plans to put a laboratory in his living room."

10   Instances of prestigious scientists behaving like ordinary mortals are noted with an air of surprise. The caption for a *New York Times* photograph of Walter Gilbert (the Nobel Prize-winning chemist who gave up his chair at Harvard to run the firm Biogen) notes his managerial skills: "[These] should not be underestimated just because he has a Nobel Prize."[5] Writing of Nobel physicist Hans Bethe's concern about the buildup of nuclear weapons, a *New York Times* reporter remarks that "he ultimately places his faith not in technology but in human beings—a remarkable stance for a man who has dedicated his life to the pursuit of science."[6]

11   While successful male scientists appear in the press as above the mundane world and totally absorbed in their work, the very few women laureates have enjoyed a very different image. Stories of female Nobel Prize winners appear not only in the science pages, but in such life style and women's magazines as *Vogue* and *McCall's*, which seldom cover science news.

12   *McCall's* described Maria Mayer, who shared the physics prize in 1963 for her theoretical work on the structure of the nucleus, as a "tiny, shy, touchingly devoted wife and mother," a woman "who makes people very happy at her home." Approaching the story in a personal style hard to imagine in the coverage of a male Nobelist, the reporter found Mayer "almost too good to be true"—"a brilliant scientist, her children were perfectly darling, and she was so darned pretty that it all seemed unfair." The reporter noted her "graceful union between science and femininity," but also emphasized the conflict between being a mother and a scientist, the guilt, the opportunities missed by not spending more time at home. Writing about Mayer's research, the journalist remarked that she explains it in a "startlingly feminine way" because she used the image of onion layers to describe the structure of the atom. The article then goes on to describe Mayer's reputation as "the faculty's most elegant hostess."[7]

13   Specialized science writers used similar stereotypes in their descriptions. A *Science Digest* article called "At Home with Maria Mayer" begins: "The first [American] woman to win a Nobel Prize in science is a scientist and a wife." It showed a picture of her, not at the blackboard, but at her kitchen stove.[8]

Similarly, the *New York Times* headlined its article on Dorothy Hodgkin, who shared the prize for chemistry in 1966: "British Grandmother Wins the Prize."

The feminist movement did little to dispel such stereotypes. 14 In 1977 Rosalyn Yalow, winner of the prize in medicine, also received extensive coverage in women's magazines. By *Vogue* she was characterized as "a wonderwoman, remarkable, able to do everything, who works 70 hours a week, who keeps a kosher kitchen, who is a happily married, rather conventional wife and mother."[9] *Family Health,* a magazine that reaches 5.3 million readers, headlined an article: "She Cooks, She Cleans, She Wins the Nobel Prize" and introduced Yalow as a "Bronx housewife." This journalist expected to meet "a crisp, efficient, no nonsense type" but discovered that Dr. Yalow "looked as though she would be at home selling brownies for the PTA fund raiser."[10]

Journalists had more difficulty fitting Barbara McClintock, 15 recipient of the 1983 Nobel Prize in medicine, into this stereotype, and this in itself became news. *Newsweek* called her "the Greta Garbo of genetics. At 81 she has never married, always preferring to be alone."[11] (This article was published in the newsmagazine's "Transition" section—a column of briefly noted milestones, including weddings and deaths, among the noteworthy—although an item on McClintock also appeared on the "Medicine" page.) The *New York Times* covered McClintock in a long feature article. Its very first paragraph observed that she is well known for baking with black walnuts.[12]

The overwhelming message in these popular press accounts 16 is that the successful woman scientist must have the ability to do everything—to be feminine, motherly, and to achieve as well. Far from being insulated and apart from ordinary mortals, women scientists are admired for fitting in and for balancing domestic with professional activities. As an exception to the usual coverage of scientists in the press, the portraits of female Nobelists only highlight the prevailing image of science as a recondite and superior profession, pointing up their lack of attention to scientific substance.

To complete the image of the esoteric scientist, journalists 17 often convey the need of money and freedom to sustain science stars. During the 1970s, *Time* attributed the prominence of American Nobel Prize winners to the "heady air of freedom in U.S. academia and the abundant flow of grants. . . . Just do your own thing, the bounteous government seemed to say."[13] According to this 1979 analysis, the American tradition of freedom is far better for science than the "rigid" British, the "ideological" Soviets, and the "herr doctor" syndrome in Germany and France. Accepting the conventional (but questionable) wisdom among many scientists, this reporter expressed concern that the pressure to apply science to practical ends and to impose "cumbersome" regulations on experimental procedures will limit future triumphs. He also argued that U.S. science gains by insulation from humanistic pursuits: "The best minds have not been overburdened with required studies that are remote from their interests." Scientists, he emphasized, do such specialized and important work that they operate outside a common intellectual or cultural tradition.

18   The message of the 1970s was that science is distinct from cultural influence and that scientists need not consider the application of their work. In some respects this message has changed. Concerns about money and oppressive regulation persist, but in the 1990s media, the model scientist looks for practical applications and watches for ethical implications. In 1993, an admiring *New York Times* article on Francis Collins, director of the Human Genome Project, praised not only his vision and skills but his "personal empathy," his broad range of interests, and his concern about the applications and implications of genomics research. A quote from Sophocles shapes this report: "It is but sorrow to be wise when wisdom profits not."[14] However, the article also emphasizes that Collins is unique, a lonely genius who had been educated at home, able to work 100 hours a week with total dedication to "unlocking the secrets of the genome."

19   Ironically, even when treating scientists as removed from the common culture, journalists often turn them into authorities in areas well outside their professional competence. Thus we frequently read of their opinions on political dilemmas that have little to do with science. The implication is that science is a superior form of knowledge, so those who have reached its pinnacle must have some special insight into every problem.

The Authority of Scientific Theory

20   Although scientific findings are reported in the press, theories are seldom newsworthy. Notably excepted are those theories of behavior that bear on social stereotypes. Thus theories of evolutionary biology and natural selection, when used to explain human differences, have had a very active press. The theory of biological determinism attracted considerable news coverage following the controversy over psychologist Arthur Jensen's claims about the relationship between race and IQ. Its reappearance as sociobiology again attracted the press. The reports

on sociobiology have been less concerned with substance than with purported applications. In selecting this subject for extensive coverage, journalists are in effect using a controversial theory to legitimize a particular point of view about the importance of biological determinism.

Sociobiology is a field devoted to the systematic study of the biological basis of social behavior. Its premise is that behavior is shaped primarily by genetic factors selected in a species over thousands of years for their survival value. Its most vocal proponent, E. O. Wilson of Harvard University, contends that genes create predispositions for certain types of behavior and that a full understanding of these genetic constraints is essential to intelligent social policy. He believes that sociobiology is "a new synthesis," offering a unified theory of human behavior. "The genes hold culture on a leash," he wrote in his book *On Human Nature*. "The leash is very long but inevitably values will be constrained in accordance with their effects on the human gene pool."[15]   21

Wilson's arguments about human behavior, extrapolated from his research on insect behavior, were widely attacked by other scientists for their apparent justification of racism and sexism, their lack of scientific support, and their simplistic presentation of the complex interaction of biological and social influences on human behavior.[16] Wilson's first book on the subject, *Sociobiology, A New Synthesis*, was welcomed in 1980 by the *New York Times* as a "long-awaited definitive book." Subsequently, sociobiological concepts appeared in popular-press articles about the most diverse aspects of human behavior—used, for example, to explain: 22

- Child abuse: "The love of a parent has its roots in the fact that the child will reproduce the parent's genes." (*Family Week*)
- Machismo: "Machismo is biologically based and says in effect: 'I have good genes, let me mate'." (*Time*)
- Intelligence: "On the towel rack that we call our anatomy, nature appears to have hung his-and-hers brains." (*Boston Globe*)
- Promiscuity: "If you get caught fooling around, don't say the devil made you do it. It's your DNA." (*Playboy*)
- Selfishness: "Built into our genes to insure their individual reproduction." (*Psychology Today*)
- Rape: "Genetically programmed into male behavior." (*Science Digest*)
- Aggression: "Men are more genetically aggressive because they are more indispensable." (*Newsweek*)

23   The press is especially attracted to sociobiology's controversial implications for understanding stereotyped sex differences. The theory, we are told, directly challenges women's demands for equal rights, since differences between the sexes are innate. *Time*, for example, tells its readers that "Male displays and bravado, from antlers in deer and feather-ruffling in birds, to chest thumping in apes and humans, evolved as a reproductive strategy to impress females."[17] And a *Cosmopolitan* reporter, citing the "weight or scientific opinion" to legitimize his bias, writes: "Recent research has established beyond a doubt that males and females are born with a different set of instructions built into their genetic code."[18]

24   Sociobiological ideas easily shift to genetic explanations. The media have readily picked up on research suggesting a genetic basis of sex differences. In 1980, for example, two psychologists, Camille Benbow and Julian Stanley, published a research paper in *Science* on the differences in mathematical reasoning between boys and girls. Their study, examining the relation between Scholastic Aptitude Test scores and classroom work, found that differences in the classroom preparation of boys and girls were not responsible for differences in their test performance. The *Science* article qualified the implication of male superiority in mathematics: "It is probably an expression of a combination of both endogenous and exogenous variables. We recognize, however, that our data are consistent with numerous alternative hypotheses."[19] But the popular press was less circumspect, writing up the research as a strong confirmation of biological differences and a definitive challenge to the idea that differences in mathematical test scores are caused by social and cultural factors. The news peg was not the research, but its implications.

25   The original authors themselves encouraged this perspective, however, in their interviews with reporters, where they were less cautious than in their scientific writing. Indeed, they used the press to push their ideas as a useful basis on which to adjust public policy. According to the *New York Times*, they "urged educators to accept the possibility that something more than social factors may be responsible. . . . You can't brush the differences under the rug and ignore them."[20] The press was receptive. *Discover* reported that male superiority is so pronounced that "to some extent, it must be inborn."[21] *Time*, writing in 1980 about the "gender factor in math," summarized the findings: "Males might be naturally abler than females."[22] In 1992, *Time* continued to explain sex differences: "Nature is more important than nurture" and it is just a matter of time until scientists will prove it.[23]

In the 1990s, the ideas of sociobiology and genetics have been   26
integrated into the media coverage of an extraordinary range of
behaviors, including shyness, directional ability, aggressive personality, exhibitionism, homosexuality, dyslexia, job success,
arson, political leanings, religiosity, infidelity, criminality, intelligence, social potency, and zest for life. These and other complex
characteristics are treated as if they were simple Mendelian disorders, directly inherited like brown hair or blue eyes.

What is striking about the many articles on genetics and socio-   27
biology is how easily reporters slide from noting a provocative
theory to citing it as fact, even when they know that the supporting evidence may be flimsy. A remarkable article called "A Genetic
Defense of the Free Market" that appeared in *Business Week*
clearly illustrates this slide. While conceding that "there is no
hard evidence to support the theory," the author wrote: "For better or worse, self-interest is a driving force in the economy because it is engrained in each individual's genes. . . . Government
programs that force individuals to be less competitive and less
selfish than they are genetically programmed to be are preordained to fail." The application of sociobiology that this author
calls "bioeconomics" is controversial, he admits; nevertheless, it is
"a powerful defense of Adam Smith's laissez-faire views."[24]

Similarly, a 1993 *New York Times* article is called: "Want a   28
room with a view? Idea may be in the genes."[25] The reporter
described "Biophilia . . . a genetically based emotional need to
affiliate with the rest of the nature world." And in 1994, media
attention is turning—albeit with caution and caveats—to controversial claims about an association between violent behavior and biological predisposition.[26]

The journalists who write about sociobiology recognize, in-   29
deed rely on, the existence of controversy to enliven their stories. Yet most articles convey a point of view by giving space to
sociobiology's advocates and marginalizing critics, who are described as "few in number but vociferous" or people who are
"unwilling to accept the truth."[27] In 1976 *Newsweek* suggested
that Wilson was a victim like Galileo: "The critics are trying to
suppress his views because they contradict contemporary or-
thodoxies."[28] In 1982 *Science Digest* compared the criticism of
sociobiology to the attack of religious fundamentalism on the
theory of evolution ("Like the theory of evolution, sociobiology
is often attacked and misinterpreted"[29])—a comparison that
places sociobiology's scientific critics, such as Stephen J.
Gould and Richard Lewontin, of Harvard University, in the
same league as William Jennings Bryan.

In the 1990s, journalists are questioning the potential abuses   30
of genetic information but not the benefits of the research or

the credibility of research claims. We read of the importance of genetic explanations but then are warned that the ability to identify genetic predisposition is far ahead of therapeutic possibilities. Stories extoll the benefits of genetic research, but then decry the risk of gathering genetic information. We are told that this is the dawn of a new genetic era, yet cautioned about an impending eugenic nightmare. An article on the genetics of violent behavior, for example, worries that people are "lulled into believing that all problems can be solved by science," but then raises few questions about the "new biological revelations."[30] A story about the "vexing pursuit of the cancer gene" laments the delays in a discovery promising therapeutic interventions, but then welcomes the delays as a "blessing" in light of the problems such knowledge will bring.[31]

31   The media response to sociobiology and, more recently, to genetic explanations of behavior, reflects the tendency to idealize science as an ultimate authority. By its selection of what theories to champion, the press in effect uses the imprimatur of science to support a particular world view. It does so, however, with little attention to the substance of science, its slow accumulative process, and the limits of its theories as an adequate explanation of complex human behavior.

The Purity of Science

32   Stories of fraud and misconduct in science appear in the media with increasing frequency. One would expect them to undercut the mystique of the authority of science, but this is not necessarily the case. On the contrary, journalists often report deviant behavior in a manner that further idealizes science as a pure and dispassionate profession.

33   Journalistic interest in scientific fraud began in the late 1970s as part of the post-Watergate preoccupation with corruption in American institutions. It has burgeoned in the 1990s as hundreds of articles report on incidents of data tampering, abuses of research subjects, and other forms of scientific misconduct. Some news articles on fraud are similar in style to reports of political or business scandals, describing particular acts of fraud, the investigations that revealed the incidents, and the institutional responses. Others discuss the issue of fraud more analytically, focusing on the causes and extent of misconduct, suggesting that particular cases are symptomatic of deeper problems. These two approaches reflect different interpretations. The first suggests that fraud is simply the deviant behavior of aberrant individuals, the second that it is a

larger phenomenon with underlying causes basic to the present organization of science. Yet both convey a mystique about science, idealizing it as a sacrosanct, if vulnerable, profession.

Incidents of scientific misconduct elicit moral outrage, especially when research institutions are reluctant to recognize fraud or unwilling to react appropriately. This was the response of investigative reporters from the *Boston Globe* in covering a case of fraud at Boston University's hospital in 1980.[32] Marc J. Straus, a research physician specializing in lung cancer, had falsified data on his research subjects in order to claim the success of his research on cancer therapy. The *Globe's* headlines focused attention on both the scandalous aspects of his behavior and the institutional failure to take action despite the seriousness of the offense, which involved human subjects. "Cancer Research Falsified," "Boston Project Collapses," "Doctor under Fire Gets a New Grant"—these articles emphasized that corruption in science was an unusual event.

Other reports of fraud use individual cases to criticize current research practices. A *New York Times* reporter, in a 1980 article entitled "The Doctor's World: How Honest is Medical Research?" called attention to competitive practices in research.[33] The *Christian Science Monitor* in 1982 interpreted fraud as part of "a larger problem," in particular the "corrosive effect of pressure to publish."[34] As incidents of fraud increased, journalists variously attributed the problem to "the pressure cooker of research," inadequate supervision of younger colleagues, or the fact that most experiments are never replicated because "you don't get a grant for repeating someone else's work."[35]

Changes in media interpretations of fraud appear when we compare the 1980 coverage of the Straus case at Boston University with the 1994 coverage of the falsification of evidence in a breast cancer study of the relative benefits of full vs. partial mastectomy. As in 1980, the disclosure of fraud brought weeks of outraged media coverage, condemning not only the incident, but also the National Cancer Institute for its extended delay in informing the public. Judging that the incident did not significantly change the research results, the NCI had simply reported the case in the Federal Register, hardly a widely circulated journal; physicians as well as patients found out about the incident much later from the press. Covering this case in the context of other incidents of fraud, journalists questioned the ability of scientific investigators to control large scale projects and of government to regulate them. Thus media disclosure of the incident brought about a profound sense of betrayal and mistrust.

In 1993, a research group at the Acadia Institute conducted a survey trying to quantify the prevalence and significance of scientific fraud.[36] Its findings—that problems were far more pervasive than many scientists believed and that the publicized cases were just the tip of a misconduct iceberg—attracted wide media attention. According to Lawrence Altman, M.D., the medical reporter of the *New York Times*, "It shattered the myth that fraud in science is a rarity." Articles today increasingly raise fundamental questions concerning the validity of certain traditional assumptions about science. Can scientific honesty be assumed? Is the scientific method adequate? Does the peer review process offer enough protection against fraud? But many reporters still avoid these structural issues, preferring to topple a few high-profile scientists through dramatic exposés.

38   Among the most visible cases involved the well-known AIDS researcher Robert C. Gallo. In 1989, John Crewdson, a reporter for the *Chicago Tribune*, accused Gallo of wrongly taking credit for discovering HIV, the virus that causes AIDS. The accusation led to a four year investigation involving the U.S. Congress, the National Institutes of Health, and Parisian researchers working on the same virus. Gallo was eventually cleared, but media reports throughout the ordeal were consistently hostile, turning Gallo, the leading American researcher on AIDS, into a villain, a symbol of "the desanctifying of the temple of science in the eyes of much of the public."[37]

39   Another much-publicized case involved Nobelist David Baltimore, president of Rockefeller University, who had been involved in the publication of a suspect paper written by a scientist in his research group. "Attack" journalism focused on individuals is relatively rate in the coverage of science, but Baltimore became a target. The media, dwelling less on the facts of the case than on his personality, portrayed the assistant who called attention to the incident as "powerless victim" with "selfless" motivations.[38] Reporters apparently took delight in toppling a star, described as "fall[ing] from a place of personal power." From most media accounts, readers would not have realized that Baltimore himself was never accused of fraud. Nor would they understand the problems of multiple authorship so prevalent in the biological sciences. The extensive coverage of this case failed to communicate the nature of scientific misconduct, behavior that can range from improper assignment of credit, to plagiarism, to the outright faking of data.

40   Whether journalists define fraud as an individual aberration or a growing problem in the contemporary practice of science, they project a coherent image of scientific ideals. The metaphors typically used to describe fraudulent data are instructive. They "contaminate," "tarnish," "besmirch," "taint," or "sully" the reputation of individual scientists, their institutions, and science

itself. Faked data must be "expunged" or "purged." Scientists who learn that one of their colleagues is involved are reported to be "shocked," "horrified," "stunned," or "reluctant to believe it." For scientific fraud is a "sin" as well as a scandal. The culprit has "fallen," "betrayed" the profession. "When a scientist succumbs to temptation and pays the price, it is always sad."

Fraudulent acts in most other fields evoke quite different   41 and less moralistic metaphors. Consumer fraud is a "ripoff" or a "crime," hardly a sin. Political scandals are abuses of trust and reported, often cynically, as critiques of political institutions. Bribery scandals or savings and loan company scams are covered as the corruption to be expected in local politics. The press is admired for exposing such incidents. But Crewdson's role in exposing Gallo was not admired by his journalist colleagues, who worried about diverting the scientist from his valuable research mission.[39]

Even in reports of scientific fraud, scientists are often ideal-   42 ized as dispassionate, objective, and with values that must remain above those in other fields. A *Newsweek* article clearly stated this view: "A perception of widespread fakery undermines the trust in others' work that is the foundation of science. More than business or law or politics, science rests on the presumption or honesty in a quest for truth. If that presumption comes into question, a backlash against science may not be far away. And that could compromise what is still one of the more objective and honest sources of information in an ever more complicated world."[40]

In the news reports of the 1990s, that backlash is increasingly   43 apparent, but it has followed less from fraud than from growing realization that science is hardly independent of political and economic institutions. The exposés of Cold War radiation experiments and reports on the commercial ties of scientists and academic institutions are changing public and media perspectives. Media attention is focused on the increased importance of industry–university collaborations, the "profiteering" of academic scientists, and the "gold-rush atmosphere" in several biomedical fields. Scientists are becoming "tycoons," "gene merchants," or "molecular millionaires." "Biology Loses her Virginity" reads a headline, as if science was ever so pure.[41]

Whether covering prizes, professional misconduct, or contro-   44 versial scientific theories, the media convey a sense of awe about science. The scientist is portrayed as a star engaged in a competitive international race for prizes or prestige. Sometimes the intensity of competition can lead to misconduct, and sometimes research choices may compromise ethics. But science remains idealized as an esoteric activity, a separate culture, a profession apart from and above other human endeavors. This is a convenient image, serving the interest of scientists seeking status and autonomy, while allowing journalists to present problematic incidents as significant "news." But by neglecting the substance of science, ignoring the process of research, and avoiding questions of scientific responsibility, the press ultimately contributes to the obfuscation of science and helps to perpetuate the distance between science and the citizen.

NOTES

1. *Nation*, January 16, 1902.
2. *Boston Globe*, October 15, 1993.
3. *Kansas City Times*, September 17, 1982.
4. *Time*, October 27, 1980.
5. *New York Times*, February 19, 1983.
6. *New York Times*, June 12, 1984.
7. *McCall's*, July 1964, pp. 38–40, 124.
8. *Science Digest* 55, February 1964, pp. 30–36.
9. *Vogue*, January 1978, p. 174.
10. *Family Health*, June 1978, p. 24.
11. *Newsweek*, October 24, 1983.
12. *New York Times*, October 11, 1983.
13. *Time*, October 29, 1979.
14. *New York Times*, November 30, 1993.
15. Edward O. Wilson, *On Human Nature* (Cambridge, Mass.: Harvard University Press, 1980).
16. For a comprehensive review of the criticism and the controversy, see Ullica Segerstrale, "Colleagues in Conflict: An In Vivo Analysis of the Sociobiology Controversy," *Biology and Philosophy* 1, 1986, pp. 53–87.
17. *Time*, August 1, 1977.
18. *Cosmopolitan*, March 1982.
19. Camille Benbow and Julian Stanley, "Sex Differences in Mathematical Reasoning: Fact or Artifact?" *Science* 210, December 12, 1980, pp. 1262–1264.
20. *New York Times*, December 7, 1980.
21. Pamela Weintraub, "The Brain: His and Hers," *Discover*, April 1981, pp. 15–20.
22. *Time*, December 15, 1980.
23. *Time*, January 20, 1992, p. 42.
24. *Business Week*, April 10, 1978.
25. *New York Times*, November 30, 1993.
26. *New York Times*, January 23, 1994.
27. See, for example, interviews in the *New York Times*, October 12, 1975, and *People Weekly*, November 19, 1975.
28. *Newsweek*, April 12, 1976.
29. *Science Digest*, March 1982.
30. *New York Times*, January 23, 1994.
31. *New York Times*, July 12, 1994.
32. *Boston Globe*, June 19, 1980.
33. *New York Times*, August 5, 1980.

34. *Christian Science Monitor*, March 10, 1982.
35. See, for example, the *Washington Post*, August 14, 1991.
36. Judith Swazey, Melissa S. Anderson, and Karen Seashore Louis, "Ethical Problems in Academic Research," *American Scientist*, 81, November–December 1993, pp. 542–53.
37. *Washington Post*, November 13, 1993.
38. See, for example, the *New York Times*, May 5, 1989; April 1, 1991; and July 22, 1991.
39. See, for example, Nicholas Wade, "Method and Madness," *New York Times Magazine*, December 26, 1993.
40. *Newsweek*, February 8, 1982.
41. For examples of the media view of industry-university relations, see Sheldon Krimsky, *Biotechnics and Society* (New York: Praeger, 1991), p. 71.

Muriel Lederman

SCIENCE IS A SOCIAL ENTERPRISE

One section in Part 1 of this book asked the question "What Does It Mean to Be Literate?" and included several definitions of literacy—the ability to read and write, access to the language of the ruling class, access to and ability to use information technology, and so forth. In this essay, Muriel Lederman adds what she calls scientific literacy: "to be able to understand and contribute to discussions of the uses of scientific knowledge, so that they can help make science socially responsible." As you read this piece, you might consider how important this form of literacy is in our own time, especially in light of the other essays in this section. Muriel Lederman is an associate professor of molecular and cellular biology at Virginia Tech. Among her recent work is an edited collection, The Gender and Science Reader *(2001), prepared with Ingrid Bartsch. This essay was first published in* The Chronicle of Higher Education, *a publication that features issues that are important for those who work in colleges and universities.*

One of the goals of science education in the United States is to   1
produce citizens who are scientifically literate—that is, able to

understand and contribute to discussions of the uses of scientific knowledge, so that they can help make science socially responsible. However, science education today reflects the biases of science itself with regard to race, class, and gender. In the West, scientists are predominantly white and male, and science values "masculine" attributes like rationality, logic, and competition. To remedy that situation, scientists need to work with nonscientists to create a better way for novices (especially future scientists) to learn about science during higher education, if not earlier. A new pedagogy should include science-and-technology studies, in which researchers look at science as a social enterprise.

2   The subject matter of a reformed science education would include the interaction of science and the society in which it is practiced—for example, how society influences scientists in choosing problems to investigate. Scientists can no longer afford to ignore the fact that science is a social activity, with norms, attitudes, and practices shaped by history, institutions, beliefs, and values. Incorporating discussions of the social dimensions of science into science courses broadens students' understanding of current theory, tools, analytical techniques, and how different disciplines investigate and interpret the natural world. In cell biology, for instance, researchers typically study only parts of cells, rarely relating their findings to the whole cell or organism.

3   One benefit of a new science pedagogy might be to encourage women and members of minority groups to study science in college and graduate school, by making its culture easier to understand and thus less forbidding. So far, strategies for increasing the number of female and minority scientists have been based on the metaphor of a leaky pipeline, with the idea that women and minorities start out studying science but leave the field throughout their education. If we assume that the pipeline and the pond into which it empties—i.e., the practice of science—have no effect on retention, we could compensate for that decline by recruiting more women and minorities early in the process, so that more would come out the far end of the pipeline in spite of continued leaks. However, Elaine Seymour and Nancy M. Hewitt pointed out in *Talking About Leaving: Why Undergraduates Leave the Sciences* that the pipeline does have an effect. Women and members of minority groups in college and graduate school have had little experience with the norms and attitudes they encounter when they enter science or engineering programs, like unnecessarily harsh grading standards or being told point-blank that they cannot succeed in those fields. Such statements may not reflect official policy but are nevertheless condoned within some departmental cultures.

Female and minority students do not know what to make of 4
the new culture that they find themselves in, nor how to respond to it; they feel alienated and lose self-confidence. If the
culture of science is responsible for the loss of many of those
students, including the social studies of science in science education may help them recognize, understand, and overcome
their estrangement.

Many factors work against reforming science education 5
along those lines. Because many professors of science are also
practicing scientists, they have internalized the culture of science. When they teach the methods and results of scientific inquiry, they unconsciously transmit that culture, presenting it
as normal and not to be questioned.

In addition, the recommendations for improving science ed- 6
ucation made by various agencies—with the exception of the
National Research Council's general call for affiliating science
with the humanities and social sciences through required
courses that link science to society—place scientists in the
position of determining what counts as science and, consequently, of limiting who gets to do science. For example, the
American Association for the Advancement of Science published its recommendations for improving science education in
a volume called *Science for All Americans*, yet Angela Calabrese
Barton and Margery D. Osborne point out in their edited volume, *Teaching Science in Diverse Settings*, that the recommendations require "all Americans" to adopt the scientist's view in
order to participate in science. Thus, scientists claim that their
work should be exempt from public debate or oversight, rather
than allowing individuals to make decisions about how science
should affect their lives.

Scientists may not have the best understanding of science. 7
And because science has so many aspects, practitioners often
don't see the big picture. Nonscientists should question scientists' agendas when their work directly affects the environment, say, or requires large amounts of taxpayers' money.
Exposure to science-and-technology studies would give nonscientists the perspective they need to participate in such debates.

The National Research Council's suggestion that all students 8
have the opportunity to do original research unfortunately
echoes the view of the AAAS: Becoming a researcher includes
learning what is an acceptable question, what are the acceptable ways in which to ask a question, and how to interpret the
results of experiments. Such uncritical acceptance, replication,
and advocacy of the paradigms of science would not lead to
the reformed science education that we need. Instead of indoc-
trinating more students in the ways of the current scientific

culture, we should have scientists work with social scientists and scholars of education to make science more welcoming to those from outside. We should break the cycle of teaching just the facts by including science-and-technology studies in teacher education, so that K-12 students will be exposed to the principles of the field. At the college level, we should provide support, information, and institutional recognition and rewards for scientists who teach the social aspects of their disciplines.

9   Commendably, the National Science Teachers Association believes that an objective of science education is "understanding the nature of science—the goals, values, and assumptions inherent in the development and interpretation of scientific knowledge," but unfortunately the association views science as more rigorous and objective than other disciplines. Decades of research in science-and-technology studies have shown instead that science is less different from other fields than scientists like to think.

10   Improved science education would teach students that science, like any other discipline, is a social enterprise. With that knowledge, even if they do not become practicing scientists, they could participate knowledgeably in public debates on scientific issues, like the use of stem cells. Science studies is a tool that we can use not only to analyze science as it is, but also to make science more equitable, more socially responsible, and more valuable to all.

L. H. Neese

SCIENCE VS. RELIGION
THE CHALLENGE OF INTERPRETATION

L. H. Neese, a retired engineer, addresses in this essay the sometimes contentious ground between religion and science. Because science relies on that which is observable (i.e., empirical evidence) and religion relies on that which often is not (i.e., faith), it is often difficult to find enough common ground to create a conversation that is sensitive to the beliefs of both. Neese attempts to do so in this essay, first published in 2001 in

USA Today Magazine. *Do you think he succeeds? In what ways does he attempt to accommodate both religious and scientific attitudes in his essay? Does he seem to side with one side or the other?*

Science and technology have become the most ubiquitous of human creations, changing how we perceive our world and shaping the way we live. We live in a home built with materials fabricated by technology. The food we eat was likely grown and processed using the tools of technology. Wherever we travel, technology provides the mode of transportation. Much of our entertainment comes to us through the medium of technology. When we seek medical care, science and technology usually provide the instruments for diagnosis and treatment, and give us the means and the information to care for our health. 1

Science serves our innate need to know, helping us to deal effectively in some measure with the forces of nature. For many, it provides meaning and understanding in facing life's realities and challenges. 2

Science coexists and competes for influence with religion, which once dominated intellectual life and explained the world. Religion no longer has the preeminence it once had in the field of learning. Science gains influence each year as it brings forth discoveries, embraces new knowledge, and abandons old inadequate concepts. 3

Science and religion have their respective reasons for being. Each stands alone as independent human endeavors, having their own culture, body of knowledge, processes and procedures for verifying truth, and ways of serving humanity. They do not have the same viewpoints about the nature of the world or agree about how truth is perceived or confirmed. 4

Traditional religion endeavors to give life meaning and reason for existence in terms of its conceptions about God's actions and His authority as the guide for human behavior. A number of religions explain the existence of the world and the universe as due to a creative act of God. Science seeks to know the world and acquire understanding in terms of the laws of nature, gaining information by observing natural phenomena, testing and experimenting, and using reason in interpreting data. 5

Science earns acceptance by pragmatic demonstration of results. Most religions do not gain believers by demonstrating through evidence, as science does, the efficacy and validity of their claims. They rely, in large measure, on the cultural identification people have with traditions as they adopt the religion 6 of their parents or community. Religions further have promotion techniques to convince uncommitted people, and those outside their cultural domain, to bring them into their fold.

7   Science is committed to furthering the advance of knowledge about the universe. It succeeds because the intellectual processes that guide those in the pursuit of scientific knowledge yield results which can be confirmed by independent investigators everywhere.

8   In contrast, the various religions do not have their beliefs confirmed by independent investigators. Instead, the authority of their belief system is independent of evidence the scientific community would regard as confirming. They promote their tenets in the context of idealized morality from God while, at the same time, promising rewards to those willing to believe.

9   Traditional religion makes no systemic effort to convey to its followers the findings of contemporary scholarship. However, it does have strict accountability to maintain consistency of its teaching with tradition. Under these conditions, tradition prevails as the measure of right and truth.

10   Science embraces a standard for verification based on evidence derived from the largest human perspectives and most comprehensive sources of information, as judged by thinking minds. In contrast, many religions demand conformity to their traditions irrespective of what critics may say or the evidence obtained outside of their traditions may indicate.

11   The confirmation process in science involves giving the mind free rein to look at all the evidence without emotional constraints to follow any specific preconceived point of view. The conception of truth in religion is derived from the authority of tradition and the emotional bonds that prevail in the religious community and society at large.

12   Much of the theological structure of traditional religion is being questioned by scholars and other thoughtful people, for it derives from the assertions of people of the past who often did not have sufficient knowledge to make confirming judgments. Their assertions merely state the cultural opinions of their time, rather than truths which can be confirmed. Many traditional ideas do have value, however, for ancient people had numerous valid insights into human behavior that remain relevant. For example, "Do unto others as you would have them do unto you" is a profound ethical principle that is still useful today. Yet, religion, although it contains within its heritage profound ethical wisdom, sometimes stifles thought, makes people unthinking conformers, and inhibits development of human potential.

13   The new knowledge that science acquires about the world and universe presents people with a vision of the world and

universe religion had never anticipated and, of course, could not foretell. It can be argued that the laws of nature determine the functions of the world and universe. In contrast, the traditional religious vision of the world and universe has them functioning as God directs. This apparent dichotomy presents a challenge to religion to reappraise its position.

Earlier challenges to religion came from the Copernican theory of the solar system and from naturalist Charles Darwin's theory of evolution. When the Copernican theory made its appearance in the 16th century, some religious leaders were so opposed to it that they forced Italian astronomer Galileo Galilei, one of its chief proponents, to recant his belief in this conception of the solar system. However, religion eventually had to accept the Copernican theory because of the overwhelming evidence supporting it.   14

When Darwin published *On the Origin of Species* (1859), outlining an evolutionary theory as an explanation for the existence of the multitude of species of life on Earth, many in the religious community look an opposition stand which, for some orthodox believers, still prevails. A number of the latter are unwilling to countenance the idea that the laws of nature, through evolutionary change, produced human beings. They are convinced that only the creation ideas which are described in Genesis are the correct explanation for the origin of mankind.   15

Belief in the creationist account in Genesis derives from adopting the ideas of culture as truth. The source of the creation story is ancient Babylon, where similar accounts have been found on clay tablets. The Genesis account reflects the myths of the ancient Babylonian legends, not truths from a creator God.   16

The content of most religions is derived from the beliefs which prevailed in the culture that gave birth to these religions. These beliefs grew out of the perceptions, judgments, and thoughts of human beings. Religious movements and institutions developed as human societies sought to give people direction and maintain authority. Religions embraced and advanced the presumption that they had the truth from God, which must be accepted and not questioned. This presumption continues today and gives tradition its longevity.   17

Despite institutional efforts to maintain belief in the traditional, it is increasingly apparent that the realities science discloses are different from what religion has espoused. Many people in the religious community have accepted the theory of evolution, but are unaware of the larger challenge spawned by science with which religion has not made an accommodation: The universe everywhere, as far as science can determine, from the smallest particle of matter to the galactic systems in the   18 vastness of outer space, including all life forms, functions because of and in accord with the laws of nature. Most religions developed and evolved before humanity became aware of the causal features of the laws of nature. The literature of most major religions explains the happenings the people observed and wrote about as being caused by God. The writers of the Bible were not aware of the laws of nature and, therefore, what they perceived occurring around them, they attributed to God. Ancient people had no other way to explain the happenings in the world. This fact alone confirms the humanity of the Bible because it reflects the limitations of knowledge of people of that era and denotes how they explained their world.

19   The scientific process of acquiring knowledge is at variance with the methodology of religion and accordingly creates cause for concern about the way religious beliefs are verified. Religion holds its beliefs came from God and therefore are true, but offers no method of verification that is universally acceptable. Tradition promoted in the name of God is no longer a convincing reason to many people for holding a belief.

20   Are God and nature the same? Is there a semantic problem here that prevents a resolution of the God vs. nature controversy? Are we using different terms for the same thing? Religion is being challenged by science to address these questions.

21   Does God really have the attributes that biblical writers gave Him and many religious people still assume He has? Does He have the image of man? Does He walk, talk, see, love, show anger, etc.? Does He hear prayers, give moral instructions to humanity, and intercede in the affairs of mankind? Is He omniscient and/or omnipotent? If we can't confirm that God has these attributes, why should people still regard them as valid?

22   Is God supernatural? The Bible does not make such a claim. The writers of the Bible accepted the ideas of their culture about the nature of God. It was a divine being, with an image of man, that made things happen in the world. The writers knew nothing about the laws of nature, so they would not have regarded God as supernatural and did not.

23   Human cultures of past ages created many gods. There were Egyptian, Greek, Roman, Hindu, Incan, and many more gods before the Judeo–Christian God came upon the human scene. The gods of ancient cultures were the means by which people explained the unknown about their world. These gods also were thought to be the source of benefits to those whose behavior and belief were in accord with the teachings of their religion. Contemporary culture is disposed to hold that only claims about current gods are valid. The ancient gods and the claims about them were all creations of uninformed people, they insist.

The secret of understanding God may depend more on ob-   24
serving and examining how the god concept has been used
throughout the ages than upon literal acceptance of what biblical literature has indicated and what its interpreters have
written about God. The plethora of documents purporting to
explain God usually omit the human contribution to explaining the God concept and assume the premise that God has an
existence beyond this human effort. When we become wise
enough to see the attributes of God that are human opinions,
we have removed an obstacle to understanding God. We can
then make an assessment of these opinions and see what the
reality is beyond them.

Will religion rise to the challenge of the vision of humanity   25
and the universe posed by science and embrace the realities
science has brought forth? Or will it continue to take refuge in
an enclave seeking more believers of its traditions? The world
needs a larger perspective to guide it through the new millennium. Will religion expand its perspective by bringing a more
reliable intellectual process to the religious community than it
has now and by embracing the content of contemporary knowledge? The world waits and watches to see what religion will do.

It seems suitable to end by quoting Albert Einstein, arguably   26
the most influential scientist of the 20th century: "Science
without religion is lame; religion without science is blind."

Is Genetic Engineering a Threat or a Moral Imperative?

Kenan Malik

THE MORAL CLONE

In May 2001, Kenan Malik, author of Man, Beast, and Zombie *and* The Meaning of Race: Race, History, and Culture in Western Society, *published the following essay in* Prospect *magazine, a British publication on public issues and contemporary culture.*

1   The Pope condemns their work as "abhorrent." Jeremy Rifkin warns that they are striking a "Faustian bargain" which could pave the way to a "commercial eugenics civilisation." The object of this hostility is two doctors, the U.S.-based Panayiotis Zavos and the Italian Severino Antinori, who, in March, declared their intention of helping infertile couples conceive through the use of cloning techniques.

2   From Aldous Huxley's picture of human production lines in *Brave New World* to Michael Marshall Smith's description in his novel *Spares* of farms where the rich keep clones of themselves so that their organs can be "harvested" for transplants, cloning has been a metaphor for the creation of an immoral, inhuman world. The birth in February 1997 of Dolly the sheep transformed such visions from the realms of science fiction to science fact. It seemed only a matter of time before humans could also be duplicated, a prospect greeted with almost universal condemnation. Even Ian Wilmut, Dolly's creator, believes that we should "reject this proposed use of cloning."

3   I want to argue that the current debate about cloning turns the ethical issues on their head. There are no reasons to regard the cloning of humans as unethical. There is, on the other hand, something deeply immoral about a campaign that seeks to block the advancement, not just of reproductive technology,

but also of other medical techniques based on cloning methods which could save countless lives.

There are three main objections to cloning: that it undermines 4 human dignity and personal identity; that it uses people as objects; and that it is unnatural. Opponents argue that it is immoral to create exact copies of people. According to the bioethicist Leon Kass, "the cloned individual will be saddled with a genotype that has already lived. He will not be fully a surprise to the world." Others worry that unethical governments, or even corporations, may institute a programme to create production line people, perhaps even a race of Adolf Hitlers.

Such arguments misunderstand both the character of cloning 5 and the nature of human beings. To clone an organism—whether Dolly or Adolf Hitler—scientists take an egg and remove its nucleus, the pail that includes, among other things, the bulk of the DNA. Next, they remove the nucleus from a cell belonging to the adult that is to be cloned and insert it into the egg. The reconstructed egg is stimulated, either electrically or chemically, to trick it into behaving like a fertilised egg. If this is successful, the egg divides and becomes an embryo, which is then transferred into the uterus of a surrogate mother. Pregnancy then follows its normal course.

Any human child conceived in this fashion will be the ge- 6 netic twin of the person who is the cell donor. But to have the same genome is not to be the same person. Genes play an important part in shaping who we are but they are not the only influence on us.

If having the same genome means being the same person, 7 then all naturally-born identical twins would be exact duplicates of each other. This is not the case. Identical twins differ in everything from their fingerprints to their personalities. Children conceived with the aid of cloning technology will be even more different from their genetic parents than are most natural twins from each other. Most naturally conceived identical twins grow up in roughly the same environment. Cloned children, on the other hand, will be born into a different family from their "twin," have different parents and siblings, and have different experiences from the day they are born. In other words they will be nothing like their parent whose genome they inherit.

Children conceived though cloning will be indistinguishable 8 from children conceived naturally, whether these happen to be identical twins or not. Each will be a unique human being with a unique identity and an unpredictable future.

What of the argument that cloning turns human beings into 9 means, not ends? Cloned children, critics say, will simply be the means for their parents' self-aggrandisement. This may

well be true, but it is also true for many children born in conventional ways. Twenty years ago opponents of the then-
nascent in vitro fertilisation (IVF) technology also argued that
"test-tube" babies were being treated as objects. Anyone who
has witnessed the emotional and financial commitment that
couples have to invest in IVF treatment will recognise, however, that such children are very much wanted and treasured
by their parents. The same will be true for any cloned child.

10   Faced with the implausibility of most of their arguments, opponents of cloning generally fall back on the claim that cloning is
repugnant because it is unnatural. "From time immemorial,"
Jeremy Rifkin says, "we have thought of the birth of our progeny
as a gift bestowed by God or a beneficent nature." According to
Rifkin, "the coming together of sperm and egg represents a moment of surrender to forces outside of our control."

11   Cloning is certainly unnatural. But then so is virtually every
human activity. The whole point of any medical intervention
from taking an aspirin to heart surgery is to ensure that humans are not at the mercy of "forces outside our control." If we
were to look upon human conception as simply a "gift from
God," then contraception, abortion and IVF would all have to
be ruled immoral. Cloning is no more unnatural than IVF. If
we are happy to accept the latter (as most people are), then
why should we not accept the former too?

12   There is only one argument against human cloning that has
any substance. Many experts believe that it is precipitous to attempt to clone human beings today because the procedure is
insufficiently safe. It remains difficult to get reconstructed eggs
to develop into embryos and many of these embryos show abnormalities. In the case of Dolly, for instance, Ian Wilmut began
with 277 reconstructed eggs, of which 29 developed into embryos. Of these 29 embryos only one resulted in a pregnancy
that went to term. Given such problems, the consensus among
most scientists is that Zavos and Antinori are being hasty in
their plans to clone humans. Cloning techniques have yet to
be fine-tuned and the risk of conceiving deformed children is
too great. The question of safety, however, is not an ethical one.
Ethical injunctions are absolute: under no circumstances
should we attempt to clone a human. Safety considerations are
relative: when the technology has become more refined, we can
proceed.

13   By preventing cloning research, opponents are preventing
the development of new treatments that draw upon cloning
techniques, and hence are allowing many people to suffer unnecessarily. A case in point is the controversy over "therapeutic
cloning." Therapeutic cloning is a means of growing human

tissue that fuses the techniques that helped create Dolly with another new medical technology: the ability to grow embryonic stem (ES) cells.

The cells of an adult human are highly specialised; under nor- 14
mal circumstances a liver cell will always stay a liver cell, and a skin cell can never become anything else. Stem cells, however, are cells that can develop into any kind of tissue: liver, skin, nerve, heart. The best source of such stem cells are tiny embryos, a few days old. If we could take the nucleus of, say, a healthy cell from a patient with Parkinson's disease and fuse it with an enucleated stem cell, we could grow brain tissue that could potentially replace the patient's damaged cells. Because such tissue would be genetically identical to that of the patient, there would be no problem of tissue rejection. Such a technique could help patients with problems from Parkinson's and Alzheimer's to diabetes, leukaemia and even heart disease.

Therapeutic cloning is a way of growing human tissues, it has 15
nothing to do with creating new human beings. The embryo is a pin-prick of about two dozen cells; because it could potentially be a human life does not mean that it *is* one. Anyone who objects to therapeutic cloning must logically object not only to all forms of abortion but to IVF too, which produces spare embryos in pursuit of a successful pregnancy.

According to the *Telegraph*, "The difference between thera- 16
peutic cloning, to create 'spare part' organs, and reproductive cloning, to create babies, is only one of purpose—a secondary distinction." In both cases "the embryo is treated as a disposable object, deprived of any humanity." The same "fundamental moral objections," the *Telegraph* claims, "apply to all human cloning."

As a result of such arguments, most European states still ban 17
research into therapeutic cloning. Britain finally licensed certain forms of cloning research last year, but only in very limited cases. In the U.S., the Bush administration is expected to ban federal funding for any form of ES-cell research. In a special report on therapeutic cloning, the journal *Nature* asked recently why it was that only a dozen or so research teams are pursuing work in such a promising area. A large part of the answer, it concluded, was the degree of political restriction.

Opponents of cloning like to present the debate as one be- 18
tween an immoral science, hell-bent on progress at any cost, and those who seek to place scientific advancement within a moral framework. But what is moral about allowing unnecessary suffering? Theologians and Luddites are using norms drawn from dogmatic and reactionary visions of life to prevent the alleviation of human suffering.

Kenneth R. Weiss

IT CAME FROM
THE GENE LAB

*Though cloning has been the highest profile issue in biotech-
nology, all the issues surrounding bioengineering seem to gravitate toward, on the one hand, the hope for a better future
through science and, on the other, fear of "playing God"—a
type of Frankenstein syndrome. Kenneth R. Weiss, a reporter
for the* Los Angeles Times *who published this piece in 2003,
here discusses the genetic engineering of fish, citing both critics who dub the product of this process "Frankenfish," and
others who liken the process to simply "tuning up your car." As
you read this piece, note the various types of arguments made
by individuals interviewed by Weiss—and how they converse
with other essays in this section. You might also consider
whether the way Weiss constructs this news story seems to
favor a specific view toward genetic engineering.*

1   One newly bioengineered salmon, endowed with a gene from
an eel-like fish, grows five times faster than its natural cousins.
Another genetically modified salmon produces antifreeze in its
blood so it can survive icy waters that swirl through oceanic
fish farms.

2   A tropical zebra fish, infused with the green fluorescent gene
of a jellyfish, glows in the dark—a living novelty that promoters hope will be a must-have for the home aquarium.

3   These experimental superfish are more than laboratory cu-
riosities. They are the progeny of genetic engineers whose skill
at mixing and matching genes is outpacing laws and regulations meant to protect the food supply and the environment.

4   None of these designer fish, being pushed by biotech entrepreneurs as potential lucrative ventures, have yet reached the
market. But the U.S. Food and Drug Administration has initiated a review of the souped-up salmon, a process that could
lead to the first approval of a "transgenic" animal—one that
has genetic material transplanted from another.

5   Although the human health implications of eating bioengineered animals remain unknown, a panel of scientists last
August reported it had "a moderate level of concern" that new
species could trigger allergic reactions. What might happen,
the scientists asked, if a gene from a shellfish were implanted

into a fish? Could it cause a reaction in consumers hypersensitive to shellfish?

The National Academy of Sciences panel, assembled at the   6
FDA's request, said its primary concern was the potential for ecological havoc should highly mobile, fast-breeding transgenic species escape into the wild.

"It is possible," the panel reported, "that if transgenic salmon   7
with genes engineered to accelerate growth were released into the natural environment, they could compete more successfully for food and mates than wild salmon."

That means these "Frankenfish," as critics have labeled   8
them, could squeeze out their wild cousins, driving them to extinction through interbreeding or by eating them.

Alarmed by the potential risks, Washington, Oregon and   9
Maryland have banned genetically enhanced fish to protect the native fish populations.

California's Fish and Game Commission, trying not to hin-   10
der scientific research or the state's burgeoning biotech industry, plans to grant permits, based on its own reviews, for each new transgenic species as it emerges under new rules that take effect today.

"We could have put up a stop sign and said 'No,'" said   11
Michael Flores, president of the Fish and Game Commission. "But then we would have crippled our university researchers and other research and development. We will look at every single species and make sure safeguards are in place."

West Coast commercial fishermen are pushing California to   12
ban genetically altered fish, arguing that the potential threat to wild salmon and other native species is too great.

"Once this genie escapes, can we put it back in the bottle?"   13
asked Zeke Grader, executive director of the Pacific Coast Federation of Fishermen's Associations. "I doubt it."

"So what happens when these fish get out in the wild? Will   14
they spread disease? Will they be predators of our native fish or interbreed with them? How can we assure the public the fish we catch are safe if transgenic fish are mixed in?"

"It's all unknown," Grader said.   15

It's the FDA's job to answer those questions. But "marine ecol-   16
ogy is not historically an area of FDA scientific strength," said Michael Taylor, a National Academy of Sciences panel member and senior fellow at the nonprofit Resources for the Future.

Taylor and others also fault the agency for closing its reviews   17
to the public to protect trade secrets.

Lester M. Crawford, deputy FDA commissioner, said the   18
agency is reconsidering its secrecy policy when weighing the food safety and ecological impact of newly designed species.

19   "We certainly have a framework to deal with environmental risks," Crawford said.

20   But new breeds of transgenic animals have prompted some internal soul-searching. "We are evaluating whether we need new regulations or new money or congressional authority to tweak the law," Crawford said.

21   He said the agency may never approve a transgenic fish or any other kind of genetically modified animal for the marketplace. But the pressure is mounting to do so, with a menagerie of them expected to arrive at the FDA's offices soon.

22   Researchers at biotech companies and universities have redesigned the genes of freshwater catfish and tilapia to make them grow faster, and those of shrimp and abalone to help them resist disease.

23   Scientists in Singapore are designing ornamental fish—such as the zebra fish—that glow green when spliced with a jellyfish gene or red when infused with the gene of a sea anemone.

24   Those same researchers are devising a fish that changes color when it passes through different temperatures. Such gene-splicing is being extended to goldfish and koi, stirring excitement in the $1-billion annual home aquarium trade.

25   Genetic manipulations are becoming so routine that an artist in Chicago has put a pair of fluorescent green zebra fish on public display, along with assorted glow-in-the-dark rodents and other creatures he calls "transgenic art" in an exhibit called "The Eighth Day."

26   "We're adding one day to the seven days of creation," said Eduardo Kac, a self-described "biotech artist" at the School of the Art Institute of Chicago.

27   "From the technical point of view, the technology is here and part of society. I'm saying, 'What are we going to do with it?'"

28   Genetically enhanced fish are just the beginning.

29   A Canadian firm has spliced a spider gene into goats so their milk is laced with spider thread that can be extracted to make bulletproof vests or surgical sutures.

30   Other animals are being tailored to the demands of factory farms, from featherless fowl that don't need to be plucked to low-emission pigs that excrete 75% less phosphorous, a key contaminant in agricultural runoff.

31   Advances in genetically modified plants are much further along, both in government approval and public acceptance. Unlike Europeans, most Americans have readily digested the idea of genetically engineered corn, soybeans and cotton that have been modified to resist insects and tolerate herbicides.

32   The first animal candidate for FDA approval is an Atlantic salmon with the transplanted gene of an ocean pout, an ugly, bottom-dwelling fish that resembles an eel.

Elliot Entis, co-founder and president of the firm that wants 33
to market the salmon, Aqua Bounty of Waltham, Massachusetts,
said the pout gene allows the salmon to produce growth hormones year-round, instead of during warmer months, so that it
grows five times as fast as a normal farm-raised salmon.

Aqua Bounty's salmon do not end up larger than their nat- 34
ural cousins. But they reach marketable size much faster, in 18
months—and do so with 10% to 25% less food, Entis said.

"It's like tuning up your car," he said. "Instead of 10 miles per 35
gallon, in the early stages it gets 40 miles per gallon."

Raising salmon on less food is an important advance. It now 36
takes about 2 1/2 pounds of wild fish ground into meal to produce one pound of farmed salmon.

For that reason, feeding salmon on those proliferating farms 37
contributes to the overfishing that is rapidly depleting the
world's oceans.

Entis said genetically enhanced fish are needed to feed a 38
growing global population. He believes the risk of the fish escaping can be all but eliminated by containing them in inland
tanks. He also proposes to make them sterile.

But scientists say fish tend to flop out of the most secure 39
pens and that no sterility technique works 100% of the time.

The FDA has brought in a team of experts from the 40
Environmental Protection Agency, National Marine Fisheries
Service and U.S. Fish and Wildlife Service to help assess the
potential ecological impact.

One of the few studies to look into the issue focused on the 41
risk of extinction of native species by what researchers at
Purdue University called the "Trojan gene" effect.

Genetics professor William Muir and biologist Richard 42
Howard, studying mating and survival rates, found that transgenic fish are typically larger than their wild cousins.

That gives them an advantage in attracting mates. If the ge- 43
netic change reduces the offspring's life expectancy, as it did in
their laboratory experiments, a transgenic fish could wipe out
a wild population in as few as 40 generations.

Worried about Northern California's salmon runs, state 44
Senator Byron Sher (D-Stanford) has asked California officials
to yank the new regulations on genetically enhanced fish, arguing that it is premature to legalize the "commercialization of
transgenic fish" with so many unknowns and potential threats.

"The FDA has not yet decided whether farm-raised trans- 45
genic fish are safe to eat," Sher wrote to California Fish and
Game Director Bob Hight.

"Equally important, there are growing concerns that FDA's 46
regulatory process does not adequately consider the potential
environmental risks to native fish species."

47   Fish and Game officials defend the regulations, saying they are designed to protect native species rather than promote genetic tinkering.

48   State officials have no idea how many bioengineered fish may exist in California.

49   The new rules are designed to help them find out and impose state controls, such as requiring secure fish tanks to prevent escape as researchers, farmers or fish sellers obtain permits to possess, transport or raise animals with altered genes.

50   Fish and Game officials expect to hear first from biomedical researchers at UCLA and UC–San Francisco, who work with genetically altered zebra fish in research on human heart disease.

51   Zebra fish, a tropical freshwater species, are gaining popularity as a lab research tool. That's partly because they reproduce quickly and are cheap to maintain, and partly because scientists are nearly done mapping the fish's genome, which has significant similarities to that of humans.

52   "Once you get the genome completed, it begs for you to do some manipulation," said Marc Aarens, UC's director of academic legislative issues.

53   Researchers tinkering with zebra fish genes declined to be interviewed.

54   "It's important work—research dealing with heart disease—and none of them want publicity," Aarens said.

55   "We might get protesters who fear they are creating 'Frankenfish' and going to ruin the environment."

David B. Sandalow

BIOTECHNOLOGY AND WORLD HUNGER

POTENTIAL BENEFITS FOR ENHANCED NUTRITION

The piece below was excerpted from a statement by David B. Sandalow, who was at the time the Assistant Secretary of the Bureau of Oceans, Environment, and Science for the U.S. Department of State. Sandalow is now a scholar at the

Brookings Institution, a Washington think tank. Consider his argument, which was published in Congressional Digest *in 2001, in light of the* Open Letter from World Scientists *that follows in this section of* Conversations. *Like many conversations, this one has strong arguments on many sides—after all, fighting hunger is a compelling argument for genetic engineering, despite the dangers cited by others. This debate also raises questions about the role of government in regulating science and industry—a question discussed in Part 5 as well.*

Every day, more than 800 million people on this planet go to 1 bed hungry. More than one billion people live in abject poverty on incomes of less than $1 per day. Poor education, pests, drought, disease, food distribution problems, and civil strife are all in part to blame. But the enormity of the problem cannot stop us from shaping a response. We must explore all means available.

In fighting hunger and poverty, modern biotechnology must 2 be part of our arsenal. In the past several months alone, the news has been filled with indications of the great promise of this technology. Researchers have found ways to enhance the vitamin A content of rice, promising great strides in the fight against blindness and other diseases around the world. A working draft of the sequence of the human genome has now been mapped, offering tremendous potential in using the science of genetics to help fight disease.

At the same time, we must proceed with wisdom and cau- 3 tion. Biotechnology presents both potential benefits and risks. In the United States, we have had a strong and effective regulatory system to address environmental and other concerns from biotechnology for many years.

As the technology advances, we will continue to refine our 4 regulatory processes. For biotechnology to do the most good for the most people, we must encourage and support credible, science-based regulatory systems around the world.

How Biotechnology Can Contribute

How do we feed a growing population—which some estimate 5 will reach 9 billion in the next 30 years—when most arable land on the planet is already under cultivation? How do we find new ways to deliver desperately needed medicines to desperately poor people? Modern biotechnology is part of the answer.

6   Among the most promising applications of modern biotechnology are those that can enhance the nutritional content of foods. Vitamin A-enriched rice has recently been developed and received much attention; other possibilities include vitamin A-enhanced oil, vitamin A-enhanced tomatoes, and iron-enriched rice. Modern biotechnology can be used to fight the many scourges that accompany malnutrition around the world, including illness, blindness, developmental problems, and death.

7   Some have questioned the need for such products, arguing that poor people need balanced diets, not vitamin-enriched rice. But we should not let the perfect become the enemy of the good. Access to balanced diets is limited in many countries by poverty, food distribution problems, and other complex and entrenched social conditions. Staple foods such as rice may be the only foods available. As we attack all causes of hunger and malnutrition, increasing the nutritional content of staple foods can make a difference in people's lives.

8   Drought and disease plague developing country farmers around the world. Here, too, modern biotechnology can make a difference. Scientists are exploring ways to make mangoes, cassava, plantains, and other tropical crops resistant to drought and virus-born diseases. Pests are also a significant barrier to agricultural productivity around the world.

9   By using modern biotechnology, scientists can insert natural pesticides such as Bt [an insecticide produced by strains of the bacterium *Bacillus thuringiensis*] into crops, reducing loss due to insect damage. This technology is already helping farmers increase productivity, while reducing pesticide usage, here in the United States. In the developing world, the technology can help promote food security and increase incomes among poor farmers.

10   Part of biotechnology's promise is to produce plants that are more productive with fewer inputs (such as chemicals and water). Such applications would reap enormous benefits for poor farmers, who could use their scarce resources to produce crops that would better feed their families while lessening or removing the need to convert new lands to agriculture.

11   These applications would help to protect farmers from environmental fluctuations, such as drought. Such vagaries of agriculture have had extremely serious impacts on the poor, as we are seeing right now in parts of Africa, where drought is again taking a terrible toll. The ability to stabilize yields will obviously offer great benefits to U.S. farmers and consumers as well.

Barriers to the Use of Modern Biotechnology in the Developing World

Many experts have noted that, as with many technologies, initial applications have primarily benefited those with purchasing power in wealthier countries. For modern biotechnology to help the poor farmer in developing countries, we must find ways to finance the use of this technology for the farmer's benefit.   12

Part of the answer lies in the public sector. We must find ways to support the work of universities, research institutions, and other organizations with expertise in this area. In particular, we must support the Consultative Group on International Agricultural Research, whose work has been instrumental in fighting hunger and poverty for many years. Part of the answer must be found in the private sector as well.   13

Private companies, of course, often have fiduciary responsibilities to shareholders and have a very different role than public sector institutions or charities. But we must find creative solutions, looking to public–private partnerships and other tools. We must find programs that improve the lives of the poor, promote long-term acceptance of this technology, and help advance the goals of all concerned. One encouraging example is the collaboration between Monsanto, the U.S. Agency for International Development (USAID), and the government of Kenya to develop a disease-resistant sweet potato that will likely be among the first genetically engineered crops tested in sub-Saharan Africa.   14

A second issue is the need for adequate regulatory structures. Like any new technology, modern biotechnology presents risks that must be managed. Environmental testing is important, for example, to ensure gene transfer issues are addressed. Issues related to pest resistance may be important.   15

A final barrier is lack of knowledge and fear. Around the world, we've seen lack of knowledge and fear emerge as major factors in the development of modern biotechnology. We should neither minimize nor bemoan this important fact. We should recognize and address it. We should work to promote scientific cooperation and reasoned dialogue on this topic. We should recognize that this topic can implicate ethical and religious issues for some. In the long run, modern biotechnology cannot promote a better tomorrow unless people from around the world understand it and have a stake in the technology's future.   16

How the United States Is Addressing the Issue

17 [The Clinton] Administration is strongly committed to finding ways for modern biotechnology to help fight hunger and poverty. Our work in this area cuts across many agencies.

18 ***U.S. Agency for International Development.*** USAID spends roughly $7 million a year on agricultural biotechnology in developing countries. USAID's work emphasizes two aspects—cooperative research and technology development, and the promotion of science-based regulatory systems. Cooperative research and technology development efforts link U.S. universities and companies with research and government institutions in developing countries. It is important that developing countries have the technical and institutional ability to access the potential of biotechnology for themselves.

19   Creating ownership over the technology helps diffuse the political issues, and provides the basis for a science-driven regulatory system. In addition, USAID supports the development of biosafety regulatory systems and legal and management policies for addressing intellectual property rights associated with biotechnology.

20 ***U.S. Department of Agriculture (USDA).*** USDA spends more than $60 million annually on biotechnology research, providing education programs to current and emerging agricultural biotechnology markets, and on cooperative efforts with researchers in developing countries. USDA has implemented special programs for a targeted group of developing countries, and it conducts training seminars, which provide a balanced view of biotechnology to selected consumer, producer, processor, trader, or regulator representatives.

21   In addition, USDA directs efforts toward educating regulators and journalists on the science-based regulatory process practiced in the United States for biotech crops and products, and it brings interested stakeholders for U.S.-based training.

22 ***The Agricultural Research Service (ARS) of USDA.*** ARS not only conducts its own research into biotechnology, it also manages a germplasm system that shares germplasm freely with developing countries. For example, USDA recently signed an agreement with sub-Saharan African countries and Tuskegee University to facilitate technology transfer related to agricultural biotechnology.

Over $280,000 is also spent annually on biotech outreach ef- 23
forts in developing countries, which includes biosafety symposia
on the potential environmental risks of biotechnology. USDA has
also implemented regulations concerning special foods or ingredients. For example, it would be misleading to state "not produced through biotechnology" on the label of green beans, when
there are no marketed bioengineered green beans.

To not be misleading, the claim should be in a context that 24
applies to the food type instead of the individual manufacturer's product. For example, the statement "green beans are
not produced using biotechnology" would not imply that this
manufacturer's product is different from other green beans.

Substantiation of Label Statements. A manufacturer who 25
claims that a food or its ingredients, including foods such as
raw agricultural commodities, is not bioengineered should be
able to substantiate that the claim is truthful and not misleading. Validated testing, if available, is the most reliable way to
identify bioengineered foods or food ingredients.

For many foods, however, particularly for highly processed 26
foods such as oils, it may be difficult to differentiate by validated
analytical methods between bioengineered foods and food ingredients and those obtained using traditional breeding methods.

Where tests have been validated and shown to be reliable they 27
may be used. However, if validated test methods are not available or reliable because of the way foods are produced or
processed, it may be important to document the source of such
foods differently.

Also, special handling may be appropriate to maintain 28
segregation of bioengineered and nonbioengineered foods. In
addition, manufacturers should consider appropriate record-
keeping to document the segregation procedures to ensure that
the food's labeling is not false or misleading. In some situations, certifications or affidavits from farmers, processors, and
others in the food production and distribution chain may be
adequate to document that foods are obtained from the use of
traditional methods.

A statement that a food is "free" of bioengineered material 29
may be difficult to substantiate without testing. Because appropriately validated testing methods are not currently available for
many foods, it is likely that it would be easier to document handling practices and procedures to substantiate a claim about
how the food was processed than to substantiate a "free" claim.

FDA has been asked about the ability of organic foods to bear 30
label statements to the effect that the food (or its ingredients) was
not produced using biotechnology. On December 21, 2000, the

Agriculture Marketing Service of the USDA published final regulations on procedures for organic food production (National Organic Program final rule: 65 FR 80548). That final rule requires that all but the smallest organic operations be certified by a USDA-accredited agent and lays out the requirements for organic food production.

31   Among those requirements is that products or ingredients identified as organic must not be produced using biotechnology methods. The national organic standards would provide for adequate segregation of the food throughout distribution to assure that nonorganic foods do not become mixed with organic foods. The agency believes that the practices and record-keeping that substantiate the "certified organic" statement would be sufficient to substantiate a claim that a food was not produced using bioengineering.

Institute of Science in Society

Open Letter from World Scientists to All Governments Concerning Genetically Modified Organisms (GMOs)

The Institute of Science and Society published this open letter from world scientists on its website, with the hope that scientists around the world would sign on to its campaign against genetically modified organisms (GMOs)—which many have. This group lays out a series of 29 carefully worded and well-documented arguments about why GMOs should be banned. As you read, you might consider the types of evidence that are valued by the scientific community as well as by the wider societies and government agencies that form their audience—and how those groups are accommodated. Think too about the ethos, or credibility, that this group musters with each name that is added to the list, especially in light of the "mystique" of science discussed in Dorothy Nelkin's essay (included in this section). And you can also think about this issue in light of the regulating role of government discussed in Part 5 or the role of activist websites like the one that published this open letter, as discussed in Part 2.

We, the undersigned scientists, call for the immediate suspension of all environmental releases of GM crops and products, both commercially and in open field trials, for at least 5 years; for patents on living processes, organisms, seeds, cell lines and genes to be revoked and banned; and for a comprehensive public enquiry into the future of agriculture and food security for all.

1. Patents on life-forms and living processes should be banned because they threaten food security, sanction biopiracy of indigenous knowledge and genetic resources, violate basic human rights and dignity, compromise healthcare, impede medical and scientific research and are against the welfare of animals.[1] Life-forms such as organisms, seeds, cell lines and genes are discoveries and hence not patentable. Current GM techniques which exploit living processes are unreliable, uncontrollable and unpredictable, and do not qualify as inventions. Furthermore, those techniques are inherently unsafe, as are many GM organisms and products.

2. It is becoming increasingly clear that current GM crops are neither needed nor beneficial. They are a dangerous diversion preventing the essential shift to sustainable agricultural practices that can provide food security and health around the world.

3. Two simple characteristics account for the nearly 40 million hectares of GM crops planted in 1999.[2] The majority (71%) are tolerant to broad-spectrum herbicides, with companies engineering plants to be tolerant to their own brand of herbicide, while most of the rest are engineered with bt-toxins to kill insect pests. A university-based survey of 8200 field trials of the most widely grown GM crops, herbicide-tolerant soya beans— revealed that they yield 6.7% less and required two to five times more herbicides than non-GM varieties.[3] This has been confirmed by a more recent study in the University of Nebraska.[4] Yet other problems have been identified: erratic performance, disease susceptibility,[5] fruit abortion[6] and poor economic returns to farmers.[7]

4. According to the UN food programme, there is enough food to feed the world one and a half times over. While world

population has grown 90% in the past 40 years, the amount of food per capita has increased by 25%, yet one billion are hungry.[8] A new FAO report confirms that there will be enough or more than enough food to meet global demands without taking into account any yield improvements that might result from GM crops well into 2030.[9] It is on account of increasing corporate monopoly operating under the globalised economy that the poor are getting poorer and hungrier.[10] Family farmers around the world have been driven to destitution and suicide, and for the same reasons. Between 1993 and 1997 the number of mid-sized farms in the U.S. dropped by 74,440,[11] and farmers are now receiving below the average cost of production for their produce.[12] The farming population in France and Germany fell by 50% since 1978.[13] In the UK, 20,000 farming jobs were lost in the past year alone, and the Prime Minister has announced a £200m aid package.[14] Four corporations control 85% of the world trade in cereals at the end of 1999.[15] Mergers and acquisitions are continuing.

5. The new patents on seeds intensify corporate monopoly by preventing farmers from saving and replanting seeds, which is what most farmers still do in the Third World. In order to protect their patents, corporations are continuing to develop terminator technologies that genetic engineer harvested seeds not to germinate, despite worldwide opposition from farmers and civil society at large.[16]

6. Christian Aid, a major charity working with the Third World, concluded that GM crops will cause unemployment, exacerbate Third World debt, threaten sustainable farming systems and damage the environment. It predicts famine for the poorest countries.[17] African Governments condemned Monsanto's claim that GMOs are needed to feed the hungry of the world: "We ... strongly object that the image of the poor and hungry from our countries is being used by giant multinational corporations to push a technology that is neither safe, environmentally friendly, nor economically beneficial to us ... we believe it will destroy the diversity, the local knowledge and the sustainable agricultural systems that our farmers have developed for millennia and ... undermine our capacity to feed ourselves."[18] A message from the Peasant movement of the Philippines to the Organization for Economic Cooperation and Development (OECD) of the industrialized countries stated, "The entry of GMOs will certainly intensify landlessness, hunger and injustice."[19]

7. A coalition of family farming groups in the U.S. have issued a comprehensive list of demands, including ban on ownership of all life-forms; suspension of sales, environmental releases and further approvals of all GM crops and products

pending an independent, comprehensive assessment of the social, environmental, health and economic impacts; and for corporations to be made liable for all damages arising from GM crops and products to livestock, human beings and the environment.[20] They also demand a moratorium on all corporate mergers and acquisitions, on farm closures, and an end to policies that serve big agribusiness interests at the expense of family farmers, taxpayers and the environment.[21] They have mounted a lawsuit against Monsanto and nine other corporations for monopolistic practices and for foisting GM crops on farmers without adequate safety and environmental impact assessment.[22]

8. Some of the hazards of GM crops are openly acknowledged by the UK and U.S. Governments. UK Ministry of Agriculture, Fisheries and Food (MAFF) has admitted that the transfer of GM crops and pollen beyond the planted fields is unavoidable,[23] and this has already resulted in herbicide-tolerant weeds.[24] An interim report on UK Government-sponsored field trials confirmed hybridisation between adjacent plots of different herbicide tolerant GM oilseed rape varieties, which gave rise to hybrids tolerant to multiple herbicides. In addition, GM oilseed rape and their hybrids were found as volunteers in subsequent wheat and barley crops, which had to be controlled by standard herbicides.[25] Bt-resistant insect pests have evolved in response to the continuous presence of the toxins in GM plants throughout the growing season, and the U.S. Environment Protection Agency is recommending farmers to plant up to 40% non-GM crops in order to create refugia for non-resistant insect pests.[26]

9. The threats to biodiversity from major GM crops already commercialized are becoming increasingly clear. The broad-spectrum herbicides used with herbicide-tolerant GM crops decimate wild plant species indiscriminately; they are also toxic to animals. Glufosinate causes birth defects in mammals,[27] and glyphosate is linked to non-Hodgkin's lymphoma.[28] GM crops with bt-toxins kill beneficial insects such as bees[29] and lacewings,[30] and pollen from bt-corn is found to be lethal to monarch butterflies[31] as well as swallowtails.[32] Bt-toxin is exuded from roots of bt-plants in the rhizosphere, where it rapidity binds to soil particles and becomes protected from degradation. As the toxin is present in an activated, non-selective form, both target and non-target species in the soil will be affected,[33] with knock on effects on species above ground.

10. Products resulting from genetically modified organisms can also be hazardous. For example, a batch of tryptophan produced by GM microorganisms was associated with at least

37 deaths and 1500 serious illnesses.[34] Genetically modified Bovine Growth Hormone, injected into cows in order to increase milk yield, not only causes excessive suffering and illnesses for the cows but increases IGF-1 in the milk, which is linked to breast and prostate cancers in humans.[35] It is vital for the public to be protected from all GM products, and not only those containing transgenic DNA or protein. That is because the process of genetic modification itself, at least in the form currently practised, is inherently unsafe.

11. Secret memoranda of the U.S. Food and Drug Administration revealed that it ignored the warnings of its own scientists that genetic engineering is a new departure and introduces new risks. Furthermore, the first GM crop to be commercialized—the Flavr Savr tomato—did not pass the required toxicological tests.[36] Since then, no comprehensive scientific safety testing had been done until Dr. Arpad Pusztai and his collaborators in the UK raised serious concerns over the safety of the GM potatoes they were testing. They conclude that a significant part of the toxic effect may be due to the "[gene] construct or the genetic transformation (or both)" used in making the GM plants.[37]

12. The safety of GM foods was openly disputed by Professor Bevan Moseley, molecular geneticist and current Chair of the Working Group on Novel Foods in the European Union's Scientific Committee on Food.[38] He drew attention to unforseen effects inherent to the technology, emphasizing that the next generation of GM foods—the so-called 'neutraceuticals' or 'functional foods,' such as vitamin A 'enriched' rice—will pose even greater health risks because of the increased complexity of the gene constructs.

13. Genetic engineering introduces new genes and new combinations of genetic material constructed in the laboratory into crops, livestock and microorganisms.[39] The artificial constructs are derived from the genetic material of pathogenic viruses and other genetic parasites, as well as bacteria and other organisms, and include genes coding for antibiotic resistance. The constructs are designed to break down species barriers and to overcome mechanisms that prevent foreign genetic material from inserting into genomes. Most of them have never existed in nature in the course of billions of years of evolution.

14. These constructs are introduced into cells by invasive methods that lead to random insertion of the foreign genes into the genomes (the totality of all the genetic material of a cell or organism). This gives rise to unpredictable, random effects, including gross abnormalities in animals and unexpected toxins and allergens in food crops.

15. One construct common to practically all GM crops already commercialized or undergoing field trials involves a gene-switch (promoter) from the cauliflower mosaic virus (CaMV) spliced next to the foreign gene (transgene) to make it over-express continuously.[40] This CaMV promoter is active in all plants, in yeast, algae and E. coli. We recently discovered that it is even active in amphibian egg[41] and human cell extract.[42] It has a modular structure, and is interchangeable, in part, or in whole with promoters of other viruses to give infectious viruses. It also has a 'recombination hotspot' where it is prone to break and join up with other genetic material.[43]

16. For these and other reasons, transgenic DNA—the totality of artificial constructs transferred into the GMO—may be more unstable and prone to transfer again to unrelated species; potentially to all species interacting with the GMO.[44]

17. The instability of transgenic DNA in GM plants is well-known.[45] GM genes are often silenced, but loss of part or all of the transgenic DNA also occurs, even during later generations of propagation.[46] We are aware of no published evidence for the long term stability of GM inserts in terms of structure or location in the plant genome in any of the GM lines already commercialized or undergoing field trials.

18. The potential hazards of horizontal transfer of GM genes include the spread of antibiotic resistance genes to pathogens, the generation of new viruses and bacteria that cause disease and mutations due to the random insertion of foreign DNA, some of which may lead to cancer in mammalian cells.[47] The ability of the CaMV promoter to function in all species including human beings is particularly relevant to the potential hazards of horizontal gene transfer.

19. The possibility for naked or free DNA to be taken up by mammalian cells is explicitly mentioned in the U.S. Food and Drug Administration (FDA) draft guidance to industry on antibiotic resistance marker genes.[48] In commenting on the FDA's document, the UK MAFF pointed out that transgenic DNA may be transferred not just by ingestion, but by contact with plant dust and air-borne pollen during farm work and food processing.[49] This warning is all the more significant with the recent report from Jena University in Germany that field experiments indicated GM genes may have transferred via GM pollen to the bacteria and yeasts in the gut of bee larvae.[50]

20. Plant DNA is not readily degraded during most commercial food processing.[51] Procedures such as grinding and milling left grain DNA largely intact, as did heat-treatment at 90°C. Plants placed in silage showed little degradation of

DNA, and a special UK MAFF report advises against using GM plants or plant waste in animal feed.

21. The human mouth contains bacteria that have been shown to take up and express naked DNA containing antibiotic resistance genes, and similar transformable bacteria are present in the respiratory tracts.[52]

22. Antibiotic resistance marker genes from GM plants have been found to transfer horizontally to soil bacteria and fungi in the laboratory.[53] Field monitoring revealed that GM sugar beet DNA persisted in the soil for up to two years after the GM crop was planted. And there is evidence suggesting that parts of the transgenic DNA have transferred horizontally to bacteria in the soil.[54]

23. Recent research in gene therapy and nucleic acid (both DNA and RNA) vaccines leaves little doubt that naked/free nucleic acids can be taken up, and in some cases, incorporated into the genome of all mammalian cells including those of human beings. Adverse effects already observed include acute toxic shock, delayed immunological reactions and autoimmune reactions.[55]

24. The British Medical Association, in their interim report (published May, 1999), called for an indefinite moratorium on the releases of GMOs pending further research on new allergies, the spread of antibiotic resistance genes and the effects of transgenic DNA.

25. In the Cartegena Biosafety Protocol successfully negotiated in Montreal in January, 2000, more than 130 governments have agreed to implement the precautionary principle, and to ensure that biosafety legislations at the national and international levels take precedence over trade and financial agreements at the WTO. Similarly, delegates to the Codex Alimentarius Commission Conference in Chiba, Japan, March 2000, have agreed to prepare stringent regulatory procedures for GM foods that include pre-market evaluation, long-term monitoring for health impacts, tests for genetic stability, toxins, allergens and other unintended effects.[56] The Cartegena Biosafety Protocol has now been signed by 68 Governments in Nairobi in May, 2000.

26. We urge all Governments to take proper account of the now substantial scientific evidence of actual and suspected hazards arising from GM technology and many of its products, and to impose an immediate moratorium on further environmental releases, including open field trials, in accordance with the precautionary principle as well as sound science.

27. Successive studies have documented the productivity and sustainability of family farming in the Third World as well as in the North.[57] Evidence from both North and South

indicates that small farms are more productive, more efficient and contribute more to economic development than large farms. Small farmers also tend to make better stewards of natural resources, conserving biodiversity and safeguarding the sustainability of agricultural production.[58] Cuba responded to the economic crisis precipitated by the breakup of the Soviet Bloc in 1989 by converting from conventional large scale, high input monoculture to small organic and semi-organic farming, thereby doubling food production with half the previous input.[59]

28. Agroecological approaches hold great promise for sustainable agriculture in developing countries, in combining local farming knowledge and techniques adjusted to local conditions with contemporary Western scientific knowledge.[60] The yields have doubled and tripled and are still increasing. An estimated 12.5 million hectares worldwide are already successfully farmed in this way.[61] It is environmentally sound and affordable for small farmers. It recovers farming land marginalized by conventional intensive agriculture. It offers the only practical way of restoring agricultural land degraded by conventional agronomic practices. Most of all, it empowers small family farmers to combat poverty and hunger.

29. We urge all Governments to reject GM crops on grounds that they are both hazardous and contrary to ecologically sustainable use of resources. Instead they should support research and development of sustainable agricultural methods that can truly benefit family farmers the world over.

NOTES

1. See World Scientists' Statement, Institute of Science in Society website <www.i-sis.org.uk>
2. See Ho, M. W., and Traavik, T. (1999). *Why Patents on Life Forms and Living Processes Should be Rejected from TRIPS—Scientific Briefing on TRIPS Article 27.3(b)*. TWN Report, Penang. See also ISIS News #3 and #4 <www.i-sis.org.uk>
3. James, C. (1998, 1999). *Global Status of Transgenic Crops*, ISAAA Briefs, New York.
4. Benbrook, C. (1999). *Evidence of the Magnitude and Consequences of the Roundup Ready Soybean Yield Drag from University-Based Varietal Trials in 1998*, Ag BioTech InfoNet Technical Paper No. 1, Idaho.
5. "Splitting Headache," Andy Coghlan. *NewScientist*, News, November 20, 1999.
6. "Metabolic Disturbances in GM Cotton Leading to Fruit Abortion and Other Problems" <bikwessex@bigfoot.com>.
7. "Genetically Altered Crops—Will We Answer the Questions?" Dan McGuire, American Corn Growers Association Annual Convention, Las Vegas, Nevada, Feb. 4, 2000; see also "Biotech News," Richard Wolfson, *Canad. J. Health & Nutrition*, April, 2000.

8. See Watkins, K. (1999). Free trade and farm fallacies. *Third World Resurgence* 100/101, 33–37; see also El Feki, S. (2000). Growing pains, *The Economist*, 25 March, 2000.

9. Agriculture: towards 2015/30, FAO Global Perspectives Studies Unit http://www.fao.org/es/esd/at2015/toc-e.htm.

10. This is now admitted in an astonishing series of articles by Shereen El Feki in *The Economist* (March 25, 2000), hitherto generally considered as a pro-business right-wing magazine.

11. Farm and Land in Farms, Final Estimates 1993–1997, USDA National Agricultural Statistics Service.

12. See Griffin, D. (1999). Agricultural globalization. A threat to food security? *Third World Resurgence* 100/101, 38–40.

13. El Feki, S. (2000). Trust or bust, *The Economist*, 25 March, 2000.

14. Meikle, J. (2000). Farmers welcome £200m deal. *The Guardian*, 31 March, 2000.

15. Farm Aid Fact Sheet: The Farm Crisis Deepens, Cambridge, Mass., 1999.

16. U.S. Department of Agriculture now holds two new patents on terminator technology jointly with Delta and Pine. These patents were issued in 1999. AstraZeneca are patenting similar techniques. Rafi communique, March, 2000.

17. Simms, A. (1999). *Selling suicide, farming, false promises and genetic engineering in developing countries*, Christian Aid, London.

18. "Let Nature's Harvest Continue," statement from all the African delegates (except South Africa) to FAO negotiations on the International Undertaking for Plant Genetic Resources, June, 1998.

19. Letter from Kilusang Mgbubukid ng Pilipinas to OECD, 14 Feb. 2000 <www.geocities.com/kmp.ph>

20. Farmer's Declaration on Genetic Engineering in Agriculture, National Family Farm Coalition, USA, <nffc@nffc.net>.

21. Farmer's rally on Capitol Hill, September 12, 1999.

22. McGuire, D. (2000). Genetically altered crops: Will we answer the questions? American Corn Growers Association Annual Convention, Las Vegas, Feb. 4, 2000.

23. MAFF Fact Sheet: Genetic modification of crops and food, June, 1999.

24. See Ho, M. W., and Tappeser, B. (1997). Potential contributions of horizontal gene transfer to the transboundary movement of living modified organisms resulting from modern biotechnology. *Proceedings of Workshop on Transboundary Movement of Living Modified Organisms resulting from Modern Biotechnology: Issues and Opportunities for Policy-makers* (K. J. Mulongoy, ed.), pp. 171–193, International Academy of the Environment, Geneva.

25. "The BRIGHT Project: Botanical and Rotational Implications of Genetically Modified Herbicide Tolerance: Progress Report, March 2000, sponsored by MAFF, SERAD, HGCA, BBRO, Aventis, Crop Care, Cyanamid, Monsanto.

26. Mellon, M., and Rissler, J. (1998). *Now or Never. Serious New Plans to Save a Natural Pest Control*, Union of Concerned Scientists, Cambridge, Mass.

27. Garcia, A., Benavides, F., Fletcher, T., and Orts, E. (1998). Paternal exposure to pesticides and congenital malformations. *Scand. J. Work Environ. Health* 24, 473–80.

28. Hardell, H., and Eriksson, M. (1999). A Case-Control Study of Non-Hodgkin's Lymphoma and Exposure to Pesticides. *Cancer* 85, 1355–1360.

29. "Cotton Used in Medicine Poses Threat: Genetically-Altered Cotton May Not Be Safe," *Bangkok Post*, November 17, 1997.

30. Hilbeck, A., Baumgartner, M., Fried, P. M., and Bigler, F. (1998). Effects of transgenic *Bacillus thuringiensis*–corn-fed prey on mortality and development time of immature Chrysoperla carnea (Neuroptera: Chrysopidae). *Environmental Entomology* 27, 480–96.
31. Losey, J. E., Rayor, L. D., and Carter, M. E. (1999). Transgenic pollen harms monarch larvae. *Nature* 399, 214.
32. See Wraight, C. L., Zangerl, R. A., Carroll, M. J., and Berenbaum, M. R. (2000). Absence of toxicity of Bacillus thuringiensis pollen to black swallowtails under field conditions. PNAS Early Edition www.pnas.org; despite the claim in the title, the paper reports toxicity of bt-pollen from a high-expressing line to swallowtail larvae in the laboratory. The issue of bt-crops is reviewed in "Swallowing the tale of the swallowtail" and "To Bt or Not to Bt," ISIS News #5.
33. Deepak Saxena, Saul Flores, G. Stotzky. (1999). Transgenic plants: Insecticidal toxin in root exudates from Bt corn. *Nature* 402, 480.
34. Mayeno, A. N., and Gleich, G. J. (1994). Eosinophilia-myalgia syndrome and tryptophan production: a cautionary tale. *Tibtech* 12, 346–352.
35. Epstein, E. (1998). Bovine growth hormone and prostate cancer; Bovine growth hormone and breast cancer. *The Ecologist* 28(5), 268, 269.
36. The secret memoranda came to light as the result of a civil lawsuit spearheaded by lawyer Steven Druker against the U.S. FDA, May 1998. For details see Biointegrity website: <www.biointegrity.com>.
37. Ewen, S. W. B., and Pusztai, A. (1999). Effects of diets containing genetically modified potatoes expressing Galanthus nivalis lectin on rat small intestine. The Lancet 354, 1353–1354; see also <http://plab.ku.dk/tcbh/ PusztaiPusztai.htm>.
38. Pat Phibbs, P. (2000). Genetically modified food sales 'dead' in EU until safety certain, says consultant. The Bureau of National Affairs, Inc., Washington, D.C. March 23, 2000.
39. See Ho, M. W. (1998, 1999). *Genetic Engineering Dream or Nightmare? The Brave New World of Bad Science and Big Business.* Gateway, Gill & Macmillan, Dublin.
40. See Ho, M. W., Ryan, A., Cummins, J. (1999). The cauliflower mosaic viral promoter—a recipe for disaster? Microbial Ecology in Health and Disease 11, 194–197; Ho, M. W., Ryan, A., Cummins, J. (2000). Hazards of transgenic crops with the cauliflower mosaic viral promoter. Microbial Ecology in Health and Disease (in press); Cummins, J., Ho, M. W., and Ryan, A. (2000). *Hazards of CaMV promoter. Nature Biotechnology* (in press).
41. Reviewed in Ho, 1998, 1999 (note 37); Ho, M. W., Traavik, T., Olsvik, R., Tappeser, B., Howard, V., von Weizsacker, C., and McGavin, G. (1998b). Gene Technology and Gene Ecology of Infectious Diseases. *Microbial Ecology in Health and Disease* 10, 33–59; Traavik, T. (1999a). *Too early may be too late: Ecological risks associated with the use of naked DNA as biological tool for research, production and therapy,* Research report for Directorate for Nature Management, Norway.
42. N. Ballas, S. Broido, H. Soreq, A. Loyter. (1989). Efficient functioning of plant promoters and poly(A) sites in Xenopus oocytes. *Nucl. Acids Res.* 17, 7891–903.
43. Burke, C., Yu, X. B., Marchitelli, L., Davis, E. A., and Ackerman, S. (1990). Transcription factor IIA of wheat and human function similarly with plant and animal viral promoters. *Nucl. Acids Res.* 18, 3611–20.

44. Reviewed in Ho, 1998, 1999 (note 37); Ho, M. W., Traavik, T., Olsvik, R., Tappeser, B., Howard, V., von Weizsacker, C., and McGavin, G. (1998b). Gene Technology and Gene Ecology of Infectious Diseases. Microbial Ecology in Health and Disease 10, 33–59; Traavik, T. (1999a). Too early may be too late: Ecological risks associated with the use of naked DNA as a biological tool for research, production and therapy, Research report for Directorate for Nature Management, Norway.

45. Kumpatla, S. P., Chandrasekharan, M. B., Iuer, L. M., Li, G., and Hall, T. C. (1998). Genome intruder scanning and modulation systems and transgene silencing. Trends in Plant Sciences 3, 96–l04.

46. See Pawlowski, W. P., and Somers, D. A. (1996). Transgene inheritance in plants. Molecular Biotechnology 6, 17–30.

47. Reviewed by Doerfler, W., Schubbert, R., Heller, H., Kämmer, C., Hilger-Eversheim, D., Knoblauch, M., and Remus, R. (1997). Integration of foreign DNA and its consequences in mammalian systems. *Tibtech* 15, 297–301.

48. Draft Guidance for Industry: Use of Antibiotic Resistance Marker Genes in Transgenic Plants, U.S. FDA, September 4, 1998.

49. See Letter From N. Tomlinson, Joint Food Safety and Standards Group, MAFF, to U.S. FDA, 4 December, 1998.

50. See Barnett, A. (2000). GM genes 'jump species barrier.' The Observer, May 28.

51. Forbes, J. M., Blair, D. E., Chiter, A., and Perks, S. (1998). *Effect of Feed Processing Conditions on DNA Fragmentation Section 5—Scientific Report*, MAFF; see also Ryan, A., and Ho, M. W. (*1999*). *Transgenic DNA in Animal Feed*. ISIS Report, November 1999 <www.i-sis.org.uk>.

52. Mercer, D. K., Scott, K. P., Bruce-Johnson, W. A., Glover, L. A., and Flint, H. J. (1999). Fate of free DNA and transformation of the oral bacterium Streptococcus gordonii DL1 by plasmid DNA in human saliva. *Applied and Environmental Microbiology* 65, 6–10.

53. Reviewed in Ho, 1998, 1999 (note 37).

54. Gebbard, F., and Smalla, K. (1999). Monitoring field releases of genetically modified sugar beets for persistence of transgenic plant DNA and horizontal gene transfer. *FEMS Microbiology Ecology* 28, 261–272.

55. See Ho, M. W., Ryan, A., Cummins, J., and Traavik, T. (2000). *Unregulated Hazards, 'Naked' and 'Free' Nucleic Acids*, ISIS Report for Third World Network, Jan. 2000, London and Penang <www.i-sis.org.uk>.

56. Viewpoint, Henry Miller, *Financial Times*, March 22, 2000.

57. See Pretty, J. (1995). *Sustainable Agriculture*, Earthscan, London; also Pretty, J. (1998). *The Living Land—Agriculture, Food and Community Regeneration in Rural Europe*, Earthscan, London; see also *Alternative Agriculture: Report of the National Academy of Sciences*, Washington D.C., 1989.

58. Rosset, P. (1999). *The Multiple Functions and Benefits of Small Farm Agriculture In the Context of Global Trade Negotiations*, The Institute for Goods and Development Policy, Policy Brief No. 4, Oakland.

59. Murphy, C. (1999). *Cultivating Havana: Urban Agriculture and Food Security in the Years of Crisis*, Institute for Food and Development Policy, Development Report No. 12, Oakland.

60. Altieri, M., Rosset, P., and Trupp, L. A. (1998). *The Potential of Agroecology to Combat Hunger in the Developing World*, Institute for Food and Development Policy Report, Oakland, California.

61. Peter Rosset, Food First Institute.

Richard Manning
SUPER ORGANICS

Though "genetic engineering" has come to mean the manipula-
tion of genes in a laboratory, raising specters of dangerous new
breeds, as Richard Manning suggests in this article, farmers
have always crossbred and attempted to help nature along.
Manning's article, first published in Wired Magazine, *tries to*
find a middle ground between the fear of all scientific manipu-
lation of organisms and the wholesale changing of genetic
codes. Consider how Manning's perspective adds depth to the
conversation, keeping it from a simple pro/con. Manning is an
environmental writer, and the author of Against the Grain:
How Agriculture Has Hijacked Civilization *and* Food's
Frontier: The Next Green Revolution.

Once upon a technologically optimistic time, the founders of a   1
swaggering biotech startup called Calgene bet the farm on a
tomato. It wasn't just any old tomato. It was the Flavr Savr, a
genetically engineered fruit designed to solve a problem of
modernity.

Back when we all lived in villages, getting fresh, flavorful   2
tomatoes was simple. Local farmers would deliver them, bright
red and bursting with flavor, to nearby markets. Then cities
and suburbs pushed out the farmers, and we began demanding
our favorite produce year-round. Many of our tomatoes today
are grown in another hemisphere, picked green, and only turn
red en route to the local Safeway. Harvesting tomatoes this
way, before they've received their full dose of nutrients from
the vine, can make for some pretty bland fare. But how else
could they endure the long trip without spoiling?

Flavr Savr was meant to be an alternative, a tomato that   3
would ripen on the vine and remain firm in transit. Calgene
scientists inserted into the fruit's genome a gene that retarded
the tendency to spoil. The gene-jiggering worked—at least in
terms of longer shelf life.

Then came the backlash. Critics of genetically modified   4
food dubbed the Flavr Savr "Frankenfood." Sparked by
the Flavr Savr's appearance before the U.S. Food and Drug
Administration, biotech watchdog Jeremy Rifkin set up the
Pure Food Campaign, stalling FDA approval for three years
and raising a ruckus that spread to Europe. When the tomato
finally emerged, it demonstrated that there was no accounting

for taste at Calgene. Flavr Savr wasn't just oddly spelled; it was a misnomer. Even worse, the fruit was a bust in the fields. It was highly susceptible to disease and provided low yields. Calgene spent more than $200 million to make a better tomato, only to find itself awash in red ink. Eventually, it was swallowed by Monsanto.

5   But the quest for a longer-lasting tomato didn't end there. As the Flavr Savr was stumbling (Monsanto eventually abandoned it), Israeli scientist Nachum Kedar was quietly bringing a natural version to market. By crossbreeding beefsteak tomatoes, Kedar had arrived at a savory, high-yield fruit that would ripen on the vine and remain firm in transit. He found a marketing partner, which licensed the tomato and flooded the U.S. market without any PR problems. The vine-ripened hybrid, now grown and sold worldwide under several brand names, owes its existence to Kedar's knowledge of the tomato genome. He didn't use genetic engineering. His fruit emerged from a process that's both more sophisticated and far less controversial.

6   Welcome to the world of smart breeding.

7   The tale of the Flavr Savr is a near-perfect illustration of the plight of genetically modified organisms. A decade ago, GMOs were hailed as technological miracles that would save farmers money, lower food prices, and reduce the environmental damage unintentionally caused by the Green Revolution—a movement that increased yields but fostered reliance on chemical fertilizers, pesticides, and wanton irrigation. Gene jocks said they could give us even greater abundance and curb environmental damage by inserting a snip or two of DNA from another species into the genomes of various crops, a process known as transgenics.

8   In some cases, GMOs have fulfilled their promise. They've allowed U.S. farmers to be more productive without as much topical pesticide and fertilizer. Our grocery stores are stuffed with cheaply produced food—up to 70 percent of all packaged goods contain GM ingredients, mainly corn and soybean. GM has worked even better with inedible crops. Take cotton. Bugs love it, which is why Southern folk music is full of tunes about the boll weevil. This means huge doses of pesticides. The world's largest cotton producer, China, used to track the human body count during spraying season. Then in 1996, Monsanto introduced BT cotton—a GMO that employs a gene from the bacterium Bacillus thuringiensis to make a powerful pesticide in the plant. BT cotton cuts pesticide spraying in half; the farmers survive.

9   But while producers have embraced GMOs, consumers have had a tougher time understanding the benefits. Environmentalists and foodies decry GMOs as unnatural creations bound to destroy traditional plants and harm our bodies.

Europe has all but outlawed transgenic crops, prompting a global trade war that's costing U.S. farmers billions in lost exports. In March, voters in Mendocino County, California, banned GMO farming within county lines.

Opponents have found an ally in crop scientists who condemn the conglomerates behind transgenics, especially Monsanto. The company owns scores of patents covering its GM seeds and the entire development process that creates them. This gives Monsanto a virtual monopoly on GM seeds for mainline crops and stifles outside innovation. No one can gene-jockey without a tithe to the life sciences giant.   10

Which brings us back to smart breeding. Researchers are beginning to understand plants so precisely that they no longer need transgenics to achieve traits like drought resistance, durability, or increased nutritional value. Over the past decade, scientists have discovered that our crops are chock-full of dormant characteristics. Rather than inserting, say, a bacteria gene to ward off pests, it's often possible to simply turn on a plant's innate ability.   11

The result: Smart breeding holds the promise of remaking agriculture through methods that are largely uncontroversial and unpatentable. Think about the crossbreeding and hybridization that farmers have been doing for hundreds of years, relying on instinct, trial and error, and luck to bring us things like tangelos, giant pumpkins, and burpless cucumbers. Now replace those fuzzy factors with precise information about the role each gene plays in a plant's makeup. Today, scientists can tease out desired traits on the fly—something that used to take a decade or more to accomplish.   12

Even better, they can develop plants that were never thought possible without the help of transgenics. Look closely at the edge of food science and you'll see the beginnings of fruits and vegetables that are both natural and supernatural. Call them Superorganics—nutritious, delicious, safe, abundant crops that require less pesticide, fertilizer, and irrigation—a new generation of food that will please the consumer, the producer, the activist, and the FDA.   13

Nearly every crop in the world has a corresponding gene bank consisting of the seeds of thousands of wild and domesticated relatives. Until recently, gene banks were like libraries with millions of dusty books but no card catalogs. Advances in genomics and information technology—from processing power to databases and storage—have given crop scientists the ability to not only create card catalogs detailing the myriad traits expressed in individual varieties, but the techniques to turn them on universally.   14

15   One of the smart breeder's most valuable tools is the DNA marker. It's a tag that sticks to a particular region of a chromosome, allowing researchers to zero-in on the genes responsible for a given trait—a muted orange hue or the ability to withstand sea spray. With markers, much of the early-stage breeding can be done in a lab, saving the time and money required to grow several generations in a field. Once breeders have marked a trait, they use traditional breeding tactics like tissue culturing—growing a snip of plant in a nutrient-rich medium until it's strong enough to survive on its own. One form of culturing, embryo rescue, allows breeders to cross distant relatives that wouldn't normally produce a viable offspring. This is important because rare, wild varieties often demonstrate highly desirable characteristics. After fertilization, a breeder extracts the premature embryo and fosters it in the lab. Another technique—anther culture—enables breeders to develop a complete plant from a single male cell.

16   The science behind some of these techniques makes transgenics look unsophisticated. But the sell is simple: Smart breeding is the best of transgenics crossed with the best of organics. It can feed the world, heal the earth, and put an end to the Big Ag monopoly.

17   Take it from Robert Goodman, the former head scientist at Calgene who now works with the McKnight Foundation, overseeing a $50 million program that funds genomics research in the developing world. "The public argument about genetically modified organisms, I think, will soon be a thing of the past," he says. "The science has moved on."

18   In the mid-'80s, a grad student in plant breeding at Cornell University was handed a task that none of her peers would take. Her name: Susan McCouch. Her loser assignment: Create a map of the 40,000 genes spread across the rice genome. In 1988, the completion of that work would be heralded as a scientific breakthrough. Sixteen years later, it's beginning to shake corporate control of science.

19   A genome map is a detailed outline of an organism's underlying structure. Until McCouch came along, rice—the most important food for most of the world's poor—was an orphan crop for research. Big Ag was interested only in the Western staples, wheat and corn. But good maps enlighten—geologists once looked at maps of South America and Africa and figured out that the edges of the two continents fit together, giving rise to the idea of plate tectonics. McCouch's map was just as revealing. Researchers compared it to the genomes of wheat and corn and realized that all three crops, along with other cereal grasses—more than two-thirds of humanity's food—have remarkably similar makeups. The volumes of research into corn and wheat

could suddenly be used to better understand developing world essentials like rice, teff, millet, and sorghum. If scientists could find a gene in one, they'd be able to locate it in the others.

By extension, characteristics of one crop should be present 20 in related plants. If a certain variety of wheat is naturally adept at defeating a certain pest, then rice should be, too; scientists would just need to switch on that ability. McCouch started her project as a way to unlock the door to the rice library; it turned out she cut a master key.

Still at Cornell, McCouch is now learning how crossbreeding 21 domesticated rice with wild ancestors can achieve super-abilities that neither parent possesses. "We're finding things like genes in low-yielding wild ancestors, which if you move them into culti-vated varieties can increase the yields of the best cultivar," McCouch says. "Or genes of tomatoes that come out of a wild background—they make a red fruit redder. We also have ways to make larger seeds, which can yield bigger fruit." Generations of unscientific plant breeding have inadvertently eliminated count-less valuable genes and weakened the natural defenses of our crops. McCouch is recovering the complexity and magic.

Food scientists around the world are picking up on her work. 22 In China, researcher Deng Qiyun, inspired by McCouch's papers, used molecular markers while crossbreeding a wild relative of rice with his country's best hybrid to achieve a 30 percent jump in yield—an increase well beyond anything gained during the Green Revolution. Who will feed China? Deng will. In India, the poorest of the poor can't afford irrigated land, so they grow un-productive varieties of dryland rice. By some estimates, Indian rice production must double by 2025 to meet the needs of an ex-ploding population. One researcher in Bangalore is showing the way. H. E. Shashidhar has cataloged the genes of the dryland va-rieties and used DNA markers to guide the breeding toward a high-yield super-rice. In West Africa, smart breeders have created Nerica, a bountiful rice that combines the best traits of Asian and African parents. Nerica spreads profusely in early stages to smother weeds. It's disease-resistant, drought-tolerant, and con-tains up to 31 percent more protein than either parent.

This is not exclusively a matter of crafting new rice varieties in 23 the developing world. Irwin Goldman, a horticulture professor at the University of Wisconsin-Madison, cites McCouch's work as critical to the progress he's made with carrots, onions, and beets. For example, he has spawned a striped beet through some sophis-ticated genome tweaking—and in the process revealed methods to improve the appearance and taste of all sorts of vegetables.

Beet genes make two pigments of a class of chemicals called 24 betalain. When both are present, the beet is red. Switch off one gene, as happens in natural mutations, and the beet is gold. Switch it on and off at different stages and the beet becomes striped. Creating a striped beet is not hugely important by itself—striped heirloom varieties date back to 19th-century Italy. What's significant is that Goldman pinpointed the genes responsible for the trait and figured out how to turn them on.

25   This type of smart breeding may one day lead to something as useful as a high-yield rice that's naturally rich in beta-carotene, which out bodies convert to vitamin A. For years, genetic engineers have been trying to introduce so-called golden rice to Asia, where vitamin A deficiency causes millions of people to go blind every year. Creating the GM version wasn't easy—it required the insertion of two daffodil genes—but it wasn't nearly as difficult as getting it to the people. As with the Flavr Savr, golden rice drew the ire of the Frankenfood crowd while running afoul of some 70 patents. A natural counterpart wouldn't encounter such problems Far-fetched? Maybe, considering that there's no known naturally occurring rice containing beta-carotene. [This is contradicted by Syngenta.] Then again, we never thought carrots had vitamin E—until Goldman found some.

26   By scouring the carrot gene bank, Goldman discovered several exotic varieties of carrots (ranging in color from yellow to orange, red, and purple) that make vitamin E. Capitalizing on that native ability is a matter of tagging the relevant genes and crossbreeding the wild relatives with ordinary, everyday carrots. Gene bank searches are also revealing a whole host of antioxidants, sulfur compounds, and tannins—chemicals that bring sharp color and strong tastes—that have been stripped out of our lowest-common-denominator crops over the centuries. Many of these qualities not only fight cancer and increase the nutritional value of our vegetables, but also make them taste better while helping plants fight disease. We now have the ability to bring these traits back.

27   And we can do it quickly. It often takes seed companies several years to establish a new variety. To recover their investment, they release seeds that don't usually pass on the parents' traits, forcing farmers to buy new seed every year. Smart breeding, by contrast, is faster and cheaper because much of it can be done in the lab—reducing the time and expense of growing countless varieties in the field. Goldman's work is funded by university dollars, which allows him to give away the spoils. He links up with local organics growers, farmers' markets, and the expanding counter-agribusiness food movement and hands out open-pollinated seeds—ag's version of open source.

28   Richard Jefferson is an iconoclastic American bluegrass musician living in Australia. He's also a brash biotechnologist

intent on wrestling control of our crops away from Big Agriculture. As head of CAMBIA (the Center for the Application of Molecular Biology to International Agriculture), a plant science think tank in Canberra, he's sowing the seeds of a revolt, citing the open source ethos of Linus Torvalds and Richard Stallman as inspiration. "In the case of almost every single enabling technology, the corporations have acquired it from the public sector," he says. "They have the morals of stoats."

If McCouch and Goldman are making an end run around GMOs by improving on methods that predate genetic engineering, Jefferson is taking a direct approach. All three scientists use an expanded knowledge of plant genomes to create new crop varieties. But where McCouch and Goldman do gene bank searches and study genome maps to figure out which plants to bring together, Jefferson digs into the genome itself and moves things around. He doesn't insert anything—he calls transgenics "hammer and tong science; as dull as dishwater"—but he's not above tinkering. His big idea: manipulate plants to teach ourselves more about them. 29

Jefferson made a name for himself as a grad student in 1985 when he discovered GUS, a clever little reporter gene that causes a glow when it's linked to any active gene. He distributed GUS to thousands of university and nonprofit labs at no cost—but charged the Monsantos of the world millions. He used the money to establish CAMBIA, which invents technologies to help developing world scientists create food varieties without violating GMO patents. 30

Transgenic researchers treat the genome like software, as if it contained binary code. If they want an organism to express a trait, they insert a gene. But the genome is more complicated than software. While software code has two possible values in each position (1 and 0), DNA has four (A,C,T, and G). What's more, a genome is constantly interacting with itself in ways that suggest what complexity theorists call emergent behavior. An organism's traits are often less a reaction to one gene and more a result of the relationship between many. This makes the expression of DNA fairly mysterious. 31

Jefferson is out to master this squishy science with a practice he calls transgenomics. You are different from your siblings because your parents' genes were unzipped during reproduction and the 23 chromosomes on each half rejoined in a unique pattern. The same thing happens in plants. Jefferson has modified native genes to act as universal switches that turn a plant's latent genes on and off. Simply put, he's rigging the reproductive shuffle. 32

In a process he calls HARTs—homologous allelic recombination techniques—Jefferson manipulates genomes (no insertions 33 allowed) to force plants to mimic other crops. "We're taking inspiration from one plant and asking another plant to make that change in itself," he says. One example Jefferson likes to talk about is sentinel corn—a plant-sized version of the GUS gene that would turn red when it needs water. It may not sound like much, but by the time a traditional corn plant wilts, it's usually too late. More efficient irrigation would mean the difference between profit and loss—or nourishment and starvation.

34   Jefferson's greatest hope to challenge Big Ag comes in what's known as apomixis—plant cloning. He wants to teach all sorts of crops to clone themselves the way dandelions and blackberries do naturally. When a plant's seeds produce genetically identical offspring, there's no need to buy hybrid seeds every year. Jefferson and rival scientists claim to have several paths to apomixis—but the race is competitive and no one's offering details. The real problem, says Jefferson, is not developing the methods, but releasing them into a world of patents. "I am not a technological optimist who thinks that if you put a technology out there, everything is going to be fine," he says. "How you put it out there matters as much or more than what it is."

35   His solution is to create an open source movement for biotechnology. In his vision, charitable foundations, which have paid for most of the world's public-interest crop science, would fund platform technologies and provide free licenses to public and private scientists. Commercial end products would be encouraged, but the basic technology, the OS, would remain in public hands. To get the whole thing started, Jefferson is offering up Cambia's portfolio of patents.

36   It's tempting to reach for the Linux versus Microsoft analogy to describe Cambia's plan to unlock some of the astounding technologies that remain dormant in labs and greenhouses. It's powerful, but also decentralized, networked, and accessible—democratic. It's like Monsanto's mainframe giving way to biotech's equivalent of the PC.

37   Agriculture is one of the most ill-conceived human endeavors. We plow down stable communities of hundreds of species of plants to get single-row crops. We replace entire ecosystems with pesticides, fertilizers, precious fresh water, and tractor emissions. Then, after every harvest, we start all over again. Organic agriculture breaks this cycle. But it's just a Band-Aid on the wound.

38   Add the knowledge and tools of biotechnology, though, and we are on the verge of something enormous. Plant genomes carry age-old records that reveal the complex manner by which nature manages itself. Researchers around the world—McCouch, Goldman, and Jefferson are a few examples—are learning to not only read those records but re-create them.

Which is not to say success is automatic. This new era of food   39
won't arrive with a technological big bang. But that's a good
thing. Single events are too easy to control and monopolize. A
steady trickle of innovation will buy time to get the marketing
right. Public perception is as complex as the genome, and just
as important to master. The science is taking hold. If the business side can clearly communicate what superorganics are—
and what they are not—these new foods will not only change
the way we eat, they'll change the way we relate to the planet.

Ron Reagan

ADDRESS TO THE 2004 DEMOCRATIC NATIONAL CONVENTION

*Ron Reagan (whose full name is Ronald Prescott Reagan) is the
son of former President Ronald Reagan and former first lady
Nancy. However, unlike his father, the younger Reagan's politics
lean toward the liberal. He worked with the late Christopher
Reeve and Susan Sarandon to found the "Creative Coalition," a
group that has attempted to involve entertainers and artists in
political causes. (Reagan himself was a dancer for the Joffrey
Ballet.) Most recently, he has worked as a journalist and political analyst. He delivered the following address during the 2004
presidential election at the Democratic National Convention as
an appeal to allow government funding for embryonic stem cell
research. Consider the* ethos *that his father's name gives to
him—as well as the fact that President Reagan died from
Alzheimer's disease, one of the disorders that researchers hope
might someday be cured by stem cell therapy.*

Thank you very much. That's very kind. Good evening, ladies   1
and gentlemen.
    A few of you may be surprised to see someone with my last   2
name showing up to speak at a Democratic Convention.
Apparently some of you are not. Let me assure you, I am not

here to make a political speech and the topic at hand should not—must not—have anything to do with partisanship.

3   I am here tonight to talk about the issue of research into what may be the greatest medical breakthrough in our or any lifetime: the use of embryonic stem cells—cells created using the material of our own bodies—to cure a wide range of fatal and debilitating illnesses: Parkinson's disease, multiple sclerosis, diabetes, lymphoma, spinal cord injuries and much more.

4   Millions are afflicted. And every year, every day, tragedy is visited upon families across the country, around the world. Now, it may be within our power to put an end to this suffering. We only need to try.

5   Some of you—some of you already know what I'm talking about when I say embryonic stem cell research. Others of you are probably thinking, that's quite a mouthful. Maybe this is a good time to go for a tall cold one. Well, wait a minute, wait a minute.

6   Let me try and paint as simple a picture as I can while still doing justice to the science, the incredible science involved. Let's say that 10 or so years from now you are diagnosed with Parkinson's disease. There is currently no cure and drug therapy, with its attendant side-effects, can only temporarily relieve the symptoms.

7   Now, imagine going to a doctor who, instead of prescribing drugs, takes a few skin cells from your arm. The nucleus of one of your cells is placed into a donor egg whose own nucleus has been removed. A bit of chemical or electrical stimulation will encourage your cell's nucleus to begin dividing, creating new cells which will then be placed into a tissue culture. Those cells will generate embryonic stem cells containing only your DNA, thereby eliminating the risk of tissue rejection. These stem cells are then driven to become the very neural cells that are defective in Parkinson's patients. And finally, those cells—with your DNA—are injected into your brain where they will replace the faulty cells whose failure to produce adequate dopamine led to the Parkinson's disease in the first place.

8   In other words, you're cured.

9   And another thing—another thing, these embryonic stem cells, they could continue to replicate indefinitely and, theoretically, can be induced to recreate virtually any tissue in your body.

10   How'd you like to have your own personal biological repair kit standing by at the hospital? Sound like magic? Welcome to the future of medicine.

11   Now by the way, no fetal tissue is involved in this process. No fetuses are created, none destroyed. This all happens in the laboratory at the cellular level.

Now, there are those who would stand in the way of this   12
remarkable future, who would deny the federal funding so
crucial to basic research. They argue that interfering with the
development of even the earliest stage embryo, even one that
will never be implanted in a womb and will never develop into
an actual fetus, is tantamount to murder.

A few of these folks, needless to say, are just grinding a politi-   13
cal axe and they should be ashamed of themselves. But many—
but many—many are well-meaning and sincere. Their belief is
just that, an article of faith, and they are entitled to it. But it
does not follow that the theology of a few should be allowed to
forestall the health and well-being of the many.

And how can we affirm life if we abandon those whose own   14
lives are so desperately at risk? It is a hallmark of human intelligence that we are able to make distinctions.

Yes, these cells could theoretically have the potential, under   15
very different circumstances, to develop into human beings—
that potential is where their magic lies. But they are not, in and
of themselves, human beings. They have no fingers and toes,
no brain or spinal cord. They have no thoughts, no fears. They
feel no pain.

Surely we can distinguish between these undifferentiated   16
cells multiplying in a tissue culture and a living, breathing
person—a parent, a spouse, a child.

I know a child—well, she must be 13 now—I guess I'd better   17
call her a young woman. She has fingers and toes. She has a
mind. She has memories. She has hopes. She has juvenile diabetes. Like so many kids with this disease, she's adjusted amazingly well. The—the insulin pump she wears—she's decorated
hers with rhinestones. She can handle her own catheter needle. She's learned to sleep through the blood drawings in the
wee hours of the morning.

She's very brave. She is also quite bright and understands full   18
well the progress of her disease and what that might ultimately
mean: blindness, amputation, diabetic coma. Every day, she
fights to have a future.

What excuse will we offer this young woman should we fail   19
her now? What might we tell her children? Or the millions of
others who suffer? That when given an opportunity to help, we
turned away? That facing political opposition, we lost our
nerve? That even though we knew better, we did nothing?

And, should we fail, how will we feel if, a few years from   20
now, a more enlightened generation should fulfill the promise
of embryonic stem cell therapy? Imagine what they would say
of us who lacked the will.

21   No, no, we owe this young woman and all those who suffer—
we owe ourselves—better than that. We are better than that.
We are a wiser people, a finer nation.

22   And for all of us in this fight, let me say: we will prevail. The
tide of history is with us. Like all generations who have come
before ours, we are motivated by a thirst for knowledge and
compelled to see others in need as fellow angels on an often
difficult path, deserving of our compassion.

23   In a few months, we will face a choice. Yes, between two
candidates and two parties, but more than that. We have a
chance to take a giant stride forward for the good of all
humanity. We can choose between the future and the past,
between reason and ignorance, between true compassion and
mere ideology.

24   This—this is our moment, and we must not falter.

25   Whatever else you do come November 2, I urge you, please,
cast a vote for embryonic stem cell research.

26   Thank you for your time.

Steven Milloy

RON REAGAN WRONG
ON STEM CELLS

*Ten days before Ron Reagan's speech on stem cell research at
the 2004 Democratic National Convention (included in this
section of* Conversations*), Steven Milloy published this "pre-
view" of the speech, an attempt to discredit the "junk science"
that Milloy believed informed Reagan's speech. Milloy, publisher of JunkScience.com and adjunct scholar at the Cato
Institute, a socially conservative think tank, is also the author
of* Junk Judo: Self-Defense Against Health Scares and Scams
*(2001). Why would Milloy publish his piece before, rather than
after, Reagan's speech?*

1   Ron Reagan, the younger son of the late Republican president,
announced this week that he would give a prime-time address

This photograph of actor Michael J. Fox (who has Parkinson's disease) and Nancy Reagan (who tended to her husband, former President Ronald Reagan, as he suffered through more than a decade with Alzheimer's disease) was taken as Reagan was being honored for her commitment to embryonic stem cell research. There is no overt mention of the issue of stem cell research in the photograph; but what do the faces say as they hold the award they have received?

in support of stem cell research at the Democratic National Convention in Boston later this month.

"Ron Reagan's courageous pleas for stem cell research add a 2 powerful voice to the millions of Americans hoping for cures for their children, for their parents and for their grandparents," said a spokesman for John Kerry to the Associated Press.

3   Reagan told the *Philadelphia Inquirer* that the speech was intended "to educate people about stem cell research" rather than be critical of President George Bush. But the Kerry campaign seems to want to scare people by having the son of the revered late President Ronald Reagan decry President Bush and his pro-life supporters as the major roadblocks to a host of supposedly just-around-the-corner miracle cures for cancer, Alzheimer's, diabetes, and other dreaded diseases.

4   It will be a junk science-fueled spectacle.

5   The controversy centers around the use of stem cells derived from destroyed human embryos. So-called "embryonic stem cells" give rise to all other cells and tissues in the human body and have been touted as possibly yielding treatments for a variety of diseases.

6   Moral concerns over the destruction of human embryos caused President Bush to limit taxpayer funding for embryonic stem cell research to stem cell lines already in existence. Researchers who were counting on taxpayer funding to conduct research on embryonic stem cells—and then rake in millions of dollars from naive investors—were enraged and began a campaign to pressure the president into opening the taxpayer spigots for embryonic stem cell research on the basis of a wide-eyed hope that cures are near at hand.

7   Though embryonic stem cell research advocates euphemistically refer to the current state of research as an "early stage," the unfortunate reality is the goal of embryonic stem cell therapies is, at this point, more accurately described as a pipe dream. No researcher is anywhere close to significant progress in developing practical embryonic stem cell therapies

8   Mouse embryonic stem cells were first grown in a laboratory in 1981. It took 20 years to make similar achievements with human embryonic stem cells—and merely growing stem cells is nowhere close to employing those cells in therapies. Embryonic stem cells must be directed to grow into specific cell types and that growth must be controlled—they can proliferate indefinitely in the lab. Uncontrolled stem cell growth may have tumor-forming potential. Because embryonic stem cells don't come from the patient being treated, there may also be problems associated with immune system rejection following transplantation of foreign stem cells.

9   The difficulty of embryonic stem cell research is underscored by the lack of progress in cancer research. Despite a 30-year, $40-billion "War on Cancer" launched by President Nixon, researchers continue to have great difficulty in controlling, let alone eradicating, the vast majority of cancer cell growth. Conceptually, controlled deployment of "good" stem

cells should be vastly more complex than simply destroying "bad" cancer cells.

None of this is to say that embryonic stem cell research can't   10 possibly lead to some improvements in biological understanding or future therapeutic treatments, but such speculative progress of who-knows-what value isn't in the foreseeable future. The only thing certain is that the cost of that research will be high. If embryonic stem cell research had real and imminent possibilities, private investors would be pouring capital into research hoping for real and imminent profits. Instead, venture capital firms are contributing to political efforts to get taxpayers to fund research.

A proposed ballot initiative in California known as   11 Proposition 71 would provide $3 billion in taxpayer money for stem cell research. Supporters hope to raise $ 20 million to get the initiative passed. What the venture capitalists seem to be hoping for is that taxpayer funding of stem cell research will increase the value of their stakes in biotech companies. The venture capitalists can then cash out at a hefty profit, leaving taxpayers holding the bag of fruitless research.

The spectacle of Ron Reagan at the Democratic Convention   12 will be sad—the disgruntled son of the beloved former president misleading the public with naive hopes while being exploited for political gain by opponents of his father's party. That cynical strategy may get John Kerry a few more votes in November, but it's not going to produce any medical miracles anytime soon, if at all.

Richard M. Doerflinger
DON'T CLONE
RON REAGAN'S AGENDA

Richard Doerflinger is Deputy Director of the Secretariat for Pro-Life Activities, U.S. Conference of Catholic Bishops. His critique of Ron Reagan's speech at the Democratic National Convention (included in this section of Conversations*) first appeared the day following Reagan's delivery of the speech in*

The Weekly Standard, *a political opinion magazine published in Washington, DC.*

1   Ron Reagan's speech at the Democratic convention last night was expected to urge expanded funding for stem cell research using so-called "spare" embryos—and to highlight these cells' potential for treating the Alzheimer's disease that took his father's life.

2   He did neither. He didn't even mention Alzheimer's, perhaps because even strong supporters of embryonic stem cell research say it is unlikely to be of use for that disease. (Reagan himself admitted this on a July 12 segment of MSNBC's *Hardball.*) And he didn't talk about current debates on funding research using existing embryos. Instead he endorsed the more radical agenda of human cloning—mass-producing one's own identical twins in the laboratory so they can be exploited as (in his words) "your own personal biological repair kit" when disease or injury strikes.

3   Politically this was, to say the least, a gamble. Americans may be tempted to make use of embryos left over from fertility clinics, but most polls show them to be against human cloning for any purpose. Other advanced nations—Canada, Australia, France, Germany, Norway—have banned the practice completely, and the United Nations may approve an international covenant against it this fall. Many groups and individuals who are "pro-choice" on abortion oppose research cloning, not least because it would require the mass exploitation of women to provide what Ron Reagan casually calls "donor eggs." And the potential "therapeutic" benefits of cloning are even more speculative than those of embryonic stem cell research—the worldwide effort even to obtain viable stem cells from cloned embryos has already killed hundreds of embryos and produced exactly one stem cell line, in South Korea.

4   But precisely for these reasons, Ron Reagan should be praised for his candor. The scientists and patient groups promoting embryonic stem cell research know that the current debate on funding is a mere transitional step. For years they have supported the mass manufacture of human embryos through cloning, as the logical and necessary goal of their agenda, but lately they have been coy about this as they fight for the more popular slogan of "stem cell research." With his speech Reagan has removed the mask, and allowed us to debate what is really at stake.

5   He claimed in his speech, of course, that what is at stake in this debate is the lives of millions of patients with devastating diseases. But by highlighting Parkinson's disease and juvenile

diabetes as two diseases most clearly justifying the move to human cloning, he failed to do his homework. These are two of the diseases that pro-cloning scientists now admit will probably *not* be helped by research cloning.

Scottish cloning expert Ian Wilmut, for example, wrote in the   6
British Medical Journal in February that producing genetically matched stem cells through cloning is probably quite unnecessary for treating any neurological disease. Recent findings suggest that the nervous system is "immune privileged," and will not generally reject stem cells from a human who is genetically different. He added that cloning is probably useless for autoimmune diseases like juvenile diabetes, where the body mistakenly rejects its own insulin-producing cells as though they were foreign. "In such cases," he wrote, "transfer of immunologically identical cells to a patient is expected to induce the same rejection."

Wilmut's observations cut the ground out from under Ron   7
Reagan's simple-minded claim that cloning is needed to avoid tissue rejection. For some diseases, genetically matched cells are unnecessary; for others, they are useless, because they only replicate the genetic profile that is part of the problem. (Ironically, for Alzheimer's both may be true—cloning may be unnecessary to avoid tissue rejection in the brain, and useless because the cloned cells would have the same genetic defect that may lead to Alzheimer's.) Reagan declared that this debate requires us to "choose between . . . reason and ignorance," but he did not realize which side has the monopoly on ignorance.

That ignorance poses an obstacle to real advances that   8
are right before our eyes. Two weeks before Ron Reagan declared that a treatment for Parkinson's may arrive "ten or so years from now," using "the material of our own bodies," a Parkinson's patient and his doctor quietly appeared before Congress to point out that this has already been done. Dennis Turner was treated in 1999 by Dr. Michel Levesque of Cedars-Sinai Medical Center in Los Angeles, using his own adult neural stem cells. Dr. Levesque did not use the Rube Goldberg method of trying to turn those cells into a cloned embryo and then killing the embryo to get stem cells—he just grew Turner's own adult stem cells in the lab, and turned them directly into dopamine-producing cells. And with just one injection, on one side of Turner's brain, he produced an almost complete reversal of Parkinson's symptoms over four years.

Turner stopped shaking, could eat without difficulty, could   9
put in his own contact lenses again, and resumed his avocation of big-game photography—on one occasion scrambling up a tree in Africa to escape a charging rhinoceros.

10   Amazingly, while this advance has been presented at national and international scientific conferences and featured on ABC-TV in Chicago, the scientific establishment supporting embryonic stem cell research has almost completely ignored it, and most news media have obediently imposed a virtual news blackout on it. That did not change even after the results were presented to the Senate Commerce Subcommittee on Science, Technology and Space this month. Pro-cloning Senators on the panel actually seemed angry at the witnesses, for trying to distract them from their fixation on destroying embryos.

11   Turner also testified that his symptoms have begun to return, especially arising from the side of his brain that was left untreated, and he would like to get a second treatment. For that he will have to wait. Dr. Levesque has received insufficient appreciation and funding for his technique, and is still trying to put together the funds for broader clinical trials—as most Parkinson's foundations and NIH peer reviewers look into the starry distance of Ron Reagan's dreams about embryonic stem cells.

12   But hey, who cares about real Parkinson's patients when there's a Brave New World to sell?

At What Price Wilderness?

John Muir

SAVE THE HETCH
HETCHY VALLEY!

*The famous nineteenth-century naturalist John Muir, founder of
the Sierra Club, wrote the following appeal a century ago. It was
an effort—an unsuccessful effort, as it turned out—to block the
construction of a dam in the Yosemite National Park area that
was designed to provide water to the San Francisco area. Muir
spent his life hiking through the American West and recording
what he saw in a way that persuaded people to preserve outstanding wilderness areas. Two of his best known books are* The
Mountains of California *(1894) and* Our National Parks
*(1901). You will hear more about him when you read William
Cronon's "The Trouble with Wilderness" later in this segment.*

Yosemite is so wonderful that we are apt to regard it as an ex- 1
ceptional creation, the only valley of its kind in the world; but
Nature is not so poor as to have only one of anything. Several
other yosemites have been discovered in the Sierra that occupy
the same relative positions on the Range and were formed by
the same forces in the same kind of granite. One of these, the
Hetch Hetchy Valley, is in the Yosemite National Park about
twenty miles from Yosemite and is easily accessible to all sorts
of travelers by a road and trail that leaves the Big Oak Flat
road at Branson Meadows a few miles below Crane Flat, and to
mountaineers by way of Yosemite Creek basin and the head of
the middle fork of the Tuolumne.

It is said to have been discovered by Joseph Screech, a hunter, 2
in 1850, a year before the discovery of the great Yosemite. After

my first visit to it in the autumn of 1871, I have always called it
the "Tuolumne Yosemite," for it is a wonderfully exact counterpart of the Merced Yosemite, not only in its sublime rocks and
waterfalls but in the gardens, groves and meadows of its flowery
park-like floor. The floor of Yosemite is about 4000 feet above the
sea; the Hetch Hetchy floor about 3700 feet. And as the Merced
River flows through Yosemite, so does the Tuolumne through
Hetch Hetchy. The walls of both are of gray granite, rise abruptly
from the floor, are sculptured in the same style and in both every
rock is a glacier monument.

3   Standing boldly out from the south wall is a strikingly picturesque rock called by the Indians, Kolana, the outermost of a
group 2300 feet high, corresponding with the Cathedral Rocks
of Yosemite both in relative position and form. On the opposite
side of the Valley, facing Kolana, there is a counterpart of the El
Capitan that rises sheer and plain to a height of 1800 feet, and
over its massive brow flows a stream which makes the most
graceful fall I have ever seen. From the edge of the cliff to the
top of an earthquake talus it is perfectly free in the air for a
thousand feet before it is broken into cascades among talus
boulders. It is in all its glory in June, when the snow is melting
fast, but fades and vanishes toward the end of summer. The
only fall I know with which it may fairly be compared is the
Yosemite Bridal Veil; but it excels even that favorite fall both in
height and airy-fairy beauty and behavior. Lowlanders are apt
to suppose that mountain streams in their wild career over
cliffs lose control of themselves and tumble in a noisy chaos of
mist and spray. On the contrary, on no part of their travels are
they more harmonious and self-controlled. Imagine yourself in
Hetch Hetchy on a sunny day in June, standing waist-deep
in grass and flowers (as I have often stood), while the great
pines sway dreamily with scarcely perceptible motion. Looking
northward across the Valley you see a plain, gray granite cliff
rising abruptly out of the gardens and groves to a height of
1800 feet, and in front of it Tueeulala's silvery scarf burning
with irised sun-fire. In the first white outburst at the head there
is abundance of visible energy, but it is speedily hushed and
concealed in divine repose, and its tranquil progress to the
base of the cliff is like that of a downy feather in a still room.
Now observe the fineness and marvelous distinctness of the
various sun-illumined fabrics into which the water is woven;
they sift and float from form to form down the face of that
grand gray rock in so leisurely and unconfused a manner that
you can examine their texture, and patterns and tones of color
as you would a piece of embroidery held in the hand. Toward
the top of the fall you see groups of booming, comet-like

masses, their solid, white heads separate, their tails like combed silk interlacing among delicate gray and purple shadows, ever forming and dissolving, worn out by friction in their rush through the air. Most of these vanish a few hundred feet below the summit, changing to varied forms of cloud-like drapery. Near the bottom the width of the fall has increased from about twenty-five feet to a hundred feet. Here it is composed of yet finer tissues, and is still without a trace of disorder—air, water and sunlight woven into stuff that spirits might wear.

So fine a fall might well seem sufficient to glorify any valley; 4
but here, as in Yosemite, Nature seems in nowise moderate, for a short distance to the eastward of Tueeulala booms and thunders the great Hetch Hetchy Fall, Wapama, so near that you have both of them in full view from the same standpoint. It is the counterpart of the Yosemite Fall, but has a much greater volume of water, is about 1700 feet in height, and appears to be nearly vertical, though considerably inclined, and is dashed into huge outbounding bosses of foam on projecting shelves and knobs. No two falls could be more unlike—Tueeulala out in the open sunshine descending like thistledown; Wapama in a jagged, shadowy gorge roaring and thundering, pounding its way like an earthquake avalanche.

Besides this glorious pair there is a broad, massive fall on the 5
main river a short distance above the head of the Valley. Its position is something like that of the Vernal in Yosemite, and its roar as it plunges into a surging trout-pool may be heard a long way, though it is only about twenty feet high. On Rancheria Creek, a large stream, corresponding in position with the Yosemite Tenaya Creek, there is a chain of cascades joined here and there with swift flashing plumes like the one between the Vernal and Nevada Falls, making magnificent shows as they go their glacier-sculptured way, sliding, leaping, hurrahing, covered with crisp clashing spray made glorious with sifting sunshine. And besides all these a few small streams come over the walls at wide intervals, leaping from ledge to ledge with birdlike song and watering many a hidden cliff-garden and fernery, but they are too unshowy to be noticed in so grand a place.

The correspondence between the Hetch Hetchy walls in their 6
trends, sculpture, physical structure, and general arrangement of the main rock-masses and those of the Yosemite Valley has excited the wondering admiration of every observer. We have seen that the El Capitan and Cathedral rocks occupy the same relative positions in both valleys; so also do their Yosemite points and North Domes. Again, that part of the Yosemite north wall immediately to the east of the Yosemite Fall has two horizontal benches, about 500 and 1500 feet above the floor,

timbered with golden-cup oak. Two benches similarly situated
and timbered occur on the same relative portion of the Hetch
Hetchy north wall, to the east of Wapama Fall, and on no other.
The Yosemite is bounded at the head by the great Half Dome.
Hetch Hetchy is bounded in the same way, though its head rock
is incomparably less wonderful and sublime in form.

7   The floor of the Valley is about three and a half miles long, and
from a fourth to half a mile wide. The lower portion is mostly a
level meadow about a mile long, with the trees restricted to the
sides and the river banks, and partially separated from the main,
upper, forested portion by a low bar of glacier-polished granite
across which the river breaks in rapids.

8   The principal trees are the yellow and sugar pines, digger
pine, incense cedar, Douglas spruce, silver fir, the California and
golden-cup oaks, balsam cottonwood, Nuttall's flowering dog-
wood, alder, maple, laurel, tumion, etc. The most abundant and
influential are the great yellow or silver pines like those of
Yosemite, the tallest over two hundred feet in height, and the
oaks assembled in magnificent groves with massive rugged
trunks four to six feet in diameter, and broad, shady, wide-
spreading heads. The shrubs forming conspicuous flowery
clumps and tangles are manzanita, azalea, spiræa, brier-rose,
several species of ceanothus, calycanthus, philadelphus, wild
cherry, etc.; with abundance of showy and fragrant herbaceous
plants growing about them or out in the open in beds by
themselves—lilies, Mariposa tulips, brodiaeas, orchids, iris,
spraguea, draperia, collomia, collinsia, castilleja, nemophila,
larkspur, columbine, goldenrods, sunflowers, mints of many
species, honeysuckle, etc. Many fine ferns dwell here also, especially the beautiful and interesting rock-ferns—pellaea, and
cheilanthes of several species—fringing and rosetting dry rock-
piles and ledges; woodwardia and asplenium on damp spots with
fronds six or seven feet high; the delicate maidenhair in mossy
nooks by the falls, and the sturdy, broad-shouldered pteris covering nearly all the dry ground beneath the oaks and pines.

9   It appears, therefore, that Hetch Hetchy Valley, far from
being a plain, common, rock-bound meadow, as many who
have not seen it seem to suppose, is a grand landscape garden,
one of Nature's rarest and most precious mountain temples. As
in Yosemite, the sublime rocks of its walls seem to glow with
life, whether leaning back in repose or standing erect in
thoughtful attitudes, giving welcome to storms and calms
alike, their brows in the sky, their feet set in the groves and gay
flowery meadows, while birds, bees, and butterflies help
the river and waterfalls to stir all the air into music—things
frail and fleeting and types of permanence meeting here and

blending, just as they do in Yosemite, to draw her lovers into close and confiding communion with her.

Sad to say, this most precious and sublime feature of the Yosemite National Park, one of the greatest of all our natural resources for the uplifting joy and peace and health of the people, is in danger of being dammed and made into a reservoir to help supply San Francisco with water and light, thus flooding it from wall to wall and burying its gardens and groves one or two hundred feet deep. This grossly destructive commercial scheme has long been planned and urged (though water as pure and abundant can be got from outside of the people's park, in a dozen different places), because of the comparative cheapness of the dam and of the territory which it is sought to divert from the great uses to which it was dedicated in the Act of 1890 establishing the Yosemite National Park.

The making of gardens and parks goes on with civilization all over the world, and they increase both in size and number as their value is recognized. Everybody needs beauty as well as bread, places to play in and pray in, where Nature may heal and cheer and give strength to body and soul alike. This natural beauty-hunger is made manifest in the little window-sill gardens of the poor, though perhaps only a geranium slip in a broken cup, as well as in the carefully tended rose and lily gardens of the rich, the thousands of spacious city parks and botanical gardens, and in our magnificent National Parks—the Yellowstone, Yosemite, Sequoia, etc.—Nature's sublime wonderlands, the admiration and joy of the world. Nevertheless, like anything else worth while, from the very beginning, however well guarded, they have always been subject to attack by despoiling gainseekers and mischief-makers of every degree from Satan to Senators, eagerly trying to make everything immediately and selfishly commercial, with schemes disguised in smug-smiling philanthropy, industriously, sham-piously crying, "Conservation, conservation, panutilization," that man and beast may be fed and the dear Nation made great. Thus long ago a few enterprising merchants utilized the Jerusalem temple as a place of business instead of a place of prayer, changing money, buying and selling cattle and sheep and doves; and earlier still, the first forest reservation, including only one tree, was likewise despoiled. Ever since the establishment of the Yosemite National Park, strife has been going on around its borders and I suppose this will go on as part of the universal battle between right and wrong, however much its boundaries may be shorn, or its wild beauty destroyed.

The first application to the Government by the San Francisco Supervisors for the commercial use of Lake Eleanor and the Hetch Hetchy Valley was made in 1903, and on

December 22nd of that year it was denied by the Secretary of the Interior, Mr. Hitchcock, who truthfully said:

> Presumably the Yosemite National Park was created such by law because of the natural objects of varying degrees of scenic importance located within its boundaries, inclusive alike of its beautiful small lakes, like Eleanor, and its majestic wonders, like Hetch Hetchy and Yosemite Valley. It is the aggregation of such natural scenic features that makes the Yosemite Park a wonderland which the Congress of the United States sought by law to reserve for all coming time as nearly as practicable in the condition fashioned by the hand of the Creator—a worthy object of national pride and a source of healthful pleasure and rest for the thousands of people who may annually sojourn there during the heated months.

13   In 1907 when Mr. Garfield became Secretary of the Interior the application was renewed and granted; but under his successor, Mr. Fisher, the matter has been referred to a Commission, which as this volume goes to press still has it under consideration.

14   The most delightful and wonderful camp-grounds in the Park are its three great valleys—Yosemite, Hetch Hetchy, and Upper Tuolumne; and they are also the most important places with reference to their positions relative to the other great features—the Merced and Tuolumne Cañons, and the High Sierra peaks and glaciers, etc., at the head of the rivers. The main part of the Tuolumne Valley is a spacious flowery lawn four or five miles long, surrounded by magnificent snowy mountains, slightly separated from other beautiful meadows, which together make a series about twelve miles in length, the highest reaching to the feet of Mount Dana, Mount Gibbs, Mount Lyell and Mount McClure. It is about 8500 feet above the sea, and forms the grand central High Sierra camp-ground from which excursions are made to the noble mountains, domes, glaciers, etc.; across the Range to the Mono Lake and volcanoes and down the Tuolumne Cañon to Hetch Hetchy. Should Hetch Hetchy be submerged for a reservoir, as proposed, not only would it be utterly destroyed, but the sublime cañon way to the heart of the High Sierra would be hopelessly blocked and the great camping-ground, as the watershed of a city drinking system, virtually would be closed to the public. So far as I have learned, few of all the thousands who have seen the Park and seek rest and peace in it are in favor of this outrageous scheme.

15   One of my later visits to the Valley was made in the autumn of 1907 with the late William Keith, the artist. The leaf-colors

were then ripe, and the great god-like rocks in repose seemed to glow with life. The artist, under their spell, wandered day after day along the river and through the groves and gardens, studying the wonderful scenery; and, after making about forty sketches, declared with enthusiasm that although its walls were less sublime in height, in picturesque beauty and charm Hetch Hetchy surpassed even Yosemite.

That any one would try to destroy such a place seems incredible; but sad experience shows that there are people good enough and bad enough for anything. The proponents of the dam scheme bring forward a lot of bad arguments to prove that the only righteous thing to do with the people's parks is to destroy them bit by bit as they are able. Their arguments are curiously like those of the devil, devised for the destruction of the first garden—so much of the very best Eden fruit going to waste; so much of the best Tuolumne water and Tuolumne scenery going to waste. Few of their statements are even partly true, and all are misleading. 16

Thus, Hetch Hetchy, they say, is a "low-lying meadow." On the contrary, it is a high-lying natural landscape garden, as the photographic illustrations show. 17

"It is a common minor feature, like thousands of others." On the contrary it is a very uncommon feature; after Yosemite, the rarest and in many ways the most important in the National Park. 18

"Damming and submerging it 175 feet deep would enhance its beauty by forming a crystal-clear lake." Landscape gardens, places of recreation and worship, are never made beautiful by destroying and burying them. The beautiful sham lake, forsooth, would be only an eyesore, a dismal blot on the landscape, like many others to be seen in the Sierra. For, instead of keeping it at the same level all the year, allowing Nature centuries of time to make new shores, it would, of course, be full only a month or two in the spring, when the snow is melting fast; then it would be gradually drained, exposing the slimy sides of the basin and shallower parts of the bottom, with the gathered drift and waste, death and decay of the upper basins, caught here instead of being swept on to decent natural burial along the banks of the river or in the sea. Thus the Hetch Hetchy dam-lake would be only a rough imitation of a natural lake for a few of the spring months, an open sepulcher for the others. 19

"Hetch Hetchy water is the purest of all to be found in the Sierra, unpolluted, and forever unpollutable." On the contrary, excepting that of the Merced below Yosemite, it is less pure than that of most of the other Sierra streams, because of the sewerage of camp-grounds draining into it, especially of the Big Tuolumne Meadows camp-ground, occupied by hundreds 20 of tourists and mountaineers, with their animals, for months every summer, soon to be followed by thousands from all the world.

21   These temple destroyers, devotees of ravaging commercialism, seem to have a perfect contempt for Nature, and, instead of lifting their eyes to the God of the mountains, lift them to the Almighty Dollar.

22   Dam Hetch Hetchy! As well dam for water-tanks the people's cathedrals and churches, for no holier temple has ever been consecrated by the heart of man.

Wallace Stegner
A WILDERNESS LETTER

Wallace Stegner (1909–93) was an important novelist in the United States after World War II. He wrote more than thirty books, including Angle of Repose, *which won the Pulitzer Prize, and* The Spectator Bird, *which won the National Book Award in 1976. Stegner was also a committed conservationist, and his books often feature American Western themes and settings. As a creative writing teacher at Stanford, he taught Edward Abbey and Wendell Barry. In 1960 he wrote the following letter, a famous argument for the spiritual values found in the wild; it helped persuade Congress to create the National Wilderness Preservation System in 1964.*

Los Altos, Calif.
Dec. 3, 1960

David E. Pesonen
Wildland Research Center
Agricultural Experiment Station
243 Mulford Hall
University of California
Berkeley 4, Calif.

Dear Mr. Pesonen:

1   I believe that you are working on the wilderness portion of the Outdoor Recreation Resources Review Commission's

report. If I may, I should like to urge some arguments for wilderness preservation that involve recreation, as it is ordinarily conceived, hardly at all. Hunting, fishing, hiking, mountain-climbing, camping, photography, and the enjoyment of natural scenery will all, surely, figure in your report. So will the wilderness as a genetic reserve, a scientific yardstick by which we may measure the world in its natural balance against the world in its man-made imbalance. What I want to speak for is not so much the wilderness uses, valuable as those are, but the wilderness *idea*, which is a resource in itself. Being an intangible and spiritual resource, it will seem mystical to the practical-minded—but then anything that cannot be moved by a bulldozer is likely to seem mystical to them.

I want to speak for the wilderness idea as something that has   2 helped form our character and that has certainly shaped our history as a people. It has no more to do with recreation than churches have to do with recreation, or than the strenuousness and optimism and expansiveness of what historians call the "American Dream" have to do with recreation. Nevertheless, since it is only in this recreation survey that the values of wilderness are being compiled, I hope you will permit me to insert this idea between the leaves, as it were, of the recreation report.

Something will have gone out of us as a people if we ever let   3 the remaining wilderness be destroyed; if we permit the last virgin forests to be turned into comic books and plastic cigarette cases; if we drive the few remaining members of the wild species into zoos or to extinction; if we pollute the last clear air and dirty the last clean streams and push our paved roads through the last of the silence, so that never again will Americans be free in their own country from the noise, the exhausts, the stinks of human and automotive waste. And so that never again can we have the chance to see ourselves single, separate, vertical, and individual in the world, part of the environment of trees and rocks and soil, brother to the other animals, part of the natural world and competent to belong in it. Without any remaining wilderness we are committed wholly, without chance for even momentary reflection and rest, to a headlong drive into our technological termite-life, the Brave New World of a completely man-controlled environment. We need wilderness preserved—as much of it as is still left, and as many kinds—because it was the challenge against which our character as a people was formed. The reminder and the reassurance that it is still there is good for our spiritual health even if we never once in ten years set foot in it. It is good for us when we are young, because of the incomparable sanity it can bring briefly, as vacation and rest, into our insane lives. It is important to us when we are old simply because it is there—important, that is, simply as idea.

4   We are a wild species, as Darwin pointed out. Nobody ever tamed or domesticated or scientifically bred us. But for at least three millennia we have been engaged in a cumulative and ambitious race to modify and gain control of our environment, and in the process we have come close to domesticating ourselves. Not many people are likely, any more, to look upon what we call "progress" as an unmixed blessing. Just as surely as it has brought us increased comfort and more material goods, it has brought us spiritual losses, and it threatens now to become the Frankenstein that will destroy us. One means of sanity is to retain a hold on the natural world, to remain, insofar as we can, good animals. Americans still have that chance, more than many peoples; for while we were demonstrating ourselves the most efficient and ruthless environment-busters in history, and slashing and burning and cutting our way through a wilderness continent, the wilderness was working on us. It remains in us as surely as Indian names remain on the land. If the abstract dream of human liberty and human dignity became, in America, something more than an abstract dream, mark it down at least partially to the fact that we were in subtle ways subdued by what we conquered.

5   The Connecticut Yankee, sending likely candidates from King Arthur's unjust kingdom to his Man Factory for rehabilitation, was over-optimistic, as he later admitted. These things cannot be forced, they have to grow. To make such a man, such a democrat, such a believer in human individual dignity, as Mark Twain himself, the frontier was necessary, Hannibal and the Mississippi and Virginia City, and reaching out from those the wilderness; the wilderness as opportunity and as idea, the thing that has helped to make an American different from and, until we forget it in the roar of our industrial cities, more fortunate than other men. For an American, insofar us he is new and different at all, is a civilized man who has renewed himself in the wild. The American experience has been the confrontation by old peoples and cultures of a world as new as if it had just risen from the sea. That gave us our hope and our excitement, and the hope and excitement can be passed on to newer Americans, Americans who never saw any phase of the frontier. But only so long as we keep the remainder of our wild as a reserve and a promise—a sort of wilderness bank.

6   As a novelist, I may perhaps be forgiven for taking literature as a reflection, indirect but profoundly true, of our national consciousness. And our literature, as perhaps you are aware, is

sick, embittered, losing its mind, losing its faith. Our novelists are the declared enemies of their society. There has hardly been a serious or important novel in this century that did not repudiate in part or in whole American technological culture for its commercialism, its vulgarity, and the way in which it has dirtied a clean continent and a clean dream. I do not expect that the preservation of our remaining wilderness is going to cure this condition. But the mere example that we can as a nation apply some other criteria than commercial and exploitative considerations would be heartening to many Americans, novelists or otherwise. We need to demonstrate our acceptance of the natural world, including ourselves; we need the spiritual refreshment that being natural can produce. And one of the best places for us to get that is in the wilderness where the fun houses, the bulldozers, and the pavements of our civilization are shut out.

Sherwood Anderson, in a letter to Waldo Frank in the 1920s, 7 said it better than I can. "Is it not likely that when the country was new and men were often alone in the fields and the forest they got a sense of bigness outside themselves that has now in some way been lost. . . . Mystery whispered in the grass, played in the branches of trees overhead, was caught up and blown across the American line in clouds of dust at evening on the prairies. . . . I am old enough to remember tales that strengthen my belief in a deep semi-religious influence that was formerly at work among out people. The flavor of it hangs over the best work of Mark Twain. . . . I can remember old fellows in my home town speaking feelingly of an evening spent on the big empty plains. It had taken the shrillness out of them. They had learned the trick of quiet. . . ."

We could learn it too, even yet; even our children and grand- 8 children could learn it. But only if we save, for just such absolutely nonrecreational, impractical, and mystical uses as this, all the wild that still remains to us.

It seems to me significant that the distinct downturn in our lit- 9 erature from hope to bitterness took place almost at the precise time when the frontier officially came to an end, in 1890, and when the American way of life had begun to turn strongly urban and industrial. The more urban it has become, and the more frantic with technological change, the sicker and more embittered our literature, and I believe our people, have become. For myself, I grew up on the empty plains of Saskatchewan and Montana and in the mountains of Utah, and I put a very high valuation on what those places gave me. And if I had not been able periodically to renew myself in the mountains and deserts of western America I would be very nearly bughouse. Even when

I can't get to the back country, the thought of the colored deserts of southern Utah, or the reassurance that there are still stretches of prairie where the world can be instantaneously perceived as disk and bowl, and where the little but intensely important human being is exposed to the five directions and the thirty-six winds, is a positive consolation. The idea alone can sustain me. But as the wilderness areas are progressively exploited or "improved," as the jeeps and bulldozers of uranium prospectors scar up the deserts and the roads are cut into the alpine timberlands, and as the remnants of the unspoiled and natural world are progressively eroded, every such loss is a little death in me. In us.

10   I am not moved by the argument that those wilderness areas which have already been exposed to grazing or mining are already deflowered, and so might as well be "harvested." For mining I cannot say much good except that its operations are generally short-lived. The extractable wealth is taken and the shafts, the tailings, and the ruins left, and in a dry country such as the American West the wounds men make in the earth do not quickly heal. Still, they are only wounds; they aren't absolutely mortal. Better a wounded wilderness than none at all. And as for grazing, if it is strictly controlled so that it does not destroy the ground cover, damage the ecology, or compete with the wildlife it is in itself nothing that need conflict with the wilderness feeling or the validity of the wilderness experience. I have known enough range cattle to recognize them as wild animals; and the people who herd them have, in the wilderness context, the dignity of rareness; they belong on the frontier, moreover, and have a look of rightness. The invasion they make on the virgin country is a sort of invasion that is as old as Neolithic man, and they can, in moderation, even emphasize a man's feeling of belonging to the natural world. Under surveillance, they can belong; under control, they need not deface or mar. I do not believe that in wilderness areas where grazing has never been permitted, it should be permitted; but I do not believe either that an otherwise untouched wilderness should be eliminated from the preservation plan because of limited existing uses such as grazing which are in consonance with the frontier condition and image.

11   Let me say something on the subject of the kinds of wilderness worth preserving. Most of those areas contemplated are in the national forests and in high mountain country. For all the usual recreational purposes, the alpine and forest wilderness are obviously the most important, both as genetic banks and as beauty spots. But for the spiritual renewal, the recognition of identity, the birth of awe, other kinds will serve every bit as well.

Perhaps, because they are less friendly to life, more abstractly nonhuman, they will serve even better. On our Saskatchewan prairie, the nearest neighbor was four miles away, and at night we saw only two lights on all the dark rounding earth. The earth was full of animals—field mice, ground squirrels, weasels, ferrets, badgers, coyotes, burrowing owls, snakes. I knew them as my little brothers, as fellow creatures, and I have never been able to look upon animals in any other way since. The sky in that country came clear down to the ground on every side, and it was full of great weathers, and clouds, and winds, and hawks. I hope I learned something from knowing intimately the creatures of the earth; I hope I learned something from looking a long way, from looking up, from being much alone. A prairie like that, one big enough to carry the eye clear to the sinking, rounding horizon, can be as lonely and grand and simple in its forms as the sea. It is as good a place as any for the wilderness experience to happen; the vanishing prairie is as worth preserving for the wilderness idea as the alpine forests.

So are great reaches of our western deserts, scarred some-   12
what by prospectors but otherwise open, beautiful, waiting, close to whatever God you want to see in them. Just as a sample, let me suggest the Robbers' Roost country in Wayne County, Utah, near the Capitol Reel National Monument. In that desert climate the dozer and jeep tracks will not soon melt back into the earth, but the country has a way of making the scars insignificant. It is a lovely and terrible wilderness, such a wilderness as Christ and the prophets went out into: harshly and beautifully colored, broken and worn until its bones are exposed, its great sky without a smudge of taint from Technocracy, and in hidden corners and pockets under its cliffs the sudden poetry of springs. Save a piece of country like that intact, and it does not matter in the slightest that only a few people every year will go into it. That is precisely its value. Roads would be a desecration, crowds would ruin it. But those who haven't the strength or youth to go into it and live can simply sit and look. They can look two hundred miles, clear into Colorado: and looking down over the cliffs and canyons of the San Rafael Swell and the Robbers' Roost they can also look as deeply into themselves as anywhere I know. And if they can't even get to the places on the Aquarius Plateau where the present roads will carry them, they can simply contemplate the *idea*, take pleasure in the fact that such a timeless and uncontrolled part of earth is still there.

These are some of the things wilderness can do for us. That is   13
the reason we need to put into effect, for its preservation, some other principle than the principles of exploitation or "usefulness"

or even recreation. We simply need that wild country available to
us, even if we never do more than drive to its edge and look in.
For it can be a means of reassuring ourselves of our sanity as
creatures, a part of the geography of hope.

Very sincerely yours,

Wallace Stegner

William Cronon

THE TROUBLE
WITH WILDERNESS

*William Cronon is a professor of history, geography, and envi-
ronmental studies at the University of Wisconsin, Madison. He
is the author of many books, including* Changes in the Land:
Indians, Colonists, and the Ecology of New England *(1983)
and* Nature's Metropolis: Chicago and the Great West *(1991).
The following essay is an excerpt from a piece that appeared in
his* Uncommon Ground: Toward Reinventing Nature *(1995).
Published in the inaugural issue of* Environmental History, *a
magazine designed for academics, in January 1996, it inspired
many responses—including the one published after it in this
book by Samuel P. Hays.*

The Time Has Come to Rethink Wilderness

1   This will seem a heretical claim to many environmentalists,
since the idea of wilderness has for decades been a fundamental
tenet—indeed, a passion—of the environmental movement, especially in the United States. For many Americans wilderness
stands as the last remaining place where civilization, that all too
human disease, has not fully infected the earth. It is an
island in the polluted sea of urban-industrial modernity, the one
place we can turn for escape from our own too-muchness. Seen
in this way, wilderness presents itself as the best antidote to our

human selves, a refuge we must somehow recover if we hope to save the planet. As Henry David Thoreau once famously declared, "In Wildness is the preservation of the World."[1]

But is it? The more one knows of its peculiar history, the   2
more one realizes that wilderness is not quite what it seems. Far from being the one place on earth that stands apart from humanity, it is quite profoundly a human creation—indeed, the creation of very particular human cultures at very particular moments in human history. It is not a pristine sanctuary where the last remnant of an untouched, endangered, but still transcendent nature can for at least a little while longer be encountered without the contaminating taint of civilization. Instead, it is a product of that civilization, and could hardly be contaminated by the very stuff of which it is made. Wilderness hides its unnaturalness behind a mask that is all the more beguiling because it seems so natural. As we gaze into the mirror it holds up for us, we too easily imagine that what we behold is Nature when in fact we see the reflection of our own unexamined longings and desires. For this reason, we mistake ourselves when we suppose that wilderness can be the solution to our culture's problematic relationships with the nonhuman world, for wilderness is itself no small part of the problem.

To assert the unnaturalness of so natural a place will no   3
doubt seem absurd or even perverse to many readers, so let me hasten to add that the nonhuman world we encounter in wilderness is far from being merely our own invention. I celebrate with others who love wilderness the beauty and power of the things it contains. Each of us who has spent time there can conjure images and sensations that seem all the more hauntingly real for having engraved themselves so indelibly on our memories. Such memories may be uniquely our own, but they are also familiar enough be to he instantly recognizable to others. Remember this? The torrents of mist shoot out from the base of a great waterfall in the depths of a Sierra canyon, the tiny droplets cooling your face as you listen to the roar of the water and gaze up toward the sky through a rainbow that hovers just out of reach. Remember this too: looking out across a desert canyon in the evening air, the only sound a lone raven calling in the distance, the rock walls dropping away into a chasm so deep that its bottom all but vanishes as you squint into the amber light of the setting sun. And this: the moment beside the trail as you sit on a sandstone ledge, your boots damp with the morning dew while you take in the rich smell of the pines, and the small red fox—or maybe for you it was a raccoon or a coyote or a deer—that suddenly ambles across your path, stopping for a long moment to gaze in your direction

with cautious indifference before continuing on its way. Remember the feelings of such moments, and you will know as well as I do that you were in the presence of something irreducibly nonhuman, something profoundly Other than yourself. Wilderness is made of that too.

4   And yet: what brought each of us to the places where such memories became possible is entirely a cultural invention. Go back 250 years in American and European history, and you do not find nearly so many people wandering around remote corners of the planet looking for what today we would call "the wilderness experience." As late as the eighteenth century, the most common usage of the word "wilderness" in the English language referred to landscapes that generally carried adjectives far different from the ones they attract today. To be a wilderness then was to be "deserted," "savage," "desolate," "barren"—in short, a "waste," the word's nearest synonym. Its connotations were anything but positive, and the emotion one was most likely to feel in its presence was "bewilderment" or terror.[2]

5   Many of the word's strongest associations then were biblical, for it is used over and over again in the King James Version to refer to places on the margins of civilization where it is all too easy to lose oneself in moral confusion and despair. The wilderness was where Moses had wandered with his people for forty years, and where they had nearly abandoned their God to worship a golden idol.[3] "For Pharaoh will say of the Children of Israel," we read in Exodus, "They are entangled in the land, the wilderness hath shut them in."[4] The wilderness was where Christ had struggled with the devil and endured his temptations: "And immediately the Spirit driveth him into the wilderness. And he was there in the wilderness for forty days tempted of Satan; and was with the wild beasts; and the angels ministered unto him."[5] The "delicious Paradise" of John Milton's Eden was surrounded by "a steep wilderness, whose hairy sides / Access denied" to all who sought entry.[6] When Adam and Eve were driven from that garden, the world they entered was a wilderness that only their labor and pain could redeem. Wilderness, in short, was a place to which one came only against one's will, and always in fear and trembling. Whatever value it might have arose solely from the possibility that it might be "reclaimed" and turned toward human ends—planted as a garden, say, or a city upon a hill.[7] In its raw state, it had little or nothing to offer civilized men and women.

6   But by the end of the nineteenth century, all this had changed. The wastelands that had once seemed worthless had for some people come to seem almost beyond price. That Thoreau in 1862 could declare wildness to be the preservation

of the world suggests the sea change that was going on. Wilderness had once been the antithesis of all that was orderly and good—it had been the darkness, one might say, on the far side of the garden wall—and yet now it was frequently likened to Eden itself. When John Muir arrived in the Sierra Nevada in 1869, he would declare, "No description of Heaven that I have ever heard or read of seems half so fine."[8] He was hardly alone in expressing such emotions. One by one, various corners of the American map came to be designated as sites whose wild beauty was so spectacular that a growing number of citizens had to visit and see them for themselves. Niagara Falls was the first to undergo this transformation, but it was soon followed by the Catskills, the Adirondacks, Yosemite, Yellowstone, and others. Yosemite was deeded by the U.S. government to the state of California in 1864 as the nation's first wildland park, and Yellowstone became the first true national park in 1872.[9]

By the first decade of the twentieth century, in the single most   7 famous episode in American conservation history, a national debate had exploded over whether the city of San Francisco should be permitted to augment its water supply by damming the Tuolumne River in Hetch Hetchy valley, well within the boundaries of Yosemite National Park. The dam was eventually built, but what today seems no less significant is that so many people fought to prevent its completion. Even as the fight was being lost, Hetch Hetchy became the battle cry of an emerging movement to preserve wilderness. Fifty years earlier, such opposition would have been unthinkable. Few would have questioned the merits of "reclaiming" a wasteland like this in order to put it to human use. Now the defenders of Hetch Hetchy attracted widespread national attention by portraying such an act not as improvement or progress but as desecration and vandalism. Lest one doubt that the old biblical metaphors had been turned completely on their heads, listen to John Muir attack the dam's defenders. "Their arguments," he wrote, "are curiously like those of the devil, devised for the destruction of the first garden—so much of the very best Eden fruit going to waste; so much of the best Tuolumne water and Tuolumne scenery going to waste."[10] For Muir and the growing number of Americans who shared his views, Satan's home had become God's own temple.

The sources of this rather astonishing transformation were   8 many, but for the purposes of this essay they can be gathered under two broad headings: the sublime and the frontier. Of the two, the sublime is the older and more pervasive cultural construct, being one of the most important expressions of that broad transatlantic movement we today label as romanticism; the frontier is more peculiarly American, thought it too had its

European antecedents and parallels. The two converged to re-make wilderness in their own image, freighting it with moral values and cultural symbols that it carries to this day. Indeed, it is not too much to say that the modern environmental move-ment is itself a grandchild of romanticism and post-frontier ideology, which is why it is no accident that so much environ-mentalist discourse takes its bearings from the wilderness these intellectual movements helped create. Although wilderness may today seem to be just one environmental concern among many, it in fact serves as the foundation for a long list of other such concerns that on their face seem quite remote from it. That is why its influence is so pervasive and, potentially, so insidious.

9   To gain such remarkable influence, the concept of wilderness had to become loaded with some of the deepest core values of the culture that created and idealized it: it had to become sacred. This possibility had been present in wilderness even in the days when it had been a place of spiritual danger and moral tempta-tion. If Satan was there, then so was Christ, who had found an-gels as well as wild beasts during His sojourn in the desert. In the wilderness the boundaries between human and nonhuman, be-tween natural and supernatural, had always seemed less certain than elsewhere. This was why the early Christian saints and mys-tics had often emulated Christ's desert retreat as they sought to experience for themselves the visions and spiritual testing He had endured. One might meet devils and run the risk of losing one's soul in such a place, but one might also meet God. For some that possibility was worth almost any price.

10   By the eighteenth century this sense of the wilderness as a landscape where the supernatural lay just beneath the surface was expressed in the doctrine of the *sublime*, a word whose modern usage has been so watered down by commercial hype and tourist advertising that it retains only a dim echo of its former power.[11] In the theories of Edmund Burke, Immanuel Kant, William Gilpin, and others, sublime landscapes were those rare places on earth where one had more chance than elsewhere to glimpse the face of God.[12] Romantics had a clear notion of where one could be most sure of having this experi-ence. Although God might, of course, choose to show Himself anywhere, He would most often be found in those vast, power-ful landscapes where one could not help feeling insignificant and being reminded of one's own mortality. Where were these sublime places? The eighteenth century catalog of their loca-tions feels very familiar, for we still see and value landscapes as it taught us to do. God was on the mountaintop, in the chasm, in the waterfall, in the thunder-cloud, in the rainbow, in the sunset. One has only to think of the sites that Americans chose

for their first national parks—Yellowstone, Yosemite, Grand Canyon, Rainier, Zion—to realize that virtually all of them fit one or more of these categories. Less sublime landscapes simply did not appear worthy of such protection; not until the 1940s, for instance, would the first swamp be honored, in Everglades National Park, and to this day there is no national park in the grasslands.[13]

Among the best proofs that one had entered a sublime land- 11 scape was the emotion it evoked. For the early romantic writers and artists who first began to celebrate it, the sublime was far from being a pleasurable experience. The classic description is that of William Wordsworth as he recounted climbing the Alps and crossing the Simplon Pass in his autobiographical Poem *The Prelude*. There, surrounded by crags and waterfalls, the poet felt himself literally to be in the presence of the divine—and experienced an emotion remarkably close to terror:

> The immeasurable height
> Of woods decaying, never to be decayed,
> The stationary blasts of waterfalls,
> And in the narrow rent at every turn
> Winds thwarting winds, bewildered and forlorn,
> The torrents shooting from the clear blue sky,
> The rocks that muttered close upon our ears,
> Black drizzling crags that spake by the way-side
> As if a voice were in them, the sick sight
> And giddy prospect of the raving stream,
> The unfettered clouds and region of the Heavens,
> Tumult and peace, the darkness and the light—
> Were all like workings of one mind, the features
> Of the same face, blossoms upon one tree;
> Characters of the great Apocalypse,
> The types and symbols of Eternity,
> Of first, and last, and midst, and without end.[14]

This was no casual stroll in the mountains, no simple sojourn in the gentle lap of nonhuman nature. What Wordsworth described was nothing less than a religious experience, akin to that of the Old Testament prophets as they conversed with their wrathful God. The symbols he detected in this wilderness landscape were more supernatural than natural, and they inspired more awe and dismay than joy or pleasure. No mere mortal was meant to linger long in such a place, so it was with considerable relief that Wordsworth and his companion made their way back down from the peaks to the sheltering valleys.

12   Lest you suspect that this view of the sublime was limited to timid Europeans who lacked the American know-how for feeling at home in the wilderness, remember Henry David Thoreau's 1846 climb of Mount Katahdin, in Maine. Although Thoreau is regarded by many today as one of the great American celebrators of wilderness, his emotions about Katahdin were no less ambivalent than Wordsworth's about the Alps.

> It was vast, Titanic; and such as man never inhabits. Some part of the beholder, even some vital part, seems to escape through the loose grating of his ribs as he ascends. He is more lone than you can imagine. . . . Vast, Titanic, inhuman Nature has got him at disadvantage, caught him alone, and pilfers him of some of his divine faculty. She does not smile on him as in the plains. She seems to say sternly, why came ye here before your time? This ground is not prepared for you. Is it not enough that I smile in the valleys? I have never made this soil for thy feet, this air for thy breathing, these rocks for thy neighbors. I cannot pity nor fondle thee here, but forever relentlessly drive thee hence to where I *am* kind. Why seek me where I have not called thee, and then complain because you find me but a stepmother?[15]

This is surely not the way a modern backpacker or nature lover would describe Maine's most famous mountain, but that is because Thoreau's description owes as much to Wordsworth and other romantic contemporaries as to the rocks and clouds of Katahdin itself. His words took the physical mountain on which he stood and transmuted it into an icon of the sublime: a symbol of God's presence on earth. The power and the glory of that icon were such that only a prophet might gaze on it for long. In effect, romantics like Thoreau joined Moses and the children of Israel in Exodus when "they looked toward the wilderness, and behold, the glory of the Lord appeared in the cloud."[16]

13   But even as it came to embody the awesome power of the sublime, wilderness was also being tamed—not just by those who were building settlements in its midst but also by those who most celebrated its inhuman beauty. By the second half of the nineteenth century, the terrible awe that Wordsworth and Thoreau regarded as the appropriately pious stance to adopt in the presence of their mountaintop God was giving way to a much more comfortable, almost sentimental demeanor. As more and more tourists sought out the wilderness as a spectacle to be looked at and enjoyed for its great beauty, the sublime in effect became domesticated. The wilderness was still sacred, but the

religious sentiments it evoked were more those of a pleasant parish church than those of a grand cathedral or a harsh desert retreat. The writer who best captures this late romantic sense of a domesticated sublime is undoubtedly John Muir, whose descriptions of Yosemite and the Sierra Nevada reflect none of the anxiety or terror one finds in earlier writers. Here he is, for instance, sketching on North Dome in Yosemite Valley:

> No pain here, no dull empty hours, no fear of the past, no fear of the future. These blessed mountains are so compactly filled with God's beauty, no petty personal hope or experience has room to be. Drinking this champagne water is pure pleasure, so is breathing the living air, and every movement of limbs is pleasure, while the body seems to feel beauty when exposed to it as it feels the campfire or sunshine, entering not by the eyes alone, but equally through all one's flesh like radiant heat, making a passionate ecstatic pleasure glow not explainable.

The emotions Muir describes in Yosemite could hardly be more different from Thoreau's on Katahdin or Wordsworth's on the Simplon Pass. Yet all three men are participating in the same cultural tradition and contributing to the same myth: the mountain as cathedral. The three may differ in the way they choose to express their piety—Wordsworth favoring an awe-filled bewilderment, Thoreau a stern loneliness, Muir a welcome ecstasy—but they agree completely about the church in which they prefer to worship. Muir's closing words on North Dome diverge from his older contemporaries only in mood, not in their ultimate content: 14

> Perched like a fly on this Yosemite dome, I gaze and sketch and bask, oftentimes settling down into dumb administration without definite hope of ever learning much, yet with the longing, unresting effort that lies at the door of hope, humbly prostrate before the vast display of God's power, and eager to offer self-denial and renunciation with eternal toil to learn any lesson in the divine manuscript.[17]

Muir's "divine manuscript" and Wordsworth's "Characters of the great Apocalypse" were in fact pages from the same holy book. The sublime wilderness had ceased to be a place of satanic temptation and become instead a sacred temple, much as it continues to be for those who love it today.

15   But the romantic sublime was not the only cultural movement that helped transform wilderness into a sacred American icon during the nineteenth century. No less important was the powerful romantic attraction of primitivism, dating back at least to Rousseau—the belief that the best antidote to the ills of an overly refined and civilized modern world was a return to simpler, more primitive living. In the United States, this was embodied most strikingly in the national myth of the frontier. The historian Frederick Jackson Turner wrote in 1893 the classic academic statement of this myth, but it had been part of American cultural traditions for well over a century. As Turner described the process, easterners and European immigrants, in moving to the wild unsettled lands of the frontier, shed the trappings of civilization, rediscovered their primitive racial energies, reinvented direct democratic institutions, and thereby reinfused themselves with a vigor, an independence, and a creativity that were the source of American democracy and national character. Seen in this way, wild country became a place not just of religious redemption but of national renewal, the quintessential location for experiencing what it meant to be an American.

16   One of Turner's most provocative claims was that by the 1890s the frontier was passing away. Never again would "such gifts of free land offer themselves" to the American people. "The frontier has gone," he declared, "and with its going has closed the first period of American history."[18] Built into the frontier myth from its very beginning was the notion that this crucible of American identity was temporary and would pass away. Those who have celebrated the frontier have almost always looked backward as they did so, mourning an older, simpler, truer world that is about to disappear forever. That world and all of its attractions, Turner said, depended on free land—on wilderness. Thus, in the myth of the vanishing frontier lay the seeds of wilderness preservation in the United States, for if wild land had been so crucial in the making of the nation, then surely one must save its last remnants as monuments to the American past—and as an insurance policy to protect its future. It is no accident that the movement to set aside national parks and wilderness areas began to gain real momentum at precisely the time that laments about the passing frontier reached their peak. To protect wilderness was in a very real sense to protect the nation's most sacred myth of origin.

17   Among the core elements of the frontier myth was the powerful sense among certain groups of Americans that wilderness was the last bastion of rugged individualism. Turner tended to stress communitarian themes when writing frontier history, asserting that Americans in primitive conditions had been

forced to band together with their neighbors to form communities and democratic institutions. For other writers, however, frontier democracy for communities was less compelling than frontier freedom for individuals.[19] By fleeing to the outer margins of settled land and society—so the story ran—an individual could escape the confining strictures of civilized life. The mood among writers who celebrated frontier individualism was almost always nostalgic; they lamented not just a lost way of life but the passing of the heroic men who had embodied that life. Thus Owen Wister in the introduction to his classic 1902 novel *The Virginian* could write of "a vanished world" in which "the horseman, the cow-puncher, the last romantic figure upon our soil" rode only "in his historic yesterday" and would "never come again." For Wister, the cowboy was a man who gave his word and kept it ("Wall Street would have found him behind the times"), who did not talk lewdly to women ("Newport would have thought him old-fashioned"), who worked and played hard, and whose "ungoverned hours did not unman him."[20] Theodore Roosevelt wrote with much the same nostalgic fervor about the "fine, manly qualities" of the "wild rough-rider of the plains." No one could be more heroically masculine, thought Roosevelt, or more at home in the western wilderness:

> There he passes his days. there he does his life-work, there, when he meets death, he faces it as he has faced many other evils, with quiet, uncomplaining fortitude. Brave, hospitable, hardy, and adventurous, he is the grim pioneer of our race; he prepares the way for the civilization from before whose face he must himself disappear. Hard and dangerous though his existence is, it has yet a wild attraction that strongly draws to it his bold, free spirit.[21]

This nostalgia for a passing frontier way of life inevitably implied ambivalence, if not downright hostility, toward modernity and all that it represented. If one saw the wild lands of the frontier as freer, truer, and more natural than other, more modern places, then one was also inclined to see the cities and factories of urban-industrial civilization as confining, false, and artificial. Owen Wister looked at the post-frontier "transition" that had followed "the horseman of the plains," and did not like what he saw: "a shapeless state, a condition of men and manners as unlovely as is that moment in the year when winter is gone and spring not come, and the face of Nature is ugly."[22] In the eyes of writers who shared Wister's distaste for modernity, civilization contaminated its inhabitants and absorbed them into the faceless, collective, contemptible life of the crowd. For all of its troubles and dangers, and despite the fact that it must pass away, the frontier had been a better place. If civilization was to be redeemed, it would be by men like the Virginian who could retain their frontier virtues even as they made the transition to post-frontier life.

19   The mythic frontier individualist was almost always masculine in gender: here, in the wilderness, a man could be a real man, the rugged individual he was meant to be before civilization sapped his energy and threatened his masculinity. Wister's contemptuous remarks about Wall Street and Newport suggest what he and many others of his generation believed—that the comforts and seductions of civilized life were especially insidious for men, who all too easily became emasculated by the femininizing tendencies of civilization. More often than not, men who felt this way came, like Wister and Roosevelt, from elite class backgrounds. The curious result was that frontier nostalgia became an important vehicle for expressing a peculiarly bourgeois form of antimodernism. The very men who most benefited from urban-industrial capitalism were among those who believed they must escape its debilitating effects. If the frontier was passing, then men who had the means to do so should preserve for themselves some remnant of its wild landscape so that they might enjoy the regeneration and renewal that came from sleeping under the stars, participating in blood sports, and living off the land. The frontier might be gone, but the frontier experience could still be had if only wilderness were preserved.

20   Thus the decades following the Civil War saw more and more of the nation's wealthiest citizens seeking out wilderness for themselves. The elite passion for wild land took many forms: enormous estates in the Adirondacks and elsewhere (disingenuously called "camps" despite their many servants and amenities), cattle ranches for would-be rough riders on the Great Plains, guided big-game hunting trips in the Rockies, and luxurious resort hotels wherever railroads pushed their way into sublime landscapes. Wilderness suddenly emerged as the landscape of choice for elite tourists, who brought with them strikingly urban ideas of the countryside through which they traveled. For them, wild land was not a site for productive labor and not a permanent home; rather, it was a place of recreation. One went to the wilderness not as a producer but as a consumer, hiring guides and other backcountry residents who could serve as romantic surrogates for the rough riders and hunters of the frontier if one was willing to overlook their new status as employees and servants of the rich.

In just this way, wilderness came to embody the national 21
frontier myth, standing for the wild freedom of America's past
and seeming to represent a highly attractive natural alternative
to the ugly artificiality of modern civilization. The irony, of
course, was that in the process wilderness came to reflect the
very civilization its devotees sought to escape. Ever since the
nineteenth century, celebrating wilderness has been an activity
mainly for well-to-do city folks. Country people generally know
far too much about working the land to regard *un*worked land
as their ideal. In contrast, elite urban tourists and wealthy
sportsmen projected their leisure-time frontier fantasies onto
the American landscape and so created wilderness in their own
image.

There were other ironies as well. The movement to set aside 22
national parks and wilderness areas followed hard on the heels
of the final Indian wars, in which the prior human inhabitants
of these areas were rounded up and moved onto reservations.
The myth of the wilderness as "virgin," uninhabited land had
always been especially cruel when seen from the perspective of
the Indians who had once called that land home. Now they
were forced to move elsewhere, with the result that tourists
could safely enjoy the illusion that they were seeing their nation in its pristine, original state, in the new morning of God's
own creation.[23] Among the things that most marked the new
national parks as reflecting a post-frontier consciousness was
the relative absence of human violence within their boundaries. The actual frontier had often been a place of conflict, in
which invaders and invaded fought for control of land and resources. Once set aside within the fixed and carefully policed
boundaries of the modern bureaucratic state, the wilderness
lost its savage image and became safe: a place more of reverie
than of revulsion or fear. Meanwhile, its original inhabitants
were kept out by dint of force, their earlier uses of the land redefined as inappropriate or even illegal. To this day, for instance, the Blackfeet continue to be accused of "poaching"
on the lands of Glacier National Park that originally belonged
to them and that were ceded by treaty only with the proviso
that they be permitted to hunt there.[24]

The removal of Indians to create an "uninhabited wilderness" 23
uninhabited as never before in the human history of the place—
reminds us just how invented, just how constructed, the
American wilderness really is. To return to my opening argument: there is nothing natural about the concept of wilderness.
It is entirely a creation of the culture that holds it dear, a product
of the very history it seeks to deny. Indeed, one of the most
striking proofs of the cultural invention of wilderness is its

thoroughgoing erasure of the history from which it sprang. In virtually all of its manifestations, wilderness represents a flight from history. Seen as the original garden, it is a place outside of time, from which human beings had to be ejected before the fallen world history could properly begin. Seen as the frontier, it is a savage world at the dawn of civilization, whose transformation represents the very beginning of the national historical epic. Seen as the bold landscape of frontier heroism, it is the place of youth and childhood, into which men escape by abandoning their pasts and entering a world of freedom where the constraints of civilization fade into memory. Seen as the sacred sublime, it is the home of a God who transcends history by standing as the One who remains untouched and unchanged by time's arrow. No matter what the angle from which we regard it, wilderness offers us the illusion that we can escape the cares and troubles of the world in which our past has ensnared us.[25]

24   This escape from history is one reason why the language we use to talk about wilderness is often permeated with spiritual and religious values that reflect human ideals far more than the material world of physical nature. Wilderness fulfills the old romantic project of secularizing Judeo-Christian values so as to make a new cathedral not in some pretty human building but in God's own creation, Nature itself. Many environmentalists who reject traditional notions of the Godhead and who regard themselves as agnostics or even atheists nonetheless express feelings tantamount to religious awe when in the presence of wilderness—a fact that testifies to the success of the romantic project. Those who have no difficulty seeing God as the expression of our human dreams and desires nonetheless have trouble recognizing that in a secular age Nature can offer precisely the same sort of mirror.

25   Thus it is that wilderness serves as the unexamined foundation on which so many of the quasi-religious values of modern environmentalism rest. The critique of modernity that is one of environmentalism's most important contributions to the moral and political discourse of our time more often than not appeals, explicitly or implicitly, to wilderness as the standard against which to measure the failings of our human world. Wilderness is the natural, unfallen antithesis of an unnatural civilization that has lost its soul. It is a place of freedom in which we can recover the true selves we have lost to the corrupting influences of our artificial lives. Most of all, if is the ultimate landscape of authenticity. Combining the sacred grandeur of the sublime with the primitive simplicity of the frontier, it is the place where we can see the world as it really is, and so know ourselves as we really are—or ought to be.

But the trouble with wilderness is that it quietly expresses 26
and reproduces the very values its devotees seek to reject. The
flight from history that is very nearly the core of wilderness
represents the false hope of an escape from responsibility, the
illusion that we can somehow wipe clean the slate of our past
and return to the tabula rasa that supposedly existed before we
began to leave our marks on the world. The dream of an un-
worked natural landscape is very much the fantasy of people
who have never themselves had to work the land to make a
living—urban folk for whom food comes from a supermarket or
a restaurant instead of a field, and for whom the wooden houses
in which they live and work apparently have no meaningful connection to the forests in which trees grow and die. Only people
whose relation to the land was already alienated could hold up
wilderness as a model for human life in nature, for the romantic
ideology of wilderness leaves precisely nowhere for human beings actually to make their living from the land.

This, then, is the central paradox: wilderness embodies a du- 27
alistic vision in which the human is entirely outside the natural. If we allow ourselves to believe that nature, to be true,
must also be wild, then our very presence in nature represents
its fall. The place where we are is the place where nature is not.
If this is so—if by definition wilderness leaves no place for
human beings, save perhaps as contemplative sojourners enjoying their leisurely reverie in God's natural cathedral—then
also by definition it can offer no solution to the environmental
and other problems that confront us. To the extent that we celebrate wilderness as the measure with which we judge civilization, we reproduce the dualism that sets humanity and nature
at opposite poles. We thereby leave ourselves little hope of discovering what an ethical, sustainable, *honorable* human place
in nature might actually look like.

Worse: to the extent that we live in an urban-industrial 28
civilization but at the same time pretend to ourselves that our
real home is in the wilderness, to just that extent we give ourselves permission to evade responsibility for the lives we actually lead. We inhabit civilization while holding some part of
ourselves—what we imagine to be the most precious part—aloof
from its entanglements. We work our nine-to-five jobs in its institutions, we eat its food, we drive its cars (not least to reach the
wilderness), we benefit from the intricate and all too invisible
networks with which it shelters us, all the while pretending that
these things are not an essential part of who we are. By imagining that our true home is in the wilderness, we forgive ourselves
the homes we actually inhabit. In its flight from history, in its
siren song of escape, in its reproduction of the dangerous

dualism that sets human beings outside of nature—in all of these ways, wilderness poses a serious threat to responsible environmentalism at the end of the twentieth century.

29   By now I hope it is clear that my criticism in this essay is not directed at wild nature per se, or even at efforts to set aside large tracts of wild land, but rather at the specific habits of thinking that flow from this complex cultural construction called wilderness. It is not the things we label as wilderness that are the problem—for nonhuman nature and large tracts of the natural world *do* deserve protection—but rather what we ourselves mean when we use the label. Lest one doubt how pervasive these habits of thought actually are in contemporary environmentalism, let me list some of the places where wilderness serves as the ideological underpinning for environmental concerns that might otherwise seem quite remote from it. Defenders of biological diversity, for instance, although sometimes appealing to more utilitarian concerns, often point to "untouched" ecosystems as the best and richest repositories of the undiscovered species we must certainly try to protect. Although at first blush an apparently more "scientific" concept than wilderness, biological diversity in fact invokes many of the same sacred values, which is why organizations like the Nature Conservancy have been so quick to employ it as an alternative to the seemingly fuzzier and more problematic concept of wilderness. There is a paradox here, of course. To the extent that biological diversity (indeed, even wilderness itself) is likely to survive in the future only by the most vigilant and self-conscious management of the ecosystems that sustain it, the ideology of wilderness is potentially in direct conflict with the very thing it encourages us to protect.[26]

30   The most striking instances of this have revolved around "endangered species," which serve as vulnerable symbols of biological diversity while at the same time standing as surrogates for wilderness itself. The terms of the Endangered Species Act in the United States have often meant that those hoping to defend pristine wilderness have had to rely on a single endangered species like the spotted owl to gain legal standing for their case—thereby making the full power of the sacred land inhere in a single numinous organism whose habitat then becomes the object of intense debate about appropriate management and use.[27] The ease with which anti-environmental forces like the wise-use movement have attacked such single-species preservation efforts suggests the vulnerability of strategies like these.

31   Perhaps partly because our own conflicts over such places and organisms have become so messy, the convergence of wilderness values with concerns about biological diversity and

endangered species has helped produce a deep fascination for remote ecosystems, where it is easier to imagine that nature might somehow be "left alone" to flourish by its own pristine devices. The classic example is the tropical rain forest, which since the 1970s has become the most powerful modern icon of unfallen, sacred land—a veritable Garden of Eden—for many Americans and Europeans. And yet protecting the rain forest in the eyes of First World environmentalists all too often means protecting it from the people who live there. Those who seek to preserve such "wilderness" from the activities of native peoples run the risk of reproducing the same tragedy—being forceably removed from an ancient home—that befell American Indians. Third World countries face massive environmental problems and deep social conflicts, but these are not likely to be solved by a cultural myth that encourages us to "preserve" peopleless landscapes that have not existed in such places for millennia. At its worst, as environmentalists are beginning to realize, exporting American notions of wilderness in this way can become an unthinking and self-defeating form of cultural imperialism.[28]

Perhaps the most suggestive example of the way that wilder- 32 ness thinking can underpin other environmental concerns has emerged in the recent debate about "global change." In 1989 the journalist Bill McKibben published a book entitled *The End of Nature,* in which he argued that the prospect of global climate change as a result of unintentional human manipulation of the atmosphere means that nature as we once knew it no longer exists.[29] Whereas earlier generations inhabited a natural world that remained more or less unaffected by their actions, our own generation is uniquely different. We and our children will henceforth live in a biosphere completely altered by our own activity, a planet in which the human and the natural can no longer be distinguished, because the one has overwhelmed the other. In McKibben's view, nature has died, and we are responsible for killing it. "The planet," he declares, "is utterly different now."[30]

But such a perspective is possible only if we accept 33 the wilderness premise that nature, to be natural, must also be pristine—remote from humanity and untouched by our common past. In fact, everything we know about environmental history suggests that people have been manipulating the natural world on various scales for as long as we have a record of their passing. Moreover, we have unassailable evidence that many of the environmental changes we now face also occurred quite apart from human intervention at one time or another in the earth's past.[31] The point is not that our current problems are trivial, or that our devastating effects on the earth's ecosystems should be accepted as inevitable or "natural." It is rather that we seem unlikely to make much progress in solving these problems if we hold up to ourselves as the mirror of nature a wilderness we ourselves cannot inhabit.

34   To do so is merely to take to a logical extreme the paradox that was built into wilderness from the beginning: if nature dies because we enter it, then the only way to save nature is to kill ourselves. The absurdity of this proposition flows from the underlying dualism it expresses. Not only does it ascribe greater power to humanity than we in fact possess—physical and biological nature will surely survive in some form or another long after we ourselves have gone the way of all flesh— but in the end it offers us little more than a self-defeating counsel of despair. The tautology gives us no way out: if wild nature is the only thing worth saving, and if our mere presence destroys it, then the sole solution to our own unnaturalness, the only way to protect sacred wilderness from profane humanity, would seem to be suicide. It is not a proposition that seems likely to produce very positive or practical results.

35   And yet radical environmentalists and deep ecologists all too frequently come close to accepting this premise as a first principle. When they express, for instance, the popular notion that our environmental problems began with the invention of agriculture, they push the human fall from natural grace so far back into the past that all of civilized history becomes a tale of ecological declension. Earth First! founder Dave Foreman captures the familiar parable succinctly when he writes,

> Before agriculture was midwifed in the Middle East, humans were in the wilderness. We had no concept of "wilderness" because everything was wilderness and *we were a part of it*. But with irrigation ditches, crop surpluses, and permanent villages, we became *apart from* the natural world. . . . Between the wilderness that created us and the civilization created by us grew an ever-widening rift.[32]

In this view the farm becomes the first and most important battlefield in the long war against wild nature, and all else follows in its wake. From such a starting place, it is hard not to reach the conclusion that the only way human beings can hope to live naturally on earth is to follow the hunter-gatherers back into a wilderness Eden and abandon virtually everything that civilization has given us. It may indeed turn out that civilization will end in ecological collapse or nuclear disaster, whereupon one might expect to find any human survivors returning to a way of life closer to that celebrated by Foreman and his followers. For most of us, though, such a debacle would be cause for regret, a sign that humanity had failed to fulfill its own promise and failed to honor its own highest values—including those of the deep ecologists.

In offering wilderness as the ultimate hunter-gatherer alternative to civilization, Foreman reproduces an extreme but still easily recognizable version of the myth of frontier primitivism. When he writes of his fellow Earth Firsters that "we believe we must return to being animal, to glorying in our sweat, hormones, tears, and blood" and that "we struggle against the modern compulsion to become dull, passionless androids," he is following in the footsteps of Owen Wister.[33] Although his arguments give primacy to defending biodiversity and the autonomy of wild nature, his prose becomes most passionate when he speaks of preserving "the wilderness experience." His own ideal "Big Outside" bears an uncanny resemblance to that of the frontier myth: wide open spaces and virgin land with no trails, no signs, no facilities, no maps, no guides, no rescues, no modern equipment. Tellingly, it is a land where hardly travelers can support themselves by hunting with "primitive weapons (bow and arrow, atlatl, knife, sharp rock)."[34] Foreman claims that "the primary value of wilderness is not as a proving ground for young Huck Finns and Annie Oakleys," but his heart is with Huck and Annie all the same. He admits that "preserving a quality wilderness experience for the human visitor, letting her or him flex Paleolithic muscles or seek visions, remains a tremendously important secondary purpose."[35] Just so does Teddy Roosevelt's rough rider live on in the greener garb of a new age.

However much one may be attracted to such a vision, it entails problematic consequences. For one, it makes wilderness the locus for an epic struggle between malign civilization and benign nature, compared with which all other social, political, and moral concerns seem trivial. Foreman writes, "The preservation of wildness and native diversity is *the* most important issue. Issues directly affecting only humans pale in comparison."[36] Presumably so do any environmental problems whose victims are mainly people, for such problems usually surface in landscapes that have already "fallen" and are no longer wild. This would seem to exclude from the radical environmentalist agenda problems of occupational health and safety in industrial settings, problems of toxic waste exposure on "unnatural" urban and agricultural sites, problems of poor children poisoned by lead exposure in the inner city, problems of famine and poverty and human suffering in the "overpopulated" places of the earth—problems, in short, of environmental

36

37

justice. If we set too high a stock on wilderness, too many
other corners of the earth become less than natural and too
many other people become less than human, thereby giving us
permission not to care much about their suffering or their fate.

It is no accident that these supposedly inconsequential envi-
38 ronmental problems affect mainly poor people, for the long affiliation between wilderness and wealth means that the only
poor people who count when wilderness is *the* issue are hunter-
gatherers, who presumably do not consider themselves to be
poor in the first place. The dualism at the heart of wilderness
encourages its advocates to conceive of its protection as a crude
conflict between the "human" and the "nonhuman"—or, more
often, between those who value the nonhuman and those who
do not. This in turn tempts one to ignore crucial differences
among humans and the complex cultural and historical reasons
why different peoples may feel very differently about the meaning of wilderness.

Why, for instance, is the "wilderness experience" so often
39 conceived as a form of recreation best enjoyed by those whose
class privileges give them the time and resources to leave their
jobs behind and "get away from it all"? Why does the protection of wilderness so often seem to pit urban recreationists
against rural people who actually earn their living from the
land (excepting those who sell goods and services to the
tourists themselves)? Why in the debates about pristine natural areas are "primitive" peoples idealized, even sentimental-
ized, until the moment they do something unprimitive,
modern, and unnatural, and thereby fall from environmental
grace? What are the consequences of a wilderness ideology
that devalues productive labor and the very concrete knowledge that comes from working the land with one's own
hands?[37] All of these questions imply conflicts among different
groups of people, conflicts that are obscured behind the deceptive clarity of "human" vs. "nonhuman." If in answering these
knotty questions we resort to so simplistic an opposition, we
are almost certain to ignore the very subtleties and complexities we need to understand.

But the most troubling cultural baggage that accompanies
40 the celebration of wilderness has less to do with remote rain
forests and peoples than with the ways we think about ourselves—we American environmentalists who quite rightly
worry about the future of the earth and the threats we pose to
the natural world. Idealizing a distant wilderness too often
means not idealizing the environment in which we actually
live, the landscape that for better or worse we call home. Most
of our most serious environmental problems start right here,

at home, and if we are to solve those problems, we need an environmental ethic that will tell us as much about *using* nature as about *not* using it. The wilderness dualism tends to cast any use as *ab*-use, and thereby denies us a middle ground in which responsible use and non-use might attain some kind of balanced, sustainable relationship. My own belief is that only by exploring this middle ground will we learn ways of imagining a better world for all of us: humans and nonhumans, rich people and poor, women and men, First Worlders *and* Third Worlders, white folks and people of color, consumers and producers—a world better for humanity in all of its diversity and for all the rest of nature too. The middle ground is where we actually live. It is where we—all of us, in our different places and ways— make our homes.

That is why, when I think of the times I myself have come closest to experiencing what I might call the sacred in nature,   41 I often find myself remembering wild places much closer to home. I think, for instance, of a small pond near my house where water bubbles up from limestone springs to feed a series of pools that rarely freeze in winter and so play home to waterfowl that stay here for the protective warmth even on the coldest of winter days, gliding silently through streaming mists as the snow falls from gray February skies. I think of a November evening long ago when I found myself on a Wisconsin hilltop in rain and dense fog, only to have the setting sun break through the clouds to cast an otherworldly golden light on the misty farms and woodlands below, a scene so unexpected and joyous that I lingered past dusk so as not to miss any part of the gift that had come my way. And I think perhaps most especially of the blown-out, bankrupt farm in the sand country of central Wisconsin where Aldo Leopold and his family tried one of the first American experiments in ecological restoration, turning ravaged and infertile soil into carefully tended ground where the human and the nonhuman could exist side by side in relative harmony. What I celebrate about such places is not *just* their wildness, though that certainly is among their most important qualities; what I celebrate even more is that they remind us of the wildness in our own backyards, of the nature that is all around us if only we have eyes to see it.

Indeed, my principal objection to wilderness is that it may teach us to be dismissive or even contemptuous of such hum-   42 ble places and experiences. Without our quite realizing it, wilderness tends to privilege some parts of nature at the expense of others. Most of us, I suspect, still follow the conventions of the romantic sublime in finding the mountaintop more glorious than the plains, the ancient forest nobler than the grasslands, the mighty canyon more inspiring than the humble marsh. Even John Muir, in arguing against those who sought to dam his beloved Hetch Hetchy valley in the Sierra Nevada, argued for alternative dam sites in the gentler valleys of the foothills—a preference that had nothing to do with nature and everything with the cultural traditions of the sublime.[38] Just as problematically, our frontier traditions have encouraged Americans to define "true" wilderness as requiring very large tracts of roadless land—what Dave Foreman calls "The Big Outside." Leaving aside the legitimate empirical question in conservation biology of how large a tract of land must be before a given species can reproduce on it, the emphasis on big wilderness reflects a romantic frontier belief that one hasn't really gotten away from civilization unless one can go for days at a time without encountering another human being. By teaching us to fetishize sublime places and wide open country, these peculiarly American ways of thinking about wilderness encourage us to adopt too high a standard for what counts as "natural." If it isn't hundreds of square miles big, if it doesn't give us God's-eye views or grand vistas, if it doesn't permit us the illusion that we are alone on the planet, then it really isn't natural. It's too small, too plain, or too crowded to be *authentically* wild.

43   In critiquing wilderness as I have done in this essay, I'm forced to confront my own deep ambivalence about its meaning for modern environmentalism. On the one hand, one of my own most important environmental ethics is that people should always be conscious that they are part of the natural world, inextricably tied to the ecological systems that sustain their lives. Any way of looking at nature that encourages us to believe we are separate from nature—as wilderness tends to do—is likely to reinforce environmentally irresponsible behavior. On the other hand, I also think it no less crucial for us to recognize and honor nonhuman nature as a world we did not create, a world with its own independent, nonhuman reasons for being as it is. The autonomy of nonhuman nature seems to me an indispensable corrective to human arrogance. Any way of looking at nature that helps us remember—as wilderness also tends to do—that the interests of people are not necessarily identical to those of even other creature or of the earth itself is likely to foster *responsible* behavior. To the extent that wilderness has served as an important vehicle for articulating deep moral values regarding our obligations and responsibilities to the nonhuman world, I would not want to jettison the contributions it has made to out culture's ways of thinking about nature.

If the core problem of wilderness is that it distances us too   44
much from the very things it teaches us to value, then the question we must ask is what it can tell us about *home*, the place
where we actually live. How can we take the positive values we
associate with wilderness and bring them closer to home?
I think the answer to this question will come by broadening
our sense of the otherness that wilderness seeks to define and
protect. In reminding us of the world we did not make, wilderness can teach profound feelings of humility and respect as
we confront our fellow beings and the earth itself Feelings
like these argue for the importance of self-awareness and
self-criticism as we exercise our own ability to transform the
world around us, helping us set responsible limits to human
mastery—which without such limits too easily becomes
human hubris. Wilderness is the place where, symbolically at
least, we try to withhold our power to dominate.

Wallace Stegner once wrote of

> the special human mark, the special record of human pas-
> sage, that distinguishes man from all other species. It is rare
> enough among men, impossible to any other form of life. *It
> is simply the deliberate and chosen refusal to make any marks
> at all.* . . . We are the most dangerous species of life on the
> planet, and every other species, even the earth itself, has
> cause to fear our power to exterminate. But we are also the
> only species which, when it chooses to do so, will go to great
> effort to save what it might destroy.[39]

The myth of wilderness, which Stegner knowingly reproduces
in these remarks, is that we can somehow leave nature untouched by our passage. By now it should be clear that this for
the most part is an illusion. But Stegner's deeper message then
becomes all the more compelling. If living in history means
that we cannot help leaving marks on a fallen world, then the
dilemma we face is to decide what kinds of marks we wish to
leave. It is just here that our cultural traditions of wilderness
remain so important. In the broadest sense, wilderness teaches
us to ask whether the Other must always bend to our will, and,
if not, under what circumstances it should be allowed to flourish without our intervention. This is surely a question worth
asking about everything we do, and not just about the natural
world.

When we visit a wilderness area, we find ourselves sur-   45
rounded by plants and animals and physical landscapes whose
otherness compels our attention. In forcing us to acknowledge

that they are not of our making, that they have little or no need of our continued existence, they recall for us a creation far greater than our own. In the wilderness, we need no reminder that a tree has its own reasons for being, quite apart from us. The same is less true in the gardens we plant and tend ourselves: there it is far easier to forget the otherness of the tree.[40] Indeed, one could almost measure wilderness by the extent to which our recognition of its otherness requires a conscious, willed act on our part. The romantic legacy means that wilderness is more a state of mind than a fact of nature, and the state of mind that today most defines wilderness is *wonder*. The striking power of the wild is that wonder in the face of it requires no act of will, but forces itself upon us—as an expression of the nonhuman world experienced through the lens of our cultural history—as proof that ours is not the only presence in the universe.

46   Wilderness gets us into trouble only if we imagine that this experience of wonder and otherness is limited to the remote corners of the planet, or that it somehow depends on pristine landscapes we ourselves do not inhabit. Nothing could be more misleading. The tree in the garden is in reality no less other, no less worthy of our wonder and respect, than the tree in an ancient forest that has never known an ax or a saw—even though the tree in the forest reflects a more intricate web of ecological relationships. The tree in the garden could easily have sprung from the same seed as the tree in the forest, and we can claim only its location and perhaps its form as our own. Both trees stand apart from us; both share our common world. The special power of the tree in the wilderness is to re-mind us of this fact. It can teach us to recognize the wildness we did not see in the tree we planted in our own backyard. By seeing the otherness in that which is most unfamiliar, we can learn to see it too in that which at first seemed merely ordi-nary. If wilderness can do this—if it can help us perceive and respect a nature we had forgotten to recognize as natural—then it will become part of the solution to our environmental dilemmas rather than part of the problem.

47   This will only happen, however, if we abandon the dualism that sees the tree in the garden as artificial—completely fallen and unnatural—and the tree in the wilderness as natural—completely pristine and wild. Both trees in some ultimate sense are wild; both in a practical sense now depend on our manage-ment and care. We are responsible for both, even though we can claim credit for neither. Our challenge is to stop thinking of such things according to a set of bipolar moral scales in which the human and the nonhuman, the unnatural and the natural, the fallen and the unfallen, serve as our conceptual map for

understanding and valuing the world. Instead, we need to embrace the full continuum of a natural landscape that is also cultural, in which the city, the suburb, the pastoral, and the wild each has its proper place, which we permit ourselves to celebrate without needlessly denigrating the others. We need to honor the Other within and the Other next door as much as we do the exotic Other that lives far away—a lesson that applies as much to people as it does to (other) natural things. In particular, we need to discover a common middle ground in which all of these things, from the city to the wilderness, can somehow be encompassed in the word "home." Home, after all, is the place where finally we make our living. It is the place for which we take responsibility, the place we try to sustain so we can pass on what is best in it (and in ourselves) to our children.[41]

The task of making a home in nature is what Wendell Berry   48
has called "the forever unfinished lifework of our species." "The only thing we have to preserve nature with," he writes, "is culture; the only thing we have to preserve wildness with is domesticity."[42] Calling a place home inevitably means that we will *use* the nature we find in it, for there can be no escape from manipulating and working and even killing some parts of nature to make our home. But if we acknowledge the autonomy and otherness of the things and creatures around us—an autonomy our culture has taught us to label with the word "wild"—then we will at least think carefully about the uses to which we put them, and even ask if we should use them at all. Just so can we still join Thoreau in declaring that "in Wildness is the preservation of the World," for *wildness* (as opposed to wilderness) can be found anywhere: in the seemingly tame fields and woodlots of Massachusetts, in the cracks of a Manhattan sidewalk, even in the cells of our own bodies. As Gary Snyder has wisely said, "A person with a clear heart and open mind can experience the wilderness anywhere on earth. It is a quality of one's own consciousness. The planet is a wild place and always will be."[43] To think ourselves capable of causing "the end of nature" is an act of great hubris, for it means forgetting the wildness that dwells everywhere within and around us.

Learning to honor the wild—learning to remember and ac-   49
knowledge the autonomy of the other—means striving for critical self-consciousness in all of our actions. It means that deep reflection and respect must accompany each act of use, and means too that we must always consider the possibility of non-use. It means looking at the part of nature we intend to turn toward our own ends and asking whether we can use it again and again and again—sustainably—without its being diminished in the process. In means never imagining that we can flee into a

mythical wilderness to escape history and the obligation to take responsibility for our own actions that history inescapably entails. Most of all, it means practicing remembrance and gratitude, for thanksgiving is the simplest and most basic of ways for us to recollect the nature, the culture, and the history that have come together to make the world as we know it. If wildness can stop being (just) out there and start being (also) in here, if it can start being as humane as it is natural, then perhaps we can get on with the unending task of struggling to live rightly in the world—not just in the garden, not just in the wilderness, but in the home that encompasses them both.

NOTES

1. Henry David Thoreau, "Walking," *The Works of Thoreau*, ed. Henry S. Canby (Boston, Massachusetts: Houghton Mifflin, 1937), p. 672.
2. *Oxford English Dictionary*, s.v. "wilderness"; see also Roderick Nash, *Wilderness and the American Mind*, 3rd ed. (New Haven, Connecticut: Yale Univ. Press, 1982), pp. 1–22; and Max Oelschlaeger, *The Idea of Wilderness: From Prehistory to the Age of Ecology* (New Haven, Connecticut: Yale Univ. Press, 1991).
3. Exodus 32:1–35, KJV.
4. Exodus 14:3, KJV.
5. Mark 1:12–13, KJV; see also Matthew 4:1–11; Luke 4:1–13.
6. John Milton, "Paradise Lost," *John Milton: Complete Poems and Major Prose*, ed. Merritt Y. Hughes (New York: Odyssey Press, 1957), pp. 280–81, lines 131–42.
7. I have discussed this theme at length in "Landscapes of Abundance and Scarcity," in Clyde Milner et al., eds., *Oxford History of the American West* (New York: Oxford Univ. Press, 1994), pp. 603–37. The classic work on the Puritan "city on a hill" in colonial New England is Perry Miller, *Errand into the Wilderness* (Cambridge, Massachusetts: Harvard Univ. Press, 1956).
8. John Muir, *My First Summer in the Sierra* (1911), reprinted in *John Muir: The Eight Wilderness Discovery Books* (London, England: Diadem; Seattle, Washington: Mountaineers, 1992), p. 211.
9. Alfred Runte, *National Parks: The American Experience*, 2nd ed. (Lincoln: Univ. of Nebraska Press, 1987).
10. John Muir, *The Yosemite* (1912), reprinted in *John Muir: Eight Wilderness Discovery Books*, p. 715.
11. Scholarly work on the sublime is extensive. Among the most important studies are Samuel Monk, *The Sublime: A Study of Critical Theories in XVII-Century England* (New York: Modern Language Association, 1935); Basil Willey, *The Eighteenth-Century Background: Studies on the Idea of Nature in the Thought of the Period* (London, England: Chattus and Windus, 1949); Marjorie Hope Nicolson, *Mountain Gloom and Mountain Glory: The Development of the Aesthetics of the Infinite* (Ithaca, New York: Cornell Univ. Press, 1959); Thomas Weiskel, *The Romantic Sublime: Studies in the Structure and Psychology of Transcendence* (Baltimore, Maryland: Johns Hopkins Univ. Press, 1976); Barbara Novak, *Nature and Culture: American Landscape Painting, 1825–1875* (New York: Oxford Univ. Press, 1980).

12. The classic works are Immanuel Kant, *Observations on the Feeling of the Beautiful and Sublime* (1764), trans. John T. Goldthwait (Berkeley: Univ. of California Press, 1960); Edmund Burke, A *Philosophical Enquiry into the Origin of Our Ideas of the Sublime and Beautiful*, ed. James T. Boulton (1958; Notre Dame, Indiana: Univ. of Notre Dame Press, 1968); William Gilpin, *Three Essays: On Picturesque Beauty; on Picturesque Travel; and on Sketching Landscape* (London, England, 1803).

13. See Ann Vileisis, "From Wastelands to Wetlands" (unpublished senior essay, Yale Univ., 1989); Runte, *National Parks*.

14. William Wordsworth, "The Prelude," bk. 6, in Thomas Hutchinson, ed., *The Poetical Works of Wordsworth* (London, England: Oxford Univ. Press, 1936), p. 536.

15. Henry David Thoreau, *The Maine Woods* (1864), in *Henry David Thoreau* (New York: Library of America, 1985), pp. 640–41.

16. Exodus 16:10, KJV.

17. John Muir, *My First Summer in the Sierra*, p. 238. Part of the difference between these descriptions may reflect the landscapes the three authors were describing. In his essay, "Reinventing Common Nature: Yosemite and Mount Rushmore—A Meandering Tale of a Double Nature," Kenneth Olwig notes that early American travelers experienced Yosemite as much through the aesthetic tropes of the pastoral as through those of the sublime. The ease with which Muir celebrated the gentle divinity of the Sierra Nevada had much to do with the pastoral qualities of the landscape he described. See Olwig, "Reinventing Common Nature: Yosemite and Mount Rushmore—A Meandering Tale of a Double Nature," *Uncommon Ground: Toward Reinventing Nature*, ed. William Cronon (New York: W. W. Norton & Co., 1995), pp. 379–408.

18. Frederick Jackson Turner, *The Frontier in American History* (New York: Henry Holt, 1920), pp. 37–38.

19. Richard Slotkin has made this observation the linchpin of his comparison between Turner and Theodore Roosevelt. See Slotkin, *Gunfighter Nation: The Myth of the Frontier in Twentieth-Century America* (New York: Atheneum, 1992), pp. 29–62.

20. Owen Wister, *The Virginian: A Horseman of the Plains* (New York: Macmillan, 1902), pp. viii–ix.

21. Theodore Roosevelt, *Ranch Life and the Hunting Trail* (1888; New York: Century, 1899), p. 100.

22. Wister, *Virginian*, p. x.

23. On the many problems with this view, see William M. Denevan, "The Pristine Myth: The Landscape of the Americans in 1492," *Annals of the Association of American Geographers* 82 (1992): 369–85.

24. Louis Warren, "The Hunter's Game: Poachers, Conservationists, and Twentieth-Century America" (Ph.D. diss., Yale University, 1994).

25. Wilderness also lies at the foundation of the Clementsian ecological concept of the climax. See Michael Barbour, "Ecological Fragmentation in the Fifties" in Cronon, *Uncommon Ground*, pp. 233–55, and William Cronon, "Introduction: In Search of Nature," in Cronon, *Uncommon Ground*, pp. 23–56.

26. On the many paradoxes of having to manage wilderness in order to maintain the appearance of an unmanaged landscape, see John C. Hendee et al., *Wilderness Management*, USDA Forest Service Miscellaneous Publication No. 1365 (Washington, D.C.: Government Printing Office, 1978).

27. See James Proctor, "Whose Nature?: The Contested Moral Teirain of Ancient Forests," in Cronon, *Uncommon Ground*, pp. 269–97.

28. See Candace Slater, "Amazonia as Edenic Narrative," in Cronon, *Uncommon Ground*, pp. 114–31. This argument has been powerfully made by Ramachandra Guha, "Radical American Environmentalism: A Third World Critique," *Environmental Ethics* 11 (1989): 71–83.

29. Bill McKibben, *The End of Nature* (New York: Random House, 1989).

30. McKibben, *The End of Nature*, p. 49.

31. Even comparable extinction rates have occurred before, though we surely would not want to emulate the Cretaceous-Tertiary boundary extinctions as a model for responsible manipulation of the biosphere!

32. Dave Foreman, *Confessions of an Eco-Warrior* (New York: Harmony Books, 1991), p. 69 (italics in original). For a sampling of other writings by followers of deep ecology and/or Earth First!, see Michael Tobias, ed., *Deep Ecology* (San Diego, California: Avant Books, 1984); Bill Devall and George Sessions, *Deep Ecology: Living as if Nature Mattered* (Salt Lake City, Utah: Gibbs Smith, 1985); Michael Tobias, *After Eden: History, Ecology, and Conscience* (San Diego, California: Avant Books, 1985); Dave Foreman and Bill Haywood, eds., *Ecodefense: A Field Guide to Monkey Wrenching*, 2nd ed. (Tucson, Arizona: Ned Ludd Books, 1987); Bill Devall, *Simple in Means, Rich in Ends: Practicing Deep Ecology* (Salt Lake City, Utah: Gibbs Smith, 1988); Steve Chase, ed., *Defending the Earth: A Dialogue between Murray Bookchin & Dave Foreman* (Boston, Massachusetts: South End Press, 1991); John Davis, ed., *The Earth First! Reader: Ten Years of Radical Environmentalism* (Salt Lake City, Utah: Gibbs Smith, 1991); Bill Devall, *Living Richly in an Age of Limits: Using Deep Ecology for an Abundant Life* (Salt Lake City, Utah: Gibbs Smith, 1993); Michael E. Zimmerman et al., eds., *Environmental Philosophy: From Animal Rights to Radical Ecology* (Englewood Cliffs, New Jersey: Prentice-Hall, 1993). A useful survey of the different factions of radical environmentalism can be found in Carolyn Merchant, *Radical Ecology: The Search for a Livable World* (New York: Routledge, 1992). For a very interesting critique of this literature (first published in the anarchist newspaper *Fifth Estate*), see George Bradford, *How Deep is Deep Ecology?* (Ojai, California: Times Change Press, 1989).

33. Foreman, *Confessions of an Eco-Warrior*, p. 34.

34. Foreman, *Confessions of an Eco-Warrior*, p. 65. See also Dave Foreman and Howie Wolke, *The Big Outside: A Descriptive Inventory of the Big Wilderness Areas of the U.S.* (Tucson, Arizona: Ned Ludd Books, 1989).

35. Foreman, *Confessions of an Eco-Warrior*, p. 63.

36. Foreman, *Confessions of an Eco-Warrior*, p. 27.

37. See Richard White, "'Are You an Environmentalist or Do You Work for a Living?': Work and Nature," in Cronon, *Uncommon Ground*, pp. 171–85. Compare its analysis of environmental knowledge through work with Jennifer Price's analysis of environmental knowledge through consumption. It is not much of an exaggeration to say that the wilderness experience is essentially consumerist in its impulses.

38. Compare with Muir, *Yosemite*, in *John Muir: Eight Wilderness Discovery Books*, p. 714.

39. Wallace Stegner, ed., *This Is Dinosaur: Echo Park Country and Its Magic Rivers* (New York: Knopf, 1955), p. 17 (italics in original).

40. Katherine Hayles helped me see the importance of this argument.

41. Analogous arguments can be found in John Brinckerhoff Jackson, "Beyond Wilderness," *A Sense of Place, a Sense of Time* (New Haven, Connecticut: Yale Univ. Press, 1994), pp. 71–91, and in the wonderful collection of essays by Michael Pollan, *Second Nature: A Gardener's Education* (New York: Atlantic Monthly Press, 1991).
42. Wendell Berry, *Home Economics* (San Francisco, California: North Point, 1987), pp. 138, 143.
43. Gary Snyder, quoted in *New York Times*, "Week in Review," September 1994, p. 6.

Samuel P. Hays

RESPONSE
TO WILLIAM CRONON

Samuel P. Hays taught history at the University of Pittsburgh before his retirement. He has published two groundbreaking books on environmental history, Conservation and the Gospel of Efficiency: The Progressive Conservation Movement, 1890–1920 *(1959) and* Beauty, Health, and Permanence: Environmental Politics in the United States, 1955–1985 *(1987; written with his wife, Barbara). He has also written dozens of articles related to environmental history and the "meanings" attached to wilderness. His response here is to the preceding essay in this book; it appeared in 1996 in the magazine* Environmental History.

Bill Cronon's "trouble with wilderness" is ostensibly an assessment of the role the wilderness idea plays for environmentalists in the United States. But his "trouble" is far less with that wilderness idea and more with his own. He is wrestling with a wilderness idea that is confined to a few writers rather than with wilderness devotees who actually do it. Hence his account is well off the mark.

For this rejoinder, I draw on two sources of evidence, quite different from Cronon's. First is my own experience in the eastern wilderness movement running through the decade of the 1970s. I was one of a considerable number of easterners who thought that there was wilderness in the East. We studied

USGS topographic maps; identified large, roadless sections; scouted them out; drew up proposals for their protection as wilderness areas; and presented the plans to our congressional delegations. Henry David Thoreau, John Muir, and Roderick Nash were never mentioned. We had no thought of preserving "virgin" forest, since almost all of it was cut-over. It was the Forest Service who argued that none of it was wilderness because it wasn't "pristine." We retorted that it wasn't how it came to be that was important but what it looked like now, and we quoted that provision of the 1964 act that spoke of wilderness as a place where "human intrusion is relatively unnoticeable." What's more, we thought of it all as part of our own "backyard," not as something far away and remote.

3   At about the same time I decided to find out about the wilderness movement in the country as a whole, joined several dozen organizations (western as well as eastern) to obtain their newsletters and documents, and proceeded to build an archive of wilderness activity. I found out that it wasn't much different "out there." People became interested in large roadless areas they knew about; they wrote about their "backyard"; they didn't try to persuade others to read "major thinkers" to get their support but, just like we did, to expose them to it through slide shows and directly by taking them there. The dynamics of human engagement with wilderness was the same: people living in an urbanized society who felt that wilderness areas would enhance the quality of their life while enjoying modern material standards of urban living. As I observe it, the dynamics of Bureau of Land Management wilderness, today's political "hot spot," are much the same.

4   This is perhaps enough to make the reader understand why I view Bill Cronon's problem as that he hasn't looked much at the wilderness movement. He has read a few writers who have much to say about wilderness philosophy, but he has not followed those active in the fray and the more day-to-day and down-to-earth ideas and actions wilderness advocates carried out. Most of those advocates have long been "going forward" to the "right nature"; Cronon just has not noticed.

5   To make several arguments in rebuttal to Cronon about the values involved in wilderness action:

6   First, most wilderness engagement does not look toward some remote area, but toward the area of one's personal experience—my backyard. People near the candidate areas undertook wilderness action, saying simply, "we have some, too, right here." This created tension between old and new advocates. The Sierra Club, for example, tried to keep Oregon wilderness confined to the Cascades. But others argued that

the Coast Range and eastern Oregon had some lively candidates. They were brought together by the Oregon Natural Resources Council that outmaneuvered the Sierra Club with its more restricted view.

Second, wilderness advocates did not point toward a "more   7
natural" past for the temporal significance of what they were doing; instead they pointed to the future. What appealed to people most was they hoped to save something they valued for those who would come later. When economists got to work to try to identify the values people placed on wilderness through contingent valuation, the idea of "return" was not among them. Instead, people spoke of "bequest value." Wilderness advocates only thought of going forward to the world of their grandchildren.

Third, the main human engagement with wilderness has   8
long been outdoor recreation, not the romanticizing of nature, and still is. Wide-ranging outdoor recreation interest grew rapidly after World War II. Wilderness guidebooks included information about distances and landmarks along the way, not about stages of forest biological change. Most units in the wilderness system were "rocks and ice" above the tree line rather than forested areas. If I am not mistaken the French Pete area in the Oregon Cascades was the first fully forested watershed to be designated wilderness, and thus the first area to have a biological content that was taken seriously. Because we had no rocks and ice, easterners helped to bring "biological nature" into the wilderness movement and even urged the Sierra Club to adopt that view of the wilderness.

Fourth, wilderness proposals are usually thought of not in   9
terms of perpetuating some "original" or "pristine" condition but as efforts to "save" wilderness areas from development. "Land saving" is the watchword of almost all "nature" programs. We enjoy wilderness today because our forebears bypassed it as "The Lands that Nobody Wanted." We now turn the past action of neglect into the present and deliberate action of "saving" for the future. The experience of rapid destruction of nature and restricting development now and in the future define the world of wilderness action.

Fifth, wilderness was not thought of as an attempt to create   10
a role for humans amid nature, but to create a role for nature amid humans. Most wilderness advocates were urbanized people who thought of wilderness as part of an urbanized society. The great majority of wilderness advocates enjoyed modern amenities of life and thought of wilderness as another such. Keep the cities and their benefits, yes, but let's add some nature to all that in order to enhance the "good life."

11   Cronon's wilderness is a world of abstracted ideas, real enough to those who participate in it, but divorced from the values and ideas inherent in wilderness action. The evidence for such values is abundant but it takes a bit of work to get it, far more time and effort than that required by the more attractive task of emphasizing ideas of "major thinkers" whose writings libraries have close at hand.

12   Human attempts to bring nature into their urbanized environment have been many and far-reaching: the conservation commissions of New England, dating from the mid-1960s; federal urban open space programs of the same era; land conservancies and land trusts, now numbering more than 1,000; wild and scenic rivers and trails programs, augmented today with the ever popular rails-to-trails; wetlands; new tropical breeding bird habitats and the currently popular "Partners in Flight"; natural area programs in almost every state; nongame programs; endangered species habitats; "Watchable Wildlife Programs"; biodiversity reserves; eastern "old growth"; state and local land-buying referenda that have increased state park acreage since 1970 by 16 percent. In all of these Cronon's wilderness idea has played a mighty limited role. However, all of these programs have one theme in common: make sure that nature will play an ever greater role in a society where urbanization is proceeding at a rapid pace.

13   Cronon succumbs to the temptation to bring in peripheral issues that are useful in advancing the polemical argument, but they actually distort history. One is the notion that wilderness is an "elitist" playground. Participation in wilderness recreation is actually middle class. Users are primarily local and daytime, and in terms of occupation and income are a cross-section of the area population. Cronon also seeks to enhance his argument by absorbing into it both biodiversity and endangered species issues. However, the recreation content of wilderness and the ecological content of biodiversity differ markedly, come from different sources, have different meanings, and it has been a bit of a wrench for the first to accept the second. Further, while some endangered species require large, intact forest habitats, most do not; they include suburban and rural habitats, streams and riparian areas, highway berms, barrens, wetlands, small woodlands, and a host of areas hardly associated with wilderness.

14   Cronon argues that the wilderness idea diverts environmentalists from the real world of environmental affairs; he appeals to the environmental justice movement's political ideology to make the case for neglect. But the blinders in this case belong to Cronon. Almost every sector of the diverse environmental community thinks that it is "neglected"; this leads to a wide range of

intra-environmental disputes. Cronon's "right nature" groups are well divorced as a whole from those groups preoccupied with urban pollution issues. By the same token, groups preoccupied with pollution issues are divorced from groups engaging in "land saving." Both groups ignore issues of population and limits. It is one thing to use the accompanying polemics to organize history; it is another to examine these intra-environmental relationships as a subject for historical analysis. Despite divergence the organizations act as if they are part of the same piece and their activities, even land saving and opposition to hazardous waste siting, frequently cross the boundaries of specialization and dispute.

Cronon's essay reflects the temptation for historians to draw   15
into their historical analyses both personal moral struggles and the ideology of contemporary debate. This tendency is more than risky. Transfer of the accompanying polemics into environmental history not only invites bad history but also the risk that it will obscure the abundant opportunities ahead in pursuing the field of environmental history.

With a degree of clear thinking and vigilance historians can   16
avoid these dangers, and bring an historical analysis shaped by an independent historical perspective to both personal and political dimensions of environmental affairs. In this case, such vigilance requires that we not be diverted into the wilderness thickets into which Cronon's "Trouble" so temptingly invites us.

VISUAL CONVERSATIONS 6

Picturing the Landscape

The wilderness and the natural environment are unquestionably among America's most treasured possessions—little need for conversation there! Despite the idealized visions of nature that we read from the likes of Wallace Stegner and John Muir, and that we see in landscape paintings, drawings, and photography, people still debate whether those idealizations are in fact part of the problem. William Cronon's "The Trouble with Wilderness" asks us to complicate our understanding of the relationship between humans and nature. It prompts us to consider whether the images we have of wild nature are accurate and, in the end, beneficial to the environment they tend to idealize. The images included here can help you to think more about the ways that the American landscape and wildlife have been presented to us through visual rhetoric. As you view these pieces, consider how they provide us with varying perspectives on nature, and whether those perspectives are meant to define, to persuade, and/or to argue on this important topic of conversation.

From Teddy Roosevelt's "teddy bear" to the various other stuffed animals that inhabit our children's rooms, wildlife has long been depicted as cute, lovable, and innocent. Discuss the features of the World Wildlife Fund's famous panda icon: how does it serve the goals of that organization?

Landscape art, like the words of those who write about nature, attempt to represent reality. At the same time, both words and images stylize reality through the artist's (or writer's) eye. Though both of these works stimulate our aesthetic sensibilities, the two landscapes above depict very different versions of natural settings. What are your emotional reactions to these pieces? What elements of the pieces account for the differing moods of each?

One way that we are asked to interact with wildlife in nature photography is through a process of personification. That is, the images ask us to see animal life in relation to human beings and their actions. What aspects of humanity are brought out in the photographs on this page? What relationship between humans and nature is suggested? And what argument might those visuals make about the status of wildlife in relation to concepts that we can understand? What particular features of these visuals are meant to create those connections?

CREDITS

INTRODUCTION

Page 1: Photodisc Blue/Getty Images. **Page 18:** *Time* Magazine © 2001 Time Inc. Reprinted by permission.

PART 1

Page 23: Bill Aron/PhotoEdit. **Pages 27–29:** "Education," from *One Man's Meat* by E. B. White. Copyright © 1939 by E. B. White. Reprinted by permission of Tilbury House Publishers, Gardiner, Maine. **Pages 29–34:** "A Liberal Case for Vouchers" by Paul E. Peterson, from *The New Republic*, October 4, 1999. Copyright © 1999 by *The New Republic*. Reprinted by permission. **Pages 34–42:** Martin Carnoy, "Do School Vouchers Improve School Performance?" Reprinted with permission from *The American Prospect*, Volume 12, Number 1: January 01, 2001. *The American Prospect*, 11 Beacon Street, Suite 1120, Boston, MA 02108. All rights reserved. **Pages 42–59:** "To Each Its Own," by Marc Fisher, from *The Washington Post Magazine* April 2001. Copyright © 2001 The Washington Post Writers Group. Reprinted with permission. **Pages 59–73:** "The New Vocationalism: What It Is, What It Could Be" by W. Norton Grubb, from *Phi Delta Kappan*, April 1996, reprinted by permission of the author. **Pages 73–81:** "Making Public Schools Business-Like . . . Again" by Larry Cuban. Copyright © 2004 by Larry Cuban, Stanford University. Reprinted by permission of the author. **Pages 81–94:** "Divide and Conquer: How Breaking Up Big High Schools Can Be the Key to Educational Reform," by Thomas Toch, from *The Washington Monthly*, May 2003. Reprinted with permission from *The Washington Monthly*. Copyright © Washington Monthly Publishing, LLC, 733 15th St. NW, Suite 520, Washington, DC 20005. (202) 393-5155. Web site: www.washingtonmonthly.com. **Pages 94–101:** "When School Choice Isn't" by Alexander Russo, from *The Washington Monthly*, September 2002. Reprinted with permission from *The Washington Monthly*. Copyright © Washington Monthly Publishing, LLC, 733 15th St. NW, Suite 520, Washington, DC 20005. (202) 393-5155. Web site: www.washingtonmonthly.com. **Pages 101–114:** "Home Schooling Debate: Is the Movement Undermining Public Education?" by Rachel S. Cox, from *CQ Researcher*. Copyright © 2004 by Congressional Quarterly Inc. Reproduced with permission of Congressional Quarterly Inc. in the format Textbook via Copyright Clearance Center. **Page 115:** *Time* Magazine © 2001 Time Inc. Reprinted by permission. **Page 116 (top):** Kate Denny/PhotoEdit. **Page 116 (bottom):** Tony Freeman/PhotoEdit. **Page 117 (top):** Susan Van Etten/PhotoEdit. **Page 117 (bottom):** Guadalupe Alternative Programs, www.gapschool.org/parents.htm. **Page 118 (top):** Spencer Ainsley/The Image Works. **Page 118 (bottom):** Paul Conklin/PhotoEdit. **Page 119:** Robert Caputo/Aurora. **Pages 120–127:** "Everyday Use" from *In Love & In Trouble: Stories of Black Women*, copyright © 1973 by Alice Walker, reprinted by permission of Harcourt, Inc. **Pages 128–133:** "College Isn't for Everyone," by W. J. Reeves, from *USA Today Magazine*, May 2003. Copyright © by the Society for the Advancement of Education, Inc., reprinted by permission. **Page 134:** *Doonesbury* Cartoon. Copyright © 1985 by Gary Trudeau. Reprinted by permission of Universal Press Syndicate. All rights reserved. **Pages 135–145:** "The Challenge of Liberty," by Ellen Condliffe Lagemann. Reprinted by permission from Liberal Education, Spring 2003. Copyright © by the Association of American Colleges and Universities. **Pages 145–151:** "A Rationale for Civic

PART 3

PART 4

PART 5

Page 611: AP/Wide World Photos. **Pages 621–630:** From Democracy *in America*, by Alexis de Tocqueville, edited by J. P. Mayer and Max Lerner. Translated by George Lawrence. English translation copyright © 1965 by Harper & Row, Publishers, Inc. Reprinted by permission of HarperCollins Publishers. **Pages 646–650:** "Letter to Lord Irwin," by Mahatma Gandhi, March 1939. Reprinted by permission of Navajivan Trust. **Pages 651–653:** "A Call for Unity," by Birmingham Clergyman, originally published in *The Birmingham News*, April 12, 1963. Reprinted by permission of *The Birmingham News*. **Page 652:** AP/Wide World Photos. **Pages 654–668:** "Letter from a Birmingham Jail," by Dr. Martin Luther King Jr., Copyright © 1963 by Dr. Martin Luther King Jr., copyright renewed 1991 by Coretta Scott King. Reprinted by arrangement with the Estate of Martin Luther King Jr., c/o Writers House as agent for the proprietor, New York, NY. **Pages 668–674:** "Motherhood, Activism, and Social Reform," by Christine Woyshner, from USA Today Magazine, March 2002. Copyright © by the Society for the Advancement of Education, Inc., reprinted by permission. **Pages 674–680:** "Let Freedom Roll," by Julie Quiroz-Martínez. Reprinted with permission from the October 27, 2003, issue of *The Nation*. **Pages 680–690:** "The Rise of the New Civic Revolutionaries: Answering the Call to Stewardship in Our Times," by Henton/Melville/Walesh, from *National Civic Review*, Spring 2004, Copyright © 2004, reprinted by permission of John Wiley & Sons. **Pages 699–704:** "Dawn of the Daddy State," by Paul Starobin. © 2004 by Paul Starobin, as first published in the June 2004 issue of *The Atlantic Monthly*. Reprinted by permission of the author. **Pages 704–711:** "Can We Curb the Privacy Invaders?" by Ray C. Spencer, from *USA Today Magazine*, March 2002. Copyright © by the Society for the Advancement of Education, Inc., reprinted by permission. **Pages 711–713:** "Resolution on the USA Patriot Act and Related Measures That Infringe on the Rights of Library Users," as adopted by the American Library Association Council, January 29, 2003. Reprinted by permission. **Pages 713–716:** "Gun Control Is Constitutional," by Robert Goldwin. Copyright © 1991 by Dow Jones & Co. Inc. Reproduced with permission of Dow Jones & Co. in the format Textbook via Copyright Clearance Center. **Pages 716–718:** Letters to the Editor of the *Wall Street Journal*: Responses to "Gun Control Is Constitutional" by Robert Goldwin, January 1992, *Wall Street Journal*. **Page 719:** Website page from Women Against Gun Control. Copyright © 2001 by Women Against Gun Control. Reprinted by permission. **Pages 720–721:** Advertisement entitled "Don't Edit the Bill of Rights." © 1991 National Rifle Association of America. Reprinted by permission. **Pages 722–724:** "The Necessity of Global Tobacco Regulations," by Douglas Bettcher and Chitra Subramaniam from the December 12, 2002, issue of *Journal of the American Medical Association*. Reprinted with permission. **Pages 724–727:** "Nazi Tactics," by Walter E. Williams, reprinted from *Ideas on Liberty*, January 2003. Copyright © 2003, Foundation for Economic Education, 30 S. Broadway, Irvington-on-Hudson, NY 10533, www.fee.org. **Page 728:** AP/Wide World Photos. **Page 729 (top):** Bettmann/Corbis. **Page 729 (bottom):** AP/Wide World Photos. **Page 730 (top):** http://furfreenyc.org. **Page 730 (bottom):** *Time* Magazine © 2001 Time Inc. Reprinted by permission. **Page 731 (top and bottom):** AP/Wide World Photos. **Pages 732–736:** "Fast Food Nation," by Eric Schlosser, published in the April © 2004 issue of *The Ecologist*. Reprinted by permission of *The Ecologist*. **Pages 736–738:** "In A Supersized World, Regulatory Indigestion," by Charles Stein. Copyright © 2003 by Globe Newspaper Co. (MA). Reproduced with permission of Globe Newspaper Co. in the format Textbook via Copyright Clearance Center. **Pages 738–741:** "Fast Food and Personal Responsibility," by Ninos P. Malek, reprinted from *Ideas on Liberty*, January 2003. Copyright © 2003, Foundation for Economic Education, 30 S. Broadway, Irvington-on-Hudson, NY 10533, www.fee.org. **Pages 741–744:** "Those Extra Pounds—Are They Government's Business?" by Susan Llewelyn Leach, from *The Christian Science Monitor* © 2004 *The Christian Science Monitor*. Reproduced with permission in the format Textbook via Copyright Clearance

PART 6

AUTHOR/TITLE INDEX